THE CANADIAN WHO'S WHO

1910

100th Anniversary Commemorative Edition

Photo: Sgt Eric Jolin (2006)

LA GOUVERNEURE GÉNÉRALE
THE GOVERNOR GENERAL

RIDEAU HALL
OTTAWA

As a celebrated reference for the past 100 years, the *Canadian Who's Who* has stood the test of time, with each successive edition portraying the people who have shaped Canada into the nation it is today.

Across its pages, a veritable parade of notable names marches through history. Names that echo throughout Canadian artistic, political, scientific and literary spheres. There is no doubt that these laudable individuals, through their accomplishments behind the scenes and in the limelight, have left an indelible mark on society.

I congratulate the University of Toronto Press on this milestone and I wish its staff continued success as they showcase exceptional Canadians.

Michaëlle Jean

February 2010

The Canadian

WHO'S WHO

London, England: The Times.
Printing House Square, E.C.

Toronto: THE MUSSON BOOK COMPANY, Limited.

Toronto Buffalo London

www.utppublishing.com

Printed in Canada

ISBN 978-1-4426-1111-5

Library and Archives Canada Cataloguing in Publication

The Canadian who's who 1910.

Reprint of the first ed. of Canadian who's who, published by the Times of London to celebrate the 2010, 100th anniversary ed. Includes t.p. of the 1910 ed.
Sponsoring editor: Elizabeth Lumley.
ISBN 978-1-4426-1111-5

1. Canada--Biography--Dictionaries. I. Lumley, Elizabeth

FC25.C342 2010 920.071 C2009-906575-4

University of Toronto Press acknowledges the financial assistance to its publishing program of the Canada Council for the Arts and the Ontario Arts Council.

University of Toronto Press acknowledges the financial support for its publishing activities of the Government of Canada through the Book Publishing Industry Development Program (BPIDP).

FOREWORD.

In the preparation of the first edition of The Canadian Who's Who, the desire has been to make it thoroughly representative of the leading men and women of Canada, whether resident in their own land or abroad. If, perchance, the biography of some prominent Canadian has been omitted, the error must not, in all cases, be ascribed to the editor, inasmuch as some gentlemen, to whom circulars were sent, failed to answer them, and consequently their biographies could not be included.

Thanks are due to Capt. Chambers, editor of the Canadian Parliamentary Guide; Dr. Doughty, Dominion Archivist; Dr. Benjamin Sulte, Dr. Wilfred Campbell, and other gentlemen for valuable data furnished.

Suggestions for future issues, corrections of errors, etc. will be gratefully appreciated by

THE EDITOR.

Press Gallery,
Ottawa, May, 1910.

INDEX TO ADVERTISEMENTS.

PAGE

Acetylene Buoys.

International Marine Signal Co., Ltd. 5

Advocates, Barristers, Etc.

Cahan, C. H. .... *xiv*
Chauvin, Baker & Walker 6
Christie, Greene & Hill 2
Code & Burritt 2
Davidson & Wainwright 6
Elliott & David 10
Gormully, Orde & Powell 6
Greenshields, Greenshields & Languedoc .... *xiv*
Lighthall & Harwood 2
McGiverin, Haydon & Greig 2
McLennan, Howard & Aylmer 6
McMaster & Papineau 6
Smith & Johnston 10
Thompson, A. T. 10
Vipond & Vipond 2

Banks.

Bank of Ottawa .... *ii*
Dominion Bank 16
Imperial Bank .... *vi*
Merchants' Bank of Canada .... *vi*

Books.

Nelson's Loose-Leaf Encyclopœdia .. 15

Brokers and Financial Agents.

Bergevin, Achille .... *viii*
Bethune, J. T. .... *xix*
Black, John .... *iv*
Browne, W. Graham & Co. .... *xiv*
Elmore, W. E. & Co. 10
Forget, Rodolphe 13
Ives, A. Scott .... *xix*
MacCuaig, W. W. 4
Meredith, C. & Co. .... *viii*
Wilson-Smith, R. .... *viii*

Canadian Government.

Canadian North-West Land Regulations 3
Royal Military College Regulations .. 1

PAGE

Fraternal Society.

Sons of England Benefit Society 14

Hotels.

Grand Union, Ottawa 8
The New Russell, Ottawa 8
St. Regis, Montreal .... *x*

Insurance Companies.

Canadian Railway Accident Insurance Co. .... *iii*
General Accident Assurance Co. of Canada .... *iv*
Law Union & Rock Insurance Co., Ltd. (The) .... *iii*
London & Lancashire Life Assurance Co. .... *xix*
Metropolitan Life Insurance Co .... *ii*
Sun Life Assurance Co. of Canada. .. *iii*

Newspapers.

The Times .... *i*
The Times Weekly 16

Railways.

Canadian Pacific Ry. Co. .... *xx*
Grand Trunk Ry. System .... *v*

Miscellaneous.

British American Bank Note Co. .... *ix*
Corticelli Silk Co., Ltd. 12
Durnford, George, Ltd. 10
Gourock Ropework Export Co., Ltd. (The) 4
Mothersill Remedy Co. .... *vii*
Robert's Counting House .... *xiv*
Thiel Detective Service Co. of Canada, Ltd., (The) 7
Todd, Frederick G. .... *xix*
Ward & Co. 4
Ware Co. (The) 4
Windsor Salt 12
Woods, Ltd. 9

ABBREVIATIONS.

A.A.G. . . . . . . Assistant-Adjutant-General.
Abp. . . . . Archbishop.
A.C.A. . . . . . . Associate of the Institute of Chartered Accountants.
Acad. . . . . Academy.
A.D.C. . . . . . . Aide-de-camp.
Adj. . . . . Adjutant
Adm. . . . . Admiral.
Adv. . . . . Advocate.
Advt. . . . . Advertisement.
A.G. . . . . Attorney-General; Adjutant-General.
Ala. . . . . Alabama (U.S.)
Alta. . . . . Alberta.
A.M.I.C.E. . . Associate Member of Institute of Civil Engineers.
A.M.I.E.E. . . Associate Member of Institute of Electrical Engineers.
Anat. . . . . Anatomy; Anatomical.
A.Q.M.G. . . . Assistant-Quartermaster-General.
A.R.A. . . . . . . Associate of the Royal Academy.
A.R.A.M. . . . Associate of the Royal Academy of Music.
A.R.C.A. . . . . Associate Royal Canadian Academy.
Archt. . . . . . . Architect.
A.R.S.C. . . . . Associate Royal College of Science.
A.R.I.B.A. . . . Associate of the Royal Institute of British Architects.
Ark. . . . . Arkansas (U.S.)
A.R.S.M. . . . . Associate Royal School of Mines.
Art. . . . . Artist.
A.S.C. . . . . . . Army Service Corps.
Ass. or Assist. Assistant.
Atha. . . . . Athabasca.
Av. . . . . Avenue.

B. . . . . Baron.
b. . . . . born; brother.
B.A. . . . . Bachelor of Arts.
Barr. . . . . Barrister.
Bart. or **Bt.** . . Baronet.
Batt. or **Batn.** Battalion.
B.C. . . . . Before Christ; British Columbia.
B.C.L. . . . . . . Bachelor of Civil Law.
B.D. . . . . Bachelor of Divinity.
Bd. . . . . Board.
B.E. . . . . Bachelor of Engineering.
Berks. . . . . . . Berkshire.
B.Litt. . . . . . . Bachelor of Letters or of Laws.
B.M.A. . . . . . British Medical Association.
Bot. . . . . Botany; Botanical.
Bp. . . . . Bishop.
Brev. . . . . Brevet.
Brig. . . . . Brigade; Brigadier.
B.S. . . . . Bachelor of Surgery.
B.Sc. . . . . Bachelor of Science.
B.Th. . . . . Bachelor of Theology.

(C.) . . . . Conservative.
c. . . . . Cents; centimes; child.
C.A. . . . . Chartered Accountant.
Calif. . . . . California (U.S.)
Capt. . . . . Captain.
Cav. . . . . Cavalry.
C.B. . . . . Companion of the Bath.
C.C. . . . . County Councillor.
C.E. . . . . Civil Engineer.
Chanc. . . . . . Chancellor; Chancery.
Chap. . . . . . . Chaplain.
Ch. Ch. . . . . . Christ Church.
Chn. . . . . Chairman.
Civ. Serv. . . . Civil Service.
C.J. . . . . Chief Justice.
Cl. . . . . Class.
C.M. . . . . Master in Surgery.
C.M.G. . . . . . Companion of St. Michael and St. George.
C.O. . . . . Commanding Officer.
Co. . . . . County; Company.
Col. . . . . Colony; Colonel.
Coll. . . . . College; Collegiate.
Comdg. . . . . . Commanding.
Comdt. . . . . . Commandant.
Com.-in-Chf. Commander-in-Chief.
Comr. . . . . . . Commissioner.
Corp. . . . . Corporal.
Corr. Mem. or **Fell.** . . . Corresponding Member or Fellow.
C.P.R. . . . . . . Canadian Pacific Raliway.
Cr. . . . . Crown.
cr. . . . . created.
C.S. . . . . Civil Service.
C.V.O. . . . . . . Commander of the Royal Victorian Order.

D. . . . . Duke.
d. . . . . Pence; died; daughter.
D.A.A.G. . . . . Deputy-Assistant-Adjutant-General.
D.A.G. . . . . . . Deputy-Adjutant-General.
D.A.Q.M.G. . . Deputy-Aissistant-Quartermaster-General.
D.C.L. . . . . . . Doctor of Civil Law.
D.D. . . . . Doctor of Divinity.
D.D.S. . . . . . . Doctor of Dental Surgery.
deg. . . . . Degree.
del. . . . . delegate.
Dep. . . . . Deputy.
Dept. . . . . Department.
Dioc. . . . . Diocese; Diocesan.
Div. . . . . Division.
D. Litt. or **D. Lit.** Doctor of Literature.
Dr. . . . . Doctor.
D.Sc. . . . . Doctor of Science.
D.S.O. . . . . . . Companion of the Distinguished Service Order.
D.Theol. . . . . Doctor of Theology.

E. . . . . East; Earl.
Eccl. . . . . Ecclesiastical.
Ed. . . . . Editor.
Edin. . . . . Edinburgh.
Educ. . . . . . . Educated.
Eng. . . . . England.
eng. . . . . Engineer.

F.C.A. . . . . . . Fellow of the Institute of Chartered Accountants.
F.C.P. . . . . . . Fellow College of Preceptors.
F.C.S. . . . . . . Fellow of the Chemical Society
F.E.S. . . . . . . Fellow of the Entomological Society.
F.F.A. . . . . . . Fellow of the Faculty of Actuaries.
F.G.S. . . . . . . Fellow of the Geological Society.
F.I.A. . . . . . . Fellow of the Institute of Actuaries.
F.I.C. . . . . . . Fellow of the Institute of Chemistry.
Fr., ... French.

F.R.A.M. . . . Fellow of the Royal Academy of Music.
F.R.A.S. . . . Fellow of the Royal Astronomical Society.
F.R.C.I. . . . Fellow of the Royal Colonial Institute.
F.R.C.O. . . . Fellow of the Royal College of Organists.
F.R.C.P. . . . Fellow of the Royal College of Physicians.
F.R.C.S. . . . Fellow of the Royal College of Surgeons.
F.R.C.V.S. . . Fellow of the Royal College of Veterinary Surgeons.
F.R.G.S. . . . Fellow of the Royal Geographical Society.
F.R.Hist. S. . Fellow of the Royal Historical Society.
F.R.Hort.S. . Fellow of the Royal Horticultural Society.
F.R.I.B.A. . . Fellow of the Royal Institute of British Architects.
F.R.M.S. . . . Fellow of the Royal Microscopical Society.
F.R.Met.S. . . Fellow of the Royal Meteorological Society.
F.R.S. . . . . . Fellow of the Royal Society.
F.R.C.S. . . . Fellow of the Royal Society of Canada.
F.R.S.L. . . . Fellow of the Royal Society of Literature.
F.S.A. . . . . . Fellow of the Society of Antiquaries.
F.S.S. . . . . . Fellow of the Royal Statistical Society.
F.Z.S. . . . . . Fellow of the Zoological Society.

G.C.B. . . . . . Knight Grand Cross of the Bath.
G.C.M.G. . . . Knight Grand Cross of St. Michael and St. George.
G.C.V.O. . . . Knight Grand Cross of Royal Victorian Order.
Gen. . . . . . . General.
G.L. . . . . . . Grand Lodge.
Gov. . . . . . . Governor.
Govt. . . . . . Government.
g.s. . . . . Grandson.
Harv. . . . . . Harvard.
H.E. . . . . . . His Excellency.
Heir pres. . . . Heir presumptive.
H.H. . . . . . . His (or Her) Highness.
H.I.H. . . . . . His (or Her) Imperial Highness.
H.I.M. . . . . . His (or Her) Imperial Majesty.
H.M. . . . . . . His (or Her) Majesty.
H.M.I. . . . . . His Majesty's Inspector.
H.M.S. . . . . . His Majesty's Ship.
Hon. . . . . . . Honourable.
Hon. . . . . . . Honorary.
H.R.H. . . . . . His (or Her) Royal Highness.

Imp. . . . . . . Imperial.
Insp. . . . . . . Inspector.
Inst. . . . . . . Instant; Institute.
I.O.O.F. . . . . Independent Order of Oddfellows.
I.S.O. . . . . . . Imperial Service Order.

J.A. . . . . Judge-Advocate.
Jas. . . . . James.
Jes. . . . . Jesus.
Joh. Jno . . . . John.
J.P. . . . . Justice of the Peace.
Jun. . . . . Junior.
K. . . . . King.

K.B. . . . . Knight Bachelor.
K.C. . . . . King's Counsel.
K.C.B. . . . . . Knight Commander of the Bath.
K.C.M.G. . . . Knight Commander of St. Michael and St. George.
K.C.V.O. . . . Knight Commander of the Royal Victorian Order.
K.G. . . . . Knight of the Order of the Garter.
Kt. or Knt. . . Knight.
Lib. . . . . Liberal.
L.C.J. . . . . . Lord Chief Justice.
L.D.S. . . . . . Licentiate of Dental Surgery.
L.F.P.S. . . . . Licentiate of the Faculty of Physicians and Surgeons.
L.H.D. . . . . . Doctor of Literature.

L.I. . . . . Light Infantry.
Lic. Med. . . . Licentiate in Medicine.
Lieut. . . . . . Lieutenant.
Lit. . . . . Literature; Literary.
Lit. D. . . . . . Doctor of Letters.
LL.B. . . . . . . Bachelor of Laws.
LL.D. . . . . . . Doctor of Laws.
LL.M. . . . . . . Master of Laws.
L.R.C.P. . . . . Licentiate of the Royal College of Physicians.
L.R.C.S. . . . . Licentiate of the Royal College of Surgeons.
L.R.C.V.S. . . Licentiate of the Royal College of Veterinary Surgeons.
Lt. or Lieut. . Lieutenant.
Lt.-Col. . . . . Lieutenant-Colonel.
Lt.-Gen. . . . . Lieutenant-General.

m. . . . . married.
M.A. . . . . Master of Arts.
Mag. . . . . Magazine.
Maj.-Gen. . . . Major-General.
Man. . . . . Manitoba.
Marq. . . . . . . Marquis.
Math. . . . . . . Mathematics; Mathematical.
M.B. . . . . Bachelor of Medicine.
M.D. . . . . Doctor of Medicine.
Me. . . . . Maine (U.S.)
Med. . . . . Medical.
Mem. . . . . . . Memorandum.
M.F.H. . . . . . Master of Foxhounds.
M.H.R. . . . . . Member House of Representatives.
M.I.E.E. . . . . Member of Institute of Electrical Engineers.
M.I.M.E. . . . . Member of Institute of Mining and Mechanical Engineers.
M.I.Mech.E. Member Institution of Mechanical Engineers.
M.I.M.M. . . . Member of Institute of Mining and Metallurgy.
Min. . . . . Minister.
M.Inst.C.E. . Member of Institution of Civil Engineers.
M.Inst.M.E. . Member of Institution of Mining Engineers.
M.L. . . . . Licentiate in Medicine.
M.L.A. . . . . . Member of Legislative Assembly.
M.L.C. . . . . . Member of Legislative Council.
Mme. . . . . . . Madame.
Most Rev. . . Most Reverend (of an Archbishop).
M.P. . . . . Member of Parliament.
M.R.C.P. . . . . Member of the Royal College of Physicians.
M.R.C.S. . . . . Member Royal College of Surgeons.
M.S. . . . . Master of Surgery.

M.Sc. . . . . . . Master of Science.
Mt. . . . . Mountain.
Mus. B. . . . . . Bachelor of Music.
Mus.D. . . . . . Doctor of Music.
Mus. M. Master of Music.
M.V.O. . . . . . Member of the Royal Victorian Order.

N.B. . . . . New Brunswick.
N.H. . . . . New Hampshire (U.S.)
N.P. . . . . Notary Public.
N.R.A. . . . . . . National Rifle Association.
N.S. . . . . Nova Scotia.
N.W.T. . . . . . North-West Territories.
N.Y. . . . . New York—City or State.
o.c. . . . . only child.

Ont. . . . . Ontario.
o. s. . . . . only son.
O.S.A. . . . . . . Ontario Society of Artists.

Parl. Agt. . . . Parliamentary Agent.
P.C. . . . . Privy Councillor.
P.E.I. . . . . . . Prince Edward Island.
Ph.D. . . . . . . Doctor of Philosophy.
Phil. . . . . Philosophical.
Phys. . . . . Physical.
Plen. . . . . Plenipotentiary.
P.M.G. . . . . . Postmaster-General.
P.M.O. . . . . . Principal Medical Officer.
P.Q. . . . . Province of Quebec.
Pres. . . . . President.
Prof. . . . . Professor.

Q. . . . . Queen.
Q.C. . . . . Queen's Counsel.
Q.M.G. . . . . . Quartermaster-General.
Que. . . . . Quebec.

R.A. . . . . Royal Academician; Royal Artillery.
R.A.C. . . . . . . Royal Agricultural College.
R.A.M. . . . . . . Royal Academy of Music.
R.A.M.C. . . . . Royal Army Medical Corps.
R. Art. . . . . . . Royal Artillery.
R.C.V.S. . . . . Royal College of Veterinary Surgeons.
R.E. . . . . Royal Engineers.
Rear-Adm. . . Rear-Admiral.
Reg. Prof. . . . Regius Professor.
Regt. . . . . Regiment.
Res. . . . . Resigned; Reserve.
Rev. . . . . Reverend.
R.F.A. . . . . . . Royal Field Artillery.
R.G.A. . . . . . . Royal Garrison Artillery.
R.I.B.A. . . . . Royal Institute of British Architects.
R.M.C. . . . . . . Royal Military Coll., Canada.
R.M.L.I. . . . . Royal Marine Light Infantry.
R.N. . . . . Royal Navy.
R.N.R. . . . . . . Royal Naval Reserve.
Roy. . . . . Royal.

Rt. Hon. . . . . Right Honourable.
Rt. Rev. . . . . Right Reverend (of a Bishop.)
R.Y.S. . . . . . . Royal Yacht Squadron.

S. . . . . succeeded; South; Saints.
s. . . . . son; shillings.
S.A. . . . . South Australia; South Africa.
Sask. . . . . Sskatchewan
Sc.D. . . . . Doctor of Science.
Sch. . . . . Scholar; School.
Sec. . . . . Secretary.
Serjt. . . . . Serjeant.
S.G. . . . . Solicitor-General.
S.J. . . . . Society of Jesus (Jesuits).
S.L. . . . . Serjeant-at-Law.
S.M.E. . . . . . School of Military Engineering
Soc. . . . . Society.
Sovs. . . . . Sovereigns.
S.P.C.C. . . . . Society for the Prevention of Cruelty to Children.
S.P.C.K. . . . . Society for Promoting Christian Knowledge.
S.P.G. . . . . . . Society for the Propagation of the Gospel.
Sq. . . . . Square.
SS. . . . . Steamship; Saints.
St. . . . . Street; Saint.
Supt. . . . . Superintendent.
Surg. . . . . Surgeon.
Surv. . . . . Surviving.
T.R.H. . . . . . Their Royal Highnesses.
Ter. or **Terr.** Terrace.
Trin. . . . . Trinity.
u. . . . . uncle.
U.K. . . . . United Kingdom of Great Britain and Ireland.
Univ. . . . . University.
U.S. . . . . United States.
U.S.A. . . . . . . United States of America.

V. . . . . Five (Roman numerals); Version; Vicar; Vicsount; Vice.
V.C. . . . . Victoria Cross.
Ven. . . . . Venerable (of an Archdeacon).
Very Rev. . . Very Reverend (of a Dean).
Vet. . . . . Veterinary.
Vice-Admn. Vice-Admiral.
Vol. . . . . Volume; Volunteers.
V.P. . . . . Vice-President.

W.I. . . . . West Indies.
W.O. . . . . War Office. Warrant Officer.
X. . . . . Ten (Roman numerals).

yds. . . . . yards.
Y.M.C.A. . . . . Young Men's Christian Association.
Yorks. . . . . . . Yorkshire.
Yrs. . . . . Years.
Y.W.C.A. . . . Young Women's Christian Association.

CANADIAN WHO'S WHO

1910.

BIOGRAPHIES.

A

ABBOTT, Harry B., C.E.; *b.* Abbotsford, Que., 14 June, 1829; *s.* of Rev. Joseph Abbott and Harriet Elizabeth Bradford; *m.* Margaret, *d.* of the late Chief Justice Sicotte, and widow of C. Freer, C.E. (*d.* 1907); two *s.* and one *d.* *Educ.*: Montreal High Sch. and McGill Univ. Commenced his career as engr. on the St. Lawrence and Atlantic Ry., now part of G.T.R. system; later was employed on the Riviere de Loup section, G.T.R.; chief engr. Brockville and Ottawa Ry. 1864; chief engr. of the Eastern Extension Ry. Co., 1876; entered service of C.P.R., 1882; gen. supt. C.P.R. in B.C., 1886; retired therefrom 1897. Assisted in formation of 11th Argenteuil Rangers, retiring with rank of major; unsuccessfully contested Brockville at Dom. g. e., 1872, and East Algoma, for Ont. Legis., 1866; has been pres. of the Vancouver club. *Address*: 720 Jervis St., Vancouver, B.C. *Clubs:* Vancouver; Union, Victoria.

ABRAMOWITZ, Rabbi Herman, B.A., L.H.D.; *b.* Russia, 28 Feb., 1880. *Educ:* College of City of N. Y., Columbia Univ. Jewish Theo. Seminary of America. Aptd Minister of the "Shaar Hashomayim" Congregation of Montreal in 1902, which pos. he still holds. *Address:* 17 Hutchison St., Montreal. *Club;* Montefiore.

ACLAND, Frederick A., Dep. Min. of Labour, Canada; *b.* Bridgewater, England, 9 Aug., 1861; *s.* of S. Acland and Mary Bryant Acland; *m.* Elizabeth Adair, Toronto, Ont.; one *s.* one *d.*; *Educ.* Bridgewater. Arrived in Canada 1883; connected with various newspapers in England, United States and Canada; Asst. Editor *The Globe*, Toronto, 1890 to 1902; Manager in London, Eng., Booklovers' Library, 1902 to 1904; Editor *Globe*, Toronto, in Western Canada, 1906 to 1907; Secretary Dept. of Labour, Canada, 1907-1908; Deputy Minister of Labour 1908. *Publications:* Pamphlets, magazine articles, and newspaper work. *Address;* 14 Somerset St., Ottawa. *Club;* Rideau, Ottawa.

ADAM, Graeme Mercer, author; *b.* Loanhead, near Roslin Castle, Scot., 25 May, 1839; *s.* of James and Margaret Adam; *m.* (1st) Jane Gibson, of Toronto, (2nd) Frances Isabel Brown, of London, Eng.; three *s.* seven *d.* *Educ:* Portobello and Edinburgh, Scot. Went to Canada in 1858 and since then engaged in literary work as publisher, author and editor. Identified with Can. Mil.; Capt. Q. O. Rifles; served during Fenian Raid. Former editor of The Canadian Monthly, and the Canada Educational Monthly; for twelve years priv. sec. to Prof. Goldwin Smith, D.C.L., at Toronto; editor of Lovell's "Gazetteer of the Canadian Dominion," Montreal, 1908. *Publications;* "The Canadian North West, its history and its Troubles, with the Narrative of Three Insurrections"; "Canada's Patriot Statesman, a life of Sir J. A. Macdonald, based on the work of Edmund Collins"; "Life of General Robert E. Lee"; "Canada from Sea to Sea"; "Toronto, Old and New"; "Outline History of Canadian Literature"; "Public School History of England and Canada", and fifty other books of biography, history, encyclopædias, etc. *Address;* 7 West 106th St., New York, N.Y.

ADAMI, John George, F.R.S., M.A., M.D. F.R.S.S., LL.D.; Professor of Pathology, McGill Univ., Montreal; *b.* Manchester, Eng., 12 Jan., 1862; *s.* of late John George Adami of Manchester and Sarah Ann Ellis, *d.* of Thomas Leech of Urmston, Lancs; *m.* 1894, Mary Stuart, *d.* of James Alexander Cantlie and Eleonora Stephen of Montreal; one *s.* one *d.* *Educ.:* Owens College, Manchester; Christ's College, Cambridge; Breslau and Paris. House Physician, Manchester Royal Infirmary, and Demonstrator of Pathology, Univ. of Camb. 1887; M.D. Cantab. 1890; John Lucas Walker Student of Pathology in the Univ. 1890; elected Fellow of Jesus Coll. Camb. 1891; head of the Pathological Department of the Royal Victoria Hospital. *Publications;* Numerous papers upon pathological subjects in various medical journals and transactions of medical journals, English, American, and French; including Observations upon the Mammalian Heart (with Professor Roy) in the Phil. Trans.; Middleton Goldsmith Lectures upon Inflammation, Trans. New York Pathological Society; Allbutt's System of Medicine; on Cirrhosis of the Liver; Inflammation, M. 4th edit. 1909; Principles of Pathology, 2 vols. *Address;* McGill Medical Coll., 331 Peel St., Montreal. *Clubs:* Saville, London; St. James's, Montreal, etc.

ADAMS, Frank Dawson, Ph.D., D.Sc., F.G.S.A., F.R.S.; Dean of the Faculty of Applied Science at McGill Univ., and Logan Prof. of Geology and Palaeontology; *b.* Montreal, 17 Sept., 1859; *m.* 1892, Mary Stuart, *d.* of the late Samuel Finlay, of Montreal. *Educ.:* Montreal High Sch., McGill Univ., where grad. from Dept. of Applied Science in the Faculty of Arts with the degree of B. Ap. Sc., 1879, and Master of Science, 1884. Studied in Sheffield Scientific Sch., Yale Coll., and at Heidelberg, Germany, Doctor of Philosophy 1892. For nine yrs. on staff of Canadian Geological Survey; apptd. Lecturer in Geology, McGill Univ., 1888; Logan Prof. of Geology and Palaeontology, 1893, and apptd. Dean. of the Faculty of Applied Science, 1908. El. Pres. Natural History Soc., 1897; apptd. a F.G.S.A., 1888; F.G.S. of London, Eng., 1895; F.R.S. of London. He is also a Fellow of the Royal Soc. of Canada; Pres. Geological and Biological Section of that organization; mem. German Geological Soc. *Publications:* Numerous papers and reports which he has submitted to the Geological Survey of Canada, the Royal Soc. of Canada, and other leading socs. "An investigation into the electric constants of rocks, more especially with reference to cubic compressibility," and a series of papers dealing with the effect of pressure on the folding and flow of rocks, a special report on the artesian wells of the Island of Montreal, 1908. *Recreations:* Camping, canoeing, and exploring new fields. *Address:* 243 Mountain St., Montreal, *Clubs:* St. James', University, Outremont Golf, Montreal.

AHEARN, Thomas; *b.* Ottawa, Ontario, 24 June, 1355; *s.* of John Ahearn and Honora Power; *m.* (1st) Lilias Mackay Fleck; (2nd) Margaret Howit Fleck. One *s.* one d. *Educ.:* University of Ottawa. Pres. Ottawa Land Association, Ottawa Gas Co., Ottawa Electric Co., Ottawa Car Mfg. Co., Ottawa Electric Railway Co., Ottawa Light, Heat and Power Co.: vice-pres. Ahearn & Soper, Ltd., The Ottawa Investment Co.; Director Canadian Westinghouse Co. *Recreation:* travelling. *Address;* Buena Vista, Ottawa. *Clubs;* Rideau, Laurentian, Golf, Hunt, and Country, Ottawa.

AHEARN, Mrs. Margaret Howit: *b.* Montreal; *d.* of Alexander Fleck, of Ottawa, and Lilias Walker; *m.* 1892, Thomas Ahearn, electrician, Pres. of the Ottawa Electric Ry. and Electric Cos. *Educ.:* McGill Model Sch., and Bute House. Active in many movements for the advancement of Women; mem. of Local Council; pres., Women's Canadian Hist. Soc., and Victorian Order of Nurses. *Address:* "Buena Vista," 584 Laurier Ave., W., Ottawa.

AIKINS, Herbert Austin, M.D., LL.D., Ph.D.; *b.* Toronto, Ont.; 1 March, 1867; *s.* of Dr. W. T. Aikins; married. *Educ.:* Toronto Univ. and Yale. Prof. Univ. Southern Calif., 1888; lecturer on history of philosophy, Yale., 1890-1; prof. logic and philosophy, Trinity Coll., N.C., 1891-3; hon. fellow Clark Univ., 1892-3; Prof. philosophy, Coll. for Women, Western Reserve Univ. since 1893; mem. Am. Psyshol. Assn., Am. Philos. Assn. *Publication:* Philosophy of Hume, 1893; author of Principles of Logic, 1903; and papers on psychol. and philos. subjects; translater of Forel's Hygiene of Nerves and Mind, 1907. *Address:* 2038 Cornell Rd., Cleveland, Ohio.

AIKINS, James Albert Manning, M.A. (Tor.), K.C.; *b.* Richview, Peel co., Ont,; *s.* of the late Hon. J. C. Aikins, P.C., and Mary Elizabeth Somerset; *m.* (1st) Mary B. McLelan; (2nd) Mary French Colby; one *s.*, two *d.* *Educ.:* Brampton Gram. Sch., Upper Can. Coll., Toronto Univ. Called to the Bar of Ontario, 1898; Manitoba, 1879; North West Territories a few yrs. later. Hon.-treas. 13 times of Manitoba Bar; mem. of Council; dir., Agricultural Coll. and Wesley Coll.; counsel at Winnipeg for C. P. Ry. Co., and other companies and banks. *Recreation:* Golf. *Address:* Winnipeg, Man. *Clubs:* Manitoba, Country, Winnipeg.

AIRD, John; Mgr. of the Canadian Bank of Commerce, Winnipeg; *b.* Longueuil, Que., 15 Nov., 1855; *s.* of William and Margaret Aird; *m.* Eleanor Lawlor Johnston; three *s.* three *d.* *Educ.:* Model Sch., Toronto. Engaged in railway work for six yrs., and in banking enterprise for thirty-one yrs. *Recreations:* golf, curling, bowling, lacrosse. *Address:* Winnipeg, Man. *Clubs:* Toronto; Manitoba, Commercial, Winnipeg.

AITKEN, Peter; *b.* Dundas, Ont., June 16, 1858; *s.* William Aitken; *m.* Florence H. Corkhill, of Brooklyn; went to the U.S., 1879; studied wood engraving several yrs.; visited Europe, 1887 and 1891, and studied in Paris, 1895. Awarded medal World's Columbian Expn., 1893; exhibited Paris Expn., 1900. V.-p. and chm'n exec. com. Radical Democracy; del. at large to City Com. of Citizens' Union of New York; mem. exec. com. Citizens' Union, Brooklyn; mem. (ex-pres.) Brooklyn Single Tax League. *Address:* 121 Pulaski St., Brooklyn, N.Y.

ALBANI, Madame (Marie Louise Cecilia Emma Lajeunesse), Ord.-Merit (England, Denmark, Coburg); Queen Victoria Jubilee Ord.; *b.* Chambly, nr. Montreal, 1 Nov., 1854; *d.* of the late Joseph Lajeunesse; *m.* 1879, Ernest Gye; one *s.* *Educ.:* Sacred Heart Convent, Montreal. Studied music in Paris and Milan. Made debut in opera at Messina, Sicily, 1870, and then was engaged at Florence and Malta. First appearance in London at Coventgarden theatre May, 1872, in "La Somnambula," and subsequently every year for twenty seasons. Has sung at all the great English festivals for many yrs., and created most of the modern orations. Has sung in Paris, Italy, Germany, Russia, United States, Canada, Holland, Belgium, India, South Africa, Australia. *Address:* 61 Trequnter Rd., London, S.W., England.

ALCORN, George Oscar, K.C.; *b.* Lennoxville, Que., 3 May, 1850; *s.* of Thomas C. Alcorn, M.D., and Martha A. Bartlett; *m.* 3 Aug., 1872, Sara J. Leavens of Belleville, Ont. *Educ.:* Toronto Gram. Sch., Model Gram. Sch., and private tuition. Called to the Bar of Ont., in Easter, 1871. Created K.C., 1890. Has been Councillor and Reeve of Picton, Ont., and Pres. Lib.-Con. Assn., Picton, for three yrs. Elected to House of Commons at *g.e.*, 1900; re-elected at g. e., 1904; unsuccessful at g. e., 1908. *Address:* Picton, Ont.

ALGER, John Lincoln, M.A.; *b.* Eaton, Que., 20 Nov., 1864; *s.* of Nathan Willis and Mary (Key) Alger; *m.* 1896, Edith Goodyear, of North Haven, Conn. *Educ.:* Brown Univ., teacher in high schs., Rutland, Vt. and Providence, R.I., 1890-2; instr. mathematics, Brown Univ., 1892-5; supt. of schs., Bennington, Vt., 1895-1900; prin. Johnson (Vt.) State Normal Sch., 1900-04, Vt. Acad., since 1904. Mem. State Normal Sch., Comm'n. Phi Beta Kappa. *Address:* Saxtons River, Vt., U.S.A.

ALLAN, Alexander Macdonald, F.R.H.S.; *b.* Stratford, Ont., 11 July, 1844; of Scotch parentage; *m.* Esther Leslie, Toronto, five *s.* one *d.* *Educ.:* Pub. Sch., and Stratford High Sch. For some yrs. ed. and prop. of the *Huron Signal*, Goderich; one of the organizers of the Ontario Fruit-growers. Assn., and pres. for some yrs,; Can. Commr. to the Indian and Colonial Exhibition, London, England, 1866. Writer on horticulture and pomology in many publications. *Recreations:* travel, bowling, curling. *Address:* Toronto.

ALLAN, Bryce James, dir. of the Allan line; *b.* Montreal, 20 Aug., 1862; *s.* of Sir Hugh and Lady Allan; *m.* Anna Palfrey. *Educ.:* Bishop's Coll. Sch., France and Germany. For many yrs. connected with management of the Allan Line; now mgr. for the Co. at Boston, Mass. *Address:* Boston. *Clubs:* St. James', Montreal; Somerset, Boston; Union and Knickerbocker, New York; Junior Carlton, London, Eng.

ALLAN, Sir Hugh Montagu, K.B,. C.V.O.; vice-chn. of the Allan Line Steamship Co., Montreal; *b.* Montreal, 13 Oct., 1860; *s.* of the late Sir Hugh Allan, one of the founders of the Allan Line Steamship Co., and Matilda Caroline Smith; *m.* 1893, Marguerite Ethel, *d.* of the late Hector MacKenzie, of Montreal; one *s.* three *d.* *Educ.:* Bishop's Coll. Sch., Lennoxville, Que., and in Paris, France. Entered the firm of H. & A. Allan, and is now vice-chn. of the line. Pres., Merchants' Bank of Can., the Can. Paper Co., Acadia Coal Co., Railway Securities Co.; director of the Montreal Rolling Mills Co., Montreal street Ry. Co., Montreal Light, Heat and Power Co., Ogilvie Flour Mills Co., Ltd., Canadian Transfer Co., Labrador Co., Dom. Iron and Steel Co., Mutual Life Ins. Co. of Can., Canadian White Co., International Banking Corporation of New York; vice-pres., Canada Car Co., and North British Development Co.; mem. of the Montreal Board of Trade. Was created a Knight Bachelor by His Majesty King Edward VII, 1904, and in 1906 was decorated Commander of the Victorian Order, C.V.O.; Order of Rising Sun (third class) conferred by the Emperor of Japan on the occasion of the visit to Can. in 1907, of His Imperial Highness General Prince Fushimi. *Address:* "Ravenscrag," McTavish St., Montreal; "Montrose," Cacouna, Que. *Clubs:* Mount Royal, St. James', Forest and Stream ,Montreal Hunt, Montreal; Toronto; Rideau, Ottawa; Manitoba, Winnipeg; Knickerkocker, New York; Junior Carlton, London, Eng.

ALLARD, Hon. Jules; Minister of Lands and Forests, Quebec; *b.* St. Francois du Lac, 21 Jan., 1859; *s.* of Louis Allard and Marie Ann Chapdelaine; *m.* 1885, Berthe Toupin, of Montreal; ten *c.* *Educ.:* Nicolet Coll. Called to the Bar, 1883. Pres. sch. commrs. of St. Francois du Lac, 1892-1898, and Mayor of the village, 1895-1898; Registrar of Yamaska Co., 1890-1897. El. to Quebec Legis. at bye-el. 22 Dec., 1898; re-el. at g. e. 1900, 1904; called to Legis. Council, 23 March, 1905, and received portfolio of Minister of Colonization and Pub. Works in Gouin Admn., apptd. Minister of Agriculture, 31 Aug., 1906; Lands and Forests, 1909. Pres. Abenakis Springs Hotel Co., St. Lawrence Telephone Co.; dir. Sorel Electric Co., St. Francois du Lac Aqueduct Co.; mem. St. Jean Baptiste Soc. of Quebec. *Recreations:* canoeing, fishing. *Address:* Quebec, Que. *Club:* St. Francois du Lac.

ALLEN, Frank, M.A., Ph.D., F.R.S.C., Prof. of Physics, University of Manitoba; Fellow American Physical Society; Fellow American Ass. for Advancement of Science. *b.* Canterbury, N.B.; *s.* of Rev. John Salter Allen and Charlotte Matilda N. Tuttle; *m.* Sarah Estelle Harper, *d.* of late D. S. Harper, Shediac, N.B.; one *s.* and one *d.* *Educ.:* Public Schools of New Brunswick, University of New Brunswick, Fredericton, N.B., and Cornell University, Ithaca, N.Y. Alumni Gold Medalist U. of N.B., 1895; principal Westmorland County Gram. Sch., 1895-1899; University Scholar in Physics, Cornell, 1900; president, A.D. White Fellow in Physics, Cornell, 1901; instructor in Physics, Cornell, 1902-1905; Professor of Physics, University of Manitoba, Winnipeg, 1905. *Publications:* papers in scientific journals on color measurements; History of color vision, efficiency of liquid air production. *Address:* 117 Harvard Av., Crescentwood, Winnipeg, and Univ. of Manitoba, Winnipeg. *Club:* University, Winnipeg.

ALLEN, Thomas Carleton, LL.B., K.C., *b.* Fredericton, N.B., 9 Nov., 1852; *s.* of Sir John Campbell and Margaret A. Allen; *m.* Louisa L. Wetmore, two *s.* one d. *Educ.:* Fredericton. Registrar Supreme Court of New Brunswick, and Clerk of the Crown; practiced law in St. John, until 1883, when appointed Registrar; Mayor of Fredericton, 1890 to 1893. *Publications:* five volumes of reports of cases in the Supreme Court. *Recreations:* golf, tennis, hunting. *Address:* Fredericton. *Clubs:* Union, St. John.

ALLEN, Thomas Grant, M.D., M.A.; *b.* Leeds Co., Ont., Oct. 14, 1863; *m.* 1890, Nettie Mabel Fralick, Toronto, Ont. *Educ.:* Queen's Univ., Kingston; demonstrator and instr. Queen's Univ., 1888-9; science master in Seaforth and Ingersoll, Ont., 1890-3; prof. chemistry Armour Inst. of Technology, 1894-8; Univ. Extension lecturer on chemistry, Univ. of Chicago, 1895-8 Instr. clinical medicine, Northwestern Univ. prof. children's diseases, Post-Graduate Med. Sch.; clinical prof. pediatries, Coll. Phys. and Surg., Chicago. *Address:* 5661 Washington Av., Chicago.

ALLNATT, Rev. Francis John Benwell, D.D., D.C.L.; vice-principal, Harrold Prof. of Divinity, and Dean of the Faculty of Theology, Univ. of Bishop's Coll., Lennoxville; Canon of Cathedral of Quebec; *b.* Clapham, Surrey, Eng., 15 Jan., 1841; *s.* of the late Rev. Francis J. Allnatt, M.R.C.S.; Vicar of Grinsdale, Diocese of Carlisle, Eng.; *m.* Jane, *d.* of the late Lieut.

Robin, and widow of Ignace Gill, M.L.A., of Quebec. *Educ.:* St. Augustine's Coll. Canterbury, Eng.; arrived Can. 1864; appointed to rectory of Drummondville where he remained for 21 yrs. with exception of an interval of two years, which he spent as a volunteer missionary in wilds of Labrador. In 1879, he was apptd. inspector of Academies and Model-Schools in Prov. of Que., which office he resigned on appointment to rectory of St. Matthew's Church in Quebec, in 1885. In 1887 was apptd. occupant of Chair of Pastoral Theology in Bishop's Univ., which he retained until 1892, when he was promoted to position of Harrold Prof. of Divinity and Dean of that Faculty, and in same year was elected to office of Vice-Principal. *Publications:* The Witness of St. Matthew. *Address:* Harrold Lodge, Bishop's Univ., Lennoxville; Cap à l'Aigle, Que. (summer).

ALLOWAY, William Forbes; *b.* Queen's Co., Ireland, 20 Aug., 1852; *s.* late Capt. Arthur Wm. Alloway, H.M. 4th (King's Own) Regt of foot, and Mary, *d.* of the late Judge Johnson: *m.* Elizabeth *d.* of late James Maclaren, of Buckingham, Que. *Educ.:* Montreal High Sch. Went to Manitoba, 1870, as private under Col. (Lord) Wolseley (Red River Expedition), and has resided in prov. ever since. For many yrs. in mecrantile life; now senior partner in private banking firm of Alloway & Champion, the largest of the kind in the Dominion; mem. of different commercial organizations; governor of Winnipeg hospital; mem. of different athletic organizations. *Addresses:* 407 Assiniboine Av., or 362 Main St., Winnipeg. *Clubs:* Manitoba, Country, Winnipeg.

AMBROSE, Paul, musical composer; *b.* Hamilton, Ont., Oct. 11, 1868; *s.* R. S. and Elizabeth Ambrose. *Educ.:* Pub. Schs.and Hamilton Collegiate Inst,; married. Organist Madison Av. M. E. Ch., 1886-90; organist and choirmaster St. James' Ch., since 1890. Teaches piano and organ at Am. Inst. of Applied Music, New York; is prof. music, N. J. State schs.; formerly for long period actively engaged as soloist and accompanist, but abandoned that work because of press of other duties. Sec. to Music Com. and Librarian Manuscript Soc. of New York; v.-p. Synthetic Guild of New York. Composer of numerous sacred and secular songs, vocal duets, part songs, piano solos, etc. *Residence:* Trenton, N.J.

AMES, Alfred Ernest; head of the firm of A. E. Ames & Co., Ltd., bankers and brokers; *b.* Lambeth, Ont., 1866; *s.* of Rev. William Ames; *m.* 1889, Mary, *d.* of Senator George A. Cox, of Toronto; one *s.* one *d.* *Educ.:* Com. Sch. and Brantford Coll. Inst. Entered Owen Sound Branch of Merchants' Bank of Can., 1881; resigned and joined staff of Imperial Bnk. of Can., at Toronto; became Act. Accnt. in Ont. Bnk., Peterborough; made accnt.; became mgr. Ont. Bnk. in Mount Forest; promoted to Lindsay branch; returned to Toronto 1889 and opened a banking and brokerage business, and founded the firm of A. E. Ames & Co.; pres. Toronto Stock Exchange 1897-1898; pres. Toronto Bd. of Trade, and Metropolitan Bnk.; vice-pres., Imperial Life Assur. Co.; dir. Robert Simpson Co., Ltd., Twin City Rapid Transit Co., ot Minneapolis and St. Paul, and other cos. *Address:* 467 Sherbourne St., Toronto.

AMES, Herbert Brown, B.A., M.P., dir. Ames-Holden Co., Ltd., Montreal; *b.* Montreal, 27 June, 1863; *s.* of Evan Fisher Ames, a native of Mnssachusetts, and Caroline Matilda Brown, a native of New York; *m.* 19 May, 1890, Louise Marion, *d.* of John Kennedy, C.E., Montreal. *Educ.:* Private and Public Schs., of Montreal, until his 15th year; three years at Williamstown and Easthampton, Mass., and four years at Amherst College, Amherst, Mass., when he graduated 1885. A member of the Council of Public Instruction for Quebec; alderman of Montreal from 1898 to 1906; first elected to the House of Commons, 1906; re-elected 1908; Presbyterian; Conservative. *Address:* Montreal.

AMI, Henry M., M.A., D.Sc., F.G.S., F.R.S.C.; late Assist. Palæontologist, Geological Survey of Canada; *b.* Belle Riviere, near Montreal, 23 Nov. 1858; 2nd *s.* of late Rev. Marc Ami of Geneva, Switzerland, and Anne Giramaire of Glay, Montbéliard, Doubs, France; *m.* 1892, Clarissa J., *e. d.* of George B. Burland, Montreal. *Educ.:* private tuition; Ottawa Public and Grammar Schools; McGill University. Redpath Exhibition; Macdonald Scholar and Dawson Prizeman; Faculty of Arts, B.A. 1882; M.A. 1885; D.Sc. (Queen's), 1892; president of the Ottawa Field-Naturalists' Club, 1899-1901; President of the Ottawa Valley Graduates' Society of McGill University, 1902-3; awarded the Bigsby Medal by the Council of the Geological Society of London, 1903; five years in "A" Company, Governor General's Foot Guards; Fellow of the Geological Societies of London, Switzerland, and America, etc. *Publications:* Resources of the Country between Quebec and Winnipeg along the line of the National Transcontinental Railway, and other Government reports; numerous papers on graptolites, palæozic faunas of Eastern Canada; publications relating to the Palæontology and Chronological Geology of Canada, issued in Canada, Britain, and the United States of America; editor of the Ottawa Naturalist 1895-1900. *Recreations:* geological excursions, golf, curling, skating, etc. *Adress:* 453 Laurier Av., East. *Clubs:* Rideau, Golf, Ottawa; Royal Societies, London Eng.

AMYOT, Lieut.-Col. (Hon.) George Elie; *b.* St. Augustine, Portneuf Co., Que., 28 Jan., 1856; *s.* Dominique Amyot; *m.* Marie Josephine Tanguay; two *s.* three d. *Educ.:* Quebec; commenced business as commercial traveller; mfgr. of corsets, Quebec, 1886; paper box factory, 1894 brewery, 1895; all three still in successful operation; ex-pres. Canadian Mfrs. Association; ex-pres. Quebec Board of Trade; director National Breweries, Ltd.; Home Life Ins. Co. *Address:* St. Foye Rd., and 45 Dorchester St., Quebec. *Clubs:* Garrison, Hunt, Quebec.

ANDERSON, Right Rev. Charles Palmerston; Bishop of the Prot. Epis.Ch. of the U.S.; *b.* Kemptville, Ont.; *s.* of Henry and Mary R. Anderson; *m.* 1899, Janet Glass, of Belleville, Ont.; *Educ.:* Trinity Coll. Sch.; Port Hope, Ont., and Trinity Univ., Toronto (grad. D.D.). Ordained 1888; in charge Beachburg, Ont., 1888-91; Grace Ch., Oak Park, Ill., 1891-1900. *Publications:* The Christian Ministry. *Address:* 1612 Prairie Av., Chicago, Ill.

ANDERSON, John; Registrar of Deeds for North Wellington; *b.* Toronto, 11 Mar., 1838; *s.* James and Susan Anderson; *m.* Emily Louise, *d.* of John B. Bagwell, of Hamilton; three *d.* *Educ.:* Toronto and Streetsville Gram. Sch. Entered mercantile life in Streetsville. Removed to Orangville, and occupied several municipal offices there. Apptd. Registrar for N. Wellington, 1871, and holds position to-day. Pres. of the Arthur Agric. Socy. for many years; chr. High Sch. Bd. ofr ten years. *Address:* "Roscrea," Arthur, Ont.

ANDERSON, Lieut. Col. William Patrick, M. Inst. C. E.; Past President Canadian Society C.E.; *b.* Levis, Que.; *s.* of Thomas Anderson, native of Newcastle-on-Tyne, England, and Adelaide Alicia, native of Dublin, Ireland; *m.* in 1876, to Dorothea S., *e. s.* of H. Beaumont Small, late Secretary Department of Agriculture; four *s.* and one d. *Educ.:* Bishop's College, Lennoxville, and Manitoba Coll.; entered Dept. of Marine as Asst. Engineer in Oct., 1874; promoted Chief Engineer in Feb., 1880, and has since occupied that position, controlling all construction work in connection with aids to navigation, and most of the technical work of the Dept. Has designed and built one 500 lighthouses and 50 fog alarm stations. A member of the lighthouse board, and of the Geographic Board of Canada. Lieut.-Colonel in 43rd Regt., Ottawa. *Publications:* Established Canadian *Military Gazette* in 1885 and edited it for two years; has contributed many papers to Can. fSoc. of C. E., and other scientific societies, and publications. *Recreations:* golf, and curling. *Address:* 64 Cooper St., Ottawa. *Clubs:* Rideau, Golf, Ottawa.

ANGLIN, Hon. Francis Alexander, K. C.; Judge of the Supreme Ct. of Canada; *b.* St. John, N.B., 2 April, 1865; *s.* of Hon. T. W. Anglin, for some time Speaker of Can. House of Commons, and Ellen McTavish; *m.* Harriet I., *y. d.* of the late Archibald Fraser, of Fraserfield, Co., Glengarry, Ont.; two *s.* three d. *Educ.:* St. Mary's Coll., Montreal, and Univ. of Ottawa Called to Ontario Bar 1888; cr. K.C., 1902; Puisne Judge, Ont. High Ct., 1904; Judge of the Sup. Ct. of Can., Feb., 1909. *Publications:* "Trustees' Limitations of Actions and other relief." *Address:* 97 St. Joseph St., Toronto. *Clubs:* Rideau, Ottawa, Toronto, Royal Can. Yacht, Toronto.

ANGLIN, Margaret Mary, actress; *b.* Ottawa, Ont., Apr. 3, 1876; *d.* Timothy Warren and Ellen Allen. *Educ.:* Loretto Abbey, Toronto, and Convent of the Sacred Heart, Montreal; grad. Empire Sch. of Dramatic Acting, New York, 1894. Made professional debut in "Shenandoah," New York, Sept., 1894; leading lady with James O'Neil, playing in "Tue Courier of Lyons," "Virginius," "Hamlet," "Monte Cristo," 1896-7; leading woman with E. H. Sothern, 1897-8, Richard Mansfield, 1898-9, and in Empire Theatre Stock Co.; starred in "Zira," 1905-6; co-star with Henry Miller, in "The Great Divide," 1906-7; starred throughout the Australian continent for six months in 1908; travelled around the world afterwards for pleasure. Her own manager Sept. 1909, when she produced "The awakeing of Helen Ritchie," with much success at Savoy Theatre, New York City. *Recreations:* golf, horse-back riding, music and sea fishing. *Address:* 25 West 42nd St., New York City.

ANGUS, Richard Bladworth; *b.* Bathgate, nr. Edinburgh, Scot., 28 May, 1831; married; three *s.* five *d.* *Educ.:* Bathgate. For several yrs. in employ of the Manchester and Liverpool Bank at Manchester; arrived in Canada, 1857, and joined staff of Bank of Montreal; placed in charge of the Chicago agency, 1861, and subsequently apptd. one of the agents at New York; became local mgr. at Montreal; gen. mpr. 1869, but retired from active connection, 1879. Dir. Canadian Pacific Ry., Bank of Montreal, the Canada North-West Land Co., the London and Lancashire Life Insur, Co., the Dom. Bridge Co., the Laurentide Paper Co.; was pres. of the Art Assn., 1888-9; pres. of the Bd. of Governors of the Royal Victoria Hospital; governor McGill Univ.; governor and pres., Fraser Inst. *Address:* 240 Drummond St., Montreal. *Clubs:* St. James, Mount Royal, Forest and Stream, Montreal; Rideau, Ottawa; Toronto; Manitoba, Winnipeg; Union, Halifax.

ANNABLE, Harry Dexter; genl. freight agent for C. P. R. in Gt. Britain and Europe; *b.* Ottawa, 6 Aug., 1871; *s.* Wm. Alva Annable and Ellen Esme MacMillan; unmarried. *Educ.:* Ottawa Coll. Inst. Entered service of the Canadian Pacific Railway Company, Montreal District Freight Office, Ottawa, Sept., 1891; transferred to General Freight Department, Montreal, Feb., 1892; appointed Travelling Freight Agent for Ontario and Quebec Division, with Headquarters at Montreal, June 1, 1898; appointed Contracting Freight Agent for Great Britain and Europe, April, 1901, with Headquarters at London; appointed General Freight Agent for Great Britain and Europe, April, 1903, with Headquarters at London. *Recreations:* golf, motoring. *Adress:* Sports' Club, St. James' Sqr., London, Eng. *Clubs:* Sports, Royal Automobile; London, Eng.

ANNABLE, Weldon Grant; genl. pass. Manager, Canadian Pacific Railway Steamship Lines; *b.* Ottawa. Ont., 3 March, 1875; *s.* of William A. and Ellen E. Annable; *m.* Florence E. McDonald, *d.* of Kenneth McDonald, Ottawa; two *s.* and one d. *Educ.:* Ottawa; entered service of Can. Pacific Ry., at Ottawa; transferred to General Passenger Dept., Jan., 1900, Montreal; appointed General Baggage Agent for all lines of company, Nov., 1905; appointed General Passenger Manager at Montreal, of the Company's Steamship lines, Jan., 1909. *Residence:* 5 Hilton Av., Montreal.

ANTLIFF, Rev. James Cooper, M.A., D. D.; *b.* Huddersfield, Yorkshire, Eng., 1 Feb., 1844; *s.* of William Antliff, D.D., and Barbara Cooper; *m.* (1st) Fanny Holden, of Dalbury Lees, Derbyshire, (2nd) Jane Elizabeth Ray Gooderham, Toronto; three *s.* and one *d.* *Educ.:* Haslingden Wesleyan

School, and Edinburgh University; arrived in Canada, 1878; methodist minister in English Conference, and since 1878 in Methodist Church in Canada; Secretary of first General Conference, 1883; President of Montreal Conference, 1890; Professor in Wesleyan College, Montreal, 1894-1910; at present Pastor of the Methodist Church, Acton, Ont. *Address:* Acton, Ont.

APOSTOLIC DELEGATION to Canada; see **Sbarretti, Most Rev. Donatus,** D. D.

ARCHAMBEAULT, Hon. Horace, D.C.L. (Laval Univ.); Judge of the Court of Appeal; *b.* L'Assomption, Que., 6 March, 1857; *s.* of the late Hon. Louis Archambeault and Elizabeth Dugal; *m.* 1882, Elizabeth, *d.* of Roger Lelièvre, of Quebec. *Educ.:* L'Assomption Coll., Laval Univ. Has practiced in Montreal since called to the Bar; became member of the firm of Rainville, Archambeault, Gervais & Rainville, 1889. Apptd. Prof. of Commercial and Maritime Law in Laval Univ., 1882; apptd. a Q.C., 1889; Attorney-Gen. of Prov. of Que., 1897-1905; apptd. to present position 16 Sept., 1908. *Address:* Pine Ave. Apts., Montreal. *Clubs:* St. James', St. Denis, Forest and Stream, Montreal.

ARCHAMBEAULT, Mgr. Joseph Alfred; Bishop of Joliette, Que.; *b.* L'Assomption, Que., 23 May, 1859; *s.* Louis Archambeault and Elizabeth Dugal. *Educ.:* L'Assomption; Montreal Seminary and Rome. consecrated first B. of Joliette, 24 Aug., 1904. *Address:* Joliette, Que.

ARCHIBALD, Peter Suthro, C. E.; member of American and Canadian Societies of Civil Engineers; *b.* Truro, N.S., 21 Mar., 1848; *s.* of William Archibald and Elizabeth Blair; *m.* Claris G. Lindsey, of Rockland, Maine, U.S.; two *s.* and two *d. Educ.:* Truro Normal School; Asst. Engineer on I. C. Ry., from 1869 to 1879; chief engineer to 1897. Has been practicing profession since, and now commissioner of railways for the New Brunswick Government, and manager of Elgin and Havelock Railway. *Recreations:* motoring and golf. *Residence:* Moncton, N.B.

ARCHIBALD, Hon. John Sprott, B.A., M.A., B.C.L., D.C.L. (McGill University); a Puisne Judge of the Superior Court of the Prov. of Que., since 1893; *b.* Musquodoboit, N.S., 8 Sept., 1843; *s.* of William Archibald and Nancy Archibald; *m.* 1871, Ellen Hutchinson of Bluevale, Ont.; four *s.* one *d. Educ.:* Presbyterian Seminary, Truro, N.S., McGill Univ., where he won the Prince of Wale's Gold Medal, 1867, and the Elizabeth Torrance Gold Medal, 1870. Called to the Bar, 1871; apptd. lecturer on Criminal Law at McGill Univ., 1871; became Prof. of Commercial Law and governor of Univ., 1894; alderman of Montreal, 1884-1890; apptd. a Revising Officer under the Electrial Franchise Act of 1885, and held office until 1896. *Address:* 113 Mackay St., Montreal. *Club:* University.

ARGUE, James, M.L.A.; *b.* North of Ireland, 1852; *s.* of Robert and Rebecca Argue; *m.* Emma Laura Sholy; one *s.* one *d. Educ.:* Ireland. Arrived in Canada, 1874; farmed in Ontario for 8 years, and in Manitoba, since 1882; was a member of Municipal Council for 15 years, and has been mem. of Leg. Assembly of Manitoba for ten years. *Residence:* Elgin Village, Manitoba.

ARMSTRONG, Bartholomew Mahon; Controller, Railway Mail Service Branch, Post Office Dept.; *b.* Lloydtown, Ont., 31 March, 1849; *s.* of the late Col. Arthur Armstrong and Olivia Mahon; *m.* 1876, Emma L., *d.* of W. J. Alexander, of Toronto, three *c. Educ.:* Com. Sch., Gram. Sch., Paris, Ont.; Toronto Military Sch. (obtained a First Grade Military Certificate, 1865). Joined Toronto Field Battery,, and served in Fenian Raids (medal and clasp); served as Lieut. of Marines on the gunboat Prince Albert; retired from the service with rank of capt., 1873. Apptd. to the Toronto Post Office as a clerk; supt., 1896; Controller of the Railway Mail Service, 1896. *Address:* 33 Cooper St., Ottawa.

ARMSTRONG, George E., M. D. (McGill); *b.* Leeds, Que., 1854; *s.* of Rev. John Armstrong; *m.* 1878, Miss Hadley. *Educ.:* Pub. Schs. and McGill Univ. Commenced practice of his profession in Montreal, and has since travelled and studied abroad principally in England, Germany and France. Mem. Medical Faculty of McGill Univ., for nearly twenty yrs,. and Prof. of Clinical Surgery that inst. since 1896; attending Surgeon at Montreal Gen. Hospital and Consulting Surgeon of Western Hospital and Protestant Hospital for Insane; past-pres., and mem. Medico-Chirurgical Soc., British Medical Assn., Canadian Medical Assn., American Medical Assn., and Assn. Internationale d'Urologie; Senator of Wesleyan Theological Coll., Montreal. *Publications:* Has contributed to several medical journals and text-books. His was the first important paper on the Surgical Treatment of Haemorrhage from the Stomach read in London, before British Medical Assn. Author of article on Surgery of the Pancreas in Buck's Reference Hand-book of the Medical Sciences: the Surgery of the Infectious Diseases in Keen's Surgery; the Surgery of the Tongue and Salivary Glands in American Practice of Surgery, Bryant & Buck. *Recreations:* horseback riding. *Address:* 320 Mountain St., Montreal. *Clubs:* Mount Royal, University, Montreal.

ARMSTRONG, Hon. Hugh, M. L. A.; Prov. Treas. for Manitoba; *b.* New York, Aug., 1858. Came to Can. with his parents in 1860, and *educ.* at Richmond, Ont.; *m.* 1885, Mary, *d.* of Henry Younghusband, of Carleton Co., Ont. Removed to Manitoba, 1883; settled in Portage la Prairie, 1886, and engaged in fish export industry. El. to Manitoba Legis, for Woodlands, at g. c., 1892; resigned, 1896, to contest Selkirk for H. of C., but unsuccessful; el. to Man. Legis. by accl. for Portage la Prairie, 7 Feb., 1902; re-el. at g. e., 1903 and 1907. *Recreation:* travel. *Address:* Portage la Prairie. *Clubs:* Manitoba, Commercial, Advance, Winnipeg.

ARMSTRONG, Joseph E., M.P.; Oil producer, manufacturer and farmer; *b.* York Co., Ont., 9 Nov., 1864; *s.* of Elijah Armstrong, and Sarah Brown; *m.* 30 Dec., 1891, Margaret J. Phipps, *d.* of James Shilly Phipps, West Chester, Pa. An unsuccessful independent candidate for H. of C., 1896, elected at bye-election, 1904; re-elected

1904 and 1908; Presbyterian; Conservative. *Address:* Petrolia, Ont.

ARNAND, Elias de Barbazau; *b.* London, Eng., 20 Oct., 1847; *s.* of Elias M. Arnand, late Controller General H. M. Customs, London, Eng., and Anna M. Norris; *m.* Constance Walcot, *e. d.* of the late Charles Walcot, Indian Dept., Ottawa, Ont.; five *s.* and four *d.* *Educ.:* Somersetshire College, Eng. Arrived in Canada, 1 July, 1868; entered Bank of British North America, at London, in 1867, and served continuously in the banking business in Canada, until 1905, when appointed Canadian Trade Commissioner in Chicago; transferred to Newfoundland, 1906, and to Bristol, Eng., 1909. *Recreations:* golf, walking. *Address:* 71 Woodland Road, Tyndalls Park, Bristol, Eng. *Clubs:* Constitutional and Liberal, Bristol, Eng.

ARNOLDI, Frank, K.C.; *b.* Montreal, 3 April, 1848; *s.* of F. C. T. Arnoldi, M.D., and Christina M. Arnoldi; *m.* Louise Fauquier, *d.* of Aemelius A. H. Fauquier, late of Woodstock, Ont.; three *s.* and two *d.* *Educ.:* Upper Canada College, Toronto, Ont. Called to the Bar, Ont., 1870; created K.C., 1889; elected a governor of Upper Canada College, 1895, and has been elected annually since. *Address:* Toronto. *Club:* National, Toronto.

ARSENAULT, Aubin Edmond, M. L. A.; Barrister-at-Law; *b.* Edmont Bay, P.E.I., 28 July, 1870; *s.* Joseph O. Arsenault, and Gertrude Gaudet; *m.* Bertha Rose, *d.* of late Capt. F. Gallant of Tiguish, P.E.I.; one *s.* *Educ.:* St. Dunstan's College, Charlottetown, P.E.I., and St. Joseph's College, Memramcook, N.B.; studied law with McLeod, Morrison and McQuarrie, Charlottetown, and Hon. Charles Russell, London, Eng.; admitted P.E.I. Bar, Nov., 1898. Practicing in Summerside, P.E.I., in partnership with Neil McQuarrie, K.C.; elected to Prince Edward Island Leg. Ass., at g. e., Nov., 1908. Liberal-Conservative in Politics. *Recreations:* fishing and reading. *Address:* Summerside, P. E. Island.

ARTHUR, Julia (Mrs. Cheney); *b.* in Hamilton, Ont., May 3, 1869, of Irish and Welsh parentage; real name, Ida Lewis, stage name being taken from her mother's maiden name of Arthur; *m.* 28 Nov., 1898, to Benjamin B. Cheney, Jr., of Boston, Mass. At 11 played in amateur dramatic club, taking part of Gamora in The Honeymoon and of Portia in The Merchant of Venice; 3 yrs. later made professional debut as the Prince of Wales in Daniel Bandmanns presentation of Richard III; remained 3 seasons with that co.; studied violin music and dramatic art in England: first New York success at Union Sq. Theatre in The Black Masque; later in A. M. Palmer's co., in several roles, notably in Mercedes, 1893; London debut, Feb. 1, 1895, in Henry Irving's co., playing roles next to Miss Terry; especially successful as Rosamond in A'Becket, with Irving and Terry in U.S., 1896. Retired from the stage after her marriage. *Addresses:* Boston, Mass.; 41 Spring St., Hamilton, Ont.

ARTHURS, James, M.P., Hardware Merchant, *b.* Toronto, Ont., 6 Oct., 1866; *s.* of John Arthurs, Belfast, Ireland, and Margaret Arthurs, Sterling, Scot.; *m.* 12 Sept., 1887, Elizabeth P. Gillespie, Orangeville, Ont.; four *s.* and three *d.* *Educ.:* Public Schools, and Hamilton Coll. Inst., first el. to H. of C., 1908; Presbyterian; Conservative. *Address:* Powassan, Ont.

ASHDOWN, J. H., Pres of the Ashdown Hardware Co., Winnipeg; *b.* London, Eng., 1844; *s.* of William Ashdown and Jane Watling; married; one *s.* three *d.* Arrived in Canada with his parents 1852. At eleven yrs. of age commenced work in his father's store at Weston, York Co. Learned trade of tinsmith at Hespeler, Ont.; went west and arrived at Red River settlement 30 June, 1868. A prisoner in Fort Garry during first Riel Rebellion. Has been active in religious political, educational and municipal life of Winnipeg; ex-pres. of the Bd. of Trade; one of the founders of Wesley Coll.; governor of the City Hospital; dir. of the Y. M. C. A.; for many yrs. a mem. of the City Council; Mayor 1906, 1907. *Address:* Winnipeg. *Club:* Manitoba, Winnipeg.

ASHLEY, Rev. Barnas Freeman; *b.* Liverpool, Nova Scotia, Nov. 27, 1833; *s.* Rev. William Washington and Hannah Kempton Ashley; *m.* Nov. 26, 1857, Caroline L. Goodspeed, Osterville, Mass. *Educ.:* public schools, Barrington, N.S.; classical and theol. course under private tutors in Boston; 3 yrs'. med. course, Ohio Med. Coll., Cleveland, Ohio. In active pastorate 43 yrs., of Bapt. chs., and later of Reformed (Dutch) Ch., New York. Began to write poems and sketches at 16; lately writer of short stories for McClure syndicate, and books for boys. *Publications:* Tan-Pile Jim; Dick and Jack's; Adventures on Sable Island; Air Castle Don., etc. *Address:* Ravenna, Ohio, U.S.A.

ASHWORTH, Alice; see **Mrs. Townley.**

ASKIN, James Wallace; Registrar of Deeds, Co. of Essex; *b.* Sandwich, Ont., 25 May, 1848; *s.* of John Alexander, and Melina Askin; *m.* Eliza Mary, *d.* of the late Charles Baby, of Sandwich, Ont.; six *d.* *Educ.:* Sandwich Coll. and St. Hyacinthe Coll., Quebec. Has been Registrar of Deeds for the Co. of Essex for thirty eight yrs., succeeding his father, who succeeded his father, the late Col. James Askin. Capt., with medal, for services in rebellions of 1866 and 1870. *Address:* Windsor, Ont.

ASSELIN, Olivar (Joseph Francois); Journalist, *b.* St. Hilarion, Charlevoix Co., Que., 9 Nov., 1874; *s.* of Rieule Asselin and Cedulie Tremblay; *m.* Alice Le Boutillier; three *s.* *Educ.:* Rimouski Coll. In varied businesses for eight yrs. in U.S.; editor of Woonsocket *Daily Tribune*, Woonsocket *Star*; served as a private in Cuban War. Returned to Canada in 1900; in journalism since, except two yrs., priv. sec. to Sir Lomer Gouin. Founded *Le Nationaliste;* one of the leaders of the Nationalist party. *Publications:* "Feuilles de combat." *Recreations:* Hand-ball, fishing. *Address:* 85 B. Drolet St., Montreal.

ATKINSON, Joseph E., managing editor, the Toronto *Star*; *b.* Newcastle, Ont., 23 Nov., 1865; *s.* John and Hannah Atkinson; *m.* Elmena Elliott; one *s.* one *d.* *Educ.:* Newcastle High School; entered newspaper work in 1884 in Port Hope "*Times;*" joined Toronto *World* in 1888; Toronto *Globe*, in

1889; appointed editor Montreal *Herald*, in 1896; joined new company purchasing Toronto Daily *Star*, in 1899, and has since had charge of that paper; was one of the Canadian delegates to the Imperial Press Conference at London, 1909. *Club:* National, Toronto.

ATKINSON, Mrs. Elmina; *b.* Oakville, Ont.; *m.* Joseph E. Atkinson, Managing editor Toronto Star; one *s.* one *d.* *Educ.:* Oakville; engaged in 1891 in journalism on the Toronto Globe, and still writes under the nom-de-plume of "Madge Merton." Has done work for many daily papers and magazines. *Address:* 64 Glen Road, Toronto.

ATKINSON, William Edwin, A.R.C.A.; *b.* Toronto, Ont., 22 March, 1862; *s.* of W. T. and Emma Atkinson; *m.* Laura Dredge; two *s.* *Educ.:* Paris, France, Philadelphia, Pa., and Toronto Ont.; landscape painter; awarded highest prlze for best picture of the year 1902, in Toronto; pictures purchased by the Canadian Government. *Residence:* 20 Durie St., Toronto.

AUDEN, Henry William, M.A. Cantab.; Principal, Upper Canada College, Toronto; *b.* 1867; *s.* of Preb. T. Auden; *m.* 1896, Constance, *d.* of Rev. F. W. Kittermaster of Meriden, Warwickshire, Eng.; two *s.* two *d.* *Educ.:* Shrewsbury School; Christ's College, Camb. (scholar and prizeman); Porteous gold medal for Latin Prose; Bell Univ. Scholar; 1st class, class Tripos, 1889; 1890; Marburg University, 1891; 6th Form Master and Librarian at Fettes College, Edinburgh, 1891-1903; came to Can. in latter year. *Publications:* editor, Cicero pro Plancio, Plautus Pseudolus, Meissner Latin Phrase Book, Higher Latin Prose, Greek Prose, Latin and Greek Unseens, Cicero in Catilinam, Greek Prose Phrase Book; The Messenian Wars; A Minimum of Greek; Member, Classical Society of Scotland; Canadian Society of Authors, etc. *Recreations:* fishing and botany. *Address:* Upper Canada College, Toronto. *Club:* Toronto.

AUDETTE, Rodolphe; pres. of La Banque Nationale, Que.; *b.* Quebec, Que., 5 Aug., 1844; *s.* of John Audette and Flore Fraser; *m.* 1867, Elise, d. of J. Morency, of Quebec; three *s.* seven *d.* *Educ.:* Thom's Academy, Quebec. Entered firm of Thibaudeau, Thomas & Co. (now Thibaudeau, Frere & Cie), as junior clerk, 1863; became a partner, 1883, and senior mem. 1894; pres. La Banque Uationale; vice-pres. Can. Electric Light Co., Levis Co., Ry. Co., Quebec Bridge Co.; mem. Quebec Bd. of Trade. *Address:* 1 Collins St., Quebec. *Club:* Garrison.

AUSTIN, Albert William; *b.* Toronto, Ont., 27 March, 1857; *s.* of James and Susan Austin; *m.* Maria R. Kerr; two *s.* three *d.* *Educ.:* Upper Canada College; vice-pres. Consumer's Gas Co., Toronto; director Dominion Bank, Toronto. Introduced the first electric over-head trolley cars into Canada, at Winnipeg, Man.; founded the Lambton Golf and Country Clubs, and for six yrs., its president; now Honorary President. *Recreation:* golf. *Address:* "Spadena," Toronto. *Clubs:* National, Lambton Golf, Toronto.

AYLMER, Hon. Henry; sheriff of the dist. of St. Francis, Que.; *b.* Melbourne, Que., 25 April, 1843; *s.* of the 7th Baron Aylmer; *m.* 1871, Louisa Blanche Fanny, d. of H. A. Howe, LL.D., Montreal. *Educ.:* Montreal High Sch., Royal Naval Coll., Portsmouth, Eng. Called to the Bar 1882, and pracitced at Richmond, Que.; mem. H. of C. for Richmond and Wolfe 1874-1878; uncuscessfully contested Richmond for seat in Que. Legis., 1880; defeated at Dom. g. e., for Sherbrooke, 1896; apptd. sheriff of dist. of St. Francis, 1900. Trustee, St. Francis Coll. and Gram. Sch.; mem. corporation Bishop's Coll., Lennoxville. Organized Richmond Field Battery of Artillery, 1876; retired Nov., 1887, with rank of Lieut.-Col; commanded Wimbledon Rifle Team, 1887; served for twelve yrs. in Royal Marine Artillery, and gazetted at Lieut. *Address:* Melbourne, Que.

AYLMER, Lord (The Right Hon. Sir Matthew), 8th Baron de Balrath, peerage of Ireland; *b.* Richmond, Que., 28 March, 1842; *s.* of Udolphus, Lord Aylmer, 7th Baron, and Mary, *d.* of Edward Journeaux, of Dublin, Irel.; *m.* 1875, Amy Gertrude, *d.* of the late Hon. John Young, of Montreal; three *s.* two *d.* *Educ.:* Montreal High Sch., McGill Univ., Dublin; served six yrs. as Lieut. in 7th Royal Fus., and 35 yrs. on staff of Can. Forces; retired from Inspector-Generalship, 1907, with rank of Major-Gen. Succeeded to title 1901. Served in Fenian Raids 1866-70. Hon.-Col. 11th Hussars, Richmond, Que., now engaged in fruit farming in British Columbia. *Address:* Queen's Bay, Kootenay, Lake B.C.

AUDETTE, Louis Arthur, B.D., LL.B. (Laval Univ.), K.C. (Que); *b.* Quebec city, 14 Dec., 1856; *s.* George Semeon Audette and Rosalie L. Mareon; *m.* Mary Grace Stuart, *d.* of late Sir Andrew Stuart, Chief Justice, Que., and Elmin C. de Gaspe; four *s.* and one *d.* *Educ.:* Seminary of Quebec and Laval University; Barrister in Pravince of Quebec; at one time deputy prothonotary Quebec; appointed Registrar Exechequer Court of Canada, 8 Nov., 1887. *Publications:* "The Practice of the Exchequer Court of Canada, first editions, 1895; 2nd edition in 1909. *Address:* 161 Daly Ave., Ottawa.

AYLESWORTH, Hon. Allen Bristol, M.A., K.C., P.C., M.P.; *b.* Newburgh, Ont., 27 Nov., 1854; *s.* John Bell Aylesworth and Catharin Bristol; *m.* Adelaide Augusta Miller; one *s.* *Educ.:* Newburgh High School, Toronto, University College; barrister and Attorney in Ontario since Aug., 1878; was one of His Majesty's Commissioners for the settlement of the Alaska Boundary, in 1903; appointed Pastmaster-General, 16 Oct., 1905; Minister of Justice, 4 June, 1906. *Residence:* Ottawa, Ont. *Clubs:* Toronto, Toronto; Rideau, Ottawa.

AYER, Albert Azro; *b.* nr. Freleighsburg, Que., 6 Feb., 1845; *s.* of George W., and Mary Ayer; *m.* Rebecca C. Hibbard; five *s.* two *d.* *Educ.:* Stanbridge Acad. and Fairfax, Vt. Commenced business as exporter of butter and cheese, 1867; now pres. A. A. Ayer & Co., Ltd.; has been connected with the dairy industry since the first cheese were exported from Canada.

Address: 388 Roslyn Av., Montreal. *Club:* Canada, Montreal.

B

BABIN, Rear Admiral Hosea John; *b.* in Can., Dec. 15, 1842. Apptd. acting asst. surgeon U.S.N., from Mass., Feb. 10, 1865; asst. surgeon, Mar. 13, 1865; passed asst. surgeon, June 23, 1869; surgeon, Mar 17, 1876; med. insp., June 22, 1894; med. dir., May 7, 1898; retired, Dec. 15, 1904; advanced to rank of rear admiral for services during Civil War. Mem. Bd. of Inspection and Survey, Jan. 23-June 22, 1894: pres. Med. Examining Bd. at New York, Oct. 5, 1897-May 7, 1898; in charge Naval Hosp., New York, 1900-4. *Address:* Care C. A. Betts, 126 Broadway, Brooklyn.

BADGLEY, Sidney Rose; *b.* Ernestown, Ont., May 28, 1850; *s.* William Edwin and Nancy Rose Badgley; *m.* (1st) 1872, Alma A. Clark (*d.* 1874); (2nd) Charlotte J. Cillo land, St. Catharines, Ont., Sept. 21, 1876; *Educ.:* pub. schs. and acad.; studied architecture under R. C. Windeyer, Toronto, Can.; went to U. S., 1887; specialist in ch. architecture; has built chs. and other bldgs. in various parts of U. S. and Can. *Address:* Springbank, Wickliffe, O. *Office:* 6110 Euclid Av., Cleveland.

BAILLIE, John; *b.* Montreal, 1858; *s.* of Andrew Baillie and Isabella Irwin; *m.* 1886, Maggie, *d.* of the late Donald Fraser, of Montreal; two *s.* two *d.* *Educ.:* private tuition, Arnold's and McGill Model Sch. In employ of a paint, oil and chemical firm for nine yrs.; estb. a similar business 1883, which he sold out in 1886, and became mgr. Dominion Oilcloth Co., Ltd.; now managing dir. Pres., Canada Linseed Oil Co.; governor Montreal Gen. Hospital, Western Hospital, Protestant House of Industry and Refuge. *Recreations:* golf, curling. *Address:* 133 Crescent St., Montreal. *Clubs:* St. James', Royal Montreal Golf, Montreal; Montreal Curling.

BAIN, John, gen. mgr. International Marine Signal Co.; *b.* Paisley, Scot., 8 June, 1869; *s.* of Robert and Agnes Bain; *m.* Maude Buckley, *d.* of P. Buckley, Paris, Ont.; two *d*; arrived in Canada, May, 1888. *Educ.:* Paisley, Scot.; private secretary to Hon. Wm. Paterson, Minister of Customs for 11 yrs.; Asst. Com. of Customs, 4 yrs.; secretary Tariff Commission, 1906-07; secretary to Canadian Ministers on trade questions at Coronation Imperial Conference, 1902; now associated with Hon. Clifford Sifton in various business enterprises; also Imperial trade correspondent at Ottawa. *Address:* 167 James St., Ottawa. *Clubs:* Laurentian, Ottawa; Ontario, Toronto.

BAIRD, Hon. George Thomas, Senator; *b.* Andover, N.B., 3 Nov., 1847; *s.* of George Baird and Frances Jane Bishop; *m.* Ida Jane Sadler; two *s.* one *d.* *Educ.:* Carleton Co. Gram. Sch; born on a farm; taught Andover Gram. Sch. for five years; carried on lumbering and general store since 1874; occupied seat in N.B. Legislature for 10 yrs.; two of which he was in Legislative Council; called to Senate 1895. *Address:* Andover, N.B.

BAKER, Alfred, M.A.; *b.* Toronto, of Yorkshire parents; *m.* 1894, Norah Kathleen, *d.* of John McCormack of Wilmette, Illinois. *Educ.:* Toronto Univ.; Mathematical Master Upper Can. Coll., 1872-5; Mathematical lecturer Univ. Coll., Toronto, 1875-87; registrar 1880-7; dean of residence 1884-90; Professor of Mathematics, 1887; elected by graduates a member of Senate of Univ. of Toronto, 1887-1906; Lieutenant and Captain, Queen's Own Rifles, 1876-83; F.R.S. Canada, member of the Societe Mathematique de France and of the American Mathematical Society; president, Ont. Educational Society, 1895; president, Section III, R. S. C., 1905; member of Executive Committee, Brit. Empire League in Canada; with Dr. John Seath re-organized geometrical teaching in schools of Ontario, 1904; *Publications:* articles relating to Quaterninous, Geometry of Position, and Foundations of Geometry (translated into Japanese) in proceedings of R. S. C.; also works on synthetic and analytic Geometry, Trigonometry, and Mechanics. *Recreations:* walking and rowing. *Addresses:* 81 Madison Av., Toronto; in summer, Ishkauqua, Lake Rosseau, Muskoka. *Club:* Canadian Military Institute, Toronto.

BAKER, Francis Spence, F.R.I. of B.A., F.R.I.C.; *b.* Co. of Halton, Ont., 21 Aug., 1867; *s.* Francis Baker of Dublin, Ireland and Sarah Georgina Spence, Co. of Halton, Ont., *m.* Florence Mary Kenrick, Shropshire, Eng.; two *s.* one *d.* *Educ.:* Hamilton, Ont.; practicing as Architect in Toronto, since 1892. *Publications:* principally magazine articles. *Recreation:* golf. *Address:* 185 Balmoral Av., Toronto. *Club:* Rosedale Golf Club, Toronto.

BAKER, Hon. George Barnard, M. A., K.C.; *b.* Dunham, Que., 26 Jan., 1834 (of U.E.L. descent). *Educ.:* Bishop's Coll., Lennoxville; Solicitor-General for Quebec, 1876-78; el. to H. of C. for Missisquoi Co., Que., 1870-74, 1878-1887, 1891-1896. Called to Senate in latter yr. for the Bedford dist. *Address:* Sweetsburg, Que.

BAKER, J. Allen, M.P. (Britain) Eastern Finsbury since 1905; member, L.C.C.; Chairman, Baker and Sons, Ltd., Willesden, *b.* Canada. *Educ.:* Trenton High Sch.; entered his father's business (engineering) in 1876, went to London in connection with his business. Has been prominently connected with tramway extension in the L.C.C.; contested East Finsbury, 1900. *Address:* Donnington, Harlesden, London, N.W.

BAKER, Lieut.-Col. Jesse Wheelock, M. L.A., J.P.; *b.* Baker Brook, Madawaska Co., N.B., 30 Nov., 1854; *s.* of Enoch Baker, of Fort Kent Aroostook Co., Maine; *s.* of Gen. John Baker of the U. S. Army, and Madeline Ouillet, of St. Paschal, Que.; *m.* Betsaide Martin; two *s.* two *d.* *Educ.:* Common Schs. of N.B.; spent his early days on his father's farm at Baker Brook; owned a small saw mill, but gave it up and became a lumber scaler and forest inspector, in which business he still continues; enlisted in 1872 in the 67th Regt., Carleton Light Infantry, and rose to the command as Lieut.-Col.; served 34 years as an officer (decoration); was Captain of G. Co., of the N.B. and P.E.I. provisional Regt., raised for service in the North West Rebellion, and commanded the Maritime Province composite Regiment at the Quebec Tercentenary; elected to the legislature of N.B. for Madawaska, March, 1908; declined nomination for legislature in 1903; also for H. of C., 1908; Conservative. *Address:* Baker Brook, Madawaska Co., N.B.

BAKER, Walter Reginald, Secy. C.P.R., Montreal; 3rd class, order of Sacred Treasure, Japan; *b.* York, Eng., 25 May, 1852; *s.* of Stephia and Priscilla Willing Kimsoll Baker, married; one *s.* three *d.* Arrived in Canada Nov., 5, 1865; *Educ.:* Privately in York and London, Eng. Had charge as the representative of the C. P. Ry. Co., of the tours through Canada, of T. R. H. The Prince and Princess of Wales in 1901; of Prince Arthur of Connaught, 1906, and Prince Fushimi, of Japan, 1907; was connected with the Allan Steamship Co., for eight years after his arrival in Canada; from 1873 to 1874, local freight and passenger agent at Ottawa, of the Canada Central Ry.; the following five years was private secretary and A.D.C., to Earl of Dufferin, Governor General; has been Asst.-Secretary Treasury Board, Ottawa; asst. to Gen'l. Supt., C. P. Ry., Western Division; Asst to Gen'l. Mgr. P. P. Ry.; Gen'l. Supt., Man. & Western Ry., Winnipeg, and later Gen'l. Manager; Executive Agent, C. P. Ry., Winnipeg; Asst. to vice-pres., C. P. Ry.; Asst. to pres., and now Secretary C. P. Ry. Co., Montreal. *Address:* 773 Sherbrooke St., Montreal. *Recreations:* golf. *Clubs:* Mount Royal, St. James', and Royal Montreal Golf, Montreal; Rideau, Country, Ottawa; Manitoba, Winnipeg.

BALFOUR, George Hopper, gen. mgr. Union Bank of Canada, Quebec; *b.* Frost Village, Que., 5 April, 1848; *s.* Rev. Andrew and Eliza Balfour; *m.* Alice Charlotte Shaw (*dec.*); two *s.* three *d.* *Educ.:* Lennoxville After some years in a merchant's and stock broker's office, joined the staff of the Union Bank in 1870, passing through all grades to position of gen. mgr; active in military affairs for many years; Fenian Raid, 1870; retired from 8th Royal Rifles (Captain), 1886; winner of P. Q. Rifle Assoc. championship, and Governor-General's prize at Ottawa, 1880; member of the Canadian Wimbledon Team, 1881, which won the Kolapore Cups. *Recreations:* golf, curling; Capt. of the Royal Montreal Club for several years; an ex-president of the Royal Canadian Golf Assn; a former president of the Can. branch of the Royal Caledonian Curling Club. *Address:* 57, The Esplanade, and Union Bank of Canada, Quebec. *Clubs:* Garrison, Quebec; St. James', Montreal; Manitoba, Winnipeg.

BALLANTYNE, Charles Colquhoun; *b.* Dundas Co., Ont., 9 Aug., 1867; *s.* of the late John Ballantyne, native of Scotland; *m.* 1901, Ethel, *d.* of Thomas A. Trenholme, of Montreal West; two *s.* *Educ.:* pub. schs. of Ont., and Montreal. In 1882, entered employ of a paint concern; 1895 became sales mgr. of the Sherwin-Williams Co., of Cleveland, Ohio, in Canada; 1898, apptd. mgr. of the entire Canadian business. Dir. Canada Consolidated Rubber Co.; mem Can. Manufacturers' Assn., and was first vice-pres., 1899 ; mem. Montreal Board of Trade, Chambre de Commerce; apptd. a Harbor Commr., 1907. *Address:* Montreal West, Que. *Clubs:* St. James', Canada, Montreal.

BALLANTYNE, Robert Mitchell, *b.* Stratford, Ont., 20 Aug., 1859; *s.* Hon. Thos. and Mary Ballantyne: *m.* Charlotte L. Scott; one *s.* two *d.* *Educ.:* Stratford schs.; ex-pres. Dairymen's Ass'n of Western Ont.; ex-pres. Montreal Produce Merchants' Assn.; second vice-pres. Montreal Board of Trade; director Lake of the Woods Milling Co., man. director, Lavell, Christmas, Ltd., Montreal. *Address:* 30 Farden Av., Westmount. *Clubs:* St. James', Montreal.

BARBER, Major John Roy, R.L.; *b.* Georgetown, Ont., 5 July, 1841; *s.* James Barber ,Co. Antrim, and Hannah Patrick, Berwickshire; widower; four *s.* two *d.* *Educ.:* Georgetown Collegiate Institute. Has been engaged in the paper and pulp business since 1861, pres. Toronto Paper Co., Cornwall, Ont.; Wm. Barber and Bros., Georgetown, Ont.; The Barber and Ellis Co., Toronto and Brantford; vice-pres. Spanish River Pulp Co., vice-pres. Canada Coated Paper Mills, Georgetown; vice-pres. Anglo American Fire Insurance Co.; Major Canadian Militia (retired); long service and Fenian Raid medals; ex-member of Provincial Parliament, and ex-Warden Co. of Halton. *Address:* Georgetown, Ont., and Mail Building, Toronto. *Club:* National, Toronto.

BARCLAY, Rev. James, D.D.; Pastor of St. Paul's Pres. Church, Montreal; *b.* Paisley, Scotland, 19 June, 1844; *s.* of James Barclay and Margaret Cochrane; *m.* Marion Simpson of Dumfrieshire; five *s.* one *d.* *Educ.:* Paisley Gram. Sch. and Glasgow Univ. Ordained in parish of St. Michaels, Dumfries, 1873. Held several pastoral charges in Scotland, and frequently preached before Queen Victoria at Balmoral. Called to pastorate of St. Paul's Church, Montreal, 1883, and inducted 11 Oct.; since then has been intimately connected with all philanthropic, religious, and patriotic movements in Montreal. Chaplain to Montreal Garrison Artillery and accompanied that corps to North West in 1885. *Recreations:* golf, curling. *Address:* 398 Dorchester W., Montreal.

BARKER, Lewellys Franklin; *b.* Norwich, Ont., Sept. 16, 1867; *s.* James F. and Sarah Jane Taylor Barker; *m.* Oct., 1903, Lilian H. Halsey, New York. *Educ.:* Ont. public schs and Pickering Coll., 1881-4; grad. med. dept. Univ. of Toronto (M.B.), 1890; house phys. Toronto Gen. Hosp., 1890-1; asst. physician, Johns Hopkins Hosp., 1891-2; fellow pathology, 1892-4; asso. anatomy, Johns Hopkins Univ., 1894-7; student Univ. of Leipzig, 1895; asst. resident pathologist, Johns Hopkins Hosp., 1894-9; asso. prof. anatomy, Johns Hopkins Univ., 1897-9; Johns Hopkins Med. Comm'r to Phillippines, 1899; asso, prof. pathology, Johns Hopkins Univ., 1899-1900; prof. and head dept. anatomy, Rush Med. Coll., Univ. of Chicago, 1900-5; grad. work univs. of Munich and Berlin, 1904; prof. medicine, Johns Hopkins Univ. and chief physician Johns Hopkins Hosp. since 1905. mem. sp'l comm'n apptd. by Secretary Treasury to determine existence or non-existence of plague in San Fransicco, 1901. *Publications:* The Nervous System and its Constituent Neurones, 1899; Translation of Werner Spalteholz's Hand Atlas of Human Anatomy, 1900; Laboratory Manual of Human Anatomy, 1904; also numerous med. papers and addresses. *Address:* 6 E. Franklin St., Baltimore, Md., U.S.A.

BARKER, Samuel, M.P.; *b.* Kingston, Ont., 25 May, 1839; *s.* of William and Annie Barker; *m.* (1st) Isabella, *d.* of John and Catherine Cruickshank, London, Ont. (*d.*); (2nd) Helen Cruickshank, *d.* of same. *Educ.:* London Gram. Sch.; was alderman and chairman of Finance, London; was solicitor and general Council G. W. Ry.; general manager N. and N. W. Ry. In 1895 was selected by both directors and malcontent proprietors of G. T. Ry., in England, to examine and analyse the accounts of that company in Canada; contested Hamilton unsuccessfully for H. of C., 1896; elected, 1900; elected for Hamilton East, 1904, and 1908; was twice pres. Hamilton Board of Trade; Church of England; Conservative. *Address:* Hamilton, Ont. *Club:* Rideau, Ottawa.

BARLOW, John Rigny, M. C. S. C. E., City Surveyor, Montreal; *b.* Stornoway, Isle of Lewis, Scotland, 29 July, 1850; *s.* of Robert Barlow, R.E., of the Geological Survey of Can., and Eliza Short; *m.* 1877, Margaret *d.* of the late Rev. William Darrach, Presbyterian clergyman; five *s.* four *d.* Arrived Can. 1855; employed by Geological Survey of Can., 1872-1875; asst. engr. by city of Montreal, 1876-1879; chief asst. to J. A. U. Beaudry, P.L., C.E., 1879-80; became asst. engr., Road Dept., of Montreal, 1880; Deputy City Surveyor; City Surveyor, 1901. *Address.* 52 Park Av., Montreal. *Club:* Engineers'.

BARNARD, George Henry, K.C., M.P.; *b.* Victoria, B.C., 9 Oct., 1868; *s.* Francis Jones Barnard and Ellen Stillman Barnard; *m.* Ethel Burnham, *e. d.* Lt.-Col. H. C. Rogers, Peterboro, Ont. *Educ.:* Trinity Coll. Sch., Port Hope, Ont.; called to the Bar, 1891; K.C. 1907; alderman in Victoria, 1902-1903; Mayor, Victoria, 1904-1905; elec. to H. of C. 1908. *Recreations:* fishing, golf. *Residence:* "Duvals," Victoria, B.C. *Clubs:* Uuion, Victoria; Vancouver; Rideau, Ottawa.

BARNES, Benjamin F., LL.B., Postmaster at Washington, D.C.; *b.* Yarmouth, N.S., Dec. 3, 1868; s. Benjamin H. and Orena Higgins Barnes; *m.* Washington, Oct. 18, 1892, Emily Frech. *Educ.:* pub. schs. of N. J., law dept. Georgetown, (D.C.) Univ.; apptd. clerk in U. S. P. O. dept., under competitive exam., Oct., 1887; pvt. sec. to 1st asst. p. m. gen., Sept., 1889; later pvt. sec. to chief P. O. insp., and to 4th asst. p. m. gen,; sec. to Hon. James S. Clarkson several yrs.; apptd. stenographer at White House, Jan., 1898; exec. clerk, July 1, 1898; apptd. by President McKinley asst. sec. to the President, May 1, 1900; re-apptd. by President Roosevelt, Apr. 22, 1902; post-master, Washington since June 23, 1906. *Address:* 48 R. St., N.E. *Office:* Post Office, Washington.

BARNES, Howard Turner, M.S., D.S.; Macdonald Professor of Physics and Director of the Physics Building, McGill Univ.; *b.* Woburn, Mass., U.S.A., 21 July, 1873; *s.* Wm. S. Barnes and Mary Alice Turner; *m.* Annie Kershaw Cunliffe; two *s.* *Educ.:* McGill Univ.; came to Canada in 1879; held Studenstship Royal Society ,London; F.R.S.C. *Publications:* various original papers, and one book on ice formation. *Address:* 239 Pine Av. West,; McGill University, Montreal.

BARNET, Alexander, lumberman; *b.* Renfrew Co., Ont., 25 Feb., 1840; of Irish descent; *m.* 1867 Jane Greene; four *s.* four *d.* *Educ.:* country sch. At age of fifteen commenced his career as a lumberman. Started business for himself 1861; formed a partnership with late William Mackay and William Bannerman, under name of Barnet, Bannerman & Co., 1865; continued the business under the name of Barnet & Mackay 1876-1884; formed another partnership with Thos. Mackie, M.P., 1869, a dir. of the Bank of Ottawa. *Address:* Renfrew, Ont. *Club:* Rideau, Ottawa.

BARR, James (Angus Evan Abbott); *b.* Wallacetown, Ont., 1862; 5th *s.* Robert Barr, Windsor, Ont., and Jane, *d.* of William Watson, West Glen, Kilmalcolm, Scot.; *m.* Elizabeth Sabel, *d.* of A. C. Wylie, Brook Green, London; three *s.* three d. *Educ.:* Canadian Public Schs.; from 16 to 21 a newspaper rep. in U.S.; since then a journalist in London. *Publications:* The Gods Give My Donkey Wings; The Gods Gave My Donkey Wings; Under the Eaves of Night; The Great Frozen North; The Witchery of the Serpent; Laughing through a Wilderness; The Grey Bat. *Recreations:* cricket, lacrosse, billiards. *Address:* 50 Cambridge Road, Gunnersby. *Club:* London Sketch.

BARR, Robert, novelist; *b.* Glasgow, 16 Sept., 1850; *m.* 1876, Miss Eva Bennett; *Educ.:* Normal Sch., Toronto, Ont.; school teacher in Canada until 1876; then joined editorial staff of the Detroit Free Press, U.S.A.; went to England in 1881; founded the Idler Magazine with Jerome K. Jerome in 1892. *Publications:* In a Steamer Chair, 1892; From whose Bourn, 1893; The Face and the Mask, 1894; Revenge; In the Midst of Alarms, 1894; A Woman Intervenes, 1896; The Mutable Many, 1897; The Countess Tekla, 1899; The Strong Arm, The Unchanging East, 1900; The Tempestuous Petticoat, 1905; A Rock in the Baltic, 1907; *Recreations:* golf, cycling, photography, travel. *Address:* Hillhead, Woldingham, Surry. *Clubs:* Devonshire, Witenagemote.

BARRON, His Hon. John Augustus, K. C., Judge of the County Court, Perth, Ont.; *b.* Toronto, Ont., 11 July, 1850; *s.* Frederick William Barron, M.A., Principal of U. C. Coll., and Eleanor Thompson; *m.* Elizabeth Caroline Clarice 4th *d.* of Hartley Dunsford, Registrar of the Co. of Victoria; two *s.* three *d.* *Educ.:* at Cobourg Gram. Sch., Laval Seminary, Que., and U. C. Coll., Toronto; was member for North Victoria in H. of C., from 1887 to 1892; called to the Bar 1873; created Q.C., in 1888; was elec. as Liberal in 1887 to H. of C.; appointed to the bench in 1897. *Publications:* Author of Barron on Bills of Sataread Chattel Mortgage, a work on Banking, and conditional sales of Chattels. A frequent writer for the Press. *Address:* Stratford, Ont.

BARRY, Mgr. Thomas Francis, D.D., Bishop of Chatham; *b.* Pokemouche, N.B., 3 March, 1841. *Educ.:* St. John Coll., Montreal Coll., and Grand Seminary, Montreal; after ordination was rector of the Cathedral at Chatham, N.B., for some yrs. then pastor of St. Basil, N.B., and Vicar General of the Diocese; afterwards pastor of Caraquet, and finally of Bathurst. Coadjutor Bishop on 11 Feb., 1900; succeeded as Bishop of Chatham, 7 Aug., 1902. *Address:* Chatham, N.B.

BARTON, George Aaron, M.A., Ph.D.; *b.* E. Farmham, Que., Can., Nov. 12, 1859; *s.* Daniel and Mary S. Bull Barton; *m.* 1884, Caroline Brewer Danforth. *Educ.:* Haverford Coll., 1882, 1885; grad. student Harvard, 1888-91. Ins. broker Boston, 1883; teacher higher mathematics and classics Friends' School, Providence, 1884-9; prof. Biblical literature and Semitic languages, Bryn Mawr Coll. since 1891; lecturer on Bible languages, Haverford Coll., 1891-5. Acknowledged minister Society of Friends (orthodox) since Aug., 1879. Dir. Am. School Oriental Study and Research in Palestine, 1902-3. Mem. Phi Beta Kappa, Am. Oriental Soc., Soc. of Bibl. Literature and Exegesis, Archæol. Inst. America, Soc. Bibl. Archæology and Victoria Inst. (London), Contb'r to Ency. Biblica and Jewish Ency. and numerous philol. and religious revs. *Publications:* A Sketch of Semitic Origins, Social and Religious, 1902; Roots of Christian Teaching as Found in the Old Testament, 1902. A Year's Wandering in Bible Lands, 1905; The Haverford Library Collection of Cuneiform Tablets, or Documents from the Temple Archives of Telloh, 1905. *Address:* Bryn Mawr, Pa.

BASTEDO, Samuel Tovel, Supt. of Canadian Government Annuities; *b.* Hamilton, Ont., 4 Dec., 1855; *s* David Bastedo and Sarah Elizabeth Bastedo; (of U. E. L. descent); *m.* Ida Virginia Straubel; two *d.* *Educ.:* Oxford Co., private sec. to Premiers of Ont., 1880-1898; Deputy Com. of Fisheries, Ont., 1898-1906; British Com. on International Fisheries Treaty with United States, 1909;resigned to accept appointment as Supt. of Canadian Govt. Annuities; *Recreations:* Outdoor and indoor games. *Address:* Ottawa, Ont.

BATE, Lieut.-Col. Henry Allan; Chevlier, Order of Leopold; *b.* Ottawa, Ont., 12 May, 1867; *s.* of Henry Newell, and Catherine Cameron Bate; *m.* Florence Mary Wilson; two *s.* three *d.* *Educ.:* Ottawa Gram. Sch., Hellmuth Coll., London, Ont. Pres. Canadian Rifle League; A.D.C. to Gen. Gascoigne, commanding Can. Forces; military attache to Sir Wilfrid Laurier, Queen's Jubliee; late commandant, The Governor General's Foot Guards; Consul Gen. for Paraguay; Consul for Belgium. *Recreations:* golf, fishing, hunting, riding. *Address:* 440 Wilbrod St., Ottawa. *Clubs:* Rideau, Country, Hunt, Golf, Ottawa.

BATE, Henry Newell; chairman of the Ottawa Improvement Commission; *b.* Truro Eng., 9 April, 1828; *s.* Henry Newell Bate, and Lizette Meyers; *m.* Catherine Cameron; five *s.* four *d.* *Educ.:* St. Catharines, Ont. Came to Canada with his parents, July, 1833; spent boyhood days in St. Catharines; paid first visit to Ottawa in 1848, and permanently settled there in 1854; with his brother, C. T. Bate, established the grocery firm now doing business as H. N. Bate & Sons, Ltd.; has been identified for half a century with every public movement in Ottawa, although shunning public office until invited (1899), by the Federal Government, to accept the position of first chairman of the Ottawa Improvement Commission, which office he still holds. In ten yrs. the commission has expended $944,423 (to Dec. 31st, 1909) in making roadways, boulevards, parkways and otherwise beautifying the capital. *Recreations:* travel, golf, fishing. *Address:* 216 Chapel St., Ottawa. *Clubs:* Rideau, Country, Hunt, Ottawa; Riviere du Loup Golf.

BATES, William Wallace, *b.* N. S., Feb. 15, 1827; *s.* Stephen and Elizabeth Bates; *m.* 1856, Marie Cole, Saratoga, N.Y. *Educ.:* in common schs., Calais, Me., beyond that self-educated; also self-educated in naval architecture. Began in shipwright trade, 1839; built first clipper schooner ("Challenge") on the great lakes, 1851; editor Nautical Mag. and Naval Jour., New York, 1854-8; capt. in Union Army, 1861-3; in shipbuilding and dry-dock business, Chicago, 1866-81; dry-dock building, Portland, Ore., 1881-3; mgr. Inland Lloyds, Buffalo, 1885-8; U.S. comm'r navigation, Washington, 1889-92; Republican. *Publications:* Rules for Shipbuilding, 1876, 1894; American Marine, 1892; American Navigation, 1902. Has issued numerous pamphlets and written many newspaper articles on the shipping question. Mem. Soc. Naval Architects and Marine Eng'rs, Shipping Soc. America (pres.). *Address:* 38 W. 2d Av., Denver, Colo.

BAUMGARTEN, Alfred, M.F., Ph.D.; Pres. of the St. Lawrence Sugar Refining Co.; *b.* Dresden, Saxony, 13 Nov., 1842; *s.* Dr. Moritz Baumgarten, physician to King of Saxony, and Emmy Zocher; *m.* Martha C. Donner, of Hamburg, two *d.* *Educ.:* Dresden High Sch. and Polytechnic Sch., where grad. as chemist. Later had two yrs. practical experience in chemical works at Schoeningen, studied at Berlin Univ., where took degree; arrived U. S., 1866, employed in different chemical works and sugar refineries. Arrived Montreal, 1873; founded, 1879, Co. of which he now is pres.; life governor of Montreal General Hospital, Western Hospital, and the Alexandra Hospital. *Recreations:* hunting, fishing. *Address:* 34 McTavish St., Montreal. *Clubs:* Mount Royal, St. James', Forest and Stream, Hunt.

BAXTER, Lieut.-Col. John Babington Macaulay, B.C.L., K.C.; Lieut.-Col. Commanding 3rd Regt., Can. Art.; *b.* St. John, N.B., 16 Feb., 1868; *s.* Wm. S. and Margaret Baxter. *Educ.:* Common Schs., St. John, N.B.; admitted Attorney, 1890; Barrister, 1891; K.C., 1909; alderman, city of St. John, 1891-1896; 1900, to present time. Has been deputy Mayor, Warden of the City and of St. John. Is now chairman of the Treasury Board, City of St. John, and a member of the Finance Committee of the Municipal Council. *Publications:* Historical records, N. B. Regiment of Artillery, 1793-1896. *Residence:* 289 Lancaster St., St. John, P. O. Box 15.

BAYLISS, Major William; *b.* Pictou, N. S., Nov. 8, 1848; *s.* John and Lillia (McKenzie) Bayliss; *m.* Providence, R. I., Dec. 18, 1872, Marion Frances, *d.* William A. Ray, of Washington. *Educ.:* pub. schs., Picton, N.S.; studied architectural drawing at night schs.; Supt. of hosp. constr'n, office of surgeon-gen., U.S.A., since 1882; invented combination steam and hot water heating system, 1893. Sovereign Grand Comdr., Sup. Council of Sovereign Grand Inspectors-Gen., 33d and last degree of A. A. S. R. Freemasonry for U.S. of America, since 1896. *Addcess:* War Dept., Washington.

BAZIN, Adolphe, K.C.; advocate and Justice of the Police Court at Montreal; *b.* Saint-Ours, nr. Sorel, Que., 27 May, 1869; *s.* of Pierre Bazin, notary, and Azilda Duhamel; *m.* 1896, Laura Beauchemin, three *d.* *Educ.:* Saint-Ours Pub. Schs., St. Hyacinthe Coll. (grad. B.A., 1890), Laval Univ. (grad. LL.B., 1894). Commenced practice of his profession in Montreal; was in partnership with Hon. Judge Piche for three yrs.; Mr. Laurendeau for four yrs.; Joseph A. Frouin and Hon. Jean Prevost, K.C., for two yrs., but has practiced alone ever since. Cr. K.C., 1906; apptd. Justice of the Police Ct., at Montreal, by Prov. Govt., 1 Aug., 1908. At one time pres. of the Cercle Ville Marie and of the Liberal Club of St. Henri. *Recreations:* shooting, fishing. *Address:* 15 St. Louis sq., Montreal. *Club:* Canadien.

BEARDMORE, Alfred Owen; *b.* Toronto, Ont., 4 March, 1859; *m.* Jeanie Torrance (*dec.*); two *s.* one *d.* Called to the Bar in 1882; gave up the practice of law in 1880, and has since been connected with the firm of Breardmore & Co. *Recreations:* Polo and Golf. *Residence:* 75 St. George St., Toronto. *Clubs:* Toronto, Hunt, Golf, Toronto; Metropolitan, New York; Sports, London, Eng.

BEATTIE, Major Thomas, M.P.; *b.* 12 Aug. 1844; *m.* Agnes M. Burwell, of Fingall (*dec.*); one *s.*; was Major in 7th Fusiliers, served with his regiment in the North West Rebellion, 1885; first elected to H. of C. for London, Ont., 1896; re-elec. 29 Oct., 1907 and 1908; Church of England; Conservative. *Address:* London, Ont.

BEAUBIEN, Hon. Louis; *b.* Montreal, Que., 27 July, 1837; *s.* Dr. Pierre Beaubien and Justine Casgrain; *m* Suzanne Lauretta, *d.* of Chief Justice Sir Andrew Stuart; four *s.* four *d.* *Educ.:* Montreal Coll.; was member of Provincial Legislature, also simultaneously member of H. of C. for Co. Hochelaga; speaker of Quebec House of Assembly, and Minister of Agriculture. *Residence:* Outremont (near Montreal) Office, 112 St. James' St., Montreal. *Clubs:* Montreal, Lafontaine, Montreal.

BEAUPARLANT, Aime Majorie, M.P.; *b.* St. Aimé, Co. of Richelieu, Que., 4 Jan., 1864; *s.* Oliver Beauparlant, farmer and Louise Beaudreau. *Educ.:* St. Aimé Coll., and St. Hyacinthe Sem.; studied law in the office of Hon. Honoré Mercier, at one time Premier of Quebec; was formerly in partnership with Hon. O. Desmarais; an advocate: elec. to the H. of C., 1904; re-elected, 1908. *Address:* St. Hyacinthe, Que.

BECK, Hon. Adam, M.L.A.; manufacturer; *b.* Baden, Waterloo Co., Ont., 20 June, 1857; *s.* of Jacob Beck and Charlotte Hespeler; *m.* 1898, Lillian Ottaway, of London, Ont. *Educ.:* Pub. Schs. of Baden, and in Galt, Ont. Entered office of his father who was engaged in the iron foundry business in Baden; removed to Galt, 1880, and commenced the manufacture of veneering and thin lumber boxes; removed his business to London, 1884, where he built an extensive plant, and estbd. branch plants in Montreal and Toronto. Master of the London Hunt Club; mem. Victoria Hospital Bd., and of the Masonic Order A. F. and A. M.; unsuccessful candidate for Legis. at g. e., 1898.; first returned to Legis. at g. e., 1902; re-el. 1905 and 1908. Apptd. Minister without portfolio in the Whitney Admn., Feb. 8, 1905; Mayor of London, 1902-1904; originated Hydro-Electric Power leg. *Address:* London, Ont. *Clubs:* St. James', Montreal; Albany, Toronto; London, London.

BECK, Hon. Nicholas Dominic, LL. B.; a Judge of Sup. Ct. of Alberta; *b.* Cobourg, Ont., 4 May, 1857; *s.* Rev. J. W. R. Beck, M.A., for years Anglican Rector of Peterboro, Ont., and Georgina Boulton; *m.* (1st) Mary Ethel Lloyd, (2nd) Louisa Teepy; two *s.* two *d.* *Educ.:* Private sch., Cobourg, Collegiate Institute, Peterboro, and Univ. of Toronto; admitted to the Bar of Ontario, 1879; Manitoba, 1883; North West Territory (now Alberta and Saskatchewan), 1889. Became a Catholic in 1893; has since been identified with Catholic Educational matters; member of Educational Council; vice-Chancellor of Univ. of Alberta. *Publications:* Sometime editor Territorial Law reports, sometime editor North West Catholic Review (now Central Catholic) of Winnipeg. *Recreations:* reading, bowling. *Address:* 469 Fifth St., Edmonton, Alta. *Club:* The Edmonton.

BEDDOE, William Arthur, F.R.G.S.; Journalist; *b.* Hill Top House, West Bromwick, Staff, Eng., 16 March, 1859; *s.* of John and Charlotte Beddoe; unmarried. *Educ.:* Marshall's High Sch. and Jackson's Coll., West Bromwich, Staff. Came to Canada, Dec., 1876. Studied law with Chancellor Cronyn, London, Ont.; dir., Press Alliance, Ltd., London, Eng. Editor, Alaska *Miner*, Juneau, Alaska; Dawson *Daily News*, Yukon *World*, and Yukon *Mining Journal*. *Publications:* writer on political subjects. *Recreations:* shooting, fishing. *Address:* 209 Wellington Street, Ottawa. *Club:* Ontario, Toronto.

BEDFORD, Spencer Argyle; *b.* Sussex Co., Eng., 1 Feb., 1851; *s.* Jacob and Elizabeth Bedford; *m.* Minnie Bolton; one *s.* three *d.* *Educ.:* Hadlow Academy, Kent, Eng.; came to Canada in 1863. Farmed in Manitoba and N. W. T.; Inspector for Can. N. W. Land Co., Scottish Ontario, and North British Co'ys.; in 1888 became supt. of Experimental Farm at Brandon; member of the N. W. Council for Moosomin district 1885 to 1888; now Professor of Field Husbandry, Manitoba Agricultural Coll. *Publications:* Frequent contributor to Agricultural Press, also issues annual reports of Experimental Farm. *Address:* Agricultural College, Winnipeg, Man.

BEGIN, Mgr. Louis Nazaire, D.D.; Archbishop of Quebec; *b.* Levis, Que., 10 June, 1840. *Educ.:* Que. Seminary, French

Seminary, Rome; ordained in Rome, 10 June, 1865; a professor at Quebec Sem.; principal of Laval Normal Sch.; Consec. Bishop of Chicoutimi, 1 Oct., 1888; coadjutor Bishop of Quebec, 22 Dec., 1891; Archbishop of Que.; 12 April, 1898. *Publications:* "The Rule of faith," "A Catechism of Controversy," "The infallibility of the Sovereign Pontiffs," etc. *Address:* Archbishop's Palace, Quebec.

BEIQUE, Hon. Frederic Ligori, LL. D., K.C.; *b.* St. Mathias, Que., May, 1845; *s.* of Louis Beique and Elizabeth d'Artois; *m.* 1875, Caroline Angeline, *o. d.* of the late Hon. L. A. Dessaulles, M.L.C.; two *d. Educ:* Coll. of Marieville. Called to Bar, 1868; cr. Q.C., by Quebec, 1885, and by Dom. Govt., 1889; one of the Dom. Counsel before the Behring Sea Claims Comm., 1896; batonnier of Montreal Dist. Bar., 1891-93; cr. LL.D. by Laval Univ., 1900; Mayor of Dorion, 1895-96; pres. of St. Jean Baptiste Assn., of Montreal, 1899-1905. Called to the Senate, 8 Feb., 1902; mem. of the Numismatic and Antiquarian Soc., of Montreal. *Address:* 540 Sherbrooke St. W., Montreal. *Clubs:* St. James', Montreal, Montreal Reform.

BEITH, Hon. Robert; *b.* 17 May, 1843; *s.* of Alexander Beith and Catharine McTaggart, Argyleshire, Scot. *Educ.:* Bowmanville Pub. Sch. and Commercial Coll., Toronto, el. to H. of C. for West Durham in succession to Hon. Edward Blake, 1891; re-el. 1896; defeated at g. e., 1900; re-el. at bye el.. 1902, but retired, 1904; called to Senate, 15 Jan., 1907. A farmer and one of the pioneer importers of thoroughbred horses, chiefly Clydesdales. *Address:* Bowmanville, Ont.

BELAND, Henri Severin, B.A., M.D., M.P.; *b.* Louiseville, Que., 11 Oct., 1869; *s.* of Henri Beland and Sophia Lesage; *m.* 1895, Flore Gerin Lajoie. *Educ.:* Three Rivers Coll., and Laval Univ.; elec. to L. A., Quebec, 1897 and 1900; elec. for H. of C. at bye elec., 1902; re-elec., 1904 and 1908; Liberal. *Address:* St. Joseph de Beauce, Que.

BELCOURT, Hon. N. A., LL.D., K. C.; 1905; Senator, P. C., *b.* 15 Sept., 1860; *e. s.* of F. N. Belcourt and Marie Ann Clair; *m.* (1st) 1889, Hectorine, *e. d.* of Hon. Joseph Shehyn, Senator, Quebec; (2nd) Mary Margaret, *e. d.* of R. H. Haycock, of Ottawa; three *s.* six *d. Educ.:* St. Joseph's Seminary of Three Rivers, Que.; Laval Univ.; admitted to Bar of Quebec, 1882; K.C., 1899; admitted to Ontario Bar, 1884; speaker of H. of C., 1904; Senator since 1907; has had extensive practice in courts of the Provinces of Ontario and Quebec, and in the Exchequer and Supreme Courts of Canada, and before Judicial Committee of Privy Council. *Recreations:* riding and amateur farming; pres. Ottawa Hunt Club; member and officer of cricket, football, and other clubs. *Address:* 489 Wilbrod St., Ottawa; in summer, Blue Sea Lake, Que. *Clubs:* Rideau, Country, Ottawa.

BELCHER, Henry Martyn; *b.* Calcutta, India, 21 Nov., 1856; *s.* of the Rev. Canon Samuel Belcher and Jane Goldsmith; m. Jessie Sloan Notman; four *s.* two d. Arrived in Canada, 1863; member of the Victoria Rifles of Canada, Montreal, from 1875 to 1885; last two years as Captain of No. 4 Co. In 1882, he was a member of the Canadian Rifle Team at Wimbledon, Eng.; connected with Galt Bros. & Co., Montreal, since 1872; now Managing Director of Galts, Limited, Winnipeg; pres. Winnipeg Board of Trade, 1908-1909; del. to Imperial congress, Chamber of Commerce, Sydney, 1909. *Recreation:* Motoring; *Address:* 37 Edmonton St., Winnipeg, Man. *Clubs:* Life Member M.A.A.A., Montreal; Manitoba, St. Charles Country, Winnipeg, Man.

BELL, Adam Carr; *b.* Pictou, Nova Scotia, 11 Nov., 1847; *s.* of Basil Hall Bell and Mary Carr; *m.* Annie Henderson; four *s.* one *d. Educ.:* New Glasgow, Sackville, N.B., Glasgow Univ., Glasgow, Scot. Was first Mayor (Warden) New Glasgow, 1876, and was again Mayor in 1884; elec. M.L.A. of N. S., g. e., 1878, and again in 1882 and 1886; was Provincial Secretary of N.S., from May to July, 1882; defeated for Federal House in 1889 and 1904, but was elec. in 1896 and 1900. *Recreation:* Farming. *Address:* New Glasgow, N.S.

BELL, Alexander Graham, LL.D., Ph. D., M.D.; *b.* Edinburgh, 3 March, 1847; *s.* of late Alexander Melville Bell; m. 1877, Mabel Gardiner, *d.* of G. G. Hubbard; two *d. Educ:* Royal High Sch., Edinburgh; Edinburgh Univ.; Univ. Coll., London; Matriculated London Univ., 1867. Arrived in Canada, 1870; became Professor of Physiology, Boston Univ.; patented invention of telephone, 1876; invented also photophone, induction balance, and telephone probe, and (with C. A. Bell) graphophone; has investigated, studied eductaion of the deaf; late president American Association to Promote Teaching of Speech to the Deaf; late President National Geographic Society; Regent Smithsonian Institute since 1898; awarded the Volta Prix by French Govt., 1881; officer of French Legion of Honour; Prince Albert Medal (London Society of Fine Arts), 1902; Founder Volta Bureau; member National Academy of Sciences; and many foreign and American Societies; in recent years, has taken great interest in the laws of flight and aviation generally. *Publications:* many scientific monographs, including Memoir on the formation of Deaf Variety in the Human Race; Census Report on the Deaf of the United States, 1906; Lectures on the Mechanism of Speech, 1906; many scientific and eductaional monographs. *Address:* 1331 Connecticut Avenue, Washington, U.S.A.; Baddeck, Nova Scotia.

BELL, His Hon. Archibald, County and Surrogate Judge of Kent Co., Ont.; *b.* Toronto, Ont., 16 Nov., 1840; *s.* of Archibald Bell and Agnes Hood; *m.* Elizabeth Cameron; two *s.* two *d.* Called to the Bar, 1886, and admitted attorney and solicitor, 1868; practiced in Chatham until 1 Oct., 1878, when he was appointed Judge of the Co. and Surrogate Courts, of the Co. of Kent, and subsequently local Judge of the High Courts of Justice, Ontario. *Address:* Chatham, Ont.

BELL, James, M.D.; Prof. of Surgery and Clinical Surgery, McGill Univ.; *b.* North Gower, Ont., 1852; *m.* 1889, Edith Mary, *e. d.* of the late J. J. Arnton of Montreal; one *s. Educ.:* local schs. and by private tuition; grad. M.D., McGill Univ.,

1877, and won the Holmes Gold Medal. House Surgeon Montreal Gen. Hospital, 1877-1880; medical supt., 1881-1885; asst. Surg., 1885; surgeon, 1886; became surgeon Royal Victoria Hospital, 1894. Apptd. Associate Prof. of Clinical Surgery, McGill Univ., 1888; asst. prof. of Surgery and Clinical Surgery, 1890; Prof. of Clinical Surgery, 1895; Prof. of Surgery and Clinical Surgery, 1907. Mem. American Surgical Assn., Canadian Medical Assn.; Surgeon to the Sixth Batt., Fusiliers, 1880 1888; Surgeon-Major in charge of the Field Hospital Corps at Riel Rebellion, 1885, and received medal for services. *Recreations:* fishing, hunting. *Address:* 409 Dorchester St., W., Montreal; summer res., Cartierville. *Clubs:* Mount Royal, St. James', Hunt, University, Montreal.

BELL, James Macintosh, M.A., Ph.D., F.R.G.S.; Dir. of the Geological Survey, of New Zealand; *b.* St. Andrew's, Que., 23 Sept., 1877; *s.* of Andrew Bell, and Marian Rosamond; *m.* 1909, Vera Margaret Beauchamp. In 1896, accompanied his uncle Dr. Robt. Bell, of the Geological Survey of Can., to Grand Lake Victoria, on the Upper Ottawa, and thence to Nimiskow Lake on Rupert River; in 1898 asst. his uncle in making a geological survey of the Michipicoten Dist.; on Mackenzie River, and made a geological resonnaissance of its North Arm; after wintering at Fort Resolution, in 1900, accompanied by Mr. Charles Camsell, travelled to Great Bear Lake and made a geological exploration of its northern shores; returned by a chain of lakes to the North Arm of Great Slave lake and during the winter reached Edmonton; in 1901-02, was geologist to the Lake Superior Corporation, with headquarters at Sault Ste. Marie; employed by the Govt. of Ont., on geological work in the region southward of James Bay, 1903; apptd. Director of the Geological Survey of New Zealand, 1904. *Publications:* Reports on Great Bear Lake, pubd. by the Geol. Survey of Can., 1901; reports for the Lake Superior Corporation in Philadelphia, and that of 1903 by the Govt. of Ont.; reports of New Zealand Geological Survey, 1904-1908, accompanied by maps, pubd. by the Govt. at Wellington. *Addresses:* Wellington, N.Z.; Blacket House, Silver Stream, North Island, N.Z. (summer).

BELL, Robert, I.S.O., M.D.C.M., D.Sc. (McGill and Cantab), LL.D., F.R.S.; late Director and Chief Geologist, Geological Survey of Canada; *b.* Toronto, Ont., 3 June, 1841; *s.* of Andrew Bell and Elizabeth Notman; *m.* Agnes Smith, of Westbourne and Auchentroig, Scot.; one *s.* three *d.* *Educ.:* Prescott County Gram. Sch., Science Dept., McGill Univ., McGill Medical Coll., Edinburgh Univ.; mem. of Am. Inst. of Mining Engrs., 1881; hon. mem. Medico-Chirurgical Soc., Montreal; Fellow Am. A. A. Sci.; one of foundation Fellows of Roy. Soc. of Can.; mem. of Govt. Geographical Bd.; joined Geological Servey of Can., 1857, and since that time has made very extensive topographical and geological surveys in nearly all parts of the Dominion. The Bell River or W. branch of Nottaway, which he surveyed, in 1895, is officially named after him; was medical officer, naturalist, and geologist of "Neptune" expedition in 1884, and of "Alert" expedition in 1885 to Hudson's Strait and Bay; was also geologist of the "Diana" expedition in 1897, when he surveyed the south coast of Baffinland and penetrated to the great lakes of its interior; among the rivers he has surveyed are the Athabasca, Slave, Beaver, Churchill, Nelson, Hayes and branches, the Winnipeg, English, Albany, Kenogami, Nipigon, Moose and its numerous branches, the Harricanaw, Broadback, Nottaway and its branches, the upper Gatineau and most of the rivers of northern Ontario; he also made the first surveys of some of the largest lakes in Canada, including Great Slave, Nipigon, Osnaburgh, Seul, and parts of Athabasca, Winnipeg, and Lake of the Woods, del. from the Dom. Govt. and the Roy. Soc. of Can. to the Intl. Geol. Congress, Vienna, 1903; has been Canadian cor. of the Royal Scottish Geographical Soc. ever since its foundation; Canadian cor. of la Société de Géographie; mem. of the Royal Ast. Sco. of Can.; was a Royal Comm. on the Mineral Resorces of Ontario, 1888-89, Hon. Chief of Algonquin Indians of Grand Lake; pres., International Congress of Americanists, 1906; King's or Patron's gold medal of the Royal Geographical Soc. of London, 1906; Callum gold medal of the Am. Geographical Soc., 1906. *Publications:* Fifty reports published by the Geological Survey of Can., 1857-1905; report of the Royal Commission on the Min. Res. of Ontario, 1890 (in part). Many papers read before the Roy. Soc. of Can., 1882-1909, the Geol. Soc. of Am., 1890-09, in the Canadian Naturalist and Geologist, Record of Science, and in the journals of other scientific societies. *Address:* 136 Maclaren St., Ottawa. *Club:* Rideau, Ottawa.

BELL-SMITH, Frederick Marlett, R.C.A.; *b.* London, 26 Sept., 1846; *s.* of late John Bell-Smith, Artist; *m.* 1871, Annie Myra Dyde; one *s.* *Educ.:* London. Member of Council of the Royal Canadian Academy of Arts; President of the Ontario Society of Artists; studied drawing at South Kensington; arrived in Canada, 1867; charter member Society of Canadian Artists, 1867; served in Volunteers in suppressing Fenian invasion, 1870 (medal); Director of Fine Arts, Alma Coll., since 1881; teacher of drawing, public sch., London, Ont., 1882-89; Director Toronto Art Sch., 1889-91; lecturer and writer on Art subjects. *Principal pictures:* Queen Victoria's Tribute to Canada (for which Her Majesty gave personal sittings); Landing of the Blenheim, National Collection, Ottawa; Whitehead, Diploma work, Nat. Coll,; Lights of a City Street, Ont. Collection; has exhibited at Royal Academy and other principal exhibitions; paints with equal facility in oils and water cloours. *Recreations:* annually visits Rocky Mountains of Canada, and has made some ascents; member of Appalachian Club. *Address:* 336 Jarvis Street, Toronto. *Club:* Arts and Letters, Toronto.

BENGOUGH, John Wilson; journalist; *b.* Toronto, 7 April, 1851; *s.* of John Bengough and Margaret Wilson; *m.* (1st) 1880, Helena Siddall, of Toronto (*d.* 1902); (2nd) 1908, Annie Robertson Matheson. *Educ.:*

Whitby Gram. Sch.; began journalistic career on Whitby *Gazette;* removed to Toronto, 1872; reporter on *Globe* for three yrs.; started *Grip* in 1873, and edited it for 21 yrs.; appeared as entertainer in 1874, and has done platform work continuously since in Canada, United States, England, Australia and New Zealand. *Publications:* 2 vols of verse; "Grave and Gay," and "In many Keys," "The up to date primer," (humorous exposition of Henry George); "The Whole Hog Book." *Address:* Toronto.

BENNETT, Mrs. Annie Dunlop ("Gena Macfarlane"); *b.* Baddeck, C.B., 12 June, 1859; *d.* of David Dunlop and Catherine McGrath; *m.* Thomas J. Bennett, 11 Jan., 1882, Baldwin, Wis.; five *s.* six *d.* *Educ.:* Baddeck Academy; Congregation de Notre Dame, Arichat C.B., River Falls (Wisconsin) Normal Sch. Joined the Roman Catholic Church at fifteen years of age; taught sch. in Cape Breton three years; two years in Wisconsin; received into the Catholic Church by His Lordship, Bishop Cameron of Antigonish; always taken an active part in charitable work; was pres. of Relief Soc.; charter member of Children's Aid Society; accompanied her husband to Regina in 1892, when he went to put the Regina Jail under Penitentiary discipline. *Publications.* For several years regular correspondent of "The *Catholic Record*," also of the N. W. *Review* during the editorship of L. Drummond, S.J.; was editor of the special edition of the Regina *Leader*, in aid of the Victorian Hospital. *Address:* 2108 Albert St., Regina, Sask.

BENNETT, William H., K.C.; *b.* Barrie, 23 Dec., 1859; *s.* of Humphrey Bennett and Annie A. Fraser; *m.* Margaret F. Cargill, *d.* of Henry Cargill (M.P. for East Bruce for many years); *Educ.:* Barrie High Sch. Called to the Bar, 1881; represented E. Simcoe in H. of C. from 1892, to 1908. *Address:* Midland, Ont.

BENOIT, Joseph Alderic, M.L.A.; agriculturist; *b.* Mount Johnson, Que., 20 Feb., 1854; *s.* of Julien Benoit and Lucie Harbec; *m.* 1874; Cath. McQuillen; one *s.* *Educ.:* County Sch. Hay dealer and farmer; Mayor, 1900-1907; warden of Co.; pres. of the St. Johns Exhibition and laureate of the Merite Agricole. El. to Quebec Legis., 1906; re-el. 1908. *Address:* Mount Johnson, Que.

BENSON, Major-General Frederick William, C.B.; Director of Transport and Remounts since 1903; *b.* St. Catharines, Ont., 2 Aug., 1849; 3rd *s.* of late Hon. J. R. Benson, Senator, and Marianne, *d.* of late Charles Ingersoll, of Ingersoll, Ont.; *m.* Caroline, *e. d.* of Sir G. E. Couper, Bart., C.B., K.C.S.I. *Educ.:* Up. Can. Coll., Toronto; R.M.C., Sandhurst; served as Volunteer during Fenian raids in Canada, 1866; joined 21st Hussars, 1869; exchanged to 12th Royal Lancers, 1876; passed Staff Coll., 1880; Captain 5th Dragoon Guards, 1880; exchanged to 17th Lancers, 1881; A.D.C. to Lieut.-Governor, N. W. Provinces, India, 1877; Brigade Major, Poona, 1882-84; Garrison Instuctor, Bengal, 1884-90; commanded Egyptian cavalry, 1892-94; D.A.A.G. (Instructor) Dublin, 1895-98; Assistant Adjutant-General, Chief Staff Officer, South-Eastern District, 1898-1900; special service S. Africa, A.A.G. 6th division S.A. Field Force, 1900-1 (despatches, medal, three clasps, C.B.); Headquarters, 1901-3. *Recreations;* shooting, fishing, riding, cycling, skating. *Club:* Army and Navy, London, Eng.

BERGERON, Joseph Gedeon Horace, B.C.L., K.C.; *b.* Rigaud, Que., 13 Oct., 1854; *s.* of the late T. R. Bergeron, N.P., of Rigaud, and Leocadie Caroline Dephine Coursol, *d.* of Gedeon Coursol, N.P., of St. Andrews, Que.; *m.* 1890, Josephine Ada, *d.* of the late Capt. Wall, of Montreal. *Educ.:* Gram. Sch. of St. Timothee, St. Mary's Coll., McGill Univ., Montreal. Called to Bar, 1877, and has since practised in Montreal; el. to Parlt., 1879; re-el. 1882, 1887, 1891, 1896; unsuccessful 1900, and at bye-el. 1902; el. at g. e., 1904; Deputy Speaker of the House of Commons, 1891-1896; defeated at g. e., 1908. Took 2nd class artillery certificate, Montreal, 1874; served in No. 1 Troop of Montreal Hussars for short period. *Address:* 76 St. James' St., Montreal. *Clubs:* St. James', Lafontaine, Canadien.

BERGEVIN, Achille; *b.* Valleyfield, Que., 3 March, 1870; *s.* of Gilbert Bergevin and Ann Daoust; *m.* Flora Faucher, of Montreal; one *s.* two *d.* *Educ.:* Model Sch. and English Acad., Valleyfield; Commercial Coll., Varennes, Que.; an investment broker doing business in Montreal; for many yrs. a newspaper editor; sec. of the Montreal Reform Club and other important organizations. First el. to Legis. at g. e., 1900; re-el. 1904; defeated 1908. *Recreations:* fishing. *Address:* 235 Board of Trade Bldg., Montreal. *Clubs:* Canadien, St. Denis.

BERNARD, Mgr. Alexis-Xyste, Bishop of St. Hyacinthe, Que.; *b.* at Beloeil, Que., 29 Dec , 1847; *s.* of Theodule Bernard and Heloise Prefontain. *Educ.:* Coll. and Seminary of Montreal, under the Sulpician Fathers; Curate; president of Sorel Coll.; Canon of the Cathedral of St Hyacinthe; Archdeacon; secretary for the Diocese ; Vicar General; Provost of the Chapter of Prothonotary Apostolic. *Publications:* Besides "Tynoral Decrees." and a summary of the "Clerical Conferences" he edited the Pastoral Letters of the Bishops of St. Hyacinthe, in nine volumes. *Address:* St. Hyacinthe, Que.

BERNARD Ludger Pierre, M.L.A.; *b.* L'Ange Gardien, Co. of Rouville, Que., 5 March, 1870; *s.* of Jean Baptiste Bernard and Julie Beaudry; *m.* Mary Racicot; one *s.* two *d.* *Educ.:* Elementary Schs. of the Province; a farmer; elec. to the Legislature of Quebec, 25 Nov., 1904; re-el. 8 June, 1908; Conservative. *Address:* Granby, Que.

BERNIER, Hon. Michael Esdras; one of the Bd. of Ry. Commrs. for Canada; *b.* St. Hyacinthe, Que., 27 Sept., 1841; *s.* of the late Etienne Bernier; *m.* 1865, Alida, *d.* of the late Simeon Marchesseault, who in 1837 was a leader in the Rebellion, and subsequently exiled to the Bermudas. El. to H. of C. at g. e., 1882, 1887, 1891, 1896, and 1900. Sworn of the Privy Council and apptd. Minister of Inland Revenue in the Laurier Admn., 22 June, 1900; apptd. one of the Bd. of Rl. Commrs. for Canada, Jan.,

1904. *Addresses:* 403 Maclaren Street, Ottawa; St. Hyacinthe, Que.

BERRY, Rev. Joseph F., D.D., LL. D.; *b.* Alymer, Ont., May 13, 1856; *s.* Francis and Ann L. B.; *Educ.:* Milton Acad., Ont.; Lawrence Univ., Upper Iowa Univ.; *m.* 1876, Olive Johnson. Entered M. E. ministry, 1874; asso. editor Mich. Christian Advocate, 1884-1890; editor Epworth Herald, 1890-1894. Elected bishop of M. E. Ch., May, 18 1904. *Address:* 455 Franklin St., Buffalo, N.Y.

BERTHIAUME, Hon. Treffle; proprietor of La Presse; *b.* St. Hughes, Que., 4 Aug., 1848; *s.* of Gédéon Berthiaume and Eléonore Normandin; *m.* 1871, Helmina Gadbois, of Montreal; three *s.* three *d.* *Educ.:* St. Hyacinthe Coll.; became partner in the Gebhardt-Berthiaume Lithographing and Printing Co., 1884, and proprietor La Presse, 1889; called to Legis. Council of Quebec, 1896. *Address:* 713 St. Urbain St., Montreal. *Clubs:* All the French clubs of Montreal.

BETHUNE, Charles James Stewart, B. A., M.A., D.C.L.; *b.* West Flamboro, Co. Wentworth, Ont., 11 Aug., 1838; *s.* of Right Rev. Alexander Neil Bethune, D.D., Second Lord Bishop of Toronto, and Jane Eliza, *e. d.* of Hon. James Crooks; *m.* 21 April, 1863, to Harriet Alice Mary, 2nd *d.* of Lieut. Col. James Furlong, K.H., H. His Majesty's 43rd Regt., Light Infantry; two *s.* three *d.* *Educ.:* Up. Can. Coll., and Trinity Univ.; ordained deacon by Bishop Strachan in 1861, and Priest in 1862; Curate to his father at Cobourg until 1866; Incumbent of Credit Mission, 1866-1870; Honorary Clerical Secretary of the Lower House of the General Synod of the Church of England in Canada, 1901-1908; Head Master of Trinity Coll. Sch., Port Hope, 1870-1899. Professor of Entomology and Zoology, Ontario Agricultural Coll., Geulph, 1906; Fellow of the American Assn. for the Advancement of Science and of the Entomological Society of America; member of Scientific Societies in Toronto, Ottawa, Boston, New York, Washington, Buffalo, Philadelphia, etc., and of the Assn. of Economic Zoologists, Eng., and of Economic Entomologists, America; Chairman of the Canadian Committee of the International Congress of Entomology, etc. *Publications:* Editor "Canadian Entomology"; reports to the Legislature of the Entomological Society of Ont.; 1886 to 1874, and 1886 to present time; author of scientific papers. *Recreations:* Study of Nature. *Address:* Ontario Agricultural Coll., Geulph, Ont.

BETHUNE, Robert Cecil, J.P.; *b.* Montreal, 10 May, 1872; *s.* of Lt.-Col. Angus Robert Bethune and Mary Elizabeth Rogers *m.* Jean Peden; three *s.* two *d.* *Educ.:* St. Johns High Sch., Montreal, Collegiate Institute, Ottawa; business, Fire Insurance; Secretary Board of Trade of the City of Ottawa; Secretary-Treasurer of Collegiate Institute Board, Ottawa. *Recreations:* fishing, shooting and rowing. *Address:* 145 Cartier St., Ottawa.

BETTS, Craven Langstroth; *b.* St. John, N.B., April 23, 1853; *s.* Hiram and Sarah Ann Purdy Betts; descended from old Colonial New England stock, and of U. E. L. *m.:* Feb. 10, 1905, Elizabeth Cushing Colby. *Educ.:* there; removed to New York, 1879; went into business life and pursued literary studies. *Publications:* Songs from Beranger (translation of 61 chansons), The Perfume Holder, A Persian Love Story, Tales of a Garrison Town (with Arthur Wentworth Eaton); a Garland of Sonnets; Freeswick's Experiment (a novel), 1907; also many poems in mags.,etc. Mem. Municipal Art Soc. *Club:* Salmagundi. *Address:* 14 Timpson Pl. *Club:* Salmagundi Club, 14 W. 12th St., New York.

BICKERDIKE, Robert, M.P.; *b.* Kingston, Ont., 17 Aug., 1843; *s.* of Thomas Bickerdike; *m.* 1866, Helen Thompson Reid (*d.* 1907); three *s.* six *d.* *Educ.:* Beauharnois County. Organized the Dom. Abattoir & Stock Yards Co., of which he was mgr. dir.; one of the founders of the Dom. Live Stock Assn., and of the Live Stock Insur. Co., of which he became pres.; was promoter and pres. of the Standard Light and Power Co., and of the Adirondack & St. Lawrence Rapids Tourist Line; pres. of the Montreal and Great Lakes Steamship Co., Ltd., and of the Robert Bickerdike Co., Ltd.; vice-pres. of the Hochelaga Bank; ex-pres. of the Montreal Bd. of Trade; 1st vice-pres. of the Western General Hospital; dir. Canadian Marconi Wireless, Western and British American Fire and Marine Insur. Co., the Imperial Guarantee & Accident Insur. Co.; a former mem. of the Montreal Harbour Comm.; life gov. of the Montreal Gen. Hospital; founder and ex-mayor of the town of Summerlea on Lake St. Louis. El. to Quebec Legis., at g. e., 1897; el. to the H. of C. at g. e., 1900, 1904, 1908. *Address:* "Elmcroft," Summerlea, Que. *Clubs:* Rideau, Ottawa; Montreal, Canada, Montreal.

BICKWELL, James, K.C.; *b.* Rottersea Park, Surrey, Eng., 26 April, 1862; *s.* of James and Annie Bickwell; *m.* Minnie Kappell; one *s.* two *d.* *Educ.:* Hamilton Collegiate Institute; arrived in Canada, 12 July, 1872; called to the Bar in Feb., 1884; practiced in Hamilton until 1894, and since that time in Toronto. *Publications:* Bickwell-Seager Division Courts, 1893, and 1900; Bickwell and Kappell's Practice, Statutes, 1900. *Address:* 37 Cherry Av., Toronto. *Clubs:* Hamilton, Hamilton, Ont. Albany, R.C.T.C., Toronto, Ont.

BIENVENU, Tancrede; Gen. Mgr., Provincial Bank of Canada, Montreal; *b.* Varennes, Que., 26 April, 1864; *s.* of the late A, Bienvenu and Octavie Larose; *m.* Clara Martin; four *s.* seven *d.* *Educ.:* Varennes Bus. Coll. Banker. *Recreations:* family, and office. *Address:* 32 Sherbrooke St., W., Montreal. *Club:* Montreal.

BIGGAR, Henry Percival B.A., B. Litt.; *b.* Carrying Place, Ont., 9 Aug., 1872; *s.* of J. Lyons Biggar and Isabella Hodgins of Dublin. *Educ.:* Belleville Public Sch.; Up. Can. Coll., and Univ. of Toronto. *Publications:* "The Early Trading Companies of New France," "The Voyages of the Cabots and of the Cote-Reds to North America and Greenland. *Address:* 34 Oxford Mansion, London W., Eng.

BIGGAR, Lieut.-Col. James Lyons, V.D., Director of Transport and Supplies and Officer Administering Canadian Army Service Corps; *b.* at the Carrying Place, Co.

Northumberland, 16 July, 1856; *s.* of James Lyons Biggar, who represented East Northumberland H. of C., from 1861-1878, and Isabella Hodgins; *m.* Mary Scott, *e. d.* of Robert W. Elliot of Toronto; two *s.* one *d.* *Educ.:* Trenton Gram. Sch., and Upp. Can. Coll.; served with the Argyll Light Infantry from 1881-1901, and as Supply and Camp Quartermaster on the District Staff from 1891-1900; on staff of Canadian Contingent at Queen Victoria's Diamond Jubilee in 1897; Jubilee Medal, South Africa, 1899-1901; during the earlier stages of the War, was with the Supply and Transport cloumn and later apptd. Staff Officer to the Oversea Colonials on Lines of Communication and Chief Base. Also acted as Red Cross Commissioner for Canada for seven months. Queen's Medal with four clasps. Apptd. to Headquarters Staff in Dec., 1901, as Deputy Adjutant General for Army Service Corps and organized the Canadian Army Service Corps; afterwards apptd. Assist. Quartermaster-General; acted as Staff Officer for Colonials at the Coronation of His Majesty King Edward VII in 1902; (Coronation Medal). Apptd. Director of Transport and Supplies in 1904; Honorary Associate of the Order of St. John of Jerusalem. *Publications:* "Hints to Quartermasters"; the "Army Service Corps Manual. *Address:* 525 King Edward Ave., Ottawa. *Clubs:* Rideau, Country, Ottawa.

BIGGAR, William Hodgins; Genl. Solicitor, Grand Trunk Pacific Ry.; *b.* Carrying Place, Ont., 19 Sept., 1852; *s.* of James Lyons and Isabella Biggar; *m.* Marie Louise Ballon; three *s.* one *d.* *Educ.:* Upp. Can. Coll. (grad. 1872). Called to the Bar of Ontario, 1880; mem. Ontario Legis., 1890-1898; cr. Q.C., 1899; asst. General counsel G.T.R., Jan. 1, 1903; genl. solicitor, Dec. 1, 1905; genl. solicitor, Grand Trunk Pacific, Dec. 1, 1905. *Recreations:* lawn bowling, curling, golf. *Address:* 726 Pine Av., Montreal. *Clubs:* Mount Royal, Canada, Montreal; Rideau, Ottawa.

BIGGER, Charles Albert, C.E., D.L.S., O.L.S., Astronomer, Dept. of Int., and in charge of Geodetic Survey of Canada; *b.* in Oakville, Ont.; 15 Aug., 1853; *s.* of Col. Chas. Bigger and Amelia Kenny; *m.* Louise Cockburn Brennan of Ottawa; one *d.* *Educ.:* pub. sch., Toronto Normal Sch., and private tuition; parents of U. E. Loyalist descent.; grad. from Military sch., Kingston, 1874; articled to Prov. Land Surveyor, 1878, and passed exams. 1882. Employed by Dom. Govt. on N. W. T. Staff of Surveyors, 1882-88; private practice as engineer and surv., until 1901, when apptd. to staff of Dom. Boundary Commission; had full charge of boundary survey on New York State line, 1902, doing astronomical work for U. S. and Can.; in charge of field work Alaska boundary survey, 1904-6; started geodetic survey of Canada, June, 1905, and now devotes all time to it. *Publications:* many reports upon engineering and surveying work. *Address:* 145 Gloucester St., Ottawa.

BIGGS, Hon. S. C., B.A., K.C.,; *b.* Ancaster, Ont., 8 Oct., 1851; *s.* Richard Biggs and Eleanor Wood; *m.* 1875, Emily Orythia, *d.* of the Rev. Thomas Atkinson; four *s.* *Educ.:* Ancaster pub. schs., Victoria Coll., Cobourg; Toronto Univ. (grad. B.A., 1872). Studied law with Charles Moss, of the firm of Harrison, Osler & Moss, now Chief Justice of the Ct. of Appeal; removed to Winnipeg, Man., 1875, and admitted to Manitoba Bar, and commenced practice of his profession; was one founder of the Winnipeg *Daily Sun*; removed to St. Paul, Minn., 1888, and engaged in practice of his profession, and large enterprises; removed to Toronto, 1892, and continued practice of his profession, where he has since remained. Formerly mem. of Legis. for St. Paul's, Man., and Minister of Pub. Works. *Address:* 55 St. George St., Toronto.

BINNING, John Russell; Gen. Mgr., Furness, Withy & Co., Ltd., steamship agents, Montreal; *b.* Hamilton, Scotland, 1866; *m.* 1891, Margaret Caird, of Montrose, Scot.; two *s.* four *d.* *Educ.:* Hamilton pub. sch., Hamilton Academy. Arrived Canada, in 1888, and entered employ of C. P. Ry. Co.; became connected with the firm of Furness, Withy & Co., Ltd., 1898; apptd. gen. mgr., 1903; Treas. Montreal Bd. of Trade, Shipping Federation of Can.; mem. Caledonian Soc., Montreal; belongs Masonic Order. *Recreations:* curling, amateur gardening. *Address:* Cote des Neiges, Montreal. *Club:* Canada.

BIRGE, Cyrus A.; Pres., Canada Screw Co.; *b.* nr. Oakville, Ont.; 7 Nov., 1867; *s.* of Herman P. Birge and Helen M. Ainslie; *m.* (1st) 1870, Rebecca J. Coote, of Oakville, (*d.* 1898); (2nd) 1902, Margaret Vanstone, of Wingham, Ont.; one *s.* one *d.* *Educ.:* Dist. Sch. and Oakville Gram. Sch. Took up study of medicine with Dr. C. H. Lusk, of Oakville; removed to Stratford, 1870, on account of ill-health, and started a grocery business; removed to Chatham, 1872; entered employ of Great Western Ry. as agent. in engrg. dept.; later removed to London and subsequently back to Hamilton; resigned position with G.W.R. 1882, to take management of the Can. Screw Co.; became vice-pres. and mgr. dir. of co. in 1883; co. removed to Hamilton, 1887; became pres., 1898. Was one of the orig. dirs. of the Hamilton Blast Furnace Co., before its amalgamation with the Hamilton Steel and Iron Co.; el. vice-pres. for Ont. of Can. Mfgrs. Assn., 1900; vice-pres. for the Dom., 1901; pres., 1902; mem. Toronto and Hamilton Bds. of Trade; vice-pres. Caledon Mountain Trout Club. *Address:* Hamilton, Ont. *Club:* National, Toronto; Hamilton.

BIRDWHISTLE, (originally BIRTWISTLE), **Captain Richard John;** *b.* Ottawa, Ont., 4 April, 1874; *s.* of Richard Birtwistle, whose father came from Lancashire, Eng., and Margaret Coughlan, of Kilkenney, Ireland; *m.* Carolyn Savage, *d.* of Samuel and Elizabeth Savage of Ottawa; *Educ.:* St. Joseph's School, Ottawa, and privately; learned the trade of Printer and Stereotyper eight years on the Ottawa Free Press; Financial, military, dramatic and special writer; Ottawa correspondent for various Canadian papers until 1902; for seven years manager of various theatrical enterprises; Broker, 1909; Captain in the 43rd Regt., D.C.O.R.; holds Subaltern and Captain's certificate, R.S.I.; Commanded Guard of Honour for H. R. H. The Prince of Wales, Quebec Tercentenary, 1908; long Service medal; originator of the "Birdwhistle System of military bookkeeping"; member of the Ottawa Board of Trade; Secretary Dominion of Canada Rifle Association; Secretary Publicity Committee of the City of Ottawa; *Publications* "History of the 43rd Regt., D. C. O.R., Rifle Association; military Correspondence under non-de Plume "Little Bobs;" dramatic sketches; *Recreation*, Walking shooting, reading. *Address;* 178 James St., Ottawa, *Club:* Commercial.

BIRKETT, H. S., M.D., C.M.; Professor of Laryngology and Otology; *b.* Hamilton, Ont., 17 July, 1864; *s.* of late William Birkett, (*d.*) Merchant, and Caroline Amelia, *d.* of late Jacob Ball of Grantham, Ont.; *m.* 1899, Margaret, *e. d.* of John MacNaughton, Glengarry, Ont.; *Educ.:* Forest House Sch., Chester, Eng.; Laryngologist and Otologist to the Royal Victoria Hospital; Consulting Laryngologist and Otologist, Alexandra Hospital; Senior House Surgeon Montreal General Hospital, 1880-87, Assist. Physician Montreal Dispensary, 1887-89; Laryngologist to Montreal Dispensary, 1889-91; to Montreal General Hospital, 1891-99; Junior Demonstrator of Anatomy McGill Univ., 1899–1890; Demonstrator, 1890-96; for some years General Secretary, Dominion Medical Association, and Montreal Medico-Chirurgical Society; vice-pres. American Laryngological Association, 1898; Montreal Medico-Chirurgical Society, 1902; Section of Laryngology British Med. Assoc. 1897; mem. American Association of Anatomists, 1890-96; Governor Montreal General Hospital; pres. Montreal Medico-Chirurgical Society; vice-pres. Section of Laryngology and Otology, British Medical Association, 1906; pres. American Laryngological Association, 1907-8; mem. Otological Society of United Kingdom. *Publications:* Hemiatrophy of the Tongue; Empyæma of the Antrum, Thyrotomy for sub cordal Sarcoma; Dermoid Cyst of the Nose; Anomalous cases of Primary Nasal Diphtheria; Carcinoma of the Larynx; Diphtheria, its treatment and Nursing; Syphilis of the Larynx, Trachea, and Bronchi; Diseases of the Oro, and Nasopharynx (Posey and Wright); Rhinoliths, Salivary Calculi, Lupus of the Oro-pharynx and Naso-pharynx; Diphtheria (Hare's System of Therapeutics) with Dr. J. C. Cameron; Perichondritis of the Larynx, from an unusual cause; Foreign Body in the Naso-pharynx; Oidium Albicans; Address to the Graduating Class of the Medical Faculty (M'Gill University); Otomycosis due to the Aspergillus Glaucus; Seventh Lecture of the Somerville Course, before the Montreal Natural History Soc.; Diseases of the Larynx (Osler's Modern Medicine). *Recreations:* golf, fishing, yachting. *Address:* 252 Mountain St., Montreal. *Clubs:* St. James', Montreal; Mount Royal, Hunt, St. Lawrence Yacht, Outremont Golf.

BIRMINGHAM, Robert; *b.* Ireland, 26 July, 1852; *s.* of Henry Birmingham and Mary Birmingham; *m.* Mary A. Fleming; three *s.* two *d.* *Educ.:* Ireland and Canada. Arrived Canada, May, 1866; political sec. of Liberal-Conservative party of Prov. of Ont. for 25 yrs. Past Grand Sec., Orangemen of British America. *Address:* 5 Harbord St., Toronto, Ont.

BIRNIE, John, B.C.L., LL.B., K.C.; *b.* Collingwood, Ont., 22 Nov., 1862; *s.* of John Birnie and Caroline Bell; *m.* 1884, Annie L., *y. d.* of the Rev. Edwin Clement, of Toronto; three *c.* *Educ.:* Pub. and High Schs. of Collingwood; Trinity Univ. (grad. B.C.L. 1884, and won silver medal); Toronto Univ. (grad. LL.B., 1886). Called to the Bar of Upper Can., 1882, and commenced practice of his profession at Collingwood, making a feature of Admiralty and Maratime Law. Apptd. K.C., by Ont. Govt., 1899; solicitor for the town of Collingwood, Bank of Montreal, Prov. Bldg., Loan Assn.; pres. Collingwood Reform Assn., West Simcoe County Liberal Assn.; Lieut. Collingwood Battery of Garrison Art. for number of yrs. *Recreation:* yachting. *Address:* Collingwood, Ont.

BLACK, Harry St. Francis,; *b.* Cobourg, Ont., Aug. 25, 1863; *s.* Capt. Thomas Black; *m.* Allen Mae, *d.* George A. Fuller. *Educ.:* Cobourg. Started business life in a gen. store; joined surveying party in Northwest and on Pacific Coast; traveller for wholesale woolen house of Chicago on Pacific Coast, 1882-92; in banking business in Wash. and later mcht. with stores at Menominee, Mich., and Tekoa, Wash.; joined George A. Fuller Co., bldg. contractors, 1896, becoming v.-p., and on its consolidation in U.S. Realty and Improvement Co. (capital $66,000,000) became chmn. bd. dirs.; also v.-p. and dir. Broad-Exchange Co.; pres. and dir. George A. Fuller Co.; dir. N. Am. Trust Co. *Clubs:* Metropolitan, Manhattan, Lawyers, Larchmont Yacht (N.Y.); Chicago. *Address:* 667 Madison Av. *Office:* 111 Broadway, New York.

BLACK, Judson Burpee, M.D., M.P.; *b.* St. Martins, N.B.; 15 Aug., 1842; *s.* Thomas Henry Black, late of Armagh Ireland, and Mary Eliza Fownes of Saint Martins; *m.* Bessie, *d.* of Senator Churchill; six *s.* four *d.* *Educ.:* Mount Allison Coll., Dartmouth Coll. and New York; post graduate Medical Sch. Has practiced medicine and Surgery since 1864; ex-vice-pres. Canadian Medical Assn.; ex-pres. N.S. Medical Society and ex-pres. of Colchester-Hants Medical Society. Twice elec. to Dom. Parliament. *Address:* Windsor, N.S.

BLACKADER, Alexander Dougall, B.A., M.D., C.M., M.R.C.S.; Professor of Pharmacology and Therapeutics, and Lecturer on Diseases of Children, McGill Univ., Montreal. *Educ.:* McGill Univ.; afterwards studied at St. Thomas's Hospital, London; Vienna and Prague. Graduated in Medicine, 1871; Surgeon on board R. M. Steamer to South American and to Chinese ports. In London, held the positions of Acting-Resident Physician to Royal Pimlico Dispensary; Resident Clinical Assistant to the Brompton Consumption Hospital; Clinical Assistant to the Royal South London Ophthalmic Hospital, and for four months acting Resident Physician to the Great Ormond Street Hospital for sick children. Began practice in Montreal, 1877; member Montreal Medico-Chirurgical Society, American Pediatric Society, American Association of Physicians, American Climatological Association, American Therapeutic Society.

Publications; Art. Variola, Keating's Cyclopædia of the Diseases of Children; Art. Gastric Catarrh, American Text-Book of Diseases of Children; Art. Hydrocephalus, Infancy, and Artificial Feeding of Infants, Reference Handbook of the Medical Sciences; and numerous articles in the Montreal Medical Journal, Archives of Pediatrics, International Medical Journal, International Clinics, and Progressive Medicine. *Address:* 236 Mountain Street, Montreal. *Club,* St. James', Montreal.

BLACKWOOD, Alexander Leslie; *b.* Huntingdon Co., Quebec, July 28, 1862; *s.* John and Ann Steell Blackwood; *m.* Hammond, Ind., Aug. 16, 1891, Helen A. Winslow (*d.* 1903). *Educ.:* Huntingdon Acad. and McGill Univ., Montreal; grad. Hahnemann Med. Coll., Chicago, M.D., 1888, New York Post-Grad. Med. Sch. and Hosp., 1889, Johns Hopkins Med. Sch., 1902; Sr. prof. materia medica and prof. clin. medicine, Hahnemann Med. Coll., Chicago. Mem. Chicago B'd Ed'n. *Author:* Diseases of the Heart, 1901; Diseases of the Lungs, 1902; A Manual of Materia Medica, Therapeutics and Pharmacology, 1906; Pancreas and Ductless Glands, 1907. *Residence:* 9128 Erie Av. *Office:* 31 Washington St., Chicago.

BLAIN, Richard, M.P.; *b.* Vienna, Ont., 8 Dec., 1857; *s.* Capt. Isaac Blair, and Mary Broderick; *m.* 19 Nov., 1884, Hattie James, Peel Co., Ont.; member of Brampton Town Council for ten years; Reeve and Deputy Reeve of Brampton, and Warden of Peel Co.; elec. to the H. of C., 1900; re-elec., 1904 and 1908; Methodist; Conservative. *Address:* Brampton, Ont.

BLAIR, Andrew George, LL.B.; *b.* Fredericton, N.B., 29 Nov., 1870; *s.* of late Hon. Andrew G. Blair and Annie E. Blair; *m.* Marjorie L. Holden of St. John N.B.; four *s.* three *d.* *Educ.:* at Collegiate Sch., and Univ. of N.B., Fredericton, and Univ. of Virginia, Charlottesville, Va.; graduated from the Law School of the Univ. of Virginia June, 1893; in October of that year, adm tted an attorney of the Supreme Court of N.B., and immediately commenced the practice of law in St. John. A year later called to the Bar of the Province and entered into partnership with the late Hon. A. G. Blair; continued to practice in St. John until the formation of the Board of Railway Commissioners for Canada, Feb. 1, 1904, when he moved to Ottawa to accept the position of law clerk of the Board, which position he fills to-day. *Recreations:* Horseback riding, golf and curling. *Address:* 331 Cooper St., Ottawa, Ont. *Clubs:* Union, St. John; Rideau, Laurentian, Golf, Ottawa.

BLAIS, Mgr. Andre Albert, LL.D., Canon of Rome, Bishop of Rimouski; *b.* St. Vallier, Que., 26 Aug., 1842; *s.* Hubert Blais and Anne Roy. *Educ.:* Quebec Seminary; for some years a prof. at Quebec Sem.; ordained Priest, 5 June, 1865; consec. bishop, 18 May, 1890. *Address:* Rimouski, Que.

BLAKE, Hon. Edward, M.A,. K.C., P. C., LL.D.; *b.* Adelaide, Ontario, 13 Oct., 1883; *e. s.* of Hon. William Hume Blake, Ont., Chancellor of Upper Canada; *m.* Margaret, *d.* of Bishop of Huron. *Educ.:* Up-Can. Coll.; Univ. of Toronto. M.P. (L.) Canada, 1867-91; M.P. (L.) Ontario House, 1867-72; Prime Minister, Ontario, 1871-72; Minister-Justice, Attorney-General, Canada, 1875-77; President of Council, 1877-78; M.P. (N.) S. Longford, 1892-1907. *Address:* Humewood, Toronto; Le Caprice, Murray Bay, Quebec.

BLANCHE, Mgr. Gustave, D.D., Titular Bishop of Sicca, Vicar Apostolic of the Gulf of St. Lawrence; *b.* Jasselin, Morlehan, France, 30 April, 1848; *s.* of L. Blanche and Marie Hayard. *Educ.:* Redon, Ile et Vilaire; Eudist fathers. Studied law in France and admitted to bar; a volunteer in the Franco-Prussian War, 1870; joined Eudist Fathers in 1873; director of l'ecole St. Jean, at Versailles, 1878-90; Superior of Acadian sch. in N.S., 1890-99; l'ecole St. Jean again 1899-1903; Provincial of the Eudist Fathers in America, 1903-9; Bishop of the Gulf of St. Lawrence, 1903. *Address:* Seven Islands, Saguenay Co., Que.

BLANCHET, Charles Albert Emile; *b.* Quebec, 1 Sept., 1862; *s.* of Francois Xavier Blanchet and Emma R. Thomas; unmarried. *Educ.:* Ottawa Univ. and Osgoode Hall; admitted to bar of Ontario, 1888, and has practised there ever since. *Recreations:* Curling, golf, angling, shooting. *Address:* 27 Central Chambers, Ottawa. *Clubs:* Rideau, Golf, Coulonge, F. & G., Ottawa.

BLIGH, Harris Harding, B.A., M.A., D. C.L., K.C.; *b.* Cornwallis, King's Co., N.S., 14 April, 1842; *s.* of James and Sarah E. Bligh; *m.* Alice T. Smith of Halifax. *Educ.:* Acadia Univ., Wolfville, N.S.; called to the bar of N.S., 1863, and practised profession in Halifax, in partnership, first, with Hon. James (now retired Chief Justice) Macdonald, and subsequently, in suceession with William A. Johnston, Q.C., and James W. (now Mr. Justice) Longley; apptd. Official Assignee under the Canadian Insolvent Act, 1879; Revising Officer under the Dominion Electoral Franchise Act, 1885, and Librarian to the Supreme Court of Canada, July, 1892, which last office he still holds; formerly a member of the Senate of Acadia Univ., and later a Senator of McMaster Univ. *Publications:* Index to the Revised Statutes of Canada, 1884. "The Consolidated Orders in Council of Canada," 1899; one of the compilers of the Dominion Law Index, 1890; compiled Statutory Indexes for the Provinces of Ont., Que., N.S., and N.B. *Recreations:* Walking, Riding and gardening. *Address:* 427 Gilmour St., Ottawa.

BLONDIN, Pierre Edouard, LL.L., N. P., M.P.; *b.* St. Francois du Lac., Yamaska Co., Que., 14 Dec., 1874; *s.* of Louis M. Blondin, and Elodie Barnard; *m.* 1901, Marie Rose Buisson; one *d.* *Educ.:* Nicolet Coll., Laval Univ. Clerk of Circuit Ct., Champlain Co.; alderman for town of Grand Mere; elec. to H. of C. for Champlain at g. e., 1908. *Address:* Grand Mere, Que.

BLOUIN, J. Cleophas, B.C.L., M.L.A.; *b.* Levis, Que., 19 Feb., 1864; *s.* of J. B. Blouin, and Adelaide Fouquet; *m.* 1887, Marie Louise Thomas; four *d.* *Educ.:* Levis Coll., Commercial and Classical courses. A boot and shoe manufacturer; mem. of the Bd. of Arts and Manufacture of the Prov. of Que.; 1900; for many yrs. vice-pres. of the Levis Bd. of Trade; dir., of the Levis City Ry.; first el. to Legis., 1901; re-el. at g. e., 1904; 1908. *Address:* P. O. Box 86, Levis, Que.

BLUE, Archibald, LL.D.; *b.* Township of Oxford, Co. of Kent, Ont., 3 Feb., 1840; *s.* John Blue and Mary MacTavish; *m.* (1st) to Mary Black, (2nd) to Amelia Brahant; three *s.* *Educ.:* in Common Sch.; Sch. Teacher for two years; newspaper writer and editor for 14 years; Secretary Bureau of Industries and Deputy Minister of Agriculture, Ont., 10 yrs.; Director Bureau of Mines, Ont., nine yrs.; chief officer of Census of Canada, from 1900 to present time; Can. del. to International Agric. Congress at Rome, Jan., 1910. *Publications:* Annual reports of Bureau of Industries, and Bureau of Mines, census reports, and various bulletins and papers on industrial subjects; also Canada year book. *Address:* The Kenniston, Ottawa.

BOGERT, Ven. Archdeacon James John, M.A., D.C.L., Examining Chaplain of Bishop of Ottawa; *b.* Brockville, Ont., 2 Aug., 1855; *s.* of John Bogert and Mary Radcliffe; *m.* Elizabeth Grant Atkinson; four *s.* and four *d.* *Educ.:* Private Sch. of Rev. A. Palmer, Guelph, and Trinity Coll., Toronto; Curate of Prescott, Rector of Napanee 19 years and Rector of St. Alban's, Ottawa 28 years. *Recreations:* Cricket. *Address:* St. Alban's Rectory, Ottawa.

BOILEAU, Philip; *b.* Quebec, Can., June 1863; *s.* Baron Charles and Susan Taylor Benton Boileau; *Educ.:* in Eng.; studied art in Italy. Began painting 1900; specialty is "Am. girl" portraits. *Address:* 305 5th Av., New York.

BOLDUC, Hon. Joseph, Senator; *b.* St. Francois de la Beauce, 22 Jan., 1847; *s.* of Capt. A. Bolduc; *m.* 1873, M.G.A., *d.* of Jean Mathieu, of St. Francois; one *s.* three *d.* *Educ.:* Ste. Marie Coll., Laval Univ., Que.; el. to H. of C. for Co. of Beauce at g. e., 1870, which seat he held until called to the Senate, Oct., 1884. When a young man went through the Military Sch. at Que., and afterwards served as a Lieut., in the volunteer militia; was mayor of the municipality of St. Victor de Tring, and Warden of the Co. of Beauce; a notary public and lumber merchant. *Address:* St. Victor de Tring, Que. *Club:* Garrison, Quebec.

BOLE, David W.; *b.* Co. of Lambton, Ont., 15 Feb., 1856; *s.* of James Bole and Ann Murdock; *m.* Isabella Lennox; two *s.* one *d.* *Educ.:* Common Sch. Wellford and Woodstock Coll.; pres. of the National Drug and Chemical Co.; was a resident of Winnipeg for many years, during which time he was alderman for two years; member of Sch. Board, eight years; chairman of Sch. Board, three years; pres. Board of Trade, one year, and represented Winnipeg for four years in H. of C. *Address:* 83 Mackay St., Montreal. *Clubs:* St. James', and Montreal,

BOLE, Hon. W. Norman; Local Judge of the Supreme Court and Judge of the Co. Court, New Westminster, B.C.; *b.* Castlebar, 6 Dec., 1844; *e. s.* of late John Bole of Lakefield, Mayo, Ireland, and Elizabeth Jane Campbell; *m.* 1881, Florence Blanchard *o. d.* of Major John Haning Coulthard, J.P.; one *s.* one *d.* Went to New Westminster, 1877; called to B.C. Bar,, 1877; Q.C. 1887; M.L.A., New Westminster, 1886-89; Captain No. 1 Battery, B.C. Brigade Artillery, 1884-89. *Recreations:* shooting, yachting. *Address:* Altamont Villa, New Westminster, B.C. *Clubs:* Terminal City, Vancouver; Royal Vancouver Yacht.

BONAR, James, M.A., LL.D., deputy Master Can. Branch of Royal Mint; *b.* Collace, Pertshire, Scot.; 27 Sept., 1852; *s.* of Andrew A. Bonar, D.D., and Isabella Dickson of Liverpool, (*d.*); two *s.* two *d.* *Educ.:* Glasgow Academy and Univ.; Lepzig and Tubviger Univ., Oxford Univ., Balloit Coll. Arrived in Canada in July, 1907; Lecturer in East London, 1877 to 1880; junior examiner in H. M. Civil Service Commission, 1881 to 1895, Senior examiner, 1895 to 1907, Deputy Master Canadian Branch Royal Mint, 1907; pres. of Section F, (Economics), British Association, 1898. *Publications* Matthus and his work, 1885; Richard's letters to Matthus, 1887; Adam Smith's Library, 1894; Richard's letters to Trower (with Prof. Hallander), 1899; Philosophy and Political Economy, 1893; Eliments of Political Economy, 1903. *Address:* The Mint, or 259 Daly Av., Ottawa, Ont. *Clubs:* Savile, London, Eng.; Rideau, Ottawa, Ont.

BONE, John Rainsford, B.A. (Univ. of Toronto); Managing Editor Toronto Daily *Star* since 1907; *b.* Huron, Ont., 25 Feb., 1877; *s.* of John Bone and Mary Oak; *m.* Edith Evans, *d.* of H. W. Evans, of Toronto; four *d.* *Educ.:* pub. sch., Coll. Inst., Clinton and London, Univ. of Toronto. Graduated from Univ., 1899, with first class honours, gen. scholarship during course. Joined staff of Toronto Daily *Star*, 1900, as reporter; asst. managing ed., 1906; managing ed., 1907, sec.-treas., Canadian Press Assn., since 1905. *Publications:* Associate Editor, "History of Canada Journalism," magazine articles. *Recreations:* lawn bowling. *Address:* 494 Brunswick Av., Toronto, Ont. *Club:* University.

BOOMER, Mrs. Harriet Ann; *b.* Bishop's Hall, Taunton, Eng., 10 July, 1835; *m.* (1st) A. R. Roche, Hon.-Sec. of Royal Colonial Institute and formerly of the Canadian Civil Service; (2nd) Very Rev. Michael Boomer, Dean of Huron, London, Ont. *Educ.:* Private Boarding Sch., at Winchester and Queen's Coll., London, Eng.; pres. London, Ont., Local Council of Women; pres. Mothers' Union, London Convalescent Home, Victorian Order of Nurses; Hon. vice-pres. Woman's Auxiliary Association. Arrived in Canada, 1858. In early girlhood with her monther, took mission work in the Red River Settlement (Winnipeg), and later with her first husband in South Africa; from 1878, associated with the National Council of Women. *Publications:* "On treck in the Transvaal," "Notes from our log in South Africa," and for the last twelve years on the Staff of the Home Magazine Department of Canada's Farmers' Advocate. *Recreations:* Reading and travelling. *Address:* 513 Dundas St., London' Ont.

BOOTH, John R.; *b.* Shefford, Que., 5 April, 1886; *s.* of John Booth and Helen Rowley; *m.* Rosalind Cook (*d.* 1886); two *s.* two *d.* *Educ.:* Waterloo, Que. Commenced business as bridge carpenter. Removed to Ottawa in late fifties; one of the pioneer lumbermen of the Ottawa Valley, his mill at Chaudiere Falls being the largest in Canada. Built the Canada Atlantic Ry. system, aggregating over 500 miles of ry., now operated as part of G. T. Ry. System. C. A. R., completed in 1882; Ottawa and Parry Sound completed in 1896. In addition to lumbering, now owns and operates a large pulp and paper mill at Ottawa, which he commenced to build at 70 yrs. of age. A dir. of the G. T. P. Ry. Co. One of the founders of St. Luke's Hospital; first pres. of Bd. of Governors and still occupies position. *Recreation:* work. *Address:* 252 Metcalfe St., Ottawa. *Club:* Rideau, Ottawa.

BORDEN, Lieut.-Col. The Honourable Sir Frederick William, K.C.M.G., P. C., B.A., M.D., M.P., Minister of Militia and Defence; *b.* Cornwallis, N.S., 14 May, 1847; *s.* of the late Jonathan Borden; *m.* (1st) Oct., 1873, Julia M., *d.* of J. H. Clark, Canning, N.S. (*d*); (2nd) June, 1884, Bessie B. Clark, Canning; two *d.* *Educ.:* King's Coll., Windsor; Harvard Medical Sch., Boston; practiced medicine at Canning, where he was also agent for Halifax Banking Co.; a member of Prov. Board of Health, 1893; apptd. Asst.-Surgeon, 68th Batt., 1869, and by promotion, Surg.-Lieut.-Col, 22 Oct., 1893. Apptd. Hon. Colonel, Army Medical Corps, 1 Aug., 1901; first returned to H. of C. for King's Co., N.S., in 1874; re-elec., 1878, but defeated in 1882; again elec. for same Co., in 1887, 1891, 1896, 1900, 1904, 1908. Sworn of Privy Council, and apptd. Minister of Militia in the Laurier Admin., 13 July, 1896; re-elec. by acclam. on appointment to office; created by King Edward, a Knight Commander of the Most Distinguished Order of St. Michael and St. George, on the occasion of His Majesty's Coronation. Is also a Knight of Grace of the Order of St. John of Jerusalem, 1902; is a mem. of the Imperial Council of Defence Can. del. to Defence Conference, 1909. *Recreations*: Walking, fishing, music. *Clubs:* Rideau, Laurentian, Ottawa; Halifax.

BORDEN, John William; *b.* Grand Pré, N.S., 10 Oct., 1856; *s.* of Andrew Borden and Eunice Jane Laird; *m.* Annie Frances Brown. *Educ.:* Arcadia Villa Academy, Hortonville, N.S.; commenced career in the Railway service, and afterwards banking; at present accountant and Paymaster General Canadian Military Forces. *Recreations:* fruit growing at his county place at Grand Pré. *Address:* 17 Blackburn Av., Ottawa, Ont.

BORDEN, Robert Laird, D.C.L., K.C., M.P., Leader of His Majesty's Opposition in House of Commons; *b.* Grand Pré, 26 June, 1854; *e. s.* of Andrew Borden and Eunice Laird; *m.* Sept., 1889, Laura, *d.* of the late T. H. Bond, Halifax, N.S. *Educ.:* Acadia Villa Academy, Horton; was professor in Glenwood Inst., N.S.; Returning to N.S., he studied law and was admitted to the Bar 1878; before removing to Ottawa, was head of the law firm of Borden, Ritchie and Chisholm, Halifax, and for ten years, pres. of the N.S. Barristers' Society; created Q.C., 1900; Hon LL.D. (Queen's) 1903; Hon. LL.D. (St. Frances Xavier) 1905; elec. to the H. of C. for Halifax, 1896 and 1900; an unsuccessful candidate for Halifax, 1904; Edward Kidd, member for Carleton, Ont., resigned, and he was elec. for that constituency by acclam., 4 Feb., 1905; at gen. elec., re-elec. in Carleton by a large Majority, and also elec. in Halifax, heading the poll; elec. leader of the Conservative party in the H. of C., 6 Feb., 1901. Has made several political tours of the Country; Church of England; Conservative. *Recreations:* Golf, cricket, fishing. *Address:* 201 Wurtemburg St., Ottawa. *Clubs:* Rideau, Laurentian, Ottawa; Halifax.

BOSTOCK, Hon. Hewitt, M.A., F.R.C. I., F.R.A.S.; *b.* The Hermitage Wallan Heath, Epson Surrey, Eng., 31 May, 1864; *s.* of Samuel Bostock and Marian Iliff; *m.* Lizzie Jean McCombie; three *s.* three *d.* Arrived in Canada, 1893; called to the Bar at Lincolns, Feb., 1888; never practiced; travelled for nearly two years on American Continent, in Australia, New Zealand, China and Japan; worked for a time on Labour Commission in 1892-1893; was elec. H. of C. for Yale Cariboo, June, 1896; called to the Senate, 1902. *Publications:* Established "*The Province*" Newspaper, first as a weekly in Victoria, afterwards as a daily in Vancouver, B.C.; now living on a ranch at Ducks, on the main line C. P. Ry. *Address:* Monts Creek, B.C.

BOSWELL, Vesey; *b.* Quebec, 5 April, 1856; *s.* of the late J. K. Boswell and Mary J. Paterson; *m.* 1879, Florence F., *d.* of Alfred E. Brown, of Sydney, N.S.; one *s.* one *d.* Has been sole proprietor and operator of the brewing and malting firm of Boswell & Bro., Quebec, since 1893. Dir. and one of the organizers of the Quebec Bridge Co.; mem. Quebec Bd. of Trade; dir. Quebec Gas Co. and of the Quebec Bank. *Address:* 46 des Carriere's St., Quebec. *Club:* Garrison, Quebec.

BOSWORTH, George Morris, Fourth Vice-Pres., Canadian Pacific Ry.; *b.* Ogdensburg, N.Y., 27 Jan., 1858; *s.* of William C. B. Bosworth, mgr. of the elevators of the Ogdensburg and Lake Champlain Ry., and Elizabeth Linton; *m.* (1st) 1887, Lucy R. (*d.* 1905), *d.* of L. O. Medbury of Detroit, Mich.; (2nd) Alleyne, *d.* of W. D. Birchall, of Montreal; one *s.* one *d.* *Educ.:* Ogdensburg Coll. Inst. Entered Ogdensburg and Lake Champlain Road, 1875; apptd. clerk of local freight office; clerk gen. frt. office; gen. Frt. Agt.; Travelling Frt. Agt. of National Despatch Line at Chicago, 1881, 1882; asst. gen. frt. agt. of Ont. and Que. lines of C. P. R., 1882-1884; gen. frt. agt. of lines east of Fort William, Ont., 1884, 1885; Asst. Frt. Traffic Mgr., 1885-1896; Frt. Traffic Mgr. of entire system, 1896-1901; apptd. 4th vice-pres., C. P. R., 1901. Dir. Provincial Bank of Can., and a number of subsidiary cos. *Recreation:* fishing. *Address:* 41 "Linton Apts." Montreal, Que. *Clubs:* St. James', Canada, Hunt, Jockey, Royal St. Lawrence Yacht, Montreal; Lachine Boating, Canadian Camp, New York; Century, Ogdensburg.

BOXER, Sidney S.; *b.* Quebec, Que, 1853; *s.* of Fred N. Boxer and Charlotte Joyce, *d.* of Rev. Robert R. Burrage. *Educ.:* Montreal and Boston priv. schs. Entered employ of John Watson & Co., wholesale crockery merchants, Montreal, 1870, and is now vice-pres. and man. dir. Watson-Foster Co., Ltd. Dir. Reg. N. Boxer Co., Ltd., Toronto; mem. Montreal Bd. of Trade, Can. Manufacturers' Assn.; life governor Montreal Gen. Hospital; hon. mem. Union Protective Co., of Halifax. *Recreations:* travelling and other outdoor diversions. *Address:* 4837 Western Av., Montreal. *Clubs:* Engineers', Montreal Jockey, Royal Yacht, Hamilton.

BOUCHETTE, Robert Errol, LL.B., F. R.S.C.; *b.* Quebec, 2 June, 1863; *s.* Robert Shore Milner Bouchette, late Com. of Customs, and Clara Lindsay; grandson of late Col. Bouchette, whose maps and geographical works are well known; great gandson of Commodore Bouchette, who commanded provincial navy on the Great Lakes (1784-1804) *m.* Alice Pacaud, *y. d.* of the late Hon. E. L. Pacaud of Arthabaska; three *s.* two *d.* *Educ.:* Laval. A barrister and well-known writer; chief clerk, Library of Parliament. *Publications:* several books on social and economic conditions in Quebec, the effect of which was to cause an economic and educational revival in that province; articles and regular contributions, both in English and French, in magazines and newspapers, Canada, U.S., and Europe. *Address:* 353 Wilbrod St., Ottawa.

BOUDREAU, L. N. H. Rodolphe, B.S., Clerk of the Privy Council; *b.* St. Gregoire, Co. of Nicolet, 19 Sept., 1865; *s.* of Dr. J. B. Boudreau, and Sarah Fortier; *m.* Annie Wensley, of Ottawa; two *d.* *Educ.:* at Nicolet Coll. *Address:* 198 Stewart St., Ottawa.

BOULTON, A. C. Forster, F.R.G.S., M. P. (L.) Ramsey Div. Hunts, since 1906; Barrister; *b.* Port Hope, Ont. *o. s.* of late Forster Boulton, barrister, Ottawa, and Moulton Lines, and Jane, *d.* of Col. Graham 75th Regiment, and *y. d.* of late General Graham, Governor of Stirling Castle; *m.* 1891, Florence (*d.* 1903), *o. c.* of late Henry Harms; two *s.* one *d.* *Educ.:* Trin. Coll. Sch. and Trinity Coll., Toronto. Called to Bar, 1888; Inner Temple, 1896; South-eastern Circuit; Counsel to the Post Office at the Central Criminal Court, 1900, has travelled extensively through United States Canada and Europe; Canadian Pacific Land Explorers, Rocky Mountains, 1885. *Publications:* The Law and Practice of a Case Stated, and various Canadian editions of English text books; Liberalism and the Empire; joint founder with the late Sir Walter Besant of the Atlantic Union. *Recreations;* cycling, angling, travelling. *Address:* 2 Pump Court, Temple, E.C.; St. Ives, Huntingdonshire. *Clubs:* National Liberal, Eighty.

BOURASSA, Henri, M.L.A.; *b.* Montreal 1 Sept., 1868; *s.* of Napoleon Bourassa, author and painter, and Azelie, *d.* of the late Hon. Louis Joseph Papineau. *Educ.:* by private tuition at Montreal. Removed to Montebello in 1886. Was Mayor of Montebello, 1890-1894, and Mayor of Papineauville in 1897. Has written for and edited one or two newspapers; now edits *Le Devoir,* founded 1910. First el. to H of C., at g. e., 1896; resigned his seat in Oct., 1899, in order to vindicate his position on the constitutional aspect of the participation of Canada in the South African War. Re-el. by accl., Jan., 1900; again el. at g. e., 1900 and 1904; el. to Quebec Legis., at g. e., 1908. Leader of Nationaliste party. *Address:* 71a St. James' St., Montreal.

BOVEY, Henry Taylor, F.R.S., D.C.L., LL.D., late Dean of the Faculty of Applied Science, McGill Univ., Montreal; *b.* Devonshire; *m. y. d.* of late John Redpath of Montreal; two *s.* three *d.* *Educ.:* private school; Camb. Univ. On graduation, took high place in the mathematical tripos, and was shortly afterwards made a Fellow of Queen's Coll.; adopting the profession of a civil engineer, he joined staff of the Mersey Docks and Harbour Works, and was in a short time appointed an assistant-engineer on this work, in which capacity he had charge of some of the most important structures then in progress; in 1887 he came to Canada on his appointment as Professor of Civil Engineering and Applied Mechanics in McGill Univ.; at that time the engineering courses in the university were managed as a branch of the Faculty of Arts, and were without buildings or equipment; the following year, however, a department of Applied Science was constituted with Professor Bovey as Dean, and to his management and advice the Science department owes its development. Rector of Imp. Coll. of Science and Technology, London, Eng., May, 1909, resigned (ill health), Dec., 1909; one of the founders of the Canadian Society Civil Engineers, and held the offices of honorary secretary, treasurer, and member of council for many years; vice-president, 1896 and 1897; president, 1900; a member of the Institution of Civil Engineers (England), and of the Liverpool Society of Civil Engineers (of which Society he was one of the founders); an Honorary Member of the National Electric Light Association of the United States; a Fellow of the Royal Soc. of Canada, in which Society he was President of Section III., 1896; vice-president of the Mechanical Section of the British Association, 1897; F.R.S., 1902; Hon. Fellow, Queen's College, Cambridge, 1906. *Publications:* Applied Mechanics, 1882; Theory of Structures and Strength of Materials, 1893, 6th edition, 1905; Hydraulics, 1895; 5th and 6th editions, 1904; also a member of papers for various scientific societies. *Recreations:* golf, lawn-tennis, boating. *Address:* Montreal; London, Eng.

BOVILLE, Thomas Cooper, B.A., deputy Min. of Finance, Canada; *b.* the Grange, County Antrim, Ireland, 14 March, 1860; *s.* of William Boville and Mary O'Neill; *m.* Margaret Caroline, Tapling Silver, *d.* of W. N. Silver, Halifax, N.S. *Educ.:* Model Sch., Belfast, Ireland. Public Sch., and Collegiate Institute, Ottawa, and Toronto Univ. Came to Canada in 1874. Entered public service, Jan., 1883, and has passed through the various grades to the post of Deputy Minister of Finance. He has served since 1882, in the Canadian Militia, and retired to the Reserve of Officers of the 43rd Regiment, with the rank of Captain. Twice one of the representatives of Canada at Bisley, and holds a Queen's Badge. *Recreations:* Shooting, curling, bowling, rowing, cricket. *Address:* Aylmer Apartments, Ottawa. *Club:* Rideau, Ottawa.

BOWELL, Hon. Sir Mackenzie, K.C.M.G., P.C., ed. and prop. Belleville *Intelligencer; b.* Rickinghall, Suffolk, Eng., 27 Dec., 1823; *s.* of John Bowell, contractor and builder; *m.* Dec., 1847, Harriet Louise, *d.* of the late Jacob G. Moore, of Belleville, (*d.* 1884). *Educ.:* Belleville pub. sch. Arrived Canada with his parents, 1832; entered office of Belleville *Intelligencer.* 1834, and remained connected with that paper until he joined Cabinet of Sir John Macdonald, in 1878. On resigning office in 1896, resumed editorship of the *Intelligencer.* Actively connected with the 15th Light Infantry and 49th Rifles, retiring with rank of Lieut.-Col.; served on frontier during American War, 1864–5, and Fenian troubles 1866. A governor of Toronto Univ., and mem. of Senate of Albert Coll., Belleville. Grand Master of the Loyal Orange Assn. of America for many yrs. El. to H. of C. for North Hastings at Confederation, and sat continuously until called to Senate, 5 Dec., 1893. Entered Macdonald Admn. as Minister of Customs, 19 Oct., 1878; Minister of Militia, Abbott Admn., 25 Jan., 1892; Minister Trade and Commerce ,Thompson Admn., 5 Dec., 1893 until 12 Dec., 1894; formed a Ministry 21 Dec., 1894; pres. of Council; reconstructed Ministry, 15 Jan. 1896; resigned 27 April, 1896. Leader Senate, 1893-1896; leader of oppos. in Senate until 1906, when retired. Organized Colonial Conference, of which was chairman, June, 1896; created K.C.M.G., 1 Jan., 1895; pres. Imperial Life Assn. of Can.; ex-pres. Belleville Hardware Mfg. Co., and Northumberland Power Co. *Address:* Belleville, Ont. *Clubs:* Rideau, Ottawa; Albany, Toronto.

BOWMAN, Charles M., M.L.A.; manufacturer and lumber merchant; *b.* St. Jacob's, Waterloo Co., Ont., 7 May, 1863; *e. s.* of the late Isaac E. Bowman; *m.* 1886, Lulu Hessen, of Howell, Mich., U.S. *Educ.:* local pub. schs. and High Sch. of Berlin, Ont. Head of a large modern tannery and a lumber business operating throughout the Bruce Peninsula; was pres. of the Southampton Bd. of Trade, and Reeve of the Municipality. El. to Ont. Leg. Assy. for North Bruce, at g. e., 1898, 1902, 1905, 1908. *Address:* Southampton, Ont.

BOWSER, Hon. William J., LL.B., K.C.; Attorney-General of B.C. since 1907 *b.* Rexton, N.B., 3 Dec., 1867; *s.* of Wm. and Margaret Bowser; *m.* 1896, Lorinda D. Doherty. *Educ.:* Dalhousie Univ., Halifax, N.S. Called to N.B. Bar, 1890; B.C. Bar, 1891; Q.C., 1900; Grand Master of Masons, 1904; el. to Prov. Leg., 1903, 1907. 1909- Apptd. Atty. Gen., 1907. *Recreation:* Riding. *Address:* Vancouver, B.C. *Clubs:* Vancouver, Vancouver, Union, Victoria.

BOWYER, Philip Henry, M.L.A.; *b.* Toronto, Ont., 1 Feb., 1860; *m.* Agnes Yocom, 9 Sept., 1882; two *d.* Elec. to Ontario Legislature, 1905 and 1908; Conservative; Editor of the Ridgetown *Dominion. Address:* Ridgetown, Ont.

BOYCE, Arthur Cyril, K.C., M.P.; *b.* Wakefield, Yorkshire, Eng , 12 Sept., 1867; *s.* Rev. John Cox Boyce, M.A., late Rector of Cornwall Oxfordshire, Eng., and Mary R. B. Boyce (*both d*). *m.* Victoria Mary Louisa, *d.* of Rev. Canon Mochen, Bac. Mus. Milford Bay, Muskoka, one *s.* three *d.* *Educ.:* in private sch. in Wakefield, York and Carlisle, Eng. Arrived in Canada, 12 Sept., 1884; called to the Bar, Osgoode Hall, Toronto, 1890 (honors and bronze medal). elec. M.P. for West Algoma, Nov., 1904 and re-elec., Oct., 1908; created a K.C., 1908: *Address:* Sault Ste. Marie, Ont., and Ottawa *Club:* Albany, Toronto.

BOYD, John; *b.* Montreal, Que., 2 May 1864; unmarried. *Educ.:* Montreal High Sch. and McGill Univ.; began newspaper work, 1881, successively connected with Montreal *Herald*, Montreal *Witness*, and Toronto *Mail and Empire.* Now occupies editorial position on Montreal *Gazette.* Author of many poems and sonnets; on occassion of Quebec Tercentenary celebration, wrote Ode "On The Quebec Battlefields," and "The Fight of the Atalante." Has translated many of leading French Canadian poems into English. In recognition of his work was honored with prominent part in great St. Jean Baptiste celebration held in Montreal, June, 1909, and read poem dedicated to Association on occasion of its seventy-fifth anniversary. Other works include sonnet on occasion of Hilton Tercenterary, sonent on Poe read at centennial celebration held by Univ. of Virginia, sonnet on death of Swinburne and poem on the centenary of the birth of Tennyson; a frequent contributor to the magazines. *Address:* Montreal Gazette, Montreal.

BOYD, Nathaniel; Pres. and Managing Dir. of the Boyd Ranching Co., Carberry, Man.; *b.* Lachute, Que., 9 July, 1853; *s.* of Hugh Boyd and Marie Kilfoyle; *m.* 1878, Miss Abbott, of Ottawa (*d.* 1886); one *s.* one *d.* *Educ.:* Ottawa pub. schs. Commenced his career as an operator in office of Montreal Telegraph; apptd. to the charge of a branch office at the Chaudiere Lumber Mills, Ottawa, 1870; apptd. operator in H. of C., 1876; became chief despatcher and confidential clerk to M. J. Haney, Ry. Contractor, 1879; engaged in building C. P. R. main line between Cross Lake and Rat Portage, 1880-81; mem. of firm of Boyd & Crowe, lumber merchants, 1881-88, when he commenced the breeding of horses and Galloway cattle, and in 1892 the Boyd Ranching Co., was formed, with a stock farm of seven thousand acres, about ten miles from Carberry, Mr. B. now being pres. and mgn. dir. of the Co. First el. to Parlt., for Marquette, 1891; for Macdonald, 1896; re-el. 1900. *Address:* Carberry, Man.

BOYER, Hon. Arthur, Senator; *b.* Montreal, 9 Feb., 1851; *s.* of the late Louis Boyer, and Amelie Mignault; *m.* 1875, Ernestine, *d.* of P. N. Barleneau, of Montreal. *Educ.:* Montreal Coll., and London, Eng.; a mercht.; first el. to Leg. Ass., 1884, and represented Jacques Cartier until g. e., 1892, when unsuccessful. A mem. of the Mercier Govt., without portfolio, 1890-1. Called to Senate, June, 1909. Rep. Canada at Internl. Agric. Congresses at Rome, 1909-10. *Addresses:* 210 Drummond St., Montreal; The Senate, Ottawa. *Club:* Rideau, Ottawa.

BOYER, Benjamin Gustave, M.P.; journalist; *b.* St. Laurent, Jacques Cartier Co., Que., 29 Nov., 1871; *s.* of Benjamin Boyer and Angelique Latour; *m.* 1907, Pamela Rheaume, of Montreal. *Educ.:* St. Laurent Coll. Pub. Lecturer on agric. for the Que. Govt. Has been connected with *La Patrie* as agricul. correspondent, and with *Le Canada*, as agric. editor. Founded the *Echo de Vaudreuil*, 1907; el. Mayor of Rigaud, 1907; Major of B. Squadron, 17th Regt., Duke of York R. C. H. El. to H. of C. for Vaudreuil at g. e., 1904; re-el. 1908. *Address:* Rigaud, Que.

BRABAZON, Gerald H., C.E., Mayor of Portage du Fort, Que.; *b.* Montreal, 7 Dec., 1854; *s.* of Samuel L. Brabazon and Margaret Clarke, *m.* 1879, Nellie Murphy of Portage du Fort. Has been mayor of Portage du Fort for 18 yrs., and Warden of Pontiac Co. for 12 yrs. Served under Middleton in North-West Rebellion, 1885, as first Lieut. in Dennis's Scouts. First ran for Parlt. in 1900, and was defeated, but was el. for Pontiac at g. e., 1900; unsuccessful at g. e., 1908. *Address:* Portage du Fort, Que.

BRADBURN, Thomas Evans, M.L.A.; *b.* Peterborough, Ont., 19 May, 1853; *s.* of Thomas Bradburn and Jane Morrow; *m.* 1874, Catherine Ormond; six *c.* *Educ.:* Pub. and Gram. Schs., Coll. Inst., Peterborough. Was a clerk in his father's store 1871-1875; removed to his father's branch store at Lindsay; purchased, with a Mr. Mason, his father's business, 1877, and continued it under the firm name of Bradburn and Mason until 1887, when returned to Peterborough and entered into the insur. and real estate business. Organized the Peterborough Sugar Co., of which he is pres. Pres. Peterborough Electric Light and Power Co., and of the West Peterborough Conservative Assn. Mem. Peterborough Town Council for three yrs., and of the Sch. Bd. for four yrs. Was for three yrs. Reeve of Monaghan tp., and mem. of the Council for six yrs. First el. to Legis. at g. e., 1905; re-el., 1908. *Address:* Belleville, Ont.

BRADBURY, George Henry, M.P.; *b.* Hamilton, Ont., 29 June, 1859, *s.* of William Murry and Matilda M. Bradbury; unmarried. *Educ.:* At Ottawa; went to Manitoba in 1881; became Managing Director of the North-West Lumber Co., 1882 to 1884; Managing Director Manitoba Pressed Brick Co.; elected to the H. of C., 1908. *Address:* Selkirk, Manitoba. *Club:* Commercial, Winnipeg.

BRADY, Frank Pierce; *b.* Hoveshill, New Hampshire, 22 June, 1853; *s.* of Patrick Brady and Hannah O'Connor; *m.* Harriet Vincent Cavanagh; two *s.* three *d.* *Educ.:* in Newbury, Vermont; and arrived in Canada, Aug., 1880. Has been train despatcher, train master, superintendent and General Superintendent C. P. Ry., from Aug., 1880, until Sept., 1907; at present a member of the Government Railways Managing Board, and General Superintendent. *Address:* Moncton, N.B.

BRAITHWAITE, Arthur Douglas; *b.* Alve, Yorkshire, 1856; *s.* Rev. Wm. Braithwaite, M.A.; *m.* Marjory Hendrill; three *d.* *Educ.:* at Reading. Has been in the service of the Bank of Montreal, since 1 June, 1873. *Recreation:* golf. *Address:* 160 St. George St., Toronto. *Club:* Toronto.

BREADNER, Robert Walker; Manager Tariff Dept. Canadian Manufacturers' Association; *b.* Athelstan, Huntingdon Co., Que., 13 Jan. 1865; *s.* of Major Joshua Breadner and Beatrice Dudgeon Walker; *m.* Nellie Fraser; one *s.* four *d.* *Educ.:* Separate Sch. of Prov. of Que., High Sch., Port Henry, N.Y. In commercial life for short period, afterwards entering Canadian Civil Service; Post Office Dept., 1884-1892; transferred to Customs Dept., 1892-1908, passing through all grades to position of Dominion Appraiser and Chief Clerk; a member of the Board of Customs for ten yrs.; apptd. Manager of Tariff Branch of the C.M.A., which he organized, the object of the department being to assist the manufacturers in obtaining proper tariff classification for imported goods and such other tariff matters as affects the members of the Association. *Recreations:* lawn bowling, angling. *Address:* 488 Brunswick Av., Toronto.

BREITHAUPT, John C.; *b.* Buffalo, N. Y., 27 Feb., 1859; *s.* of the late Louis Breithaupt and Miss Hailer; *m.* 1892, Caroline C., *d.* of John S. Anthes, of Berlin; three *s.* two *d.* *Educ.:* Pub. and High Schs. of Berlin, Northwestern Coll., Napierville, Ill. Removed to Berlin in his early childhood, where he has since been engaged, with one of his brothers, in the leather business, now known as the Breithaupt Leather Co., Ltd. Mem. Berlin Town Council for seven yrs.; Mayor, 1896-1897; reeve for two yrs.; mem. of the Berlin Bd. of Water Commrs,; pres. Berlin and Waterloo Hospitals; mem. Bd. of Publication, Publishing House of the Evangelical Assn., of Cleveland. President Berlin Bd. of Trade in 1895; mem. of the Toronto Bd. of Trade since 1891. *Address:* Berlin, Ont.

BRENT, Rev. Charles Henry; *b.* Newcastle, Ont., Apr. 9, 1862; *s.* Rev. Canon Henry and Sophia Frances Cummings. *Educ.:* Univ. Trinity Coll., Torono; unmarried. Ordained Deacon, 1886, Priest, 1887; Asst. Minister, St. Paul's Cathedral, Buffalo, 1887; St. John Evangelist, Boston, 1888-91; asso. rector St. Stephen's, Boston, 1891-1901; elected by Gen. Conv., 1901, consecrated, Dec., 1901, Bishop of the P. I. On editorial staff of The *Churchman*, New York, 1879-1900; mem. Philippine Opium Comm'n, 1903-4; William Belden Noble Lecturer, Harvard, 1907. *Publications:* With God in the World, 1899; The Consolations of The Cross, 1902; The Splendor of the Human Body, 1904; Adventure for God (Paddock lectures delivered at Gen. Theol. Sem.), 1904; Liberty and other Sermons, 1906; With God in Prayer, 1907. *Address:* 253 Calle Nozaleda, Manila, P. I.

BREYNAT, Mgr. Gabriel, Bishop, Vicar Apostolic of Mackenzie, O.M.I., D.D.; *b.* Saint-Vallcir, France, 5 Oct., 1867. *Educ.:* Seminary of Valence, France; arrived in Canada, 1888; ordained Priest, 21 Feb., 1891; Missionary among the Indians in Mackenzie District until named Titular Bishop and Vicar Apostolic of Mackenzie, on 22 July, 1901. *Address:* Providence, Mackenzie, N.W.T.

BRIERLY, James Samuel; *b.* London, Ont., 4 March, 1858; *s.* James B. Brierly and Jane M. Brierly; *m.* Alison Bosworth Gossage; one *s.* one *d.* *Educ.:* at London, Ont. Publisher and Editor, St. Thomas *Journal*, 1881 to 1905, and Chatham *Banner*, 1894 to 1896. Since that date has been conncteed with the Montreal *Herald*. Del. to Imp. Press Conference, London, 1909. *Address:* 147 Cote St., Antoine Rd., Montreal. *Club:* Montreal.

BRIGGS, Rev. William, D.D., book Steward of the Methodist Book and Publishing House, Toronto; *b.* Banbridge, Co. Down, Ireland; *m.* Rosalie M. Clarke, of Melbourne, Australia; one *s.* *Educ.:* Liverpool, Eng.; arrived in Can., 1859; preached successively in Montreal, London, Cobourg, Belleville and Toronto. Apptd. to present position, 1879. Degree of D. D. conferred by Victoria Univ. *Address:* 21 Grenville St., Toronto.

BRILL, Hascal R., LL.D.; *b.* Que., Aug. 10, 1846; *s.* Thomas R. and Sarah Sager Brill. *Educ.:* pub. schs., Can. and Minn., Hamline Univ. and Univ. of Mich. Studied law in St. Paul. *m.* Niagara Falls, N.Y., 1873, Cora A. Gray. Admitted to bar, 1870; judge probate court, Ramsay Co., Minn., 1873-4; judge common pleas court, Ramsay Co., 1875-6; judge dist. court, 2d jud. dist., Minn., since 1876 (present term expires 1913); Republican. *Address:* 471 Laurel Av., St. Paul.

BRISTOL, Edmund, B.A. (Univ. of Toronto), K.C., M.P.; *b.* Napanee, Ont., 1 Sept., 1861; *s.* of A. S. Bristol, M.D. (McGill Univ.), and Sarah M. Everett; *m.* Mary Dorothy ,*d.* of the late Mr. Justice Armour of the Supreme Court of Canada. *Educ.:* Napanee High Sch., Upper Can. Coll., Toronto Univ. Graduated from Toronto Univ. in 1883 with first class honors in classics; called to the Bar in 1886; el. by accl. to Parlt. for Centre Toronto, 11 April, 1905; re-el. at g. e., 1908; created King's Counsel by Dom. Govt., 1896, and by Ont. Govt., 1907. Specialty corporation law. *Recreations:* hunting, golf. *Address:* Res., 179 Beverley St.; postal, 103 Bay St., Toronto. *Clubs:* Toronto, Albany, National, Royal Canadian Yacht, Toronto Hunt; Rideau, Golf, Ottawa.

BRITTON, Hon. Byron Moffatt, M.A., K.C.; *b.* Ganonoque, Ont., 3 Sept., 1833; *s.* of Daniel Freeman Britton; *m.* Mary Eliza Halton, *d.* of late Hon. C. H. Halton (*d.*); three *s.* six d. *Educ.:* Victoria Coll., Cobourg. Called to the Bar, Sept., 1859; Mayor of Kingston, 1876; Co. Attorney, 1882; elec. to H. of C., 1896, and re-elec. 1900; apptd. Judge of the High Court of Justice, Prov. of Ont., Sept., 1901. *Address:* Osgoode Hall, Toronto, Ont.

BROCHU, Michael Delphus, B.A. (Que. Seminary), M.D. (Laval Univ.); Medical Supt. of the Beauport Asylum, *b.* Ste. Lazarre, Bellechasse Co., Que., of French Canadian descent; *m.* (1st) 1878, Eugenie Mava (*d.* 1879); 1894, Miss Fortin, of Que.; eight *c.* *Educ.:* Quebec Seminary, Laval Univ. Commenced practice in Quebec; apptd. Prof. of Hygiene of the Faculty of Médicine, Laval Univ., 1884; Prof. of Internal and Nervous Diseases, 1829; Prof. of Mental Diseases since 1903; apptd. Medical Supt. of the Beauport Asylum, 1903; el. vice-pres. Medical Council of Prof. of Quebec, 1902; pres. Quebec Medical Assn., 1904. *Address:* 63 St. John St., Quebec.

BROCK, Henry, B.A., D.C.L.; *b.* Township of Walfagar, Ont., 14 May, 1859; *s.* of William Rees Brock, ex-M.P. for Toronto, and Margaret Anna Diamond, *d.* of Capt. John S. Diamond of Queen's Co., Ireland; *m.* Anna Maude, *e. d.* of H. Cawthra, Toronto. *Educ.:* Up. Can. Coll. and Toronto Univ., Toronto; one *d.* Retired with rank of Major, in the Canadian Militia; served in the North-West campaign, 1885; (medal and clasp); mentioned in despatches; retired Barrister; Director in the W. R. Brock Co., Ltd., the Dominion Fire Insurance Co., The Standard Granite Co. *Recreations:* rifle shooting, riding. *Address:* 216 Beverly St., Toronto. *Clubs:* Toronto, Hunt, Toronto.

BROCK, Reginald Walter, M.A., F.C.S., F.G.S.A., Director Geo. Survey of Canada; *b.* Perth, Ont., 1874; *s.* Rev. Thomas Brock and Marianne Jenkins; *m.* Mildred G., *d.* of Hon. Mr. Justice Britton. *Educ.:* Ottawa Collegiate Institute and Mount Forest High. Sch., Toronto Univ., Sch. of Mining Kingston, and Heidelberg Univ. Vice-Pres., Am. Assn. Advancement of Science, and Chairman Section E. Councillor Can. Mining Institute; mem. Mining Institute;Mining and Metallurgical Society, and National Geographical Society. In 1897, was appointed to the technical staff of the Geological Survey of Canada, and from 1902 to 1907, was Professor of Geology and Petrography, School of Mining, Kingston. In 1907, was apptd. Director of the Geological Survey of Canada. *Publications:* Reports of the Geological Survey, and in Scientific Journals. *Recreations:* Open air sports, exploration and mountaineering. *Address:* Ottawa. *Club:* Rideau, Ottawa.

BROCK, William Rees; *b.* Eramosa, Ont., 14 Feb., 1836; *s.* of Thomas Rees Brock, and Eleanor Thompson; *m.* Margaret Anna, *d.* of Captain John Sigur Diamond of Queen's Co., Ireland, 23 Sept., 1857; three *s.* three *d.* *Educ.:* Guelph Gram. Sch.; studied law and then went into business. Pres. of the W. R. Brock Co., Ltd., Toronto, Montreal, and Calgary; Pres., The Canadian General Electric Co.; Vice-Pres., The Western, and British America Assurance Companies; Director Dominion Bank; The Toronto General Trust. *Recreation:* travel. *Address:* 21 Queen's Park, Toronto. *Clubs:* Toronto, Hunt; Albany, Toronto; St. James', Montreal.

BRODER, Andrew, M.P.; *b.* Franklin Centre, Que., 18 April, 1845; *s.* of William Broder; *m.* Carrie Summers; three *s.* one *d.* *Educ.:* Malone N.B., and Huntingdon,Academy, Que. A farmer and merchant until 1982, when he became collector of Customs at Morrisburg, Ont.; resigned in 1896, to become candidate for H. of C.; elec. 1896, 1904, 1908; represented Dundas in the Ontario Legislature, 1875-1886. *Address:* Morrisburg, Ont.

BRODEUR, Hon. Louis Philippe, K.C., LL.D.; Minister of Marine and Fisheries; *b.* Beloeil, Que., 21 Aug., 1862; *s.* Toussaint Brodeur and Justine Lambert; *m.* Emma Brillon; four *s.* and one *d.* *Educ.:* St. Hyacinthe Coll. and Laval Univ. Admitted to the Bar in 1884; elec. to Commons in 1891, re-elected in 1896, when he became Deputy Speaker of the H. of C. and Chairman of Committees. After election of 1900, was apptd. Speaker of the House, and in 1904 entered the Laurier Cabinet with the portfolio of Minister of Inland Revenue. Accompanied Sir Wilfrid Laurier to England, as a delegate to the Colonial Conference of 1907. In Jan., 1906, assumed portfolio of Minister of Marine and Fisheries; delegate to Imperial Defence Conference, 1909. *Address:* 169 Daly Av., Ottawa, Ont. *Clubs* Rideau, Hunt, Ottawa; Montreal, St. Denis, Canadien, Montreal.

BRODRICK, Arthur Bentley; Mgr. Molson's Bank, Ottawa; *b.* Jersey, Channel Islands, 9 Nov., 1858; *s.* of Charles Cumberland Brodrick and Mary Anne Balleine; *m.* Julia Alice Travis. *Educ.:* Christ's Hospital, Victoria Coll., Jersey. Arrived Can., 1876; with Molson's Bank at Brockville, Toronto, Montreal, Ingersoll, Exeter, Smiths Falls; now mgr. of the Ottawa branch. *Recreation:* golf. *Address:* 473 Wilbrod St., Ottawa. *Club:* Rideau, Ottawa.

BRONSON, Mrs. Ella Hobday Webster; *b.* Portsmouth, Va., U.S.A., 1 Sept., 1846; *d.* of Nathan B. Webster, and Isabella Hobday Webster; *m.* Erskine Henry Bronson, of Ottawa; one *s.* one *d.* *Educ.:* Portsmouth, Va.; arrived in Can., Sept., 1874. Active in charitable work in Ottawa; mem. of Nat. Council of Women. *Recreations:* driving, automobiling. *Addresses:* 75 Bronson Av., Ottawa; Kennebunkport, Me., U.S.A.

BRONSON, Hon. Erskine Henry; Pres. The Bronson Co., Ottawa; *b.* Bolton, Warren Co., N.Y., 1844; *s.* of Henry Franklin Bronson and Editha Pierce; *m.* 1874, only *d.* of Prof. N. B. Webster, of Norfolk, Va.; one *s.* one *d.* In 1867 was given an interest in his father's business, the Bronson-Weston Lumber Co., and is to-day pres. of the Bronson Co., of Ottawa. Pres. Ottawa Carbide Co., and the Ottawa Power Co. Was one of the inaugurators of the Ottawa Electric Co., one of its directors. Was for fourteen yrs., mem. Ottawa Pub. Sch. Bd.; mem. of the Ottawa City Council, 1870-1878; unsuccessful candidate for H. of C. in Carleton Co., 1882; mem. for Ottawa in Ont. Legis., 1886-1898; joined the Mowat Govt., without portfolio, 10 Sept., 1890, and held a similar position in the Hardy Govt. *Address:* 75 Bronson Av., Ottawa.

BROOME, Isaac; *b.* Valcartier, Que., May 16, 1835; *s.* Isaac and Annie Broome. *Educ.:* Phila. until 1850; art at Pa. Acad. Fine Arts, Phila., and pvt. tutors; *m.* Feb. 9, 1856, Victoria Myers, Washington. Worked on Crawford statues for pediment of U.S. Capitol, 1855-6; executed statue for W. W. Corcoran's Mausoleum at Georgetown, D.C., 1857; established studio at Rome, Italy, 1858; executed many works in sculpture; mfd. art tiles extensively; now living in Southern climate for health; devoted to ideal sculpture. Elected academician Pa. Acad. Fine Arts, 1860; dir. life and antique dept., 1860-3. Medals for ceramic arts, Centennial Exp'n, 1876. Paris Exp'n, 1878; sp'l. comm'r on ceramics, Paris Exp'n, 1878 by United States Government and State of N.J.; dir. many schs. for teaching fine and industrial arts and the sciences. Active in edn'l, polit. and industrial reforms lectured extensively on these subjects; was mem. Ruskin Industrial Co-operative Assn. Chautauqua lecturer on ceramic arts, etc. *Publications:* The Brother, 1890; Last Days of the Ruskin Cooperative Association, 1902 Extensive contb'r to mags. and newspapers. Invented the Perfected Rotary Press, 1906-7. *Address:* Jonesboro, Ga.

BROPHY, George Patrick, J.P.; Superintending Engr. of the Ottawa River Works; *b.* Carillon, Argenteuil Co., Que., 24 Feb., 1848; *m.* 1870, Elizabeth M., *d.* of M. Clarke, of Quebec; one *s.* four *d.* *Educ.:* Ottawa Pub. Schs. One of the founders of the Ottawa Street Ry., in 1893; a dir. of the Co.; was one of the promoters of the Chaudiere Electric Co., and is also interested in the Ontario Graphite Co. Vice-Pres., Ottawa Trust and Deposit Co.; dir. Ottawa Gas Co. *Address:* 320 Chapel St., Ottawa. *Club:* Rideau, Ottawa.

BROSSEAU, Toussaint, K.C.; *b.* Chambly, Que., 21 Sept., 1857; *s.* of Louis Brosseau and Celina Senical; *m.* Eugenie Brais; two *s.* *Educ.:* Jesuits Coll., Montreal. *Address:* Montreal, Que. *Clubs:* St. James', Hunt, Montreal.

BROUGHALL, Frederick William; *b.* Toronto, 12 Aug., 1867; *s.* Rev. A. J. and Mrs. Broughall; *m.* Miss Strathy; three *s.* one *d.* *Educ.:* Trinity Coll. Sch., Port Hope. Entered service of Dominion Bank, 1885, and passed through all grades, until apptd. mgr. of the Sterling Bank of Can., 1896. *Address:* 1 Elmsley Pl., Toronto. *Clubs:* Toronto, National, Albany, Toronto.

BROWN, Adam, Postmaster of Hamilton, Ont.; *b.* Edinburgh, Scotland; *s.* of William and Elizabeth Brown; *m.* (1st) Marian Evath, and (2nd) Mary Kough; nine *s.* two *d.* *Educ.:* Montreal, in the private sch. of Rev. Edward Black, D.D. Has always been connected with mercantile pursuits; removing to Hamilton, Ont., in 1850; member of H. of C., 1886-1891; commissioner for the Government to Jamaica; Chairman of Hamilton Water Works. Presented the address to H. R. H. the Prince of Wales (now King Edward VII), at the opening of the Water Works in 1860. *Address:* Hamilton, Ont.

BROWN, David Robertson; architect; *b.* Montreal, 1869; *s.* of James Brown and Elizabeth Robertson; *m.* 1900, Harriet Fairbairn, *s. d.* of William Robb, City Treas. Montreal. *Educ.:* Montreal High Sch., and studied architecture in Montreal and Boston. Commenced practice in Montreal, 1892; entered into partnership with Hugh Vallance, firm being David R. Brown & Hugh Vallance. Pres. Quebec Assn. of Architects. Designed Bd. of Trade Bldg., Montreal, M.A.A.A., Olivet Baptist Church, new Medical Bldg., of McGill Univ., Children's Memorial Hospital, the Standard Shirt Bldg., Southam Bldg., etc. Member Montreal Bd. of Trade, Architectural League of New York. *Address:* 729 Pine Av., W., Montreal. *Clubs:* Canada, St. Lawrence Yacht, Beaconsfield Golf.

BROWN, Gerald H.; *b.* Ottawa, Ont., 30 July, 1875; *s.* of Horace Taylor Brown and Minnie McLardy, both of Ottawa; *m.* Eva Isabella Sharpe *e. d.* of Mr. and Mrs.

John Sharpe of Ottawa; one *d.* *Educ.:* pub. sch. and Collegiate Institute, Ottawa. For many years a newspaper man; was resident correspondent in Ottawa, from 1893 to 1909, representing various Canadian and British papers, including, Montreal *Witness*, Toronto Daily *Star*, Manitoba *Free Press*, Vancouver *Province*, The *Tribune* and *Daily News* of London, Eng., and "*Canada*"; also published in London, Eng.; was attached also for a time, to Ottawa *Free Press*, and Ottawa *Evening Journal*. President Press Gallery, Dominion Parliament, 1900; apptd. Assistant Deputy Minister of Labour for Canada, March, 1909; Hon. Secretary (1906-1909), First Vice-President (1909), of Canadian Club of Ottawa. *Address:* 6 McLeod St., Ottawa, Ont. *Clubs:* Ottawa Golf Club, Ottawa, Ont.

BROWN, Miss Edith; *b.* Wolfville, N. S., 1874; *d.* John Lothrop and Elizabeth Whidden Brown; ed. Acadia Sem. to 1890. *Educ.:* Boston Mus. of Fine Arts Sch., 1895. Teacher of clay modeling and drawing in Miss Pierce's pvt. sch., Brookline, Mass.; Miss Hazard's pvt. sch., Boston, and N. Bennet St. Industrial Sch., Boston. First illustrating done for The Churchman about 1899. Mem. Copley Soc., Boston. *Illustrator:* Folk-lore Stories and Proverbs (Miss S. E. Wiltse), 1900; Wonderfolk in Wonderland (Edith Guerrier), 1903; Stella's Adventures in Starland (Elbridge H. Sabin), 1907; The Cheerful Cricket (Jeanette Marks), 1907. *Address:* Chestnut Hill, Mass.

BROWN, George Mackenzie; *b.* Canada, 1869; *s.* of Hon. George Brown of Toronto, many yrs. leader of the Liberal Party in Canada; *m.* 1901, Mary Elinor, *y. d.* ol late Thomas Nelson, St. Leonard's, Edinburgh. *Educ.:* Up. Can. Coll., Toronto; Merchiston Castle Sch., Edinburgh; King's Coll., Cambridge; M.P. (L.) Central Edinburgh, 1900-1906. *Address:* 20 Moray Place, and Parkside Works, Edinburgh. *Clubs:* Royal Societies; University, Edinburgh.

BROWN, George McLaren; Gen. Traffic Mgr. (in Europe) for the C. P. R.; *b.* Hamilton, Ont., 29 Jan., 1865; *s.* of Adam Brown and Mary Kough; *m.* 1890, Eleanor Graham *d.* of John Crerar, K.C., of Hamilton. *Educ:* Priv. Sch. at Shrewsbury, Eng., Hamilton Gram. Sch., Up. Can. Coll. Became clerk in freight dept. of Northern and Northwestern Ry., in Hamilton; employed in G. T. R. System at Hamilton, 1883-1887; became agt. of the C. P. R., at Vancouver, 1887; asst. gen. passngr. agt. of C. P. R., for Western Div., 1892-1897, apptd. executive agt. of Western lines, 1897; transferred to Montreal 1902, as mgr. of Atlantic Steamship line; present position, 1908. *Address:* 62 Charing Cross, London, S.W., Eng.

BROWN, James Pollock, M.P.; *b.* Beau River, 4 April, 1841; *s.* of David Brown and Jean Pollock, both of Renfrewshire, Scot.; *m.* 19 Feb., 1869, Margaret Stewart. *Educ.:* Elimentary Sch., and Business Coll., New Haven, Conn.: elec. to H. of C., 1891, 1896, 1900, 1904, and 1908; Liberal. *Address:* St. Chrysostome, Que.

BROWN, Mrs. Margaret Adeline; wife of J. Y. Brown, of Brantford, Ont.; *b.* Huron Co., 3 Dec., 1867; *d.* Richard Porter and Margaret McKee. *Educ.:* Goderich Coll. Inst. and honour graduate of Toronto Normal Sch.; one *d.* *Publication:* "My Lady of the Snows." *Recreations:* Painting in oils, water colours and china; wood carving. *Address:* Court House, Brantford; Country home, Brant Co.

BROWNE, William Graham, B.A.; *b.* Galt, Ont., 28 May, 1874; *s.* of Dr. J. Price of Toronto, and Agnes Cranston Graham; *m.* Edna Carlyle, two *s.* *Educ.:* Galt Coll. Inst., Jarvis St. Coll. Inst., Toronto Univ. Entered service of Can. Bank of Commerce in Galt; afterwards in Toronto and New York; now dealer in bonds, etc., in Montreal under firm name of W. Graham Browne & Co. *Address:* 297 University St., Montreal. *Clubs:* St. James, Hunt, University, Canada, Montreal; Toronto, National, Toronto; Garrison, Quebec.

BROWNELL, Franklin, R.C.A.; *b.* New Bedford, Mass., U.S.A., 28 July, 1857; *s.* of Leander and Annice Brownell; *m.* 1889, Louise, *d.* of John W. Nickerson of New Bedford; one *d.* *Educ.:* Public Schs. of Mass. Studied art at Sch. of Boston Museum, of Art., and at Paris with Bougureau and Fleury; Head Master of Ottawa Art Association, 1885-98; present work principally portraits, combined with some genre and landscape painting; exhibited at Paris salons and principal exhibitions of U.S. and Canada; bronze medal, Paris Exposition of 1900; representative works at the Canadian National Gallery. *Recreations:* rod and gun *Address:* 124 Wellington St., Ottawa, Ont.

BROWNLEE, Walter George; *b.* Lawrenceville, Illionois, U.S.A., 9 Sept., 1858; *s.* of William and Sarah Brownlee; *m.* May Adele Cunningham; one *s.* *Educ.:* Public Sch. Arrived in Canada, 1 Feb., 1899; has been telegraph operator; train despatcher, train master, and superintendent; now gen. transportation mgr. for G. T. R. *Address:* 419 Lansdowne Av., Montreal. *Club:* Canada, Montreal.

BRUCE, Alexander, M.A., K.C.; *b.* Langside, Aberdeenshire, Scot., 23 March, 1836; *s.* of William and Isabella Bruce: *m.* Agnes Robb, *d.* of Rev. Ralph Robb; two *s.* four *d.* *Educ.:* Langside Parish Sch., Aberdeen Gram. Sch., and Aberdeen Univ.; arrived in Canada in 1854; studied law in the office of the late Sir George Britton, and was partner of his, until elevated to the bench, in 1874; since then head of the firm in Hamilton, Ont.; removed to Toronto in 1905. *Recreations:* Walking and travelling *Address:* 91 Bedford Road, Toronto. *Clubs:* Toronto, R. C. Y. C., Toronto and Hamilton.

BRUCHESI, Rt. Rev. Mgr. Paul, Archbishop of Montreal; *b.* Montreal, 29 Oct., 1855; *s.* of Paul Bruchési and Caroline Aubrey. *Educ.:* at Montreal Coll., and Montreal Seminary, also Paris and Rome. Ordained Priest, 21 Dec., 1878; Archbishop of Montreal, 8 Aug., 1897. *Publications:* Religious Essays, Sermons, and Pastoral Letters. *Address:* Archbishop's Palace, Montreal.

BRUNTON, David William; *b.* Ayr, Can., June 11, 1849; *Educ.:* Toronto; course mining. eng'ring Univ. of Mich.; in Colo., since 1875; now mine mgr. and president. Taylor & Brunton Sampling Works Co., of Aspen, Colo.; v.-p., 1897, Am. Inst. Mining Eng'rs.; life mem. Inst. of Civ. Eng'rs.; and

Royal Geog. Soc.; mem. Colo. Scientific Soc., etc. *Address:* 865 Grant Av., Denver, Colo.

BRYCE, Rev. George, M.A., D.D., LL.D., F.R.S.C.; *b.* Mount Pleasant, Brantford, Ont., Can., 22 April, 1844; *s.* of George Bryce, J.P., and Katherine Henderson, natives of Perthshire, Scotland, and early settlers in Brant County, Ontario; *m.* 1872, Marion Samuel of Broom House, Kirkliston, West Lothian, Scotland. *Educ.:* Brantford High Sch.; Univ. of Toronto; Knox Coll., Toronto. A founder, councillor, and examiner of Univ. of Manitoba, 1877-1907; Head of Faculty of Science and Lecturer in Biology and Geology in Manitoba Univ., 1891-1904; Senior Professor and Financial Agent of Manitoba Coll., Winnipeg; also Professor of English Literature. Took numerous scholarships, etc.; Examiner in Natural History in Toronto Univ., 1870-72; selected by General Assembly of Presbyterian Church of Canada to proceed to Winnipeg to organize a church and coll., 1871; organized Manitoba Coll., 1871; organized Knox Church, Winnipeg, 1872; first Moderator of Synod of Manitoba, 1885; Moderator General Assembly of Presbyterian Church in Canada, 1902-3; Chairman of Winnipeg Public Library, 1893-1903. *Publications:* Manitoba; Infancy, Progress, and Present Condition, 1882; Short History of Canadian People, 1887; The Apostle of Red River, 1898; Remarkable History of the Hudson's Bay Company, 1900; Makers of Canada (series), 1906; articles in Ency. Brit.; Nar. and Crit. Hist. of America; Canadian Encyclopedia and numerous transactions and pamphlets. *Recreations:* in college days, Captain Univ. of Toronto Football Club; 1861-68, a volunteer officer of Univ. Co. (Queen's Own); in Ridgeway fight against Fenians, 1866. *Recreation:* curling. *Address:* Kilmadock, Winnipeg.

BRYCE, Peter Henderson, M.A., M.D., L.P.C.P. & S. (Edin.); Chief Medical Officer, Dept. of Interior and Dept. of Ind. Affairs, Ottawa; *b.* Mount Pleasant, Brant Co., Ont., 17 Aug., 1853, of Scotch parentage; *m.* K. Lynde Pardon, of Guelph; four *s.* two *d.* *Educ.:* Mount Pleasant Gram. Sch. and Up. Can. Coll., Toronto. After teaching in a pub. and gram. sch. one yr., went to Toronto Univ., in 1872 (grad. 1876); Gold Medal in Science and the McMurrich Medal for essay on Geology of the Grand River; Literary and Scientific Society's prize for best Literary Essay. In 1876, was apptd. to Natural Science Professorship, Guelph Agrig. Coll. After two yrs., resigned to continue medical studies, grad. 1880 from Toronto Univ., with Sch. Scholarship and the Univ. First Silver Medal and Star Medal for special pathology. Received the same yr. degree L.P.C.P. & S., Edinburgh, and continued studies there and in Paris. Returning, practiced in Guelph. In 1882, accepted the position of Sec. to Bd. of Health of Ont., just organized and removed to Toronto. Continued practice as well as Pub. Health Work, till 1888. In 1892, had the additional duties of Dep. Registrar Gen. added, and continued in the position till Jan., 1904, when he was offered and accepted his present position. A mem. of the American Public Health Assn., since 1885; pres. 1900; for yrs. a mem. of the Royal Sanitary Inst., of Great Britain. *Publications:* Annual Address on "History of the Progress of Public Health during the Century 1800-1900;" "The Science of the Preservation of Food by Cold." Among the most important of his papers is "Climates and Health Resorts of Canada," prepared for the British Medical Assn., meeting in Montreal in 1896, published by the C. P. Ry., and has been distributed by hundreds of thousands; at present editing the Report of the Committee of Public Health of the Senate of Canada. *Address:* Lisgar Road, Rockliffe, Ottawa.

BRYMNER, William; Pres. R.C.A. of A.; *b.* Greenock, Scot., 14 Dec., 1855; *s.* of Dr. Douglas Brymner, late Dominion Archivist; unmarried. *Educ.:* St. Frances Coll., Richmond, Que.; St. Therese Coll., St. Therese, Que.; and studied art in Paris, under W. A. Bouguereau and T. Robert Fleury. Arrived in Canada, 1857; received Gold Medal for painting at the Pan American Exhibition, Buffalo, N.Y., and at the Louisanna Purchase Exhibition, St. Louis, Mo. He has conducted the Advanced Art Classes of the Art Association of Montreal, since 1886. *Address:* 255 Bleury St., Montreal, Que. *Club:* St. James', Montreal.

BRYSON, Hon. Geo.; *b.* Fort Coulonge, Que., 20 July, 1872; *s.* George Bryson Paisley and Robina Cobb, Glasgow, Scot.; *m.* Helen Craig; one *s.* four *d.* *Educ.:* Commercial Coll., Ottawa, and Toronto. Has been a lumberman all his life. Apptd. to Legislative Council of Quebec in 1887; is vice-pres. and dir. of the Bank of Ottawa. *Recreations:* Fishing and Hunting. *Club:* Rideau, Ottawa.

BUCHANAN, James Isaac; *b.* Hamilton, Ont., Aug. 3, 1853; *s.* Isaac and Agnes (Jarvie) Buchanan; *m.* Eliza Macfarlane, Pittsburgh. *Educ.:* in schs. of Hamilton and Tassie's Collegiate Inst., Galt, Ont.; Trustee estate of J. J. Vandergrift, deceased, founder of town of Vandergrift, Pa.; pres. Pittsburgh Trust Co., Pittsburgh Terminal Warehouse and Transfer Co.; sec. and treas. Keystone Commercial Co.; dir. Keystone Nat. Bank of Pittsburgh, Natural Gas Co., of W. Va. Presby'n; ex-pres. Presby'n Union of Pittsburgh and Allegheny. Chmn. Orchestra Com., Pittsburgh Art Soc.; mem. Bot. Soc. of Western Pa., Pittsburgh Acad. of Science and Art, A. A. A. S. *Clubs:* Duquesne Country, Oakmont Country, Thousand Islands Yacht. *Address:* 6108 Walnut St. *Office:* 323 4th Av., Pittsburgh.

BUCKINGHAM, William; *b.* Crediton, Eng., 3 Dec., 1832; *s.* of Robert and Jane Buckingham; *m.* Martha Phelps; six *s.* four *d.* *Educ.:* in the pub. sch. at Crediton, Eng. Arrived in Canada, in 1857, when he joined the staff of the Toronto *Globe.* In 1859, he inagurated the first newspaper, "*The Nor' Wester,*" in the North West Territories, at Fort Garry. He has since owned the Norfolk *Reformer,* and the Stratford *Beacon.* Joint author (with Hon. Geo. W. Ross), of "The Life and Times of Hon. Alexander Mackenzie, the first Liberal Premier of Canada. He has written for various publications, sketches of other Canadian Statesmen. *Address:* Stratford, Ont.

BUCKNAM, Ransford D., naval adviser and a.-d.-c. to H. I. M. The Sultan; *b.* Hansport, N.S., 1869; *s.* Ezra Taylor and Isabella Roscoe Bucknan. *Educ.:* pub. schs. of Me. and N.Y.; *m.* Phila., Jan. 2, 1904, Rose Thayer. Removed with parents to Me., when an infant; lived nr. Bucksport; went to sea in merchant sailing ship at 14 yrs. of age; comd. merchant steam and sailing ships on both Atlantic and Pacific Coasts and Great Lakes. Supt. Am. Steel Barge Co. of N.Y.; supt. Pacific Mail Steamship Co. at Panama; supt. Cramps' shipyards, Phila.; trial comdr. U.S. S. "Maine," and Imperial Ottoman steamship "Medjidia," comd. latter from Phila. to Turkey, and apptd. naval adviser and personal a.-d.-c. to the Sultan, Apr. 19, 1904. Decorated with Turkish Order of Osmanieh, and distinguished service medal; mem. Boston Marine Soc., Republican. *Clubs:* Lotos (New York), Art, Pen and Pencil (Phila), International (Panama), Constantinople). *Address:* Rue Marlian, 38. *Office:* Navy Dept., Constantinople, Turkey.

BULLOCK, Thomas Harrison, Mayor of St. John, N.B.; *b.* Wentworth Co., Ont., 14 Feb., 1862; *s.* Joseph and Elizabeth Bullock; *m.* Jeannette Chestnut; two *s.* three *d.* *Educ.:* Pub. Sch. terminating at St. John Gram. Sch.; was two years as Mayor of St. John, the second term by acclam.; five yrs. as alderman and Co. Councillor. He has made a special study of municipal work, which resulted in the improvement and advancement of all departments during his term of office. Refused nominations for both Provincial and Federal Houses. Has been associated with his father in the oil business in the Maratime Provinces, and is now manager of the Imperial Oil Co. He is a director in several large enterprises and takes a deep interest in the Sch. Board, Board of Trade, Tourist Association, Industrial Home for Boys, Seaman's Mission; Associated Charities, Victorian Order of Nurses, etc. *Address:* 183 Germain St., St. John.

BULYEA, Hon. George Headley Vickers, B.A., LL.D., Lieut.-Gov. of Alberta; *b.* Gagetown, Queen's Co., N.B.; *s.* of James A. Bulyea and Jane Blizzard; *m.* Annie Blanche Babbit (*d.*); one *s.* *Educ.:* Queen's Co. Gram. Sch. and Univ. of N.B. Was Principal of Sunbury Co. Gram. Sch., from Sept., 1878, to May, 1882. Arrived in Winnipeg, 14 May, 1882, and went to Qu' Appell the following spring, and engaged in business until 1897. He was a candidate for the North West Council in 1892, but was defeated. Was elec. in 1894; selected as a member of the first Executive Council, 1892; special representation to the Yukon, in 1896; re-elec. in 1898, and 1902. Commissioner of Agriculture and Commissioner of Public Works in Territorial Government, until apptd. first Lieut.-Governor of Alberta 1 Sept., 1905. *Recreations:* Driving and travelling. *Address:* Edmonton, Alta.

BUMBRAY, J. E. C.; advocate; *b.* Hochelaga, Que., 1879; *s.* of Ald. Bumbray and Elise Masson; *m.* (1st) Eva (*d.* 1902), *d.* of Mr. C. H. Laurier; (2nd) M. L., *d.* of Prof. Hervieux, of Laval Univ., Montreal. *Educ.:* St. Mary's Coll., Laval Univ. Called to Bar, 1902, and has since practiced in Montreal. Del., Laval Univ., to Exposition at Paris, France, 1900. *Address:* 56 Prefontaine St., Montreal.

BURGESS, T. J. W., M.D., F.R.S.C.; Professor of Mental Diseases, McGill Univ., Montreal; *b.* Toronto, Canada, 11 March, 1849; *y. s.* of Thomas Burgess and Jane Rigg, both natives of Carlisle, Cumberland; *m.* 1875, Jessie, 2nd *d.* of late Lieut.-Col. Alex. Macpherson, of Whitby, Ont.; three *d.* *Educ.:* Up. Can. Coll. and Toronto Univ. Graduated in medicine as Starr gold medallist and 1st Univ. silver medallist, 1870; appointed surgeon to H.M's British North American Boundary Commission, 1872, and served as such until the close of the work, being thanked by H. M.'s Government for the efficient way in which he had carried out the duties; took up the study of mental diseases and became assistant physician of the London Asylum for Insane, 1875; assistant supt. of Hamilton Asylum, 1887; medical supt. of the Protestant Hospital for the Insane, Montreal, since 1890; Fellow of the American Association for the Advancement of Science, 1886; hon. sec. for Canada of the Pan-Am. Medical Congress, Mexico, 1896; President American Medico-Psychological Association, 1904-5. *Publications:* The Beneficent and Toxic Effects of the Various Species of Rhus; A Botanical Holiday in Nova Scotia; Canadian Filicinæ; Recent Additions to Canadian Filicinæ; How to Study Botany; Orchids; Notes on the Flora of the 49th Parallel; The Lake Erie Shore as a Botanising ground; Art in the sick room; Ophioglossaceae and Filices; A Historical Sketch of Canadian Institutions for the Insane; The Insane in Canada, etc., etc. *Recreations:* botany, golf, cricket, philately. *Address:* Protestant Hospital for the Insane, Box 2381, Montreal, Canada.

BUREAU, Hon. Jacques, LL.B. (Laval Univ.), M.P., Solicitor-General; *b.* Trois-Rivieres, Que., 9 July, 1860; *s.* of J. Napoleon Bureau, lawyer, and Sophie Gingras; *m.* 15 July, 1884, Ida Beliveau, *d.* of U. Beliveau and Delphine Prince, of Arthabasca; one *s.* one *d.* *Educ.:* Nicolet Coll., Laval Univ., Que. El. to H. of C. for Three Rivers and St. Maurice, at g. e., 1900, and re-el. at g. e., 1904. In 1907 was sworn in as Solicitor-General of Canada, and at the subseqeunt election was returned by acclm.; re-el. at g. e., 1908. *Address:* Windsor Hotel, Ottawa; Three Rivers. *Clubs:* Laurentian, Ottawa; Canadien, St. Denis, Montreal.

BURKE, Very Rev. Alfred Edward, D. D., LL.D.; *b.* Georgetown, P.E.I., 8 Sept., 1862; *s.* of James Burke and Mary Moar. *Educ.:* Gram. Sch., St. Dunstan's Coll., and Laval Univ.; ordained Cardinal Taschereau, Que., 1885; was seceretary to Bishop of Charlottetown, P.E.I., for two and a half years; Pastor in Alberta for 19 years; Pres. Catholic Church Extension Society of Canada, Toronto, Ont. *Publications:* A whole series of Monographs, Forestry, Agriculture, Horticulture, Historical, regligious, etc. *Recreations:* boating, swimming. *Address:* 119 Wellington St., W., Toronto, Ont.

BURK, Daniel Francis; *b.* Bowmanville, Ont., 1848; *s.* of William K. Burk and Clara

Coryell; *m.* 1873, Annabelle Ida, *d.* of James H. Gerrie; seven *s.* *Educ.:* Pub. and High Schs. of Bowmanville. At nineteen yrs. of age entered service of Ontario Bank, Whitby; apptd. mgr. Port Arthur Branch, 1875; resigned 1884 to become financial mgr. for his brother Marvin, contractor for the C. P. R. Has since been actively connected with every movement for the development of New Ontario. Vice-Pres. and Gen. Mgr. of the Port Arthur, Duluth and Western Ry., until 1898, when it became merged in the C. N. R. A Dir. of the Port Arthur Light and Power Co., afterwards acquired by the town; Pres. of the St. Joe Ry. Co.; for many yrs. Pres. of the West Algoma Agricultural Soc,; owner of the Port Arthur *Herald;* gen. mgr. of the New Ontario Colonization Assn. *Address:* Port Arthur, Ont.

BURK, Frederic Lister, B.L., A.M., Ph. D.; *b.* Blenheim, Ont., Sept. 1, 1862; *s.* Erastus and Matilda Turner Burk; *m.* Oakland, Calif., 1898, Caroline Frear. *Educ.:* Univ. of Calif., Leland Stanford Jr. Univ., Clark Univ. In journalism, San Francisco, 1883-9. Teacher in pub. and pvt. schs., Calif., 1889-91; supt. schs., Santa Rosa, Calif., 1892-6, Santa Barbara, Calif., 1898-9; pres. State Normal Sch., San Francisco, since 1899. Pres. Calif. State Teachers' Assn., 1899; chmn. Calif. Council of Ed'n., 1002-1904. *Publications;* A Study of the Kindergarten Problem, 1899. Contb'r. to mags. on edn'l. pedagog, and psychol. subjects. *Address:* Ross, Marin Co., California.

BURLAND, Lieut.-Col. Jeffrey Hale, B. A.Sc., (McGill), F.C.S.; *b.* Montreal, 19 March, 1861; *s.* of George B. Burland and Clarissa H. Cochrane, *m.* Isabel May, *d.* of the late Henry Megarry, of Lurgan, Irel. *Educ.:* Montreal Acad., and McGill Univ. For yrs. associated with his father in business, and in addition to his connection with the B. A. Bank Note Co., is pres. of the Consolidated Lithographing and Manufacturing Co.; Chn. of the Eastern Canada Manufacturers' Mutual Fire Insur. Co.; dir. of the Central Canada Manufacturers' Mutual Fire Insur. Co., Mount Royal Spinning Co., Noiseless Typewriter Co., etc.; mem. of the Council of the Bd. of Trade; a life-gov. of the Montreal Gen. Hospital, of the Protestant Hospital for the Insane, Western Hospital and County Carleton Hospital; 1stVice-Pres. of the Royal Edward Inst. for the study, prevention and cure of Tuberculosis, Protestant House of Industry and Refuge; mem. of the Committee of the Alexandra Hospital for Infectious Diseases, Advisory Committee of the Montreal Foundling Hospital, Protestant Industrial Rooms, Young Women's Christian Assn., Protestant Infants' Home, the Montreal Charity Organization, Parks and Playgrounds Committee, McGill Conservatorium of Music; Vice-Pres. of the Montreal Technical Inst.; 1st Vice-Pres. Citizens' Assn. for securing good government for the City; a fellow of the Chemical Soc. and Soc. of Chemical Industry, of London, Eng., of the Royal Geographical Soc. and British Assn. for the Advancement of Science; mem. of the Decimal Assn. of London, Eng. Holds a first class R. S. I. certificate and succeeded to the command of the 6th Fusiliers, Dec. 16, 1892. Awarded the Colonial Officers decoration for 20 yrs. service, 1902; held presidency of the Montreal Amalgamated Rifle Assn., in 1895; Montreal Military Inst., 1897. Chn. of the Council of the Dominion Rifle Assn.; mem. of the Coun., Prov. of Quebec Rifle Assn.; apptd. a mem. of the Standing Small Arms Committee of the Dom., 1907. Gazetted, 1905, Hon. Lt.-Col. 1st Prince of Wales Fusiliers of which His Majesty is Hon. Colonel. One of the originators of the movement for sending a Canadian Battalion to England in connection with the celebration of the Queen's Diamond Jubilee, 1897; engaged in the organization of a regt. for that purpose when the Govt. decided to send a composite contingent; selected by the Govt. to proceed to England on that occasion. Commandant of the Can. Rifle Team at Bisley, when it won the Mackinnon Challenge Cup in 1902. Presented to Her Late Majesty during the Diamond Jubilee public ceremonies; presented to Prince and Princess of Wales, at St. James' Palace, July, 10 1902; present by invitation at the Coronation of Their Majesties at Westminster Abbey on Aug. 9th, 1902. With his sisters, erected, equipped and donated the building for the Royal Edward Inst., Montreal, for the study, prevention and cure of Tuberculosis; devised the electrical appliances and arranged for the use of the cables so that it was possible for His Majesty, King Edward, on 21 Oct., 1909, by pressing a telegraph key at West Gean Park, a distance of 4,225 miles, to open the doors of the Inst., turn on the lights in the building, and hoist the Royal Standard on the flag staff. *Publication*: A chart of the Metric System. *Addresses:* 342 Sherbrooke St. W., Montreal; "Kilmarth," Little Metis Que. (summer). *Clubs:* Mount Royal, St. James', Royal Montreal Golf, Hunt, Racquet, Montreal, Rideau, Golf, Country; Ottawa; Toronto; Garrison, Quebec; Royal Societies', London, Eng.

BURN, George; Gen. Mgr. Bank of Ottawa; *b.* Thurso, Scot., 10 April, 1847; *s.* of Rev. David Burn, and Anne Macleod; *m.* Kate Fraser Drummond; one *s.* four *d.* *Educ.:* Scot. Arrived in Canada, 1866; served four years in Royal Bank of Scot., and various Canadian Banks; cashier and latterly General Manager, Bank of Ottawa since 1880; Actuary and Treasurer for many charitable organizations. *Publications:* Articles in relation to Canadian Banking. *Recreations:* sailing, golf. *Address:* 255 Metcalfe St., Ottawa; Cushing's Island, Maine, U.S. (Summer). *Clubs:* Rideau, Golf, Country, Ottawa, Ont.

BURPEE, Lawrence Johnston, F.R.G. S., Public Librarian of the City of Ottawa; *b.* Halifax, N.S., 5 March, 1873; *s.* of Lewis Johnston Burpee and Alice De Mille; *m.* Maude, *d.* of Rev. Canon Hannington; one *s.* and two *d.* Private Secretary to Minister of Justice in two Dominion Administrations, afterwards accepted Librianship Ottawa Public Library. *Publications:* The Search for the Western Sea; Canadian Life in Town and Country; Flowers from a Canadian Garden," "A little book of Canadian Essays," "By Canadian Streams," etc. *Re-*

creation: chess. *Address:* 22 Rideau Terrace, Ottawa.

BURRELL, Martin, M.P.; *b.* Faringdon, Berks, Eng., 15 Oct., 1858; *s.* of Edward Burrell and Jane Harmer; *m.* Sara B. Armstrong, 2nd *d.* of the late Jos. Armstrong of Swindon, Wilts, Supt. of the G. W. Ry. *Educ:* St. John's Coll., Hurstpierpoint. Arrived in Canada, June, 1885; engaged in Horticulture work from 1883 to 1899, in the Niagara Pininsula, Ont.; went to British Columbia in 1900; apptd. member of Board of Horticulture. In 1907-08, was in England as Fruit Commissioner and lecturer for the B. C. Government; contested Yale-Cariboo in the Conservative interest for the H. of C., in 1904, but was defeated; elec. in 1903. *Address:* Grand Forks, B. C.

BURROWES, Edward Thomas; *b.* Sherbrooke, Que., July 25, 1852; *s.* Ambrose and Jane Hall Burrowes; since May 24, 1867, resident of Portland, Me.; *m.* Portland, Oct. 4, 1880, Frances E. Norcross. *Educ.:* Me. Wesleyan Sem., and Wesleyan Univ.; Began mfr. of wire screens in 1873; now pres. E. T. Burrowes Co., Portland; also pres. of Curtain Supply Co., Chicago; has taken out many patents; trustee Boston Univ. *Address:* Portland, Me.

BURROWES, Miss Katharine; *b.* Kingston, Ont.; *d.* Edwin Annesley and Florinda Anne Radcliffe Burrowes. *Educ.:* by teachers at home and in Europe; settled in Detroit; specialized in piano under Prof. J. C. Batchelder, Detroit, and Prof. Karl Klindworth, Berlin. Mem. faculty Detroit Conservatory of Music, several yrs.; organired Burrowes Piano Sch., 1895-1903. Invented several appliances to aid in teaching of beginners. *Publications:* Burrowes course of Music Study for Beginners (kindergarten) 1895 (2 U.S. parents and 26 copyrights); Manual for Teachers, 1901; Kindergarten Class Songs, 1901; Modern Music Methods (read before Music Teachers' Nat. Assn.), 1902; The Note Gatherers, 1903; Short Pieces for Small Hands, 1904; Forty Reading Studies, 1904; Playtime Pieces, 1904; Musical Puzzle Stories, 1905; The Doves and the Squirrels, 1905; Some of the Knowldgde which a Music Teacher of Children should Possess, 1906; contb'r. to mus. magazines. *Address:* Detroit.

BURROWS, Theodore Arthur; lumber manufacturer; *b.* Ottawa, 15 Aug., 1857; *s.* of Henry J. Borrows, of Ottawa, grandson of Capt. John Burrows of the Royal Engineers, who came from Eng. in 1809, the first settler on the present site of Ottawa City, and patentee of the farm which is now known as the Sparks Estate in Ottawa, and who had charge of construction of the Rideau Canal, under Col. Bye about 1830; *m.* 1899, Georgina K. Creasor, *y. d.* of the late D. A. Creasor, K.C., of Owen Sound. *Educ.:* Ottawa Pub. and High Schs., Manitoba Coll. Has lumbering mills in Dauphin, and extensive lumber interests in other parts of the West. Mem. of Manitoba Legis., 1892-1903 for Dauphin. El. to H. of C., same constituency at g. e., 1904; unsuccessful at g. e., 1908. *Address:* Winnipeg, Man.

BURWASH, Nathanael, M.A., S.T.D., LL.D., F.R.S.C.; *b.* Argenteuil, Que', 25 July, 1839; *s.* Adam Burwash and Annie Taylor; *m.* Margaret Proctor; four *s.* *Educ.:* Victoria Coll., Yale Univ., Garratt Biblical Institute; ordianed Clergyman, 1864; apptd. Professor in Victoria Coll., 1886; Dean of faculty of Theology, 1873; Pres. of Victoria Univ., 1887. *Publications:* Wesley's Docternal Standards; Commentary on Romans; Inductive studies in Theology; Manual of Christian Theology; Life and work of Egerton Ryerson; History of Univ. of Toronto; various Biographical Sketches: *Recreations:* boating and fishing. *Address:* Victoria College, Queen's Park, Toronto.

BUTLER, Matthew Joseph, LL.B., O.L.S., D.L.S., C.M.G., Gen'l. Mgr. Dom. I. & S. Co.; *b.* Deseronto, Ont., 19 Nov., 1856; *s.* of Tobias Butler and Elizabeth McVey; *m.* Lorretto M. J. Shelby; two *d.* *Educ.:* Pub. Sch., Toronto Univ., Kent Coll. of Law, Chicago; mem. Inst. C. E., Mem. Am. S.C.E., Mem. C.S.C.E., Mem. R. Ass'n. S. Can., Mem. Am. Ass'n. for the Advancement of Science; Mem. A. Geo. Soc. Was on Govt. Surveys, 1878 to 1883; K. and P. Ry., 1884; Chief Engineer, Thousand Island Ry., 1884-1885; Chief Engineer, N. T. Q. Ry., 1885. Building Water Service, 1886-1887; Chief Engineer Bay of Quinte Ry. and Nav. Co., 1890 to 1899; Chief Engineer Locomotive and Machine Co., Montreal, 1900-1903; Asst. Chief Engineer Eastern Division National Transcontinental Railway. In 1908, apptd. to the position of Deputy Minister and Chief Engineer, Dept. of Railways and Canals, Canada. From April 1909 to Jan., 1910, was Chairman of the Board of Management of the Canadian Government Railway, in addition, now Gen'l. Manager, Dom. I. & S. Co. *Address:* 5 Wurtenburg St., Ottawa, Ont. *Club:* Rideau, Ottawa.

C

CALDER, Hon. Jas. Alexander, B. A., LL.D., M.L.A.; Commr. of Education, Prov. Treas. and Railway Commr. for Prov. of Saskatchewan; *b.* Oxford Co., Ont., 17 Sept., 1868; *s.* of James Calder and Johanna McKay; unmarried. *Educ.:* Ingersoll pub. schs., pub. and high schs., Winnineg; Manitoba Coll. Hon. grad. in science, Manitoba Univ., 1888 (silver medalist). Called to Bar of N. W. T., 1906. Principal of Moose Jaw High Sch., 1891-1894; inspector of schs., N. W. T., 1894-1900; Dep. Commr. of Educ., N. W. T., 1901-1905. El. to Sask. Ass. at first g. e., 1905; apptd. Prov. Treas., and Commr. of Educ. upon formation of the Scott Ministry, 5 Sept., 1905; unsuccessful can. for Milestone div. at g. e., 1908; el. for Saltcoats at bye-el., 7 Dec., 1908. *Address:* Regina, Sask.

CALDERON, Alfred Merigon, F.R.A.S.I.; *b.* Hampton Court Village, Middlesex, England, 7 June, 1861; *s.* of Philip H. Calderon, R.C., and Clara Nareau Storey; *m.* Helen May Bate, of Ottawa, Ont. *Educ.:* Sevenacks, Kent, and London Univ. Coll. Sch., also Royal Academy Schools, Burlington House. Arrived in Canada, 3 Oct., 1887; pupil for five years in office of late George Edmond Street, R. A. Architect for New Law Courts and English and American

Cathedrals in Rome and Paris, also with Charles J. Ferguson, Architect, Carlisle, England; associated as Architect with Sir L. Alma Tadema, R. A., in building his residence. Partner for eight years, with late King Arnoldi, Architect, Ottawa, Ont. Acquired experience of high buildings, by working in offices in New York, Washington and Baltimore. Practiced Architecture two years in London, 15 years in Ottawa, and four years in Edmonton, Alta. Recently Secretary of the Edmonton Conservative Association. *Address:* 523 Fourth Street, Edmonton. *Clubs:* Edmonton, Elks, Edmonton; Rideau, Ottawa.

CALDWELL, James Ernest; *b.* City View, Ont., 1 Aug., 1862; *s.* James Caldwell and Ellen Neilson; *m.* 1895, Mary Caldwell McCurdy, 1901, Rhoda I. Percival. *Educ.:* pub. schs. Engaged in farming and dairying in view of Capital; candidate for H. of C., Co. Carleton, 1904, 1908; Pres. of C. of C. Farmers' Institute. *Publications:* Songs of Pines, 1895; Castle on the Hill, 1899; The Yellow Bag, 1907. *Address:* City View, Ont.

CALDWELL, Thomas Boyd; woollen manufacturer; *b.* Lanark, Ont., 22 Feb., 1856; *s.* of Boyd Caldwell and Dinah Waugh *m.* 22 Jan., 1879, Jeanette Falconer. *Educ.:* Lanark Pub. Sch., Kingston Coll. Institute. Liberal candidate for H. of C., 1900, but defeated; el. at g. e., 1906; unsuccessful at g. e., 1908. *Address:* Lanark, Ont.

CALGARY, Bishop of; see under Pinkham.

CALLAWAY, William Rodger, Gen. Passngr. Agt., Minneapolis, St. Paul and Sault Ste. Marie Ry.; *b.* Toronto, 31 Aug., 1852; *s.* of the late Frederick Callaway; *m* 1875, Elizabeth Ecclestone, of Hamilton. *Educ.:* Pub. Sch. Entered Ry. Service, 1870, as agent G. T. Ry. at Craig's Rd., Quebec, since which he has been consecutively 1873-1875, agent Great Western Ry. of Can.; 1875-1877, purser Beatty Line of Steamers at Sarnia, Ont.; 1877-1878, gen. agt. same Co., at Toronto; April to Nov., 1878, Passngr. Agt., Canada Southern Ry., at Toledo, O.; Nov., 1878-1880, passngr. agt. Wabash St. Louis and Pacific Ry., at St. Louis, Mo.; 1880-1882, dist. agt. Credit Valley Ry. at Toronto; 1882-1895, dist. agt., C. P. Ry., at Toronto; 1895 to date, gen. passngr. agt., Minneapolis, St. Paul & Sault Ste. Marie Ry. *Address:* Minneapolis Minn.

CALVERT, William Samuel; Trans-continental Ry. Commissioner; *b.* Tp. of Warwick, Lambton Co., Ont., 3 March, 1859; *s.* of David Calvert and Anna Macdonald Calvert; *m.* Cora, *d.* of James D. Sutherland of Napier; one *s.* four *d.* *Educ.:* Public Sch., Tp. of Warwick, and Watford Seminary. Elected to H. of C., 1896, re-elec., 1900, 1904 and 1908; elected Chief Liberal Whip, H. of C., Feb., 1901, and again Jan., 17, 1909; apptd. by Canadian Govt., to position of Comr. of National Transcontinental Ry., Oct. 21st, 1909; Pres. and Vice-Pres., of several industrial and insurance corporations; a former Warden of Middlesex Co., Ont. *Address:* Ottawa.

CALVIN, Hiram Augustus; Mgr. of the Calvin Co., Shipbuilders and Forwarders; *b:* Garden Island, Ont., 6 April, 1851; *s.* of Dileno Dexter Calvin and Marion M. Breck; *m.* 1879, Annie W., *d.* of the Rev. D. Marsh, of Quebec; five *s.* two *d.* *Educ.:* Woodstock Coll., Queen's Univ., Kingston. For many yrs. Reeve of the Village of Garden Island; was mem. Frontenac Co. Council for twelve years. First el. to H. of C. at bye-el., 1892; re-el., 1900. Trustee of Queen's Univ., gov. Mining Sch., and of the General Hospital; dir. of the Y. M. C. A. *Address:* Garden Island, Ont.

CAMERON, Miss Agnes Deans; *b.* Victoria, B.C., 20 Dec., 1863; *d.* of Duncan Cameron and Jessie Anderson. *Educ.:* Victoria. Began teaching at age of fifteen and for quarter of century closely identified with pub. schs. of Province. During last ten yrs. of service was Principal of South Park Pub. Sch., Victoria. As result of dispute with trustees, resigned position, and ran for Sch. Bd., and was el. Trustee. Took up journalistic work, writing on "The Wheat Fields of Western Canada," for the Century, Atlantic Monthly, and Saturday Evening Post. In 1908, journeyed from Chicago to rim of Artic Ocean by way of Athabaska, Slave and Mackenzie Rivers, journey lasting six months and covering ten thousand miles. Has lectured extensively in U.S. and Can., on "Journeys through unknown Canada." *Publications:* "The New North" (Appleton & Co., N.Y., 1909). *Recreation:* travel. *Address:* 64e Government St., Victoria, B.C. *Club:* Canadian Women's Press.

CAMERON, Allan; Gen. Agt. C.P.Ry., New York; *b.* 14 March, 1864. *Educ.:* Ryerson Sch., Toronto. Entered Ry. service 1879, since which he has been consecutively to July 31, 1882, Messenger and Clerk Great Western Ry. of Can., at Toronto; Aug. 7, 1882 to May 1, 1883, Baggage Master Northern Ry. of Can. at Orillia, Ont.; June 1, 1883, to June 1, 1887, clerk local freight office C. P. Ry. at Vancouver, B.C.; June 1, 1887, to Feb., 1890, Clerk Gen. Freight and Passngr. Dept.; Feb., 1890 to July 1, 1893, Freight and Passngr. Agt. at Victoria, B.C.; July 1, 1893 to Sept. 30, 1896, Freight and Passngr. Agt. at Portland Ore.; Oct. 1, 1896, to July 1, 1899, Dist. Freight Agt.; July 1, 1899, to Dec., 1900, Asst. Gen. Freight Agt., same road at Vancouver; Jan., 1901, to Sept. 1, 1905, in charge of Asiatic business Oregon Rd. & Nav. Co's line of steamers as Gen. Agt., at Hong Kong, China; Sept. 27, 1905, Gen. Traffic Agt., C. P. Ry., for Great Britain and Europe; 1908, Gen. Agt., New York. *Address:* 458 Broadway, New York.

CAMERON, Edward Robert, K.C.; Registrar, Supreme Court of Canada; *b.* London, Canada, 18 Mar., 1857; *s.* of late Daniel Cameron, merchant, and Louisa, *d.* of late Major John Parke; *m.* 1866, Carrie A., *d.* of late John Emerson of Boston, U.S.A. *Educ:* Woodstock Coll.; Univ. of Toronto. Gold Medalist in Natural Sciences and B.A., 1879, M.A., 1881; called to Bar of Ontario, 1882; one of the Commissioners for the Revision of the Statutes of Canada, 1902. *Publications:* The Vansittart Memoirs, 1902; a volume of unreported judgments of the Supreme Court of Canada, 1905; a work on the practice and jurisprudence of the same Court, 1906. *Recreation:* fishing.

Address: 457 Laurier Av., Ottawa. *Club:* Rideau, Ottawa.

CAMERON, James Chalmers, M.D.; *b.* 1852; *s.* of the late Rev. James Y. Cameron and Charlotte Ault; *m.* 1880, Elizabeth Dakers, of Montreal. *Educ.:* Upper Can. Coll., Toronto; McGill Univ., and pursued his prof. duties in Great Britain and on continent of Europe for several yrs. Commenced practice in Montreal, where he has remained since. Dux of Upper Can. Coll., 1870. For many yrs. on staff of Montreal Gen. Hospital, and acted as Surgeon of Sixth Fusiliers; apptd. Prof. of Obstetrics and Diseases of Infants, McGill Univ., 1886. Medical Dir. and Physician Accoucheur of Montreal Maternity Hospital; at one time pres., Montreal Chirurgical Soc.; apptd. hon. pres. of section on Pediatrics at second Pan-American Congress at Mexico, 1896. *Publications:* Numerous papers on Obstetrics and Medical Jurisprudence. *Address:* 605 Dorchester St. W., Montreal. *Clubs:* St. James', University, Montreal.

CAMERON, Right Rev. John, D.D., Ph.D., Bishop of Antigonish; *b.* South River Antigonish Co., N.S., 11 Feb., 1824; *s.* of John Cameron and Mary McDonald. *Educ.:* Urban Coll. of Propaganda Fide, Rome. Parish Priest of Antigonish; Prof. in Francis Xavier's Coll., Antigonish in 1887; Parish Priest of Arichat and Vicar General; coadjutor Bishop of Arichat; Bishop of Antigonish. *Recreations:* walking, riding. *Address:* Bishop's House, Antigonish, N.S.

CAMERON, John Robson; Chief Editor of the *Spectator*, Hamilton; *b.* Perth, Ont., Can., 19 April, 1845; 2nd *s.* of late Alexander Cameron. *Educ.:* Brockville, Ont., and Quebec. In his profession as a journalist has been employed upon several Canadian and American newspapers. Has been with the Hamilton Spectator since 1880. Was at the Canadian front as a militiaman at the time of the Fenian raid into Canada, 1866-was a member of the Red River Expeditionary Force, 1st Ontario Rifles, under (then) Col. Wolseley, 1870. *Address:* Hamilton.

CAMERON, Ludwig Kribbs; King's Printer, Province of Ontario; *b.* Stouffville, Tp. Markham, 30 Jan., 1854; *s.* of William and Elizabeth Cameron; *m.* Lillie Graves Harwood, May 23, 1879; two *s.* five *d.* *Educ.:* London, Ont. Learned the trade of printer; afterwards became Pres. and Man. London "*Advertiser*"; founded the "*North West Farmer*," in Winnipeg in 1882, and "*Outdoor Canada*," in 1904. *Recreations:* fishing, bowling, and curling. *Address:* 390 Markham St., Toronto. *Club:* R. C. Y. C., Toronto.

CAMERON, Ossian; *b.* Montreal, Mar. 22, 1868; *s.* Colin Cameron and Annie Munro. *Educ.:* St. Louis pub. schs., 1876-84; grad. Chicago Coll. of Law (Lake Forest Univ.), 1893. Admitted to Ill. bar, June, 1893; Republican. *Publications:* Illinois Criminal Law and Practice, 1898; Illinois City and Village Laws, 1905. Revised and enlarged Jones' and Binmore's General Legal Forms and Precedents, 1902. *Address:* 5160 Indiana Av., Chicago.

CAMPBELL, Alexander Colin; Official Reporter, House of Commons; *b.* Shannonville, Ont., 26 Sept., 1857; *s.* of William Stewart Campbell, and Margaret Brough; *m.* Jerusha Hawks Leggo; one *s.* two *d.* *Educ.:* Toronto pub. schs., Coll. Inst. For many yrs. a journalist; now official reporter H. of C. *Publication:* "Insurance and Crime." *Address:* The Firs, Aylmer E., Quebec.

CAMPBELL, Hon. Archibald; Senator; *b.* Ridgetown, Co. Kent, Ont., 27 April, 1854; *s.* Neil Campbell and Flora Johnson; *m.* Merretta Burke; three *s.* three *d.* *Educ.:* in the pub. and High Sch.; merchant and miller. Elected member of the Dominion House for Kent, 1887-1888, 1891-1896; contested West York unsuccessfully in 1900, but upon the death of Hon. Mr. Wallace, was elected for that constituancy in 1901. Re-elec. in 1904; resigned in 1904, and was called to the Senate in the same year; was Chairman of Banking and Commerce Committee of the H. of C. for several years, and for the last three yrs., Chairman of Railway Committee. *Address:* 333 Annette St., W. Toronto. *Club:* Ontario, Toronto.

CAMPBELL, Archibald William, C.E.; *b.* Wardsville, Ont., 1863; *s.* of Cameron John, and Elizabeth McLaughlin Campbell; unmarried. *Educ.:* Wardsville and St. Thomas Collegiate Inst.; grad. in Engineering at Toronto. From 1886 to 1901, conducted local practice. Until 1896, was City Engineer of St. Thomas, and afterwards Commissioner of Highways for Ont. In 1902, was apptd. to the position of Deputy Minister of Public Works for Ont. *Publicaitons:* Many public reports and pamphlets on the science of road and street construction. *Address:* King Edward Hotel, Toronto. *Clubs:* Toronto, Victoria, and R. C. Y. C., Toronto.

CAMPBELL, Hon. Colin H., K.C., F.R. C.I., Attorney-General of Manitoba; *b.* Burlington, Ont., 25 Dec., 1859; *s.* of John H. and Jane Kennedy Campbell; *m.* 16 July, 1884, Minnie Julia Beatrice Buck, *d.* of Anson Buck, M.D., M.R.C.S., and Ketural Adelaide Howell, of Palermo, Ont.; one *s.* one *d.* *Educ.:* Public Schs., Burlington High Sch., Oakville and Toronto Law Sch. Barrister of Ont., 1881; of Manitoba, 1882. *Address:* "Inverary," Winnipeg. *Clubs:* Manitoba, Advance, Country, Albany and Grosvenor, Winnipeg.

CAMPBELL, Major Duncan John D'Urban; *b.* St. Hilaire, Que., 16 July, 1885; *s.* of Major T. E. Campbell and Henreitta Duchesnay; *m.* Eleanor MacRubin Wood; three *s.* one *d.* *Educ.:* Lennoxville, Que.; High School, 1873; entered Bank of Montreal, 1874; went to the North West, 1882; was Postmaster, MacLeod, Alberta, and Sheriff since 1883. Major, Commanding 23rd Alberta Rangers. *Address:* MacLeod, Alberta. *Club:* MacLeod.

CAMPBELL, Glen, M.P.; *b.* Fort Pelly, Sask., 23 Oct., *s.* of Robert Campbell, Chief Factor, Hudson Bay Co., and Elleonora Stirling, both from Perthshire, Scot.; *m.* 1 April, 1884, Harriet Burns, of Okansase; four *c.* *Educ.:* Glasgow Academy, and Merchiston Castle School, Edinburgh, Scot.; Captain in Boulton's Scouts, 1885; unsuccessful candidate for local house in 1892 and 1896; elected 1902 and 1907. First elected to the H. of C. for Dauphin, 1908. Presbyterian; Conservative. *Address:* Gilbert Plains, Man.

CAMPBELL, John A., B.A., M.L.A.; *b.* Clinton, Ont., 19 April, 1872; *s.* of John and Mary Campbell; unmarried. *Educ.:* Winnipeg pub. schs., Manitoba Univ. (grad. 1900). For five yrs. Principal of Boissevain Sch., Man.; now mem. of the legal firm of Campbell & Simpson. Unsuccessful can. to Man. Leg., 1903; el. 1907. *Recreation:* curling. *Address:* Dauphin, Man. *Clubs:* Dauphin; Commercial, Winnipeg.

CAMPBELL, Rev. John Lorne, B.A., D.D.; *b.* Dominionville, Ont., Jan. 14, 1849, *s.* Peter Campbell and Flora McLean; *m.* Aug. 27, 1868, Maggie C. McIntyre, Dominionville. *Educ.:* Woodstock Coll., 1868; Bapt. Theol. Sem., same, 1868; Toronto Univ., 1883; Central Univ. of Iowa, 1893; McMaster Univ., Toronto. Ordained, Chatham, Ont., Aug. 14, 1868, to Bapt. ministry; in addition to pastorate also sec. Bapt. For. Missionary Soc. of Ontario and Quebec, 1872-9; took large party of tourists through Egypt, Palestine, Asia Minor, Constantinople, Greece, Italy, etc., 1898; preached in London, Eng., summer, 1899, 1901 and 1902; pastor Lexington Av., Bapt. Ch., New York, 1889-1904, First Bapt. Ch., Cambridge, Mass., since 1904. Republican. *Publications:* Heavenly Recognition and other Sermons, 1895; Sanctification, 1903. *Address:* Cambridge, Mass.

CAMPBELL, Captain Kenneth Rankin, D.S.O., *b.* Quebec; 3rd *s.* of late Archibald Campbell, Thornhill; *m.* 1900, Edith, *e. d.* of late Thomas Riley Bannon; one *d.* *Educ.:* Royal Military College, Kingston. Entered army, 1883; Lieutenant, 1886; Captain, 1895; Adjutant Gold Coast (Hausa) Constabulary, 1890-91; apptd. Deputy-Commissioner and Vice-Consul in the Oil Rivers Protectorate and adjoining Native Territories, 1891; Acting Commissioner and Consul-General, 1893; served in operations against Chief Nanna in Benin River, 1894; employed with forces of Protectorate (medal with clasp); resigned, 1895; served in Carabiniers, and left army, 1897; now in Army Reserve; accompanied Naval Brigade in China (1900) from taking of Taku Forts until relief of Tienstin and capture of Tientsin native city by the Allied Forces, as correspondent. *Decorated* for various services West Coast of Africa on special service; awarded bronze medal of Royal Humane Society for saving a native from the Vice-Consulate hulk in a river where crocodiles abound. *Recreations:* yachting, automobiling, canoeing, swimming, and driving, etc. *Address:* 171 Queen's Gate, S.W. *Clubs:* Army and Navy, Ranelagh, R. C. Y.

CAMPBELL, Hon. Philip Pitt, B. A.; Mem. of U. S. House of Representatives for 3rd Dist. of Kansas; *b.* Nova Scotia; *m.* 1892, Helen Goff. When four yrs. of age moved with his parents to Kansas, and has resided there ever since. Grad. of Baker Univ. Read law on the farm, and called to Bar of Kansas, 1889. First el. to 58th Congress; re-el. 59th, 60th and 61st Con. *Addresses:* The Capitol, Washington, D.C.; Pittsburg, Kan., U.S.A.

CAMPBELL, Rev. Robert, M.A., D.D.; *b.* Township of Drummond, Ont., 21 June, 1835; *s.* of Peter Campbell, and Margaret Campbell; *m.* Margaret Macdonnell; three *s.* two *d.* *Educ.:* Local Sch., and Queen's Univ. Taught sch. for six yrs.; clerk of Gen. Assembly since 1892; minister of St. Andrew's Church, Galt, Ont., for four yrs.; Minister of St. Gabriel Church, Montreal, for 42 yrs. In 1870, won prize essay on Union of Presbyterians in Canada. Moderator of Gen. Assemb,y, 1907; pres. of Nat. Hist. Soc. 1895-98. *Publications:* History of St. Gabriel Church, 1887; Union or Co-operation, 1906; numerous articles in reviews and periodicals. *Recreations:* golf, curling, botany. *Address:* St. Gabriel Ch. Manse, 68 St. Famille St., Montreal.

CAMPBELL, Robert Henry; Superintendent of Forestry; *b.* Ailsa Craig, Ont., 26 May, 1867; *s.* of James Campbell, Canadian Parliamentary Library, and Dorothy Campbell; unmarried. *Educ.:* Strathroy and Ottawa Collegiate Inst. Entered Government service in Secretary's branch, in 1887; served as private Sercetary to Deputy Minister and Minister, and Secretary of Canadian Forestry Association. Apptd. Superintendent, 1907. *Publications:* Departmental reports, magazines and newspaper articles. *Recreations:* Football, mountainering. *Address:* 225 Clemow Av., Ottawa.

CAMPBELL, Wilfred, LL.D. (Aberdeen), F.R.S.C.; lyric and dramatic poet; *b.* Berlin, Ont, 1 June, 1861; *s.* of Rev. Thos. Swainston Campbell and Matilda Frances, *d.* of late Major Francis Wright of Walworth Manor House, Surrey; *m.* Mary Louisa, *o. d.* of late D. M. Dibbie, M.D., and Louisa Mackenzie Macdonald, senior representative of the ancient Barons Mackay of Strathy, and Derlot, N. Britain, and 10th in descent through her maternal grandfather, 11th through her maternal grandmother from Robert Stuart, Earl of Orkney, son of James V. of Scotland; also through the same 9th and 10th, from Lady Jane Gordon, *e. d.* of 17th Earl of Sutherland. *Educ.:* privately High Sch.; Univ. of Toronto; Cambridge, Mass.; F.R.S., Canada; Vice-Pres. Eng. Sec. R. S., 1899-1900; President, 1900. Studied for Church of England; retired from Church to enter Civil Service of Canada and devote life to literature, 1891; holds position in Dominion Archives Office; writer of verse for American and English periodicals and of several poetical dramas. *Publications:* Lake Lyrics, 1889; The Dread Voyage Poems, 1893; Mordred and Hildebrand Tragedies, 1895; Beyond the Hills of Dream Poems, 1899; Collected Verse, Sagas of Vaster Britain, 1906; Ian of the Orzades, a historical novel, 1906; Canada, 1907; Poetical Tragidies, 1908; a beautiful rebel, a historical novel of Up. Can. in 1812, (1909); "Life and Letters," "Canadian Seasons and Woods"; The University and The Natural Life; "Imperialism in Canada"; "The Canadian Lake Region"; Shakespeare and the Modern Drama; "A sheaf of winter Lyrics, 1908; Carnagie Edition of his poems, issued in 1906, by Andrew Carnegie the great philanthropist; has written much Imperial verse. *Recreations:* walking, skating, tennis, golf. *Address:* 24 Lisgar St., Ottawa.

CAMPBELL, William B.; *b.* Shannonville, Ont., 17 July, 1854; *s.* of William Camgbell and Margaret Brough; *m.* Jessie G. L. Rose, *d.* of late Geo. Maclean Rose of Toronto, Ont. *Educ.:* Toronto and Montreal Sch.; after several years service in the offices of three Insurance Companies, branched out as Publisher of *The Budget and Insurance Journal*; afterwards established *Office and Field*, now the only weekly journal in the world devoted to Life Insurance; five months ago commenced publication of "*Fire Insurance*," devoted to fire indemnity and reducing of fire waste, the only journal of its kind published. *Address:* 84 Victoria St., Toronto, Ont.

CANADA, Archbishop and Metropolitan of ; See Sweatman.

CANNIFF, William, M.D.; *b.* Ontario, 20 June, 1830; *s.* Jonas Canniff, a U. E. L., and Letta Flagler; *m.* (1st) Grace Hamilton, (2nd) Elizabeth Foster; six *s.* one *d.* *Educ.:* Common Sch., Univ. of Victoria Coll., Cobourg, Ont. Born and brought up on a farm, working until about 18 years of age; went to school in winter; Student at Victoria Coll.; Student at Toronto Medical School; at Univ., New York. Home Surgeon, N. Y. State Hospital for 14 months; Surgeon on board a vessel to London, Eng. Entered St. Thomas Hospital; passed Army Medical Board; apptd. Acting Asst. Surgeon Royal Artillery; retired from the Army at the close of the War; travelled through Great Britain, Germany, and France; Hospital work in Paris; returned to Canada; apptd. Professor of Surgery and General Pathology, Victoria Coll., Toronto; Dean of Medical Faculty; retired to general practice; organized Medical Health Dept., Toronto, and was the first Medical Health Officer. *Publications:* Principles of Surgery; The Settlement of Upper Canada; "The Medical Profession in Upper Canada, 1783-1850"; "Canadian Nationality, its growth and development"; "Early Steam Navigation in the Dominion;" Historical Sketch of the County of York; "Account of the Upper Canada Rebellion, 1837." *Address:* Belleville, Ont.

CANNON, Hon. Lawrence John, LL.B., LL.L., D.C.L., (Laval Univ.); a Puisne Judge of the Superior Court of Que., for the Dist. of Three Rivers, since 1905; *b.* Quebec, 18 Nov., 1852; *s.* of L. A. Cannon and Miss Cary; *m.* 1876, Aurelie (*d.* 1905), *d.* of J. G. Dumoulin, Prothonotary of the Superior Ct., Arthabaska; five *s.* three *d.* *Educ.:* Quebec Seminary, Laval Univ. Admitted to the Bar, 1874; commenced practice of his prof. at Arthabaskaville; apptd. Asst. Attorney-Gen. for the Prov. of Que., 1891; cr. Q.C., 1897, and in same yr. acted as counsel for the Prov. of Que. in the Fisheries case before the Judicial Committee of the Privy Council in Eng.; unsuccessful candidate for H. of C. at g. e., 1882. *Address:* Three Rivers.

CANTLIE, Lieut.-Col. George Stephen; Supt. of the Car Service of C. P. Ry.; *b.* Montreal, Que., 2 May, 1867; *s.* of James A. Cantlie, wholesale drygoods merchant, Montreal, and Eleanora Simpson Stephen, sister of Lord Mount Stephen; *m.* 1896, Beatrice, *d.* of the late W. Darling Campbell, of Quebec. *Educ.:* By private tuition, Montreal High Sch., McGill Univ. Entered Audit Dept. of C. P. R., 1885; apptd. chief clerk in office; asst. gen. mgr.; gen. baggage agt., and supt. of the car service, 1896. Joined 5th Royal Highlanders, 1885; gazetted Lt.-Col. in 1906, when regt. formed into two batt. Mem. Montreal Bd. Trade. *Address:* 338 Mountain St., Montreal. *Clubs:* Mount Royal, St. James, Montreal Hunt.

CANTLIE, James Alexander; senior mem. of firm of James A. Cantlie & Co., *b.* Mortlach, Banffshire, Scotland, 5 June, 1836; *s.* of the late Francis Cantlie and Mary Stuart; *m.* 1866, Eleanora Simpson, *o. d.* of the late William Stephen; two *s.* one *d.* *Educ.:* Mortlach. Arrived Can., 1863; estd. firm of Cantlie, Ewan & Co., 1868, which was reorganized under the name of James A. Cantlie & Co., 1893, Mr. C. becoming head of the concern, which position he now holds. Pres., Dom. Travellers' Assn., 1880; Pres. Montreal Bd. of Trade, 1885; Vice-Pres., Dom. Transport Co.; mem. of the St. Andrew's Soc. and a Governor of Montreal General Hospital and Western Hospital. Served in First Aberdeenshire Regt., 1859-1863; attended Royal Review before late Queen Victoria, 1861; served two yrs. in Victoria Rifles of Montreal. *Address:* 131 Crescent St., Montreal.

CAPPON, James, M.A.; *b.* 8 Mar., 1854; *s.* of Thomas Cappon and Ellen M. O'Brien; *m.* Mary Elizabeth Macnee. *Educ.:* Broughty Ferry Parish Sch., Dundee High Sch., and Glasgow Univ., Scot. Arrived in Canada, 1888; was Bursar and Medalist in Philosophy (Glasgow); Correspondence tutor in English at Queen Margaret Coll., Glasgow; Lecturer in English History for Glasgow Univ. Extension; Prof. of English in Queen's University (1888), and of Arts Faculty (1906). For some years Prof. Cappon took an active part in the University Extension Movement in Canada, and for four winters, gave courses in English literature at Ottawa, under the auspices of Government House. He has also given courses in the Normal Sch., at the request of the Education Department. *Publications:* Victor Hugo; a memoir Britain's title in South Africa; studies in Canadian Poetry; The Secretarian Principle in the Constitution of Canada; What Classical Education means. *Recreation:* golf. *Address:* "Fairnook," Kingston, Ont.

CARLING, Hon. Sir John, K.C.M.G., P.C.; *b.* in Tp. of London, Middlesex, Ont., 23 Jan., 1828; *s.* of the late Thomas Carling, of Yorkshire, Eng., who came to Canada in 1818; *m.* Hannah, *d.* of the late Henry Dalton, London, Ont. *Educ.:* London; el. to the London Sch. Board, 1850, and served for four years; City Council, 1854, and served for four years; member of Old Can. Legislature, from 1857 to 1867; Receiver General in Cartier-Macdonald Govt., 1862; at Confederation, was elec. for London to H. of C., and also to Ontario Legislature; Commissioner of Agriculture and Public works in Sandfield-Macdonald Govt., from July, 1867, until Dec., 1871; re-elec. in 1872, but defeated 1874; elec., 1878; entered Sir John Macdonald's Administration as Postmaster General 23 May, 1882; Minister of Agriculture, 25 Sept., 1885; defeated for London 1891; apptd. to the Senate, 27 April, 1891; resigned in Feb., 1892, to contest bye-elec. in London for H. of C., and was successful; ceased to be Min. of Agriculture on dissolution of Abbott Ministry, 5 Dec., 1892; member of Sir John Thompson's Cabinet, without portfolio same date; re-apptd. to the Senate, 23 April, 1896; in 1892 was offered position of Lieut.-Governor of Ontario, but declined, and in the following year declined the proffered appointment of Honorary Commissioner for Canada at the World's Fair, Chicago; created Knight Commander of the Order of St. Michael and St. George, 3 June, 1893; in march, 1893, the Standing Committee on Agric. of the House of Commons adopted a resolution recording its appreciation of the services rendered by him to the Agricultural interests of the Dominion. Is Pres. of the Carling Brewing and Malting Co. *Address:* London, Ont.

CARMAN, Rev. Albert, D.D., LL.D.; General Supt. of the Methodist Church; *b.* Iroquois, Dundas Co., Ont., 27 June, 1833; *s.* of Philip Carman, Warden of Cos. of Stormont, Dundas and Glengarry, and Emmaline Carman, *d.* of Peter Shaver; *m.* Mary Jane, *d.* of Capt. Jas. Sesk; three *s.* one *d.* *Educ.:* Dundas Co. Gram. Sch., Victoria Univ., Cobourg, now Toronto. Head Master, Dundas Co. Gram. Sch., 1853-57; Chancellor of Albert Univ., 1857-74 (confederated with Victoria Coll.); Bishop of Methodist Episcopal Church, 1874-84; Gen. Supt., Methodist Church since 1884. *Publications:* Activities of Calling, and several pamphlets. *Address:* 42 Murray St., Toronto.

CARMAN, Albert Richardson, B.A.; Journalist; *b.* Belleville, Ont., 8 Feb., 1865; *s.* of Rev. Dr. Carman, Gen. Supt. of the Methodist Church, and Mary Sisk; *m.* Gertrude Walker, of Belleville. *Educ.:* Albert Coll., Belleville. On staff of Toronto *Globe*, 1887-1891. Parliamentary Correspondent, 1890-1; Chief Editorial Writer, Montreal *Star*, from 1891 to date. *Publications:* Two novels, "The Preparation of Ryerson Embury," and "The Pensionnaires;" one economic work, "The Ethics of Imperialism;" magazine stories and review articles. *Recreation:* golf. *Address:* Star Office, Montreal.

CARMAN, Bliss, B.A., journalist; *b.* Fredericton, N.B., 15 April, 1861; *e. s.* of William Carman and Sophia Mary, *d.* of George P. Bliss. *Educ.:* Collegiate Sch. and Univ. of N.B.; Edinburgh and Harvard. Office editor, the *Independent*, New York, 1890-92. *Publications:* Low Tide on Grand Pré, 1893; Behind the Arras, 1895; A Seamark, 1895; Ballads of Lost Haven, 1897; Songs from Vagabondia (with Richard Hovey), 1894; More Songs from Vagabondia (with Richard Hovey), 1896; by the Aurelian Wall, 1898; A Winter Holiday, 1899; Last Songs from Vagabondia, 1900; Christ m s Eve at St. Kavin's, 1901; Ode for the Coronation, 1902; Pipes of Pan, No. 1, 1902; Pipes of Pan, No. II, 1903. *Recreation:* canoeing. *Address:* 70 Fifth Avenue, New York.

CARNEY, Michael; West India merchant; *b.* Waterford, Irel., 11 May, 1839; *s.* of Edmund Carney and Margaret Carney; *m.* 25 Aug., 1873, Sarah Richardson. El. to H. of C., at g. e., 1904; unsuccessful at g. e., 1908. *Address:* Halifax, N.S.

CARON, Hon. Joseph Edouard, M.L.A., Min. of Agric. for Prov. of Que.; *b.* Ste. Louise, Que., 10 Jan., 1866; *s.* of Edouard Caron and Desanges Cloutier; *m.* (1st), 1888 Leopoldine Castonguay, of St. Roch des Aulnaies (*d.* 1894); (2nd), 1897, Matilda Destroismaisons; two *s.* one *d.* *Educ.:* Ste. Ann's Coll. An Agriculturist. Sec.-Treas. of Co. Council, Municipality of Ste. Louise; sch. commr. of Ste. Louise and Agric. Soc. of L'Islet Co., since 1893. Unsuccessful can. for H. of C. at g. e., 1900, and at bye-el., 1902; first returned to the Legis, by accl., at bye-elec., 20 Sept., 1902; re-elec. at g. e., 1904 and 1908. *Address:* Ste. Louise, Que.

CARREL, Frank; Ed. and Prop. of Quebec *Telegraph;* *b.* Quebec, 7 Sept., 1870; *s.* of James Carrel and Josepha Butchart; unmarried. *Educ.:* Quebec, and Stanstead Coll. In journalism for many yrs. Owner of *Quebec Telegraph;* pres. "Frank Carrel, Limited." *Publications:* "Carrel's Guide to Quebec;" "Tips;" "History of Quebec Tercentenary." *Recreations:* tennis, fishing, hunting. *Address:* Chateau Frontenac. *Clubs:* Garrison, Hunt, Turf, Quebec.

CARRIER, Louis Auguste, B.A., M.P.; *b.* Levis, Que., 24 May, 1858; *s.* of Antoine Carrier, and Helen Caroline Sheppard; *m.* 6 Oct., 1892, Angeline C. Hamel; two *s.* *Educ.:* Levis Coll. and High Sch. of Quebec and Poughkeepsie, N.Y.; Provincial Dir. Quebec Central Ry.; elec. to H. of C., bye-elec., 6 June, 1905, by acclam.; re-elec., 1908; Liberal; Catholic. *Address:* Levis.

CARRIQUE, William Jeffrey; *b.* Halton Co., Ont., 19 Aug., 1872; *s.* of William Carrique, and Martha Marlowe; *m.* 1909, Mabel Gascoyne. *Educ.:* Georgetown High Sch., formerly Advertising Manager, Hamilton *Spectator*, and afterwards the Ottawa *Citizen*. Pres. and Gen. Man., Canadian Street Car Advertising Co., which controls the advertising in all the Street Cars in the Dominion. *Recreations:* motoring and fishing. *Addresses:* Bank of Ottawa Building, St. James St., "The Sherbrooke," Montreal. *Clubs:* National ,Toronto; Canada, R. St. L. Y. C., and Military Club, Montreal.

CARROLL, Hon. Henry George, LL.B., D.L., Judge of the Superior Court, Quebec; *b.* Kamouraska, 31 Jan., 1865; *s.* of M. B. Carroll; *m.* 1891, Amazelie, *d.* of L. Boulanger, Merchant of Ste. Agathe de Lotbiniere.. *Educ.:* Ste. Anne's Coll., and Laval Univ., Quebec. Admitted to the Bar, 1889; grad. at Laval Univ., practised his profession at Fraserville, Quebec; K.C., 1899; Crown Attorney for Kamouraska district; elected to Parliament, 1891, 1896, and 1900; Solicitor-General, Canada, 1902-4; Director of the Quebec and Lake Huron Railway Co. *Publications:* President of Le Soleil Publishing Co. *Address:* 6 Brebae St., Quebec. *Clubs:* Rideau, Ottawa; Garrison, Quebec.

CARRUTHERS, James; *b.* Toronto, Ont., 1853; *s.* of George Andrew Carruthers and Janet Carruthers; two *s.* *Educ.:* Toronto. Entered office of T. C. Chisholm, grain merchant, Toronto; partner of the firm of Crane and Baird; estb. offices of his own in Montreal, Toronto, and Winnipeg. Pres. Toronto and Montreal Steamboat Co., United Supply and Contracting Co.; Hiram L. Piper Co.; Montreal and Lake Erie Steamboat Co.; Dir., Dominion Bank of Can., St. Lawrence and Chicago Steam Navigation Co., Royal Marine Insur. Co., Winnipeg Elevator Co.; ex-pres., Montreal

Bd. of Trade, Corn Exchange; Governor Montreal Gen. Hospital, Western Hospital. *Address:* Montreal.

CARSON, Lieut.-Col. John, J.P., Mem. Carson Bros., fire insur. agts., Montreal; President of the Crown Reserve Mining Co., Cobalt; *b.* Montreal, Que., 13 Oct., 1884; *s.* of William Carson and Mary Johnston; *m.* 1885, Minnie R., *d.* of the late Henry Corran, of St. John's, Que.; one *s.* one *d.* *Educ.:* Pub Schs., Montreal. At age of sixteen yrs., entered employ of the Royal Insur. Co., and has remained in the insur. business ever since. Mem. Montreal Board of Trade. Entered Fifth Royal Scots, now Fifth Royal Highlanders, as second Lieut., 22 May, 1891; Capt., 1894; Major, 1898; Lieut.-Col., 1902; Lieut.-Col. Commanding, 1906, when Regt. organized into two batt. *Address:* 4113 Sherbrooke St., Montreal. *Club:* Canada.

CARSWELL, Robert; *b.* Colborne, Ont., 19 July, 1838; *s.* of Hugh and Margaret Carswell, of Glasgow, Scot.; *m.* (1st), Milicent A. Carmen, sister of Rev. Dr. Carmen; (2nd) Martha Swan; (3rd) Sophia Frankish; one *s.* three *d.* *Educ.:* Grammar Sch., Brighton; Belleville Seminary and Middlesex Univ. course. Taught School at 18 years of age, during which time he attended Seminary and Coll., at intervals until 1864, when he removed to Toronto, and entered into Lawbook selling and publishing. Has published over 200 different volumes of Law Books. His life's ambition has been to become informed in the life and doctrine and theology of the New Jerusalem. *Recreations:* chess, drafts., etc. *Address:* 1534 King St., West, Toronto, Ont.

CARTER, Col. James Colebrooke, J.P.; *b.* Fredericton, N.B., 22 Nov., 1844; *s.* of Sir James Carter, for many years Chief Justice of N.B., and Mary Anne Elizabeth Carter; *m.* (1st) Frances Katherine Jones; (2nd) Eleanor Frances Oswall; four *s.* one *d.* *Educ.:* King's Coll., N.B.; Vice-Chairman Berkshire Territorial Association; served in the 43rd Light Infantry, and Commanded the 1st V. B. Royal Berkshire Regiment. *Address:* Ardington, Wantage, Berkshire, Eng. *Clubs:* Naval and Military, London, Eng.

CARTER, Rev. John, M.A.; Bursar of Pusey House, Oxford; *b.* 7 Nov., 1861; *s.* of John Carter, Toronto. *Educ.:* Up. Can. Coll., and Trinity Univ., Toronto; Exeter Coll., Oxford (Exhibitioner), 2nd class Lit, Hum. 1887. Curate of Limehouse Parish Church, 1887-89; Resident at Pusey House since 1889; Assistant Chaplain Exeter Coll., Oxford, 1890-95; Hon. Secretary of the Christian Social Union from its foundation in 1889; Editor of the Economic Review since 1891. *Address:* Pusey House, Oxford.

CARTER, John William; Supreme Sec., S.O.E.; *b.* Cheltenham, Eng., 30 June, 1839; *s.* of John and Sarah Carter; *m.* Jane Honan. *Educ.:* Cheltenham, Eng. Arrived Canada, May, 1870. Unsuccessful candidate for West Toronto at Prov. elec., 1883. Has been Sup. Sec. of the Sons of England, B. S. for 27 yrs. *Address:* 64 Macpherson Av., Toronto.

CARTER-COTTON, Hon. Francis L., M. L.A.; Ed. and Prop. of Vancouver *News Advertiser;* *b.* Yorkshire, Eng., 1847. First el. to B.C. Leg. for Vancouver, 1890; re-el. 1894, 1896; defeated 1900; el. for Richmond at g. e., 1903. Prov. Min. of Finance from Aug., 1898, to Feb., 1900; Chief Commr. of Lands and Works from March, 1899, to Feb., 1900. Apptd. Pres. of the Ex. Coun., June, 1904. *Address:* Vancouver, B.C.

CARTWRIGHT, Alexander Dobbs; Sec. to the Bd. of Ry. Commrs. for Canada; *b.* Kingston, Ont., 20 Sept., 1864; *s.* of Sir Richard Cartwright and Frances Lawe; *m.* A. E. S. Hart; one *s.* *Educ.:* Queen's Coll., Kingston (Grad. 1885). Called to the Bar, 1888; practiced in Toronto until 1904, when apptd. to his present position *Recreations:* golf, angling, rifle shooting. *Address:* 354 Stewart St., Ottawa. *Clubs:* Rideau, Golf, Country, Ottawa; Toronto, Toronto.

CARTWRIGHT, Captain Francis Lennox, D.S.O.; *b.* 27 March, 1874; 5th *s.* of Rt. Hon. Sir R. J. Cartwright, G.C.M. G., P.C.; *m.* 1901, Ada Marion Carlos, *e d.* of Augustus F. Perkins of Oak Dene, Holmwood. Surrey. *Educ.:* Bishop Ridley Coll.; St. Catherine's; Queen's Univ., Kingston. Capt. 14th Batt. Princess of Wales Own Rifles, Canadian Militia, 1896; joined North West Mounted Police, 1897, served in Yukon and North-West Territories; was seconded to serve in Strathcona's Horse, 1900; served in S. Africa with that corps till its return to Canada; returned to N. W. M. P., 1901; retired, 1904; Captain 5th Field Battery, C. A., 1906. *Decorated* for distinguished service in S. Africa throughout the campaign. *Recreations:* shooting, riding, yachting, swimming, football, hockey. *Address:* Kingston, Ont.

CARTWRIGHT, Rt. Hon. Sir Richard John, P.C.; G.C.M.G., *cr.* 1897; K.C. M.G., *cr.* 1879; Senator, Minister of Trade and Commerce and leader of the Senate of Canada; *b.* Kingston, Ont., 14 Dec., 1835; *s.* of late Rev. R. D. Cartwright, Chaplain to the Forces, Kingston, Ont., and Harriet, *d.* of Conway Edward Dobbs, of Dublin, Ireland; *g. s.* of Hon. Richard Cartwright, formerly a Judge of Common Pleas in Up-Canada, and afterwards a member of the Legislative Council of that Province; *m.* 1859, Frances, *d.* of Col. Alexander Lawe, of Cork, Ireland; six *s.* three *d.* *Educ.:* Trinity Coll., Dublin. Became President of the Commercial Bank of Canada; is Pres. Director, or Trustee of several commercial and financial corporations; during its existence was Pres. of the Reform Club, Toronto; Pres. of the Eastern Ont. Liberal Association, formed in 1897; elected to Parliament of Old Canada, for Lennox and Addington, 1863, and continued to sit for that constituency until 1867; from Confederation down to 1878, represented Lennox in House of Commons; defeated in Lennox, 1878; was returned for Centre Huron at bye-election on resignation of H. Horton; contested Centre Wellington, 1882; elected S. Huron, 1883; S. Oxford, 1887, 1891, 1896; Finance Minister, 1873-78; Chief Financial Critic, and one of the Leaders of the Opposition in Parliament, 1879-96; Acting-Premier and Leader in the House of Commons, 1897; went to Washington, 1897, to promote better relations between Canada and the United States; proposed a Joint Commission, and represented Canada on the Anglo-

American Joint High Commission when it sat at Quebec in the summer of 1898, and Washington in the winter of 1898-99; Acting Premier during Premier's absence at Colonial Conference, 1907. A Liberal. *Address:* 276 O'Connor St., Ottawa. *Club:* Rideau, Ottawa.

CARTWRIGHT, Lieut.-Col. Robert, C. M.G., 1900; formerly Assistant Adjutant-General for Musketry, Headquarters, Can.; *b.* 1 Nov., 1860; *s.* of Rt. Hon. Sir R. Cartwright; *m.* 1885, Ivy Maria Russell, *d.* of Benjamin C. Davy; two *d.* Com. and School of Musketry; A.A.G. Militia Force of Canada; Major and Brevet Lieut.-Col., Royal Canadian Regiment. Served North West Rebellion, 1885 (Medal); South Africa Canadian Contingent (Medal, four clasps); now engaged in fruit farming. *Address:* Summerlands, B.C. *Club:* Rideau, Ottawa.

CARVELL, Frank Broadstreet, LL.D., M.P.; *b.* Bloomfield, Co. Carleton, N.B., 14 Aug., 1862; *s.* of Bishop Carvell and Margaret Lindsay; *m.* Carrie B. Packs, 28 July, 1887; one *d.* *Educ.:* in the Com. Sch., and Boston Univ.; graduated from Boston Univ., June, 1890. Admitted Attorney, Oct., 1890. Elec. to the H. of Assembly of New Brunswick, Feb., 1889, and resigned in Oct., 1900; unsuccessfully contested Carleton, N.B., for the H. of C. in 1900, but was elec. in 1904 and 1908. *Address:* Woodstock, N.B.

CASEY, Right Rev. Timothy, D.D., Bishop of St. John; *b.* Charlotte Co. N.S., 20 Feb., 1862; *s.* of Jere. Casey and Catherine Casey. *Educ.:* St. Joseph's Coll., and Laval Univ., Quebec.; ordained Priest, 29 June, 1886. Bishop, 30 Sept., 1899. *Address:* St. John, N.B.

CASGRAIN, Hon. Joseph Philippe Baby, C.E., Senator; *b.* Quebec, Que., 1 March, 1856; *s.* of P. B. Casgrain, K.C., for 19 yrs. mem. of Parlt., and Mathilde Perrault; grandson of the late Col. C. E. Casgrain, mem. of the Legislative Assembly, 1830-1834; g. grandson of the late Hon. James Baby, at one time Speaker of the Legislative Assembly of Up. Can.; *m.* 1885, Ella, *d.* of the late J. W. Cook, four *s.* two *d.* *Educ.:* Seminary of Quebec. Has followed prof. of Civil Engineer in Montreal, since 1888; admitted as a Provincial Land Surveyor, 1878, and as a Dom. Land Sur., 1881, and is also an Ont. and Manitoba Land Surv. Director Richelieu and Ont., Navigation Co. Called to the Senate, Jan. 27, 1900; mem. of the Ottawa Improvement Com., since 1903; Chairman of Railway Committee of the Senate. *Address:* 180 St. James St., Montreal, Que. *Clubs:* St. James', Montreal; Rideau, Ottawa.

CASGRAIN, Major Philippe Henri du Perron, R.E.; *b.* Quebec, 31 May, 1864. *Educ.:* Royal Military Coll., Kingston. Served North-West Territory, throughout Rebellion, as Adjutant 9th Rifles, 1885 (medal; joined R. E., 1885; qualified as an Interpreter in Russian, 1893; Captain, 1894; Major, 1902; served Manipur Expedition, 1891, (medal and clasp); Ordnance Survey, Bedford, 1891-95; served S. African War (despatches, two medals, and five clasps). *Address:* 8 St. James's Square, S. W. Eng.

CASGRAIN, Thomas Chase, K.C., LL. D.; *b.* Detroit, Mich., U.S.A., 28 July, 1852; *s.* of Hon. C. E. Casgrain and Charlotte Mary Chase; *m.* Marie-Louise Le Moine; one *s.* *Educ.:* Quebec Sem. and Laval Univ., Que.; member of the Que. Legis., 1886-1896; Attorney-General for Que., 1891 1896; member of the H. of C., 1896-1904. *Address:* Montreal. *Clubs:* Mount Royal; St. James', Montreal; Garrison, Quebec, and Rideau, Ottawa.

CAHAN, Charles Hazlitt, B.A., LL.B., K.C.; *b.* Yarmouth, N.S., 31 Oct., 1861; *s.* of Charles and Theresa Cahan; *m.* Mary J. Hetherington; two *s.* one *d.* *Educ.:* Yarmouth Seminary; Dalhousie Univ., Halifax. Grad. Dalhousie Univ. in Arts, 1884, in Law, 1890; called to the Bar of N.S., 1893, and subsequently called to the Bar of Que., apptd. K.C. for N.S., 1907; K.C. for Que., 1909.; Pres. of the Canada Cement Co., el. to the N.S. Legis. for Shelburne, 1890; Leader of Conservative Party in N.S. Legis., 1890-94. *Address:* 37 Royal Insurance Bldg., (bus.); 198 University St., Montreal. *Clubs:* Halifax, Halifax; Jockey, Mexico; Mount Royal, Montreal.

CAINS, Fred. L.; *b.* Tp. of Lochiel, Glengarry Co., Ont., 19 Feb., 1862; *s.* of Henry Cains and Ann Lighthall; *m.* 1884, Frances Pulsford, of London, Eng.; two *s.* two *d.* *Educ.:* McGill Coll.; commenced mercantile career with Greenshield's Ltd., Montreal; estab. firm Brophy, Cains & Co., wholesale dry goods, 1888; remained with firm until 1908, and then organized "F. L. Cains, Ltd.", wholesale dry goods; Pres., Commercial Travellers' Assoc. of Can., 1905. *Recreations:* golf. *Address:* 41 Hampton Court, Montreal; 301 St. James St., Montreal (bus.) *Clubs:* St. James', Canada, Forest and Stream, Royal Montreal Golf, Montreal. Laurentian, Ottawa; (Life Mem. M.A.A.A., Montreal.)

CASH, Edward L., M.D., M.P.; *b.* Markham, Ont., 26 Dec., 1849; *s.* of David Cash and Elizabeth Eckardt; *m.* Mary V. Simpson; one *s.* two *d.* *Educ.:* Markham High Sch. and Victoria Univ,; Graduated in Medicine at age of 21; went to U.S.A., and remained for 25 yrs., returning to Canada in 1890 and was el. to Parlt. for Mackenzie, Sask., in 1904, and again in 1908. *Address:* Yorkton, Sask.

CASSELS, Hon. Walter Gibson Pringle, B.A., K.C., Judge of the Exchequer Court of Canada; *b.* Quebec, Que., 14 Aug., 1845; *s.* of Robert Cassels and Mary Macnab; *m.* Susie Hamilton; two *s.* four *d.* *Educ.:* Quebec High Sch., and Toronto Univ.; member of the law firm of Blake, Lash and Cassels, Toronto, for many years, during which he held briefs as Councel for the C. P. Ry., in the famous Onderdonk Arbitration, and for the Province of Ont., Queen's Council, 1883; apptd. Judge of the Exchequer Court, 2 March, 1908. *Recreations:* salmon fishing, golf and curling. *Address:* 21 Blackburn, Av., Ottawa. *Clubs:* Toronto, Toronto Hunt, Toronto, Ont.; Rideau, Golf and Country, Ottawa, Ont.; Halifax, Halifax.

CASSILS, Charles; merchant; *b.* Renton Dumbartonshire, Scotland, 16 June, 1841; *s.* of John Cassils and Margaret Murray; *m.* (1st) 1865, Agnes Shearer, of Rutherglen (*d.* 1868); (2nd) Miss Cochrane, *d.* of the late Senator Cochrane of Hillhurst, Que.; three *s.* four *d.* *Educ.:* Rutherglen, near Glasgow. On arrival Can., joined firm of Cochrane, Cassils & Co., boot and shoe mnfrs., Montreal. Represents English House of Messrs. Bolckow, Vaughan & Co., Ltd., of Middlesboro', Yorkshire. Acted as chief rep. in Can., of the Carnegie Steel Co., for many yrs., until formation of the U.S. Steel Trust. Pres., Dom. Transport Co.; dir., Bell Telephone Co., Northern Electric and Mnfg. Co., Dominion Bridge Co., Wire and Cable Co., Windsor Hotel Co., Canadian Transfer Co. International Nickel Co., of New York, and various other Cos.; mem. Masonic fraternity and life governor of Montreal General Hospital; Pres., St. Andrew's Soc. of Montreal. Was Pres., Montreal Philharmonic Soc. for several yrs. *Recreation:* music. *Address:* 209 University St., Montreal, Que. *Clubs:* Mount Royal, St. James', Forest and Stream, Montreal, Hunt, Canada, Royal St. Lawrence Yacht, Jockey.

CATTO, Charles James, Captain 48th Regt., Highlanders; *b.* Toronto, Ont., 14 Nov., 1868; *s.* of John Catto and Margaret Mundee; *m.* Leila Alice Taylor; five *s.* Merchant, Junior Partner of John Catto & Son, Toronto. *Address:* 46 Breadalbane St., Toronto. *Club:* Canadian Military Institute, Toronto.

CATTO, Dr. William; *b.* Aberdeenshire, Scotland, 1867. *Educ.:* Aberdeen Univ., and later at Edinburgh; completed his medical educ., Berlin, Germany. Went by sea from Liverpool to Dawson at height of Klondike fever. In addition to large medical practice has taken a great interest in mining operations; operated first mill on a quartz deposit at Klondike. *Address:* Dawson, Y.T.

CAVERHILL, George; mem. of the firm of Caverhill, Learmont & Co., Hardware Merchants; *b.* Beauharnois, Que., 18 Oct., 1858; *s.* of Thomas Caverhill and Elizabeth Spiers Buchanan; *m.* 1887, Emily Margaret, *d.* of John Caverhill; one *s.* one *d.* *Educ.* Montreal High Sch., Coll. Inst. of Galt, McGill Univ. Entered the employ of Crathern & Caverhill, 1877; joined his bro. the late Frank Caverhill, J. B. Learmont. and T. H. Newman in organizing the firm of Caverhill, Learmont & Co. Was Pres., Montreal Bd. of Trade; Vice-Pres., Montreal Loan and Mortgage Co.; dir., Dominion Iron and Steel Co., Montreal Street Ry. Co., Royal Victoria Life Ins. Co., Richelieu and Ont. Nav. Co., Canadian Colored Cotton Mills Co.; governor, Montreal General Hospital. *Address:* 166 Drummond St., Montreal, Que. *Clubs:* St. James', Mount Royal, Montreal, Canada, Forest and Stream, Royal Montreal Golf, Montreal Hunt, Montreal Jockey, Royal St. Lawrence Yacht.

CEPERLEY, Henry T.; real estate agent *b.* Oneonta, N.Y., 10 Jan., 1851; *s.* of Martin Ceperley and Desiah Winnie; one *s.* one *d.* *Educ.:* Pub. Schs. and secured teacher's certificate. Taught sch. in New York State, until 1875, when he removed to Minnesota and later to Montana, where he engaged in real estate. Became resident Vancouver, 1886, where has built up extensive business as real estate and insur. agent, also mining broker. Dir. of the British America Development Co., the British Columbia Building Assn., and the Carter River Power Co. *Address:* Georgia St., Vancouver, B.C. *Clubs:* Vancouver, Terminal City, Vancouver.

CHADWICK, His Hon. Austin Cooper, Judge of the County Court, Wellington County, and local Judge High Court of Justice, Ontario; *b.* Tp. of Ancaster, Wentworth Co., Ont., 18 Nov., 1842; *s.* John Craven Chadwick, originally of Ballmora Co., Tipperary, Ireland, and Louisa, *d.* of Jonathan Bell, Kensington, Eng.; *m.* Caroline Christie, *d.* of Ralph Charles Nicholson, late of Toronto and Lewes, Eng.; one *s.* one *d.* *Educ.:* at Private Sch. in Clapham, Eng., and the Guelph Grammar Schs. Called to the Bar, 1864; apptd. Junior Judge of the County of Wellington, Jan., 1873; Local Judge, H. C. J., March, 1882; Judge Wellington, 1891. *Recreations:* field sports, fishing, shooting. *Address:* Guelph, Ont.

CHALLENER, Frederick Sproston, R. C.A.; *b.* Whetstone, England, 1869; *s.* of Edwin and Emma Jane Wood, London; *m.* 1902, Ethel White, Oshawa, Ont.; one *s.* two *d.* *Educ.:* St. Paul's Sch., Stratford, Essex. Arrived in Canada, 1883; studied at Ontario School of Art, and with G. A. Reid, R.C.A., Toronto; also in England, Italy, Egypt, and Syria; A.R.C.A.; received medal, Pan-American Exposition, Buffalo; mem. of Council, Toronto Guild of Civic Art.; Ont. Society of Artists, and Royal Canadian Academy of Art. *Principal works:* National Gallery, Ottawa—Workers of the Fields (Diploma work); A Song at Twilight. Provincial Art Gallery, Toronto—The Milkmaid; When the Lights are Low; A Quiet Old Road; mural decorations—Russell Theatre, Ottawa; King Edward Hotel, Toronto; and C. P. R. Hotel, The Alexandra Winnipeg; steamers of the R. and O. Nav. Co.; medal at Louisiana Purchase Exposition, 1904. *Address:* Old Court House, Toronto.

CHAMBERLAIN, Montague; *b.* St. John, N.B., April 5, 1844; *s.* Samuel M. Chamberlain and Catherine W. Stevens. *Educ.:* pvt. schs., St. John, until 1858; unmarried. Bookkeeper 18 yrs., and partner 1885-7, firm of J. & W. F. Harrison, wholesale grocers, St. John; asst. sec., 1889-93, sec., 1893-1900, Lawrence Scientific Sch. For 10 yrs. was active mem. of Canadian Militia; retired with rank of Capt. Mem. Natural History Soc., of N.B., Boston Natural History Soc., Am. Ornithol. Union, Nuttall Ornithol. Club, Victorian Club (Boston), Boston Folk Lore Soc., and Indian Industries League. *Publications*: Canadian Birds, 1870; Systematic Table of Canadian Birds, 1887; Nuttall's Ornithology, revised and extended, 1891 and 1896; Birds of Greenland, 1892; Some Canadian Birds, 1895; The Church Army, 1897; Maliseet Vocabulary, 1899; The Penobscot Indians, 1899; also various bulls., etc. *Address:* Felton Hall, Cambridge, Mass.

CHAMBERLAYNE, Miss Catharine Jane, B.A.; *b.* Toledo, Can.; *d.* Ashley Taylor Chamberlayne and Cynthia Sheffield Thompson. *Educ.:* Elmira Coll. for Women, 1865; studied literature and French, in Paris. Lady prin., Lasell Sem., 9 yrs., Cincinnati Wesleyan Coll., 6 yrs., Wilbraham Acad., 7 yrs.; founded, 1892, and since prin., Miss Chamberlayne's School for Girls. *Address:* The Fenway, Boston, Mass.

CHAMBERS, Edward Thomas Davies; *b.* Saffron Walden, Eng., 26 June, 1852, *s.* of Edward Thomas Chambers and Louisa Percy Davies; *m.* Margaret, *d.* of the late James Jamieson, J.P.; three *s.* one *d.* Arrived in Canada, May, 1870; in the seventies was Principal of the Granby and St. Andrew's Academies. In journalism and literary pursuits ever since. For many years editor Quebec *Chronicle.* For ten years a member of the Quebec City Council, and for sometime Pro. Mayor. Past-Grand Master Masonic Grand Lodge, Que. *Publications:* The Ouananiche and its Canadian Environments; Illustrated Quebec, The Port of Qubec; Chambers Guide to Quebec; The Anglers Guide to Eastern Canada; The Sportsman's Companion, etc. *Recreation:* Angling and gardening. *Address:* 274 Grand Allee, Quebec. *Club:* Garrison, Quebec.

CHAMBERS, Captain Ernest John; Gentleman Usher of the Black Rod, the Senate of Canada; *b.* Penkridge, Staffordshire, Eng., 16 April, 1862; *s.* of Edward Thomas Chambers, and Louisa Percy Davies (both Eng).; *m.* 1898, Bertha Macmillan, of Kingston, Ont.; one *s.* one *d.* *Educ.:* Prince Albert Sch., St. Henri, Que., and Montreal High. Sch. Came to Canada with his parents, 1870. Father was for most of his life engaged in educational work in Eng. and Prov. of Que. An ancestor on father's side (Rear Admiral Thos. Chambers) served in Saunders' fleet at Quebec, 1759, and during the Revolutionary War commanded the British Squadron on Lake Champlain and George. Until apptd. to the Senate, was actively engaged in journalism, most of the time in Montreal. In 1888 and 1889, was Managing Director and Editor of the Calgary *Herald*, the pioneer daily newspaper in the then Northwest Territories. Was for two years joint proprietor and editor of the Canadian Military Gazette. Has contributed to a variety of publications on historical, military, hunting and] yachting subjects. Among his books are the following: "Suburban Montreal," six editions (published at Montreal, 1890-96); "The Origin and Services of the Prince of Wales' Regiment" (Montreal, 1897); "The Third (Montreal) Field Battery, its Origin and Services" (Montreal, 1898); "History of the Queen's Own Rifles of Canada," (Toronto, 1903); "The Montreal Highland Cadets, a Corps History" (Montreal, 1901); "The Governor General's Body Guard, Canada" (Toronto, 1902); The Duke of Cornwall's Own Rifles," (Ottawa, 1903); "The Book of Montreal" (Montreal, 1903); "The Royal Grenadiers, a Regimental History" (Toronto, 1904); "The 5th Regiment, Royal Scots of Canada (Highlanders)" (Montreal, 1904); "The Book of Canada" (Montreal, 1905); "A Great Building Firm of a Great City" (Montreal, 1905); "The Canadian Marine, a History of the Department of Marine and Fisheries" (Toronto, 1905); "Regimental History of the 90th Winnipeg Rifles" (Winnipeg, 1905); "Encyclopedia of Canadian Biography," Volumes I and II (Montreal and Toronto, 1904 and 1906); "Histoire du 65eme Regiment Carabiniers Mont Royal" (Montreal, 1906); "History of the Royal Northwest Mounted Police" (Montreal and Ottawa, 1906); "A History of the Canadian Militia" (Ottawa, 1907) "Canada's Fertile Northland," three editions (Govt. Printing Bureau, Ottawa, 1907, 1908, 1909); "The Settler's Guide," (Winnipeg, 1908); "The Great Mackenzie Basin" (Govt. Printing Bureau, Ottawa, 1908); "The Allan Line" a history and guide book (London, Eng., 1909); "The Canadian Parliamentary Guide," editions of 1908, 1909, and 1910 (Ottawa). Has been connected with Canadian Militia for many yrs. As a boy commanded the Montreal High Sch. Cadet Rifles, and later was Adjutant of the 6th Fusiliers, now the Prince of Wales' Fusiliers. At present Capt. of the Corps of Guides, on special service, attached to Intelligence Branch at Headquarters. *Recreations:* shooting, fishing. *Addresses:* The Senate, Ottawa; 325 Daly Ave., Ottawa

CHAMBERS, Rev. James, B.A., M.A., D.D.; *b.* Holbrook, Ont., Mar. 1, 1851; *s.* Robert Chambers and Katharine Lucas Nesbitt; *m.* 1877, Jessie Irene Buell. *Educ.:* Princeton, 1872; Princeton Theol. Sem., 1875' Ordained to Presby'n Ministry,1875; pastor Sherburne, N.Y., 1875-1882; Calvary Presby'n Ch., New York, 1882-1900; delivered sermon in 1894 that started campaign against Tammany; 3 times moderator Presbytery of New York; mem. 5 Gen Assemblies, Presby'n Ch.; editor Church Work, 12 yrs.; writer of religious, critical and reform articles. Connected with Nat. Bank of Norwich, N.Y., since 1900. Life mem. A. B. C. F. M., Am. Home Missionary Soc., Am. Tract Soc., Am. Bible Soc. *Clubs:* Presby'n Union (New York), Norwich. *Address:* Norwich, N. Y.

CHAMPAGNE, Albert, M.P.; *b.* Ottawa, Ont., 23 June, 1867: *s.* of Seraphin Champagne and Melina Ducharme; *m.* 29 Sept., 1895, Ester Oliver. *Educ.:* Christian Bros. Sch., Ottawa; constable in the R. N. W. M. P., for 10 years, stationed at Battleford in "C" Division; was elec. first Mayor of the town of Battleford, July ,1904; was elec. a member of Legislature of Saskatchewan; elec. to H. of C., 1908; a brother of Controller Champagne, Ottawa; Roman Catholic; Liberal. *Address:* Battleford, Sask.

CHAMPAGNE, Napoleon; Controller of Ottawa; *b.* Ottawa, Ont., 4 May, 1862; *s.* of Seraphin Champagne and Melina Ducharme. *Educ.:* Christian Brothers Sch., Ottawa, and Law Sch.; alderman for Ottawa for fifteen years; Controller for three years; Acting Mayor; unsuccessful candidate for H. of C., three times, and once for the Legislature in the Conservative interests. *Address:* 48 Sparks St., Ottawa. *Club:* Elks, Ottawa.

CHAPAIS, Jean Charles, LL.B.; *b.* St. Denis de la Bouteillerie, Kamouraska Co., Que., 6 March, 1850; *s.* of Hon. Jean Charles Chapais, Senator of Canada, and Georgina Dionne, *d.* of Hon. Lunable Dionne, a mem. of the Legislative Council of Quebec, before Confederation; *m.* Henrietta *d.* of Alexis Thomas Mechaud, M.D., on of the Governors of the Coll. of Medicine, of Quebec; one *s.* one *d.* *Educ.:* Coll. of St. Ann de la Pocatiere, Kamouraska County, Que., and

Laval, Que.; admitted to the Barr, 1870; practised law for two years; has since devoted all his time to agriculture; was Associate Editor of the official Journal of Agriculture of the Province of Quebec, from 1879 to 1890; also official Agricultural Lecturer. Is at present, since 1890, Assist. Dairy Commissioner, Canada; was Secretary the first Quebec Forestry Association; Dir., Vice-Pres. and Pres. of the Pomological and fruit growing Soc., of the Prov. of Que.; and since 1879, Agricultural Lecturer in all the French Sections of the Dominion; colloborator and correspondent of the French and English Agricultural Press for 30 years. *Publications:* Book on Forestry "The Canadian Foresters' Illustrated Guide," in French and English, 1883. *Address:* St. Denis de la Bouteillerie, Kamouraska, Co., Quebec.

CHAPAIS, Hon. Joseph Amable Thomas LL.D., M.L.C.; *b.* St. Denis de Kamouraska, 23 March, 1858; *s.* of the late Hon. J. C. Chapais and Henriette Georgina Dionne; *m.* Hectorine, *e. d.* of Sir Hector Langevin, formerly Min. of Pub. Works for Canada. *Educ.:* at Coll. of St. Anne de la Pocatiere. Studied law and called to the Bar of Que., 1879. From 1884 to 1890, was Chief Editor, and from 1890-1901, Proprietor and Editor of *Le Courrier du Canada.* Unsuccessful can. for H. of C. at g. e., 1891. Appd. to Legis. Coun., March, 1892; Jan., 1893, Min. without portfolio in Taillon Govt., and Leader of Govt. in Legis. Coun.; Pres. of Legis. Coun., 1895; Pres. of the Council, May, 1896; Min. of Colinization and Mines in Flynn Govt., 1897. *Publications:* "Le serment du Roi, 1900; Jean Rolin, Intendant of New France, 1904; Melanges, 1905, etc. *Address:* 3 Ursulines St., Quebec.

CHAPLEAU, Major Samuel Edmour St. Onge; Clerk of Senate of Canada and Clerk of Parliaments of Canada, since 1900; *b.* Syracuse, N.Y., 1839; 2nd *s.* of Pierre Chapleau, builder, Montreal; *m.* Caroline K; 3rd *d.* of Lt.-Col. Geo. W. Patten, U.S. Army; one *s.* *Educ.:* Coll. of Terrebonne. Went to U.S., 1860; entered regular army, 1861. Received brevet rank of Capt. for gallant and mertiorious services at battle of Murfreesboro', Tenn., and that of Brevet-Major for gallant services during Atlanta campaign and at battle of Jonesboro,' Ga.; was also at battle of Shiloh, Tenn., the siege of Corinth, Miss., and battles of Chickamauga and Chattanooga, Tenn,; sent to Memphis during the riots in that city, 1866; in command of the troops at Augusta, Ga., during the riots, 1868. Retired from U.S. Army, 1871; entered Civil Service of Can., 1873; Secretary of Department of Public Works, Sheriff of North West Territories, and Clerk of the Crown in Chancery. *Recreations:* Reading, camping, fishing, shooting, horseback riding, etc. *Address:* The Senate, Ottawa, Canada. *Clubs:* Rideau, Ottawa; Army and Navy, New York.

CHAPLEAU, Samuel Jefferson, C.E.; *b.* Atlanta, Ga., 1 Jan., 1869; *s.* of Major S. E. Chapleau, clerk of the Can. Senate, and Carrie K. Patten; *m.* Mary Edith, *d.* of James Gouin, Postmaster of Ottawa; one *s.* one *d.* *Educ.:* Ottawa Coll. Inst. and Rensselaer Poly. Inst., Troy, N.Y. (grad., 1891). Member of Can. and Amer. Socs., Civil Engrs. Summers 1889-1890, instrument man and draughtsman on municipal and general engineering for P. H. Baerman, C.E., Troy, N.Y.; Nov., 1890, transitman, Hudson River Impvt. Commission U.S. Corps Engrs.; July to Sept., 1891, transitman preliminary location for proposed railway form Greenwich, N.Y., to Rutland, Vermont; Sept., 1891, to May, 1892, General Engr. practice office of P. H. Baerman, Troy, N.Y.; May, 1892, to Jan., 1894, Assistant to Div. Engr., Eastern Div., C. P. R., general maintainance of way, yards surveys, &c.; Jan. to Aug., 1894, private practice Ottawa, Canada; Aug., 1894 to Feb. 1895, in charge topographic party on Hydrographic Survey of Fraser River, B.C., for Dept. Public Works, Can.; May to Sept., 1895, structural draftsman Soulanges Canal construction. Coteau Landing, Que.; Sept., 1895 to June, 1896, Asst. Engineer on adjustment of final estimates, Canadian Ship Canal, Sault Ste. Marie, Ont; June, 1896 to June, 1900, structural draftsman, later Assist. Engr. Soulanges Canal construction, Coteau Landing, in responsible charge of design of working drawings, construction estimates, &c., Dept. of Railways and Canals, Canada; June, 1900 to March, 1901, Ass't. Engr., N.Y. State Barge Canal survey in charge of designs and estimates of locks and their equipment and construction proposed 12′ Canal, Buffalo to Albany, and on Champlain Canal improvement; March, 1901, to June, 1904, Asst. Engr., Dept. Public Works Engineer in charge Hydro-graphic investigation, Middle Channel River, St. Lawrence Kingston to Brockville, Ont., for 14′ navigation, also surveys and improvements of harbor and chanels upper St. Lawrence Dist., June to Oct., 1904, Prin. Asst. Engr. in organization of Canadian Hydrographic office and in charge district Montreal to Great Lakes, Dept. of Marine, Can. To date, Engr. in charge Nipissing Dist. (Mem. of Board of Advisory Engrs.), Geo. Bay Ship Canal survey for Dept. Public Works, Can. *Recreations:* Motor boating, canoeing, hunting. *Address:* P. O. Box 203, Ottawa. *Clubs:* Yacht, Canoe, Gananoque, Ont. Rowing, Ottawa.

CHAPPLE, His Hon. Thomas William, Judge of the District of Kenora; *b.* Kilkenny Ireland, 10 Feb., 1813; *s.* of Capt. William Chapple and Entychia McNaughton; *m.* Lucy Ann French, of Oshawa; one *s.*; *Educ.:* Newcastle and Toronto, Ont.; arrived in Canada, 9 Oct., 1858; called to the Bar of Ontario, 1883; elected M.P., 1894; apptd. Judge, 1898. *Recreations:* Baseball and boating. *Address:* Kenora, Ont. *Club:* Lake of the Woods.

CHAPUT, Charles; head of the firm of L. Chaput, Fils & Cie, wholesale grocers, Montreal; *b.* Montreal, Que., Nov., 1841; *s.* of the late Leandre Chaput, founder of the firm of L. Chaput, Fils & Cie, and Helene St. Denis; three *s.* two *d.* *Educ.:* French and English Schs., Montreal. Joined father's firm as clerk, 1857; made partner 1862, head of the firm, 1878. Mem. of the Council of Montreal Bd. of Trade. Dir., Canada Life Ass. Co.; Vice-Pres., Montreal Business Men's League; Gov., Notre Dame

Hospital and Mem. Montreal Dispensary. *Address:* 349 Sherbrooke St. E., Montreal.

CHARBONNEAU, Hon. Napoleon, K.C.; a Puisnie Judge of the Superior Court of the Prov. of Que., since 1903; *b.* Cote des Neiges, Que., 12 Feb., 1853; *s.* of Augustin Charbonneau and Julienne Dufort. *Educ.:* Montreal Coll. Admitted to the Bar, 1879, and practiced prof. in Montreal. Unsuccessful candidate for H. of C., at g. e., 1887; elec. 1895. *Address:* 36 Simpson St., Montreal.

CHARLTON, Alexander Drysdale, Asst. Gen. Passngr. Agt., Northern Pacific Ry.; *b.* Hamilton, Ont., 15 Nov., 1859. Entered Ry. service, Feb., 1876, since which he has been consecutively to June, 1877, Clerk, Auditor's office Great Western Ry. of Can.; June 8, 1877, to Feb. 15, 1884, with Chicago & Alton Rd., successively in charge return ticket dept., and of issuing tickets and rate clerk; Feb. 15, 1884, to date, successively gen. western passngr. agt. and asst. gen. passngr. agt., Northern Pacific Rd. and its successor, the Northern Pacific Ry. *Address:* Portland, Ore.

CHARLTON, George James, Gen. Passngr. Agt., Chicago & Alton Ry.; *b.* Hamilton, Ont., 9 Sept., 1860. *Educ.:* Pub. and Priv. Schs. Entered Ry. service 1875, as Messenger Boy, Gen. Passngr. Dept., Chicago & Alton Rd., since which he has been consecutively to March, 1895, successively Junior Clerk, Conductor's Clerk, Ticket Stock Clerk, Rate Clerk and Ticket Accnt. same Dept.; March 14, 1885 to Jan. 1, 1900, Asst. Gen. Passngr. Agt., and Jan. 1, 1900, to date, Gen. Passngr Agt.; entire service with the Chicago & Alton Rd. and its successor, the Chicago & Alton Ry. *Address:* Chicago, Ill.

CHARLTON, Harry Ready; *b.* St. Johns, Que., 9 Feb., 1866; *m.* R. L. Edith Osgoode; one *s.* *Educ.:* St. John's High Sch.; started in 1881, with the St. Johns *News*, and was afterwards with the Montreal *Herald* for five years; C. P. R. Co., for five years, and Davis and St. Lawrence Co. for two years. Entered the service of the G. T. Ry. System, 1 Jan., 1898, as Advertising Agent; now General Advertising Agent for G. T. Ry. System and G. T. Pacific Ry.; *Address:* 8 Sussex Av., Montreal. *Clubs:* Transportation, Buffalo; Press Club, Chicago.

CHATEAUVERT, Victor; *b.* Quebec, Que., 1841; *s.* of Pierre Chateauvert and Angele Rousseau; *m.* Virginie Dussault, of Quebec; four *s.* three *d.* *Educ.:* Christian Brothers' Sch., William Thom's English Academy, Quebec. Entered employ Louis Renaud & Frere (now J. B. Renaud & Co.), flour, grain and provision merchants, 1885; became a partner, 1879; bought out the bis. together with Gaspard Lemoine, 1884. Pres. Renaud & Co., Ltd., Dir. La Banque Nationale; Pres. Quebec Bd. of Trade, 1891-1893. Served as Harbor Commr. of Que. El. to Que. Legis. Assembly, 1892; retired on dissolution that Parlt. *Address:* St. Foy Rd., Quebec.

CHAUSSE, Alcide; Supt. of Bldgs., Montreal; *b.* Saint Sulpice, l'assomption Co., Que., 7 Jan., 1868; *s.* of Edouard Chausse, lumber merchant, and Rose de Lima Rivet; *m.* 1894, Rose de Lima Renaud; two *s.* *Educ.:* St. Mary's Academy, Montcalm Sch., Montreal. Studied architecture in Montreal, Chicago, and Milwaukee, U.S. Practiced as an architect in Montreal for twelve yrs.; apptd. head of the Bureau of Bldg. Inspection, Montreal, 1900. Mem. of the Council of the Chamber of Commerce commr. of the Superior Ct.; Vice-Pres. of International Soc. of Inspectors of Bldgs.; Sec. Architectural Inst. of Can.; past Pres. Prov. of Que. Assn. of Architects; corres. mem. National Socs. of Architects of U.S., France, Belgium, Holland, England, Spain, Portugal, etc. Mem Council of the Permanent Committee of International Congresses of Architects, British Fire Prevention Com., Comite Technique contre les Accidents et les Incendies (France). Pres. Fire Prevention Committee of the American Soc. of Municipal Improvements; was mem. of the Congresses of Architects of Paris, 1889; Brussels, 1897; Paris, 1900; Madrid, 1904; London, 1906; Vienna, 1908; Congress of Civil Engineering at St. Louis, U.S., 1905; Congress of Fire Prevention, London, Eng., 1903, when awarded a silver medal; Congress of Sanitation in Houses, Geneva, 1906; Congress, Chambers of Commerce of the Empire, in London, 1906. *Publications:* Building Inspector's Handbook, Code of Building Laws, both in English and French; contributions to several technical publications and reviews. *Address:* 1433 St. Hubert St., Montreal.

CHAUVEAU, Hon. Charles F. X. Alexandre, LL.D., K.C.; Chev. Leg. Hon. (France); Vice-Pres. La Banque Nationale; *b.* Quebec, 23 Feb., 1847; *s.* of Hon. P. J. O. Chauveau, former Premier of Quebec, and Flore Masse; *m.* Marie Adele, *d.* of Hon. Judge Tessier; two *s.* *Educ.:* Jesuit's Coll., Coll. St. Sulpice, Montreal; McGill and Laval. Descendant of an old family of lle d'Oleron, France, whom emig. to Canada, about 1720. Called to Bar of Que., 1868; el. to Leg. Ass., 1872; Solicitor General, 1878; Prov. Sec., 1879; Judge of Sessions, 1880; Prov. of Criminal Law at Laval Univ.; Quebec for 15 yrs.; Director and Vice-Pres. La Banque Nationale. *Address:* Chateau Frontenac, Quebec; Rimouski, (Summer).

CHEW, Thomas Edward Manley, M.P.; *b.* Rugby, Ont., 11 Aug., 1874; *s.* of Geo. Chew, and Sophia Lawrence; *m.* 1 March, 1899, Effie Williams; one *d.* *Educ.:* Midland Ont., first returned to H. of C., 1908; Methodist; Liberal. *Address:* Midland, Ont.

CHISHOLM, Alexander W., M.D., M.P.; *b.* Margard Forks, C.B., 24 Jan., 1869; *s.* of William and Mary Chisholm, both Scotsh; *m.* 27 Jan., 1904, Clara Le Brun. *Educ.:* Margard Forks High Sch., St. Francois Xavier Coll., Antigonish. Was a candidate in a three cornered contest in the Co. of Inverness, 1904, but was defeated; first elec. to H. of C., 1908; Roman Catholic; Liberal. *Address:* Margard Harbour, N.S.

CHISHOLM, Hon. Christopher P.; Com. of Works and Mines of Nova Scotia; *b.* Clydesdale, Antigonish Co., N.S., April, 1854; of Scottish parentage; *m.* 1890, Sarah Campbell, of Antigonish. *Educ.:* St. Francois Xavier Coll., Antigonish. Called to Bar of N.S., 1883. Apptd. Notary, 1884. El. to N.S. Ass., 1891, and has represented Antigonish continuously since. Called to the Prov. Cabinet without portfolio, 16

Feb., 1903. Apptd. Com. of Public Works and Mines, 23 March, 1907; re-el. by accl. at bye-el., 9 April, 1908. *Address:* Halifax, N.S.

CHISHOLM, Hugh J.; *b.* Niagara-on-the-Lake, Ont., May 2, 1847; *m.* 1872, Henrietta Mason, Portland, Me. Was train newsboy on G. T. Ry., at 13; studied in evening classes at a business coll. in Toronto, gradually secured control of news routes on trains of G. T. Ry., east to Portland, Me., taking his brothers into partnership and steadily added to this business. Sold out Canadian business and purchased his brothers' interests in New England; located in Portland and added publishing. Became interested in wood-pulp business late in '70s; began mfr. of indurated fibre ware; organized Somerset Fibre Co.; mfg. wood-pulp at Fairfield; established, 1881, Umbagog pulp mill at Livermore Falls on Androscoggin River, and later organized the Otis Falls Pulp Co.; developed water power at Rumford Falls, organizing Rumford Falls Power Co.; became largely interested in mfg. enterprises there and established there a community of model homes for mill operatives, known as Strathglass Park; organized and is Pres. Portland and Rumford Falls Ry., Rumford Falls and Rangeley Lakes R. R.; with William A. Russell and others organized International Paper Co., and on death of Mr. Russell, became its Pres., and Nov., 1907, chmn. b'd. dirs.; also Pres. or Dir. various other corp'ns. *Address:* 813 5th Av. *Office:* 30 Broad St., New York.

CHISHOLM, Joseph Andrew, B.A., M. A., LL.B., K.C.; *b.* St. Andrews, Antigonish Co., N.B., 9 Jan., 1863; *s.* of William Chisholm, J.P., and Flora Mackintosh; *m.* Frances Alice Afflick, *d.* of James Afflick; five *d.* *Educ.:* St. Francis Xavier Coll., Antigonish, and Dalhousie Coll., Halifax; admitted to the Bar, 1886; contested Antigonish for the H. of C., 1895 and 1896, but was defeated; President North British Soc. of Halifax, 1889; apptd. K.C., 1907; Pres. Canadian Club, 1908; Mayor of Halifax, 1909-10. *Publications:* Joseph Howe, a Sketch (1909); speeches and public letters of Joseph Howe (1909); contributor to the Catholic Encycleopedia. *Recreations:* Walking. *Address:* Hillside Hall, Halifax, N.S. *Club:* Halifax.

CHISHOLM, Thomas, M.B., M.D., C.M., M.P.; *b.* Glenwilliams Co. Halton, Ont., 12 April, 1842; *s.* John Chisholm, and Jane McClure; *m.* Margaret Gerrie; two *s.* one *d.* *Educ.:* Self-eductaed, and finished at Toronto Univ.; spent his early life on a farm where he had hired out, after loosing his mother; studied at night without a teacher. Taught pub. sch., then High Sch.; studied medicine; lectured in Western Univ., London, Ont. Practiced medicine for 30 yrs. Elec. member of Parlt., 1894, and in 1898. *Publications:* Rhyming history of England, in 100 lines; Dialogues on English History and "The Hunter's Adventures in the Canadian Wilderness. *Address:* Wingham, Ont.

CHISHOLM, William, B.A., M.P.,; *b.* Heatherton, Antigonish, Co., N.S., 8 Dec., 1870; *s.* of John and Isabella Chisholm; unmarried. *Educ.:* at St. Francis Xavier Univ., Antigonish, N.S.; has been a Town Councillor in Antigonish for two terms. First elec. to Federal Parlt., at bye-elec. in 1905; re-elec. at g. e., 1908. *Address:* Antigonish, N.S. *Clubs:* Antigonish, and Neptune, Antigonish; Laurentian, Ottawa.

CHOQUET, Francois Xavier, B.C.L. (McGill); *b.* Varennes, Que., 8 Jan., 1851; *s.* of Jean Baptiste Choquet and Adeline Provost; *m.* Mary Caroline Barry, of Trois Pistoles, Que. *Educ.:* L'Assomption and Montreal Colls.; studied law under Sir L. A. Jette and Senator Beique in firm of Jette and Beique; took a law course at McGill Univ., from which he grad. B.C.L., 1874. Called to the Bar, 10 Jan., 1875, and commenced practice of his profession in Montreal; partner in firm of Jette and Beique for four yrs.; practiced alone for six yrs.; partner in the firm of Mercier, Beausoleuil and Choquet, 1884-1892, when name of the firm was changed to Beausoleil & Choquet; cr. K.C., 7 March, 1893; mem. of Council of Montreal Bar, 1894-1897; apptd. a del, to Gen. Council of Bar, of Prov. of Quebec; apptd. Judge of the Sessions of the Peace, License Commr., Police Magistrate 24 Dec., 1889, and Extradition Commr. under the Extradition Act of 1901. Pres., Montreal Children's Aid Soc. *Recreations:* hunting, fishing. *Address:* 814 Dorchester St., W., Montreal. *Clubs:* Engineers', Montreal, Winchester, Shawinigan.

CHOQUETTE, The Hon. Philippe Auguste, LL.D., Senator; *b.* at Beloeil, Que., 26 Jan., 1854; *s.* of Joseph Choquette, a farmer, and Dame Marie F. Audet; *m.* Aug., 1883, Marie Bender, *d.* of A. Bender, Prothonatary of the Superior Court of the District of Montmagny, and Grand *d.* of the late Sir. Eteanne Pascal Tache, Prime Minister of Canada before Confederation; five *s.* three *d.* *Educ.:* at the Coll of St. Hyacinthe and Laval Univ. Obtained his degree as Advocate in 1880, also the silver medal offered by Marquis of Lorne, then Governor General; Private Secretary to the late Hon. Mr. Mercier; founded the "*Sentinelle*" of Montmagny, in 1883, which still exists in the name of "*Courrier de Montmagny.*" In 1896, founded at Montreal, the journal "*Le Soir.*" Entering political life in 1882, was defeated, but was elec. for H. of C. for same Co., in 1887, re-elec. in 1891, and 1896. Apptd. Judge of the Supreme Court for the Province of Quebec; resigned, 1904, as Judge to accept a Senatorship, and to take charge of the general elections in the District of Quebec and its environs; edited "*Le Soleil,*" French Liberal organ, of Quebec, 1905-1906. President, The Boston Asbestos Co., Ltd.; President of the Ha Ha Bay Ry., and ex-President, and now legal advisor of the Canada and Gulf Terminal Ry., both under construction *Address:* Quebec. *Clubs:* St. Louis, and Garrison, Quebec.

CHRISTIE, Major Albert Edward, D.S. O., 16th Mounted Rifles; *b.* 3 Dec., 1860; *s.* of late Charles Robertson Christie, of Toronto; *m.* 1902, Mary Ludlow, *d.* of Hon. Mr. Justice Wetmore; two *s.* Served North West Rebellion, 1885; South Africa, 1900. *Address:* Brandon, Man.

CHRISTIE, John, K.C.; *b.* Ottawa, Ont. 21 Jan., 1847; *s.* of Alexander and Susannah Christie; unmarried. *Educ.:* Ottawa and

Philadelphia, Pa. Called to the Bar of Ont., 1878; joined the legal firm of Pinhey, Christie & Hill; now head of the firm of Christie, Greene & Hill. *Recreation:* reading. *Address:* 211 Bronson Av., Ottawa. *Clubs:* Rideau, Golf, Country, Ottawa.

CHRYSLER, Francis Henry, B.A., K. C.; *b.* Kingston, Ont.; *s.* of Gordon Harvey Chrysler, *s.* of Colonel John Chrysler, Chrysler's Farm, and Jane Mackenzie, *d.* of Capt. James Mackenzie, R.N.; *m.* Margaret Grant; two *s.* two *d.* *Educ.:* at Queen's Coll., Kingston; engaged in practice of law at Ottawa, since 1872. *Publications:* Edgar and Chrysler Insolvent Act, 1875. *Address:* 87 Catherine St., Ottawa. *Clubs:* Rideau, Country, Golf, Ottawa.

CLARE, George A., M.P. for South Waterloo; *b.* Preston, Ont., 6 June, 1854; *s.* of John and Marguerite Clare; *m.* Catherine Fink; one *s.* three *d.* *Educ.:* Preston Com. Sch. A mfr. of Stovers and furnaces; Pres. Clare Bros. & Co., of Preston; Pres. Can. Office and School Furniture Co. Ten years Reeve of Preston; first Mayor; ten yrs. a member of Waterloo County Council; one yr. Warden. First el. to H. of C., 1900; re-el. 1904 and 1908. *Address:* Preston, Ont. *Clubs:* Albany, Toronto; Waterloo Co. Golf, Galt.

CLARKE, Hon. George Johnson, K.C.; Speaker of N. B. Legislature; *b.* St. Andrews, N.B., 10 Oct., 1857; *s.* of Nelson and Mary Clarke; *m.* Bessie, *d.* of the late Rev. Hezekiah McKeown, of St. John, N.B.; two *d.* *Educ.:* St. Andrews and Fredericton. Editor of St. Croix *Courtier*, 1882; admitted Attorney, 1885; called to Bar, 1886; unsuccessful can. for H. of C., 1891; unsuccessful can. for N.B. Legis., 1899, el. to Legis., 1903; re-el., 1908; apptd. K.C., 1907; Speaker of Legis., 1909. *Address:* St. Stephen, N.B.

CLARK, Rev. Francis E., M.A., D.D., LL.D.; President World's Christian Endeavour Union since 1895; editor in chief of the Christian Endeavour World since 1886; *b.* Aylmer, Que.; *m.* Harriet E. Abbott, Andover, Mass., U.S.A., 1876; three *s.* one *d.* *Educ.:* Kimball Union Academy; Dartmouth Coll., N.H., U.S.A.; Andover Theolog. Seminary; Dartmouth Coll., 1887; grad. at Dartmouth Coll., 1873; at Andover Theol. Sem., 1876; Pastor of Williston Church, Portland, M., 1876; founded Christian Endeavour Soc., 1881; Pastor of Phillips Church, Boston, 1883; President United Soc. of C.E., 1887-1907; four times around the world, etc. *Publications:* Christian Endeavour in All Lands; Ways and Means; The Children and the Church; Young People's Prayer Meetings; Our Journey around the World, World-Wide Christian Endeavour; The Great Secret; Fellow Travellers; a New Way around an Old World; Old Lanterns for New Paths; Training the Church of the Future; Christian Endeavour Manual, and several other volumes, large and small. *Recreations:* fishing in the Main woods, outdoor sports, etc. *Address:* Tremont Temple, Boston, Mass.

CLARK, George Harold; *b.* Brantford, Ont., 1872; *s.* of James and Sarah Clark; *m.* R. Irene Fault; two *s.* one *d.* *Educ.:* Brantford Com. Sch., and High Sch., and Ontario Agricultural Coll., Guelph. Farmed until 21 years of age; grad. from O. A. C., in 1908; apptd. on the staff of Guelph in the same year. In 1902, was apptd. Chief of the seed division of the Federal department, and in 1905, promoted seed Commissioner. Organized the seed branch of the Department of Agriculture, and instituted the work of seed testing and control of the seed trade of Canada, under the Hon. S. A. Fisher. *Publications:* Farm needs of Canada; and numerous reports and bulletins of the department. *Address:* 501 O'Connor St., Ottawa.

CLARK, Lieut.-Col. Hugh, M.L.A.; *b.* Kincardine, 6 May, 1867; *s.* of Donald and Mary Clark; *m.* Kate Ross, *e. d.* of H. M. Ross., M.D., of Richard's Landing, Ont.; one *s.* *Educ.:* Kincardine High Sch.; taught Sch. for three years, after which he edited the Walkerton *Herald;* in 1890, purchased the Kincardine *Review*; in 1897-8, edited the Ottawa *Citizen*. Is still owner and Editor of the Kincardine *Review*; was elec. to the Legisltaure at the g. e., 1892, but was unseated; was afterwards elected in a bye-election in 1903, and also in 1905 and 1908. Joined the militia in 1892, and became Lieut.-Col. of the 32nd Regt., 1906. *Recreations:* bowling and golf. *Address:* Kincardine, Ont.

CLARK, John Murray, K.C., M.A., LL. B.; *b.* St. Mary's, Ont., 6 July, 1860; *s.* of James and Isabella Clark; *m.* Anne M. Anderson; three *d.* *Educ.:* Univ. of Toronto; prize in Logic, McMurrich Medal in Natural Science, Gold Medal in Mathematics and Physics. Called to Bar with Honours and Law Society's Gold Medal; has been Counsel in many *causes celebres*, such as the Quaker Case, the Ontario Express Co., the Fisheries Case, and the Ophir Case; Pres. of the Toronto Branch of the British Empire League in Canada. *Publications:* The Law of Mines in Canada; Company Law; The Ontario Mining Law; International Arbitration; The Future of Canada; Thermotics; the History of the Theory of Energy *Address:* 16 King St. West, Toronto. *Clubs:* Toronto, R. C. Y. C., Toronto; Rideau Ottawa.

CLARK, Joseph Thomas; *b.* Flesherton, Grey County, Ont., 4 Sept., 1866; *s.* of William Mathewson Clark and Phyllis McConkay Clark; *m.* Sarah Louise Greig of Pickering, Ont.; three *s.* one *d.* *Educ.:* in the Public Sch; Journalist; for many years editor of *Saturday Night*; now editorial writer Toronto *Star*. *Recreations:* golf and angling. *Address:* 66 Howland Av., Toronto. *Clubs:* National, Lambton Golf and Country Clubs, Toronto.

CLARK, Michael, M.B., C.M., M.P.; *b.* Belford, Northumberland, Eng., 12 May, 1861; *s.* of Michael Clark and Jane Hall, Belford, Northumberland; *m.* Elizabeth, *e. d.* of George Smith, late of Cherrybank Farm, near Hamilton, Ont., formerly of Scot.; four *s.* *Educ.:* Elmfield Coll., York, Eng., and Univ. of Edinburgh; arrived in Can., Jan., 1902. Gold medal in languages at School; also Scholarship for head boy of the year; made and sold County and Town practices in the Old Country; former member of Newcastle School Board; farming and ranching successfully with sons in Western Canada. First elec. to H. of C,

1908. *Recreations:* cricket, walking. *Address:* Belford Glen Ranch, Olds, Alberta.

CLARK, Sir William Mortimer, Kt.; cr. 1907., W.S., K.C., LL.D.; Barrister, Chairman, Knox College, Toronto, since 1880; *b.* Aberdeen, Scotland, 24 May, 1836; *s.* of John Clark, manager, Aberdeen Insurance Company; *m.* 1866, Helen, *d.* of Gilbert Gordon, Caithness; one *s.* John Gordon, President, Toronto Gray and Bruce Railway; two *d.* *Educ.:* Grammar Sch. and Marischal Coll., Aberdeen; Univ. of Edinburgh; Life Member of General Council of latter Univ. Admitted W.S., 1859; settled in Toronto, Ont., same year; called to Bar of Ontario, 1869; Q.C., 1890; for fifteen yrs. Senator of Univ. of Toronto; LL.D. Toronto 1902, Kingston, 1903; President Toronto Mortgage Company; Director Metropolitan Bank of Canada; solicitor for various public companies and charities; President, St. Andrew's Society, for two years; for five years Secretary. Canadian Institute; for two years President, County of York Law Association. *Publications:* numerous contributions to Toronto press on public, educational, and literary questions. *Recreations:* travelled largely on American Continent, in Africa, Asia, and almost every country in Europe. *Address:* 303 King St., Toronto.

CLARK, Prof. William Robinson, M.A., D.D., LL.D., D.C.L., F.R.C.S.; Professor of Philosophy, Trinity Coll., Toronto, since 1882; *s.* of Rev. James Clark, Daviot, Aberdeenshire, and Catherine Lyon; *b.* Inverurie, 26 March, 1829; *m.* Louise, *o. c.* of Hon. James Patten, LL.D.; five *s.* four *d.* *Educ.:* Grammar Sch., Old Aberdeen; King's Coll., Aberdeen; Hertford Coll., Oxford. Ordained Deacon, 1857; Priest, 1858; Curate of St. Matthias's, Birmingham, 1857; St. Mary Magdalene, Taunton, 1858; Vicar, 1859; Prebendary of Wells, 1870; Baldwin Lecturer in the Univ. of Michigan, U.S.A., 1887; Slocum Lecturer in the Univ. of Michigan, 1899; President of the Royal Society of Canada, 1910; Hon. Canon of St. Alban's Cathedral, Toronto, 1907. *Publications:* The Redeemer, 1863; The Comforter, 1864; The Four Temperaments, 1874; Witnesses to Christ (Baldwin Lectures), 1888; Savonarola; His Life and Times, 1892; The Anglican Reformation, 1896; The Paraclete (Slocum Lectures), 1900; Pascal and Port Royal, 1902; translated and edited Hagenbach's History of Christian Doctrine; Hefele's History of the Councils. *Recreation:* literature. *Address:* 53 Beverley Street, Toronto.

CLARKE, Alfred Henry, LL.B. (Toronto Univ.), K.C., M.P.; *b.* Manilla, Ont., 25 Oct., 1860; *s.* of John Clarke and Ann Clarke; *m.* 8 Aug., 1888, Margaret Gibson, *d.* of D. Z. Gibson, of Brantford, Ont. *Educ.:* Manilla Pub. and Gram. Sch., Oakwood High Sch., Toronto Univ. A bencher of the Law Society of Upper Canada; has been Co. Crown Attorney and Clerk of the Peace; also Local Master in Chancery, Co. Essex; elec. M.P. for South Essex at g. e., 1904; re-elec. at g. e., 1908. *Address:* Windsor, Ont.

CLARKE, Charles Kirk, M.D., LL.D.; *b.* Elora, Ont., 16 Feb., 1857; *s.* of Hon. Chas. Clarke, and Emma Kent; *m.* (1st) Margaret De Veber Andrews, 1880; (2nd) Theresa Gallagher, 1904; four *s.* two *d.* *Educ.:* Elora Grammar Sch. and Univ. of Toronto; Dean of Medical Faculty, Univ. of Toronto; Prof. of Univ. of Toronto; Medical Supt., Hospital for Insane, Toronto. was Asst. Physician in Toronto Hospital for Insane, under Dr. Joseph Workman; Asst. Supt. of Hospital for Insane, Hamilton; Supt. of Rockwood Hospital for Insane, Kingston, and Supt. of H. for Insane, Toronto. *Address:* 999 Queen St. West, Toronto. *Club:* University, Toronto.

CLARKE, Hugh Archibald; *b.* Canada, Aug. 15, 1839; *m.* 1859, Jane M. Searle, Toronto; *Educ.:* Knox Coll. (Mus. Doc., Univ. of Pa., 1861). Resided in Phila. since 1860.; Prof. of Music Univ. of Pen., since 1875. *Publications:* The Scratch Club, 1888; Music and the Comrade Arts, 1900; Highways and Byways of Music, 1901. *Address:* The Sherwood, 38th and Chestnut Sts., Philadelphia.

CLARKE, John Duncan; *b.* Belhelvie, Aberdeenshire, Scot., 13 Aug., 1854; *s.* of Peter Clarke, and Helen Grey; *m.* Jennie Armstrong, *d.* of the late J. W. Armstrong, J.P., Flecherton, Ont.; two *s.* one *d.* *Educ.:* Belhelvie and Arbroath, Scot.; arrived in Canada, 1 June, 1875; was connected with newspaper work since boyhood, until entering into the Civil Service; served on the Arbroath and Dundee *Courier* as reporter; in 1875, joined the staff of the London, Ont. *Free Press*; in 1878, became City Editor of the Hamilton *Spectator*; apptd. Managing Editor of the Hamilton *Times*, in 1879; on the retirement of the Hon. David Mills, from the London Daily *Advertiser*, in 1889, succeeded him as Editor; in 1898, joined the Civil Service at Secretary to the Minister of Justice, which position he has held under succeeding Ministers. *Recreation:* bowling. *Address:* 10 Somerset St., Ottawa.

CLEAVE, Arthur Harold Wyld, M.I.M. E., C.E., F.R.M.S.; *b.* Putney, England, 8 June, 1868; *s.* of John Cleve, I.S.O., and Martha Cleve; *m.* *d.* of the late George Caxon, of Beddington, Northumberland. *Educ.:* Battersea Grammar Sch., King's Coll., Devonport. Arrived in Canada, Sept. 1906; engineer at sea for five years; entered Royal Mint, London, Jan., 1893; Supt. of Royal Mint, Canada, 1907. *Recreations:* Microscopy, and Astronomy. *Address:* "Royston," 446 Daly Av., Ottawa. *Club:* Rideau, Ottawa.

CLORAN, Hon. Henry Joseph, B.C.L., K.C.; *b.* Montreal, 8 May, 1855; *s.* of Joseph Cloran and Ann Kennedy; *m.* (1st) Agnes N. Donovan (*d.* 1896); (2nd) 1906, M. Inez, *d.* of George Goodwin, of Ottawa. Editor of Montreal *Post* and *True Witness*, 1882-87; pres. of leading Irish Canadian Literary, Athletic and National Assns. of Montreal, 1880-1892; past pres., Canadian Press Assn. Crown Prosecutor, 1890-92; Prof. of English, Montreal Coll., 1879-80; Reeve and Mayor of Hawkesbury, 1894-1901. Unsuccessful candidate for H. of C., at four g. e., 1887-1901. Called to Senate, 1903. A mem. of the Knights of Columbus; a warm supporter of athletic sports. *Addresses:* Montreal; The Senate, Ottawa. *Club:* St. Denis, Montreal.

CLOUSTON, Sir Edward, Bart.; *b.* Moose Factory, Can., 9 May, 1849; *s.* James Stewart Clouston and Margaret Miles; *m.* Annie Easton; one *s.* *Educ.:* Montreal High Sch.; Vice-Pres. and Gen. Mgr. of the Bank of Montreal; entered Bank of Montreal, in 1865; Assist. Inspector, 1877; Manager Montreal Branch, 1881; Asst. Gen. Mgr., 1887; Gen. Mgr., 1890. *Recreations:* yachting and golf. *Address:* "Boisbriant," St. Anne de Bellevue, Que., and 362 Peel St., Montreal. *Clubs:* Mount Royal and St. James', Montreal; Toronto, Toronto; Rideau, Ottawa; Manhattan, New York; Bath, London, Eng.

CLOUTIER, Mgr. Francois Xavier, M. A., Bishop of Three Rivers, Que.; *b.* Three Rivers, 2 Nov., 1848; *s.* of Jean Cloutier & Olive Rivard. *Educ.:* at Seminary of native City. Has made two visits to Rome, and one to Palestine. Curate of Three Rivers for 15 yrs; consec. Bishop, 1899. *Publications:* Two vols. of Pastoral Letters; several discourses. *Address:* Bishopric of Three Rivers.

COATS, Robert Hamilton, B.A. (Toronto Univ.), Assoc. editor of The *Labour Gazette; b.* Clinton, Ont., 25 July, 1874; of Scottish and American parentage; *m.* Marie Halboister, of Pairs, France. *Educ.:* Toronto Univ.; served on Toronto *World* and Toronto *Globe*. Sec. of the Civil Service Assn., of Ottawa; sec., Civil Service Federation of Canada; apptd. Assoc. ed. of The *Labour Gazette*, 1902. *Publications:* Life of Sir James Douglas in "Makers of Canada" series. *Recreations:* canoeing, skeing. *Address:* "The Nook," Rockliffe Park, Ottawa. *Club:* Ottawa Canoe.

COATSWORTH, Emerson, LL.B.; *b.* Toronto, 9 March, 1854; *s.* of Emerson Coatsworth, for 30 years City Commissioner of Toronto; *m.* 1883, Helen, *d.* of late John Robertson, De Cew Falls, Ont.; two *s.* two *d.* *Educ.:* Toronto Pub. Sch.; Br. Am. Com. Coll.; Up. Can. Law School, and Toronto Univ. Called to Bar, 1879; M.P. (Conservative), East Toronto, 1891-1896; Alderman for Ward 2, 1904 and 1905; Mayor, 1906 and 1907; Methodist. *Address:* 1 May Place, Toronto. *Clubs:* Albany, Royal Canadian Yacht.

COCHRANE, Hon. Francis, M.L.A.; Min. of Lands and Mines for Ontario; *b.* Clarenceville, Que., 18 Nov., 1852; *s.* of Robert Cochrane, and Mary Ann Hunter; *m.* 1882, Alice Levina Dunlop; two *s.* one *d.* *Educ.:* sep. sch. in the parish of St. Thomas, Que. For many yrs. a resident of Sudbury, Ont., where he still has important business interests. First el. by accl., to Ass. for electoral dist. of E. Nipissing at bye-el., 30th May, re-el. at g. e., 1908 for newly created constituency of Sudbury. Apptd. Min. of Lands and Mines, 30 May, 1905, now known as the Dept. of Lands, Forests and Mines. *Address:* 15 Maple Av., Rosedale, Toronto.

COCKBURN, George Ralph Richardson, M.A.; *b.* Edinburgh, Scot., 15 Feb., 1832; *m.* Mary E. Lane, of Louisville, Kentucky; one *s.* one *d.* Son is Major C. Cockburn, V.C., and daughter Mrs. Thomas Tait, wife of Thomas Tait, Chief Commissioner of Government Railways, Victoria, Australia. *Address:* Toronto, Ont., Varona Lake, Rosseau, Muskoka. *Clubs:* Toronto, Albany, R. C. Y. C., Toronto.

COCKSHUTT, Harry; Mng. dir. of the Cockshutt Plow Co., Ltd.; *b.* Brantford, Ont., 8 July, 1868; *s.* of Ignatius and Elizabeth Foster Cockshutt; *m.* Isabelle Rolls; two *d.* *Educ.:* Brantford Pub. and High Schs. Entered factory of the Cockshutt Plow Co., Ltd., 1884; became Sec.-Treas., 1888; made Mgr. Dir. of the Company, 1893. Mayor of Brantford, 1899 and 1900; Pres., Brantford Bd. of Trade, 1898; Pres., Can. Manufacturers Assn., 1906; Vice-Pres., Frost & Wood Co., Smith Falls; Dir. of the Canada Iron Corporation, Montreal; Dir., Ont. Portland Cement Co., Brantford, and others *Recreations:* hunting, fishing. *Address:* Dufferin Av., Brantford, Ont. *Clubs:* Brantford, Toronto, National, Toronto; Manitoba, Winnipeg.

COCKSHUTT, William Foster; merchant and manufacturer; *b.* Brantford, Ont., 17 Oct., 1855; *s.* of I. Cockshutt, Yorkshire, Eng., and Elizabeth Foster, Lancashire, Eng.; *m.* 8 Aug., 1891, Minnie Turner Ashton, of Brantford, Ont. *Educ.:* Brantford and Galt Coll. Institutes. An unsuccessful candidate for H. of C., at g. e., 1887. Pres. Bd. of Trade, Brantford; member of Council of Toronto Bd. of Trade; Pres. Bell Memorial Assn.; mem. of Ont. Power Commission; mem. of Huron Synod and Executive; delegate to several congresses of Chambers of Commerce of the Empire. el. to H. of C., at g. e., 1904; unsuccessful at g. e., 1908. *Address:* Brantford, Ont.

CODE, Robert George, K.C.; Counsel at Ottawa for the Ontario Govt.; *b.* Junisville, Lanark Co., Ont., 20 Oct., 1858; *s.* of William Code and Elizabeth Code; unmarried. *Educ.:* Perth Coll. Inst., Hamilton Coll. Inst., Ottawa Normal Sch. Barrister-at-law and solicitor; Legal rep. in Ottawa, for the Ontario Govt. *Recreations;* golf, hunting, fishing. *Address:* 45 Slater Street, Ottawa. *Clubs:* Rideau, Golf, Ottawa; Coulonge Fish and Game.

CODERRE, Louis, B.A., (St. Sulpice Coll.), LL.B. (Laval Univ)., head of the firm of Coderre, Cedras and Goderre; *b.* St. Ours, nr. Sorel, Que., 1 Nov., 1865; *s.* of Alfred Coderre, at one time supt. of St. Ours Lock, St. Ours, Que.; *m.* 1895, Marie Anne Ste. Marie. *Educ.:* St. Sulpice Coll., Laval Univ.; called to the Bar, 1892, and practiced with the firm of Primeau & Goderre, until 1904, when became a partner in the firm of Coderre, Cedras and Magnan; now head of the firm of Goderre, Cedras and Coderre; acted as City Attorney for the Town of St. Henri, 1896-1905; Syndic of the Montreal Bar Assn., since 1904; unsuccessful candidate for H. of C. at g. e. 1908. *Recreations:* piscatorial pursuits, hunting. *Address:* 31 Laporte Av., St. Henri, Montreal. *Club:* La Fontaine.

CODY, Very Rev. Henry John, B.A., M. A., D.D. (Queen's Univ.), LL.D. (Univ. of Toronto); Rector of St. Paul's Church, Toronto; Canon of St. Alban's Cathedral; Archdeacon of York; *b.* Embro, Ont., 6 Dec., 1868; *s.* of E. J. Cody and Margaret L. Torrance; *m.* Florence L. Clarke, *d.* of late H. E. Clarke, M.L.A. of Toronto; one *s.* *Educ.:* Galt Grammar Sch., Univ. of Toronto, Wycliffe Coll., Toronto; after graduating from Univ., was classical master of Ridley Coll., St. Catharines, then Prof. of Church history, and afterwards of systematic thealogy in Wycliffe Coll., Toronto; Rector of St. Paul's Church, Toronto, and Archdeacon of York. In 1904, elected Bishop of N.S., but declined; member of Royal Com. on Reorganization of Univ. of Toronto, 1905-6; member of General Synod and of Executive Committee of Anglican General Board of Missions. *Publications:* sermons and magazine articles. *Address:* 603 Jarvis St., Toronto. *Clubs:* Lambton Golf, Country, Queen City Bowling, Toronto.

COFFEE, George Thomas; hydraulic engr. for Yukon Gold Co.; *b.* Nevada, Co., Cal., 1871. First went to Yukon, 1908. *Publications:* several reports on mining properties. *Address:* Dawson, Y.T.

COFFEE, Hon. Thomas, Senator; *b.* Co. Tipperary, Ireland, 12 Aug., 1843; *s.* of Patrick and Ellen Coffee; *m.* Margaret Hevey; one *d.* *Educ.:* Montreal; arrived in Canada, 1 June, 1852; Printer and publisher of the *Catholic Record*; called to Senate, 1903. *Address:* London, Ont. *Club:* London.

COLBY, Charles William, M.A., Ph.D., D.C.L., F.R.S.C.; *b.* Stanstead, Que., 25 March, 1867; *s.* of Hon. Charles Carroll Colby and Harriet Child Colby; *m.* Emma Frances Cobb, *d.* of the late Walter Balfour Cobb; one *s.* one *d.* *Educ.:* Stanstead Coll., McGill Univ., Harvard Univ.; Professor of History, McGill Univ. *Publications:* Selections from the sources of English History" Canadian Types of the Old Regime. *Recreations:* Hill climbing, gardening, fishing. *Address:* 560 Pine Av., Montreal; Willock Birches, Georgeville, Que. *Club:* University, Montreal.

COLDWELL, Hon. George Robson, B. A., K.C., Minister of Education of Manitoba and Municipal Commissioner of Manitoba; *b.* Tp. Clarke, Co. of Durham, Ont., 4 July, 1858; *s.* of William Edward Caldwell and Mary Robson; *m.* Ann Anderson; four *s.* one *d.* *Educ.:* in Kinburn Pub. Sch., Ont.; Clinton Grammar Sch., Trinity Coll., Sch., Port Hope, Ont., and Trinity Coll., Toronto, Ont.; practiced law in Brandon, Manitoba, since Feb., 1883; member of Brandon Municipal Council for 20 years. *Address:* 122 Eighteenth St., Brandon, Man. *Clubs:* Brandon, Manitoba; Commercial, Winnipeg.

COLEMAN, Arthur Philemon, M.A., Ph. D.; *b.* Lachute, Que., 4 April, 1852; *s.* of Francis Coleman, and Emmeline Adams. *Educ.:* Cobourg Collegiate Institute, Victoria Univ., and Breslau Univ.; Professor of Geology, Victoria Univ., Cobourg, 1882; Professor of Geol., Univ. Toronto, 1891; Geologist Bureau of Mines, Toronto, 1893-1910. *Publications:* Reports. *Recreations:* canoeing and travel. *Address:* 476 Huron St., Toronto, and Pinehurst Island, Gananoque, Ont.

COLMER, Joseph Grose, C.M.G.; *b.* London, Eng., 3 Jan., 1856; *m.* Margaret Cox Black, *g. d.* of Professor T. R. McCulloch; one *s.* one *d.* *Educ.:* City of London Sch.; arrived in Canada, 1878; served in Merchants Bank of Canada, as Secretary to the General Manager; Secretary to Mr. J. J. C. Abbott, (afterwards Sir John Abbott); Secretary High Commissioners, office, London, 1880-1903; Secretary Colonization Board, 1889-1909; now partner in Coates & Son, London, Eng.; member of Council, Royal Colonial Institute; Executive Committee, British Empire League; Council, London Chamber of Commerce. *Publications:* many contributions to magazines, Reviews and the Press on Canadian and economic questions;divided 1000 guinea purse offered by The Sketch, in 1896, for the best essay on the Commercial Federation of the Empire. *Address:* 29 Eldon Road, Kensington, London, and 99 Gresham St., London, Eng. *Clubs:* Constitutional, Grosvenor, Canada and Midsummer Golf Club, Eng.

COLQUHOUN, Arthur H. U., B.A., LL. D., Deputy Minister of Education for Ontario; *b.* Montreal, 2 Dec., 1861. *Educ.:* Cornwall Pub. Sch., Montreal High Sch., and McGill Univ.; for many years in journalism; on staff of Montreal *Star*, Ottawa *Journal*, and Toronto *Empire*; apptd. Depy. Minister of Education, 1906. *Address:* 59 Borden St., Toronto. *Clubs:* Toronto, Lambton Golf, and Country, Toronto.

COLSON, Frederick; *b.* Shedfield, Hants, Eng., 23 July, 1854; *s.* of J. H. Passingcombe Colson, and Emily Henly; *m.* (1st) Rosalind M. Bell (*d.*); (2nd) Elizabeth Partie Brymner, *d.* of Douglas Brymner, LLD., F.R.S.C., First Dominion Archivist. *Educ.:* Sherborne Dorset; arrived in Canada, 1871; was for many years City Editor Montreal *Gazette;* Correspondent New York *Times;* apptd., 1885, to Dept. of Secretary of State of Canada, of which he is now Chief Clerk and Accountant; was pres. of the Montreal Press Club, and Ottawa Amateur Athletic Club; also one of the early Governors of St. Luke's Hospital; is a water colour painter, and frequent exhibitor at the Royal Canadian Academy, and Montreal Spring Exhibitions. *Publications:* A Winter's Night," and "The Rain", two plays successfully produced in Montreal, and a number of short stories. *Address:* 466 Besserer St., Ottawa. *Club:* Golf, Ottawa.

COMEAU, Hon. Ambrose H., Senator; *b.* Meteghan River, N.S., 27 Sept., 1860; *s.* of Hilaire J. Comeau, and Madeleine LeBlanc; *m.* Louise D'Entremont; five *s.* one *d.* *Educ.:* Pub. Schs. Senior mem. of the firm of H. H. Comeau & Co. Councillor, 1884-1890; warden of the Municipality of Clare, 1889-1890. El. to Legis of N.S., May, 1890, 1894, 1897, 1902, 1907. Mem. of Ex. Coun., from 1894, until apptd. to Senate in 1907. *Address:* Meteghan River, N.S.

CONGDON, Frederick Tennyson, B.A., LL.B., K.C., M.P.; *b.* Annapolis, N.S., 16 Nov., 1858; *s.* of Hinkle Congdon; *m.* Louisa Gladwin; one *s.* two *d.* *Educ.:* Yarmouth High Sch., Yarmouth, N.S.; mem. of Bar of N.S., Yukon, Alberta, and Sask.; contested Shelbourne, N.S., in 1888; Yukon, 1904; first el. to H. of C., 1909. *Publications:* Digest Nova Scotia Reports, 1890; member of Commission to Revise Statutes of N.S. *Recreations:* music, literature, hunting. *Address:* Dawson Y. T. *Club:* Zero Club, Dawson.

CONMEE, James, M.P.; *b.* Sydenham, Ont., 13 Oct., 1848; *s.* of the late Matthew

Conmee and Rosanna O'Shaughnessy, *m.* 1874, Emily Florence, *d.* of Joseph Cox, Meaford, Ont.; *Educ.:* Owen Sound Gram. Sch.; served in the 8th New York Cavalry, under General Custer, during the American Civil War; largely interested in mining and lumbering; built several sections of the C. P. Ry., and also the Algoma Central; in 1886 projected the Atlantic and Pacific Ry. to get to a winter port on Lake Superior; built portions of what is now the C. N. Ry., and is now interested in the construction of the Nepigon Ry.; a strong advocate for the Transcontinental Railway, and of development of mineral resources of the north; was the first President of the Ontario Mining Institute, 1894; Pres. of the Ont. Mines Development Co., 1896; has been Mayor of Port Arthur; was a delegate to the deep waterways commission, Sept., 1894; elec. to Legislature of Ont., 1885, 1886, 1890, and 1894; resigned to contest Nipissing for the H. of C., 1896, but resignation not having been technically effected, he on being defeated, reclaimed his seat in the Legislature; was re-elec., 1898 and 1902; resigned again to contest Thunder Bay and Rainy River ,1904, and was successful; re-elec. 1908; Roman Catholic; Liberal. *Address:* Port Arthur.

CONNELL, William; *b.* Cape Breton, N.S., Sept. 10, 1827; self-ed.; taken in infancy by parents to what is now Hazleton, Pa.; worked in mines as driver boy; rose steadily; became mgr. of mines of Susquehanna & Wyoming Valley R. R. and Coal Co.; purchased the plant, 1870, and organized firm of William Connell & Co.; has other large industrial and commercial interests; pres. 3d Nat. Bank of Scranton; delegate to Nat. Rep. Conv., 1896; mem. Pa. Rep. Com,; mem. Congress, 1897-1903, 11th Pa. dist.; Republican. *Address:* Scranton, Pa.

CONSTANTINEAU, His Hon. Albert, B.A., D.C.L. (Laval), senr. Judge of united Counties of Prescott and Russell; *b.* St. Engene, Ont., 16 April, 1866; *s.* of George Constantineau and Josephine Roy; *m.* Alice McLaughlin, M.D., C.M.; one *d.* *Educ.:* Rigaud Coll., Laval Univ., Osgoode Hall; called to Bar of Ont., 1890; Junior Judge of United Counties, 1900; Senr. Judge, March, 1904. *Address:* Ottawa, Ont.

COOK, Herman Henry; Pres. of the Ontario Lumber Co.; *b.* Tp. of Williamsburg, Dundas Co., Ont., 26 April, 1837; *s.* of the late Capt. George Cook, who served in American War of 1812-15, and Sarah Castleman; *m.* 1861, Lydia, *d.* of James White; two *d.* *Educ.:* Iroquois Gram. Sch. Entered lumber business, 1858; later became Pres. of the Ontario Lumber Co.; was one of syndicate that offered to build the C. P. Ry., 1880. Mem of the H. of C. for North Simcoe, 1892-1898; mem. Ont. Legis., 1879-1882, when he resigned; returned to H. of C. for East Simcoe, which constituency he represented until 1890. *Address:* 20 Dowling Av., Toronto.

COOK, John Stanley Alexander; Asst. Sec., Montreal Bd. of Trade; *b.* Montreal, 18 Jan., 1876; unmarried. *Educ.:* Pub. Schs.; entered service of Montreal Bd. of Trade, 1892; became Asst. Sec., 1898. *Address:* 9 York St., Westmount. *Club:* Canada, Montreal.

COOK, Samuel A.; *b.* Ont., Jan. 28, 1849; *m.* 1876, Jennie Christie (*d.* 1895); removed with parents to Wis., 1855; common school ed'n.; worked as farm boy, mill hand and clerk; engaged in mercantile business; was mayor of Neenah, Wis., 1889; mem. legislature, 1890-91; delegate Rep. Nat. Conv., 1892; mem. Congress, 6th Wis. dist., 1895-7; declined renomination; candidate for U.S. senator from Wis., 1898, receiving 2nd highest number of votes (five prominent candidates in the contest). Served in Civil War, Co. A, 2d Wis. Vol. Cav. Pres. S. A. Cook Mfg. Co.; pres. Alexandria Paper Co. Republican. *Address:* Neenah, Wis.

COOKE, Edmund Vance; *b.* Canada 1866; *s.* Edmund Cooke and Matilda Vance. *Educ.:* principally in Cleveland schs.; *m.* Chicago, 1897, Lilith Castleberry. Platform lecturer, with lecture-entertainments. Contributor to leading mags. and weeklies of poems, stories and occasional articles. *Publications:* A Patch of Pansies, 1894; Rimes to Be Read, 1897 (revised edit.); Impertinent Poems, 1903, 1907; Chronicles of the Little Tot, 1905; Told to the Little Tot, 1906. *Address:* 30 Mayfield Rd., S. E., Cleveland, Ohio.

COPP, Arthur Bliss, LL.B., M.L.A.; *b.* Jolicure, Westmoreland Co., N.B., 10 July, 1870; *s.* Harvey and Frances Brennan Copp; *m.* 1904, E. Margaret Bell. Taught in the public Sch. of Westmoreland for two yrs.; practiced law in Sackville, since 1895; contested Westmoreland Co., in 1895, and was defeated, but was elec. by acclamation the following year, for the Provincial House. re-elec. in 1904 and 1908; was Liberal organizer for N.B., from 1904 to 1908. *Address:* Sackville, N.B.

CORBOULD, Gordon Edward, K.C.; *b.* Toronto, 2 Nov., 1847; *s.* of Charles and Mary Corbould; *m.* (1st) Arabella Almond, 4th *d.* of Major W. Dion of 1st Madras Fusiliers in 1877; (2nd) Charlotte M. E. Cameron, 2nd *d.* of Sir Matthew Cameron, Chief Justice of Ont.; two *s.* five *d.* *Educ.:* Model Grammar Sch., Toronto, and Up. Can. Coll., admitted to practice in Ont., 1872; went to British Columbia, 1890; called to the B.C. Bar in 1882; elected to H. of C. for New Westminster, 1890; re-elec., 1891; Conservative. *Address:* New Westminster, B.C. *Clubs:* Westminster and Terminal City, Vancouver.

CORBY, Henry; *b.* Belleville, Ont., 2 May, 1851; *s.* of the late Henry Corby; *m.* 1872, Maria, *d.* of the late John Courtenay. *Educ.:* Belleville Pub. Schs., Rockwood Academy, Toronto; entered offices of his father, miller, distiller and importer of wines, which business he succeeded on the death of his father. Was for many yrs. Asst. Chief of the Fire Dept., Pres. Belleville branch of the St. John Ambulance Assn., Belleville Natural Gas Co., Bay of Quinte Bridge Co.; Dir. Agricultural Exhibition Assn. of his dist.; elec. to H. of C. for West Hastings, 1888, retired 1901. Was for many yrs., pres. of the Conservative Assn. *Address:* Belleville, Ont.

CORRIVEAU, Apollinaire, K.C., LL.L. (Laval Univ.); *b.* Quebec, July, 1862; *m.*

1889, Leda Dufresne, of Quebec; one *s.* *Educ.:* Laval Univ., Grad. 1885, winning medal for general proficiency and Tessier Prize of thirty dollars in gold. Called to Bar, 1886, and has practiced in Quebec ever since. Cr. K.C., 1906. Mem. of the Council of Quebec Bar Assn. for many yrs.; Pres. St. Jean Baptiste Soc. of Sauveur, 1892. *Address:* 632 St. Valier St., Quebec.

CORY, William Wallace; Deputy Minister of the Interior; *b.* Strathroy, Ont., 16 June, 1865; *s.* of Thomas Cory and Margaret Garrett; *m.* Laura Watson of Kirton, Lincolnshire, England; two *s.* one *d.* *Educ.:* St. John's Coll., Winnipeg. Inspecting officer, Y.T., 1901-4; Dept. Min. of Interior, 1 Jan., 1905. *Address:* 212 Argyle Av., Ottawa, Ont. *Club:* Rideau, Ottawa.

COSTE, Louis, B.S., M.I.C.E., London, Eng.; mem. Can. Soc. C.E.; *b.* Amherstburg, Essex Co., 31 July, 1857; *s.* of Hon. H. Alexandre Coste and Mathilde Robidoux; *m.* Marie Therese d'Esterre. *Educ.:* France, England. Chief Engineer Public Works of Can. 1892-1800; now consulting engr.; one of the International Deep Waterways Commissioners for Can. *Address:* 242 Charlotte St., Ottawa. *Club:* Rideau, Ottawa.

COSTIGAN, Hon. John, P.C.; *b.* St. Nicholas, Levis, Co. Que., 1 Feb., 1835; *s.* of John Costigan and Bridget Costigan; *m.* 1855, Harriet S. Ryan, of Grand Falls, N.B.; two *s.* three *d.* *Educ.:* Grand Falls and St. Ann's Coll., Quebec.; was mem. of New Brunswick Legislature, 1861-1867; elec. to H. of C., 1867, and held seat continuously, until apptd. to the Senate, 1907; Min. of Inland Revenue, 1882-1892; Sec. of State, 1892-94; Min. of Marine and Fisheries, 1894-96. *Recreations:* angling, hunting. *Address:* 232 Cooper St., Ottawa; Edmundston, N.B.

COTE, Narcisse Omer; Chief of Land Patents Branch, Dept. of Interior, Ottawa; *b.* Quebec, 14 Sept., 1859; *s.* of Joseph Olivier Cote, formerly Clerk of the Queen's Privy Council for Canada, and Marie Julie Leocadie Leprohon; *m.* 1907, Mabel Edna, *d.* of Hon. Justice Girouard, of the Supreme Ct. of Canada; one *s.* *Educ.:* Commercial Acad., Ottawa Univ.; entered the Civil Service of Can. in 1879, as Clerk in the Dept. of the Interior; sec. in 1885 to the Royal Com., apptd. to investigate and adjudicate upon the claims of the half-breeds of the North-West Territories; apptd a mem. of said Com., 1887; in 1900, apptd. chn. of a similar com. to deal with the claims of the Half-breeds of the Dist. of Sask., and of persons who had served as scouts, or otherwise, during the Rebellion of 1885; apptd. chief clerk in the Dept. of the Interior, 1904; Register of Dom. Lands Patents and Chief of Land Patents Branch, 1906; Capt., Can. Mil., retired list. *Publications:* "Political Appointments, Parliaments and the Judical Bench in the Dominion of Canada, 1867 to 1895," pub. 1896, and a supplement thereto covering the period from 1896 to 1903. *Address:* 27 Cooper St., Ottawa. *Clubs:* Rideau, Golf, Ottawa.

COTE, Captain Thomas, B.A.; *b.* Trois Pistoles, Que., 22 Sept., 1869; *s.* of Theophile Cote and Flavia Laxrive. *Educ.:* Quebec Seminary and Laval University; in journalism in Quebec for several years; Private Secretary to the Minister of Public Works for Canada, three years; Managing Editor *La Presse* for nine years; Secy. International Deepwaterways Com., 1905-9; Commissioner to Brussels Exposn., 1910. *Address:* 728 Elgin St., Ottawa. *Clubs:* St. Denis, Military Institute, Montreal; Laurentian, Golf, Ottawa.

COTTON, Brig.-Gen. William Henry, Commanding Western Ontario; *b.* Montreal, 7 Jan., 1848; *s.* of Henry Cotton of S. Petersburg, and Eleanor Ross, of Montreal; *m.* Jessie Penner; four *s.* three *d.* *Educ.:* Quebec High Sch.; continuous military service in Canada since 1866; 2nd Lieut., Quebec Garrison Art., in that yr.; Lieut. Ottawa Garrison Art., Aug., 1868; Capt. in the Sch. of Gunnery, 1871; Capt. and Brev. Major, Can. Art., 1872; Lieut.-Col. and Commandant, R.C.A., 1882; Col., 1900; Brig. General, 1907; D.O.C., M.D. No. 3, 25 Aug., 1893; D.O.C., M.D. No. 4, 29 Apr., 1897; A.A.G., for Art., H.Q., 15 July, 1897; O. C. Ottawa Brig., 1 Nov., 1897; Q.M.G., 1 July, 1901; M.G.O., 15 Nov., 1904; Comdg. Western Ontario, 1 April, 1908. *Recreation:* golf. *Address:* 84 St. George St., Toronto. *Clubs:* Rideau, Ottawa; Toronto, Golf, Toronto.

COTTON, William Lawson; *b.* New London, P.E.I., 23 July, 1848; *s.* of Rev. Richard Cotton and Marie Lawson; *m.* Margaret Ellen Harris, *d.* of W. C. Harris, four *s.* three *d.* Editor of the *Examiner* since 1875; *Publications:* many essays and papers on historical, political and social topics. *Address:* Charlottetown, P.E.I.

COULTER, Dr. Robert Millar; Deputy Postmaster-General of Canada; *b.* York Co., 1857; of Scotch and Irish parentage; *m.* 1887, Emma, *d.* of the late J. P. Wells, of Aurora. *Educ.:* Toronto Univ. (M.B. 1882); Victoria Univ. (M.D., 1882); commenced practice of medicine at Aurora, Ont.; apptd. Deputy Postmaster-Gen., 1897. Was for many yrs. Health Officer and Physician of the County Industrial Home of Aurora, and served in the Municipal Council and Sch. Bd.; organized the Young Liberal Club of North York, and was Vice-Pres. of the North York Reform Assn., for several yrs. Mem. Ontario Medical Soc. and Dominion Medical Soc. *Address:* 190 Cooper St., Ottawa. *Club:* Rideau, Ottawa.

COURTLEIGH, William Louis; *b.* Guelph, Ont., June 28, 1869; *s.* Stephen Courtleigh and Elizabeth Phelan; *m.* Mar. 17, 1890, Helen Cross, Cleveland. Began career as actor, Sept. 1, 1888; mem. Actors Order of Friendship; pres. Actors Soc. of America. *Clubs:* Players, Lambs, Greenroom. *Address:* 304 2d Av., New York.

COURTNEY, John Mortimer, C.M.G., I.S.O., formerly Deputy Minister of Finance and Receiver-Gen., and Sec. of the Treasury Board of Canada (now retired); *b.* Penzance, Cornwall, 22 July, 1883; 2nd *s.* of John Sampson Courtney of Alverton House, Penzance, and Sarah, *d.* of John Mortimer; *m.* 1870, Mary Elisabeth Sophia, 2nd *d.* of late Fennings Taylor, Clerk Assistant of the Senate of Canada; one *s.* *Educ.:* Penzance. After several years spent in banking, came to Canada, in 1869, to become the Chief Clerk of the Treasury; has served on several

Commissions; was Hon. Treasurer in Canada for the Indian Famine Fund; Hon. Treasurer of Canadian Patriotic Fund and of Canadian Association for Prevention of Tuberculosis; mem. of the Quebec Battlefields Com. *Recreation:* reading. *Clubs:* Rideau, Golf, Ottawa.

COUSINEAU, Philemon, B.A., L.L.D. (Laval), K.C., M.L.A.; *b.* St. Laurent, Que., 25 Oct., 1874; *s.* of Gervais Cousineau and Angelique Gould; *m.* 1897, Helmina Gendron; five *d.* *Educ.:* Ste. Therese Coll.; Professor of constitutional and municipal law at Laval Univ., Montreal; Pres., Mount Royal Tel. Co.; dir., Saguenay Light and Power Co., St. Lawrence Tobacco Co.; elec. to Legis. Assn. for Co. of Jacques Cartier, 1908. *Address:* St. Laurent, Que. *Club:* Lafontaine.

COUTLEE, Lieut.-Col. Louis William, K.C., B.C.L., Civil Law Reporter of the Supreme Court of Canada; *b.* Oakland Hall, Hull, Que., 17 Dec., 1851; *m.* Charlotte, *d.* of late Wm. Wilson, H.M. Customs, Belleville, Ont.; one *s.* four *d.* *Educ.:* Aylmer Academy; Masson Coll., McGill Univ., Montreal; admitted to Bar of Quebec, 1873; Bar of Ontario, 1875; Bar of Manitoba, 1882; Deputy Attorney General of Manitoba, 1883-1887; Municipal Commissioner to organize Manitoba Municipal System, 1887; Registrar-General of Manitoba, 1887-1890; Law Clerk, Manitoba Legislative Assembly, 1883-1888. *Publications:* Concordance to Code of Civil Procedure of Quebec (1870), Torrens System of Registration by Title in Manitoba and Northwest Territories of Canada (1890), Digests of Decisions of Supreme Court of Canada, 1898, 1903, and 1908, also Collection of Unreported Supreme Court Cases, 1906. Served in Canadian Militia since 1866, has been three times on active service, holds Imperial War Medal for Fenian raids with clasps for 1866 and 1870, and Medal for Saskatchewan Campaign, 1885, with clasp, was praised by Major General Middleton for services in last campaign as second in command of Winnipeg Field Battery of Artillery; Asst. Adjt. Gen. of Arty., 1899, 1900 and 1901, during annual trainings, under Cols. Montizambert and Stone, and Brig. Gen. Drury, C.B.; has held present office on staff of Supreme Court, since 1895. *Recreations:* hunting, fishing, skatng, curling. *Address:* Ottawa. *Club:* Rideau, Ottawa.

COWAN, George Henry, M.P., B.A., K.C.; *b.* Warwick, Ont., 17 June, 1858; *s.* of William Cowan, and Anne King; *m.* Josephene Irene Downie, *d.* of Canon Downie of Port Stanley, Ont.; one *s.* four *d.* *Educ.:* Strathroy and Brantford Collegiate Inst., Toronto Univ., and Osgoode Hall, Toronto; graduated B.A., in 1884; called to the Bar of Ont., in 1889, and B.C. Bar in 1893; apptd. Q.C. by Dom. Govt., 1896; K.C. by B.C. Govt., 1905; unsuccessful conservative candidate in 1896; elected in 1908. *Publications:* The Chinese question in Canada, in Canadian Encyclopaedia, vol. 5; Better terms for British Columbia, in pamphlet form. *Recreations:* Horses, hunting, bowling billiards. *Address:* 1225 Davis St., Vancouver B.C. *Clubs:* Vancouver and Terminal City, Vancouver; Union, Victoria; Albany, Toronto.

COWAN, Mahlon K., K.C.; *b.* Blytheswood, Essex Co., Ont., 10 May, 1863; *s.* of Walter Cowan, and Mary Ann Cowan; *m.* Clara S. Pilkey. *Educ.:* Brantford and Collingwood Collegiate Institutes; elec. to H. of C.. 1896; re-elec. in 1900; refused to run in 1904; joined the G. T. Ry. in Dec., 1904; as Assistant Solicitor. *Recreations:* hunting, golf. *Address:* Montreal, Que. *Clubs:* St. James', Canada, Royal Montreal Golf, Beaconsfield Golf, Westmount Golf, Montreal, Que., and Windsor, Windsor, Ont.

COWIE, Frederick William, B.A.S., M. Inst. C.E., M. Can. Soc. C.E., Chief Engineer Harbour Commissioners, Montreal; *b.* Green wood Farm, Caledonia Co., Haldimand, Ont., 27 March, 1863; *s.* John Cowie, Esq.; *m.* in 1895, Katherine Greenough, *d.* of William Parker Greenough, of Boston, U.S. A., and Seigneur of Perthuis, Portneuf, Que., one *s.* two *d.* *Educ.:* Public and High Sch. in central Ont.; Woodstock Coll., Woodstock; McGill Univ., Montreal; graduating in 1886 with honors in Civil Engineering; after leaving McGill Univ., accepted position under John Kennedy, C.E., Chief Engineer, Montreal Harbor Commissioners to 1892; in 1982 was Assistant Engineer Public Works of Canada, to 1897; in 1897, was resident Engineer, River St. Lawrence Ship Canal to 1903, from 1904 to 1908, Supt. Eng.; afterwards and at present Chief Engineer, Montreal Harbour, Trustee of the Seigniory of Perthuis, from 1900 to the present time. *Publications:* River St. Lawrence official reports; winter navigation in Canada; British and Continental Ports, 1908; (Jointly with Major G. W. Stephens). *Recreations:* Polo, big game hunting and fishing. *Address:* 49 "The Linton," Montreal. *Clubs:* Rideau, Ottawa; Engineers, and Canada, Montreal.

COWLES, Eugene; *b.* Stanstead, Que.; *s.* Dr. C. W. Cowles; *m.* May 23, 1898, Louise Cleary. Went to Chicago in 'teens; was clerk in 1st Nat. Bank; sang in ch. choirs, quartets, etc.; Nov., 1888, joined the Bostonians, at Ford's Theatre, Baltimore, making debut as Squire Bantam in Dorothy; was for 10 yrs. mem. of that organization, singing premier basso roles, his most noted part being Will Scarlett in Robin Hood; became leading man in Alice Nielsen Opera Co., Sept., 1898, playing The Fortune Teller; later appeared in London in opera; has sung in concerts and various operas, composed several songs. *Address:* Derby Line, Vt.

COX, Hon. George Albertus; Senator; *b.* Colborne, Northumberland Co., Ont., 7 May, 1840; *s.* of Edward W. Cox, and Jane Tanner; *m.* 1862, second *d.* of the late Daniel Hopkins, Peterborough (*d.* Jan 1905). *Educ.:* Public and Grammar Schs., Colborne, Ont.; from 1858 to 1871, engaged in life insurance business in Peterborough; in 1871, secured control of and was elected pres. and Genl. Mgr. of the Midland Ry., which he retained until the road became part of the G. T. Ry. in 1884; is now Pres. of the Canada Life Assurance Co.; Central Loan and Savings Co., Western Assurance Co., British American Assurance Co., and the Toronto Savings and Loan Co., and is a Director of the Canadian Bank of Commerce, The National Trust Co., Can. General Electric Co., The Dominion Iron and Steel Co., The Toronto Railway Co., and the Grand Trunk Pacific Ry.; is also Bursar of Victoria Univ., Toronto; called to the Senate, 13 Nov., 1896. *Address:* Toronto.

COX, Palmer, author and artist; *b.* Granby, Que., 28 April, 1840; 5th *s.* of Michael Cox, farmer, and pensioner of the English army; unmarried. *Educ.:* Granby Academy; went to California, 1863; followed railroading, contracting, etc.; wrote for newspapers; came to New York, 1875; took up writing and illustrating for children's magazines, and also humorous books. *Publications:* Squibs of Everyday Life, 1874; Hans Von Pelter's trip to Gotham, 1878; How Columbus found America, 1878; That Stanley, 1878; The Brownies, their Book, 1887; Queer People with Wings and Stings, 1888; Comic Yarns (revision of Squibs), 1888; another Brownies' Book, 1890; Brownies at Home, 1893; Brownies around the World, 1894; Palmer Cox's Brownies, a spectacular play in three acts, 1894; The Brownies ln Fairyland, a musical cantata, 1894; Brownies through the Union, 1895; Brownies abroad, 1899; Brownies in the Philippines, 1904; Palmer's Cox's Brownie Primer, 1906. *Recreations:* rifle target shooting, fishing, cycling. *Address:* 134 West 23rd Street, New York.

COX, Robert N., M.L.A.; *b.* Charlottetown, P.E.I., 12 Oct., 1850; *m.* Elizabeth Sutherland; three *s.* three *d.* *Educ.:* Prince of Wales Coll., Charlottetown, P.E.I. In commercial business at Morell since 1869. *Recreations:* fishing, and shooting. *Address:* Morell, P.E.I.

COYLE, Rev. Robert Francis, D.D., LL.D.; *b.* Roseneath, Ont., July 28, 1850; *s.* James and Ann Coyle; *m.* June 4, 1885, J. Adella Haviland, Fort Dodge, Ia. *Educ.:* in Can., 1856-64; grad. Wabash Coll., Westminster Coll.; sudied theology, Auburn, N.Y.; Theol. Sem., 1878-9; ordained to Presby'n ministry, Ft. Dodge, Ia., 1879; pastor there, 1879-85, Fullerton Av. Presby'n Ch., Chicago, 1885-91, 1st Presby'n Ch., Oakland, Calif., 1891-1900, Central Presby'n Ch., Denver, since 1900. Moderator Presby'n Gen. Assembly at Los Angeles, Calif., 1903. *Publications:* Foundation Stones, 1887; Workingmen and the Ch., 1896; The Christianity of Christ, 1892; The Church and the Times (sermons), 1905. *Address:* 1650 Sherman Av., Denver, Col.

COYNE, James Henry, B.A., M.A., LL.D., F.R.S.C.; *b.* St. Thomas, Ont., 3 Oct., 1849; *s.* of William and Christina Coyne; *m.* Matilda, 3rd *d.* of the late John George Brown, of Toronto, who for several years was Mayor and M.L.A. for that city; four *s.* two *d.*; *Educ.:* St. Thomas common and grammar Schs., Univ. of Toronto; Matricufated, Toronto Univ., 1864; volunteered and saw service at London, Port Stanley, Sarnia and Thorald, 1866, as private in St. Thomas Rifles (Medal). In 1870, B.A. at Univ. of Toronto, and gold medal. During four years, won four scholarships. Studied law at St. Thomas; Meadmaster at Cornwall High School, in 1871, and returned to law studies, in 1872; from this date he took all active part in Provincial and Dominion Politics; admitted to the Bar at Attorney, 1874; was defeated for the Provincial House in 1886; organized the Elgin Historical and Scientific Institute; became first Pres., and still holds that post. *Publications:* 1893, The Southwold Earthwork and the Country of the Neutrals (in Boyle's Archaeological Reoport); 1895, The Country of the Neutrals from Champlain to Talbot, (St. Thomas); 1899, First Steps in the Discovery and Exploration of Ontario (Ontario Educational Association Transactions); 1899, A Century of Achievement (Hamilton); 1901, A Century of Achievement (Hamilton), reprinted with alterations and additions in Methodist Magazine for Jan. and Feb.; 1903, Exploration of the Great Lakes, 1669-1670, by Dolliee de Casson and De Bréhaut de Galinée; Galinée's Narrative and Map, with an English Version, including all the Map Legends. Translator and Editor, James H. Coyne; 1906, Richard Maurice Bucke, a sketch; 1908, The Talbot Papers, edited with preface, introduction and some annotations; 1898-1902, Presidential address to The Ontario Historical Society. *Recreations:* golf and curling. *Address:* "Woodlands," Metcalfe St., St. Thomas. *Clubs:* County Club, St. Thomas, Ont.

COYNEY, Weston; editor Dawson *Daily News*; *b.* Birmingham, Eng., 1849; commenced his newspaper career under late George Dawson, editor Birmingham *Morning News;* engaged for several years the *Tribune*, New York; Secy. to American Minister of Paris; worked on Panama Canal, under Count de Lesseps; returned to New York and joined staff of *Herald*; correspt. of that paper to Yukon, 1898, and has remained there ever since. *Address:* Dawson, Y.T.

CRAICK, William Arnot, B.A.; editor of *Busy Man's Magazine*, Canadian *Bookman* and *Bookseller & Stationer* of Canada; *b.* Port Hope, Ont., 19 Sept., 1880; *s.* of James and Jean Kyle Craick; *m.* Hilda M. Bingay, of Yarmouth, N.S. *Educ.:* Port Hope Sch., and Toronto Univ.; for seven yrs. associated with the Maclean Pub. Co. of Toronto, and now editor of *Busy Man's Magazine*, *Canadian Bookman*, and *Bookseller & Stationer*, of Canada. *Publication:* "History of Port Hope," 1901. *Recreation:* pedestrianism, mem. Champlain Soc. *Address:* 79 Walker Av., Toronto. *Club:* Toronto Press.

CRAIG, Hon. James, K.C.; Judge of the Territorial Court, Yukon; local Judge in Admiralty; *b.* Invernrie, Scot., 31 July, 1851; *s.* of late Geo. Craig, Police Magistrate of Arnprior, Ont., and Annie Clark; *m.* Lizzie Olivia, *d.* of Edwd. S. Macpherson, barr., of New York; one *d.* *Educ.:* McGill Univ., Osgoode Hall. Practiced Law in Renfrew after grad. in 1878; Warden of Renfrew Co., 1896; Capt. and Paymaster, 42nd Batt., 1879; apptd. Judge, 26 April, 1900. *Recreations:* fishing, shooting, curling. *Address:* Dawson, Y.T. *Club:* Zero, Dawson.

CRATHERN, James; *b.* Montreal, Que., Feb., 1830. *Educ.:* Montreal; was mem. of the firm of Crathern & Caverhill, wholesale dealers in hardware; director of the Canadian Bank of Commerce, the St. Lawrence

Sugar Refining Co., Dominion Coal Co., National Trust Co., Liverpool, London, and Globe Ins. Co.; Pres. Kewatin Flour Milling Co., and the Royal Victoria Life Ins. Co., Montreal General Hospital; Governor of the McGill Univ., and member of the Governing Committee of the Alexandra Hospital. *Address:* 32 Macgregor St., Montreal. *Clubs:* Mount Royal, St. James', Montreal.

CRAWFORD, Hon. Thomas; Speaker of the Legis. Ass. of Ontario; *b.* Co. Fermanagh Irel., 14 Aug., 1847; *s.* of Jaes and Jane Crawford; *m.* Isabella Fyfe, of Toronto; five *c.* *Educ.:* in Ireland and Toronto. Came to Canada with his parents, 1865. Commenced work in the Can. Northern Ry. Co.; in 1868, joined his father in the cattle business and has been a successful dealer for many yrs., exporting many thousand heads to Great Britain and U.S.; for three yrs., mem. Toronto City Council; elec. to Legis at g. e., 1894, 1898, 1902, 1905, 1908; after death of Hon. J. W. St. John, was elec. Speaker, 8 April, 1907, re-elec. 1909; Pres. of the Equity Fire Insur. Co.; Pres. of the Metropolitan Sch. of Music; Vice-Pres. of the Bd. of Governors of the Western Hospital.

CRAWFORD-FROST, Rev. William Albert, M.A.; *b.* Owen Sound, Ont., Oct. 29, 1863; *s.* of William and Louisa Crawford; *m.* Aug. 28, 1889, Damaris Constance, *d.* John Ings.; prep. ed'n. public schs. and Collegiate Inst., Owen Sound; grad. Toronto Univ., 1884; grad. divinity, Wycliffe Coll., Toronto, 1887; sp'l. course Baltimore Med. Coll., 1897; was on staff of Toronto *Globe* while attending Univ. of Toronto; ordained deacon, 1888, priest, 1889; curate, St. Paul's, Charlottetown, P.E.I., 1888; rector St. George's New Glasgow, N.S., 1889-92; Ch. of the Redeemer, Merrick, L.I., 1892-6; Memorial Ch. of the Holy Comforter, Baltimore, 1896-1903; Instructor of Chemistry in Baltimore Med. Coll., 1904-1906; founder Young Men's Liberal Club, Toronto; invented a thought recorder, 1902. Former mem. Canadian Inst., Toronto; mem. Soc. of Am. Authors, astrom. sect. Md. Acad. Science, Soc. Arts. England, Transatlantic Soc., etc. *Publications:* Old Dogma in a New Light, 1896; The Philosophy of Integration, 1906; also an anthem "Columbia," 1907. *Address:* 2120 Chelsea Terrace, Baltimore, Ind.

CREELMAN, Adam Rutherford, K.C.; General Counsel of C.P.R.; *b.* Richibucto, Kent Co., N.B.; *s.* of James Rutherford Creelman, and Isabella Christina Patterson; *m.* 1878, Margaret Cummings, *d.* of Rev. John Jennings, D.D., of Toronto; four *s.* one *d.* *Educ.:* Richibucto Gram. Sch., Chatham Acad.; studied law in Toronto; mem. of the legal firm of McCarthy, Osler, Hoskin & Creelman, 1878-1901; gen. counsel of C.P.R. since that time. For four yrs. in Can. Militia. *Address.* 45 "The Sherbrooke" C.P.R. Co's Office, Windsor St., Montreal. *Clubs:* Mount Royal, St. James, Royal Montreal Golf, Forest and Stream, Montreal Toronto, Granite, Toronto Hunt, Cricket, Toronto; Rideau, Golf, Country, Ottawa; New York City, N.Y.

CREELMAN, James, F.R.G.S.; associate editor Pearson's Magazine (American); *b.* Montreal, 1859; *m.* 1891, Alice L. Buell of Ohio; one *s.* two *d.* Editorial writer and correspondent, New York *Herald*, 1877-89; editor London edition, 1890; editor Paris edition, 1891-92; editor New York Evening *Telegram*, 1893; late European editor of New York *Journal:* has interviewed the Pope, King George of Greece, Emperor of Corea, President Faure, Prince Bismarck, H. M. Stanley, Louis Kossuth, Count Tolstoi; British editor Cosmopolitan Magazine, 1893; war correspondent for New York World, Japanese War, 1894; war correspondent New York *Journal*, Græco-Turkish War, 1897; Cuban War, 1898; Philippine War, 1899; was Aide on General Lawton's staff, Philippines; captured Spanish flag, and was shot after he received surrender of Spanish commandant at El Caney, 1898. *Publications:* On the Great Highway, 1901; Eagle Blood, 1902. *Recreations:* fencing, *Address:* 67 West 94th Street, New York. *Clubs:* National Liberal; Lotos, Authors', Explorers,' Democratic, New York.

CREIGHTON, David; *b.* Glasgow, Scot., 1 April, 1843; *s.* of Abraham Creighton and Margaret Bonar; *m.* to Jennie Elizabeth Kramer, 15 Oct., 1873; one *s.* and four *d.* *Educ.:* Glasgow Scotland and Owen Sound, Ont.; learned the printing business and in 1864, became publisher of the Owen Sound *Times*, which he continued until 1887, when at the request of Sir John A. Macdonald, he founded *The Empire*, at Toronto, continuing its publication until 1895, when it and "*The Mail*" were amalgamated under the title of *The Mail and Empire.*" He then became Assist. Receiver General at Toronto, which office he still holds. In 1875 he was elected to represent North Grey in the Ontario Legislature, which he continued to represent until 1890. *Address.* 26 Spadina Road, Toronto.

CRIDGE, Rt. Rev. Edward, B.A., D.D., Bishop; *b.* Bratton-Heming of Devonshire, Eng., 17 Dec., 1817; *s.* John and Grace Cridge; *m.* Mary Winnelle, *d.* of George Winnelle of Boniford, Essex; four *s.* five *d.* *Educ.:* North Molton, Devon, Eng., and Gram. Sch., Sault Moulton; arrived in Canada, Fort Victoria, Vancouver Island, 31 March, 1855; from 1836 to 1842, was third master at the Gram. Sch. Oundle, Northamptonshire; B.A., St. Peter's Coll., Cambridge, 1848; one of the students, soliciting aid for the Great Irish famine; ordained the same year on appointment as Asst. Curate, and 2nd Master, Grammar Sch., in Walsham, Norfolk; in 1851, apptd. to incumbency of Christ Church, West-Ham London; Sept. 1854, apptd. Chaplain to Hudson Bay Co., and District Minister of Victoria, Vancouver Island. Left Engand with his bride, and arrived six months later, going around cape Horn, in the sailing Ship, Marquis of Bute; apptd. Bishop, in 1876; one of the original provisional Committee appointed by Governor Douglas, to arrange for the building of an Hospital, afterwards called the Royal Jubilee Hospital; also one of the originators for the erection of an Orphans' Home; said the opening prayers at the first parliament in Vancouver Island, 1856; addressed the Crowds on Beacon Hill on the occasion of Queen Victoria's Jubilee; Pronounced benediction upon soldiers at the farewell given to the South African Contingent, Oct., 1899; now in his 92nd year, he does not take an active part in the Ministry, but lives on the homestead. *Publications:* Tract on spiritualism; a book "As it was in the beginning;" pamphlet, "Life after death." *Recreations:* Music. *Address:* Hudson Bay Co., Fort Victoria; Christ Church Parsonage, Victoria, B.C.; 238 Government Street, Victoria, B.C.

CROCKET, Oswald Smith, B.A., M.P.; *b.* Chatham, N.B., 13 April, 1868; *s.* of William Crockett, LL.D., formerly Chief Supt. of Educ. in N.B., and Mary Crocket; both Scotch; *m.* (1st) 2Q July, 1893, A. Bersa Stanger, *d.* of the late Thomas Stanger, Merchant, Fredericton (*d.*); (2nd) 6 Sept., 1905, Clarine M. Stevenson, *d.* of the late Chas. M. Stevenson, M.P., Coaticook, Que. *Educ.:* Com. Sch. and High Sch., Fredericton, and Univ. of N.B.; admitted Attorney, Supreme Court of N.B., 15 Oct., 1891; Barrister, 20 Oct., 1892; first elec. to H. of C., 1904; re-elec., 1908; was Pres. of Fredericton Soc. of St. Andrew for five yrs., 1900-1905; Chairman of N.B. Burns Memorial Com., through whose efforts the statue of Robert Burns was erected, 1906; Presbyterian; Conservative. *Address:* Fredericton, N.B.

CROFTON, Francis Blake, B.A.; *b.* Cronboyne, Mayo, Ireland, 1841; *s.* of Rev. Wm. Crofton, Rector of Skreene, Sligo; *m.* in 1872, Emma Katherine Bradshaw of Que.; two *s.* two *d.* *Educ.:* Royal School Dungannon and Trinity Coll., Dublin, with honors in classics and English Literature; also passed for Indian Civil Service, but did not go to India. Arrived in Canada in 1864; was professor in Bishop's Coll., Lennoxville, 1864 to 1865, but removed to N.S. in 1877, after some years spent in New York, in Educational work; from 1882 to 1906, was Librarian to Legislature of N.S. *Publications:* The Bewildered Quereste, "The Major's Big Talk Stories," "Is it too late," and other pamphlets. *Address:* Halifax, N.S. *Clubs:* Halifax, Halifax, N.S., and Authors, London, Eng.

CROOK, James Walter; *b.* Bewdley, Ont., Dec. 21, 1858; *s.* Richard and Jane Sackville; *m.* 1883, Miss Eva M. Lewis. *Educ.:* Oberlin Coll., 1891; studied Univ. of Wis., 1892-3, Univ. of Berlin, Germany, 1893-4, Columbia, 1894-5 (Ph. D., 1898; Prof. economics, Amherst Coll., since Sept., 1895; lecturer on economic, social and edn'l. subjects. *Publications:* German Wage Theories, 1898. *Address:* Amherst, Mass.

CROSBY, A. B., M.P.; *b.* Belfast, Ireland, 5 May, 1859; *s.* of Adam Crosby and Mary J. Crosby Brown; *m.* 15 Jon., 1885, Mamie F. Cody, Hailfax; five *s.* three *d.* *Educ.:* Pub. Schs. Cape Breton, Commercial Coll., Halifax, N.S.; Pres. Arena Rink Co., Vice-Pres., Cheticamps Copper Co.; alderman in Halifax for one year; following year elec. Mayor, and continued in office for three years, when disqualified by the law of limitation; again elec. Mayor, which office he now holds; first elec. to H. of C., 1908. Roman Catholic; Conservative. *Address:* P.O. Box, 108, Halifax.

CROSS, Hon. Charles Wilson, B.A., LL. B.; Attorney General of Alberta; *b.* Madoc, Ont., 30 Nov., 1872; *s.* of Thomas Cross and Marie Cross; *m.* Annie Louisa Lynde; one *s.* two *d.* *Educ.:* Upper Can. Coll., Toronto Univ., Osgoode Hall, Toronto; appted. Attorney General in the first Alberta Govt., 6 Sept., 1905, and el. to Leg. Ass. at the first g. e., same yr.; re-elec. 1909. *Recreation:* golf. *Address:* Edmonton, Alta.

CROSSEN, William James; Gen. Mgr. of the Crossen Car Mnfg. Co. of Cobourg, Ltd.; *b.* Cobourg, Ont., 1857; *m.* 1880, Minnie, *d.* of S. Stanley Howell; two *s.* one *d.* *Educ.:* Cobourg pub. schs.; joined his father in the management of the business of building Ry. Cars, 1870; became head of the business on the death of his father, 1890; organized it into a joint Stock Co., the following year and became Gen. Mgr. of the Co. *Address:* Cobourg, Ont.

CRCTHERS Thomas Wilson, B.A., K. C., M.P.; *b.* Northport, 1 Jan., 1850; *s.* of William Crothers and Nancy Gray; *m.* Mary E. Burns. *Educ.:* Pub. Sch. and Victoria Coll.; Public Sch. teacher one yr.; Head Master High Sch., Wardsville, Ont., three years; unsuccessful Conservative candidate for Ont. Legislature for W. Elgin, 1879 (defeated by 7); studied law in the office of Messrs. Foy, Tupper and Macdonell, and Messrs. Bethune, Olser and Moss, Toronto; practiced law at St. Thomas, Ont., since 1880; first elec. to H. of C., 1908. *Recreation:* gardening. *Address:* St. Thomas Ont.

CROUTER, A. L. Edgerton, M.A., LL. D.; *b.* Belleville, Ont., Sept. 15, 1846; *s.* Abraham Lewis and Elizabeth Eliza German Crouter; *m.* 1895, June Yale. *Educ.:* pub. and pvt. schs.; studied Franklin Inst. and Univ. of Pa.; (M.A., Gallaudet Coll., Washington, 1886; LL.D., Ill. Coll., Jacksonville, 1894). Teacher, 1867-84, Supt. since 1884, Pa. Inst'n for the Deaf and Dumb, Mt. Airy, Pa. Pres. Am. Assn. to Promote Teaching Speech to Deaf; mem. Am. Acad. Polit. and Social Science, Pa. Hist. Soc., Conv. Am. Inst'rs of Deaf; U.S. del. Internat. Conf. Teachers of Deaf, Edinburgh, 1907. Republican. Episcopalian. Contributor to literature instr'n deaf. *Address:* 7406 Germantown Av., Mt. Airy, Philadelphia.

CROWE, George Reading; *b.* Clifton, Colchester Co., N.S., 22 Oct., 1852; *s.* of James and Harriet N. Crowe; *m.* Mary Elizabeth Alexander; one *s.* two *d.* *Educ.:* Common Sch., Colchester Co. Grain dealer since 1885. *Address:* 125 Hargrave St., Winnipeg, Man. *Club:* Manitoba, Winnipeg.

CROWE, Lieut.-Col. John Henry Verender, R.A.; commandant of the Royal Military College, Kingston, Ont.; *b.* 1682; *m.* Mary Margaret, widow of Wilfred Walls-Russell; one *s.* one *d.* *Educ.:* at Charterhouse, R. M. Coll., Woolwich, and Staff Coll.; arrived in Canada, Oct., 1909; commissioned as Lieut., 1882; Captain, 1890; Major, 1899; Lieut.-Col., 1907; Private Secretary to the Governor of Punjab, 1892-7; D.A.Q.M.G. Intelligence Dept., of the War Office, 1899-1902; chief instructor in military topography and military history and tactics at the R. M. Academy, Woolwich, 1904-08; Knight Commander of the Danebrog (Denmark); Order of Merit (Spain); officer of the Order of S. Bente de Aviz (Portugal). *Publications:* "Problems in manoeuvre tactics; "Epitome of the

Afghan War, 1878-1880; "Epitome of the Russo-Turkish War ,1877-8;" Handbook of the armies of Sweden and Norway," and Translator of Drill Regulations of the German Field Artillery, from the German of Count Sternberg. *Address:* Royal Military College, Kingston, Ont. *Clubs:* Naval and Military, and Grosvenor, London, Eng.

CRUIKSHANK, Lieut.-Col. Ernest Alexander, F.R.S.C., D.O.C. Mil. Dist. No. 13; *b.* Tp. of Bertie, Welland Co., Ont., 29 June, 1854; *s.* of Alexander Cruikshank, and Margaret Milne (both Scotch); *m.* Julia E. Kennedy, of Buffalo, N.Y. *Educ.:* St. Thomas Gram. Sch., Upper Can. Coll.; mem. of Welland Co. Coun., 1879-1903; Warden, 1886; police Magistrate, Niagara Falls, 1903-8; joined 44th Reg., in 1881, and served through all ranks to position of Lieut.-Col., Comdg.; now Hon. Lieut.-Col. of Regt.; commanded 5th Infan. Brig.; apptd. D. O. C., No. 13 Dist., 1 May, 1909. Has written voluminously upon historical matters. *Publications:* Documentary History, War of 1812; Battle of Lundy's Lane; Battle of Queenston Heights; Story of Butler's Rangers; Siege of Fort Eric; Hist. Records of Can. Regiments; Hist. of Welland Country. *Recreations:* riding, walking, mouutaineering. *Address:* Marlborough Mansions, Calgary, Alta.

CULLEN, Thomas Stephen, M.D.; *b.* Bridgewater, Ont., Nov. 20, 1868; *s.* Rev. Thomas and Mary Greene; *m.* 1901, Emma Jones Beckwish. *Educ.:* Collegiate Inst., Toronto; grad. med. dept., Toronto Univ., 1890; Specialist in abdominal surgery; asso. prof. gynecology, Johns Hopkins; asso. in gynecology, Johns Hopkins Hosp.; Hon. mem. La Societa Italiana Ostetricia Ginecologia, Rome; corr. mem. Gesellschaft fur Geburtshulfe, Leipzig. Contb'r. to med. jours. on gynecol. pathology and abdominal surgery. *Publications:* Cancer of the Uterus, 1900; Adeno-myoma des Uterus, Verlag von August Hirschwald, 1903. *Address:* 3 W. Preston St., Baltimore, Md.

CUMBERLAND, Frederic Barlow, M.A. (Trin. Coll.); *b.* Portsmouth, Eng., 5 Aug., 1846; *s.* of F. W. Cumberland, and Wilmot Mary Bramley; *m.* Seraphina Fraser, of Port Hope; one *d.* *Educ.:* Model Gram. Sch., Toronto; Cheltenham Coll., Eng.; Trin. Coll., Toronto. Came to Can. with his parents in 1847; studied law in Toronto, but abandoned it in 1870 to enter railway service; served in many capacities on Great Western and Northern Rys. With Sir Frank Smith, estbd., 1880, Niagara Nav. Co.; Vice-Pres. of Co. since formed Collingwood Lake Superior Line to Port Arthur and Duluth, 1881. Placed S. S. Campana on Upper Lakes, first twin screw steamer on Upper Lakes, and first vessel to be cut in two to be taken through Canadian Canals. conducted general tourist and ticket office in Toronto, 1870-1902; Pres. or Dir. of many important business organizations; mem. of Corporation of Trinity Coll.; mem. of Senate, Toronto Univ.; was a priv. in Cheltenham Coll. Rifle Corps, and best shot in Wimbledon Team; served in Fenian Raid.in Can., 1866; has been Pres. of St. George's Soc., Toronto, and Pres. of National Club; Supreme Pres., S. O. E., 1896. Has steadily refused nomination for public office; mem. of Colonial Committee of the Tariff Reform League; resided in England, 1903-4, but returned to Canada, 1905. *Publications:* "The Northern Lakes of Canada;" "History of the Union Jack and Flags of the Empire;" "The Navies on Lake Ontario in 1812." Mem. of the Authors' Soc., England; Champlain Soc., Canada; is pres. of the Ontario Historical Soc. *Addresses:* "Dunain," Port Hope, Ont.; c|o Niagara Nav. Co., Toronto. *Clubs:* Toronto; Royal Col. Inst., London, Eng.

CUMMINGS, Mrs. Willoughby Emily; *m.* to Willoughby Cummings of Willoughby Hall, Chippawa; active for many years in the National Council of Women; Corresponding Secretary thereto; Convener of Press Committee of the International Council, Toronto, June, 1909. *Address:* 44 Dewson St., Toronto.

CUMMISKEY, Hon. James H.; Commr. of Pub. Works of Prince Edward Island; elec. for the 3rd dist. of Queen's Co., on the Councillor list at g. e., 1897; re-el. at g. e., 1900, 1904 and 1908; apptd. to Ex.-Coun., and made Commr. of Pub. Works, 28 Dec., 1900, which he stll holds; Speaker of the House of Ass., 8th Legis., 1888–1900. *Address:* Charlottetown, P.E.I.

CURRIE, Major John Allison, M.P.; *b.* Nottawa, Simcoe Co., Ont., 25 Feb., 1862; *s.* of John Currie and Catherine McAllister; *m.* E. Helen Sparks; one *d.* *Educ.:* Pub. Sch. and Coll. Inst., Collingwood; on staff of the Toronto *News* and Toronto *Mail:* left journalism to enter business; now pres. of the Imperial Steel and Wire Co.; first elec. to H. of C., 1908; Major, 48th Highlanders, Canada; Pres., Toronto Garrison Indoor Baseball League. *Publications:* Articles to magazines and reviews. *Address:* 39 Howland Av., Toronto; Collingwood, Ont. *Clubs:* Albany, Can. Mil. Inst., Toronto; Collingwood.

CURRIE, Morley, B.A., M.D., M.P.; *b.* Picton, Ont., 1869; *s.* of Geo. C. Currie and Catherine Richards; *m.* Clara Clarke; one *d.* *Educ.:* Pub. Sch. and High Sch. of Picton. Ont., and Univ. of Toronto; a physician; surgeon with rank of Capt. in the 16th Regt.; elec. to the Ont. Legislature, 1902 and 1904; elect. to the H. of C., 1908. *Address:* Picton, Ont.

CURRY, Nathaniel; *b.* Kings County, N.S., 26 March, 1851; *s.* of Charles Curry and Eunice Davidson; *m.* Hary M. Hall; four *s.* *Educ.:* Pub. Sch. of N.S.; spent some years in the United States with Railway and Mining Companies; established business in Amherst, N.S., 1877; Pres., Rhodes, Curry Co., Ltd., Canada Car and Foundry Co., Canada Land Co.; Dir. Bank of Nova Scotia, Canada Cement Co., Canadian Light and Power Co., and 15 other companies. *Recreations:* yachting, shooting, fishing, curling. *Address:* Amherst, N.S. *Clubs:* Marshlands, Amherst, N.S.; Albany, Toronto, Ont., Engineers, and St. James', Montreal.

CUSHING, Hon. William Henry, M.L. A.; Min. of Pub. Works of Alberta; *b.* 21 Aug., 1852; of English and Irish parentage; *m.* 1877; two *d.* *Educ.:* Ontario Pub. Schs. A manufacturer; apptd. Min. of Pub.

Works in the first Alberta Govt., 6 Sept., 1905; elec. to Alberta Leg. for Calgary, at g. e., 1905; re-elec. 1909. *Address:* Calgary, Alta.

D

DAFOE, John W., Man. Ed. Manitoba *Free Press; b.* Combermere, Ont., 8 March 1866; *s.* of C. W. Dafoe, now of Killarney, Man., and Mary, *d.* of the late John Elcome, of Kent, Eng.; *m.* Alice, *d.* of W. G. Parmelie of Ottawa; three *s.* four *d. Educ.:* Arnprior Pub. and High Schs.; connected with the Montreal *Star* from 1883 to 1885; first editor of the Ottawa *Journal,* 1886; editorial staff of the Manitoba *Free Press,* 1886-92; editor Montreal *Herald,* 1892-1895; editorial staff of Montreal *Star* 1895 to 1901; editor in Chief, Manitoba *Free Press,* 1901, to the present time. *Address:* 509 Spence St., Winnipeg. *Club:* Manitoba, Winnipeg.

DAFOE, Samuel Wallace; *b.* Hastings Co., Ont., 9 Jan., 1874; *s.* of Calvin Wesley and Mary Dafoe; *m.* Amy Templeton King, Ottawa; one *s. Educ.:* Killarney and Winnipeg, Man.; reporter for the Winnipeg *Free Press,* 1890-1893; sporting and city editor *Nor. Wester,* 1893-1895; Parliamentary reporter Ottawa *Journal,* 1896; Telegraph editor Montreal *Herald,* 1897-1898; Saturday Editor Montreal *Star,* 1899; Telegraph Editor Montreal *Star,* 1900 to 1905; Press Correspondent at Ottawa, from 1905 to the present date, representing London *Daily Mail,* Montreal *Witness,* Toronto *Star. Address:* 21 Waverly St., Ottawa.

DAGGER, Francis; *b.* Liverpool, Eng., 3 June, 1865; *s.* of Henry Dagger, *s.* of the Superviser of H. M. Customs, and Frances, *d.* of John Henry Hopkins, Seaforth, Liverpool; *m.* Emma *d.* of Charles and Harriet Holland, Bristol Eng.; one *s.* two *d. Educ.:* Farndon Hall Academy, Cheshire, Eng.; arrived in Canada, Aug., 1899; eighteen years in the telephone service of Great Britain, holding various positions in the Lancashire & Cheshire Telephonic Exchange Co., the Western Counties & South Wales Telephone Co., and the National Telephone Co., in Lancashire, Bristol, Plymouth, Birmingham, and Sheffield. came to Canada in 1899, and made a special study of telephone conditions on the North American continent with a view to determining the relative merits of public ownership, private monopoly, and competition; in 1903, prepared a report for the Postmaster-General (Sir William Mulock), upon this subject, which resulted in the appointment in 1905, of a parliamentary Select Committee to inquire into and report regarding the various public telephone systems in operation in Canada, and else where; was apptd. to assist this Committee during its inquiry. In 1906, was called upon by the Government of Manitoba to conduct an educational campaign throughout the province, resulting in an affirmative vote of the people in favour of public ownership of the telephone service; in 1907, was commissioned by Government of Saskatchewan to submit recommendations enabling Government to enact legislation dealing with the telephone service. *Address:* 63 Thorold Av., Toronto.

DAIGNEAULT, Frederic Hector, M.D., C.M., M.L.A.; *b.* Chambly, Que., 19 May, 1860; *s.* Joseph Daigneault, and Henrietta Lachapelle; *m.* Catherine Jane McGrail; two *s.* one *d. Educ.:* St. Hyacinthe oll. and Victoria Medical Sch.; was elected to the Quebec Legislature, 1900; re-elec. 1904 and 1908. *Address:* Acton Vale, Que.

DALE, James Alfred, M.A. (Oxon); Prof. of Educ., McGill Univ.; *b.* Birmingham, Eng., 21 June, 1874; *s.* of J. A. Dale, of Birmingham, and Eliz. Holmes, of Manchester; *m.* Margaret Butler; two *s. Educ.:* King Edward VI Sch., Camp Hill; Mason Univ., Coll., Birmingham; Weston Coll., Oxford; came to Canada, Aug., 1908 to assume pres. pos. at McGill. Open Classical Exhibitioner of Merton, tutor at Borough Road Training Co., London, 1902-3; Oxford Univ. Extension lecturer, 1904-8. *Publications:* History of Englsh Literature; contributions to various periodicals chiefly on literary and educational subjects. *Address:* 260 University St., Montreal.

DALY, Hon. Thomas Mayne, P.C., K. C.; *b.* Stratford, Ont., 16 Aug., 1852; *s.* Thomas Mayne Daly, for many years member of Parliament for Perth County, and Mayor of Stratford, and Helen Wharen; *m.* Margaret A. Jarvis, *d.* of P. R. Jarvis, J.P., Stratford, Ont.; two *s. Educ.:* Up. Can. Coll., Toronto; first Mayor of Brandon, 18$2; Mayor of Brandon, 1887 to 1896; Minister of Interior and Superintendent of Indian Affairs in Government of Sir John Abbott, and Sir John Thompson and Sir McKenzie Bowell, Oct., 1892 to April, 1896; Rossland, B.C., 1897 to 1902; Police Magistrate, 1901, and Judge Juvenile Court, Winnipeg, 1909; Senior mem. of law firm of Daly and Crichton, Winnipeg, *Address:* 901 Dorchester Avenue, Winnipeg. *Club:* Manitoba, Winnipeg.

DANDURAND, Hon. Raoul, P.C., LL. D., Kt. Legion of Honor (France), Senator; *b.* Montreal, 4 Nov., 1861; *s.* of the late O. E. Dandurand, Merchant, Montreal, and Marie Marguerite Roy; *m.* in 1886, Josephine, *d.* of the late Hon. F. G. Marchand. *Educ.:* Montreal Coll. and Laval Univ.; called to the Bar in the Prov. of Quebec., Jan., 1883; became a partner of the late Joseph Dautre, Q.C.; later he formed a partnership with Mr. (now Hon.) L. P. Brodeur, and is now practicing law as head of the firm of Dandurand, Hibbard, Boyer and Gosselin; was made a K.C., in 1898; created a Knight of the Legion of Honor, by the French Government, in 1891, and promoted to the rank of officer, 1907; called to the Senate, Jan., 1898; Speaker, Jan., 1905; sworn of the Privy Council, Jan., 1909. *Publications:* conjointly with Mr. Charles Lanctot, now Deputy Attorney General, Que., a treatise on Criminal Law, and Manuals for Justices of the Peace and Police Officers.

DANDURAND, Madame Josephine; *b.* Montreal; *d.* of the late Hon. F. G. Marchand, Premier of Quebec; *m.* Hon. Rauol Dandurand; Vice.-Pres. of the National Council of Women of Canada, and of the Woman's Canadian Club of Montreal; has published "Les Contes de Noel," a volume of essays, three comedies "Rancune," "La Carte Postale," and "Le Langage des Fleurs," which were played in Montreal and Quebec; another comedy, "Victimes de l'Ideal," in verse, was played in Ottawa. A frequent contributor to periodicals; was appointed Lady Commissioner for Canada, to the Paris Exhibition in 1900; presided in Paris over a number of meetings of the International Council of Women; was the first Canadian Woman to be honoured with the decoration of "Officier d'Académie" by the French Government in 1899; founded "L'oeuvre des Livres Gratuits" in 1892, which circulates yearly, many thousands of books to people in need, and more especially to the female teachers in the rural parts of Quebec. *Address:* 548 Sherbrooke St. W., Montreal.

DANIEL, John Waterhouse, M.R.C.S., M.P.; *b.* St. Stephen, N.B., 27 Jan., 1854; *s.* of Henry and Honor Daniel, natives of Cornwall, Eng.; *m.* 15 Oct., 1890, Jessie Porteous Ennis, *d.* of the late John Ennis. *Educ.:* New Kingswood Coll., Bath, Somersetshire, Eng., and at New York and London, Eng.; first elec. to the H. of C. at bye-election, 16 Feb., 1904; re-elec. 1904 and 1908; has been Surgeon Lt.-Col. in the Militia (Long Service decoration); an alderman for three years; Warden of the Co. one year; Mayor two years; past Pres., St. George's Society; Past Pres. Council of Physicians and Surgeons; mem. Board of Health; Commr. and Consulting Surgeon, General Public Hospital; Methodist; Conservative. *Address:* St. John, N.B.

DANIELS, Hon. Orlando T., B.A., M.L.A.; Mem. of the Ex. Coun. of Nova Scotia; *b.* Laurencetown, Annapolis Co., N.S., 20 March, 1860; *s.* of Wellington Daniels, and Lavinia Daniels; *m.* 1893, Mary L. Muir; one *d.* *Educ.:* Laurencetown Pub. Sch., Univ. of Acadia Coll., Wolfville, N.S.; Barrister-at-law; apptd. mem. of the Ex. Coun. of N.S., 16 March, 1907; first elec. to Leg. Ass. at bye-el. 6 March, 1906; re-el. at g. e., 20 June, 1906. *Address:* Bridgetown, N.S.

DANSEREAU, Clement Arthur, B.C.L.; editor-in-chief of *La Presse*, Montreal; *b.* Contre Coeur, Que., 5 July, 1844; *s.* of Clement Dansereau and Louise Fiset; *m.* (1st) Marie Cordelie Hurteau (*d.* 1879); (2nd) Stephanie, *d.* of Stephen McKay (*d.* 1897). *Educ.:* Vercheres and L'Assomption Coll.; studied law under Mr. Justice Girouard, now of Sup. Ct.; grad. McGill, 1865; did not practice legal prof., but entered into journalism; from 1873, onward one of the editors of *La Minerve;* joined staff of *La Presse*, 1880; accepted Postmastership of Montreal, 1891, but resigned 1899, to return to journalism; has been editor-in-chief of *La Presse* since that date. *Publications:* Annales Historiques College de L'Assomption. *Address:* 1028 Dorchester St., W., Montreal. *Clubs:* St. James', Canada, Montreal, Montreal.

DARGAVEL, John Robertson, M.L.A.; *b.* Elgin, Ont., 3 May, 1846; *s.* of Robert Dargavel and Miriam Robertson Dargavel; *m.* Mary Jane Hopkins, one *s.* two *d.* *Educ.:* in Pub. Schs.; engaged in the mercantile business since 1868, also in farming and dairying; Pres. of the Eastern Ontario Dairymen's Ass.; first elec. to Ontario Legislature, 1905, and re-elected 1909; Conservative. *Address:* Elgin, Leeds Co., Ont.

DAVID, Hon. Laurent Olivier; Senator; Clerk of the City of Montreal; *b.* Saint-au-Recollet, nr. Montreal, 24 March, 1840; *s.* of the late Major Stanislas David and Elizabeth Tremblay; *m.* (1st) 1868, Albina Chenet (*d.* 1887); (2nd) 1892, Ludivine Garceau; one *s.* nine *d.* *Educ.:* St. Therese Coll.; called to the Bar, 1864; assisted to estb., and was chief editor of *L'Opinion Publique*, an illustrated weekly, 1870. In 1874, in conjunction with Mr. Beausoleil, M.P., founded *Le Bien Public;* was a translator and Asst. Clerk of the votes and deliberations of H. of C. during the Mackenzie regime. Unsuccessful can. for local Legis. at g. e., 1867, and 1875, and for H. of C. at g. e., 1878 and 1891; elec. to local Legis. at g. e., 1886; delegate to the French-Canadian National Convention at Nashua, N.H., in 1888, apptd. City Clerk of Montreal, 1892; Pres., Ste. Jean Baptiste Soc., Montreal, 1887-8; Fellow of the Royal Soc. of Canada; apptd. to the Senate, 19 June, 1903. *Publications:* "Biographies et Portraits," "Les Heros de Chateauguay," "Les Patriotes, de 1837-38," "Mes Contemporains," "Les Deux Papineau," "L'Union des Deux Canadas (1841-1867)," "Le Drapeau de Carillon," "Laurier et son temps," "Le Clergé Canadien; Sa Mission et Son Oeuvre" *Addresses:* 391 St. Hubert St.; City Hall, Montreal.

DAVIDSON, Colonel Andrew Duncan; *b.* Glencoe, Ont., 18 May, 1853; *s.* of Scotch and Irish Parents; *m.* Ella F. McRae, Glencoe; one *d.* *Educ.:* Glencoe; raised on a farm in Western Ontario; went to Wisconsin at age of 19; after taking a course in Business College, took up railroad work; after serveral years moved to Minnesota, where he became engaged in the land business, which he has followed ever since; returned to Canada in 1902 and inagurated what is known as the American Invasion, he and his associates having purchased 1,250,000 acres of land; also had a colonization agreement with the Dominion Government, by which he was to settle a large tract of country in the Saskatchewan Valley; brought 350 bankers, grain buyers and newspaper men from the U.S., and showed them the country; their reports were so favourable that 1,000,000 acres of land were sold actual settlers from the U.S. in the next 8 months; carried through his colonization agreement to successful completion; later took over the land grant of the C. N. Ry.; has sold 12,000,000 acres of land during his career; is interested in lumbering business in B.C.; Vice-Pres. Columbia River Lumber Co., and also of the Fraser River Lumber Co., the latter having the largest saw mill in the British Empire; also interested in Grain Elevator Companies in the Western Canada Flour Mills; Land Commissioner of the Canadian Northern Ry., and closely identified and interested with Mackenzie and Mann, in many of their enterprises; senior mem. of the firm of Davidson and McRae; is a member of the Boards of Directors of 44 companies. *Address:* Toronto, Ont. *Clubs:* National, Toronto; Rideau, Ottawa, Manitoba, Winnipeg.

DAVIDSON, Hon. Charles Peers, Puisne Justice Superior Court, Province of Que.; Professor of Criminal Law, McGill Univ., Montreal; *b.* Huntingdon, Que., Jan. 1841; *s.* of Captain Alexander Davidson; *m.* 1868, Alice, *d.* of William Mattice, Cornwall, Ontario. *Educ.:* Victoria College, Cobourg; McGill Univ., Montreal; called to Bar of Que., 1885; Q.C., 1878; Bench, 1887; on service during Fenian raids, 1866-67, and holds medal; Lieut.-Col. Victoria Rifles, Montreal, 1887; president Montreal Snow Shoe Club, 1871-77; president Victoria Skating Club, 1879-83; commodore Royal St. Lawrence Yacht Club, 1902. *Publication:* Banking Laws of Canada. *Recreations:* throughout life has been ardent sportsman, running, lacrosse, yachting, and winter sports of all kinds. *Address:* Minto Apts., Montreal. *Clubs:* St. James', Royal St. Lawrence Yacht, Forest and Stream, Montreal.

DAVIDSON, James; *b.* Montreal, 1854; *s.* of the late Thomas Davidson and Marie Ritchie. *Educ.:* Montreal priv. schs.; at age of eighteen entered the establishment of Thomas Davidson Mnfg. Co., founded by his father in 1860; became a partner, 1880; 1894, on the death of his father, assumed full control of the business, which was incorporated in 1895, under the name of the Thomas Davidson Mnfg. Co., Ltd., and has been Pres. ever since; Vice-Pres., Brome Lake Electric Co.; mem. Montreal Bd. of Trade, Chambre de Commerce. *Recreation:* trout fishing. *Address:* 292 Stanley St., Montreal. *Clubs:* St. James', Montreal Hunt Beaconsfield Golf.

DAVIDSON, Peers, M.A., B.C.L., K.C.; *b.* 17 Nov., 1870; *s.* of Mr. Justice Charles Peers Davidson; *m.* 1895, Harriet Louise, *d.* of Rt. Hon. Sir William Whiteway, C.P., K.C.M.G., formerly Premier of Newfoundland; two *s.* one *d.* *Educ.:* Montreal High Sch., McGill Univ.; called to the Bar, 19 Sept., 1893; cr. K.C., 6 July, 1906; now senior mem. of the firm Davidson & Wainwright, barristers and solicitors, Montreal. *Publication:* "Canadian Law of Partnership," in collaboration with Mr. R. B. Henderson, barrister. *Addresses:* 7 Selkirk Av.; 224 St. James' St., Montreal. (Bus.) *Clubs:* St. James', Canada, Hunt, Royal St. Lawrence Yacht, Montreal.

DAVIES, Acton; *b.* St. Johns, Que. Joined staff of New York *Evening Sun*, May, 1890; dramatic critic since 1893; was Corr., New York *Sun* in Cuba and Porto Rico, and was with the marine corps during the fight at Guantanamo. *Address:* Evening Sun, New York.

DAVIES, Hon. Sir Louis Henry, K.C.; one of the Judges of the Supreme Court of Canada; K.C.M.G., 1897; *b.* Prince Edward Island, 4 May, 1845; *s.* of Hon. Benjamin Davies; *m.* Susan *d.* of Rev. Dr. Wiggins, 1872; one *s.* three *d.* *Educ.:* Prince of Wales Coll. Barr. Prince Edward Island, 1867; Solicitor-General, 1869 and 1871-92; Leader of the Opposition, 1873-76; Premier and Attorney-General, Prince Edward Island, 1876-79; Q.C. 1880; elected to Dom. H. of C., 1882, and re-elec. continuously until his appointment to Supreme Court; Counsel for Great Britain before the International Fisheries Arbitration at Halifax in 1877, between Great Britain and United States of America; P.C., Canada, 1896; Joint Delegate to Washington with Sir Wilfrid Laurier 1897, on Behring Sea seal question; one of Joint High Commissioners on part of Great Britain in 1898 for settlement of all differences with U.S.A. in respect of Canada; Minister of Marine and Fisheries, Canada, 1896-1901. *Recreations:* golf, driving. *Address:* 236 Metcalfe St., Ottawa. *Clubs:* Rideau, Golf, Ottawa.

DAVIS, Edward Pease, B.A., K.C.; *b.* King, Ont., 1860; *s.* Andrew Davis and Elizabeth Pease; *m.* Adelia Oouise Davis; two *s.* one *d.* *Recreation:* bridge, yachting. *Address:* 1115 Seaton St., Vancouver, B.C. *Clubs:* Vancouver, Royal Yacht, Jericho, Vancouver; Union, Victoria; Toronto; United Empire, London, Eng.

DAVIS, Rev. Evans, M.A., D.D., Dean of the Diocese of Huron; *b.* in Ireland, of Welsh extraction, 20 May, 1848; *s.* of the late Rev. W. Davis; *m.* Louisa Victoria Greenwood; three *s.* one *d.* *Educ.:* in Quebec, Toronto, and London; arrived in Canada when very young; ordained deacon, by Bishop Cronyn, 3 June, 1871; Priest by Bishop Hellmuth, 5 Nov., 1875; apptd. to the Bayfield, Co. Huron, 5 June, 1871; apptd. to St. James', London, Feb., 1894, where he still is in charge as rector; was apptd. Canon of the Cathedral, 2 May, 1888; apptd. Archdeacon of London, 26 Sept., 1894, and Dean of the Diocese, 16 Oct., 1905. *Address:* London, Ont.

DAVIS, Mortimer B.; Pres. Imperial Tobacco Co. of Canada; *b.* Montreal. *Educ.:* High Sch.; entered firm of S. Davis & Sons, Cigar Manufacturers, his father's business, at an early age, became manager, and on formation of the American Tobacco Co., of Can., became Pres., 1895; Pres. Imperial Tobacco Co., of Can.; Dir. Union Bank of Can.; Man. Dir. Corby Distillery Co., Belleville, Ont.; Dir. B. Houde Tobacco Co., Quebec.; Pres., Baron de Hirsch Inst.; founded a law chair in Laval Univ., 1900; mem. Montreal Bd. of Trade. *Address:* 516 Pine Av., W., Montreal. *Clubs:* Mount Royal, St. James', Montreal Hunt, Jockey.

DAVIS, Hon. Thomas Osborne; Senator *b.* Sherrington, Que , 16 Aug., 1856; *s.* of Samuel and Anne Davis; *m.* Rebecca Jennings; five *s.* three *d.* *Educ.:* at home; Councillor and Mayor of Prince Albert; Pres. of the Board of Trade and Chairman of Public Sch. Board; elected to the H. of C. for Saskatchewan, 19 Dec., 1896, in place of Sir Wilfrid Laurier, who vacated the seat to accept Quebec East; re-elected 1900; elec. Whip for the West, 1901; apptd. to the Senate, 30 Sept., 1904. *Address:* Prince Albert, Saskatchewan. *Club:* Prince Albert.

DAVY, John M.; *b.* Ottawa, Ont., June 29, 1835; removed to Rochester with his parents when a child; brought up on farm; *Educ.:* com. schs. and Monroe Acad., E. Henrietta, N.Y.; studied law; was law student when Civil war broke out; assisted in raising and became 1st Lieut., 108th N.Y. Vols.; served until 1863, when he was honorably discharged because of illness; resumed law study; admitted to bar, 1863; dist. atty., Monroe Co., 1868-71; collector of customs, Rochester, 1872-5; mem. Congress, 1875-7; Judge Supreme Court, 7th jud, dist., N.Y., 1889-1905; retired; Republican. *Address:* Rochester, N.Y.

DAWSON, Samuel Edward, C.M.G., Litt.D., F.R.S.C.; *b.* Halifax, N.S., 1833; *m.* 1858, Annie, *d.* of late Gilbert Bent, of St. John, N.B.; went to Montreal in 1847, where he was for forty years a publisher and bookseller, first with his father Benjamin Dawson (*d.*), and then as senior mem. of Dawson Brothers,—a firm very widely known; went to Ottawa, in 1891, on appoinment as King's Printer and Controller of Stationary for the Dominion of Canada, which position he held until 1909; is a mem. of the Royal Society of Canada and (1907), President. Is Docteur es-Lettres of Laval Univ.; has been Sch. Commissioner and Pres. of the Board of Arts, and Manufactures at Montreal; has written much on Canadian subjects. *Publications:* "A Study of Lord Tennyson's Princess," (Montreal, 1884); "Canada and Newfoundland," (Stanford, 1896); "The Voyages of the Cabots," (1894-97); "The St. Lawrence Basin and its Borderlands," (London and New York, 1905), and other works on the history and geography of Canada. *Address:* 136 Bay Street, Ottawa.

DAWSON, William Bell, M.A., Ma.E., M. Inst. C.E., P.S.L., F.R.S.C., Supt. of tidal serveys, Canada; *b.* Picton, N.S., 2 May, 1854; *s.* of late Sir J. W. and Lady Dawson; *m.* Florence, *d.* of Commissary Gen. Elliott (Eng); three *s.* one *d.* *Educ.:* McGill Univ., and Ecole des ponts et Chaussées, Paris (grad. 1878); in the summer of 1873, inspected the works of the Intercolonial Railway, then inp rogress, between Riviere du Loup and Bathurst; following summer was employed on the construction of the Louisburg Railway, Cape Breton; in 1875, travelled in England, and on the continent of Europe, visiting Scientific Schools, Workshops, and Museums; 1876, was employed on the Quebec Montreal, Ottawa, and Occidental Railway, infield and office work; 1877, visited the Canal de l'Est, then under construction; and examined the works at the summit near Epinal, in the vicinity of Nancy, and along the Meuse to Namur in Belgium; also availed himself of the opportunity to examine the Harbor Improvements in progress at Havre. From the notes, plans and drawings made regarding these works, prepared papers on the Paroy Reservoir, and on the Canal de l'Est, for the Institution of Civil Engineers, London; for which was awarded a Miller Scholarship; admitted 1878, as a Provincial Land Surveyor in the Province of Quebec; in December, 1879, was elected an Associate mem. of the Inst. of Civil Engineers; and in the following year passed for Degree of Master of Engineering; 1882, was apptd. one of the Examiners in the Faculty of Applied Science of McGill Univ., specially in the subjects of Applied Mechanics, Construction, Hydraulics, and the Steam Engine; Asst. Mgr. with the Dominion Bridge Company, 1882; entered the service of the Canadian Pacific Railway Co., as Assist. Engineer, 1884; amongst other work, organized a testing laboratory for the Company, to examine into the qualities of materials, including burning oils, lubricating oils, fuel, metals, axles, rails, and other supplies largely dealt in; since 1893, has been in charge of Survey of tides and currents for Canada. *Publications:* various technical and engr. papers; series of reports on investigation of currents; annual tide-tables for Atlantic and Pacific coasts of Can. *Address:* 436 Gilmour St., Ottawa.

DAY, Mrs. Lilla; *b.* Ireland; *d.* of Rev. William Swanton and Rizia Collins, *e. d.* of the late Capt. Francis Collins, 11th Huzzars, Prince Albert's Own; *m.* Robert Scott Day, C.E., April, 1888; four *s.* three *d.* *Educ.:* Ireland and England; arrived in Canada, June, 1891; visited Australia, when two years old with her parents and brother, but having lost her father on the voyage, the family returned; the remaining years of her childhood were spent with her grand father in Cork, Ireland. As a result of the land league agitation, her family lost all their property and income; she married in Cork, Ireland, and the first three years of her married life were spent in Kimberley, South Africa, where she took an active part in social, religious and philanthropic life of the diamond fields, and was instrumental in forming the Kimberley Benevolent Society; on the organization of a branch of the Woman's Council, by Lady Aberdeen in Victoria, B.C., became its first Vice-Pres.; has continued in the work ever since; in 1904, was elected Pres. of the Victoria and Vancouver Island Local Council of Women, retiring after four years to accept the Vice-Pres. of the National Council of Women of Canada; originator the club idea in Victoria, and with Mrs. Dewdney, wife of the then Lieut.-Governor, and Miss Perrin, sister of the Lord Bishop of Columbia, organized the Alexandra Club, which was for many years the only Woman's Club west of Toronto. *Address:* Rockland Avenue, Victoria, B.C. *Club:* Alexandra.

DEANE, John Hall; *b.* Canada; went to U.S. in boyhood; entered Rochester Univ., but left to enlist; private Union army, 1862; captured at Gettysburg, and for some time in C. S. prison; after being exchanged, served in navy to end of war; studied law; practiced in New York; gave $100,000 to Univ. of Rochester; has made other noteworthy gifts to Bapt. Instns. *Address:* 62 E. 78th St. *Office:* 135 Broadway, New York. *Clubs:* Union League.

DE BLAQUIERE, Baron William, J.P.; *b.* Woodstock, Ont., 5 Sept., 1856; *s.* of 5th Baron William Barnard de Blaquiere, Capt., R.N., and Anna Maria Wormald; *m.* 1888, Lucianne, *e. d.* of George Desbarats, of Montreal; two *s.* one *d.* Baronetcy created, 16 July, 2874; barony, 30 July, 1800; succeeded his cousin as 6th baron 1889. *Addresses:* Brockworth Manor, Gloucestershire (seat); 3 Circus, Bath, Eng. *Club:* White's.

DE BLAQUIERE, The Baroness Lucianne; *b.* Quebec, 1865; *d.* of the late George E. Desbarats and Lucianne Bosse; *m.* 1888, William de Blaquiere, of Woodstock, Ont., who succeeded to the peerage as 6th Baron in 1889; two *s.* one *d.* *Educ.:* Sacred Heart Convent, Montreal; is on the "Britannia roll" of the Imperial Federation

League. *Addresses:* Brockworth Manor, Gloucestershire (seat); 3 Circus, Bath, Eng.

deBOUCHERVILLE, Hon. Charles Eugene Boucher, M.D., C.M.G.; *b.* Montreal, 4 May, 1822; *s.* of late Hon. P. B. Dd Boucherville, M.L.C. and Amelie de Bleury; *m.* (1st) Susanna, *d.* of th late R. M. Morrough, Montreal; (2nd) *d.* of the late Felix Lussier, Seigneur of Varennes (*d.* Jan., 1892). *Educ.:* St. Sulpice Coll., Montreal and McGill Univ. (M.D.); sat in Can. House of Assembly for Chambly, 1861, until Confederation, when called to Legis. Council, of which he has been a mem. since. Speaker of Council in Chauveau Admn.; Premier of Quebec, Sept., 1874; dismissed by Lieut.-Governor, March, 1878; called to Senate of Can. for Montarville div., 1879; cr. C.M.G., May, 1894. *Address:* Montreal.

DE BRUMATH, Adrien Leblond, B.A.; Director of the Catholic Commercial Academy of Montreal; *b.* Schlestadt, Alsace, 16 April, 1854; *s.* of Pascal de Brumath, dir. of Insane Asylums of France, and Kt. of Legion of Hon., and Blanche, *d.* of D. Dispot, King's Attorney, France; *m.* J. Nolan; two *s.* two *d.* *Educ.:* Jesuits Coll., Amiens, France; studied law in France; was pupil of the Military Riding Sch. at Saumuir, France; non. com. officer of Cuirassiers, at Paris; came to Canada 1877; in addition to present position, is examiner on Bd. for Vet. Surgeons; del. for the Central Bd. of Examiners; Corresponding mem. Geographical Soc. of Lille, France. *Publications:* History of Canada; Life of Bishop Laval; Life of Mlle. Mance; Life of Mr. Olier; Life of Bishop Bourget. *Addresses:* 85 St. Catharine St., West, 355 St. Denis St., Montreal.

deBURY, Major Visart Henry Robert; *b.* Constance, Germany, 11 June, 1872; *m.* Agnes May Robertson; two *d.* *Educ.:* Stonehurst, England, and Royal Military Coll., Kingston, Ont.; arrived in Canada, 1876; Commission in the Royal Artillery, 1892; Adjutant Ceylon Mauritus Batt., R. A., 1898; command St. Luci Co. R. A., 1900; Garrison Adjutant, St. Luci, 1902; Professor of Artillery, Strategy and Tactics, Royal Military Coll., Can., 1905. *Recreations:* golf, tennis, cricket and rifle shooting; *Address:* Royal Military Coll., Kingston, and Chateau de Bury, Hamault, Belgium.

DECARIE, Hon. Jeremie L., LL.D., K.C., M.L.A.; Prov. Sec. for Quebec; *b.* Notre-Dame de Grace, 1870; *s.* of D. Jeremie, Decarie, and Philomene Leduc; *m.* (1st) his cousin, *d.* of A. C. Decary; (2nd) 1907, Juliette, *d.* of Hon. H. B. Rainville. *Educ.:* Montreal Coll., St. Mary's Coll., Laval Univ. (grad. LL.B.); studied law in office of the late Hon. Honore Mercier, and Hon. Messrs. Gouin and Lemieux; practised in Montreal in partnership with Hon. Messrs. Gouin and Lemieux; now in partnership with his cousin, Alphonse Decary, K.C.; first el. to Leg. Ass. at g. e., 1904, in succession to his father, who represented Hochelaga from 1897 until his death; re-el. at g. e., 1908, and by accl. 1909; sworn of the Ex. Coun. as Min. of Agric., 19 Jan., 1909; Prov. Sec., Dec., 1909. *Addresses:* Notre Dame de Grace, Que.; 415 New York Life Bldg., Montreal. (Bus.)

DE CAZES, Paul, Litt. D. (Laval), F. R.S.C.; *b.* St. Harblon, France, 16 June, 1840; *s.* of Charles de Cazes; *m.* Hermaine St. Denis (*d.* 1905). *Educ.:* L'Institution Loriol, Paris; came to Can., 1858; in journalism, 1863-1872; called to the Quebec Bar 1869, and entered into practice with late Hon. Mr. Mercier; Dom. Govt. rep., at Paris, 1874-9; an officer of Pub. Instruction of France; ex-sec. of the Dept. of Pub. Instruction of Quebec; ex-sec. of the Council of Catholic Pub. Instruction, Quebec; vice-pres. sec. I of the Roy. Soc. of Can., 1884-6. *Publications:* "Notes sur le Canada;" "Code of Public Instruction for Quebec;" many contributions to the proceedings of the Royal Soc. *Address:* Neuilly-sur-Seine, nr. Paris, France.

DE CELLES, Alfred D., LL.D., C.M.G. Chevalier de la Legion d'Honneur, F.R.S. C.; Librarian of Parliament; *b.* St. Laurent, nr. Montreal, 15 Aug., 1844; *s.* of Augustin de Celles; *m.* Eugenie Dorion; one *s.* *Educ.:* Laval Univ., Quebec; lawyer; editor of *Le Journal de Quebec; La Minerve,* Montreal; *L'Opinion Publique,* Montreal. *Pubications:* La Crise du regime parlementaire; A la conquete de la liberte en France et au Canada; Les constitutions du Canada; Les Etats Unis; Papineau (Political History of Canada); Papineau and Cartier (in English); La Fontaine, Cartier (in French). *Address:* 71 Russell Ave., Ottawa, Ont.

DELAMERE, Thomas Dawson, M.A., K.C.; *b.* Co. Down, Ireland, 25 March, 1874; *s.* of Dawson Delamere and Jane Delamere; *m.* Grace, *e. d.* of the late E. O. Bickford, of Toronto; three *s.* three *d.* *Educ.:* Up. Can. Coll. and Univ. Coll., Toronto; arrived in Canada in 1855; Barrister at Law, 1870; served ten years in the Queen's Own Rifles, and Fenian Raid (Medal); retired with rank of Captain. *Recreations:* Gardening, canoeing, Fishing, shooting. *Address:* 39 Heath St., Toronto.

DELISLE, George Isidore, M.L.A.; *b.* Sherbrooke, Que., 29 June, 1856; *s.* of Augustine Delisle and Carmel Gauthier; *m.* 1884, Leda, *d.* of George Felix Heroux; three *s.* three *d.* *Educ.:* Three Rivers Coll.; Pres., La Fonciere Fire Assur. Co., Montreal Pres., St. Maurice and Champlain Tel. Co., of the Protectrice du Colon Fire Assur. Co. at Yamachiche; of the Dumoulin Council of L'Alliance Nationale Life Assur. Co.; first el. to Legis. Ass. at g. e., 1908. *Address:* Yamachiche, Que.

DELISLE, Michael Simeon, M.P.; *b.* at Point aux-Trembles, Portneuf, Co. 27 Sept., 1856; *s.* of Albert Delisle and Dina Bertrand *m.* 19 Sept., 1881, to Elmena Poliquin. *Educ.:* at Quebec; a merchant; has been Mayor for fiye years, and was elected to the H. of C. in 1901-1904, and 1908 as a Liberal. *Address:* Portneuf, Que.

DE LORIMIER, Hon. Chas. Chamilly, LL.D., Judge of the Superior Court at Montreal; *b.* Dubuque, Iowa, U.S.A., 13 Sept., 1842; *s.* of J. B. Chamilly de Lorimier and Rachel de Courville; *m.* M. de Serre; two *s.* two *d.* *Educ.:* St. Mary's Coll.; Jesuits' Coll., Montreal; called to bar of Que., 1865; Q.C., 1882; Prof. at Laval, 1880-1908; Judge of Sup. Ct. at Joliette, 1889-1909; transferred to Montreal, 6 Sept., 1909. *Publications:* Library of the Code Civil (21 vols).; La Revue de Jurisprudence (15 vols. to date). *Address:* 54 Cherrier St., Montreal.

deLOYNES, Marie-Joseph, Consul General of France in Canada; *b.* Blois, France, 8 Aug., 1857; *s.* of C. A. deLoynes and M. J. T. Naudin; *m.* Yvonne Adam; one *d.* *Educ.:* Pont-Levoy Sch., France; arrived in Canada, 5 May, 1908; entered the French diplomatic Service, 1881; Sec. to the Ambassador in Madrid, Spain and St. Petersburg, Russia; attache at the Minister of Foreign Affairs; Consul General of France in Canada, 28 Dec., 1907. *Address:* 71 Viger Av., Montreal; 1 Rue de la Mage, Versailles, France. *Clubs:* Hunt, Montreal; Cercle de l'Union Evelistique, Paris, France.

DEMERS, Joseph, LL.B., K.C., M.P.; *b.* at Henryville, Co. Iberville, 31 May, 1871; *s.* of Alexis Louis Demers, M.L.A., and Marie Goyette; *m.* 8 Jan., 1896, to Bertha Gravel of Arthabaska; three *s.* one *d.* *Educ.:* at St. Hyacinthe Sem. and St. Mary's Coll., Montreal; Liberal; Catholic; first elec. to the H. of C., 1906 (bye election); re-elec. in 1908, both times by accla. *Address:* St. Jean, Que.

DeMILLE, Rev. Alban Bertram, M.A., *b.* Halifax, N.S., 1873; *s.* of James de Mille, Professor of English, Dalhousie Coll., Halifax, N.S., and Annie, *d.* of Rev. John Pryor, D.D., first Pres., Acadia Coll., Wolfville, N.S.; *m.* Miss Barker, *d.* of Chief Justice Barker, St. John, N.B.; one *s.* *Educ.:* King's Coll., Windsor, N.S., Harvard Univ., Cambridge Mass.; Professor of English and History, King's Coll.; head of History Dept., Milton Academy, Milton, Mass.; head of History Dept., Belmont Sch., Belmont, Calif. *Publications:* "School edition of Longfellow's Evangeline;" "Literature in XIX Century;" Articles and poems in magazines. *Recreations:* rowing, tennis, sailing, golf. *Address:* Belmont, California. *Clubs:* Harvard Union, Cambridge, Mass.

DENISON, Lieut.-Col. Clarence Alfred, Comdg. 1st Cavalry Brigade, Western Ont.; *b.* Toronto, Ont., 9 April, 1851; *s.* Colonel Geo. T. Denison (Rusholm); *m.* Harriet Wallbridge; one *s.* one *d.* *Educ.:* Up. Can. Coll.; served during the Fenian Raid, 1866, and North West Rebellion, 1885 (medals). *Recreations:* golf, riding. *Address:* 55 Prince Arthur Av., Toronto. *Club:* Military Institute, Toronto.

DENISON, Lieut.-Col. George Taylor, L.L.B., F.R.S.C., Hon. Lieut.-Col. Governor General's Body-Guard; Police Magistrate of Toronto; *b.* Toronto, 31 Aug., 1839; *s.* of late Col. George T. Denison; *m.* (1st) 1863, Caroline (*d.* 1885), *d.* of late Oliver Macklem; (2nd) 1887, Helen, *d.* of late James Mair, of Perth, Ontario; three *s.* four *d.* *Educ.:* Upper Can. Coll., Toronto; Univ. of Toronto, (LL.B.); ex-President of the Royal Soc. of Canada, 1903; served 44 yrs. in the Canadian Militia; commanded the Governor-General's Bodyguard in the Fenian Raid on Fort Erie, 1866 (medal and clasp); and in the North-West Rebellion, 1885 (medal); President of the Imperial Federation League in Canada in 1893-95; President of the British Empire League in Canada since 1896; a mem. of the Quebec Battlefields Com. *Publications:* Manual of Outpost Duties, 1866; The Fenian Raid on Fort Erie, 1866; Modern Cavalry, 1868; History of Cavalry, 1877; Soldiering in Canada, 1900; Struggles for Imperial unity, 1909; also magazine articles. *Address:* Heydon Villa, Toronto. *Club:* National, Toronto.

DENISON, Rear Admiral John; *b.* Rusholme, Toronto, Ont., 25 May, 1853; *s.* of Colonel George Taylor Denison; *m.* Florence Ledgard; two *s.* two *d.*; entered Navy, April, 1867; Sub-Lieut., Dec., 1873; Lieut., April, 1879; Commander, Dec., 1891; Captain, May, 1896; Rear Admiral, Sept., 1906; Flagship Leviathan; as Captain of "Niobe." escorted H.I.M. the German Emperor from the Nore to Flushing in his Imperial yacht, 6 Feb., 1901; Commander of Royal Yacht, prom. to Captain; Captain of "Niobe," 1901, escorted "Ophir" from Canada to England; Aide-de Camp to the King, 13th July, 1905, to 1 July, 1906, when he was promoted to Rear-Admiral. *Address:* Alverstoke, England. *Club:* United Service, London, Eng.

DENISON, Lieut.-Col. Septimus Julius Augustus, C.M.G.; *b.* 3 Sept. 1859; 7th *s.* of late Col. George T. Denison of Rusholme, Toronto; *m.* 1881, Minnie Clarke, *d.* of late James Lowe, two *d.* *Educ.:* Upper Can. Coll., Toronto; Royal Military Coll., Kingston, Canada; served in 4th Batt. S. Staffordshire Regt., retiring with rank of Major, and joined the Royal Canadian Regt., 1888; served as A.D.C. to Earl of Aberdeen when Gov.-Gen. of Canada, and in the South African Campaign as A.D.C. to Field Marshall Earl Roberts (despatches twice, medal with four clasps, C.M.G., Brevet of Lieut.-Col.); A.D.C. to H.R.H. The Prince of Wales during his tour through Canada, 1901; chief staff officer, West. Ont. Com., 1 May, 1905. *Recreations:* tennis, golf, hunting. *Address:* Toronto. *Clubs:* Toronto, United Service, London, Eng.

DENNIS, William, Prop. of the Halifax *Herald:* *b.* Cornwall, Eng., 4 March, 1856; *s.* of John Dennis and Mary Ann Parnell; *m.* Agnes Miller; two *s.* five *d.* Came to Canada in 1873; joined staff of The Halifax *Herald*, as reporter when it started in 1875; now owns it; was for some years engaged in journalism in Winnipeg; raised through the medium of the *Herald*, over $15,000 for the Japanese Famine Fund in 1906. *Address:* *Herald* Bldg., Halifax, N.S. *Club:* Halifax.

DENNIS, Mrs., wife of above. Pres. of Halifax Local Council of Women for five years; active in work for the feeble-minded, children's hospital, home gardens for sch. children, supervised playgrounds, industrial educ. for girls. Asstd. in organizing V. O. N.; Pres. of Local Com., 6 yrs.; an active mem. of Bd. of Women's Foreign Miss. Socy (Presby.) *Address:* Halifax, N.S.

DERBYSHIRE, Hon. Daniel, Senator; *b.* Leeds County, Ont., 11 Dec., 1846; *s.* of Harry and Mary Derbyshire; *m.* Mary Ann Cawley; one *s.* *Educ.:* Farmersville High Sch., and Pub. Sch.; Reeve of Bastard and Burgess; Mayor of Brockville, and mem. of the H. of C. for Brockville; Pres. Eastern Ontario Dairyman's Assn. for 25 years. *Address:* Brockville, Ont. *Club:* Brockville.

DERICK, Miss Carrie Matilda, M.A. (McGill), Asst. Prof. of Botany, McGill Univ.; *b.* Clarenceville, Que., 14 Jan., 1862; *d.* of Frederick Derick, *g. d.* of Philip

Derick, a U. E. Loyalist, who came to Canada from Brunswick, N.Y., March, 1784, and Edna Cotton, descendant of one of earliest settlers in Clarenceville. *Educ.:* Clarenceville Acad., McGill Normal Sch. (P. of Wales Medalist), McGill Univ. (Logan Gold Medalist); later carried on research work at Maime Biol. Stu., Woods' Hall, Mass.; at the Royal Acad. of Science, London, Eng., and at Bonn Univ., Germany; apptd. demonstrator in Botany, McGill Univ., in 1891 (the first woman on the staff); in 1896, promoted to a lectureship; in 1906, Asst. Prof. of Botany; Chairman of the Montreal Local Council of Women; Vice-Pres. of the National Council of Wom. of Canada; Vice-Pres. of the Natural History Society, Montreal; Hon. Pres. of the Woman's Committee of the Missisquoi Co. Historical Society; member of the Women's Canadian Club, Montreal, of the Botanical Soc. of America, of the Am. Assoc. for the Advancement of Science, of the McGill Alumnae Society; Convener of the Section "Education" of the Quinquennial Congress of the International Council of Women, Toronto, June, 1909. *Publications:* "The Hold fasts of the Florideae, "Flowers of the Field and Forest;" many popular essays and sketches. *Address:* 85 Crescent St., Montreal; Clarenceville, Que. (summer).

DEROCHE, His Hon. George Edward, Judge of the County Court, Hastings Co., Ont.; Local Judge of the High Court; *b.* Newburg, Ont., 25 Jan., 1869; *s.* Edward A. Deroche and Clarice Eakins; *m.* Bertha E. McCulloch, *d.* of Rev. Robt. McCulloch, Methodist Minister; one *s.* two *d.* *Educ.:* Newburgh Academy and Osgoode Hall, Toronto; Taught shcool for three years; grad. in Law with honours from Osgoode Hall; practiced Law in Toronto for eleven years, when apptd. Judge; unsuccessful candidate for H. of C., Nov., 1904; has held every office in the gift of the Methodist Church. *Address:* Belleville, Ont.

DESBARATS, George J., B.Ap.Sc., C. E., Deputy Minister of Marine and Fisheries; *b.* Quebec, 27 Jan., 1861; *s.* of George E. Desbarats, and Lucianne Bosse; *m.* Lilian, *d.* of Sir Richard Scott; two *s.* two *d.* *Educ.:* Montreal Pub. Schs., Terrebonne Coll., and Montreal Polytechnic Sch. (grad. with honours, 1879, winning gold medal); entered the Govt. service as an engineer on canal construction and other public works; for some yrs. asst. to Mr. Page, the then Chief Engr. of Canals; Inspector of railway construction in British Columbia 1892-1896; engr. in charge of the building of the Galops Canal 1896-1899; for three yrs. employed in the Hydrographic Survey work on the St. Lawrence River; rebuilt and enlarged the Govt. shipyard at Sorel, 1901, and continued as agent for the Dept. there, until 1908, when he came to Ottawa as Acting Deputy Minister; Vice-Pres. of the Can. Soc. of Civil Engineers. *Address:* 330 Wilbrod St., Ottawa. *Club:* Rideau, Ottawa.

DESCARRIES, Joseph Adelard, K.C.; *b.* St. Timothee, Co. Beauharnois, Que., 7 Nov., 1853; *s.* of Pierre Descarries and Elizabeth Geugon; *m.* 1881, Marie Celine Ellmore, *e. d.* of Alfred Barcisse Le Pailleur, of Chateauguay; five *s.* one *d.* *Educ.:* McGill and Laval Univs.; studied law under Hon. Sir Alexander Lacoste; called to the Bar, 1879; has built up a large practice, holding several large legal appointments; Mayor of Lachine for many yrs. El. to Leg. Ass. for Jacques Cartier Co., 1892; resigned 1896, to run for H. of C., but unsuccessful; Pres. of the Equitable Mutual Fire Insur. Co. and St. Jean Baptiste Soc. of Lachine. *Address:* 50 Notre Dame St., W., Montreal.

DESJARDINS, Hon. Alphonse, P.C.; *b.* Terrebonne, Que., 6 May, 1841; *s.* of E. Desjardins and Josephine Panneton; *m.* Hotense Barsalon; five *s.* eight *d.* *Educ.:* Terrebonne Coll., Nicolet Seminary; an Advocate and Journalist; M.P. for Hochelaga, 1874-1893; Senator 1893-1896; Minister of Militia, 1896; Min. of Pub. Works, 1896; Mayor of Montreal, 1893-4. *Address:* Terrebonne, Chateau, Que.

DESJARDINS, Louis Edouard, M.D.; oculist; *b.* Terrebonne, Que., 10 Sept., 1837; *s.* of Edouard Desjardins and Josephine Panneton; *m.* 1867, Emilie Zaide, *s. d.* of Hubert Pare, of Montreal; two *s.* four *d.* *Educ.:* Masson Coll., Terrebonne; Nicolet Seminary, Victoria Coll. (grad. M.D., 1872); went to Europe to study ophthalmology 1870, and again in 1872; returned to Montreal, 1873, and founded the Ophthalmic Inst. of the Nazareth Asylum. One of the founders of the journal L'Union Medicale, L'Etendard, and Societe Medicale; has been surgeon-oculist to Hotel Dieu Hospital since 1870; prof. of Ophthalmology at the Sch. of Medicine and Surgery (now Laval Univ.), 1872-1908; mem. of the Societe Francaise D'Ophthalmologie of Paris since 1900; a great lover of music and has harmonized nearly one hundred popular Canadian airs. *Address:* 696 St. Hubert St., Montreal.

DESSAULES, Hon. Georges Casimir; Senator; *b.* St. Hyacinthe, Que., 29 Sept., 1827; *s.* of Hon. Jean Dessaules, and Rosalie Papineau, sister of Hon. L. J. Papineau; *m.* (1st) 1857, Emilie *d.* of Judge Mondelet, of Three Rivers (*d.* 1864); (2nd) 1869, Frances Louise, *d.* of Dr. Denis Leman; three *s.* four *d.* *Educ.:* St. Hyacinthe Seminary; mem. of St. Hyacinthe City Council, 1858-68; Mayor 25 yrs.; el. to Leg. Alss., 1897; called to Senate 12 March, 1907; a Roman Catholic. Liberal. *Address:* St. Hyacinthe, Que.

DE STRUVE, Hon. Nicholas; Officer of the Russian Foreign Office, Councillor of State, and Imperial Consul for Russia in Canada; *b.* Chateau Fall, nr. Reval, Esthonia, Russia, 5 July, 1862; *s.* of Bernhard de Struve, and Anna, Baroness de Rosen; *m.* Mortha Wisznewski; one *s.* two *d.* *Educ.:* Pub. Sch. of Odessa, Royal Coll., Stuttgart, Germany, Imperial Univ., St. Petersburg (Let. Doc). Commenced his career in the Dept. of Pub. Instruction, and was sent to Sweden, Denmark and Holland, to study the systems of educ.; on the completion of this mission, he was entrusted with the education of His Imperial Highness, Prince Alexander Romanoffsky, Duc of Leuchtenberg; transferred to Foreign Office, 1894; apptd. Vice-Consul at Frankfort-on-the-Main, Germany; cr. Councillor of State, 1900, and selected Minister of

Foreign Affairs, to establish the first Imperial Russian Consulate in Can.; arrived Canada, 1899; mem. of the Neophilogical Soc. of St. Petersburg, and Goethe Soc. of Weimar. The following decorations were conferred upon him: the Order of St. Stanislas and Medal of Merit for services under the Tzar Alexander III, by the Emperor of Russia; Order of Medjidie, from the Sultan of Turkey; Order of St. Daniel, from Prince of Montenegro; the Order of the Crown of Wenden, from the Grand Duke of Mecklenburg Schwerin; apptd. a Commander of the Order of St. Stanislas since coming to Can. *Address:* Russian Consulate, Montreal.

DE VARENNES, Hon. Ernest F., B.A. (Que. Seminary), B.C.L. (Laval Univ.); mem. of the Legis. Council of the Prov. of Quebec; *b.* Quebec, Que., 8 Feb., 1865; *s.* of Ferdinand de Varennes and Ide Bertrand *m.* 1890, Josephine Marie Louise, *d.* of Sheriff Cimon, of Murray Bay; two *s.* five *d.* *Educ.:* Quebec Seminary, Laval Univ., Que.; commenced practice as N.P. at Waterloo, Que.; Sec. and Treas. of Waterloo; Apptd. mem. of Que. Legis. Council, 1904; Dir. La Cie O. Poirier, Limitée, Quebec, Le Comptoir Mobilier Franco-Canadian, Montreal; Strathcona Fire Ins. Co. *Address:* Waterlee, Que. *Clubs:* Garrison, Quebec; Canadien, Montreal.

DE VEBER, Hon. Leverett George, M. D., Senator; *b.* St. John, N.B., 10 Feb., 1849; *s.* of Richard and Caroline De Veber; *m.* Rachael Frances Ryan; one *s.* *Educ.:* College Sch., and King's Coll., Windsor, N.S.; Univ. of Penna and Bartholomew's Hospital, London, Eng.; el. by accl. to Northwest Assem., 1898; re-el. 1902; was Govt. Whip in Assem.; on creation of Prov. of Alberta, 1 Sept., 1905, entered Cabinet as Min. without portfolio; called to Senate, 1906; Was for some yrs. surgeon to N.W.M. P.; is Health Officer for Lethbridge. *Recreations:* cricket, rowing, hunting, fishing, curling. *Addresses:* Lethbridge, Alta.; The Senate, Ottawa. *Clubs:* Chinook, Lethbridge; Elks, Ottawa.

DEVINE, Major J. A., D.S.O. Professor of Therapeutics and of Clinical Medicine, Manitoba Medical College; member of Council and Examiner in Materia Medica and Therapeutics, and Clinical Medicine, Univ. of Manitoba; Physician to Winnipeg General Hospital; Senior Physician to Isolated Wards, St. Boniface Hospital; *b.* 9 Nov., 1869; *s.* of Capt. Devine, late Deputy Surveyor-General, Ontario; unmarried. *Educ.:* Cardinal Manning's Coll. West Kensington, London; Trin. Coll., Dublin (M.A., M.B., B.Ch., B.A.O., M.D.); served South Africa with two Canadian Contingents, the 1st Canadian Mounted Rifles and the 2nd Canadian Mounted Rifles (despatches twice, D.S.O., Queen's medal with five clasps); Permanent Army Medical Staff (Canada); Principal Medical Officer, Military Districts 10 and 11 (Manitoba, N.W.T., and British Columbia); *Address:* Osborne Place, Osborne Street, Winnipeg. *Club:* Manitoba, Winnipeg.

DEVITT, John Henry, M.L.A.; *b.* Cartwright Tp., Durham Co., Ont., 1 Feb., 1851; *s.* of Thomas Devitt and Jane McKee; *m.* Elizabeth Watson; two *s.* three *d.* *Educ.:* Pub. Sch. of Cartwright. Dir., Cartwright Agric. Soc. for 32 yrs., and Pres. in 1907 and 1897; mem. of Sch. Bd. S. S. No. One, Tp. Cartwright for 15 yrs.; Sec.-Treas. of same for ten yrs.; mem. of Municipal Council of Cartwright, 1882-1890; Dept. Reeve, 1891-1895; Reeve, 1896; Co. Commr. Div. No. 6, Durham Co., 1897-1902, making 21 yrs. in municipal service; Warden of the United Counties of Northumberland and Durham, 1889; el. to Leg. Ass. for West Riding of Durham, 25 Jan., 1905; re-el. at g. e., 1908. *Address:* Blackstock, Ont.

DEVLIN, Hon. Charles Ramsay; Min. of Colonization, Mines and Fisheries for the Prov. of Quebec; *b.* Aylmer, Que., 29 Oct., 1858; *m.* 1893, Blanche, *d.* of Major de Montigny, of Ste. Scholastique, Terrebonne, Que. *Educ.:* Montreal Coll., Laval Univ.; for many yrs. engaged in newspaper work; M.P. for Co. of Ottawa, 1891-96; M.P. for Co. of Wright, 1896-97; Can. Commr', Ireland, 1897-1903; el. M.P. by accl. (British H. of C.) for Galway City, 1903; re-el. by accl., 1906; el. M.P. for Nicolet Co., 29 Dec., 1906; called to Ex. Coun. of the Prov. of Quebec, and sworn as Min. of Colonization, Mines and Fisheries, 17 Oct., 1907; resigned seat H. of C., and returned for Nicolet Co., in Leg. Ass. at bye-el., 4 Nov., 1907; re-el. at g. e., 1908. *Address:* 126 St. Augustin St., Quebec.

DEVLIN, Emmanuel B., K.C., B.A., M. A., B.C.L., M.P.; *b.* Aylmer, Que., 24 Dec., 1872; *s.* of Charles Devlin and Helen Roney; *m.* Cecile, *d.* of the late Hon. L. R. Masson, Senator, one time Minister of Militia for Canada, and Lieutenant-Governor of Quebec; one *d.* *Educ.:* St. Mary's Montreal, Mount St. Mary's, Derbyshire, England; McGill Univ., Montreal; practiced law in Montreal, 1895-1901; at the present time in the district of Ottawa, Hull; elec. to succeed Sir Wilfrid Laurier, as M.P. for Wright, 1905; re-elec. 1908. *Address:* 523 Besserer St., Ottawa.

DEWART, Herbert Hartley, B.A., K.C.; *b.* St. Johns, Que., 9 Nov., 1861; *s.* of Edward Hartley Dewart, D.D., and Matilda Hunt Dewart; *m.* Emma Smith, *Educ.:* Model School, Toronto Collegiate Inst., Toronto Univ., and Osgoode Hall Law Sch.; Examiner in English, Toronto Univ., 1886-1890; County Crown Attorney, York, 1891-1904; Pres. Young Men's Liberal Club, Toronto, 1889; an active political speaker; Liberal candidate S. Toronto, 1904. *Recreations:* fishing, golf. *Address:* 5 Elmsley Place, Toronto, Ont. *Clubs:* Toronto, Ontario, Hunt, Golf, Toronto; Rideau, Ottawa.

DEXTER, David; *b.* St. Thomas, Ont., 4 April, 1854; *s.* of Ransom and Margaret Dexter; *m.* Isabella McLachlin; two *s.* *Educ.:* St. Thomas, Ont.; Insurance and Loan business in earlier years, and Manager of a Loan Company afterwards; organized the Federal Life Assurance Co., in 1882; has been Managing Director of this Company since its organization, and for the past six years, Pres. also. *Recreations:* bowling and curling. *Address:* Hamilton, Ont. *Clubs:* Hamilton, Commercial, Royal Hamilton Yacht, Jockey, Hamilton; National, Toronto.

D'HELLENCOURT, Henri M. V. L.; *b.* Paris, France, 12 Sept., 1862; *s.* of Henri

Lefebvre d'Hellencourt, and Louise Kreusler; *m.* Louise Eugenie Belard. *Educ.:* Lycee Henri IV, du Coll. Millitaire St. Cyr. Previous to arrival in Can., 1891, was officer in French Army for ten yrs.; resided in Manitoba, 1891-1905. Ed. "*L'Echo" du Manitoba*, for eight yrs.; chief ed. "Le *Soleil*," Quebec since 1906.; del. to Imperial Press Conference, 1909. *Address:* Le Soleil, Quebec.

DICKSON, George, M.A.; *b.* Tp. of Markham, York Co., Ont., 1846; *m.* 1882, Mary H., *d.* of Capt. Thomas Fleck, of Hamilton, Ont. *Educ.:* Richmond Hill Gram. Sch., Markham, Whitby, and Toronto Univ.; Asst. Master of Chatham Gram. Sch., 1868; later on staff of Woodstock Coll.; Principal of Hamilton Coll. Inst., 1873-1885; Principal of Upper Can. Coll., 1884-1895; organized St. Margaret's Coll. for Girls, 1896, of which Mrs. D. became Lady Principal; mem. of the Senate, Toronto Univ., and of Knox Coll., for several yrs.; mem. of the Bd. of Trustees of St. Andrew's Coll. *Recreation:* golf. *Address:* St. Margaret's Coll., 144 Bloor St., E., Toronto.

DICKSON, Walter Brittain, M.L.A.; *b.* St. John, N.B., 26 Dec., 1847; *s.* of Richard S. and Eleanor Dickson; *m.* Margaret Hunter; four *s.* four *d.* *Educ.:* Kingston Gram. Sch., King's Co., N.B., and Sackville Academy; is engaged in the lumber business first elec. to the Provincial Legis. (N.B.), March, 1908. *Address:* Hillsborough, N.B.

DIGGS, Mrs. Annie L.; *b.* London, Ont., 1853; *m.* A. S. Diggs, Lawrence, Kan.; was chmn. of delegation from D. C., National People's Party Conv., Omaha, 1892 (first time a woman worker for temperance; speaker for People's Party in nearly every state and Territory; state librarian of Kan., 1898-1902; Ex-Pres. Kan. State Woman Suffrage Assn,; Pres. Kan. Woman's Press Assn.; lecturer on sociology; del. Internat. Cooperative Congress, Manchester, Eng., 1903; Peace Congress, Rouen, France, 1904. *Publications:* Little Brown Brothers; cont'b. to mags.; writer of short stories; asso. editor The *Advocate*, Topeka. *Address:* Topeka, Kan.

DIGNAM, Mrs. Mary Ella; *d.* of Byron Williams and Margaret Ellenor Ferguson, both U. E. Loyalists; *m.* John Sifton Dignam; two *s.* one *d.* *Educ.:* Paris, France, and Italy; Artist; Exhibitior in European and American Exhibitions; Pres. of the Woman's Art Association of Canada; mem. of New York Art Club, and International Art Club, London, Eng.; associate mem. Can. Soc. of Authors. *Publications:* criticisms and special articles on Art. *Address:* 284 St. George St., Toronto. *Clubs:* Toronto Lady's Club, Lyceum Club and Woman's Institute, London, Eng.

DIMOCK, Wilbert David, B.A.; Ed., Truro *News; b.* Onslow, N.S., 27 Nov., 1870; *s.* of Rev. D. W. C. Dimock, M.A., and Ellen Delaney Dimock; unmarried. *Educ.:* Truro, and Acadia Coll., Wolfville; for some yrs. principal of the North Sydney Acad., and of the Normal Schs. at Truro; apptd. Sec.-Treas. of the Can. Dept., at the Internl. Fisheries Exhn., London, 1883; agt. for N.S. at the Ind. and Col. Exhn., London, 1886; mgr. of the Maritime Provinces Exhn., Moncton, N.B., 1889; supt. of the Can. Sec. at the Jamaica Exhn., 1891; sec. of the Ca. Sec. at the World's Fair, Chicago, 1893; el. to the N.S. Ass. for Colchester at g. e., 1894; resigned June, 1896; returned to H. of C. for same constituency, 1896, but unseated 1897. *Address:* "Forest Lawn," Truro, N.S.

DINGMAN, William Smith; Ed. and prop. *Daily Herald*, Stratford, Ont.; Mayor of Stratford, 1909-10; *b.* Sarnia Tp., Lambton Co., Ont., 9 May, 1858; *s.* of Absalom and Emma Adelaide Dingman; *m.* Margaret E., *d.* of Rev. Dr. McDonagh; two *s.* one *d.* *Educ.:* Sarnia pub. and gram. sch.; of U. E. Loyalist descent, family having settled in Bay of Quinte dist., about 1783. A journalist; conducted Strathroy *Dispatch* until 1884; *Daily Sentinel*, Port Arthur, 1884-5; founded Daily *Herald*, of Stratford (1886 to present); Pres. of Can. Press Assoc., 1899; ten yrs. mem. and one yr. chmn. of Coll. Inst. Bd.; three yrs. alderman; elec. Mayor of Stratford, 1909. *Address:* 196 Cambria St., Stratford, Ont.

DINNICK, Wilfrid Servington; *b.* Guildford, Eng., 1876; *Educ.:* Elmfield Coll., Yorkshire, Eng.; came to Canada to assume position as Insp. of the Canadian Birkbeck Investment Security and Savings Co.; now mgr. of the Standard Loan Co. and Dir. of the Canadian Casualty Co. *Address:* 24 Adelaide St. E., Toronto; Clinton Ave., Deer Park, Toronto. *Clubs:* National, Albany, Toronto.

DION, Francois Napoleon, M.L.A.; *b.* Trois Pistoles, Que., 6 May, 1849; *s.* of Thomas Dion, and Mathilde Nadeau; *m.* (1st) widow of Elise Lebel; (2nd) Aurelie Fortin. A manufacturer of stoves and kitchen utensils. First el. to Leg. Ass., 1900; re-el. 1904, 1908; for many yrs. a mem. of the Fraserville Town Council; Pres. of the Ste. Jean Baptiste Soc. *Address:* Fraserville, Que.

DIONNE, Narcisse Eutrope, B.Sc., M. D., LL.D., Provincial Librarian of Quebec; *b.* St. Denis, Co. Kamouraska, Que., 18 May, 1848; *s.* of Narcisse J. Dionne and Elizabeth Bouchard; *m.* Marie Emma Bidegare; five *s.* one *d.* *Educ.:* Coll. Ste. Anne de la Pocatiere, Laval Univ.; practised medicine in Quebec, 1873-80; editor of *Courrier du Canada*, 1880-4; Federal License Inspector, 1884-5; editor of *Courrier* 1886-92, when apptd. Librarian of the Prov. Leg. *Publications:* Lives of "Jacques Cartier," "Champlain," and "Abbe Pamchaud," "Quebec under two flags," "New France from Cartier to Champlain," and many other historical works. *Address:* 29 Couillard St., Quebec.

DOBELL, William Molson; *b.* Quebec, 1867; *s.* of the late Hon. Richard Dobell and Elizabeth Frances Macpherson; *m.* 1895, Constance May, *d.* of Lieut.-Col. Sewell, of Quebec; four *s.* *Educ.:* Charterhouse Sch., Surrey Eng.; enter employ of the firm of Dobell, Beckett & Co., exporters of timber and lumber, founded by his father in 1856; admitted a partner 1895; took the leading part in the management of the firm on the death of his father in 1902, but retired 1907; mem. Que. Harbor Com. since 1903; Sch. Commr. and mem. of the Council of the Municipality of St. Colomba of Sillery, nr. Quebec; for several yrs. officer in the 8th Royal Rifles, of Quebec; retired with rank of Capt. *Address:* St. Louis Rd., Quebec. *Clubs:* Garrison, Turf, Quebec; Rideau, Ottawa; Montreal Hunt, Mount Royal, St. James', Montreal; Junior Athenaeum, London, Eng

DOHERTY, Hon. Charles Joseph, D.C.L.; LL.D., K.C., M.P.; *b.* Montreal, Que., 11 May, 1855; *s.* of Hon. Marcus Doherty, Judge of the Supreme Court, and Elizabeth O'Halloran; *m.* Catherine Lucy Barnard, *d.* of Edmund Barnard, K.C. *Educ.:* St. Mary's Coll., and McGill Univ., Montreal; grad. in Law, McGill Univ., 1876 (Elizabeth Torrence Medalist); admitted to the Bar, 1877; K.C. in 1887; apptd. Judge of the Superior Court, Prov. of Que., Oct., 1891; retired Nov. 1906; elec. M.P. for St. Ann's Division, Montreal, Oct., 1908; served as Captain in the 65th Batt., through the North West Rebellion, 1885; apptd. Professor of Civil Law, McGill Univ., 1800, which chair he still holds as well as the chair of International Law. *Address:* 282 Stanley St., Montreal. *Clubs:* St. James', University, Lafontaine, Montreal; Catholic Club, New York; Rideau, Ottawa.

DOHERTY, William; *b.* nr. Bradford, Ont., 21 March, 1841; *m.* 1870, Aggie, *d.* of Peter Depew, of Clinton, Ont.; six *s.* six *d.* Removed to Claude, Ont., 1856, where he worked on a farm and pursued his sch. studies at night; spent three yrs. in Petrolia; removed to Clinton, Ont., 1868, and estbd. a furniture and music store; now manfr. the "Doherty Organ." Mayor of Clinton for three yrs. *Address:* Clinton, Ont.

DOMVILLE, Lieut.-Col. Hon James, F.R.C.I., Senator; *b.* Belize, British Honduras 29 Nov., 1842; *s.* of Lt.-General James Wilson Domville, Royal Artillery and Fanny Blind Domville; *m.* 1867 to Ann Isabella, *d.* of the late William Henry Scovil, of St. John, N.B.; *Educ.:* Woolwich, Eng.; arrived in Canada, 1866; organized the 8th Hussars, which Regiment he commanded for 20 years, was one of the officers who accompanied Sir Wilfrid Laurier to England on the occasion of the late Queen's Jubilee (Medal); alderman for the City of St. John and Chairman of Finance Committee; founded the Free Public Library; was President of Kings Co. Board of Trade; elec. to the H. of C., 1872-1874; defeated 1882 by Hon. Geo. E. Foster, unsuccessful also in bye-elections and in general elections of 1887 and 1891; elec. 1896; defeated 1900; was four years chairman of the Standing Committee on Banking and Commerce; Apptd. to the Senate, 20 April, 1903; connected with many industries. Chairman General Oil Trades Co., of Canada Limited. *Recreations:* travel and science. *Address:* Rothesay, N.B. *Clubs:* Rideau, Laurentian, Ottawa; Military Institute, Montreal; Union Club, St. John.

DONALDSON, Lieut.-Col. the Rev. James Ball; *b.* Dublin, Ireland, 5 Aug., 1842; *s.* of William Alfred Donaldson and Mary Ann Ball; *m.* (1st) Elizabeth Lambert; (2nd) Janet Ann Wylie Bell, *d.* of Wm. Ralph Bell, M.D., *g. d.* of late William Bell, Brook House, Sutton, under White House Cliff, nr. Thirsk, Yorkshire and *g. g.* niece of Sir James Wylie, who was physician to Emperors Paul and Alexander of Russia. *Educ.:* Private Schs. in Dublin; arrived in Canada, May, 1868; served apprenticeship to late Pattison Jolly, Printer, Dublin; joined Royal Artillery in 1859; came to Canada when schools of Gunnery were organised in 1872; apptd. to Stores Branch, Militia Department, Ottawa, in 1883; Asst. Dir., Gen. of Ordnance and 2nd in command Ordnance Stores Corps, 1903; Dir. of Clothing and Equipment and Officer administering Ordanance Corps, Quartermaster General's Branch, Headquarter's Staff, 1904; retired after 49 years service, in 1908; Ordained Presbyter in Reformed Episcopal Church, and is now Rector of St. David's Parish; served as alderman for Rideau Ward, Ottawa, 1896-7-8; was chmn. Water Works Committee; was Secretary Treasurer of Canadian Artillery Association for 28 years, resigning on appointment to headquarters' staff. *Address:* 197 Mackay St., Ottawa.

DONEGALL, The Marchioness of (Violet Gertrude); *o. d.* of the late Henry St. George Twining, of Halifax, N.S.; *m.* 23 Dec., 1902, the 5th Marquess of Donegall (*d.* 13 May, 1904), heir Edward Arthur Donald St. George Hamilton, 6th and present Marquess, *b.* 7 Oct., 1903. *Address:* Isle Magee, Co. Antrim, Ireland.

DONLY, Augustine William; Canadian Trade Comr. to Mexico; *b.* Simcoe, Ont., 6 May, 1866; *s.* of the late Augustine James Donly and Maria Harrison; *m.* Ava Maria Brook. *Educ.:* Pub. and High Sch., Simcoe and Victoria Univ., Cobourg; High Sch. Teacher, Woodstock, Ont., 1889; merchant in Mexico 1889-1904; Canadian Trade Comr., Mexico, 1905-1909. *Recreations:* golf, gardening. *Address:* P. O. Box 91 B., Mexico, Mex. *Clubs:* Mexico Country; University, Mexico.

DONLY, Harrison B.; *b.* Simcoe, Ont., 4 Jan., 1862; *s.* of A. J. Donly, and Maria Harrison Donly; *m. y. d.* of the late Joseph Brook, "Elmhurst," Simcoe; two *s.* one *d.* *Educ.:* Public and High Schs., Simcoe, succeeded his father as editor and proprietor of the Simcoe *Reformer*, in 1881, and still continues as editor; helped to found the Canadian Wheelman's Association, in 1882, and was its Secretary-Treasurer for 18 years; editor and publisher "*The Canadian Wheelman*," from 1890 to 1898; Secretary of the Reform Association of Norfolk, 1884 to 1903; Pres. from 1903 to date; Liberal candidate in the general elec. 1904 and 1908, for the H. of C.; member of the Board of Education for Simcoe for 18 years; Chairman for two years; Pres., 1908-09, of the Weekly Section of the Can. Press Assn. *Recreations:* golf, gardening. *Address:* Simcoe. *Clubs:* Phoenix, Simcoe; Ontario and R.C.Y.C., Toronto.

DONNELLY, James J., M.P.; *b.* Tp. Greenock, Bruce Co., Ont., 14 Nov., 1866; *s.* of James Donnelly and Ellen Desmond; *m.* Julia C. McNat; three *s.* two *d.* *Educ.:* Pinkerton Public School; Reeve of Greenoch Tp. for two years, and a member for

Bruce County for four years; Warden of the Co. of Bruce, 1902; elected to the H. of C. for E. Bruce, in bye-elec., Feb., 1904; unsuccessful candidate in S. Bruce, g. e., Nov., 1904; elec. for S. Bruce in g. e., Nov., 1908; Catholic; Conservative. *Address:* Pinkerton, Ont.

DOUGALL, John Redpath, M.A.; Prop. the Montreal *Witness; b.* Montreal, 17 Aug., 1841; *s.* of John Dougall and Elizabeth Ridpath; unmarried. *Educ.:* High Sch. and McGill Univ.; Journalist since 1860; publisher of the Daily and Weekly *Witness*, and Editor and Publisher of other publications. *Address:* Montreal.

DOUGALL, Miss Lily; *b.* Montreal; *d.* of John Dougal, *g. s.* of John Dougal, of the Porter Hall, Paisley, Scot., and Elizabeth Redpath, *d.* of John Redpath, of Terrace Bank, Montreal; *Educ.:* Brooklyn and Edinburgh Univ.; since 1891, when she first wrote "Beggars all," has lived in Eng., except for the years, 1897-1903, when she resided in Montreal; obliged to leave on account of the climate. *Publications:* "Beggars all," "What Necessity knows," "Question of Faith," "The Madonna of a day," "A Dozen Ways of love," "The Woman Prophet," "The Earthly Purgatory," "The Spanish Dowry," "Paths of the Righteous." *Address:* East Undercliff, Exmouth, Eng. *Club:* University Club for Ladies, George St., Hanover Square, London, Eng.

DOUGHTY, Arthur, C.M.G., 1905; M. A., Lit.D. (Laval), F.R.Hist. S.; F.R.S.C., Dominion Archivist; *b.* Maidenhead, Berks; 2nd *s.* of William James Doughty, formerly of Grantham; widower. *Educ.:* Pub. Schs., Maidenhead; Eldon Sch., London; New Inn Hall, Oxon. Came to Canada, 1886, and entered the service of the Legal and Commercial Exchange at Montreal; apptd. clerk in Dept. of Inland Revenue, Que., 1896; Private Secretary to Minister of Public Works, 1897; Private Secretary to Treas. of Province, 1899; Joint-Librarian of Legis. of Province of Quebec, 1901-4; has devoted much time to the illumination of books on vellum. *Publications:*Life and Works of Tennyson, 1893; Rose Leaves, 1894; The Song Story of Francesca and Beatrice, 1896; Nugæ Canoræ, 1897; with Dr. Parmelee) The Siege of Quebec and the Battle of the Plains of Abraham (6 vols. 1901-2); Quebec under Two Flags, 1903; The Fortress of Quebec, 1904; documents relating to the Constitutional history of Canada (edited with Prof. Shortt), 1907; The Cradle of New France, 1908; contributor to the American Historical Review, Encyclopedia Britannica; The Battle of the Plains, 1898; mem. of Geographic Board of Canada, 1909. *Recreations:* lawn tennis, golf. *Address:* 168 Cobourg St., Ottawa; *Clubs:* Rideau, golf, Ottawa.

DOUGLAS, Campbell Mellis, V.C., M. D., L.R.C.P.; *b.* Quebec; *s.* of Dr. Geo. M. Douglas; *m.* Eleanor Annie McMaster, *niece* of late Sir Edward Belcher, R.N.; three *s.* one *d.* *Educ.:* St. John's; Laval Univ.; Edinburgh; joined 24th Regt., 1863; Medical Officer to expedition to Little Andaman Islands, 1867; Medical Officer in charge of Field Hosp. 2nd Riel expedition, 1885; retired 1882; *Decorated* for relieving 17 officers and men from a position of danger on the coast of Little Andaman Island. *Publications:* pamphlet relating to Boat Service of Vessels, papers on Physical Education, The Recruit, Nervous Degeneration, etc. *Recreations:* bicycling, boating. *Address:* Dunmow, Essex, Eng.

DOUGLAS, Howard; Commissioner of Dominion Parks; *b.* Halton Co., Ont., 8 May, 1853; *s.* of Thomas Douglas and Charlotte Ross; *m.* Alice Maud Johnson; three *s.* one *d.* *Educ.:* Waterdown, Wentworth Co.; on father's farm until twenty-one; kept general store in Bronte, Halton Co., for four yrs.; engaged in wood and coal business in Hamilton until 1882; in general cartage and coal business in Calgary until 1897; was for ten yrs. Supt., National Park, Banff; apptd. to present position, 1907. *Address:* Banff, Alta. *Club:* Ranchmen's, Calgary.

DOUGLAS, James, LL.D., B.A.; *b.* Quebec, Canada, 1837; *s.* of James Douglas, M.D., and Elizabeth Ferguson; *m.* 1860, Naomi Douglas; two *s.* four *d.* *Educ.:* Queen's Univ., Kingston,; Edin. Univ.; mem. of the Iron and Steel Inst. of Great Britain; the North of England Society of M. E.; the American Geographical Society, N.Y.; the Philosophical Society, Phil.; the Society of Arts, London; formerly Professor of Chemistry, Morrin College, Quebec; pres. and business manager of the Copper Queen Mining Company, Detroit Copper Company and others in Arizona, and of the Nacozari Copper Mining Company, Mexico; president of the El Paso and S.W.R.R., the El Paso and N.E.R.R., and the Nacozari R.R. Companies; twice president of the American Institute of Mining Engineers; president of the Can. Society of New York; representative of the U.S. at the Mining Congress in Paris, 1900; mem. and Vice-President, American Institute Mining Engineers, New York. *Publications:* Old France in the New World; Biography of Dr. T. Sterry Hunt, F.R.S.; Canadian Independence; Imperial Federation and Annextation; Untechnical addresses on Technical Subjects; a Cantor Lecturer, Society of Arts. *Recreation:* fishing. *Address:* 99 John Street, New York; Spuyten Duyvil, New York. *Clubs:* Century Association, Engineers, City, Westchester Country, New York.

DOUGLAS, Hon. James Moffat; Senator; *b.* Linton, Bankhead, Roxborough, Scot., 26 May, 1839; *m.* 1861, Jane, *d.* of Geo. Smith, Darlington, Ont. *Educ.:* Scot., and Toronto Univ., Knox Coll., Toronto and Princeton Sem.; ordained to the Ministry, 1865; was Pastor at Uxbridge and Cobourg Presbyterian Churches; a Missionary to India, and Chaplain to the British troops at Mhow, 1876-1882; returned to Canada, and became Minister at Brandon, Man., and at Moosomin, N.W.T.; retired from the Ministry, 1896, and devoted himself to farming; has been a mem. of the Ontario Board of Public Instruction; Inspector of Common Schs., Chairman of High School Board, and Pres. of Evangel. Alliance; elec. to H. of C., 1896-1900; called to the Senate, 8 March, 1906. *Address:* Tantallon, Sask.

DOUGLAS, J. M., M.P.; *b.* Lanark, Ont., 1868; *s.* of Rev. James Douglas, a pioneer Presby. Missionary to Western Can.; *m.* 1890, Miss Pickerton, of Glasgow, Scot. *Educ.:* Morris, Man. and Winnipeg; went west with parents in 1878; taught sch. in Man. for some years; entered mercantile life in 1886; removed to Edmonton, 1893; formed partnership with his brother, 1897, as gen. merchants in Strathcona; Pres. of Strathcona Bd. of Trade, two years; mem. of City Council two yrs.; first el. to H. of C., 1909, at bye-el., caused by death of Dr. McIntyre. *Address:* Strathcona, Alta.

DOUGLAS, William James, J.P.; *b.* Hamilton, N.Y., 28 May, 1846; *s.* of James S. Douglas, A.M., M.D., Ph.D.; *m.* Eliza Riordon, *d.* of Jeremiah Riordon, late Surgeon Royal Navy; three *s.* one *d.* Arrived in Canada, 1877; has been connected with the *Mail and Empire* since its inception; now General Manager; is a trustee of the Toronto General Hospital. *Address:* 62 St. Alban's Street, Toronto. *Clubs:* National and Albany, Toronto.

DOWNEY, Joseph Patrick, M.L.A.; *b.* Puslinch, Wellington Co., Ont., 17 Jan., 1865; *s.* of Patrick Downey and Miss McTague; *m.* 1893, Ellen Josephine, *d.* of Thomas Coghlan, of Guelph; four *c.* *Educ.:* Pub. Sch., Puslinch. At age of fifteen entered the service of the Guelph *Herald;* apptd. editor, 1885; el. to Ont. Legis., 9 May, 1902; re-el. 1905 and 1908; mem. of the C.M.B.A., A.O.U.W., I.O.F. *Address:* Guelph, Ont.

DREWRY, Edward Lancaster; *b.* London, Eng., 6 Feb., 1851; *m.* Eliza, *d.* of Capt. James and Sarah Ann Starkey; three *s.* four *d.* *Educ.:* St. Paul, Minn.; engaged in the brewing business at St. Paul; removed to Winnipeg, 1872; is now Pres. of the E. L Drewry Redwood Factories; mem. Winnipeg City Council, 1883-4; M.L.A. 1886-8; Pres. of Winnipeg Bd. of Trade, 1899; chairman of the local bd. of the Crown Life Insur. Co.; Vice-Pres. Havergal Coll. Co.; Vice-Pres. of the Western Implement Co.; Pres. Winnipeg Rifle Range Co.; Vice-Pres. Winnipeg Gen. Hospital; mem. of the Advisory Bd. of the Children's Home; a warm supporter of all manly sports. *Recreations:* Motoring, golf, boating. *Address:* "Redwood" Winnipeg. *Clubs:* Manitoba, Commercial, St. Charles Country, Winnipeg.

DREWRY, Frederick William; Vice-Pres. Winnipeg Bd. of Trade; *b.* Newport, Eng., 1855; *s.* of Edward and Caroline Drewry; *m.* Augusta E., *d.* of Col. A. R. Keifer, of St. Paul, Minn., U.S.A. *Educ.:* Pub. Sch. and Bus. Coll., St. Paul, Minn.; arrived Can., 1881; takes active interest in business and public affairs; Vice-Pres. Bd. of Trade; Past Pres., Winnipeg Exhibition Assn.; mem. Pub. Parks Bd.; mem. Roy. Soc. of Arts, London, Eng. *Recreations:* golf, motoring, travel. *Address:* "Redwood," Winnipeg, Man. *Clubs:* Manitoba, Commercial, Clef, St. Charles Country, Adanac, Travellers', Winnipeg.

DRUMMOND, Lady (Grace Julia); *b.* Montreal; *d.* of the late Alexander Davidson Parker and Grace Gibson; *m.* (1st) Rev. George Hamilton, M.A., of Quebec; (*d.* 1880); (2nd) 1884, Sir George Alexander Drummond, Senator, and Pres. of the Bank of Montreal (*d.* 1910). *Educ.:* Montreal; has taken an active part in all movements for the uplifting of women. One of the founders and first Pres. of Canadian Women's Club of Montreal, the first organization of its kind in Canada; a Dir. of the Women's Historial Soc.; also of the Home of Incurables, founded by Sir George, and conducted by the Sisters of St. Margaret; Mem. of the Ex. Committee of the Aberdeen Assn., of the Victorian Order of Nurses, and of the Advisory Bd. of the Parks and Playgrounds Assn. of Montreal; First Pres. of the Montreal Branch of the National Council of Women, and has taken great interest in this organization; an active mem. of the League for the Prevention of Tuberculosis; on occasion of visit to England in 1900, had the honour of being received by the late Queen Victoria; presented to the Duchess of Cornwall and York, the jewel furnished by the citizens' reception Committee on the visit of the Prince and Princess to Canada, in 1901. *Address:* 448 Sherbrooke St. W., Montreal; Gadshill, Cacouna, Que.

DRUMMOND, George Edward; Consul General for Denmark; *b.* Tawley, Irel., 21 Oct., 1858; *s.* of George, and Elizabeth Morris Soden Drummond; *m.* Elizabeth Foster, *d.* of the late Ignatius Cockshutt, of Brantford, Ont.; two *s.* two *d.* Arrived in Can., 1865. *Educ.:* Montreal. Estab. the firm of Drummond, McCall & Co., 1881; their iron and steel interests in Nova Scotia, New Brunswick, Quebec and Ontario, merged into the Canada Iron Corporation, Ltd., 1908; Pres., Montreal Bd. of Trade, 1904-5; Pres., Can. Manuf. Assn., 1904-5; Vice-Pres., Can. Mining Inst., 1908-9; Dir. of the Molsons Bank, of the Liverpool, London and Globe Insur. Co., the Canada Car Co., Ltd., the Canada Cement Co., Ltd.; mem. of the managing bd. of the Montreal General Hospital; Montreal Bd. of Trade rep. at the Con., Chambers of Com. of Empire, Montreal and London, Eng.; apptd. Consul Gen. for Denmark, 1909. *Publications:* "The Iron Industry in Canada;" "Fiscal and Imperial Defence questions." *Recreations:* fishing. *Address:* 15 Macgregor St., Montreal. *Clubs:* Mount Royal, St. James, Montreal, Canada, Montreal.

DRUMMOND, Thomas J.; *b.* Tawley, Ireland, 26 Sept., 1860' *s.* of George and Elizabeth Morris Soden Drummond; *m.* Edith Chetlain; two *s.* *Educ.:* Montreal; arrived in Canada with parents, 1865; joined Drummond, McCall Co., 1882; Pres., Lake Superior Corporation; Pres., Canada Iron Corporation, Ltd.; Dir., Royal Bank of Canada. *Address:* 512 Sherbrooke St., Montreal, and Montarville, St. Bruno, Que. *Clubs:* Mount Royal, St. James', Canada, Montreal; Toronto, Toronto.

DRURY, Brig.-Gen. Charles William, C.B., A.D.C., Colonel commanding Maritime Provinces; *b.* 18 July, 1856; *e. s.* of W. C. Drury, Newlands, and St. John, N.B.; *m.* 1880, Mary Louise, *d.* of James A. Henderson, D.C.L.; two *s.* four *d.* *Educ.:* St. John, N.B.; Lieut., 1874; Capt., 1881; Major, 1889; Lieut.-Col., 1899; Col., 1901; Commandant, R.S.A., Kingston, 1893; Asst. Inspector Artillery, 1898; Inspector Field

Artillery, 1901; served with the R.F.A., North West Rebellion, actions Fish Creek and Batoche (medal and clasp, despatches); South Africa, 1900 (despatches, brevet Colonel, Queen's medal, 3 clasps, C.B.) *Address:* Citadel, Halifax, N.S. *Club:* Halifax.

DRYSDALE, Hon. Arthur, K.C.; a Puisne Judge of the Superior Ct. of Nova Scotia; *b.* New Annan, Colchester Co., N.S., 5 Sept., 1857; *s.* of George Drysdale and Margaret Shearer; *m.* 1887, Carrie, *d.* of George P. Mitchell, of Halifax; one *d.* *Educ.:* New Annan pub. sch.; studied law at Windsor, N.S.; called to the Bar in Nova Scotia, 1883; removed to Halifax same yr., and is a mem. of different legal firms acquiring a extensive practice; el. to Legis. Assem., N.S., for Hants Co., 1891, and at succeeding g. e., apptd. Commr. of Pub. Works and Mines, 1901; apptd. to present position, 1907. *Address:* Halifax, N.S. *Club:* Halifax.

DUBEAU; Joseph Adelard, B.Sc., M.P.; *b.* St. Ambrose de Kildare, Joliette, Que., 25 March, 1873; *s.* of Joseph Dubeau, and Salomee Brulé; *m.* 1904, Eva Rivard, Three Rivers, Que. *Educ.:* Jolliette Coll.; studied law in office of J. M. Tellier, M.L.A. for Joliette; first elec. to H. of C., 1904; re-elec. 1908; Liberal. *Address:* Joliette, Que.

DUBORD, Hon. C. Eugene, M.L.C.; *b.* Champlain, Que., 16 Sept., 1856; *s.* of Louis Edouard Dubord, M.D., and Josephine Martineau; *m.* 1882, Marie Chabot, of Que.; two *s.* two *d.* *Educ.:* Com. Sch. of Champlain, Commercial Academy of St. Anne de la Perade.; commenced a grocery business in Montreal, and in 1898 started vegetable farming; apptd. to Que. Legis. Council, 1907, for La Salle Div.; Pres., Beauport Brewery Co., Island of Orleans Ry. Co., Que., Exhibition Co.; Pres., of the Agricultural Council of Quebec. *Address:* Beauport Rd., Quebec. *Club:* Garrison, Quebec.

DUBUC, Hon. Joseph, B.C.L. (McGill), L.L.D. (Tor.), late Chief Justice of Ct. of Kings Bench for Manitoba; *b.* Ste. Martine, Que., 26 Dec., 1840; *s.* of Joseph Dubuc and Phebie Garand; *m.* 1872, Marie Anne, *d.* of H. B. Henault, of St. Cuthbert, Que.; five *s.* five *d.* *Educ.:* Sulpician Coll., Montreal; admitted to Que. Bar, 1869; went to Manitoba, 1870; admitted to Manitoba Bar, 1871; el. to first Leg. Assem. of Man., 1870; Supt. of Cath. section of Prov. Bureau of Educ., 1872; mem. Ex. Com. of N.W.T. and Legal Adviser, 1872-4; Atty. Gen., Man., 1874; speaker of Leg. Assem., 1875-8; el. to H. of C., 1878; Judge of Queen's Bench, Man., 13 Nov., 1879; Chief Justice, 8 Aug., 1903; retired on full salary after 30 yrs. Judicial service. Nov., 1909; a mem. of the Council of Man. Univ., since its foundation in 1877, and Vice-Chancellor since 1888. *Address:* 72 Donald St., Winnipeg.

DUBUC, Julien Edouard Alfred; Managing Dir. and Sec., Chicoutimi Pulp Co.; *b.* St. Hugues, Bagot Co., Que.; *s.* of Joseph Alfred Dubuc and Marie Blanchard; *m.* 1892, Amie Marie, *d.* of Dr. J. M. Palardy, of St. Hugues; two *c.* *Educ.:* Sherbrooke Seminary; entered Sherbrooke Branch of Bank National at age of sixteen; apptd. mgr. of branch in Chicoutimi, 1892; became Mgr. Dir. and Sec. of Chicoutimi Pulp Co., 1897; became principal owner of the Chicoutimi Water-power Co., 1896; one of the chief organizers of the Chicoutimi Pulp Co.; Pres. of the Chicoutimi Waterworks and Electric Co. *Address:* Chicoutimi, Que.

DUCHARME, Guillaume Narcisse; Pres. La Sauvegarde Life Ins. Co.; *b.* Chateauguay, Que., 3 Jan., 1851; *s.* of Vincent Valiere Ducharme and Marie St. Denis; *m.* 1880, Marie Mathilde Delia, *d.* of Leon Rivet five *s.* one *d.* Clerk in gen. store, Quebec, until 1870, when removed to Montreal and entered firm of Jas. Williamson & Co.; Sec.-Treas. of the Sch. Municipality of St. Cunegonde, 1878-1884, when became postmaster; apptd. clerk and treas. of the Town 1884, but resigned 1893; mem. St.Conegonde (which became annexed to Montreal) Council, 1893-1899; Mayor, 1899-1902; Dir. of La Banque Provinciale du Can.; mem. Montreal Bd. of Trade and La Chambre du Commerce. *Ahdress:* 504 Lindsay Bldg., Montreal, Que. *Club:* Montreal.

DUCKWORTH, Rev. Henry Thomas Forbes, M.A., Oxon; *b.* Aigburth, Liverpool, Eng.; *s.* of Henry and Mary Jane Duckworth, of Chester, Eng.; *m.* Hope Holland, *d.* of the late Wellington Hunt, of Brantford, Ont. *Educ.:* Birkenhead Sch., and Morton Coll., Oxford; arrived in Can., 9 Nov., 1901; Postmaster of Merton Coll., 1893-6; Assistant Chaplain in Cypress, 1896-1901; Assistant Chaplain All Saints, Cairo, 1901; Professor of Divinity, Trinity Coll., Toronto, Ont., 1901; Dean of Residence, Trinity, 1903; Prof. of Classics, 1906. *Publications:* Greek Manuals of Church Doctrine; Pages of Levantine History. *Recreation:* Canoeing. *Address:* Trinity Coll., Toronto.

DUFF, Hon. James Stoddart; Min. of Agric. for the Prov. of Ont.; *b.* nr. Cookstown, Ont., 20 June, 1856; *s.* of John Duff, and Eliza Jane Stodders; *m.* Jane Bell, *d.* of the late John E. Stoddart, of W. Gwillimbury. *Educ.:* Pub. Sch. and Collingwood Coll. Inst.; a farmer; mem. of the Council of the tp. of Essa, since 1888; elec. to Leg. Ass. at g. e., 1898; re-el. at g. e., 1902, 1905, 1908; apptd. Min. of Agric. in the Whitney Govt., 6 Oct., 1908; re.el. by accl. *Address:* Cookstown, Ont.

DUFF, Hon. Lyman P., K.C., B.A., LL. B. (Toronto Univ.), Judge Supreme Court of Canada; *b.* Meaford, Ont., 7 Jan., 1865; *s.* of Rev. Charles Duff, M.A., and Isabella Johnson; *m.* Elizabeth Eleanor, *d.* of Henry Bird. *Educ.:* Toronto Univ.; called to Bar in 1893; Judge of Supreme Court of British Columbia, 1904; Judge of Supreme Court of Canada, 1906. *Address:* 413 Laurier Ave., Ottawa. *Clubs:* Union, Victoria; Vancouver; Rideau, Country, Ottawa.

DUGAS, Hon. Francois Octave, B.C.L., K.C., Judge of the Superior Court of the Province of Quebec; *b.* St. Jacques, Que., 12 April, 1857; *s.* of Aime Dugas, and Sophia Poirier; *m.* Marie Alex. Godin; two *s.* *Educ.:* St. Mary's College and McGill University, Montreal, Que.; B.C.L., McGill Univ., 1880; admitted to the Bar of Que., 1880; Town Councillor for Joliette, Que., 1890-1900; Crown Prosecutor from 1887 to 1892, and from 1897; K.C., 1898; mem. H. of C. for Montcalm, from 1900, until his appointment as Judge in Sept., 1909. *Address:* Joliette, Que.

DUGGAN, George Herrick; Consulting Engr., Dominion Iron and Steel Co., and Dominion Bridge Co.; *b.* Toronto, Ont., 1862; *s.* of John Duggan, Q.C., and Amelia Fulton; *m.* Mildred S. Stevenson; two *s.* one *d.* *Educ.:* Upper Can. Coll., and Ontario Sch. of Science; Engineering Department, Can. Pac. Ry.; Chief Engineer, Dominion Bridge Co., 1891 to 1901; Asst. to Pres., Dominion Iron and Steel Co.; Dominion Coal Co., Ltd., 1901 to 1903; was 2nd Vice-Pres. and General Manager, Dominion Coal Co. *Recreations:* yachting, winner Seawanhaka International Cup, 1896-97-98-99-1900 and 1901. *Address:* Montreal. *Clubs:* St. James', R. St. L. Y. C., Montreal; R. Cape Breton Yacht Club, Sydney, C.B.; R. Can. Y. C. Toronto, Ont.; R. Halifax Y.C. and Halifax Club, Halifax.

DUNBAR, Ulric Stonewall Jackson; *b.* London, Ont., Jan. 31, 1862; *s.* Alexander and Susannah Jackson Dunbar; *m.* Washington, Sept. 17, 1892, Mary John Davis. *Educ.:* common schs. in Canada and Rockwood Acad. Professionally engaged as sculptor since 1880; did figures for Atlanta, Buffalo and St. Louis exp'ns, for which received medals and diplomas; executed over 100 portrait busts, principally of prominent men, for U. S. Capitol and Corcoran Gallery of Art, Washington, State Capitol, St. Paul, Minn., Union Club, New York, etc.; also several monuments; bronze statue of late Gov. Alex. R. Shepherd for front of new Municipal Bldg., Washington. Served in Canada 3 yrs. in vol. service. Episcopalian-Theosophist.; mem. Nat. Art Assn., Soc., Washington Artists; Nat. Soc. Fine Arts. *Address:* 60 V. St., N. W., Washington.

DUNCAN, Norman; *b.* Brantford, Ont., 2 July, 1871; *s.* Robert Augustus, and Susan (Hawley) Duncan. *Educ.:* Univ. of Toronto; journalist 1895 to 1900; on the staff of the New York *Evening Post*, 1897-1900; Professor of Rhetoric, Washington and Jefferson Coll., 1901-04; Adjunct Professor of English Literature, Univ. of Kansas, 1906. *Publications:* "Doctor Luke of the Labrador;" "The Way of the Sea;" "The Soul of the Street;" "The Cruise of the Shining Light;" "Gowing down from Jerusalem;" "The Suitable Child"; "Dr. Grenfell's Parish;" "The Mother;" "The Adventures of Billy Topsail;" "Every man for Himself." *Recreations:* fishing. *Address:* North East Pa. *Club:* City, New York.

DUNCAN, Robert Kennedy, B.A., Prof. of Ind. Chemistry, Univ. of Kansas; *b.* Brantford, Ont., Nov. 1, 1868; *s.* Robert Augustus and Susan (Hawley) Duncan; *m.* 1899, Charlotte M. Foster. *Educ.:* grad. Univ. of Toronto, (with 1st class honors in physics and chemistry), 1892; follow in chemistry, Univ. of Chicago and Clark Univ. 1892-3; grad. student in chemistry, Columbia, 1897-8: Instr. physics and chemistry, Auburn (N.Y.) Academic High Sch., 1893-5; Dr. Julius Sach's Collegiate Inst., New York, 1895-8; The Hill Sch., Pottstown, Pa., 1898-1901; Prof. Chemistry, Washington and Jefferson Coll., 1901-6; Discoverer and patentee of new process for mfg. phosphorus. of a new low-melting glass and of processes of decorating glass; consultant in the chemistry of glass; contb'r to New York Evening Post, 1900; sent abroad by McClure's Mag., summer of 1901, to study radio-activity, by A. S. Barnes & Co., summer of 1903, for material for The New Knowledge; by Harper's Mag., 1905-6, to study relations of modern chemistry to industry; mem. Am. Chem. Soc., A. A. A. S., Kan. Acad. Science, Sigma Xi; fellow Chem. Soc. of London. *Publications:* The New Knowledge, 1905, and numerous articles in Harper's Monthly. *Editor:* New Science Series, *Address:* Lawrence, Kan.

DUNLOP, Hon. John, K.C.; Superior Court Judge; *b.* Clober, Stirlingshire, Scot.; *m.* 1863, Eleanor, *d.* of the late David Bellhouse; two *s.* three *d.* *Educ.:* Edinburgh Academy, Edinburgh Univ., McGill Univ., Montreal; arrived in Can., 1857; admitted to the Bar, 1861; apptd. a Puisne Judge of the Superior Ct. of the Prov. of Que., 1894; Batonnier of the Bar of Montreal, 1891-2. *Address:* 200 Peel St., Montreal. *Clubs:* Mount Royal, University, Montreal.

DUNN, Rt. Rev. Andrew Hunter, M.A. (Camb.), Lord Bishop of Quebec; *b.* Saffron Walden, Essex, Eng., 16 Oct., 1839; *s.* of Hannehal Dunn and Mary Ann, *d.* of William Hunter, Alderman, Sheriff and Lord Mayor of London; *m.* Alice, *o. d.* of William Hunter, of Parley Lodge, Croydon; five *s.* two *d.* Arrived Can., Sept., 1892; Curate of St. Mark's, Notting Hill1864-70; Curate of Acton, 1870-1872; vicar of All Souls, Acton, 1872-92; cons. Lord Bishop of Quebec, 1 Sept., 1892; Hon. D. D. of Univ. of Bishop's Coll., Lennoxville, Que., 1893; Hon. D.C.L.; Vice-Pres. of the Univ. of Bishop's Coll., Lennoxville, 1892-1906; Pres., 1906. *Publications:* "Helps by the Way;" "Our Church Manual;" "Holy Thoughts for Quiet Moments;" "Our Only Hope." *Address:* Bishopthorpe, Quebec.

DUNSMUIR, Hon. James; *b.* Vancouver, Wash., U.S.A., 8 July, 1851; *e. s.* of the late Hon. Robert Dunsmuir and wife, both natives of Scotland; *m.* 1876, Laura Miller, *d.* of W. B. Suoles, of North Carolina; nine *c.* *Educ.:* Nanaimo, B.C., and Dundas, Ont.; later took a course at the military sch., Blackburg, Va., U.S.A.; at age of seventeen worked in the several depts. of the extensive mining operations carried on by his father, in order to master all the details; Pres. and chief stock-holder of the Wellington Colliery Co., which owns and operates coal mines at Wellington, Comox, and Alexandria, Vancouver, Island, and in which 3,500 men are employed; was Pres. and chief stock-holder of the E. and N. Railway, previous to its transfer to the C.P.R.; large real estate interests in Ladysmith, Cumberland, Newcastle and Nanaimo; first el. to the B.C. Legis. at g. e., 1898, and held seat until Nov., 1902, Then he resigned; called upon to form an admn., and was Premier and Pres. of the Council from June 15, 1900, until his resignation; apptd. Lieut.-Gov. of B.C. in succession to Sir Henry Joly, Lotbiniere, 11 May, 1906; resigned Nov., 1909. *Address:* Victoria, B.C. *Club:* Union, Victoria.

DUPUIS, Nathan P., M.A., F.R.S.C.; Professor of Mathematics and Mechanism, and Dean of Practical Science Faculty,

Queen's Univ., Kingston; *b.* Frontenac Co., 1836; father a French Canadian of Norman stock; mother of English and Irish extraction, *d.* of a united empire loyalist; *m.* 1861, Amelia A. McGinnis of Watertown, N.Y.; one *s.* one *d.* *Educ :* Queen's Univ.; private study; has taught almost continually since about eighteen years old, with the exception of three years spent in acquiring a knowledge of handicraft; began teaching in Queen's Univ., 1867, and for thirteen years taught the subjects of chemistry and natural science to both arts and medicals; is a first-class mechanic, and has built several (all different) and peculiar astronomical clocks; is somewhat of an artist, and a fair performer on the violin. *Publications:* Treatise on Geometrical Optics, 1868; Geometry of Point, Line, and Circle, 1889; Principles of Algebra, 1893; Elements of Syn. Solid Geometry, 1893; Elements of Trigonometry for Practical ScienceStudents, 1902; numerous periodical articles. *Recreations:* principally boating, wheeling, and travelling. *Address:* 144 University Av., Kingston, Ont.

DURNFORD, George; chartered accountant; *b.* Toronto, Ont., 1838; *s.* of the late Capt. Durnford of His Majesty's 68th Regt., Durham Light Infantry, and Augusta Sewell, *d.* of the late Stephen Sewell, K.C., of Montreal; *m.* 1856, Melanie, *o. d.* of the late George Vardon, at one time Supt. of Indian Affairs; four *d.* *Educ.:* private schs., Montreal; in employ Lomis & Sewell, shipbuilders Quebec, 1854-1856; entered Up. Canada Bank, Montreal; later Bank of British North America, and Mgr. Kingston Branch, 1874-1880; Sec.-Treas. Canada Cooperative Assn., 1880-1886; estb. himself in business as chartered accnt., 1886; mem. Montreal Bd. of Trade; a J.P.; Treas. Anglican Synod of the Diocese of Montreal; Treas. Homeopathic Hospital; Historical Landmark Assn., Numismatic and Antiquarian Soc. *Recreation:* Sketching. *Address:* "The Sherbrooke," Montreal, Que. *Club:* Junior Conservative, London, Eng.

DU VERNET, Rt. Rev. Frederick Herbert, D.D., Bishop of Caledonia; *b.* Hemmingford, Que., 20 Jan., 1860; *s.* of Rev. Canon Edward Du Vernet, M.A., and Frances Eliza Ellegood; *m.* Stella Yates, *d.* of Honatio Yates, M.D., Kingston, Ont.; one *s.* one *d.* *Educ.:* King's Coll., Windsor, N.S.; Univ. of Toronto, and Wycliffe Coll., Toronto; Mission preacher for Diocese of Montreal, 1883-1885; Professor of Practical Theology, Wycliffe, 1885-1897; Rector, St. John's Toronto Junction, 1895-1904; Bishop of Caledonia, 1904; *Publications:* Editorial Secretary of Can. C. M. S., 1896-1904; Editing "Can. C. M. S., Gleaner." *Address:* Prince Rupert, B.C.

DYDE, Samuel Walters, M.A., D.Sc., LL.D.; *b.* Ottawa, Ont., 11 March, 1862; *s.* of Samuel Dyde, and Jane Christina Wardrope; *m.* Jane Farrell, *d.* of the late J. W. Farrell, Detroit, Mich.; two *s.* two *d.* *Educ.:* Ottawa Coll. Inst., Queen's Univ., and in Germany; Prof. in Univ. of N.B., 1886-9; Prof. in Queen's, Kingston, 1889, up to the present. *Publication:* Hegel's Philosophy of Right (translation); magazine articles. *Recreations:* tennis, camping, curling. *Address:* Queen's College, Kingston.

DYKE, Joshua, B.A., B.D.; *b.* Wednesfield, Wolverhampton, Staffordshire, Eng., 15 Sept., 1849; *s.* of John Dyke and wife; *m.* (1st) Bella, *d.* of the late John Park, of London, Ont.; (2nd) Sophia, *d.* of John Fox, of Chatham, Ont.; two *s.* two *d.* *Educ.:* Pub. Schs., and Divinity Coll.; transferred to Canada by the British Methodist Conference; ordained at Toronto, 1874, and stationed many points in Ontario; retired from the Ministry and settled in Fort William, 1890; was mem. of the Municipal Council; Mayor for several yrs.; active mem. of Union of Can. Municipalities; takes a leading part in charitable works. *Address:* Fort William, Ont.

DYMENT, Albert Edward, Hon. Lieut.-Col., 77th Regt., *b.* Lynden, Wentworth County, Ont., 23 Feb., 1868; *s.* of Nathaniel Dyment and Annie McRae; *m.* Edith Frances Chapman, of Hamilton, Ont.; one *d.* *Educ.:* Barrie Coll. Inst., and Up. Can. Coll.; in 1896, was elec. to the H. of C. as a supporter of the Liberal Covernment, remaining until 1908; in the lumber business in Algoma for 15 years; afterwards moving to Toronto; entered 1909, into stockbrokerage business in the firm of Dyment, Cassels & Co.; Director of a number of financial and industrial companies. *Recreations:* Thorobred horse breeding and racing. *Address:* The Dale, Toronto, Ont. *Clubs:* Toronto, Mount Royal, Montreal; Rideau, Ottawa.

E

EARLE, William Edward; Mgr. Western Union Telegraph Co., North Sydney, N.S.; *b.* St. John's, Nlfd., 29 April, 1847; *s.* of H. and C. Earle, Dartmouth, Devon, Eng.; *m.* Eliza Primrose Hadley of Mulgrave, N.S.; two *s.* two *d.* *Educ.:* Church of England Acad., St. John's; arrived in Can. in 1869; in 1852 entered the service of the New York, Newfoundland and London Tel. Co., at St. John's, contemporary with the laying of the first Atlantic Cable in that yr., and was present at the celebration of that event held at St. John's; apptd. mgr. at Brigus repeating station in 1862, remaining there till the second Atlantic cable was laid in 1866; was at Heart's Content, Nfld., and acted as sec. for Cyrus W. Field on board the Great Eastern, and received his personal thanks for services during the first two weeks' rush of traffic. In 1866 apptd. mgr. at Grandy's Brook, Nfld, repeating station and promoted to mgr. at Placentia, Nfld. cable station in 1868; promoted asst. mgr. of main cable station at Port Hastings, N.S., 1869; in 1875, New York, Nlfd., and London Tel. Co., amalgamated with Anglo-American Cable Co., lines and staff of former in Cape Breton passing under control of latter; in August, 1875, the Western Union Tel. Co. assumed control of lines and staff in Cape Breton and moved their headquarters from Port Hastings, N.S., to North Sydney, W.F.; apptd. mgr., 1899. *Address:* Pleasant St., North Sydney.

EASTWOOD, Miss Alice, F.A.A.S.; *b.* Toronto, Ont., Jan. 19, 1859; *d.* Colin Skinner and Eliza Jane Gowdey; *Educ.:*

E. Denver High Sch., 1879; Teacher E. Denver High Sch., 1879-89; curator of herbarium, Calif. Acad. of Sciences, since 1892; Fellow A. A. A. S., Calif. Acad. of Sciences. *Publications:* Popular Flora of Denver, Colo., 1893; Popular Flora and Pacific Coast Edit., Bergen's Botany, 1897 Popular Flora and Rocky Mountain Edit., Bergen's Botany, 1900; Hand-Book of Trees of California, 1905; also writer of many papers on systematic botany and articles for scientific mags. *Address:* 2705 Hearst Av., Berkeley, Cal.

EATON, Rev. Arthur Wentworth Hamilton, D.C.L.; *b.* Kentville, N.S.; *s.* late William and Anna Augusta Willoughby Hamilton; unmarried. *Educ.:* Harvard; Ordained Deacon, 1884, priest, 1885, in New York; Priest in charge of Parish, Chestnut Hill, Mass., 1885-6. *Publications:* The Heart of the Creeds; Historical Religion in the Light of Modern Thought, 1888; Acadian Legends and Lyrics, 1889; Letter Writing, its Ethics and Etiquette, 1890; The Church of England in Nova Scotia and the Tory Clergy of the Revolution, 1891; Tales of a Garrison Town (with Craven Langstroth Betts), 1892; College Requirements in English, 1900; also many poems, historical monographs and mag. articles. Edited, with introductions, Recollections of a Georgia Loyalist, written in 1886 by Mrs. Elizabeth Lichtenstein Johnston, 1901; Pope's "Rape of the Lock," 1901; Arcadian Ballads, 1905; Poems of the Christian Year, 1905; The Lotus of the Nile and other Poems, 1907. *Address:* 20 E. 50th St., New York.

EATON, Seymour; *b.* Epping, Ont., 1859; *m.* Jan. 15, 1884, Jennie V. Adair, Winnipeg, Manitoba. Resident Boston, 1886-92; founder Booklovers and Tabard Inn libraries in U.S. and Great Britain and of The Booklovers Magazine; for 5 yrs. Dir. Drexel Inst.; daily contb'r Chicago Record, 4 yrs. *Publications:* Dan Black Editor and Proprietor; The Roosevelt Bears; The Teddy Bears Musical Comedy; The Telepath (drama); Sermons on Advertising; also several coll. text-books. Creator of the famous Teddy Bears. *Address:* Lansdowne Pa.

ECREMENT, Arthur, B.A., M.P.; *b.* St. Gabriel de Brandon, 29 June, 1879. *Educ.:* Montreal College and Laval Univ., Montreal; Secretary for five years to Hon. R. Dandurand, Speaker of the Senate; Secretary of the Liberal organization of the District of Montreal; first el. to H. of C., 1908. *Address:* Montreal.

EDWARDS, John Wesley, B.A., M.D., C.M., M.P.; *b.* Tp. Storrington, Co. Frontenac, Ont. 25 May, 1865; *s.* of George Edwards, Co. Norfolk, Eng., and Elizabeth Jane Lyon, of U. E. Loyalist descent, Frontenac, Ont.; *m.* Hester Jane, Purdy, Frontenac Co.; one *s.* four *d.* *Educ.:* Public Sch., Sydenham High Sch., Ottawa Normal Sch., Queen's Univ., Kingston, Ont.; School Teacher for 10 years; Co. Clerk, Frontenac, 10 years; Gaol Surgeon, two years; elec. to the H. of C., Oct., 1908, as Liberal Conservative; Methodist. For many years Sec.-Treas. of the Tp. of Kingston Agricultural Society. *Address:* Cataraqui, Ont.

EDWARDS, Hon. William Cameron, Senator; *b.* Tp. Clarence, Russell, Ont., 7 May, 1844; *s.* of the late William Edwards, of Portsmouth, Eng., who came to Canada about 1820, and Ann Cameron, a native of Fort William, Scot.; *m.* Jan., 1885, Catherine M., *e. d.* of the late Wm. Wilson, Cumberland, Ont. *Educ.:* Grammar Sch., Ottawa; an extensive lumber manufacturer, and stock raiser; has taken a practical interest in agriculture; for many years Pres. Russell Agric. Society; is a Director Canadian Bank of Commerce, Trusts Corporation, Toronto, and other companies; established the lumber firm of W. C. Edwards Co., in 1868; an unsuccessful candidate for H. of C. in Russell, 1882; elec. 1887; seat declared void, but was re-elec., and again in 1891-1896 and 1900; called to the Senate, 17 March, 1903. *Address:* Ottawa, *Clubs:* Rideau, Ottawa.

EDWARDS, Gordon C.; *b.* Thurso, Que., 17 Nov., 1867; *s.* of John C. Edwards and Margaret Cameron; *m.* Edna S. Meighen, of Perth, Ont.; one *s.* one *d.* *Educ.:* Thurso Sch., and Ottawa Coll. Inst. Commenced in lumber industry with the Canada Lumber Co., of Carleton Place, Ont., later joined firm of W. C. Edwards & Co., Ltd., Ottawa; now mgr. of Company's New Edinburgh Mills. Pres. of the Capital Planing Mill Co., Ottawa; Treas. of the Library Bureau of Canada; dir., Cobalt Lake Mining Co., and many other similar concerns. First Pres. of the Canadian Lumbermen's Assn., and now one of Directors; Pres. of the Y. M. C. A., Ottawa; dir., Perley Home, Ottawa. *Address:* 55 MacKay St., Ottawa. *Clubs:* Rideau, Laurentian, Golf, Country, Hunt, Ottawa.

EDYE, Lieut.-Col. Lourenco; *b.* Rio de Janeiro, Brazil, 1848; *m.* Clara Frances, *o. d.* of the late Richard Willoughby Laws; one *s.* *Educ.:* England and France; joined Royal Marines Light Infantry, as second Lieut., 1866; promoted Lieut., 1867; Capt., 1881; brevet Major, 1887; Major, 1888; brevet Lieut.-Col., 1894; Lieut.-Col., 1895, retired from service, 1898; served in China, 1869-1872, on board Her Majesty's Ship "Ocean," bearing the flag of Vice-Admiral Sir Henry Keppel, K.C.B.; served on staff of batt. of Royal Marines during Egyptian campaign, 1882, and received the Egyptian medal, clasps for Tel-el-Kebir, Khedive's Bronze Star; also served in the Eastern Soudan, 1884-5; was mem. of Naval Intelligence Dept., and is barrister-at-law of the Middle Temple, Eng.; arrived Can., 1899; apptd. Comm. of the Trust and Loan Co., of Can., at Toronto, 1899; apptd. Commissioner at Montreal, 1900, which position he now occupies; mem. Montreal Bd. of Trade. *Address:* 131 Stanley St., Montreal, Que. *Clubs:* St. James, Montreal; United Service, London, Eng.

EILBECK, Robert James; Sheriff of the Yukon Territory; Marshal, Exchequer Court, Yukon Admiralty Dist.; *b.* Newcastle Ont., 20 June, 1859; *s.* of James Eilbeck and Christina Eilbeck; *m.* Annie Vanderwater; one *s.* one *d.* *Educ.:* Newcastle, 1865-6, was newsboy on G. T. Ry.; lived with uncle on farm in Zorra, Oxford Co., Ont., 1867-8, in 1868 became telegraph operator and asst. postmaster at Newcastle; promoted to mgr. of Dom. Telegraph Company's office at Belleville, Ont.; promoted to mgr.

of office at Kingston, Ont., in the winter of same yr.; in 1880, built steamer grain elevator at Kingston and was actively engaged in the grain trade for five yrs. In 1886, went west and was engaged in mining in Arizona, U.S.A.; 1892, agent for the Crawford Gold Mill, a pulverizor at Helena, Montana, U.S.A.; 1895, agent for the Crawford Stamp Mill for the whole of the Western States, including Old Mexico; in 1894, went on prospecting trip through Yellow Head Pass in Rocky Mountains; apptd. by Dom. Govt. as Sec. to Royal Com. to investigate into Canadian Penitentaries, 1896; apptd. to present position as Sheriff of the Yukon Territory and Marshal of the Exchequor Ct., Yukon Admiralty Dist., 1899. *Publications:* "Government Ownership of Public Utilities"; "Action Organization Remedy." *Recreations:* baseball, curling. *Address:* Dawson, Y.T. *Clubs:* Zero, Dawson Amateur Athletic Assn.

ELIOT, Lieut.-Col. Charles Algernon; *b.* Fort George, North Britain, 9 March, 1857; *s.* of Capt. William H. Eliot, formerly 15th Foot; *m.* Frances Ellen Wood Hamilton; two *s.* two *d.* Arrived in Canada, 1859; in Bank of Montreal service. *Recreations:* fishing, golf. *Address:* 148 Elgin St., Ottawa, and Evandale Cottage, Fernbank, Brockville, Ont. *Clubs:* Rideau, Golf, Ottawa.

ELLEGOOD, Rev. Jacob, B.A., D.C.L.; *b.* near Fredericton, N.B., March, 1824; *s.* of Margaret and Jacob Ellegood; widower. *Educ.:* King's Coll., N.B.; clergyman; Rector of Church of St. James' the Apostle, Montreal; associated as Rector with the building of five places of worship besides sch. buildings, parsonages; travelled extensively; visited Egypt, Palestine, Constantinople, Asia Minor, Athens, Rome, etc. lectured on these countries; been upwards of 61 years in the Ministry; said to be the oldest rector in Canada; was one of the visiting clergymen at Point St. Charles, in 1848, when thousand of Irish immigrants died of ship fever; the deaths followed so quickly that 6000 were burried in one grave; seven Anglican clergymen gave up their lives in their devotion of these friendless strangers. *Recreation:* golf. *Address:* 697 St. Catherines St., Montreal. *Club:* Dixie Golf, Montreal.

ELLIOT, James; Gen. Mgr. of the Molson's Bank; *b.* Montreal Que., 2 June, 1840; *s.* of Andrew Elliot. *Educ.:* Montreal High Sch.; entered the service of Molson's Bank, at age of 19, and worked through the various grades until assuming his present position of General Manager. *Recreations:* books, pictures, horticulture and gardening. *Address:* 515 Cote des Neiges Road, Westmount, Que.

ELLIOTT, Dawson Kerr; *b.* Pakenham. Ont., 11 July, 1853; *s.* of John and Margaret Elliott; *m.* Mary Alice McCreary; four *s.* four *d.* Entered into the dry goods business at Arnprior, Ont., 1871; settled in Winnipeg, 1879, and with the late R. J. White, founded the wholesale dry goods business of which he is now President. *Address:* 35 Kennedy St., Winnipeg, *Club:* Manitoba, Winnipeg.

ELLIOTT, John Campbell, D.C.L., M.L.A., Barrister; *b.* Ekfrid, Ont., 25 July, 1872; *s.* of George Campbell Elliott, and Jane Gunn Elliott. *Educ.:* Glencoe, Ont., and Osgoode Hall, Toronto; grad. with honours from Osgoode Hall, in 1898; practiced law in Glencoe since that date; solicitor for the County of Middlesex; Dir. of the Equity Life Ins. Co.; elected to the Ontario Legis., 8 June, 1908. *Address:* Glencoe, Ont.

ELLIOTT, Rev. John Henry; *b.* Trafalgar, Ont., 6 Mar., 1853; *s.* William and Mary (Kentner) Elliott; *m.* Beulah Clemence. *Educ.:*Brampton, Ont. High Sch.; studied theology under Dr. Robert Boyle in Can.; Gen. Sec. Y.M.C.A., Augusta, Ga., 1877-9, Nashville ,1879-81, Albany, 1881-3, Minneapolis, 1883-93; evangelist with Moody at Columbian Exp'n meetings, 1893; Ordained to Presby'n Ministry, 1894; asso. Pastor Central Presby'n Ch., Rochester, N.Y., 1896-8; Pastor 34th St. Reformed Ch., New York, 1898-1903; evangelistic work under Presby'n Gen. Assembly, 1904-7; Trustee United Soc. Christian Endeavor; twice pres. New York Christian Edneavor, *Publications:* Notes and Suggestions for Bible Readings, 1877; Outline Bible Studies and Bible Readings, 1883; Workers Weapon, 1895; Brook in the Pasture, 1903. *Address:* 219 S. Kenilworth Av., Oak Park, Ill.

ELLIOTT, William, M.B., M C P & S., M. L.A.; *b.* Mitchell, Ont., 1863; *s.* of James Elliott, and Eleanor Durnin; *m.* Jennie M. Carter. *Educ.:* Mitchell High Sch. and Toronto Univ.; grad. in medicine, 1893; removed to the N.W.T.; elected to the Legislature, 1898; re-elec. 1902, 1903, 1905, and 1908; mem. of the Government of Premier Haultain, as Minister of Agriculture, 1903-1905. *Address:* Wolseley, Sask. *Clubs:* Assiniboia, Regina, Sask.

ELLIS, James Fraser, M.D., M.L.A.; *b.* Upper Stewiacke, N.S., 11 June, 1870; *s.* Wm. Ellis and Margaret Ellis; *m.* Ethel, *d.* of Alexander Anderson, of Sherbrooke, N.S.; one *s.* one *d.* *Educ.:* Pub. Schs., Western Univ.; left home when 18 years of age for Canadian North-west; spent five yrs. in Manitoba; taught school and homesteaded; graduated in medicine with honours in 1898; returned same yr. to N.S., settled in Sherbrooke, and was elec. by acclamation to the local Legislature in 1904; re-elec. in 1906; prominent in Masonic circles, also an Odd Fellow. *Address:* Sherbrooke, N.S.

ELLIS, Hon. John Valentine; Senator; *b.* Halifax, N.S., 14 Feb., 1835; *s.* of Michael Ellis and Margaret Walsh; *m.* 1864, Mary Caroline, *e. d.* of S. W. Babbitt; five *s.* two *d.* *Educ.:* Halifax, N.S.; editor of St. John (N.B.) Daily *Globe* since 1861; elec. to Provincial Legislature of N.B., 1882 and 1886; and H. of C., 1886-90, 1896-1900. *Publications:* New Brunswick as a Home for Immigrants; Address on Canada before the Canadian Club, Boston; and on Reciprocal Relations with the United States. *Recreations:* fishing, golf. President of the Natural History Society of N.B. *Address:* The Senate, Ottawa; St. John, N.B. *Clubs:* Union, St. John; Rideau, Ottawa.

ELLIS, Philip William; *b.* Toronto, Ont, 11 Sept., 1856; *s.* of William Henry Ellis, C.E., Liverpool, Eng., and Susan Jane Ellis, of Cambletown Isle of Man; *m.* Elizabeth Kate Gooderham; two *s.* four *d.* *Educ.:*

Model and High Schs., Toronto; President, Canadian Manufacturers' Association, 1901; Treasurer and Vice-Chairman Ontario Power Commission; was mem. of the Hydro Electric Commission; Deputy Chairman Queen Victoria Niagara Falls Commission; Pres., Central Canada Manufacturers; Montreal Fire Insurance Co.; Westmount Silver Mining Co., and Ellis Silver Mining Co., of Slocan; President P. W. Ellis Co., Ltd. *Recreations:* golf, curling. *Address:* 66 Glen Road, Rosedale, Toronto. *Club:* Rosedale Golf, Toronto.

ELLIS, William Hodgson, M.A., M.B., F.R.S.C., F.I.C.; *b.* Bakewall, Derbyshire, Eng., 1845; *s.* of J. E. Ellis, M.R.C.S., and Eliza Hodgson; *m.* Ellen Maude, *d.* of C. Mickle, Guelph, Ont.; two *s.* one *d.* *Educ.:* Toronto, and St. Thomas Hospital, London; arrived in Canada, 1860; Lecturer on Chemistry, School of Practical Science; Professor of Chemistry, Trinity Medical Faculty; Professor of Applied Chemistry and Toxicology, Univ. of Toronto; until 1907, was District Analyst for Inland Revenue District of Toronto. *Publications:* reports Food Adulteration and contributions to Scientific Journals, *Address:* 74 St. Alban Street, Toronto.

ELLISON, Hon. Price, M.L.A.; Chief Commr. of Lands for B.C.; *b.* England, 1862; now a farmer on the Okanagan Dist., B.C., where he has 11,000 acres of land; for yrs. has been the largest grower of wheat in B.C.; first to urge the importance of irrigation; mem. of the B.C. Legis. since 1898; apptd. Commr. of Lands, 1909. *Address:* Victoria, B.C.

ELLISON, William Bruce; *b.* St. Thomas, Ont., July 17, 1857; *s.* Richard and Sarah Eleanor Arthurs. E. *Educ.:* Ont. Pub. Schs.; *m.* St. Thomas, Ont., Sept. 5, 1883, May Alma Jackson; admitted to Canadian Bar, 1880, New York Bar, 1882; mem. N.Y. legislature, 1893; Comm'r. water, gas and electricity, New York, 1906; corp'n counsel, 1907; Dir. Tefft-Weller Co. Democrat; Episcopalian; mem. Am. Acad. Polit. and Social Science, Am. Bar Assn., N.Y. State Bar Assn., New York City Bar Assn. *Publications:* Unification of the United States and Canada; The Canadian American Fisheries. *Address:* 900 West End Av. New York. *Clubs:* Manhattan, Nat. Democratic, Merchants, Fordham (Fordham).

ELLS, Robert Wheelock, B.A., M.A., LL.D., F.R.S.C.; *b.* Cornwallis, King's Co., N.S., 26 July, 1845; *s.* of Robert and Catherine Ells; *m.* Harriet Newell Stevens of Onslow, N.S.; two *s.* *Educ.:* Acadia Coll., N.S., and McGill Univ., Montreal; joined the Geological Survey of Canada, 1872; has been constantly engaged in the work of that department, as Geologist. *Publications:* numerous reports on the Geology of Canada, also in New Foundland and the British West Indies. *Address:* 204 O'Connor St., Ottawa.

ELSON, Peter, M.P.; *b.* London, Co. of Middlesex, 18 Jan., 1841; *s.* of Joseph Elson, a U. E. Loyalist of German descent, and Samantha, of American parentage; *m.* 25 Sept., 1872, Rebecca Wood. *Educ.:* public Sch., Middlesex and Hamilton; was deputy Reeve, London Tp. for two years; Reeve for Eight years; Co. Councillor for 18 yrs.; Warden of Middlesex Co. for one year; for many years Director in the London Tp. Mutual Fire Inst. Co.; also in Proof Line Road Co.; first elec .to the H. of C., 1904; re-elec. 1908. Mothodist; Conservative. *Address:* London, Ont.

EMARD, Mgr. Joseph Medard, D.D.; First Bishop of Valleyfield, Que.; *b.* St. Constant, Laprairie Co., Que., 1 April, 1853; *s.* of Medard Emard and Mathilde Beaudin. *Educ.:* Ste. Therse Coll. and Petit Seminaire, Montreal; ordained Priest, 1876, took degrees at French Seminary at Rome, returning to Can. and was Secretary to the Archbishop; consec. Bishop of Valleyfield, 9 June, 1892. *Publications:* "Messages." "At London, Lourdes and Rome in 1908;" many pastoral letters. *Address:* Valleyfield, Que.

EMARD, J. U., K.C.; *b.* St. Constant, Que., 27 March, 1855; *s.* of Medard Emard, and Mathilde Beaudin; *m.* 1890, Josephine Ada Wall, of Montreal; when quite young removed with his parents to St. Hubert, Chambly Co., and attended the gram. sch., which was conducted by his father; at age of seventeen removed to Montreal, and secured a position in a wholesale establishment; then took up a literary course, and admitted to the study of law, 1878; obtained the degree of Licentiate in Law, Laval Univ., 1881, and admitted to Montreal Bar; pracitced with Messrs. Beiqu and Choquet for five yrs.; a partner of Hon. J. A. Ouimet, 1880-1896, until later apptd. to the Bench; he then formed the firm of Emard & Emard, taking in his son, Charles who was admitted to the Bar, 1902; cr. K. C., 1903. *Address:* 6 Park Av., Montreal. *Clubs:* St. Denis, St. James, Lafontaine, Montreal.

EMERY, Very Rev. Joseph Edward, O. M.I., D.D., Rector University of Ottawa, since 1901; *b.* New Glasgow, Que.; 1885. *Educ.:* Coll. of Assumption, St. Josephs Coll. (now Univ. of Ottawa), 1877; entered congregation of Oblate Missionaries of Mary Immaculate, 1873; ordained a Priest, 1881; Missionary to Western Canada, 1881-64; Master of Novices and Superior of Oblate Coll., Tewksburg, Mass., 1884-93; Missionary in Texas, 1893-94; Assistant Pastor Holy Angels Church, Buffalo, N.Y., 1895-1901. *Address:* University of Ottawa.

EMMERSON, Hon. Henry Robert, K. C., M.A., LL.D., D.C.L., P.C., M.P.; *b.* Maugerville, Sunbury Co., New Brunswick, 25 Sept., 1853; *m.* 1878, Emily C. (*d.* 1901), *d.* of C. R. Record of Moncton, iron-founder; one *s.* four *d.* *Educ.:* several provincial academies and high schs.; Acadia College in N.S.; and Boston, Univ. of Massachusetts. Admitted as an Attorney of the Supreme Court of New Brunswick, 1877; sworn as a Barrister, 1878; elected a member of Legislature of N.B., 1888; Chief Commissioner of Public Works. 1892; Attorney-General and Premier of New Brunswick, 1897-1900; member of the Legislature for Albert Co., to 1900; P.C., Can., 1904; M.P. Westmorland County, New Brunswick, 1900-07; Minister of Railways and Canals, Canada, until April, 1907, when he resigned to engage in private enterprises; now President of Acadia Coal and Coke Co., N.B., and President of Sterling Coal Co., Cleveland, Ohio; a Director of the Record Foundry and

Machine Co., Ltd., of Moncton, N.B., and Montreal, Que.; a member of the Board of Governors of Acadia University, Wolfville, Nova Scotia. *Publications:* The Legal Condition of Married Women; pamphlets and lectures. *Recreations:* fishing and golf. *Address:* Dorchester, New Brunswick; 16 Delaware Av., Ottawa, Ont. *Club:* Rideau, Ottawa.

ENGLAND, Mrs. Octavia Grace, B.A., M.D.C.M.; *b.* Montreal, Que.; *d.* of Thomas Weston Ritchie and Jessie Torrance Fisher; *m.* Frank Richardson, England, M.D.; one *d. Educ.:* Montreal, Que.; one of the first class of ladies who grad. at McGill Univ., in 1888; took first class honors in Natural Science in addition to her B.A.; took post-graduate course in Vienna, and later commenced general practice in Montreal; a prominent worker in the Montreal Local Council of Women. *Address:* 126 Bishop Street, Montreal.

ENGLEHART, Jacob Lewis; Chn. T. & N. O. Ry. Commission; *b.* Cleveland, U.S.A., Nov., 1847; *s.* of John Joel and Hannah Englehart; widower. *Educ.:* Cleveland, Ohio; arrived in Canada, Jan., 1869; his business career was made up of manufacturing, oil refining and Railroading; Vice-President, of Crown Savings and Loan Association, Petrolia, Ont.; London and Western Trust Co., London, Ont.; Imperial Oil Co., Ltd.; Chairman Government of Prov. of Ont. Railway—Temiskaming and Northern Ontario Railway. *Address:* Glenview, Petrolia, Ont.; Queen's Hotel, Toronto; office, 25 Toronto St., Toronto.

ERMATINGER, His Hon. Charles Oakes Zaccheus, K.C.; Junior Judge of the Co. Ct. of the Co. of Elgin, Ont., Local Judge H.C.J.; *b.* St. Thomas, Ont., 5 Feb., 1851; *s.* of Edward Ermatinger, M.P. for Middlesex, 1844, and Achsah, *d.* of Hon. Zaccheus Burnham of Cobourg, Ont.; *m.* Charlotte, *d.* of Hon. Hugh Richardson of Ottawa, retired Justice of Supreme Court of North West Territories; one *s.* one *d. Educ.:* St. Thomas and Galt Grammar Schs. Osgoode Hall; called to Bar, 1873; apptd. K.C., 1885, Judge, 1880; member Ont. Prov. Assem. for East Elgin, 1882-1886. *Publications:* Canadian Franchise and Election Laws, 1886; The Talbot Regime or The First Half Century of the Talbot Settlement, 1904. *Recreations:* golf. *Address:* "Bella Vista," 48 Stanley St., St. Thomas, Ont. *Clubs:* Elgin Golf, Country, St. Thoms.

ETHIER, Joseph Arthur Calixte, K.C., M.P.; *b.* St. Benoit, Two Mountains Co., Que., 26 May, 1868; *s.* of J. B. Ethier, and Julie Boyer; *m.* Therese, *d.* of Dr. L. A. Fortier; two *d. Educ.:* Montreal Coll.; Dep. Prothonotary of Dist. of Terrebonne, 1888-1895; Crown Pros. of Dist. of Terrebonne; Mayor of the village of St. Scholastique for two terms; Sec.-Treas. of Schs. rural muns. of St. Scholastique and St. Columbin; Sec. of "La Compagnie d'Assurance Mutelle de la paroisse de St. Scholastique." Dir., Central Ry. Co. of Can.; pres., Ontario Cobalt Min. Co., Ltd.; first el. to H. of C., at g. e., 1896; re-el., 1900; re-el. at bye-el. 1903; re-el. at g. e., 1904, 1908; el. chmn. of Com-on Miscellaneous Priv. Bills at Session of 1907. *Address:* St. Scholastique, Que.; *Club:* Canadien, Quebec.

EVANS, Frederick William; head of the firm of Evans & Johnson, Insur. Agents, Montreal; *b.* Montreal, 1850; *s.* of William Evans and Miss Wood; *m.* 1877, Mary L., *d.* of Arthur Wilcocks, Mayor of Richmond, Que. *Educ.:* Montreal High Sch.; employed in a wholesela dry goods house, 1865–1868; joined firm of which he is now senior partner, about 1868; became a Council mem. Bd. of Trade, 1897; Treas., 1899, first Vice-Pres., 1910; Pres., Dominion. Guarantee Co., Canada Envelope Fo., West End Land Co.; Treas., Montreal Gen. Hospital; became a Councillor for Cote St. Antoine, Ot.; 1899; re-entered Council, 1893; and served until 1902; Mayor, 1896-97. *Address:* 26 St. Sacrament St., Montreal. *Clubs:* Montreal, Westmount Bowling.

EVANS, Miss Marguerite; *b.* Georgetown, Ont., 19 Sept., 1876; *d.* of John Evans. *Educ.:* Georgetown and Toronto; spent some yrs. on ranch in North West and contributed series of sketches to Toronto *Globe*, illustrative of prairie life; went to Victoria in 1908, and now a mem. of the staff of the Victoria *Times*. *Publications:* novels, "A Prairie Rose;" "The Lost Baby;" "After the Storm." Has written considerable poetry, short stories, travel sketches, and stories for children. *Recreations:* motoring, travelling, canoeing, riding, driving. *Address:* 115 Croft St., Victoria, B.C. *Clubs:* Ladies' Musical; Alexandra, Women's Canadian, Victoria; Women's Press Assn.

EVANS, William Sanford, M.A.; Mayor of Winnipeg; *b.* Spencerville, Ont., 18 Dec., 1869; *s.* of Rev. J. S. Evans, D.D., and Mary Jane Vaux; *m.* Irene Gurney, of Toronto; one *s.* two *d. Educ.:* Pub Schs. and Coll. Inst. of Hamilton; Victoria Univ., Cobourg; Columbia Univ., New York, U.S. A.; engaged in newspaper work 1897-1905; editor, Winnipeg *Telegram*, 1901-1905; has since been in brokerage and investment agency business as W. Sanford Evans & Co., mem. Winnipeg Bd. of Trade; Mayor of Winnipeg, 1909; re-el. 1910; unsuccessful can. for Dom. Parlt., for Winnipeg, 1904. *Publication:* "The Canadian Contingents and Canadian Imperialism." *Address:* Winnipeg, Man. *Clubs:* Manitoba, Commercial, Winnipeg.

EWAN, John Alexander; Asst. Editor, Toronto *Globe; b.* Aberdeen, Scotland, 14 Feb., 1854; *s.* of Peter Ewan and Margaret Stewart Smith; *m.* Elizabeth A. O'Neil; one *d. Educ.:* Toronto and Scotland. Has always been engaged in newspaper work; was correspondent for the Toronto *Globe* in South Africa; now asst. editor, *Globe. Recreations:* riding, golf. *Address:* 10 Victoria Av., Toronto. *Clubs:* National, Ontario, Rosedale Golf, Toronto.

EWART, John Skirving, K.C.; *b.* Toronto, 11 Aug., 1849; *s.* of Thomas Ewart, and Catharine S. Skirving; *m.* 1873, Jessie Campbell; two *d. Educ.:* Upper Can. Coll.; called to Bar of Ont., 1871, and Manitoba, 1882; resided in Winnipeg for several yrs., and was prominently connected with Manitoba sch. legis. as rep. of Catholic minority; removed to Ottawa in 1905; Assoc. Counsel in preparation of British case in connection with North Atlantic Coast Fisheries Arbitration at the Hague, necessitating several months' residence in England in 1909. *Publications:* "Index to the Statutes" "Manual of Costs," The Manitoba School Question." *Recreation:* golf. *Address:* 400 Wilbrod St., Ottawa. *Clubs:* Rideau, Golf. Ottawa.

EWING, Samuel H.; *b.* Londonderry, Ireland, 10 May, 1834; *s.* of Samuel Ewing and Margaret Hamilton; *m.* (1st) Caroline Wilson Cheese, of London England (d. 1872) (2nd), Margaret Anna Knight, of Glasgow, Scotland (*d.* 5 March, 1908); three *s.* three *d.* *Educ.:* Londonderry and Montreal; arrived in Can. with parents 1845; joined father in establishing coffee and spice business, now conducted by H. Ewing Sons; Pres. of Montreal Cotton Co.; Vice-President Molson Bank; Director Canada Accident Assurance Co., Sun life Assn. Co., and other important corporations. A governor of Montreal General Hospital and of Protestant Hospital for the Insane. *Address:* 100 Cote des Neiges, Rd., Montreal. *Clubs:* St. James' Canada.

F

FABRE, Hector, F.R.S.C., C.M.G.; *b.* Montreal, 9 Aug., 1834; *s.* of the late E. R. Fabre, and Luce Perrault; *m.* 1864, Flore, *d.* of Adolphus Glein, of Arthabaskaville. *Educ.:* L'Assomption Coll., St. Hyacinthe Coll., Seminary of St. Sulpice, Montreal. studied law with his brother-in-law, Sir Geo. E. Caritier; called to Bar of Quebec, 1856. Engaged in journalism for many yrs.; unsuccessful can. for H. of C., 1873; called to the Senate, 1875; apptd. agent for the Dom. Govt. at Paris, 1882, and thereupon resigned his seat in the Senate. In 1886, apptd. C.M.G. in recognition of his services as a Commr. to the Colonial Exhibition, London. *Address:* 10 Rue de Rome, Paris. France.

FAIRBANK, J. H.; oil operator; *b.* Rouse's Point, N.Y., U.S., 21 July, 1831; *s.* of Asa Fairbank and Mary Oliver (both American born); *m.* 1885, Edna, *d.* of Hermann Crysler, of Niagara Falls, Ont. (*d.* 1896); one *s.* one *d.* *Educ.:* Village schs., and Chaplain Acad., N.Y.; arrived Canada, 1853, and engaged in surveying in Ontario; located at Oil Springs, Ont., 1861; one of the first to promote the oil industry in Canada; removed to Petrolea, 1865, where he has since been a large operator. Owns and operates many wells in the oil belt of Ontario; Pres., Crown Loan and Savings Co., of Petrolea; partner in the firm of Van Tuyl & Fairbank, of Petrolea, dealers in hardware and oil well supplies; mem. of the firm of Vaugh & Fairbank, private bankers; owner of the Stephenson Boiler Works and Foundry, and is interested in several large other concerns in Petrolea; mem. of the H. of C. for East Lambton, 1882-1887. *Address:* Petrolea, Ont.

FALCONBRIDGE, John Delalie, B.A., M.A., LL.B.; *b.* Toronto, Ont., 7 June, 1875; *o. s.* of the Hon. Sir Glenholme Falconbridge Chief Justice of the King's Bench (Ontario); *m.* to Elizabeth Porten, Hamilton, *d.* of the Rev. S. M. Hamilton, D.D., of New York, and *g. d.* of the Hon. Wm. Panter, sometime Judge of the Supreme Court of Pennsylvania, U.S.A. *Educ.:* Univ. Coll., Toronto, Ont.; Barrister at-Law; called to the Bar 1899; mem. of firm of Cassels, Brock, Kelly and Falconbridge; Lecturer in Equity to the Law Society of Up. Can. *Publications:* Law Books on Banking and Bills of Exchange, and articles on legal subjects in the Canadian Law Times. *Recreations:* sailing and canoeing. *Address:* 22 Chestnut Park, Toronto; Business, 19 Wellington St. West, Toronto, Ont. *Clubs:* Toronto and R. C. Y. C., Toronto, Ont.

FALCONBRIDGE, Hon. Sir William Glenholme, B.A., LL.D., K.C., Chief Justice of the Court of King's Bench for Ontario; *b.* Drummondville, Ont., 12 May, 1846; *s.* of John Kennedy Falconbridge (Irish); *m.* 1873, Mary, *y. d.* of the late Mr. Justice Sullivan; one *s.* five *d.* *Educ.:* Barrie Gram. Sch.; Model Gram. Sch. for Upper Canada & Toronto Univ. (grad. B.A., 1866); filled chair of Modern Languages at Yarmouth Seminary, N.S. for one yr.; lecturer in Spanish and Italian at Toronto Univ., 1868; studied law and called to Bar of Ontario, 1871; an examiner for Univ. of Toronto for several yrs.; Registrar, 1872-1881; mem. of Senate of Univ., 1881-1896; el. Bencher of the Law Soc. in 1885; apptd. a Judge of the Queen's Bench, Div. in Ontario, Nov. 21, 1887; Chief Justice, 1900. Has served on many important commissions: one of revisers of Statutes of Ontario, 1896-97; commr. to investigate alleged election frauds, 1900; a commr. for revision and consolidation of Imperial Statutes in force in Ontario. *Publications:* Many translations from foreign writers. *Address:* 80 Isabella St., Toronto. *Club:* Toronto.

FALCONBRIDGE, Lady Mary Phœbe, (nee Sullivan); *b.* Toronto, Ont., 2 May, 1850; *d.* of the Hon. Robert Baldwin Sullivan, Judge of the Court of Queen's Bench for Up. Can., and Emily Louisa De Latre, a *d.* of Lieut.-Col. Philip DeLatre, *m.* Hon. Sir Glenholm Falconbridge; one *s.* five *d.* *Educ.:* Villa Marie Convent, Montreal, Que.; the greater portion of her life devoted to various religious and charitable organizations, and social duties. *Recreations:* music and Art. *Address.* 80 Isabella St., Toronto. *Club:* Toronto Ladies'.

FALCONER, Kenneth; Canadian manager, Gunn, Richards & Co., production engineers and accountants; *b.* Chicago, Ill., 1863; *s.* of William Falconer and E. Chambers; *m.* 1889, Ida Frances Smith, of Whitensville, Mass.; two *s.* one *d.* *Educ.:* Pub. and High Sch., Montreal; arrived Can., with his parents when very young; filled sev. commercial positions, 1880-1896; made a specialty of electrical accounting, 1896-1899; a consulting cost accnt. in Montreal, 1899-1904, and has been connected with the firm of Gunn, Richards & Co., since 1904; was Associate Editor of the Journal of American Foundrymen's Assn., 1899-1904; mem. Can. Manufacturers' Assn., Brass Founders' Assn., American Foundrymen's Assn. *Publications:* Contributions to Cassier's Engineering Magazine, American Machinist, Brass Founder. *Address:* 34 Staynor Av., Montreal. *Club:* Engineers'.

FALCONER, Robert Alexander, B.A., M.A., B.D., D.Litt., D.D., LL.D., Pres. of

Toronto Univ., *b.* Charlottetown, P.E.I., 10 Feb., 1867; *s.* of Rev. Alexander Falconer, D.D., and Susan Douglas; *m.* Sophie *d.* of Rev. I. Gaudier; two *s. Educ.:* Queen's Royal Sch., Trinidad; B.W.J. The Univ. of Edinburgh, Leipzig, Berlin, Marburg; Gilchrist Scholar for West Indies, 1885; apptd. on graudation in 1892, Lecturer in New Testiment Greek in Pine Hill Coll., Halifax; Professor in 1895 and Principal in 1904; apptd. President of Univ. of Toronto, in June, 1907. *Publications:* numerous articles on New Testiment subjects in English and American Encyclopoedies and Reviews. *Recreations:* travel, walking. *Address:* 69 St. George St., Toronto. *Clubs:* Toronto, Golf.

FALCONER, Walter George; solicitor; manager, Gen. Accident Assurance Co. of Can. and the Canadian Casulty and Boiler Insurance Co.; *b.* Bathgate, Scot., 30 Aug., 1875; *s.* of Duncan Stewart Falconer and Isabella Mathew Falconer, both of Edinburgh, Scot.; *m.* Alice Margaret Farquharson; *Educ.:* George Watson's Coll., Univ. of Edinburgh; qualified as solicitor in Edinburgh in Jan., 1902; joined head office staff of Gen. Accident Fire & Life Assurance Corporation of Perth, Scotland in Perth in April, 1902; came to Canada, 15 Sept., 1904; promoted to Associate Managership of General Accident Assurance Co. of Can (subsidiary Company to Perth), July, 1906; President of the Watsonian Club of Canada, formed of old pupils of Geo. Watson's College, now res. in Dominion. *Recreations:* golf, bowling. *Address:* 6 Oakland Av., Toronto. *Clubs:* National, Victoria; Commercial, Hamilton.

FALLON, Right Rev. Michael Francis, B.A., D.D., O.M.I., Bishop of London, Ont.; *b.* Kingston, Ont., 17 May, 1867; *s.* Dominick Fallon. *Educ.:* Christian Bros. Sch.; Coll. Inst., Kingston, Ottawa Univ. (grad. 1889); Gregorian Univ., Rome, Italy (grad. D.D.. 1894); ordained Priest, 1894, and apptd. Professor of Eng. Lit. at Ottawa Univ., editor of *The Owl;* Parish Priest of St. Joseph's Parish, Ottawa, 1898-1901; transferred to Holy Angel's Parish, Buffalo, N.Y., in latter year; Provincial of the Oblat Order. *Address:* London, Ont.

FANE, Admiral Sir Charles George, K.C.B.; *b.* 13 Nov., 1837; *m.* 1875, *d.* of Sir Edward Kenney of Halifax, N.S.; entered navy, 1853; Lieut., 1859; Commander, 1868. Captain, 1877; Rear Admiral, 1890; Vice-Admiral, 1896; served Crimea (Crimea and Turkish Medals and clasp), and Baltic attack on Sieborg; Chairman of Admiralty Committee for reorganizing Ordanance and Constructive Department, Admiralty; 1st Lieut. "Galatia," under H. R. H. Duke of Edinburgh; A.D.C. to Queen, 1888-90; Captain Superintendent of Sheerness Dockyard, 1888-90; Admiral Superintendent, Portsmouth Dockyard, 1892-96; retired 1902; J.P.; Aberdeenshire. *Address:* Balnacoil Aboyne, N.B.

FAREWELL, Lieut.-Col. John Edwin Chandler, LL.B., K.C.; *b.* Tp. of East Whitby, Co. of Ontario, 18 Feb., 1840; *m.* (1st) Mary J. Shmitliff, (2nd) Mrs. Melinda Wolfenden. *Educ.:* Whitby Collegiate Inst., Barrie Gram. Sch., and Univ. Coll., Toronto; graduate in Agriculture: late Commanding 34th Regt.; enlisted as a private, Univ. Rifles, Q.O.R., 1862; served during Fenian Raid, 1866 (Medal and one clasp); retired from Command of 34th Regt., 1902; Long Service Medal; Barrister-at-Law, 1864; County Crown Attorney, 1872; Q.C. in 1889; Bencher Law Society, 1906. *Publications:* Historical Notes Co. of Ontario; Prize Essay "Relation of Science to Agriculture. *Address* Whitby, Ont. *Club:* Can. Military Institute, National, Toronto, Ont.

FARMER, Jones Hughes, B.A., LL.D.; *b.* Perth, Ont., 28 Jan., 1858; *s.* of Thomas Farmer and Mary Jones; *m.* Cora Cutten; four *s.* one *d. Educ.:* Perth Pub. and High Sch.; University of Toronto, Southern Baptist Theological Seminary, studied in Berlin and Germany; taught London Collegiate Institute as Classical Master, 1879-1881; Classical Master, Woodstock Coll., 1881-1888; Principal Woodstock Coll., 1888-89; Professor of New Testament and Greek in McMaster Univ., since 1889; Dean in Theology since 1905. *Publications:* articles in various papers and magazines; contributions to Hastings Dictionary of the Gospels; Life of E. W. Dodson, D.D. *Recreations:* Camping, walking and gymnasium. *Address:* 750 Bathurst St., Toronto.

FARRELL, Hon. Alexander Gray, B. A., *b.* Detroit, Mich., U.S.; *s.* of James William Farrell, Belfast, Ireland, and Isabel Grey, Aberdeen, Scot.; *m.* Isabella, *d.* of William John Dick of Kingston, Ont.; two *s.* one *d. Educ.:* Privately, Ont. Public Sch., Detroit High Sch., and Queen's Univ., Kingston; Major in the 42nd Regt., Lanark and Renfrew Infantry, Canadian Militia; many years a mem. of the Council of Queens Univ.; arrived in Canada at the age of three, on the death of his mother, returned to Detroit at 6 years of age, but returned at 9 on death of his father; grad. in Arts, 1885; studied law in the office of G. W. MacDonnell, K.C.; admitted to the Bar of Osgoode Hall, 1888; Practiced law in Smith's Falls; next year with J. R. Lavell, and continued there until 1906, when he went to Moose Jaw, Sask., and formed a law partnership with W. E. Knowles, M.P.; elevated to the bench for the judicial district of Moosimin, Nov., 1907; member of Council of Univ. of Sack.; Mayor, 1894-1900; Chairman board of Education from 1901, until he left for Moosimin in 1906; contested South Lanark, unsuccessfully in Liberal interests in 1904; saw service in North West Rebellion, 1885. *Recreations:* boating and canoeing. *Address:* Moose Jaw, Sask. *Clubs:* Moose Jaw.

FARRELL, Hon. Edward Matthew; Senator; *b.* Liverpool, N.S., 31 March, 1854; *s.* of Patrick Farrell, and Mary Ann Shea. *Educ.:* Liverpool Com. Schs.; a printer and publisher; returned to H. of Ass. by accl., 1896; re-el. at g. e., 1897, 1901, 1906; Chief Dep. Sheriff for Queen's Co., 1888-1896, when resigned to run for the Legis.; elec. Speaker of the Ass., 9 Feb., 1905; re-el. 14 Feb., 1907; called to the Senate, Jan., 1910. *Address:* Liverpool, N.S.

FARRER, Edward; *b.* England, 1850, of Irish descent; *m.* Miss A. Peters, Toronto. *Educ.:* England and the Continent; arrived in Canada in 1870; journalist; formerly editor of the Toronto *Mail:* Canadian correspondent for the London *Economist*. *Recreations:* walking. *Address:* 488 Wilbrod St., Ottawa, Ont.

FARTHING, Right Rev. John Cragg, M.A. (Cantab)., D.D. (Trinity and Lennoxville), D.C.L. (King's, Windsor, N.S.); *b.* Cincinnati, U.S.A., 13 Dec., 1861; *s.* of Richard and Rose Farthing; *m.* Elizabeth Kemp, two *s.* *Educ.:* Liverpool and Cambridge, Eng.; came to Can., 1888; Rector of Woodstock, Ont., until 1906, when apptd. Dean of Anglican Diocese of Kingston; Lord Bishop of Montreal, 1909. *Address:* 42 Union Av., Montreal.

FARWELL, Charles Franklin, K.C.; *b.* Oshawa, Ont., 24 Dec., 1860; *s.* of Charles Farwell and Mary McGill; *m.* to Dora Stuart, McGill; two *s.* *Educ.:* Oshawa High Sch., Ont. Law Sch.; graduated in law, 1885, spent two years in Toronto; removed to Sault Ste. Marie, Ont., May, 1887, where filled several municipal offices; elec. to Ont. Leg. Ass. at g. e., June, 1894; re-elected March, 1898; retired to private practice, 1902. *Recreations:* fancy stock raising, horticulture. *Address:* Oshawa and Sault Ste. Marie, Ont. *Club:* Sault Ste. Marie.

FARWELL, William, D.C.L. (Bishop's Coll.), Pres. of the Eastern Townships Bank *b.* Compton, Que., 20 Sept., 1835; *s.* of William Farwell and Harriet Carr; *m.* Elizabeth Jane Winn; two *s.* *Educ.:* Sherbrooke and Hatley High Schs. As a young man was engaged in mercantile business for some yrs.; joined staff of People's Bank of Derby Line, Vermont, Vt., as Asst. Cashier in 1859; apptd. Asst. Cashier of Eastern Townships Bank, 1860, and filled different offices to gen. managership until 1902; since then he has continuously discharged duties of Pres.; a Dir. of several Cos.; Trustee of Bishop's Coll. *Recreations:* golf, motoring. *Address:* 60 Dufferin Av., Sherbrooke, Que. *Club:* St. George's. Sherbrooke.

FASKEN, Rev. George Robert, B.A.; *b.* Elora, Ont., 18 April, 1863; *s.* George Fasken and Sarah Carder; *m.* Ida J. Gray, of Elora; one *s.* one *d.* *Educ.:* No. 4 Pilkington Wellington Co., Com. Sch.; Elora High Sch., Toronto, Univ. and Knox Coll.; farmer, teacher in Com. Sch. for three years; in Univ., for four years; in Collegiate Inst., Owen Sound, one year; London, two yrs.; Knox Coll., three yrs.; Mission Work in B.C.; President Knox Coll. Missionary Soc., 1895; graduated from Knox Coll., 1896; St. Paul's Presbyterian Church, Toronto, Feb. 1897 to the present date. *Recreations:* gardening, fishing, hunting, curling, bowling. *Address:* 60 Howland Av., Toronto, Ont. *Clubs:* Victoria Toronto; Baconian, London Eng.

FAULKNER, Rev. John Alfred, D.D.; Prof. Drew Theol. Sem.; *b.* Grand Pré, N.S., July 14, 1857; *s.* John L. and Elizabeth Faulkner; *m.* 1887, Helen Underwood. *Educ.:* Acadia Coll., Wolfville, N.S., 1878, M.A., 1890; grad. Drew Theol. Sem., 1881; post-grad. studies Andover Theol. Sem., Univ. of Leipzig and Bonn. Entered M. E. Ministry, 1883; served at Beach Lake, Pa., Yatesville, Taylor, Great Bend, Pa., and Chenango Street, Binghamton, N.Y.; wrote articles in Hist. Theology in Bibliotheca Sacra, Meth. Rev. (Nashville), Meth. Rev. (New York), Andover Rev., Reformed Quarterly Rev., Am. Journal of Theology; Papers of Am. Soc. of Church History; also a large portion of Hurst's History of the Christian Church, and article, "Methodism" in New Internat. Ency. *Publications:* The Methodists, in the Story of the Churches series, 1903; Cyprian the Churchman, in Men of the Kingdom, series, 1906. *Address:* Madison, N.J.

FEATHERSTONHAUGH, Edward Phillips, B.Sc., Mem. Can. Soc. C.E., Mem. A.I.E.E.; *b.* Montreal, Que., 20 July, 1879; *m.* Ruth Harrington, Montreal. *Educ.:* High Sch. and McGill Univ., Montreal, Que.; grad. from McGill, 1899; Draughtsman; Featherstonhaugh & Co., until 1900; Manager Ottawa Branch till 1904; Lecturer and Demonstrator, McGill Univ., 1905-1907 Westinghouse Electric and Man'fg. Co., Winnipeg Branch, 1907-1909; Professor of Electrical Engineering, Univ. of Manitoba, 1909. *Address:* 119 Betourney St., Fort Rouge, Winnipeg.

FERGUSON, Alexander Hugh, M.D., C. M.; *b.* Ontario Co., Ont., Feb. 27, 1853; *s.* Alexander and Annie McFadyen Ferguson; *m.* 1882, Sarah Jane Thomas, of Nassagaweya, Ont. *Educ.:* Rockwood Acad. and Manitoba Coll.; honor grad., Med. Coll.; of Trinity Univ., Toronto, 1881; visited Am. hosps., 1881, London, Edinburgh, Glasgow and Berlin hosps., 1889, taking a course at Koch's laboratory in Berlin; Practiced at Winnipeg, 1882-94; took active part in founding Manitoba Med. Coll., in which was 3 years prof. of physiology and histology, and prof. surgery, 1886-1894; was mem. gen. staff of Winnipeg Gen. Hosp., surgeon in chief St. Boniface Hosp. and chief operator at Brandon and Morden hosps., Manitoba; 1st Pres., Manitoba branch, British Med. Assn. and mem. Provincial B'd. of Health; Prof. clin. surgery, Coll. Phys. and Surg., Chicago, since 1900; Prof. Surgery, Chicago Hosp.; Surgeon to Cook Co. Hosp. for the Insane. *Address:* 4619 Grand Boul. Chicago, Ill. *Clubs:* South Shore Country, Press.

FERNIE, William; *b.* Kimbolton, Huntingdonshire, 1837; *s.* of Thos. P. Fernie and Elizabeth Ladds. As lad of fourteen, went to Australia and began career as miner at Bendigo; went to Peru, 1856, and worked in mines; later became quartermaster on U.S. Mail Steamer, plying to South American ports; removed to B.C., 1860, and for many yrs. engaged in mining in Cariboo country; apptd. gold commr. for Canada, 1873, and held office until 1882; joined with Col. Baker in securing charter of B.C. Southern Ry., now Crow's Nest Pass Div. of C. P. R.; located Crow's Nest Coal deposits, 1887. Fernie, the centre of a coal mining dist. of Crow's Nest, is named after him. *Address:* Victoria, B.C.

FIELD, Frederick William; *b.* Twickenham, Eng., 4 April, 1884; *s.* of Frederick Field and Amelia Parsons; *m.* Frances Annie Farrant; one *s.* *Educ.:* Tiffin's Sch., Kingston-on-Thames, Eng.; arrived Can., 1905; "Free Lance" writer, England; asst. editor, Monetary Times of Canada, 1906; apptd. mgr. editor July, 1907; also holds position of Imperial Trade Correspondent at

Toronto, to His Majesty's Govt. *Address:* 380 Victoria St., Toronto.

FIELDING, Hon. William Stevens, D. C.L., LL.D., P.C., Minister of Finance and Receiver General; *b.* Halifax, N.S.; *s.* of Charles and Sarah Fielding; *m.* 7 Sept., 1876, to Hester, *d.* of Thomas A. Rankine, St. John, N.B.; one *s.* four *d.* A journalist; entered the office of the Halifax "*Morning Chronicle,*" in 1864; ultimately became Managing Editor; retired from journalism in 1884, upon his accepting responsibility of the Premiership of the Province of Nova Scotia; was for some years connected with the Toronto "*Globe,*" as Halifax Correspondent; entered active political life in 1882, when he contested the City and County of Halifax and was elec. The Government of Mr. (afterwards Sir John) Thompson, was defeated at that election. A Liberal Convention called to arrange the formation of a new administration offered Mr. Fielding the Premiership, which he declined. The administration was formed under the leadership of Mr. Pipes, and some months later Mr. Fielding entered it as member without portfolio. The Pipes administration resigned in July, 1884, whereupon Mr. Fielding became Premier and Provincial Secretary, which positions he continued to hold until July, 1896. He was in the meantime re-elec. for Halifax at successive elec. of 1884, 1886, 1890 and 1894. On the formation of the Laurier administration in Federal affairs, July, 1896, was chosen Minister of Finance and thereupon retired from the N.S. Govt.; elec. to the H. of C. for the Counties of Shelburne & Queens, August 5th, 1896, by acclam.; re-elec. at the g. e., of 1900, 1904, at a bye-elec., 1906, and g. e., 1908. Introduced in the H. of C. in 1897, and subsequent years the various measures which form the British preferential tariff; has presented the annual Canadian Budget uninterruptedly from 1897, to the present time. The Act to establish a Canadian Branch of the Royal Mint and important amendments to the Banking and Insurance Acts are among the most prominent measures initiated by him; was Acting Minister of Railways for some months in 1903, and in that capacity conducted the negotiations which resulted in the agreement for the construction of the National Transcontinental Railway, the contract between the Government and the Grand Trunk Pacific Railway being signed; by him. Has placed several large loans on the London money market on favourable terms. Was a del. to the Colonial Conference held in London, 1902, and attended the coronation of the King. Was apptd. one of the delegates to the Imperial Conference of 1907, but owing to pressure of business in the Can. Parlt., which was then sitting, was unable to attend; was one of the Plenipotentiaries apptd. by His Majesty in 1907, to negotiate a commercial treaty between France and Canada, and also for the supplementary treaty of 1908; a member of the British Royal Commission, apptd. in Aug., 1909, to inquire into trade relations between Canada and the West Indies. A Governor of Dalhousie Univ., Halifax, N.S.; Pres. of St. George's Society of Halifax, for some years. *Publications:* Chiefly of a political character. *Address:* 216 Metcalfe Street, Ottawa. *Clubs:* Halifax and City, Halifax; Rideau, Golf, Country, Ottawa.

FIFE, Captain Alexander John; King's Royal Rifle Corps; *b.* Sherbourne, Dorsetshire, Eng., 13 Aug., 1880; *s.* of Major D. H. Fife. *Educ.:* Harrow and Sandhurst; arrived in Canada, 1908; A.D.C. to His Excellency the Governor General, Earl Grey. *Address:* Government House, Ottawa; Langton Hall, Northalburton, Yorkshire. *Clubs:* Junior Naval and Military, London; Rideau, Ottawa.

FINLAY, William Thomas, M.L.A.; *b.* Lisborn, Antrim Co., Irel., 13 July, 1854; *s.* of John Finlay; *m.* 1883, Miss Catherine Allott, of Newark, five children. *Educ.:* priv. sch. in Lisburn. Came to Canada in 1878, engaged as cashier with a boot and shoe manufacturing establishment; removd to Toronto, 1880; Winnipeg, 1882; estbd. a lumber business for himself at Medicine Hat, and has also identified himself with ranching, being treas. of the Medicine Hat Ranching Co.; was Mayor of Medicine Hat for several yrs. Has been twice elec. to the Legislature of Alta.; Pres., Medicine Hat Gen. Hospital. *Address:* Medicine Hat, Alta.

FINLAYSON, Hon. Duncan, B.A., LL. B.; Barrister; *b.* Grand River, N.S., 12 Sept., 1867; *s.* of Donald Finlayson and Annabelle Murchison; *m.* 1905, Ethel M., *d.* of the late William G. Bullan of Arichat, N.S. *Educ.:* Sydney Acad., Dalhousie Univ. Halifax. Mem. of the Legis. Ass. of Nova Scotia, 1897-1904. Elec. to H. of C. at g. e., 1904; unsuccessful at g. e., 1908. apptd. Co. Judge of Cape Breton County. *Recreations:* yachting, fishing. *Address:* Sydney, N.S. *Club:* Royal Cape Breton Yacht.

FINLEY, Frederick Gault, M.D. (McGill Univ.), Prof. of Medicine and Clinical Medicine, McGill Univ.; *b.* Australia, 1861; *s.* of Samuel Finley and Emma Gault; *m.* 1898, Emily, *d.* of John Levell. *Educ.:* Montreal High Sch., McGill Univ.; brought to Can. by his parents when very young. Apptd. asst. prof. of Medicine and Clinical Medicine McGill Univ., 1894, and Professor, 1907; Past Pres., Montreal Chirurgical Soc.; mem. American Soc. of Physicians. *Recreations:* reading, fishing. *Address:* 729 Dorchester St., W., Montreal.

FINNIE, David Maclachlan; asst. gen. Manager, Bank of Ottawa; *b.* Peterhead, Scotland, 10 July, 1849; *s.* of Robert Finnie, and Mary Smith; *m.* Caroline Nicholson Sterling; four *s.* one *d.* *Educ.:* Parish Sch., Peterhead. Five yrs. with A. W. Boyd, solicitor and agent for Union Bank of Scotland, Peterhead, Bank of British North America, London, Eng., Montreal, Hamilton and Arnprior; with Bank of Ottawa, Arnprior and Ottawa. *Recreations:* golf, curling. *Address:* 329 Chapel St., Ottawa. *Clubs:* Rideau, Country, Golf.

FINNIE, John T., M.D., L.R.C.S. (Edinburgh), M.L.A.; *b.* Peterhead, Aberdeenshire, Scot., 14 Sept., 1847; *s.* of Robert Finnie; *m.* 1874, Amelia, *d.* of Christopher Healy, of Montreal; five *s.* one *d.* *Educ.:* Parish Sch., Peterhead, High Sch., Montreal; grad. McGill Univ., 1869, and in same yr. passed exam. in Royal Coll. of Surgeons,

Edinburgh; visited hospitals of London and the continent for some months; returned to Montreal, where he has since practiced. Elec. to Legis. Assembly for St. Lawrence Div. at g. e., 8 June, 1908; was Pres. Caledonian Soc., Montreal Swimming Club. *Recreations:* hunting, fishing. *Address:* 35 Park Ave., Montreal.

FISET, Col. Eugene, D.S.O., A.D.C., Deputy Minister of Militia; *b.* Rimouski, Que., 1874; *s.* of Hon. J. B. R. Fiset, M.D., now a Senator, and Aimee Plamondon; *m.* 1902, Stella, *d.* of L. Taschereau, K.C., of Quebec; two *d.* *Educ.:* Rimouski Coll., Laval Univ., Quebec (grad. B.A. and M.D.) Was House Surgeon in the London Throat Hospital, London, Eng., 1901; practiced his profession at Rimouski for eight mos.; joined 89th Regt., as Lieut., 1894; Major, 1896; Surgeon-Major, 1898; transferred to newly organized Army Medical Corps, with rank of Major, 1890. Took part in South African War as Asst. Surgeon of first Canadian Contingent, the second (Special Service) Battalion of Royal Canadian Regt. (despatches, D.S.O. Brevet of Lieut.-Col., A.M.S., Medal with 4 clasps). Promoted Lieut.-Col., 1900; apptd. staff Adjutant for Medical Service at headquarters, 1902; joined Permanent Branch of Army Medical Corps; promoted Col.; apptd. Dir.-Gen. of Medical Service; apptd. Deputy Minister of Militia and Defence, and Vice-Pres., Militia Council, 1906; has been Hon. Surgeon to Governor-General since 1904, and Hon. A.D.C., since 1905. Mem. Visiting Bd. of Royal Military Coll.; associate mem. United States Military Assn. of Surgeons; mem. Canadian Medical Assn., Ottawa Medico-Surgical Soc. *Address:* 470 Wilbrod St., Ottawa. *Clubs:* Rideau, Golf, Laurentian, Ottawa; hon. life mem. Garrison, Quebec.

FISET, Hon. Jean Baptiste Romuald, M.D., Senator; *b.* St. Cuthbert, Que., 7 Feb., 1843; *s.* of Henri Fiset of St. Cuthbert; *m.* 1869, Aimee, *d.* of late Honore Plamondon of Quebec; five *s.* three *d.* *Educ.:* Montreal Coll. classical course; Laval Univ., Quebec, as M.D., 1868. Is a Governor of the Coll. of Physicians and Surgeons of Quebec; has been Councillor and subsequently Mayor of Rimouski, Quebec, 1871; took his certificates of Captain, Military School, Quebec, 1865; was appointed Surgeon of 89th Batt. Rimouski, 1871; elevated to rank of Surgeon Major, 1895; retired, 1899; with rank of Lieut.-Col.; elected as Member for Rimouski Quebec, to H. of C., 1872; sat until 1882, when defeated; re-elec. 1887; defeated, 1891 re-elec. 1896; called to the Senate, 1897—a Liberal. *Recreations:* hunting and fishing. *Address:* Rimouski, Que.

FISHER, Lieut.-Col. Alson Alexander; *b.* Athens, Leeds Co., Ont., 9 Dec., 1863; *s.* Duncan Fisher and Helen Mitchell; *m.* Mary Edith, *d.* of Rich'd. Brown, Pres. Brown Bros., Ltd., Toronto; two *s.* two *d.* *Educ.:* Athens High Sch., Osgoode Hall. After graduating in law, commenced practice at Brockville; Chr. Brockville Pub. Sch. Bd., 1903; Pres. Brockville Gen. Hospital, 1902; Pres. Brockville Can. Club, 1909-10. *Recreations:* golf, acquatic sports. *Address:* Brockville, Ont. *Clubs:* Brockville; Can. Military Inst., Toronto.

FISHER, Carl Eugene; registrar of deeds for Lincoln Co., Ont.; *b.* St. David's Ont., 3 Sept., 1852; *s.* of Charles and Lavina Fisher; *m.* S. Dora Forbes; two *s.* *Educ.:* St. David's Pub. Sch. Mcht. in Queenston, Ont., for 17 years; fruit grower for 20 years; Registrar for Lincoln Co. since 1902; Sec.-Treas., Niagara Pinensula Fruit Growers' Assoc., since organization in 1896. *Address:* 21 Chestnut St., St. Catharines, Ont.; Dulverton Fruit Farm, Queenston, Ont.

FISHER, Hon. Charles Wellington; Speaker of the Alberta Leg. Ass.; *b.* Hyde Park, London, Eng., 4 Aug., 1866; *s.* of James and Eliza Fisher; *m.* 1907, Helen Marjorie Powell, of Ottawa. A merchant. El. mem. of the Leg. Ass. of N.W.T., for Banff at bye-el., 26 Jan., 1903- El. for same constituency to Leg. Ass. of Alta. at first g. e., 1905; el. Speaker of the House at the first Session. Major in 15th Light Horse. *Address:* Cochrane, Alta.

FISHER, Edward, Mus. Doc.; Dir. of the Toronto Conservatory of Music; *b.* Jamaica, Vt., U.S.A., 11 Jan., 1848; *m.* 1876, Florence E. Durgan, of Boston, Mass. *Educ.:* Boston; musical education completed at Berlin, Germany. Apptd. Musical Dir. of the Ottawa Ladies' Coll., 1875; removed to Toronto, 1879, to become Organist of St. Andrew's Church; Conductor of the Toronto Choral Soc. for several yrs.; founded Toronto Conservatory of Music, 1886; since opening of institution in Sept., 1887, thousands of students have received musical training there. *Address:* 11 Bedford Rd., Toronto.

FISHER, John H., M.L.A.; *b.* Paris, Ont., 23 April, 1855; *s.* of Robert Fisher and Mary A. Hunter; *m.* Jessie D. Martin, in 1883; one *s.* *Educ.:* Paris Public and High Sch.; Reeve of Paris three yrs.; Mayor five years; Warden, Co. of Brant; first elec. to Ontario Leg., 1905; re-elec. in 1908; Conservative. *Address:* Paris, Ont. *Clubs:* Albany, Toronto.

FISHER, Joseph Priestley; Barrister-at-law; Registrar of Deeds for the City of Ottawa; *b.* Montmorency Falls, Que., 8 May, 1852; *s.* of Benjamin and Eliza Benson Fisher; *m.* Edith Annie Perceval. *Educ.:* Ottawa Gram. Sch. and N. B. Webster's Sch. Dir. County of Carleton Gen. Protestant Hospital and of Protestant Home for the Aged; mem. Ottawa Bd. of Trade; apptd. Registrar, 1907. *Address:* 322 Gilmour Street, Ottawa.

FISHER, Hon. Sydney Arthur, B.A., M.P., Minister of Agriculture; *b.* Montreal, Que., 12 June, 1850; *s.* of Dr. Arthur Fisher, F.R.S.C., Edinburgh, and Susan Corse; unmarried. *Educ.:* High Sch. and McGill Coll., Montreal; Trinity Coll., Cambridge. Farmer, at Knowlton, in Eastern Townships, Que.; entered Parliament of Canada as M.P. for County Brome, 1882; re-elec. 1887, 1896, 1900-04 and 08; defeated, 1891, by one vote. *Recreations:* riding and cricket. *Address:* Alva Farm, Knowlton, Que., 286 Charlotte St., Ottawa. *Clubs:* Rideau, Ottawa.

FITCH, C. Russell, Ph.B., LL.B.; appointed District Judge, and local Judge of the High Court of Justice and Surrogate Judge, June, 1909; *b.* Brantford, Ont., 22 Feb., 1866; *m.* Ida Main, *d.* of the late Henry

Main, Private Banker of Galt, Ont.; *Educ.:* Brantford, Toronto, and Bloomington, Ill.; President East York Liberal Ass'n.; Vice-Pres. North York Liberal Assn.; Chairman of Pub. Sch. Bd. for 8 years. *Recreations;* bowling, and hunting. *Address:* Brantford, Ont. *Club:* Ontario, Toronto.

FITZHUGH, Earl Hopkins; First Vice-Pres., Grand Trunk Ry. System; *b.* Montgomery Co., Mo., U.S.A., 1 Feb., 1853. *Educ.:* St. Louis Pub. Schs. Entered Ry. service in 1873, as clerk in the office of the Master car builder of the St. Louis, Kansas City and Northern Ry.; afterwards served in the car mileage office of the same Co., and when the road was absorbed by the Wabash System, he became chief clerk to the supt. of the Western Div., of the latter; Master of transportation on the Wabash Ry., at Moberly, 1889-1896; joined the G. T. R., Jan., 1896, and served as Supt. of the middle div., with headquarters at Toronto, until May, 1899; acted as Vice-Pres. and Gen. Mgr. of the Central Vermont Ry., 1899-1901; employed as Asst. to Pres. of Southern Pacific Ry. from May, 1901, until Dec. of the same yr.; returned to G. T. R., Feb., 1902, and acted as Vice-Pres. and Gen. Mgr. of the Central Vermont at St. Albans, until 1904; promoted to third Vice-Presidency of G. T. R., and Vice-Pres. of the Central Vermont Ry., 1 Jan., 1905; apptd. Vice-Pres. G. T. R., Jan., 1910. *Address:* 690 Sherbrooke St., Montreal. *Clubs:* St. James', Canada, Montreal.

FITZPATRICK, Rt. Hon. Sir Charles, B.A., D.L., Privy Councillor (G.B.), K.C.M.G.; *b.* Quebec, 19 Dec., 1853; *s.* John Fitzpatrick and Mary Connolly; *m.* Corinne Caron, *d.* of the late Hon. R. E. Caron; one *s.* four *d.* *Educ.:* St. Ann's Coll. and Laval Univ.; admitted to the Bar in 1876; Crown Prosecutor for City and District of Quebec, 1879; M.L.A. for County of Que., 1890; resigned as Provincial Member in 1896, and was elected to sit as member for the same County in Dominion Parliament; Solicitor General, 1896; Minister of Justice, 1902; Chief Justice of Canada, June, 1906; K.C.M.G., 1907, and P.C., 1908; mem. of the Hague Tribunal of Arbitration, 1908-10. *Address:* 240 Daly Av., Ottawa. *Clubs:* Garrison, Quebec; St. James', Montreal; Rideau, Ottawa.

FLAVELLE, John D., Managing dir. of the Flavelle Milling Co., Ltd.; *b.* nr. Peterborough, Ont., 18 July, 1850; *s.* of John Flavelle and Dorothea Dundas; *m.* 1873, Minnie, *d.* of Joseph Cooper. of Lindsay; three *d.* *Educ.:* Pub. and Gram. Schs. of Peterborough; settled in Lindsay, 1864, and ent. into business in the dry goods trade as mem. of the Dundas & Flavelle Bros. In 1884, became mgr. of the milling interests of the firm. Company incorporated 1894 Cold storage plants now operated at several points in Ontario. *Recreation:* curling. Has skipped rinks from his club on six dilferent tours through Canada and the States. *Address:* Lindsay, Ont.

FLAVELLE, Joseph Wesley, LL.D.; *b.* Peterborough, Ont., 15 Feb., 1858, *s.* John Flavelle and Dorothea (Dundas) Flavelle; *m.* Clara Ellsworth, Sept., 1882; one *s.* two *d.* Clerk and later Merchant in Peterborough; started business in Toronto in 1887, and is now Pres. and Genl. Manager, The William Davis Co., Export and Domestic Bacon Curers; Pres. National Trust Co.; Director Canadian Bank of Commerce; Chairman Board of Trustees, Toronto General Hospital, and Governor of the Univ. of Toronto. In 1906, was Chairman of Royal Commission to report scheme of reorganization, Univ. Toronto. *Address:* "Holmwood," Queen's Park Toronto, Ont. *Club:* Toronto.

FLECK, Andrew Walker; *b.* Montreal, 17 October, 1848; *m.* Helen Gertrude Booth; two *s.* and two *d.* *Educ.:* in Montreal. Was for 21 years Secretary-Treasurer Canada Atlantic Railway System; at present in brokerage. *Address:* 500 Wilbrod St., Ottawa. *Clubs:* Rideau, Golf, Country, Hunt, Ottawa.

FLEMING, Rev. John Dick, M.A., D.D.; Professor of Systematic Theology and Lecturer in Philosophy, Manitoba College, Winnipeg; *s.* of late Rev. James Fleming of Whithorn, one of the Moderators of the U. P. Church. *Educ.:* U.P. Theological Hall, Univ. of Edinburgh, Berlin, Heidelberg, Gottingen, Leiden, and Paris. Studied for four years in Germany, France, and Holland; travelled in Holland, Germany, Italy, etc.; had experience of Home Mission work in Grassmarket, Edinburgh; assistant to Rev. Dr. Muir at Egremont, Liverpool, 1893; member of the "97 Theological Club," composed of young ministers all over Scotland, for advanced theological study; Minister of Wishart U. F. Church, Tranent, East Lothian, 1894-1907; apptd. to present position, 1907. *Publications:* articles in the Expository Times since 1899, chiefly on the new Evangelical School of Paris; also criticisms of German and Dutch literature; Israel's Golden Age, 1907. *Address:* Manitoba College, Winnipeg.

FLEMING, Sir Sandford, K.C.M.G., LL.D., M.I.C.E.; Chancellor of Queen's Univ., Canada; *b.* 1827; *s.* of late Andrew Greig Fleming, Kirkcaldy; *m.* Ann Jean, *d.* of late Sheriff Hall, Co. Peterborough, 1855; lived in Canada since 1845; extensive practice as Chief Engineer of Railway and other public works; constructed the Intercolonial Railway through provinces of N.S., N.B., and Que.; Engineer in Chief C. P. R., 1871-80; President R. S. C., 1888-89; has for many years taken a special interest in the movement for establishing the Pacific cable and a Pan-Britannic telegraph service, having State-owned telegraph communicattions encircling globe, and constituting a great Imperial Intelligence Union, in the unification of Time Reckoning throughout the world, and more recently in the Atlantic Steamship Service of Canada. *Publications:* The Intercolonial; a History, 1832-76; England and Canada; Old to New Westminster; Time and its Notation; Memoirs on Universal Time and a Prime Meridian for all Nations; The New Time Reckoning. *Recreations:* curling, golf, bowls. *Address:* Winterholm, Chapel St., Ottawa; The Lodge, Halifax. *Clubs:* Rideau, Ottawa; St. James, Montreal; Halifax.

FLEMMING, Hon. James Kidd, M.L.A., Provincial Secretary, N.B.; *b.* Woodstock, N.B., 27 April, 1868; *s.* of Thomas Flemming and Sarah A. Kerr; *m.* Helena Flemming;

three *s.* two *d.* *Educ.:* Common Sch., and Provincial Normal Sch.; taught in Provincial Sch. for two years, afterwards engaging in Mercantile persuits; for a number of years been a Manufacturer and dealer in lumber; was unsuccessful candidate for Carleton Co., N.B., in 1895 and 1899; elec. at bye-elec. in Jan., 1900; re-elec. in 1903 and 1908; entered Hazen Administration in March, 1908, as Provincial Secretary and Receiver General. *Address:* Hartland, N.B.

FLINT, Thomas Barnard, M.A., LL.B., D.C.L.; Clerk of the House of Commons of Canada; *b.* Yarmouth, N.S., 28 April, 1847; *s.* of late John Flint, Shipowner, and Anne Barnard Flint of Yarmouth, N.S.; *m.* 1874, Mary Ellen, *d.* of late Thos. B. Dane, of Yarmouth. *Educ.:* Mt. Allison Univ., Sackville, N.B.; Harvard Univ., Cambridge, Mass., U.S.A. Admitted to the Supreme Court Bar of N.S., 1871; Commissioner of the Supreme and County Courts and in Admiralty, 1873; High Sheriff of the County of Yarmouth, N.S., 1884-87; Assistant Clerk of the Provincial Assembly, 1887-91; mem. for the County of Yarmouth, H. of C., 1891; re-elec., 1896 and 1900; Chief Government Whip for Maritime Provinces, 1896-1900; Chairman of the Committee on Standing Orders of the House, 1898-1902; Grand Master of the Grand Lodge of N.S., A.F. and A.M., 1897, 1898, and 1899. *Publications:* editor 3rd edition Bourinot's Parliamentary Practice and Procedure. *Recreations:* travel and research. *Address:* 67 Somerset St., Ottawa.

FLUMERFELT, Alfred Cornelius; *b.* Markham, Ont., 29 Sept., 1856; *s.* of George Flumerfelt and Cynthia Barnes; *m.* 1881, Ada Kilvingston; two *d.* *Educ.:* Markham Village Sch. Engaged in mercantile pursuits at Cobourg, until 1870, when removed to Winnipeg. Sold out boot and shoe business to Ames Holden & Co., of Montreal; removed 1886, to Victoria, B.C., to become manager of Company's Branch. Became greatly interested in mining developments; Asst. Gen. Mgr. and Dir., Granby Consolidated Mining, Smelting & Power Co., Ltd.; Dir. Ames, Holden Co., Ltd., Montreal, Eastern Townships Bank, at Grand Forks, Redmond & Co., Ltd., of Montreal and Winnipeg; Pres. Hutchison Co., Ltd., Victoria, B.C.; Patterson Shoe Co., Victoria, B.C.; mem. of Council, Pres. or Vice-Pres. of Victoria Bd. of Trade for ten yrs.; Pres. Grand Forks Bd. of Trade, 1901; was Vice-Pres. Union Club, Jubilee Hospital, and Treas. Protestant Orphans' Home of Victoria; mem. Royal Comm. on Forestry resources of B.C., 1910. *Address:* Victoria, B.C.

FLYNN, Hon. Edmund James, LL.L., LL.D., (Laval Univ.), Prof. of Roman Law, Laval Univ.; *b.* Perce, Gaspe Co., Que., 16 Nov., 1847; *s.* of James Flynn and Elizabeth Tostevin or Tautevin; *m.* Mathilde Augustine, *d.* of the late Augustin Cote, for many yrs. proprietor of Le Journal de Quebec; three *s.* two *d.* *Educ.:* Quebec Seminary, Laval Univ.; called to the Bar, 1873, and has practiced in Quebec ever since; cr. a Q.C. by Marquis of Lansdowne, 1887, and Que. Govt., 1st June, 1899; Dep. Registrar, Dep. Prothonotary, Dep. Clerk of Circuit Ct. of the Crown and Peace for the Co. of Gaspe, prior to admission to the Bar; now Batonnier of the Quebec Bar; Prof. of Roman Law in Laval Univ., since 1874, and became a mem. of the Council of the Univ. about 1884, unsuccessful candidate for Legis. Assembly in Gaspe Co., 1875; had the election annulled 1877; defeated 1877; returned to Legis. at g. e., 1878; unsuccessful for Quebec Co., at g. e., 1891; el. to Legis at g. e., 1892 for Gaspe and Matane Cos., but sat for Gaspe; el for Gaspe at g. e., 1897 and for Co. of Nicolet, 13 Dec., 1900; retired from politics 1904; Commr. of Crown Lands, under Chapleau Govt., 1879-1882; Commr. of Rys.; Solicitor-Gen. in Dr. Ross' Cabinet, 1884-1887; Commr. of Crown Lands under de Boucherville and Taillon Admns., 1891-1896; Premier of the Prov. of Que., and took office of Commr. of Pub. Works, 1896-1897, then became leader of the Opposition. *Address:* 9 Hamel St., Quebec. *Club:* Garrison.

FOLGER, Benjamin Webster; mem. of the firm of Folger Bros., bankers and proprietors of extensive ry., mining and shipping interests; *b.* Cape Vincent, N.Y., 24 April, 1841; *s.* of H. A. Folger and Laura Breck; *m.* 1861, Louisa Jones, of Cape Vincent, N.Y.; two *s.* two *d.* *Educ.:* New York State. Removed to Kington, 1862, and engaged in banking business with his brother; Dir. Thousand Island Steamboat Co., Ltd.; Mgn. Dir., Kingston, Portsmouth and Cataraqui Ry.; Vice-Pres., Kingston Light, Heat and Power Co., Dir., St. Lawrence River Steamboat Co., Canadian Lake and Ocean Navigation Co.; was one of the chief projectors of the Kingston and Pembroke Ry., which was acquired by C. P. R., 1901; Folger Bros., are also greatly interested in mineral lands along the line of the K. and P. Ry and Rainy River Dist., of New Ont.; apptd. mem. of comm. to build the Temiskaming and Northern Ont. Ry., 1902. *Address:* 123 King St., Kingston, Ont.

FORAN, Joseph Kearney, LL.B., Lit. D., Asst. Law Clerk, H. of C., of Canada; *b.* Aylmer, Que., 5 Sept., 1857; *s.* of John Foran and Catharine F. Kearney; *m.* 1892, Louisa Davis; one *s.* one *d.* *Educ.:* Ottawa Univ., and Laval Univ., Que. In July, 1877, commenced study of law in office of Andrews, Caron, Andrews & Fitzpatrick, of Quebec; attending the lectures at Laval; grad. June, 1881; addmitted to Bar of Quebec, 1882; from 1884 to 1886, spent the winters in the woods of the North, winding up his father's lumbering business and incidentally hunting with the Indians of that region; wrote there a series of magazine articles of Canadian Backwoods Life, and the novel "Simon the Abenakis." From the summer of 1886 to that of 1888, on the editorial staff of the Montreal *Star*. From 1888 to 1892, practised Law in the district of Ottawa; in 1892, took the editorship of the Montreal "*True Witness.*" Edited the paper for eight years, giving several series of lectures for different societies, on all manner of subjects, historical, literary, &c. In 1899, established the "Pen," an historical, scientific and literary review; written, and published weekly by himself; continued the publication until 1902, when apptd. Chief English Translator of the House of Commons, Ottawa; in 1905, became Law

Secretary of the House of Commons, and in 1908, Assistant Law Clerk. Has published a volume of poems, and since the appearance of that work has written some two hundred other poems, principally on Canadian and patriotic subjects. Has delivered lectures for almost every institution in Ottawa, and for all classes and denominations. In French for the Institut Canadien Francais, the St. Jean Baptiste Society and other French literary bodies; in English for the Y. M. C. A., the Roman Catholic Convents and Colleges, the St. Andrew's and Caledonian Societies, both in Ottawa and Montreal. *Publications:* The Spirit of the Age, 1886; Simon the Abenakis, a tale of Canadian Shanty Life, 1887; Lyrics and Poems, 1896; many magazine articles. *Recreations:* hunting, baseball, poetry, history, law. *Address:* 1034 St. Hubert St., Montreal and House of Commons, Ottawa.

FORBES, John Colin, R.C.A., and Union International des Beaux Arts and des lettres (Paris); *b.* Toronto, 23 Jan., 1846. *s.* of late Duncan Forbes, Doune, Perthshire Scot.; *m.* 1888, Laura Gertrude, *d.* of George M. Holbrook, Ottawa. *Educ.:* U.C. College, Toronto; R. A., and South Kensington Museum. studied at Royal Academy, London; Portraits of King Edward and Queen Alexandra, for H. of C., Ottawa; Queen Alexandra (painted at Her Majesty's command); in possession of Queen Maud of Norway; W. E. Gladstone, National Liberal Club, London, and Glasgow Liberal Club; Sir Henry Campbell-Bannerman (Prime Minister), National Liberal Club, London; Lord Dufferin, Parlt. Buildings, Canada; Sir Wilfrid Laurier, Presentation, Ottawa; Sir John Macdonald, and many other noted Canadians; General Benjamin Harrison, President of the United States and many other noted Americans; has recently painted a large picture entitled, "Christ or Barabbas." *Recreations:* curling, golf, camping. *Address:* 9 St. Paul Studios, West Kensington, London, Eng. *Clubs:* National Liberal Club; Atlantic Union, Yorrick Club, United Arts, St. Johns Wood, Wimbleton Golf, all of London, Eng.

FORGET, Hon. Amedee Emmanuel; First Lieut.-Gov. of Prov. of Sask.; *b.* Ste. Marie de Monnoir, Que., 12 Nov., 1847; *s.* of Jeremie Forget and Marie Guenette; *m.* 1876, Henriette A. Drolet. *Educ.:* Village Sch. Studied law under the late Hon. J. A. Chapleau. Called to Bar of Quebec, 1871; Sec. to Bar, 1873; Sec. of Manitoba half-breed comm., 1875; clerk of the North-west Council, 1876-88; asst Indian commr. for Manitoba and the Territories, 1888-93; commr. 1895-8; Lieut.-Gov. of the Territories of N. W. T., 1898-1905; apptd. Lieut.-Gov. of Sask., 1 Sept., 1905, on creation of that Province. *Address:* Government House, Regina, Sask.

FORGET, Madame A.E.; *b.* St. Hyacinthe, Que., 29 Sept., 1853; *d.* of the late Lieut.-Col. C. E. Drolet and Helene Duvert; *m.* Oct., 1876, Hon. A. E. Forget, Lieut.-Gov. of Sask. *Educ.:* Hochelaga Convent. Has travelled extensively through Western Canada with her husband. Had honour of entertaining at Government House, Regina, Duke and Duchess of Cornwall and York in 1901. Hon. Pres. Daughters of the Empire and of Nat. Coun. of Women. Takes great interest in work of V. O. N., and Aberdeen Assn. *Address:* Government House, Regina, Sask.

FORGET, Hon. Louis J.; Senator; *b.* Terrebonne, 11 March, 1853; *s.* of French parents, who came from Normandy, France, about 1600; *m.* 2 May, 1876, Marie Raymond, Montreal. *Educ.:* Masson Coll.; a Banker and Stockbroker; Pres., Montreal Street Railway, Vice-Pres., Dom. Textile Co.; Vice.-Pres., Dom. Steel Co., Vice-Pres., Victoria Life Ins. Co., Dir. Montreal L. H. & P. Co.; Director, Rich. and Ont. Nav. Co., and is Pres. of the Board of Governors of Laval Univ.; called to the Senate, June, 1896; Conservative. *Address:* 545 Sherbrook St., W., Montreal. *Clubs:* Mount Royal, St. James', and Hunt, Montreal.

FORGET, Lieut.-Col. Hon. Rodolphe, M.P.; *b.* Terrebonne, Que., 10 Dec., 1861; *s.* of David Forget, and Angele Limoges; *m.* (1st), 1885, Alexandra Tourville, (2nd) 1894, Blanche McDonald; three *s.* two *d.* *Educ.:* Masson Coll., Terrebonne. A stock broker; first el. to H. of C. at g. e., 1904; re-el. at g. e., 1908; Pres., Richelieu & Ontario Nav. Co.; Vice-Pres., Montreal Light, Heat and Power Co.; Dir. Can. Gen. Electric Co., Toronto Railway Co., Can. Cement Co. *Addresses:* 361 Sherbrooke St., E.; 83 Notre Dame St., W. Montreal (Bus.) *Clubs:* Mount Royal, Lafontaine, St. James, Montreal, Canadien, St. Denis, Montreal.

FORIN, His Hon. John Andrew; Judge of the Co. Ct. of West Kootenay; Senior Co. Ct. Judge, Prov. of British Columbia; *b.* Belleville, Ont., 20 July, 1861; *s.* of John Forin, and Jane Forin; *m.* 1895, May Dunn; two *s.* two *d.* *Educ.:* Albert Coll., Belleville, Osgoode Hall, Toronto. Barrister, Provs. of Ont. and B.C.; apptd. Co. Ct. Judge, 1896. *Publications:* Essays on legal and sociological subjects. *Recreations:* cricket, golf, curling, lawn bowling, fishing, skating, boating. *Address:* Nelson, B.C. *Clubs:* Vancouver, Rossland, Nelson.

FORNERET, Very Rev. Archdeacon George Augustus, B.A., M.A., Rector All Saints' Church, Hamilton, Ont., Diocese of Niagara; Archdeacon of Wellington; *b.* Berthier-en-Haut, Que., 25 Sept., 1851; *s.* of Lt.-Col. Chas. Alexander Forneret, J.P., and Elizabeth Barbier; *m.* Adelaide Robbins; one *s.* one *d.* *Educ.:* Berthier Gram. Sch., Bishop's Coll. Sch.; McGill Univ.; Montreal Diocesan Theol. Coll.; began life in a Stock Brokers office, Montreal, 1869; took 2nd class certificate, Military Sch., Montreal, 1871; Curate Christ Church Cathedral; Missionary to Saskatchewan; Rector, Dunham, Que.; Curate, St. Catherines; in charge Dundas; Rector, All Saints', Hamilton, 1886. *Publications:* "How shall I give," (Am. Tract Society). *Address:* All Saints' Rectory, Hamilton, Ont.

FORTIER, Edmond Louis Phileas, M. P.; *b.* St. Gervais, Co. Bellechasse, Que., 10 April, 1849; *s.* of Octave Cyrille Fortier, and Henriette Emilie Ruel; *m.* Elizabeth Lesieur. *Educ.:* Laval Normal Sch., Que.; farming in Co. of Beauce for 26 years; Mayor of Lambton; Pres. of the Court of Commissioners; Director, Organizer and Sec.-Treas. of Agricultural Societies of

Beauce Co.; was Capt. in the 23rd Regt., serving 19 years in the Militia; elec. to the H. of C., 25 Jan., 1900; re-elec. Nov., 1900, 1904-1908. *Address:* Ste. Croix Co. Lotbinière, Que.

FOSTER, Hon. George Eulas, B.A., Ph. D., LL.D., P.C.; *b.* Carleton Co., N.B., 3 Sept., 1847; *s.* of John Foster and Margaret Foster; *m.* Adeline C., *d.* of Milton Davies, banker, Hamilton. *Educ.:* Common and Superior Schs., King's Co., N.B., Univ. of New Brunswick, Edinburgh Univ., Heidelberg Univ.; entered Univ. of N.B. in 1865, where he won the King's County Scholarship and various honours and medals, and took his degree of B.A. in 1868; taught in various High Schs. and seminaries of learning, and in 1871, was apptd. prof. of classics and ancient literature in the Univ. of N.B. Shortly afterwards studied in Edinburgh, Scot., and Heidelberg, Germany, resuming his duties at N.B. Univ., in 1873; resigned in 1879. El. to H. of C. for King's Co., as Ind.-Con., at g. e., 1882; became mem. of Sir John Macdonald's Govt., 10 Dec., 1885, as Minister of Marine and Fisheries; re-el. at g. e., 1891; returned for York, N.B., at g. e., 1896; unsuccessfol can. for St. John City, at g. e., 1900 and at bye-elec. in North Ont., 10 March, 1903; elec. for present seat at g. e., 1904, re-el. g. e., 1908. Succeeded Sir Charles Tupper, Bart., in the office of Minister of Finance, 29 May, 1888, and remained in that office in the Abbott admn., the Thompson admn., the Bowell admn., and the Tupper admn.; resigned, 8 July, 1896. with the Govt. Was leader in the H. of C. during session of 1905, and in session of Jan., 1896, up to the re-entry of Sir Charles Tupper, Bart.; resigned from Govt., 4 Jan., 1896, and was re-apptd. to office on the 15 of same month. In 1892, visited the West Indies in the interest of reciprocal arrangements for extension of trade; visited Eng. twice as Minister of Finance for the purpose of effecting loans. Mem. of the advisory bd. of the Lib.-Con. Assn. of Can. Has been pres. of several mining and development Cos., and first vice-pres. and gen.-man. of the Union Trust Co., of Toronto. Has held important positions in various temperance organizations of the Dom. Visited Great Britain in 1903, on the invitation of Mr. Chamberlain, and delivered 28 addresses on Imperial Preference. *Publications:* Numerous speeches on Political, Imperial, Social and Economic questions. *Recreations:* bicycling, angling, walking. *Address:* 67 McDonald St., Ottawa; Toronto. *Club:* National, Toronto.

FOSTER, George Green, K.C.; mem. of the firm of Foster, Martin, Mann & McKinnon, advocates, Montreal; *b.* Knowlton, Que., 21 June, 1860; *s.* of Samuel Willard Foster and Ellen Green; *m.* 1896, Mary Maud, *o. d.* of the late Hon. Mr. Justice Buchanan; one *s.* one *d.* *Educ.:* Knowlton, Academy. Grad. B.C.L., McGill Univ., 1881. Called to the Bar 1882; has been connected with a number of Montreal legal firms and is now head of the firm of Foster, Martin, Mann & McKinnon; apptd. K.C., 1896; acted in the case of Robert vs. Montreal Light, Heat and Power Co., which involved over three hundred thousand dollars. Pres. St. Lawrence Power Co.; dir. Eastern Townships Bank, George Hall Coal Co., Dominion Guarantee Co., Aluminum Co., of America. Unsuccessfully contested Brome Co., 1896. El. pres. Eastern Townships Cons. Assn., 1894; Lieut. in the Victoria Rifles of Montreal, 1889. *Address:* 8 Edgehill Av., Montreal. *Clubs:* Mount Royal, Hunt, Montreal; Rideau, Ottawa.

FOSTER, Col. the Hon. John Gilman, B.A., Consul-General for the United States at Ottawa; *b.* Derby Line, Vt., 9 March, 1850; *s.* of Austin T. Foster and Sarah H. Gilman; *m.* 1886, Clara S. Merriman, *d.* of Judge Amos Lee Merriman, of Peoria, Ill.; two *s.* one *d.* *Educ.:* Goddard Seminary, Barre, Vt., Tuft's Coll., Mass. (B.A., 1880). Called to Bar of Vt., 1881; el. to Vt. Leg. for Derby, 1892-3; Colonel on staff of Governor Levi K. Fuller, of Vt., 1892-4; apptd. Consul General at Halifax, N.S., 23 June, 1897; transferred to Ottawa in like capacity, 18 June, 1903, which postition he still holds; Dir. Eastern Townships Bank, 1893-7; Vice-Pres. National Bank of Derby Line. *Address:* (Consulate) Thistle Block, Wellington St. (Residence) The Cecil, Ottawa; Derby Line, Vt. *Clubs:* Rideau, Golf, Hunt, Ottawa.

FOURNIER, Jules; *b.* Coteau du Lac, Que., 23 Aug., 1884. *Educ.:* Valleyfield Coll. A journalist; first on staff of *La Presse;* two yrs. political ed. and parlt. corr, for *Le Canada.* Edited *Le Nationaliste* since Feb., 1908, until its transformation to daily paper *Le Devoir* in Jan., 1910. Condemned in June, 1909, to three months' imprisonment by Judge Langelier, for publishing an article against the Judge, but liberated after sixteen days' detention. *Publications:* many essays on sociological and literary subjects. *Address:* 648 City Hall, Av., Montreal.

FOWKE, Frederick Luther, M.P.; *b.* Harmony, East Whitby, Ont., 27 May, 1857; *s.* Job. Wilson and Adeline Perkins (Stone) Fowke. *Educ.:* Oshawa High Sch.; started work with his father after leaving sch. and in 1880, began business in Oshawa as General Merchant, and dealer in grain, seeds, etc.; continued this business ever since; eight years Mayor of Oshawa; elec. M.P. for South Ontario, 1908; Liberal; Baptist. *Address:* 270 Gladstone Ave., Oshawa, Ont.

FOWLER, George W., K.C.; *b.* Hammond Vale, King's Co., N.B., 1859; *s.* of Werden Fowler and Harriet Fownes; *m.* 1897, Ethyl G., *e. d.* of Capt. John Wilson; one *s.* one *d.* *Educ.:* Varley Sch., St. John, Dalhousie Univ.; called to the Bar of New Brunswick, 1884, and began practice at Sussex, N.B.; Warren of King's Co., 1889; el. to N.B. Legis., 1895; el. to H. of C. 1900; re-el. 1904; unsuccessful 1908; for many yrs. an enthusiastic militia man, retiring from 8th Hussars, 1898, with rank of Capt. Has large lumber and mining interests in British Columbia. *Address:* Sussex, N.B.

FOWLER, Rev. James, M.A., LL.D., F.R.S.C., *b.* Bartibog, Miramichi, N.B., 16 July, 1829; *s.* George Fowler and Jane McKnight (both scotch); *m.* Mary Ann McLeod, Truro, N.S. (*deceased*); two *d.* *Educ.:* Gram. Sch., Chatham, N.B., and Coll., Halifax, N.S.; ordained to Presbyterian Ministry, May 19, 1857; apptd. Science

Master in the Prov. Normal Sch. at Fredericton, 1878; Lecturer on Natural Science in Queen's Univ., Kingston, Ont., 1880; Professor of Botany, Queen's Univ., 1902; retired 1907. *Publications:* A Plea for the Study of Natural History, in Stewart's Quarterly, April, 1870, St. John, N.B.; list of New Brunswick Plants, 1879; additions to the List of N.B. Plants, 1880; A Preliminary list of the Plants of N.B., compiled with assistance of members of the N.B. Natural History Society, 1885; Arctic Plants growing in N.B., with notes on their distribution, Transactions R. S. C., vol. IV, 189-1887; Vegetable Physiology, Queen's Quarterly, III, 1, 199-208; How Plants use Animals, a chapter in Ecology, Queen's Quarterly, VI, III, 188-203; report on the Flora of St. Andrew's, N.B. supplement to the Thirty-second Annual Report of the Department of Marine and Fisheries, Ottawa, 1901; Report on the Flora of Canso, N.S., 39th Annual Report of The Department of Marine and Fisheries, 1907. *Recreation:* walks. *Address:* 121 Union St., Kingston, Ont.

FOY, Hon. James Joseph, K.C., M.L.A., LL.D., Atty. Gen. for Ontario; *b.* Toronto, 22 Feb., 1847; *s.* of Patrick Foy; *m.* Marie Couvillier, of Montreal; two *s.* three *d.* *Educ.:* St. Michael's Coll., Toronto and Ushaw Coll., Eng.; called to Bar of Ont., 1871, Q.C., 1883; mem. for South Toronto, 1898-1910 in Leg. Ass.; Commr. of Crown Lands for Ont., 8 Feb., 1905; Atty. Gen., 30 May, 1905 to date. *Address:* 90 Isabella St., Toronto. *Clubs:* Toronto, Albany, Royal Can. Yacht, Toronto.

FOX, Samuel J., M.L.A.; *b.* Bowmanville, Durham Co., Ont., 28 Sept., 1854; *s.* of Thomas R. Fox, a native of London, Eng.; *m.* 1887, Rosanna Free, of Seymour Tp., Ont. *Educ.:* Bowmanville pub. and gram. Schs.; removed to Lindsay, 1869, where he commenced work as a printer; went to work with his father at brickmaking 1871, and is now engaged in farming and brick and tile making about two miles south of Lindsay. Dep. Reeve of Ops. Tp., 1895-1896. El. to Co. Council, 1897. One of the supts. of The Lindsay Central Exhibition for number of yrs. Pres. of "Watchman-Warder" Printing and Pub. Co., Lindsay; Vice-Pres., Madison William Mfrs. Co., Lindsay; pres. The Canadian Clay Product Mfrs. Assn., 1906, elec. to Legis. for W. Victoria at g. e., 1898; re-elec. at g. e., 1902, 1905, 1908. *Address:* Lindsay, Ont.

FRALICK, His Hon. Edison Baldwin, B.A., Junior Judge of the Co. of Hastings; *b.* near Belleville, Tp. of Sidney, Co. Hastings, Ont., 6 Feb., 1841; *s.* Thomas Tillotson Fralick, and Hannah Nicholson; *m.* Jane E. Judd, *d.* of Wm. Judd, Sterling, Ont.; two *s.* three *d.* Lieutenant in 49th Regt., Hastings Rifles for seven years; studied law in the office of Hon. Stephen Richards, Q.C.; called to the Bar, Easter Term, 1868 at Osgoode Hall, Toronto; revising officer for 15 years; apptd. County Junior Judge, 28 Dec., 1881; member of Queen's Univ., Council for 20 years. *Publications:* Articles for magazines, etc. *Recreation;* canoeing. *Address:* Belleville, Ont.

FRANCOEUR, Joseph Napoleon, M.L.A.; *b.* Cap St. Ignace, Montmagny, Que.; 13 Dec., 1880; *s.* of Auguste Francoeur and Marie Avila Caron. *Educ.:* Laval Normal Sch., Quebec; Quebec Seminary; Laval Univ.; an advocate. Lieut. in the 9th Quebec, Regt.; first elec. to Leg. Ass. of Quebec, at g. e., June, 1908. *Address:* 72½ St. Peter St., Quebec.

FRASER, Alexander, F.R.S.C., F.F.S.C., M.A., Prov. Archivist for Ontario; *b.* Invernesshire, Scot., 2 Nov., 1860; *s.* of Hugh Fraser and Mary Mackenzie; *m.* Christina Frances Ramsay; five *s.* five *d.* *Educ.:* Inverness, Perth, Glasgow. Came to Canada, 1886; for fifteen yrs. on staff of *Toronto Mail*, and *Mail and Empire;* editor of the Massey Illustrated; Presbyterian *Review*; Scottish Canadian; apptd. Prov. Archivist for Ontario, 1903; for four yrs. pres. Gaelic Soc. of Can.; grand chief Sons of Scotland fourteen yrs.; one of founders 48th Regt., "Highlanders," and of Empire Club, Toronto. Life Mem. Caledonian Soc., Past Master St. John's Lodge, A.F. & A.M.; Past Chn. of Coll. Inst. Bd., Toronto; Pres. of the Can. Folklore Soc.; taught gaelic at Knox Coll., Toronto for three winters; past pres. Toronto Shinty Club; Pres. Scottish Can. Assn.; pres. Can. Fraternal Assn.; past pres. Burns' Lit. Soc., of Toronto; Hon. Sec. and Librarian, Gaelic Soc. of Can. *Publications:* "Practical lessons in Gaelic Grammar;" "Short Scottish Canadian Biographies;" "The Last Laird of Macnab"; "Essays on Celtic Literature," "Antiquities and Art;" "History of Toronto;" "Guide to Toronto;" "The Mission of the Scot in Canada;" "The Clan Fraser in Canada; "History of the 48th Highlanders," and many contributions on Celtic, Scottish, and Canadian historical subjects. *Addresses:* Legislative Bldgs., Toronto; Woodlawn Av., Toronto.

FRASER, Angus William, K.C.; *b.* Glengarry, Ont., 22 Aug., 1859; *s.* Jane and Isabella Fraser; *m.* Mary Bromley; two *d.* *Educ.:* Alexandria, Ont., and Osgoode Hall, Toronto; called to the Bar in May, 1887; created Queen's Council, May, 1899; formerly High Chief Ranger, I.O.F. *Address:* 157 Gilmour St., Ottawa. *Club:* Rideau, Ottawa.

FRASER, Austin L., B.A., M.P.; *b.* Vernon River, P.E.I., 17 March, 1868; *s.* of Edward and Flora Fraser; *m.* Maude A. Moar; two *s.* one *d.* *Educ.:* Prince of Wales Coll., and St. Dunstan's Coll.; taught sch. eight years; studied law and admitted to the Bar, 6 Nov., 1900; candidate for local house in 1904, and was elec.; first elec. to the H. of C., at g. e., 1908; Conservative; Roman Catholic. *Address:* Souris, P.E.I.

FRASER, Hon. Duncan Cameron, B.A., D.C.L., LL.D.; Lieut.-Governor of Nova Scotia; *b.* New Glasgow, N.S., 1 Oct., 1845; *s.* of Alex. Fraser and Ann Chisholm; *m.* 1878, Bessie G., *d.* of Wm. Graham, of New Glasgow. *Educ.:* Pub. and Normal Schs., Truro; Dalhousie Univ. (grad. B.A., 1872); taught sch. for several yrs.; called to the Bar, 1873; twice elec. Mayor of New Glasgow; called to N.S. Leg. Council, Feb., 1878, and entered N.S. Govt., but resigned same yr. to run for the Assembly. Called to Leg. Coun. and Ex-Coun., Feb., 1888, becoming Govt. leader in Leg. Coun.; elec. to H. of C. for Guysborough, at g. e., 1891; re-el. at

g. e., 1896-1900; resigned his seat Feb., 1904, and in same month apptd. to the Bench of the Supreme Ct. of Nova Scotia; Grand Master of Free Masons of N.S., 1892, 1893; has been pres. of the Alumni Assn., Dalhousie Univ., Commr. of Schs., Pictou Co., and Govr. Halifax Ladies' Coll., and Dal. Coll. D.C.L., St. Francois-Xavier; D.C.L., King's Coll.; LL.D., Dal.; Chn. Pub. Accounts Com., H. of C. *Address:* Government House, Halifax, N.S.

FRASER, James Dewar; *b.* St. Andrews Que., 26 March, 1851; *s.* of Andrew Fraser and Jane Walker; unmarried. *Educ.:* Pub. Schs. Sec. Treas., The Ottawa Electric Ry. Co., and The Ottawa Car Co., Ltd., also a Director of latter Co.; Past Pres., Ottawa Amateur Athletic Club. *Recreation:* golf. *Address:* 451 Albert St., Ottawa. *Clubs:* Rideau, Golf, Ottawa.

FRASER, Miss Jane Wells; *b.* Toronto, Ont., 20 Dec., 1877; *d.* Rev. R. Douglas Fraser and Elizabeth Wilson; one of the editors of the Presbyterian Sabbath Sch. Publications; Recording Sec., Canadian Women's Press Club, 1909-10. *Address:* Presbyterian Publications, Toronto. *Club:* Heliconian.

FRASER, John, I.S.O.; Auditor General, Dominion of Canada; *b.* Loch Garry, Co. of Glengarry, Ont., 13 Dec., 1852; *s.* James Fraser and Isabella Macdonald; *m.* Mary J. Atchison; six *s.* three *d.* In mercantile business from 1869 to 1874; entered Civil Service of Canada as Clerk in the Finance Department, 1875; chief clerk and Dominion Bookeeper, 1902; apptd. Auditor General of Canada, 1 Aug., 1905. *Recreations:* Lawn bowling and motor boating. *Address:* 64 Carling Av., Ottawa, Ont.

FRASER, Malcolm; *b.* Montreal, April 19, 1868; *s.* W. Lewis Fraser; *m.* 1897, Katharine Church. *Educ.:* New York; studied art under Wyatt Eaton, at Art Students' League; under Carrol Beckwith, Gotham Art Students; under Walter Shirlaw, and in Paris, at Ecole Julien, under Boulanger and Lefebre. Black and white work in Century, St. Nicholas, Ladies' Home Journal, etc. Illustrator of Richard Carvel, Caleb West, Bret Harte stories, etc. *Address:* 14 W. 12th St., New York. *Club:* Salmagundi, New York.

FRASER, Hon. Simon; Mem. of the Senate of Australia; *b.* nr. Hopewell, N.S., 21 Aug., 1834; *s.* of W. F. Fraser, of Pictou, N.S.; *m.* Three *s.* three *d.* *Educ.:* East River Acad. Went to Australia in 1852; a squatter, with extensive interests in Victoria, New South Wales and Queensland. First el. to Leg. Ass. of Victoria, 1874; Leg. Council, 1886; since 1901, one of the six Senators to the Commonwealth Parlt. from Victoria. Del. to Colonial Conserence at Ottawa, 1894. *Address:* Toorak, nr. Melbourne, Australia. *Club:* Melbourne.

FRASER, William Henry, M.A.; Professor of Italian and Spanish, Univ. of Toronto; *b.* Bond Head, Ont., 1853; 5th *s.* of late Rev. William Fraser, D.D.; *m.* 1883, Helene Zahm. *Educ.:* Bradford Gram. Sch.; Toronto Univ. After graduation in 1880, taught as resident master in Up. Can. Coll., for three years; and was French and German master there, 1884-87; lecturer in Italian and Spanish in the Univ. of Toronto, 1887-92; associate-professor, 1892-1901; Prof., 1901. *Publications:* joint author with Professor Van der Smissen of High School German Grammar, 1887, and with Professor Squair of High School French Grammar, 1891; various papers on literary and educational subjects. *Address:* 67 Madison Ave., Toronto.

FRECHETTE, Achille; chief translator to the H. of C. of Can.; *b.* Levis, Que., 13 Oct., 1847; *s.* Louis Frechette and Marguerite Martineau; *m.* Annie Thomas Howells, sister of W. Dean Howells, the well-known novelist; one *s.* one *d.* *Educ.:* Levis College and Quebec Seminary; a lawyer and a journalist; law translator and Chief of Translation Branch, H. of C., was Chn. French Sep. Sch. Bd., Ottawa; for 18 years, one of the Directors, and for five years, Sec'y. to the Art Assn. of Ottawa. *Publications:* many magazine articles. *Recreations:* painting and modelling. *Address:* H. of C.; 87 Mackay St., Ottawa.

FRECHETTE, Mrs. Annie Thomas Howells; *b.* Hamilton, Ohio, U.S.A.; *d.* Hon. Wm. Cooper and Mary Dean Howells; *m.* Achille Frechette, of Ottawa, Ont.; one *s.* one *d.* *Educ.:* Jefferson, Ohio. For some time literary editor of the Chicago *Inter-Ocean;* later correspondent for New York *Tribune*, N. Y. *Graphic, Hearth and Home*, Chicago *Tribune*, Cleveland *Herald;* Buffalo *Courrier*, Ohio *State-Journal*, &c.; actively engaged in philanthropic work. *Publications:* "Reuben Dale," "Popular Sayings from Old Iberia," (in collaboration with El Conde de Premis—Real); "On Grand father's farm," "The farm's Little People"; short stories and sketches in magazines. *Address:* 87 Mackay Street, Ottawa.

FREDERICTON, Bishop of; see **Richardson, Rev. John Andrew.**

FRIPP, Alfred Ernest, K.C., M.L.A.; *b.* Ottawa, Ont., 29 June, 1866; *s.* of Sidney Bowles Fripp, and Mary Eaton; *m.* Clementina, S. Bell; one *d.* *Educ.:* Collegiate Inst., Ottawa, and Osgoode Hall, Toronto; called to the Bar, Province of Ont., Trinity Term, 1893; apptd. K.C., 20 Jan., 1908; elec. to Legislature for West Ottawa, 8 June, 1908. *Recreations:* golf, curling. *Address:* 407 Queen St., Ottawa. *Clubs:* Rideau, Golf, Ottawa.

FRIZELL, Joseph Palmer; *b.* Barford, Que., Mar. 13, 1832; *s.* Oliver and Mary S. Beach Frizell. *Educ.:* in Canada; sp'l. studies in civ. eng'ring; *m.* Boston, Oct., 1864, Julia A. Bowes. Was engaged in construction of fortifications on Gulf Coast in Civil war in U.S.; since employed in pub. service in improvement of rivers and harbors; especially in charge system of reservoirs on head waters of the Mississippi; chief eng'r bd. pub. works, Austin, Tex., 1890; since 1892 in Boston engaged in hydraulic engineering mainly in line of water power. Mem. Am. Soc. Civ. eng'rs. Contb'r. to eng'ring jours. *Publications:* Water Power, 1901. *Address:* 75 Linden St., Dorchester Dist., Boston.

FROST, Hon. Francis Theodore; Senator; *b.* Smiths Falls, Ont., 20 Dec., 1643, of American parents; *m.* 1868, Maria E. Powell of Madrid, New York. *Educ.:* Smiths Falls Gram. Sch.: St. Lawrence Academy, Potsdam, New York. Smiths Falls first mayor; M.P., 1896-1900; a Trustee on the Sch. Bd. of Smiths Falls, 1893-98; a Director of the manufacturing business of the Frost and Wood Co.; a mem. of the Ottawa Imp. Comm., since 1903. *Address:* Smiths Falls, Ont. *Club:* Rideau, Ottawa.

FULTON, Hon. Frederick John, B.A., K.C.; *b.* Bedlington, Eng., 8 Dec., 1862; *s.* of Alexander and Barbara Fulton; unmarried. *Educ.:* Heversham Gram. Sch., and Magdalene Coll., Cambridge. A barrister. El. to B.C. Legis. at g. e., 1900, 1903 1907. Sworn and apptd. pres. of Council in McBride Admn., Nov., 1903; Prov. Sec. and Min. of Education, May, 1904; Attorney Gen., 1906; Chief Commr. of Lands and Works, 1907. Resigned from Ministry, 1909. *Address:* Victoria, B.C. *Club:* Union, Victoria.

FUTCHER, Thomas Barnes; *b.* St. Thomas, Ont., Jan. 1, 1871; *s.* Thomas and Susan Northwood Futcher. unmarried. *Educ.:* Ontario pub. schs.; grad. Univ. of Toronto Med. Sch., 1893; house officer, Toronto Gen. Hosp., 1893-4; asst. resident physician, 1894-8, resident physician, 1898-1901, Johns Hopkins Hosp., Baltimore; student Univ. of Graz, Asutria, 1896, Univ. of Strassburg, 1898; Instr. in medicine. 1896-7, asso. in medicine, 1897-1901; asso-prof. medicine since 1901, Johns Hopkins Univ.; also asso. in medicine, Johns Hopkins Hosp., and engaged in gen. med. practice in Baltimore. Mem. Assn. Am. Physicians. Episcopalian. *Address:* 3 Franklin St., W., Baltimore.

G

GADSBY, Henry Franklin, B.A.; *b.* St. Catherines, Ont., 5 April, 1869; *s.* of James Gadsby and Margaret Owen Smiley; *Educ.:* Stratford Ont. pub. sch., Woodstock, Ont., Coll., and Univ. of Toronto. Honours in classics and English at Toronto Univ.; reporter on Chicago newspapers; edited St. John *Telegraph*; editorial writer, Toronto *Star;* editor *Colliers| Weekly* (Canadian edition). *Publications:* Poems, short stories, Parliamentary sketches from Ottawa Gallery of Notables (public men of Canada), Gallery Clock; Political Skit at Ontario Legislature. *Address:* 82 Howard Street, Toronto, Ont. *Clubs:* Arts and Letters, Toronto.

GAGE, William James; Pres. of the Toronto Bd. of Trade, 1910; *b.* nr. Brampton, Ont.; *m.* Ida Burnside. Pres. of the W. J. Gage Co., one of the leading book and stationery firms in Canada. An ardent social reformer; conceived the plan of establishing a sanatorium for the treatment of consumptives, and for this purpose visited similar institutions in Europe and the U.S., and brought this knowledge to bear on the Ont. situation. The Muskoka Cottage Sanatorium, the Muskoka Free Hospital, the King Edward Sanatorium and the Toronto Free Hospital for consumptives were created mainly by his efforts. Has offered a series of six scholarships of $100.00 each, together with gold medals, to be given in connection with the early diagnosis of tuberculosis; el. pres. Bd. of Trade, 1910. *Address:* 434 Bloor St., West, Toronto. *Club:* National, Toronto.

GAGNE, Hon. Jean Alfred, K.C.; Judge of the Superior Court of the Prov. of Que.; *b.* Murray Bay, Que., 17 April, 1842; *s.* of Jean B. Gagne, and Christine Blackburn; *m.* Marie Emilie Guay; five *s.* *Educ.:* Que. Seminary. Admitted to the Bar, 1864; el. to H. of C., 1882; Dir. of the Quebec and Lake St. John Ry.; apptd. Judge of the Superior Ct. of Quebec for the dists of Chicoutimi and Saguenay, 1889. *Address:* 18 Mount Carmel St., Quebec.

GAGNON, Mgr. Charles Octave; *b.* Quebec, 23 Dec., 1857; *s.* of Charles Gagnon and Hortense Caron. *Educ.:* Quebec Sem., Laval Univ. (B.A., 1878). Was ordained Priest in 1882, and apptd. Sec. of the Archives and Master of Ceremonies to the Archbishop of Quebec, 1882-7; Treas. of St. Charles Hospital, 1898-1909. Chaplain of the Ste. Jean Baptiste Soc., Quebec since 1890. A prelate of His Holiness the Pope; one of the promoters of the first Plenary Council in Canada, 1909. *Publications:* Conjointly with Mgr. Tetu, published the Pastoral Letters to the Bishops of Quebec, 1659-1887 (6 vols.) *Address:* St. Charles Hospital, Gignac St., Quebec.

GAGNON, Ernest (Frederick Ernest Amedee), F.R.S.C., Litt.D.; *b.* Louiseville, Que., 7 Nov., 1834; *s.* of Charles Edward Gagnon, and Julia Jane, *d.* of Colonel Durand, of Plattsburgh, U.S.; *m.* (1st) Caroline Nault; (2nd) Emma Cimon; two *d.* *Educ.:* Joliette Coll.; studied music in Paris, 1857-58, and became organist of Basilica, Quebec, 1864; made a trip to Europe in 1873, as special correspondent of *Le Courrier du Canada;* apptd. Sec., Dept. of Pub. Works, Que., 1876, and held position for over thirty yrs. *Publications:* 12 vols. of a historical character, including "Chansons populaire du Canada;" "Lettres de Voyage;;" "Le Comte de Paris a Quebec;" "Le Fort et le Chateau St. Louis;" "Government Buildings in Quebec;" "Louis Joliet, discoverer of the Mississippi." "Pages d'Histoire." *Address:* 164 Grande Allee, Quebec.

GALIBERT, Paul; *b.* France, 1856; *m.* Ealadie Galibert; five children. *Educ.:* Montreal pub. schs. Arrived Canada with his parents, 1863. At age of fourteen entered his father's establishment to learn the tanning trade; commenced a business of his own 1880, and now owns one of the largest plants in this line in the Prov. of Quebec. Chairman Montreal Turnpike Trust since 1896; mem. Montreal Bd. of Trade, executive bd. of Can. Manfrs. Assn.; dir. Suburban Power and Tramway Co., Montreal Street Ry., Co., Laprairie Brick Co.; chairman Montreal Terminal Ry. Co. Was Mayor of Longue Pointe Municipality for five yrs. Governor Montreal Gen. Hospital Notre Dame Hospital, Western Hospital, Montreal. *Recreations:* outdoor amusements and sports, travelling. *Address:* 81 Cherrier St., Montreal. *Clubs:* Canada, St. Denis, Canadien, Montreal.

GALLIHER, Hon. William Alfred; Judge of the Court of Appeal for B.C.; *b.* Bruce Co., Ont., 1860; *s.* of Francis Galliher and Sarah Kirkpatrick; *m.* 17 April, 1907,

Margaret Louise, *d.* of Charles Brown, formerly of Toronto. *Educ.:* Pub. and High Schs., Walkerton, and Coll. Inst., Collingwood; is a Barrister-at-law, entitled to practice in Manitoba, North-West Territories, and British Columbia; elec. to H. of C. at g. e., 1900; re-elec. at g. e., 1904; apptd. one of the first Judges of the B.C. Court of Appeal, 29 Nov., 1909. *Address:* Victoria, B.C.

GALLINGER, Hon. Jacob Harold; member of U.S. Senate for New Hampshire; *b.* Cornwall, Ont., March 28, 1837; *s.* Jacob and Catharine Cook; *m.* 1860, Mary Anna Bailey, Salisbury, N.H. Graduated in Med. 1858, and practiced until he entered public life. Mem. N. H. legislature, 1872 3, 1891; State constitutional conv., 1876; State senator, 1878, 1879, 1880; Pres. State Senate, 1879, 1880. Surgeon-gen. of State. with rank Brig.-Gen., 1879-80. Chmn. Rep. State Com., 1882-90, 1898-1907; mem. Congress, 1885-9; Senator, 1891; term exp., 1915. *Address:* Concord, N.H.

GALT, Alexander Casimer, B.A., K.C.; *b.* Toronto, Ont., 15 March, 1853; *s.* Sir Thomas Galt, and Lady Galt; *m.* Ella Grace Vivian, 17 June, 1885; four *s.* two *d.* *Educ.:* Hellmuth Coll., London, Ont., and Toronto Univ.; Barrister and Solicitor; member of firm of Tupper, Galt, Tupper, etc., Winnipeg. *Publications:* Contributions to *Canada Law Journal* and *Canadian Law Times. Recreations:* tennis, fishing and shooting. *Address:* 219 Gale Ave., Winnipeg, Man. *Clubs:* Manitoba, Winnipeg, Man.

GALT, Elliott Torrance; *b.* Sherbrooke, Que., 24 May, 1850; *s.* Sir Alexander T. Galt, K.C.M.G., and Elliott Torrance. *Educ.* Lennoxville, Que., and Harrow, Eng.; asst. Indian Commissioner, N.W.T., in 1881. Manager Alberta Ry. and Coal Co., 1882-1893, and President, 1894 to 1903; President of the Alberta Ry. and Irrigation Co., in 1904. *Address:* St. James' Club, Montreal. *Clubs:* St. James', Mount Royal, Montreal; Metropolitan, New York; Wellington, London, Eng.

GALT, George Frederick; *b.* Toronto, 1 March, 1855; *s.* of the late Chief Justice Galt and Frances Louisa, *d.* of the late James Perkins, R.N.; *m.* 1883, Margaret, *d.* of Richard Smith, of Montreal; four *d.* *Educ.:* Galt Coll. Inst.; entered into commercial life and in 1882 formed a partnership with his cousin, John Galt, *s.* of late Sir Alexander Galt, under the firm name of G. F. and J. Galt, importers of teas and groceries, Winnipeg. Business developed so rapidly as to necessitate opening up branches in Toronto, Calgary, Edmonton, Prince Albert and Vancouver. A dir. of the Canada Permanent and Western Canada Loan Corporations; Vice-Pres. Great West Life Insur. Co. Actively interested in charitable institutions of Winnipeg; an ardent supporter of manly sport, especially rowing. *Address:* Winnipeg. *Clubs:* Manitoba, Commercial, Winnipeg.

GAMBLE, Francis Clarke; Pub. Works Engr., Prov. of British Columbia; *b.* Toronto 23 Oct., 1848; *s.* of Clarke Gamble, Q.C., and Harriet Eliza Boulton; *m.* Sarah Eleanor, *d.* of William E. Clark, formerly a mem. of the P.E.I. Legis., and afterwards Collector of Customs of the same Prov.; one *s.* *Educ.:* Upper Can. Coll. and private tutors. Chairman on Intercolonial Ry. 1869-70; Rodman on Great Western Ry. of Can. 1871; Asst. Engr. on Great W. Ry., 1871-72; Renn selaer, Polytechnic Inst., Troy, N.Y. (short course) 1872-73; Resident Engr. for Contractor, P.E.I. Ry., 1873-75; Asst. Engr. Intercolonial Ry., 1876; Asst. Mgr. Georgian Bay Ry., C.P.R. 1876-77; Asst. Engr. Q.M. and Ottawa Ry., 1877-78; private practice, 1879; first Asst. Engr., Contract No. 42, C.P.R., 1879-80; first Asst. Engr., C.P.R., in B.C., 1880; Asst. Engr., Dept. of Pub. Works, Can., in B.C., 1881-87. Govt. Agt. and Resident Engr. of Dept. of Pub. Works, Can., in B.C., 1887-97; private practice, 1897; Pub Works Engr., prov. of B.C., 1897 to date. *Recreation:* golf. *Address:* 820 Pemberton Road, Victoria, B.C. *Club:* Union, Victoria.

GANONG, William Francis, Ph.D., Professor of Botany in Smith College; *b.* St. John, N.B., 19 Feb., 1864; *s.* James Harvey Ganong and Susan Elizabeth Brittain; *m.* Jean Murray Carman, *d.* of Bliss Carman. *Educ.:* Pub. Sch. of St. John and St. Stephen, N.B.; Univ. of N.B., Harvard Univ., and Univ. of Munich, Germany. For five years, Asst. Instructor in Harvard Univ. Since 1894, Professor of Botany in Smith Coll. *Publications:* Many special papers in Scientific and Historical Journals, and transactions of the R.S.C.; "The Teaching Botanist," Labratory Cruise in Plant Physiology, Dering's description and Natural History of Arcadia; Toronto Champlian Society, 1908. *Address:* Massasoit St., Northampton, Mass., U.S.A.

GARDEN, James Ford, C.E., D.L.S., M.L.A.; *b.* Woodstock, Ont., 19 Feb., 1847; *s.* of H. W. G. Garden and E. Jane Gale, U. E. Loyalists. *Educ.:* Charlotte Co. Gram. Sch., N.B.; was Lieut. in Intelligence Corps in North West Rebellion, 1885; wounded at Batoche; (Medal); Mayor of Vancouver, B.C., 1898-99-1900; member of British Columbia Legislature, 1900 to 1909. *Address:* Vancouver, B.C. *Clubs:* Vancouver, B.C.

GARDINER, Herbert Fairbairn, B.A., M.A.; *b.* Brockville, Ont., 21 Aug., 1849; *s.* Rev. James Gardiner, D.C.L., and Matilda Fairbairn; *m.* Margaret Ellen Morden, of London, Ont.; one *s.* two *d.* Newspaper work from 1870 to 1903; editor of Hamilton *Times*, 1880 to 1903; Principal Ont. Inst., for Blind, from 15 July, 1903, to present time. *Publications:* Book on Origin of names of Ont. Counties and Tps.; "Nothing but Names;" annual reports of Ont. Inst. for Blind, 1903-1909. *Recreations:* Lawn bowling. *Address:* "Sardarghar," Brantford, Ont. *Clubs:* Brantford, Hamilton.

GARDNER, Lieut.-Col. Robert; *b.* Montreal, Que.; *s.* of the late Robert Gardner. *Educ.:* Montreal. At age of sixteen entered machinery establishment, founded by his father, 1850; became a partner, 1869, and head of the firm on the death of his father, 1890. Entered 6th Fusiliers (now 1st Prince of Wales Fusiliers), 1886; Lieut.-Col., 1878; retired 1886. Took part in Fenian Raids of 1866 and 1870 (medal with two clasps, and Victoria decoration). mem. Montreal Bd. of Trade, Canadian Mfgrs. Assn., Can. Soc. of Civil Engrs.; Pres.,

Mount Royal Foundry Co.; Vice-Pres., St. Andrew's Soc.; Gov. Montreal Gen. Hospital and Montreal Dispensary; mem. M.A.A.A. *Address:* St. Luke and St. Matthew St., Montreal. *Clubs:* Engineers', St. James' Royal Montreal Golf, Montreal Curling, Royal St. Lawrence Yacht.

GARNEAU, Hon. Edouard Burroughs, M.L.C.; *b.* Quebec, 18 Jan., 1859; *s.* of Hon. Pierre Garneau, and Cecile Burroughs; *m.* 1882, Laura Braun; two *s.* three *d.* *Educ.:* Com. Acad., Quebec High Sch., Eastman's National Bus. Coll., Poughkeepsie, N.Y. A wholesale drygoods merchant, Pres., Garneau, Ltd., Quebec Land Co.; ex-Pres., Quebec Bd. of Trade; Dir., Richelieu and Ont. Nav. Co., National Tel. Co., Quebec Cartage and Transfer Co.; apptd. to Leg. Coun., 6 April, 1904. *Recreations:* hunting, fishing. *Address:* 102 Grande Allee, Que. *Club:* Garrison, Quebec.

GARNEAU, Hon. Nemese, M.L.C.; *b.* Ste. Anne de la Perade, Que., 15 Nov., 1847; *s.* of Dr. J. B. Garneau, and Marie Nathalie Rinfret; *m.* Marie Eulodie, *d.* of J. Petrus Plamondon; one *s.* *Educ.:* St. Cyr Acad. A merchant. First el. to Leg. Ass., 1897; Leg. Coun., 1901; Min. of Agric., 1905; mem. of Council of Agric.; Pres. of Chicoutimi Pulp Co.; Pres. of Les Prevoyants du Canada Ass. Co. Takes great interest in agric.; awarded medal of agric. merit. *Address:* 10 Av. St. Denis, Quebec.

GARRETT, R. W., M.A., M.D., C.M.; Professor of Obstetrics, Queen's Univ., Kingston; *b.* Tp. of Brock, Co. of North Ont., 31 May, 1853; father English, and mother Irish; *m.* 1887, M. L., *d.* of A. S. Kirkpatrick, Co. Crown Attorney; two *s.* one *d.* *Educ.:* Preliminary Ont. Coll., Picton; M.A. Trinity Coll., Toronto; M.D. Queen's Univ., Kingston. After securing his degree in medicine, 1882, commenced the practice of his profession in Kingston, where he has remained ever since; first appointment was Professor of Anatomy in the Women's Medical School; afterwards appointed Demonstrator of Anatomy in the Royal Coll. of Physicians and Surgeons, and later filled the chair of Professor of Anatomy; Senior Surgeon in the Kingston General Hospital, and Surgeon-Major in the 14th Batt. Princess of Wales' Own Rifles. *Publications:* Medical and Surgical Gynæology; editor, Kingston Medical Quarterly. *Recreations:* boating, fishing, and cycling; also very fond of photography, and has a large collection of his own work. *Address:* 52 Johnson Street, Kingston, Ont.

GARTSHORE, Lieut.-Col. William Moir; *b.* Dundas, Ont., 3 April, 1853, of Scotch parents; *m.* Catherine McClary; one *d.* *Educ.:* Dundas, and Dr. Tassie's, at Galt. Manufacturer; at present Vice-Pres. McClary Mfg. Co.; Director Ontario Loan and Debenture Co.; formerly of the 18th Hussars, and Commanding 1st Brigade Cavalry; North West 1885, as Major 7th Fusiliers (Medal). *Recreations:* riding, cricket and baseball. *Address:* London, Ont.

GARVIN, John Anketell, B.A.; *b.* Montreal, 4 Nov., 1866; *s.* of John Garvin, Glaslough, Monaghan, Ireland, and Martha Pedlar, St. Blazey, Cornwall; *m.* Florence Cameron, *d.* of the late John A. Cameron, Stadacona Hall, Ottawa; one *d.* Ottawa Correspondent, Toronto *News*, 1890, 1891, 1892, 1899, 1900, 1904; Managing Editor Montreal *Herald*, 1895-1896; Assistant Editor, Ottawa *Journal*, from 1905; visited Great Britain and Ireland in 1888 as a member of the Toronto Amateur Lacrosse team, on tour for the purpose of introducing the game; President Press Gallery, Dominion Parliament, 1909. *Address:* The Journal, Ottawa.

GAULT, A. Hamilton; Dir. Gault Bros. & Co.; *b.* England, 1882; *s.* of Leslie H. Gault, and Marion A. Davidson; *m.* 1904, Marguerite, *d.* of the late Hon. G. W. Stephens. *Educ.:* Bishop's Coll., Lennoxville and McGill Univ. Was officer in the 5th Royal Highlanders, and served in Boer War as subaltern in the 2nd Canadian Mounted Rifles. Joined firm of Gault Bros. & Co., of which he is now a dir. Dir. Montreal Cotton Co., Van Allen Co., Trent Valley Woollen Mills, Crescent Mnfg. Co., Gault Bros., Winnipeg; Gault Bros., Vancouver. *Address:* 595 Sherbrooke St., W., Montreal. *Clubs:* Mount Royal, St. James', Hunt, Racket, Royal St. Lawrence Yacht, Jockey, Montreal.

GAULT, Major Charles Ernest, M.L.A.; *b.* Montreal, Que., 19 Sept., 1861; *s.* of Matthew Hamilton Gault, and Elizabeth J. Bourne; *m.* Florence Fairbanks. *Educ.:* Montreal High Sch. and preparatory Coll.; Major in 5th Royal High., Canadian Militia; elec. to represent St. Antoine Division,, Montreal, in Jan., 1907, and again in June 1908. *Address:* 128 Mackay St., Montreal. *Clubs:* Mount Royal, Montreal; Club and Hunt Club, Montreal.

GAULT, Leslie Hamilton; Pres. Gault Bros. & Co.; *b.* Montreal, Que., 1855; *s.* of Matthew H. Gault, of Strabane, Ireland, and Elizabeth I. Bourne, of England; *m.* Marion A. Davidson, of Eastwoodhill, Giffrock, Renfrewshire, Scotland; three *s.* one *d.* *Educ.:* Montreal High Sch., Galt Coll. Inst. Entered firm of Gault Bros. & Co., dry goods merchants, 1871; became a partner, 1883; director 1896; president, 1903. Is connected with the cotton industry of Can.; dir. Gault's Ltd., of Winnipeg; Gault Bros., Ltd., Vancouver; Crescent Mnfg. Co., Montreal; Van Allen Co., Ltd., Hamilton; Gov. Montreal Gen. Hospital, Montreal Diocesan Theological Coll.; life mem. M.A.A.A. *Address:* 148 McTavish Street, Montreal, Que. *Clubs:* St. James', Canada, Hunt, Montreal.

GAUTHIER, Most Rev. Mgr. Charles Hugh, Archbishop of Kingston; *b.* Alexandria, Ont., 13 Nov., 1843; *s.* of Gabriel Gauthier and Mary McKinnon; *Educ.:* Regiopolis Coll., Kingston. Consecrated Archbishop of Kingston, 18 Oct., 1898. *Address:* Archbishop's Palace, Kingston, Ont.

GAUTHIER, Miss Josephine Phœbe Eva; *b.* Ottawa, Ont., 20 Sept., 1885; *d.* of Louis Gauthier, C.E., and Parmelia Agnes Laporte. *Educ.:* Rideau St. Convent, Ottawa Coll. Inst. Obtained musical educ. in Ottawa; Paris, France, London, Eng.; Milan, Italy. Operatic, oratorio and concert singer. Made debut in Paris, 1904, London, 1905. Toured England, Scotland, and Canada in 1905, 1906, 1907; in New York, 1907. Made debut at Pavia, Italy, in opera, 28 April, 1909, at Scheveningen,

Holland, Aug., 1909, at Ostende, Belgium, 9 Sept., 1909. *Recreations:* outdoor exercises. *Addresses:* 31 Mutchmor St., Ottawa. Piaza Cavour–5, Milano, Italy.

GAUVREAU, Charles Arthur, B.A. (Laval), M.P.; *b.* Isle Verte, Temiscouata Co., Que., 29 Sept., 1860; *s.* of Louis N. Gauvreau, N.P., Seigneur of Villeray, and Gracieuse Gauvreau; *m.* 1887, Gertrude Gauthier of Montreal; three *s.* one *d.* *Educ.:* Coll. of Rimouski, Laval Univ. Commr. Superior Ct.; made N.P., 1885. El. to H. of C. at bye-el., 1897; re-el. at g. e., 1900, 1904, 1908. *Address:* Stanfold, Que. *Club:* Fraserville, Que.

GAYS, Henry W.; Gen. Mgr. of the New York & Ottawa Ry.; *b.* Brant, Erie Co., N.Y., 21 March, 1849. *s.* of William and Sarah W. Gays; *Educ.*: Dunkirk, N.Y.; *m.* Nannie Keigiven: two *s.*: arrived in Canada, February, 1899. Entered Ry. service, 1 Jan., 1861, since which he has been consecutively to Dec. 31, 1862, messenger, and 1863-1864, telegraph operator Erie Ry. at Dunkirk, N.Y.; 1864-1867, Asst. Cashier, and 1867-69, cashier, Buffalo & Erie Ry. same place; 1869-1874, cashier, and 1874-77, gen. agt., Louisville & Cincinnati Mail Line Steamers; 1877-79, gen. agt., and 1879-85, asst. gen. frt. agt., Cleveland Columbus Cincinnati & Indianapolis Ry.; 1881-85, also gen. frt. agt. Indianapolis & St. Louis Ry.; 1 July to 31 Oct., 1885, in charge traffic; 1885-1886, supt.; 1886-89, mgr. Wiggins Ferry Co., and East St. Louis Connecting Ry., and operated lines at St. Louis; 1889-94, gen. mgr. St. Louis Merchants Bridge & Terminal Ry.; 1894-96, traffic mgr. St. Louis Chicago & St. Paul Ry.; 1896-99, gen. mgr. same road, and Chicago Peoria & St. Louis Ry.; 1899-1900, gen. mgr. New York & Ottawa Rd.; 1899-1900 also pres., and 1900-1905, receiver same road; 1 March, 1905, to date, gen. mgr. New York & Ottawa Ry., successor to the New York & Ottawa Rd. *Address:* Alexandra Hotel, Ottawa.

GEARY, George Reginald, K.C.; Mayor of Toronto; *b.* Strathroy, Ont., 12 Aug., 1873; *s.* of Theophilas Jones Geary and Mary Goodson Geary, unmarried. *Educ.:* Up. Can. Coll., and Univ. of Toronto; called to the Bar, 1894; practices in Toronto; Counsel for Prov. of Ont., in insurance investigation; School Trustee, 1903; Alderman in 1904-5-6-7; Candidate for Mayor in 1908, but was second in a field of five, Controller, 1909, and elected by the largest vote yet recorded for that office; elec. Mayor, 1910. *Address:* Wellesley St., Toronto. *Clubs:* Toronto Golf, Albany, Toronto.

GEDDES, George; *b.* Glenmorris, Co. Brant, Ont., 20 Sept., 1860; *s.* of George Geddes and Jane Ann Forbes; *m.* Margaret Alexander, Galt, Ont.; one *d.* *Educ.:* Glenmorris Pub. Sch.; farmer, then Mill Mgr., and now personal agency. Has been Trustee 5 years; at present time, Mayor of St. Thomas, Ont.; Pres., Ontario Municipal Association; Grand Councellor, K. of P. *Recreations:* bowling and curling. *Address:* St. Thomas, Ont. *Clubs:* Elgin Country Club, Golf.

GEIKIE, Walter B., M.D., LL.D., C.M., D.C.L.; *b.* at Edinburgh, Scotland, 8 May, 1830; *m.* Feb., 1854, to Frances M. Woodhouse; two *s.* two *d.* *Educ.:* Edinburgh, Scotland; Toronto, Philadelphia; post grad. work in London and Edinburgh; arrived in Canada, July, 1843; life spent in general practice and as a Medical Professor; has at different times been in Victoria Medical Dept. and in Trinity Medical Coll.; many years on the Consulting Staff of Toronto General Hospital; Founder Trinity Medical Coll., 1870, and its Executive Officer from 1871 to 1903; representative of Trinity Medical Coll., on Council of Physicians and Surgeons of Ont. from 1877 to 1902. *Recreations:* travel. *Address:* Holywood Villa, 52 Maitland St., Toronto.

GEOFFRION, Victor, B.C.L., K.C., M.P.; *b.* St. Simon, Bagot Co., Que., 23 Oct.' 1851; *s.* of Felix Geoffrion, and Catherine Brodeur; *m.* 1884, Francesca, *d.* of the late Hon. Senator Paquet, of St. Cuthbert. *Educ.:* St. Hyacinthe Coll., McGill Univ. Practicing lawyer of the legal firm of Geoffrion & Cusson, of Montreal. M.P. for Chambly and Vercheres since 1899. *Address:* 234 Mountain St., Montreal. *Clubs:* Canada, Montreal.

GERALD, William John, I.S.O., Deputy Minister of Inland Revenue, Can.; *b.* Prescott, Ont., 27 July, 1850; *s.* of William and Charlotte Gerald; *m.* Elizabeth Hamsworth Billyard; two *d.* *Educ.:* St. Joseph's Coll., St. Laurent, Montreal; entered Inland Revenue Dept., 4 April, 1867; was collector at Brantford and London; Chief Inspector; Asst. Commissioner, now Deputy Minister. *Address:* 336 Metcalfe St., Ottawa.

GERMAN, William Manley, K.C., M.P.; *b.* Prince Edward Co., Ont., 26 May, 1851; *s.* of George German and Susan Garrett; *m.* Henrietta Macdonnell; four *s.* one *d.* *Educ.:* Common Sch., and Victoria Coll., Cobourg; called to the Bar, 1881; and began practice of law in Welland; was Deputy Reeve of Welland; elec. to the H. of C., 1891 and at elec. since that time. *Address:* Welland, Ont. *Club:* Rideau, Ottawa.

GERVAIS, Honore Hippolyte Achille, K.C., LL.D., M.P.; *b.* Richelieu, Co. Rouville, Que., 13 Aug., 1864; *s.* of Charles Gervais and Adele Monty; *m.* 17 May, 1887, Albina Robert, Montreal; *d.* of Joseph Robert. *Educ.:* Petit Seminaire of Sainte Marie de Monoir, and Laval Univ., Montreal. Has been for 20 years in partnership with Hon. H. B. Rainville, K.C.; Speaker for some years of the Quebec Leg.; now with Hon. Horace Archambault, K.C., Attorney General and Speaker and Mr. Paul Rainville, LL.L., under the name of Rainville, Gervais and Rainville; a candidate for the Liberal party in St. James' Division, Montreal, bye election, 16 Feb., 1904, against J. H. G. Bergeron, and elected; re-elec. 1904 and 1908; has been a member of the Council of the Montreal Bar and Batonnier General of the Bar of the Prov. of Que.; Governor of "l'EcolePolytechnique; Promoter and Governor of l'Ecole des Hautes Etudes Commerciales of the Prov. of Que.; A Gov. of Laval Univ.; Professor of International Law and Civil Procedure at Laval Univ.; membre-correspondant de la Société de Législation comparé de France;" is a writer of several legal works; elec. chmn. of Debates. Com. of H. of C.,

1905, and since; Liberal. *Address:* 181 Berri St., Montreal. *Clubs:* St. Denis, Montreal; Rideau, Ottawa.

GIBBENS, William; editor and proprietor of Cornwall *Standard;* *b.* London, Eng., 7 June, 1854; *s.* of William J. and Emma Gibbens; *m.* Florence S. Culbert, of Lindsay, Ont.; one *d.* *Educ.:* Priv. Sch., Dorking, Surrey, and London. Came to Canada, July, 1869. First engaged in commercial work; newspaper experience commenced on the Brockville *Recorder;* joined staff of the Ottawa *Citizen*, 1875, and filled positions of local reporter and city editor until 1880; 1880-1884, Rapid City *Standard* and Minnedosa *Tribune* in Manitoba, the *Standard* being the first newspaper pubd. in the Canadian Northwest, west of Portage la Prairie, with the exception of the Battleford *Herald;* returned to Ottawa, 1884, and was mng. dir. of the *Citizen* Pub. Co., until 1888; editor and publisher of the Cornwall *Standard* since Aug., 1888; became proprietor, 1907. *Address:* Cornwall, Ont. *Club:* Cornwall.

GIBSON, Col. Hon. John Morrison, M. A., LL.D., K.C., A.D.C., Lieut.-Governor of Ontario; *b.* 1 Jan, 1842; *m.* (1st) Emily Annie, *d.* of late Ralph Birrell, London; (2nd) Caroline, *d.* of Hon. Adam Hope, Senator; (3rd) Elizabeth, *d.* of late Judge Malloch, of Brockville; four *s.* two *d.* *Educ.:* Central Sch., Hamilton; Univ. of Toronto. (Prince of Wales Prize, medals in Classics and Modern Languages, LL.B., with gold medal, 1869; LL.D. *honoris causa*, 1903). Barr. (U.C.), 1867); Prov. Sec. of Ont., 1889; Comm. of Crown Lands, 1896; Attorney-Gen. 1899-1905; Q.C. 1890; Bencher of Law Society of Up. Can., 1899; Lieut.-Col. 13 Regt., Canadian Militia, 1876; Hon. Lieut.-Col. 13th Regt., 1895; Hon. Col., 1901 Colonel, Reserve of Officers, 1902; Colonel Commanding 15th Brigade, Canadian Militia, 1903; Pres. Dominion of Canada Rifle Association; Prince of Wales Prize, Wimbledon, 1879; Commander Canadian Rifle Team to Wimbledon, 1881, and to Bisley, 1907; President Canadian Branch Red Cross Society; President Dominion Power and Transmission Company; Hon. A.D.C. to Their Excellencies the Earl of Aberdeen and the Earl of Minto, Governors-General of Canada; Past Grand Master Grand Lodge of Canada, A.F. and A.M.; Grand Commander A. and A.S. Rite for Canada. *Address:* Government House, Toronto. *Clubs:* Toronto, National, Toronto; Hamilton.

GIBSON, Thomas William; Deputy Minister of Mines for Ontario; *b.* Wroxeter, Ont., 19 Feb., 1859; *s.* Alexander L. Gibson and Janet F. Gibson; *m.* Jessie E. Brown; two *s.* and four *d.* *Educ.:* Wroxeter pub. sch., Rockwood, Ont. (Academy). Clerk, bookkeeper, journalist, manufacturer, Sec. Bureau of Mines; Director, Bureau of Mines, Deputy Minister of Mines; *Publication:* Official Reports. *Recreations:* canoeing, gardening. *Address:* 84 De Lisle St., Toronto.

GIBSON, Hon. William, Senator; *b.* Peterhead, Scot., 7 Aug., 1849; *e. s.* of the late William Gibson and Lucritia Gilzeau; *m.* 1876, Jennie Hill (*d.* 1902), *d.* of the late John F. Davidson, of Hamilton, Ont.; (2nd) Margaret E., *d.* of the late Alex. Mackie, merchant of Peterhead, Scot,; five *d.* *Educ.:* Peterhead Acad. Railway Contractor, and mem. Can. Soc. of Civil Engrs.; owns and operates two of the most extensive limestone quarries in Canada near Beamsville and Crookston, Ont. Pres. of the Bank of Hamilton, of the Hamilton Gas Light Co., the Keewatin Lumber and Mfg. Co., the Keewatin Power Co.; dir. of the Canada Screw Co., the Canada Life Assur. Co., of the Hamilton Provident and Loan Soc. First returned to H. of C., at g. e., 1891, for Lincoln and Niagara; unseated, but re-el. at bye-elec., 28 Jan., 1892; re-elec. at g. e., 1896; defeated at g. e., 1900; Chief Whip, Liberal Party for some years. Called to the Senate, 11 Feb., 1902. Past Grand Master, A.F. and A.M.; 33° active mem. of the Supreme Council of Canada and Deputy for Ontario. *Recreation:* travel. *Address:* Beamsvill, Ont. *Clubs:* Hamilton, Commercial, Hamilton; Toronto, National, Toronto; Rideau, Ottawa.

GIGAULT, George Auguste, N.P., Dep. Min. of Agric., for Prov. of Quebec; *b.* St. Mathias, Co., Rouville, Que., 23 Nov., 1845; *s.* of Pierre Gigault, and Marguerite Wait; *m.* Isabella Dillon; two *s.* five *d.* *Educ.:* St. Hyacinthe Sem. Admitted to profession of notary in 1867; apptd. Dep. Min. of Agric. for Quebec, 1892. Represented Rouville Co. in H. of C., 1878-1891. In 1884, moved for special Committee of which he was chmn., whose report led to establishment in 1886 of Dom. Experimental Farms. *Publications:* Report on a trip to Denmark; report on establishment of Agricultural Clubs in Prov. Quebec. *Address:* Ste. Foy, Que.

GILBERT, Alexander Glen; *b.* Georgetown, Demerara, 31 Dec., 1840; of Scotch parentage; *m.* Susan Chamings, of Devon., Eng. *Educ.:* Glasgow, Scot. Came to Canada in 1860. Was engaged in Journalism, chiefly on staff of Montreal *Gazette*, for many years. Apptd. poultry expert at Central Experimental Farm, which position still holds. *Publications:* Many pamphlets and reports on Poultry keeping; "Montreal and Maritime Provinces;" (pamph). *Address:* Central Experimental Farm, Ottawa, Ont.

GILL, Robert; *b.* Dundas, Ont., 30 Sept. 1851; *s.* of William and Alison Sanderson Gill; *m.* (1st) Caroline Gilmour, *e. d.* of the late John Gilmour, of Marchmount, Que., (*d.* 1884); (2nd) Anna Louisa Thistle, *d.* of the late W. R. Thistle, P.L.S., of Ottawa; four *s.* *Educ.:* Up. Can. Coll., Toronto. Has been Manager of the Canadian Bank of Commerce, Ottawa, since 1887; previously Manager of other branches, and Chief Inspector for six years. *Address:* 281 O'Connor St., Ottawa. *Clubs:* Rideau, Golf, Country, Ottawa; St. James', Montreal.

GILLIES, Joseph Alexander, M.A., K. C.; *b.* at Irish Cove, Cape Breton, 17 Sept., 1849; *s.* of John Gillies and Mary Isabella Maclean; *m.* Josephene E. Bertrand; one *s.* *Educ.:* St. Frances Xavier Coll., Antigonish; graduated M.A., in 1871; Registrar of probate, Cape Breton Co., from 1872 to 1887, when he resigned; elec. M.P. in 1891, and sat in H. of C., until 1900. *Address:* Parklands, Sydney, Cape Breton. *Clubs:* R.C.B.Y.C., Sydney, C.B.

GILLMOR, Hon. Daniel; Senator; *b.* St. George, N.B., 1 July, 1849; *s.* of the late Hon. A. H. Gillmor, Senator, and Hannah Dawes Gillmor; *m.* Nov., 1877, Catherine Sophia Duffy. *Educ.:* St. George Sch.; a merchant; mem. of the firm of O Brien and Gillmor, St. George, and of the firm of Chase and Sanburn, Montreal; Liberal. *Address:* 4149 Dorchester St. W., Montreal.

GILMOUR, John; Pres. of the Gilmour & Hughson, Lumber Co.; *b.* Quebec, 22 April, 1849; *s.* of the late John Gilmour, a native of Scotland; *m.* 1874, Jessie Miller McLimont; six *s.* one *d.* Succeeded to control his father's extensive lumber business, and is now Pres. of the Gilmour & Hughson Lumber Co., which owns extensive limits on the Gatineau and operates a large steam sawmill on the Ottawa River, near the mouth of the Gatineau. *Address:* 29 Cartier St., Ottawa. *Club:* Rideau, Ottawa.

GILPIN, Edwin, B.A., M.A., Hon. Dr. Sc., Hon. LL.D. (Dalh.); I.S.O., F.R.S.C.; *b.* Halifax, N.S., 28 Oct., 1850; *s.* of Edwin Gilpin, Dean of N.S., and Amelia, *y. d.* of the Hon. Justice Haliburton, "Sam Slick;" *m.* Florence Ellen, *e. d.* of Lewis Johnstone, M.D., of Stellarton N.S.; one *s.* two *d.* *Educ.:* Halifax Gram. Sch. and King's Coll., Windsor, N.S.; apptd Inspector of Mines, N.S., 1879; a member and Secretary, Board of Examiners of Collery Officials, N.S., 1881; Deputy Commissioner of Pub. Works and Mines, N.S., 1886; member of many English, Canadian and American Societies. *Publications:* numerous and valuable papers and books on the Geology, etc., of N.S., and on mining subjects. *Recreations:* Boating. *Address:* Edgemere, Halifax, N.S. *Club:* Halifax.

GIRARD, Joseph, M.P.; *b.* St. Urbain, Charlevoix Co., Que., 2 Aug., 1854; *s.* of Patrice Girard, and Marie Tremblay; *m.* 1875, Emma Cote; three *s.* *Educ.:* Quebec Seminary. An argiculturist. Pres., Agric. Soc. of Lake St. John; Sec. of the Farmers' Club; Pres. of the Dairy Soc. of Quebec Prov. El. to Quebec Leg. Ass., at g. e., 1892; re-el. at g. e., 1897. El. to H. of C. at g. e., 1900, for Chicoutimi and Saguenay; re-el. at g. e. 1904, 1908. *Address:* St. Gedeon, Que.

GIRDWOOD, Gilbert P., Emeritus Professor of Chemistry, McGill Univ., *b.* London, Eng., 22 Oct., 1832; *s.* of G. F. Girdwood, M.D., Edinburgh, and *d.* of Rev. Thos. Bazely, Rector of Lavenham, Suffolk; *m.* 1862, M. M., *d.* of late T. E. Blackwell, C.E., Managing Director G. T. R.; five *s.* three *d.* *Educ.:* private sch., and St. George's Sch. of Medicine, London. Passed Coll. of Surgeons, London, 1854; House Surgeon Liverpool Infirmary, 1854, joined 1st Battalion Grenadier Guards, as Asst. Surgeon, 1854; came to Canada with 1st Battalion; at Trent Affair, 1862; stationed in Montreal; left the service on the Regt., returning to England; joined the Victoria Volunteer Militia as surgeon; served during Fenian Raid, 1866 (medal); promoted to Medical Staff Officer of Militia of Canada; took degree of M.D., C.M. at McGill Univ., 1865; apptd. Lecturer in Practical Chemistry in Medical Faculty of McGill Univ., 1869; Professor of Practical Chemistry, 1872-94; Professor of Chemistry, 1879-1902; emeritus prof., 1902 to date; 12 years Surgeon to Montreal Dispensary, and for 12 years Surgeon to Montreal General Hospital and is now Consulting Surgeon to both institutions; is Director of Electrical Treatment and X-Rays in Royal Victoria Hospital, Montreal; ex-President of the Roentgen Society of America; Vice-President, Canadian Branch Society of Chemical Industry; Fellow of the Chemical Society of the Chemical Institute of Great Britain of the Society of Public Analysts, of the Society of Chemical Industry, of the Royal Society of Canada, of the Natural History Society and Microscopical Society of Montreal. *Publications:* on Testing for Strychine, in the Lancet, 1856; on Dislocation of Phalanges, Montreal Medical Journal; on a case of Poisoning by Strychnine, Montreal Medical Journal, 1865; on Stereoskiagraphy and Stereoscopic Vision, Montreal Medical Journal, 1900; Address as Pres. of Chemical Section of R. S. C., vol. xii., 1894; on Stereomicropaphy in Transactions of Royal Microscopical Society, Feb., 1901, etc. *Recreations:* won mile race open to all officers in British Army, Aldershot, 1856; athletic exercise; boating. *Address:* 111 University Street, Montreal. *Club:* St. James', Montreal.

GIROUARD, Hon. Desire, B.C.L., D.C.L. (McGill); Judge of the Supreme Court of Canada; *b.* St. Timothee, Que., 7 July, 1836; *s.* of Jérémie Girouard and Hyppolite Picard; *m.* 1862, Marie Mathilde, *d.* of the late John Pratt, of Montreal. *Educ.:* Montreal Coll., studied law under the late Edward Carter, Q.C. Unsuccessful Can. for H. of C. at g. e., 1872 for constituency of Jacques Cartier; 1874, for Beauharnois; 1876, 1878, for Jacques Cartier, but thereafter el. and held seat for Jacques Cartier until 1895. In latter yr. refused seat in the Dom. Cabinet, on personal grounds. In collaboration with the late W. H. Kerr, Q.C., Sir Louis Jette, the late H. F. Rainville and Mr. J. A. Perkins, K.C.; carried on "La Revue Critique," which forced the downfall of the Que. Court of Appeals, 1874. Apptd. 28 Sept., 1895, to the Supreme Ct. of Can., of which he is now Senior Judge. *Publications:* Considerations sur les Lois Civiles du Marriage, also an essay on Insolvent Act of 1868; a work on Bills of Exchange; "Lake St. Louis, Old and New," and "Chevalier de la Salle." *Address:* 398 Wilbrod St., Ottawa; "Quatre Vents," Dorval, Que. (Summer). *Clubs:* Rideau, Golf, Ottawa; Royal Montreal Golf, Royal St. Lawrence Yacht, Dorval.

GIROUARD, Lieut.-Col. Sir Edouard Percy Cranwell, R.E., K.C.M.G., C.B., D.S.O.; Governor and Commander-in-Chief of Northern Nigeria; *b.* Montreal, 26 Jan., 1867; *s.* of Hon. D. Girouard, one of the Judges of the Supreme Court of Canada; *m.* 1903, Mary Gwendolen, *o. c.* of Sir Richard Solomon, K.C.M.G., C.B., Attorney-General for the Transvaal. *Educ.:* Royal Military Coll., Kingston. Entered British Army, 1888; Major, 1899; served Dongola Expeditionary Force, 1896 (despatches brevet of Major, D.S.O., British medal, Khedive's medal with two clasps); Nile Expedition, 1897 (despatches, clasp); railway traffic manager, Royal Arsenal, Woolwich, 1890-95; Director of Soudan railways, 1896-98; President of Egyptian Railway Board, 1898-99 (2nd class Medjidie); Director of Railways, South Africa, 1899-1902 (despatches); Commissioner of Railways, Transvaal and Orange River Colony, 1902-4; A.Q.M.G., Western Command, Chester, 1906; apptd. to present position, 1907. *Publication:* History of the Railways during the War in South Africa. *Address:* St. James's Court, Buckingham Gate, S.W. *Clubs:* Brooks's, Army and Navy.

GIROUARD, Hon. Jean, M.D., M.L.C.; *b.* St. Benoit, Que., 7 March, 1856; *s.* of Jean Joseph Girouard, notary, and Marie Emelie Berthelot; *m.* 1883, Lydia, *d.* of Hon. M. Laviolette, former Legis. Councillor for Delorimier: two *s.* two *d.* *Educ.:* St. Sulpice Seminary, Montreal. Apptd. Legis. Councillor for Delorimier, 27 Mar., 1897; a physician; has practised for thirty years. *Recreations:* hunting and fishing. *Address:* 54 St. Charles St., Longueuil, Que.

GISBORNE, Francis Hernaman; *b.* Brigus, Newfoundland, 19 May, 1858; 2nd *s.* of the late Frederick Newton Gisborne, the well known Electrical Engineer; *m.* Edith D. Himsworth, 2nd *d.* of Frederick H. Himsworth, barrister; four *s.* two *d.* *Educ.:* London, Eng., Coll. Sch., Windsor, N.S., and private tutor; called to the Bar of N.S., in 1880; for two years Asst. Engr. of Govt. Telegraphs; associate member of the Inst. of Elec. Engineers. Apptd. to the legal staff of the Dept. of Justice of Canada in 1882, and Secretary of the Department in 1909; Counsel to the Canadian Commissioners at the making of the International regulations for the protection of the fisheries under the treaty with the U.S. A member of the Diocesan, Provincial and General Synods of the Church of England in Canada, and Registrar of the General Synod. A member of the Board of the Missionary Society, and a member of the Anglican Executive of the Layman's Miss. Movement, and also Sunday School Commission. *Recreations:* canoeing, horticulture *Address:* 110 Cartier St., Ottawa.

GLADU, Joseph Ernest Oscar, B.A., M.P., *b.* St. Francois du Lac, Yamaska Co., 25 Oct.. 1870; *s.* of Victor Gladu and Mary Gill; *m.* 15 Nov., 1900, Isabella Boucher (*deceased*). *Educ.:* St. Mary's Coll., Montreal; elec. to the House of Commons, 1904-1908; Roman Catholic; Liberal. *Address:* St. Francois du Lac, Que.

GOBEIL, Antoine, B.A., I.S.O.; *b.* St. Jean, Island of Orleans, Que., 22 Sept., 1854; *s.* of Antoine Gobeil and Eléonore Pouliot; *m.* Blanche Gingras; two *s.* two *d.* *Educ.:* Seminary of Quebec; Laval Univ., entered the Civil Service in 1872, and retired 1st January, 1908; admitted to the bar, Province of Quebec, in 1902; now practicing in Montreal; was Law Clerk of Department of Public Works at Ottawa, from 1880 to 1885; Secretary from 1885 to 1891, and Deputy Minister, 1891 to 1908, when accepted pension. *Address:* The Marlborough, Montreal; "Aux Quartre Vents," St. Laurent, Island of Orleans, Que. *Club:* Rideau, Ottawa.

GODBOUT, Hon. Joseph, M.D.; Senator; *b.* St. Vital de Lambton, Co. of Beauce, Que.; *m.* (1st) Rachael Audet, Que., 8 Oct., 1878 (*d.* 21 Jan., 1881); (2nd) Mrs. G. N. Fauteaux (nee St. Pierre). *Educ.:* Laval Univ. and Quebec Seminary; graduated in medicine, 1877, and moved to St. Francois, when he followed his profession for 21 yrs. Elected Governor of the Bureau of Physicians, Que., July, 1895; Mayor of St. Francois, Beauce, Jan., 1898; first elec. to the H. of C., 1887, and re-elec., 1891-1896-1900; called to the Senate, 4 April, 1901; Liberal. *Address:* St. Francois, Beauce, Quebec.

GODBOUT, Joseph Arthur, LL.B., M.L.A.; *b.* 13 Dec., 1872, Lambton, Beauce Co., Quebec; *s.* of Joseph Godbout and Lucil Roy; *m.* Corinne Poulin; five *s.* one *d.* *Educ.:* Seminary of Quebec, and Laval Univ., Quebec. An advocat, 1898. Elec. to Leg. Ass. of Que., 1902; re-elected by acclam. 1904, and 1908. *Address:* St. George's, Beauce Co., Que.

GOOD, Henry John Prescott Wilshere; *b.* Solihull, nr. Birmingham, Eng., 22 Nov., 1848; *s.* of John Presley Good, M.A., and Clara Louise Rogers; *m.* Helen MacClude; three *s.* two *d.* *Educ.:* privately, Shoreham, and King's Coll. Arrived Canada, 30 June, 1869. For many years sporting editor *Mail and Empire;* editor, *Sunday World*, Canadian *Sportsman*. *Publications:* Many short stories. *Recreations:* racing, bowling, curling. *Address:* 644 Manning Ave., Toronto. *Club:* Albany, Toronto.

GOODERHAM, George Horace, M.L.A.; *b.* Toronto, 18 April, 1868; *s.* of George Gooderham, one of the founders of the distillery firm of Gooderham & Worts; *m.* Maude, *d.* of late H. S. Northrup. *Educ.:* Toronto Model Sch., and Jarvis Street Coll. Inst. A manufacturer and capitalist. Mem. of the Toronto Sch. Bd., 1899-1903; Chn. of the Bd. of Education, 1904. First el. to Ont. Legis. at g. e., 1908. *Addresses:* 49 Wellington St (Bus.); 204 St. George St., Toronto.

GOODEVE, Arthur Samuel, M.P.; *b.* Guelph, Ont., 15 Dec., 1860; *s.* of Arthur H. Goodeve, and Caroline Higginson; *m.* Ellen E. Spence; four *s.* two *d.* *Educ.:* Guelph Pub. and High Sch. Medalist, Ont. College of Pharmacy; Mayor of Rossland, B.C., 1899-1900; Provincial Secretary, McBride Government, 1902; Provincial Forestry Commissioner, 1909. *Address:* Rossland, B.C. *Club:* Rossland.

GOODWIN, William Lanton, B.Sc., D. Sc.; F.R.S.C.; *b.* Baie Verte, New Brunswick, 30 April, 1856; *s.* of Edward Chappell Goodwin (descended from a Massachusetts family of that name, members of which came to New Brunswick with Monckton's army, 1754), and Margaret Carey, *g. d.* of John Carey, an officer in a Highland Regt.; m. 1885, Christina Murray, *d.* of Rev. Wm. Murray, of Earlton, N.S., and of Kingston, Jamaica. *Educ.:* Mount Allison Academy and Univ., Sackville, N.B.; Edinburgh Univ.; Heidelberg; London. Canadian Gilchrist Scholar, 1877-80; Demonstrator of Chemistry in Univ. of Edinburgh, 1879-80; Demonstrator of Chemistry with Prof. Wm. Ramsay, Univ. Coll., Bristol, 1881-1882; Prof. of Chemistry, etc., Mount Allison, 1882-83; Professor of Chemistry, Queen's Univ., 1883-92; Director of the Sch. of Mining, Queen's Univ., Kingston.

1893-1906. *Publications:* A Text-book of Chemistry; papers in Transactions of R. S., Edinburgh; Berichte der deut. chem. Gesellsch.; Chemical News; Nature; Canadian Mining Review, etc. *Recreations:* fishing, music, study of birds and their songs. *Address:* 3 Alice St., Kingston, Ont.

GORDON, Rev. Charles William ("Ralph Connor"), B.A., D.D., LL.D., F.R.S.C.; *b.* Indian Lands, Glengarry Co., Ont., 13 Sept., 1860; *s.* of Rev. Daniel Gordon and Mary Robertson; *m.* Helen King, B.A., *d.* of Rev. Principal King of Manitoba Coll., Winnipeg; one *s.* four *d.* *Educ.:* Pub. Sch., Athol, Ont., and Harrington, Ont. High Sch., St. Mary's Ont., Univ. of Toronto; Theological Coll., Knox, Toronto, and Edinburgh. In Glengarry Co. until 11 yrs. of age; Oxford Co., High Sch. until 1879; grad. from Toronto Univ., 1883, and from Knox Coll., Toronto, 1887; New College, Edinburgh, 1887-1888; continental bicycle tour with five companions, 1888; missionary in the Rocky Mountains, until 1893; represented the Canadian Church in Great Britain, in 1893; St. Stephen's Church, Winnipeg, 1894, until the present time. *Publications:* "Black Rock," 1898; "Sky Pilot," 1899; Man from Glengarry," 1906; "Glengarry School Days," 1902;" "The Prospector," 1904; "Beyond the Marshes," 1900; "The Pilot at Swan Creek," 1903; "The Doctor," 1906; "The Angel and the Star," 1907; "Life of James Robertson," 1908; "The Foreigner," 1909. *Address:* 567 Broadway, Winnipeg, Man.; Kenora, Lake of the Woods, Ont.

GORDON, The Very Rev. Daniel Miner, M.A., B.D., D.D., LL.D., Principal of Queen's University, Kingston; *b.* Pictou, N.S., 30 Jan., 1845; *s.* of William Gordon and Amelia Miner; *m.* Eliza *s. d.* of Rev. John Maclennan (*d.* 1910); three *s.* two *d.* *Educ.:* Pictou Academy, Univ. of Glasgow, and Univ. of Berlin; ordained to the Ministry of the Church of Scot., Aug., 1866; Pastor of St. Andrew's Church, Ottawa, 1867-1882; of Knox College, Winnipeg, 1882-1887; Hon. Chaplain of 90th Regt., Winnipeg Rifles, through North-West Rebellion campaign in 1885, accompanying the fighting column under Gen'l. Middleton; Pastor of St. Andrew's Church, Halifax. 1887-1894; apptd. Professor of Systematic Theology in Presbyterian Coll., Halifax. In 1903, succeeded the late Principal Grant as Principal of Queen's Univ., Kingston. *Publications:* In 1880, "Mountain and Prairie." *Recreations:* boating, golf and skating. *Address:* Queen's Univ., Kingston. *Club:* Frontenac, Kingston.

GORDON, David Alexander, M.P.; *b.* Wallaceburg, Ont., 18 Jan., 1858; *s.* of Aaron Gordon and Jane Steinhoff; *m.* 8 April, 1884, Rose Fox, Bay City, Mich. *Educ.:* Wallaceburg Pub. Sch. Has been Town Councillor and was Mayor of Wallaceburg for three years in succession; elec. to the H. of C., 1904 and 1908; Church of England; Liberal. *Address:* Wallaceburg, Ont.

GORDON, George, M.P.; *b.* Pakenham, Ont., 2 May, 1865; *s.* of Alexander Gordon, and Elizabeth Fraser; *m.* 30 Aug., 1894, A. E. Parry, Dunnville, Ont.; three *d.* *Educ.:* Pembroke High School and Pub. Schs. Dir. Temagami Lumber Co., Ltd., Cache Bay Lumber Co., Ltd., A. J. Young Co., Ltd., Strong Lumber Co., Ltd., Lovering Lumber Co., Ltd., and George Gordon & Co. Contested Nipissing in 1904, but was defeated; first elec. to H. of C., 1908; Presbyterian; Conservative. *Address:* Sturgeon Falls, Ont.

GORDON, Henry Bauld, F.R.A.I.C., O.A.A.; *b.* Toronto, Ont., 30 Jan, 1854; *s.* Thomas and Elizabeth Hamilton; *m.* (1st) Mary Reynolds; (2nd) E. L. Skinner, two *s.* and one *d.* *Educ.:* Model School; studied with late Henry Langly; spent three years in Far East practicing Architecture. *Address:* 467 Spadina Ave., Toronto, Ont.

GORDON, James T., M.L.A.; *b.* Hastings Co., Ont., 24 Dec., 1859; *s.* of John and Sarah Gordon; *m.* 1880, Merle Baldwin, of King, Ont. *Educ.:* Com. Sch., Tweed, Ont. Removed to Winnipeg in 1880, and commenced to work in a lumber yard. Subsequently went into business of cattle exporting with Robt. Ironside. First built and owns largest abattoir west of St. Paul, and has cold storage plants at Kenora, Fort Winnipeg, Sault Ste. Marie, and Montreal. Company's ranches on Little Bow River, Alta.; employs some 1,600 or 1,700 men during season. El. to Manitoba Legis. at bye-el., 1901; re-el. at g. e., 1903, and 1907. *Address:* Winnipeg.

GORMAN, Michael James, LL.B., K.C.; *b.* Pembroke, Ont., 10 Sept., 1856; *s.* of James Gorman and Mary Ouellette; *m.* Mary Frances O'Meara, of Pembroke; three *d.* *Educ.:* Ottawa Univ., Toronto Univ. Admitted to the Bar 30 Jan., 1880. *Publication:* "Gorman's County Court Manual." *Address:* 291 Nelson St., Ottawa.

GORMULLY, Joseph James, K.C.; *b.* England, 1845; widower; one *s.* two *d.* *Educ.:* in England, a leading barrister in Ottawa. *Address:* 138 Daly Ave., Ottawa, Ont. *Clubs:* Rideau, Country, Ottawa; Mount Royal, Montreal.

GOSNELL, R. Edward; Sec. of Forestry Comn. for B.C.; *b.* Lake Beauport, Seigniory of St. Francis, Que., 1860; *m.* 1887, Agnes Wilson (*deceased*); one *d.* Taught sch. for a short time, and then entered into journalism, joined the staff of the Chatham *Tribune*, and subsequently ed. the Port Hope *Times*. and the Chatham *Planet*; removed to B.C., 1888, and joined staff of the Vancouver *News Advertiser;* apptd. Commr. of the B.C. Exhibit. Assn., 1890; apptd. Census Commr. for the New Westminster Dist., 1891; made Librarian and Sec. of the Bureau of Statistics and Historical Information for B.C.; for many yrs. editor of the Victoria *Colonist*, and Assoc. editor of the Winnipeg *Commercial;* now Sec. of the B. C. Forestry Comn., 1909-10. *Publications:* A year Book of B.C., 1896; an occasional contributor to mags. *Address:* Victoria, B.C.

GOSSELIN, L'Abbe Auguste Honore, Lit.D. (Laval), LL.D. (Ottawa), F.R.S.C.; *b.* St. Charles de Bellechasse, Que., 29 Dec., 1843; *s.* of Joseph Gosselin, and Angele Labrie. *Educ.:* Laval Univ., Quebec. Ordained to priesthood, and for some time was sec. to the Archbishop of Quebec; then curé for 25 yrs. Retired from ministry, 1893, to devote himself to literary work.

Publications: Life of Mgr. de Laval, first Bishop of Quebec; Le Docteur Labrie; Champlain on the Hudson; Abbe Picquet, founder of Ogdensburg, and many other historical works. *Address:* St. Charles de Bellechasse, Que.

GOUIN, Sir Lomer, B.C.L. (Laval Univ.); Premier of the Prov. of Quebec; *b.* Grondines, Que., 19 March, 1861; *s.* of J. Gouin, M.D., and Victoire Seraphine Fugere; *m.* 1888, Eliza, *d.* of the late Honore Mercier; two *s.* *Educ.:* Sorel Coll., Levis, Coll., Laval Univ., Montreal. Studied law under Sir John Abbott and afterwards under Hon. R. Laflamme, formerly Minister of Justice; called to the Bar, 1884. Unsuccessfully contested Richelieu Co. at g. e., in 1891; was returned for the St. James Division of Montreal for the local House in 1897; el. to Montreal City Council, 1900, but receiving the portfolio of Public Works in the Parent admn., he resigned from the Council; resigned from Ministry, 1905, and called upon to form a cabinet by the Lieut.-Gov.; was sworn in as Prime Minister in 1905; mem. of the Council of Public Instruction, Board of Control of La Banque Provinciale du Canada; director of Mount Royal Fire Ins. Co.; Knighted by Prince of Wales on occasion Quebec Tercentenial, 1908. *Address:* Quebec. *Clubs:* Canadien, St. Denis, Reform, Canada, Montreal; Garrison, Quebec.

GOULD, Ashley Mulgrave; *b.* Lower Horton, N.S., Oct. ,1859; s. Charles Edward and Mary Jane Fuller Gould; *m.* 1888, Margaret, *d.* Horace J. and Flora M. Gray. Early ed'n pub. and high schs., Northampton, Mass.; graduated Amherst, 1881, Georgetown Univ. Law Sch., 1884; admitted to bar of D. C., Apr., 1884. Was mem. Md. Ho. of Dels., 1898 (Rep. caucus nominee for speaker); since May, 1901, U.S. atty. for D. C. Prof. law of contracts, domestic relations and criminal law in law dept. Georgetown Univ. Apptd. Asso. Justice Supreme Court., Dist. of Columbia, Dec. 8, 1902. *Address:* 1931 16th St., N. W., Washington, D.C.

GOULD, Elgin R. L., B.A., Ph.D., *b.* Oshawa, Ont., 15 Aug., 1860; *s.* of John T. and Emily Adelaide Gould; *m.* 1887, Mary Hurst, *d.* ol late Lyttleton B. Purnell, Baltimore; three *s.* one *d.* *Educ.:* Toronto (private school); Victoria Univ., Johns Hopkins Univ., Baltimore; Pres. City and Suburban Homes Company, New York, and 34th St., National Bank; formerly statistical expert in charge of various investigations for the U.S. Department of Labour; formerly Lecturer at Johns Hopkins and Professor Chicago Universities; Chamberlain of city of New York, 1902-1904; takes an active interest in public, religious, and philanthropic affairs; prominent in Citizen's Union, New York's reform municipal party, Vestryman and Treasurer, St. Bartholomew's Church. *Publications:* The Gothenburg System of Liquor Traffic; Housing of the Working People; Public Control of the Liquor Traffic; The Social Condition of Labour; Civic Reform and Social Progress. *Recreations:* golf, fishing. *Address:* 301 West 77th Street, New York. *Clubs:* City, Century, National Arts, St. Andrew's Golf, Baltimore Country.

GOULD, Harvey James; *b.* Uxbridge, Ont., 1 May, 1857; *s.* Joseph Gould, ex-M.P. *m.* Martha Sharp, sister of S. Sharp, M.P., and Wm. Sharp, M.P.; four *s.* two *d.* *Educ.:* Uxbridge, Toronto, and Rockwood; Alderman, Reeve and Mayor of Uxbridge and Warden of Ont. Co.; President of Board of Trade; President of Midland Coal Ass'n.; Chairman of Presbyterian Church Board; P.D.D.G.M. of A.F. and A.M. *Address:* Uxbridge, Ont.

GOURDEAU DE BEAULIEU, Lieut.-Col. Francois F. E.; *b.* Quebec, 16 Oct., 1846; *s.* of Francois Gourdeau de Beaulieu, and Thesille Marcoux; *m.* Clara Paston, Quebec; one *d.* *Educ.:* Quebec Seminary. In pub. service of Canada for over 45 yrs.; Dep. Min. of Marine and Fisheries, 1896-1909, when request for superannuation granted. An officer of the Legion of Honour of France, 1905; a Dom. Commr. to Paris Exhibition, 1900; hon. Col. of Princess Louise Dragoon Guards, Ottawa. *Recreation:* hunting. *Address:* 27 Goulbourn Av., Ottawa. *Clubs:* Rideau, Elks, Hunt, Ottawa; Montreal; Century, Ogdensburg, N.Y.

GOWER; *see* Leveson-Gower.

GRACE, John D. G.; *b.* Almonte, Ont., Sept., 1870; *s.* of James Grace, and Mary Foley; unmarried. *Educ.:* Almonte; Ramsay; Ottawa; in journalism in Ottawa for many yrs. on the staff of the *Free Press* and *Journal;* editor and prop. of *United Canada*, which he founded in 1888; ex-pres., St. Patrick's Lit. Soc. Is an ardent supporter of all athletic sports. *Address:* 31 Slater St., Ottawa.

GRAHAM, Lieut.-Col. Alexander Petrie, Pres. of Canadian Club of Boston, Mass.; *b.* Hamilton, Ont., 18 March, 1864; *m.* Blanche Adams of Haverhill, Mass.; one *s.* *Educ.:* Hamilton. Served with Q.O.R., in N. W. Rebellion, 1885. In business at Boston, Mass, since 1889; Past Commander, British Naval and Mil. Veterans of Mass., and headed del. which presented address to Duke of Cornwall and York at St. John, N.B., 1901; mem. Ancient and Hon. Arty. Co. of Mass., and accompanied Regt. in its visit to England some yrs. ago; one of the founders of the Can. Club of Boston. *Recreations:* Lacrosse, horses, tennis. *Address:* 275 Main St., Haverhill, Mass., U.S.A.

GRAHAM, Hon. George Perry, M.P., LL.D., Minister of Railway and Canals; *b.* Eganville, Ont., 31 Mar., 1859; *s.* of late Rev. W. H. Graham and late Eleanor Stevenson; *m.* Carrie L. Southworth; two. *s.* *Educ.:* High Sch., Iroquois; Morrisburg Collegiate Inst. Taught school; received a practical business training; journalist for 25 years; editor of *Daily Recorder*, Brockville; elected to Ontario Legislature, 1898; made Provincial Secretary, 1905; Government defeated six months later. Became Leader of the Opposition shortly after. In Aug., 1907, called to Federal Government by Sir Wilfrid Laurier, as Minister of Railways and Canals. *Address:* Ottawa and Brockville, Ont. *Clubs:* Brockville; Laurentian, Ottawa; Ontario, Toronto.

GRAHAM, Sir Hugh, LL.D. (Glasgow), K.B.; *b.* Athelstan, Quebec, 1848; *s.* of Robert Walker Graham and Marion Gardner; *m.* Annie Beekman Hamilton; one *d.*

Educ.: Huntingdon, Que. Founder and proprietor of Montreal Daily and Weekly *Star*, two of the most successful newspapers in Canada; Knighted, 1908, by His Majesty in recognition of eminent services in many philanthropic enterprises. Leader in suppression of smallpox epidemic, 1885; initiated Fresh Air Fund in Montreal; insured lives of members of First Canadian Contingent to South Africa, 1899, each in $1,000.00 for benefit of their families; organized children's Patriotic Fund for families of British soldiers, delegate to imp. press confce, 1909; and chairman of Canadian section. *Address:* 538 Sherbrooke St. W., Montreal. *Clubs:* Mount Royal, St. James', Montreal.

GRAHAM, Robert James; *b.* Belleville, Ont., 2 April, 1860; *s.* of Kitchan Graham and E. A. Roblin; *m.* Grace A. Roblin; four *s.* three *d.* *Educ.:* Belleville, Ont. Mayor of Belleville, 1901-03; Pres., Board of Trade, 1907-08; Pres. of Canadian Club on organization; Pres., Y.M.C.A., for several years; Pres. New Brunswick Cold Storage Co., and several other industrial concerns. *Recreations:* travels abroad. *Address:* Belleville, Ont. *Clubs:* Imperial Belleville; Union, St. John, N.B.

GRAHAM, Hon. Wallace, B.A., K.C., Judge in Equity of Supreme Court and of Court for Divorce in N.S.; *b.* Antigonish, N.S., 15 Jan., 1848; *s.* of David Graham and Mary Elizabeth Bigelow; *m.* Annie Lyons, of Cornwallis, N.S.; one *s.* two *d.* *Educ.:* Acadia Coll. Called to Bar, 1871; Q.C., 1881; standing counsel in N.S. for Govt. of Canada 8 yrs.; apptd. on Commission to revise Statutes of Canada, 1888; and to revise Statutes of N.B., 1898. Governor of Dalhousie Coll., Halifax. *Address:* 37 South Park Street, Halifax. *Club:* Halifax.

GRANGE, Edward Wilkinson, B.A. (Toronto); journalist; *b.* Napanee, Ont., 4 July, 1876; *s.* of A. W. Grange and Annabella Daly; unmarried. *Educ.:* Napanee Coll. Inst., Victoria Univ. On staff of Toronto *News*, 1899-03; *Mail and Empire*, 1903-06; Ottawa corr. Toronto *Globe* since Jan., 1907; also Ottawa Corr. for the Winnipeg *Free Press*, Halifax *Chronicle*, St. John *Sun*, Montreal *Le Canada*, Vancouver *World*, Victoria *Times*, The *Standard*, and *Standard of Empire*, London, Eng.; Chicago *Tribune*, etc. *Address:* Gloucester Apts.; Press Gallery, Ottawa.

GRANT, George Davidson; Barrister-at-Law; *b.* Waterdown, Wentworth Co., Ont., 25 June, 1870; *s.* of Rev. Robert N. Grant, D.D., and Marian E. McMullen; unmarried. *Educ.:* Com. Sch., Coll. Inst., and Osgoode Hall. First el. to H. of C., 10 March, 1903; elected again at g. e., 1904 for newly constituted riding of N. Ontario; el. in Jan., 1905; Liberal Whip for Ont.; elec. Chairman of Comm. on Standing Orders; unsuccessful at g. e., 1908. *Address:* Orillia, Ont.

GRANT, Gordon, C.E., Chief Engineer National Transcontinental Railway Commission; *b.* Dufftown, Banffshire, Scotland, 2 Jan., 1865; *s.* Peter Grant, C.E., and Helen Gordon; *m.* Katherine McCarthy, *d.* of late Wm. McCarthy, C.E.; two *d.* *Educ.:* Ottawa Bus. Coll. and Ottawa Univ.; arrived Can., Sept., 1872; 1881-7, engaged on railway construction in Argentina; 1887-90, similar work on Intercolonial Ry., Canada, Cape Breton branch; 1890-93, Can. Pac. Ry.; 1893-95, East Coast Florida Ry., U.S.A.; 1895-1905, Can. Pac. Ry.; 1905 to date, Nat. Trans. Ry.; apptd. chief engineer, 1909. *Address:* 58 Sweetland Av., Ottawa. *Club:* Rideau, Ottawa.

GRANT, Sir James Alexander, M.D., K.C.M.G.; *b.* Inverness, Scot.; 1831, *m.* Maria, *d.* of Edward Mallock, *Educ.:* Queen's Coll., Kingston, Ont.; London; Edinburgh. M.P. for Co. of Russell, 1863-73; Ottawa, 1892-96; introduced Pacific Railway Bill to construct the present Trans-continental Railroad, 1892; President Tuberculosis Association of Canada, 1901-2; President R.S.C., 1903; hon. phy., Govs. Gen. of Canada, Knighted 1885. *Publications:* Essays on Medical, Surgical, and Scientific Subjects in the Journals of Canada, United States, and England; Organic Heart Disease. *Recreations:* chiefly in field of Geology; has made a large collection Silurian fossils. *Address:* 150 Elgin Street, Ottawa. *Club:* Rideau, Ottawa.

GRANT, William Lawson, M.A.; *b.* Halifax, N.S., 2 Nov., 1872; *s.* of George Monro Grant and Jessie Lawson. *Educ.:* Kingston Collegiate Institute, Queens' Univ., Kingston, Balliol Coll., Oxford and Univ. of Paris. Graduated Oxford, 1898; Master at Up. Can. Coll., Toronto, 1898-1902; Master at St. Andrew's Coll., Toronto, 1902-04; studied in Paris, 1904-06; Lecturer in Colonial History at Oxford, 1906. *Publications:* Principal Grant, a biography (in colloboration with C. F. Hamilton), 1904; Voyages of Samuel de Champlain (1907); Lescarbot's History of New France (1908-09), Canadian Constitutional documents (with H. E. Egerton) 1908; Acts of the Privy Council (Colonial Series), 1908-10, various magazine articles. *Address:* 10 Park Terrace, Oxford; Balliol Coll., Oxford, Eng.

GRASETT, Lieut.-Col. Henry James; Chief Constable of Toronto; *b.* Toronto, 18 June, 1847; *s.* of the Very Rev. the Dean of Toronto; *m.* Miss Parke, of London, Eng.; *Educ.:* Leamington Coll., England. Served with Q. O. R., in 1866; present at the battle of Lime Ridge; joined the 100th Prince of Wales Royal Can. Regt. (now Leinsters) as ensign in 1867; retired 1875; apptd. Lieut.-Col. of the Royal Grenadiers, 1880, and commanded that Corps throughout the N. W. Rebellion, being present at the engagements of Fish Creek and Batoche (mentioned in despatches). Apptd. Chief Constable of Toronto, Dec., 1886, which position he still holds. *Address:* 66 St. Patrick St., Toronto. *Clubs:* Toronto, Royal Canadian Yacht, Hunt, Military Inst., Toronto.

GREEN, Robert Francis; *b.* Peterborough, Ont., 14 Nov., 1861; *s.* of Benjamin Green and Rebecca A. Lipsett; *m.* 1889, Celia, *d.* of P. Macdonnell, of Erie, Pa. *Educ.:* Pub. and High Schs., Peterborough. Removed to Erie, Pa., when nineteen yrs. of age. Joined C. P. R. staff at Winnipeg, 1882. Served in North-West Rebellion, 1885; opened general store at Revelstoke, B.C. that yr., and later engaged actively in mining. First el. to B. C. Legis. for Slocan,

1898; apptd. chief commr. of Lands and Works, 5 Nov., 1903; resigned 1907. *Address:* Kaslo, B.C.

GREENWOOD, Hamar, B.A.; *b.* Whitby, Ont., 1870; *s.* of John Hamar Greenwood (*deceased*), Barr.-at-Law, Whitby, Ont., and Charlotte Hubbard (*deceased*), of United Empire Loyalist stock; unmarried. *Educ.:* Whitby Collegiate Inst. and Toronto Univ. Eight years Lieut. in Can. Militia; sometime in Department of Agriculture of Ontario. Went to England, 1885; joined Gray's Inn; now practicing Barrister, specializing in Privy Council Appeals; active Liberal speaker; declined an invitation to contest Grimsby, 1900; became Senior M.P., York, Eng., 1906; unsuccessful can. 1910. Parliamentary Private Secretary to Winston Churchill. *Recreations:* riding, shooting and fishing. *Address:* St. James' Court, Buckingham Gate, London, 4 Crown office Row, Temple, London, Eng. *Clubs:* Eighty, London, Eng.

GREGORY, Charles Ernest, LL.B., K.C.; *b.* Fredericton, N.B., 5 May, 1856; *s.* of Charles Curier Gregory, C.E.; *m.* Maude Charlotte Graham, *d.* of David Graham, Esq.; one *s.* *Educ.:* King's Coll., Windsor, Dalhousie Coll., Halifax, N.S.; candidate for H. of C. for Guysboro Co., in Conservative interest, 1896-1900. *Address:* Antigonish, N.S. *Clubs:* Halifax, N.S.

GREGORY, Hon. F. B.; one of the Judges of the Supreme Court of British Columbia; *b.* Fredericton, N.B., 1862; *s.* of Hon. Mr. Gregory, a former Judge of the Supreme Ct. of N.B. *Educ.:* Collegiate Sch., Fredericton, and Harvard Univ., where grad. 1884. Called to Bar of N.B., 1884, and practiced law at Fredericton, until 1890, when he removed to Victoria, B.C. For many yrs. a partner in the firm of Fell & Gregory; took an active part in the cases arising out of the seizure of B.C. sealing schooners by U.S. revenue cutters; apptd. to his present position Nov., 1909. Has taken great interest in military affairs, and was Col. of the 5th Regt., C.G.A. retiring with rank of Lieut.-Col. *Address:* Victoria, B.C.

GRENFELL, Wilfred Thomason, C.M.G., M.D., M.R.C.S., L.R.C.P., London; J.P., Newfoundland; Superintendent of Labrador Medical Mission of Royal National Missions to Deep Sea Fishermen; *b.* 28 Feb., 1865; *s.* of Algernon Sydney and Jane Georgina Grenfell; *m.* 1909, Anna MacClanahan, of Chicago, Ill. *Educ.:* Marlborough; Oxford; London Hospital. Entered service of R.N.M.D.S.F., 1889; after leaving Oxford, where he played for the Univ. at Rugby football, he was House Surgeon to Sir Frederick Treves, Bart., at the London, Hospital; fitted out the first hospital ship for the North Sea fisheries, and cruised with the fishermen from the Bay of Biscay to Iceland; established homes for them on the land and arranged mission vessels for them at sea; came to Labrador, 1892, where he built four hospitals, a series of co-operative stores, and an orphanage, and started numerous small industrial schemes. *Publications:* Vikings of To-day; The Harvest of the Sea; Off the Rocks; Labrador and its possibilities; many articles and monographs on deep-sea fisheries, fishermen, and work among them. *Recreations:* shooting, fishing, ski-ing. *Address:* 181 Queen Victoria St., London, E. C. Eng., or Harrington, Labrador, via St. John's, Nfld.

GRENIER, Gustave, I.S.O., J.P.; Clerk of the Executive Council, of Quebec; Deputy Lieutenant-Governor for signing warrants; *b.* Montreal, June, 1847; *m.* (1st) 1879, Kate Winfred Heatley of Quebec, (*d.* 1880); (2nd) 1889, Helen, d. of late Hon. F. G. Marchand, Premier of the Province; one *s.* three *d.* *Educ.:* Toronto and Quebec. Entered Civil Service of Province, 1867, as a junior clerk in the Executive Council Dept.; apptd. to present position, 1886. *Address:* 107 Grande Allée, Quebec.

GREY, The Earl, Albert Henry George, 4th Earl), G.C.M.G. (*cr.* 1904), LL.M., J.P., Governor-General and Commander-in-Chief of Canada; *b.* 28 Nov., 1851; *s.* of General Hon. Charles Grey and Caroline, *d.* of Sir Thomas Harvie Farquhar, Bt.; *S. u.*, 1894; *m.* Alice, 3rd *d.* of Robert Stayner Holford, M.P., Westonbirt, Gloucestershire, 1877; one *s.* two *d.* *Educ.:* Harrow; Trin. Coll. Camb. (Senior in Law and History Tripos, 1873); M.P. (L) S. Northumberland, 1880-85; Northumberland (Tyneside), 1885-86; Administrator of Rhodesia, 1896-97; Director of British South Africa Company, 1898-1904; apptd. Gov. Gen. of Canada, 1904; owns obaut 17,600 acres. *Publication:* Hubert Hervey. a Memoir, 1899. *Heir:* Viscount Howick. *Address:* Government House, Ottawa; Howick House, Lesbury, Northumberland. *Club:* Brooks's, London, Eng.

GRIER, Edmund Wyly, artist; *b.* Melbourne, Australia, 26 Nov., 1862; *s.* of Chas. Grier, L.R.C.P., M.R.C.S., and Mrs. (nee Morris) Grier; *m.* Florence Grale Dickson; three *s.* two *d.* *Educ.:* Bristol, Eng., and Up. Can. Coll.; arrived in Canada, 1876; exhibited at the Royal Acadmey, London, 1886 to 1895; studied under Legros, Bouguereau, Flewry, Gold Medal, Paris Solon, 1890; silver medal, Pan American Exhibition, 1901; Pres. Ont. Soc. Artists; mem. R.C.A. *Recreations:* shooting and fishing; *Address:* 73 Gormley Ave., and Imperial Bank Chambers, Toronto, Ont. *Clubs:* National, Toronto, Ont.

GRIFFIN, Frederick Thomas; Land Commr. of the Canadian Pacific Ry. Co.; *b.* Waterdown, Ont., 29 Oct., 1853; *m.* 1878, Edna E., *d.* of Charles Walker, of Toronto, Ont.; three *s.* *Educ.:* Pub. and High Schs., of Hamilton, Ont. Employed in a law office in Hamilton; entered Govt. services of Ont., in Dept. of Education, 1875; entered service of Canada North-West Land Co., 1882; entered Land Dept., of C.P.R., at Winnipeg, 1883; Asst. Land Commr., 1890; Land Commr., 1900. *Address:* Winnipeg. *Club:* Manitoba.

GRIFFIN, Martin Joseph, LL.D., C.M.G.; Parliamentary Librarian; *b.* St. John's, Nfld., 7 Aug., 1847; *s.* of Capt. P. Griffin, *m.* 1872, Harriet Staratt; three *s.* two *d.* *Educ.:* Halifax, N.S. Arrived in Canada, 1854; barrister, solicitor, civil servant; for some yrs. editor of the Halifax *Herald*, and Toronto *Mail;* apptd. Parliamentary Librarian, 6 Aug., 1885. *Publications:* contributions to Blackwood's, and many other periodicals. Has for many yrs. edited the literary column "At Dodsley's," a feature of the Montreal *Gazette's* Saturday edition. *Address:* 319 Daly Ave., Ottawa. *Club:* golf Ottawa.

GRIFFITH, William Lenny; *b.* Bangor, North Wales, 16 Aug., 1864; *s.* of John Griffith, a well known public speaker and lecturer, and Mary Elizabeth Rowlands; *m.* J. Ruth Sutherland, Huron Co., Ont.; four *s.* two *d.* *Educ.:* Grocers' Company Schs.; City of London, Coll.; arrived in Canada, 1882; took an active part in Manitoba politics from 1886 to 1896; one of the first wheat exporters from Manitoba to England; Canadian Agent in Wales; delegate Canadian Government to Patagonia; Permanent Secretary, Canadian High Commissioners' Office in London, since 1903. *Recreations:* Cricket, gardening. *Address:* White Lodge, 60 Tulse Hill, London, S.W. Eng. and Emerson, Man. *Clubs:* Devonshire, Canada, Royal Colonial Institute, London, Eng.

GRIGG, Richard; His Majesty's Trade Commissioner to the Dominion of Canada; J.P. for Counties of Durham and Devonshire, Eng.; *b.* Plymouth, Eng., 6 Sept. 1847; *s.* of Richard Grigg and Matilda Clara Lethbridge; *m.* Clara, *d.* of Adolphus Ayer of Plymouth; one *s.* one *d.* *Educ.:* Elmira, New York. Visited Canada, 1872; engaged in manufacturing and commercial pursuits in England, until 1904; special com. to Canada for H. M. Board of Trade in 1906. *Publications:* Conditions and prospects of British Trade in Canada (Blue Book). *Address:* The New Sherbrooke, Montreal; Wingfield, Devonport, Eng. *Clubs:* Royal Western Yacht, Pylmouth; St. James', Montreal; Constitutional, London.

GRIMMER, Hon. Ward Chipman Hazen, M.A., M.L.A.; Surveyor-General of New Brunswick; *b.* St. Stephen, N.B., 31 Oct., 1858; *s.* of George S. Grimmer, and Mary A. Grimmer; *m.* 1884, Bessie E. Gove. A lawyer; Mayor of St. Stephen; warden o Charlotte Co.; an unsuccessful can. for Charlotte Co., at g. e., 1899; first returned to the Legis. at g. e., 1903; re-el. at g. e., 1908. Sworn of the Ex. Coun. as Surveyor-General in the Hazen Govt., 24 March 1908; re-el. by accl., 7 April. *Address:* St. Stephen, N.B.

GRISDALE, Right Rev. John, D.D., D.C.L., Lord Bishop of Qu'Appelle, Sask.; *b.* Bolton, Lancashire, Eng.; *s.* of Robert and Alice Grisdale; *m.* Anne Chaplin, Leicestershire, Eng.; one *s.* one *d.* *Educ.:* Church Miss Coll., London, Eng. Arrived in Canada, 1873: Canon of St. John's Catherral, Winnipeg, 1874 to 1878; Dean, 1878-96; Rector of Qu'Appelle, 1896; Prof. of Theology, St. John's Coll., Winnipeg, 1874-1878; Prof. of Past. Theology, 1878-1890, Prol of General Synod; Bishop of Qu'Appelle, 1896. Examiner of Univ. and one of the original members of the Senate of the Univ of Saskatchewan, *Recreations* chess. *Address:* Bishop's Court, Indian Head Sask.

GRISDALE, Joseph Hiram, B.Agr.; *b.* St. Marthe, Que 18 Feb, 1870; *s* of Albert B. Grisdale and Elizabeth Simpson; *m.* Laura Vipond of Hudson Que., two *s.* two *d* *Educ.:* Vankleek Hill Albert Coll., Belleville Toronto Univ., Ont. Agric Coll., and Iowa Agricultural Coll. A farmer's son Taught school for a few years to earn money for education; Gold Medalist at O. A. C., Guelph; first class honors in Agriculture and Live Stock, Guelph and Iowa. *Publications:* reports, etc. *Recreations:* carpentry. *Address:* Experimental Farm, Ottawa, Ont.

GROUARD, Right Rev. Mgr. Emile, O. M.I., D.D., Vicar Apostolic of Athabasba; *b.* Sablé (Mans), France, 2 Feb., 1840. *Educ.* Little Seminary of Le Mans and Grand Seminary in Quebec; arrived in Canada, 1860; ordained Priest, 3 May, 1862; entered community of Oblate Fathers, 21 Nov., 1863; Missionary among Indians of Canadian North West; named Titular Bishop of Ibora, and Vicar Apostolic of Athabaska, 18 Oct., 1890. *Address:* Lesser Slave Lake, Alta.

GROVES, Abraham, M.D.; *b.* Peterborough, Ont., 8 Sept., 1847; *s.* of Abraham Groves and Margaret Gibson; *m.* Jennie Gibbon (*deceased*); one *s.* one *d.* *Educ.:* Fergus High Sch, and Toronto Univ.; founded Royal Alexandra Hospital, Fergus; Director of Farmer's Bank; Pres. Munro Mines. *Address:* Fergus, Ont.

GUERIN, James John Edmund, M.D.; Mayor of Montreal, 1910-11; *b.* Montreal, 4 July, 1856; *s.* of Thomas Guerin, C.E., and Mary Maguire (both Irish); widower. *Educ.:* Montreal Coll., and McGill Univ. (grad. in Med., 1878); Clinical Prof. in Laval Univ. A Commr' to settle the claims arising from the North West Rebellion, 1885. First el. to Quebec Leg. Ass. for Montreal Centre, 1895; re-el. at g. e., 1897. A mem. of the Marchand Admn. without portfolio. Has been Pres. of St. Patrick's Soc., Shamrock Lacrosse Club, and many other organizations. El. Mayor of Montreal, Feb., 1910, as head of the Citizen's slate. *Address:* 4 Edgehill Av., Montreal.

GUISE, Arthur; Comptroller to His Excellency's Household; *b.* Gorey, Wexford Co., Irel., 20 Feb., 1868; *s.* of Lieut.-Gen. J. C. Guise, V.C., C.B. *Educ.:* Wellington Coll., Berks. Asst. Priv. Sec. to Lord Houghton, Lord Lieut. of Irel., 1892; Comptroller to Lord Minto, Gov.-Gen. of Can., 1898; priv. Sec. to Mr. W. Astor, 1904; Priv. Sec. to Lord Rosebery, 1906; Comptroller to Lord Grey, Gov.-Gen. of Can., 1909. *Address:* St. Valeran, Irel. *Club:* Wellington, London, Eng.; Rideau, Ottawa.

GURD, Charles; *b.* Edgeworthstown, Irel., 1842. *Educ.:* Watson's Academy, Montreal; McGill Univ. Arrived in Canada with his parents in early childhood. Entered firm of which he is now Pres., about 1868. Mem. Montreal Bd. of Trade. Can Manufacturers' Assn.; life governor Montreal Gen. Hospital, Western Hospital Protestant Hospital for Insane: officer of Dom. Commercial Travellers' Assn.; Treas Dom. Commercial Travellers' Mutual Benefit Soc. *Address:* 65 McGill Coll. Av Montreal.

GURNEY, Edward: Pres. of the Gurney Foundry Co.: *b.* Hamilton. Ont 4 August, 1845; *s.* of Edward Gurney: *m* 1868, Mary Frances, *d.* of William A. Cromwell, of Ingersoll, Ont; two *s.* three *d.* *Educ.:* Hamilton pub. schs. Admitted a mem of his father's firm which was converted into a joint-stock Co under the name of The Gurney Foundry Co. 1891 of which he was made Pres. Estbd. a foundry in Boston, Mass., 1887. El. Vice-Pres. of the Toronto Bd. of Trade, 1895; Pres. 1896. Mem. Ex-Committee of the National Sanitarium Assn. *Address:* 44 Walmer Rd., Toronto.

GUSSOW, Hans. Theodor, botanist, Central Exp. Farm, Ottawa; *b.* Breslau, Silesia, 24 Aug., 1879; *s.* of Ernest Gusson, City Architect, Breslau and Helene Sirgel; *m.* Jenny Maria Hilzegrath; one *s.* *Educ.:* Breslau, St. Elizabeth Pub. Sch., Botan Inst., Univ. Breslau, Leipzig; arrived in Canada, 19 July, 1909. Asst. to Consulting Botanist Royal Agricultural Society of England, 1903-1909. Botanist to the Dominion Experimental Farm. F.R.M.S., M.T. de la S.T. de France; mem. of Assoc. of Economic Biology; mem. of Assoc. of Botany; mem. of American Assn. for Advancement of Science; Corr. mem. Royal Hort. Soc., London. *Recreations:* Microscopy and Philately. *Address:* 83 Fairmount Ave., Ottawa, Ont.

GUTHRIE, Donald, K.C.; Inspector of Registry Offices for Ontario; *b.* Scotland, 1840; *s.* of Hugh Guthrie and Catherine MacGregor; *m.* Eliza Margaret MacVicat (*d.* 1900); four *s.* three *d.* *Educ.:* Scotland and Canada. Came to Canada, 1854; called to Bar of Ont., 1866; apptd. Q.C. by Lieut.-Gov. of Ont., 1876, and by Gov.-Gen., 1885. Mem. of H. of C. for South Wellington, 1876-1882, and of Ont. Leg. Ass. 1886-1894; Bencher of Law Soc. of Upper Can. since 1882; apptd. to his present position 1895. *Recreation:* gardening. *Address:* "Ardmay," Guelph, Ont. *Club:* Priory, Guelph.

GUTHRIE, Hugh, K.C., M.P.; *b.* Guelph, Ont., 13 Aug., 1866; *s.* of Donald Guthrie and Eliza Margaret Guthrie; *m.* Maude Henrietta Scarff; three *s.* one *d.* *Educ.:* Guelph Collegiate Inst., Osgoode Hall, Toronto. Called to Bar, Ontario, Jan., 1888; created K.C. June, 1902; elected to H. of C. for South Wellington at g. e., 1900-1904-1908; chairman Railway Committee H. of C. since 1907. *Address:* Guelph, Ont.

GZOWSKI, Casimir S.; *b.* Toronto, Ont. 2 Dec., 1847; *s.* of Col. Sir Casimir, K.C.M.G., and Lady Gzowski, *m.* Mary Bell, Buffalo, N.Y., U.S.A.; seven *s.* three *d.* *Educ.:* Leamington Coll., Eng., and Toronto Univ., Toronto, Ont. *Address:* 60 Glen Road, Rosedale, Toronto.

H

HACKETT, James Keteltas; *b.* Wolfe Island, Ont., 6 Sept., 1869; *s.* James Henry and Clara C. Hackett; *m.* 1897, Mary Mannerin. Grad. Coll. of City of New York, 1893; studied New York Law School. Made his debut on stage in Palmer's Stock Co., 1892; leading man New York Lyceum at 26; most notable success, Prisoner of Zenda, and its sequel, Rupert of Hentzau, and The Pride of Jennico; now one of the few actor-managers in America. *Clubs:* The Players. *Address:* 38 E. 33d. St., New York.

HADRILL, George; Secy. Montreal Bd. of Trade; *b.* London, Eng., 2 Aug., 1848; of English parentage; *m.* Emmeline L., *d.* of J. Albert Copland, solicitor of Chelmsford, Eng.; one *s.* *Educ.:* at Dr. Pinche's Sch., George Yard, Lombard St., London. Came to Canada, in 1874, but spent following two yrs. in Eng., in mercantile life. Entered service Montreal B. of T., 1877; Asst. Secy., May, 1880; Secy. since 1886. Has been del. of Bd. to several Congresses of Chambers of Com. of Empire, including Australia, 1909. *Address:* 632 Dorcester St. W., Montreal. *Club:* Canada, Montreal.

HAGGART, Alexander, B.A., LL.B., K.C., M.P.; *b.* Peterborough, Ont., 1850; *s.* of Archibald Haggart and Elizabeth McGregor; *m.* 1888, Elizabeth Littlenales. *Educ.:* Victoria Univ., Cobourg, Ont.; studied Law in Toronto, shortly afterwards leaving for Manitoba ,and practiced in Winnipeg; first el. to H. of C., 1908. *Address:* 229 Kennedy St., Winnipeg. *Clubs:* Manitoba, Commercial, Advance, Winnipeg.

HAGGART, Hon. John Graham, M.P.; *b.* Perth, Ont., 14 Nov., 1836; *s.* of the late John Haggart, a native of Breadalbane, Scot., and Isabella Graham of the Isle of Skye; *Educ.:* Perth; was Mayor of Perth, 1867, 1869 and 1871; an unsuccessful candidate for the Ontario Legislature; elec. to the H. of C. for S. Lanark, 1872, and each subsequent election; entered Sir John A. Macdonald's Cabinet as Postmaster Gen'l., 3 Aug., 1888, and re-appointed to the same office in the Abbott Administration; until 11 Jan., 1892, when he became Minister of Railways and Canals; held the same portfolio in the Thompson, Bowell and Tupper Administrations, retiring with the latter 8 July, 1896; resigned from the Bowell Ministry, 4 Jan., 1896, and was re-apptd. to the same office, 15 Jan., 1896; was elec. Chairman of the Executive of the Liberal Conservative Union of Ont., Oct., 1896. Presbyterian; Conservative. *Address:* Perth Ont.

HAGUE, Rev. Canon Dyson, M.A.; Canon of St. Paul Cathedral, London, Ont.; *b*, Toronto, Ont., 1857; *s.* of George Hague. Esq., Montreal (late Gen'l. Manager, Merchants Bank, Montreal); *m.* J. Baldwin, *d.* of Robert Baldwin and *g. d.* of late Hon. Robt. Baldwin; two *s.* two *d.* Curate, St. James' Cathedral, Toronto; first Rector of St. Paul's, Brockville; 7th Rector St. Paul's, Halifax, 1890-97; Professor of Liturgies, Wycliffe Coll., 1897-1902; since 1903, Rector Memorial Church, London, Ont. *Publications:* Protest of Prayer Book (3rd ed., Can. and 2 English); Church of England before the Reformation; Confirmation. *Address:* Memorial Church Rectory, London, Ont.

HAGUE, George; *b.* Rotherham, Yorkshire, Eng., 13 Jan., 1825; *s.* of John Hague, draper and tailor, Rotherham; *m.* (1st) Miss Cousins, *d.* of Jax M. Cousins, of Sheffield, Eng.; 2nd, Miss Matcheson, of Philadelphia, Pa. *Educ.:* Moorgate Acad., Rotherham. Arrived in Can., 1854; for 25 years gen. mgr. of the Merchants Bank of Can.; a governor of McGill Univ.; Vice-Pres., Montreal Diocesan Coll. For many years has taken an active part in the development of religious life and work in Canada through medium of Anglican Church and Y.M.C.A. *Publications:* Many articles on banking in financial journals, covering a long series of years; a practical treatise on banking and Commerce; 3 vols. of Studies in the Biography and History of the Old Testament. *Recreations:* art, literature. *Address:* "Rotherwood," Redpath St., Montreal; Fairmount Lodge, Ste. Agathe des Monts, Que.

HALE, Edward John; *b.* Quebec, Que., 1833; *s.* of the late Hon. Edward Hale; *m.* 1866, Miss Sewell, of Quebec (now deceased) one *s.* *Educ.:* Bishop's Coll., Sch., Lennoxville. Removed to Sherbrooke with his parents in early childhood; Boston, Mass. 1853, and entered office of J. M. Forbes & Co., china merchants, as junior clerk; returned to Quebec, 1875; acts as executor of his father's estate. Dir. Union Bank of Can.; Treas., Finlay Asylum of Quebec, and St. George's Soc., for many years. *Recreations:* boating, shooting, fishing. *Address:* 50 des Carrieres St., Quebec. *Clubs:* Garrison, Quebec, Stadacona Fish and Game.

HAM, George Henry; *b.* Trenton, Ont., 23 Aug., 1847; *s.* of John Vandal Ham, and Eliza A. E. Clute Ham; *m.* Martha Helen Blow; one *s.* two *d.* *Educ.:* Whitby Gram. Sch., Ontario; went to Winnipeg in 1875, was alderman and School Trustee of Winnipeg for several years; Correspondent for Toronto *Mail* and St. Paul Minn., *Pioneer Press*, during the rebellion of 1885; City editor, Winnipeg *Free Press;* managing editor Winnipeg *Tribune* and Winnipeg *Times;* member Parliamentary Press Gallery, Ottawa, for several years. In 1891, went on the staff of the C. P. Ry. Co., with which he still continues as publicity agent. *Publications:* The New West (1884); The Flitting of the Gods (1906). *Address:* 4132 Western Av., Westmount, Que.; *Clubs:* Montreal; Laurentian, Ottawa.

HAMILTON, Most Rev. Charles, M.A. (Oxford); D.D. (Bishop's Coll.),D.C.L. (Trinity); Archbishop of Ottawa and Metropolitan of Canada; *b.* Hawkesbury, Ont., 6 Jan., 1834; *s.* George Hamilton, of Que. and Hawkesbury, and Susan Craigill Hamilton; *m.* Frances Louisa Hume Thomson four *s.* five *d.* *Educ.:* Montreal High Sch., Univ. Coll., Oxford, Eng. Ordained Deacon, St. Matthew's Cath., Quebec, 21 Sept., 1857; ordained Priest, 1858; enthroned as Bishop of Hamilton, Ont., 20 May, 1885, translated to Ottawa Diocese, 1896; chosen as Metropolitan of Canada, by the House of Bishops, in the Ecclesiastical Prov. of Can., 1909; Archbishop of Ottawa, 1909. *Recreations:* reading, walking. *Address:* 495 Wilbrod St., Ottawa, Ont.

HAMILTON, Charles Frederick, M.A.; *b.* Roslin, Hastings Co., Ontario, 7 Dec., 1869; *s.* Charles Samuel Hamilton, M.D., C.M., and Alice, *d.* of Geo. Edward Jaques, Montreal; *m.* (1st) Clarissa, *e. d.* of Donald Wilson Ross, barrister-at-law, sometime of Walkerton, Ont.; (2nd) Eliza Henrietta, *d.* of the Rev. James Mockridge, Belleville, sometime Rector of St. George's Church, Belleville; one *d.* *Educ.:* Picton and Campbellford High Sch., Queen's University, Kingston, Ont.; employed on Toronto *Globe*, 1893 to 1903, serving as its correspondent in South Africa; connected with Toronto *News* since 1903; its resident correspondent at Ottawa, since 1904. Corr. *Morning Post*, London, Eng. *Publications:* colloborated with W. L. Grant in writing the life of Principal G. M. Grant. *Address:* 9 Cliff St., Ottawa, Ont. *Club:* Rideau, Ottawa.

HAMILTON, Rev. Harold Francis, M. A., B.D., *b.* Quebec, 1876; *s.* Charles Hamilton, Archbishop of Ottawa, and Frances Louisa Hamilton. *Educ.:* Trinity Coll. Sch., Port Hope, Ont., and Christ Church, Oxford Eng. Curate St. Matthew's Church, Que., 1900-1902; Lecturer Bishop's Coll., 1902-1906; Instuctor General Seminary, New York, 1906-1907; Professor Bishop's Coll. 1907. *Recreations:* Tennis, golf, hockey. *Address:* Bishop's Coll., Lennoxville, Que.

HAMILTON, John, M.A., D.C.L., Chancellor, Univ. of Bishop's Coll., Lennoxville, Que.; *b.* Quebec, 7 Sept., 1851; *s.* of Robert Hamilton and Isabella H. Thomson; *m.* Ida M., *d.* of A. C. Buchanan, *g. d.* of Chief Justice Bowen; four *d.* *Educ.:* Bishop's Coll., School; Trinity Coll., Toronto. Merchant, retired. *Recreations:* yachting, golf. *Address:* 48 Rue des Carrieres, Quebec. *Clubs:* Garrison, Quebec; Royal Canadian Yacht, Toronto.

HAMILTON, Miss May; *d.* of the late James Cleland Hamilton, B.A., Honor grad. of the Toronto Conservatory of Music; organist of Cook's Church, Toronto, and mus. teacher; Canadian representative of the New York *Musical Courier.* For three yrs. edited the Toronto Conservatory Bi-monthly Magazine. Returned to Canada after being on the staff of the *Musical Courier* in Chicago and New York. Removed to Victoria, and continued musical career, giving piano lessons. *Publications:* A poem on "Sir Henry Irving," printed in the Vancouver *News Advertiser*. A number of poems tending to uphold the superiority of the soul. *Address:* 1020 Cullinson St. Victoria, B.C. *Club:* Ladies' Musical.

HAMILTON, Lieut.-Col. Robert Baldwin; *b.* Toronto, Ont., 10 Oct., 1847, *s.* Sidney Smith and Ann Coulthard Hamilton; *m.* Mary Kate Pellatt; one *s.* *Educ.:* Model and Model Gram. Sch., Toronto. On leaving sch., joined his father in business. Inspector of vital statistics for 13 years; resigned and now engaged as Mining broker and in machinery business. For several yrs. mem. of Toronto City Coun. and Public Sch. Bd. Served 31 years continuously in 2nd Queen's Own Rifles; rose from the ranks and was Commanding Officer for 8 years, retiring in 1897; Commanding Officer Boys' Brigade for some years; was an active lacrosse player for years, captain of his team for 13 years, and President for three years; Pres. of National Amateur Lacrosse Assn., twice, and one of the founders and first Pres., Canadian Lacrosse Association; a Liberal. *Address:* 267 Sherbourne Street. *Office:* 24 Aberdeen Chambers, Toronto.

HANBURY-WILLIAMS, General Sir John, K.C.M.G., C.V.O.; *b.* 19 Oct., 1859; *y. s.* of late Ferdinand Hanbury-Williams of Coldbrook Park, Monmouthshire; *m.* 1888, Annie Emily, *e. d.* of Emile Reiss; two *s.* three *d.* *Educ.:* Wellington Coll. Joined 43rd Light Infantry, 1878; apptd. A.D.C. to Lt.-Gen. Sir E. Hamley, commanding 2nd Div. in Egypt, 1882; battle of Tel-el-Kebir, horse shot (despatches, medal with clasp, bronze star, 5th class Medjidie); extra A.D.C. to Sir M. E.

Grant Duff, Governor of Madras, 1884, and again 1885; apptd. extra A.D.C. to Lt.-Gen. Sir H. Macpherson, Burma, 1886; adjutant 3rd Oxford Light Infantry, 1892-97, Military Sec. to His Ex. Sir A. Milner, 1897-1900; Secretary to Secretary of State for War, 1900-3; served South Africa, 1899-1900 (despatches, medal and 3 clasps, promoted Lieut.-Col., half-pay). Military Secretary to His Excellency Earl Grey, 1904-9; Brigadier-General, Scottish Command, 1909 *Recreations:* hunting, golf, shooting. *Address:* Edinburgh, Scot. *Clubs:* Army and Navy; Travellers, London, Eng.

HANCE, James Busick, artist; *b.* England, 19 Jan., 1847; of English parentage; *m.* Emily, *d.* of the late I. W. Ritchie; one *s.* *Educ.:* England. Visited France and Italy in order to advance his artistic education; finally settled in Canada, 1895. Devotes himself principally to the scenery of the Prov. of Que., and esp. the Lower St. Lawrence. *Addresses:* Morrin College, Quebec; Murray Bay, Que.

HANEY, Michael John, C.E., contractor; *b.* Galway Co., Irel., 5 Sept., 1854; *s.* of Peter Haney and Bridget Ruddy; *m.* 1881, Margaret Godfrey, of Kingston, Ont.; five *d.* *Educ.:* Watertown, N.Y. Came to Canada, May, 1873. First worked on the farm; in 1872, was Asst. Engr. at the building of the Kingston and Pembroke Ry.; Divisional Engr. on the Lake Ontario Shore Road in 1877; supt. of the Pembina branch of the C.P.R., 1879, being first Supt. on the C.P.R.; Supt. of construction of secs. 14 and 15 of the C.P.R., which cost $4,000,000, 1881; Divisional Supt. of the lines west of Winnipeg, 1882; Mgr. of construction for Andrew Onderdonk, of 370 miles of the C.P.R. in British Columbia, 1883-1887. Was the first contractor of the Red River Valley Ry. from Winnipeg to West Lynn, now part of the Mackenzie & Mann system, 1886; was contractor of the Sault Ste. Marie Canal, 1889-1896; Mgr. of the construction work of the C.P.R., 1897. Also built the Crow's Nest Pass Ry., and the Hillsborough Bridge, P.E.I.; in 1903 built the Locomotive and Machine Works at Longue Pointe, Montreal. Since 1904 has built the Toronto tunnel, several break-waters, and other contracts with the Dom. Govt. Is associated with the Montreal Locomotive and Machine Co., Montreal; Canadian Locomotive Co., Kingston; Pres. Canadian Portland Cement Co.; Dir., Home Bank, and North American Life Insur. Co.; mem. of the Toronto and Canadian Soc. of Civil Engineers. Pres., Ontario Club; founder and mem. of the Bd. of Governors of the Catholic Church Extension Soc. of Can. *Recreations:* fishing, motoring, riding. *Addresses:* Home Bank Bldg. (Bus.); Clifden Hall, Rosedale, Toronto. *Clubs:* National, Ontario, Toronto; Rideau, Ottawa; Manitoba, Winnipeg.

HANNA, D. Blyth; *b.* Thornliebank, Scot., 20 Dec., 1858; *s.* of William and Janet Blair Hanna; *m.* Maggie Garland, Portage La Prairie, Man.; one *s.* two *d.*; *Educ.:* Thornliebank and Glasgow, Scot.; arrived in Canada, 1882; began as a junior clerk on the Glasgow, Barrhead and Kilmarnock Railway, 1874; entered Grand Trunk Auditing Department, Montreal, 1882; from 1884 to 1886 in Audit Department of New York West Shore & Buffalo Railway, at New York. Went to Portage La Prairie in 1886 as chief accountant of the Manitoba & Northwestern Railway; apptd. Treasurer in 1892, and land commissioner in 1893. Became first Gen. Supt. of the Can. Nor. Ry., at its inception in 1896, remaining with headquarters at Winnipeg till 1902, when he became third Vice-Pres. and was transferred to Toronto. Still holds that office Apptd. Pres. of the Can. Northern Que. Ry. in 1903, and Pres. of the Quebec & Lake St. John Railway in 1907. Is also third Vice-Pres. of the Can. Northern Ont. Ry., and third Vice-Pres. of the Halifax & South Western Ry. Apptd. a receiver of the Chicago & Milwaukee Electric Ry. in 1908. Director of many companies, including Winnipeg Electric Ry.; Manufacturers' Life Assurance Co.; London and Canadian Loan and Agency Co.; Canadian Northern Prairie Lands Co.; Western Fire Insurance; British Empire Trust Co. *Address:* Toronto, Ont. *Clubs:* Toronto, Albany, Toronto; Winnipeg, and Brandon.

HANNA, Hon. William John, K.C.; Prov. Sec. and Registrar-General of the Prov. of Ontario; *b.* Adelaide, Middlesex Co., Ont., 13 Oct., 1862; *s.* of George Hanna and Jane Murdock; *m.* (1st) 1891, Jean G. Neil; (2nd) Maud MacAdams, of Sarnia, Ont.; one *s.* two *d.* *Educ.:* Pub. Sch., Brooke Tp., Lambton Co. A barrister. An unsuccessful can. for H. of C. for West Lambton at g. e., 1896 and 1900. First el. to Legis. at g. e., 1902; re-elec. at g. e. 1905. Apptd. Prov. Sec. in Whitney Admn. 8 Feb., 1905; re-el. by accl. at bye-el., 21 Feb., 1905; re-el. at g. e., 1908. *Address:* Toronto, Ont.

HANNAH, George Weir; Passr. Mgr. of the Allan Steamship Line, Montreal; *b.* Glasgow, Scot., 5 Dec., 1847; *s.* of William and Margaret Hannah; *m.* Cora A. Kissam; one *s.* one *d.* *Educ.:* Glasgow, and Brooklyn L. Coll., New York. (Grad. 1874). Came to Canada, 1893; has for forty-two years been continuously connected with the North Atlantic Passenger business; Associated with the Inman Steamship Co., New York, for twenty-five years., and passenger mgr. of the Allan Line, Montreal, for seventeen yrs. *Address:* 186 Mansfield St., Montreal. *Clubs:* St. James', Canada, Montreal.

HANNON, James Willson, Judge of the District Court of the Judicial District of Regina, in the Prov. of Sask.; *b.* Hamilton, Ont., 11 Oct., 1870; *s.* Rev. James Hannon, D.D., and Sarah Margaret Willson; *m.* Emma Orilla Woods. *Educ.:* Schs. of Ont. Taught Sch. and studied law; went west; Crown Prosecutor for Sask.; Town Solicitor at Prince Albert; Agent of Dominion Lands and Crown Timber Agent at Prince Albert; Registrar of Land and Titles at Battleford. *Address:* 2276 Lorne St., Regina, Sask.

HARCOURT, Hon. Richard, M.A., LL. D., D.C.L., K.C., M.L.A., Ontario, continuously from 1878 to 1905; Member of Cabinet since 1888 to 1905; late Minister of Education; *b.* 17 March, 1849; *s.* of late Michael Harcourt, M.P., *m.* Augusta H. Young; three *s.* *Educ.:* Toronto Univ. Barr., 1876; Q.C., 1890; D.C.L., Trinity Univ.; LL.D., Univ. of Toronto; Treasurer of Province, 1888-98; a Liberal. *Address:* Welland, Ontario.

HARDING, His Hon. John Elley, K.C.,Co. Ct. Judge of the Co. of Victoria; *b.* Beverley Tp., Wentworth Co., Ont., 29 May, 1840 *s.* of John Harding and Jane Talbot; *m.* 1866, Mary, *d.* of George Stevenson, of Sarnia, Ont.; two *s.* three *d.* *Educ.:* Com. Schs., private tuition, Caradoc Acad., nr. London, Ont. At age of seventeen commenced study of law in office of Richard Bayley, K.C., London, Ont., and later in office of Eccles & Carroll, Toronto; called to Bar of Upper Can., 1866, and began practice in St. Mary's, Ont.; removed to Stratford, Ont., 1884, where he practiced for fourteen yrs. Apptd. Q.C., 1899, and Local Master of the High Ct. at Stratford, in 1890; apptd. to his present position, 1898. Chr., Coll. Inst. Bd. of St. Mary's for two yrs., and a mem. for thirteen yrs. A distinguished mem. of the Masonic Order, in which Order he has held important offices. Grand Master of the Grand Lodge of Canada, 1902-03. *Address:* Lindsay, Ont.

HARDING, Right Rev. Malcolm Taylor McAdam, D.D., coadjutor Bishop of Qu'Appelle, Sask. For twenty three years in the service of the Canadian Anglican Church. Very early in his career he was stationed at Mattawa, from which he was transferred to Brockville, Ont. Called to the West, and became Rector of St. Mathew's, Brandon, Man.; Archdeacon of the Diocese; Co-adjutor Bishop of Qu'Appelle. *Address:* Qu'Appelle, Sask.

HARDER, Worth Cleland, Can. Corr., the Chicago *Tribune*; *b.* Niles, Mich., U.S.A., 27 Aug., 1881; *s.* of James E. and Florence M. Harder; *m.* Caroline Selden Gale. Engaged in newspaper work in the U.S.A. since 1901; Washington corr. Minneapolis *Tribune*, 1907; apptd. Can. corr. Chicago *Tribune*, 1909. *Address:* 162 Daly Ave., Ottawa. *Club:* National Press.

HARDY, His Hon. Alexander David, County Judge of Co. of Brant, and local Judge of the High Court of Justice; *b.* Brantford, Ont., 13 July, 1859; *s.* of Russell Hardy and Juletta Sturges, both of U. E. L. descent; *m.* Mary Elomabet Curtis, *e. d.* of David Curtis, Esq., Collector of Customs; one *s.* one *d.* *Educ.:* Brantford and London, Ont. Called to the Bar 1886; first practiced at London, Ont., and in 1890 became member of firm of Hardy, Wilkins and Hardy at Brantford. Apptd. to the Bench, 23 April, 1897; has been active in extending the usefulness of Public Libraries, and Ex-Pres. of the Ontario Library Assn. *Recreation:* golf. *Address:* 56 Wellington Street, Brantford, Ont. *Club:* Brantford.

HARE, John James, M.A., Ph.D., *b.* in Tp. of Nepean, six miles from Ottawa, 3 Oct., 1847; *s.* of Robert Hare and Barbara Shillington Hare; *m.* Katherine Isabella McDowell, *d.* of the late Rev. D. C. McDowell; two *s.* *Educ.:* Victoria Univ. Entered the ministry of the Methodist Church in June, 1867, and was stationed at Chatham, Ont.; Smith's Falls, and London, Ont.; was called to the Principalship of the Ontario Ladies' Coll., Whitby, Ont., in Sept., 1874; became governor as well as Principal in 1879. both of which positsion he still holds. *Address:* Ontario Ladies' College, Whitby, Ont.

HARKNESS, James, M.A., F.R.S.C.; *b.* Derby, England, 24 Jan., 1864; *s.* of the late John Harkness of Derby; *m.* Katharine E. Cam, *d.* of Rev. W. H. Cam. Birchanger Rectory, Herts. *Educ.:* Derby Sch.; arrived in Canada, 1903; scholar of Trinity Coll., Cambridge, 1882-8; Professor of Maths. at Brynmaur Coll., Pennsylvania for a number of years. From 1903, Prof. at McGill Univ.; mem. Royal Society of Canada; Am. Math. Soc., London Math. Soc.; recently Vice-Pres., American Math. Society. *Publications:* joint author with Prof. Frank Morley of two treatises on the Theory of Tunneling. *Address:* 23 Lorne Av., Montreal.

HARLING, Thomas; *b.* Liverpool, Eng., 5 July, 1859; *s.* of Mark and Agnes Harling; *m.* Grace Parry, 1884; two *s.* three *d.* *Educ.:* St. Peter's Church Sch. and Liverpool Coll.; arrived in Canada, 1895; received training in shipping office of Wm. Hunter & Co., from 1873; succeeded to firm in 1883; in business on his own account as ship broker in Liverpool, until 1895, when he joined Elder Dempster & Co., and opened office for them in Montreal; The Elder Dempster Co. sold out to the C. P. Ry., when he joined Fred. Leyland & Co., as their agent in Canada, until absorbed by American combine; now in business on his own account and agent for Bristol docks. *Address:* 105 St. Antoine Road, Westmount Que.; 406 Board of Trade Bldg., Montreal. *Club:* Canada.

HARRINGTON, B. J., B.A., Ph.D., LL. D., Director, Macdonald Chemistry and Mining Building, and Macdonald Professor of Chemistry, McGill Univ., Montreal; *b* St. Andrews, Que., 5 August, 1848; *s.* of William Harrington and Laura Seymour, both born in Canada; *m.* 1876, Anna Lois Dawson, *e. d.* of late Sir J. W. Dawson, Principal McGill Univ.; three *s.* four *d.* *Educ.:* early education mostly by private tuition; McGill Univ., 1865-69; Yale Univ., 1689-71. Obtained First Rank Honours in Natural Science and Logan Gold Medal on graduation, 1869, and later the Mineralogy Prize at Yale. Apptd. Lecturer in Chemistry at McGill, 1871, and the following year succeeded Dr. T. Sterry Hunt as Chemist and Mineralogist to the Geol. Survey of Canada; discharged duties of both positions for seven years, and then retired from Geol. Survey in order to devote entire time to teaching work at McGill; apptd. David Greenshields Professor of Chemistry and Mineralogy in 1883; for many years also lectured on both mining and metallurgy; has been President of the Nat. Hist. Soc. of Montreal, President of the Chemical and Physical Section of the Royal Soc. of Can.; Vice-President, Chemical Section of British Association (Toronto), etc. *Publications:* Notes on Dawsonite, a new Carbonate; Notes on the Iron Ores of Canada and their Development; The Minerals of some of the Apatite-bearing Viens of Ottawa County, Que.; the Sap of the Ash-leaved Maple; etc., etc.; Life of Sir William Logan, First Director of the Geol. Survey of Canada. *Recreations:* gardening and music. *Address:* 295 University St., Montreal.

HARRIS, Mrs. Dennis R. (Martha Douglas); *b.* Victoria, B.C., 8 June, 1854; *d.* of the late Sir James Douglas, K.C.B., and Lady Douglas; *m.* Dennis Reginald Harris, C.E.; two *s.* two *d.* *Educ.:* Victoria and England. *Publication:* Indian Legends. *Recreations:* riding, driving, physical culture, painting, music, gradening. *Address:* 603 Superior St., Victoria, B.C.

HARRIS, Lloyd, M.P.; *b.* Beamsville, Ont., 14 March, 1867; *s.* of John and Alice Jane Harris; *m.* Evelyn F. Blackmore; one *d.* *Educ.:* Brantford Pub. Sch., Woodstock Coll., and Brantford Collegiate Inst. Pres., Brantford Screw Co., Ltd.; Pres. Brantford Bd. of Trade, 1903; Director Dominion Power and Transmission Co., Underfeed Stoker Co., of America; Trust and Guarantee Co., of America; mem. of Brantford City Council, 1905-6; Ont. Vice-Pres., Can. Manufacturer's Assn., 1906; First elec. at g. e., to H. of C., 1908; a Liberal. *Address:* 110 Brant Av., Brantford, Ont. *Clubs:* Brantford, Toronto, National, Ontario, Toronto Hunt, R.C.Y.C., Toronto; Rideau, Ottawa; Sports, London, Eng.

HARRIS, Robert, C.M.G., R.C.A.; *b.* Wales, 1849; *s.* of William Critchlow Harris; *m.* Elizabeth Putnam; *Educ.:* Prince of Wales Coll., Charlottetown, P.E.I.; arrived in Canada, 1856; has received gold medals and other awards at several art exhibitions, including International ones at Chicago, Buffalo, St. Louis, and Paris; when quite young was a Provincial Land Surveyor; after practicing, and self-teaching went to Europe for study; paints figure subjects and occasionally landscapes; chiefly portraits; was Pres., R.C.A. for 15 years. Chef d'oeuvre "The Fathers of Confederation" now hanging in Parlt. Bldgs., at Ottawa. *Address:* 11 Durocher St., Montreal; Art Gallery Bldg., Philip's Square, Montreal, Que.

HARRIS, Robert Edward, K.C., D.C.L.; *b.* Annapolis, N.S.; *s.* of Robert J. Harris and Rebecca (Ditmars) Harris; *m.* Minnie L., *d.* of James Horsfall of Annapolis Royal. *Educ.:* at Annapolis Royal; studied Law with J. M. Owen at Annopolis and afterwards with Messrs. Thompson and Graham (Right Hon. Sir J. S. D. Thompson, Hon. Mr. Justice Graham); admitted to the Bar in 1882; Q.C., in 1889; practiced law in Yarmouth, N.S., and in 1892, joined firm of Henry, Harris and Henry, Halifax; Pres. of the Council of the N.S. Bar Society; apptd. Chancellor, Diocese of N.S., in 1905; Pres. of the N.S. Steel Co., and Eastern Trust Company; Director of Trinidad Electric Co., Acadia Sugar Refining Co., etc. *Address:* 15 South Park St., Halifax, N.S. *Club:* Halifax.

HARRISON, William S., M.D.; *b.* Milton, Co. Halton, Ont., 10 Aug., 1864; *s.* of William Harrison, a farmer, and Hannah Hessey. *Educ.:* Milton Public Sch., and Toronto Univ.; a Controller of the City of Toronto; head Physician, Canadian Order Woodmen of the World, since 1894; graduated in Medicine, 1880; practiced in Brantford, in 1896; since that time in the City of Toronto. Elec. Alderman, Ward 4, Toronto, 1903, 1904, 1905, 1906; Controller, 1907, 1908, 1909. *Address:* 32 Borden St., Toronto. *Club:* Ontario, Toronto.

HARRISS, Charles Albert Edwin, Mus. Doc., Cantuar; F.R.A.M. (hon.); composer, conductor; *b.* London, Eng., 17 Dec., 1892; *s.* of Edwin Harriss and Elizabeth Duff; *m.* Ella Beatty-Shoenberger, of Scarlet Oaks Cincinnati, O., and Earnscliffe, Ottawa. *Educ.:* St. Michaels Coll., Tenbury, Eng., Came to Can., Dec., 1882. Ouseley scholar, 1875; organist and rector of the choir, Montreal Cathedral, 1883; conductor state concerts to His Excellency the Gov.-Gen.; ex-dir., McGill Univ. Conservatorium of Music; hon.-dir., Associated Bd. Exams., Royal Coll. and Royal Acad.; Director, Empire Concerts, London; Liveryman of the Worshipful Co. of Musicians; life mem., Roy. Soc. of Musicians; mem. Soc. of British Composers; life mem. Union of Graduates in music of G.B.; mem., British Musical Assn.; advisor in Can. to Roy. Coll. of Organists; directed first Cycle Musical Festivals of British compositions throughout the Dom., 1903; directed Canadian British Festival, London, in the presence of H.M. The King, 1906; guest conductor at London Symphony Orchestral Concert, given in honour of Premiers of Empire attending Colonial Conference, London, 1907; brought 200 members of the Sheffield Choir to Can., 1908; apptd. del. for Can., to National Congress and Hayden Centenary, Vienna; guest conductor, Cape Town Municipal Musical Festival, 1909; visited and lectured in England, Canada, Fizi, Australia, Tasmania, New Zealand, and South Africa, in the interest of musical reciprocity, 1909. *Publications:* "Daniel before the King;" "Torquil;" "The Admiral;" "Festival Mass;" "Pan;" "Coronation Mass, Edward VII;" "The Sands of Dee;" Empire choruses, songs, organ and pianoforte pieces, anthems etc. *Recreations:* big game shooting, fishing, poultry raising. *Addresses:* "Earnscliffe," Ottawa; "Earnscliffe Lodge," Banff, Alta. 160 Wardour St., London, W., England. *Clubs:* Rideau, Hunt, Golf, Ottawa; Savage, German Athenaeum, London, Eng.; York Lodge, Manitoba.

HART, Rev. Thomas, M.A., D.D.; *b.* Paisley, Scot., 6 Sept., 1835; *s.* of John Hart and Jean Mason Simple; *m.* Isabella Margaret Malloch, *y. d.* of Judge Malloch, Perth, Ont.; four *s.* two *d.* *Educ.:* Perth, Ont., Queen's Univ., Kingston, and Edinburgh Univ., Scot. Arrived in Canada, 1842; graduated as B.A. in 1860; M.A.,1868; B.D., 1880; D.D., 1902; made licentiate of Presbyterian Church, 1864; Professor of Classics in Manitoba Coll., 1872. *Address:* 448 Qu'Appelle, Av., Winnipeg,

HARTNEY, Edward Patrick; *b.* Toronto, Ont., 6 March, 1851; *s.* of Henry and Sarah Hartney; *m.* Laura Weston of Toronto; one *s.* one *d.* *Educ.:* High Sch., Que.; entered Pub. Service of Canada in 1872, in the Private Bill branch of the H. of C.; drafted the first model railway bill, adopted by the House in 1887, and was appointed Examiner of private bills in 1887, and Registrar of private bills, in 1907. *Publications:* a manual showing the private bill practice of the Parliament of Canada, 1882, *Address:* 357 Sparks St., Ottawa. *Clubs:* Rideau, Country, Lttawa.

HARTY, William, M.P.; *b.* Biddolph, County of Middlesex, Ont., 8 March, 1847; *s.* of John Harty and Elizabeth Heenan; *m* Catherine M. Bermingham, of Ottawa; three *s.* one *d.* *Educ.:* Christian Brothers' Sch. and Regeopolis Coll., Kingston, Ont. mem. of Administration, Ontario Legislature for over 5 years; in mercantile and manufacturing business. El. to H. of C., 1902; re-elected 1904-1908. *Address:* Kingston, Ont. *Clubs:* Frontenac, Kingston; Rideau, Ottawa.

HARVEY, Henry Allen; *b.* Edgebaston, Warwickshire, Eng., 24 April, 1852; *s.* of Henry Logan Harvey, Apothecary to the forces, Woolwich, Eng.; *m.* Kate Alley; one *s.* eight *d.* *Educ.:* High Sch., Quebec, and King's Coll. Sch., London, Eng.; arrived in Canada, 1862; entered service of Bank of British North America in 1873; Manager at Kingston, Ont., 1890; St. John, N.B., 1891-1900; Ottawa, 1901. *Address:* Ottawa. *Clubs:* Rideau, Ottawa.

HARVEY, Hon. Horace, B.A., LL.B., Puisne Judge of the Superior Court of Alberta; *b.* Malahide Tp. Elgin Co., Ont., 1 Oct., 1863; *s.* of Wm. Harvey and Sophrainia Mack; *m.* Louise Palmer of Toronto; one *s.* *Educ.:* Univ. Coll., Toronto Univ., called to the Bar, Ont., 1889; practiced in Toronto, until 1893; went to Calgary and called to the Bar of N. W. T.; in 1896, apptd Registrar of Land Titles for South Alberta Land Registration District, at Calgary; in 1900, apptd. Deputy Attorney General of N. W. T. at Regina. In June, 1904, apptd. puisne Judge of Superior Court of N. W. T., and on organization of the Province of Alberta and Saskatchewan, and establishment of Provincial Courts, apptd. puisne Judge of the Superior Court of Alberta, in 1907, which he now holds. *Address:* Calgary, Alta.

HASZARD, Hon. Francis Longworth, K.C.; Premier and Attorney-General of Prince Edward Island; *b.* Bellevue, P.E.I. 20 Nov., 1849; *s.* of Charles Haszard and Margaret Longworth; *m.* ElizabethDes-Brisay; three *s.* five *d.* *Educ.:* Prince of Wales Coll., Charlottetown, P.E.I.; called to the Bar, 1872, and commenced practice of his profession in Charlottetown; cr. Q.C., 1894; apptd. Judge of the City Ct. of Charlottetown, Feb., 1895. First el. to Leg. at g. e., 1904; became Premier 1 Feb., 1908; apptd. Attorney Gen., Oct., 1908; re-el. at g. e., 1908. *Recreation:* golf. *Address:* Charlottetown, P.E.I.

HAULTAIN, Frederick William Gordon, B.A., K.C.; *b.* Woolwich, Eng., 25 Nov., 1857; *s.* of Lieut.-Col. W. F. Haultain, R.A. *Educ.:* Montreal High Sch., Peterborough Coll. Inst., and Toronto Univ. Called to the Ontario Bar, 1882. El. mem. ofthe Northwest Assembly, 1888, and at each succeeding el. until its dissolution; became Territorial Premier, Oct., 1897, and remained in power until dissolution of old Northwest Govt., by creation of the two new provinces. El. at first g. e., for Saskatchewan Legis Assem., 1905, and re-el. at g. e., 1908, represented Northwest Territories at Coronation of His Majesty, Aug., 1902. *Address:* Regina, Sask.

HAULTAIN, Theodore Arnold, M.A., *b.* Cannamore, India, 3 Nov., 1857; *s.* of General Francis Mitchell Haultain, and Isabella Thomas; *m.* Amy Millicent Fraser; one *s.* one *d.* *Educ.:* Private Sch., Brighton Eng.; Bedford Gram. Sch., Eng.; Univ. of Toronto; Journalist; for many years private Secretary to Goldwin Smith. *Publications:* "Two country walks in Canada"; "The mystery of golf;" "Hints for Lovers, etc." *Address:* 49 Springhurst Ave., Toronto. *Club:* Toronto Golf.

HAVERSON, James Percival; *b.* Toronto, Ont., 3 Oct., 1880; *s.* James Haverson, K.C.; *m.* Jessie Hodson, one *d.* *Educ.:* Model Sch., Toronto; Ridley Coll., St. Catharines, Ont., and Ontario Law Sch. Toronto. *Publications:* "Sour Songs of a Sorehead," and other songs of the street; also magazine and newspaper stories; articles and verse; newspaper work. *Address:* The *World*, Toronto. *Club:* Press, Toronto.

HAWKE, John Thomas, proprietor The Moncton *Transcript*; *b.* Plymouth, Devon, Eng., 30 April, 1854; *s.* of J. P. Hawke and M. A. Harvey; *m.* Della Thornton; three *d.* *Educ.:* Plymouth Free Schs. Arrived Can., 1873. On several leading Canadian newspapers, including the Toronto *Globe* and Ottawa *Free Press;* chairman Moncton Sch. Board for ten yrs. Presdt. Moncton Liberal Assn. for nine yrs., besides other public positions. *Address:* Moncton, N.B.

HAWKES, Arthur; *b.* Aylesford, Kent Eng., 15 Dec., 1871; *s.* of William and Sarah Hawkes; *m.* Augusta Josephine, *d.* of the late John Anderson, Borgstena, Sweden; four *d.* *Educ.:* Private Sch., at Maidston and Kent Coll., Canterbury; graduated from weekly journalism to staff of Manchester *Guardian*, Daily *Mail*, Daily *Despatch* (London edition), and *Review* of *Reviews*. Three months trip throughout Dominion; returned to Canada permanently Dec., 1905, as managing editor, Toronto *World*, became editor *Monetary Times*, leaving to take charge of publications dept., Can. Northern Ry. System; made special journey in 1903 to South Africa, France, Austria, Germany, and the United States, to enquire into methods of leading publications. *Recreation:* gardening. *Address:* 142 Beech Ave., Toronto.

HAWKINS, Frank, secy. Can. Lumbermen's Assn.; *b.* Rochdale, Eng.; *s.* of Joseph S. Hawkins and Eliza Illingworth; *m.* 1885, Isabel M. Campbell, of Toronto; two *s.* *Educ.:* Rochdale. Came to Canada, 1881. In business in Toronto for some years; with the Pullman Co., at Chicago for 6 years; Private Secy. to Hon. Mr. Dobell, mem. of Laurier Ministry, 1896-1902; subsequently with Dobell, Beckett & Co., at Quebec, until 1908; also Secy.-Treas. Manicouagan & English Bay Export Co. Apptd. to present position, August, 1908. *Address* 320 Cooper St., Ottawa.

HAY, George Upham, Ph.B., M.A., D. Sc., F.R.S.C.; *b.* Norton, N.B., 18 June, 1843; *s.* of William and Eliza Hay; *m.* Francis Annetta Hartt. *Educ.:* Pub. Schs. of N.B., and Cornell Univ.; Teacher and Journalist; for 34 years teacher in Pub. Schs., last 10 of which Principal of Victoria and Girls' High Sch., St. John, N.B.; for past 23 years editor Educational *Review*, St. John, N.B. *Publications:* editor Canadian History Readings; author School Histories of Canada. *Recreation:* plant study *Address:* 31 Leinster St., St. John, and Ingleside, N.B. (Summer).

HAYES, Mrs. Kate Simpson ("Mary Markwell"); *b.* Dalhousie, N.B., 1856. For many yrs. actively connected with Press of Canada. Staff writer on Manitoba *Free Press;* at one time librarian of Legis. Library at Regina. *Publications:* "Prairie Pourri;" "Shanty Songs and Stories," "The Legend of the West;" other works of fiction, drama, and poetry. *Address:* Victoria, B.C.

HAYS, Charles Melville, Pres. and Gen. Mgr., Grand Trunk Ry. System; *b.* Rock Island, Ill., 16 May, 1856; *m.* Clara J., *d.* of William H. Gregg, of St. Louis, Mo.; four *d.* *Educ.:* Pub. Schs. and High Sch., Rock Island. Entered passenger dept. of the Atlantic and Pacific Railroad Co., at St Louis, Mo.; transferred to auditor's dept.; promoted to supt's office; Sec. to Gen. Mgr. of Missouri Pacific, 1878-1884; Sec. to Gen. Mgr. of the Wabash, St. Louis & Pacific Railroad Co., 1884-1886; became Asst. Gen. Mgr. to Wabash Western Ry. Co. 1886; Gen. Mgr. six months later; apptd. Vice-Pres. and Gen. Mgr. of the reorganized Wabash Ry., 1st Feb., 1894; resigned, 1887; accepted position of gen. Mgr. of G. T. R. Co. at Montreal; became Pres. of the Southern Pacific Co., and its allied lines at San Francisco; resigned following autumn; apptd. 2nd V.P. and Gen. Mgr. G. T. R., 1 Jan., 1902. Pres. Grand Trunk Pacific Ry., Central Vermont Ry., Grand Trunk Western Ry., and numerous other subsidiary lines of G. T. R.; Dir., Royal Trust Co., Merchants Bank of Canada, and many other large enterprises; Vice-Pres. St. John Ambulance Assn.; Gov. Royal Victoria Hospital, Montreal Gen. Hospital; Gov. McGill Univ. *Address:* 27 Ontario Avenue, Montreal. *Clubs:* St. James, Mount Royal, Forest and Stream, Montreal Hunt, Jockey, St. Maurice, Laurentian, Montreal; Rideau, Ottawa.

HAYWARD, Charles, J. P.; *b.* Stratford, Essex, Eng., 12 May, 1839; *s.* of Charles Hayward and Harriet Tomlinson; *m.* Sarah *s. d.* of the late John McChesney, of London, Eng.; two *s.* one *d.* *Educ.:* Salem Coll., Bow, Middlesex, Eng. Has large interests in Victoria, and is prominently identified with building, contracting, mining and manufacturing. Served several terms as alderman of Victoria, and was Mayor for three yrs.; was Presdt. of the Provincial Royal Jubilee Hospital, and for ten years Chairman of the School Board; is now Presdt. of the B.C. Protestant Orphan's Home; and of the Children's Aid Soc.; is an active mem. of the Masonic, Oddfellows, Foresters and Pioneer Socs. *Address:* 1003 Vancouver St., 1010 Government St., Victoria, B.C. *Club:* Pacific, Victoria.

HAZEN, Hon. John Douglas, B.A., B. C.L.; Premier and Attorney-General of New Brunswick; *b.* Oromocto, Sunbury Co., N.B. 6 June, 1860; *s.* of James K. Hazen and Mrs. Hazen, *d.* of the late Hon. John A. Beckwith; *m.* 1884, Ada *s. d.* of James Tibbits, of Fredericton. *Educ.:* Coll. Sch., Fredericton; Univ. of N.B. Called to the Bar, 1883. A mem. of the Senate of Univ. of N.B., and Registrar and Treas. of the Univ., 1882-1890; Ald. of Fredericton for three yrs. and Mayor for two yrs, Removed to St. John, 1890. Returned to H. of C. for St. John City, and Co. at g. e., 1891; an unsuccessful can. at g. e., 1896. El. to N. B. Legis. for Sunbury at g. e., 1899; re-el. at g. e., 1903, and 1908. In 1899, chosen Leader of the Opposition; summoned by His Honour the Lt.-Gov. to form a Govt., which he did, and assumed the portfolio of Premier and Attorney-General. The Cabinet was sworn in March 24, 1908, all the members re-el. by accl., April 7. *Address:* St. John, N.B.

HEARST, William Howard, K.C., M.L. A.; *b.* Tp. of Arran, Co. of Bruce, Ont., 15 Feb., 1864; *s.* William Hearst and Margaret McFadden; *m.* Isabella Jane Dunkin; two *s.* two *d.* *Educ.:* Tara pub. schs. and Collingwood Collegiate Inst. Called to the Bar in 1888; K.C. in 1908; senior member of the law firm of Hearst, Darling and Brown; contested riding of Sault Ste. Marie in Conservative interest at g. e., in 1908, and was elected. *Recreations:* driving and boating. *Address:* Sault Ste. Marie Ont.

HEBDEN, Edward F., Gen. Mgr. of the Merchants Bank of Canada; *b.* Hamilton, Ont., 29 April, 1851; *s.* of the Rev. Canon Hebden, M.A., F.C.D., Rector of Church of the Ascension, Hamilton, and Catherine Pilkington, of the Pilkingtons of York, Ireland; *m.* Mary Henderson, *y. d.* of James Henderson of Hanley Castle, Worcestershire two *s.* three *d.* Thirty-eight years of service in the Merchants Bank of Canada *Address:* 445 Sherbrooke St. West, Montreal *Clubs:* Mount Royal, St. James, Hunt and Royal Montreal Golf, Montreal; Toronto.

HEBERT, Louis Philippe, C.M.G., Sculptor; *b.* Prov. Quebec, 27 Jan., 1850; *m.* 1879, Marie, *d.* of Thomas Roy, Montreal. In early days worked on a farm; obtained prize at Provincial Exhibition, Montreal, for wood-carving in 1873; afterwards studied in Paris; won prize given by Dominion Government for full-length statue of George Cartier. *Principal Works:* Statues, among which are those to Champlain at Quebec, Maisonneuve and Chenier, Montreal. *Address:* 217 Berri St., Montreal.

HELMER, Major Alexis Richard, Assistant Adjutant General for Musketry (Canada); *b.* Russell, Ont., 12 Oct., 1864; *s.* of Nathaniel Helmer and Melissa Johnson; *m.* Elizabeth S. Hannum; one *s.* *Educ.:* Ottawa and Toronto; Chemist of Prov. of Ont. and Que. Officer of the Canadian Militia, 1892; twice Mayor of Hull, Que.; Adjutant Canadian Rifle Team, 1899; Palma Team, 1901; Sea Girt, 1903; Ottawa, 1906; Commandant Canadian School of Musketry, since 1907. *Recreations:* rifle shooting. *Address:* Ottawa, Ont. *Club:* Laurentian, Ottawa.

HEMING, Arthur Henry Howard; *b.* Paris, Ont., Jan. 17, 1870; *s.* George Edward and Frances Ann Morgan Heming. *Educ.:* pub. schs.; taught Hamilton Art Sch., 1887-90; illustrator on Canadian publs. till 1899; studied at Art Students' League under Frank Brangwyn, A.R.A., London, 1904 Contb'r of illustrated articles and stories to leading newspapers and mags. in Europe and America, and illustrator of many books on animal and wild life. Student, by personal contact, of phases of life in Canadian wilderness. Mem. Soc. of Illustrators. Episcopalian. *Publications:* Spirit Lake, 1907. *Address:* 33 W. 67th St., New York.

HENDERSON, Major Alexander, B.A., K.C., Commissioner of the Yukon; *b.* Oshawa, Ont., 1861; *s.* of Alexander Henderson and Grace Kilpatrick; *m.* Susan Crawford, *d.* of William McCraney, ex-M.P. for Co. of Halton, Ont., one *d*; grad. B.A., 1884; admitted solicitor, Ont., 1889; called to Bar of B.C., 1892; mem. of Legislature for New Westminster, B.C., 1898, created Q.C., same year; Attorney General, B.C., 1899 Judge of County Court, Vancouver,1901; resigned Jan., 1907; practiced law, Vancouver; apptd. Commissioner of the Yukon 18 June, 1907. *Recreations:* rifle shooting principally; was Adjutant Canadian Rifle Team, Bisley, in 1901. *Address:* Dawson Y.T., and 1424 Burnaby St., Vancouver, B.C. *Clubs:* Vancouver and United Service Club, Vancouver, B.C.

HENDERSON, David, M.P.; *b.* Tp. of Nelson, Co. of Halton, Ont., 18 Feb., 1841; *s.* John Henderson and Isabella Davidson, both from Roxburgh, Scot.; *m.* Alison Christie, *d.* of Chas. Christie; six *s.* one *d.* *Educ.:* Milton Gram. Sch. and Normal Sch., Toronto; a pub. sch. teacher for 5 years, Deputy Registrar for Halton for seven yrs.; M.P. for 21 sessions; contested nine elections, and successful seven times. *Recreation:* travelling. *Address:* Acton, Ont.

HENDERSON, George F., B.A. (Queens, K.C.; *b.* Kingston, Ont., 17 Feb., 1864; *s.* of Peter Robertson Henderson and Henrietta Sweetland; *m.* Margaret Eglinton Brown, of Ottawa; one *d.* *Educ.:* Private Schs. Kingston Coll. Inst., Queen's Univ. Called to Bar of Ont., 1887, and has since practised at Ottawa; mem. of the firm of MacCracken, Henderson, McDougall and Greene; apptd. drainage referee for Eastern Ont., June, 1906; K.C., 1907. *Publications:* "The Ditches and Watercourses Act," 1907. *Recreations:* golf, curling. *Address:* 184 Somerset St., Ottawa. *Clubs:* Rideau, Golf, Hunt, Ottawa; Brockville; Cornwall.

HENDERSON, Rev. James, D.D. (Vic. Univ.); *b.* Airdrie, Scot., 1851; *m.* 1876, Mary, 2nd *d.* of James Gillespie, of Quebec. *Educ.:* Glasgow, Scot. Came to Canada in 1870, and was ordained to the Methodist Ministry in 1876. Had several important stations in the Prov. of Quebec, including three pastorates in Montreal. Went to Toronto in 1891, and held the pastorates of Carlton St. and Sherbourne St. Churches in 1896, apptd. Asst. Sec. of Methodist Missions, and hold that position until 1907, when called to the pastoral charge of the Dominion Methodist Church, at Ottawa. *Address:* 243 Lisgar St., Ottawa.

HENDERSON, Robert, Asst. Govt. Mining Engr. for Yukon; *b.* Nova Scotia. Went to Yukon, 1893. Found gold on Quartz Creek and Gold Bottom Creek, 1894, and has been mining in Yukon ever since. Claimed that was first discoverer of gold on Klondike, but this is disputed. *Address:* Dawson, Y.T.

HENDRIE, Lieut.-Col. John Strathearn, M.L.A., member of Executive Council of Ontario; Com. Royal Victorian Order; *b.* Hamilton, 15 Aug., 1857; *s.* William Hendrie and Margaret Walker Hendrie; one *s.* one *d.* *Educ.:* Hamilton sch. and Up. Can. Coll.; elec. to Ontario Legislature, 1902; re-elected 1905 and 1908; Lt.-Col., lately in command, 2nd Brigade, C.F.A.; Ex-Mayor of Hamilton, Ont. *Recreations:* racing, fishing, shooting. *Address:* Hamilton, Ont. *Clubs:* Toronto, Hamilton, Albany, Ontario Jockey.

HENDRY, John; *b.* Billedune, Gloucester Co., N.B., 20 Jan., 1843; *s.* of James Hendry and Margaret Wilson from West Kilbride, Ayrshire, Scot.; *m.* Adeline McMillan, of Pictou, N.S.; one *d.* *Educ.:* In N.B.; Pres., Canadian Manufacturers' Association; Commissioner of Conservation of Natural Resources of Canada; Pres., Vancouver, Westminster and Yukon Railway Co.; Pres., Nicola Valley Coal and Coke Co.; Chairman, Burrard, Westminster and Boundary Ry. and Navigation Co. After completing education in the Pub. Sch., studied and practised saw mill and flour-mill engineering and followed this for some time in the Maritime Provinces; shortly after B.C. had joined confederation, moved to the Pacific Coast, landing in Victoria, B.C. in 1872, afterwards spent some time in California and State of Washington; located in British Columbia, in 1874; went to Winnipeg in 1875; returned to British Columbia in 1875; was interested in the pioneering of the timber interests, saw-milling and factories and general utalizing of lumber. *Recreations:* motoring, yachting, fishing. *Address:* Cor. Burnaby and Jervis St., Vancouver, B.C. *Clubs:* Vancouver, Terminal City, Jericho Country, Vancouver B.C.; Westminster, New Westminster, B.C.; Union, Victoria, B.C.; Rideau, Ottawa.

HENRY, William Alexander, K.C., LL. B.; *b.* Antigonish, N.S., 19 March, 1863; *s.* of William Alexander and Christianna Henry; *m.* Minna H. Troop, Halifax; two *s.* one *d.* *Educ.:* Halifax Schs.; Lycee de Tours, France; Merchiston Castle Sch., Edinburgh; Dalhousie Univ., Halifax; Harvard Univ., Cambridge, Mass., U.S.A. Admitted to Nova Scotia Bar, 1887; apptd. K.C., June, 1907. *Recreations:* golf, badminton, photography, bicycling, billiards, bridge. *Address:* 16 South St., Halifax, N. S. *Club:* Halifax.

HEROUX, Omer; journalist; *b.* St. Maurice, Champlain Co., Que., 8 Sept., 1876; *s.* of Louis-Dollor Heroux, and Marie-Adelaide Neault. *Educ.:* Christian Bros. Sch., and Coll. of Three Rivers, Que. In newspaper work in Quebec and Montreal for some yrs.; one of the editors of *Le Nationaliste,* and one of the editors of *Le Devoir.* *Address:* 71a St. James St., Montreal.

HERRIDGE, Rev. William Thomas, Pastor of St. Andrew's Presbyterian Church Ottawa; *b.* Reading, Eng., 14 Jan., 1857; *o. s.* of the Rev. W. Herridge, and Emma Barkshire; *m.* 1885, *d.* of Rev. Thos. Duncan, D.D.; two *s.* two *d.* *Educ.:* Model Sch., Toronto; Hamilton Coll. Inst., Galt Coll. Inst., Toronto Univ. Inducted as Pastor of St. Andrew's Presbyterian Church, Aug., 1883, before completing his studies. Spent a yr. abroad, returning to Can. in 1884. Mem. of Senate of Toronto Univ.; Trustee of Queen's Univ., Kingston. *Publications:*

"The Coign of Vantage and other Essays." *Recreations:* golf, curling. *Address:* 293 Somerset St., Ottawa.

HERRON, John, M.P.; *b.* County of Carleton, Ont., 15 Nov., 1853; *s.* of John Heron and Margaret Crain; *m.* Ida Lake; three *d.* *Educ.:* Pub. Sch., Ashton, Ont. A license Commissioner and Stock Inspector in Alberta; first elec. to H. of C., 1904; re-elec., 1908. *Address:* Pincher Creek, Alta.;

HERVIEUX, Henri, M.D., Prof. of Internal Pathology at Laval Univ.; *b.* St. Jerome, Que., 1862; *s.* of Joseph A. Hervieux and Virginie Lachine; *m.* 1886, Minnie Vallee, of Montreal. *Educ.:* Ste. Therese, studied philosophy at Ste. Mary's Coll., and medicine Sch. of Medicine and Surgery, Montreal (M.D., 1886, and the Prize Hourget). Practiced in Massachusetts, U.S., for one yr. Went to Montreal, 1893, where he has since practiced. Won the vacant Chair of Therapeuties in the Medical Faculty of Laval Univ., 1894; apptd. Prof. Titulaire of Materia Medica, 1900. El. life mem. Medical Faculty, Laval Univ ; was first pres. of La Societe Medicale de Montreal; Dir. of St. Justine Hospital for Children; Dir. and Associate editor of L'Union Medicale du Canada. *Address:* 490 St. Denis St., Montreal.

HESPLER, Wilhelm, late Imperial German Consul, and Speaker of Legislature of Manitoba; *b.* Baden-Baden, Germany, 29 Dec., 1830; *s.* Johnna Glory Hespler, and Barbara Anna; *m.* Katherine R. Keachie; one *s.* one *d.* *Educ.:* Grand Duchy of Baden; arrived in Canada, October, 1850; formerly of Hespeler, but moved to Winnipeg 1873. *Address:* Wardlow Building, Fort Rouge, Winnipeg. *Club:* Manitoba, Winnipeg.

HEWARD, Lieut.-Col. Edward H. T., Staff Officer to Inspector-Gen. Can. Militia; *b.* Toronto, 17 Jan., 1852; *s.* J. H. and Eliza Heward; *m.* Louisa, *y. d.* of Sir Wm. Collis Meredith, late C.J., Prov. Que., one *s.* one *d.* *Educ.:* Upper Can. Coll., Toronto. Joined Can. Militia, 1866; apptd. Lieut. in G. G. Body Guard, 1879; apptd. Lieut. and Adjt., Permanent Cav. Sch. Corps (now R. C. Dragoons, 1883); Commandant R. C. Mounted Rifles, Winnipeg, 1891-6; Brevt. Capt., 1888; A.D.C. to G.O.C., Can. Mil., 1901-3; Staff Officer to Inspector General at headquarters, with rank of Major, 1904; Lieut.-Col., 1906. Served in Fenian Raid, 1866; N.W. Rebellion, 1885. *Address:* 415 Laurier Av., Ottawa.

HEWARD, Stephen Beverley, Kt. of Order of Orange Nassau, of Holland; *b.* Montreal, Que., 7 Nov., 1843; *s.* of Francis Harris Heward and Eliza Paul; *m.* Alice Graham; one *s.* two *d.* *Educ.:* Up. Can. Coll., Toronto, Ont. For 30 yrs. Vice-Consul of the Netherlands; served on the Canadian Frontier in 1864 and 1866; (Fenian Raid Medal). *Address:* 55 St. Francois Xavier St., and 10 Park Ave., Montreal. *Club:* St. James', Montreal.

HEWITT, Charles Gordon, D.Sc., (Univ. of Manchester, Eng.); Fellow of the Entomological Soc., Eng.; *b.* nr. Macclesfield, Eng., 23 Feb., 1885; *s.* of Thomas Henry Hewitt and Rachael Hewitt; unmarried. *Educ.:* Macclesfield Gram. Sch., Univ. of Manchester. Obtained first class honors in Zoology, Manchester Univ.; University prizeman and scholar; asst. lecturer in Zoology, 1904; Lecturer in Economic Zoology in Univ. of Manchester, 1906; arrived Can., 16 Sept., 1909; apptd. Dominion Entomologist, 1909. *Publications:* numerous articles on pure and economic Zoology, especially Entomology in various scientific journals, the most important being a monograph on The House-fly."" *Address:* The Sherbrooke, 90 O'Connor St., Ottawa.

HEWSON, His Hon. Charles Edward, District Judge of Manitoulin, Judge of the Surrogate Court, and local Judge of the High Court of Justice; *b.* Township of Innisfil, Co. of Simcoe, Ont., 23 Oct., 1856; *s.* of William and Abigail M. Hewson; *m.* Julia, *y. d.* of Henry Creswicke, P.L.S., late of the Town of Barrie; three *s.* seven *d.* *Educ.:* Barrie Collegiate Inst.; entered law office of late Mr. Justice Lount, Jan., 1874; admitted to Bar, May, 1880; commenced practice in Barrie, and formed partnership with A. E. H. Creswicke, K.C.; appointed District Judge, Dec., 1908. *Address:* Gore Bay, Ont.

HIEBERT, Cornelius, M.L.A.; *b.* South of Russia, 2 Aug., 1862; *s.* Johun Hiebert and Helma Tows; *m.* Anganetha Dick; one *s.* two *d.* *Educ.:* Village Sch. in Russia; arrived in Canada, 2 Aug., 1876; settled in Manitoba; a Lumber Merchant; up to 21 years was farming; since then in commercial business; Director of the Knee Hill Coal Co.; overseer for Didsbury Village for past three years. *Address:* Didsbury, Alta.

HIGGINS, Charles Herbert, B.S., D.V.S.; *b.* Newtownville, Mass., 23 Feb., 1875; *s.* of Eben Higgins and Sarah A. Goulding; *m.* Jane Ruth Hall; one *s.* one *d.* Arrived in Canada, Oct., 1894; practicing Veterinarian, Island of Jamaica, 1896; Asst. Pathologist, Dept. of Agriculture, 1899; Pathologist since 1902. *Publications:* "Canadian Chicken Cholera, 1896," etc., and yearly Government reports. *Address:* 73 Fairmount Ave., Ottawa, Ont.

HILL, George Griswold; *b.* Montreal, 24 April, 1868; *s.* George William and Frances Harriet Griswold Hill; *m.* 1893, Frances Mary Chaffee. *Educ.:* pub. schs., Englewood (now Chicago) and St. Ignatius Coll., Chicago. Began newspaper work on The *Farmer*, St. Paul, Minn., 1886; mng. editor, Am. *Farmer*, Chicago, 1890-7, of Produce *Trade Reporter*, Chicago, 1895-7; Washington corr. Johnstown *Democrat*, Crawfordsville *Journal* and other papers, 1900-2; mem Washington Bureau, New York *Tribune*, since 1902; represented New York *Tribune* at Russo-Japanese peace conf., 1905. Republican. Roman Catholic. *Author:* Marketing Farm Produce, 1897; Practical Hints for Farm Buildings, 1901. *Address:* 1322 F St., Washington, D.C.

HILL, Rev. James Edgar, M.A., D.D.; *b.* Glasgow, Scot., 18 Oct., 1841; *s.* James Hill and Catherine Hunton; *m.* Mariann Fletcher Philip; three *s.* three *d.* *Educ.:* Univ. of Edinburgh, 1863-72; Minister in Scot., 1873 to 1882; since of St. Andrew's Church, Montreal (Church of Scotland); Major, 5th Royal Highlanders. *Address:* 267 Peel St., Montreal.

HILL, James J., President of the Gt. Northern Ry. of the United States; *b.* nr. Guelph, Ont., Sept. 16, 1838; *s.* James and Ann Dunbar Hill; *m.* St. Paul, Aug. 19, 1867, Mary Theresa Mehegan. *Educ.:* Rockwood Acad.; left his father's farm for business life in Minn.; was in steamboat offices in St. Paul, 1856-65; Agt. Northwestern Packet Co., 1656; later established gen. fuel and transportation business on his own account; head of Hill, Griggs & Co., same line, 1869-75; established, 1870, Red River Transportation Co., which was first to open communication between St. Paul and Winnipeg. organized, 1875, the Northwestern Fuel Co., and 3 yrs. later sold out his interest, in the meantime having organized a syndicate which secured control of the St. Paul & Pacific R. R., from Dutch owners of the securities; reorganized system as St. Paul, Minneapolis & Manitoba Ry. Co., and was its gen. mgr., 1879-82, v.-p., 1882-3, pres. since 1883; it became part Great Northern system, 1890; interested himself in building the Great Northern Ry., extending from Lake Superior to Puget Sound, with northern and southern branches, and a direct steamship connection with China and Japan, 1883-93; pres. entire Great Northern system, 1893; retired Apr., 1 1907, and became chmn. bd. dirs. same; chief promoter and now pres. Northern Securities Co.; dir. C., B. & Q. R. R. Co., C., B. & O. Ry. Co., St. Paul, Minneapolis & Manitoba Ry. Co., Manhattan Trust Co., Chase Nat. Bank, 1st Nat. Bank of City of N. Y., 1st Nat. Bank of Chicago. *Address:* 240 Summit Ave., St. Paul, Minn.

HILLIARD, Thomas; *b.* Tanilagh, Co. Fermanagh, Ireland, 9 April, 1841; *s.* John Hilliard and Ann Hutchison; *m.* Catherine Lauder; six *s.* six *d.* *Educ.:* Public Sch., Bolton, Ont., and Normal Sch., Toronto, Ont. Arrived in Canada, July, 1847; teacher in pub. sch., 5 years, 1683 to 1867; publisher of country neswpapers, *Maple Leaf* and Waterloo *Chronicle*, 1867 to 1888; founded Dominion Life Assurance Co., of Waterloo Ont., and was Managing Director until 1907, then elected President and holds both offices to date. Pres., Waterloo Board of Trade; Methodist; has been six times elected member of General Conference, and has been a member of most of the boards which administer the affairs of the denomination. *Address:* Waterloo, Ont.

HILTON, Alexander; *b.* Hamilton, Ont., June 19, 1864; *s.* Edward and Harriet Hale Hilton; *m.* Hamilton, May 10, 1886, Grace Barr. *Educ.:* Hamilton pub. schs.; Clerk Great Western Ry., Hamilton, 1878-9; clerk gen. ticket office, Chicago, 1879-84; city pass. and ticket agt., Kansas City, 1884-7; Pacific coast agt., San Francisco, 1887-8; gen. agt. pass. dept., Kansas City, 1888-1901, C. & A. R. R.; asst. gen. pass. agt., Kansas City, Fort Scott & Memphis Ry., Kansas City, 1901, and since consolidation in 1901, gen. pass. agt. S. L. & S. F. R. R. *Address:* 11 Colchester Apartments, St. Louis, Mo., U.S.A. *Clubs:* Mo. Athletic Mercantile.

HIMSWORTH, William, Secretary Inland Revenue Dept., *b.* Montreal, 23 Dec., 1847; *s.* of William Alfred Himsworth and Louisa Morrison; *m.* Julia Emily Easton, of Belleville (*deceased*); three *s.* one *d.* *Educ.:* Toronto private sch. (Frank's) and Queen's High Sch.; entered the service of the Government, Inland Revenue Dept., 30 June, 1868. *Address:* 81 Somerset St., Ottawa.

HINSHAW, Matthew Cochrane, Canadian Mgr. of the Atlas Assur. Co. of London, Eng.; *b.* Glasgow, Scot., 21 June, 1853; *s.* of Andrew Hinshaw and Helen Watt; *m.* Edith Gertrude, *d.* of Dunbar Browne, of Montreal. *Educ.:* Glasgow. Trained in insurance work in the Glasgow office of the Atlas Assur. Co., Ltd. Came to Canada, 1891, to assume present position. *Recreations:* general. *Address:* The "Denbigh, Western Av., Montreal. *Clubs:* St. James, Montreal, Montreal; Albany, Toronto.

HOBART, George Vere; *b.* Cape Breton, Jan. 16, 1867; *m.* 1897, Sarah H. de Vries. *Educ.:* Nova Scotia. Became mng. editor, 1895, Sunday *Scimitar*, Cumberland, Md.; a yr. later went to Baltimore, 1st on *Morning Herald*, then as sp'l. humorous writer on the Baltimore *American;* originated the "Dinkelspiel" papers on Baltimore *News;* since 1899 has written "Dinkelspiel" exclusively for the New York *American* and other Hearst papers, Chicago and San Fransico. *Club:* Lambs. *Author:* John Henry, 1901; Down the Line, 1901; Its Up To You, 1902; Back to the Woods, 1903; Out for the Coin, 1903; I Need the Money, 1704; I'm from Missouri, 1904; You Can Search Me, 1905; also 3 Dinkelspiel books; Gonversationings Mit Dinkelspiel, 1902; Heart to Heart Talks Mit Dinkelspiel, 1901; Eppy Grams, 1904; Jim Hickey, 1904; Li'l Verses for Li'l Fellers, 1903; Get Next, 1905; Silly Syclopedia, 1905; Skiddoo, 1906; Beat It, 1907, Cinders, 1907; Ikey's Letters to His Father, 1907; *Plays:* Broadway to Tokio; After Office Hours; Sally in Our Alley; The Ham Tree; The Sleepy King; Morning Glory; Mrs. Black Is Back (for May Irwin); Smiling Island; Peaches; Coming Thru the Rye; The Song Birds; Mrs. Wilson (for May Irwin); and numerous others. *Address:* Ruraldene, Pelham Manor, N.Y.

HOBBS, Thomas Saunders; *b.* Langtree, Devon, Eng., 1856; *s.* of Thomas and Mary Hobbs; unmarried. *Educ.*. Methodist Coll., Shebbear, Devon, Arrived Can., 1873. Rep. London in Ont. Leg., 1894-98; retired for business reasons. Pres., Hobbs Manufacturing Co., Toronto; Independent Cordage Co., London, Ont.; Hobbs Hardware Co., Winnipeg. *Recreations:* baseball, fishing, farming, travel. *Address:* London, Ont. *Clubs:* London, London; Toronto Hunt, National, Ontario, Toronto.

HOCKEN, Horatio Clarence; *b.* Toronto, 12 Oct., 1857; *s.* of English parents; *m.* Isabella Page; two *s.* two *d.* *Educ.:* Pub. Sch., Toronto; learned trade of compositor on *Globe;* commenced reporting on the *News*, in 1893; managing editor, Evening *News*, from Sept., 1895, to April, 1901. Editorial writer on the *News*, with Mr. Willison, until 1905; purchased *Sentinel and Protestant Advocate* from E. F. Clarke Estate, 1905. For several yrs. a mem. of Toronto City Council; unsuccessful can. for Mayoralty, 1910. *Recreations:* gardening and boating. *Address:* 563 Euclid Ave., Toronto, Ont.

HODGETTS, Charles Alfred, M.D., C. M., L.R.C.P., Chief Health Officer, Prov. of Ontario and Deputy Registrar General; *b.* Toronto, 23 Aug., 1859; *s.* of George and Susan Hodgetts; *m.* Elizabeth B. Salter. St. John's, Nfld. (*deceased*); two *s.* three *d.* *Educ.:* Provincial Model Sch., Toronto; Toronto Medical Coll.; first Dufferin Medalist, Prov. Model Sch.; Grad. Ont. Coll. of Pharmacy; mem. and Secy. Prov. Board of Health for Ont., since 1902; mem. R. Sanitary Inst.; F.R.I. of P.H.; Hon. Vice-Pres.. Assn. of Public Vaccinators of Great Britain; Major A.M.C., Canada; Hon. Secy. Can. Red Cross Society; Hon. Associate Order of Jerusalem in England. *Publications:* "Smallpox," "Vaccination." *Address:* Parliament Buildings, Toronto.

HODGINS, George Frederick, M.P.; *b.* Shawville, Que., 17 Dec., 1865; *s.* of James and Sarah Hodgins; *m.* Georgina R. E. Thomas; two *s.* two *d.* *Educ.:* Shawville Academy; M.P. for Pontiac Co., Que.; engaged in mercantile business, also flour milling, and lumber manufacturing. *Address:* Shawville, Que.

HODGINS, John George, M.A., LL.B., LL.D., M.R.G.S., I.S.O.; *b.* Dublin, Ireland. 12 Aug., 1821; *m.* (1st) Frances Rachel Doyle; (2nd) Helen Fortescue Scoble; four *s.* one *d.* *Educ.:* Up. Can. Academy, Victoria Univ., and Toronto Univ.; called to the Bar in 1870. *Publications:* Lovell's General Geography," "First steps in General Geography," "School History of Canada and of the other British N. A. Provinces," "The Canadian School Speaker and Reciter," "The School Manual," "Lectures on School Law," "Sketches and Anecdotes of the Queen," "The School House and its Architecture." Has been an officer in the Queen's Own Rifles. *Address:* 92 Pembroke St., Toronto, Ont.

HODGSON, Jonathan, merchant; *b.* Clintonville, N.Y., 15 April, 1827; *s.* of Thomas Hodgson; *m.* 1854, Margaret, *d.* of the late John Cassels, of Glasgow, Scotland; five *s.* one *d.* *Educ.:* pub. schs. of Lacolle. In 1845, became a clerk in a general store at Napierville, Que.; removed to Montreal, 1850. and seven yrs. later formed a partnership with John Foulds, under the firm style of Foulds & Hodgson, wholesale dry goods and smallwares merchants; 1870, on retirement of Mr. Foulds, the firm was reorganized, Mr. Hodgson becoming senior partner of Hodgson, Sumner & Co., Ltd.; mem., Montreal Board of Trade, and of the Dry Goods Assn.; director of the Almonte Knitting Co., Victor Hudon Cotton Co., Montreal Cotton Co., Paton Woollen Mills, of Sherbrooke, Que.; is connected with the directorate of the Royal Victoria Life Ins. Co., and Alliance Assurance Co.; Vice-Pres., Merchants' Bank of Can. *Address:* 340 Peel St., Montreal.

HOGG, William Drummond, K.C.; Bencher of the Law Soc. of Upper Canada; *b.* Perth, Ont., 29 Feb., 1848; *s.* of David Hogg, manufacturer; *m.* Louisa Agnes, *d.* of Dr. Charles Rattray, of Cornwall, Ont.; two *s.* *Educ.:* Perth Gram. Sch. and by priv. tuition. Studied law at Perth and Toronto. Called to the Bar, 1874; has practiced in Ottawa since 1875. Engaged in many important cases on behalf of Dom. Govt. *Recreation:* walking. *Address:* 221 Somerset St., Ottawa. *Club:* Rideau.

HOLGATE, Henry, C.E.; *b.* Milton, Ont., 14 Sept., 1863; *s.* of John Halgate and Jane Brown; *m.* Bessie Bell Headley of Milford Deleware; two *s.* *Educ.:* Toronto; spent 13 years in Railway construction and maintenance; followed by bridge and structure designing. For the past 8 years, principally engaged in general engineering; practice, particularly in Hydro Electric Power development, and consulting. *Publications:* contributions to Engineering Society; report on the collapse of the Quebec Bridge, as Chairman of the Royal Commission of Enquiry. *Address:* 44 Rosemount Ave., Westmount, Que. *Club:* Engineers', Montreal.

HOLLAND, Andrew; *b.* Ottawa, 11 Aug. 1844; *s.* of W. L. Holland, and Charlotte Clarke; *m.* 1875, Margaret, *d.* of James Gibson, contractor, Ottawa; four *s.* three *d.* *Educ.:* Ottawa Pub. Schs. Commenced journalistic career, 1870, on Ottawa *Evening Mail*, subsequently with *Free Press;* with brother became joint editor and proprietor of *Citizen;* with bro. has been contractor for reporting and publishing Senate Debates since 1875. Official reporter for Dom. Bd. of Trade during its existence. Reported I.C.R., Welland Canal, and first series of C. P. R. cases. Has travelled extensively; visited Australia in 1892, and again in 1896. First visit led to inauguration of Can. Australian Steamship service between Vancouver and Sydney. An active mem. of Bd. of Trade. *Addresses:* The Senate; 47 Vittoria St., Ottawa.

HOLLAND, George Clarke; *b.* Ottawa, Ont., 5 March, 1846; *s.* of William Lewis Holland and Charlotte Clarke; *m.* Alison Hilson Robinson; two *s.* three *d.* *Educ.:* Ottawa. Has been connected with the *Press* in Ottawa, Toronto, Chicago, Ill., St. Louis, Mo., Nashville, Tenn., New York and Washington; was official reporter in H. of C., 1875, 1876, when apptd. official reporter of the Senate. *Publications:* "O Canada," a national anthem for Lavallee's harmonized by A. Trembley. *Address:* 117 Frank St., Ottawa.

HOLMAN, Charles J., M.A., LL.D., K. C.; *b.* Cobourg, Ont., 1852; *s.* of John Holman and Mary Webster Holman; *m.* Carrie Haigh, *d.* of Rev. W. M. Haigh. D.D., Chicago, Ill. *Educ.:* Victoria Univ. Formerly of Blake, Lash, Cassels and Holman, Barristers, and now Holman, Drayton and Bessett, Toronto. *Address:* "Holmhurst," 75 Southern Ave., Toronto. *Club:* Toronto.

HOLMES, Robert; *b.* St. Catharines, Ont., 14 Sept., 1852; *s.* of Edmund Holmes and Mary Watson; *m.* 1877, Emma L., *d.* of Edward L. Leavenworth, of St. Catharines; two *s.* six *d.* *Educ.:* Pub. Schs. of Hamilton, Ont. Began to learn the trade of a printer and compositor at age of twelve; bought an interest in the Clinton *New Era*, 1885. Was Mayor of Clinton for four yrs.; mem. Sch. Bd. for six yrs. Elec. to H. of C. for West Huron at bye-elec., 1899; re. elec. at g. e., 1900. Surveyor of Customs, Toronto, 1909. Pres., Can. Press Assn., 1897. *Address:* Toronto, Ont.

HOLT, Charles Macpherson, K.C., LL. D.; *b.* Quebec, *s.* Judge C. G. Holt, and

Margaret Macpherson; *m.* Mabel, *d.* of late Senator Cochrane; three *s.* one *d.* *Educ.:* at High Sch., Quebec, Lennoxville, and Laval Univ.; now in active practice as mem. of Montreal Bar; Library Committee of Bar; Lecturer in Post Graduate course, McGill Univ.; Director of Charity Organization Society; Royal Edward Institute; Montreal General Hospital; Legal mem. of Royal Commission on Tuberculosis. *Publications:* Holt's Insurance Law of Canada, and articles in legal periodicals. *Address:* 281 University St., Montreal. *Clubs:* Royal, Montreal Golf, Hunt, Canada, St. James, Montreal.

HOLT, Herbert S.; *b.* Dublin, Ireland, 1856; *s.* of the late William Robert Grattan Holt, of King's Co., Ireland; *m.* 1890, Jessie, *d.* of the late Andrew Paton, of Sherbrooke, Que.; three *s.* *Educ.:* Dublin, Ireland. Arrived Can., 1875. Acted as engineer for the Credit Valley, Victoria, Lake Simcoe Junction, Ont. & Que. and other Rys. in Ont., 1875-1883; removed to North-West where he engaged in engineering and construction work. Built a large part of the Can. Pac. Ry. through the Ste. of Maine, the Regina, Long Lake and Saskatchewan Calgary and Edmonton, and other railways. El. member of American Soc. of Civil Engineers, 1889; became Pres. of Montreal Gas. Co., 1894; Montreal Park and Island Ry. Co., 1896; Montreal Light, Heat and Power Co., 1900, which office he still holds; Kaministiqua Power Co., Imperial Writing Machine Co.; Royal Bank of Can; Can. Paper Co.; Director Dominion Textile Co., Ogilvie Flour Mills Co., Canadian General Electric Co.; National Trust Co.; Canada Car Co.; Monterey Ry. and Light Co. *Address:* 297 Stanley St., Montreal. *Clubs:* Mount Royal, St. James', Forest and Stream Royal St. Lawrence Yacht, Royal Montreal Golf, Montreal Hunt, Montreal.

HOOPER, James; *b.* Hatherleigh, Devonshire, Eng., 23 March, 1855; *s* of John and Susannah Hooper; *m.* Emma Johnston of London, Ont.; one *s.* four *d.* *Educ.:* Parochial Sch., Hatherleigh, Eng. Arrived in Canada in the fall of 1868, settling in London, Ont.; was apprenticed as printer in *Mercury* office, Plymouth, and sometime after arrival, took up reporting; went to Manitoba, 1880, and started a paper at Morris; later was identified with Winnipeg newspapers until 1889, when he became Managing Editor of the *Telegram;* apptd. Deputy Provincial Secretary and King's Printer, in Feb., 1900. *Address:* 195 Nassau St., Winnipeg, Manitoba. *Club:* Advance, Winnipeg.

HOPKINS, John Castell, F.S.S.; *b.* Dyersville, Iowa, U.S.A., 1 April, 1864, *s.* of John Castell Hopkins and Phila (Hendebourck) Hopkins; *m.* Annie Beatrice Bernner; one *d.* *Educ.:* Bowmanville, Ont. Entered Imperial Bank in 1883. In 1886, formed at Ingersol the first branch of thel Imperial Federation League in Ontario and apptd. member of the Council of the League in England. Became Honorary Secretary of the League in Canada, in 1889; apptd. in 1890, associate editor Toronto *Daily Empire.* In 1891-2, was President of Toronto Young Men's Conservative Assn., also Pres. of the Ontario Con. Assn. the same term. In 1892, was apptd. a mem. of Toronto High Sch. Board; Hon.-Secy., Sir John Macdonald Memorial Com., in 1893-4; in 1894, was apptd. mem. of the Council of the British Empire League in Canada; commenced literary work with the publication of a "Life of Sir John Thompson," in 1895. In 1896, was delegate to the Canadian Manufacturers Assn. at the Congress of Chambers of Commerce of the Empire, in London. Has been at one time or another a Fellow of the Royal Statistical Society, and the Royal Historical Society; a member of the American Historical Association, the Executive of the Can. Soc. of Authors, the Ont. Historical Society, the Niagara Historical Society, &c. *Publications:* include an immense amount of contributions to History, Biography and Current Literature. *Recreation:* Reading novels. *Address:* 8 Oaklands Ave., Toronto. *Clubs:* Albany, R.C.Y., Toronto, Ont.

HORNING, Lewes Emerson, B.A., Ph. D.; *b.* Norwich, Ont., 2 April, 1858; *s.* James and Eliza Macklem Horning; *m.* Beatrice Lillian Nixon; one *s.* two *d.* *Educ.:* Brantford Coll. Inst., Victoria Univ., Univ. of Breslau, Goettinger and Leipzig (German); Taught in Peterborough Coll. Inst., 1884-86, adjunct Prof. Classics and Theories, Victoria Univ., 1886-91; Prof. of German and Old English, 1891-1905; Prof. of Teutonic Philology, 1905. *Publications:* several schoolbooks for German Classes; translation of Wilkonski, History of German Training of 19th Century, 1909; numerous articles on Canadian Literature and on German Life and Times. *Recreations:* golf and gardening. *Address:* Toronto and Cobourg.

HOSKIN, John, LL.D., K.C., D.C.L.; *b.* Holsworthy, Devon, May, 1836; *s.* of Richard Hoskin; *m.* 1866, Mary Agnes, *d.* of late Walter Mackenzie, Barrister-at-Law, of Castle Frank, Toronto. *Educ.:* London. Arrived in Canada, 1854; called to Bar, 1863; Q.C., 1873; elected a Bencher of the Law Society of Up. Can., 1876; Senator of Toronto Univ., Trinity Univ.; Chairman of Board of Trustees of Univ. of Toronto until its reorganization in 1906, and then apptd. by the Government of the Province Chairman, of the New Board of Governors; head of the firm of McCarthy, Osler, Hoskin, and Harcourt; Guardian *ad litem,* and Official Guardian of Infants, 1874-1904; Advisory Counsel to his successor in office since 1904; on the directorate of Canadian Life Assurance Company, of the Bank of Commerce. and of the British American Assurance Co.; a Vice-President of the Canadian Landed and National Investment Company; Pres, of the Toronto General Trusts Company; and a Director of the Toronto Gas Company; Chairman of the Board of Governors of University of Toronto. *Address:* The Dale Rosedale, Toronto. *Clubs:* Grosvenor, Toronto.

HOSMER, Charles Rudolph; *b.* Coteau Landing, Que., 12 Nov., 1851; *s.* of Hiram Pratt Hosmer and Mary Briggs; *m.* Clara Jane Bigelow; one *s.* one *d.* *Educ.:* Coteau Landing, Que. At the age of fourteen commenced the study of telegraphy with the G.T.R. Co.; was given charge of telegraph office 1866; became mgr. of the office of the Dom. Tel. Co. at Kingston,

1870; transferred to Buffalo, N.Y., 1871; apptd. supt. of the Co. at Montreal, 1873; remained with the Dom. Tel. Co. until it was merged with the G. N. W. Tel. Co.; in 1881 effected the organization of the Can. Mutual Tel. Co., of which he remained pres. and mgr. until he engaged with the C. P. R. Co. as head of the tel. dept., in Jan., 1886; retired from the management of the C. P. R. Tel. system, 1899. Dir., Bank of Montreal; of the C. P. Ry.; Vice-Pres. and Dir. of the Commercial Cable Co.; Dir., Postal Tel. Cable Co., Montreal Light, Heat and Power Co., the Halifax and Bermudas Cable Co., the London and Lancashire Life Assur. Co. the Laurentide Paper Co., the Canada Paper Co., the Royal Trust Co., the West Kootenay Power and Light Co., the Acadia Coal Co., the Edwardsburg Starch Co., the Dom. Express Co., the Direct West India Cable Co.; pres., the Ogilvie Flour Mills Co., (President), and of the E. N. Heney Co., Ltd.; gov., Royal Victoria Hospital, Montreal Gen. Hospital, Western Hospital. *Recreation:* motoring. *Address:* 302 Drummond St., Montreal; St. Andrews, N.B, (summer). *Clubs:* Mount Royal, St. James, R. St. L. Yacht, Royal Montreal Golf, Forest and Stream, Montreal.

HOUSTON, Edward Strachan, Mgr. Ottawa Branch, Imperial Bank of Canada; *b.* Waterdown, Ont., 14 July, 1875; *s.* of Stewart Houston, Dean of Niagara, and Fanny S. Houston; *m.* Errol Louise Boulton *d.* of Samuel Nordheimer, "Glen Edyth," Toronto. *Educ.:* Drummondville Gram. Sch. Entered service of Imperial Bank of Canada at Niagara Falls, 1892. Stationed at Toronto, and Montreal. Manager at Niagara Falls Branch before transferred to Ottawa. *Address:* 508 Besserer St., Ottawa. *Clubs:* Rideau, Ottawa; Hunt, Toronto.

HOUSTON, Mrs. Stewart, née **Augusta Louise Beverly Robinson;** *b.* Toronto, Ont.; *d.* of Hon. John Veverly Robinson, formerly Lieut.-Gov. of Ontario; *m.* Stewart Field Houston; one *d.* *Educ.:* in Toronto. During her father's term as Lieut.-Governor amid the many duties of that position, found time to cultivate an admirable voice which she had inherited from her mother. She went to New York at that period to study under Signor Agramonte. Studied in Paris, under Madame La Borde, and London, where she completed her vocal training with Randeggar and Henschel. Was associated with Maud Valerie White, in a number of recitals in London, and also made a number of appearances at St. James' Hall, Queen's Hall, and other principal concerts. On tour with Plunket Greene, Ben Davies, Marie Brema and other notable artists. Returning to Canada in 1895, achieved great success in Massey Hall in "The Creation." In 1896-7, was a member of Madame Albani's concert party on her tour of Canada and the United States. In 1899, sang on tour with Plunket Greene in Canada. 1899-1900, sang on behalf of the Dominion patriotic fund of the South African War in a large number of cities and as a result of this series of entertainments arranged by Mr. Stewart Houston, some $10,000 was obtained for patriotic purposes. Then retired from the concert stage; is interested in the work of the Soc. for Prevention of Cruelty to Animals, and has latterly delivered addresses in several cities on the subject. *Address:* 5 Cluny Avenue, Toronto. *Clubs:* Toronto Ladies', Ladies' Empire, London, Eng.

HOUSTON, William Robert; *b.* Mount Forest, Ont., 2 Oct., 1866; *m.*; four *s.* one *d.* *Educ.:* Trinity Coll. Sch. Entered banking profession, 1893, and spent fifteen yrs. with the Dominion Bank. Founded Houston's Standard Publications, 1901, being editor of The Annual Financial *Review* (Canadian), and the Bank Directory of Canada. *Addresses:* 7-9 King E.; 8 Elmsley Place, Toronto. *Clubs:* Toronto Hunt, Victoria, Toronto.

HOWARD, Hon. Mrs. Robert (Margarat Charlotte Smith); heir presump. to the Barony of Strathcona and Mount Royal; *o. c.* of the 1st Baron Strathcona, and Isabella Sophia Hardisty; *m.* Robert J. B. Howard, M.D., F.R.S.C. *Address:* 31 Queen Anne St., Cavendish Square, London, W.

HOWE, Clifton Durant, B.A., M.S., F. E., Ph.D.; *b.* Newfalls, Vermont, U.S.A., 30 July, 1874; *s.* of Marshall O. Howe and Gertrude Q. Dexter. *Educ.:* Univ. of Vermont., Univ. of Chicago. Arrived in Canade, Oct., 1908; associate director of Beltmore Forest Sch. and Assistant Forester to the Beltmore Estate, Beltmore, N.S., 1900-1908; Lecturer in Botany and Forestry, Univ. of Toronto, since Oct., 1908. *Recreations:* anything in the "bush." *Address:* 11 Queen's Park, Toronto, Ont.

HOYLES, Newman Wright, B.A., LL. D., K.C.; *b.* St. John's, Nfld., 14 March, 1844; *s.* of Sir Hugh William Hoyles, Chief Justice of Newfoundland, and Jean Liddell; *m.* Georgina Martha, *d.* of the late Lewis Moffatt, of Toronto; two *s.* two *d.* *Educ.:* Upper Can. Coll., Toronto; King's Coll., Windsor, N.S.; Trinity Coll., Cambridge. Called to Bar of Ontario, 1872; cr. Q.C., 1889; principal of the Law Sch., Osgoode Hall, Toronto, 1894. Pres., Wycliffe Coll., Toronto and Havergal Coll., Toronto; Vice-Pres., British and Foreign Bible Soc. and Church Missionary Soc. of England; Pres., Upper Canada and Canadian Bible Socs. *Publications:* articles in legal journals. *Recreation:* rowing. *Address:* 567 Huron St.; The Law School, Osgoode Hall, Toronto.

HUDON, Lieut.-Col. Joseph A. G., C.M. G.; *b.* Quebec, 7 June, 1858; *s.* of Francois Etienne Hudon, Esq., and Henrietta Couillard Dupuis; *m.* Alphonsene, *d.* of Charles Joncas, Esq., Quebec; two *s.* two *d.* *Educ.:* Elementary Sch., Seminary and Commercial Academy; joined Milita, Quebec Garrison Artillery, as Lieutenant, 1878; "A" Battery, R.C.A., 1883; served in the North-West Rebellion, 1885; present at actions of Fish Creek and Batoche (medal with clasp); in South Africa as Major in Command of "C" Battery, R.C.F.A.; present at relief of Mafeking, and operations in Orange Free State, Transvaal and Rhodesia (despatches, medal with clasp), 1902. *Address:* 158 Earl St., Kingston, Ont.

HUGHES, Hon. James Anthony, Mem. of U. S. House of Representatives for 5th Dist. of West Virginia; *b.* Corunna, Ont., 27 Feb., 1861. Moved with his parents to

Ashland, Ky., where educ. and entered on business career. Mem. of Legis. of Kentucky, 1887-88. Removed to West Virginia, and el. to State Senate, 1894-98. First el. to 57th Congress; re-el. 58th, 59th, 60th, and 61st Con. *Addresses:* The Capitol, Washington, D.C.; Huntington, West Va., U.S.A.

HUGHES, James Laughlin; *b.* Durham County, Ont., 20 Feb., 1846; *s.* of John Hughes and Caroline Laughlin; *m.* (1st) Annie Agnes Sutherland; (2nd) Ada Marian Hughes; one *s.* three *d.* Lived in the country till he was twenty years of age, and worked his father's farm till he was nineteen, when he became a teacher. After teaching one year, went to the Normal Sch. in Toronto, and remained till he secured the highest grade of certificate issued by the Education Department of Ontario. After leaving the Normal School, taught in Frankford for six months, and was then apptd. to a position in the Model Training School in connection with the Normal School, Toronto. Received this appointment on his twenty-fifth birthday; became principal of the school. In 1874, he was elected to his present position as Chief Inspector of Schools for the city of Toronto. *Publications:* Frobel's Educational Laws," "Dickens as an Educator," "Mistakes in Teaching, "Teaching to Read," "How to secure and retain attention." *Recreation:* lacrosse. *Address:* 47 Dundonald St., Toronto.

HUGHES, Miss Katherine, Prov. Archivist for Alberta; *b.* Melbourne, P.E.I.; *d.* of John Wellington Hughes and Anne O'Brien, *d.* of the late Terence O'Brien, of New Glasgow, P.E.I. *Educ.:* Notre Dame Convent, and Prince of Wales Coll., Charlottetown, P.E.I. Upon leaving Coll., was actively engaged for a few yrs. in work for the uplift of native Indian races; in 1903 joined the editorial staff of the Montreal *Star*, and in 1906, the staff of the Edmonton *Bulletin;* representative of the *Bulletin* in Press Gallery of Alberta Legislature; appointed Provincial Archivist for Alberta in 1908; in summer of 1909 to secure material for the Alberta Archives made a tour alone of the Peace River and Athabasca districts by frontier stage, canoe, river-boats and scows; elec. Vice-President of the Canadian Women's Press Club in 1909. *Publication:* "Archbishop O'Brien," Man and Churchman. Short stories and articles in Canadian and American Magazines; contributed Forest and Timber section to Canadian Encyclopedia, Vol. V; wrote and edited Christmas magazines of Edmonton *Bulletin*, 1906-07-08; at present engaged upon a "Life of Pere Lacombe." *Recreations:* riding, canoeing, walking. *Address:* 150 Bellamy St., Edmonton, or Government Buildings, Edmonton, Alta.

HUGHES, Colonel Samuel, M.P.; *b.* Darlington, Co. Durham, Ont., 8 Jan., 1853; *s.* of John Hughes, a native of Tyrone, Ireland, and Caroline Laughlin, of Scotch-Irish-Huguenot descent; *m.* (1st) 1872, Caroline J., *d.* of the late Major Preston, Vancouver, B.C. (*deceased*) (2nd) 1875, Mary, *e. d.* of H. W. Burk, ex-M.P., West Durham. *Educ.:* Pub. Sch., Toronto Model and Normal Sch., and Toronto Univ. Lecturer in English Language, Literature and History in Toronto Collegiate Institute, until 1885, when he purchased the Lindsay *Warder*, which he edited until 1897; was prominently identified with Amateur Athletics; has been in the Active Militia since his fourteenth year; declined position of Deputy Minister of Militia, in 1891, and of Adjt.-Gen'l., Canada, 1895; apptd. Lt.-Col., Commanding 45th Batt., 9th June, 1897; took part in the Queen's Jubilee celebration, 20 June, 1897 (medal); President of the Dominion of Canada Rifle Association; President, Small Arms Committee, Canada; Chn. Board of Visitors, Royal Military Coll., Kingston; Railway Intelligence Officer, Headquarters' Staff; served in the Fenian Raids, 1870 (medal); since 1872, has strongly advocated and made personal offers of Colonial Military Assistance to the Empire in Imperial Wars; personally offered to raise corps for the Egyptian and Soudanese campaigns, the Afghan Frontier War, and the Transvaal War; visited Australia and New Zealand in 1897-98 in the interest of Colonial assistance in Imperial Wars; served in the South African Transvaal War, 1899-1900, (1) on railway transport, (2) as Assist. to Inspector General Settle on the lines of communication; (3) as Chief Intelligence Staff to General Settle in the Gordonia and Prieska campaign; and (4) in similar position on Staff of Gen'l. Sir Charles Warren in the Griqualand West, and Bechuanaland campaigns; (5) Commander of the Mounted Brigade in same campaign; mentioned several times in despatches; an unsuccessful candidate for the H. of C. for N. Victoria, 1891; elec. bye-election 1892, and re-elec. 1896 and 1900; elec. for Victoria and Haliburton, 1904 and 1908; member of the Orange Order, Foresters and Masonic Order; Methodist; Conservative. *Address:* Lindsay, Ont.

HULL, William Roper; *b.* Somersetshire, Eng., 20 Dec., 1857; *s.* of Arthur Hull and Honora Roper; *m.;* *Educ.:* Dorchet and Bridgeport, Eng. For many yrs. sole owner of Hull Bros. & Co., ranches, abattoirs and meat agencies in Alberta, but recently sold out to P. Burns & Co. A large owner of real estate in Calgary. Built and owns the Calgary Opera House, Victoria Block, Hull Block, and many private residences; dir. of the Calgary Brewing Co. *Address:* Calgary. *Club;* Ranchmen's.

HUMPHREY, Lieut.-Col. William Marshall, District Officer Commanding Military District, No. 8; Hon. Lieut.-Col., 66th Regt., "Princess Louise Fusiliers;" *b.* Halifax, N.S., 8 July, 1852; *s.* of William and Merian Humphrey, fomerly of Illmunster, Somerset, Eng.; *m.* Eva, *e. d.* of the late Andrew Mitchell of Halifax, N.S.; one *s.* one *d.* Identified with the Militia of Canada for 40 years; first commission as Ensign, 66th Regt., 1869; was present at Queen Victoria's Diamond Jubilee in London, 1897, as representative from N.S. *Recreations:* cricket, walking, reading. *Address:* 19 Wellington Row, St. John, N.B. *Clubs:* Halifax; Union, St. John, N.B.

HUNT, Aylmer Byron, M.P.; *b.* Bury, Que., 26 April, 1864; *s.* James and Jane Hunt; *m.* Annie Dawson; two *s.* five *d.* *Educ.:* Bury Model School; carriage maker and lumber dealer and also largely interested in timber lands; defeated as a Liberal candidate for Quebec Legislature; elected to the Federal House in 1904; election annulled in 1905; successful in the bye-election and also in g. e. in 1908. *Address:* Robinson, Bury, Prov. Que.

HUNT, Rev. Thomas Henry, M.A., D. D.; *b.* St. Eleanor's P.E.I., 7 Nov., 1865; *s.* of William Thomas De Vere Hunt, and Isabella Fortune Mackenley. *Educ.:* St. Peter's Boys' Sch., Charlottetown, P.E.I., and King's Coll., Windsor, N.S.; ordained Deacon in 1888; Priest in 1889; Master St. Peter's Boys' Sch., 1888 to 1904; Assistant Priest St. Peter's Cathedral, 1889 to 1904 (both at Charlottetown, P.E.I.;) Lecturer in Divinity, Trinity Coll., Toronto, 1904 to 1907; Alexandra Professor of Divinity, King's Coll., Windsor, N.S., 1907. *Address:* King's College, Windsor, N.S.

HUNTER, Hon. Gordon, Chief Justice of the Supreme Court of British Columbia; *b.* Beamsville, Ont., 4 May, 1863; *o. s.* J. Howard Hunter, M.A., Govt. Inspector of Insurance for Ontario, and Anne Gordon; *m.* 1896, Mrs. Ida Nelson, *d.* of Chas. F. Johnson, of Portland, Ore. *Educ.:* Brantford, Coll. and Toronto Univ., where he grad. 1885, winning Lorne silver and Lansdowne gold medals for general proficiency. Studied law in office of Messrs. McCarthy, Hoskins & Creelman, and called to Ontario Bar, 1888. Removed to B.C., 1891, and apptd. first official law reporter to Supreme Court. Later became Crown Solicitor; sworn 18 March, 1902 as Chief Justice of B. C. A charter mem. and one of organizers of the Young Men's Liberal Assn. of Toronto in 1887, first organization of the kind in Canada. *Address:* Victoria, B.C. *Club:* Union, Victoria.

HUNTER, James Blake, B.A.; Deputy Minister of Public Works, Canada; *b.* Waterdown, Ont., 31 Aug., 1876; *s.* of the late David Hamilton Hunter, Principal of Woodstock (Ont.) Collegiate Institute, and Eunice Kitchen, *d* of the late J. B. Kitchen, Esq., J.P. of St. George, Ont.; *m.* Helena Augusta Calvert, *d.* of W. S. Calvert, Railway Commissioner, formerly M.P. for West Middlesex; one *d.* Entered pub. service in 1899, in the Privy Council department, as private secretary to late Hon. James Sutherland; Private Secretary, 1900, to Acting Postmaster General during the absence of Sir Wm. Mulock, in Australia; in 1901, Private Secretary to the Minister of Marine and Fisheries; in 1902, Private Secretary to the Minister of Public Works; Jan. 1st, 1908, apptd. Asst. Deputy Minister of Public Works, and July 1st, 1908, apptd. Deputy Minister. *Address:* 752 Maclaren St., Ottawa, Ont.

HUNTER, John Howard, Prov. Inspector of Insurance for Ontario, M.A., K.C.; *b.* near Bandon, Ireland, 22 Dec., 1839; *s.* of William Hunter and Charlotte Howard; *m.* Annie Gordon, *d.* of John Gordon, Inverness, Scot.; two *s.* three *d.* *Educ.:* Queen's Univ., Ireland. and Univ. of Toronto; arrived in Canada, 1859; Principal of Collegiate Institute, St. Catharines, 1871; Inspector of Insurance for Ont. since 1881; also Registrar of Loan Companies, and Trust Companies, and Registrar of Friendly Societies. *Publications:* articles in "Picturesque Canada; in conjunction with his sons H. H. and A. T. published treatises on Insurance and Property Law; formed the Ontario Statute relating to insurance, and the law of loan corporations; in 1896 he computed from the Canada Life Mortality, the minimum table of premium rates, which is the statutory standard in Ontario, and Quebec for Friendly Societies, and which became the basis for the fraternal congress table in the United States. *Address:* 82 St. Mary St., Toronto, Ont.

HUNTER, John Kelso, barrister, City Clerk of Regina, Sask., and Secretary-Treasurer for the Union of Sask. Municipalities; *b.* Glasgow, Scot., 18 Nov., 1856; *s.* of John Kelso Hunter and Margaret Goldie; *m.* Elizabeth W. Walker, Sunderland, Eng.; *Educ.:* Kirkwall Gram. Sch. and Glasgow Univ.; arrived in Canada, July 1892; since coming to Canada has been farming, Teacher, Barrister, Deputy Registrar for the Assiniboia Land Registration District, and City Clerk of Regina. *Publications:* Regina Municipal Manual." *Recreations:* cricket and golf. *Address:* 2330 Victoria St., Regina. *Clubs:* Assinaboia, Regina.

HUNTER, Samuel, cartoonist; *b.* Millbrook, Co. of Durham, Ont., 3 March, 1858; *s.* of John Hunter, and Jane O'Brien; *m.* Jeanette Brayley, of Toronto. *Educ.:* Millbrook Public Sch.; during the past twenty-five years, has been cartooning on the Toronto press. *Recreations:* interested in plant and bird life. *Address:* 158 Springhurst Av., Toronto, and Stony Lake, Ont. (Summer).

HUTCHISON, Alexander Cooper, architect; *b.* Montreal, 1838; *s.* of William Hutchison and Helen Hall; *m.* 1862, Margaret Burnet, of Cobourg, Ont.; two *s.* one *d.* *Educ.:* Sch. of the late C. P. Watson; night schs., and devoted his spare time to self study. Attended drawing classes conducted at the Mechanics' Inst. At age of twelve, began to learn the trade of stone-cutter. Had charge of the stone cut work of the eastern block of the Parlt. Bldgs. at Ottawa, and Christ Church Cathedral. Conducted the drawing classes in connection with the Mechanics' Inst. at Montreal, for some time; apptd. mem. R.C.A. by Marquis of Lorne, 1880, and vice-pres. that Assn. for twenty yrs. One of the founders and Pres., Prov. of Quebec Assn. of Architects. For several yrs. mem. of the Council and second Mayor of Cote St. Antoine; School Trustee for eighteen yrs. Mem. No. 5 Queen's Company. Volunteer Fire Brigade for number of yrs.; first company of Rifles, also an officer in a Rifle Company in Ottawa and afterwards with the Montreal Engineers, retiring with rank of Lieut. Took part in Fenian Raids in 1866 and 1870 (medal); life gov. Montreal Gen. Hospital, Hospital for the Insane, Protestant House of Industry and Refuge; ex-Pres. Canadian Branch of Royal Caledonian Curling Club, Montreal Caledonian Curling and Heather Curling Club, of Westmount. *Address:* 240 Kensington Av., Montreal.

HUTCHISON, Dr. James Alexander; *b.* Montreal, 12 June, 1863; *s.* of the late Matthew Hutchison and Helen Ogilvie; *m.* 1891, *o. d.* of the late Thomas Caverhill (*d.* 1899); three *s.* one *d.* *Educ.:* Montreal, Goderich,

Univ. of Montreal (grad. 1884), and prosecuted his studies in Edinburgh and London qualifying Licentiate of the Royal Coll. of Physicians and Surgeons in Edinburg. On return to Can., commenced practice in Montreal. In 1885 became a mem. of surgical staff of G. T. Ry.; apptd. Asst. Surgeon, Montreal Gen. Hospital, 1891; attend-Surgeon, 1894. Is at present Asst. Prof. of Surgery and Clinical Surgery, McGill Univ.; promoted Chief Medical Officer of G. T. R., about 1894, later receiving the entire control of the medical services of the G. T. R. System, including the Central Vermont Ry. and later of the G. T. P. Ry. Pres., Montreal Medico-Chirurgical Soc.; mem. Can., Ontario and National Ry. Medical Assns.; life mem. M.A.A.A. *Publications:* has contributed valuable surgical papers to Canadian and U.S. medical journals. *Address:* 70 Mackay St., Montreal. *Clubs:* St. James, University, Royal St. Lawrence, Yacht, Royal Montreal Golf.

HUTCHISON, William, Ex-M.P.; Order of the Rising Sun (Japan); Colonel (Japan); Commissioner of Dominion Exhibitions; *b.* Ottawa, Ont., 25 Dec., 1843; *s.* of Robert and Mary Hutchison; *m.* E. B. Willet; two *s.* *Educ.:* Ottawa Grammar Sch.; was representative for the Capital in the H. of C. for one term; president of the Central Canada Exhibition for many years; now Commissioner of Exhibitions for the Dominion of Canada; decorated by the Emperor of Japan for services at Osaka. *Address:* Ottawa, Ont. *Club:* Rideau, Ottawa.

HUYCKE, His Hon. Edward Cornelius Stanbury, B.A., LL.B., K.C.; County Judge of Peterborough, Ont.; *b.* Percy Tp., Northumberland Co., Ont., 10 March, 1860; *s.* of James Kemp Huycke, P.J., and Annie Stanbury; *m.* Rose Meredith Field; four *s.* two *d.* *Educ.:* Percy, Campbellford, Cobourg, Toronto. Taught classics before study of law. Called to the Bar, 1886; cr. K.C., 1902; elevated to the Bench, 1909. *Address:* Peterborough, Ont. *Club:* Citizens, Peterborough.

HYMAN, Hon. Charles Smith, P.C.; *b.* London, Ont., 31 Aug., 1854; *s.* of Ellis W. Hyman and Anna M. Niles; *m.* Elizabeth Birrell; one *d.* *Educ.:* Hellmuth Coll.; Mayor of London, 1884; Chairman Board of Trade, 1886; elec. member of H. of C. for London, 1891; defeated 1892, and 1896; relec. 1900, 1904 and 1905; Chairman Railway Committee, 1903, 1904, 1905; Chairman Redistribution Committee, 1903; Minister of Public Works, 1905; resigned owing to ill health, 1907. *Address:* London, Ont. *Clubs:* London; St. James, Montreal; Toronto, Toronto; Rideau, Ottawa; and Union, St. John, N.B.

I

IDINGTON, Hon. John, LL.B., K.C.; a Judge of the Supreme Court of Canada; *b.* Wellington, Ont., 14 Oct., 1840; *s.* of Peter Idington and Catherine Stewart; *m.* Margaret Cotelengh, *d.* of the late George Cotelengh of Mount Forest, Ont.; four *s.* four *d.* Called to the Bar, Trinity Term, 1864; Q.C. in Ont., 1876; Dominion, 1885; practiced in Stratford, Ont.; apptd. County Crown Attorney for Perth, 1879; continued as such until apptd. Puisne Judge, Exchequer Division of High Court of Justice for Ontario, 15 March, 1901; and Supreme Court of Can., 10 Feb., 1905; has been President of North Simcoe Reform Assn. *Address:* 325 Stewart St., Ottawa, Ont. *Club:* Rideau, Ottawa.

INCH, James Robert., M.A., LL.D.; Chief Supt. of Educ. for the Prov. of New Brunswick; *b.* Petersville, Queen's Co., N.B., 29 April, 1835; *s.* of Nathaniel Inch and Ann Armstrong; *m.* Mary Alice Dunn; one *d.* *Educ.:* Gagetown Gram. Sch., Mt. Allison Univ. Taught in pub. schs., 1850-54, in Mt. Allison Acad., 1854-64; principal Mt. Allison Ladies' Coll. 1864-1878; Pres. of Mt. Allison Univ., Sackville, N.B., 1878-1891; apptd. Chief Supt. of Educ. for the Prov. of N.B., 1891. *Address:* Sackville, N.B.

INGRAM, Andrew B., Vice Chairman Ontario Railway, and Municipal board; *b.* Strabane, Ont., 23 April, 1885; *s.* of Thomas and Mary Ann Ingram; *m.* Elizabeth McIntyre; three *s.* one *d.* Represented West Elgin in the Legislative Assembly of Ont., for four years, and East Elgin in the H. of C. for seven years. *Address:* 322 Palmerston Boulevard, Toronto, Ont.

INNIS, Hugh Paterson, K.C., M.L.A.; *b.* Dundas, Ont., 14 Sept., 1870; *s.* of William Patrick Innis, founder of the Simcoe Canning Company, and Marian Livingstone. *m.* Mabel Margaret, *e. d.* of the late Judge R. T. Livingstone; two *s.* three *d.* *Educ.:* Simcoe Pub. and High Sch. Admitted to the Bar, 1893; created K.C., 1908. elected to Ontario Legislature, June, 1908. *Address:* Simcoe, Ont.

INWOOD, Frederick George, Gen. Sec. the Reform Assoc. for Ontario; *b.* Kingston on Thames, England, 20 Sept., 1854; *s.* of Geo. and Susanna Inwood; *m.* Annabel Sutherland, of Napier, Ont.; two *d.* *Educ.:* Ont. Pub. and High Schs., Ont. Com. Coll., Belleville. Came to Can. with parents in 1857. In commercial life for many yrs., until apptd. to present position. Past G. M. and Treas. A.O.U.W., P.D.D.G.M., A.F. & A.M., Past Pres., Can. Fraternal Assocn. *Address:* 63 Glen Rd., Toronto. *Club:* Ontario, Toronto.

IRVIN, Joseph Samuel; *b.* Belle Plain, Marshall Co., Illinois, U.S.A., 6 May, 1862; *s.* of Col. Joseph Irvin, 77th Illinois Volunteers, and Elizabeth M. Irvin; *m.* (1st) Martha A. Barnard (2nd) Miss Wright, of Ottawa; one *s.* Arrived in Can., January, 1900. *Educ.:* Pub. Sch. of Illinois; employed on his father's farm until he was seventeen years of age, when he accepted a position with Scott, Arnold & Company, of Bloomington, Ill., as salesman. Two yrs. later, was offered and accepted a position with the Plano Harvesting Machine Co., of Chicago, as travelling expert and salesman. The following year, and before twenty-one years of age, he was promoted to the position of general manager for the State of Michigan and placed in charge of branch house at Jackson, Mich., a position held by him for seven years. Enjoyed the distinction of being the youngest general manager in this business in the United

States. At the end of this period of service, accepted a position with the McCormick Harvesting Machine Company of Chicago, Ill., remaining with them until October, 1898, when he resigned his position and became associated with Jackson and Detroit capitalists, and at once distinguished himself in the organization of the Peninsular Portland Cement Company of Cement City, Mich. At the first annual Meeting of this Company, was unanimously elected a member of the Board of directors. Assisted in the promotion of and served as a director of the Southern States Portland Cement Company of Atlanta, Ga., and the Western States, Portland Cement Co., of Independence, Kansas. In 1902, promoted and built the works of the International Portland Cement Company of Ottawa, Canada, and is at present its managing director. In 1905, promoted and built the big works of the Western Canada Cement & Coal Company at Exshaw, Alberta. The International and Exshaw Plants are conceded by experts to be models in design and equipment and economically produce the very highest grade cement. A leading spirit in the early promotion of the big $30,000,000 Cement Merger, known as the Canada Cement Company, Limited, and one of its first Directors. *Publications:* several books on Cement; its production and method of manufacture. *Address:* Suite 401, Aylmer Apartments, Ottawa.

IRVING, Sir Aemilius, Kt., K.C.; barrister; *b.* Leamington, Eng., 1823; *s.* of the late Jacob Aemilius Irving, Mem. Legis. Coun., Canada, and Catherine Diana, *d.* of Sir Jere Homfray, of Llandaff, House Glamorganshire; *m.* 1851, Augusta Louisa (*d.* 1892), *d.* of Col. Gugy, Quebec; five s. two *d.* *Educ.:* Upper Can. Coll. Called to Bar, 1849; cr. Q.C., 1864; cr. Kt., 1906. Mem. of H. of C. for Hamilton, 1874-1878; Treas. of Law Soc. of Upper Canada, first el. 1893 and re-el. annually since; Hon. LL.D., Univ. of Toronto, 1905. *Address:* 19 Russell St., Toronto. *Clubs:* Toronto, Victoria, Toronto, Hamilton.

IRVING, Major Lewis Erskine Wentworth, D.S.O., M.D., C.M., Royal Canadian Artillery; *b.* Hamilton, 16 Aug., 1868; 5th *s.* of Sir. Æmilius Irving. *Educ.:* Up. Can. Coll., Toronto; McGill Coll. Montreal; Trinity Univ., Toronto. Capt. Canadian Artillery, 1891; Lt. Royal Canadian Artillery, 1899; served South Africa (Rhodesian Field Force), 1899-1900; Beira to Mafeking, etc. (despatches, D.S.O., Brevet of Major, 1901, Queen's medal, 4 clasps). Treas. Law Society of Up. Canada. *Address:* Walton, Ont. *Clubs:* Canadian Military Institute, Victoria, Toronto.

IRVING, David Purdy, M.L.A.; *b.* Cherry Valley, P.E.I., 6 April, 1841; *s.* of James Irving and Anne MacKenzie; *m.* Anne Tweedy; six *s.* six *d.* *Educ.:* Prince of Wales Coll., Charlottetown, P.E.I. Taught in the pub. schools for six yrs., then went to New York where he filled an important position in office of New York and Erie Railroad; returned to P.E.I., to take up life of country gentleman at Vernon; elected Liberal for East Queens, in 1900; re-elected in 1904, again elected in 1908; colleague of Hon. T. L. Haszard, Premier of Pr.ovince *Recreations:* walking, culture and care of fruit. *Address:* Vernon, P.E.I.

IRVING, Hon. Paulus Æmilius, M.A., D.C.L., a Judge of the Supreme Court of B.C.; *b.* 3 April, 1857; 3rd *s.* of Sir Æmilius Irving, Toronto; *m.* 1883, Diana, *d.* of Hon. W. Hamley; two *s.* two *d.* *Educ.:* Trinity Coll. Sch., Port Hope; Trinity Coll., Toronto Called to Bar of Ont., 1880; B.C., 1882; Deputy Attorney-General, B.C., 1888-90; Puisne Judge, British Columbia, 1897; as special commissioner he settled mining disputes in Atlin, B.C., 1899; his services on this occasion were acknowledged in the speech from the throne. *Address:* Halwyn, 29 Richardson Street, Victoria, B.C. *Clubs:* Union, Victoria; Vancouver.

IRWIN, Lieut.-Col. De la Cherois Thomas, C.M.G.; Hon. A.D.C. to Governor-General; retired Colonel, Royal Canadian Artillery; Lt.-Col. (retired) Royal Artillery; *b.* Armagh, Ireland, 31 March, 1843; *m.* 25 April, 1867, Isabella *d*, of Robert Hamilton of Hamwood, Quebec; three *s.* one *d.* *Educ.:* privately; Royal Military Academy, Woolwich; arrived in Canada, Dec., 1861; entered Royal Artillery, 1861; retired as Lt.-Col., 1882; sent to Canada at the time of the Trent affair; marched with the 10th Brigade to Quebec, March, 1862; entered Canadian Military Service, 1872; on reserve list, 1897; on retired list with rank of Colonel, May, 1909; R.M. Staff College, 1871-72; Inspector of Artillery for Dominion of Canada, 1882-98; commandant Royal School of Artillery, 1873-82; commanding Royal Canadian Artillery, 1883-97; President Dominion Artillery Association, 1900-1901; Secy. of the Can. Patriotic Fund Assocn. *Recreations:* golf, curling, angling. *Address:* 170 Cooper St., Ottawa; Carnagh, Co. Armagh. Ireland. *Clubs:* Rideau, Golf, Ottawa.

IRWIN, May; *b.* Whitby, Ont., 1862; *d.* Robert E. and Jane Draper Campbell; *m.* 1878, Frederick W. Keller, St. Louis (*d.*) 1886. Debut Adelphi Theatre, Buffalo, Feb., 1876; mem. of Tony Pastor's Co. (with her sister Flora), 1877-83; Augustin Daly.s Co., 1883-7; later with Charles Frohman and Rich. & Harris; subsequently starring in "The Widow Jones," "The Swell Miss Fitzwell," "Courted into Court," "Kate Kip-Buyer," "Sister Mary," "Belle of Bridgeport," "Madge Smith, Attorney," "Mrs. Black is Back," "Mrs. Wilson—Andrews," "Mrs. Peckham's Carouse," etc. *Address:* Irwin Island, Clayton, N.Y.

IRWIN, Robert, M.L.A.; *b.* Shelburne, N.S., 17 January, 1865; *s.* of Robert Gore Irwin and Isabel Muir Archer; *m.* Mary Prescott McGill, *d.* of James P. McGill of Shelburne, N.S.; two *s.* *Educ.:* Shelburne Academy; followed commercial life; elect. to Legislature of Nova Scotia, 1906. *Address:* Shelburne, N.S.

J

JACKSON, Rev. George, B.A.; *b.* Grimsby, Eng., 15 Oct., 1864; 2nd *s.* of William and Eliza Jackson; *m.* 1892, Annie, *d.* of J. Hyslop Bell, J.P., Darlington; three *s.* one *d.* *Educ.:* Collegiate Sch., Grimsby; Wesleyan Methodist Coll., Richmond; London Univ.

Entered Wesleyan Methodist ministry, 1887 one year in the Clitheroe Circuit; superintendent of the Wesleyan Methodist Mission, Edinburgh, 1888; held several important pastoral charges in Canada, including Sherbourne St. Church, Toronto; apptd. Prof., English Bible, Victoria College, Toronto, 1909. *Publications:* First Things First, 1894; The Table Talk of Jesus, 1896; Judgment, Human and Divine, 1897; The Ten Commandments, and a Young Man's Book Shelf, 1898; a Young Man's Religion, 1900; Memoranda Paulina, 1901; The Old Methodism and the New, 1903; The Teaching of Jesus, 1903; The fact of conversion, 1908; studies in the Old Testament, 1909. *Recreations:* walking, cycling, cricket, *Address:* 115 Wellesley St., Toronto.

JACKSON, Samuel Jacob, farmer; *b.* Stradbally, Ireland, 18 Feb., 1848; *s.* of Samuel Jackson and Elizabeth Sutcliffe; *m* 28 Feb., 1878, Ida Isabella Clarke, of London, Ont.; six children. *Educ.:* Common and Grammar Schs., Brampton, Ont.; and Brantford Grammar Sch. Apptd. Inspector of Indian Agencies, 6 Dec., 1902, and resigned 3 Oct., 1904. El. to Manitoba Legis. in 1883, 1886, 1888, 1892, 1896, defeated in 1899. El. Speaker Man. Legis., Feb., 1891. Was three times a candidate for alderman in the city of Winnipeg, and el. 1877, 1878, 1883. Has been pres. of the Rockwood Agric. Soc. for a number of yrs. Elected to H. of C. at g. e., 1904. Unsuccessful at g. e. 1908. *Address:* Stonewall, Man.

JAFFRAY, Hon. Robert, senator; *b.* near Bannockburn, Scotland, 1832; *s.* of William Jaffray and Margaret Heugh; *m.* 1860, Sarah (*d.* 1906), *d.* of John Bugg, Toronto. *Educ.:* Stirling Academy. Served apprenticeship in Edinburgh, emigrated to Toronto, 1852; in business in Toronto until 1883, and since then director of numerous railways, insurance companies, land corporations, and other enterprises, President of the *Globe*, (Toronto) Newspaper, since 1888; member of the Commission of Queen Victoria Niagara Falls Park, since 1890 Vice-President, Crow's Nest Pass Coal Co. since 1898; vice-president Imperial Bank of Canada since 1906. *Address:* Surrey Lodge, Grenville Street, Toronto. *Clubs*: Ontario; Toronto; Rideau, Ottawa.

JAMESON, Clarence, M.P.; *b.* Badeque, P.E.I., 12 June, 1872; *s.* of the late J. H. Jamieson, M.D., Shipharbour, N.S., and Sophie, *d.* of the late Rev. Charles J. Shreve, Chester, N.S. *Educ.:* Prince Co. Academy; studied law, 1893; apptd. town clerk and Treasurer of Digby, 1895; Deputy Magistrate, Digby, 1900; Magistrate, 1903; Surrogate of Probate, 1904; fellow R.C.I., London, Eng., and member of the N.S. Historical Society; elec. to the H. of C., 1908; Ch. of England; Conservative. *Address:* Digby, N.S.

JAMIESON, James Alexander; *b.* Peterborough, Ont., Dec., 1859; *s.* of John Jamieson and Elizabeth Mason; *m.* Miss Mathews, of London, Eng. *Educ.:* Peterborough pub. and high schs. Studied architectural and mechanical draughting, and engaged on plans and construction of the original elevator at Midland, Ont. Employed on engineering staff of C.P.R. on construction of Ry., 1883; transferred to Owen Sound, 1884; transferred to engineering dept. at Montreal, 1885, and apptd. Supt. of elevators. Estb. a business in Montreal as a designing and contracting engr., making a specialty of grain elevators, 1895. Mem. Council, Can. Soc. of Civil Engineers, American Soc. of Civil Engineers. Designed and constructed Govt. elevator at Port Colbourne, Ont., Welland Canal. *Publications:* a paper entitled "Grain Pressures in Deep Bins," submitted to the Can. Soc. of Civil Engrs.. Dec., 1903. *Address:* 585 Dorchester St., W., Montreal. *Club:* Engineers.

JAMIESON, His Hon. Joseph; County Judge of Wellington; *b.* Tp. of South Sherbrooke, Co. of Lanark, Ont., 15 March, 1839; *s.* of William Jamieson and Margaret Molyneux; *m.* Elizabeth Carss, *d.* of the late Robert Carss, J.P., of Fitzroy, Carleton County; four *s.* *Educ.:* Perth Grammar Sch.; called to the bar, Ontario, 1869; practiced in Almonte for 25 years; represented North Lanark in the H. of C. from 1882, until 1891, when apptd. Junior Judge of the County of Wellington, which position he occupies at present. *Address:* Guelph, Ont.

JAMIESON, Reuben Rupert; *b.* Westover, Ont., 12 Dec., 1856; *s.* of John and Mary Jamieson; *m.* Alice J. Jukes; two *s.* two *d.* *Educ.:* pub. schs. in Railway service from 1873 to 1908; commenced as telegraph operator and ended as General Superintendent; all on Can. Pac. Ry.; Mayor, City of Calgary, 1909. *Address:* Calgary, Alberta. *Clubs:* Ranchmens', Calgary.

JARVIS, Aemilius; head of the firm of Aemilius Jarvis & Co., bankers and brokers, *b.* Toronto, Ont., 25 April, 1860; grandson of Col. Samuel Peter Jarvis, after whom is named Jarvis St., Toronto, and great-grandson of William Jarvis, the first Prov. Sec. of Upper Can.; *m.* 1886, Augusta, *d.* of Aemilius Irving, K.C., of Hamilton; two *s.* three *d.* *Educ.:* Upper Can. Coll. Gained his first business experience in the Bank of Hamilton at Hamilton; estbd. the banking and broking firm of Aemilius Jarvis & Co., 1892, of which he is head; has been financially connected with the Hamilton, Grimsby and Beamsville Electric Ry. Co., the Hamilton Iron & Steel Co., the Toronto Hotel Co., the Niagara, St. Catharines and Toronto Ry. Co., Trenton Electric and Water Power Co., and many other large institutions. Is well known throughout Canada as a yacht skipper and skilful helmsman, and in 1896, was chosen by the North American Yacht Racing Assn., to represent them at a conference held in London, 1897, with the Yacht Racing Assn. of Great Britain. *Address:* 34 Prince Arthur Av., Toronto. *Clubs:* Toronto, National; Toronto.

JARVIS, Lt.-Col. Arthur Leonard Fitz-Gerald, I.S.O.; *b.* Toronto, Ont., 17 June, 1852; *s.* of George Murray, and Elizabeth Arnold Jarvis; *m.* Frances Geraldine Fitzgerald. *Educ.:* Toronto and Quebec. Entered the Government service in 1868; Secretary, Department of Agriculture, 1896. Assistant Deputy Minister, 1908; commanded the Governor-General's Foot Guards, 1899 to 1904. *Recreations:* curling and golf.

Address: 365 Daly Avenue, Ottawa, Ont. *Club:* Rideau.

JARVIS, Ernest Frederick, Asst. Dep. Min. of Militia and Defence; *b.* St. Eleanors, P.E.I., 16 Sept., 1862; *s.* of Henry Fitzgerald Jarvis, physician and surgeon, and Lucy Des Brisay Jarvis; *m.* Ethel Colborne, *d.* of the late E. A. Meredith, LL.D., Toronto; one *s.* three *d.* *Educ.:* P.E.I. Pub. Schs. Apptd. asst. third class clerk, P.O. Dept., 23 March, 1881; priv. sec. to the Hon. J. C. Patterson, Sec. of State, and subsequently Min. of Militia and Defence, Jan., 1892, to March 1895; permanently transferred to Dept. of Militia and Defence from P. O. Dept., 1 July, 1893; apptd. chief clerk, 1 Jan., 1903; sec. of the Militia Coun., 28 Nov., 1904; Asst. Dep. Min., 1 Sept., 1908. *Address:* 347 Stewart St., Ottawa.

JETTE, Hon. Sir Louis Amable, K.C.M.G., K.C., LL.D., (Laval Univ.), Chief Justice of the Superior Court, of the Prov. of Que.; *b.* L'Assomption, 15 Jan., 1836; *s.* of Amable Jette and Caroline Gauvreau; *m.* 1862, Berthe, *d.* of Toussaint Laflamme, of Montreal; one *s.* *Educ.:* L'Assomption Coll. Called to the bar in 1857, and commenced the practice of his profession in Montreal; at on time was ed. of "*La Revue Critique de Legislation et de jurisprudence du Canada,*" and correspondent of "*La Revue de Droit International de Gand, Belgium;*" for some months was ed. of the paper "*L'Ordre.*" Was Treas, of the Bar Assn.; apptd. a Puisne Judge of the Superior Court of prov. of Que., and in same yr., was apptd. Prof. of Civil Law in Laval Univ., and later became Dean of the Faculty of Law; was mem. of the Provincial Council of Public Instruction, 1878-1898; in 1898 was apptd. Lieut.-Gov., and in 1903, was re-apptd., retiring from Office in August, 1908; Chief Justice, 1909; in 1898, was made a Commander of the Legion of Honour, and in 1901, cr. K.C.M.G. In 1903 was apptd. one of the British Commissioners representing the Dom. of Can. on the Alaska Boundary Com., convened in London, Eng.; Returned for Montreal East to H. of C., 1872. *Publication:* Observations relatives au Code de Procedure, in conjunction with his fellow commissioners who were apptd. for the revision of the Quebec Code of Civil Procedure. *Address:* 71 d'Auteuil Street, Quebec. *Club:* Garrison, Quebec.

JOBIN, Patrick Joseph, Inspector of Industrial establishments and public edifices. *b.* Quebec, 26 Oct., 1854; *m.* t o Elizabeth Dowling; one *s.* two *d.* *Educ.:* Com. Sch. and Christian Brothers; a labour leader; ex-president of the Trades and Labour Congress, and active in the Canadian Labour Movement for the last twenty-five years. *Address:* 116 Scott Street, Quebec.

JOHNSON, George, D.C.L.; *b.* Annapolis Royal, N.S., 29 Oct., 1836; *s.* of George Johnson, Yorkshire Eng., and V. M. Cater, London, Eng.; widower. *Educ.:* at Sackville, N.B. Has been editor *News*, Toronto; editor Toronto *Mail;* Reuters Agent; Statistican of the Dominion of Canada; Hon. mem. Royal Statistical Society, London; Hon. mem. Manufacturers' Assn. of Canada. *Publications:* statistical year book of Canada; Handbook of Canada; pulp wood resources of Canada; Forest Wealth of Canada; Historical papers in magazines. *Recreations:* orchardist, studies of place names of Canada, walking. *Address:* Grand Pre, N.S.

JOHNSON, George Balfour, M.L.A.; *b.* Romano Bridge, Peebleshire, Scot., 21 March, 1865; *s.* of John Johnson, and Anna M. L. L. Donald; *m.* Frances M. Hayward; three *d.* *Educ.:* Aberdeen, Scot.; arrived in Can., 1884. A general merchant. Mayor of Melfort, 1907-08. Mem. Sask. Leg. Ass. *Address:* Melfort, Sask.

JOHNSON, Gordon Bennett; *b.* Belleville, Ont., 18 Nov., 1880; *s.* J. W. Johnson, M.L.A., Belleville, Ont., and Sarah L. Johnson (*deceased*), *d.* of Dr. P. W. Smith, Montreal. *Educ.:* Pub. and high schs., Belleville; Royal Military Coll., Kingston, and School of Military Engineering, Chatham, Eng.; graduated of the R. M. C. of Canada, 1900; received commission in the Royal Engineers, June, 1900; Lieut., School of Military Engineering, 1900 to 1902; attached 55th Field Co., R.E., Colchester, Eng., 1902-1903; first Lieutenant, 1903; stationed at Ceylon, 1903-1905; retired, 1905. Assistant-Engineer on Construction Shanghai, Nanking Railway, China; a retired Lieut. of the Royal Engineers; Assoc. mem., Can. Soc., C.E.; *Canadian Address:* c|o J. W. Johnson, M.L.A., Belleville, Ont.

JOHNSON, Hon. James, M.L.A.; *b.* Mitchell, Ont., 18 Nov., 1855; *s.* of John Johnson and Martha Bainbridge Johnson (English); *m.* 1879, Susana Oliver; three *s.* *Educ.:* Pub. Schs., Mitchell. At age of twenty, bought and worked a small farm in Logan tp.; purchased a farm between Brandon and Boissevain, 1882; removed to Boissevain, 1894, and devoted his attention largely to buying and shipping of wheat and operating of elevators at Boissvain and Minto; has also a general mercantile business at Minto. Pres. of the Boissevain Land Co.; reeve and coun. of mun. of Riverside; reeve and coun. of mun. of Morton; mayor and coun. of town of Boissevain. El. to Manitoba Legis. Assem., for Turtle Mountain, 1897, and has been successful in every el. since; now Speaker. *Address:* Boissevain, Man.

JOHNSON, John Wesley, F.C.A., M.L.A.; *b.* Antrim, Ireland, 17 Jan., 1846; *s.* of William Mary Johnson; *m.* (1st) Sarah, *d.* of W. P. Smith, M.D., of Montreal; (2nd), Mary, *d.* of Rufus Sawyer, Picton, Ont.; four *s.* five *d.* *Educ.:* Ireland and Canada. Arrived in Can., Sept., 1864; Principal of the Ont. Business Coll., Belleville, since 1877; was Mayor of Belleville, 1897-1900; was Pres. of the Institute of Chartered Accountants of Ont., in 1908; now mem. of the Ont. Legislature for West Hastings. *Recreation:* golf. *Address:* Belleville, Ont. *Club:* Albany, Toronto.

JOHNSON, Thomas Herman, B.A., M.L.A.; *b.* Iceland, 12 Feb., 1870; *s.* of John and Margaret Johnson; *m.* Aurora Frederickson; two *s.* one *d.* *Educ.:* Public Sch. of Winnipeg and Gustavus Adolphus Coll., St. Peter, Minn.; arrived in Canada, August, 1879; School Trustee, Winnipeg, 1904-1907; elec. to Manitoba Legislative Assembly, 7 March, 1907. *Address:* Winnipeg, Man. *Club:* Commercial, Winnipeg.

JOHNSTON, His Hon. Frederick William; Senior Judge of District of Algoma, Ont.; Judge of the Surrogate Court and Local Master; *b.* Goderich, Ont., 6 April, 1849; *s.* of Hugh Johnston and Matilda, *d.* of W. B. Rich of Kent Co., Eng.; *m.* Sept., 1890, Elizabeth S., *d.* of Thomas Graham, of Goderich; three *s.* two *d.* *Educ.:* Public and grammar sch., Goderich. Studied law in office of the late Judge Sinclair, of Hamilton, who formerly practiced law in Goderich; called to the bar in 1872; carried on the practice of law in Goderich for 20 yrs. with John Davison, Q.C.; apptd. Junior Judge of Algoma, 18 June, 1890; was revising officer for Western Algoma, Senior Judge, 9 July, 1892, succeeding the late Hon. W. McCrae; served in Goderich as Alderman, Deputy Reeve, Reeve and Warden of the Co. of Huron, 1882; unsuccessfully contested riding of Huron for local legislature in 1882. *Address:* Sault Ste. Marie, Ont.

JOLY DE LOTBINIERE, Major Alain Chartier, R.E., C.I.E.; *b.* Quebec, 31 Oct., 1862; *s.* of Sir Henry Joly de Lotbiniere; *m.* 1887, Marion Helen Campbell. *Educ.:* R. M. Coll., Kingston. Entered R. E., 1886; Captain, 1895; Major, 1903; proposed and carried out the first large Hydro Electric Transmission Power Scheme in the East, *i.e.* the Cauvery Falls transmission of power to the Kolar Goldfields in Mysore, Ind.; for a short time this was the longest power transmission line in the world; at present engaged as chief engineer in constructing a large Hydro Electric Power Installation on the River Shelum in Kashmir; this power will be used for the Abbotabad Srinagar Railway, dredging of the River Shelum in Kashmir, and for industrial purposes in Kashmir and the Punjab. *Recreations:* golf, fishing, shooting. *Address:* Srinagar, Kashmir, India.

JOLY DE LOTBINIERE, Major Henri Gustave, D.S.O., R.E.; *b.* 10 March 1868; *s.* of Sir Henry J. de Lotbiniere; *m.* 1902, Mildred Louisa, *d.* of C. S. Grenfell. Entered Army, 1888; Captain, 1899; Major 1900; served N.W. Frontier, India, 1897-98 (medal with 3 clasps); S. Africa, 1899-1902 (despatches twice, brevet of Major, Queen's and King's medals, 5 clasps, D.S.O.) *Address:* Quebec.

JONES, Frank Percy; Gen. Mgr. of the Canada Cement Co.; *b.* Brockville, Ont., 5 Nov., 1869; *s.* of Chillion Jones, and Eliza M. Harvey; *m.* Helen Stevens, of Brockville. *Educ.:* Brockville High Sch. and R. M. C., Kingston. Was sales mgr. of the Nova Scotia Steel Co.; similar position with Dom. Iron and Steel Co.; mgr. of same co.; mgr., Canada Cement Co., 1909. *Recreations:* Yachting, riding. *Address:* Imperial Life Bldg., Montreal.

JONES, George Burpee, M.L.A.; *b.* Springfield, King's Co., N.B., 9 Jan., 1866; *s.* of Stephen and Eliza Jones; *m.* Melissa J. Fowler, in 1889, one *s.* one *d.* *Educ.:* Apohaqui Superior sch. At 12 years of age, entered employ of late J. A. Sinnott, and after 6 years resigned and accepted position of general manager with Hugh McLean, of Salmon River, Queen's County, in general business and lumbering. Mem. of N.B. Legis Ass. for some yrs. *Address:* Apohaqui, N.S.

JONES, Lt.-Col. Guy Carleton, G.G.H.S., M.D., C.M., M.R.C.S., Director General of Medical Services, Canada; *b.* Halifax, N. S., 28 Dec., 1864; *s.* of Hon. A. G. Jones, and Margaret, *d.* of Hon. W. J. Stairs; *m.* Susan, *d.* of the late Robert Morrow. *Educ.:* Merchester Castle, Edinburgh; Galt. Coll. Inst. Surgeon-Lieut., 1st Regt., C.A., 1696; Major Halifax Bearer Co., 1899; Lt.-Col., A.M.S., 1 June, 1904; P. A.M.C., 1 Oct., 1905, D.G. M.S., 22 Dec., 1906 to date. Served during South African War, 1902 (medal with two clasps); *Address:* Ottawa, Ont. *Clubs:* Halifax, Halifax, N.S.; Rideau, Ottawa.

JONES, Hon. John Edward, M.D., LL. B.; B.A.; U.S. Consul General, at Winnipeg; *b.* Virginia, U.S.A., 21 Feb., 1869; *s.* of John W. Jones and Kate J. Williams; *m.* Hilda Virginia Tyssowski; one *s* two *d.* *Educ.:* Columbia Univ., and National Law School; arrived in Canada, May, 1907; was delegate to Republican National Convention, 1900, representing Washington, D.C.; Asst. Sec'y., Republican National Committee. Consul General to and opened Dalny, Manchuria; a graduate of both medicine and law; now consul General at Winnipeg, Man; for 18 years a member of the editorial staff of the Washington *Star;* fond of amateur athletics; a member of the Executive of the Manitoba Game Protective Association. *Address:* 264 Edmonton Av., Winnipeg, Man. *Clubs:* University, Washington; Manitoba, Winnipeg.

JONES, Hon. Lyman Melvin; *b.* in York Co., Ont., Sept. 21, 1843; of Welsh-Scotch descent; *s.* of Norman Jones and Therese Jane Patterson; *m.* in 1873, Louise, *d.* of Thomas Irwin; one *d.* In 1886, alderman Winnipeg, and Chairman of Finance Com.; in 1887, Mayor of Winnipeg and Vice-Pres. of Board of Trade; in 1888, re-elec. Mayor of Winnipeg; in January, 1888, accepted portfolio in Manitoba Government as Provincial Treasurer, and, during the year, negotiated in London, England, first Provincial loan to build railway; represented constituency of Shoal Lake; re-elec. at the g. e., in 1888 to represent North Winnipeg; resigned office of Provincial Treasurer in 1889, though retaining seat in Legislature until end of term and returned to Eastern Canada to devote his time to private business. Upon amalgamation of the Massey and Harris Companies in 1891, removed to Toronto, and became Managing Director of consolidated Companies; member of Senate of Dominion of Canada since Jan'y., 1901; liberal. Is (since 1902) Pres. and Gen. Man. of Massey-Harris Co., Ltd.; Pres., Bain Wagon Co., Ltd., Woodstock; Vice-Pres., Ont. Jockey Club; Director Canadian Bank of Commerce; Verity Plow Co., Ltd.; Nova Scotia Steel & Coal Co., Ltd., Canada Cycle & Motor Co., Ltd. *Recreations:* driving, golf, motoring. *Address.* Llawhaden, St. George St., Toronto, Can. *Clubs:* Toronto, National, Toronto Hunt, R. C.Y.C.; Rideau, Ottawa.

JONES, Wendell Phillips, K.C.; *b.* Woodstock, N.B., 25 Nov., 1866; *s.* of Randolph K., and Gertrude H. Jones; *m.* Grace J. Jordan; five *s.* five *d.* *Educ.:* Woodstock Gram. Sch., Dalhousie Coll., Halifax; Boston Univ. Law Sch.; member of the Legislature of N.B., from 1903 to 1908; solicitor General for New Brunswick, 1905 to 1908. *Recreation:* golf. *Address:* Woodstock, N.B.

JORDAN, Rev. W. G., B.A., D.D.; Professor of Hebrew and Old Testament criticism, Queen's Univ., Kingston; *b.* Whitby, Yorks, 1852; *s.* of Dennis Jordan and Elizabeth Batty; *m.* 1880, Marianne *d.* of J. B. Taylorson, Sunderland, England; three *s.* two *d.* *Educ.:* National Sch., Whitby, prepared for London Univ., by private study, tuition, etc.; also attended classes in Airedale Coll., Bradford; later a graduate in Theology of the Presbyterian College, London (England). Minister in United Methodist Free Churches (England), 1872-85; joined the communion of the Presbyterian Church of England; minister at Dudley (Worces.) about two years; came to Canada, 1889; minister for about nine years of Presbyterian congregation, Strathroy, Ont.; Chancellor's Lecturer, 1906-7; Prof. of Hebrew since 1899. *Publications:* articles in American Journal of Theology, Biblical World, etc; literary editor of Dominion Presbyterian; Prophetic ideas and Ideals, 1902; The Philippian Gospel, 1904; Biblical Criticism and Modern Thought, 1909. *Address:* 76 Sydenham Street, Kingston, Ont.

JOUSSARD, Right Rev. Celestin, O.M.I. D.D., Coadjutor Bishop to the Vicar Apostolic of Athabaska; *b.* Grenoble, France, 1851. *Educ.:* Seminary of Grenoble and France; arrived in Canada, 1880; ordained priest in 1876; for 28 years was missionary among the indians in the district of Athabaska; in 1909 was named Coadjutor to the Vicar Apostolic of Athabaska and was consecrated Bishop in Sept. of the same year. *Address:* Lesser Slave Lake, Alta.

K

KAINE, Hon. John C.; Mem. of the Ex. Council of Quebec; *b.* Quebec, 18 Oct., 1854; *s.* of John Kaine and Ellen McGowan; *m.* (1st), 1879, Theresa Maria Tucker; (2nd), 1904, Helen Smith. *Educ.:* Commercial Acad., Quebec. Head of the Kaine and Bird Transportation Co., Ltd., Quebec. First el. to Legis. at g. e., 1904; re-el. at g. e., 1908. Called to the Prov. Cabinet as a Minister without portfolio, 3 Jan., 1906. *Addresses:* 111 Mountain Hill (Bus.) 5 St. Ursule St., Quebec.

KARN, Dennis Weston, J.P.; pres. of Karn-Morris Piano and Organ Co., of Woodstock, Ont.; *b.* Tp. of Oxford, Oxford Co., Ont., 6 Feb., 1843; *s.* Peter Karn and Priscilla Thornton; *m.* Elizabeth Hannah Featherston; one *s.* two *d.* *Educ.:* Common Sch. and Woodstock Coll. Engaged in farming until 1869, and then removed to Woodstock to become partner with Mr. Miller, an organ maker; this led to the foundation of the business of the Karn Piano & Organ Co., which to date has shipped 75,000 instruments to all parts of the world. Recently retired from active business on organisation of present Co. Was Mayor of Woodstock; unsuccessful candidate for H. of C., 1892 and 1896; Vice-Pres., Dominion Permanent Loan Co. and People's Life Ins. Co.; Dir., Home Life Ins. Co.; has been Pres., Woodstock Board of Trade and Can. Mfrs. Assoc.; member of Senate of McMaster University. *Recreations:* curling, lawn bowling, golf, gardening, fishing, *Address:* Woodstock, Ont.

KAULBACH, Ven. Archdeacon James Albert; *b.* Lunenburg, N.S., 30 Aug., 1839; *s.* of John Henry and Sophia Frederica *m.* Mary Sophia Bradshaw; one *s.* *Educ.:* King's Coll., Windsor, N.S.; Curate of River John, 1864-1870; Vicar of Truro, N.S., 1870-1903; Rector of Truro, 1903; Archdeacon of N.S., 1889; Examining Chaplain to Bishop of N.S., 1896; Canon of St. Luke's Cathedral, 1899. *Address:* Truro, N.S.

KEATING, Edward Henry, C.E.; *b.* Halifax, N.S., 7 Aug., 1844; *s.* of Wm. H. and Eliza Walford Keating; *m.* Mary Little Beauchard, *d.* of the late J. Fleming Beauchard, of Truro, N.S.; one *s.* three *d.* *Educ.:* Dalhousie Coll., Halifax, N.S.; studied his profession under Geo. Whiteman, C.E., Government Engineer for the Province of N.S., and subsequently under Sir Sandford Fleming; was engaged in laying out and construction of several railways in N.S., N.B., and Quebec, including the Intercolonial Ry., and also in the Exploration Surveys for the C. P. Ry. Served for a number of years as City Engineer and Engineer of the Waterworks, Halifax; also acted as resident Chief Engineer in the construction of the Halifax graving dock. In 1890-91, was City Engineer of Duluth, Minn.; in 1892 became City Engineer of Toronto, subsequently assuming the additional duties of Engineer of the Toronto Waterworks, in which capacity he recommended several extensive enlargements and improvements in the waterworks including a tunnel under Toronto harbour all of which were subsequently investigated and endorsed by the late Jas. Mansergh, President of the institution of Civil Engineers, and have since been carried to successful completion. Resigning in 1898 he became Chief Engineer and Manager of the Toronto Electric railway system, which position he relinquished in 1904 and has since been engaged in the private practice of his profession in Canada, and in the republic of Mexico. In 1901, he was elected Pres. of the Can. Soc. of C. E., and is a member of the British Institution of Civil Engineers and also a mem. of the American Society of C. E. *Address:* 99 Elm Avenue, Rosedale, Toronto, Ont. *Club:* Toronto.

KEEFER, George Alexander, resident Engr., Dep. of Pub. Works of Canada, in B.C.; *b.* Cornwall, Ont., 10 Sept., 1836; *s.* of George Keefer and Margaret Keefer; *m.* Charlotte Maude MacMartin, of Perth, Ont.; three *s.* one *d.* *Educ.:* Grantham Acad., St. Catharines, Ont. On survey G. T. Ry., 1853-57; architects office and Victoria Bridge, 1857-61; Brockville and Ottawa Ry.; Belleville Grand Junction, and Belleville and North Hastings Rys., 1867-75; C. P. Ry. surveys in Rocky Mountains and construction Fraser River Canon, 1875-85; Ry. Insp. for Govt. in B.C., 1886-87; priv. practice 1887-99; Resident Engr. for B.C. in Dept. of Pub. Works of Can., 1900 to date. *Addresses:* Victoria, B.C.; New Westminster, B.C. *Clubs:* Union, Victoria; Westminster, New Westminster.

KEEFER, Thomas Coltrin, C.M.G., M.I. C.E., Canal and Ry. Engr.; *b.* Thorold, Ont., 4 Nov., 1821; *s.* of Geo. Keefer, and Jane McBride; *m.* (1st) 1848, Elizabeth (*d.* 1870), *d.* of the late Hon. Thos. McKay, M.L.C., of Rideau Hall, Ottawa; (2nd) 1873, Annie, widow of the late John MacKinnon, of Ottawa; one *s.* *Educ.:* St. Catharines Acad. and Upper Can. Coll., Toronto. At age of 17 commenced his career as an engr.; employed on Erie and Welland Canals, 1838-45; chief engr. of Ottawa River Works, 1845-48; won Lord Elgin's prize for best essay on "The Influence of the Canals of Can. on her Agriculture." Charged with surveys for nav. of rapids of St. Lawrence, etc.; was sent by Can. Govt. to assist U.S. Consul to report on Can. trade with U.S., 1850; asst. in a second report 1852, which reports led to the Reciprocity Treaty of 1854; engaged in making preliminary surveys for the G. T. Ry., between Montreal and Toronto, and for ry. bridge over St. Lawrence at Montreal; apptd. Can. Comnr. for Interl. Exhn. at London, 1851; apptd. engr. to Montreal Harbour Comnrs., 1853. In 1853, advocated "Stephenson" gauge for G. T. Ry. of Can., adopted much later; has constructed water works for cities of Montreal, Hamilton and Ottawa; for some time chief engr. to railways in Upper and Lower Can.; comnr. to Interl. Exhn., 1862, and ex. comnr. for Paris Exhn., 1878, when made a mem. of the Internl. Jury for Architecture and Engineering; cr. an officer of the Legion of Honour; cr. C.M.G., 1878. Pres., Rideau Club, Ottawa, 1881; Vice-Pres. of Am. Soc. of C. E. of New York; chn. of Roy. Comn. at Montreal, on Ice Floods, 1886; Pres. of Can. Soc. of C. E., 1887; Pres., Am. Soc. of C.E., 1888; el. mem. Roy. Soc. of Can., 1891; Internl. Comnr. for "Deeper Water Ways between the Great Lakes and the Atlantic seaboard" 1895; Vice-Pres., Roy. Soc. of Can., 1897-98; Pres., 1898-99; LL.D., McGill Coll., 1905. *Publications:* "Philosophy of Railways," 1849; a series of letters advocating the Canadian Pacific Railway, 1869-70; various essays, lectures, reports and papers. *Address:* "Manor House," Rockcliffe, Ottawa. *Club:* Rideau, Ottawa.

KEHOE, His Hon. John James, LL.D. (Ottawa Univ.), Judge of Dist. of Sudbury; *b.* Ottawa, Ont., 2 Sept., 1854; *s.* John Kehoe; *m.* Marian Gravelle, one *s.* one *d.* Crown Atty. for Algoma Dist., 1884-1904; unsuccessful can. for West Algoma, 1904; apptd. County J., 1908. *Publications:* "Treatise on law of Choses in Action"; "Municipal Councillors Handbook." *Address:* Sudbury, Ont.

KELLY, John Hale, B.A., M.L. (Laval) M.L.A.; *b.* St. Godfrey, County of Bonaventure, 1 Sept., 1879; *s.* of Maucer James Kelly and Bridget Hall; *m.* Marie Adel Dionne, *d.* of C. E. L. Dionne, K.C., Quebec; one *s.* one *d.* *Educ.:* Univ. of St. Josephs, N.B., classical course, Law; Laval Univ., Que.; admitted to the bar in 1903; elected to the Quebec Legislature in 1904, by 1500 majority; re-elected at g. e., 1908; Liberal; organized Bonaventure and Gaspe Telephone Company, in 1905, of which he is Pres. *Address:* New Carlisle, Bonaventure Co., Que.

KELLY, Robert; *b.* Russell, Ont., 15 Aug., 1862; *s.* of James Kelly and Sarah Mills; *m.* 1892, Lillian, *d.* of Alexander Craig, of Russell, Ont.; two children. *Educ:* Russell pub. sch. Commenced business in a general store at Russell; mgr. of a store and telegraph office at South Finch, Ont.; 1884-1888; removed to California, and became mgr. of a gen. store and telegraph office at McPherson; removed to Vancouver and opened a gen. store, but sold it out and engaged with Oppenheimer Bros., wholesale grocers; was travelling representative for this firm, 1889-1896. With F. R. Douglas, organized the present firm of Kelly & Douglas, wholesale grocers and tea importers, of which he is now Pres. and Mgr. Dir.; Treas. and Hon. Pres., Vancouver Liberal Assn. *Address:* Vancouver, B.C. *Clubs:* Vancouver, Terminal City, Western.

KELSO, John Joseph, Superintendent of neglected and dependent children of Ontario; *b.* Dundalk, Ireland, 31 March, 1864; *s.* of George Kelso; *m.* Irene Martin of Nashville, Tenn.; one *s.* one *d.* Founder of Toronto Humane Society, Children's Fresh Air Fund, and Children's Aid Society. *Publications:* author of many reports and pamphlets on social reform work and the care and protection of children. *Address:* 21 Prince Arthur Ave., Toronto, Ont.

KEMP, Albert Edward, manufacturer; *b.* Clarenceville, Que., 11 Aug., 1858; *s.* of Robert Kemp and Sarah A. Kemp; *m.* 1879, Miss Wilson, of Montreal. *Educ.:* Clarenceville, Que., and Lacolle Acad.; was Pres. of the Canadian Manufacturers. Assn. and Toronto Bd. of Trade; el. to H. of C. at g. e., 1900; re-el. at g. e., 1904; unsuccessful at g. e., 1908. *Address:* Toronto. *Clubs:* Toronto, Toronto; Rideau, Ottawa.

KENDALL, Arthur Samuel, M.D., M.L. A.; *b.* Sydney, N.S., 25 March, 1861; *s.* of Rev. S. F. Kendall and Emily Long; *m.* 1886, Mary, *d.* of the late Rev. A. R. Crawley; one *s.* one *d.* *Educ.:* Sydney Academy, Mount Allison Coll., Bellevue Hospital Medical Coll., N.Y., and Guy's Hospital Medical Sch., London. Town coun. for Sydney, 1888, unsuccessful candidate for H. of C., 1896; mem. of N.S. Legis, for Cape Breton Co., 1897-1900; mem. of the Prov. Bd. of Health, and Commr. of Schs. for Cape Breton. El. to H. of C. at g. e., 1900; again el. to N.S. Legis., 1904; re-el., 1906. Has taken great interest in mining legislation; secured the establishment of bait cold storage plants; projector of the fruit demonstation stations in Nova Scotia. *Address:* Sydney, N.S. *Club:* Royal C.B. Yacht.

KENNEDY, James Buckham; *b.* Bytown (now Ottawa), 23 Feb., 1844; *s.* of Donald Kennedy and Janet Buckham; *m.* (1st) Josephine E. D. Beck; (2nd) Mrs. D. Lloyd; one *s.* *Educ.:* in Bytown before his 12th year; started work on a farm at 12 years of age; left it at 23 years of age, and went into the lumber business, in which he has continued; moved out West; at New Westminster, B.C. has been on the Sch. Board for many years; City Council 2 years; Provincial Legislature, 4 years, and H. of C., four years; now a member of the New

Westminster Pilot Board, and also on the Board of Control. *Address:* 45 Columbia St., East, New Westminster, B.C.

KENNEDY, William, Jr., C.E.; *b.* Charleston, Ont., 4 Jan., 1848; *s.* of Wm. Kennedy and Agnes Stark Kennedy; *m.* Eliza Ann Brown. *Educ.:* Owen Sound, Ont.; has built seven city water works systems, and a few sewerage works; also a number of important Hydro Electric and other power developments. *Address:* 79 St. Matthew St., Montreal.

KENT, James, mgr. C.P.R. telegraphs; *b.* Montreal, Que., 15 Jan., 1854; *s.* of Robert Kent and Eliza Burchell; *m.* Evaline Elizabeth Vipond; seven *s.* six *d.* *Educ.:* at Montreal; has always been in the telegraph business, having entered the service of the C.P.R. Telegraph Dept., in 1886; now Mgr. *Recreations:* bowling and curling. *Address:* 458 Wood Av., Westmount, Que., and 4 Hospital St., Montreal. *Club:* Montreal.

KENT, Lt.-Col. Robert Edwin; *b.* Kingston, Ont., 6 Oct., 1861; *s.* of Rubert Kent; *m.* Isabella C. Sinclair, of Halifax, N.S.; three *d.* *Educ.:* Kingston Schs., Royal Mil. Coll. Apptd. Brig.-Major, 7th Inftry. Brig., 18 Jan., 1903; Lieut.-Col., Comdg., 7th Infantry Brig., 18 Jan., 1909. *Address:* 85 King St., Kingston, Ont. *Club:* Frontenac, Kingston.

KER, David Russell; *b.* Victoria, B.C., 2 Oct., 1862; *s.* of Scotch parents; *m.* Laura Agnes Heisterman; two *s.* two *d.* *Educ.:* in Victoria, B.C.; a manufacturer. *Address:* Kershaugn, Victoria, B.C. *Club:* Union, Victoria, B.C.

KER, Venerable John, D.D.; *b.* Monaghan, Ireland, 22 April, 1848; *s.* of Robert and Elizabeth Ker; *m.* Mary T. Easters; three *s.* one *d.* *Educ.:* Trinity Coll., Toronto; ordained Deacon, 1876; Priest, 1879; Incumbent, Glen Sutton, 1876-1881; Rector of Dunham, 1881-1889; Rector, Grace Ch., Montreal, 1889; Hon. Canon, Christ Church Cathedral, Montreal, 1900; Archdeacon of St. Andrew's, 1901. *Address:* Grace Church Rectory, 879 Wellington St., Montreal.

KER, Newton James; city engineer of Ottawa, *b.* at Brantford, Ont., 6 May, 1866. *Educ.:* Brantford Coll. Inst. Was engaged in construction C. P. R. into Montreal from Lachine to Windsor Street; C. P. R. esplanade entrance into Toronto; construction of the C. P. R. bridge over the Thames and approaches at London, Ont.; the Detroit extension at Windsor; was on his way to accept a position on the Virginia, Roanoke & Ironton Railway, Virginia, when offered a position on staff of City Engineer of Toronto; had charge of the reconstruction of the street ry. system from a horse-car to an electric system, acting as engineer for both the Toronto Railway Company and the city. During his ten years' service in Toronto, filled the position of engineer in charge of roadways, engineer in charge of sewers, assistant engineer on waterworks, engineer in charge of the Queen street subway and Island survey, lake undercurrent observation; chart of Toronto Bay, and many other works of importance. In 1899, was apptd. Assistant City Engineer of Ottawa and engineer in charge of the main drainage system, a work which was built within the estimated cost of $500.000. In 1900, was appointed City Engineer of Ottawa and during his regime, under which great improvements have been made in Ottawa. has spent over $5,000,000 on civic works. This embraces permanent pavements, drainage systems, subways, bridges, the establishment of the civic asphalt plant and blacksmith shops, and other works, all by the day labor system; is manager of the by Ottawa Waterworks, which has a capacity of 32,000,000 gallons per day at the main pumping station. Has been offered, at different times, the City Engineership of Victoria, B.C., and Vancouver, B.C.; also positions on the National Transcontinental Railway, but has always decided to continue his work in endeavouring to make the Federal capital one of the most beautiful cities in the Dominion. Captain of the Corps of Guides since the Corps was founded; at one time District Intelligence Officer for the Ottawa District. *Address:* 315 MacLeod St., Ottawa.

KERGIN, William Thomas, M. D.; *b.* St. Catharines, Ont., 17 May, 1876; *s.* of William Henry and Margaret Kergen; *m.* Fannie A. Stevenson; two *s.* one *d.* *Educ.:* St. Catharines Coll. Institute and Toronto Univ.; grad. in medicine, Univ. of Toronto, 1902, and located in Port Simpson the same year; el. to Legislature Assembly of British Columbia, 1907. *Recreations:* Motoring, boating, and hunting. *Address:* Sea View, Port Simpson, B.C.

KERNIGHAN, Robert Kirkland, "The Khan of Khanada;" *b.* Rushdale Farm, Wentworth Co., Ont., 25 April. 1857; *s.* of Andrew and Jane Kernighan; (unmarried). *Educ.:* Rockton pub,ic sch.; a free-lance newspaper man all over the North American continent. *Publications:* "The Khan's Canticles," a book of poems. *Recreation:* tree planting. *Address:* The Wigwam, Rushdale Farm, Rockton P. O., Ont.

KERR, Hon. James Kirkpatrick, K.C., Speaker of the Canadian Senate; *b.* Tp. of Puslinch, Ont., 1 Aug., 1841; *e. s.* of Robert Warren Kerr, Sligo, Ireland, and Jane Hamilton, *d.* of James Kirkpatrick, Wentworth County, Ont.; *m.* (1st) 1864, Anne Margaret (d. 1882); *d.* of late Hon. William Hume Blake, and sister of Hon. Edward Blake; (2nd) 1883, Adelaide Cecil, *d.* of late Rev. George Stanley-Pinhorne, and niece of late Rt. Hon. A. Staveley Hill, P.C., M.P. *Educ.:* Doctor Tassie's School, Galt; called to Bar, 1862; a bencher of Law Society of Up. Can., 1879; Q.C., 1876; Member of Senate since 1902; apptd. Speaker for 11th Parlt., 13 Jan., 1909. Pres., Ont. Reform Association, 1892-1903; contested Central Toronto, 1891; Grand Master of the Masonic Grand Lodge of Canada, 1874-77; Knight Grand Cross of the Temple, 1883. *Recreations:* riding and driving. *Address:* Rathnelly, Toronto. *Clubs:* Toronto, Hunt, Jockey, Toronto; Rideau, Ottawa.

KEYS, David Reid, M.A.; *b.* Louisville, Ky., 1856; *s.* John Wesley Keys and Caroline Johnston Keys; *m.* Erskine I. I. Maclean, of Edinburgh; three *s.* three *d.* *Educ.:* Up. Can. Coll.; Univ. of Toronto; Leipsic, Columbia (N.Y.) Law School; Geneva, Switzerland, Univ. of Halle; Associate Prof. of Anglo-Saxon Univ., Coll.; Univ. of Toronto. Studied in Germany after grad. in

Toronto, 1878; returned to New York and studied law; taught in Peekskill Military Academy, 1880-1882; called to Univ. Coll., Toronto, in 1882, as lecturer on English and History. Became lecturer on Italian, 1880-87; in 1902 was apptd. Associate Professor of Anglo Saxon. *Publications:* various articles in periodicles; chapters in History of U. C. Coll. *Recreations:* rowing, walking, golf. *Address:* 87 Avenue Road, Toronto, Ont., and Go Home Bay. *Clubs:* Rosedale Golf, Toronto; Deutscher Virein, Alliance Francaise; Dante Alighiei.

KING, Hon. George Gerald, senator; *b.* Springfield, N.B.; *s.* of Malcolm King of Fintry, Scot., and Elizabeth Hickson, Miltown, Ireland; *m.* 23 Oct., 1860, Esther, *d.* of Ebenezer Briggs. *Educ.:* at Springfield; is a lumber merchant; was Warden of Queen's Co., in 1877; member of H. of C., 1878 to 1886; at last election had majority of votes, but lost his seat through action of the returning officer; re-elected 1891 and 1896; resigned in 1896 and was called to Senate, Dec. of the same year; Liberal. *Address:* Chipman, N.B.

KING, John, K.C. (Dominion and Provincial); member of the law firm of King & Sinclair; Lecturer to the Law Society of Ontario, Law School, Osgoode Hall, Toronto since 1893; *b.* Toronto, 15 Sept., 1843; only son of John King of Fraserburg, Tyrie, Aberdeenshire, subaltern R. H. A., and of Christina Macdougall, *e. d.* of Alexander Macdougall of Oban, Argyllshire; *m.* Isabel Grace, *y. d.* of William Lyon Mackenzie, M.P.; two *s.* two *d.* *Educ.:* Upper Canada Grammar Schools, University of Toronto, B.A., 1864, M.A., 1865; prizeman in Univ. College and the Univ.; editor *Telegraph* newspaper, Berlin, county of Waterloo, 1864-65; ex-member Univ. Company, Queen's Own Rifles, Toronto, medal for military services; Fenian Raid, 1866; Law Clerk *pro tem.* Legislative Assembly of Ontario, 1868; in active professional practice at Berlin, 1869-1893, and subsequently at Toronto; solicitor at Berlin for Consolidated Bank of Canada, Canadian Bank of Commerce and for county of Waterloo; conducted Crown prosecutions for many years in different parts of the country, ex-president, North Waterloo Liberal Association; president University College Literary and Scientific Society, and secretary University Association, 1866-68; member Senate of University of Toronto since 1879; honorary member Canadian Press Association. *Publications:* The Other Side of the "Story" a review and criticism of J. C. Dent's story of the Upper Canadian Rebellion, 1837; contributions to the *Canadian Monthly*, the *Nation*, the *Week* and the *Varsity*, of which he was one of the projectors; The Law of Defamation; Slander and Libel in Canada; papers and pamphlets on the History of Newspaper Libel, Canadian Criminal Law of Libel, Ontario Law of Libel, the Newspapers and the Courts; articles in Canadian and United States law periodicals; editor Canadian cases in American Law Book Co's. Cyclopaedia of Law and Procedure; (in the press), The Criminal Law of Libel in Canada; a treatise on the prosecution of Libel by Criminal Information and by Indictment; The law of Contempt in Canada, comprising (1) contempts of the Federal and Provincial Legislatures, their Committees and Members; and (2) Contempts of Court by wrongful interference with the administration of justice. *Address:* 4 Grange Road, Toronto.

KING, William Frederick, C.M.G., LL. D., Chief Astronomer of the Dept. of the Interior, and Supt. of the Geodetic Survey of Can.; *b.* Stowmarket, Suffolk, Eng., 19 Feb., 1854; *s.* of William King and Ellen Archer; *m.* 1881, Augusta Florence, *d.* of John Allen Snow, of Ottawa; three *s.* two *d.* *Educ.:* Gram. Sch., Port Hope, Ont.; Univ. of Toronto (Grad. B.A., 1875). Dom. Land and Topographical Surveyor, 1876; Inspector of Surveys, Dept. of the Interior, 1881; Chief Inspector, 1886; H. M. Commr. for the International Boundary between Canada and the U.S., under treaties of 1892, 1903, 1906, 1908; also under agreements, entered into in 1899, 1901, and 1906; mem. of International Waterways Com., 1904-7; Dir. of Dom. Astronomical Observatory from its opening in 1905; Fellow (and Hon. Pres. since 1906) of the Roy. Astronomical Soc. of Can.; Fellow of the Roy. Soc. of Can., and of the American Assn. for the Advancement of Science; cr. C.M.G., 1908; Supt. of the Geodetic Survey of Can., 1909. *Publications:* various scientific papers. *Recreation:* riding. *Address:* 127 Gloucester St., Ottawa. *Clubs:* Rideau, Laurentian, Ottawa.

KING, Hon. William Lyon Mackenzie, C.M.G., M.P., M.A., Ph.D., LL.B., P.C. (Canada), Minister of Labour; *b.* Berlin, Ont., 17 Dec., 1874; *s.* of John King, K.C., Professor of Law, and Isabella Grace Mackenzie, *d.* of William Lyon Mackenzie, M.P.; unmarried. *Educ.:* Univ. of Toronto, Univ. of Chicago; Harvard Univ., Cambridge, Mass.; abroad; winner of Blake Scholarship in Arts and Law Univ. Toronto, 1893; Fellow in Political Economy, Univ. of Chicago, 1896-97, in Harvard Univ., 1897 1900. Apptd. Instructor in Political Economy Harvard Univ., 1900; editorial staff "The *Globe*," Toronto, 1895-96; special Commissioner of Government of Canada, to inquire into methods of carrying out Government contracts in Canada and Europe, 1898-1900; editor of labour *Gazette* and Deputy Minister of Labour from 1900 to Sept., 1908; Registrar of Boards of Conciliation and Investigation, Canada, 1908-9; Secretary Royal Commission to inquire into industrial disputes in B.C., 1903; Government conciliator in over forty important industrial strikes in Canada between 1900-7; represented Canadian Government in England on question of false representations to emigrants, 1906, mission resulted in legislation by British Parliament; chairman Royal Commission to inquire into conditions of employment of telephone operatives 1907; Royal Commissioner to assess losses of Japanese residents of Vancouver, B.C., in anti-Asiatic Riots, 1907; Royal Commissioner to inquire into the methods by which Oriental labourers had been induced to come to Canada, 1907; Royal Commissioner to assess losses of Chinese residents of Vancouver, B.C., in anti-Asiatic Riots, 1908; representative of Canadian Government sent to England for the purpose of conferring with British authorities on the subject of immigration to Canada, from the Orient and immigration from India in particular, 1908; Royal Commissioner to inquire into conditions of employment of operatives in the Cotton Industry, 1908; Author of special report on the need for the suppression of the opium traffic in Canada, 1908; also the author of important reports to the Government of Canada with recommendations for legislation subsequently enacted, *e. g.*—An Act to prevent false representations to immigrants, 1904; the Industrial Disputes Investigation Act, 1907. The Act to prohibit the importation, manufacture and sale of opium in Canada for other than medicinal purposes, 1908; apptd. by the Imperial Government one of the British delegates on the International Opium Commission, held in Shanghai, China, 1909; member of Canadian Society of Authors, the Champlain Society, and American Economic Association; Pres. of Canadian Club of Ottawa, 1904-5; elected to H. of C. as member for the riding of North Waterloo, Oct., 1908; apptd. Minister of Labour for Canada, June 2, 1909; re-elec. in bye-election by acclam., June, 1909. *Publications:* The Secret of Heroism, 1906; several special reports to Government of Canada; contributions to magazines, etc. *Recreations;* country and woods. *Addresses;* Berlin, Ont., and Ottawa, Ont. *Clubs:* Rideau, Golf, Ottawa; Ontario Club, Toronto; Berlin Club, Berlin, Ont.

KINGSMILL, Rear Admiral Charles Edmund, officer commanding Marine Service of Canada; *b.* Guelph, Gnt.; 7 July, 1855; *s.* of John Juchereau Kingsmill and Ellen 'Diana Grange, *d.* Sheriff Grange, Guelph, Ont.; *m.* Frances Constance, *d.* of Walter Beardmore, Esq., Toronto; two *s* one *d.* Served in the Royal Navy until May, 1908, when he accepted command of the Marine Service of Canada, and subsequently retired from the active list in order to retain appointment; Egyptian medal, bronze star; officer of the Legion of Honour. *Recreations:* riding, golfing and boating. *Address:* Ottawa, Ont. *Clubs:* United Service, Royal Navy, London, Eng.; Country, Club Ottawa.

KINGSTON, Archbishop of, see Most Rev. Mgr. Charles Hugh Gauthier.

KIRCHHOFFER, Hon. John Nesbitt, Senator; *b.* Ballygowney, Co. Cork, Ireland, 5 May, 1848; *s.* of Rev. Richard B. Kirchhoffer, Rector of Ballygowney and Isabella Kirchhoffer; *m.* (1st) Ada, *d.* of W. Smith, Port Hope, Ont; (2nd) Clara Louisa, *d.* of Rev. T. B. Howard; one *s.* three *d.* *Educ.:* Marlbourough Coll., Eng.; arrived in Canada, 1 Oct., 1864; settled originally in Port Hope, Ont., where he studied law under his uncle the late Nesbitt Kirchhoffer, Q.C., whose partner he subsequently became; called to the bar in 1870; in 1880 founded the well known Souris settlement in Manitoba, where he moved in 1883; was elected reeve 1884; apptd. a member of the Western Judicial District Board in 1885, of which he became Chairman in 1886; elected to the Man. Legislature in 1886 for South Brandon; moved to Brandon in 1889; apptd. to the Senate in 1891; Chairman of Internal. Economy Com., in 1892; Chairman Divorce Com., 1898, which he still retains; was Capt. of a Co. in the 46th Batt., and served through the Fenian Raid (medal). In his day, was one of the best known athletes in Canada; played football for Canada vs. U.S., in 1868. In cricket he played against Wilspers' prof. team in Montreal, in 1869, and between 1870 and 1880, he captained the Canadian elevens against Dafts professional team, against W. G. Grace's team; twice against the U.S., and against the Australians. Is a noted wing shot, and has a famous duck shooting preserve on Lake Manitoba, well known to a large number of English sportsmen and to successive Governors General, who were always warmly welcomed to "York Lodge," so named by the Prince of Wales, whom he entertained for three days of unexcelled duck shooting during the Royal tour in 1901. *Address:* Brandon, Man., and the Senate, Ottawa. *Clubs:* Brandon; Manitoba, Winnipeg, Man.; Toronto, Toronto; Rideau, Ottawa; Mount Royal, Montreal.

KIRKPATRICK, Capt. Arthur James Ernest; *b.* Toronto, Ont., 29 April, 1876; *s.* of George Brownly Kirkpatrick and Mary Francis Morris; *m.* Ethel Mulock, *d.* of Sir Wm. Mulock, K.C.M.G.; one *d.* Captain in the 2nd Regt., Queen's Own Rifles, Toronto; manager for Canada, "The United States Fidelity and Guarantee Co., of Baltimore, Md. *Recreations:* rifle shooting horseback riding, fox and drag hunting. *Address:* 123 Bedford Road, Toronto. *Clubs:* Toronto, Hunt, R. C. Y. C., Can. Military Institute, Toronto.

KITTSON, Rev. Canon Henry, M.A., D.D., Rector of Christ Church Cathedral, Ottawa; *b.* Pembina, Minn., U.S.A., 15 Nov., 1848; *s.* of Norman W. Kittson, a former member of the Minnesota State Legis. and Mayor of St. Paul, Minn., and Elise Marion, of St. Boniface, Man.; *m.* 1875, Flora Macdonald Grant, of St. Johns, Que., (*dec.*) *Educ.:* Berthier, Que., and Bishops Coll., Lennoxville. Ordained Priest, 1871; engaged inmissionary work for seven years; rector of St. John's Church, St. Paul, Minn., for four yrs.; Asst. rector, Church of Ascension, Philadelphia, 1888-92; later rector of the Church of the Advent, Westmount, Que.; apptd. Rector of Christ Church Cathedral, Ottawa, 1901. *Address:* "Church Hill," Sparks St., Ottawa.

KLEIN, His Hon. Alphonse Basil, K.C., Junior Judge County Bruce, Local Master High Court at Walkerton; *b.* Berlin, Ont., 11 Sept., 1851; *s.* John Klein, and Ludonka Lang; *m.* (1st) Sophia Amelia Morden; (and) Clara Elizabeth May; two *d.* *Educ.:* in his fathers sch. and Berlin Gram. Sch.; Mayor of Walkerton, in 1883-1884; Reeve in 1892-1893; Paymaster, 32nd Regt., from 1881 to 1894; contested South Bruce in 1886, for the local house; apptd. Q.C. in 1889; was youngest Mayor Walkerton ever had; has been Chairman, Secretary and member of the public sch. board at different periods, covering some years. *Recreations:* hare hunting, fishing, bowling. *Address:* Walkerton, Ont.

KLOCK, James Bell; *b.* Aylmer, Que., 5 Oct., 1854; *s.* Robert H. Klock and S. A. Murphy; *m.* Alice McDougall, *d.* of late Judge McDougall of Aylmer. *Educ.:* Aylmer Academy and Berthier Academy. Formerly M.P. for Nipissing; actively engaged in lumbering operations in the Upper Ottawa; *Address;* Mattawa, Ont.

KLOTZ, Otto Julius, LL.D., F.R.A.S., Dominion Astronomer, *b.* Preston, Ont., 31 March, 1852; *s.* of Otto and Elise Klotz; *m.* Marie Widenmann; three *s.* Hon. mem. New Zealand Inst., etc. Explorations and Surveys, 1875 to 1885, from Atlantic to the Pacific; Astronomer for Dominion Government since 1885; completed first astronomic girdle of the world, 1903-1904; Canadian delegate at International Seismological Congress at the Hague, 1907, and Zermatt, 1909. *Publications:* many articles on surveying, astronomy, gravity, terrestial force, and seismology. *Address:* 437 Albert St., Ottawa, Ont. *Club:* Rideau, Ottawa.

KNIGHT, John Thomas Philip, Sec.-Treas. and Currency Inspector, Canadian Bankers' Assn.; *b.* Deal, Kent Co., Eng., 27 Oct., 1851; *s.* of David Knight and Olympia Butt; *m.* Emma B. Harris, of Nova Scotia (*dec.*); three *s.* *Educ.:* Royal Asylum of St. Ann's Soc., Streatham, Eng.; arrived Can., 1871. Engaged in law, banking, and journalism; manager, Montreal Clearing House; editor, Canadian Bankers' Journal. *Publications:* Canadian Banking Practice. *Recreations:* canoeing, yachting. *Address:* 22 "Linton Apts.," Montreal.

KNOWLES, Farquhar McGillivray Strachan Stewart, R.C.A.; *b.* Syracuse, 22 May, 1860; *s.* of William and Jessie Knowles; *m.* Elizabeth A. Beach. *Educ.:* Toronto, Philadelphia, England, France. Arrived Canada, 1862. A well known Canadian artist; a frequent contributor at annual exhibitions. *Recreations:* yachting, motoring. *Address:* 340 Bloor St. W., Toronto. *Clubs:* Arts & Letters, Golf, Toronto.

KNOWLES, Mrs. F. McGillivray (Elizabeth Annie Beach), A.R.C.A.; *b.* Ottawa, 8 Jan., 1866; *d.* of William Gedkin and Emily Dyde Beach; *m.* F. McGillivray Knowles, a well-known landscape painter and Assoc. of the Canadian Acad. of Arts. *Address:* 340 Bloor St., W., Toronto.

KNOWLES, Rev. Robert Edward, B.A., Pastor of Knox Church, Galt, Ont.; author, *b.* Feversham, Co. Grey, Ont., 30 March, 1868; *s.* Rev. Robert Knowles and Frances Tyner; *m.* Emma Katherine Jones, of New Berne, North Carolina; one *s.* *Educ.:* Queen's Univ., Kingston and Manitoba Coll., Winnipeg. Ordained, 1891, as Minister of Stewarton Pres. Church, Ottawa; called (1898) to the pastorate of Knox Church, Galt, the largest Presbyterian Church in Canada, which position he still holds. Has travelled extensively in Europe; greatly in demand as lecturer, his "Abraham Lincoln," being probably the best known. *Publications:* "St. Cuthbert's," (ten ed.); "The Undertow," "The Dawn at Shanty Bay," "The Web of Time," "The Attic Guest." *Recreations:* golf, curling. *Address:* Knox Manse, Galt, Ont. *Club:* Waterloo Golf and Country.

KNOWLES, William Erskine, M.P.; *b.* Allison, Ont., 29 Nov., 1872; *s.* of Rev. Robert Knowles and Frances Tyner; *m.* *Educ.:* Almonte High School, McGill Univ., and Osgoode Hall, Toronto, Ont.; elec. by acclam. to H. of C. for Assiniboia in bye-elec. caused by the resignation of Hon. Walter Scott, who was accepting Premiership of Sask., Sept., 1905; re-elec. 1908, for Moose Jaw. *Address:* Moose Jaw, Sask. *Clubs:* Laurentian, Ottawa; Moose Jaw, Moose Jaw, Sask.

KNOX, Miss Ellen Mary, Principal of Havergal Ladies' Coll., Toronto; *b.* Waddon, Surrey, Eng., 4 Oct., 1858; *d.* of Rev. George Knox and Frances Reynolds. *Educ.:* by private tuition, and at St. Hugh's Hall, Oxford, and Ladies' Coll., Cheltenham. Obtained first class honours in final exam. at Oxford; Cambridge Univ. diploma in teaching. Came to Can. in 1894, to assume principalship of Havergal, which is now one of the largest Ladies' colleges in Can. Sir George Knox, of the Sup. Ct., Allahabad, India, and Right Rev. A. Knox, D.D., Bishop of Manchester, are brothers. *Publications:* Bible Lessons for Schools, 3 vols.; Acts, Genesis, Exodus, and articles in magazines. *Address:* Havergal College, Jarvis St., Toronto; Bishops' Court, Manchester, Eng. *Club:* Alliance, Eng.

KUNG, Hon. Hsin Chao, His Imperial Chinese Majesty's Consul General for Canada; *b.* Anhui, China, 1873; *s.* of Kung, Ta Jen, Chinese Minister at St. James, also Minister in France, Belgium and Italy; *m.* Li Flory; one *s.* Arrived in Canada June, 1909; assisted in parental Embassy and was afterwards attaché and Secretary to Li Hung Chang; several times examiner for final Imperial Examination in Literature. *Publications:* Chinese Essays and Poems; translated, "English Grammar," "Julius Ceasar," "English local Government," Apiculture, into Chinese. *Recreations:* fishing, philately, numismatics. *Address:* The Imperial Chinese Consulate-general, 283 Somerset St., Ottawa, Ont., also 1 Tang Shau Road, Shanghai, China.

KYDD, George, Mgr. of the Royal Bank of Canada, Ottawa; *b.* Carnoustie, Scot., 17 Aug., 1859; *s.* of David and Susan Carrie Kydd; *m.* Emily Helen Sharpe; one *s.* three *d.* *Educ.:* Scotland. Arrived in Canada, Sept., 1892. Engaged in banking business in Dundee, London, New York, and Canada, now being mgr. of the Royal Bank of Canada, Ottawa. *Recreation:* lawn bowling. *Address:* 190 James St., Ottawa. *Clubs:* Rideau, Country, Ottawa.

KYDD, Samuel L.; *b.* Scot., 26 March, 1853; *s.* of David Kydd, and Margaret Gillies; *m.* M. Allan; three *s.* one *d.* *Educ.:* Ontario Pub. Sch. Arrived in Canada, 1857; began newspaper work in 1867 at Lindsay, Ont.; apptd. editor Montreal *Gazette,* Jan., 1906. *Address:* 237 University St., Montreal.

KYLIE, Edward, M.A.; Assoc. Prof. of History, Univ. of Toronto; *b.* Lindsay, Ont., 1880; *s.* of R. Kylie. *Educ.:* Coll. Inst., Lindsay; Univ. of Toronto; Balliol Coll., Oxford. Hon. Exhibitor of Balliol Coll.; first Flavelle scholar from Univ. of Toronto to Oxford; first class, Modern Hist. Sch., 1903; Assoc. Prof. of History in Univ. of Toronto; editor of Univ. of Toronto *Monthly.* *Publication:* The English Correspondence of Saint Boniface. *Address:* Univ. of Toronto. *Clubs:* Toronto Golf, Arts and Letters, Toronto.

KYTE, George William, K.C., M.P.; *b.* St. Peters, Richmond Co., N.S., 10 July, 1864; *s.* of John Kyte, and Elizabeth Robertson; *m.* Tena Chisholm, of Heatherton, N.S., on the 5 July, 1893; one *s.* nine *d.* *Educ.:* Univ. of St. Francais Xavier Coll., Antigonish, N.S.; called to the bar, 16 Nov., 1891; apptd. clerk assistant Legislative Assembly of N.S., Feb., 1892; reapptd. 1895, 1898, 1902; apptd. clerk, 3 Dec., 1903; resigned, 12 Oct., 1908, to become a candidate for the H. of C. for Richmond Co. and was elected. Liberal; Roman Catholic. *Address:* St. Peter's, Nova Scotia.

L

LABATT, John, proprietor of the London Brewery; *b.* nr. London, Ont., 11 Dec., 1838; *s.* of John K. Labatt and Eliza Kell. *Educ.:* Caradoc Acad., of Caradoc. Entered employ of his father and learned the trade of a brewer; removed to Wheeling, W. Va., 1859, where he carried on a brewing business, but it was completely destroyed by the Civil War in the U.S., in 1864. Returned to London, and joined the business of his father; became proprietor on death of his father, 1866. Vice-Pres., London & Western Trust Co.; dir., Huron & Erie Loan Co., London. *Address:* London, Ont.

LABATT, Theodore, Vice-Pres. St. Lawrence Sugar Refining Co., Montreal; *b.* New York; *m.* 1878, Marie Ribighini, of Ancona, Italy. *Educ.:* Hamburg and Germany. Came to Montreal, 1869, and entered business house of Thos. May & Co., estb. himself in tobacco business, 1870; joined the De Castro Syrup Co., 1878; founded (with Mr. A. Baumgarten) the St. Lawrence Sugar Refining Co., 1879, of which he is now Vice-Pres. Life Governor, Montreal General Hospital. *Recreations:* music, chess, billiards. *Address:* 208 Drummond St., Montreal. *Clubs:* St. James, Mount Royal, Montreal Hunt, Forest and Stream.

LABELLE, Lieut.-Col. Alfred Eugene; Local Manager, Ogilvie Flour Mills Co., Ltd. Montreal, *b.* Montreal, 1866; *s.* of Hospice Labelle and Leocadie Masson; *m.* 1890, *d.* of Hon. Judge Sicotte, of Montreal; five *s.* one *d.* *Educ.:* Archbishop's Academy and Commercial Sch., Montreal. Entered in employ of the firm of A. W. Ogilvie & Co., now the Ogilvie Flour Mills Co., about 1883; apptd. mgr. of Sales Dept., 1897, and has held position of local mgr. at Montreal since 1894. Joined 65th Batt. "Mount Royal Rifles," 1882; Lieut-Col., 1897; transferred to reserve of officers and apptd. Brig. Commander of 19th Infantry Brigade; took part North West campaign, 1885, (medal), Queen's Diamond Jubilee celebration, London, 1897; commanded Bisley Team, from Can., 1908. Mem. Montreal Military Inst. *Address:* 23 Laval Av., Montreal. *Clubs:* St. James, Canadian, Lafontaine, Montreal.

LaBILLOIS, Charles H., M.L.A.; *b.* Dalhousie, N.B., 18 Dec., 1856; *s.* of Joseph H. LaBillois, merchant; *m.* Charlotte, *d.* of the late John McNaughton, of Quebec; two *s.* two *d.* *Educ.:* Dalhousie Gram. Sch. and at Carleton Model Sch. In mercantile business at Dalhousie. First el. to Legis. Assem., 1882, and at each succeeding el.; commr. of Agriculture, 1897; chief commr. of Pub. Works, 1900, which position he retained until defeat of Robinson Govt., 1908. *Address:* Dalhousie, N.B.

LABRECQUE, Mgr. Michel Thomas, D. Theol.; Bishop of Chicoutimi, Que.; *b.* St. Anselme, Que., 30 Dec., 1849; *s.* of F. X. Labrecque, and Emelie Lemelin. *Educ.:* Quebec Sem., and Rome. After ordination was prof. of rhetoric and theology at Quebec Seminary; consec. Bishop of Chicoutimi, 8 April, 1892. *Publications:* "Catechisme de la Perfection Religieuse; (1 vol.); "Circular Letters and Mandements," (2 vols.) *Address:* Chicoutimi, Que.

LACHANCE, Arthur, K.C., LL.B., M.P. *b.* Quebec, 22 June, 1868; *s.* of F. X. Lachance and Eulalie Jobin; *m.* Marie Ann Routhier. *Educ.:* Christian Brothers' Sch., Quebec Seminary, Laval Univ. An advocate. Crown Attorney for three yrs. for dist. of Montmagny, and since 1905 for city and dist. of Quebec. First el. to H. of C., 1905; re-el., 1908. *Recreations:* reading, music. *Address:* 79 d'Aiguillon St., Quebec. *Club:* Garrison, Quebec.

LACHAPELLE, Emmanuel Persillier, M.D., Knight of the Legion of Honor (France); *b.* Sault au Recollet, Que., 21 Dec., 1845; *s.* of Pierre Persillier-Lachapelle and Marie Zoe Toupin, descendents of some of the earliest settlers of New France. *Educ.:* Montreal Coll., Montreal Sch. of Medicine and Surgery. Founder of the Notre Dame Hospital; Pres. of Board of Health, Province of Quebec; Surgeon of the 65th Regt., 1872-1886; in 1878, was elec. a Governor and Treasurer of the Coll. of Physicians and Surgeons of the Province of Quebec, and was for years Pres.; in recognition of his services to the cause of hygienic science in Canada, was made, in 1889, Knight of the Legion of Honor, by the Government of France, and elec. Associate mem. of the Société Francaise d'Hygiene of Paris; from 1876 to 1882, was proprietor and editor of "*L'Union Medicale.*" *Address:* 267 Prince Arthur St., Montreal. *Clubs:* St. James. University, Hunt, Montreal.

LACKNER, Henry George, M.D., L.C.P. S., M.L.A.; *b.* Hawksville, Ont., 25 Dec., 1851; *s.* of William and Juliana Lackner; *m.* in 1880, Helen Allister Mackie, of Berlin, Ont.; one *s.* one *d.* *Educ.:* Hawksville Pub-Sch.; Berlin Gram. School, Toronto Univ.; M.B., Toronto Univ., and star gold and first Univ. silver medalist, 1876; Mayor of Berlin, 1886-1887; and 1893; elec. to the Legislative Assembly as a Conservative for North Waterloo, 1898-1902, 1905 and 1908. *Address:* Berlin, Ont. *Clubs:* Berlin; Grand River Country.

LACOMBE, Very Rev. Father Albert, Catholic Missionary in Western Canada (Alta).; *b.* St. Sulpice, L'Assomption Co., Que., 28 Feb., 1828; *s.* of Albert Lacombe, and Agathe Duhamel. *Educ.:* L'Assomption Coll. Ordained Priest, 1849, and proceeded to present Prov. of Manitoba. Mem. of Bd. of Educ., Man., 1880; missionary to Territories, 1881; Vicar Gen. of the Diocese of St. Albert. For yrs. has studied languages and traditions of Indians of Plains. *Publications:* Dictionaries and grammars, and other works referring to language of

Cris and Objibway Indians. *Addresses:* Calgary; Pincher Creek, Alta.

LACOSTE, Hon. Sir Alexander, LL.D., D.C.L., K.C., P.C., formerly Chief Justice of the Court of Appeal of Quebec; *b.* Boucherville, Que., 12 Jan., 1842; *s.* of Hon. Louis Lacoste, Senator, and Thois Proulx; *m.* Marie Louise Globensky; two *s.* seven *d.* *Educ.:* St. Hyacinthe Seminary and Laval Univ. Advocate, 1863; K.C. (Federal), 1876; Province of Quebec, 1880; Batonnier of the Montreal bar, 1879-1880; Councillor in the Legislature of the Province of Que,. 1882-1884; Senator, 1884-1891; Speaker of the Senate, 1891; Chief Justice of the Court of Appeal, 1891-1907. *Address:* 191 St. Hubert St., Montreal. *Clubs:* Mount Royal, Lafontaine, Montreal.

LAFONTAINE, Joseph, M.L.A.; *b.* St. Barthelemi, Que., 25 Nov., 1865; *s.* of Annable Lafontaine, and Julie Lincourt; *m.* Juliette Mousseau; four *s.* two *d.* *Educ.:* Joliette Coll., L'Assomption Coll. First el. to Quebec Leg. at bye-el., 1904; returned by accl. at g. e., 1904; re-el. at g. e., 1908. *Address:* St. Barthelemi, Que.

LAFRAMBOISE, Louis, B.C.L.(Victoria Univ.); Chief Translator, H. of C.; *b.* St. Hyacinthe, Que., 10 July, 1848; *s.* of Hon. M. Laframboise, former Min. of Pub. Works, and Judge of the Superior Ct. of the Prov. of Quebec, and Rosalie Eugenie Dessaulles; *m.* Alphonsine St. Jean, of Ottawa; four *s.* five *d.* *Educ.:* Coll. St. Marie (Jesuits), Montreal. Called to the bar of the Prov. of Quebec, 1871; editor and prop. of *Le National*, Montreal, 1873-1876; priv. sec. to Hons. F. Geoffrion and R. Laflamme, 1876-77; apptd. French translator, H. of C., June, 1877. *Address:* 206 Nelson St., Ottawa.

LAIDLAW, John Baird; *b.* Toronto, 31 March, 1866; *s.* of John Laidlaw, Toronto, formerly of Douglas, Lanarkshire, Scot., and Catherine Agnes Laidlaw; *m.* Bertha Fredericka Gunther; two *s.* two *d.* Was for a time in wholesale millinery office; clerk in office of City of London Fire Ins. Co.; chief clerk for eight years in Norwich Union Fire Ins. Society, Toronto; two years Inspector of the Lancashire Ins. Co.; since Feb., 1895, manager of the Norwich Union Fire Ins. Society, and chief agent for Can.; past Pres. of Canadian Fire Underwriters' Assn. *Publications:* various contributions to insurance papers; pamphlet "The Protection of Vertical openings in mercantile establishments," "History of Conflagrations." *Recreations:* sailing, golf. *Address:* 7 Clarendon Crescent, College Heights, Toronto. *Clubs:* National, R.C.Y.C., Lambton Golf and Country, Rosedale; Golf, Toronto.

LAIRD, Alexander, gen. mgr. Can. Bank of Commerce; *b.* Ballater, Scot., 25 Nov., 1853; *s.* Francis O. Laird and Eliza Paterson; *m.* Mary E. Sharrar, of Dixon, Ill.; two *s.* one *d.* *Educ.:* Gram. Sch., Sarnia, Ont., and Aberdeenshire, Scot. Came to Can. with his parents, 1854. Wide experience in banking in Scotland, U.S.. and Can.; now gen. mgr., Canadian Bank of Commerce. *Recreations:* golf, motoring, hunting. *Address:* "Craig-en-darroch," 48 Cluny Ave., Toronto. *Clubs:* Toronto, York, Golf, Toronto; St. James, Montreal.

LAIRD, Hon. David, P.C.; *b.* New Glasgow, P.E.I., 12 March, 1833; *s.* of Hon. Alexander and Janet Orr Laird; *m.* Louisa Owen; four *s.* two *d.* Established a newspaper in Charlottetown, in 1861, which is still published, though he ceased connection with it in 1898; was a member of the P.E.I. Legislature, 1872-3; elec. to H. of C., in the latter year, and on the 7 Nov. of the same year, was apptd. a member of the Privy Council, and Minister of the Interior; continued in the office until apptd. Lieut.-Governor of the N.W.T., 7 Oct., 1876; when term ended in 1871, resumed newspaper work in Charlottetown, P.E.I., which he continued until apptd. to his present position of Indian Commissioner for the Western provinces and Territories in Oct., 1908. *Address:* Dept. of Indian Affairs, Ottawa.

LAKE, Maj.-Gen. Sir Percy Henry Noel, K.C.M.G., C.B.; *b.* Tenby, Wales, 29 June, 1855; *s.* of Lt.-Col. Percy Lake, late 100th Regt., and Margaret, *d.* of William Phillips of Quebec; *m.* Hester F., *d.* of H. Woodger of Grantham, Surrey, Eng. *Educ.:* Uppingham, Eng.; arrived in Canada, 13 Oct., 1894; Chief of General Staff, Canadian Militia; Chief Military adviser to the Minister of Militia; Afghan war, 1878-79; Asst. Field Engineer with the Southern Afghanistan Field Force (medal); Soudan Expedition, 1885; Suakin; D.A.A. and Q.M.G., Intell. Dept., Actions of Hasheen and Tofrek, and advances on Tamai (medal with two clasps; bronze star). *Recreations:* shooting, fishing, tennis. *Address:* 115 Vittoria St., Ottawa. *Clubs:* United Service, London, Eng.; Rideau, Ottawa.

LAKE, Richard Stuart, M.P.; *b.* Preston Lancashire, Eng., 10 July, 1860; *s.* of Lt.-Col. Percy Lake, late 100th Regt., and Margaret, *d.* of Wm. Phillips of Quebec; unmarried. *Educ.:* Heversham School, Westmoreland; arrived in Canada, June, 1883; was in British Civil service in Admiralty at Cyprus, 1878-1883; has been farming in the North West since 1883; represented Grenfell Constituency in Legislative Ass. of N.W.T., 1898-1904; represented Qu'Appelle in H. of C., from 1904 to present time; re-el. 1908. *Recreations:* shooting and cricket. *Address:* Winmarleigh Grange, Grenfell, Sask. *Club:* Rideau, Ottawa.

LALIBERTE, J. B.; *b.* St. Rochs, Que., 24 March, 1843; *s.* of Jean Baptiste Laliberte and E. Labrecque; *m.* 1871, E. Emond (*d.* 1895); two *s.* *Educ.:* parochial and Quebec Normal Schs. Entered employ of V. Nichol, a furrier, St. Rochs, Que., 1856; commenced business on own account as furrier in 1867. Dir., La Banque Nationale, Quebec Bridge Co.; chn. of the Quebec Harbor Com. since 1896. *Address:* 182 des Fosses St., Quebec.

LALOR, Francis Ramsey, M.P.; *b.* St. Catharines, Ont., 14 Nov., 1856; *m.* 28 June, 1883, Annie L. Stevens. *Educ.:* Dunnville, Pub. and High Sch. First elec. to H. of C., 1904; re-elec. 1908. Church of England; Conservative. *Address:* Dunnville, Ont.

LAMBE, Lawrence M., F.G.S., F.R.S.C. *b.* Montreal, 27 Aug., 1863; *s.* of William Bushby Lamb, Worstershire, Eng., and Margaret Morris, *d.* of Hon. William Morris, M.L.C., Perth, Ont.; *m.* Mabel Maude, 3rd *d.* of Collingwood Schriber, C.

E., C.M.G., Ottawa; one *s.* three *d.* *Educ.:* Private Sch., Montreal; R.M.C., Kingston; In December, 1884, was apptd. to the permanent staff of the Geological Survey of Canada; since then engaged in Palaeontological and Zoological research. At present holds the position of Vertebrate Palaeontologist to the Geological Survey; has given much time to field work in the middle and far west and in British Columbia, as well as in Ontario and the Eastern provinces of Quebec, New Brunswick and Nova Scotia. In 1890, was elected a Fellow of the Geological Society of London (Eng). In 1901, elec. a Fellow of the R. S. of Canada; mem. of the Council since 1903, first as Secretary of the Geological and Biological Section, (1903-1907), and later as Honorary Treas. of the Society (1907 to present date). In 1903, elected an original member of the American Society of Vertetrate Palaeontologists (member of Council for 1906); for a number of years held a commission as Lieut. in the Governor General's Foot Guards, Ottawa. At present is on the Reserve of Officers (Engineers) of the Militia of Canada, holding the rank of Lieut. *Publications:* chiefly on paleontological and zoological subjects. *Address:* 226 Agryle Avenue, Ottawa. *Club:* Rideau, Ottawa.

LAMONT, Hon. John Henderson, B.A., LL.B., K.C.; a Judge of the Sup. Ct. of Saskatchewan; *b.* Dufferin Co., Ont., 12 Nov., 1865; *s.* of Duncan C. Lamont and Margaret Robson; *m.* Kargaret M. Johnston one *d.* *Educ.:* Orangeville High Sch. and Toronto Univ. Studied law in Toronto; admitted to the bar, 1893; practised in Toronto, until 1899, when removed to Prince Albert, N.W.T. El. to H. of C., 1904, but resigned following year to become first Atty. Gen., Prov. of Sask.; apptd. to present position, Sept., 1907. *Address:* Reniga, Sask.

LANCASTER, Edward Arthur, K.C., M.P.; *b.* London, Eng., 22 Sept., 1860; *s.* of Frederick Wm. Lancaster and Emma A. Lister; *m.* to Mary H. C., *d.* of A. H. Pettit, Grimsby, Ont.; two *s.* one *d.* Arrived in Canada, April, 1871. *Educ.:* English Private Sch.; High Schs. at London, Ont., and Osgoode Hall, Toronto; practiced law at Grimsby, Ont., 1882 to 1890, and at St. Catherines since 1890; M.P. since 1900, having been elec. at three successive g. e. *Recreation:* cricket. *Address:* St. Catherines, Ont.

LANCTOT, Adelard, M.P., Advocate; *b.* St. Philippe, Co. Laprairie, Que., 13 Feb., 1874; *s.* of Louis Lanctot and Rosalie Robidoux; *m.* 2 June, 1902, Sarah Dery, Quebec. *Educ.:* Normal Sch. and Laval Univ., Montreal; practices his profession at Sorel; has been in politics for 10 years; elec. to H. of C., 7 March, 1907, at a bye-elec.; re-elec., 1908; Roman Catholic; Liberal. *Address:* Sorel, Que.

LANCTOT, Charles, K.C., Asst. Law Clerk of the Leg. Ass., Quebec.; *b.* Lapprairie, Que., 19 Oct., 1864; *s.* of Edmond Lancot, and Elizabeth Roy; *m.* Donalda Sariof. *Educ.:* Ste. Marie Coll.; Laval Univ. Practised law in Montreal for some yrs., until apptd. to present position. *Publications:* Theory and Practise of Criminal Law; Manuel for J.P's.; Annotated Criminal Code of Canada. *Address:* 9 Haldimand St., Quebec. *Club:* Garrison, Quebec

LANCTOT, Roch, M.P.; *b.* St. Constant, Que.; *s.* of Hormidas Lanclot; *m.* 25 Oct., 1887, Delphine Toissant. *Educ.:* Coll. of Ottawa, and Ottawa Com. Coll.; Mayor of his parish; elec. to the H. of C., 1904 and 1908. Liberal. *Address:* St. Constant, Que.

LANDRY, Col. the Hon. Charles Philippe Augustue Robert, B.A., Senator; *b.* Quebec, 15 Jan., 1846; *s.* of Dr. J. E. Landry and Caroline Lelievre; *m.* (1st), Wilhelmina, *d.* of Capt. E. Couture (*dec*).; (2nd), Amelia, *d.* of late Hon. E. Dionne, M.L.C.; one *s.* one *d.* *Educ.:* Quebec Seminary. An agronomist; was pres. of the Council of Agric. of Quebec; commr. for the Prov. to Chicago World's Fair, 1893. Takes great interest in military affairs. Brig. Comdr. of the 10th Infantry Brigade; for seventeen yrs. Col., commandant 61st "Montmagny" Regt. Was hon. A.D.C. to Lord Stanley of Preston and Lord Aberdeen Served in Fenian Raid (medal); a kt. comdr. Order of St. Gregory the Great; kt. comdr. of the Military Order of the Holy Sepulchre. First el. to Quebec Legis. Ass., 1875. El. to H. of C. at g. e., 1878 and 1882. Called to Senate, Feb., 1892. *Addresses:* Candiac, Que.; The Senate, Ottawa.

LANDRY, Hon. David V., M.D., C.M., M.A., M.L.A., Commr. of Agric. for New Brunswick; *b.* Memramcook, Westmoreland Co., N.B., 14 July, 1866; *s.* of Vital J. Landry, and Matilda D. Cormier; *m.* Annie Michaud; one *s.* four *d.* *Educ.:* St. Joseph's Univ., N.B. A physician; mem. Mun. Coun. for the parish of Wellington, Kent Co., N.B., 1899-1900. El. to N.B. Legis. for Kent Co., 3 March, 1908; apptd. Commr. of Agric. for N.B., 24 March, 1908. *Address:* Bouctouche, N.B.

LANESBOROUGH, The Earl of (Charles John Brinsley Butler, 7th Earl), M.V.O., 1909; Baron of Newtown Butler, 1715; Vicount Lanesborough, 1728; *b.* 12 Dec., 1865; *e. s.* of 6th Earl and Anne, *d.* of Rev. John Dixon Clark, Bedford Hall, Northumberland; *m.* 1891, Dorothea Gwladys, *e. d.* of Maj.-Gen. Sir Henry Tombs, K.C.B., V.C.; one *s.* two *d.* *Educ.:* Eton. Entered Coldstream Guards, 1888; Captain, 1898; Major, 1904; Asst. Mil. Sec. to Duke of Connaught, Commander-in-Chief and High Commr., Mediterranean, 1908; served in South Africa, 1899-1902; apptd. Mil. Sec. to His Ex. Earl Grey, Gov.-Gen. of Canada, Dec., 1909. *Recreations:* shooting, fishing. golf, cricket. *Addresses:* Rideau Cottage, Ottawa; Swithland Hall, Loughborough; Lanesborough Lodge, Belturbet, Co. Caven; Irel.; 1 Cadogan Terrace, London, S.W. *Clubs:* Wellington, Carlton, Guards', London, Eng.; Rideau, Ottawa.

LANG, W. R., D.Sc., Professor of Chemistry, Univ. of Toronto; unmarried. *Educ.:* Univ. of Glasgow and Paris. Graduated at the former B.Sc., 1890; D.Sc., 1889; Asst. and lecturer there, 1890-1900; first chairman of Canadian Section of the Society of Chemical Industry; fellow of the Chemical Society, and of the institute of Chemistry of Great Britain and Ireland; member of the Royal Philosophical Society of Glasgow, the Canadian Institute. The Franco-Scottish Society. Major of R. E. (vols.) and Canadian Militia. *Publications:* author of various papers on chemical subjects published in the Jour. Chem. Soc., Jour. Soc. Chem. Ind.; Comptes Rend. (Paris); Jour. Amer Chem. Soc., etc.; also articles on the production of low temperatures, on explosive on the chemical industries of Canada, etc. *Address:* University of Toronto. *Clubs:* Caledonian, Scottish, Conservative, Edinburgh; Toronto, Hunt; Toronto.

LANGELIER, Charles, K.C., Sheriff of Quebec; *b.* Ste. Rosalie, Co. of Bagot, Que., 23 Aug., 1852; *s.* of Capt. Louis S. Langelier, and Julie Esther Casault; *m.* Lucille La Rue; one *d.* *Educ.:* Quebec Sem. An advocate. Mem. of Quebec Leg. Ass. and H. of C. for 15 yrs.; Min. in Mercier Cabinet, 1890; Vice Pres. of the Garrison Club; Pres. of Canadian Club. *Publications:* Souvenirs Politiques. *Address:* 63 St. Ursule St., Quebec. *Club:* Garrison, Quebec.

LANGELIER, Sir Francois Zavier, Kt.; Acting Chief Justice of Superior Court of Quebec for Que. div.; *b.* 24 Dec., 1838; *m.* (1st), 1864, Virginie Sarah Sophie (*d.* 1891), *d.* of late J. Legare, Quebec; (2nd), 1892, Marie Louise Adelaide Braun; two *s.* two *d.* *Educ.:* St. Hyacinthe Coll.; Laval Univ. (B.C.L., LL.D.); Law Faculty of Paris. Professor of Roman Law, and afterwards of Civil Law and Political Economy, Laval Univ.; Dean of Faculty of Law since 1892, and Member of Council of Univ.; M.L.A., Que., 1873-75; H. of C., 1884-98; Minister of Crown Lands, Que., 1878-79; Provincial Treasurer, 1879-80; Q.C., 1878; Mayor of Que., 1882-90; Roman Catholic. *Publications:* De la Preuve en matiere Civile et Commerciale; Commentarie du Code Civile de la Province de Que. *Address:* 217 Grande Allée, Quebec. *Club:* Garrison.

LANGEVIN, Most Rev. Louis Philippe Adelard, D.D., O.M.I.; Archbp. of St. Boniface, Manitoba; *b.* St. Isidore, Laprairie, Que., 23 Aug., 1855; *s.* of Francois Theophile Langevin, a near relation of Sir Hector Langevin, formerly Minister of Public Works at Ottawa, and Pamela Racicot, sister of the Right Rev. Zotique Racicot, Bishop of Pogla and Vicar-General of the diocese of Montreal. *Educ.:* Montreal Coll. Studied theology at the Sulpician Grand Seminary, Montreal; completed the course of his theology (moral) at St. Mary's Coll. (Jesuits), Montreal; entered the order of Oblates of Mary Immaculate, 1881; ordained priest, 1882; preacher for diocesan missions, 1882-85; Professor of Moral Theology in the Catholic Univ. of Ottawa, where he soon became Vice Dean of the Theological Faculty, 1885; D.D., 1892; went to Manitoba as Superior of the Oblates in the Archdiocese of St. Boniface, and Rector of St. Mary's Church, Winnipeg, 1893; has battled on the Manitoba School Question; has visited England, France, Belgium, Germany in 1890; Rome and the Holy Father thrice, in 1896, 1898, and 1904, and the latter year visited the Holy Land. He also visited Austria in the interest of Galicians, Poles, and Ruthenians coming to Canada; has founded 28 parishes, 24 educational convents, 3 hospitals, 2 orphanages, 6 Indian boarding-schools; has doubled the number of priests and the number of missionary stations among the Indians. *Publications:* some 20 pastoral charges and many circular letters. *Address:* Archbishop's Palace, St. Boniface, Man.

LANGLOIS, Joseph Godfroy, B.L., M.L.A., Canadian Secy. of the International Commission on Deep Waterways; *b.* St. Scholastique, Que., 26 Dec., 1866; *s.* of Joseph Langlois and Olympe Clemant; *m.* to Marie Louise Herbour of Butte, Montana; one *d.* *Educ.:* St. Therese Seminary and St. Laurent Coll.; elec. member of Quebec Legislature in 1904; re-elec. in 1908; chief editor of *La Patrie* for ten years; managing director of *Le Canada*, 1903-10; apptd. to Waterways Commission, Jan., 1910. Has fought for years for better education in the Province of Quebec. *Publications:* "Sus au Seuet," "La Republique de 1848. *Recreations:* yachting and gardening. *Address:* 58 Laval Avenue, Montreal. *Club:* St. Denis, Montreal.

LANGMUIR, John Woodburn; *b.* Ayrshire, Scot., 6 Nov., 1834; *m.* (1st), Emma Lucretia, *d.* of the late Dr. Fairfield; (2nd), Elizabeth Harriest, *d.* of the late John Ridout; (3rd), Catharine Mary Bloodgood, of New York; five *s.* four *d.* *Educ.:* Osborne's Acad., Kilmarnock, Scot. Arrived Canada, 1869, and engaged with the firm of Miller Bros., Picton, Ont. El. Mayor of Picton, 1858; apptd. Isnp. of Prisons and Pub. Charities for the Prov. by Stanfield Admn., 1868; resigned 1882; and associated himself with a group of prominent gentlemen in formation of the Toronto Gen. Trusts Co., now the Toronto Gen. Trusts Corporation, of which he is mng. dir.; apptd. Chr., Royal Com. on the Prison and Reformatory System of Ont., which sat in 1891. Pres. Homewood Retreat Assn., a private asylum estbd. at Guelph, Ont.; vice Pres., Toronto Hotel Co., Ltd. Was Major of 16th Batt., while Regt served in Fenian Raids of 1866. *Address:* 11 Roxborough St., E. Toronto. *Clubs:* Toronto; Grosvenor, London, Eng.

LAPOINTE, Ernest, B.A., B.C.L. (Laval Univ.), M.P., *b.* St. Eloi, Que., 1876; *s.* of S. Lapointe and Adele Lavoie (*deceased*); *m.* 1904, M. E., *d.* of J. A. Pratte, of Fraserville. *Educ.:* Rimouski Coll., Laval Univ., Quebec. Called to the bar, 1898; practised in Quebec for one yr., then removed to Fraserville, and formed a partnership with Mr. Adolphe Stein, being head of the firm. Town Attorney for Fraserville and Crown prosecutor for dist. of Kamouraska. El. to H. of C., for Kamouraska, at g. e., 1904, 1908. *Address:* Fraserville, Que.

LAPOINTE, Louis Audet; *b.* Contrecour, Vercheres Co., Que., 16 May, 1869; *s.* of Louis Audet Lapointe, farmer, and Marguerite Dupre; a widower; two *s.* *Educ.:* Masson Coll., Terrebonne, and Varennes Coll. For many yrs. a mem. of the Montreal City Council; chn. of Finance Com.; mem. of the Catholic Sch. Comn. *Recreations:* hunting, fishing. *Address:* 208 Champ de Mars, Montreal.

LAPORTE, Hormisdas; *b.* Lachine, 7 Nov., 1850; *s.* of J. B. Laporte and Marie Berthiaume; *m.* Onesime Mirsa Gervais; one *s.* one *d.* *Educ.:* Sault au Recollet Sch. Senior partner in wholesale grocery firm of Laporte Martin & Co.; Pres. Provincial Bank of Can., and several other Cos., a founder of Chambre de Commerce, of which was Pres. Entered City Council, 1896; el. Mayor, 1904. Did excellent work as leader of reform movement in city Council. A life governor of Notre Dame Hospital and Montreal General Hospital. *Address:* 812 Dorchester W., Montreal.

LARIVIERE, Alphonse Alfred Clement, Immigration Commr. for Manitoba, at Montreal; *b.* Montreal, 24 July, 1842; *s.* of Abraham C. La Riviere and Adelaide Marcil; *m.* 1867, Marie Melvina Bourdeau (*d.* 1885); three *s.* two *d.* *Educ.:* St. Mary's Coll., Montreal. For 16 years editor and prop. of *Le Manitoba,* published at St. Boniface, Man. Former mem. of the Man. Govt. Rep. in the Leg. Ass. of Man., 1878-88; rep. for Provencher, Man. in N. of C., 1889-1904; now Immigration Commr. for Manitoba at Montreal. *Address:* Room 22, Royal Trust Bldg., 107 St. James St., Montreal.

LARKE, John Short, one of the Canadian Trade Commrs. for Australasia; *b.* Cornwall, Eng., 1840; *s.* of Charles and Grace Larke; *m.* Elizabeth, *d.* of Wm. Bain, of Darlington, Ont.; three *s.* one *d.* Came to Can., 1844 and *educ.* at pub. and priv. schs., Oshawa, and Victoria Univ., Cobourg. Publisher of newspapers and Pres. of Mfg. Coys.; Executive Commr. for Canada at Columbian Exposition, Chicago, 1893. Apptd. trade commr. to Australia, 25 Aug., 1894. Promoted Pacific Cable in Australia, and on invitation of Colonial Govts. or municipal bodies delivered addresses in the interest of Australian Federation. *Address:* Royal Exchange, Sydney, N.S.W.

LAROCQUE, Rt. Rev. Paul, B.S., D. Theol. and Canon Law (Rome), Bishop of Sherbrooke, Que.; *b.* Sainte Marie de Monnoir (Marieville), Que., 28 Oct., 1846; *s.* of Albert LaRocque and Genieve Daigneault. *Educ.:* St. Hyacinthe and Ste. Therese Coll. Ten years missionary in Florida; nine years Rector of St. Hyacinthe Cathedral; sixteen years Bishop of Sherbrooke. *Publications:* two volumes of Pastorial letters. *Address:* Sherbrooke, Que.

LASCELLES, Viscount (Henry George Charles); *b.* London, Eng., 9 Sept., 1882; *s.* of Earl and Countess of Harewood. *Educ.:* Eton; R.A.C., Sandhurst; in the Grenadier Guards; attache British Embassy, service; A.D.C. to His Excellency the Governor General, Earl Grey. *Address:* Government House, Ottawa, and Harewood House, Leeds, England. *Clubs:* Rideau, Golf and Country, Ottawa.

LATCHFORD, Hon. Francis Robert, B.A., K.C., a Judge of the High Court of Justice for Ontario; *b.* Ottawa Co., Que., 30 April, 1856; *s.* of James Latchford and Mary Young; *m.* 1890, Frances Agnes O'Brien; six *c.* *Educ.:* Aylmer Sep. Sch., and Ottawa Univ. (grad. 1882 with honors), Gov. Gen's. Medal for best English essay, Archbishop's medal for essay on Christian doctrine; the Pope's medal for best Latin essay on a philosophical subject. Called to the bar of Ont., in 1886. Was solicitor for the Sep. Sch. Bd. of Ottawa, the C.M.B. of Canada, the Railway Trackmen, and other bodies. On Law Faculty of Ottawa Univ., 1895; pres. St. Patrick's Asylum of Ottawa for eight years; pres., Reform Club of Ottawa; vice-pres., Reform Assn., apptd. Minister Pub. Works in the Ross Ministry, Oct. 21, 1899, and el. to Ont. Legis. for South Renfrew, Nov. 14; re-el. at g. e., 1902; unsuccessful at g. e., 1905; apptd. to High Ct. of Ont., 1908. *Address:* 6 Elmsley Place, Toronto.

LATULIPE, Rt. Rev. Elec. A., Bishop of Catenna, Vicar Apostolic of Temiskaming; *b.* St. Anicet, Que., 3 Aug., 1859; *s.* of Antoine Latulipe and Lucie Bonneville. *Educ.:* Montreal Coll.; Professor in Montreal Coll. two years; Curate, St. Henry, Montreal, three yrs.; Chaplain Good Shepherds, Montreal, St. Anne's, Lachine, for six years; Rector Pembroke Cathedral, 11 years; apptd. Bishop of Temiskaming, 1 Oct., 1908. *Address:* Haileybury, Ont.

LAUDER, Thomas, Registrar of Deeds, South Riding, Grey Co., Ont.; *b.* Bewcastle, Cumberland Co., Eng., 8 Nov., 1828; *s.* of Thomas Lauder and Elizabeth Forrester; *m.* Susan Grabelle, of Port Colborne, Ont.; three *s.* five *a.* *Educ.:* Crookgate Sch., Bewcastle, Eng. Arrived Canada, May, 1875. Engaged in mercantile business in Port Colborne, Ont., until 1856; removed to Grey Co., and engaged in farming until 1871, when apptd. Registrar for South Grey. *Recreations:* reading, farming. *Address:* Durham, Ont.

LAURIER, Rt. Hon. Sir Wilfrid, P.C., C.M.G., D.C.L., LL.D., K.C., Premier of Canada; *b.* St. Lin, Que., 20 Nov., 1841; *s.* of the late Carolus Laurier, P.L.S. and Marcelle Martineau; *m.* in 1886 to Loe, *d.* of G. N. R. Lafontaine of Montreal. *Educ.:* Pub. Sch. of his native parish, L'Assomption Coll., and McGill Univ.; law student in the office of the late Hon. R. Laflamme, 1860; called to the bar 1864; created Queens Council, 1880; was for a short time engaged in journalistic work in his earlier years; first elec. to Legislative Assembly of Quebec, in 1871, representing Drummond, and Arthabaska; elec. for the same constituency to the H. of C. in 1874; member of the Mackenzie Govenrment as Minister of Inland Revenue, 1877; defeated in 1878; was elec. in Quebec East, to succeed I. Thibaudeau, who resigned to open the constituency re.el. in 1878, 1882, 1887, 1891, 1896, 1900, 1904, and 1908; in three different elections, he was chosen for two separate constituencies; chosen leader of the Liberal party in opposition, 1887, and in 1896, was called upon on defeat of the Conservative party, by Lord Aberdeen, Governor General, to form a Ministry; sworn in as pres. of the Privy Council July 11, same year; represented Canada at the Diamond Jubilee celebration of Her Late Majesty, Queen Victoria, London, Eng., at which time he was created a Knight Grand Cross of the Most Distinguished Order of St. Michael and St. George; was accorded an audience by Her Majesty, and given the place of honor in the Jubilee State Procession; received degrees D.C.L. at Cambridge and Oxford; Imperial Privy Councillor, 6 July, 1897; made honorary member and received gold medal from Cobden Club in recognition of his services for International free exchange; Star of Grand Officer of the Legion of Honour (1897) at Havre, France;

hon. LL.D., Toronto Univ. and Queen's Univ.; received the Duke of Cornwall and York, 1901, and accompanied the Royal Party across the Dominion; present at the Coronation of His Majesty King Edward VII, 1902; received freedom of City of Edinburgh, receiving degree LL.D., from Edinburgh Univ.; attended Imperial Conference, London, 1907, receiving freedom of London, Bristol and Liverpool. *Address:* 335 Laurier Ave., Ottawa. *Clubs:* Rideau, Ottawa; St. James, Montreal.

LAUT, Miss Agnes C., authoress; *b.* Stanley, Ont., 1871; *d.* of John and Eliza George Laut. *Educ.:* Manitoba Univ., became an editorial writer on the Manitoba *Free Press*, 1895; later was correspondent for U.S., Canadian, and English publications; a frequent contributor to American magazines; now on the staff of *Outing*. *Publications:* "Lords of the North," 1900; "Heralds of Empire," 1902; "Story of the Trapper," 1902; "Path-finders of the West" 1904; "Vickings of the Pacific," 1906; "The Conquest of the Great North-West," 1908; "Canada, Empire of the North." *Address:* Wassiac, Duchess Co., N.Y.

LAVELL, John Reeve, B.A.; *b.* Peterboro, Ont., 11 Dec., 1857; *s.* of M. Lavell, M.D., LL.D., and B. B. Reeve (both Canadian born); *m.* 1838, Ursula P., *d.* of Alexander MacAlister, of Kingston; two *s.* two *d.* *Educ.:* Queen's Univ., Kingston (Grad. B.A., 1877). Began study of law in Kingston; became a solicitor 1880; barrister, 1881. Commenced the practice of his profession in Smith's Falls, 1881, and is now a partner of the firm of Lavell, Farrell & Lavell. Has held the office of Reeve, Councillor and Sch. Trustee in Smith's Falls. Pres., Perrin Plow Co., Ltd., Smiths Falls; mem. Methodist General Conference since 1885; mem. Council of Queen's Univ., Canadian Manufacturerers' Assn.; unsuccessful candidate for H. of C. at g. e., 1890, el. to H. of C. at g. e., 1900; went West, 1905. *Address:* Strathcona, Ont.

LAVERGNE, Armand Renaud, B.L., M.L.A.; *b.* Arthabaska, Que., 21 Feb., 1880; *s.* of Hon. Joseph Lavergne, and Emilie Louise Barthe; *m.* 1904, Georgetta Roy, of Montreal. *Educ.:* Arthabaska Coll., Quebec Sem., Laval Univ., Quebec; an advocate and journalist. El. to H. of C. for Montmagny, at bye-el., 1904; re-el. at g. e., 1904; resigned his seat in H. of C., 25 May, 1908. El. to Que. Leg. Ass. at g. e., 1908. One of the editors of *Le Devoir*. *Address:* 71a St. James St., Montreal. *Club:* Garrison, Quebec.

LAVERGNE, Hon. Joseph, a Judge of the Court of the King's Bench for the Province of Quebec; *b.* 29 Oct., 1847, *s.* of late Louis David Lavergne, J.P., and Marie Genevieve Delagrave; *m.* 1876, Marie Louise Emilie, *d.* of late J. G. Barthe, M.P., barrister and writer; one *s.* one *d.* *Educ.:* St. Ann's Coll., Que. Admitted at bar, 1871; practised law for twenty-six years in partnership with Sir Wilfrid Laurier in Arthabaska; was Mayor of town of Arthabaska, and Warden of County of Arthabaska for some years; during same period edited a weekly newspaper, and was a member of H. of C., 1887-97, representing the constituency of Drummond and Arthabasca; Judge of Superior Court for district of Ottawa, 1897; Montreal, 1901. *Publications:* Le Journal d'Arthabaska; L'Union des Cantons de l'Est. *Recreations:* books, billiards, cards. *Address:* 4378 Western Ave., Westmount, Que. *Club:* Rideau, Ottawa.

LAVERGNE, Louis, N.P., M.P.; *b.* St. Pierre, Montmagny Co., Que., 1 Dec., 1845; *s.* of the late David Lavergne, and Marie Genevieve Delagrave; *m.* (1st) 1878, Eugenie (*d.* 1887), d. of L. E. Landry, of Becancour; (2nd) [illegible], widow of the late William Duval; one *s.* one *d.* *Educ.:* St. Anne's Coll., Kamouraska. Chn. of the Bd. of Notaries of the Prov. of Quebec, 1903-6. El. to H. of C. at bye-el., 1897; re-el. at g. e., 1900, 1904, and 1908. El. Liberal Whip for the Prov. of Quebec, session of 1901; re-el. Whip for Quebec, 1905 and 1908. *Address:* Arthabaska, Que.

LAVOIE, Napoleon, gen. mgr. La Banque Nationale; *b.* L'Islet, Que., 5 Aug., 1860; *s.* of Dr. N. Lavoie and Josephine Casgrain; *m.* Marie Elmire Morin; four *s.* four *d.* *Educ.:* Ste. Anne de la Pocatiere Coll. Has been in the banking business for 35 years; ten yrs. with La Banque du Peuple; twenty-five yrs. with La Banque Nationale. *Recreations:* all athletic sports; squash racket and handball champion. *Address:* 25 Mt. Carmel St., Quebec; L'Islet (summer). *Club:* Garrison, Quebec (vice-pres).

LAW, Andrew Bonar, M.P. for Dulwich, Eng.; *b.* N.B., 16 Sept., 1858; *s.* of Rev. James Law, M.A., of New Brunswick, and Eliza Anne, *d.* of William Kidston of Glasgow; *m.* 1891, Annie Pitcairn, *d.* of Harrington Robley of Glasgow; four *s.* two *d.* *Educ.:* N.B., Gilbert Field Sch, Hamilton; High Sch., Glasgow. Parliamentary Sec. of the Board of Trade, 1902-6; M.P. (U.) Blackfriars Div. of Glasgow, 1900-6; mem. (U.) Dulwich Division of Camberwell, since 1906; re-el. at g. e., 1910; chairman of Glasgow Iron Trade Association; was a member of William Kidston and Sons, iron merchants, Glasgow, and William Jacks and Co., iron merchants, Glasgow. *Recreations:* golf, chess. *Address:* Pembroke Lodge, Kensington London W., Eng. *Club:* Carleton, London, Eng.

LAW, Bowman Brown, M.P.; *b.* Douglas, Mass., U.S.A., 29 July, 1855; *s.* of William and Mary A. Law; *m.* Agnes M. Lovitt; one *d.* *Educ.:* Yarmouth, N.S.; arrived in Canada, 1885; Town Councillor for over six years; member of H. of C. since 1902. *Address:* Yarmouth, N.S.

LAW, Frederick Charles, R. N.; *b.* Brent Somerset, Eng., 27 March, 1841; *s.* of the Hon. William Towny Law, and the Hon. Augusta Champagne, *d.* of His Hon. John Crawford, formerly Lieutenant Governor of Ontario; five *s.* one *d.* Arrived in Canada April, 1874; twenty years on active service, Royal Navy; in Baltic Sea during Russian War in H.M.S. Hannibal; for 20 years official secretary to Lieut. Governor of Ontario; practiced as an architect for some time. *Recreations:* painting and carving. *Address:* 504 Sherbourne St., Toronto; Crawford Island, Muskoka Lake, Ont.

LAWLESS, Thomas, Sup. Treas., Independent Order of Foresters; *b.* Beech Ridge, Chateaugnay Co., Que., 23 Jan.,

1844; *s.* of John Russell Lawless (Irish), and Sarah Robinson (English); *m.* (1st) Sarah Matilda Glover (*d.* 1876); (2nd) Sophia Tranwich Miller (*d.* 1909); four *s.* two *d.* *Educ.:* Chateauguay Co. Engaged in commercial pursuits until 21st year, then entered journalism and continued in it actively for upwards of 25 years and as a secondary occupation since; has engaged actively in fraternal insurance work for the past 20 years. Apptd. Supreme Auditor of the I. O. F., 1 Aug., 1885; asst. Sup. Chief Ranger; editor, *The Forester;* now Sup. Treasurer. *Recreations:* travel, photography, gardening. *Addresses:* Parkdale, Toronto, and Oakville, Ont.

LAWRENCE, Hon. Frederick Andrew, K.C., Judge of Supreme Court of Nova Scotia; *b.* Port Hood, Inverness Co., C.B., 23 April, 1843; *s.* of Geo. C. Lawrence and Helen Lawrence; *m.* Isabella Flemming; one *d.* *Educ.:* Normal Sch., Truro; Dalhousie Univ. Recorder of Truro for a time; member of Nova Scotia Legislature, 1886-1904, during which period was Speaker for eight yrs.; elected to H. of C. 1904; apptd. a Judge, 1907. *Recreations:* golf. *Address:* Halifax, N.S.

LAWSON, Miss Maria, editorial writer, Victoria (B.C.) *Colonist; b.* New London, P.E.I., 15 Dec., 1852; *d.* Henry Lawson and Flora McKenzie. *Educ.:* P.E.I dist. Sch., Normal Sch., Charlottetown. Father was ed. of Charlottetown *Patriot;* asst. ed. Toronto *Globe* and Montreal *Herald;* editor Victoria *Colonist.* Miss L. taught sch. in P.E.I. for some yrs.; removed to B.C. with her parents in 1900. Was principal of the Girl's Sch., Nanaimo, teacher in Girls' Sch., Victoria; now conducts the Woman's Realm a daily feature of the *Colonist,* and edits a weekly children's page. *Publications:* a school history of Can. (Gage & Co., Toronto) a sketch of B.C. Member of the Canadian Women's Press Club. *Address:* 1809 Fernwood Rd., Victoria, B.C.

LEACOCK, Stephen Butler, B.A., Ph. D.; *b.* Swanmoor, Hants, Eng., 30 Dec., 1869; *s.* of W. P. Leacock of Oak Hill, and Agnes, *d.* of Rev. Stephen Butler of Subarton, Hants; *m.* to Beatrix, *d.* of R. B. Hamilton, of Toronto. *Educ.:* Up. Can. Coll., Univ. of Toronto. Arrived in Canada, 1876; on staff of Up. Can. Coll., 1891-1899; graduate of Sch. of Chicago Univ., 1899-1902; at present head of department of Economics and political science, McGill Univ., 1907-1908, tour of the British Empire, delivering lectures on Imperial problems, under the auspices of the Rhodes Trust. *Publications:* Elements of Political Science; Baldwin, Lafontaine and Hicks (Makers of Canada series, 1907) and pamphlets, etc. *Address:* Cote des Neiges, Montreal. *Club:* University, Montreal.

LEBEUF, Hon. Calixte, B.C.L., K.C., Chief Justice of Circuit Ct., Dist' of Montreal; *b.* St. Timothée, Beauharnois Co., Que., 23 May, 1850; *s.* of Joseph LeBeuf, and Judith Picard; *m.* (1st) Laura Brunelle; (2nd) Rebecca Brunelle; one *s.* two *d.* *Educ.:* St. Timothee Sch., and Ste. Therien Coll. Practised legal profession at Montreal for 35 yrs. Frequent contributor to press for 20 yrs. Judge, 1907. *Recreations:* boating, racquets. *Addresses:* 1005 Dorchester St., W., Montreal; Batiscan (summer).

LEBLANC, Hon. Henry S., M.L.C.; *b.* East Pubnico, Yarmouth Co., N.S., 4 Sept., 1865; of French-Canadian parentage; *m.* 1891, Agnes D'Entremont. Is engaged in mercantile business at West Pubnico. Was coun. for the municipality of Argyle. El. to Legis. at g. e., 1897; re-el. 1901, and 1908. Mem. of the Executive Com. of Nova Scotia, without portfolio. *Address:* Yarmouth, N.S.

LEBLANC, Oliver J., M.P.; *b.* Memramcook, N.B., 27 Nov., 1830; *s.* of Jos. J. Leblanc and Victoire Girouard, both French Acadians; *m.* (1st) 17 Nov., 1871, Olive Cormier (*deceased;* (2nd) 17 Nov., 1879, Suzanne Allain. *Educ.:* Public Sch.; a member of N.B. Legislature for ten yrs.; of the Executive Council for two yrs., and a Legislative Councillor for two sessions; first elec. to the H. of C., 1900; re-elec. 1904 and 1908. Roman Catholic; Liberal. *Address:* St. Mary's, N.B.

LEBLANC, Pierre Evariste, K.C.; *b.* St. Martin, Laval Co., Que., 20 Aug., 1854; *s.* of Joseph Leblanc and Adele Belanger. *m.* Hermine, *d.* of the late T. Beaudry. *Educ.:* St. Martin Academy, and Jacques Cartier Normal Sch., Montreal. For many yrs. a teacher. Called to Bar of Que., 1879. El. to Legis. 1882, but was unseated; re-el. 1884, 1886, 1888, 1890, 1892, 1897, 1900, 1904; defeated by four votes, 1908. Speaker of the Legis. Assem. under the de Boucherville, Taillon and Flynn Govt. *Address:* 352 St. Denis St., Montreal. *Club:* St. James, Montreal.

LECKIE, John Edwards, B.Sc., D.S.O.; *b.* Acton Vale, Que., 19 Feb., 1872; *s.* Major R. J. Leckie and Sarah Edwards; unmarried *Educ.:* Bishop's Coll. Sch., Lennoxville, and R. M. C., Kingston. Practices the profession of Mining Engineer; commanded a troop in "Strathcona's Horse," (D.S.O)., and afterwards a Squadron in 2nd C. M. R. during the South African war. *Publications:* contributions on technical subjects to periodicals. *Recreations:* riding, shooting. *Address:* Cobalt, Ont. *Club:* Can. Mil. Inst., Toronto.

LECKIE, Major Robert Gilmour Edwards, B.Sc., M. Can. Soc. C.E.; *b.* Halifax, N.S., 4 June, 1869; *s.* Major R. J. Leckie, of Sudbury, Ont., and Sarah, *d.* of Rev. John Edwards; unmarried. *Educ.:* Bishop's Coll. Sch., Lennoxville, and R.M.C., Kingston, graduating with honours and winning the "sword of honour" and one of Gov. Gen'ls. medals. Practiced for several years the profession of Civil and Mining Engineer; commanded a Squadron of 2nd C.M.R., in South Africa; conducted explorations in British Somaliland, East Africa, at time of "Mad Mullah" war. Returned to Canada, 1896. *Publications:* contributions to publications of technical societies; articles on travel in many magazines. *Recreations:* big game hunting, fishing, shooting, golf. *Address:* Vancouver, B.C. *Clubs:* United Empire, London, Eng. Canadian Mil. Inst., Toronto.

LECKIE, Major Robert Gilmour, M.A. I.M.E.; *b.* Renfrewshire, Scot., 23 Aug., 1833; *s.* of Robert Leckie, and Margaret Gilmour; *m.* Sarah, (*d.* 1894), *d.* of late Rev.

John Edwards; two *s.* six *d.* *Educ.:* Glasgow High Sch., Glasgow Tech. Coll. Came to Can. in 1856. Has been prominently associated with the mining industry; formerly mng. dir. of the Orford Nickel and Copper Co.; mgr. dir. of the Cumberland Coal and Ry. Co., and gen. mng. of the Londonderry Iron Co. Has examined professionally mines in Norway, Sweden, Australia, Tasmania, New Caledonia. One of founders and first chn. of Federated Mining Inst.; past v. p. of the. American Inst. Mining Engrs.; mem. Can. Mining Inst. *Publications:* Numerous technical contributions to mining journals. *Recreations:* riding, fishing, hunting. *Address:* Sudbury Ont. *Clubs:* Engineers', New York; Can. Military Inst., Toronto.

LEET, His Hon. Seth Penn., K.C., B.C. L. (McGill), a Police Magistrate for the City and District of Montreal; *b.* nr. Danville, Que., 26 April, 1851; *s.* of George W. Leet and Lucina Williamson; *m.* in 1874, Catharine Olivia Colwell, *d.* of Rev. B. T. Colwell; one *s.* *Educ.:* Danville Academy and McGill Coll., Montreal. Studied law with the firm of Trenholme & Maclaren, now Judge Trenholme of the Court of Appeals, of Que., and Judge Maclaren of the Court of Appeals of Ont. After graduating he entered into partnership with Mr. Maclaren and remained with firm for several yrs.; practiced until apptd. one of the Collectors of Provincial Revenues for the District of Montreal, subsequently being named one of the Police Magistrates for the city and district, which position he now holds. Chairman for one term of the Congregational Union of Ont., and Que., and has been for many yrs. the representative of the Prov. of Que. on the Executive Committee of the International Sunday School Assn.; one of the Executive Committee of the World's Sunday School Assn. *Address:* 166 Villeneuve St., Montreal Annex, Que.

LEFEVRE, Mrs. Lily Alice, ("Fleurange"); *b.* Kingston, Ont.; *d.* of the late R. P. Cooke, C.E., and Anna Plunkett, formerly of Castlemore, Irel.; *m.* Dr. John M. Lefevre. Has been a resident of Vancouver for some yrs., and a frequent contributor to the press of Montreal and Vancouver; winner of the Montreal *Witness'* prize of $100.00 for the best poem with reference to the first winter carnival. *Publications:* "The Lion's Gate and Other Verses," 1895; several lyrics which have been set to music. *Address:* Vancouver, B.C.

LEFROY, A. H. F., M.A., Professor of Roman Law and Jurisprudence, Univ. of Toronto; *b.* Toronto, 21 June, 1852; *s.* of late General Sir J. H. Lefroy, K.C.M.G., etc., and Emily Merry, *d.* of late Sir John Beverley Robinson, 1st Bt., Chief Justice of Up. Can.; *m.* 1884, Mary Theodora, *d.* of Henry S. Strathy, Toronto; three *s.* *Educ.:* Rugby; New Coll. Oxford. 2nd Class Honours in Literæ Humaniores, 1873; called to English bar, 1877; called to bar of Up. Can., 1878; has since then practised as barrister and solicitor in Toronto; Prof. Toronto Univ., 1900. *Publications:* Legislative Power in Can., 1897-98; article on The Dom. of Can., in American and English Encyclopedia of Law; joint translator with J. H. Cameron of Short History of Roman Law, by P. F. Girard, 1906; and writer of numerous articles in the Law Quarterly Review. *Recreations:* golf and bicycling. *Address:* Traders Bank Building, Toronto. *Clubs:* Toronto University, Toronto.

LEFURGEY, Alfred Alexander, B.A., LL.B.; *b.* Summerside, P.E.I., 22 April, 1871; *s.* of John Lefurgey and Dorothea Read; unmarried; *Educ.:* St. Dunstan's Coll., Charlottetown, Mount Allison Univ., Harvard Univ. Entered into mercantile life at Summerside and Sydney, C.B. First el. to P.E.I. Legis., 1897. El. to H. of C. g. e., 1900; re-el. 1904; defeated 1908. Conservative Whip for Maritime Provinces, 1901-8; now in commission business at Vancouver. *Address:* Vancouver, B.C.

LEGAL, Rt. Rev. Bishop Emile J., O.M. I., Bishop of Pogla, and Coadjutor of the Bishop of St. Albert, Alta., 1897; *b.* St. Jean de Boisseau, diocese of Nantes, France, 9 Oct., 1849. *Educ.:* Nantes, classical and theological courses. Ordained, 1874; taught sciences in colleges and seminary in France for 4 years; became a member of the Congregation known as the Missionaries Oblates of Mary Immaculate; was sent to the missions of Western Can., 1895, where he ministered to the Blackfeet tribes of Southern Alberta (Blackfeet proper, Peigans and Blood Indians); was consecrated Bishop in the same diocese, and became the titular Bishop of St. Albert on the death of his predecessor, 1902. *Address:* St Albert, Alta.

LEGER, Clement M., M.L.A.; *b.* Memramcook West, N.B., 14 Feb., 1865; *s.* of Marcel I. Leger and Rosalie P. Leger; *m.* 1891, Catherine D. Gaudet; four *s.* five *d.* *Educ.:* Pub. Schs., Memramcook West. A manufacturer and gen. merchant. First returned to Leg. at g. e., 1903; re-el. at g. e., 1908. *Recreation:* travel. *Address:* Memramcook West, N.B.

LEGRIS, Hon. Jos. Hormisdas, Senator; *b.* River du Loup, Que., 7 May, 1850; *s.* Antoine Legris and Leocadu Beland; *m.* Emma Champagne; four *s.* four *d.* *Educ.:* Pub. Schs. of Louiseville, Que.; a farmer member of the Provincial Legislature 1888; member of the H. of C., 1891-1896, 1903; apptd. to the Senate, 1903. *Address:* Louiseville, Que.

LEMAY, Leon Pamphile, Lit. D., Librarian of the Leg. of Quebec.; *b.* Lotbiniere, 5 Jan., 1837; *s.* of Leon LeMay, and Marie Louise Auger; *m.* Solina Robitaille; four *s* seven *d.* An advocate and litterateur. *Publications:* The Discovery of Canada; Evangeline (trans);. National Hymn Les Vengeances (poem); several novels. Trans. Kirby's novel "Le Chien d'or" into French. *Address:* 118 Cote d'Abraham, Quebec.

LEMIEUX, Hon. Rodolphe, K.C., LL. D., F.R.S.C.; Postmaster-General of Canada; *b.* Montreal, 1 Nov., 1866; *s.* of Mr. H. A. Lemieux, Inspector of Customs at Montreal, and Philomene Bisaillon; *m.* 1894, Berthe, *d.* of the Hon. Sir Louis Jette, K.C. M.G., Chief Justice of the Ct. of Appeal for Quebec; one *s.* two *d.* *Educ.:* Nicolet Seminary, Laval Univ. Called to the Bar in 1891, and entered into partnership with Messrs. Mercier and Gouin; Dir. in Law,

1896; Prof. of Law at Laval Univ., 1897; cr. Q.C., Quebec, 1898, and K.C., Ottawa, 1904. Mem. of Parlt. for Gaspe, 1896, 1900, 1904, 1905, also for Nicolet 1904. Represented Canada before the Privy Council in England, 1904; apptd. substitute to the Attorney General for the dist. of Montreal. Was sworn in as Solicitor-General, 29 Jan., 1904, and apptd. Postmaster General, 4 June, 1906. Cr. a Chevalier of the Legion of Honor by the French Govt., 1906; officer, 1909; author of the Lemieux Law, to settle labour disputes; report on Japanese Immigration. *Publications:* two works on law, 1896, and 1900. *Address:* 265 O'Connor St., Ottawa. *Clubs:* Rideau, Ottawa; St. James, Montreal; Garrison, Quebec; Eighty, London, Eng.

LEMOINE, Gaspard, LL.B., M.A.; *b.* Quebec City, 12 March, 1848; *s.* of Alexander Le Moine and Henrietta Massue; *m.* (1st) Emma Renaud; (2nd) Margaret Revell; two *s.* one *d.* After receiving his law degrees, entered the firm of J. B. Renaud & Co., wholesale flour, grain and provisions, and still continues the same business. *Recreations:* fishing and camping *Address:* 9 Ramparts, Quebec. *Club:* Garrison, Quebec.

LEMOINE, Sir James MacPherson, Kt., D.C.L., F.R.C.S.; *b.* Quebec, 24 Jan., 1825; *s.* of Benjamin Le Moine and Mary A. Macpherson; *m.* 1856, Harriet Mary, *d.* of late Edward Atkinson, Past Pres., of R.S.C.; two *d.* *Educ.:* Petit Seminaire de Quebec. Barr. 1850; Lieut.-Colonel, Militia *Publications:* L'Ornithologie du Canada, 1861; Les Pecheries du Canada, 1862; Maple Leaves, 1863-94 (6 vols.); The Tourist's Note Book, 1870; Quebec Past and Present, 1876; The Scot in New France, 1879; The Chronicles of the St. Lawrence, 1879; Picturesque Quebec, 1882; Canadian Heroines, 1887; The Birds of Quebec, 1891; Monographies et Esquisses; Legends of the St. Lawrence, 1898; The Annals of the Port of Quebec, 1901; *Address:* Spencer Grange, Quebec. *Club:* Garrison, Quebec.

LE MOINE, J. de St. Denis, I.S.O., Sergeant-at-Arms of the Canadian Senate; *b.* 13 July, 1850; *m.* Margaret Louise Mackey of Ottawa; two *d.* First apptd. to civil service of Canada, 18 May, 1869; Sergeant-at-Arms of the Senate since June, 1887. *Address:* 505 Wilbrod St., Ottawa. *Clubs:* Rideau, Golf, Gountry, Ottawa.

LENNIE, Robert Scott.; *b.* Smiths Falls, Ont., 16 Aug., 1875; *s.* of Rev. Robert Lennie, B.D., and Catharine Harcus; *m.* Edith Louise Douglas; two *s.* one *d.* Admitted to the bar of B.C., Jan., 1891, elec. Bencher of the Law Society, March, 1906, and annually since then; practiced in Nelson, B.C. only; for six consecutive years, Pres. of the Conservative Association of Nelson and in 1908, was elec. Pres. of District Association comprising nine electoral ridings; declined nominations for Mayor, Provincial and Dominion Houses on account of legal practice. *Address:* 416 Hoover St., Nelson, B.C. *Clvbs:* Union, Victoria; Nelson.

LENNOX, Haughton, K.C.; M.P.; *b.* Tp. of Innisfil, Co. of Simcoe, Ont.; 28 Feb., 1850; *s.* of Wm. Lennox and Maria Haughton; *m.* Margaret Whitaker; three *s.* one *d* *Educ.:* Barrie Gram. Sch. Has practiced law since 1875; exceptionally successful in criminal cases; entered politics in 1900, when he was elected a member of the H. of C.; re-elec. in 1904 and 1908. Introduced amendment to Ry. Act to prevent companies from contracting themselves out of liability to employes, and successfully defended constitutionality of statute before Judicial Committee of Privy Council. *Address:* Barrie, Ont.

LENNOX, Thomas Hubert, K.C., M.L.A., Tp. of Innisfil, Co. of Simcoe, Ont., 7 April, 1869; *s.* of Thomas and Margaret Lennox; *m.* Louise Ether Meeking; one *s.* Barrister at Law; served as Sch. Trustee, and in the Council at Aurora; elec. to Ont. Legislature, 1905 and 1908 as representative of North York; Conservative. *Address:* Aurora, Ont. *Clubs:* Albany, and Military Institute, Toronto, Ont.

LEONARD, James William, Gen. Mgr. of the Eastern Lines of C. P. Ry. Co.; *b.* Epsom, Ont., 1858; *s.* of Thomas Leonard and Catherine Shaw; *m.* 1881, Elizabeth Maguire of Franklin, Ont.; one *s.* *Educ.:* pub. sch. of Bethany, Ont. Entered service of Midland Ry. Co. at age of fourteen. Received an agency of the Victoria Ry. Co., 1877; apptd. asst. mgr., 1878; supt. of C. P. Ry's. Eastern lines, 1884; gen. supt. of the Ont. and Que. Div. of C. P. R., 1893; gen. supt. of the Western Div., 1901; apptd. mgr. of Construction in Toronto, 1904. Asst. mgr. of Eastern lines, 1905; gen. mgr. of Eastern lines of C. P. R., 1908. Dir. of Guelph and Goderich Ry., Berlin, Wellesley and Waterloo Ry., Walkerton and Lucknow Ry.; Georgian Bay and Seaboard Ry. *Recreations:* fishing, hunting. *Address:* 420 Cote St. Antoine Rd., Montreal. *Clubs:* St. James', Montreal. Toronto.

LESSARD, Col. Francois Louis, C.B., Adjutant General, Canadian Militia; A.D.C. to Gov.-General; *b.* 9 Dec., 1860; *m.* 1882, Florence, *d.* of Thomas Conrad Lee, Quebec; three *d.* *Educ.:* Coll. St. Thomas, Que.; Commercial Academy, Que. 2nd Lieut., Que. Gar. Art., 1880; transferred to 65th Batt. Infantry, Montreal, 1884; North-West Rebellion, 1885 (medal); apptd. to Cavalry Sch. Corps, 1884; Captain Royal Canadian Dragoons, 1888; Major, 1894; Lieut.-Col., 1898; South African war 1899-1900, commanding R.C.D. (despatches), (Queen's medal, five clasps); Brevet Colonel, 1901; Adjutant General, Canadian Militia, and Substantive Colonel, 1907. *Recreations:* hunting, polo, and golf. *Address:* 519 King Edward Av., Ottawa. *Clubs:* Rideau, Country, Hunt, Ottawa; Hunt, Polo, Military Inst., Toronto.

LE SUEUR, Ernest Arthur, B.Sc.; *b.* Ottawa, 3 Feb., 1869; *s.* of Wm. D. Le Sueur and Ann Jane Foster; *m.* Maude Sinclair Drummond; one *d.* *Educ.:* Ottawa Public Sch., Ottawa Coll. Inst., and Massachusetts Inst. of Technology; grad. in 1890; developed Caustic Soda Electrolyter process, 1891-1894; general manager Electrochemical Co., 1895-1899; Low temperature physical research work, Lake Superior Corporation, 1889-1902, and the same with George Westinghouse, 1902-1905; research work on explosives and commercial development of the same, 1905-1909. *Recreations:* motoring, canoeing and skating. *Address:* 50 McLaren St., Ottawa. *Clubs:* Rideau, Golf, Ottawa.

LE SUEUR, William Dawson, B.A., LL.D., F.R.S., Hon. Secretary R.S.C., 1908; *b.* Quebec 19 Feb., 1840; *s.* of Peter Le Sueur, chief supt. M. O. Branch, P. O. Dept., afterwards Secretary Civil Service Board, and Barbara Dawson, *e. d.* of Wm. Dawson of Quebec; *m.* Anne Jane Foster, *d.* of James Foster, Montreal; one *s.* one *d.* *Educ.:* Montreal High Sch.; entered Post Office Dept. of Canada, 23 Feb., 1856; Asst. Secy., 1880; Secretary, 1888; retired 1 July, 1902. *Publications:* Life of Count Frontenac (Makers of Canada series). *Address:* 478 Albert St., Ottawa. *Club:* Rideau, Ottawa.

LETELLIER, Hon. Blaise F., M.L.C.; *b.* Levis, Que.; 1862; *s.* of Blaise Letellier and Emma Lacombe; *m.* 1889, Elmira Angers; two s. three *d.* *Educ.:* Quebec Seminary. Grad. LL.B., Laval Univ., 1886. Practiced his prof. in Quebec, 1886-1896, when removed to Beauceville. Founder of the journal "*La Justice,*" and later became a dir. of "*L'Union Liberale.*" Apptd. mem. Legis. Council, 1905. *Address:* Beauceville, Que.

LETOURNEAU, Louis, M.L.A.; *b.* Ste. Famille, Orleans Island, 7 Aug., 1872; *s.* of F. X. Letourneau, and Philomene Boucher des Morency; *m.* 1899, Ludevene Letourneau; three *s.* four *d.* *Educ.:* Ste. Famille. A merchant. Mem. of the firm of Paradis & Letourneau; mem. of the firm of Quebec Preserving Co. First el. to Quebec. Legis. at g. e., 1908. *Address:* 12 Smith St., Quebec.

LEVESON-GOWER, Clement Edward Gresham; *b.* Tilsey Place, Lempsfield, Surrey, Eng., 28 Dec., 1878; *s.* of the late Granville Leveson Gower, of Tilsey Place, and the Hon. Sophia Leveson Gower, *d.* of Baron Leigh of Hookwood, Lempsfield, Surrey. *Educ.:* Winchester Coll.; arrived in Canada, Oct., 1905; formerly Lieut., Royal Sussex Militia and Lieut. Prince Albert's Somerset L. I.; served in South Africa (medal and five clasps); late comptroller of the Household to H. E. Earl Grey, Governor General of Canada. *Recreations:* cricket, golf, shooting. *Address:* Government House, Ottawa, Ont.; Nookwood, Lempsfield, Surrey, Eng. *Clubs:* Grosvenor, London; Rideau, Ottawa, Ont.

LEVY, Miss Beatrice A.; *b.* Montreal, 27 Dec., 1890; *d.* Lewis & Bella R. Levy. *Educ.:* Montreal. Engaged in journalism and magazine work, latterly in B.C. Published poetry and prose at age of 13. Issued Collector's Companion at age of 14, while still attending school. Commenced publication of Levy Magazine, when 16 years old. Recently incorporated her venture under name of Beatrice A. Levy, Ltd., with capitalisation of $50,000. *Recreations:* Literature, music, canoeing and driving. *Address:* 570 Granville St. (bus.); 956 Bidwell St., Vancouver, B.C. *Club:* Canadian Women's Press.

LEWIS, Edward Norman, M.P.; *b.* Goderich, Ont., 18 Sept., 1858; *s.* of Ira Lewis, LL.B., and Julia L. Dwight; *m.* 9 Nov., 1888, Ida Howard Shaw. *Educ.:* Goderich Gram. Sch. Has been Mayor of Goderich, and acting Crown Attorney and Clerk of the peace for Huron Co.; first elec. to H. of C., 1904; re-elec. 1908; Church of England; Conservative. *Publications:* "The Mariners' Manuel," Index to Ont. Statutes," Magistrates Manuel and Criminal Law Index," "Lewis's Law of Shipping." *Address:* Goderich, Ont.

LEWIS, John; *b.* Toronto, 17 Jan., 1858; *s.* of Richard and Mary Emmett Lewis; *m.* Eliza Garwood, *d.* of late Robert Garwood, of Winnipeg; one *s.* two *d.* *Educ.:* Toronto Pub. Schs., and Collegiate Inst.; studied law from 1874 to 1889; entered journalism, 1881; member Press Gallery, H. of C., 1884, and several years afterwards Has been editorial writer on the *Globe*, *News World* and *Star*. *Publications:* Life of George Brown, (Makers of Canada series); Canada Stories. *Address:* 125 Beach Ave., Toronto, and Balmy Beach, Ont.

LEWIS John Travers, M.A., K.C., D.C.L.; *b.* Brockville, Ont., 29 Oct., 1857; *e. s.* of His Grace the late Archbishop of Ontario; *m.* Mary Ethel, *d.* of Collingwood Schrieber, Esq., C.M.G.; two *s.* three *d.* *Educ.:* Bishops Coll. Sch., Lennoxville, Que.; Trinity Coll. Sch., Port Hope Ont.; Trinity Univ., Toronto; Dickson Scholarship, 1876; Burnside Scholarship, 1877; admitted to practice in 1882; K.C., in 1908; has practiced continuously in Ottawa since 1882; first in partnership with Hon. James Cockburn, Q.C., afterwards with F. H. Chrysler, Esq., until 1896; and for the last 13 years, senior partner of the firm of Lewis & Smellie. Has for many years been a member of the Corporation of Governors of Trinity Univ., Torotno. In 1896, was elec. Chancellor of the Diocese of Ottawa, and since 1902 he has been an elec. delegate to the General Synod of the Church of England in Canada. For the past two years, has been pres. of the Rideau Club, Ottawa. Is one of the elec. Governors of St. Luke's General Hospital, Ottawa, and a member of the Executive Council of the Victorian Order of Nurses, and Solicitor for both. Has on many occasions acted as counsel before the Imperial Privy Council, and practices in both the Supreme Court of Canada, and the Exchequer Court. Represents the Official Guardian for Infants in the Ottawa District, and is solicitor for the Imperial Bank, the Union Bank, the Anglican Synod, and other Corporations; has represented large interests at the Parliamentary Bar. *Address:* 250 Cooper St., Ottawa. *Clubs:* Rideau, Golf, Country, Ottawa.

LEWIS, Lansing, Captain, R.L.; *b.* Montreal, 7 March, 1854; *s.* of John and Caroline Lewis; *m.* Katherine Bate, of Ottawa; one *s.* one *d.* *Educ.:* Montreal, Liverpool and Paris; A.D.C. to the Lieut. Governor of Manitoba in 1881; Secretary Board of Trade of Winnipeg, 1882; alderman and chairman of Finance, Winnipeg, 1887; manager Caledonia Insurance Co., 1892; lay Pan-Anglican delegate for Montreal, 1908; grandson of Col. Snowden, who, with Sir John Colbourn, rode at the head of the Royal troops in the rebellion of 1837; *Address:* 9 Ontario Av., Montreal; and Winnipeg Cottage, St. Patrick, Que. *Clubs:* St. James, Dixie Golf, Montreal.

LIDDELL, His Hon. James William, K.C., County Court Judge for Stormont, Dundas and Glengarry; *b.* Cornwall, Ont., 2 Nov., 1852; *s.* of David and Caroline A. Liddell; *m.* Margaret Sophia, *o. d.* of the late Lt.-Col. Ronal l Macdonell; one *s.* two *d.* *Educ.:* Cornwall Gram. Sch.; Osgoode Hall, Toronto. Admitted to the Bar, 1876; cr. Q.C., 1899; made County Ct. Judge for Stormont, Dundas and Glengarry, 2 Jan., 1901. *Address:* Cornwall, Ont.

LIGHTHALL, William Dover, K.C., M. A., F.R.S.C.; F.R.S.L.; *b.* Hamilton, Ont., 27 Dec., 1857; *s.* of W. F. Lighthall, Notary, Montreal, and Margaret Wright; *m.* Cybel I. John, *g. d.* Rev. Hy. Wilkes, D.D.; one *s.* two *d.* *Educ.:* High Sch. and McGill Univ., Montreal; called to bar, 1881; Mayor of Westmount, Montreal, 1900-1-2; founded the Union of Canadian Municipalities, 1901; Hon. Pres., 1904; now Hon. Secretary; founder of the Society of Can. Lit., Can. National League, etc.; originated Chateau de Ramezay Historical Museum, etc.; Vice-Pres. Antiquarian Society of Montreal, Canadian Society of Authors, etc.; Corresponding Member, Literary and Historical Society of Quebec, etc.; has introduced much municipal legislation into Parliament. *Publications:* Thoughts, Moods, and Ideals (verse 1887; The Young Seigneur, or Nation-Making, 1888; originated and edited Songs of the Great Dominion (Windsor Series), 1891, and Canadian Poems (Canterbury Poets), 1891; Montreal after 250 Years, 1892; The False Chevalier, 1898; The Glorious Enterprise, 1902; Canada a Modern Nation, 1904; and many ethical, historical, and literary pamphlets. *Recreations:* camping, antiquarianism. *Address:* Chateauclair, Westmount, Que.; Camp Beartracks, Lac Tremblant, Que. *Clubs:* Canada; Reform, Montreal; Royal Societies, London, England.

LINDSEY, George Goldwin Smith; B.A. (Tor.), K.C., *b.* Toronto, 19 March, 1860; *s.* of Charles Lindsey & Janet Mackenzie; *m.* Cora, *d.* of late James Bethune, Q.C., two *s.* *Educ.:* Upper Can. Coll., Toronto Univ., Osgoode Hall. Called to bar of Ont., 1886 and became partner in firm of Lount, Marsh, Lindsey & Lindsey; and is now sr. partner in firm of Lindsey, Lawrence & Wadsworth; was pres. and mgr. dir. Crow's Nest Pass Coal Co., until 1909; dir. Crow's Nest Electric Light and Power Co.; the Morrissey, Fernie and Michel Ry.; one of the founders of *Varsity;* founder (1882), of *The Cricket Field.* Took to England (1887) a team of Can. cricketers. Alderman of Toronto, two yrs. Unsuccessful can., 1894, for Ont. Leg. Ass. for West Toronto in Lib. interest; pres., 1900-1, Toronto Reform Ass. *Publications:* cricket across the Sea, Life of Wm. Lyon Mackenzie (1908, Makers of Can. series). *Recreations:* cricket, golf. *Address:* 145 Tyndall Ave., Toronto. *Clubs:* Toronto, National, Royal Can. Yacht, Toronto.

LITHGOW, John Thomas; late Comptroller, Territorial Treasurer, Supt. of Works & Bldgs., Chief License Inspr. and City Assessor and Tax Collector, Yukon Territory; *b.* Halifax, N.S., 25 Jan., 1856 *s.* of James R. Lithgow and Marion Drew Lithgow. Apptd. to Asst. Receiver Gen'ls. Office, Halifax, Oct., 1880. Transferred to Yukon Territory as Comptroller, July, 1898. Apptd. a mem. of the Yukon Council, 8 Jan., 1904. Apptd. Acting Commr. 2 Feb., 1906; again apptd. Acting Commr. 14 Nov., 1906. *Recreations:* horsemanship, curl ing, fishing. *Address:* Dawson, Y.T. *Clubs:* Zero, Dawson Amateur Athletic Assn.

LLOYD, Rev. George Exton, M.A., Principal of the Divinity Coll., Saskatoon; *b.* London, Eng., 6 Jan., 1861; *s.* of William J. Lloyd, and Elizabeth A. Brown; *m.* Marion Tuppen, of Worthing; three *s.* two *d.* Came to Can., 1880, and educ. at Wycliffe Coll., Toronto and Univ. of New Brunswick. Ordained by Archbishop of Rupertsland, 1885; founder and principal of Rothesay Coll. for Boys in N.B., 1890; Archdeacon, diocese of Saskatchewan, 1905 resigned to become principal of the Divinity Coll., of the Diocese of Sask., June, 1909. *Address:* Emmanuel Coll., Saskatoon, Sask.

LOCKE, Corbet, K.C.; *b.* Barrie, Co. of Simcoe, Ont., 9 Feb., 1854; *s.* of Joseph and Mary Locke; *m.* (1st), in 1882, Esther Alice, *d.* of the late Richard Holland of Oshawa; (2nd) in 1901, Ruby Louise, *d.* of A Percy Brown, Peterboro. two *s.* two *d.* *Educ.:* Barrie Gram. Sch. Called to the bar of Ont., 1877; man., 1882; Q.C., 1893; apptd. to the Co. Court bench, Man., 1894; prior to going to the bench took an active part in politics of Manitoba; pres. of Liberal Conservative Assn. for 13 years. *Recreation:* cricket, tennis, curling, fishing. *Address:* Morden, Man.

LOCKE, George Herbert, M.A.; *b.* Beamsville, Ont., 29 March, 1870; *s.* Rev. Joseph A. Locke and Bessie Mackay Loche; *m.* Grace Isabel Moore, Toronto; one *d.* *Educ.:* Ryerson Pub. Sch., Toronto; Brampton and Collingwood Collegiate Inst., Victoria Coll., Toronto University, and Univ. of Chicago; Professor in Univ. of Toronto, Chicago, Harvard, and McGill for seven years; editor of the *School Review,* the leading journal of secondary education in America; Associate editor with Green & Co., of Boston, members of a number of learned societies; now chief librarian of the Public Libraries of Toronto. *Address:* 29 Cecil St., Toronto. *Club:* Ontario, Toronto.

LOCKHART, F. A. Lawton, M.D. (McGill), M.B., F.M.; *s.* of W. A. Lockhart and Mary E. Lawton; *m.* 1892, Mabel B. Thomas *Educ.:* Gram. Sch., St. John, N.B.; Merchiston Castle Sch., Edinburgh, Scot.; Edinburgh Univ. (grad. 1889); returned to Montreal, 1890, and grad. M.D., McGill Univ., 1900. Apptd. Asst. Gynaecologis at Montreal Gen. Hospital, 1894, became gynaeclologist; apptd. Prof. of Gynaecology, Univ. of Bishop's Coll., Lennoxville, Que., 1893, but resigned 1894. Acted as Prof. of Gynaecology at Univ. of Vermont, U.S.A., 1906-1908; has been Gnyaeologist at the Protestant Hospital for the Insane at Verdun, since 1894. Mem. Edinburgh Obstetrical Assn., British Medical Assn., Canada Medical Assn., Montreal Medical and Chirurgical Soc. *Publication:* Diseases of the Ovaries." pub. in the Reference Handbook of Medical Sciences in 1904. *Address:* 38 Bishop St., Montreal. *Clubs:* University, St. Lawrence Fish and Game, Outremount Golf.

LOFTHOUSE, Right Rev. Joseph, D.D.; *b.* Wadsley, Yorkshire, Eng., 18 Dec., 1855; *s.* of Francis and Mary Lofthouse; *m.* Bessie Falding; one *d.* *Educ.:* C.M.S. Coll., Islington; arrived in Canada, 16 Aug., 1882; Missionary to the Eskimos at Churchill, Hudson's Bay; also at York Factory; Bishop of Keewatin, 1902. *Recreations:* boating and travel in the Northland. *Address:* Kenora, Ont.

LOGAN, Hance James, LL.B.; *b.* Amherst Point, N.S., 26 April, 1869; *s.* of James A. Logan; widower. *Educ.:* Model Sch., Truro, Pictou Academy, and Dalhousie Univ. Called to the Bar of Nova Scotia, 1892. First el. to H. of C. at g. e. 1896; re-el. 1900 and 1904; retired 1908. Was asst. chief Liberal Whip and chm. of Parliamentary Committee on Privileges and Elections. *Address:* Amherst, N.S.

LOGAN, Robert Samuel; *b.* St. Louis, Mo., U.S.A., 13 Feb., 1864; *s.* of Samuel Logan and Mary Cooper McCleverly, both Canadians; *m.* Anne Rankin; three *s.* two *d.* *Educ.:* St. Louis Gram. Sch.; arrived in Canada, 6 July, 1896; entered railway service with General Manager of the Wabash Railroad, 1 Oct., 1885; Grand Trunk Ry., 6 July, 1896, as Assistant and Secretary to the General Manager. *Recreations:* walking and golf. *Address:* 12 Aberdeen Ave., Westmount, Que.

LOGGIE, William Stewart, M.P.; *b.* Burnt Church, N.B., 10 Aug., 1850; *s.* of George Loggie and Ann Morrison; *m.* Elspeth B. Kerr; six *s.* seven *d.* *Educ.:* Gram. Sch., Chatham, N.B., Pres. and mng. dir. of the W. S. Loggie Co., Ltd., wholesale and dry goods mfgrs., and packers of canned lobsters. Mem. N.B. Leg. for Northumberland Co., 1903-1904. El. to H. of C. at g. e., 1904 and 1908. Has been mayor and alderman for town of Chatham. *Address:* Chatham, N.B.

LONG, Thomas; *b.* Co. of Limerick, Ireland, 7 April, 1838; *s.* of Thomas Long and Margaret Fanel; *m.* (1st) Annie Patton; (2nd) Elizabeth Kealy; two *s.* two *d.* *Educ.:* Ireland and Canada; arrived in Canada, Oct., 1850; general merchant; member of the Ontario Legislature for North Simcoe, for eight years. *Address:* Collingwood, Ont., 513 Jarvis St., Toronto. *Clubs:* Toronto, Albany, Toronto.

LONGLEY, Hon. James Wilberforce, M.A., D.C.L., LL.D., F.R.S.C., a Judge of the Supreme Court of Nova Scotia; *b.* Paradise, N.S., 4 Jan., 1849; *m.* (1st), 1877, Annie, *y. d.* of N. Brown; two *s.* one *d.*; (2nd) 1901, Lois E., *y. d.* of late George Fletcher; five *s.* one *d.* A lecturer and public speaker, and a regular contributor to the magazines; is a Liberal in politics, and an advanced thinker on social and religious questions; graduated from Acadia Univ., 1871; admitted to the Bar of N.S., 1875; first elec. to Parliament, 1882; entered Government, 1884; Attorney-General, 1886-1905; Judge of Supreme Court 1905; Q.C., 1892; D.C.L., 1897; elec. Fellow of the Royal Society of Canada, 1898. *Publications:* Love; Socialism, its Truths and Errors; The Greatest Drama; A Material Age; Canada and Imperial Federation; Religion in 19th Century; Life of Joseph Howe, etc. *Address:* 18 Green Street, Halifax, N.S. *Clubs:* City Club, Royal Yacht, Halifax.

LORANGER, Hon. Louis Onesime, Puisne Judge of the Superior Court of the Prov. of Quebec since 1882; *b.* Yamachiche, Que., 7 April, 1837; *s.* of the late Joseph Loranger and Marie Louise Dugal; *m.* (1st. 1867, Marie Anne Rosalie (*d.* 1883), *d.* of the late Hon. Justice Laframboise; (2nd) 1888, Mad. Antoinette Varois, widow of Eugene Varois, and *d.* of the late S. Valois; three *s.* three *d.* *Educ.:* St. Mary's Coll., Montreal. Called to the Bar, 1858; commenced practice with his bro. the late Hon. Mr. Justice T. J. J. Loranger; created a Q.C., 1881. El. to Legis. Assembly for Co. of Laval, 1875, and retained seat until 1882, when apptd. Puisne Judge of Que.; Attorney-Gen., 1879-1882; pres., St. Jean Baptiste Soc., of Montreal, 1895-96; Pres., Notre Dame Hospital; a governor of the Laval Univ. *Address:* 230 Prince Arthur St. West, Montreal.

LORRAIN, Right Rev. Narcisse Zephirin, Bishop of Pembroke, Ont.; *b.* St. Martin, Laval Co., Que., 13 June, 1842; *s.* of Narcisse Lorrain and Sophie Goyer. *Educ.:* Ste. Therese Coll. *Address:* Pembroke, Ont.

LORTIE, Joseph Arthur, B.A., M.D., M.P.; *b.* Ste. Justine of Newton, Co. of Vaudreuil! *s.* of Joseph Lortie and Julienne Montpetit. French Canadians; *m.* 8 Oct., 1900, Marie Anna *d.* of L. A. Gladu, N.P. of St. Polycarpe; three *s.* one d. *Educ.:* Bourget Coll., Rigaud, and Laval Univ., Montreal. Has been a municipal councillor; first elec. to the H. of C., 1908; Roman Catholic; Conservative. *Address:* St. Polycarpe, Soulanges Co., Que.

LOUDON, James, M.A., LL.D., D.C.L., F.R.S.C.; *b.* Toronto, 1841, of Irish parentage; *m.* 1872, Julia, *d.* of John Lorn McDougall of Renfrew; three *s.* one *d.* *Educ.:* The Toronto Gram. Sch., Up. Can. Coll., and Univ. of Toronto. B.A., M.A., LL.D., Univ. of Toronto; LL.D., Queen's, Princeton, Johns Hopkins, and Glasgow Universities; D.C.L., Trinity University (Toronto); F.R. Soc. of Canada; Pres. R.S.C. (1901-2). Math. Tutor in Univ. Coll. Toronto, 1863; Classical and Math. Tutor, 1864, Math. Tutor and Dean of Residence, 1865; Prof. of Mathematics and Natural Philosophy, 1875; Pres., Toronto Univ., 1892-1906. *Publications:* various Mathematical and Physical papers in Journal of Canadian Institute, the Philosophical Magazine, the American Jour. of Math. and the Trans. of Roy. Soc. of Canada. *Address:* 83 St. George St., Toronto.

LOUGHEED, Hon. James Alexander, K.C., Leader Opposition in Senate of Canada; *b.* 1 Sept., 1854; *m.* 1884, *e. d.* of late Chief Factor William L. Hardisty of the Hon. Hudson Bay Co.; four *s.* two *d.* *Educ.:* Toronto, Ont. Practised law in city of Toronto, 1881; moved to North-West Territories, 1883; Q.C., 1889; called to Senate of Canada, 1889. *Address:* Calgary, Alberta. *Clubs:* Rideau, Country, Ottawa; Ranchmens', Calgary; Albany, National, Toronto.

LOVELL, Charles Henry, M.P.; *b.* Barnston, Que., 12 Nov., 1854; *s.* of the late Henry Lovell and Artemessa Merriman; *m.* 2 Aug., 1879, Ada Bush, Coaticook; two *s.*

one *d.* *Educ.:* Coaticook Academy; first elec. to the H. of C., bye-elec., Jan., 1908, after the death of his father; re-el. at g. e., 1908. Liberal. *Address:* Coaticook, Ont.

LOW, Albert Peter, B.Ap.S., LL.D.; Deputy Minister of Dep. of Mines, Canada; *b.* Montreal; 24 May, 1861; *m.* Isabella Cunningham; one *s.* one *d.* *Educ.:* McGill Univ., Montreal; connected with the Geological Survey since 1881; Deputy Min., 3 May, 1907; has made geological explorations in all parts of Canada, but especially in Labrador, Niagara and around the shores of Hudson's Bay. *Publications:* numerous reports. *Recreation:* curling. *Address:* 154 McLaren St., Ottawa. *Clubs:* Rideau, Country, Ottawa.

LOW, Thomas Andrew, M.P.; *b.* Quebec, 17 March, 1871; of Scotch parentage; *m.* 30 Nov., 1904, Mary G. Dean; one *s.* *Educ.:* Pembroke Ont., pub. and high schls.; moved to Pembroke with his parents when a child; pres., Renfrew Roller Mills Co., Ltd.; Pres., Logan Bros., Ltd.; director, Renfrew Mfg. Co., Ltd.; warden Co. Renfrew; member Co. Council for four years; first el. to H. of C. for South Renfrew, 1908; Methodist; Liberal; *Address:* Renfrew, Ont.

LOWE, John; *b.* Warrington, Lancashire, Eng., 20 Feb., 1824; *s.* of James Lowe and Anne Clarke; *m.* Almira Chamberlin of Freleghsburg, Missisquoi Co., Que.; two *s.* two *d.* *Educ.:* In the Sch. of Warrington, and Latchford, until 16 years of age; arrived in Canada, July, 1840; when first came to Canada, was employed as bookkeeper in Montreal fur house; reporter on Montreal *Gazette,* 1846; left Montreal in 1852, to edit the *Colonist* in Toronto, when that paper became the first daily, all-the-year-round newspaper ever published in Canada; in 1853 returned to Montreal to become partner in ownership of *Gazette,* and joint editor with Col. Chamberlin, M. L.A., C.M.G.; advocate of the railway to the North-West and the Allan Line, at that time; entered civil service as assistant Depty. Minister of Agriculture, with title of Secretary in 1869, having in charge immigration to Canada; Depty. Min. of Agriculture for several yrs. *Publications:* Editorial articles and year book; *Recreations:* gardening and vine culture. *Address,* Ottawa, Ont.

LOWE, Robert, Pres. of Yukon Council, *b.* nr. Toronto, 1869. Mem. for Whitehorse in Territorial Council; engaged in freighting business; part owner Whitehorse Tramway. A leading merchant and mining operator. Unsuccessful condidate for H. of C., at g. e., 1908. *Address:* Dawson, Y.T.

LOWRIE, William Hugh, Registrar of Deeds for the Co. of Russell; *b.* Carp, Carleton Co., Ont., 14 April, 1849; *s.* of James Lowrie and Sarah Ronan; *m.* R. S. Wilson; two *s.* one *d.* *Educ.:* Pub. Sch., Cumberland. Brought up on farm. Engaged in real estate business for 25 yrs. before receiving present appointment. Has always been active in public life. Pres. of Conservative Assn. for 18 yrs.; pres., Agricultural Soc. for several yrs. High Chief Ranger of the I. O. F. *Address:* Russell, Ont.

LUCAS, Rev. Daniel Van Norman, D.D. *b.* Hamilton, Ont., 12 July, 1834; *s.* of Capt. John Lewis; *m.* E. Adelia Reynolds; three *s.* *Educ.:* Victoria Univ., Ont.; reformer, traveller and author. *Publications:* "Australia and Homeward," "All about Canada" "The British Empire and Imperial Federation," and a score of smaller publications. *Address:* St. Catharines, Ont., and Cricklewood, London, Eng.

LUCAS, Hon. Isaac Brock, K.C., M.L. A.; *b.* Warwick, Tp. Lambton, Co., Ont., 1867; *s.* of George Lucas and Elizabeth Cowan, of Irish descent; *m.* Elizabeth E. Richardson, *d.* of M. K. Richardson, Ex-M.P. for South Grey; two *s.* *Educ.:* Strathroy Collegiate and Toronto Univ.; a member of the firm of Lucas, Wright and McArdle, Barristers; elec. to Legis. of Ont., 1898, 1902, 1905, nd 1908; chairman of Private Bills Committee; Minister without Portfolio in Ontario Cabinet. *Address:* Markdale, Ont. *Club:* Albany, Toronto.

LUMSDEN, Hugh David, C.E.; *b.* Belhelvie Lodge, Aberdeenshire, Scot., 7 Sept., 1844; *s.* Colonel Thomas Lumsden, C.B., and Hay Burnet; *m.* in 1885, Mary F., *o. d.* of J. W. G. Whitney, Toronto; four *s.* Arrived in Canada, 26 April, 1861. *Educ.:* Belleview Academy; Aberdeen and Wimbledon Sch., Surrey, Eng.; O.L.S., M.I.C.E., M.C. Soc., C.E.; in practice as O.L.S. until 1871; since then he has been employed constantly in the location and construction of Railways in many parts of the Dominion; chief engr., National Transcontinental Ry. Comn., but resigned, 1909. *Recreations:* shooting and fishing. *Address:* 152 Argyle Ave., Ottawa; and Bay St., Orillia. *Clubs:* Toronto; Rideau, Golf, Ottawa; Engineers, Montreal.

LYNCH, Hon. William Warren, B.C.L., K.C., LL.D., Judge of the Quebec Superior Court; *b.* Bedford, Missisquoi Co., Que., 30 Sept., 1854; *s.* of Thomas Lynch and Charlotte R. Williams; *m.* 25 May, 1874, Ellen Florence Pettes; two *s.* *Educ.:* Stanbridge Academy, Missisquoi Co.; Univ. of Vermont, and McGill Univ.; practiced law in Bedford District from 1868 to 1887, and in Montreal, from the latter year to 1889. when apptd. Judge; elec. member of Quebec Legislature for Brome Co. in 1871, and continued as such until appointment; member of Quebec Government from 1879 until 1887. *Address:* Knowlton, Que.

M

MABEE, Hon. James Pitt, K.C., Chief Commr., Bd. of Ry. Commrs. for Canada; *b.* Port Rowan, Ont., 5 Nov., 1859; *s.* of Simon Pitt Mabee and Fannie Leaton; *m.* Mary Thorald, of Port Rowan; one *s.* one *d.* *Educ.:* Port Rowan High Sch., Toronto Univ. After graduating in law practised profession at Listowel for some yrs., later at Stratford and Toronto. Apptd. one of the Judges of the High Ct. of Justice for Ontario, King's Bench Div., 21 Nov., 1905; apptd. Chief Commr., Bd. of Ry. Commrs., 28 March, 1908, in succession to the late Commr. Killam. *Addresses:* Railway Commission Office, Queen St., Ottawa; 15

Scarth Rd., Toronto. *Clubs:* Rideau, Ottawa; Toronto.

MACALLUM, Archibald Byron, M.A., M.B.; Ph.D., Hon. Sc. D.; Hon. LL.D., F.R.S.C., F.R.S., Professor of Physiological Chemistry in the Univ. of Toronto; *b.* Belmont, Ont., 1859; *s.* of Alexander Macallum, of Kilmartin, Argyleshire, and Anna, *d.* of Neil Macalpine, Parish of Knapdale, Argyleshire, Scot.; *m.* Minnie Isabel, *d.* of the late John Strachan Bruce, of Cornwall, Ont.; three *s.* *Educ.:* Univ. of Toronto, and Johns Hopkins Univ., Baltimore; apptd. lecturer in Physiology in the Univ. of Toronto in 1887; Professor in 1891. *Publications:* numerous papers (research chiefly on Physiology and Biochemistry, in English and American Scientific Journals. *Recreations:* golf and walking. *Address:* 59 St. George St., Toronto. *Club:* Golf, Toronto.

MACAULAY, Charles Daniel, K.C.; Judge of the Territorial Court, Yukon; *b.* Township of Sidney, Hastings Co., Ont., 20 Oct., 1863; *s.* of Daniel Macaulay and Elizabeth Macdonnell; *m.* Mary C. P., *d.* of Robert P. Davy, of Belleville, Ont.; one *s.* *Educ.:* Frankfort Pub. Sch.; Albert Coll., Belleville; Osgoode Hall. After grad., practised law at Belleville, until May, 1901, when apptd. to present office. *Address:* Dawson, Y.T. *Club:* Zero, Dawson.

MACAULAY, Robertson; Pres. Sun Life Ins. Co.; *b.* Fraserburgh, Buchan, Aberdeenshire, Scotland, Jan., 1833; *m.* 1859, Barbara Reid of Edinburgh; two *s.* one *d.* *Educ.:* Stornoway, Lewis Isd. Arrived in Can., 1854. Apptd. acct. in the Canada Life Ass. Co., 1855, but resigned in 1871 to accept Secretaryship of the Mutual Life Ass of Can., at Hamilton. Became Sec. of the Sun Life in 1874, and moved to Montreal; promoted to managership of Co., 1876 and man. dir., 1887., and two yrs. later el. pres. Resigned position of man. dir., 1906, in favor of his son, Mr. T. B. Macaulay. *Address:* 4005 Dorchester St., Montreal.

MACAULAY, Thomas Bassett, F.I.A. (G.B.), F.A.S. (Am.); F.S.S. (G.B.), Managing Dir., Sun Life Insur. Co. of Canada; *b.* Hamilton, Ont., 6 June, 1860; *s.* of Robertson Macaulay and Barbara Marie Reid; *m.* Henrietta M.L., *d.* of late Dr. T. Bragg, New Orleans, and step *d.* of Rev. J. Lawson Forster, D.D., now of London, Eng.; two *s.* three *d.* *Educ.:* Hamilton, Ont., and Montreal, Que. Entered service of the Sun Life Insur. Co., 1877; actuary, 1880; secretary, 1891; director, 1898; mng. dir., 1906; supervisor at Montreal in connection with the examinations of the Inst of Actuaries of G.B.; chapter mem. of the Actuarial Soc. of America; pres. two terms; corr. mem. of the Inst. des Actuaries Francais, Paris; rep. at the International Congress of Actuaries at Brussels, 1895; London, 1898; Paris, 1900; Berlin, 1906; vice pres. at Paris and Berlin congresses respectively for the U.S. and Canada. *Recreation:* farming (Hudson Heights, Que.) *Address:* 4007 Dorchester St., Montreal.

MacBRIDE, Ernest William, M.A. (Cantab), D. Sc. (London, F.R.S., Strathcona Prof. of Zoology, McGill Univ.; *b.* Belfast, Ireland, 12 Dec., 1866; *s.* of Samuel MacBride, of the firm of Robert MacBride & Co., linen manufacturers; *m.* Constance Harvey, *d.* of F. H. Chrysler, K.C., of Ottawa; one *s.* *Educ.:* Queen's Coll., Belfast, St. John's Coll., Cambridge; London Univ. (Univ. scholarship in Zoology, 1889). 1891. 1892, studied at Zoological Laboratory, at Naples. Apptd. Univ. demonstrator in Animal Morphology at Cambridge, 1892; made a Fellow of St. John's Coll., 1893, and obtained medal for research in Biology, same yr. Was pres. and vice-pres. of Cambridge Union, apptd. to chair of Zoology, McGill Univ.; el. mem. American Soc. of Zoologists, 1898. Mem. Royal Soc., London. *Publications:* Text-Book of Zoology, 1908; the development of Asterina Gibbosa, 1896; the early development of Amphioxus, 1898; the development of Echinus Esculentus; the development of Ophiothrix Fragilis. *Recreations:* golf, tennis. *Address:* Montreal. *Club:* University, Montreal.

MacCLEMENT, William Thomas, M.A.; D.Sc.; *b.* Inverary, Ont., 29 Jan., 1861; *s.* of David and Nancy Bruce MacClement; *m.* Mary Guthrie Freeman; one *s.* and one *d.* *Educ.:* Ont. Pub. Schs., Frontenac High Sch., Queen's University, Kingston, Ont., Chicago Univ., Chicago, Ill.; Pub. Sch. teacher for four years, and High Sch. teacher for six years; Professor of Chemistry, Armour Institute of Technology, Chicago, for five years; Professor of Chemical Engineering for five years; at present Professor of Botany, Queen's Univ., Kingston, Ont. *Publications:* Manual and Laboratory Note Book, in chemistry; Text Book and Manual of Chemistry; magazine articles on Botany. *Recreations:* golf, fishing, photography. *Address:* County House, Collins Bay, Bay of Quinte. *Club:* Saturday Club, Kingston, Ont.

MACDIARMID, Finlay George, M.L.A.; *b.* New Glasgow, Aldboro' tp., Elgin Co., Ont., 11 Oct., 1860; *s.* of Finlay Macdiarmid and Margaret Munro; *m.* Mary Isabell McGugan; one *s.* *Educ.:* Pub. Sch., Ridgetown Coll. Inst. Mem. of Tp. Coun. of Aldboro' for four yrs. First el. to Ont. Legis. at g. e., 1898; re-el. at each succeeding g. e. *Address:* Aldboro', Ont.

MacDONALD, Right Rev. Alexander, D.D., LL.D., Bishop of Victoria, B.C.; *b.* Mabou, Inverness Co., Cape Breton, 18 Feb., 1858; *s.* of Finlay MacDonald and Catherine Beaton. *Educ.:* St. Frances Xavier's Antigonish, N.S., and Propaganda, Rome; ordained priest, 8 March, 1884; Vicar General of Antigonish, 1900-1908; Bishop of Victoria, B.C., 1 Oct., 1908. *Publications:* The Symbol in Sermons; The Sacrifice of the Mass, The Symbol of the Apostles, Questions of the Day, (2 vols.); The Mercies of the Sacred Heart; The Sacraments. *Address:* Victoria, B.C.

MACDONALD, Hon. Andrew Archibald, Senator; *b.* Brudenell, P.E.I., 14 Feb., 1829; *e. s.* of Hugh and Catherine Macdonald, both natives of Inverness-shire, Scotland; *m.* 1863, Elizabeth Owen (*d.* 1901); four *s.* *Educ.:* High Sch., Georgetown, P.E.I., and by private tutor. Was in business as a general merchant till 1873, when he retired; Provincial Legislature, 1853-58 and 1863-74; a delegate to the Quebec conference on Union of the Provinces, 1864; Provincial

Postmaster-General, 1873, and Acting Post-Office Inspector till 1884; Lieutenant-Governor of the Province, 1884-1889; called to Dominion Senate, 1891; one of the only two surviving fathers of the Canadian Confederation. *Recreations:* boating, fishing, shooting. *Address:* Charlottetown. *Club:* Charlottetown.

MACDONALD, A. F., B.A., B.C.L.; Editor of the Halifax *Chronicle; b.* Hopewell, Pictou Co., N.S. *Educ.:* Pictou Acad., and Dalhousie Univ., Halifax. Joined the staff of the *Morning Chronicle* as reporter, 1897: promoted news editor 1900; editor, 1905. Was the Nova Scotia del. at the Imperial Press Conference in London in June, 1909, when sixty representative journalsits from the oversea dominions participated in a series of memorable functions. *Address:* Halifax, N.S.

MACDONALD, Archibald John, M.L.A.; *b.* Panmure, King's Co., P.E.I., 10 Oct., 1834; *s.* of Hugh and Catherine Macdonald; *m.* Marion Murphy; four *s.* three *d. Educ.:* at Georgetown and Charlottetown, P.E.I.; was collector of Customs at Georgetown for several years; member of the Provincial Legislative and Provincial Government; Master in Chancery; Consular Agent of the United States. *Recreations:* fishing, farming and boating. *Address:* Georgetown, P. E.I.

MACDONALD, Hon. Daniel Alexander; Judge of the Court of King's Bench for Manitoba; *b.* P.E.I., 17 Aug., 1858; *s.* of Alexander Macdonald and Mary McRae; *m.* Helen St. Luke Rogers; one *s.* three *d. Educ.:* Prince of Wales Coll., P.E.I.; admitted to the bar of P.E.I., in 1883; bar of Manitoba in 1885; after practising his profession in Winnipeg for some years was apptd. Judge. *Recreations:* golf, curling. *Address:* 107 Stradbrooke Place, Winnipeg. *Clubs:* Manitoba, St. Charles Country, Winnipeg.

MACDONALD, Br-General Donald Alexander, I.S.O. 1903; Quartermaster General of Ordnance, Canada, since 1904; *b.* 1845; *s.* of late Alexander Eugene Macdonald, Deputy Clerk of the Crown and Registrar of the Surrogate Court of Cornwall, Ont.; *m.* 1876, Mary, 2nd *d.* of Mr. Justice Hugh Richardson, formerly of the Supreme Court of the North-West Territories of Canada; one *d. Educ.:* County High Sch. Served during Fenian Raids, 1866; Red River Expedition, 1870 (medal, two clasps); North-West Rebellion, 1885 (medal); holds Long Service Decoration; sometime Chief Superintendent Military Stores; Director-General of Ordnance, Canada, 1903-4. *Address:* The New Russell, Ottawa. *Clubs:* Rideau, Golf, Ottawa.

MACDONALD, Edward Mortimer, B.L., K.C., M.P.; *b.* Pictou, N.S., 16 Aug., 1865; *s.* John D. and Mary Isabel Macdonald; *m.* Edith Lilian Ives; two *s.* one *d. Educ.:* Pictou Academy and Dalhousie Univ.; for seven years member for Pictou in Provincial Legislature of N.S.; member of H. of C. since 1904; re-el., 1908. Career confined to politics and law. *Recreations:* curling, and cricket. *Address:* Limehurst, Pictou, N.S. *Clubs:* Rideau, Ottawa; Halifax.

MACDONALD of Earnscliffe, The Baroness; *b.* Jamaica, 24 Aug., 1836; *d.* of Hon. T. J. Bernard, a member of the Privy Council of Jamaica, and Theodora Foulks; *m.* 16 Feb., 1867, Right Hon. Sir John A. Macdonald, Prime Minister of the Dominion, who *d.* 6 June, 1891; one *d.*, the Hon. Mary Theodore Margaret. *Educ.:* England. Cr. (14 Aug., 1891) first Baroness by H.M. Queen Victoria, in recognition of Sir John Macdonald's great services to Canada and the Empire. In 1887, headed a movement for the establishment of an Art Museum and Industrial Coll., as a memorial of Queen Victoria; was present i. Westminster Abbey at the Corontaion of the King and Queen; in the same yr. took charge, with Lady Strathcona, of the Canadian stall at the Imperial Coronation Bazaar. *Publications:* many articles for the English press on Canada and her resources. Resides chiefly abroad. *Address:* c|o Canadian High Commissioner, 17 Victoria St., London, S.W., England.

MACDONALD, Hon. Hugh John, M.A., K.C., P.C.; *b.* Kingston, Ont., 13 March, 1850; *s.* of the Rt. Hon. Sir John Macdonald for many yrs. Prime Minister of Canada, and Isabella Clark; *m.* (1st) 1876, Jean, King, *d.* of the late W. A. Murray, of Toronto; (2nd) 1883, Agnes Gertrude, *d.* of the late S. J. Van Koughnet, Q.C. *Educ.:* Queen's Coll., Kingston, Toronto Univ. (Grad. 1869). Called to Ontario bar, 1872; and practiced in Toronto for ten yrs. Removed to Winnipeg, 1882, and formed partnership with J. Stewart Tupper, *e. s.* of Sir Charles Tupper, Bart. El. to H. of C. as mem. for Winnipeg, 1891; accepted portfolio of Dept. of Interior in Tupper Ministry, 1896, but resigned office with his leader 8 July, same yr. Accepted Conservative leadership in Manitoba, and formed an admn. after defeat of Greenway Govt., Dec., 1899. Resigned office, Oct., 1900, to contest Brandon for H. of C., but was defeated. Is senior of the legal firm of Macdonald, Haggart, Sullivan and Tarr. *Address:* Winnipeg. *Club:* Manitoba, Winnipeg.

MACDONALD, Hon. James Alexander, LL.B., K.C., Chief Justice of the Court of Appeal for British Columbia; *b.* Huron Co., Ont., 1858. *Educ.:* Pub. Schs. and Coll. Inst., Stratford; Toronto Univ. and Osgoode Hall. Entered the law firm of Fullerton, Cook, Wallace & Macdonald, of Toronto, 1890, removing to Rossland, B.C., 1896, where he took up practice of his profession. First pres. of the Rossland branch of the Prov. Min. Assn. of B.C. First el. to B.C. Legis., 1903, and re-el. 1907. Leader of the Liberal Opposition in the Legis., but resigned this position previous to his appointment as Chief Justice of the B.C. Ct. of Appeal. *Address:* Victoria, B.C.

MACDONALD, John, J.P.; head of the firm of John Macdonald & Co., wholesale dry goods; *b.* Oaklands, nr. Toronto, Ont., 4 Nov., 1863; *s.* of the late Hon. John Macdonald. *Educ.:* Upper Canada Coll. When quite a young lad entered the dry goods firm of John Macdonald & Co., which was founded by his father; received a sound business training, and on the death of his father, undertook the management of the business. Mem. Toronto Bd. of Trade, Commercial Travellers' Assn., British Empire League. Was one of orig. promoters, and is now a dir. of the Annual Horse Show at Toronto; mem., Horse Breeders' Assn. and of the Hackney Horse Assn. *Address:* 116 Farnham Av., Toronto. *Club:* National Toronto.

MACDONALD, John Alexander, M.L.A. *b.* Tracadie, P.E.I., 12 April, 1874; *s.* of John Charles and Mary Elizabeth Macdonald; *m.* Marie Josephine MacDonald; one *s.* two *d.* *Educ.:* Tracadie pub. schl., merchant and shipowner; exporter of grain and produce; member of Legislative Ass., of P.E.I. *Address:* Cardigan, P.E.I.

MACDONALD, John Archibald, M.L.A.; *b.* Winnipeg, Man., 6 Aug., 1865; *s.* of Archibald Macdonald, chief factor, Hudson Bay Co., and Ellen Inkster, both Scotch; *m.* Elleonora Catherine Campbell, *d.* of the late Robt. Campbell, F.R.G.S.; three *s.* one *d.* *Educ.:* St. John's Coll., Winnipeg. Up to 1893, with the Hudson Bay Co., but since a member of the firm of H. McDonald Co., Bankers, Fort Qu'Appelle, Sask. *Recreations:* motoring, tennis, and shooting. *Address:* Sterling, Fort Qu'Appelle, Sask. *Club:* Manitoba, Winnipeg.

MACDONALD, J. A., LL.D. (Glasgow); Managing Editor of The Globe, Toronto; *b.* Middlesex Co., Ont., 22 Jan., 1882; *s.* of late John A. Macdonald, a native of Pictou Co., N.S.; *g.-g. s.* of James Macdonald, a soldier of the 84th Highland Regiment; *m.* 1890, Grace Lumsden Christian; two *s.* one *d.* *Educ.:* Hamilton and Toronto, Ont.;Edinb. Scot. Graduated at Knox Coll., Toronto, 1887; edited the Knox Coll. Monthly during Coll. course and until 1891; ordained to ministry of the Presbyterian Church, and inducted pastor of Knox Church, St. Thomas, Ont., 1891; resigned pastoral charge, 1896, and removed to Toronto to become first editor of The Westminster, a religious monthly magazine; subsequently acquired the Canada Presbyterian, The Presbyter, The Presbyterian Review, and The Western Presbyterian, which were consolidated under his editorship and issued as The Presbyterian, a weekly devoted to Presbyterian Church interests; principal of the Presbyterian Ladies' Coll., 1896-1901; apptd. by Ont. Government to serve on first Board of Governors of the Univ. of Toronto, 1906; LL.D. (Glasgow, 1909) del. to Imp. Press confce., 1909. *Publications:* From Far Formosa, volume on life-work of late Dr. G. L. MacKay; "What a newspaper man saw in Britain;" many fugitive articles on literary, social, political and religious subjects. *Recreations:* making speeches. *Address:* The *Globe*, Toronto. *Club:* National, Toronto.

MACDONALD, Hon. Lauchlin, M.L.A.; *b.* East Point, P.E.I., 25 March, 1844; *s.* of Ronald and Catherine Macdonald; *m.* Theresa McLean; one *s.* one *d.* *Educ.:* District Sch. and St. Dunstan's Coll.; first elec. a member of the legis. of P.E.I., 1875; elec. by acclam., 1876; elec. in 1879; retired in 1882; unsuccessful candidate in 1900; elec. 1908; a member of the Executive Council; pres. of the East Point Farmers' Institute; pres. of the Cheese Board of Trade, P.E.I.; pres. of the Dairy Men's Assn P.E.I.; Secretary and managing director of the East Point Dairy Assn. for 13 years. *Address:* East Point, P.E.I.

MACDONALD, Sir William Christopher, Kt., cr. 1898; *b.* Glenaladale, P.E.I., 1831; *y. s.* of late Hon. Donald Macdonald, President Legislative Council of P.E.I. Governor of McGill Univ., Montreal, to which he has given large endowments; Director of the Bank of Montreal; Governor of Montreal General Hospital; established and endowed the Macdonald Agric. Coll. at Ste. Anne de Bellevue, at a cost of $5,000,000. *Educ.:* Central Academy, Charlottetown, P.E.I. *Address:* 891 Sherbrooke St., Montreal. *Clubs:* Mount Royal, St. James', Montreal.

MACDONALD, Hon. William John, Senator; *b.* Skye, 1830; 2nd *s.* of Alexander Macdonald of Valley; *m.* Catharine Balfour, *d.* of Capt. Murray Reid of the Hudson Bay Coy.; three *s.* three *d.* *Educ.:* private tutor. Elected to Legislative Assembly of Vancouver Island, 1859; called to Legislative Council of B.C., 1866; Mayor of Victoria on two occasions; called to Senate of Canada, 1871; Captain of Militia in the early days of the Colony of Vancouver Island, 1851-58; acted as Gold Commissioner, Collector of Customs, and Postmaster; has been in public life forty-eight years; served the Hudson's Bay Company for eight years. *Recreations:* fishing, driving, riding, boating. *Address:* Armadale, Victoria, B.C.; The Senate, Ottawa.

MACDONELL, Major Archibald Cameron, D.S.O.; *b.* Windsor, Ont., 6 Oct., 1864; *s.* of S. S. Macdonell, K.C., and Ellen Broadhead; *m.* 1890, Mary Maud Flora 3rd *d.* of late Lieut.-Col. J. T. Campbell, late of the 72nd Highlanders and Royal Fusiliers; one *s.* one *d.* *Educ.:* Trin. Coll. School, Port Hope, Ont.; R.M.C., Kingston. Gazetted Lieut. Canadian Mounted Infantry Permanent Corps, 1888; apptd. Adjutant and Quartermaster, 1888; exchanged into North-West Mounted Police, 1889; volunteered into 2nd Batt., Canadian Mounted Rifles, for service in South Africa, Jan., 1900, as Captain; Major, 20 May, 1900; commanded four troops Canadian Mounted Rifles and two guns D Battery, Royal Canadian Artillery, with advanced column Sir Charles Parson's Field Force, in the operations in Kenhardt District; took part in general advance from Bloemfontein; in command of D Squadron Canadian Mounted Rifles; present at actions; was in command of Canadian Squadron that went through the Boer lines the night of the Vet River fight and blew up culvert and cut the telegraph near Smaldeel; Vet River, Zand River (two days); operations around Kroonstadt, Johannesburg, and Pretoria, including two days' action at Klip River; present at battle of Diamond Hill, 11 and 12 June, 1900 (dangerously wounded, despatches, S. African medal, 4 clasps); D.S.O.; organised and commanded the 5th (or Western) Regiment, Canadian Mounted Rifles, 1902, for active service in South Africa (arrived in Durban, Natal, after declaration of peace was signed); commanded Depot, and until lately commanded "C" Division Royal North-West Mounted Police, Canada, and Battleford District; transferred to R. C. Mounted Rifles at Winnipeg, 7 March, 1907. *Recreations:* football and cricket. *Address:*

Fort Osborne Barracks, Winnipeg. *Club:* Manitoba.

MACDONELL, Angus Claude, D.C.L., K.C., M.P.; *b.* Toronto, 23 June, 1861; *s.* of Angus Duncan Macdonell, a U.E.L., and Pauline Rosalie De-La-Haye (French descent); unmarried. *Educ.:* Toronto Model Sch. and Univ. Barrister-at-law, of Osgoode Hall; member H. of C. since 1904; Conservative. *Recreations:* aquatics and general field athletics. *Address:* Toronto. *Clubs:* Toronto, Albany, Hunt, R. C. Y. C., Toronto; Rideau, Ottawa.

MACFEE, Kutosoff Nicolson, B.A.; *b.* St. Chrysostome, Que.; *s.* C. McFee and Cath. McNaughton; *m.* 1910, Janet Louisa, *e. d.* of Hon. W. S. Fielding, P.C., Min. of Finance of Canada. *Educ.:* McGill Univ. Called to the bar of Quebec and practiced his profession in Montreal, Winnipeg and Minneapolis, U.S.A. Removed to London, Eng., in 1889 and has been very successful as a financial agent; active in all movements for furthering the interests of Canada and the Motherland; del. to commercial congresses of Empire. *Publications:* "A practical scheme of fiscal union for the purposes of defence and preferential trade from a Colonist's Standpoint." *Address:* 49a Pall Mall, S.W.; 73 Gracechurch St., E.C., London, England.

MACGILL, Mrs. Helen Gregory M.A., Mus. Bac.; *b.* Hamilton, Ont.; *d.* of Silas and Emma Gregory; *m.* (1st) Dr. F. C. Flesher (*dec.*); (2nd) J. H. MacGill; two *s.* two *d.* *Educ.:* Trinity Univ., Toronto. First woman to graduate in music (1886) and Arts (B.A., 1889), M.A. (1890), from Trinity Univ. A frequent contributor to magazines and newspapers; active member of National Council of Women. *Address:* 1492 Harwood St., Vancouver, B.C. *Clubs:* University Woman's, Women's Canadian, Vancouver.

MACGILLIVRAY, Angus, M.A.; *b.* Baileys Brook, Pictou Co., N.S., 22 Jan., 1842; *s.* John and Catharine MacGillivray; *m.* (1st) Maggie MacIntosh; (2nd) Mary E. Doherty; three *s.* five *d.* *Educ.:* Com. Sch. and St. Francais Xavier Univ.; admitted barrister and attorney, 1974; elec. to Legislative Assembly, 1878; Speaker, 1883-6; member of Executive Council 1886-1891, and 1896 1902; member of Legislative Council, 1892; re-elec. to Assembly 1895; apptd. Co. Court Judge, 1902; unsuccessful candidate for H. of C., 1887 and 1891; lecturer on Constitutional History, St. Francis Xavier Univ. *Recreations:* gardening. *Address:* Antigonish, N.S.

MACGILLIVRAY, Prof. John, B.A., Ph. D., *b.* Ontario, 1855; parents of Scotch origin; *m.* 1892, Annie G. Campbell of Perth, Ont.; two *s.* one *d.* *Educ.:* local public sch.; Coll. Inst., Collingwood, Ont.; Univ. of Toronto; Univ. of Leipzig. Prof. of Modern Languages at Albert College, Belleville, 1882-84; post-graduate studies at Leipzig and Paris, 1884-88; examiner in French and German for the Ontario Departmental leaving and univ. matriculation Examinations, and appellate examiner for the Normal Coll.; Professor of modern languages, Queen's University, Kingston, 1888-1902, and since professor of German. *Publications:* Graduation Thesis at Leipzig, Life and Works of Pierre Larivey; annotated editions of Sardou's La Perle Noire, Xavier de Maistre's Le Vovage autour de ma Chambre, Feu illet's La Fee, and De Peyrebrune's Les Freres Colombe (in collaboration); Storm's Schimmelreiter, annotated and containing practical exercises. *Recreation:* gardening. *Address:* Albert St., Kingston, Ont.

MacGREGOR, Robert Malcolm, B.A., M.L.A.; *b.* New Glasgow, N.S., 9 Jan., 1876; *s.* of Hon. James D. MacGregor (Senator), and his first wife, Elizabeth McColl.; *m.* Laura, only *d.* of the late Robert McNeil, for many years Warden of Pictou Co.; one *s.* one *d.* *Educ.:* New Glasgow High Sch. and Dalhousie Coll.; first elec. to Provincial Legislature in 1904; re-elec. at g. e., 1906; apptd. a Governor of Dalhousie Coll., in 1908. *Recreations:* tennis and curling. *Address:* New Glasgow, N.S.

MACHADO, Jose Antonio, B.A.; *b.* Puerto Principe, Island of Cuba, 20 Jan., 1862; *s.* Juan Francisco Machado, Puerto Principe, Cuba, and Elizabeth Frances Jones, Salem Mass., U.S.; *m.* Eleanor Esmond, *d.* of Alfred Whitman, of Annapolis, N.S.; two *s.* four *d.* *Educ.:* Pub. Sch., Salem, Mass., and Harvard Coll., Cambridge; arrived in Canada, Jan., 1902; after grad. from Harvard in 1883, took a special course in mechanical engineering, followed by business training in New York City; since 1902, general manager of American Bank Note Co., Ottawa. Has travelled extensively, visiting Europe, West Indies and Mexico. *Recreations:* golf, fishing. *Address:* 222 Somerset St., Ottawa. *Clubs:* Harvard, New York; Rideau, Golf, Ottawa.

MACHAR, Agnes Maud; *b.* Kingston, Ont.; *d.* Rev. John Machar, D.D., 2nd Principal, Queen's Univ.; has from early youth, been a student and a writer in prose and verse; a contributor to periodical literature at home and abroad. Among the periodicals occasionally written for, have been the "*Canadian Monthly,*" *Century* Magazine, *Andover Review, Westminster Review, Good Words,* and various minor magazines and journals. To *Good Words,* contributed poem entitled "Canada the Laureate," in acknowledgement of his "Ode to the Queen" in return for which had the honour of receiving from Lord Tennyson, an autograph letter of thanks. *Publications:* "For King and Country," "Katie Johnson's Cross," and "Lucy Raymond" (stories for girls); "Memorials of Rev. Dr. Machar;" "Lost and Won," "Stories of New France," Marjorie's Canadian Winter," "Heir of Fairmount Grange," "Roland Gramel, Knight," "Lays of the True North," (vol. of poems); "The Story of Old Kingston." *Recreations:* reading, drawing, gardening and boating. *Address:* 25 Sydenham St., Kingston, Ont.

MACKAY, Alexander Grant, M.A., K.C., M.L.A.; *b.* Sydenham, Grey Co., Ont., 7 March, 1860; *s.* of Hugh Mackay and Catherine McInnis. *Educ.:* Sydenham Pub-Sch., Owen Sound High Sch., High Sch. of Mount Forest, Toronto Univ. (grad. B.A., 1883, M.A., 1885). Taught dist schs., 1877-1879; principal of High Sch. of Port Rowan, Ont., 1883-1887; studied law and called to Ontario bar, May, 1891; Crown Attorney for Grey Co., 1894-1901. El. to Ont. Legis. for North Grey at g. e., 1902, and re-el. 1905, 1908. Leader of the Opposition; cr. K.C., 1902. Dir. of the Imperial Cement Co.; pres., Owen Sound Dredging and Construction Co. Actively interested in Canadian Militia. Capt. of the 31st Regt.; pres. Young Men's Liberal Assn., 1890-1894; sec. North Grey Reform Assn., 1888-1894; mem. of the Owen Sound Bd. of Educ. for six yrs. *Address*: Owen Sound, Ont.

MACKAY, Angus; Supt. of the Experimental Farm, Indianhead; *b.* Pickering, Ont., 3 Jan., 1840; *s.* of Donald Mackay and Margaret Broadfoot; *m.* 1874, Elizabeth, *d.* of Dr. R. J. Gunn, of Whitby, Ont.; three *s.* one *d.* *Educ.*: Pickering Scho., and Whitby Gram. Sch. In 1882, purchased 640 acres of land in the N.W.T.; became one of the most successful farmers in the West. Accepted position of Supt. of the Experimental Farm at Indian Head for the N.W. T., 18 July, 1887. Dir., Agricultural Soc. of Central Assiniboia, and the Canadian Shorthorn Cattle Assn. *Address*: Indian Head, Sask.

MACKAY, Lieut.-Col. Francois Samuel, N.P.; *b.* Papineauville, Que., 1 Feb., 1865; *s.* of Francois Samuel Mackay and Seraphine Julie, *d.* of D. B. Papineau; *m.* 1887, Marie Hillman; eight *c.* *Educ.*: Papineauville, Regaud, Laval Univ., and McGill Univ. (Grad. D.C.L., 1886). Practiced as N.P. in Montreal until 1891, when he retired to Papineauville, through failing health, to follow agricultural pursuits. Mayor of Papineauville, 1892-93. Returned to Montreal and resumed practice of his prof. Joined 65th Regt. and passed through every rank (Lieut.-Col., March, 1902); now commands 19th Infantry Brigade. Served in North-West Rebellion, 1885. *Address*: 275 St. Denis St., Montreal. *Clubs*: Canadien, Reform, Montreal Military Inst.

MACKAY, Mrs. Isabel Ecclestone; *b.* Woodstock, Ont., 25 Nov., 1875; *d.* of Donald MacLeod Macpherson and Priscilla Ecclestone; *m.* P. J. Mackay; two *d.* *Educ.*: Woodstock, Ont., Coll. Inst. Mem., Canadian Soc. of Authors, and of the Canadian Women's Press Club. *Publications*: volume of poetry "Between the Lights," 1904; winner of "*Globe* Prize," for best Canadian Historical Poem, 1907; poetry and short stories in American, Canadian and British magazines. *Address*: 1034 Denman St., Vancouver.

MACKAY, John Fields; *b.* Toronto, Ont. 7 April, 1868; *s.* Rev. W. A. MacKay, D.D.; *m.* Mary Doyle; two *s.* *Educ.*: Woodstock, Ont., Coll. Inst., and Woodstock Coll.; practical printer and business journalist; member of Canadian Conservation Commission; business manager, "The *Globe*," Toronto. *Recreations*: rowing and fishing. *Address*: 88 Walmer Road, Toronto. *Clubs*: National, Ontario, Toronto.

MACKAY, Kenneth Weir; *b.* St. Thomas, Ont., 4 Aug., 1862; *s.* of William Mackay and Susan Sells; *m.* Alma Scott; one *s.* one *d.* *Educ.*: at St. Thomas. Ont. In addition to other municipal affairs, has been clerk of the County of Elgin since 1882; is editor of the *Municipal World*, established in 1881; was Secretary to the Good Roads Association of Ont., formed in 1894; a member of the Royal Commission on Assessment and Taxation for Ont., apptd. in 1900; Secretary of the Ont. Municipal Association since 1906. *Publications*: pamphlets referring to the history and development of the Co. of Elgin and of several treatises on Municipal affairs, notably Municiapal organization in Ont. *Recreations*: horticulture, boating. *Address*: 19 Margaret St., St. Thomas, Ont. *Club*: St. Thomas.

MACKAY, Hon. Robert; Senator; *b.* Caithness, Scot., 1840; *s.* of Angus and Euphemia MacKay; father identified with agricultural interests in Scot.; *m.* in 1871, Miss Baptist, Three Rivers; four *s.* two *d.* *Educ.*: in Scot. and Phillips Sch., Montreal. Arrived in Canada, 1855; entered business life with his uncles Joseph and Edward Mackay; in 1867, was admitted to partnership; in 1875 his uncles withdrew, and were succeeded by Hugh Mackay, member of legislature, and his two brothers, James and Robert; retired from business, 1893; director Bank of Montreal, City and District Savings Bank, the C. P. Ry., the Montreal L. H. & P. Co., the Dom. Textile Co., the Dom. I. & S. Co., The Shedden Forwarding Co., Ltd., The Montreal Rolling Mills, the Royal Trust Co., the Canada Starch Co., the Port Hood Richmond Railway and Coal Co., Ltd., the Shawinigan Carbide Co., the St. Maurice Valley Railway, the Canada Paper Co., the Royal Victoria Life Ins. Co., Vice-Pres., Bell Telephone Co., the Lake of the Woods Milling Co., the Paton Manufacturing Co., and Pres., the Shawinigan Water and Power Co., and the St. Jerome Power and Electric Light Co.; was Pres. of the Montreal Harbour Board, 1890-1907; was formerly Pres., Montreal Board of Trade, and St. Andrew's Society; is Vice-Pres. of the Mackay Inst., which was founded by the family; Governor of the Montreal General Hospital, the Notre Dame Hospital, and the Western Hospital; unsuccessfully contested Montreal West for the H. of C., 1896 and 1900; Hon. Lieut.-Col. of the 5th R. H.; called to the Senate, 1901; Liberal. *Address*: 681 Sherbrooke St. W., Montreal. *Clubs*: Mount Royal, St. James, Montreal; Rideau, Ottawa.

MACKEEN, Hon. David; Senator, *b.* Mabou, N.S., 20 Sept., 1839; *s.* of late Hon. Wm. MacKeen, N.S.; *m.* (1st) Isabel, *d.* of late Henry Poole of Derby, Eng. (*dec.*); (2nd) 1877, Frances M., *d.* of late Wm. Lawson, Halifax (*dec.*); (3rd) 1888, Janie K., *d.* of late John Crerar, Halifax; was Treas. and Agent of the Caledonia Coal and Ry. Co., also resident Manager of Dominion Coal Co., during the first years of its operations at Cape Breton. Has held several public offices, such as U.S. Consular Agent, Sub. Collector of Customs, Municipal Councillor, and Warden of Cape Breton; elec. to H. of C., 1887 and 1891; resigned, Jan., 1896 called to the Senate, 21 Feb., 1896; Conservative. *Address*: Halifax.

MACKENZIE, Arthur Stanley, B.A., Ph.D., F.R.S.C., Professor of Physics, Dalhousie Coll.; *b.* Pictou, N.S., 26 Sept., 1865; *s.* of George Augustus Mackenzie, barrister, and Catherine Denoon Fogo; *m.* Mary Lewis (*dec.*); *d.* of Franklin Taylor, of Indianapolis, Ind.; one *d.* *Educ.*: Pub.

Schs., of Pictou, New Glasgow and Halifax, N.S.; Dalhousie Univ., Halifax; Johns Hopkins Univ., Baltimore, Md. (grad. 1885, winning gold medal). Teacher in Yarmouth, N.S. Academy, 1886-7; tutor in Mathematics, Dal. Coll., 1887-9; Scholar and Fellow Johns Hopkins Univ., 1889-93. Associate, Prof., and Prof. of Physics, Bryn Mawr Coll., 1891-1905; apptd. Prof. of Physics, Dal. Coll., 1905. *Publications:* "The Laws of Gravitation," 1900. Various papers in scientific journals. *Recreations:* golf, shooting, fishing, skating. *Address:* 58 Robie St., Halifax, N.S.

MACKENZIE, Duncan Stewart; Dep. Min. of Educ. for Alberta; *b.* Holyrood, Bruce Co., Ont., 21 Feb., 1868; *s.* of Donald MacKenzie and Margaret McDiarmid; *m.* Mary Walker, *e. d.* of the late Rev. Hugh Currie; one *s.* *Educ.:* Pub. Sch., High Sch.; Collegiate training obtained in various educational institutions in Ontario. Taught sch. in Ontario for several yrs.; principal of schs. in Strathcona, Alta. for eight yrs.; apptd. Chief Clerk in the Territorial Dept. of Educ.; became Dep. Commr. of Educ., 1905; apptd. Dep. Min. of Educ. upon the formation of the Prov. of Alberta, Sept., 1905. *Address:* 636 Fourth St., Edmonton, Alta.

MACKENZIE, Prof. J. J., B.A., M.B.; *b.* 1865; a Canadian by birth, of Scottish parentage. *Educ.:* Univ. of Toronto; Univ. of Leipzig and Berlin. Sometime Fellow in Biology, Univ. of Toronto; subsequently Bacteriologist to the Ont. Provincial Board of Health; Professor of Pathology and Bacteriology, Univ. of Toronto, since 1900; has written on bacteriological and pathological subjects; member of the American Public Health Association, the Society of American Bacteriologists, and American Association of Pathologists and Bacteriologists; Secretary of the Canadian Institute. *Address:* 41 Chestnut Park Rd., Toronto.

MACKENZIE, Peter Samuel George, B.C.L., K.C.; *b.* Cumberland House, N.W. T., 19 Dec., 1862; *s.* of Roderick and Jane Mackenzie. *Educ.:* High Sch., Montreal; St. Francis Coll., Richmond, McGill Univ., Montreal; called to Quebec bar, 1884; created King's Council, 1903; elec. to Provincial Legislature, 1900, for Richmond Co., and re-elected by accl., g. e., 1904 and 1908; created a member of the Council of Public Instruction of Que., in 1906, and is a trustee of the Corporation of Bishop's Coll. Univ., Lennoxville, Que. *Address:* Melbourne, and Richmond, Que. *Clubs:* Garrison, Quebec; University and Montreal, Montreal.

MACKENZIE, William; Pres. of the Canadian Northern Ry. System; *b.* Kirkfield, Ont., 30 Oct., 1849; *s.* of English parents; *m.* Margaret, *d.* of late John Merry of Kirkfield, Ont.; two *s.* six *d.* *Educ.:* Public Schools and Lindsay Gram. Sch. Began life as school teacher; then kept store, and contracted on the G. T. R.; went west and became a contractor on the Canadian Pacific, doing much work in the Rocky Mountains; his association with Mr. D. D. Mann, his position in the firm of Mackenzie, Mann & Co., Limited, began in 1886; they built, among other important works the Calgary and Edmonton Railway; the Qu'Appelle, Long Lake and Sask. Ry., and the C. P. short line through Maine. Commenced railway building on own and partner's account in 1896, with 100 miles of the Lake Manitoba Railway and Canal Company, which has become the Canadian Northern Railway System, operating in 1909, over 5000 miles between the Atlantic coast and Edmonton; is president of the Canadian Northern Railway proper, and of the Canadian Northern Ontario Ry., the Halifax and Southwestern Railway and the Inverness Railway. The Canadian Northern also controls the Duluth, Rainy Lake, and Winnipeg Railway, and is building to Duluth. Has financed all the Canadian Northern lines in London; obtaining money at the lowest rates ever paid by a pioneer railway in undeveloped agricultural country. President of the Toronto Street Railway, and Radial Railways; President, Winnipeg Electric Railway; controls the Electrical Development Company of Ontario, which has immense works at Niagara Falls; is largely interested in many other Canadian enterprises of first importance. President of the Sao Paulo Tramway Light & Power Co., Chairman of the Rio de Janeiro Tramway Light & Power Co., and President of the Monterey (Mexico) Water Works & Power Co. Director of many other Companies. Visits London twice a year on financial business. *Recreations:* travel, golf and motoring. *Address:* Benvenuto, Toronto, Ont., and Kirkfield, Ont. *Clubs:* Toronto, Albany, National and Hunt, Toronto; Rideau, Ottawa.

MACKENZIE, William; Secretary for Imperial and Foreign Correspondence, Privy Council; *b.* Advie Strathope, Scot., 16 April, 1851; *s.* of John and Elsie Mackenzie; *m.* Bella MacLean, Inverness, Scot.; two *d.* Arrived in Canada, 24 May, 1874; was engaged in journalism for over 30 yrs., being resident correspondent for many English, American, and Canadian papers at Ottawa. Apptd. to his present position 1908. *Address:* 1 McLeod St., Ottawa.

MACKINNON, Hon. Donald Alexander, K.C., LL.B.; Lieut.-Governor of Prince Edward Island; *b.* Uigg, Belfast, P.E.I., 21 Feb., 1863; *s.* of William Mackinnon, and Katherine Nicholson; *m.* 1892, Adelaide Beatrice Louise, *d.* of Charles Owen, of Georgetown; two *s.* one *d.* *Educ.:* Uigg Gram. Sch., Dalhousie Univ., Halifax Law Sch. Taught sch. at Guernsey Cove, 1877-8; principal Springtown High Sch., 1880, and Uigg, 1881. Admitted to Bar of P.E.I. 1887. First el. to Legis. Assem., 1893; re-el. 1897; Attorney-General for Prov., 1899. El. to H. of C. at g. e., 1900. Election declared void and re-el. 1901. Apptd. Lieut.-Governor, 3 Oct., 1904. *Address:* Government House, Charlottetown, P.E.I.

MACKINNON, James; Gen. Mgr. of the Eastern Townships Bank; *b.* Londonderry, Irel., 1850; *s.* of James and Mary Mackinnon *m.* 1876, Emily S. Robinson, of Waterloo, Que.; one *s.* *Educ.:* St. Francis Coll., Richmond, Que. Entered office of Walter Beckett, wholesale hardware merchant, Sherbrooke, at age of nineteen; later with Passumpsic Ry. Co. (now part of the Boston and Maine); joined Eastern Townships Bank at Sherbrooke, Oct., 1871; mgr. of the branch at Cowansville, 1876; transferred to Grand Forks, B.C., 1900; aptd. assist. gen. mgr. at Sherbrooke, 1901; gen. Mgr., 1902. Apptd. Pres. Sherbrooke Bd. of Trade, 1908; a trustee of Bishop's Coll. Univ., Lennoxville; dir. Bishop's Coll. Sch., Lennoxville; trustee and Treas. of King's Hall, Compton; took part in Fenian Raid, 1866, with 54th Regt. (medal). *Address:* Sherbrooke, Que. *Club:* St. George's, Sherbrooke; Montreal, Montreal.

MACKINNON, William Arkell, B.A.; *b.* Brampton, Ont., 28 Feb., 1874; *s.* of Donald James Mackinnon, and Hattie M. Greig; *m.* Bertha H. Sampson, *d.* of the late W. A. Sampson, Toronto; two *d.* *Educ.:* Brampton High Sch., Toronto Univ., Parkdale Coll. Inst., and Osgoode Hall; barrister; Secretary to the Canadian Commission at Paris Exposition, 1900; chief of fruit division, Dept. of Agriculture, 1901-1904; Trade Comm. at Bristol, 1904-1909; now Canadian Trade Commissioner at Birmingham, Eng. *Publications:* Pamphlets on "The Export Apple Trade," and "The Export Pear Trade." *Recreations:* lacrosse, tennis, golf, chess. *Address:* 30 Wheeley's Road, Edgbaston, Birmingham, Eng.

MACKINTOSH, Hon. Charles Herbert; *b.* London, Ont., 1843; *s.* of late Wm. Mackintosh, a native of Wicklow, Ire.; *m.* 1868, Gertrude Cook, of Strathroy, Ont. *Educ.:* Galt Gram. Sch., After leaving school, entered upon journalistic career, and served on staffs of several newspapers in Western Ontario; acquired, 1874, Ottawa *Citizen*, and was its managing editor until 1892; Mayor of Ottawa, 1879-80. First el. to H. of C., 1882; re-el. 1887; apptd. Lieut.-Gov. of the N.W.T., 1893; on retirement in 1898, became gen. mgr. in Canada of the British Am. Mining Corporation with headquarters at Rossland, B.C. In recent years has been acting as broker and financial agent in Victoria. *Publications:* Can Parliamentary Companion, 1877-82; "British America's Golden Gateway to the Orient;" many magazine articles on the development of Western Canada. *Address:* Victoria, B.C. *Club:* Union, Victoria.

MACKLEM, Rev. Thomas Clark Street, M.A., D.D., LL.D., D.C.L., Provost of Trinity Coll., Toronto; Canon and Chancellor of St. Alban's Cathedral, Toronto; *b.* Chippawa, Ont., 25 Nov., 1862; *s.* of Olive Tiffany Macklem and Julia Ann Street; *m.* Mary Elizabeth Raymond. *Educ.:* Up. Can. Coll., Toronto; St. John's Coll., Cambridge, Eng. *Address:* Trinity Coll., Toronto.

MacLACHLAN, Daniel P., M.L.A.; *b.* Chatham, N.B., 26 Jan., 1861; *s.* of Donald and Matilda MacLachlan; *m.* Isabella K. Edgar; four *d.* *Educ.:* Chatham. Alderman for three years, 1903-06; and Mayor of Chatham two years, 1907-1908; elec. to the N.B. Legislature, 3 March, 1908. *Address:* Chatham, N.B.

MACLAREN, Albert; Pres. and Mgr. dir. of the James Maclaren Co., Ltd., of Buckingham, Que.; *b.* Buckingham, 16 July, 1870; *s.* of James Maclaren and Ann Sully; *m.* Lilian Edith Moody, of Terrebonne, Que.; two *s.* three *d.* *Educ.:* Buckingham, and Upper Can. Coll. Acquired thorough knowledge of lumber and pulp business. Company operates extensive saw mills, planing mills, and pulp mills at Buckingham, drawing its supplies from 2,600 square miles of timber limits in Prov. Quebec; a dir. of the North Pacific Lumber Co. *Recreations:* fishing, motoring, hunting, golf. *Address:* "Auchterarder," Buckingham, Que. *Clnbs:* Rideau, Laurentian, Hunt, Golf, Country, Ottawa.

MACLAREN, Alexander; Pres. of the North Pacific Lumber Co.; *b.* Tp. of Masham Ottawa Co., Que., 27 Feb., 1860, *s.* of James Maclaren and Ann Sully; *m.* Annie F. Reid; one *s.* three *d.* *Educ.:* Wakefield, Ottawa, Upper Can. Coll., and Sch. of Prac. Science, Toronto. Joined his father's business in 1884, and is now Vice-Pres. of the James Maclaren Co., Ltd. Pres. of the North Pacific Lumber Co., with mills at Barnet, B.C.; a dir. of the Keewatin Power Co.; Vice-Pres., Nicola Valley Coal Co. Owns and operates at Wakefield, Que., a general store, saw mill and woolen mill. Is a devoted horseman, and for many yrs. engaged in the breeding of American standard bred trotting horses. *Recreations:* golf, hunting, fishing, driving. *Address:* Neralcam Hall, Buckingham, Que. *Clubs:* Rideau Laurentian, Ottawa; Vancouver, Vancouver.

MACLAREN, Alexander Ferguson; *b.* Lanark, Ont., 3 Feb., 1854; *s.* of the late John MacLaren; *m.* 1885, Janet, *d.* of James McLeod, of Woodstock, Ont.; one *s.* *Educ.:* Pub. Sch. Took up the study of cheesemaking at Fullerton's Corners, Perth Co., and eventually became mgr. of the cheese factories in Middlesex and Waterloo Cos. In 1891, commenced exporting cheese as MacLaren Bros., and in 1892 initiated the manufacture of MacLaren's Imperial cheese, which now has a world-wide reputation. In 1900 the A. F. MacLaren Imperial Cheese Co., Ltd., was formed. Was one of the judges at the World's Fair, Chicago, 1895. Sole judge dairy products at Toronto and Ottawa fairs. Pres., Young Conservative Assn. of Stratford, 1894-1895; Pres. Dairymen's Assn. of Western Can., Imperial Plaster Co., Summit Lake Mining Co., Peterson Lake Mining Co., Imperial Veneer Co.; Vice-Pres., Ontario Curling Assn., National Portland Cement Co., International Portland Cement Co.; dir. Equity Fire Insur. Co. Mem. Toronto Industrial Exhibition Assn. El. to H. of C. for North Perth, at g. e., 1896; re-el., g. e., 1900, 1904; unsuccessful 1908. *Recreations:* lawn bowling, curling. *Address:* 86 Chestnut Park Rd., Toronto. *Clubs:* Albany, Granite, Toronto.

MACLAREN, David; Pres. of the Bank of Ottawa; *b.* Tp. of Masham, Ottawa Co., Que., 5 Oct., 1848; *s.* of James Maclaren, and Ann Sully; *m.* Catherine Amelia McGillivray, of Whitby, Ont.; four *s.* two *d.* Associated in lumbering and manufacturing with his father, James Maclaren, one of the pioneer lumbermen of the Ottawa Valley. Became sole mgr., in 1874, of the Gatineau and Ottawa River branches of his father's business. Pres. of the Bank of Ottawa; dir. of the North Pacific Lumber Co.; dir. of the James Maclaren Co., of Buckingham, Que. *Recreations:* riding, motoring, fishing. *Address:* "Strathearn,"

Frank St., Ottawa. *Clubs:* Rideau, Laurentian, Golf, Hunt, Country, Ottawa.

MACLAREN, James Barnet; *b.* Buckingham, Que., 22 Sept., 1866; *s.* of James Maclaren and Ann Sully; *m.* Harriet M. Kenny; two *s.* *Educ.:* Buckingham, and Upper Can. Coll. A lumber manufacturer; dir. of the North Pacific Lumber Co. and the James Maclaren Co. *Recreations:* fishing, hunting, golf. *Address:* 40 Nepean St., Ottawa. *Clubs:* Rideau, Laurentian, Golf, Hunt, Country, Ottawa; Vancouver.

MACLAREN, Hon. John James, B.A., LL.D., B.C.L., D.C.L.; *b.* Lachute, Que., 1 July, 1842; *s.* of John and Janet Maclaren; *m.* (1st) Margaret G. Matthewson; (2nd) Mary E. Matthewson; one *s.* two *d.* *Educ.:* Victoria Univ., McGill Univ.; Advocate, Montreal, 1868 to 1884; barrister, Toronto, 1884 to 1902; since 1902, Justice of the Court of Appeal, Ontario; Prince of Wales Gold Medalist, Victoria Univ. *Publications:* bills, Notes and Cheques, 4th edition, 1909; Banks and Banking, 3rd edition, 1908; Roman Law in English Jurisprudence. *Address:* 80 Roxborough St. East, Toronto.

MACLEAN Hon. Alexander K., LL.B.; Attorney-Gen. of Nova Scotia; *b.* Upper North Sydney, C.B., 18 Oct., 1869; *s.* of Murdock Maclean, of Upper North Sydney; *m.* 1890, Edith Finck, of Lunenburg, N.S. *Educ.:* Dalhousie Univ., Halifax, El. to N.S. Leg. Ass., 1901; resigned to contest seat for the H. of C. at g. e., 1904, and was el.; re-el. 1908; resigned 1909, on appt. as Attorney-Gen. of Nova Scotia. *Address:* Halifax, N.S.

MACLEAN, Major Donald Hector, B.A.; County Solicitor for the Co. of Carleton, Ont.; *b.* King, York Co., Ont., 18 June, 1865; *s.* of Hector Maclean, of Mull Scot., and Sarah Frith, of London, Eng.; *m.* Edith, *d.* E. C. Fry, of Quebec; one *s.* one *d.* *Educ.:* Woodstock Coll., and Toronto Univ. Reeve of Hintonburg, 1897-1900; mem. of Carleton Co. Council, 1900-1903; unsuccessful candidate for Leg. Ass., 1902. Apptd. County Solicitor, 1903; takes an active int. in military affairs; Major G. G. F. G. *Recreations:* rifle shooting, riding. *Address:* 31 Fairmont Av., Ottawa. *Club:* Laurentian, Ottawa.

MACLEAN, Lieut.-Col. John Bayne; *b.* Crieff, Ont., 26 Sept., 1862; *s.* Rev. Andrew Maclean and Catherine Cameron; *m.* Anna P. Slade; one *s.* *Educ.:* Pub. Sch. and Coll. Inst. Journalist and publisher; commenced his newspaper career on the Toronto *World*, 1882; asst. financial ed., Toronto *Mail;* financial ed. *The Empire.* Founded the Canadian *Grocer*, *Hardware*, the *Dry Goods Review*, *Printer and Publisher*, *Canadian Bookman*, and many other influential trade papers; one of the props. of the *Financial Post of Canada;* 27 years in the Militia. *Recreations:* riding, hunting and fishing. *Address:* 13 Queen's Park, Toronto. *Clubs:* St. James, Hunt, Montreal; Toronto and Hunt, Toronto; Constitutional, London Eng.

MACLEAN, William Findlay, B.A., M. P., editor and prop. of The Toronto *World;* *b.* Township of Ancaster, Ont., 10 Aug., 1854; *e. s.* of late John Maclean and Isabella Findlay; *m.* Catherine Gwynne, *d.* of late Richard Lewis of Toronto; one *s.* one *d.* *Educ.:* pub. sch. of Hamilton and Univ. Coll., Toronto. M.P. for South York in H. of C. of Canada since 1892. Founded the Toronto World, 1880, and has been identified with it ever since; contested East York with the late Hon. Alex. Mackenzie (ex-Premier of Can.), 1891, and was defeated by 26 votes. *Recreations:* farming, motoring and hunting. *Address:* Donlands Farm, nr. Toronto. *Clubs:* Hunt, Toronto; Rideau, Ottawa.

MacLEOD, John Robert, M.D., M.L.A.; *b.* Tp. of Zorra, Oxford Co., Ont., 20 Jan., 1872; *s.* of William C. MacLeod and Mary MacKay; *m.* Grace Victoria Bentley of Clifford Mich.; two *s.* *Educ.:* Pub. Sch., Tp. of Zorra, and Woodstock Coll. Inst.; taught pub. Sch., 1890, 1892, in Oxford Co., Ont.; grad. Detroit Coll. of Medicine, 1896; edited the Coll. Magazine, 1895-1896; practiced medicine in Michigan until 1901, when he removed to Alberta; Licentiate College of Physicians and Surgeons, N.W.T. 1906; active practice; elec. to the first Alberta Legislature for Ponoka as a Liberal, 1905. *Recreation:* owns a 320 acre farm which he looks after. *Address:* Edberg, Alta.

MACLEOD, Robert Murdoch; *b.* Baddeck, N.S., 11 Oct., 1861; *s.* of late John Hugh MacLeod of Pictou, N.S., Secretary Agriculture Committee, H. of C., Ottawa, and Annie C., *d.* of late Capt. Geo. Old, Shipbuilder; *m.* Josephine Ayotte. *Educ.:* North Sydney, N.S. High Sch.; news editor, Ottawa *Free Press*, 1882-1887; spent two years travelling in Central and South America; employed for some months on Panama Canal, under De Lesseps; on returning to Ottawa, joined staff of *Daily Citizen* as city editor, and since connected with that paper; Ottawa correspondent, New York *Herald*, from 1890 until 1909; Canadian representative Reuter's Telegram Co., London, Eng., since 1894; Pres., Parliamentary Press Gallery, 1896. *Recreations:* shooting and fishing. *Address:* 228 Charlotte St., Ottawa.

MACMAHON, Hon. Hugh; Judge of the Court of Common Pleas, Ont.; *b.* 6 March, 1836, of Irish parentage; *m.* 1864, Isabel Janet, *e. d.* of late Simon Mackenzie, Belleville, Ont. Called to the bar, 1864; Q.C., 1876; Puisne Judge of Common Pleas Division of High Court of Justice, Ont., 1887; Roman Catholic. *Address:* 185 Beverley Street, Toronto. *Club:* Toronto.

MACMASTER, Donald, K.C., D.C.L., M.P. for Chertsey Div. of Surrey, Eng.; *b.* Williamstown, Ont., 3 Sept., 1846; *o. s.* of Donald Macmaster and Mary Cameron; *m.* (1st) 1880, Janet (*d.* 1883), *d.* of Ronald Sandfield Macdonald, of Lancaster, Ont.; (2nd) 1890, Ella Virginia, *d.* of Isaac Deford of Baltimore, Md.; one *s.* two *d.* *Educ.:* Gram. Sch., Williamstown, Ont.; McGill Univ., Montreal (Elizabeth Torrance gold medal prize essayist and vaeldictorian. 1871; D.C.L., 1894; barrister, Quebec, 1871; Ontario, 1882; cr. Q.C., 1882; Lincoln's Inn, 1906. Served as Crown Pros. in several Canadian *causes celebres*, and as Arbitrator between Newfoundland Govt. and Reid-Newfoundland Ry., 1904-5; Counsel for U. S. Govt. in Gaynor and Green Extradition Inquiry and Appeals thereon to Judicial

Committee of Privy Council; apptd. on Royal Comn. to inquire into matters concerning good govt. of Quebec, 1892; declined seat on Bench, 1893; pres. of Montreal bar, 1904; twice el. pres. of McGill Soc. and pres. St. Andrew's Soc., Montreal. Mem. for Glengarry in Ont. Legis., 1879-82; mem. of the H. of C., 1882-86; Unionist can. for Leigh Div. of Lancashire, 1906, but unsuccessful; el. M.P. for Chertsey Div. of Surrey, Eng., Jan., 1910. *Publications:* The Seal Arbitration at Paris, 1894. *Recreations:* golf, travel. *Addresses:* 1a Cockspur St., London, S.W., England; Mayhurst, Maybury Hill, Woking, Surrey. *Clubs:* Mount Royal, St. James', Montreal; Carlton, Constitutional, Ranelagh, London, Eng.

MACMILLAN, John, B.A., LL.D.; *b.* Campbelltown, Argyleshire, Scot., 26 Dec., 1836; *s.* of Donald Macmillan and Catherine Morrison; *m.* Catherine Kennedy; two *s.* one *d.* *Educ.:* Dalintober Sch., Campbelltown; Normal School, Toronto, and the Univ. of Toronto. Arrived in Canada, July, 1854; taught for a year and a half near Chatham, Co. of Kent. Went to Ottawa on 31 Dec., 1856; taught three and a half years in the pub. schs. of Ottawa; Matriculated at Univ. of Toronto in 1860; grad. June, 1864; taught in Collegiate, Ottawa, from 1864; apptd. Head Master, 1882, and continued as such until 1904. Is now Honorary Vice-Principal at the Coll. Institute. *Address:* 49 Frank St., Ottawa.

MacMURCHY, Archibald, B.A., L.L.D.; *b.* Kyntire, Argyleshire, Scot.; *m.* Marjory Jardine Ramsay of Linlithgow, Scot.; three *s.* three *d.* *Educ.:* Parish Sch., Scot., Rockwood Academy, Up. Can., Normal Sch., Toronto, and Univ. of Toronto. Arrived in Canada in 1840, when a young lad, speaking gaelic only; worked on the farm, and taught in town schools; for more than 28 years was principal and rector of the Collegiate Inst., Toronto. *Publications:* Six books on Arithmetic, two of them as joint author, with the Rev. Bernard Smith, M.A., both of which were authorized for use in Schs. of Up. Can., by the Council of Public Instruction. *Publication:* Handbook on Canadian Literature. *Recreation:* golf. *Address:* 133 East Bloor St., Toronto.

MacMURCHY, Miss Helen, M.B., M.D.; *b.* Toronto, Ont., *d.* of Archibald MacMurchy, and Marjory Jardine Ramsay. *Educ.:* Toronto Coll. Institute, The Woman's Medical Coll., Univ. of Toronto, the Johns Hopkins Univ.; taught for some years; now engaged in the practice of Medicine; apptd. Commissioner of the feeble minded in Ont. *Publications:* occasional papers in Educational Magazines; also in the Lancet (London, Eng.) British Medical Journal, the Practitioner, the Canadian Journal of Medicine and Surgery; editor of the reports to the Ontario Government. *Recreation:* reading and travel. *Address:* 133 Bloor St. E., Toronto. *Clubs:* Toronto Ladies' Club, University Woman's Club, Toronto.

MacMURCHY, Miss Marjory; *b.* Toronto onto, Ont.; *d.* of Archibald MacMurchy, LL.D., and Marjory, *d.* of James Ramsay, of Linlithgow, Scot. *Educ.:* Jarvis Street Coll. Inst., Toronto Univ. Literary editor of the *News*, Toronto; contributes editorials to same publication; Pres. of Canadian Women's Press Club, 1909-10; has had stories and Essays published in Univ. Magazines, *Canadian Magazine*, *Harper's Bazaar*, the *Lamp*, *Short Stories*, the *Bohemian*, and in the Christmas number of the Toronto *Globe* and *Saturday Night*. *Address:* 133 Bloor St. E., Toronto. *Clubs:* Toronto Ladies', Canadian Women's Press.

MACNAB, Brenton Alexander; *b.* Wallace, N.S., 21 Jan., 1865; *s.* of William and Mary Macnab; *m.* Catherine Helen Macquarrie; one *s.* *Educ.:* Com. Schs., Pictou Academy; in journalism for 21 years; previously connected with railways and telegraphs; now managing editor, Montreal *Daily Star*; *Recreations:* fishing. *Address:* 46 Sussex Ave., Montreal. *Clubs:* Canada, Montreal; Albany, Toronto.

MACNAMARA, Thomas James, LL.D., M.A., M.P. (British); *b.* Montreal, 31 Aug., 1861; *s.* of Sergt. Thomas Macnamara of the old 47th "Wolfe's Own," *m.* Rachel, *e. d.* of the late Angus Cameron; three *s.* one *d.* *Educ.:* St. Thomas Sch., Exeter Borough Road, Waining Coll. for teachers; Ely Sch. Teacher, Huddersfield and Bristol; Pres. of Teachers' Union; editor of "*Schoolmaster;*" member of London Sch. Board, 1894-1903; M.P. for North Camberwell, from 1900; Parlty. Secretary to local Government Board, 1907-08; Parly. and Financial Secretary to Admiralty, from 1908. *Recreation:* golf. *Address:* 31 Rollscourt Ave., Herne Hill, London, Eng. *Clubs:* Eighty, National Liberal, London, Eng.

MacNUTT, Thomas, M.P.; *b.* Campbellton, N.B., 3 Aug., 1850; *s.* Charles S. MacNutt, and E. A. Sims; *m.* Margaret McFadyen; three *s.* one *d.* *Educ.:* Ottawa, Ont.; went west 35 years ago on staff of a special survey, and has been farming and contracting ever since; member of the Territorial Leg.; speaker of the first Legis. Assembly of Sask.; re-el.. Aug., 1908, but resigned to contest constituency for H. of C. Pres., Saltcoats District Telephone Co.; Pres., Saltcoats Agricultural Society; served in the North-West Rebellion and during Fenian Raid, 1866. *Recreations:* hunting and shooting. *Address:* Saltcoats, Sask.

MACOUN, William Tyrrell; Horticulturist and Curator of the Arboretum and Botanic Gardens, Central Experimental Farm, Ottawa; *b.* Belleville, Ont., 1869; *s.* of John Macoun and Ellen Terrill; *m.* Elizabeth Macoun; one *s.* two *d.* *Educ.:* Belleville and Ottawa. Has been in the Government service at Central Experimental Farm, Ottawa, for 25 yrs. *Publications:* Annual reports and bulletins on the apple, plum, bush fruits, potato and herbaceous perennials. *Recreation:* gardening. *Address:* Experimental Farm, Ottawa.

MACPHAIL, Prof. Andrew, B.A., M.D., M.R.C.S., Eng.; *b.* Orwell, P.E.I., 24 March, 1864; *s.* of William Macphail and Catherine Smith; *m.* Georgina Burland (*dec.* 1902); one *s.* one *d.* *Educ.:* Prince of Wales' Coll., McGill Univ., London Hospital. Professor of the History of Medicine, McGill Univ.; editor Univ. Magazine, Montreal Medical Journal; Pres. Royal Montreal Golf Club. *Publications:* "Essays on Puritanism,"

"Essays on Politics," "Essays on Fallacy." *Recreations:* golf, farming. *Address:* 216 Peel St., Montreal. *Clubs:* Mount Royal, St. James, University, Pen and Pencil, Montreal; Lotos, New York.

MACPHERSON, Duncan, C.E., D.L.S.; *b.* Bath, Ont., 2 Feb., 1858; *s.* of Peter MacPherson and Clarissa Bristol; *m.* Emma Rose Owen, *d.* of the late Rev. John Wilson of Preston, Eng.; one *s.* and one *d.* *Educ.:* Napanee High Sch. and Royal Military Coll., Kingston, Ont.; from 1880 to 1905, with the C. P. Ry., in various capacities from rodman to divisional Engineer in charge of 1500 miles of line, including bridge building; 1905, to date Asst. Chief Engineer, National Transcontinental Ry. *Recreation:* golf. *Address:* 548 Besserer St., Ottawa. *Clubs:* St. James. Montreal; Rideau, Ottawa.

MACPHERSON, Robert George; Postmaster of Vancouver, B.C.; *b.* Co. of Wellington, Ont., 28 Jan., 1866; *s.* Archibald H. Macpherson of Islay, Scot.; and Janet Hall, of Wellington Co., Ont.; *m.* Susie M. Vanaken, *d.* of J. H. Vanaken, of Coldwater, Mich.; one *s.* two *d.* *Educ.:* Arthur Public Sch. and Galt Coll. Inst.; went West to New Westminster in 1888, and from there to Vancouver, in 1895; conducted a drug business; was elec. to the H. of C., 1903; re-elec. 1904; apptd. Postmaster of Vancouver, 9 Sept., 1908. *Recreations:* reading, walking and shooting. *Address:* Vancouver, B.C. *Clubs:* Vancouver, Terminal City, Vancouver, B.C.

MACPHERSON, William Molson, J.P.; Pres. of the Molson's Bank; *b.* Montreal, 24 Sept., 1848; *e. s.* of the late Sir D. L. Macpherson, K.C.M.G., and Elizabeth Sara Macpherson; *m.* 1878, Marie Stuart, *d.* of the late D. T. Wotherspoon, of Quebec. *Educ.:* Leamington Coll., and Hastings, Eng. Received his business training under A. F. & R. Maxwell, merchants, Liverpool; returned to Canada, 1870, formed the Dom. Steamship Co., and has been mgr. of the Co. at Quebec ever since; became partner in the firm of David Torrance & Co., gen. mgrs. of the line in Can.; apptd. Harbor Commr. at Que., 1896. Dir., the Molson's Bank, and Pres. since June, 1897; dir. Phoenix and British Empire Life and Investment Co., Montreal Trust and Deposit Co.; hon. Lieut.-Col., 8th Royal Rifles of Que.; Vice-Pres., Provincial Rifle Assn.; Governor, Montreal Gen. Hospital. *Address:* 53 Ste. Ursule St., Quebec. *Clubs:* St. James, Mount Royal, Montreal, Montreal Hunt; Garrison, Quebec; Toronto; Restigouche Salmon, Metapedia; Junior Athenaeum, London, Eng.

MACTAVISH, His Hon. Duncan B., M. A. (Queen's), K.C., Senior Judge of the Co. Ct. of Carleton; *b.* Osgoode, Carleton Co., Ont., 21 April, 1850; *s.* of Alexander MacTavish and Mary MacLaren (both Scotch); *m.* Flora Stewart; two *s.* one *d.* *Educ.:* Ottawa Gram. Sch., Metcalfe High Sch., Queen's Univ., Osgoode Hall, Toronto. Studied law under Sir Oliver Mowat; for many yrs. practiced law in Ottawa; City Solicitor, 1882-1897. Represented Dominion on sev. occasions before Judicial Committee; apptd. Judge, 1897. *Address:* 314 Frank St.; Court House, Ottawa. *Clubs:* Rideau, Golf, Country, Ottawa.

MACTIER, Anthony Douglas; Asst. to Vice-Pres. of C. P. Ry. Co.; *b.* Perthshire, Scot., Dec., 1867; *s.* of W. F. MacTier and Miss Bayley; *m.* 1894, Miss Waddell of Montreal. *Educ.:* Edinburgh and Sedbergh, Yorkshire, Eng. Arrived in Can., 1887, and entered service of C. P. R., where he has remained ever since, being apptd. to his present position as asst to Vice-Pres., 1907. Governor of Montreal Gen. Hospital mem. St. Andrew's Soc., Montreal. *Address:* 474 Sherbrooke St. W., Montreal. *Clubs:* Mount Royal, St. James', Forest and Stream, Royal Montreal Golf, Hunt, Racket, Jockey, Montreal.

MACWATT, His Hon. Daniel Fraser; *b.* Nairn, Scot., 9 July, 1853; *s.* of Charles WacWatt, M.A., and Mary Fraser; *m.* Elizabeth Helen, *d.* of the late Lt.-Col. John McWatt, J.P., Barrie, Ont.; two *d.* *Educ.:* Academy Naino, Scot.; arrived in Canada, Jan., 1873; admitted to Ontario bar in 1881; Senior Co. Judge of Lambton Co.; grand Master, A.F. & A.M., 1909-10. *Address:* Sarnia, Ont.

MADDIN, James William, LL.B. (Dalhousie Coll.); M.P.; *b.* Westville, Pictou Co., N.S., 8 Sept., 1874; *s.* of William and Agnes Goode Maddin; *m.* Maud Isabella McDonald; one *s.* three *d.* *Educ.:* Pictou Academy, Dalhousie Coll., Halifax, N.S.; Barrister for 9 yrs. Defeated as a Lib. Con. candidate for N.S. Legislature, 20 June, 1906; elected to H. of C., g. e., 1908. *Address:* Sydney, N.S. *Club:* Sydney.

MAGANN, George Plunkett; railway contractor; *b.* Dublin, Irel., 7 Sept., 1849; *m.* 1891, Mlle. Graziells Leona, *d.* of Joseph Loranger. of Montreal; four *s.* one *d.* *Educ.:* Central Sch., Hamilton, Ont., and by priv. tuition. Arrived Canada, when very young first engaged in the drug business, but later entered into railway contracting, in which capacity is still engaged. Has carried out several important contracts for the Fed. Govt., C. P. Ry. and G. T. Ry. Was one of orig. promoters of water route between Owen Sound and Port Arthur, and is largely interested in the lumber industry. Pres., Haliburton Lumber Co., Magann-Hawke Lumber Co., Magann Air Brake Co. *Address:* 119 Wellington St., W., Toronto. *Clubs:* Royal Canadian Yacht, Country and Hunt, Toronto.

MAGEE, Charles; *b.* Nepean Tp., Co. of Carleton, 16 Aug., 1840; *s.* of the late Charles Magee, and Frances Delamere; *m.* Frances, *d.* of T. M. Blasdell, of Ottawa. *Educ.:* Ottawa. After leaving school, entered mercantile life and later was the senior partner of the firm of Magee and Russell, dry goods merchants; retired in 1871. In 1872, was apptd. administrator and sole trustee of the Sparks Estate; in 1876, together with the late Robert Blackburn and the late James MacLaren, acquired the vacant land in Ottawa, owned by the estate of the late Col. By; one of the organizers of the Bank of Ottawa, and was successively Vice-Pres. and Pres.; was Pres. of the Central Canada Exhibition Assn., and for one year a member of the City Council of Ottawa; Pres. of the Union Trust Co., Toronto; Director of the Northern Crown

Bank, Windsor and Essex Railway, Ha Ha Bay Railway Co., and is a large owner of stock in the Bristol Iron Co.; Conservative in politics and was for two years (1895-1897), Pres. of the Ottawa Association. *Address:* Cor. Cartier and Lisgar Sts., Ottawa. *Clubs:* Rideau and Golf, Ottawa; National and Albany, Toronto.

MAGRATH, Charles Alexander, M.P.; *b.* Augusta, Ont., 22 April, 1860; *s.* of late Bolton Magrath; *m.* (1st) Margaret Muir (one *s.*); (2nd) Mabel Galt (two *d*). A Dom. topographical surveyor. Has lived in the Northwest for 30 yrs. Was a mem. of the N. W. Legis. Ass. for two terms. First el. to H. of C. at g. e., 1908. *Address:* Lethbridge, Alta.

MAHAFFY, Arthur Arnold, K.C., M.L.A.; *b.* Co. of Grey, Ont., 31 Dec., 1861; *s.* of John and Mary Mahaffy; *m.* Alice Rosalie Thomson; two *s.* one *d.* Was a candidate for the Legislature of Ontario from Muskoka, in 1898, but was unsuccessful; elec. at bye-election, 1903; re-elec. in 1905, and 1908 by acclam. *Address:* Bracebridge, Ont.

MAIR, Charles; *b.* Lanark, Ont., 21 Sept., 1838; *s.* of late James Mair, one of the pioneers of the square timber trade in the Ottawa Valley, and Margaret Holmes; *m.* 1869, Elizabeth Louise MacKenney, *niece* of late Sir John Schultz; one *s.* three *d.* *Educ.:* Gram. Sch., Perth, Ont.; Queen's Univ., Kingston. Paymaster for Dom. Govt. to men engaged in opening snow road from Fort Garry to Lake of the Woods, 1868; prisoner in the hands of the insurrectionists, 1869-70; sentenced to death, but escaped, and joined expedition from Portage la Prairie to Fort Garry; one of the founders of the "Canada First" party; acting Quartermaster of the Gov.-Gen's. Body Guard; North West Rebellion of 1885. Can. Govt. Immigration Agt., in charge of the Lethbridge Dist., Southern Alberta, N.W.T., since 1903; an ex-Fellow of the Roy. Soc. of Can. *Publications:* Dreamland and other poems, 1868; Tecumseh, 1886. *Address:* Coutts, Alta.

MAJOR, Charles B., M.P.; *b.* Ste. Scholastique, Co. Two Mountains, 17 March, 1851; *s.* of Joseph B. Major, one of the leaders in the rebellion of 1837-38, and Elmire Lafleur; *m.* 29 Feb., 1876, Cymodocie Trudel; one *s.* four *d.* *Educ.:* local schs. and afterwards studied law; called to the bar of Que., 1877; organizer and dir. of the Northern Colonization Railway; now practices law in Hull, and Papineauville, Co. of Ottawa. Elec. to Quebec Leg., for Ottawa County, 1897 and 1900; elec. by acclam. to H. of C., 23 Dec., 1907; re-elec. 1908; Catholic; Liberal. *Address.* Papineauville, Que.

MALOUIN, Hon. Albert, K.C.; a Judge of the Superior Ct. of the Prov. of Quebec; *b.* Quebec, 13 March, 1857; *s.* of late Jacques Malouin, mem. of the H. of C., 1877-1882, and Marie A. Suzor; *m.* 1907, Marie Louise Lavergne. *Educ.:* Normal Sch., Quebec Seminary, Laval Univ. Admitted to the bar 1882, and commenced the practise of his prof. in Quebec; mem. of the Coun. of the Quebec bar Assn. for several yrs., and for some time Crown Prosecutor for the Dist. of Quebec. El. to H. of C. for Quebec Centre at bye-el., 1898; re-el. at g. e., 1900, and 1904; apptd. Judge, 1904. *Address:* Arthabaska, Que. *Club:* Garrison, Quebec.

MANN, Donald D.; *b.* Acton, Ont., 1853; *Educ.:* Pub. Sch.; *m.* in 1887, J. E. Williams, of Winnipeg; one *s.* Early abandoned farming for lumbering; foreman for a lumber Company, at 21 years of age; went to Winnipeg, in 1879; became a contractor in the C. P. R. in 1880; was continuously on contracts between Whitemouth, east of Winnipeg, and the Selkirk mountains until 1885; the firm of Mackenzie, Mann & Co., Ltd., was established in 1886 and built among other important works, the Calgary and Edmonton Ry., the Qu'Appelle, Long Lake and Sask. Ry., and the C. P. short line through Maine. In 1888 and 1889, Mr. Mann visited Panama, Ecuador, Peru and Chili, it having been proposed that the firm should build railways for the Chilian Government. He declined the proposal. A trip to China resulted in an equally unfavorable judgment; took the initiative in purchasing the charter of the Lake Manitoba Ry. and Canal Company in 1895, from which has grown the Canadian Northern Railway System of upwards of 5000 miles of lines in the provinces of Alberta, Sask., Manitoba, Ont., Que., and N.S.; Vice-Pres. of the Canadian Northern, the Canadian Northern Ontario and the Halifax and Southwestern Railways; his work has chiefly consisted in directing construction in which he has a unique reputation for speed, efficiency and economy; and in convincing public opinion that legislative aid to his railway projects would be to the public benefit; during 1909, secured bond guarantees from the Governments of Alberta and Sask. for branch lines in those provinces, and negotiated an agreement with the Government of British Columbia, for the guaranteeing of the Canadian Northern funds for $35,000 per mile from Yellowhead Pass to Vancouver on which the Government successfully went to the country. Director of many other companies, including Atikokan Iron Company, of which he is President, Moose Mountain Iron Mines, Ltd.; Winnipeg Electric Railway. *Publications:* articles on "The case for a Canadian Navy," and the Tariff relations of Canada and the United States." *Address:* Fallingbrook, Scarboro Heights, Toronto, Ont.

MANUEL, John; capitalist; *b.* Muirhead, Scot., 7 March, 1830; *s.* of James Manuel and Janet Dalziel; unmarried. *Educ.:* Showts Sch., Scot. Arrived, Canada, 1854, and engaged in lumber business with Gilmour & Co., of Ottawa. Acquired an interest in firm but retired therefrom with Col. Allan Gilmour to manage the latter's private interests. An ardent supporter of all athletics sports; erected the finest curling rink in Canada at cost of $25,000, and leased it to Ottawa Curling Club at a nominal rental; pres. of the Long Point Club, Lake Erie; part owner of the Godbout River, one of the finest salmon streams on the North shore of the St. Lawrence. *Recreations:* curling, salmon fishins. *Address:* 36 Vittoria St., Ottawa. *Club:* Rideau, Ottawa.

MARCEAU, Ernest, C.E.; Supt. Engr. of Canals in the Prov. of Que.; *b.* Danville, Que., 26 Dec., 1852; *s.* of Joseph Marceau and Marie O. Morrier; *m.* 1879, M. E., *d.* of the late Dr. F. Z. Tasse, ex-M.P., and dir. of Asylums and Penitentiaries. *Educ.:* Danville Schs., took a commercial course at Napierville, Que., a classical course at Montreal Coll., 1866; studied engineering at Polytechnic Sch., obtaining diploma of C. E., June, 1877. Entered Dept. of Pub. Works, 1877; was asst engr. on Grenville canal Construction; entered Dept. of Rys. and Canals, 1879; apptd. asst. to Suptg. engr. of the Ottawa River Canals; acting suptg. engr. of the canals in Prov. of Que., 1893, and Superintending Engr., 1894. Is principal of Polytechnic Sch., a branch of Laval Univ. and affiliated with the Faculty of Arts. Admitted a mem. of Can. Soc. of Civil Engrs., 1887. Was for some yrs. Can. correspondent of "La Revue Litteraire et Politique," of Bordeaux, France, and "Le Travailleur," of Worchester, Mass., U.S.A. *Publications:* Many articles which have appeared in "La Revue de Montreal." *Address:* Place Viger Hotel, Montreal. *Club:* Engineers', Montreal.

MARCHAND, Gabriel; Proprietor of "*Le Canada Francais;*" *b.* "Beauchamp," nr. St. Johns, Que., 29 Jan., 1859; *s.* of the late Hon. F. G. Marchand, Premier of Quebec, and Marie Herselie Turgeon, of Terrebone; *m.* 1891, Rose Ann Chaput, of Montreal; one *s.* two *d.* *Educ.:* Montreal Coll., St. Hyacinthe Seminary, Laval Univ., Quebec. Studied law in St. Johns; called to the bar, 1885. Founded a French paper "*Le Railiement,*" in Holyoke, Mass., which he conducted for about twenty yrs. Returned to Can. and became sec. to his father, then Speaker of the Quebec Legis. Assembly; apptd. Prothonotary for dist, of Iberville, Que., 1888; proprietor of "*Le Canada Francais,*" since 1897. El. to Quebec Legis. Assembly for St. Johns Co. at g. e., 1908; el. a mem. of the town council, 1908, and apptd. a Sch. Commr. *Publications:* A comedy in French, Le Timide, produced at the Theatre des Nouveautes, Montreal. Was decorated by the French Govt., with the Order of Les Palmes Academiques. *Address:* St. John's. Que. *Club:* St. John's Yacht.

MARCIL, Hon. Charles; Speaker of the H. of C. of Canada; *b.* Ste. Scholastique, Que., 1 July, 1860; *s.* of the late Charles Marcil, advocate, and Maria Doherty; *m.* 1892, Marie Louise Pearson, of Montreal; two *d.* *Educ.:* Com. Schs. and Ottawa Coll. A journalist; connected with Montreal press since 1880. Unsuccessful can. in Gaspe, 1887, for Quebec Leg. Ass.; unsuccessful can. for Assm. in Magdalen Islands, 1897; returned to H. of C. for Bonaventure, at g. e., 1900; re-el. 1904, 1908. El. Dep. Speaker of the H. of C., 16 Jan., 1905; Speaker, 20 Jan., 1909. *Recreation:* walking. *Address:* House of Commons, Ottawa.

MARCILE, Joseph Edmond, M.P.; *b.* Contrecoeur, Que., 22 Oct., 1854; *s.* of Vital Marcile, and Elizabeth Jacques; *m.* (1st) 1880, Malvina Masse (*d.* 1882); (2nd) 1884, Gracia Courville; four *s.* six *d.* *Educ.:* Acton Vale, Que. Academy, Que. A merchant. Has been Mayor of Acton Vale, councillor, and chn. of the Sch. Bd. First el. to H. of C. at bye-el., 14 Dec., 1898; re-el. at g. e., 1900, 1904 and 1908. *Address:* Acton Vale, Que., *Club:* Musical, Acton Vale.

MARKEY Frederick Henry, K.C.; *b.* Bath, Eng., 8 June, 1870; *s.* of J. Markey and Ellen Sheppard of Oldfield Park, Bath; *m.* Laura Howland Toller of Ottawa; one *s.* *Educ.:* Weston, Somersetshire. Arrived in Canada, 18 May, 1887; called to bar of Quebec, July, 1895. *Address:* 975 Dorchester St. W., Montreal. *Clubs:* Rideau, Ottawa; Garrison, Quebec; Engineers, Montreal; Engineers, New York.

MARLER, Waterford Lake; *b.* Nicolet, Que., 13 May, 1844; *s.* George Leonard Marler, who was born at Chateau de Ramezay, Montreal, and Mary Ann Collins, of Woodward; *m.* Eleanor Leo. Sinnott. *Educ:* McGill Coll., Montreal. With the Merchants Bank of Canada for 38 years; was 34 years Manager as St. Johns, Que., and Ottawa, Ont.; retired 1906, under superannuation. *Recreations:* golf, fishing and hunting. *Address:* 495 King Edward Ave., Ottawa. *Clubs:* Rideau, Golf, Ottawa.

MARQUIS, Thomas Guthrie, B.A.; *b.* Chatham, N.B., 4 July, 1864; *s.* of Hugh and Mary McIndoe Marquis. *Educ.:* Chatham High Sch., and Queen's Univ., Kingston, Ont.; English Master, Coll. Inst., Stratford, 1892-1896; Kingston, 1896-1897; Principal Brockville Coll. Inst., 1897 to 1902; was editor of the Ottawa *Free Press* for a short time. *Publications:* "Stories of New France," "Life of Earl Roberts," "Canada's Sons on Kopje and Veldt," "Presidents of United States," "Naval battles of Nineteenth Century," (in collaboration with Admiral Higginson, U.S.N.) *Address:* Brantford, Ont.

MARSH, William Alfred; *b.* Quebec, 16 April, 1848; *s.* of Rev. David Marsh and Marion Exchells; *m.* Annie, *d.* of John Glass of Quebec; five *s.* four *d.* *Educ.:* Quebec High Sch.; Boot and Shoe Manufacturer; Director Quebec Bank; Governor Jeffery Thoms Hospital; 2nd Vice.-Pres. Quebec Board of Trade. *Recreations:* curling, golf. *Address:* 131 Grande Allee, Quebec. *Club:* Garrison, Quebec.

MARSHALL, David, M.P.; *b.* Halton Co., 26 Oct., 1846; *s.* of Alexander Marshall, and Alicia Locker; *m.* 1873, Eleanor Beamer one *d.* *Educ.:* Public Schs. Elec. to H. of C., at bye-elec., 4 Oct., 1906; re-elec. 1908; was Manager of the Aylmer Canning Co., for 20 years, one of the first factories in Canada; Gen. Mgr. of the Canadian Canners for three years, and Pres. of the Aylmer Condensed Milk Co.; Church of England; Conservative. *Address:* Aylmer, Ont.

MARSHALL, Duncan McLean; Minister of Agriculture and Prov. Secretary for Alberta; *b.* Elderslie tp., Bruce Co., Ont., 24 Sept., 1872; *s.* of John Marshall and Margaret McMurchy (both Highland Scotch) *m.* 1899, Tena McIsaac, of Charlottetown, P.E.I.; two *s.* *Educ.:* Walkerton High Sch., and Owen Sound Coll. Inst. Spent most of first 20 yrs. on farm. Owner and operator of large farm in Olds dist., also prop. of Olds *Gazette.* Was one of the best known organizers and workers in the Patron of Industry movement in Ont., 1891-1898;

was prop. of Thornbury *Standard*, Clarksburg *Reflector* and Bracebridge *Gazette*, Ont. Removed to Alberta, 26 June, 1905; and became Mgr. of Edmonton *Daily Bulletin*. Unsuccessful can. for H. of C. in Muskoka, at g. e., 1904; el. to Alberta Leg. Ass. for Olds dist., at g. e., 1909; sworn in Minister of Agric. and Prov. Sec., 1 Nov., 1909; re-el. at bye-el., 23 Nov., 1909. *Address:* Olds, Alta.

MARSHALL, Noel George Lambert; *b.* London, England, 30 Dec., 1852; *s.* of Kenric R. and Charlotte A. Marshall; *m.* Harriette Isabel, *d.* of John Hogg, J.P. (*dec.*); two *s.* *Educ.:* Toronto; arrived in Canada, 1856; entered coal trade with Geo. Chaffey Bros., 1870, remaining in that business ever since; Pres., the Standard Fuel Co., Ltd.; Pres., the Faramel Co.; Pres., Dominion Automobile Co.; Vice-Pres., Imperial Guarantee and Accident Co.; Director of the Sterling Bank of Canada; for many years a member of the Board of Trade of Toronto, and Director of the Canadian National Exhibition; Warden of St. Matthew's Church, Toronto, for over 20 years. *Address:* 623 Sherbourne St., Toronto. *Clubs:* National, Albany, R.C.Y.C., Hunt, Toronto.

MARTIN, Alexander Munro, M.P.; *b.* Fergus, Ont., 21 Dec., 1852; *s.* of John Martin and Jean Munro; *m.* Margaret Broadfoot; five *s.* three *d.* *Educ.:* Mount Forest, Ont. Removed to Mount Forest with his parents, 1856, where he has since resided, and has for a number of yrs. conducted a milling and grain business. Served on High Sch. Bd. and Town Council for a long period. El. to H. of C. for N. Wellington at bye-el., 1907; re-el. at g. e., 1908. *Recreation:* lawn bowling. *Address:* Mount Forest, Ont.

MARTIN, Hon. Archer Evans Stringer; Justice of the Court of Appeal for British Columbia; *b.* Hamilton, Ont., 6 May, 1865; *e. s.* of Edward Martin, Q.C., D.C.L.; *m.* 1889, Emily Mary Read, of Toronto; two *s.* *Educ.:* Trinity Coll. Sch., Port Hope, and Ghent, Belgium. Called to the bar, 1887, and has acted on many occasions for Dom. Govt. in important cases. In 1896, was apptd. counsel for the Dominion Government and representative of the Minister of Justice in Vancouver Island, and in the following year, was made a special commissioner to inquire into and to report upon the affairs of the British Columbia Crown Timber Lands Agency; in 1898, was made a Puisne Judge of the Supreme Court of British Columbia, and in the following year 1899, a deputy Judge in Admiralty for British Columbia; in 1900, special commissioner to settle mining disputes in the Porcupine district, arising out of the British-United States Treaty on the Canada-Alaskan Boundary. In 1902, was apptd. Judge in Admiralty for British Columbia. *Publications:* A Genealogy of Martin of Ballinahinch Castle; The Hudson's Bay Company's Land Tenures; Chart of the Judges of Vancouver Island and British Columbia and Martin's Mining Cases, Vols. I and II. *Recreations:* golf, croquet, gardening. *Address:* Victoria, B.C. *Club:* Union, Victoria.

MARTIN, Chester, M.A.; Prof. of History in the Univ. of Manitoba; *b.* St. John, N.B., 1882. *Educ.:* Univ. of New Brunswick, and Balliol Coll., Oxford. First Rhodes scholar from Prov. of N.B. On the completion of his course at Oxford, where he gained the Brassey scholarship and Beit prize, he entered the service of the Dom. Govt. as asst. editor in the Archives Branch; apptd. to present position, Oct., 1909. *Publications:* A volume on the Selkirk settlement; a frequent contributor to the press. *Recreations:* tennis, boating. *Address:* University of Manitoba, Winnipeg.

MARTIN, Miss Clara Brett, B.C.L., LL.B.; *b.* Toronto; *d.* of the late Abram Martin, and Elisabeth B. Brett. *Educ.:* Privately, and at Trinity Univ. (Grad. 1897). Called to the bar of Ontario, 1897, and has practised in Toronto since. Has been for some yrs. a mem. of the Bd. of Education. *Address:* Continental Life Bldg. Toronto.

MARTIN, Edward Daniel; *b.* Milton, Ont., 30 Sept., 1856; *s.* of Edward Martin and Mary Ann Fleming, *m.* Agnes Jane Perry; two *s.* six *d.* *Educ.:* Milton Pub. Sch. Graduated in pharmacy at the Ont. Coll. of Pharmacy, 1876. In business in Ottawa, 1877-1890. Was Pres., Liberal Assn. of Winnipeg in 1898, and was an unsuccessful candidate for the H. of C. in 1899. Pres. of the Young Men's Christian Assn. of Winnipeg for six yrs. Presdt. of the Manitoba Pharmaceutical Assn. for two yrs. Was respresentative in City Council for two yrs. Mem. of the Council of the Univ. of Manitoba. Mem. of the Council of St. John's Coll. Pres. of the Martin, Bole & Wynne Co., wholesale druggists. Director of the Great West Permanent Loan Co. Pres. of the Winnipeg Board of Trade; delegate to Congress of Chambers of Commerce of the Empire, Sydney, Australia, 1909. *Address:* 223 Colony St., Winnipeg. *Club:* Manitoba.

MARTIN, Joseph, M.P. for East St. Pancras (Brit.); *b.* Milton, Ont., 24 Sept., 1852; *s.* of Edward Martin and Mary Ann Fleming. *Educ.:* Milton Pub. Sch. and Toronto Normal Sch. Commenced work as a telegraph operator; afterwards obtained a first class teacher's certificate, and was apptd. Principal of the Pub. Sch., New Edinburgh, (Ottawa); afterwards entered upon the study of law in Ottawa, but removed to Portage la Prairie, Man., early in 1882, and in August of the same year was called to the bar of Man. In January, 1883, was elec. a mem. of the Manitoba Legis. and sat continuously until 1982, when he retired; from Jan., 1888, until May, 1891, was Attorney-General and Railway Commissioner of the Province; as Attorney-General, introduced and carried through the School Act of 1890, abolishing Separate Schs. in the Province of Man.; was also responsible for the Act doing away with the official use of the French language in the Province; argued the question of the constitutionality of the School Act of 1890 before Judge Killam in the first place, before the full Court of Queen's Bench in Manitoba and before the Supreme Court of Canada; also appeared with Sir Horace Davey and Mr. D'Alton McCarthy before the Judicial Committee of the Privy Council in the same case. For a time he had charge of the

Provincial Department of Education under the new arrangements. In Feb., 1891, temporarily retired from the Manitoba Cabinet to contest Selkirk for the H. of C.; was defeated, and shortly afterwards re-elec. to the Local Legislature; in Nov., 1893, contested Winnipeg for the Dominion House and was elected. During the general elections of 1896, was beaten by Hon. Hugh John Macdonald. Went to B.C. in 1897, and was shortly afterwards elec. as one of the representatives in the local Legislature for the City of Vancouver; became Attorney General and afterwards Premier of the Province; gave up the practice of his profession in Vancouver early in 1909, and went to live in London; contested the election for the H. of C. for the constituency of Stratfort-on-Avon, but was defeated; elec. for East St. Pancras, Jan., 1910. *Address:* 89 Upper Tolie Hill Rd., London. *Clubs:* National Liberal Club, London, Eng.; Vancouver; Terminal City, Vancouver.

MARTIN, Mederic, M.P.; *b.* St. Eustache, Que., 22 Jan., 1869; *s.* of Solomon Martin and Virginie Lafleur; *m.* 1893, Clarinda, *d.* of late F. X. Larochelle. *Educ.:* Coll. of St. Eustache. Cigar manufacturer. An alderman for the City of Montreal. El. to H. of C. for St. Mary's Div., 1906; re-el. at g. e., 1908. *Address:* 919 Logan St., Montreal.

MARTIN, Thomas M., R.C.A.; *b.* London, Eng., 5 Oct., 1838; *s.* of Ed. H. Martin, Treasurer of the Inner Temple until his death, for nearly 30 years, and Susannah Martin; *m.* Emma Nichols of Stratford, Eng.; four *s.* five *d.* *Educ.:* Military Academy, Enfield; arrived in Canada, 1862; charter member of Ontario Society of Artists; member of R.C.A., 1879; elected to the Royal British Colonial Society of Artists, 1909; painted large Canadian Landscape, now in Windsor Castle; also in Government Collection at Ottawa and Toronto. *Recreations:* camping, fishing, outdoor sketching. *Address:* 255 Cottingham St., Toronto.

MARTIN, William Melville, M.L.A.; *b.* Norwich, Co. Oxford, Ont., 23 Aug., 1877; *s.* of William, and Christian Martin; *m.* Sept. 26, 1906, Violette Florence Thomson of Mitchell, Ont.; one *s.* *Educ.:* Clinton Coll. Inst., and Toronto Univ. Entered Toronto Univ., 1894; graduate, 1898; taught classics in Harrison High Sch., 1899-1901; went west in 1903, and settled in Regina and practised law there ever since; offered the Liberal nomination for Western Assinaboia, May, 1906, to succeed Hon. Walter Scott, but declined; re-nominated for new constituency, and elected 1908. *Address:* Regina, Sask.

MARTY, Miss Aletta Elise, M.A. (Queen's); *b.* Mitchell, Perth Co., Ont.; *s.* Frederick Marty and Magdalena Joss (both natives of Switzerland). *Educ.:* Mitchell High Sch., Hamilton Coll. Inst., Queen's Univ., Kingston. Taught in the Pub. and High Schs. of Ont.; has specialized in Modern Languages; in 1902, visited some of the leading secondary schs. in Europe with a view to investigating the teaching of modern languages. Is at present head teacher of Modern languages in the Ottawa Coll. Inst.; in 1905 was el. a mem. of the Council of Queen's Univ., being the second woman el. to this position. *Publications:* "Principles and Practice of Reading," the authorized text-book on reading for the High Schools of Ontario. *Address:* Collegiate Institute, Ottawa.

MASON, Colonel James; Gen. Mgr. and a Dir. of the Home Bank of Canada; *b.* Toronto (of Irish parentage), 25 Aug., 1843; *m.* 1873, Elizabeth, *d.* of James Cooper. *Educ.:* Toronto Model Sch., of which he was head boy. After leaving sch., entered the service of the Toronto Savings Bank, which later became the Home Savings and Loan Co.; mng. dir.; five yrs. ago, Co. evolved into the Home Bank of Can., of which he is gen. mgr. An ardent military man, serving for three years in the Queen's Own Rifles during the Fenian Raid troubles. In 1882, was gazetted Captain in the 10th Royal Grenadiers. During the North-west Rebellion of 1885, commanded a service Company, which was the first Company to cross the Saskatchewan at the Fish Creek fight and then volunteered to rush with his Company the final position held by the rebels in the coulee, all previous attempts to carry it having failed, but General Middleton refused to allow the charge. At Batoche, the seat of the rebellion, was severely wounded. Became Lieut.-Colonel, and in command of Regiment, 1893; one of the Canadian officers sent to the Queen's Diamond Jubilee in 1897, and second in command. Presented to Queen Victoria, and received from her an autograph photogravure in the dress worn by her at the procession on the 22nd of June; retired from the command of the Grenadiers in 1899, and apptd. to the command of the 4th Infantry Brigade, which he has held ever since, and from which has just retired with the rank of full Colonel. Commanded a composite brigade of infantry at the Quebec Tercentenary; general service medal with clasp and many others; one of the founders of the Canadian Military Institute, and for two years its Pres.; an ardent Imperialist, and one of the founders of the Empire Club. *Address:* 43 Queen's Park, Toronto. *Club:* National, Toronto.

MASON, Major James Cooper, D.S.O.; *b.* Toronto, 1875; *e. s.* of Col. James Mason; *m.* 1904, Jean Florence, *d.* of late Alexander MacArthur. *Educ.:* Toronto Coll. Inst. Served as Lieutenant and Captain Royal Canadian Regiment, South Africa, 1899-1900; operations in Orange Free State, including action at Paardeberg (severely wounded); operations in Orange River Colony and Western Transvaal; in Transvaal, East of Pretoria (despatches, brevet of Major, D.S.O., medal and three clasps); a banker. *Recreations:* chiefly rowing, won Junior and Intermediate Championships, Single Sculls, Canada and the United States (North-Western), member of Argonaut eight, champion crew of United States and Canada, 1901; one of Argonaut eight at Henley, 1902. *Address:* 203 Madison Avenue, Toronto. *Club:* National, Toronto.

MASON, John Herbert; *b.* Ivy Bridge, Devon, Eng., 10 July, 1827; *s.* of Thomas and Mary Mason; *m.* Elizabeth Campbell; one *s.* five *d.* *Educ.:* London and Plymoutb

Eng. Arrived in Canada, 1842; founder and for 50 years Manager of the Canada Permanent Loan and Savings Co. (now the Canada Permanent Mortgage Corporation). For many years Pres. of the Ontario Land Mortgage Association; Pres. from its inception of the Land Law Amendment Association, which introduced the Torrens System to Canada; three times Pres. of St. George's Society; Pres. of the St. George's Union of North America in 1883; Pres. of Ridley Coll., St Catharines; Vice-Pres. of Havergal Ladies. Coll.; Commodore and Pres. of the Muskoka Lakes Association, 1902, 1905; now Hon. Pres. *Publications:* Treaties on Land Transfer Reform. *Address:* Armeleigh; 477 Sherbourne St., Toronto; Chief's Island, Lake Joseph, Muskoka.

MATHERS, Hon. T. G.; Chief Justice of Manitoba; *b.* Lucknow, Ont., 1859. Settled in Manitoba in 1883; edited the Manitoba *Liberal* at Portage la Prairie same yr.; took up study of law, 1884; called to the bar of Manitoba, 1890; in partnership with Hon. Joseph Martin, 1895-98; alderman of Winnipeg, 1898-99; apptd. Puisne Judge of the court of King's beach for Manitoba, 1905; promoted Chief Justice, 7 Feb., 1910. *Address:* Winnipeg, Man.

MATHESON, Hon. Arthur James, Provincial Treasurer of Ont.; *b.* 8 Dec., 1845; *s.* of late Col. Hon. Roderick Matheson, Senator, formerly Lieut. and Paymaster, Glengarry Light Infantry, during War of 1812, and Anna, *d.* of Rev. James Russell, minister of Gairloch, Scotland. *Educ.:* Up. Canada Coll.; Trinity Univ., Toronto (M. A.) Barrister-at-law, 1870; Lieut.-Col. 42nd Regt. (V.M.), 1886-98; Lieut.-Col. Reserve of Officers, 1898; Brigadier Commdg. Brigade (V.M.), 1900; elected to Ontario Legislature, 1894, 1898, 1902, 1905, 1908. Treasurer in the Whitney Min., 1905. *Address:* Perth, Ont.; Toronto, Ont. *Clubs:* Toronto; Albany, Toronto.

MATHESON, Most Rev. Samuel Pritchard, D.D.; Archbishop of Rupert's Land and Primate of all Canada; *b.* Manitoba, 20 Sept., 1852; *s.* of John Matheson and Catherine Pritchard; *m.* (1st) 1879, Seraphine Marie Fortin (*d.* [illegible]); two *s.* three *d.*; (2nd) 1906, Alice E. Talbot; two *d.* *Educ.:* St. John's Coll. Sch., St. John's Coll., Winnipeg (B.D., 1882). Ordained Deacon, 1875; Priest, 1876; Master, St. John's Coll. Sch.; Prof. of Exegetical Theology, St. John's Coll.; Canon of St. John's Cathedral; Dean of St. John's Cathedral; Dep. Warden and subsequently Warden and Chancellor of St. John's Coll.; Dep. Headmaster, then Headmaster, St. John's Coll. Sch. Sec. of Prov. Synod of Rupert's Land; Prolocutor of same. Grand Master of Grand Lodge of Manitoba, A.F. and A.M. Prolocutor of General Synod of Canada, 1902; Primate of all Canada, 1909. *Publications:* official addresses. *Recreations:* grouse shooting, horseback riding. *Address:* Archbishop's Palace, Winnipeg.

MATHEWS, Richard G.; *b.* Montreal, 16 July, 1870; *s.* of Richd. Mathews and Sarah Ahern; unmarried. *Educ.:* Montreal Public Schs. For 14 years artist of the Montreal *Star*, also illustrator of books and magazine articles. Removed to London, Eng., 1908, and at present drawing for the *Graphic, Bystander, Cassell's Magazine, The New Magazine, The World and his Wife;* also making portraits in pastel, samples of which are on exhibition at the Stafford galleries, Bond St. *Recreation:* golf. *Address:* 11a Parkhill Road, Haverstock Hill, London, N.W. *Club:* Savage, London.

MATHIESON, John Alexander, K.C., M.L.A.; *b.* Harrington, P.E.I.; 19 May, 1863 *s.* of Ronald Mathieson and Annie Stewart; *m.* Mary Laird, *d.* of Hon. David Laird; one *s.* three *d.* *Educ.:* Harrington Gram. Sch. and Prince of Wales Coll.; teacher; barrister 1894; M.L.A., 1900, 1904 and 1908; became leader of the opposition, 1903; created K.C., 1905. *Address:* Charlottetown, P.E.I.

MATHIEU, Hon. Michael, D.C.L. (Laval); a Puisne Judge of the Superior Court of the Prov. of Quebec for the Dist. of Montreal; *b.* Sorel, Que., 20 Dec., 1838; *s.* of Joseph Mathieu and Edwidge Vandal; *m.* (1st) 1863, Marie Rose Delina Thirza, (*d.* 1870), *d.* of Capt. St. Louis, of Sorel; (2nd) 1871, Marie Amelie Antoinette, *d.* of the late Hon. D. M. Armstrong, M.L.C.; two *s.* two *d.* *Educ.:* St. Hyacinthe Coll. Studied law under George Isidore Barthe. Admitted a Notary Public, 1864; called to the bar, 1865; apptd. Sheriff of Richelieu Dist., 1866; unsuccessful can. for H. of C. at g. e., 1874; returned by accl. to Legis. Ass. of Quebec, 1867, of which body he remained a mem. until 1881, when apptd. a Puisne Judge of the Superior Ct. of the Prov. of Quebec; cr. a Q.C., 1880; apptd. Dean of the Faculty of Law, Laval Univ., 1898. *Publications:* La Revue Legale, and several vols. of annotated reports. *Address:* 13 "The Marlborough," Montreal.

MATHIEU, Mgr. Olivier Elzear, D.D., C.M.G.; Professor and Superior of Quebec Seminary; *b.* Quebec, 24 Dec., 1835; *s.* of Joseph Mathieu and Marguerite Latouche. *Educ.:* Quebec Seminary. Grad. a Doctor of Theology, Laval Univ., 1878. Ordained a priest by Cardinal Taschereau 2 June, 1878, and apptd. Prof. of Philosophy at Laval Univ. Received degs. of Doctor of Philosophy and Doctor of the Academy of Saint Thomas at Univ., Rome, Italy, 1882; returned to Quebec 1883, and continued to act in Chair of Philosophy of Laval Univ.; took M.A., 1889; Prof. of Laval Univ. and Superior of the Seminary, Que., 1899. Nominated Apostolic Prothonotary by His Holiness Pope Leo XIII, 1902; made C.M. G. on visit of Their Royal Highness the Duke and Duchess of York to Can., 1901; cr. a Kt. of the Legion of Honor by the Pres. of the French Republic. *Address:* The Seminary, Quebec.

MATHISON, Robert, M.A.; *b.* Kingston, Ont., 9 Jan., 1843; *s.* of George Mathison, of Berwick, Scot., and Ann Miller, of Londonderry, Ire.; *m.* Isabella Christie, of Hamilton, Ont.; two *s.* two *d.* *Educ.:* Brantford, Ont. Reporter on the staff of the Hamilton *Times*, and subsequently editor and part prop. of the Brantford *Expositor*, a relation that was relinquished upon being apptd. Bursar of the Asylum for the Insane at London, Feb., 1872. In 1878, became Manager of Industries and Bursar of Central Prison, Tronto, which position he held until 1879, when he was apptd. Superintendent and Principal of the Instutition for the Deaf and Dumb, at Belleville, which he held up to the time of his appointment to the Supreme Secretaryship of the Independent Order of Foresters in October, 1906. Gave much attention to the education of the Deaf and Dumb, and his services and merits in that direction were recognized by the National (Gallaudet) College for the Higher Education of the Deaf at Washington, D.C., of which the President of the United States is Patron and Honorary President, which among other honors conferred upon him the degree of M.A. A graduate student of Prof. Alexander Melville Bell (father of Dr. Bell, of telephone fame) author of "Visible Speech;" was Vice-Pres. of the Association of American Instructors of the Deaf, a body composed of Superintendents, Principals and Teachers, about 800 in all—in the Institutions of Canada and the United States. *Recreations:* bowling, travel. *Addresses:* Temple Bldg., Toronto, and Belleville, Ont. *Club:* Royal Canadian Yacht, Toronto.

MATTHEWS, George; Pres. The George Matthews Co., Ltd.; *b.* Birmingham, Eng., 18 Sept., 1834; *s.* of Ezra Matthews and Frances Litchfield Matthews; *m.* 1859, Ann Smithson; six *s.* four *d.* *Educ.:* Birmingham High Sch. Came to Canada, 1851. Farmed in Peterborough County until 1860, when removed to Lindsay, and founded the pork packing business, now "The George Matthews Co., Ltd." with establishments at Hull, Peterborough and Brantford. Has always taken deep interest in Baptist denominational work. *Address:* Lindsay, Ont.

MATTHEWS, Wilmot D.; *b.* Burford, Brant Co., Ont., 22 June, 1850; *s.* of Wheeler D. and Maria Matthews; *m.* to Annie J. Love; two *s.* two *d.* *Educ.:* Model School; commenced business, 1873; Pres. Toronto Board of Trade, 1887; Director, Can. Pac. Ry.; Vice-Pres., Dominion Bank. *Recreations:* golf, fishing. *Address:* 89 St. George St., Toronto. *Clubs:* Toronto, Golf, Hunt, Toronto; Mount Royal, Montreal; Manitoba Winnipeg.

MATTHEWS, Wilmot Love; *b.* Toronto, Ont., 29 Jan., 1879; *s.* of Wilmot D. and Annie D. Matthews; *m.* Annabel Margaret Osler; one *s.* one *d.* *Educ.:* Bishop Ridley Coll. and R. M. C., Kingston, Ont.; Vice Pres., Canada Casting Co.; Director, Canadian Portland Cement Co. *Recreations:* tennis, golf. *Address:* Toronto, and Beachcroft. *Clubs:* Toronto, Toronto Hunt, Golf, Toronto; Manitoba, Winnipeg, Man.

MAVOR, Prof. James; *b.* Stranraer, Scot., 8 Dec., 1854; *s.* of late Rev. James Mavor, M.A., and Mary Ann Taylor Bridie; *m.* Christina, *d* of P. B. Watt, London, 1883; two *s.* one *d.* *Educ.:* High Sch. and Univ. of Glasgow. Assis . editor of Industries, edit. Scottish Art Review; Univ. Extension Lecturer in Political Economy; Prof. of Political Economy, St. Mungo's Coll., Glasgow, 1888; Professor of Political Eeconomy in the Univ. of Toronto since 1892. *Publications:* Wages Theories and Statistics, 1888; Economic Theory, and History Tables and Diagrams, 1890; Scottish Railway Strike, 1891; Currency Reform, 1891; Economic Study, and Public and Private Charity, 1892; report on Labour Colonies in Germany, etc., to H.M. Board of Trade, Parliamentary Paper, 1893; English Railway Rate Question, 1894; edited Handbook of Can., 1897; Notes on Art, 1898; Report on Immigration into Can., from Europe (to Canadian Government), 1900; report on Workmen's Compensation Acts (to Provincial Government of Ont.), 1900; Papers on Municipal Affairs, 1904; report to H.M. Board of Trade on the North-West of Can.; Parliamentary Paper, 1905; Taxation of Corporations in Can.; Rly. Transportation in America, 1909. *Recreations:* chess. *Address:* 8 University Crescent, Toronto. *Clubs:* Toronto; City, New York; Savile, London, Eng.

MAXWELL, Hon. Robert, M.L.A.; *b.* Fredericton, N.B., 17 June, 1858; *s.* of John and Eliza Maxwell; *m.* 1878, Pamilea T. McConnell, of St. John, N.B. *Educ.:* Fredericton Gram. Sch. A contractor and builder. Was an alderman for the city of St. John for seven yrs., dep. mayor for one yr.; warden of the mun. of the city and Co. of St. John, for one yr. Mem. of the St. John Bd. of Sch. Trustees for 12 yrs.; first el. to Legis. at bye-el., 1904; re-el. at g. e., 1908. Selected as Min. without portfolio upon the formation of the Hazen Cabinet, and was sworn in with the other ministers, 24 Mar., and el. Pres. of the Ex. Coun. *Address:* St. John, N.B.

MAY, George Samuel; *b.* Montreal, 18 Jan., 1858; *s.* of George May and Elizabeth N. Cobb; *m.* Mattie Elizabeth Taylor; two *s.* *Educ.:* Pub. Schs. and Coll. Inst., Ottawa; member of the Pub. Sch. Board for 16 yrs.; was chairman for two years; represented Ottawa in the Ontario Legislature for four years. *Address:* 306 Frank St., Ottawa. *Clubs:* National, Toronto; Laurentian, Hunt Ottawa.

MAYNARD, Hormidas, M.P.; *b.* St. Leon, Que., 5 Aug., 1858; *m.* Marie Anna Milot, 31 Jan., 1883. *Educ.:* in the Parish Model School; has been Mayor of the parish of St. Leon and Warden of the County; first elected to the H. of C., 3 March, 1903. re-elected 1904 and 1908. Liberal. *Address:* St. Leon, Que.

McALLISTER, D. H., B.A., M.D., M.P.; *b.* Belleisle, N.B., 18 Jan., 1872; *s.* of Walter and Margaret McAllister; *m.* 12 Jan., 1898, Isabel Reid. *Educ.:* Sussex High Sch.. Pictou Academy, Dalhousie and McGill Univ. Alderman of Sussex, 1902-6; unsuccessful candidate for Prov. Legislature, 1908; elected to the H. of C., 1908; Presbyterian; Liberal. *Address:* Sussex, N.B.

McBRIDE, Hon. Richard, K.C., LL.B., M.L.A., Premier of the Province of British Columbia; *b.* New Westminster, B.C., 15 Dec., 1870; *s.* of Arthur Hill and Mary D'Arcy McBride; *m.* Margaret McGillivray; five *d.* *Educ.:* Public and High Schs., New Westminster, B.C.; elec. to the B.C. Legislature for the riding of Dewdney, 1898; in 1900-1901, Minister of Mines in Dunsmuir Cabinet; Leader of Opposition, in 1902; Premier of British Columbia, since June, 1903; his railway policy received the overwhelming endorsation of the electors of the Province, Dec., 1909. *Address:* Victoria, B.C.

McCALL, Alexander, M.P.; *b.* Charlotteville, 21 Oct., 1841; *s.* of David and Harriet McColl, Scotch; *m.* 3 Oct., 1872, Sarah McInnis; one *s.* and three *d.* Mayor of Simcoe, 1893-94; first el. to H. of C., 1908; Church of England; Conservative. *Address* Simcoe, Ont.

McCART, William John, M.L.A.; *b.* Port Henry, N.Y., 7 Aug., 1872; *s.* of John McCart and Flora Stark; *m.* Wilmina Steel; three *s.* one *d.* *Educ.:* Berwick, Ont., and Brockville Business Coll.; arrived in Canada 1883; elec. to Council of Glengarry and Stormont, 1900; elec. member of Ont. Legislature, 1902; defeated in 1905; re-elec. in 1908; engaged in mercantile business. *Address:* Avonmore, Ont.

McCARTHY, Most Rev. Edward J.; Archbishop of Halifax; *b.* Halifax, N.S., 25 Jan., 1850; *s.* of Patrick McCarthy and Margaret McCarthy. *Educ.:* Halifax and Montreal. Ordained priest, 9 Sept., 1874; consecrated Archbishop of Halifax, 0 Sept., 1906. *Address:* Dresden Row, Halifax.

McCARTHY, Leighton Goldie, K.C.; *b.* Walkerton, Ont., 15 Dec., 1869; *s.* of John Leigh Goldie McCarthy and Francis Olivia Irwin; *m.* Muriel Drummond Campbell. *Educ.:* Barrie Coll. Inst. A barrister. Was pres. of the Osgoode Legal and Literary Soc. El. to H. of C., at bye-elec. 1898; re-el. at g. e., 1900, 1904; retired 1908. *Address:* 45 Walmer Rd., Toronto. *Clubs:* National, Ontario, Toronto; Rideau, Ottawa.

McCARTHY His Hon. Maitland; County Judge of Dufferin Co., Ont.; *b.* Oakley Park, Dublin, Irel., 5 May, 1838; *s.* D'Alton & Zona McCarthy; *m.* Jennie F. Stewart; three *s.* *Educ.:* Barrie Gram. Sch. Came to Can. with parents in 1846; commenced practice of law, March, 1861; Reeve & Mayor of Orangeville for some years. Apptd. Judge, 5 Feb., 1881. *Address:* Orangeville, Ont.

McCARTHY, Maitland Stewart, B.A., M.P.; *b.* Orangeville, Ont., 5 Feb., 1872; *s.* of His Hon. Judge McCarthy, and Jennie Frances Stewart (both Irish); *m.* 1900, Eva Florence, *d.* of late James Watson, of Hamilton, Ont.; two *s.* one *d.* *Educ.:* Trinity Coll. Sch., Port Hope, and Trinity Univ., Toronto. Called to bar of Ontario, 1897. Went West in 1903, and settled in Calgary, Alta., in Sept. of that yr. El. at g. e., 1904 to H. of C. for Calgary; re-el. at g. e., 1908. A mem. of the corporation of Trinity Coll. Sch. and of the Western Canada Coll., Calgary; chn. of the Amateur Ath. Assn. for Alberta. Was offered the Cons. leadership in Alberta, March, 1909, but declined. *Recreations:* all outdoor sports. Church of England; Conservative. *Address:* Calgary, Alta. *Clubs:* Ranchmen's, Calgary; Rideau, Ottawa.

McCLARE, Charles Herbert; architect; *b.* Sackville, N.S., 15 Feb., 1861; *s.* of Josiah McClare, and Annie S. McKay; *m.* Ella Gertrude Johnstone, of Halifax, N.S.; one *s.* three *d.* *Educ.:* Nova Scotia Pub. Schs., Lawrence Scientific Sch., Harvard Univ., Cambridge, Mass. Removed to Massachusetts, 1884. Has been a practising architect since 1888, having erected many public and private buildings from South Carolina to Nova Scotia; Fellow of the Boston Soc. of Architects; mem. of the American Inst. of Architects. El. sec. of the Canadian Club of Boston, 1909. *Recreation:* farming. *Addresses:* 211 Pleasant St., Arlington, Mass.: Lakelands, Hants, Mt. Uniacke, N.S. (summer); 649 Massachusetts Ave., Cambridge, Mass. (bus.)

McCLELAN, Hon. Abner Reid, D.C.L., LL.D.; *b.* Hopewell, N.B., 1831; *y. s.* of late Peter McClelan, a Justice of the Court of Common Pleas; *g. s.* of Peter McClelan, who, with Miss Wilson, whom he subsequently married, came to N.S. from Londonderry, Ireland; *m.* Anna B., *d.* of late W. J. Reid, Collector of Customs at port of Harvey. *Educ.:* Mount Allison, Sackville; Univ. of New Brunswick. Elected to Provincial Parliament of N.B., 1854, and each subsequent election till 1867, when he resigned seat and portfolio of Chief of Public Works in the Government to enter Senate of Canada. Lieut.-Gov. of New Brunswick, 1896-1902; a governor of Mt. Allison Acad. *Address:* Riverside, Albert County, N.B. *Club:* Union, St. John.

McCLUNG, Mrs. Nellie Letitia Mooney; *b.* Chatsworth, Ont., 20 Oct., 1873; *d.* of John Mooney and Letitia McCurdy of Dundee, Scotland; *m.* 25 Aug., 1896, Robert Wesley McClung, Manitou, Man.; three *s.* one *d.* *Educ.:* Northfields Sch., Man., and Collegiate Inst., Winnipeg; wrote short stories for newspapers; editorials for Sunday School periodicals; taught school for five years previous to her marriage. *Publications:* "Sowing Seeds in Danny," published in Canada, U.S. and England. *Address:* Manitou, Man.

McCOIG, Archibald Blake, M.P.; *b.* Tilbury East, Kent Co., 8 April, 1874; *s.* of David McCoig and Christie Martin, both Scotch; *m.* 25 Jan., 1898, Addie M. Demarse, Chatham, Ont.; one *s.* *Educ.:* Tilbury East, and Chatham Sch.; was alderman, Chatham, 1900-4; elected to Ont. Legislature, 1905; first el. to H. of C., 1908; Presbyterian; Liberal. *Address:* Chatham, Ont.

McCOLL, John B., M.P.; *b.* Tp. Murray, Co. Northumberland, Ont., 26 Jan., 1861; *s.* of John H. McColl, and Martha McColl; unmarried. *Educ.:* Pub. Sch., Tp. Murray, and High Sch., Trenton, Ont.; member of Town Council, Cobourg, one year; Deputy Reeve, one year; commissioner of town trust, one year; Secretary, Separate Sch. Board, six years; unsuccessful candidate for Northumberland W., 1896; elected to H. of C., 1900; re-el. 1904 and 1908; Catholic; Liberal. *Address:* Cobourg, Ont.

McCONNELL, John Bradford, M.D., C.M., D.C.L.; *b.* Chatham, Argenteuil Co., 28 Aug., 1851; *m.* 1895, Theodora Lovell, *d.* of Robert Miller; two *s.* four *d.* *Educ.:* McGill Univ. (M.D., 1873), Univ. of Bishop's Coll. (D.C.L., 1905). Apptd. to chair of Botany in Faculty of Medicine, Univ. of Bishop's Coll.; Chairs of Materia Medica, Histology, Pathology, and Principles and Practice of Medicine; for many yrs. Vice-Dean of the Faculty; now senior physician Montreal Western Hospital, and for many yrs. has been Medical Examiner for the Aetna Life Ins. Co. and Mutual Life Ins. Co. of Can. Was Lieut. in the 11th Batt., "Argenteuil Rangers," and Surgeon to

Prince of Wales Fusiliers, Montreal for eight yrs. *Address:* 234 Bishop St., Montreal.

McCONNELL, Richard George, B.A.; Geologist; *b.* Chatham, Que., 26 March, 1857; *s.* of Andrew McConnell, and Martha Bradford; *m.* Jeannie T. Botterell; one *s.* one *d.* *Educ.:* Wanless Academy and McGill Univ. For many years on staff of Geological Survey; principally employed in exploring the Western and Northern parts of Canada, and reporting on their resources; *Publications:* reports. *Recreations:* golf, curling. *Address:* Edgehill, Rockcliffe, Ottawa. *Clubs:* Rideau and Golf, Ottawa.

McCORKILL, John Charles, B.C.L.; Major, R.L., Canadian Militia; *b.* Farnham, Que., 31 Aug., 1854; *s.* Robert McCorkill and Margaret Meighen; *m.* Apphia Mary, *y. d.* of Hon. E. Leonard, of London, Ont. *Educ.:* McGill Model, and Normal Sch., and McGill Univ. Taught as assistant to Principal, and as Principal under Protestant Sch. Commissioners, Montreal; admitted to bar, Jan., 1878; practiced in Montreal and district of Bedford; unsuccessfully contested Co. of Missisquoi as a Liberal in Provincial General Elec., 1886; elec. in 1888, and 1897; apptd. to Legislative Council for Bedford District, in 1898; resigned 1903, to accept office in the Government of the Province as Treasurer, and to contest the vacant seat of Brome; was elec. and re-elec. by acclam., 1904; resigned in 1906; apptd. Puisne Judge of Superior Court of Que., in the District and City of Quebec. In the session of 1906, prepared the bills, revising the taxation laws (banks, corporations, successions, etc.), whereby the revenue was so improved that there was a surplus of one half million without disposing of any timber lands. Held a commission in the 5th Royal Scots (now Royal Highlanders), April, 1879; in 1887, retired with rank of Major. *Address:* Braeside, 189 Grande Allee, Quebec, and Fairfield, Cowansville, Que. (summer). *Clubs:* St. James, Montreal; Garrison, Que.

McCOWAN, Alexander, M.L.A.; *b.* Scarboro Tp., York Co., 27 May, 1853; *s.* of James W. McCowan and Martha Weir of Lancashire, England; *m.* (1st) Georgianna Ashbridge; (2nd) Mary Marshall; one *s.* one *d.* *Educ.:* No. 8 Sch., Scarboro Tp. Twenty-five years Secretary-Treas. of Scarboro Agric. Society; was four years Township Councillor; Secy.-Treas., Toronto Milk Producers' Assn. for eight years; elec. to Ont. Legis., 1905 and re-el., 1908 for East York, being the first Conservative elected to the Legislature from that riding. *Recreations:* bowling and curling. *Address:* 20 Lyall Ave., Toronto, Ont.

McCRANEY, George Ewan, B.A., LL.B. M.P.; *b.* Bothwell, Ont., 23 July, 1868; *s.* of the late Daniel McCraney; *m.* 1906, Elizabeth, *d.* of the late David Cowan, Toronto. *Educ.:* Up. Can. Coll. and Toronto Univ.; called to the Ontario bar in 1895; practiced at Milton, Ont., and removed to Sask., 1902; elected to the H. of C. at bye-election, 6 Feb., 1906; re-elec., 1908; Liberal; Presbyterian. *Address:* Rosthern, Sask.

McCREADY, John Elias Blakeney; journalist; *b.* Penobsquis (near Sussex), N.B., 4 April, 1839; *s.* of Charles McCready and Jerusha Blakeney; *m.* (1st) Alice M. Freeze (*dec.* 1883); (2nd) Louise, *d.* of Rev. Dr. James Bennett, St. John; two *s.* three *d.* *Educ.:* Superior Sch., Penobsquis, and Ottawa Business Coll.; early life spent on farm; entered newspaper work, 1867; unsuccessful candidate for H. of C., 1874; Clerkship, H. of C., 1867-1872; Pres., Press Gallery, Dominion Parliament, 1882; served two terms as Councillor for Cardwell in Municipal Council of Kings Co., N.B.; was official assignee for Kings Co., under Insolvent Act., 1875-9; member of Senate of Univ. of N.B., 1886-1893; editor Moncton *Transcript*, 1882-3; St. John *Telegraph*, 1883-1893, and Charlottetown *Guardian*, 1896 to date; Ottawa Correspondent, Toronto Globe, 1881-1882. *Address:* Charlottetown, P.E.I.

McCURDY, John Alexander Douglas, M.E.; *b.* Baddeck, N.S., 2 Aug., 1886; *s.* of Arthur W. McCurdy and Lucy Obrine. *Educ.:* Baddeck Academy and Toronto Univ.; a student of aviation; Inventor of the "Silver Dart," and "Baddeck No. 2," both of which made several successful flights in 1909. *Address:* Baddeck, N.S.

McCURRY, His Hon. Patrick; Judge of the dist. of Parry Sound; *b.* Belfast, Irel., 1838; *m.* 1864, Emily, *d.* of Hon. M. H. Foley, of Guelph, Ont.; two *s.* three *d.* *Educ.:* St. Michael's Coll., Toronto. Arrived Canada at an early age. Estbd. a law practice in Guelph, 1861, and apptd. Stipendiary Magistrate, Judge of the Div. Ct., and Registrar of dist. of Parry Sound the same yr.; apptd. to his present position 1898. Was chief promoter of Parry Sound Colonization Ry. from Parry Sound to main line of G. T. R., at Scotia, and was Pres. of Co. until its amalgamation with the Can. Atlantic Ry. *Address:* Parry Sound, Ont.

McDONALD, His Hon. Herbert Stone, M.A., D.C.L., Judge of the Co. Court of the United Counties of Leeds and Grenville. Ont.; *b.* Gananoque, Ont., 23 Feb., 1842; *s.* of Hon. John McDonald, Gananoque, and Henrietta Maria McDonald; *m.* Emma Matilda (*deceased*), *d.* of David Jones, Registrar of the Co. of Leeds; one *d.* Called to the bar, 1863; elec. to the Legislative Assembly for Ont., March, 1871, for South Leeds; apptd. Junior Judge of the Co. Court in Oct., 1873, and Senior Judge, 1878. *Address:* Woodlawn, Brockville, Ont.

McDONALD, Hon. James, K.C., P.C.; formerly Chief Justice of the Supreme Ct. of Nova Scotia; Pres. Judge of the Vice Admiralty Ct.; *b.* East River, Pictou Co., N.S., 1 July, 1828; *m.* 1856, Jane, *d.* of late William Mortimer. *Educ.:* New Glasgow. Called to bar of N.S., 1851; cr. Q.C., 1857. Mem. of N.S. Leg. Ass., 1859-67; Chief Ry. Commr. for N.S., 1863-64; Financial Sec. in Tupper Govt. First el. to H. of C., 1872; apptd. Min, of Justice in 2nd Macdonald Min., Oct., 1878; Chief Justice of N.S., 1881; resigned, 1904, but retained Vice Admiralty Judgeship. *Address:* 327 Quinpool Road, Halifax, N.S. *Club:* Halifax.

McDONALD, Hon. William; Senator; *b.* Inverness Co., N.S., 1837; *s.* of Allan and Mary McDonald of Invernessshire, Scot.; *m.* Catherine Macdonald; three *s.* three *d.* *Educ.:* St. Francois Xavier Coll., Antigonish, N.S.; school teacher for six years; in commercial business for 14 years, and public life, 37 years; has held several Municipal, Provincial and Federal offices; elec. to the H. of C. for Cape Breton, 1872, 1874, 1878, and 1882; was for several years Chairman of the Committee on Immigration and Colonization; called to the Senate, 1884. *Address:* Glace Bay, C.B. *Clubs:* R.C.B.Y.C., Sydney, C.B.

McDOUGALD, John; Commissioner of Customs; *b.* Blue Mountain, Pictou Co., N.S., 13 March, 1848; *s.* of Dougald McDougald, and Elizabeth Fraser; *m.* to Margaret Jane McLeod of Westville, N.S.; two *s.* *Educ.:* Gram. Sch., New Glasgow, N.S.; merchant; Justice of the Peace and Co. Councillor for Pictou Co.; mem. of Parliament for Pictou from 1881 to 1896; apptd Commr. of Customs, 1 May, 1896. *Address:* 149 Daly Av., Ottawa, Ont.

McEACHRAN, Duncan McNab, LL.D., D.V.S., F.R.C.V.S., Hon. Veterinary adviser to the Government of Canada; *b.* Campbelltown, Argyleshire, Oct. 1841; *o. s.* of David McEachran and Jean Blackney; *m.* 1868, Esther, 3rd *d.* of T. Plaskett of St. Croix, West Indies; one *d.* *Educ.:* Edinburgh. Lectured for two yrs., 1862-3, at Toronto on Veterinary Science, under the auspices of the Board of Agriculture of Ontario; removed to Montreal, where he inaugurated the Montreal Veterinary College in connection with the Medical College of McGill Univ., 1866, which, 1890, became the Faculty of Comparative Medicine and Veterinary Science, of which he became Dean, and held that position till his retirement, 1903; organised the Cattle Quarantine System of Canada, which he has conducted so successfully that contagious diseases of animals are practically unknown in Canada, 1876; after twenty-six years he resigned the active duties of the position and became Hon. Veterinary Adviser to the Government; has repeatedly represented Canada at scientific congresses, at Baden Baden, at London (Tuberculosis Congress, 1901), and in all international discussions and agreements bearing on animal diseases; President of the New Walrond Cattle Ranch in the Rocky Mountain region of Canada. Retired from prof. work in 1909, to his model stock farm at Ormstown, where he imports and breeds Clydesdales. *Publications:* Handbook on the Diseases of Horses, 1866; Notes of a Trip to Bow River, 1881; notes of a visit to the Scientific Institutions of France, Germany, and Denmark, 1898; numerous scientific bulletins on Contagious Diseases for the information of agriculturists and stock-breeders, issued by the Government. *Recreations:* two or three months annually in the Rocky Mountains. *Address:* Ormsby Grange, Ormstown, Que.; 142 Notre Dame St., Montreal. *Clubs:* St. James, Forest and Stream, Montreal Hunt; Manitoba, Winnipeg.

McEVAY, Most Rev. Fergus Patrick; Archbishop of Toronto; *b.* Lindsay, Ont., 8 Dec., 1852; *s.* of Michael McEvay, and Mary Lehane *Educ.:* St. Michael's Coll., Toronto; Grand Seminary, Montreal. Ordained priest, 1882, with charge at Fenelon Falls; later Rector of St. Peter's Cathedral, Peterborough; Rector and Vicar General of Hamilton, 1889; admin. of diocese 1894-5; later was apptd. Bishop of London; Archbishop of Toronto, 1908. *Address:* 510 Sherbourne St., Toronto.

McEVOY, Bernard; journalist and author; *b.* Birmingham, Eng., 7 Feb., 1842; *s.* of Henry McEvoy, Birmingham manufacturer, and Naomi McEvoy, *d.* of T. Lindley Greaves; *m.* Susan Isabelle, *d.* of W. J. Halmden, Plymouth, Eng.; seven *s.* *Educ.:* Birmingham, Eng. Trained as mechanical engineer, but gravitated to newspaper work; editorial position on Toronto *Mail and Empire*, ten years; publishers' literary manager, about four years; for the last three years on the staff of the Vancouver *Daily Province;* in 1899, went to the United States to make a report on institutions of technical education for the Ontario Government; in England, 1905-6; correspondent of various Canadian newspapers. *Publications:* Away from Newspaperdom and other poems, 1898; From the Great Lakes to the Wide West, 1902. *Recreations:* landscape painting. *Address:* 12th Ave., W., Vancouver, B.C.

McEVOY, James, B.A.Sc. (McGill); *b.* Carleton Co., Ont., 7 Feb., 1862; *s.* of James McEvoy, and Margaret Macnamara (both of Ireland); *m.* Florence A. Ray, of Ottawa; one *d.* *Educ.:* Ottawa Coll., McGill Univ. (grad. 1883). Joined Geological Survey staff in 1885; served eight yrs. as asst. to the late Dr. George M. Dawson; afterward did geological explorations till 1901, when became geologist for the Crow's Nest Pass Coal Co., Ltd.; remained with Co. for seven yrs. as geologist, land commr., and chief engr.; became certificated colliery mgr. for B.C. and Alberta, 1902; became British Columbia land surveyor (B.C.L.S.,) 1904; for the last two seasons has been examining, testing, and reporting on coal properties in Alberta for the German Development Co., Ltd., and other work as consulting mining engr. Mem. Canadian Mining Inst. *Publications:* Report on Yellow Head Pass Route, and other reports of Geological Survey of Canada. *Recreation:* curling. *Addresses:* 611 Jarvis St.; 26 Manning Arcade, King St., Toronto (bus.). *Club:* Canadian Alpine.

McFEE, Alexander; grain merchant; *b.* St. Chrysostome, Que.; *s.* Col. McFee, and Catherine McNaughton. *Educ.:* Beauharnois, Que., pub. schs., Coll. of St. Timothee; Commercial Coll., Montreal. In business with his father, a gen. merchant at Beauharnois. Removed to Montreal, 1872, and estb. a grain business. Was pres., Montreal Bd. of Trade, and was present at coronation of King Edward VII, and opening new bldg. of Chamber of Commerce, New York, in 1902. Was pres. Corn Exchange Assn. for two yrs. and representative of that assn. on Bd. of Harbor Commrs. for four yrs. Pres., Montreal Technical Inst.; mem. St. Andrew's Soc., and Caledonian Soc. of Montreal. *Recreations:* curling, golf. *Address:* 159 Stanley St., Montreal. *Clubs:* Canada, Thistle Curling, Outremont Golf, Montreal.

McGIBBON, Douglas Lorne; Pres. Canadian Consolidated Rubber Co., Ltd.; Vice-Pres. and Man. Dir., The Canadian Rubber Co. of Montreal, Ltd.; Pres., LaRose Mining

Co.; *b.* Montreal, 24 Nov., 1870; *s.* of the late Major Alexander A. McGibbon and Harriet Davidson; *m.* 1897, Ethelwyn Waldock, of Woodstock, Ont. *Educ.:* Montreal High Sch. Entered fire ins. business at age of thirteen; removed to U.S. three yrs. later and engaged in the coal business; returned to Can., 1893, and settled in Medicine Hat, N.W.T.; organized the Medicine Hat Trading Co., 1895, becoming its first man. dir. Ayptd. Purchasing Agent of the Laurentide Pulp and Paper Co., of Grande Mere, Que., 1897, promoted gen. man., 1898. Apptd. gen. man., The Canadian Rubber Co., of Montreal, Ltd., 1902; mem. Montreal Bd. of Trade; Vice-Pres., Canadian Manufacturers' Assn., and dir. in many Co's.; mem. Caledonian Soc.; life mem., St. Andrew's Soc.; mem. M.A.A.A. *Address:* 20 Ontario Ave., Montreal. *Clubs:* St. James, Canada, Royal Montreal Golf, Racquet, Back River Polo, Montreal.

McGILL, Anthony, B.A., B.Sc. (Toronto), F.R.S.C., Chief Analyst, Dept. of Inland Revenue, Ottawa; *b.* Rothesay, Buteshire, Scot., 18 April, 1847; *s.* of Rev. A. McGill, M.A., and Catherine Ross; *m.* Mary Jane, *d.* of Capt. Stephen Davidson, and *g. d.* of Rev. J. Davidson, Rector, Barnard Castle; one *s.* three *d.* Came to Canada, 1860, and educ. at Hamilton Gram. Sch., Toronto Normal Sch., and University Coll. Taught in pub. schs., 1866-1870; fellow and tutor in chemistry at Univ. Coll., Toronto, 1876-1878; Coll. Inst., Ottawa, 1882-1886; Asst. Analyst, Dept. of Inland Revenue, Ottawa, 1886-1907; Chief Analyst, 27 July, 1907. *Publications:* Contributions to Proceedings, Royal and other Societies; Paper in Journal Soc. Chem. *Recreations:* chess, music, photography. *Address:* 352 Maclaren St., Ottawa.

McGIVERN, Harold Buchanan, M.P., Barrister-at-Law; *b.* Hamilton, Ont., 4 Aug., 1870; *s.* of Lieut.-Col. Wm. McGivern, ex-M.P., and Emma Counsell; *m.* Alice Maude, *d.* of Hon. C. H. Mackintosh; one *s.* *Educ.:* Upper Canada Coll., and Osgoode Hall; el. to H. of C. for Ottawa, at g. e., 1908; *Recreations:* nearly all sports, especially cricket and football. *Address:* 361 Daly Ave., Ottawa. *Clubs:* Rideau, Laurentian, Golf and Country, Ottawa; M.C.C., London, Eng.

McGOUN, Archibald, M.A., B.C.L., K.C.; Professor of Civil Law, McGill Univ., Montreal, since 1888; *b.* Montreal, 15 Dec., 1853; *s.* of Archibald McGoun, a native of Douglas, Lanarkshire, Scot., and Jane Mackay, *d.* of Samuel Mackay of Ayr, Scot.; *m.* 1887, Abigail, *d.* of Thomas Mackay of Toronto; one *s.* one *d.* *Educ.:* McGill Univ. Montreal; L'Ecole de Droit, Paris, France. Twice President Univ. Literary Society, 1884-85; one of the founders of the Imperial Federation League in Canada, 1885; delegate to Imperial Federation Council in London, 1886; Vice-Pres. of League (now the British Empire League) in Canada; Fellow R.C.I.; Chairman of meeting, Montreal, to promote Free Trade within the Empire, 1907; President Graduates' Soc., McGill Univ., 1887; course of lectures on Constitutional Law, 1897; now lectures on Corporations and on Agency and Partnership; Q.C. 1899; attorney as practising advocate for various commercial corporations; Pres. Political Econ. Club, Montreal, 1908-9. *Publications:* Federation of the Empire, Address as President of University Literary Society, 1884; Economic Study, Commercial Union with the United States, with a word on Imperial Reciprocity, 1886; A Federal Parliament of the British People, 1890; article on Imperial Reciprocity in Canadian Encyclopaedia; articles in The Commonwealth, Ottawa, 1900-1; A Revenue Tariff within the Empire, 1905. *Address:* Standard Building, 157 St. James St., Montreal.

McGREGOR, Hon. James Drummond; senator; *b.* New Glasgow, N.S., 1 Sept. 1838; *s.* of Roderick McGregor and Janet Chisholm; *g. s.* of Rev. James McGregor, D.D., who came to Pictou in 1786, and was the pioneer minister of Eastern N.S.; *m.* (1st) 1867, Elizabeth McColl, Guysboro, (*dec.* 1891); (2nd) 1894, Roberta Ridley, Peterboro, Ont. A merchant and ship-owner; twice elec. to N.S. legislature and once defeated; unsuccessful candidate for H. of C., 1900; was twice Mayor of New Glasgow; is a director of the Nova Scotia Steel and Coal Co., Ltd.; apptd. to the Senate, 24 April, 1903; Presbyterian; Liberal. *Address:* New Glasgow, N.S.

McGUIGAN, F. H.; Pres. of the F. H. McGuigan Construction Co., Toronto; *b.* Cleveland, O., 1850. Entered Ry. service, 1863 as water boy Erie & Pittsburg div. Pennsylvania Rd., since which he has held consecutively to 1874, various minor positions same rd.; roadmaster same rd., 1874-80; foreman construction train St. Louis & Omaha div. Wabash Rd., 1880; division roadmaster same rd., 1880-65; gen. roadmaster lines west of Mississippi River, 1885-88; supt. Western div. same rd. at Kansas, Mo., 1888-95; gen. supt., G.T. Ry., 1896-02; manager, 1902-05; fourth vice-pres., 1905-08; organized the F. H. McGuigan Construction Co., and has contract for building lines in Western Ontario for Prov. Hydro-Electric Comn. *Address:* Continental Life Bldg., Toronto.

McGUIRE, George Albert, D.D.S., M.L.A.; *b.* Mount Forest, Ont., 7 April, 1871; *s.* of George McGuire and Henrietta Gardiner; *m.* Jennie McLean; two *d.* *Educ.:* Mt. Forest, and Univ. of Maryland, Baltimore. Removed to B.C. in 1892, where he has since practised dentistry. El. to B.C. Leg., Feb., 1907. *Recreations:* tennis, shooting, horseback riding. *Address:* 2031 Westminster Av., Vancouver, B.C. *Clubs:* Western, Vancouver; Union, Victoria.

McGUIRE, Hon. Thomas Horace, LL.D.; *b.* Kingston, Ont., 21 April, 1849; *s.* of James B. McGuire, and Mary Brady (both Irish); *m.* 1877, Mary Victory, *e. d.* of John Cunningham, Kingston. *Educ.:* Kingston Coll. Inst., and Queen's Univ. Called to bar of Ont., 1875; Q.C., 1833; Judge of the Supreme Ct. of the N.W.T., 1887; later Chief Justice, but retired, 1903. Was an alderman of Kingston; Pres., of the Mech. Inst., and of several Catholic Socs. Edited the Kingston *Daily News*, and also *Canadian Freeman*. Before apptd. Chief Justice, was stationed at Dawson, Y.T. Now Chn. of Educational Council of Saskatchewan; mem of the Senate of Saskatchewan Univ. *Address:* Prince Albert, Sask.

McHUGH, Hon. George; senator; *b.* Co. of Victoria, Ont., 7 July, 1845; *s.* of Peter McHugh and Ann Walker; *m.* Margaret *d.* of James O'Neill, of Peterborough; two *s.* one *d.* Member of pub. sch. Bd. for some years; member of Separate Sch. Bd., Town of Lindsay, and Chairman for several years; has been Pres. of Reform Assn. of South and West Victoria; elec. member of the H. of C., 1896; defeated at g. e., 1900; called to the Senate, 21 Jan., 1901. *Address:* Lindsay, Ont.

McHUGH, His Hon. Michael Andrew; County Court Judge of the Co. of Essex; *b.* Maidstone Cross, Essex Co., Ont., 19 Feb., 1853; *s.* Patrick and Catherine McHugh; *m.* Marie Louise Cottee, *d.* of the late James Cottee, London; four *s.* two *d.* Admitted to the bar, 1879; in partnership with Hon. J. C. Patterson; Minister of Militia, with Government of Sir John Thompson. *Recreation:* bowling. *Address:* Windsor, Ont. *Club:* Windsor.

McILWRAITH, Miss Jean N.; *d.* of Thomas and Mary McIlwraith. *Educ.:* pub. schs. and Ladies' Coll., Hamilton; studied singing afterwards in London, and also modern literature in correspondence class of Queen Margaret's Coll., Glasgow; first work published in 1895; last in 1904; since then doing editorial work in New York. *Publications:* Shakespeare for Young People 1898; Canada, Children's Study, 1899; The Span o' Life (with Wm. McLennan), 1899; a book about Longfellow, 1900; The Curious Career of Roderick Campbell, 1901; The Life of Governor-General Sir Frederick Haldimand (Makers of Canada), 1904. *Recreations:* cycling, boating, swimming, golf, etc. *Address:* 100 Waverly Place, New York.

McINNIS, John Kenneth; *b.* Strathroy, P.E.I., 29 April, 1854; *s.* of John McInnis and Isabel Ross; *m.* Jane Carr, Rustico, P.E.I.; four *s.* three *d.* *Educ.:* District Sch. and Charlottetown Central Academy; Sch. teacher in P.E.I., and in Sask.; editor and proprietor the *Regina Standard,* since 1891; operates several farms in Regina District, making specialties of grain and stock; was independent candidate for H. of C. in 1896, against late Nicholas Flood Davin, resulting in a tie, returning officer giving casting vote to Mr. Davin. *Address:* Regina, Sask.

McINNES, William, B.A., F.G.S.A.; geologist; *b.* Fredericton, N.B., 1858; *s. s.* of John McInnis and Rachel Jane, *d.* of Wm. McBeath. *Educ.:* Collegiate Sch., Fredericton; Univ. of N.B., joined Geological Survey of Canada, 1861, as Assistant Geologist; now Geologist, Dept. of Mines; extensive explorations in new Ontario lying between Fort William and Manitoba boundary. *Publications:* reports. *Address:* Victoria Chambers, Ottawa. *Clubs:* Rideau, Golf, Ottawa.

McINNES, His Hon. William Wallace Burns, B.A.; *b.* Dresden, Ont., 8 April, 1871, *s.* of Hon. Thomas R. (*deceased*) and Martha E. McInnis; *m.* Dorothea B. Young, of Victoria, B.C., Nov. 7, 1894; one *s.* one *d.* *Educ.:* Toronto Univ. and Osgoode Hall; mem. H. of C., 1896-1900; M.L.A., British Columbia, and Provincial Secretary, 1900-1905; Commissioner of the Yukon, 1905-1907; County Judge Co. of Vancouver, B.C., from April, 1909. *Address:* Vancouver. *Club:* Terminal City and Commercial, Vancouver, B.C.

McINTYRE, Alexander Fraser, K.C.; *b.* Williamstown, Glengarry, Ont., 25 Dec., 1847; *s.* of Daniel Eugene McIntyre, M.D., and Annie Fraser, *d.* of Col. the Hon. Alexander Fraser, of Fraserfield, Glengarry; *m.* 5 Sept., 1877 to Helen Sandfield Macdonald (*dec.*), *d.* of Ronald Sandfield Macdonald, Esq., of Lancaster, Glengarry; two *s.* three *d.* *Educ.:* Gram. Sch., Cornwall, Univ. of McGill, Montreal, and Osgoode Hall, Torgnto; served as Captain in No. 3 Co., Cornwall Infantry; on the frontier, 1866; elec. as an Independent Liberal to the Leg. Ass. of Ont., in 1875, but unseated on petition; unsuccessful Liberal candidate for Ottawa, for H. of C., 1882 and 1887; eleven years Pres. of Liberal Assn. of Ottawa; Pres. Young Liberal Assn. of Ontario, at Toronto, 1885, and Vice-Pres. Dominion Liberal Assn., Montreal, 1868. *Recreations:* fishing and shooting. *Address:* Ottawa, Ont.

McINTYRE, His Hon. Duncan John, K.C., Junior Judge for the Co. of Ontario; *b.* Tiree, Argyleshire, Scot., 22 Oct., 1841; *s.* of John McIntyre, and Margaret McIntyre; *m.* (1st) Margaret M., *d.* of R. F. Whitesior; (2nd) Ethel M., *d.* of J. W. Jenney, of Southampton; one *s.* two *d.* Arrived in Can., 1847, and educ. at pub. sch. in the tp. of Mariposa and Toronto Gram. and Normal Schs. Taught sch. for three yrs.; called to the Bar, 1871, and commenced practice of his profession in Lindsay, Ont.; mem. of Ont. Leg. Ass., 1883-6; apptd. Police Magistrate of Lindsay, 1892; cr. Q.C., 1890; apptd Junior Judge, Co. of Ont., 10 Sept., 1898. *Address:* Whitby, Ont.

McINTYRE, Gilbert Howard, M.P.; *b.* St. Mary's, Ont., Deputy Speaker of the Canadian H. of C.; *s.* of George McIntyre and Mary Howard; *m.* Belva, *d.* of Wm. Stevenson, Maple Bank, Guelph, Ont.; one *s.* *Educ.:* St. Mary's Gram. Sch.; el. mem. for South Perth to H. of C., 1904; re-el. 1908; el. Deputy Speaker of the House, 1908 a Methodist; a Liberal. *Address:* St. Mary's, Ont.

McISAAC, Colin Francis, K.C.; member of National Transcontinental Ry. Commission; *b.* Antigonish, N.S., 1854; *s.* of Donald McIsaac and Katherine McGillivray *m.* Mary Helena Houlett of Halifax, N.S.; three *s.* two *d.* *Educ.:* St. F. X. Coll., Antigonish, N.S., admitted to the bar, 1880; elected to the Provincial Assembly of N.S., in 1886, 1890 and 1894; apptd. member of Executive Govt. without portfolio in 1891; resigned in 1895 to contest Antigonish Co. at bye election for H. of C. on death of Sir John Thompson in 1895; elected then and at gen. elections of 1896, 1900 and 1904. Apptd. Com. of Nat. Trans. Ry., in 1905. *Address:* 255 Cooper St., Ottawa. *Club:* Rideau, Ottawa.

McKAY, Alexander; *b.* Hamilton, Ont., 19 April, 1843; *s.* of William McKay and Jane Reid; *m.* Catherine Marshall, of Barton Tp., Ont.; two *s.* two *d.* *Educ.:* Pub. Schs., Hamilton. Was alderman for Hamilton, 1879-1885; Mayor, 1886, 1887. Mem. of Dominion H. of C., 1887-1896; retired voluntarily, 1896. Now Inspector, His Majesty's Customs. *Address:* 42 Grove Av., Hamilton. *Clubs:* Hamilton, Royal Hamilton Yacht, Jockey.

McKAY, Alexander Charles, B.A., LL. D.; *b.* Beamsville, Ont., 2 June, 1861; *s.* of Alexander John McKay and Susan McCordick; *m.* Eleanor Price; two *s.* one *d.* Mathematical Master of Port Hope High Sch.; also Up. Can. Coll. and Jameson Av. Coll. Institute, Toronto; Fellow in Physics, Univ. of Toronto; Lecturer in Physics (Med. Fac.) Univ. of Toronto; Prof. of Mathematics and Physics, McMaster Univ., Toronto; Chancellor of McMaster Univ., 1905; member of Educational Council of Ont.; mem. of Advisory Council, Educational Department of Ontario. *Publications:* several elementary text books on Mathematics. *Address:* 13 Prince Arthur Ave., Toronto.

McKAY, His Hon. John; Junior Judge District of Thunder Bay; *b.* Tp. of Sydenham, Co. of Grey, Ont., 27 Feb., 1863; *s.* of Angus and Elizabeth McKay; *m.* Annie Langston; two *s.* two *d.* *Educ.:* Coll. Inst., Owen Sound and Brantford; called to the bar, 1887; practiced law at Sault St. Marie, Ont., from 1887 to 1909, during which time was actively identified with the mining and railway interests of the District of Algoma, and Secretary of the Ontario, Hudson Bay and Western Railway Co.; the Manitoulin and North Shore Mining Association, and Pres. of the Algoma Sunday Sch. Assn. *Address:* Port Arthur, Ont.

McKAY, Hon. Thomas; senator; *b.* Pictou, N.S., 8 Jan., 1839; *s.* of late Wm. McKay, Sutherlandshire; *m.* 1868, Jessie, *d.* of the late John Blair, Truro. *Educ.:* Pictou; a merchant; elec. to the H. of C., 1874; unseated on petition, but re-elec. and sat from Dec., 1874, to May, 1881; called to the Senate, Dec., 1881; Conservative. *Address:* Truro, N.S.

McKENNA, James Andrew Joseph; *b.* P.E.I., 1 Jan., 1862; *s.* of James McKenna and Rose Duffy, of Ireland; *m.* Mary Josephine Ryan; three *s.* five *d.* *Educ.:* St. Dunstan's Coll., P.E.I.; on leaving Coll., engaged in journalistic work; entered Indian Service of the Canadian Government in 1886; was for a time assistant secretary to the late Sir John Macdonald; in 1897 acted for the Dominion Government in effecting an arrangement with the Government of Brltish Columbia for the administration of the Railway Belt lands; was one of the Commissioners who, in 1899, made the treaty with the Indians under which the Peace River and Athabasca country was surrendered to the Crown, and in 1906, negotiated the treaty under which the Indians relinquished their claims to the country about Buffalo Lake, Churchill River and Reindeer Lake; was Commissioner for the settlement of the claims of the half-breeds of the North-West in 1900 and 1901; drafted the Act, now in force, which consolidated and amended the laws in respect to the public lands of Canada. *Publications:* The Hudson Bay Route, 1908;" "Sir John Thompson, a study;" "Canada's Indian Policy;" "The Indians of Canada," and other essays in magazines and reviews. *Address:* P.O. Box 1287, Winnipeg, Man.

McKENZIE, Donald Duncan, K.C., M.P.; *b.* Lake Ainslie, C.B., 8 Jan., 1859; *s.* of Duncan McKenzie and Jessie McMillan; *m.* Florence N. McDonald; one *s.* A barrister-at-law; admitted to bar of N.S., in 1889; created K.C., 1908; was Judge of County Court of N.S., from 1905 to 1908; M.L.A. of N.S. from 1900 to 1904; elec. to the H. of C. 1904 and 1908; mayor of North Sydney, N.S., from 1898 to 1904. *Address:* North Sydney, C.B.

McKEOWN, Harrison Andrew, B.A., LL.B., K.C., M.L.A.; *b.* St. Stephen, N.B., 28 Nov., 1863; *s.* of Rev. H. McKeown and Elizabeth Harrison; *m.* Edith A. Perkins, *d.* of George Perkins. *Educ.:* Univ. of Mt. Allison, Sackville, N.B.; Toronto Univ. Was first elected to the Provincial Legislature, 1890, representing St. John City and County; became a member of the Government of New Brunswick, 1899, entering the Cabinet without portfolio; Atty. Gen. for N.B., 1907-8; re-el. at g. e. 1908, but resigned portfolio on defeat of Robinson Ministry; admitted to the bar of New Brunswick, 1884; practises law in St. John. *Address:* St. John, N.B. *Club:* Union, St. John.

McKERGOW, John; mem. of the firm of A. A. Ayer & Co., Ltd., wholesale provision merchants, Montreal; *b.* Berkshire Co., England, 1847; *m.* 1868, Laura Goadby. five *s.* two *d.* *Educ.:* Model Sch., Montreal. Brought to Can. by his parents when about two years of age. Entered Stores Dept., of the G. T. R. at age of sixteen. Entered firm of Messrs. A. A. Ayer & Co., Ltd., 1868; made a partner, 1872. El. pres., Montreal Bd. of Trade, 1897. Apptd. Sch. Commr. of Westmount, 1901; Chmn. of the Bd. of Sch. Commrs., 1907; Pres., Montreal Lumber Co.; dir. Sun Life Insur. Co., Laprairie Brick Co. *Recreation:* bowling. *Address:* 13 Rosemount Av., Montreal. *Clubs:* Montreal, Canada.

McKINLAY, Hon. Duncan E.; mem. of U.S. House of Representatives for 2nd Dist. of California; *b.* Orillia, Ont., 6 Oct., 1862; married; four *c.* *Educ.:* until twelve yrs. of age at Orillia Pub. Sch. Learnt trade of carriage painter and worked in Flint, Mich.; at 21 yrs. of age went to San Francisco, and worked at his trade until 1884; spent one yr. at Sacramento, then moved to Santa Rosa, where he studied law while carrying on his business as carriage painter. Admitted to the bar of California, 1892; elector at large on the Republican ticket in McKinley's first Presidential campaign, 1896; apptd. by President McKinley as asst. U.S. Attorney at San Francisco, 1901. El. to 59th Congress; re-el. to 60th and 61st. *Address:* The Capitol, Washington, D.C.; San Francisco, Cal., U.S.A.

McKINNON, Robert Lachlan, B.A., LL.B.; *b.* Wellington County, Ont., 5 Jan., 1872; *s.* John and Annie McKinnon; *m.* Annie W. Fleming; one *s.* *Educ.:* Public Schs., Coll. Inst., Guelph and Owen Sound; Toronto Univ. and Law Sch.; Osgoode Hall, Toronto. Barrister, etc.; in practice of law at Guelph since 1898; examiner at law sch. of Law Soc. of Up. Can., 1905-09. *Address:* College Heights, Guelph, Ont.

McKNIGHT, Robert; Registrar of Deeds for North Grey; *b.* Kilkeel, Co. Down, Irel., 24 Oct., 1836; *s.* of Robert McKnight and Eliza Gray; widower; three *s.* two *d.* *Educ.:* Irish National Schs. Arrived Canada, 16 June, 1856. Engaged in a sawmill for two yrs.; taught sch. six yrs.; later in gen. business twenty-eight yrs. Unsuccessful candidate for H. of C. twice, and Leg. Ass. once. Apptd. Registrar, 10 Nov., 1875. A school trustee for thirty yrs. *Recreations:* horticulture, bookkeeping, pheasant breeding. *Address:* Owen Sound, Ont.

McLAGAN, Mrs. Sara Anne; *b.* Ireland, 1855; *d.* of John Maclure and Martha McIntyre; relict of John Campbell McLagan, who died 1903; one *s.* three *d.* Came to Canada with her parents in 1855; *Educ.:* at New Westminster, B.C. Father was one of pioneer surveyors in British Columbia and with Royal Engrs. assisted in first telegraph construction. Husband estabd. Vancouver *World,* in 1886, and on his demise, Mrs. McLagan became pres. of the World Printing and Publishing Co., and for four yrs. managed the paper. An active mem. of the Women's Council in Vancouver, and pres. three yrs.; Prov. Vice-Pres. for B.C. for three yrs. and sole Provincial del. to National Council meetings. Organized the Local Council of Women in New Westminster; assisted in organizing the Art Historical Scientific Assn., the Young Women's Christian Assn., the first Chapter of the Daughters' of the Empire and the Victorian Order of Nurses at Vancouver. *Address:* "Hazelbrae," Clayburn, B.C.

McLAY, Walter Scott Williams, M.A.; *b.* Bryanston, Middlesex Co., Ont., 19 Dec., 1870; *s.* of Dr. and Mrs. A. McLay, Woodstock, Ont.; *m.* Margaret *d.* of Sir John A. Boyd, K.C.M.G., Chancellor of Ontario; one *s.* two *d.* *Educ.:* Woodstock Coll.; Univ. of Toronto, Harvard Univ.; Lecturer in English, 1894; Professor, 1901; Dean in Arts, 1905, McMaster Univ., Toronto. *Address:* 3 Sultan St., Toronto.

McLEAN, Lieut.-Col. Hugh Havelock, K.C., M.P.; *b.* Fredericton, N.B., 22 March, 1855; *s.* of Lauchlin McLean and Sophia Marsh; *m.* 1879, Jennie Porteous; two *s.* one *d.* *Educ.:* Fredericton Gram. Sch. A barrister-at-law; Pres., New Brunswick Southern Ry. Co., the Fredericton Ry. Co., Carleton Electric Light Co., the Grand Falls Water Power & Boom Co., the New Brunswick Prov. Rifle Assn., and the Alexander-Gibson Ry. and Mfg. Co.; vice-pres., St. John Ry. Co., the New Brunswick Fish and Game Corporation, the New Brunswick Ry. Co.; dir. and treas. of the St. Andrew's Land Co., the St. John Bridge and Ry. Extension Co., the Algonquin Hotel Co., the Inglewood Pulp and Paper Co. For several yrs. commanded the 62nd St. John Fusiliers as Lt.-Col.; has been Lt.-Col. commanding 12 Infan. Brig. since 1892; was Capt. and Adjt. of the N.B. and P.E.I. Provisional Batt., raised at the time of the North West Rebellion; commanded the Maritime Prov. Brig, at the Que. Tercentenary; first el. to H. of C., 1908. *Address:* St. John, N.B. *Clubs:* Union, Golf, St. John; St. James, Mount Royal, Montreal; Rideau, Ottawa.

McLEAN, Munro Young, M.P.; *b.* Dumfries, Waterloo, Co. Ont., 7 Feb., 1846. *Educ.:* pub. sch., Ayr, Waterloo Co.; learned trade of printer in Paris, Ont.; has edited and published Huron *Expositor,* Seaforth, for 39 years; served one term in the Ontario Leg., and has at various times filled all municipal positions from sch. trustee to Mayor; first el. to H. of C. at bye-elec., Jan., 1908; re-el. at g. e., 1908. *Address:* Seaforth, Ont.

McLEAN, Simon James, M.A., LL.B., Ph.D.; *b.* Quebec, 14 June, 1871; *s.* of James and Mary McLean; *m.* Helen Baillie, *d.* of the late John Lorn McDougall, first Auditor Gen. of Canada; one *s.* one *d.* *Educ.:* Quebec; Cumberland, Ont.; Ottawa; Univ. of Toronto, Chicago Univ., Chicago, Ill., New York. Prof. of Economics, Univ. of Arkansas, 1897-1902; head of the Dept. of Economics and Social Science, Leland Stanford Junior Univ., 1902-05; Assoc. Prof. of Political Economy, Toronto Univ., 1906-08; has specialized in Economics of Transportation; presented a special report to the Hon. A. G. Blair, Min. of Rys. and Canals, on the question of Ry. Comn. Legislation, 1898-99; conducted the investigation, as commr., on Ry. Rate grievances in Canada, the report of which led to the organization of the Bd. of Ry. Commrs., 1901-02; acted as export agt. for the U.S. Bureau of the Census and the Interstate Commerce Comn. in charge of Ry. valuation in Pacific Coast States, 1904-05; apptd. a mem. of the Bd. of Ry. Commrs. for Canada, Sept., 1908. *Publications:* articles dealing with problems of transportation and commerce contributed to various periodicals in Canada, U.S., England, and Belgium; also articles on transportation and other subjects to the Montreal *Star,* Manitoba *Free Press,* Toronto *Globe.* *Address:* 220 Argyle Ave., Ottawa. *Clubs:* Rideau, Country, Ottawa; University, Toronto.

McLENNAN, Prof. John Cunningham, B.A., Ph.D., F.R.S.C., F.A.A.S.; *b.* Ingersol, Ont., 14 April, 1867; *s.* of David McLennan of Aberdeenshire, Scot., and Barbara Cunnigham of Ayrshire, Scot. *Educ.:* Univ. of Cambridge; Professor of Physics and Director of the Physical Laboratory, Univ. of Toronto; Demonstrator in Physics, 1892-to 1902; Assoc. Prof. of Physics, 1902-1907; Director, 1904; Professor, 1907; Secretary of Univ. Alumni Assn., 1900 to 1908; Secretary of Faculty Union, 1900. *Recreation:* golf. *Address:* The Dean's House, Univ. of Toronto, Toronto. *Club:* Golf, Toronto.

McLENNAN, Roderick; contractor; *b.* Woodstock, Ont., 19 March, 1866; *s.* of Alexander McLennan and Mary McInnes; *m.* 1895, Lizzy McDonald, of Seaforth, Ont.. two *s.* two *d.* *Educ.:* Seaforth High Sch; Settled in Manitoba in 1896, and has been engaged as contractor since. *Recreations:* lacrosse, curling. *Address:* 219 Colony St., Winnipeg, Man. *Club:* Commercial, Winnipeg.

McLEOD, Clement Henry, B.Sc., Ma.E., F.R.S.C.; Vice-Dean of the Faculty of Applied Science, McGill Univ.; *b.* Cape Breton, N.S., 20 Jan., 1851; *s.* of Isaac McLeod and Euphemia Laurence. *Educ.:* Model and Normal Schs, Truro; McGill Univ. (grad. from Faculty of Applied Sc., 1873). Apptd. asst. engr. in charge of construction on Intercolonial Ry., and later res. engr. construction P.E.I. Ry.; engr. of pub. wks. in Newfoundland. Apptd. Supt. of the Observatory at McGill Univ., 1874; Prof. in the Faculty of Applied Sc., 1888; Vice-Dean, 1908. Sec. Can. Soc. of Civil Engrs. since 1887. Fellow of the Royal Astronomical Soc., *Publications:* Transit of Venus, 1882; a re-determination of the longitudes of Montreal and Cambridge and of Montreal and Toronto. Contributions to the Transactions of the R.S.C. on astronomical, meteorological and physical subjects, and to Can. Soc. of Civil Engrs. *Recreations:* all athletic sports. *Address:* McGill Univ., Montreal. *Club:* University, Moutreal.

McLEOD, Hon. Ezekiel; Judge Supreme Ct., and Judge, Vice-Admiralty, N.B.; *b.* 29 Oct., 1840. *Educ.:* High Sch., Caldwell, King's Co., N.B.; Harvard. Called to the bar, 1868; cr. Q.C., 1882. Mem. Prov. Legis., 1882-86; Attorney-Gen., 1882-83. Mem. of the H. of C., 1891-96; a Senator of the Univ. of N.B. *Address:* St. John, N.B. *Club:* Union, St. John.

McLEOD, Henry Collingwood; banker; *b.* New London, P.E.I.; *s.* of Capt. John McLeod. *Educ.:* Charlottetown; commenced business in a law office, and then joined the staff of the Bank of P.E.I., later Bank of B.N.S., when it absorbed the Bank of P.E.I.; mgr. of different branches of the Bank in the U.S.; became gen. gmr. of the Bank on the resignation of Mr. Fyshe, in 1897; removed gen. mgr's. office from Halifax to Toronto; one of the aggressive forces in Canadian banking; formerly Vice-Pres. of the Can. Bankers' Assn. Resigned gen. managership, Jan., 1910, but continues as director. *Publications:* Pamphlet favouring an independent audit by Govt. Inspectors of all banks. *Recreation:* yachting, motoring *Address:* 8 Beaumont Rd., Rosedale, Toronto. *Clubs:* Toronto, National, Toronto.

McLEOD, Hon. Harry Fulton, B.A., M.L.A.; Solicitor General of New Brunswick; *b.* Fredericton, N.B., 14 Sept., 1871; *s.* of Rev. Joseph McLeod, D.D., and Jane McLeod; *m.* 1908, Ina F., *d.* of Major W. Mersereau. *Educ.:* Univ. of N.B.; Mayor of Fredericton, 1907-8; Major 71st Regt.; Grand Master, L.O.L., N.B., 1906-7. Unsuccessful can. for Legis. at g. e., 1903; el. for York Co., at g. e., 1908. A Baptist; Conservative. *Address:* Fredericton, N.B.

McMAHON, Mrs. Margherita Arlina; *b.* St. Stephens, N.B., 29 Apr., 1871; *d.* Rufus La Fayette and Almenia Spencer Hamm. *Educ.:* Convent of the Sacred Heart, Carleton, N.B.; Emmerson Coll., Boston; New York Univ. Law Sch., Royal Coll., Hong-Kong; summer lecture course, Oxford, Eng.; *m.* Aug. 1, 1902, John Robert McMahon. Newspaper reporter and author since 1887; traveled in U.S., Hawaii and W. Indies in '90s for *Sun*, *Herald* and *Mail*, New York; later visited Japan, China, India, Egypt and Russia for same papers; made maps for Geog. Soc.; war corr. Chinese-Japanese War and Spanish-Am. War; also mil. nurse without salary; made hon. mem. of several regiments; decorated by Pres. Palma of Cuba; was comm'r to England for Atlanta Exp'n. Mem. Geog. socs., London, and Hong-Kong; was librarian Medico-Legal Soc., New York; mem. Am. Civics Club, Coll. Woman's Club, Professional Woman's League; hon. v.-p. Writers' Club, London. Protestant; Episcopalian. Contb'r. to mags *Publications:* Chinese Legends, 1893; Corean Journeys, 1893; Manila and the Philippines, 1897; Porto Rico, 1898; Life of Dewey, 1898; American New Possessions, 1898; Christmas Poems, 1900; Eminent Actors in their Homes, 1902; Builders of the Republic 1902; Ghetto Silhouettes, 1902; Famous Families, of New York, 1903. *Address:* The Independent, New York.

McMICHAEL, Isaac; Gen. Mgr. of the Gt. North West Tel. Co. of Canada; *b.* Brantford, Ont., 7 Jan., 1840, *s.* James and Caroline McMichael; *m.* Margaretta P. Brock, Cleveland, Ohio; one *s.* one *d.* *Educ.:* Brantford, Ont., in 1856 he entered the service of the Buffalo and Lake Horun Ry. Co., remaining until 1860; from this date until 1865, was engaged in U.S. Military Telegraph service in Missouri, Arkansas, and Indian Territory; from 1865, until 1903, in service of the Western Union Tel. Co in the United States, and from 1903 to date, manager of the Great North West ern Tel. Co., at Toronto. *Address:* 123 St. Clair Ave., Toronto. *Clubs:* National, and R.C.Y.C., Toronto.

McMICHAEL, Solon William, I.S.O.; *b.* Waterford, Ont., 18 Nov., 1848; *s.* of Aaron McMichael, J.P., and Emily Campbell; *m.* 1873, Josephine, *d.* of Charles Shoemaker, of Muncy, Pa., U.S.A.; one *s.* one *d.* *Educ.:* Simcoe Gram. Sch. Chief and General Inspector of Customs; entered Canadian Customs, 1873; apptd. Financial Inspector of Customs for the Dominion, 1885; Chief Inspector of Customs for Canada, 1894; member of the Board of Customs, 1895; Chief and General Inspector, 1909; was Captain in the Dufferin Rifles of Canada, 1882-5; created a companion of the Imperial Service Order, 1903. *Address:* 101 St. George St., Toronto. *Clubs:* National, Lambton Golf and Country; Can. Military Institute, Toronto.

McMILLAN, Hon. Donald, M.D., senator; *b.* Tp. of Lochiel, Co. Glengarry, Ont., 5 March, 1835; *s.* of Duncan McMillan and Mary McDonell; *m.* Amy Ann, *d.* of the late Amasa Lewis, J.P., Aylmer, Ont.; seven *s.* five *d.* *Educ.:* Lochiel, by private tuition; Victoria Coll., Toronto; grad. in medicine in 1865; was for many years on town, township and county council; apptd. Coroner, in 1869; apptd. to the Senate in Jan., 1884; is a director of the Trusts Guarantee Co., Toronto, and of the Merchants' Fire Ins. Co., of Toronto; a life member of the Celtic Soc. of Montreal, and of the Gaelic Soc., Toronto. *Address:* Alexandria, Ont.

McMILLAN, J. A., M.P.; *b.* Alexandria, Ont., 11 June, 1874; *s.* of Duncan McMillan and Julia Campbell (both Scotch); *m.* 1906, Flora McDonald. A furniture merchant. El. to Ont. Legis. for Glengarry, Jan., 1905. First el. to H. of C. at g. e., 1908. A Roman Catholic. Liberal. *Address:* Alexandria, Ont.

McMULLEN, Hon. James; senator; *b.* Co. Monaghan, Ireland, 29 Nov., 1836; *s.* Archibald and Mary Jane McMullen; *m.* Mary Ann Dunbar, Guelph, 28 Sept., 1858; three *s.* and one *d.* *Educ.:* Pub. Sch. and Gram. Sch., Fergus. Ont.; arrived in Canada

12 June, 1843; was Councillor and Reeve of Mount Forest several years; director and Vice-Pres., Georgian Bay and Wellington Ry.; director Grand Trunk, Georgian Bay and Lake Erie Ry.; director and Vice-Pres. Dominion Life Assurance Co.; elec. to the H. of C. in 1882; sat for 18 years and was defeated in 1900; apptd. to the Senate, 1902. *Recreation:* cricket. *Address:* Mount Forest, Ont. *Club:* National, Toronto.

McNAB, Hon. Archibald Peter, M.L.A.; Min. of Pub. Works for Saskatchewan; *b.* Glengarry, Ont., 29 May, 1864; *s.* of Malcolm McNab and Margaret McCrimmon (both Scotch); *m.* 1893, Edith Todd; four *s.* two *d.* *Educ.:* Glengarry. A miller and grain merchant. Pres. of the Saskatoon Milling and Elevator Co. First el. to Sask. Legis. at g. e., 1908. Apptd. to Cabinet as Municipal Commr., 8 Dec., 1908; re-el. by accl. 30 Dec., 1908; apptd. Min. of Pub. Works, Jan., 1909. *Address:* Saskatoon, Sask.

McNAIR, James A.; Pres. and Gen. Manager of the Hastings Shingle Manufacturing Co.; *b.* nr. Dalhousie, N.B., 11 Aug., 1865; *s.* of Nathaniel McNair and Martha Archibald; *m.* Minnie G. McKay. *Educ.:* Jacquet River, N.B. Engaged in mercantile life in N.B., and Que., until 1892, when he removed to B.C. With his brother Robert built a small shingle mill at Hastings which has developed into the present concern with capacity of 1,250,000 shingles a day. Company also owns mills in Whatcom Co., Wash. Actively interested in Y.M.C.A. work; for several yrs. pres. of the Vancouver Assn. *Address:* Vancouver, B.C.

McNAUGHT, William Kirkpatrick, M.L.A.; *b.* Fergus, Ont., 6 Sept., 1845; *s.* of John McNaught and Sarah McNaught (both Scotch); *m.* 1872, C. E. Lugsdin, of Toronto; three *s.* one *d.* *Educ.:* Com. Sch. and Coll. Inst., Brantford. A manufacturer. Pres. of the Glenavy Co., Ltd.; American Watch Case Co. of Toronto, Ltd.; Vice-Pres., Canadian Elgin Watch Co., of Toronto, Ltd.; dir., Porto-Rico Electric Ry.; hon. pres., Canadian National Exhn.; mem. Hydro-Electric Comn. of Ontario. Was a Lieut., 12th Regt. of Militia; pres. of the Canadian National Exhn., 1901-1905; pres., National Club, Toronto, 1897-1901; pres., Canadian Mfgrs. Assn., 1888-9; Chn., Tariff Committee Can. Mfgrs. Assn., 1896-1906. First el. to Ont. Legis., 1906; re-el. at g. e. 1908. *Address:* Alexandra Apts., Toronto.

McNEE, Archibald; *b.* Perth, Ont., 1845; *s.* of Arch. McNee and Janet Ferguson; *m.* Isabella Campbell. *Educ.:* Perth Gram. School. On staff of Manitoba *Free Press* for some years; managing ed. for short period; five years in Parlt. Press Gallery and pres., 1885; started Daily *Evening Record* at Windsor, Ont., 1890, and still conducts it. Pres. of Can. Press Assn., 1905; Moderator Baptist Convention of Ont. and Que., 1901; alderman Winnipeg, and Windsor; member of Board of Td. in both cities; pres. Windsor Bd. of Trade, pres. St. Andrew's Soc.; Deacon, Baptist Church, Windsor, for 20 years. Has always taken an interest in affairs of church and state. *Recreations:* curling, bowling and quoiting. *Address:* 85 Victoria Ave., Windsor, Ont.; Record office. *Club:* Windsor.

McNEIL, Right Rev. Neil; Archbishop of Vancouver, B.C.; *b.* Hillsborough, N.S., 21 Nov., 1851; *s.* of the late Malcolm McNeil and Ellen Meagher. *Educ.:* St. Francois Xavier Coll., Antigonish, and in 1873 was sent to the Coll. of the Propaganda in Rome, where he remained for over six yrs. Ordained priest, April, 1879, in the Basilica, of John Latern, by the late Cardinal Patrizzi, and in same yr. received the degree of Doctor in both Philosophy and Divinity; joined the teaching staff of St. Francis Xavier Coll., 1880; in 1881 assumed the editorship of the *Aurora* newspaper; rector of the Coll., 1884-1891; became Bishop of Nilopolis and Vicar Apostolic of St. Georges, west coast of Nfld.; consec. at St. Ninan's Cath., Antigonish, 20 Oct., 1895; apptd. Archbishop of Vancouver, Jan., 1910. *Address:* Vancouver, B.C.

McPHERSON, Hon. David, M.L.C.; *b.* Jordan River, Shelburne Co., N.S., 1 Aug., 1832; *s.* of John and Elizabeth McPherson; *m.* Susan McDaniel, of Halifax. *Educ.:* Gram. Sch., Shelburne Co., N.S. A shipbuilder; an ald. for the city of Halifax for 14 yrs. Commr. of Pub. Charities for three yrs. El. to Legis. at g. e., 1897; re-el. at g. e., 1901, and 1906. A mem. of the Murray Admn., without portfolio. *Address:* Halifax, N.S.

McPHERSON, George Gordon, K.C.; *b.* Stratford, Ont., 1 Oct., 1859; *s.* of Rev. Thomas McPherson, and Sarah Gordon; *m.* Susie Hamilton; one *s.* three *d.* *Educ.:* Stratford Gram. Sch. Has practised law in Stratford since 1872. *Recreations:* riding, fishing. *Address:* 326 Erie St., Stratford, Ont.

McPHERSON, William David, K.C., M.L.A.; *b.* village of Moore, Lambton Co., 22 Aug., 1863; *s.* of William McPherson and Sarah Courtney; *m.* Nettie Batten; five *s.* four *d.* *Educ.:* Strathroy Collegiate Inst., Osgoode Hall, Toronto. Member of the Ontario Legislative Assembly for West Toronto. *Publications:* Law of Mines in Canada, 1898; Parliamentary Elections in Canada, 1905. *Recreations:* yachting, cricket. *Address:* 6 Meredith Crescent, Toronto. *Clubs:* Albany, Royal Canadian Yacht, Toronto; Rideau, Ottawa.

McPHILLIPS, Capt. Albert Edward, M.L.A.; *b.* Richmond, Co. York, Ont., 21 March, 1861; *s.* of George McPhillips, and Margaret Lavin (both *dec.*); *m.* Emily Sophia Davie, *d.* of the late Hon. A. E. B. Davie, Q.C.; Premier of B.C.; two *s.* one *d.* *Educ.:* St. Boniface, and Manitoba Coll.; barrister at law; called to the bar of Manitoba, 1882; of British Columbia, 1891; retired from Militia with rank of Captain; holds military sch. certificate; served with General Middleton in North West Rebellion (medal); was Attorney General in first Conservative Government of B.C., in 1903; mem. of the Provincial Legislative Assembly for the Islands' electoral district; fellow Royal Colonial Institute; Pres. Canadian Club, Victoria' B.C.; director B.C. Market Co.; *Recreations:* cross country and high jumping contests. *Address:* Cloonmore House, Rockland Ave., Victoria, B.C. *Club:* Union, Victoria, B.C.

McRAE, Alexander Duncan; *b.* Glencoe, Ont., 17 Nov., 1874; *s.* of Duncan and Mary

McRae; *m.* Blanche Latimer Howe, of Duluth, Minn.; three *d.* *Educ.:* High Sch., Glencoe, Ont., and Coll. in London, Ont. Was for seven yrs. engaged in banking business in the U.S., and for five yrs. in immigration and land business in Winnipeg; now devoting entire time to lumber business. *Recreation:* horses. *Address:* 1960 Robson St., Vancouver, B.C. *Clubs:* Manitoba, St. Charles Country, Winnipeg; Vancouver.

McSWEENEY, Hon. Peter; Senator; *b.* Moncton, N.B., 11 April, 1842; *s.* of Peter McSweeney and Joanna Downing; *m.* Wilhelmina Peters Fisher; one *s.* two *d.* *Educ.:* Moncton, N.B.; went to St. John at an early age. Returned to Moncton in 1868, and went into business with his brothers Edward and Thomas as dry goods merchants; started for himself in 1877; took an active part in promoting the incorporation of Moncton, as a town; was alderman for two years and chairman of Finance- Pub. Sch. Trustee, and mem. of Board of Health; called to the Senate 15 Mar., 1899. *Recreations:* hunting, fishing. *Address:* Moncton, N.B.

McVEIGH, Thomas, Jr., M.A.; *b.* Bryson, Que., 2 Oct., 1868; *s.* of Thomas McVeigh and Margaret T. Hughes; *m.* Feb. 1898 to Katharine B. Blake, Detroit, two *s.* three *d.* *Educ.:* Bryson Pub. Sch. and Detroit Coll.; grad. Detroit Coll., 1888; admitted to the bar, State of Michigan, 1891; practiced in Detroit to 1897; editor on the New York *World* from Sept. 1891 to date; active since 1885 as pub. and political speaker, under auspices of Republican party. *Recreations:* tennis, golf, horseback riding. *Address:* World office, New York; Northvale Farm, N.J. *Clubs:* Republican, New York; Rockland County Golf.

MEIGHEN, Arthur, B.A., M.P.; *b.* St. Mary's, Ont., 15 June, 1874; *s.* of Joseph and Mary Meighen; *m.* Jessie Isabel, *d.* of late Charles Cox of Granby, Que.; two *s.* *Educ.:* St. Mary's Coll. Inst. and Toronto Univ. Farmer; teacher; barrister; first el. to H. of C., 1908, for Portage la Prairie; went to Manitoba in 1898; Winnipeg; Portage la Prairie, 1901. *Address:* Portage la Prairie. *Clubs:* Portage Club, P. la P.; Advance Club, Winnipeg.

MEIGHEN, Robert; Pres and managing director, Lake of the Woods Milling Co.; *b.* Dungiven, nr. Londonderry, Ireland, 18 April, 1839; *s.* of Robert Meighen and Mary McLeghan; *m.* 1868, Elsie, *y. d.* of the late William Stephen, formerly of Dufftown, Scotland; one *s.* two *d.* *Educ.:* Dungiven pub. sch. Entered firm of Meighen & brother at age of 14; removed to Montreal in 1879, and became associated in business with Sir George Stephen, now Lord Mount Stephen. Founded the Lake of the Woods Milling Co., with mills at Keewatin and Portage la Prairie; director, Canadian Pacific Ry., Montreal Street Ry., Canadian North-West Land Co., Bank of Toronto, Dominion Transport Co.; mem. of the Montreal Board of Trade and Corn Exchange. *Address:* 140 Drummond St., Montreal. *Clubs:* Mount Royal, St. James', Montreal.

MEIGS, Daniel Bishop, M.P.; *b.* Henryville, Iberville Co., Que., 1 June, 1835; *s.* of Daniel Meigs and Caroline Lasalle; *m.* (1st) 1866, Louise Allsop; (2nd) 1871, Rosa Faulkner. *Educ.:* Bedford, Que. A farmer and lumberman. Mayor of Farnham for several yrs. El. to H. of C. at bye-el., 1888; unsuccessful can. at g. e., 1891; el. at g. e. 1900, 1904 and 1908. *Address:* Farnham, Que.

MEREDITH, Hon. Richard Martin; *b.* London, Ont., 27 March, 1847; *s.* of John Wallingham Cooke Meredith and Sara Pegler; unmarried. *Educ.:* London, Ont. One of the Judges of Appeal for Ontario; Chancellor of the Western Univ., Ont. *Address:* 565 Talbot Street, London, Ont., and Osgoode Hall, Toronto.

MEREDITH, Thomas Graves, K.C.; *b.* London, Ont., 16 June 1853; *s.* of the late John W. C. Meredith, and Sarah Pegler; *m.* 1882, Jessie, *d.* of Sir John Carling, of London, Ont.; two *s.* *Educ.:* Pub. and Gram. Schs., Hellmuth Coll., London; Galt Coll. Inst.; Toronto Univ. Studied law in the office of Thomas Scatcherd, of London, Ont.; called to the bar of Ont., 1878, and commenced practice of his profession in conjunction with the firm of Meredith and Scatcherd; apptd. K.C., by Ont. Govt., 1902; city solicitor for London since 1894. Was one of the organizers of the London and Western Loan Co., in 1896, of which he is now a dir. *Address:* London, Ont.

MEREDITH, Hon. Sir William Ralph, LL.D., K.B.; *cr.* 1896; Chief Justice of Common Pleas, Ontario; *b.* 31 Mar., 1840; *s.* of John Cooke Meredith, London, Ont.; *m.* Mary, *d.* of Marcus Holmes, Ont., 1862; one *s.* three *d.* *Educ.:* London, Ont.; Univ. of Toronto. Member of Legislative Assembly for London, Ont., 1872-96; and leader of the Oppos'n.; Chancellor of the Univ. of Toronto; apptd. Chief Justice, 1904. *Address:* Binscarth Rd., Toronto, Ont. *Club:* Toronto.

MICHAUD, Pius, M.P.; *b.* St. Leonard, Madawaska Co., N.B., 28 Aug., 1870; *s.* of Felix Michaud and Marguerite Violette; *m.* Marie Hebert. *Educ.:* Univ. of St. Joseph, N.B. An advocate. Sec.-Treas. of Co. Coun. of Madawaska Co.; Judge of Probate for the Co. of Madawaska. First el. to the H. of C. by accl., at bye-el., 1906; re-el. at g. e., 1908. *Address:* Edmundston, N.B.

MICHELL, William Arthur Rupert, M. D.; *b.* Perth, Ont., 18 Oct., 1879; *s.* of F. L. Michell, Public Sch. Inspector, Lanark Co., *Educ.:* Perth Coll. Inst., Toronto Univ.; grad. at Toronto in Medicine, 1902; practiced for 3 years in Ontario; went abroad for post-graduate work in Sept., 1905; studied at Dublin, Glasgow, and London Hospitals; went first to sea in merchant service in Dec., 1906; joined the British Antarctic Ship 'Nimrod," in June, 1907, sailing from Torquay in early Aug., 1907; made two trips to Victoria Land on Nimrod returning in June, 1909; returned to Canade in Sept., 1909; located in Toronto. *Address:* Perth, Ont.

MICKLE, His Hon. Charles Julius; Co. Judge of the Northern Judicial Dist. of Manitoba; *b.* Stratford, Ont., 22 July, 1848; *s.* of Alexander D. Mickle (English), and Elizabeth A. Linton (Scotch); *m.* 1889, Mary A. Ross, of Stratford, Ont. *Educ.:*

Stratford Gram. Sch. Admitted to the practice of law, 1872; removed to Manitoba 1882. El. to Man. Legis., 1888; re-el. at g. e., 1892, 1896, 1899, 1903 and 1908. Entered the Greenway Govt. as Prov. Sec., Nov., 1896; resigned 6 Jan., 1900; el. leader of the Opposition, 5 Dec., 1904, which position he later resigned. Apptd. Co. Judge of the Northern Judicial Dist. of Man., 29 May, 1909. *Address:* Minnedosa, Man.

MIDDLEBRO, William Sora, M.P.; *b.* Orangeville, Ont., 17 Oct., 1868; *s.* of John and Margaret Middlebro; *m.* Laura S. Trethewey, 2 Sept., 1903 (*dec.*) *Educ.:* Coll. Inst., Owen Sound, and Osgoode Hall, Toronto. Barrister; Mayor of Owen Sound 1905-1909; first el. to H. of C. for North Grey, 1908. *Address:* Owen Sound, Ont.

MIGNAULT, Pierre Basile, M.A., LL.D., K.C., F.R.S.C.; *b.* Worcester, Mass., U.S.A., 30 Sept., 1854; *s.* of Dr. P. B. Mignault and Catherine O'Callaghan; *m.* Marie Elizabeth Blanchaud, of Beauharnois; two *s.* one *d.* *Educ.:* Coll. Ste. Marie, Montreal; McGill Univ. Came to Can. in 1868. Called to bar, 1878; Q.C., 1893; batonnier of the bar of Montreal, 1906-7; el. to Roy. Soc., 1908. Pres. of the Bar. Assn., of Montreal. *Publications:* Manuel of Parliamentary Law, 1888; Code of Civil Procedure, 1891; Parish Law, 1893. Canadian Civil Law, commenced in 1895, of which 8 vols. have appeared. *Recreations:* golf, yachting. *Address:* 124 Crescent St., Montreal. *Clubs:* Montreal, Club Lafontaine, Beaconsfield Golf.

MILES, Henry; Pres. Leeming Miles Co., importers, Montreal; *b.* Lennoxville, Que., May, 1854; *s.* of Dr. Henry Miles, Canadian historian, of Quebec; *m.* 1875, Miss MacGregor, of Montreal; two *d.* *Educ.:* Bishop's Coll., Laval Univ., Quebec. Entered firm of Lyman Sons & Co., wholesale druggists; became a partner, 1885; retired as managing dir., 1895. Estb. the Leeming-Miles Co., Ltd., wholesale druggists, 1896, of which he is still pres. Pres. Philip Morris & Co., Ltd.; Gen. Mgr., Eastern Drug Co., Ltd., of Montreal; prop. and editor, Montreal Pharmaceutical Journal; pres., Montreal Business Men's League; hon. pres., Proprietary Articles Trade Assn. of Can.; mem. of the executive of Montreal Bd. of Trade, 1895-1908; treas., Montreal Bd. of Trade, 1898, and el. pres., 1901; hon. sec.-treas., Montreal Industrial Exhibition Assn.; was a del. from Bd. of Trade, to International Congress Chambers of Commerce of the world at Philadelphia, 1898; now consul in Canada for Paraguay; gov. Montreal Gen. Hospital; Past Master of Mount Royal Lodge of Masons; mem. I.O. O.F., A.O.U.W. *Address:* 1040 Dorchester St. W., Montreal. *Club:* Canada, Montreal.

MILLER, Henry Horton, M.P.; *b.* Owen Sound, Co. Grey, Ont., 10 Jan., 1861; *s.* Robert B. and Victoria Miller; *m.* M. Ellen Armstrong; two *s.* one *d.* *Educ.:* Owen Sound Public and High Sch. Elec. to H. of C. at g. e., 1904; re-el. 1908; Chairman of Banking and Commerce Committee from 1905, to the present time. *Recreations:* fishing, gardening and horses; *Address:* Hanover, Ont.

MILLER, Lieut.-Col. John Bellamy; *b.* Athens, Ont., 20 July, 1862; *s.* of John Clausin and Adelaide A. Miller; *m.* (1st) Hannah P. Hunter; (2nd) Jessie Thomson; one *s.* one *d.* *Educ.:* Model Sch. and Up. Can. Coll., Toronto; a lumber manufacturer since he left sch.; also in vessel building and iron business; Parry Sound Lumber Co.; man. dir., Polson Iron Works. *Recreations:* hunting, shooting, fishing, yachting. *Address:* 98 Wellesley St., Toronto. *Clubs:* National, Ontario, R.C.Y.C., and Rosedale Golf, Toronto; Rideau, Ottawa.

MILLER, Robert; *b.* Thistle Farm, Ontario Co., Ont., 15 July, 1856; *s.* of John Miller and Margaret Whiteside; *m.* Josephine B. Harding, of Waukesha, Wis.; one *s.* Family engaged for many yrs. in importing and breeding pure bred livestock; has crossed Atlantic 23 times in quest of high-class animals; imported and exported thousands of sheep and cattle. Prominent in live stock affairs; materially assisted to nationalize the "Live Stock Records of Canada;" chn. of Committee conducting these records. *Address:* "Burnbrae," Stouffville, Ont.

MILLER, Willet G., M.A., LL.D.; Provincial Geologist of Ontario; *b.* Charlotteville, Norfolk Co., Ont.; of Canadian parentage; unmarried. *Educ.:* Port Rowan High Sch.; University of Toronto. Fellow 1890-93, and Examiner in Mineralogy and Geology, 1893-95; assistant in field geology, Geological Survey of Can., in the region north of Lake Huron, 1891-93; Lecturer in Geology in Queen's Univ., Kingston, 1893; in charge of field work in geology in Eastern Ont. for the Bureau of Mines, 1897-1901; has been a post-graduate student at the American Universities, Chicago and Harvard, and at Heidelberg, Germany; apptd. to present position, 1902; pres., Can. Mining Inst., 1908-9. *Publications:* writings chiefly on the Archæan and Economic Geology of Eastern Ont.; Papers and Reports on Corundum-bearing Rocks, Iron Ores, Gold Deposits, Cobalt-Silver Ores, etc., in Annual Reports of Ont. Bureau of Mines, American Geologist, Canadian Mining Institute, etc., etc. *Recreations:* canoeing and exploring. *Address:* Bureau of Mines, Toronto. *Clubs:* National, Victoria, Toronto.

MILLER, Hon. William, K.C., P.C.; Senior Senator of Canada; *b.* Antigonish, N.S., 12 Feb., 1834; of Irish parentage; called to the bar of N.S., May, 1860; apptd. Q.C., 1872; sat in the N.S. Assembly from 1863 until Confederation, and while a mem. of the Legislature, rendered important assistance to the Union cause; was in favour of Confederation, but opposed to the financial conditions and other details of the Quebec scheme; on his initiative, the delegation to England was apptd. in 1866, in order to secure modifications more satisfactory to N.S.; nominated delegate to London Colonial Conference in 1866-67, but declined appointment; called to the Senate in 1867, and is now the Senior Senator; has been chairman of all leading standing committees, and of many important special committees; apptd. a mem. of Privy Council for Canada, 30 May, 1891; Speaker of the Senate from 17 Oct., 1883 to

4 April, 1887; a Conservative. *Address:* Arichat, N.S.

MILLICHAMP, Reuben, J.P.; *b.* Birmingham, Eng., 3 Feb., 1842; *s.* of Joseph Millichamp and Catherine Wainwright; *m.* Elizabeth E. Williams; one *s.* two *d.* Arrived in Can., 1855, and educ. in Toronto. Merchant and manufacturer. Pres., Merchants Union Co., the Irving Umbrella Co.. the Coatimental Costume Co.; vice-pres., Anglo Am. Fire Insur, Co.; vice-pres;, Montreal-Canada Fire Insur, Co.; hon, treas., Havergal Ladies Coll., Toronto. pres., Victoria Club, Toronto. *Recreations:* fishing, hunting. *Addresses:* 68 Prince Arthur Ave.; McKinnon Bldg., Toronto. (bus). *Clubs:* National, Lambton Golf, Rosedale Golf, Glen Major Angling, Toronto.

MILLMAN, Thomas, M.D.; Supreme Physician of the I.O.F.; *b.* East Zorra tp., Oxford Co., Ont., 14 Feb., 1850; *m.* 1881, Helen Dick, *d.* of John Craig, of Woodstock, Ont.; one *s.* four *d.* *Educ.:* Woodstock Gram. Sch.; grad. M.D., 1874, Trinity Med. Coll., Toronto. Apptd. Asst. surgeon of British North American Boundary Com.; remained on Com. until 1875; further studied his profession in the hospitals of London, Eng. and Edinburgh, Scot., 1875-76; became mem. R.C.S.E. and a Licentiate of the Roy. Coll. of Physicians and Surgeons, Edinburgh; returned to Can., and commenced practice of his profession in Woodstock, Ont.; asst. physician of the Asylum for the Insane at London, Ont., 1879-1885; asst. supt. of Asylum for Insane at Kingston Ont., 1885-1889; resigned latter position and removed to Toronto, where he has since resided. Has been sup. physician and sec. of Medical Bd. of I.O.F. since 1891. *Address:* 490 Huron St., Toronto, Ont.

MILLS, James, M.A., LL.D.; Member of Railway Commission for Canada; *b.* nr. Bond Head, Co. of Simcoe, Ont., 24 Nov., 1840; *s.* of John Mills, farmer and Ann Stinson, *d.* of a farmer; *m.* 1869, Jessie Ross of Cobourg, Ont.; two *s.* five *d.* *Educ.:* public schs. of Ont.; Bradford Gram. Sch., Simcoe Co., Victoria Univ., Cobourg. (Prince of Wales's Gold Medal for highest General Proficiency), 1868; worked on his father's farm till 21 years of age, when he lost his right arm in a thrashing machine. Took his first lesson in English Grammar at 21, his B.A. degree at 28, and his M.A. at a later date. His LL.D. was conferred *honoris causa.* Taught an academy in the Eastern Townships, Que., for one year; was classical master of Cobourg Coll. Inst. for 3½ years; headmaster of Brantford Coll. Inst. for 6¼ years, teaching Latin and and Greek, and for a time, French and German, in that school; was pres. of the Ontario Agricultural College, Guelph, for 25 years, an institution which has done so much for the farmers of Ontario; organized the most useful agricul ural institution in Canada, The Farmers' Institutes; and managed them for 10 years, till a special superintendent was apptd. to take charge of the work; also organized and supervised the work of the travelling dairies throughout the Province of Ont.; is now, and has been for 6 years, a member of the Board of Railway Commissioners for Canada. *Publications:* "The first principles of Agriculture," (Mills & Shaw), for use in the Public Schools of the Province of Ontario. *Address:* 241 Gilmour St., Ottawa. *Clubs:* Rideau, Country, Ottawa.

MILLS, John Burpe, M.A., K.C.; *b.* Annapolis Co., N.S., 24 July, 1850; *s.* of John Mills and Jane McCormick; *m.* (1st) 1878, Bessie B. Corbett (*dec*).; (2nd) 1896, Agnes Katherine Rose, Ottawa; three *s.* two *d.* *Educ.:* Common Sch., Horton Academy, Acadia Univ., and Harvard Law Sch.; called to the Nova Scotia Bar in 1875; apptd Q.C., 25 June, 1890; represented Annapolis Co., in the H. of C., continuously from o2 Feb., 1887, to Nov., 1900; called to the bar of B.C., 25 Aug., 1905. *Recreations:* cricket. *Address:* 1171 Nelson St., Vancouver, B.C.

MILLS, T. Wesley, M.A., M.D., F.R.S.C. *Educ.:* Toronto Univ.; McGill; after special study abroad, became Professor of Phys. in McGill Univ.; has always taken a deep interest in education; member of many learned Societies, and Fellow of the Roy. Soc. of Canada, of which he has twice been a president of Section iv.; founder of the Society for the Study of Comparative Psychology of Montreal; formerly President of Natural Hist. Soc., Montreal, and Vice-Pres. of Soc. of Am. Naturalists; Professor of Physiology, MeGill Univ., Montreal. *Publications:* Animal Physiology; Voice Production; Comparative Physiology; The Dog in Health and in Disease; The Nature and Development of Animal Intelligence; papers giving results of original researches. *Address:* McGill University, Montreal.

MILLS, Right Rev. William Lennox, D.D., LL.D., D.C.L., Bishop of Ontario; *b.* Woodstock, Ont., 27 Jan., 1846; *s.* of William and Elise Mills; *m.* Katharine S., *d.* of the late Stanley Clark Bagg, Montreal; one *s.* *Educ.:* Woodstock Gram. Sch.; Hara Coll., and Western Univ., London, Ont.; Trinity Coll., Toronto; Incumbent of Trinity Church, Norwich; St. Thomas Church, Seaforth; Rector of St. John's, Que.; Trinity Church, Montreal; lecturer on Old Testament exegises, and Scripture History, Diocesan Theological Coll., Montreal; examining Chaplain to the Bishop of Montreal, Canon of Christ Church Cathedral; Archdeacon of St. Andrew's Div. of Montreal; Bishop of Ontario. *Address:* Bishop's Court, Kingston, Ont.

MILNE, George Lawson, M.D., C.M.; *b.* Garmouth, Morayshire, Scot., 19 April, 1850; *s.* of Alexander and Isabella Milne; *m.* Ellen Catherine Kinsman; *Educ.:* Toronto Med. Sch.; Toronto Univ. Arrived in Canada, Sept., 1857; M.L.A. for Victoria, 1890-1894; Dominion Medical Inspector and Immigration Agent. *Recreations:* fishing, motoring. *Address:* 618 Dallas Road, Victoria, B.C. *Club:* Pacific, Victoria.

MITCHELL, Robert Menzies, M.D., C.M., M.L.A.; *b.* York County, Ont., 28 Oct., 1865; *s.* James Mitchell and Elizabeth Rogers, Scot.; *m.* Margaret McKinnon; two *s.* *Educ.:* Orangeville High Sch. and Trinity Medical Coll.; mem. C.P. & S. (Sask. Alberta, Ont).; taught sch. for 3 years in Ontario; grad. M.D., 1892; practiced in Dundalk until 1899; practiced in Weyburn, Sask., 1889 to present time; Quarantine Inspector at North Portal, 1901-1902; el.

mem. of the Leg. Assem. of Sask., for Weyburn in Aug., 1908. *Address:* Weyburn, Sask.

MITCHELL, Hon. William; Senator; *b.* Durham tp., Ont., 14 March, 1851; *s.* of Thomas Mitchell, and Margaret Patrick (both Irish); *m.* 1876, Dora A., *d.* of George H. Goddard, of Danville, Que. *Educ.:* Durham Pub. Schs. In his youth employed in railway work in Maine, U.S.; returned to Durham and engaged in the lumber business; removed to Drummondville, Que., and engaged in the same business. Gen. Mgr. and Dir. of the Drummond Co. Ry.; pres., Drummondville Bridge Co., Drummond Lumber Co.; dir., Richmond, Drummond, Yamaska Fire Insur. Co.; chn., Protestant Bd. of Sch. Commrs., and a J.P. Called to the Senate, 5 March, 1904. *Address:* Drummondville, Que.

MOBERLY, Frank; *b.* Barrie, Ont., 19 July, 1845; *s.* John (Capt. R. N.) and Mary Moberly; *m.* (1st) Georgina McIntyre, *d.* of John McIntyre, Factor in H. B. Co.; (2nd) Mary Violet, *e. d.* of same; three *s.* two *d.* *Educ.:* England and Canada; Police Magistrate, Ont.; Provincial Magistrate, Provinces of Que. and B.C.; has spent 45 years on railway work, including survey and construction of Union, Northern and Can. Pac.; Can. Northern and Transcontinental Rys. *Address:* Barrie, Ont. *Club:* Engineers, Toronto.

MOLLOY, John Patrick, V.V.S., M.P.; *b.* Arthur, Ont., 13 March, 1873; *s.* of John and Mary Alice Molloy; *m.* 1903, Frances H. Keeley; three *d.* *Educ.:* Emerson, Man., and Toronto. A Veterinary Surgeon; unsuccessful can. for Man. Legis., 1907; first el. to H. of C., 1908. Roman Catholic. Liberal. *Address:* Morris, Man.

MOLSON, Harry Markland; *b.* Montreal, 9 Aug., 1856; *s.* of William Molson and Helen Converse. *Educ.:* Montreal, Germany and Paris; a dir. of the Molson's Bank; dir., Canadian Transfer Co. *Address:* 2 Edgehill Ave., Montreal; summer residence, Dorval, Que. *Clubs:* Mount Royal, St. James, R. St. L. Y. C. Royal Montreal Golf, Montreal Jockey, Hunt, all of Montreal; Junior Athenaeum, London, Eng.

MOLSON, William Alexander, M.D., C.M. (McGill), M.R.C.S., England; physician; *b.* Montreal, 27 Aug., 1852; *s.* of the late John Molson and Anne Molson; *m.* Esther Edith, *d.* of the late Capt. R. W. Shepherd; one *s.* one *d.* *Educ.:* Montreal High Sch., McGill Univ. (M.D., C.M., 1874), and studied at the Royal Coll. of Surgeons, England. Served one yr. in St. Thomas Hospital, London, and completed his studies in Vienna and Edinburgh. Has practiced in Montreal since 1877. Senior physician, Montreal Gen. Hospital; was examining surgeon in Montreal Garrison Art. during North West Rebellion. *Recreations:* travelling, outdoor sports. *Address:* 384 Sherbrooke St. W., Montreal. *Clubs:* St. James', Montreal Hunt, Mount Royal.

MONAGHAN, Michael B.A. (Royal Univ., Irel.); Gen. Agent Mutual Life Assur. Co. of Canada, at Quebec; *b.* Killucan, Westmeath, Irel., 1857; *m.* 1890, Margaret Harney, of Quebec; five *s.* one *d.* *Educ.:* French Coll., Blackrock, Dublin; Royal Univ., Ireland. Taught in Blackrock Coll. for several yrs. Arrived Canada, 1888; taught sch. at Ottawa for one yr.; conducted highest classes in Latin and Greek in St. Thomas Coll., St. Paul, Minn. for five yrs.; returned to Ottawa and again taught sch.; apptd. gen. agt., Mutual Life Assur. Co., of Can., at Que., 1898. Mem. Que. Assn. of Life Insur. Underwriters. *Address:* 71 Lachevrotiere St., Quebec.

MONET, Hon. Dominique, K.C., B.C.L. (Laval Univ.); a Puisne Judge of the Superior Ct. of the Prov. of Quebec for the Dist. of St. John's since 1908; *b.* St. Michael de Napierville, Que., 2 Jan., 1865; *s.* of Dominique Monet, and Marguerite Remillard (both French-Canadians); *m.* 1887, Marie Louise La Haye; three *s.* two *d.* *Educ.:* L'Assomption Coll., Laval Univ. Unsuccessful can. for the H. of C. at bye-el. 1890; el. at g. e., 1891; re-el. at g. e., 1896, and 1900. El. to Leg. Ass. at g. e., 1904; became Mem. without portfolio in the Parent Govt., 1905; apptd. Acting Min. of Pub. Works and Colonization, 23 Feb., 1905; apptd. Prothonotary of the Superior Ct. of Montreal, 1905, which position he held until elevated to the Bench. *Recreations:* literature, angling, hunting. *Address:* St. John's, Que.

MONK, Frederick Debartzch, K.C., B. C.L., D.C.L., M.P., Professor of Constitutional Law, Laval Univ., Montreal; *b.* Montreal, 6 April, 1856; 4th *s.* of late Hon. Samuel Cornwallis Monk, a Judge of the Court of Queen's Bench, and Rosalie Caroline Debartzch; father of English descent (Devonshire); mother French descent; *m.* 1880, Marie-Louise, *o. d.* of late D. H. Senecal, advocate. *Educ.:* Montreal Coll., McGill Univ. Called to bar, 1878; Q.C., 1893; uas been twelve years a School Commissioner for the City of Montreal; el. to H. of C. at g. e., 1896; re;el. at g. e., 1900, 1904, and 1908; el. Opposition Leader for Prov. of Quebec, in H. of C., 1901, but resigned position, 1903. *Address:* 58 St. Francois Xavier, Montreal.

MONTAGUE, Hon. Walter Humphries, M.D., C.M., P.C.; *b.* Canada, 21 Nov., 1858; *s.* Joseph I. and Rhoda Montague; *m.* Augie Furry; two *s.* two *d.* *Educ.:* Canadian Coll., Royal Coll. of Physicians, Edinburgh; a member of the Canadian H. of C. for about 15 years; was Secretary of State for Canada and Minister of Agriculture until defeat of Conservative party in 1896. *Recreations:* golf. *Address:* Evergreen Place, Roslyn Road, Winnipeg, Man. *Clubs:* Rideau, Ottawa; Manitoba, Winnipeg.

MONTIZAMBERT Frederick, I.S.O., M.D. (Edin.), F.R.S.C.E., D.C.L. (Bishop's Coll. Univ.), Director-General of Public Health for the Dominion of Can.; *b.* Quebec, 3 Feb., 1843; *s.* of Edward Louis Montizambert, late Law Clerk of the Senate, and Lucy Irwin, *d.* of the late Chief Justice Bowen; *m.* June, 1865, Mary Jane, *d.* of the late Hon. W. Walker, M.L.C.; two *s.* five *d.* *Educ.:* High Sch. of Montreal, Gram. Sch. at St. John's Que., Upper Can. Coll., Toronto, Laval Univ., Edinburgh Univ. Admitted a L.R.C.S., Edinburgh, 1864; practiced at Que. until apptd. to Can. Quarantine Service, May, 1866. El. Pres. of the Canadian Medical Assn., 1907, of which he was one of original founders; was vice-pres. of American Pub. Health Assn., 1889-90, and pres. 1891. Mem., British Medical Assn., Council of Can. Branch, Red Cross Soc., Council of Can. Assn. for Prevention of Tuberculosis; Que. Literary and Historical Soc.; of the Que. Geological Soc.; hon. mem. of the Academy National de Mexico; was el. Fellow of the Royal Coll. of Surgeons, 1888; el. Fellow of the Royal Sanitary Institute, 1907; del. of Dom. Govt. to the International Cholera Conferences at Washington, D.C., 1884, and New York, 1893. Apptd. Gen. Medical Supt. of Canadian Quarantines, 1894, and has served as med. asst. since, 1866, and as supt. of the St. Lawrence Quarantines since 1869. Was made Director-Gen. of Pub. Health, 1899, and created a Deputy Minister by statute in 1905. *Address:* 123 Cooper St., Ottawa. *Clubs:* Rideau, Ottawa; Toronto.

MONTPLAISIR, Hon. Hypolite; Senator; *b.* Cap de Madeleine, Que., 7 May, 1840; *s.* of Paschal Montplasir, and Victoria Crevier; *m.* E. M. Ayer. *Educ.:* Three Rivers Academy; has been Mayor of his native parish 25 years, consecutively, and Warden of Champlain Co. six years; has been Secretary-Treas. of School Comn. for 38 years; a farmer; apptd. to the Senate, 9 Feb., 1891; Conservative. *Address:* Three Rivers, Que.

MONTREAL Arch. of (Roman Catholic.) (See **Most Rev. Paul Bruchesi**).

MOORE Colonel Frederick Strong; *b.* Charlottetown, P.E.I., 13 Aug., 1846; *s.* of George Moore and Eliza Chappele; *m.* Eliza Bouyer; one *s.* one *d.* *Educ.:* Pub. Schs. Commenced business life as a clerk in Bank of P. E. Island, afterwards with the Merchants Bank of P.E.I. Was Treasurer of Charlottetown for some years. Apptd. a Lieut. in Provincial Militia in 1867, and promoted Captain in 1868. Organized No. 2 Battery, 4th Regt., C.A., in 1882, which he commanded until 1887, when he was promoted to command the Regiment. Under his command the Battery was the most efficient in Canada, taking 1st prize for General Efficiency in competition with all the Garrison Artillery of Canada, for five years consecutively; was a Vice-Pres. of "Canadian Artillery Association," for several years, and President of Provincial Rifle Association for a number of years. Holds first class certificates from Royal Schools of Artillery and Cavalry; was apptd. district officer commanding in 1894, and commanded Military District No. 12 for 15 years, when he retired, retaining rank in 1909; was Pres. of Y.M.C.A. for 5 years, and Superintendent of Sabbath School, First Methodist Church, for 5 years. *Address:* 17 Upper Prince St., Charlottetown, P.E.I.

MOORE, Henry Philip; *b.* Acton, Ont., 18 Oct., 1858; *s.* Edward Moore and Elizabeth Hemstreet; *m.* Harriet Isabella Speight, 3 Dec., 1879; one *s.* *Educ.:* Acton Pub. Sch., Rockwood Academy, and Albert Coll., Belleville, Ont.; pres., Canadian Press Association, 1891-1892; pres., Ont. Sunday Sch. Association, 1896; is a member of the Board of Management of Albert Coll.; a member of the Committee of Management of the Methodist Book and Publishing House, Toronto, for the past 15 years. *Publications:* Editor and publisher of the Acton *Free Press* since 1878. *Recreations:* lawn bowling and fishing. *Address:* Acton, Ont.

MOORE, Samuel John; *b.* Doddington, Northamptonshire, Eng., 3 Aug., 1859; *s.* of Isaac and Louisa Moore; *m.* Matilda Anne, *d.* of Alexander Lang, Barrie; one *s.* three *d.* *Educ.:* by priv. tuition in England. Came to Can., 1874, and spent five yrs. in the office of the Barrie *Gazette;* became mem. of publishing firm of Bengough, Moore & Co., of Toronto, 1879. Now pres. of the W. A. Rogers, Ltd., of Toronto; gen. mgr. of the Carter-Crume Co.; pres. of the Kidder Press Co., of Boston, Mass.; a dir. of the Imperial Life Assur Co., Toronto; a dir. of the Metropolitan Bank; a trustee of the Massey Music Hall Trust. *Address:* 142 Jameson Ave., Toronto. *Club:* National.

MOORE, William Henry, B.A.; *b.* Stouffville, Ont., 19 Oct., 1872; *s.* James Beach, and Hannah Greenwood Moore; *m,* Christine Mabee Bertram; two *s.* one *d.* *Educ.:* Woodstock Coll., Toronto Univ. Secretary, Canadian Northern Railway Co.; General Manager, Toronto and York Radial Railway Co.; Director of several industrial undertakings. *Address:* 15 Cluny Avenue, Toronto, Ont. *Clubs:* Toronto, Toronto Hunt, Toronto; Garrison, Quebec.

MORANG, George Nathaniel; *b.* Eastport, Maine, U.S.A., 10 March, 1866; *s.* of George Nathaniel Morang and Adeline Emery; *m.* Sophia Longworthy Heaven; two *s.* two *d.* *Educ.:* Eastport Maine; arrived in Canada, 1888. A publisher, especially of Canadian works. *Address:* Toronto, Ont. *Clubs:* Toronto, Toronto Hunt, R.C. Y.C., Toronto, Ont.; Manitoba Club, Winnipeg.

MORGAN, James C., M.A.; *b.* St. Vincent, West Indies, 20 May, 1846; *s.* of Rev. Canon Edward Morgan and Mary Morgan; *m.* Kate McVittie; one *s.* one *d.* *Educ.:* Barrie Gram. Sch. and Toronto Univ. Arrived Canada, 1856. Headmaster of a Church Sch., and Inspector of Educ. in Ont., for 36 years; at present supt. of Orphans' Home Fund of I.O.F. *Publications:* musical and masonic. *Recreations:* music, floriculture. *Addresses:* Barrie, Ont; 22 Hazelton Ave., Toronto.

MORICE, Rev. Adrian Gabriel, O.M.I.; *b.* St. Mars-sur-Colmont, Dept. of Mayence, France; *s.* of Jean Morice and Virginie Seigneur. *Educ.:* Christian Brothers' Sch. of Oisseau, and the ecclesiastical colls. of Mayence, N.D. de Sion (Lorraine), and Autun. Entered the Order of the Oblates of Mary Immaculate, 9 Oct., 1879. Came to Canada, 1880. Ordained 2 July, 1882, and put in charge of the Chilcotin Indians in British Columbia; transferred to Stuart Lake Mission, Aug., 1885. In 1885 invented the Déné Syllabary, which soon spread among the northern Indians of B.C. Printed many books in the new syllabics, and for two yrs. published a monthly magazine in the same. Mem. of the Philological Soc. of Paris; American Anthropological Assn.; Canadian Institute; Natural History Soc. of British Columbia; Art. Historical and Scientific Assn. of Vancouver; Historical and Scientific Soc. of Manitoba; Historical Soc. of St. Boniface, Man.; Geographical

Soc. of Neufchatel (Switzerland); Ethnological Committee, B.A.A.S. *Publications:* a vol. of travel, "Au Pays de l'Ours Noir," (Paris, 1897); "The History of the Northern Interior of British Columbia," (Toronto, 1904); "Aux Sources de l'Histoire manitobaine (Quebec, 1907); Dictionnaire historique des Canadiens et des Metis francais de l'Ouest (Quebec, 1908); "History of the Catholic Church in Western Canada," (Toronto, 1909), in two vols.; two large vols. intitled "The Great Déné Race," now being serially issued in Vienna, Austria. Published in Neufchatel, Switzerland, a map of the valley of the Nechaco River (1904), for which he was awarded a silver medal by the Geographical Soc. *Address:* St. Mary's Church, Winnipeg, Man.

MORIN, Victor, B.A., LL.B. (Laval); *b.* St. Hyacinthe, Que., 1865; *s.* of Jean Baptiste and Aurelie Cote; *m.* (1st) 1893, Fannie Cote, of Biddeford, Me., (*d.* 1894); (2nd) 1896, Aphonsine Cote, of St. Hyacinthe; four *s.* five *d.* *Educ.:* St. Hyacinthe Coll., Laval Univ., B.A., 1884, LL.B B., 1888. Studied law in office of Papineau, Morin & MacKay; admitted to practice of notarial prof., 1888, and removed to Actonvale, Que.; returned to Montreal, 1890, and is now head partner of the firm of Morin & MacKay. Treas. Bd. of Notaries of Prov. of Que.; Notary of Corporation of City of Montreal; pres., Montreal Real Estate Assn., Petroleum Co., Federal Real Estate and Trust Co.; dir. Prudential Life Insur. Co., Montreal; Eastern Land Co.. Canadian Chrome Co.; gen. sec., Montreal Anti-Alcoholic League; Past Sup. Chief Ranger, I.O.F.; sec. Maison d'Etudians, *Recreation:* books. *Address:* 1110 St. Denis St., Montreal. *Clubs:* Montreal Polo, St. Denis, Reform, Montreal.

MORINE, Alfred Bishop, LL.B. (Dal.), K.C.; *b.* Port Medway, N.S., 31 March, 1857; *s.* of Alfred and Mary Morine; *m.* Alice M. Mason; one *s.* two *d.* *Educ.:* Dalhousie Univ., Halifax. In 1883, after completing his Univ. course, went to St. John's, Nfld., and engaged in jouranlism. In 1886, was el. to Leg. of Nfld. and sat continuously for Bonavista until 1906. Chosen, with two others, as a del. to London to represent the sentiments of the people of Nfld., concerning French Treaty rights in the Island; in reference to which subject he and his co-delegates prepared and published a pamphlet dealing with the whole question; one of five delegates sent by the Legislature on the same mission in 1891. On this occasion the delegates were received at the Bar of the House of Lords and presented an address prepared by Mr. Morine; apptd. Colonial Sec. of Newfoundland in 1894; Minister of Finance in 1897; Min. of Marine and Fisheries in 1898. In the latter yr., represented the Govt. of the colony at London, in a successful effort to procure from the British authorities, the appointment of Commissioners to enquire and report on the effect of French rights in the colony. As Min. of Marine and Fisheries, accompanied the delegates around the French treaty coast. As a result of the enquiry and report of the Commrs., the rights so injurious to Nfld. were terminated by arrangement between France and Great Britain. During the mission to London, in 1898, obtained from the British Govt., a promise to estab. in Nfld. a branch of the Naval Reserve, which promise was fulfilled. Removed to Toronto in 1900, and admitted to bar of Ontario; K.C., 1907. An unsuccessful can for H. of C. for Queens-Shelburne, N.S. *Publications:* The Mining Law of Canada, Canadian Notes to Russell on Crimes. *Recreations:* angling, bowling, golfing, motoring. *Address:* 546 Sherbourne St., Toronto. *Clubs:* Albany, Toronto; Lambton Golf.

MORISSET, McMahon Alfred, M.D., M. L.A.; *b.* St. Henedine, Dorchester Co., Que., 4 July, 1874; *s.* of Alfred Morisset, and Aglae Dion; *m.* Fabiola Vezina; one *s.* four *d.* *Educ.:* Laval Univ. Has been practising his profession at St. Henedine for some yrs. Mem. of the Medical Soc. of Beauce and Dorchester; mem. of the Medical Soc. of Quebec. First el. to the Leg. Ass., 1904; re-el. 1908. *Address:* St. Henedine, Que.

MORRICE, David; head of the D. Morrice Co., Ltd., general merchants and manufacturers' agents; *b.* St. Martin's, Perthshire, Scotland, 11 Aug., 1831; *m.* 1881, Annie S., *d.* of John Anderson, of Toronto; three *s.* *Educ.:* St. Martin's Perthshire Engaged in mercantile pursuits in Dublin, Irel.; Liverpool, London, and Manchester, Eng. Arrived Canada, 1855; went to Toronto and removed to Montreal, 1862, and estabd. the firm of D. Morrice & Co., gen. merchants and manufacturers' agents, a few yrs. ago controlling over forty cotton and woollen mills, but now confine their attention to the four largest, the Canadian Colored Cotton Mills Co., the Gibson Mill Co., Penman's Ltd., of Paris, Ont.; the Auburn Co., of Peterboro. The business is now conducted under the style of the D. Morrice Co., Ltd.; Dir., Bank of Montreal, Royal Trust Co.; Pres., Canadian Colored Cotton Mills Co., Penman's Ltd., Montreal Investment and Freehold Co.; dir. Dom. Textile Co., Royal Victoria Life Insur. Co.; mem. Montreal Bd. of Trade; life gov. and mem. bd. of management, Montreal Gen. Hospital; pres. MacKay Instit; mem. Council of Montreal Art Assn. *Address:* 10 Redpath St., Montreal *Clubs:* St. James, Mount Royal Forest and Stream, Huntreal.

MORRIS, Clara (Mrs. Harriott); *b.* Toronto, Ont., 1849; lived there until 3 months old, then to Cleveland and grew up there; became mem. of ballet in Acad. of Music, Cleveland, 1861, rapidly advancing to leading lady; in 1869 became leading lady at Wood's Theatre, Cincinnati; became mem. Daly's Fifth Av. Co., New York, 1870; soon became prominent in emotional roles and has appeared as star in prin. Am. theatres. Leading roles: Camille; Alixe; Miss Multon; Mercy Merrick in "The New Magdalene;" Cora, in "L'Article 47;" etc.; *m.* 1874, Frederick C. Harriott. Contributor to St. Nicholas, Century Mag., Pearson's, Leslie's Woman's Companion, N. Am. Rev., Ladies' Home Journal, etc. *Publications:* A Silent Singer, 1899; My Little Jim Crow, 1900; Life on the Stage, 1901; A Paste-Board Crown (novel), 1902; Stage Confidences, 1902; The Trouble Woman,

1904; Life of a Star, 1906. *Address:* Riverdale-on-Hudson, N.Y.

MORRIS, Edmund Montague; artist; *b.* Perth, Ont., 1871; *s.* of late Hon. Alexander Morris, P.C., D.C.L. *Educ.:* Art Students' League, New York; L'Academie Julian, and the Deux Arts Paris, A.R.C.A., 1897. Painted for the Ontario Govt., a series of portraits representing the best types to be found amongst the tribes of Ont., Man., Sask., and Alta. Commissioned to make Indian portraits for the Parliament Bldgs. of Sask. and Alta. Landscape purchased by Dom. Govt.; medal Pan-American Exhn., Buffalo, 1901. A founder of the New Canadian Art Club, 1908. *Address:* 43 Victoria St., Toronto, Ont. *Club:* Canadian Art, Toronto.

MORRISON, Lieut.-Col. Edward W. B. D.S.O.; Editor of the Ottawa *Citizen; b.* London, Ont., 6 July, 1865; *s.* of Alexander Morrison; unmarried. *Educ.:* Pub. Schs., and Tassie Institute, Galt, Ont. Commenced journalistic career on the staff of the Hamilton *Spectator;* ed. of the Ottawa *Citizen.* An ardent military man. Joined 4th Hamilton Field Battery, but on removal to Ottawa, transferred to 2nd Field Battery; served in South African War, 1899-1900. Operations in the Transvaal, east of Pretoria, from July to 29 Nov., 1900, including action at Belfast, 26 and 27 Aug., 1900. Operations in Orange River Colony, May to 28 Nov., 1900. Operations in Cape Colony, south of Orange River, 1899-1900. *Despatches.* Brevet of Captain.; D.S.O. Queen's Medal with three clasps; organized 1905, 23rd Field Batt., Gttawa, which in first yr. of its existence, captured the first prizes for efficiency and firing; promoted Lieut.-Col., comdg. 8th Brig., Field Art., 1909. *Recreation:* horseback riding. *Addresses:* 19 Delaware Av.; The Citizen, Ottawa. *Club:* Rideau, Ottawa.

MORRISSY, Hon. John, M.L.A.; Chief Commr. of Pub. Works, New Brunswick; *b.* Newcastle, N.B., 13 Aug., 1855; *s.* of Patrick Morrissy and Rose Carrell (Irish); *m.* 1879, Joanna A. Dunn; two *s.* one *d.* *Educ.:* Newcastle. A merchant; Dep. Sheriff, 1880-81; Veterinary Surgeon, 12th Field Battery of Newcastle, 1885-1897; mem. Co. Coun., 1882-83. Unsuccessful can. for Legis. at bye-el., 1888; el. for Legis., 1889; defeated at g. e., 1890; defeated at bye-el., 1890; defeated at g. e., 1894; an unsuccessful can for H. of C. at g. e., 1896; defeated for Legis. at g. e., 1898; defeated for H. of C., at g. e., 1900; el. for Legis., at g. e., 1903; re-el. at g. e., 1908. Sworn of the Ex. Coun. as Chief Commr. of Pub. Works in Hazen Cabinet, 20 March, 1908; re-el. by accl., 7 April, 1908. *Address:* Newcastle,'N.B.

MORSE, Charles, D.C.L., K.C.; *b.* Liverpool, N.S., 24 Dec., 1860; *s.* Charles Morse, K.C., and Margaret Henderson; *m.* Susan Mary Peters; two *s.* one *d.* *Educ.:* Liverpool Academy, Dalhousie Univ., and Trinity Univ., Toronto. Admitted to bar of N.S., in 1885; apptd. Deputy Registrar, Exchequer Court of Canada in 1889. *Publications:* "Apices Juris," and other legal essays; founded (with C. H. Masters, K.C.) "Canadian Annual Digest," in 1896; is now literary editor of the Canadian Law Times. *Recreations:* lawn bowling and rowing. *Address:* 44 Macleod St., Ottawa. *Club:* Halifax.

MOSS, Hon. Sir Charles, K.B., LL.D.; Chief Justice of the Ontario Court of Appeals; *b.* Cobourg, Ont., 8 March, 1840; *s.* of John Moss, and Cordelea Ann Ouigley; *m.* Emily, 2nd *d.* of the Hon. Robert B. Sullivan, Justice of the Court of Queen's Bench for Up. Can.; three *s.* two *d.* While student at-law, gained the Law Society Scholarship; called to the bar of Ont., Nov., 1869; lecturer and examiner to Law Society of Up. Can., 1872-79; apptd. Bencher of law Society, 1880; re-el. in 1881 and thereafter at each succeeding election; apptd. Queen's Council, 1881; represented Law Society in Senate of Toronto Univ., 1884-1897; Pres. York Law Assn., 1891-1892; Vice-Chancellor Univ. of Toronto, 1900-1906; member of Board of Governors and Vice Chairman, 1906; Pres. of Havergal Ladies' Coll.; apptd. Justice of the Court of Appeal for Ont., 1897; apptd. Chief Justice of Ontario, 1902; several times administrator of the Government of Ontario; knighted, 1907. *Publications:* Handbook of Commercial Law in colloboration with the late Robert Sullivan, barrister; *Recreations:* bowling, croquet. *Address:* Roseneath, 547 Jarvis St., Toronto, Ont. *Clubs:* Toronto, R.C.Y. C., Toronto.

MOTHERSILL, Thomas Barton; *b.* Arkona, Lambton Co., Ont., 22 Oct., 1859; *s.* of Joseph Mothersill, M.D., and Mary Darlington; *m.* Maud Louise Henderson; three *s.* one *d.* *Educ.:* Stratford Collegiate. Secretary and managing director "Mothersill Remedy Co., Ltd.," a well known preventative of sea sickness. *Recreations:* riding. *Address:* 64 Victoria Av., Windsor, Ont.

MOTHERWELL, Hon. W. R., M.L.A.; Commr. of Agric., and Prov. Sec. of Saskatchewan; *b.* Perth, Lanark Co., Ont., 6 Jan., 1860; *s.* of John and Eliza Motherwell; *m.* 1884, Adeline Rogers, of New Boyne, Ont.; two *d.* *Educ.:* Perth Coll. Inst. and Guelph Agric. Coll. (A.A.C. of Guelph Agric. Coll.) A farmer. Pres. of the Imperial Temperance Hotel. An unsuccessful can. for North Qu'Appelle, 1904, and 1906; el. to Sask. Legis. at first g. e., 1905. Apptd. Commr. of Agric. and Prov. Sec. upon the formation of the first ministry of Sask. by Hon. Walter Scott, 5 Sept., 1905 defeated in Qu'Appelle, at g. e., 1908; el. in Humbolt, at bye-el., 7 Dec., 1908. *Address:* Regina, Sask.

MOUNTAIN, George Alphonso, C.E.; Chief Engr., Bd. of Railway Commrs. for Canada; Pres. and mem. of the Canadian Soc. of Civil Engrs.; *b.* Quebec, 28 Sept., 1869; *s.* of the late Matthew G. Mountain, and Isabella Peek; *m.* 1891, Kate Damoreau, of Montreal; one *d.* *Educ.:* Quebec. Civil Engr. on suryevs of the Quebec & Lake St. John Ry., and the Quebec Graving Docks, Newfoundland Ry., Can. Atlantic Ry. for 23 yrs., the last ten as chief engr.; apptd. Chief Engr. of Bd. of Ry Commrs.. for Canada, 1904; mem. Am. Ry. Engineering & Maintenance of Way Assn.; mem. Assn. of Ry. Supts.'of Bridges and Buildings; Dom. Land Surveyor; mem. Royal Astronomical Soc. of Canada. *Recreations:* shooting, fishing, golf. *Address:* 336 MacLaren St., Ottawa. *Clubs:* Rideau, Golf, Ottawa; National, Toronto.

MOUNT-STEPHEN, Baron (Sir George Stephen), G.C.V.O., D.L.; *b.* 5 June, 1829; *s.* of William Stephen, of Dufftown, Banffshire, and Elspet Smith; *m.* (1st) 1853, Charlotte Annie (*d.* 1896), *d.* of Benjamin Kane; (2nd) 1897, Gian, *d.* of late Capt. Robert George Tufnell, R.N. Came to Canada, 1850; became director, vice-Pres. and Pres. of Bank of Montreal; Pres., St. Paul and Manitoba Ry.; head of the C. P. Ry. until 1888; cr. a baronet, 1886; mem. of House of Lords, 1891; G.C.V.O., 1905. Conservative; Presbyterian. *Addresses:* 17 Carlton House Terrace, S.W.; Brocket Hall, Hatfield, Hertfordshire; Grand Metis, Quebec. *Clubs:* Carlton, Arthur's, London, Eng.

MOWAT, Herbert Macdonald, K.C., LL.B.; *b.* Kingston, Ont., 9 April, 1860; *s.* Rev. Professor Mowat, D.D., of Queen's University and Emma, *d.* of Hon. John McDonald, of Gananoque; *m.* Mary, *d.* of John Skeaff, of Aberdeen. *Educ.:* Queen's Univ. Called to the bar of Ontario, 1886; apptd. Q.C. in Oct., 1899. *Address:* 10 Wellesley St., Toronto, Ont. *Club:* Toronto.

MOWAT, John McDonald, B.A.; *b.* Kingston, Ont., 17 Feb., 1873; *s.* of Rev. John Bower Mowat, M.A., D.D., Prof. of Oriental Languages in Queen's Univ., and Emma, *d.* of the late Hon. John McDonald. *Educ.:* Kingston Coll. Inst., Queen's Univ., Osgoode Hall, Toronto. Mayor of Kingston, 1906-07. *Recreations:* canoeing, fishing, motoring. *Address:* Kingston, Ont. *Clubs:* Frontenac, Kingston Yacht, Kingston Golf and Country, Kingston; Ontario, Can. Mil. Inst., Toronto.

MULOCK, Hon. Sir William, K.C.M.G., *cr.* 1902; M.A., K.C., LL.D.; Chief Justice of the Exchequer Division of the High Court of Justice for the Province of Ontario; *b.* Bond Head, Ont., 19 Jan., 1843; *s.* of Thomas Homan Mulock, M.D.; *m.* 1870, Sarah Ellen, *d.* of James Crowther, barrister Toronto. *Educ.:* Newmarket Gram. Sch.; Univ. of Toronto. Graduated in Arts, 1863; barr., 1868; Q.C., 1888; first elected to Dominion Parliament 1882; re-elected 1887, 1891, 1896, 1900, and 1904; Vice-Chancellor of Univ. of Toronto from 1881 until 1900, when he resigned in consequence of his public duties; Postmaster-General of Canada, 1896-1905, and Minister of Labour, 1900-5; on his suggestion, the Inter-Imperial Postal Conference adopted Penny Postage within the Empire, 1898; introduced and carried through H. of C., a bill establishing the Department of Labour, 1900; for some years was lecturer on Equity and Law Examiner for the Law Society of Up. Can.; representative of Canada, at inauguration of Federal Parliament of Australia; apptd. Chief Justice, 1905. *Address:* 518 Jarvis St., Toronto. *Club:* Toronto, Toronto; Rideau, Ottawa.

MUNRO, Lieut.-Col. James; President of the Farmers' Bank of Canada; *b.* Embro, Ont., 24 June, 1846; *m.* Agnes Orr Holmes; two *s.* three *d.* *Educ.:* Embro pub. sch. Banker and farmer; Warden of the Co. of Oxford, in 1885; member for North Oxford in the Ontario Legislature, 1904; re-elec. 1905; joined 22nd Batt., The Oxford Rifles, in 1864 as a private; became Lt.-Col., commanding the Regiment, in 1885; was paymaster of the Queen's Diamond Jubilee Contingent, in 1897, and was Brigadier of the 1st Infantry Brigade from 1905 to 1909; is now Hon. Lt.-Col., of the 22nd Regt.; Pres. of the Farmers' Bank of Canada; Liberal; Presbyterian. *Address:* Embro, Ont. *Clubs:* Can. Military Institute, and Ontario Club, Toronto.

MUNRO, William Bennett, M.A., Ph. D., LL.B., Assistant Professor of the Science of Government in Harvard Univ., U.S.; *b.* Almonte, Ont., 5 Jan., 1875; *s.* of John McNab Munro, late of H. M. Customs, and Sarah Bennett; unmarried. *Educ.:* Queen's Coll., Kingston; Univ. of Edinburgh; Harvard Univ.; Univ. of Berlin. After graduating from Queen's Coll., took law course in Univ. of Edinburgh, then entered upon special study of history and political science at Harvard; obtained degree of Doctor of Philosophy, 1900, and spent a year at Univ. of Berlin, as Parker Travelling Fellow of Harvard Univ.; Instructor in Political Science, Williams Coll., Mass., 1901-04; a mem. of Faculty of Harvard Univ., since 1904; Pres. of Harvard Co-operative Society (dealers in students' supplies). *Publications:* Canada and British North America, 1905; the Seigniorial System in Canada, 1907; Documents relating to the Seignoirial Tenure, 1907; frequent contributor to historical and political reviews. *Address:* 37 Dana Chambers, Cambridge, Mass. *Club:* Colonial, Cambridge, Mass.

MURPHY, Hon. Charles, P.C., M.P., Secretary of State for Canada; *b.* Ottawa, Ont., 8 Dec., 1864; *s.* James Murphy and Mary Conway. *Educ.:* Ottawa Primary Schools; Ottawa Univ., and Osgoode Hall, Toronto; practices Law in Ottawa; a mem. of the Privy Council and Secretary of State Oct., 1908; elected to the H. of C. as member for Russell, 26 Oct., 1908. *Address:* Ottawa. *Club:* Laurentian, Ottawa.

MURPHY, David Richard, K.C., B.A., LL.B.; *b.* St. Stanislas, Champlain Co., Que., 1 Dec., 1862; *s.* of Nicholas Murphy and Mary Sammon; *m.* 1888, Genevieve Neil Kennedy. *Educ.:* St. Laurent Coll., Laval Univ. Admitted to bar, 1886; was partner with the late L. W. Sicotte, and later with W. G. Cruikshanks, K.C., Montreal; became mem. of the firm of Gouin,-Lemieux, Murphy & Bernard, 1907. Created a K.C., 1903. Was sec. of the Montreal bar for three terms. *Recreation:* literature. *Address:* 1215 Dorchester St., Montreal.

MURPHY, Denis; one of the Commrs. of the Temiskaming and Northern Ontario Ry.; *b.* Cork, Irel., 2 April, 1842; *s.* of Jeremiah Murphy and Ellen Sullivan; *m.* Annie Patterson; one *s.* two *d.* Came to Can., 1849. *Educ.:* at Chatham, Que. Commenced life as purser on an Ottawa River steamboat; settled in Ottawa, 1866, as agent of the Montreal and Ottawa Forwarding Co.; in 1880, entered into partnership with the late Mr. J. W. McRae, in the forwarding business, under the name of D. Murphy & Co.; in 1892 amalgamated the different steamboat lines on the Ottawa River, into the Ottawa Transportation Co., with Mr. M. as pres. A dir. of the Bank of Ottawa; pres. of the Canadian Ry. Accident Insur. Co.; vice-pres. of the C. Ross Co.; dir. of the Shawinigan Water and Power Co. First el. to the Ont. Legis., 1902; unsuccessful, 1905; apptd. T. & N. O. Ry. Commr., 1905. *Address:* Tara Hall, Metcalfe St., Ottawa. *Clubs:* Rideau, Laurentian, Golf, Country, Ottawa; National, Albany, Toronto.

MURPHY, His Hon. Denis, B.A.; a Judge of the Supreme Court of British Columbia; *b.* Lac la Hache, B.C., 20 June, 1870; s. of Denis Murphy and Helen White; *m.* 1900, Maud Cameron, of Cornwall, Ont. *Educ.:* Ottawa Univ.; el. to B.C. Legis., 1900; apptd. to present position, Nov., 1909. *Address:* Victoria, B.C.

MURPHY, Martin, C.E., D.Sc., I.S.O.; *b.* Ballendaggen, Enniscorthy, Ireland, 11 Nov., 1832; *s.* of Thomas Murphy and Mary Conroy; *m.* Maria Agnes Buckley, Banteer, Ireland; eight *s.* three *d.* *Educ.:* Ballindaggin, Enniscorthy, Dublin, Ireland; studied Civil Engineerlng on the railways and other public works constructed by the late William Dargan, in Ireland, 1852, to 1862; resident engineer of the Dublin, Wicklow and Wexford Ry., 1862 to 1867. Came to Canada, April, 1868. Made preliminary surveys for projected lines of railway for the Provincial Government of N.S.; City Engineer for Halifax, N.S., during next two years. Contractor for the substructure of heavy bridge work on the Intercolonial Railway, 1872-4; Provincial Government Engineer of N.S., 1875-1903; was consulted on construction of public works, railways, hydographic improvements, etc., by the Governments of Newfoundland, Bermuda and N.B.; Pres. of the N.S. Institute of Science, 1882-3; Pres. of the Canadian Society of Civil Engineers, 1902-3; apptd. Government Inspecting Engineer on the Western Division of the National Transcontinental Railway, in 1906, a position which he holds at present. *Publications:* many on Science and Civil Engineering. *Address:* Edmonton, Alta.

MURRAY, Hon. George Henry, K.C.; Premier of Nova Scotia; *b.* Grand Narrows, N.S., 7 June, 1861; *s.* of the late William Murray and wife; *m.* 1889, Grace E., *d.* of John B. Moore, of North Sydney; three *c.* *Educ.:* local schs. and Boston Univ. Called to Nova Scotia bar, 1883, and commenced practice of law in North Sydney; cr. K.C., 1895, and is now head of the firm of Murray, McKenzie, McMillan & Phalen. Apptd. to Legis. Coun. of N.S., 1 March, 1889; unsuccessful candidate for H. of C. in Cape Breton, g. e., 1887 and 1891, and at bye-el., Feb., 1896. Apptd. a mem. of the Fielding Admn., without portfolio, 11 April, 1891. Called on by Lt.-Gov. Daly, to form admn., upon the resignation of Mr. Fielding, 17 July, 1896, which he succeeded in doing taking the portfolio of Prov. Sec. Was re-el. by accl. Appealed to the people 20 April, 1897, and was sustained by a large maj., and again in 1901 and 1906. El. for Victoria at g. e., 1897, 1901, 1906. *Address:* Halifax, N.S.

MURRAY, Gilbert Mackintosh, B.A.; *b.* Strathroy, Ont., 14 Jan., 1876; *s.* W. H. and Kate G. Murray. *Educ.:* Strathroy Coll. Inst,; Toronto Univ.; Ont. Normal Coll., Hamilton; Secretary Canadian Manufacturers' Assn., (Incorporated); after graduation one year tutorial work in Toronto; three years with Mining Exploration Companies in Western and Northern Ont.; five years with Can. Man. Assn.; Asst. Secy, and finally as Secretary; *Address:* National Club, Toronto. *Clubs:* National and R.C.Y. C., Toronto; Lambton Golf and Country Club, Lambton; Laurentian, Ottawa.

MURRAY, Howard, LL.D.; Dean of Dalhousie Coll., Halifax, N.S.; member of Advisory Board of Education for N.S., since 1906; *b.* New Glasgow, N.S., 1859; *e. s.* of late George Murray, M.D.; *m.* 1890, Janet, *d.* of late George Hattie. *Educ.:* New Glasgow High Sch. and Dalhousie Coll., N.S.; Univ. Coll., London; Edinburgh Univ. Principal of Stellarton High Sch., 1877-78; Guysboro' Academy, 1880; New Glasgow High Sch., 1880-81; won Canadian Gilchrist Scholarship, 1881, and proceeded to England; Tutor in Classics, Dalhousie Univ., 1887-89; Classical Master in Halifax Academy, 1889-94; Lecturer in Classics, Dalhousie Univ., 1890-94; Principal of Halifax Academy, 1891-94; Professor of Classics, Dalhousie Univ., 1894; Dean of the Coll., 1901. *Publications:* The classics, their use, present pos. and future prospects; Reform in the N.S. High Sch. Course. *Recreations:* quoiting, curling. *Address:* 15 Spring Garden Road, Halifax, N.S.

MURRAY, James Peter, J.P., F.S.A. (Lon.); President of the Toronto Carpet Mfg. Co.; *b.* Limerick, Ire., 17 Oct., 1852; *s.* Wm. A. Murray (Scotch), and Jane Anne McNamara (Irish); *m.* (1st) Marie Emelie Caron; (2nd) Nanno Josephine Hayes; three *s.* three *d.* *Educ.:* St. Michael's Coll., Toronto, and St. Hyacinthe Seminary, Que. Came to Canada with his parents when two years of age. Entered father's business in Toronto in 1867; founded Toronto Carpet Mfg. Co., 1891; took an active part in reorganizing Can. Mfgrs. Assn., 1899; founded Employers' Assoc. of Toronto, 1902; a provisional gov. of the Toronto Museum of Art, 1900; Canadian Sec. British Weights and Measures Assn; vice-pres. for Ontario, of the Canadian Mfrs. Assocn.; one of the first members of the Imperial Fed. League, 1884; a vice-pres. of the Can. branch of the Brit. Empire League; a founder of the Toronto Empire Club. A warm supporter of all forms of athletics, especially rowing; an hon. life mem. of tue Argonaut Rowing Club. *Publications:* "Labour in relation to capital;" "Apprenticeship," and kindred subjects. *Address:* 445 Euclid Ave., Toronto *Clubs:* National, Argonaut, Toronto.

MURRAY, Sir John, K.C.B., F.R.S., LL.D., D.Sc., Ph.D.; *b.* Coburg, Ont., 3 Mar,. 1841; 2nd *s.* of Robert Murray, accountant; *m.* Isabel, *d.* of late Thomas Henderson, shipowner, 1889; two *s.* three *d.* *Educ.:* pub. sch., London, Ont.; Victoria Coll., Coburg, Ont.; High Sch., Stirling, Scotland; Edinburgh Univ. Cuvier Prize, Institut de France; Humboldt Medal, Gesellschaft fur Erdkunde, Berlin; Royal Medal, Royal Society; Founder's Medal, R.G.S.;

Neill and Makdougall-Brisbane medals of Royal Society, Edinburgh; Cullum Medal, American Geographical Society; Clarke Medal, Royal Society of New South Wales; Lutke Medal, Imperial Rossian Society of Geography. Hon. mem. of a large number of British and Foreign scientific Societies. Knight of the Prussian Order Pour le Merite, 1898; naturalist; formerly member of the Fishery Board for Scotland; is now engaged in a bathymetrical, physical, and biological survey of the fresh-water lakes of the United Kingdom. Visited Spitzbergen and Arctic regions as a naturalist on board a whaler, 1868; one of the naturalists H.M. S. "Challenger," during exploration of physical and biological conditions of great ocean basins, 1872-76; first assistant of staff apptd. to undertake publication of scientific results of "Challenger" Expedition, 1876-82; apptd. editor, 1882; took part in "Triton" and "Knight Errant" explorations in Faroe Channel, and other deep-sea and marine expeditions; at one time scientific member of the Scottish Fishery Board; British delegate to the International Hydrographic Conference at Stockholm, 1889; has made numerous explorations in tropical oceanic islands and travelled in nearly all parts of the world. *Publications:* editor of Report on the Scientific Results of the "Challenger" Expedition, published by H. M. Stationery Office in fifty royal quarto volumes; author of a Summary of the Scientific Results of the "Challenger" Expedition; joint-author of The Narrative of the Cruise of the "Challenger" and of a Report on Deep-Sea Deposits; author of numerous papers on subjects connected with geography, oceanography, marine biology, and limnology; Report on Scientific Results of Scottish Lake Survey, 6 vols., 1909. *Recreations:* yachting, accompanied with sounding, dredging, and other scientific observations; has a large collection of marine deposits, of which he makes a special study; golf, cycling, shooting and motoring. *Address:* Challenger Lodge, Wardie, Edinburgh; Challenger Farm, Boden, Alta., Canada. *Clubs:* Athenaeum, Royal Societies, Automobile; United Service, Edinburgh; Royal and Ancient, St. Andrew's, New, North Berwick.

MURRAY, Rev. John Oswald, M.A., T.C.D., *b.* Ballymona, Ireland, 1869; *s.* The Very Rev. T. W. Murray, LL.D., Dean of Connor, and Margaret Moyers; *m.* Ada, *d.* of John Marwood R.N *Educ.:* Gram., Sch., Ballymona, and Trinity Coll., Dublin. Arrived in Canada, 1902; Canon of St. John's Cathedral, Winnipeg, and Professor of Systematic Theology in St. John's Coll.; First classical scholar, T.C.D., 1889; Vice-Chancellor's Gold Medalist, 1890; ordained Deacon, 1896; Priest, 1897; Dio. of London; Curate of St. Martin-in-the-Fields, London, 1896-1902. *Publications:* Christianity and Human Thought, London S.P.C.R., 1909. *Recreations:* walking and reading. *Address:* The Retreat, St. Johns, Winnipeg, Man.

MUSSEN, Joseph Missett; *b.* Cayuga, Co. of Haldimand, Ont., 17 Dec., 1863; *s.* of William Mussen, Belfast; unmarried. *Educ.:* Public and High Sch. of Cayuga, Ont., and Osgoode Hall, Toronto; Barrister-at-Law; after practicing law for a time travelled extensively in India and the far east; became Canadian Trade Commissioner for Leeds and Hull, Eng.; in August, 1909. *Recreations:* riding, golf. *Address:* Cromer Hall, Leeds, Eng.; Oakleigh, Cayuga, Ont.

MYERS, His Hon. Robert Hill; Co. Ct. Judge; Past Grand Master Masonic Order, for Manitoba; Past Grand Master of Oddfellows; *b.* Oxford, Ont., 30 March, 1856; *s.* of Robert Myers of Leeds, Yorkshire, and Margaret Hill of Fifeshire, Scotland; *m.* 25 Nov., 1885, Annie, *d.* of James McLeod of Woodstock, Ont.; one *s.* one *d.* *Educ.:* Stratford; Toronto, Ont. Called to bar at Osgoode Hall, Toronto, 1880, and to Manitoba bar, 1882; mem. of Manitoba Legislature, 1892-1903; apptd. to the bench, 1903; mem. of Manitoba College Senate and Board of Management and Manitoba Univ., Rhodes Scholarship Committee. *Recreations:* golf, lawn bowling. *Address:* 99 Roslyn Rd., Winnipeg, Man. *Clubs:* Manitoba, St. Charles, Country, Rockwood, Coledyke, Winnipeg.

N

NAKAMURA, Hon. Takashi; Consu General for Japan; *b.* Yuasamachi, Ku, Japan, 3 July, 1870; *m.* Mitsuyo Miura; two *s.* one *d.* *Educ.:* Japan. Came to Can. 18 May, 1909. Diplomatic and consular service for Japan in Corea, China and the U.S., 1895-1906; apptd. Sec. to the Foreign Dept. in 1906; promoted to Consul General in Canada, 1909. *Address:* 385 Laurier Av. E., Ottawa. *Club:* Rideau, Ottawa.

NANTEL, Wilfrid Bruno, LL.D. (Laval) K.C., M.P.; *b.* St. Jerome, Que., 8 Nov., 1857; *s.* of Guillaume Nantel and Adelaide Desjardins; *m.* 1885, Georgianna Gauthier, of St. Jerome; three *s.* one *d.* *Educ.:* Sem. of Ste. Theresse de Blainville. Has been mayor of the town of St. Jerome for the past six yrs., and alderman since 1894. Unsuccessful can. for H. of C. for Terrebonne at g. e., 1904. First el. to H. of C. at g. e., 1908. *Address:* St. Jerome, Que.

NANTON, Augustus Meredith; *b.* Toronto, 7 May, 1860; *s.* of Augustus Nanton, of Toronto; *m.* (1st) 1886, Georgina Hespeller (*d.* 1887); (2nd) 1893, Ethel Clark, of Winnipeg. *Educ.:* Toronto Model Sch. Commenced work at thirteen yrs. of age in office of a real estate broker, and two yrs. later entered employ of financial firm of Osler & Hammond. At age of 24, became a junior partner, and opened branch house at Winnipeg. Dir. of the Great West Life Insur. Co., Winnipeg Street Railway Co.; governor of the Winnipeg General Hospital ex-pres. of the Bd. of Trade. *Address:* Fort Rouge, Winnipeg. *Clubs:* Manitoba, Commercial, Winnipeg.

NEELY, Charles Hoffman; *b.* Iowa, U. S.A., 10 June, 1866; of American parentage. Arrived Canada, 1902; has always been engaged in the insurance business: now manager for Canada and Newfoundland, of the Ocean Accident & Guarantee Corporation. *Recreations:* golf, yachting. *Address:* 111 Crescent Road, Toronto. *Clubs:* Royal Canadian Yacht, Lambton Golf and Country, National, Toronto; New York Athletic, New York.

NEELY, David Bradley M.B. (Toronto, 1899), M.C.P. & S.O., M.P.; *b.* Harkaway, Grey Co., Ont., 18 Dec., 1873; *s.* of Thomas Neely and Jane Neely; *m.* Laura Amelia Hill, of Markdale, Ont.; two *s.* *Educ.:* Owen Sound Coll. Inst., Toronto Univ. Practiced medicine in Colborne and Markdale, Ont., till 1904, and since then in Humboldt, Sask. Elected by accl. in Humboldt to first Prov. Legislature of Sask., Dec., 1905; re-elected, Aug., 1908; resigned and el. for H. of C., Oct., 1908. *Address:* Humboldt, Sask.

NEILL, Charles Ernest; *b.* Fredericton, N.B., 25 May, 1873; *s.* of James S. Neill, and Eliza Caroline Neill; *m.* Mary L. Crerar. Manager Royal Bank at Vancouver for some years; Asst. General Manager of the Royal Bank of Canada. *Address:* 242 Sherbrooke St. West, Montreal. *Clubs:* Mount Royal, St. James, Hunt, Royal Montreal Golf, Montreal.

NELSON John, mang. dir. Victoria (B.C.) *Times; b.* Paisley, Ont., 8 March, 1872; *s.* of John and Eliza Nelson; *m.* Clara Armstrong; two *s.* two *d.* *Educ.:* Public and High Sch. of Ont.; has been a newspaper man all his life; reporter; special writer, and now managing director of the *Times*, Victoria, B.C.; del. to the Imp. Press Confce., at London, 1909. *Address:* 1034 Linden Av., Victoria, B.C.

NESBITT, Edward Walter, M.P.; *b.* North Norwich, Co. of Oxford, 15 July, 1857; *s.* of John W. and Mary Wallace Nesbitt; *m.* Mary Elizabeth *d.* of Andrew Ross, Sheriff of Oxford; two *s.* four *d.* Has been a member of the Woodstock board of Education for several years; was a member of the Co. Council for several years, and also Chairman of the Board of Trade; now engaged in manufacturing; farming and general agency business; first el. to H. of C., 1908; a Liberal. *Address:* Woodstock, Ont. *Clubs:* Rideau, Ottawa, and National, Toronto.

NESBITT, Sam. Grierson Murray, M.L.A.; *b.* Brighton, Ont., 23 Nov., 1859; *s.* of James Nesbitt, and Agnes Clarke; *m.* Eleanor Morris Bibby; one *s.* three *d.* *Educ.:* High Sch., Brighton; grocer for 12 years; manufacturer of canned goods for seven years; exporter of green apples for 18 years; pres., Can. Canners'; Gordon Pulp and Paper Co., Dryden, Ont.; Pres., Ontario Apple Shippers' Assn.; pres., Brighton Board of Trade; first el. to Ontario Leg. Ass., for East Northumberland, 1908. *Recreations:* cricket, yachting. *Address:* Brighton, Ont. *Club:* Albany, Toronto.

NESBITT, Hon. Wallace, K.C.; *b.* Woodstock, Ont., 13 May, 1858; *s.* of late John W. Nesbitt and Mary Wallace; *m.* (1st) Louise, *d.* of A. F. Elliott, of New Orleans, U.S.A.; (2nd) Amy Gertrude, *d.* of W. H. Beatty, Toronto; one *s.* *Educ.:* Woodstock; called to the bar, 1881; practised in Hamilton, Ont., for a short time; removed to Toronto and joined the firm of McCarthy, Osler, Hoskin & Creelman; in 1892, became a mem. of the firm of Beatty, Blackstock, Nesbitt, Chadwick & Riddell; in 1894 acted as senior counsel for Toronto in the investigation before Judge McDougall, to ascertain if any ald. or officials had accepted bribes or been guilty of malfeasance; apptd. a Q.C., 1896; was pres. of the Osgoode Legal and Lit. Soc.; apptd. a Judge of the Supreme Ct., 16 May, 1903; resigned 4 Oct., 1905, to resume legal practice. *Recreations:* golf, fishing, horseback riding. *Addresses:* Home Life Bldg. (bus.); 25 St. Vincent St., Toronto. *Clubs:* Toronto, Golf, Ontario Jockey, Toronto; Rideau, Golf, Ottawa; Garrick, Cecil, London, Eng.

NESBITT, William Beattie, B.A., M.D.; *b.* Vandecar, Oxford Co., Ont., 23 May, 1866; *s.* of Dr. F. L. Nesbitt and A. J. Meek; *m.* 1888, Clara Louise Hubbard; one *d.* *Educ.:* Angus Pub. Sch., Pickering Coll., and Barrie High Sch.; Grad. Toronto Univ., 1887; Trinity Univ., M.D., 1887. Practiced his profession in Toronto for several yrs., but later became connected with several corporations and manufacturing institutions, including the People's Life Insur. Co., Toronto Cold Storage Co., and the Canadian Kodak Co.; later was mgr. of the C. H. Hubbard Co. Active as a Cons. in politics. El. to Prov. Legis. for North Toronto, 1902; re-el. at g. e., 1905; retired 1908. *Address:* 71 Grosvenor St., Toronto. *Club:* Albany, Toronto.

NEWCOMBE, Edmund Leslie, C.M.G., K.C., M.A., LL.B., Deputy Min. of Justice for Canada; *b.* Cornwallis, N.S., 17 Feb., 1859; *s.* John Cumming Newcombe, and Abigail H. Calkin; *m.* Annie E. Freeman; one *s.* *Educ.:* Dalhousie Coll., Halifax. Called to the bar of N.S., 1883; bar of Ont., 1893; Q.C., 1893; Deputy Minister of Justice 1893; Governor of Dalhousie Coll., 1887-1893; Lecturer on Insurance Law, Dalhousie Coll., 1892-3; Canadian delegate to Gt. Britain on copyright question, 1905; Commissioner for Revision of Statutes of Canada 1902-1906. *Publications:* A Handbook of the British North America Act. *Recreation:* shooting. *Address:* 63 Laurier Ave. W., Ottawa. *Clubs:* Rideau, Golf, Hunt, Country, Ottawa; Halifax, N.S.

NEWNHAM, Right Rev. Jervois Arthur, M.A., D.D.; Bishop of Saskatchewan; *b.* Bath, Somerset, Eng., 15 Oct., 1852; *s.* of Rev. George William Newnham, M.A., Vicar of Combe Down, and Catherine Pennock Read; *m.* 1892, Letitia Anges, *d.* of Rev. Wm. Henderson, D.D.; five *d.* Received early educ. at Bath Coll.; came to Canada, 1 June, 1873, and entered McGill Univ. (B.A. with honours, 1878; M.A., 1883), and the Montreal Diocesan Coll. A missionary at Onslow, Que., 1878-82; curate of Christ Ch. Cath., Montreal, 1882-86; rector Westmount, Montreal, 1886-90; consec. in Winnipeg, 1893; and in same yr. received degree of D.D. from St. John's Coll., Man.; Bishop of Moosonee, 1893-04; transferred to Saskatchewan, 1904; has travelled much by canoe and on snowshoes round Hudson's Bay as Missionary Bishop. *Recreations:* cricket, tennis, riding. *Address:* Bishops thorpe, Prince Albert, Sask.

NEWNHAM, Mrs. Letitia Agnes; *b.* Pembroke, Ont., 14 April, 1865; *d.* of Rev. Wm. Henderson, D.D., and Mary Agnes Burgen; *m.* 1892, Right Rev. Jervois Arthur Newnham, Bishop of Saskatchewan; five *d.* A devoted companion and assistant of her husband in his missionary labours around the shores of Hudson's Bay, and now in Saskatchewan. *Address:* Bishopsthorpe, Prince Albert, Sask.

NEWTON, Denzil Onslow Cochrane, M.V.O.; *b.* England, 17 Oct., 1880; *s.* of George Onslow and Lady Alice Newton. *Educ.:* Eton, and Royal Military Coll. Arrived in Canada, 1902; gazetted to Middlesex Regt., 1899; A.D.C. to Earl of Dundonald, 1902-1906; A.D.C. to His Excellency the Governor General, 1904-1909; now a member of the firm of C. Meredith & Co., Ltd., bond brokers, Montreal. *Address:* 720 Cooper St., Ottawa. *Clubs:* Rideau, Golf, Ottawa.

NICHOL, Walter Cameron; Prop. Vancouver *Daily Province; b.* Goderich, Ont., 15 Oct., 1866, *y. s.* of the late Robert K. Addison Nichol, barrister, who was the eldest son of the late Lt.-Col. Robert Nichol, Q.M.G., of H.M. Militia; *m.* Odita Josephine, *d.* of the late Charles Greenwood Moore, M.D., of London, Ont.; one *s.* one *d.* *Educ.:* at home; journalist; edited the Hamilton (Ont). *Herald* for some years, and is now publisher, proprietor and editor-in-chief, of Vancouver B.C. *Daily Province.* *Recreations:* driving and motoring. *Address:* Vancouver, B.C. *Club:* Vancouver.

NICHOLLS, Albert George, M.A., M.D., C.M., D.Sc., F.R.S.C.; *b.* England, 16 April, 1870; *s.* of Rev. John Nicholls and Mary Elizabeth Harland; *m.* Lucia Pomeroy Van Vliet; one *s.* *Educ.:* Montreal High Sch.; McGill Univ.; Erlanger, Prague, Vienna. Arrived in Canada, 1874; grad. from Montreal High Sch. with Davidson Gold medal, and Lansdowne Silver medal for English History and Literature; Chapman Gold Medal and first rank honor in classics, McGill Univ.; Final prize in Medicine; Post Grad. course in Medicine in Germany and Austria. *Publications:* various articles in the reference handbook of Medical Science; part author American Text Book of Pathology and of the American Practice of Surgery; part author with Prof. J. G. Adami, of "The Principles of Pathology. *Address:* 972 St. Catherine St. West, Montreal. *Club:* University, Montreal.

NICHOLLS, Frederic; Vice-Pres. and Gen. Mgr. of the Can. Gen. Electric Co., Ltd., Toronto; *b.* England, 23 Nov., 1856; *m.* Florence, *e. d.* of late Commander Graburn, R.N. (*dec.*) *Educ.:* Stuttgart, Wurtemberg. Came to Can., 1874, and has since taken an active interest in many mining, insur., publishing and other concerns. Organizer of the Toronto Incandescent Electric Light Co., which adopted the underground system of electric light distribution. Founder, and until 1893 was ed. and prop. of the *Can. Manufacturer.* For seven yrs. sec. of the Can. Mfgrs. Assn.; vice-pres. of the Toronto Press Club, 1890 pres., Athenaeum Club, 1893. Dir., Toronto Electric Light Co., the Manufacturers' Life Insur. Co.; Electrical Development Co., of Ontario, the Sao Paulo Tramway, Light and Power Co., Brazil, and many other commercial concerns; a life mem. of the Toronto Bd. of Trade. *Recreations:* motoring, yachting (at one time commodore R. C. Y. C.) *Address:* "The Homewood," 13 Homewood Place, Toronto. *Clubs:* National, Toronto, Albany, Royal Can. Yacht, Golf, Toronto; St. James', Montreal.

NICHOLSON, Byron; *b.* Hamilton, Ont. 27 Jan., 1852; *s.* of William Manley, and Elizabeth Andry Nicholson; *m.* Mary Penberthy, *e. d.* of Chas. V. Berryman, M.D., M.A.; one *s.* *Educ.:* Public Sch. and High Sch.; journalist for many years; collector of Crown Timber Dues at the Port of Quebec up to 1909; clerk of the Senate Committees, at Ottawa, 1909. *Publications:* "Impressions Abroad," "The French Canadian" (translated into French,) "In Old Quebec." *Address:* Ottawa, Ont.

NICHOLSON, Charles Howard, Gen. Mgr. of G. T. P. Steamships; *b.* Belleville, Ont., 28 Jan., 1868; *s.* of Samuel and Nancy Nicholson, U. E. Loyalists; *m.* Lillie V. Williams, of Cobourg; one *s.* *Educ.:* Queen's Univ., Kingston, and Univ. of Maryland, Baltimore, Md.; Master Mariner; Traffic Manager, Nor. Nav. Co.; now Mgr. of G. T. Pacific lines on the Pacific. Began steamboating as Cabin boy, 1881; Purser, 1882-1884; Captain, 1885 to 1890; General Freigh and Passenger Agent, 1891 to 1903; Mgr. for the U.S., 1894 to 1902; General Mgr., Muskoka Nav. Co., 1903; Traffic Mgr., Nor. Nav. Co., 1904-09; apptd. to pres. pos. Dec., 1909. *Address:* Vancouver, B.C.

NICKERSON, Moses Hardy, M.L.A.; *b.* Clark's Harbor, Shelburne Co., N.S., 10 Sept., 1848; *s.* of Pheneas and Jane Nickerson; *m.* Mary E. Duncan; two *s.* two *d.* *Educ.:* at Clark's Harbour, by private study. Sch. teacher for 15 years; journalist, 20 years; member of the N.S. Legislature since 1902. *Publications:* "Corals of the Coast," a vol. of verse, 1892; The Coast Guard, weekly newspaper established 1897. *Recreation:* translating from the Classics. *Address:* Clark's Harbor, N.S.

NICKLE, William Folger, B.A., K.C., M.L.A.; *b.* Kingston, Ont., 31 Dec., 1869; *s.* of William Nickle, (Scotch,) and Ellen Mary Folger; *m.* Agnes Mary McAdam (*dec.*); two sons; one *d.* *Educ.:* Private tuition, Kingston Coll. Inst., Queen's Univ., and Osgoode Hall; grad. Queen's, 1892; Osgoode Hall, 1895; elec. to the Kingston Sch. Board, 1905; City Council, 1906; and again 1907 for three years; elec. to the Ont. Legislature in 1908 for the City of Kingston. *Recreation:* gardening. *Address:* Kingston, Ont. *Clubs:* Frontenac, Country, Kingston; R.C.Y.C., Toronto.

NICOLAS, Frank James; *b.* Calcutta, 1865; *s.* of English parents; *m.* Bertha Clarke; three *d.* *Educ.:* Rossal, Eng., and King's Coll., London, Eng. Arrived in Canada, Nov., 1904; Mining Engineer, Bengal, Australia, Malay Peninsula, and West Africa. *Publications:* Analytical Index to Geological Survey Publications of the Dominion Government, and of the Ontario Government; held 30 mile bicycle world's record in 1885. *Address:* 322 Gilmour St., Ottawa. *Club:* Rideau, Ottawa.

NOONAN, Daniel; Vice-Pres. and Gen. Mgr., Rideau Lakes Nav. Co.; *b.* Troy, N.Y., U.S.A., 24 Sept., 1853; *s.* of Anthony and Sarah Noonan; *m.* Mary Fleming; one *s.* one *d.* *Educ.:* Pub. Sch. Arrived in Can., May, 1856. Prominent in the forwarding business in Canada for many years. *Pub-*

lication: Rest and Sport among the Rideau Lakes. *Address:* 95 William St., Kingston, Ont. *Club:* Frontenac, Kingston.

NORDHEIMER, Samuel; Consul for Ontario, for the German Empire; *b.* Memsdorf, Bavaria, Germany, 1824; *m.* 1871, Edith Louise, *d.* of late Jas. Boulton, of Toronto; one *s.* seven *d.* Came to America with his brother in 1839, and learned the business of piano making; removed to Canada and founded the firm of A. & S. Nordheimer, at Kingston. Subsequently removed to Toronto, the firm now being known as the Nordheimer Piano & Music Co., Ltd. Was for many yrs. pres. of the Philharmonic Soc. of Toronto; vice-pres. of the Canada Permt. Loan Co.; apptd. Consul for Ont., for the German Empire, 1889. *Addresses:* 15 King St. E. (bus.); "Glen Edyth," Davenport Rd., Toronto. *Club:* Toronto.

NORDHEIMER, Mrs. Edith Louise; *b.* Toronto; *d.* of late James Boulton, barrister, and Margaret Melina Fortye; *m.* 1871, Samuel Nordheimer, Consul for the German Empire. Active in charitable and benevolent work; pres. of the Imperial of the Daughters of the Empire; has instituted many chapters of the Order. *Address:* "Glen Edyth," Davenport Road, Toronto.

NORIE-MILLER, Claud; *b.* London, Eng., 6 March, 1885; *s.* of Francis Norie-Miller, J.P., Cleese, Perth, Scot., and Grace Harvey Day, Eng. *Educ.:* Trinity Coll., Glenalmond, Scot.; now mgr. of the General Accident Ass. Co of Canada; has been since 1903 with General Accident Fire, and Life Co. of Perth, Scot., in European and Canadian branches of the Company; arrived in Canada, June, 1906. *Recreation:* golf. *Address:* 2 Bloor St., Toronto. *Clubs:* Albany, Toronto; Auxiliary Forces, London.

NORTHCOTE, Baroness (Alice), C.I., Lady of Grace of St. John of Jerusalem; adopted *d.* of 1st Lord Mount Stephen (George Stephen, of Montreal; *m.*) Montreal, 2 Oct., 1873, Sir Henry Stafford Northcote of Exeter (cr. 1900). *Educ.:* England, but spent many yrs. in Canada. Husband, Governor of Bombay, 1900-03, and Gov.-Gen. of Australia, 1903-8; in each country dispensed hospitality as mistress of Government House. *Address:* 25 St. James's Place, London, S.W., England.

NORTHRUP, William Barton, M.A., K.C., M.P.; *b.* Belleville, Ont., 19 Oct., 1856; *s.* of Anson Gilbert Northrup, and Jane C. Balster; *m.* Mary S. Fitch, of Toronto; one *s.* *Educ.:* Belleville Gram. Sch.; Up. Can. Coll.; Univ. of Toronto; head boy, U.C.C., 1874; Capt. Coll. cricket eleven, 1873-1874; championship cup races, 1873-1874; first elec. to H. of C., 1892; defeated in 1896; elec. 1900-1904-1908. *Addresses:* Belleville, and Ottawa. *Clubs:* Rideau, Golf, Ottawa; Albany, R.C.Y.C., Toronto.

NOVA SCOTIA, Bishop of; *see* Right Rev. Clarendon L. Worrell.

O

O'BEIRNE, William Mark; Editor and proprietor of the Stratford *Daily Beacon;* *b.* Cavanville, Durham Co., Ont., 26 April, 1854; *s.* of P. H. and Henrietta O'Beirne; *m.* Luella Georgina, *e. d.* of Damon S. Warner, of Napanee, Ont.; three *s.* two *d.* *Educ.:* Lindsay, Ont. Published Napanee *Express*, 1881-85; was representative of Toronto *Globe* in Montreal, 1885-88; editor and proprietor of Daily and Weekly *Standard*, Woodstock, Ont., 1888-91. Acquired the Weekly Beacon, Stratford, April, 1891, re-established the Daily *Beacon* same yr., and has been editor and proprietor since that time. Past Pres., Daily Sec., Canadian Press Assn.; mem. of executive of Can. Press Assn. *Address:* Stratford, Ont.

OBORNE, James; *b.* Montreal, 19 Sept., 1861; *s.* of John Oborne, and Annie Hilliard; *m.* (1st) Alice M. Barrie (*dec.*); (2nd) Edith M. Simpson; five *s.* three *d.* *Educ.:* Montreal Pub. Sch. Commenced railroading at 13 years of age; now General Supt., Can. Pac. Ry., at Toronto. *Address:* 175 Dowling Av. *Club:* Toronto.

O'BRIEN, Arthur Henry, M.A.; Law clerk of the H. of C.; *b.*fToronto; *s.* of Hy. O'Brien, K.C. *Educ.:* Galt and Toronto Coll. Inst., Univ. of Toronto; Trinity Univ. Unmarried. Called to the bar of Ontario, 1890; was formerly one of the editors of the *Can. Law Journal*, and is a frequent contributor to legal periodicals; entered Canadian Militia, 1886, 35th Batt., 1887 to 1897; Major, 1897; transferred to Gov. Gen'ls. Foot Guards, Ottawa, 1897; on reserve with rank of Major, 1904; for some years Secretary of the York Law Assn.; apptd. Asst. Law Clerk, of the H. of C., April, 1896, and Law Clerk, Aug., 1908. Life member of Argonaut Rowing Club. *Publications:* Digest of the Fish and Game Laws of Ont.; O'Brien's Conveyance," (now in its 4th ed.); "Chattle Mortgages and Bills of Sale," "Haliburton," a sketch and Bibliography (R.S.C. trans). *Recreation:* aquatics. *Address:* 237 Lisgar St., Ottawa. *Club:* Rideau, Ottawa.

O'BRIEN, Henry, K.C., *b.* "The Woods' Shanty Bay, Ont., 1836; 3rd *s.* of Edward George O'Brien, a retired naval and military officer, who was in charge of the first settlement in Simcoe district at Shanty Bay and Barrie, and Mary Sophia, *d.* of Rev. Edmund Gaffer, Somerset, Eng.; *m.* in 1859, Elizabeth, *d.* of Rev. S. B. Ardagh, M.A., Rector of Barrie; one *s.* two *d.* *Educ.:* Church Gram. Sch., Toronto. Called to the bar of U.C., in 1861; practiced in partnership with Mr. Christopher Robinson, K.C., until the latter's death in 1906; at present a member of the firm of O'Brien & Lundy; took an active part in 1885-6 in the movement for municipal reform in Toronto, which resulted in the elec. of the late Wm. H. Howland as Mayor, he being chairman of his Committee; devotes much time to Mission work among the poor of Toronto; chairman of the Toronto Mission Union. A Conservative; he became associated in 1888, with the "Equal Rights" movement of which his brother Col. W. E. O'Brien and D. Alton McCarthy, M.P., were leaders; since that time he has taken no part in politics. *Publications:* editor of "*Canada Law Journal.*" since 1863; author of O'-Brien's Division Court Manual," compiler of Harrison and O'Brien's digest of Ontario

Reports; was for sometime editor of Ontario Practice Reports. Founded Argonaut Rowing Club, 1872, and was its first stroke, and pres. for 16 years; was the first pres. of Canadian Assn. of Amateur Oarsmen; in 1863, raised and commanded an independent rifle co., which afterwards was incorporated in the Queen's Own Rifles, Toronto. *Address:* Dromoland, 383 Sherbourne St., Toronto.

O'BRIEN, Lieut.-Col. William Edward, LL.B.; *b.* Thornhill, Ont., 10 Mar., 1831, *s.* of Edward Georgia and Mary Sophia O'Brien; *m.* Elizabeth, relict of John F. Harris, of London, Ont., and *d.* of Colonel Loring of Toronto; one *s.* three *d.* *Educ.:* Up. Can. Coll.; after some years spent in journalism, was called to the bar, and practiced in Barrie, Ont. Later devoted himself to farming on the estate at Shanty Bay, which had been settled on by his father; contested Muskoka and Parry Sound in 1878 and was defeated; elec. in 1882 to H. of C., and held seat until 1895; joined the active militia at the time of the "Trent Affair," and retired as Lieut.-Col., after 30 years service; medals for Fenian Raid, North West Rebellion, and long service; Canadian Commissioner at Glasgow Exhibition in 1901, and was one of the officers sent to represent the Canadian militia at the Diamond Jubilee of H.M. in 1897. *Address:* The Woods, Shanty Bay, Ont.

ODLUM, Edward, M.A., B.Sc.; *b.* Tullamore, Peel Co., Ont., 27 Nov., 1850; *s.* of John A. Odlum and Margaret McKenzie; *m.* (1st) Mary E. Powell, who died in Tokio, Japan; (2nd) Martha M. Thomas of St. Catherines, Ont.; five *s.* *Educ.:* Tullamore, Goderich, and Victoria Univ, Coburg, Ont. Pres., Central Executive of Vancouver Rate Payers' Association; pres., British Tract Assn.; pres. Permanent Co-operating Board of the Laymen's Missionary Movement in Vancouver; Chairman Pub. Library Board, Vancouver; Sec., Grand View Progress Assn.; on executive of the Art Historic and Science Assn., Vancouver; member of Vancouver Board of Trade; on executive of Trustee Co. Limited; member of B.C. Oil Refining Co., Ltd.; Can. Pacific Oil Co.; Hygienic Dairy Co., Ltd.; Thomson's Stationery Co., Ltd.; Orange Hall Assn., Ltd.; Central City Mission Co., Ltd.; Dominion Trust Co., Ltd.; National Insurance Co. *Recreations:* gardening, mountain climbing, boating, camping. *Address:* 1710 Grant St., Vancouver, B.C.

OGDEN, Isaac Gouverneur; Third Vice-Pres., Canadian Pacific Ry.; *b.* New York; *s.* of Isaac Gouverneur Ogden, banker, and Elizabeth Katherine Williamson; *m.* 1884, Julia M., *d.* of the late Mr. Baker of Quincey, Ill. *Educ.:* pub. schs. of New York. Commenced his business career in a mercantile house in 1861; entered ry. service, 1871, as paymaster and accnt. of Chicago and Pacific Ry.; auditor of road, 1876-1881. Apptd. auditor of Western Div. of C. P. Ry., 1881; auditor, 1883; comptroller, 1887; third vice-pres., 1901. Dir. of various subsidiary lines of the C. P. R.; life governor of Montreal Homeopathic Hospital; pres., Coll. of Homeopathic Physicians and Surgeons of Montreal. *Recreation:* fishing. *Address:* 135 Mackay St., Montreal. *Clubs:* Mount Royal, St. James, Forest and Stream, Royal St. Lawrence Yacht, Montreal; Manitoba, Winnipeg; Anglers' Club of Rideau Lake; Lotus, Transportation, New York.

OGILVIE, William, D.L.S.; *b.* Ottawa, Ont., 7 April, 1846; *s.* James Ogilvie and Margaret Halladay; *m.* (1st) M. A. Sparks; (2nd) O. P. Richardson; five *s.* one *d.* *Educ.:* in common sch., and afterwards by study, was on several exploratory surveys, determination of boundary line, Canada and Alaska; Commissioner of the Yukon for two and a half years; engaged on exploratory work in the Yukon during the year of the gold discoveries in the Klondike river, and as a Dominion Magistrate, had to assume judicial authority in the territory; his firm administration tended to make the Klondike camp one of the most law abiding. *Publications:* official reports; "official guide to Klondike," and magazine articles. *Recreations:* shooting and fishing, en route. *Address:* (temporarily), Paris, Texas, U.S.A.

O'HALLORAN, George Finley, B.A., B.C.L., Deputy Min. of Agriculture; *b.* Cowansville, Que., 11 Oct., 1862; *s.* James O'Halloran, K.C., and Mary Ann Finley; *m.* Maude Monica, *d.* of Sir Melbourne Tait, Chief Justice of the Province of Quebec; two *s.* one *d.* *Educ.:* McGill Univ.; practiced law in Montreal with W. J. White, K.C., and A. W. P. Buchanan, K.C., until received appointment to his present position of Deputy Minister of Agriculture, and Deputy Commissioner of Patents. *Recreations:* shooting, fishing, golf. *Address:* 408 Queen St., Ottawa. *Clubs:* Rideau, Golf, Ottawa.

O'HARA, Francis Charles Trench, Dep. Min. of Trade and Commerce; *b.* Chatham, Ont., 7 Nov., 1870; *s.* of Robert O'Hara, Master in Chancery, Chatham, and Maria S. Dobbs; *m.* Helen, *d.* of H. Corby, formerly M.P.; one *d.* *Educ.:* Chatham pub. sch., and Coll. Inst.; entered Can. Bank of Commerce in 1888; resigned 1890, and went to Baltimore, Md.; joined staff of "The *World*," short period and subsequently "The *Herald*;" returned to Canada, 1896; private sectretary to Hon. Sir Richard Cartwright, 1898; supt. of commercial agencies; Deputy Minister of Trade and Commerce, Aug. 1, 1908. *Publications:* "Snap Shots from Boy Life." *Recreations:* golf, fishing. *Address:* 25 Wurtemburg St., Ottawa. *Clubs:* Rideau, Golf, Hunt, and Country, Ottawa.

O'HARA, Henry; *b.* Newry, Down Co., Irel., 20 April, 1833; *s.* of Robert O'Hara (Irish); *m.* (1st) 1859, Janet, *d.* of John Mair (*dec.*); (2nd) 1889, *d.* of Seymour Bennett, of Buffalo; three *s.* three *d.* Came to Canada, 1844, with his parents and settled at Bowmanville, Ont. *Educ.:* at Bowmanville pub. schs. Organized the Dominion Organ & Piano Co. Later became mgr, of the Sun Life Assur. Co., with headquarters at Toronto; resigned to estb. present business. Vice-Pres. of the Colonial Loan & Investment Co.; ex-pres. of the Irish Protestant Benevolent Soc.; dir. of the Home for Incurables, trustee of the House of Industry; ex-pres. of the Toronto

Dist. Assn. of the Congregational Church; formerly Grand Worthy Patriarch of the Sons of Temperance of Ontario. *Address:* 30 Toronto St. (bus.), 2 Dunbar Rd., Toronto. *Clubs:* Toronto, National, Toronto

O'KEEFE, George; Police Magistrate of the city of Ottawa; *b.* Bombay, N.Y., U.S.A., 1849. Taught sch. for number of yrs. Mem. of Ottawa City Council, as alderman, 1876-1879, and 1885-1887. Unsuccessful candidate for Prov. Legis., 1883; el. to Ontario Leg. Ass., 1894; defeated 1898; apptd. Police Magistrate, 1899; a member of the Ottawa Improvement Commission since 1903. *Address:* 229 Wilbrod St., Ottawa.

OLIVER, Hon. Frank, M.P., P.C., Minister of the Interior, Canada; *b.* Peel Co., Ont., 1853; *m.* 1881, Harriet, *d.* of Thos. Dunlop, Prairie Grove, Man.; one *s.* three *d.* Went to the North West at an early age, and became member of the North West Council in 1883, and was also elec. to the Legislative Assembly, which succeeded the Council, 1888-1896; elec. to the H. of C., 1896 as an Independent Liberal, and re-elec. 1900 and 1904, when he was the Liberal candidate; established, in the early 80's, and still owns the Edmonton *Bulletin*, now one of the most successful dailies in Western Canada, but for some yrs., by reason of his public duties, has been precluded from taking an active part in its management. Sworn of the Privy Council, and apptd. Minister of the Interior in the Laurier Administration, 8 April, 1905; re-elec. 25 April, by acclam.; re-elec. 1908. *Address:* 181 Somerset St., Ottawa. *Club:* Rideau, Ottawa.

OLIVER, John; *b.* Hartington, Derbyshire, Eng., 31 July, 1856; *s.* of Robert T. (of Derbyshire), and Emma Lomas Oliver, of Staffordshire; *m.* Elizabeth Woodward, 20 June, 1886; five *s.* three *d.* *Educ.:* Parish Sch., Hartington, Eng.; member of the Council of Delta for a number of years; elected to British Columbia Legislature in 1900, 1903, and 1907; leader of Liberal Opposition in Legislature in 1909; unsuccessful Dec., 1909. *Address:* Delta, B.C.

O'MEARA, Rev. Canon Thomas Robert, LL.D., Principal of Wycliffe Coll., Toronto; *b.* Georgetown, Ont., 16 Oct., 1864; *s.* of Rev. Frederick A. O'Meara, LL.D., late rector of Port Hope, Ont., Canon of St. Alban's Cathedral, Toronto, and Margaret Johnson Dallas; *m.* Harriett Mary Sophia *d.* of the late Justice Boyd of Toronto, three *d.* *Educ.:* High Sch., Port Hope; Univ. Toronto, Wycliffe Coll., Toronto; graduate of Wycliffe Coll.; Principal of Wycliffe Coll.; Canon of St. Alban's Cathedral, Toronto; Pres. of the Church of England; Deaconess Missionary Training Home, Toronto; vice-pres. Upper Can. Bible Soc., and Upper Canada Tract Society, Toronto; formerly Asst. at St. Philip's Church, Toronto; Dean of Wycliffe Coll.; Professor of Practical Theology, Wycliffe. *Address:* Wycliffe College, Toronto.

ONTARIO Bishop of, *see* Rt. Rev. Wm. Lennox Mills.

ORDE, John Fosberry, K.C.; *b.* Great Village, N.S., 8 May, 1870; *s.* Francis William Orde, *s.* of Capt. George Frederick Orde, and Elizabeth Margaret, *d.* of His Honor George Baker Hall, County Judge; *m.* Edith Catherine Mary, *d.* of Francis Henry Cooper Cox; two *s.* one *d.* Called to the Bar at Osgoode Hall, Toronto. May, 1891; created K.C., Jan., 1908; practiced in Ottawa since 1891; Hon. Lay Secretary of Synod of Diocese of Ottawa. Chairman Board of License Commissioners for Ottawa. *Recreations:* golf, canoeing, fishing. *Address:* 155 McLaren St., Ottawa. *Clubs:* Rideau, Golf, Ottawa.

O'REILLY, Charles, M.D., C.M.; *b.* Hamilton, Ont., 1846; *s.* of Gerald O'Reilly, M.D., L.R.C.S., Irel., and Henrietta Watts, Sussex, Eng; *m.* Sophia E. Ralph, *d.* of late George Ralph, barrister, Dundas, Ont.; one *s.* *Educ.:* Hamilton, Ont.; was resident physician, city hospital, Hamilton from 1867 to 1876; Medical Supt., Toronto General Hospital, from Jan. 1876 to 31 Dec., 1905; having always had charge of hospitals he is the oldest Hospital Physician in the British Empire; 38 years in Hospital life. *Address:* Erin Lodge, 52 College St., Toronto. *Clubs:* Toronto, R.C.Y.C., Toronto, Ont.

O'REILLY, His Hon. James Redmond, B.A., K.C.; *b.* Kingston, Ont., 14 Feb., 1862; *s.* of James O'Reilly, Q.C., and Mary I. Redmond; *m.* Rose Mary Bermingham, 4th *d.* of late James Bermingham; two *s.* *Educ.:* Regiopolis Coll., Kingston; Jesuits Coll., Montreal; Queen's Univ., Kingston; called to the bar and admitted as solicitor 1885; created Q.C., 1898; apptd. Senior Judge, County Court, United Counties, Stormont, Dundas and Glengarry, March, 1900. *Address:* Cornwall, Ont. *Club:* Cornwall.

OSLER, Edmund Boyd, M.P., Pres. of the Dominion Bank; *b.* Tp. of Tecumseh, Simcoe, Co., 1845; *s.* of the late Rev. F. L. Osler and Ellen Pickton; *m.* Anna F. Cochran, Aberdeen, (*dec*). *Educ.:* Dundas Gram. Sch. Head of the firm of Osler and Hammond, Toronto, financiers and stock brokers; pres. of the Ontario and Quebec Ry. Co., and a director of the C. P. Ry.; director, Toronto General Trust Co., the North West Land Co.; pres. Ont. Rifle Assn.; pres., Dominion Bank; was pres., Toronto Board of Trade, 1896; and was one of the representatives of Canada at the Congress of the Chambers of Commerce, London, Eng., 1896; unsuccessful candidate for Toronto Mayoralty, 1892; elec. to the H. of C., for W. Toronto, 1896, 1900, 1904, 1908. Church of England; Conservative. *Address:* 13 Beau Rd., Rosedale, Toronto. *Clubs:* Toronto, Albany, Toronto; Rideau, Ottawa.

OSLER, Hon. Featherston, D.C.L. (hon. Trinity), late Judge of the Ct. of Appeal for Ontario; *b.* Newmarket, Ont., 1838; *s.* of late Rev. F. L. Osler and Ellen Pickton; *m.* 1861, Henrietta, *d.* of the late Capt. Henry Smith, of Glanford, Ont. *Educ.:* Barrie Gram. Sch.; Osgoode Hall. Called to bar of Ontario, 1860, and practiced his profession in Toronto until apptd. a Puisne Judge of Common Pleas, 1879; transferred to Appeal Ct., 1883, and sat as a member of that Court for nearly 27 yrs., resigning in March, 1910. Bencher of the Law Soc. of Ontario, 1875; Commissioner for the Revision of the Ontario Statutes 1885, and similarly in 1896; a trustee of

Trinity Univ. *Address:* 60 Crescent Rd., Toronto. *Club:* Toronto.

OSLER, William, LL.D., McGill, Toronto, Univ. of Edinburgh, Univ. of Aberdeen, Harvard, Yale, Johns Hopkins; D. Sc., Oxford); fellow Royal Soc., Royal Coll. of Physicians, London; *b.* Bond Head, Ont., 12 July, 1849; *s.* of Rev. F. L. Osler, M.A., and Ellen Pickton. *Educ.:* High Schs., Barrie and Dundas, Trinity Coll. Sch., Western Trinity Coll., Toronto Sch. of Medicine, McGill Univ., London, Berlin and Vienna. Prof. institutes of medicine, McGill Univ., 1874-84; prof. clin. medicine, Univ. of Pa., 1884; prof. medicine, Johns Hopkins Univ., 1889-1905; Regius prof. medicine, Oxford Univ., since 1905. Student of Christ Church, Oxon. *Publications:* The Cerebral Palsies of Children, 1889; Chorea and Choreiform Affections, 1894; Lectures on Abdominal Tumors, 1895; Angina Pectoris and Allied States, 1897; The Principles and Practice of Medicine (6th edit.), 1906; Cancer of the Stomach, 1900; Science and Immortality (Ingersoll lecture, Harvard Univ.), 1904; Æquanimitas, and other addresses, 2nd edit., 1900; Counsels and Ideals, 1906. Editor of System of Medicine (Vols. I and II), 1907. *Recreation:* bibliography. *Address:* 13 Norham Gardens, Oxford, Eng. *Clubs:* Atheneum, London; University, New York.

OTTAWA, Archbishop of; *see* Most Rev. Charles Hamilton, D.D.

OTTER, Brig.-Gen. William Dillon, C. V.O., C.B., A.D.C.; Chief of the General Staff at Militia Headquarters; *b.* nr. Clinton, Ont., 3 Dec., 1843; *s.* of Alfred W. Otter, and Anna, *d.* of the Rev. James De la Hooke; *m.* 1865, Mary, *s. d.* of the late Rev. James Porter, of Toronto. *Educ.:* Goderich, Gram. Sch., Toronto Model Sch., and Upper Can. Coll. Joined Canadian Militia, 1861; Lieut., Q.O.R., 1864; served during Fenian raids, and present at action at Ridgeway; Major, 1869, and Lieut.-Col., 1864; commandant Wimbledon Team, 1883; commandant R.S.I., Dec., 1883; commandant, Battleford column during Riel Rebellion, 1885 (action at Cut Knife); D.O.C., No. 2 Dist., 1 July, 1886; In. Infy. 1896-05; Comdg. Western Ontario, 1905-8; Chief of the General Staff, 1908. During S. A. War, commanded special service Batt., Royal Can. Infantry (took part in many actions and mentioned in despatches, Queen's medal with four clasps). *Address:* Militia Headquarters, Ottawa. *Club:* Rideau, Ottawa.

OUIMET, Hon. Joseph Aldric, B.C.L. (Victoria Coll.); ex-Judge of the Court of Queen's Bench; *b.* Ste. Rose, Laval Co., Que., 20 May, 1848; *s.* of Capt. Michael Ouimet and Elizabeth St. Louis; *m.* 1874, Therese, *d.* of the late J. F. Chartier La Rocque, of Montreal; three *s.* three *d.* *Educ.:* Seminary of St. Therese de Blainville, Que., Victoria Coll., Cobourg, Ont. Practiced with the firm of Ouimet, Cornelier & Emard. created a Q.C., by Marquis of Lorne in 1880; apptd. member Privy Council, 1891. El. to H. of C. for Laval, at g. e., 1873., and held seat continuously for 24 yrs. Speaker H. of C., 1887-1891; apptd. Minister of Pub. Works, 1892; apptd. Puisne Judge of the Court of Queen's Bench for Prov. of Que., 1896, which position he resigned in 1906; unsuccessful can. for H. of C., 1908. Pres. Montreal City and District Savings Bank; vice-pres. Credit Foncier Franco-Canadien and La Sauvegarde. *Address:* 500 Sherbrooke St., Montreal. *Clubs:* Mount Royal, St. James, Forest and Stream, Hunt, Lafontaine, Royal St. Lawrence Yacht, Montreal.

OUSELEY, Frederick Arthur Gare; *b.* Windsor, Hants Co., N.S., 27 Dec., 1872; *s.* of John Ouseley, K.C., who was clerk of House of Assembly, N.S., for 21 years, and Rosina M. Ouseley; *m.* Mary Carmichael Campbell, of Baddeck, C.B.; one *d.* *Educ.:* Coll. Sch. and High Sch., Windsor, N.S.; practiced law in his father's office; admitted as barrister in 1897; District Judge of the Judicial District of Moose Jaw; is probably the youngest Canadian Judge. *Recreation:* tennis. *Address:* Moosejaw, Sask.

OWEN, Charles Lewis, M.P.; *b.* 15 July, 1852; of Welsh parentage; *m.* 1875, Mary Eliza Bain; one *s.* four *d.* For many years identified with the woollen industry, now retired; in 1894 was Warden of the United counties of Northumberland and Durham; Reeve of Campbellford for four years, and Councillor for eleven years; chairman of Sch. Board for two years; pres., Public Library for six years; elec. to the H. of C., for East Northumberland at bye-elec., 29 Oct., 1907; re-elec., 1908; Conservative; Presbyterian. *Address:* Campbellford, Ont.

OWEN, Lemuel Cambridge; *b.* Charlottetown, P.E.I., 28 Jan., 1866; *s.* Lemuel Cambridge Owen, first Premier of P.E.I., after Confederation in 1873, and Lois Welsh; *m.* Sinclair, *d.* of the late Hector Fraser, of Pembroke, Ont. *Educ.:* Normal Sch., St. Peter's Sch., and Prince of Wales Coll., Charlottetown, P.E.I., and Upper Can. Coll., Toronto; entered Union Bank of P.E.I., at Charlottetown, 1882; and in 1884, joined the Bank of Ottawa, at Ottawa Ont.; apptd. Asst. Manager at Ottawa, Dec., 1901; Inspector, 1903; Manager at Toronto, 1905. *Recreations:* canoeing, golf, bowling and billiards. *Address:* 74 Grenville St., Toronto. *Clubs:* Toronto, National, Hunt, Toronto, Ont.; Laurentian and Rideau, Ottawa.

OWENS, Hon. William; senator; *b.* Co. of Argentueil, Que., 15 May, 1840; *s.* of Owen Owens and Charlotte Lindley; *m.* Margaret C. McMartin, *d.* of John McMartin; one *s.* two *d.* Was postmaster, Councillor and Mayor of Chatham, Co. of Argenteuil; Lieut. in the Militia; general merchant; member of Leg. Ass., Quebec, from 1881 to 1891; called to the Senate, 2nd Jan., 1896; member of Board of Trade, Montreal. *Address:* 4026 Dorchester St., Montreal. *Club:* Rideau, Ottawa.

P

PANET, Major Henri Alexandre, D.S.O. *b.* Quebec, 24 July, 1869; *s.* of late Col. Charles C. Eugene Panet; *m.* 1902, Mary A., *y. d.* of late Mrs. M. A. Bermingham, Kingston, Ont. *Educ.:* Roy. Mil. Coll. Served in South African War, 1899-900, with 2nd Battalion Royal Canadian Regiment of

Infantry. Advance on Kimberley, Dec., 1899, to Feb., 1900; transferred to "C" Battery, Royal Canadian Field Artillery. Relief of Mafeking, (May 17, 1900). Operations in Rhodesia, April-May, 1900; operations in the Transvaal in May and June, 1900; operations in the Transvaal, east of Pretoria, July to Nov. 25, 1900; operations in the Transvaal, west of Pretoria, July to Nov., 25 1900; operations in Orange River Colony (May to Nov. 15, 1900); *despatches, London Gazette*, April, 15, 1901. Brevet of Major. D.S.O. Queen's Medal with four clasps. Late Staff Adjutant, Royal Military Coll., of Canada, Kingston; asst. Adjt.-General, 1905-07; Deputy Adjutant-General Can. Militia, 1907-07; Major Commanding "B" Battery, Royal Canadian Horse Artillery. *Address:* 254 King St., Kingston, Ont. *Clubs:* R.M.C., Frontenac, Kingston, Ont.

PAPINEAU, Louis J., B.C.L. (Laval), K.C., M.P., Recorder of Valleyfield; *b.* Ste. Genevieve, Jacques Cartier Co., 3 Jan., 1861; *s.* of Narcisse Papineau and Adele Gaucher; *m.* Blanche Gervais. *Educ.:* Montreal and Joliette. Practiced at the bar since 1883; Recorder of Valleyfield, 1895-1909. First el. to H. of C. for Beauharnois, at g. e., 1908. *Address:* Valleyfield, Que.

PAQUET, Eugene, M.D., M.P.; *b.* St. Agapit, Lotbiniere Co., Que., 23 Oct., 1867; *s.* of Francois Paquet, farmer, and Clarisse Bergeron; *m.* 1893, Elise Lafrance, of Quebec; one *s.* *Educ.:* Quebec Sem., Laval Univ. Has practised medicine at St. Aubert, L'Islet Co., since 1892. El. to H. of C. at g. e., 1904; re-el. 1908. A frequent contributor to *Le Peuple de Montmagny.* a Conservative. *Address:* St. Aubert, Que.

PARDEE, Frederick Forsyth, M.P.; *b.* Sarnia, Ont., 29 Dec., 1867; *s.* of Hon. Timothy Blair and Emma Kirby Pardee; *m.* Mary Eleanor Johnston; one *d.* *Educ.:* Pub. Sch., Sarnia, and Up. Can. Coll.; member of the Ontario Legislature, 1898-1902; first el. to H. of C., 1905; re-el., 1908; chief whip of the Liberal party, 1909. *Recreations:* yachting, shooting, curling. *Address:* Sarnia, Ont.

PARDOE, Avern; *b.* Stratford-on-Avon, Eng., 1845; *s.* of William and Henrietta Pardoe; *m.* Mary Sprague of Andover, Conn. two *s.* two *d.* Arrived in Canada, 1872; spent early years in a law office, subsequently in journalism in England and United States; joined staff of Toronto *Globe* in 1875; managing editor, 1882-1889; Librarian of Legislative Ass., of Ont., 1895. *Recreation:* woodworking. *Address:* 15 Elgin St., Toronto.

PARENT, George, B.A., LL.L., M.P.; *b.* Quebec City, 15 Dec., 1879; *s.* of Hon. S. N. Parent, Chairman of the National Transcontinental Railway Commission, and ex-Premier of the Prov. of Quebec, and Marie Louise Gendron; unmarried. *Educ.:* Ste. Anne de la Pocatiere; Laval Univ.; first elec. to the H. of C. for Montmorency Co., in 1904, and seconded address in reply to speech from Throne; re-elec. 1908. *Address:* Quebec. *Clubs:* Garrison and Hunt, Quebec; Laurentian, Hunt, Ottawa.

PARENT, Hon. Simon Napoleon, L.L.D., D.C.L., K.C., Chairman of the National Transcontinental Ry. Com., since Aug., 1905; *b.* Beauport, Que., 12 Sept., 1855; *s.* of Simon Polycarpe Parent and Lucie Belanger; *m.* 17 Oct., 1877, Clara Gendron; four *s.* four *d.* *Educ.:* Laval Normal Sch., Laval Univ. Admitted to the bar, 1881. Elected alderman for the city of Quebec, 1890; Mayor 1894-1906. Mem. of Legis. Assembly for Que., 1890. Called to Provincial Cabinet as Minister of Lands, Mines & Forests, 1897, and chosen Premier of Prov. of Quebec, Oct., 1901; resigned, Mar., 1905. *Address:* 485 King Edward Av., Ottawa. *Clubs:* Garrison, Quebec; Rideau, Laurentian, Hunt, Ottawa.

PARKER, Archibald Gibson; Mgr. of the Bank of Montreal, Ottawa; *b.* Montreal, 6 April, 1858; *s.* of A. Davidson Parker and Grace Gibson; *m.* Mabel Chester, of Buffalo, N.Y.; two *s.* three *d.* *Educ.:* Montreal High Sch. In mercantile life until 1876; joined staff of Bank of Montreal at Montreal in latter yr., passing through the several grades and subsequently mgr. of branches at Peterboro, Belleville, Hamilton and Brantford; took an active and leading part in musical affairs in these cities; pres. of the Schubert Choir at Brantford. Apptd mgr. of the Bank of Montreal, at Gttawa, 1909. *Recreations:* golf, tennis, curling. *Address:* 146 Wellington St., Ottawa. *Club:* Rideau, Ottawa.

PARKER, Sir Gilbert, Kt., D.C.L., M.P. (C.) Gravesend since 1900; *b.* Belleville, Ont., 23 Nov., 1862; *s.* of late Captain J. Parker; *m.* 1895, Amy, *d.* of Ashley Van Tine, New York. *Educ.:* Trin. Coll., Toronto. Associate-ed., Sydney Morning *Herald*, Sydney, Australia, 1886; travelled among South Sea Islands and extensively in Far East, in Europe, Egypt, and Northern Can.; initiated and organized the first Imperial Universities Conference in London, 1903; Hon. Col., 1st Kent Volunteer Art. *Publications:* Poems A Lover's Diary, 1896; Plays: adaptation of Faust, 1888; The Vendetta, 1889; No Defence, 1889; The Seats of the Mighty, 1897; Travels; Round the Compass in Australia, 1892; Stories and Novels: Pierre and his People, 1892; Mrs. Falchion, 1893; The Trespasser, 1893; The Translation of a Savage, 1894; The Trail of the Sword, 1894; When Valmond came to Pontiac, 1895; An Adventurer of the North, 1895; The Pomp of the Lavillettes, 1897; The Battle of the Strong, 1898; The Lane that had no Turning, 1900; The Right of Way, 1901; Donovan Pasha, 1902; History of Old Quebec, 1903; A Ladder of Swords, 1904; The Weavers, 1907; Northern Lights, 1909. *Recreations:* golfing, riding. *Address:* 20 Carlton House Terrace, London, S.W., Eng. *Clubs:* Carlton, Garrick, London, Eng.

PARKIN, George Robert, LL.D., C.M. G.; *b.* Salisbury, Westmoreland Co., N.B., 8 Feb., 1846; *m.* 1878, Annie Connell, *d.* of William Fisher of Fredericton; one *s.* four *d.* *Educ.:* Pub. Schs., Normal Sch., St. John; Univ. of New Brunswick. Was Headmaster of Bathurst Gram. Sch., 1868-72, and then proceeded to Oxford for course in Classics and History. Returning to Canada, was Principal of the Coll. Inst., Fredericton. An ardent Imperial Federationist; visited (1889-90), all the principal colonies of the Empire and delivered addresses on the subject of Imperial Federation; special corr. for *The Times* at the Intercolonial Conference, Ottawa, 1894, and again at the Quebec Tercentenary, 1908; Principal of Upper Can. Coll., Toronto, 1895-1902. In the latter year, was apptd. organising rep. of the Rhodes Scholarship Trust, and has visited different portions of the Empire again in that capacity. *Publications:* Imperial Federation, 1892; Round the Empire, 1892; The Great Dominion, 1895; Life and Letters of Edward Thring, 1898; Life of Sir John A. Macdonald, Prime Minister of Canada. *Addresses:* Seymour House, Waterloo Place London, S.W., England. *Club:* Royal Societies.

PARLOW, Miss Mary Kathleen; *b.* Calgary, Alta., 20 Sept., 1890; *d.* of Charles Henry Parlow and Minnie B. Wheeler. *Educ.:* California and Russia. When but five yrs. of age, commenced study of violin with F. J. Conrad and Henry Holmes, San Francisco; removed to St. Petersburg, 1906, and continued musical studies with Leopold Auer. Since 1908, has played in Germany, Russia, Scandinavia, Holland, Belgium and the British Isles, appearing before many of the crowned heads, notably the Queen of England, the King and Queen of Denmark, King and Queen of Norway, and other members of the Royal families. *Recreations:* reading, walking, motoring. *Address:* c|o Concert Direction, Thomas Quinlan, 318 Regent St., London, W.; Gt. Central Hotel, Marylebone, London, Eng.

PARMELEE, Charles Henry; King's Printer and Controller of Stationery for Canada; *b.* Waterloo, Que., 1 June, 1855; *s.* of Rufus E. Parmelee, and Eliza I. McVicar; *m.* 1887, Christina McLean, *d.* of Henry Rose; three *s.* three *d.* *Educ.:* Waterloo Acad. Was ed. of the Waterloo *Advertiser.* 1875-80; financial and commercial ed., Montreal *Herald*, 1880-83; again managed the *Advertiser.* Was a Town Councillor of Waterloo, a mem. of the Prov. Coun. of Agric., Sec. and Chn. of the Bd. of Sch. Commrs., and Pres. Eastern Tp. Press Assn. Pres., Dairy Assn. of the Prov. of Que. El. to H. of C., at g. e., 1896; re-elec. at g. e., 1900, 1904 and 1908. Was Chn. of Joint Com. on Printing of Parliament; apptd King's Printer and Controller of Stationery for Can., 1 Feb., 1909. *Address:* 56 Cooper St., Ottawa. *Club:* Laurentian, Ottawa.

PARMELEE, William Grannis, I.S.O. *b.* Waterloo, Que., Aug., 1833; *s.* of Rotus Parmelee, M.D., and Sara M. Grannis; *m.* (1st) Marcella A. Whitney, of Montpelier, Vermont; (2nd) Jessie B. Christie of Ottawa Ont.; four *s.* four *d.* *Educ.:* Waterloo, Que. Engaged for several years in Insurance Railway and Banking institutions; entered the Can. Civil Service in 1876, as chief clerk and accountant of the Customs Dept.; Asst. Commissioner of Customs, Deputy Minister of Trade and Commerce, which department he organized in 1892; chief controller of chinese immigration, from 1884; retired in 1908; has been connected with a number of Royal Commissions. *Address:* 387 Frank St., Ottawa, Ont.

PARROCK, Rev. Richard Arthur, M.A., LL.D., D.C.L., *b.* Shrewsbury, Eng., 11 Dec., 1869; *s.* of Richard Parrock, "The Beeches," Shrewsbury, Eng.; *m.* Annie Louise, *y. d.* of the late C. S. Parke, M.D., of Quebec; three *d.* *Educ.:* Shrewsbury Sch., Pembroke Coll., Cambridge. Arrived in Canada, in 1893; Chaplain to Bishop of Ontario, 1893; Professor of Classics, Bishops Coll., Lennoxville, 1895; Principal of Bishop's Coll.; Vice-Chancellor to the Univ., 1907; Chairman of the Coll. Council; clerical delegate to General and Provincial Synods of the Church of England in Canada; Deacon, 1893; Priest, 1894, Quebec. *Recreation:* golf. *Address:* Lennoxville, Que.

PARSON, Henry George, M.L.A.; *b.* London, Eng., 13 Sept., 1865; *s.* of George Fry Parson and Ann Baxter; *m.* Mary Jane Reid; one *s.* one *d.* *Educ.:* Cooper's Co. Gram. Sch., London, Eng. Arrived in Canada, 1883; was a member of the Parliamentary Press Gallery, Canada, on the staff of the Toronto *Mail*, sessions 1883 to 1885; removed to Regina, 1885, and worked on construction of Long Lake Ry., moving West to Banff same year; afterwards at Field, and Golden, B.C.; pres., of H. G. Parson, Ltd., Columbia Wine and Spirit Co., Ltd., Golden; Revelstoke Wine and Spirit Co., Ltd.; Revelstoke, and is dir. of several other Companies; first elec. to B.C. Legislature for Columbia District, in 1907, as a Conservative, defeating Hon. W. C. Wells, formerly Chief Commissioner of Lands and Works; re-el. 1909. *Address:* Golden, B.C. *Recreations:* curling, lawn tennis, cricket. *Clubs:* Union, Pacific, Victoria, B.C.

PASCAL, Right Rev. Albert, O.M.I., D.D., Bishop of Prince Albert; *b.* Saint Genest de Beauson, Viviers, France, 3 Aug., 1848. *Educ.:* Little Seminary of Aubenas, and Grand Seminary of Montreal; arrived in Canada, 1870, ordained priest, 1873; missionary among the Indians, North West, until 1891, when he was consecrated titular Bishop of Yosynopolis, and Vicar Apostolic of Sask.; became Bishop of Prince Albert, Dec., 1907. *Address:* Prince Albert, Sask.

PATCHIN, Robert Hasley; journalist and chief of the Ottawa Bureau of the New York *Herald;* *b.* Des Moines, owa, U.S.A., 6 Feb., 1881; *s.* of Robert A. Patchin, and Calista Halsey; *m.* Mary Curtis Lee Carter. *Educ.:* Iowa State Coll.; joined staff of Des Moines *Leader*, 1899; Washington, D.C., *Times*, 1900-1902; Washington staff of New York *Herald*, 1902-1909, writing on naval, political and international affairs; *Herald* correspondent with President Roosevelt in Panama 1906, and with U.S. battleships in cruise around the world, Dec., 1907-Feb., 1909; Ottawa bureau, Oct., 1909. *Recreations:* riding, golf. *Address:* Wellington St., Ottawa. *Clubs:* National Press, Washington, D.C.

PATENAUDE, Esuff Leon, B.A., M.L.A.; *b.* St. Isidore, Co. of Laprairie, Que., 12 Feb., 1875; *s.* of Hilaire Patenaude, and Angele Trudeau; *m.* Karie Georgiana Denigler; one *s.* one *d.* *Educ.:* Montreal Coll. and Laval Univ.; first el. to Leg. Ass. of Quebec, 1909; a Cons.-Nat. *Address:* 766 St. Denis St., Montreal.

PATERSON, Hon. William, P.C., M.P.; Minister of Customs, Canada; *b.* Hamilton, Ont., 19 Sept., 1839; *s.* of the late James and Martha Paterson, of Aberdeen, Scot.; *m.* Sept., 1863, Lucy Olive, *d.* of T. C. Davies

Brantford. *Educ.:* Hamilton, and at Caledonia, Haldimand Co., Ont.; removed to Brantford; Mayor, 1872; defeated Sir Francis Hincks, Minister of Finance, in South Brant., 1874, for H. of C., and continued to represent that constituency until 1896, when he was defeated by 91 votes; entered the Laurier Admn., 13 July, 1896, as Controller of Customs; elected for N. Grey at bye-elec., 25 Aug., 1896; sworn of the Privy Council, and apptd. Minister of Customs, 30 June, 1897, the office of Controller having been abolished by Parliament; elec. for Wentworth, N., and Brant, 1900; elect. for new constituency of Brant, 1904 and 1908; was one of the Canadian delegates to the Colonial Conference in London, June, 1902; British Commissioner on improved trade relations between Canada and the West Indies, 1909-1910. *Address:* The New Russell, Ottawa.

PATON, Hugh; *b.* Johnstone, Renfrewshire, Scot., 5 Oct., 1852; *s.* of William Paton and Mary Shedden, Kilburnie, Scot.; *m.* 1884, Isabella Robertson. *Educ.:* Gram. Sch., Paisley, Scot.; arrived in Canada in 1871; joined his uncle, the late Mr. John Shedden, in Toronto, a prominent railway contractor, who built the Toronto and Nipissing Railway, the Union Station in Toronto, and other public works; in October, 1873, removed to Montreal, taking up the business of his late uncle under the title of The Shedden Company, Limited; now the principal proprietor of this Corporation; also a director of several large corporations, principal of which are the Bell Telephone Co., the Royal Bank of Canada, The Sincennes-McNaughton Line, Ltd., The Canadian Transfer Co., and the Wire and Cable Company; lover of turf sports, having been Secretary-Treasurer of the Province of Quebec Turf Club for several years, and holding the same office in the Montreal Tandem Club for two years; sec.-treas. of the Montreal Hunt from 1879 to 1886; Master of the Hunt, 1887; won three Queens Plates, and one Hunt Cup; a lover of agricultural pursuits, and takes great pleasure in superintending the work of his farms near Montreal; has travelled considerably, having made several extended tours through Canada, the United States, and the Continent of Europe; a Governor of the Montreal General, Notre Dame and Western Hospitals, Montreal. *Address:* 507 Sherbrooke St. W., Montreal. *Clubs:* Mount Royal, St. James, Montreal; Toronto, Toronto; Manitoba, Winnipeg, Manhattan, New York; Junior Atheneum, London, Eng.

PATRIARCHE, Mrs. Valance St. Just; *b.* Toronto, Ont., 1875; *d.* of Prof. Charles Valance Berryman, M.A., M.D., and Julia Caroline Brondgeest; relict of Hugh Racey Patriarche, manager of Canadian Freight Assn., Western Lines; one *s.* *Educ.:* Toronto, Ont. *Publications:* "Tag, or the Chien Boule Dog;" newspaper articles, magazine stories, and a few poems. *Recreations:* reading, canoeing, cailing, photography. *Address:* 108 Cauchon St., Fort Rouge, Winnipeg, Man.

PATRICK, William, M.A., D.D.; *b.* Glasgow, Scot., 1852; *s.* of Robert and Kargaret Patrick. *Educ.:* Glasgow Univ.; T. C. Coll., Heidelburg; arrived in Canada, 1900; principal of Man. Coll., since 1900. *Address:* Manitoba Lodge, Winnipeg.

PATTERSON, Hon. James Colebrooke, P.C.; *b.* Armagh, Irel., 1839; *s.* of late Rev. James Patterson, formerly of Kingston, nr. Dublin; *m.* 1865, Katharine Dorothea, *d.* of the late Major John F. Elliott. *Educ.:* Dublin. Came to Can., 1857; entered the civil service of Ottawa, and was for some time priv. sec. to W. H. Griffin, late Dep. Postmaster-General of Can.; resigned, and studied for legal prof. Called to the bar, 1876; practised law at Windsor, Ont.; Reeve of Windsor for ten yrs.; Warden of Essex Co.; later was Inspr. of Schs., Windsor; rep. N. Essex in Ont. Legis., 1874-78; Co. of Essex in H. of C., 1878-82; N. Essex in H. of C., 1882-91; defeated at g. e., 1891; el. for W. Huron, 1892; Min. of Militia in the Thompson Admn., and also in the Bowell Ministry; was Pres. of the Ont. Conservative Union; became Sec. of State in the Abbott Admn., 25 Jan., 1892; Lieut.-Gov. of Manitoba, 1895-1900; one of the founders and first Pres., "Canadian Magazine" Co. *Address:* Ottawa. *Club:* Rideau, Ottawa.

PAUL, Charles Frederick; editor of Toronto *Saturday Night; b.* Saratoga Springs N.Y., Jan., 1866; *s.* of Charles F. Paul of New York City, and Esther Provondia of Montreal; *m.* Mary Costigan, of Montreal. *Educ.:* Dowd's Inst., Saratoga, N.Y.; began newspaper work in New York and Pennsylvania; moved to Montreal in 1883; Montreal *Star* as financial writer; served some years as city editor and resigned to take up managing editorship, Toronto *Saturday Night. Publications:* short stories published in England, the United States and Canada. *Address:* Alexandra Apartments, Toronto. *Clubs:* National, Ontario, Toronto., Ont.

PAYETTE, Louis; Mayor of Montreal; 1908-9; *b.* Montreal, 25 Dec., 1854; *s.* of Louis Payette and Odile Gauthier; *m.* Marie Louise Falardeau; one *d.* *Educ.:* Commercial Academy of Christian Brothers, Montreal. A gen. contractor in building construction. Erected Place Viger Station, Montreal; Chateau Frontenac, Quebec; C. P. R. Telegraph Bldg.; La Presse Bldg., and other important structures. Life governor of Notre Dame Hospital; mem. of the Catholic Sch. Bd., Chambre de Commerce and Bd. of Trade; director of several insurance, navigation and other important Co's. *Address:* 92 Laval Av., Montreal.

PAYNE, John Lambert; Controller of Statistics, Dept. of Railways and Canals; *b.* Markham, Ont., 24 Oct., 1859; *s.* of John Payne and Ellen Hollingshead; *m.* Agnes Scott; two *s.* one *d.* *Educ.:* New Hamburg, Ont. Graduated as a dispensing chemist, 1876; took up journalism in 1877 on the *Free Press*, London, Ont.; private sec. to six Dominion Ministers, including two Prime Ministers, 1885-1906; Joint Sec. of Colonial Conference of 1894 and Sec. of the Newfoundland Conference of 1895. *Recreations:* lawn bowling, general athletics. *Address:* 47 James St., Ottawa.

PAYZANT, John Young, K.C., M.A.; *b.* Falmouth, N.S., 9 Feb., 1837; *s.* of Peter and Catharine Payzant; *m.* Frances E. Silver; five *s.* three *d.* *Educ.:* University of Acadia Coll.; barrister-at-law; pres. of the Bank of N.S.; the N.S. Fire Ins. Co.; vice-pres., Eastern Trust Co., Halifax Elec-ectric Tramway Co., N.S. Telephone Co., and the Trinidad Consolidated Telephone Co.; *Address:* Halifax, N.S. *Club:* Halifax.

PEARSON, Hon. Benjamin Franklin, K.C., M.L.A., Mem. of the Ex. Council of Nova Scotia; *b.* Masstown, Colchester Co., N.S., 4 April, 1855; *s.* of Frederick M. Pearson and Eliza Crowe; *m.* Julia Reading, of Truro, N.S.; one *s.* three *d.* *Educ.:* Pictou Acad., Dalhousie Coll., Halifax. For some time mem. of the Halifax City Coun. as alderman; pres., *Chronicle* Publishing Co., Halifax; pres., *Sun* Pub. Co., St. John. El. to Leg. Ass., of N.S., at g. e. 1901 and 1906; entered the prov. cabinet as Min. without portfolio, 22 Dec., 1906. *Address:* "Eamscotte," Halifax, N.S. *Clubs:* Halifax, City, Halifax; St. James, Montreal.

PEASE, Edson L.; Vice-Pres. and Gen. Mgr., Royal Bank of Can.; *b.* Coteau Landing, Que.; entered Bank of Commerce, Montreal, 1874; joined Merchants Bank of Halifax, now Royal Bank of Can., as Accnt., 1883. Removed to Montreal, 1887, and became branch mgr. of the Royal Bank; apptd. asst. gen. mgr., 1899; gen. mgr., 1900; dir., 1906. Dir., London and Lancashire Life Ass. Co., Canada Car Co., and other important corporations. *Address:* 718 Sherbrooke St. W. Montreal. *Clubs:* Mount Royal, St. James, Canada, Montreal.

PEDLEY, Francis, B.A.; Deputy Supt. Gen. of Indian Affairs, Canada; *b.* St. John's, Newfoundland, 25 June, 1858; *s.* of Rev. Charles Pedley of Hawley, Staffordshire, Eng., and Sarah Stomill, *d.* of Rev. William Stomill, Principal Rotherham Coll., Sheffield, Eng.; *m.* Helen Louise, *d.* of Sidney and Mary Ann Hobart, of Cobourg, Ont. *Educ.:* Pub. Sch., St. Johns, Nfld., and Northumberland Co., Ont., Coll. Inst., Cobourg, Ont., and McGill Univ., Montreal. Arrived in Canada, 1864; practiced law in Toronto, 1890-1897; apptd. Supt. of Immigration for Canada, 1897, and organized the Immigration System now in operation in Canada; apptd. Deputy Supt. General Indian Affairs, Nov., 1902. *Address:* 483 McLaren St., Ottawa. *Club:* Rideau, Ottawa.

PEDLEY, Rev. Hugh, B.A.; *b.* Chester-le-Street, Durham, Eng.; *s.* of Rev. Chas. Pedley and Sarah Stowell; *m.* Eliza Locke Field; three *s.* one *d.* *Educ.:* Protestant Acad., St. John's, Nfld.; Cobourg High Sch., McGill Univ., Congregational Coll. Came to Canada in 1864; ordained in 1877; filled the following charges in the Cong. body; Cobourg, 1877-88; Winnipeg, 1888-90; Emmanuel Ch., Montreal, 1900 to date. *Recreations:* curling, canoeing and sailing. *Addresses:* 177 Drummond St., Montreal; Kenora Lodge, Brockville, Ont. (summer).

PELISSIER, Ernest, K.C.; *b.* Yamaska, Que., 24, June, 1864. *Educ.:* Sorel Coll., St. Mary's Coll., Montreal, Laval Univ.; admitted to bar, 1887, and practiced in Montreal for several years. In 1890, became head of the firm of Pelissier & Wilson, now Pelissier, Wilson & St. Pierre; cr. a K.C., 1902. Unsuccessful can for Yamaska at el., 1904. *Publication:* A vol. covering the law pertaining to builders and architects, 1902. *Address:* 151 St. James St., Montreal. *Clubs:* Lafontaine, St. Denis, Canadien, Royal St. Lawrence Yacht, Montreal.

PELLATT, Colonel Henry Mill, A.D.C.; Lieut.-Col. Commandant of the 2nd Regt., "Queen's Own Rifles of Canada"; *b.* Toronto 1860; *s.* of Henry Pellatt; m. 1887, Mary, only *d.* of John Dobson, Bewcastle, Cumberland, Eng.; one *s.* *Educ.:* Upper Canada Coll. Entered father's office when fifteen yrs. of age, and later formed partnership with his father under firm name of Pellatt & Pellatt; associated with many industrial undertakings; a dir. of the Crow's Nest Pass Co.; pres., Toronto Electric Light Co., and the Toronto & Niagara Power Co.; pres. of the Cobalt Lake Mining Co.; vice-pres. of the Manufacturers Life Insur. Co., dir., Toronto Ry. Co., the Richelieu & Ontario Nav. Co., the Dominion Iron & Steel Co., the British America Assur. Co., and other corporations; a trustee of Trinity Univ.; a governor of Grace Hospital. Joined the Queen's Own Rifles, and passed through all commissioned ranks to the command of the regt., which now consists of two batts.; Major of the Queen's Jubilee Contg. to Eng., 1897; commanded Can. contg. at Coronation of His Majesty, and took with him then at his own expense Queen's Own Bugle Band, which was an actractive feature of the pageant. Proposes to take 300 mem of regt. to Eng., 1910. *Addresses:* Traders Bank Bldg. (bus.); "Casa Loma," Walmer Rd., Davenport, Toronto. *Clubs:* Toronto, National; Toronto; Rideau, Ottawa.

PELLETIER, Sir Charles Alphonse Pantaleon, K.C.M.G., LL.D., K.C., P.C.; Lieut. Gov. of the Prov. of Quebec; *b.* Riviere Ouelle, 22 Jan., 1837; *y. s.* of late J. M. Pelletier and Julie Painchaud; *m.* (1st) Suzanne, *d.* of late Hon. C. E. Casgrain 1862; (2nd) Virginie, *d.* of late Hon. M. P. de Sales de La Terriere, 1866; one *s.* *Educ.:* Ste. Anne de la Pocatiere Coll.; Laval Univ; Bar, 1860; Q.C., 1879; Batonnier of Quebec Bar, 1892; twice elected president of Society of St. Jean Baptiste (National Society of French Canadians); several years Major of 9th Batt. or "Voltigeurs de Queber," which battalion he commanded during Fenian raid in 1866; sat for Kamouraska in the Commons, 1869-77; for Quebec East in Quebec Legislative Assembly, 1873-74; P. C. of Canada, 1877, as Minister of Agriculture, and called to the Senate for Grandville Division; was sometime Hon. Pres. of Dominion Board of Agriculture, and Pres. of Canadian Commission to Paris Universal Exhibition of 1878; Speaker of the Senate of Canada, 1896-1901; resigned seat in Senate, 1902, and apptd. Justice of the Sup. Ct. of Quebec. *Decorated* C.M.G., for services as Canadian Commissioner at Paris Universal Exhibition of 1878; K.C.M.G., 1898; apptd. Lieut.-Governor, 15 Sept., 1908. *Address:* Spencerwood, Quebec.

PELLETIER, Hon. Joseph Pantaleon, M.D., Speaker of the Leg. Ass. of Quebec; *b.* Riviere Ouelle, 27 July, 1860; *s.* of Joseph Pelletier and Henriette Martin; *m.* Alice Hudon. *Educ.:* Coll. of Ste. Anne de la Pocatiere, Que., Laval Univ., Que.; studied in hospitals in Paris and then took up practice of his profession in Sherbrooke. Served in Northwest campaign of 1885 as Lieut. of the Students' Co. of the 9th Batt., Quebec; was for 12 years coroner of the dist. of St. Francis; dir., Eastern Tps. Agric. Exposition; apptd. mem. of the Quebec Prov. Bd. of Health, 1897; for four yrs. chief physician to the Order of Catholic Foresters for Prov. of Quebec. El. to Quebec Leg. Ass. at g. e., 1900, 1904, 1908; elec. speaker, 1908. *Address:* 79 Bowen Av., Sherbrooke, Que., *Club;* Garrison, Quebec.

PELLETIER, Hon. Louis Philippe, B.A. LL.L., LL.D. (Laval Univ.); *b.* Trois Pistoles, Que., 1857; *s.* of Hon. Thos. P. Pelletier and Caroline Casault; *m.* 1883, Adele, *d.* of the late R. Lelievre, of Quebec. *Educ.:* Ste. Anne Coll. Grad. 1876, and won Prince of Wales gold medal, studied law, Laval Univ., grad., 1880, winning Marquis of Lorne gold medal. Called to bar, 1880, and commenced practice in Quebec, where he has since practiced; was pres., National Conservative Assn. of the Prov. of Quebec. Founded *La Justice,* in conjunction with Col. Amyot, M.P.; unsuccessful candidate for Temiscouata Co., at Prov. g. e., 1886; for Three Rivers, at Dom. g. e., 1887; called to Legis. Council, May 11, 1888; resigned, but was returned to Legis. Assembly, by accl. for Dorchester Co.; apptd. Provincial Sec., Dec., 1891, on formation of de Boucherville govt.; acted as Attorney-General, under Mr. Flynn, 1896, 1897; re-el. for Dorchester Co., at each succeeding el. until 1904, when retired from politics. Defeated for Legis. Assembly, Dorchester Co., 1908 and at g. e., 1908 for Lotbiniere. Pres., Canadian Electric Light Co.; dir. Manufacturers' Life Insur. Co. Served with the 9th Voltigueurs de Quebec for several yrs. *Recreations:* hunting, fishing, yachting. *Address:* 38 Garden St., Quebec. *Clubs:* Garrison, St. Louis, Quebec.

PELLETIER, Lieut.-Col. Oscar Charles Casgrain; Commandant Military District, No. 7; Chevalier of the Legion of Honour; *b.* Quebec, 3 May, 1862; *s.* Sir Alphonse Pelletier, and Suzanne Casgrain; *m.* Marie a Melle Alice Archer; three *s.* six *d.* Started his military career in 1883; participated in the North West campaign, 1885 and severely wounded at Cut Knife; mentioned in despatches; South African War, 1900. Operations in Orange Free State, Feb. to May, 1900, including operations at Paardeberg (17-26 Feb.); slightly wounded, 27 Feb,); actions at Hout Nek (Thoba Mountain), (1 May) and Zand River (10 May). Operations in the Transvaal in May and June, 1900, including actions near Johannesburg (29 May) and Pretoria (4 June). Operations in Orange River Colony and western Transvaal, August, 1900; in Transvaal, east of Pretoria, July-October, 1900. (Despatches, London Gazette, 8 Feb., 1901) Brevet of Lieut.-Col. Queen's Medal with three clasps. *Recreations:* aquatics. *Address:* 17 St. Louis St., Quebec. *Club:* Garrison, Quebec.

PELLETIER, Hon. Thomas Philippe, M.L.C.; *b.* Ste. Anne de la Pocatiere, Que., 20 Dec., 1823; *s.* of Germain Pelletier and Marie Martha Pelletier;f*m.* 1854, Caroline Casault. *Educ.:* Coll. of Ste. Anne de la Pocatiere. Taught sch. for some time and then opened a general merchandise business at Trois Pistoles, Que., and has also held the position of postmaster of Trois Pistoles for 53 yrs.; apptd. mem. of the Quebec Legis. Council, 1892. *Address:* Trois Pistoles, Que.

PEMBERTON, Frederick B., C.E., P.L. S.; *b.* Victoria, B.C., 26 April, 1865; *s.* of J. D. and Theresa Pemberton; *m.* Mary A. D. Bell, three *s.* three *d.* *Educ.:* Univ. Coll., London, Eng.; senior partner in firm of Pemberton & Son, Victoria and Vancouver, est. 1887; real estate, financial and investment agents. *Recreations:* riding, shooting, boating, motoring. *Address:* Mountjoy, Victoria, B.C. *Club:* Union, Victoria.

PEMBROKE, Bishop of; *see* Rt. Rev N. Z. Lorrain.

PENHALLOW, David Pearce, B.Sc., M.Sc., D.Sc., F.R.S.C., F.G.S.A.; *b.* Kittery Point, Maine, U.S.A., 25 May, 1854; *s.* of Andrew Jackson and Mary Ann Josepha Pickering;*m*' Sarah A. Dunlop; one *s.* *Educ.:* Boston Univ. Prof. Botany and Chemistry, Imperial College of Agriculture, Sappore, Japan, 1876-1880, and pres. 1879-1880; Botanist to Houghton Farm Experiment Station, 1882-83; Professor of Botany, McGill Univ., since 1883; ed. Canadian Record of Science, 1888-1890; associate editor of American Naturalist, 1897-1907; editor for Paleobotany of Botanisches Central-blatt, 1902-07; British Association Committee on Canadian Ethnology 1897-1904 and Chairman 1902-04; Chairman, Royal Society of Canada Committee on Ethnology, 1902-1904; Special Commissioner World's Industrial and Cotton Centennial Exposition, 1884; Society of Plant Morphology and Physiology and President for 1899; New England Botanical Society; corresponding life mem. Mass. Hort. Soc.; associate mem. of the Natural History Soc. of Boston; fellow of the R. S. C. from 1883; (pres. of Section 4, 1896-97; life mem. of N. S. Fruit Growers' Association; pres., Dominion Pomological Society, 1890; Fellow American Association for Advancement of Science, 1882-86, and from 1905 (vice-pres. for Section G, 1908-09); fellow of the Royal Microscopical Soc. of London, 1892-1902; Montreal Horticultural Society, 1883-1982; (Pres. 1888-1892; Fellow Botanical Soc. of America; American Soc. of Naturalists (Pres., 1908-09); Trustee Marine Biological Laboratory, Woods Hole, Mass.; Director and Secretary Biological Stations of Canada; Director, Atlantic Coast Biological Station, St. Andrews, N.B., 1907; Chairman of Association of American Biological Research Stations, 1908-09; British Association Committee on Pleistocene Fauna and Flora of Canada, 1897-1901; Natural History Society of Montreal, (pres., 1802); Governors Fellow on Corporation of McGill Univ., Montreal; Champlain Society of Canada; Fellow Geological Society of America, 1907. Paleontological Society of America, 1909; National Geographical Society of America, 1905; American Forestry Association 1906; New England Botanical Society; several years mem. and Pres. of the Montreal

Branch American Folk Lore Society; American Academy of Political and Social Science, 1900. *Publications:* on botanical subjects, chiefly on Paleobotany, about 150 titles. *Address:* 82 The Linton, Montreal, and 86 Bay State Road, Boston, Mass., U.S.A.

PENNINGTON, David Henry, M.L.A.; *b.* Quebec, 14 Feb., 1868; *s.* of W. Pennington and Jessie E. Smith; *m.* Mary M. Stewart; three *s.* one *d.* Lumber Merchant; first el. to Leg. Ass., Quebec, for Megantic Co., 1909; largely interested in asbestos; pres., Robertson Asbestos Mining Co., Thetford Mine; pres., Standard Bedstead Co., dir. Richmond and Drumsville Fuel Co.; *Address:* Lyster, Que.

PENSE, Edward John Barker; editor and proprietor of British *Whig*, Kingston, Ont.; *b.* Kingston, Ont., 3 June, 1848; *s.* of L. M. Pense and Harriet Barker Pense; *m.* (1st) Cornelia Vaughn; (2nd) Elizabeth Hamilton; one *s.* five *d.* *Educ.:* Kingston Academy. Was chairman of Sch. Board, also alderman and mayor, and presdt, of a number of socs.; M.L.A., 1901-1908. Publisher of the *Whig*, Kingston, and also of *Church Life* and Ontario *Churchman*. *Address:* "Ongwanda," King St., Kingston. *Club:* Frontenac, Kingston.

PERLEY, George Halsey, B.A., M.P.; *b.* Lebanon, New Hampshire, 12 Sept., 1857; *s.* of William Goodhue Perley and Mabel E. T. Stevens; *m.* Annie Hespler Bowlby; one *d.* *Educ.:* Ottawa Gram. Sch., St. Paul's School, Concord, N.H., and Harvard Univ. Father was for years one of the largest lumber operators on the Ottawa, and one of the builders of the C. A. Ry.; has always been in the lumber business and was a partner in the firm of Perley and Pattee, of which his father was senior partner; is now head of the G. H. Perley Co.; also vice-pres., Hull Lumber Co., Ltd.; Director of the Bank of Ottawa; past-pres. of the Rideau Club and the Ottawa Golf Club; along with the other heirs of his father he made a donation of the beautiful homestead in Ottawa, to the city, as a hospital for incurables, now known as the Perley Home; chairman of the fund for the relief of sufferers by the forest fires in Prescott and Russell Counties; chairman of the Ottawa and Hull Fire Relief Fund, distributing about $1,000,000 among the sufferers by the fire of April 29, 1900; defeated for H. of C. for Russell, in 1900; defeated in bye-election in Argenteuil, Que., 1902; elec. to H. of C. in 1904; re-elec. 1908. *Address:* 232 Metcalfe St., Ottawa, Ont. *Clubs:* Rideau, Golf, Ottawa.

PERODEAU, Hon. Narcisse, M.L.C. Quebec; *b.* St. Ours, Richelieu Co., Que., 26 March, 1851; *s.* of Paul Perodeau and Modeste Arpin; *m.* 1883, Mary L., *d.* of the late Dr. Charles Duckley, of St. Hyacinthe, Que., four *s.* one *d.* *Educ.:* St. Hyacinthe Coll. Grad. B.C.L., McGill Univ., 1876. Admitted a N.P., 1876, and commenced practice of his prof. with the firm of Jobin, Coutlee & Perodeau, but for the past fiye or six yrs. has practiced alone. Sec. of Prov. Bd. of Notaries at Montreal, since 1880; apptd. a Prof. of the Faculty of Law of Laval Univ., LL.D., 1902. Apptd. to Legis. Council of Quebec., 1897; dir. of "La Sauvegarde" Ins. Co., and life governor of Notre Dame Hospital. *Address:* 57 Viger Av., Montreal. *Clubs:* Mount Royal, St. James, Montreal.

PERRAULT, Maurice, M.L.A.; *b.* Montreal, 12 June, 1857; *s.* of Henri Maurice Perrault and Octavie Masson; *m.* 1879, Sara Hebert of Montreal; three *d.* *Educ.:* Montreal Coll. Has practiced his prof. as architect and C. E. in Montreal since 1878; acted as official architect for dist. of Montreal, 1888-1892; Expropriation Commn. for Montreal, 1889-1895, and architect 1889-1901. Represents Dept. of Pub. Works. of Fed. Govt. as local architect for Montreal. Mem., Architects' Assn. of Prov. of Quebec. since 1890, of which was one of organizers; American Pub. Health Assn. since 1894, Civil Engrs' Soc. of Can. since 1898; vice-pres., Architectural Inst.; governor Notre Dame Hospital. Mayor of Longueuil, Que., 1898-1900. El. to Que. Legis. by accl. at g. e., 1900; re-el. for Chambly Riding, 1904, 1908. Served as officer in 65th Regt. for about ten yrs.; retired about 1888 with rank of Capt. *Address:* 15 St. Lawrence Boulevard, Montreal.

PERRIN, Right Rev. Bishop William Willcox, D.D.; *b.* Westbury on Tyne, Somersetshire, Eng., 11 Aug., 1848; *s.* of Thomas and Margaret Perrin, *m.* Harriet Moore; one *s.* one *d.* *Educ.:* King's Coll., London, and Trinity Coll., Oxford Eng.; arrived in Canada, May, 1893; Bishop of British Columbia, 1893; formerly Curate of St. Mary's, Vicar of St. Luke's, Southampton Eng.; at the wish of the Synod of the Diocese, consecrated in Westminster Abbey. *Address:* Victoria, B.C., *Club:* Westminster, London, Eng.

PERRY, Lieut.-Col. Aylesworth Bowen; Commr. of the Royal Northwest Mounted Police; *b.* Lennox Co., Ont., 21 Aug., 1860; of U.E.L. descent; *m.* 1883, Emma, *d.* of G. L. Meikle, of Lachute, Que., one *s.* two *d.* *Educ.:* Napanee High Sch., and Royal Military Coll., Kingston; mem. of first graduating class, 1880, taking high honours. Apptd. July, 1880, a Lieut. in Royal Engrs., but had to resign his commission the following yr. on account of illhealth. Gazetted Inspector of N.W.M.P., 24 Jan., 1882; served in two NorthWest Rebellions, and mentioned in despatches; promoted to rank of Supt. 1 Aug., 1885; apptd. Commr., 1900. Commanded mounted police contingent at Diamond Jubilee of Queen Victoria (Jubilee medal). *Address:* Regina, Sask.

PERRY, Oscar Butler; mining engr. and Supt. Yukon Gold Co., Dawson; *b.* Indiana, 1873. *Educ.:* Indiana Univ. and Columbia Coll. Sch. of Mines, New York. Has been with the Guggenheim Exploration Co. for six yrs.; designed gold dredges now used by Yukon Co.; planned and constructed the seventy mile ditch and pipe line of the Yukon Gold Co. *Address:* Dawson, Y.T.

PETERSON, William, M.A., LL.D. (St. Andrew's Univ.), C.M.G., Principal and Vice-Chancellor of McGill Univ.; *b.* Edinburgh, Scotland, 29 May, 1856; *s.* of the late John Peterson and Grace M. Anderson; *m.* 1885, Lisa, *e. d.* of the late William Ross, of 12 Hyde Park Gardens, London, W., and Glenearn, Perthshire, Scotland; two *s.*

Educ.: Edinburgh High Sch.; grad. Edinburgh Univ., with first-class honors in Classics, 1875; studied at Univ. of Gottingen; gained an open scholarship at Corpus Christi Coll., Oxford, and in 1896, the Gerguson Scholarship in Classics. For two yrs., Asst. Prof. of Humanity in Edinburgh Univ. Cr. LL.D., St. Andrew's Univ., 1885, and by Princeton Univ., 1896; received hon. degrees from Univ. of New Brunswick, 1900; Yale, 1901; Johns Hopkins, 1902; Pennsylvania and Queen's 1903; Aberdeen, 1906; Toronto, 1907; Principal of McGill Univ. since 1895; mem. Protestant Committee of Council of Pub. Instruction; a trustee of the Carnegie Foundation for the Advancement of Teaching in U.S., Canada, and Newfoundland; a gov. Royal Victoria Hospital. Cr. C.M.G., 1901. *Publications:* editor of the Tenth Book of Quintilian's "Institute of Oratory;" Tactitus's "Dialogue on Oratory; Cicero's speeches in defence of Cluentius and against Veres; has contributed to numerous publications. Canadian ed. of Nelson's perpetual looseleaf Encyclopaedia. *Recreations:* walking, golf, curling. *Address:* 447 Sherbrooke St., W. Montreal. *Clubs:* St. James, Mount Royal, University, Montreal.

PETTYPIECE, Henry John; owner of the Forest *Free Press: b.* Anderdown Tp., Essex Co., Ont., 11 Nov., 1855; *s.* of Anthony and Ann Pettypiece; *m.* 1879, Mary M. Meloche, of Amherstburg; two *s.* one *d. Educ.:* Ont. Pub. Sch. Was raised on the farm, but in April, 1879, joined staff of Amherstburg Echo; in 1883, purchased the Forest *Free Press*, which he has since edited. Town Councillor of Forest, 1888; a dir of the Lambton Farmers' Inst.; for two yrs. a license commr. for East Lambton. El. to Leg. Ass. at g. e., 1898 and 1902; unsuccessful, 1905. *Recreations:* cricket, curling. *Address:* Forest, Ont.

PEUCHEN, Major Arthur Godfrey; *b.* Montreal, 18 April, 1859; *s.* of Godfrey Peuchen, Prussia, and Eliza Clark, Hull, England; *m.* Margaret Thomson; one *s.* one *d.* President of the Standard Chemical Co., Major Queen's Own Rifles; ex-vice Commodore, R. C. Y. C., Toronto. *Recreations:* yachting, hunting, militia. *Address:* 599 Jarvis St., Toronto, and "Woodlands," Barrie, Ont. *Clubs:* National, Hunt, Ontario Jockey, R.C.Y.C., Albany, and Military Institute, Toronto.

PHILLIPPS-WOLLEY, Clive, J.P., F.R.C.S.; *b.* Wimborne, Dorsetshire, Eng., 3 April, 1852; *s.* of R. A. L. Phillipps, M.A., F.R.C.S.; *m.* Jane, *d.* of Admiral Fenwick, R.N.; one *s.* three *d. Educ.:* Rossall, Eng. Arrived in Canada, 1884; vice consul at Kertch; inherited the Wolley property, Hanwood, Salop, took name and arms of Wolley; retired from foreign office service; called to the bar, Middle Temple and Oxford circuit; Capt. 4th Batt., S.W.B.; vice-pres., Navy League, England; pres., V. & E. Navy League, B.C. *Publications:* Big Game Sport in Crimea and Caucasus; Songs of an English Esau; Boys' Books, Snap, and novels. Chicamore Stone, etc. *Recreations:* shooting and fishing. *Address:* Coefields, B.C. *Clubs:* Shropshire Country, Eng., and Union Club, Victoria, B.C.

PICKTHALL, Miss Marjorie Lowrey Christie; *b.* London, Eng., 14 Sept., 1883; *d.* of Arthur C. Picthall and Helen Mallard. *Educ.:* The Bishop Strachan Sch. Toronto. Arrived in Canada, 1890; *Publications:* Chiefly magazine work, verse and fiction; some boys' books. *Recreations:* gardening, rowing. *Address:* 537 Euclid Avenue, Toronto. *Clubs:* Woman's Press Club, Toronto; Society of Authors.

PICKUP, Samuel Walter Willett, M.P.; *b.* Granville Ferry, Annapolis Co., N.S., 1 March, 1859; *s.* of Samuel Pickup, and Cylina G. Willett; *m.* Lillie L. E. Troop, 31 Oct., 1883; three *s.* three *d. Educ.:* Com. Sch. and Mount Allison, Sackville; merchant, shipbuilder and farmer; was 18 yrs. in the Municipal Council of his Municipality, and was for three yrs. Warden of the Co.; first el. to the H. of C. in 1904; re-el. 1908; a Liberal. *Address:* Granville Ferry, Annapolis Co., N.S. *Club:* Laurentian, Ottawa.

PIGOTT, Augustus Charles Doyne; Sheriff, Southern Judicial Dist. of Manitoba; *b.* Chatham, Kent, Eng., 1 Jan., 1862; *s.* Major General H. de Rinzey Pigott, of Co. Galway, Ireland, and Frances Catherine, *d.* of Capt. Powlett Doyne, Queen's Co., Ireland; *m.* Florence Harriet, third *d.* of Alex. Buchanan, of Omagh, Co. Tyrone, Ire.; two *s.* one *d. Educ.:* Marlborough Coll., Eng., and Bonn, Germany. Came to Can., 1880; commenced business as real estate and insurance agent; has been farmer in Man., 14 yrs.; Lieut. in Boulton's Scouts, 1885 *Address:* Morden, Man.

PINHEY, John Charles; artist; *b.* Ottawa, Ont., 24 Aug., 1860; *s.* of John Hamnett and Constance Pinhey of England; *m.* Amelia P. Rhynds; three *s.* two *d. Educ.:* Coll. Inst., Ottawa, and Julian's Academy, Paris, France; began to study art in Toronto, at the age of 19, and at 21 went to Paris; studied for 5 years in Julian's Academy, under Boulanger and Lefebore, and also at Beaux Arts; criticised by Jerome; elec. a mem. of R.C.A., and in 1897 was made an academican; exhibited at World's Fairs at Chicago and Buffalo. *Address:* Wolfenden, Hudson Heights, Que. *Club;* Pen and Pencil, Montreal.

PINKHAM, Right Rev. William Cyprian D.D., D.C.L.; *b.* 1844; *s.* of William Pinkham, Teignmouth, Devon, and St. John's, Newfoundland; *m.* 1868, Jean Anne, 2nd *d.* of late William Drever, Winnipeg; three *s.* three *d. Educ.:* St. Augustine's Coll., Canterbury. Incumbent of St. James's, Manitoba, 1868-82; Superintendent of Education for Protestant Public Schs. of Manitoba, 1871-83; Archdeacon of Manitoba and Canon of St. John's Cathedral, Winnipeg, 1882-87; Secretary of Synod, 1882-1887; Bishop of Saskatchewan, 1887 to date; Hon. D.C.L. Trinity Univ., Toronto; Hon. D.D. Univ. of Manitoba. *Address:* Bishop's Court, Calgary, Alta.

PLANTE, Michael Henri Arthur, LL.B., K.C., M.L.A.; *b.* Valleyfield, Que., 29 Sept., 1870; *s.* of Moise Plante ex-M.L.A., and Hermine Langevin Bergevin; unmarried. *Educ.* at the Elementary Sch., Valleyfield; Jesuites Coll., Montreal; Advocat; admitted to the bar, 1894; first el to Leg. Ass., 1898; unsuccessful 1900 and 1904; re-el. 1908; a

Conservative. *Address:* Valleyfield, Que.. *Club:* Montreal.

PLASKETT John Stanley, B.A., F.R. A.S.C.; *b.* Strathallan, Oxford Co., Ont., 17 Nov., 1865; *s.* of Joseph and Annie Plaskett; *m.* Rebecca Hope Hemley; two *s.* *Educ.:* Pub. Sch., Woodstock High Sch., Toronto Univ.; employed with Edison Electrical Co., 1888-1889; Asst. in dept. of Physics, Toronto Univ., 1890-1903; Astronomer, Dept. of Interior, 1903 to date. *Publications:* on Orthochromatic Colour Photography; Mathematics in the mechanical trades; thirteen complete papers and numerous shorter notes on various astronomical subjects. *Recreation:* photography. *Address:* "Cedarhurst" Fairmount Ave., Ottawa.

POIRIER, Hon. Pascal, B.A.; Senator; *b.* Shediac, N.B., 15 Feb., 1852; *m.* 1897, Anna Lusignan. *Educ.:* St. Joseph's Coll., Memramcook, N.B.; was postmaster, H. of C., from 1872 to 1885; pres. of a section of St. Jean Baptist Society, of Ottawa; pres., Canadian Institute, 1881-2; pres. of the Mineralogical Soc. of Ottawa Univ.; pres. of La Societe de l'Assomption for twelve yrs.; is a barrister for both N.B. and Que. *Publications:* "L'Origine des Acadiens," "Le Pére Lefebvre et l'Acadie," Fellow R. S.C.; Knight of the Legion of Honour, called to the Senate, 9 March, 1885; a Conservative. *Address:* Shediac, N.B.

POLLARD, Rev. Henry; *b.* Exeter, Eng., 1 Nov., 1830; *s.* of William Carss and Mary Pollard; *m.* Annie M. Porter, *d.* of W. Porter, M.P., St. Stephen, N.B. *Educ.:* Gram. Sch., Exeter, and St. Augustus Coll., Canterbury, Eng.; arrived in Canada, 14 Feb., 1858; Curate of St. Stephen's N.B.; Rector of Mangerville and Burts, dioceses of Fredericton; Curate of Christ Church, Ottawa; Rector of St. John's Church, Ottawa; senior Canon of Christ Church Cathedral, Ottawa. *Address.* St. John's Rectory, Ottawa.

POLLOK, Rev. Dr. Allan; *b.* 1829. *s.* of late Dr. Pollok, of Kingston. *Educ.:* Glasgow Univ. Licensed by Presbytery of Dunoon, 1852; went to N.S., 1852; in New Glasgow, 1852-73; Professor of Ecclesiastical History and Practical Theology, 1876; Principal of Presby., Theological Coll., Halifax, since 1886. *Publications:* Studies in Practical Theology, 1907. *Address:* Halifax, N.S.

PONTON, Lieut.-Col. William Nisbet, M.A., K.C.; *b.* Belleville, Ont., 1856; *s.* James Wemyss Ponton and Anna Hutton Ponton; *m.* May E. Sankey; three *s.* two *d.* *Educ.:* Up. Can. Coll., and Univ. of Toronto; barrister-at-law, 27 yrs.; commandant of 15th Regt., seven yrs., (long service decoration); represented Belleville Board of Trade at Chambers of Commerce of Empire, Toronto, 1906. *Address:* Belleville, Ont.

POOLE, Henry Skeffington, M.A., D. Sc., F.R.S.C., F.C.S.; *b.* Stellarton, N.S., 1 Aug., 1844; *s.* of Henry Poole, and Elizabeth N. Leonard of Sydney, C.B.; *m.* Florence H. G. Gray, *d.* of Hon. J. H. Gray, C.M.G., Charlottetown, 1876; four *s.* four *d.* *Educ.:* King's Coll., Windsor. N.S., and Royal School of Mines; Asst. Manager, Caledonia Mines, C.B.; Assayer Utah Silver Mines; Secretary Japanese Commission, Washington; Government Inspector of Mines, N.S., 1872-1878, when he suggested and drafted first mines regulation Act in Canada, and first special legislation on submarine coal mining; General Manager of Acadia Coal Company, N.S., 1879-1900; reported on mining for the Canadian Geological Survey, reports, 1885-1906. Asso. Royal School of Mines; Hon. mem. Fed. of Mining Engineers; founder M. Can. Soc., C.E., first pres. Mining Soc. of N.S.; past pres., N.S. Institute of Science. *Publications:* Transcations R.S.C.; Mining Soc., N. S.; The N.S. Inst. of Sc.; The Federated Inst'n.; reports. *Address:* 60 Bedford Row, Halifax, N.S. *Club:* Halifax.

POPE, Miss Georgina Fane; Royal Red Cross; *b.* Charlottetown, P.E.I., 1 Jan., 1862; *d.* of the late Hon. W. H. Pope, and Helen Des Bresay. *Educ.:* P.E.I.; served two years in South African campaign as Nursing Sister; at present Matron of the Permanent Army Medical Corps. *Address:* Military Hospital, Halifax, N.S.

POPE, Joseph, C.V.O., C.M.G., I.S.O., Japanese Order of the Sacred Treasure; Under Secy. for External Affairs, Canada; *b.* Charlottetown, P.E.I., 16 Aug., 1854; *e. s.* of late Hon. W. H. Pope and Helen Des Brisay; *m.* 1884, Marie Louise Josephine Henrietta, *e. d.* of Chief Justice H. T. Taschereau of the Superior Court of Lower Can., Montreal; five *s.* one *d.* *Educ.:* Prince of Wales Coll., Charlottetown; from 1870 to 1878, banking. Entered Civil Service of Canada, 1878; Private Secretary to Minister of Marine and Fisheries; was Private Sec. to Rt. Hon. Sir John Macdonald, Prime Minister of Canada, 1882-91; apptd Asst. Clerk of the King's Privy Council for Canada, 1889; Under Secretary of State and Deputy Registrar General of Canada, 1896; Under Sec. for External Affairs, 1908; attached to the staff of the British Agent on the Behring Sea Arbitration at Paris, 1893; was Agent of the Canadian Government at the proceedings of the Joint High Commission which met at Quebec and Washington, 1898-90; Associate Secretary to the Alaska Boundary Tribunal, London, 1903; deputed by the Government to make arrangements for the tour of the Prince and Princess of Wales in Canada in 1901, and for his services in that capacity received a C.M.G. *Publications:* Memoirs of Sir John Macdonald; The Royal Tour in Canada, 1901; "Champlain;" "Cartier." *Recreations:* astronomy. *Address:* 286 Stewart Street, Ottawa. *Club:* Rideau, Ottawa.

PORTER, Edward Guss, K.C., M.P.; *b.* Cousicon, Prince Edward Co., Ont., 28 May, 1859; *s.* of Robert and Hannah Porter; *m.* Annie A. Morrow; one *s.* *Educ.:* at Albert Univ., Belleville, Ont.; a barrister; has been alderman and Mayor of the City of Belleville, Ont.; first elec. to the H. of C., Jan., 1901, at bye-elec.; re-elec. in 1904 and 1908. *Address:* Belleville, Ont.

PORTER, John Bonsall, Ph.D., D.S.C.; Prof. of Mining Engineering, McGill Univ.; *b.* Glendale, Ont., 1861; *s.* of John Henry Porter and Lydia Bonsall; *m.* Ethel Hardinge, *d.* of Chas. H. Going; one *d.* *Educ.:* Privately and at Columbia Univ., New York. In educational work, 1882-1885;

mining and economic geology, 1885-88; engineering practice in mines and railways; prof. of mining engineering at McGill Univ., 1896. *Publications:* Numerous papers on educational and engineering subjects; economic minerals, etc. *Recreations:* yachting, angling; open air sports in general. *Addresses:* 130 McTavish St., Montreal, and Long Beach Lodge, Guysboro, N.S. *Clubs:* University, and Engineering, Montreal; Imperial and Colonial, London; Royal N.S., Yacht Squadron, Halifax.

POTTINGER, David, I.S.O.; Asst. Chn. of the Govt. Railways Managing Board; *b.* Pictou, N.S., 7 Oct., 1843; of Scottish parentage; *m.* Mary Louise, *d.* of the late William Fisher, of Fredericton, N.B., and widow of F. W. Reid; two *s.* one *d.* *Educ.:* Pictou Acad., N.S. Entered the Government railway service, at Halifax, N.S., as clerk, 1863; became cashier 1871; station master, 1872; gen. storekeeper, 1874; chief supt. 1879; gen. mgr. of Government railways, 1892; mem. of the Government Railways Managing Board, 1909; Asst. Chmn., 1910. *Address:* Moncton, N.B. *Club:* Rideau, Ottawa.

POUPORE, William Joseph; *b.* Allumette, Island, Que., 29 April, 1846; *s.* of Wm. Poupore and Susan McAdam; *m.* Barbar Eleonore, *d.* of late Hon. John Poupore; five *s.* four *d.* *Educ.:* Com. Sch., and Ottawa Commercial College; member of Leg. Ass. of Quebec from 1882 to March, 1892; member of H. of C. for Pontiac, from 1896 to 1900; studied law for two years and then went into business as General Contractor, Railways and Public works, including harbours and rivers; now pres. of the W. J. Poupore Co., Limited, Montreal; an ardent advocate of the construction of the Montreal, Ottawa & Georgian Bay Ship Canal. *Address:* 388 Wood Ave., Westmount, Que. *Clubs:* Laurentian, Ottawa; Engineers', Montreal.

POWELL, Charles Berkeley; *b.* Port Dover, Ont., 19 Aug., 1858; *s.* of Col. Walker Powell, former Adjt.-Gen. of the Militia of Can.; *m* Helen Louise, *d.* of Gordon B. Pattee, of Ottawa; two *d.* *Educ.:* Galt Coll., McGill Univ., Montreal. A mechanical engr. Served an apprenticeship in the shops of the G. T. R., in Montreal, as machinist. Was a mem. of the Ottawa City Coun., and a partner in the lumber firm of Perley & Pattee. Pres. or Dir. of several local manufacturing Cos. El. to Ont. Legis. for Ottawa at g. e., 1898; re-el. at g. e., 1902. *Address:* 283 Metcalfe St., Ottawa. *Clubs:* Rideau, Golf, Country, Laurentian, Ottawa.

POWER, Augustus, K.C., I.S.O.; *b.* Quebec, 22 Dec., 1847; *y. s.* of late Mr. Justice Power and Suzanne Aubert de Gaspe; *m.* 1885, Laleah, *d.* of late Rev. Edmund Crawley, D.D., of N.S., and relict of late Seymour Tobin, R.N.; one *s.* one *d.* *Educ.:* St. Mary's Coll. and McGill Univ., Montreal. Called to bar of Quebec, 1869; practised at Montreal, until 1874; entered Department of Justice, 1874; employed on revision of Dominion statutes, 1887; apptd. a Commissioner for revision of Statutes in 1902. Chief Clerk, Dept. of Justice since 1879. *Address:* 196 Wilbrod Street, Ottawa.

POWER, Hon. Lawrence Geoffrey, P.C., LL.D., Senator: *b.* Halifax, N.S., 9 Aug., 1841; *s.* of Patrick Power and Ellen Gaull, both of Waterford, Irel.; *m.* 23 June, 1880, Susan, 4th *d.* of M. O'Leary, of West Quoddy, Halifax Co., two *d.* *Educ.:* St. Mary's Coll., Halifax; Carlow Coll., Catholic Univ., Irel.. and Harvard Law Sch., Cambridge, Mass.; a scholar of Catholic Univ., Ireland; B.A., of St. Mary's; admitted to the bar, 1866; is a barrister and solicitor; alderman in Halifax for six years, and member of Board of Sch. Comm. for 13 years; a member of the Senate of Halifax Univ. *Publications:* pamphlet "The Manitoba Sch. Question from the Point of View of a Catholic member;" "Richard John Uniacke;" a sketch "The Irish Discovery of America;" called to the Senate, 2 Feb., 1877; apptd. Speaker, Jan., 1901; sworn of Privy Council, Jan., 1905; a Liberal; *Address:* Halifax N.S.

POWER, William; mem. of the firm of W. & J. Sharples, lumber merchants, Quebec; *b.* Sillery, Que., 21 Feb., 1849; *s.* of the late William Power, one of the mgrs. of the firm of W. & J. Sharples, and B. Fitzgerald; *m.* 1881, Winnifred Susan, *d.* of James Rockett, lumberman of Quebec; five *s.* two *d.* *Educ.:* Sillery pub. schs. Has been connected with the W. & J. Sharples firm since 1860, finally becoming a partner. Owns large timber lands and is one of the principal owners of the River Ouelle Pulp and Lumber Co. At one time pres. Bd. of Trade, and for past ten yrs. has been Sch. Commr. of the city of Quebec. Returned to H. of C. for Quebec West, bye-el., 1902, by accl.; re-el. at g. e., 1904; unsuccessful at g. e., 1908. *Address:* 75 St. Ursule St., Quebec. *Club:* Garrison, Quebec.

PREFONTAINE, Isaie; *b.* Beloeil, Que., 1861; *m.* 1883, Eliza, *d.* of Olivier Pigeon, of Vercheres. *Educ.:* Montreal Coll., from which he grad. with honors. Pres., Chambre du Commerce, Montreal, and l'Ecole des Hautes Etudes Commerciales. *Address:* Salaberry Apts., Montreal, Que.

PRENDERGAST, Hon. James Emile Pierre; one of the Judges of the Kings Bench, Manitoba; *b.* Quebec, 22 March, 1858; *s.* of late James Prendergast and Emilie Gauvreau; *m.* 1886, Olivina, *d.* of late Francois Mondor, of St. Boniface, Man. *Educ.:* Quebec Seminary and Laval Univ. Called to bar of Quebec, 1881, Manitoba, 1882; sat in Manitoba Leg. Ass., 1885-92; Prov. Sec. in the Greenway Admn., Jan., 1888 to Ang., 1889, when he resigned; mem. of the Catholic section of the board of education, 1884-90; mem. of the Manitoba Univ. Council since 1895; Mayor of St. Boniface, 1893-96; Co. Ct. Judge, 1897-1905; Judge of the Supreme Ct. of Saskatchewan, 1905-10; apptd. to present position, 7 Feb., 1910. *Address:* Winnipeg, Man.

PRENTICE, James Douglas, J.P.; Man. Dir. Western Canadian Ranching Co., Ltd.; *b.* "The Grange," Lanarkshire, Scot., 3 Feb., 1861; *s.* of Andrew Prentice; *m.* Mabel Clare, *d.* of T. D. Gilpin, of Bristol House, Roehampton, Surrey, Eng. *Educ.:* Fettes Coll., Edinburgh. Arrived in Canada, 1882 as an official in the Bank of B.N. A., and first employed at Halifax, N.S. In

1888, was transferred to the branch at Victoria, B.C., but resigned to assume his present position with the Western Canadian Ranching Co. El. to B.C. Legis. at g. e., 1898, 1900; apptd. Provincial Secretary later yr.; became Finance Minister, 1901; resigned from Legis., 1903. *Address:* Victoria, B.C.; Chilcoten, B.C. *Club:* Union, Victoria.

PRESTON, Josiah Johnston, M.L.A.; *b.* Manvers, Co. Durham, Ont., 7 June, 1855; *s.* of James Preston and Jane Johnston. *Educ.:* in the Public Schs.; was Deputy Reeve and Reeve of Township of Manvers, and Co. Councillor for 10 years, 1888 to 1897; elec. eight times by acclam.; Warden of united Counties of Northumberland and Durham in 1897; clerk, 1898, until date; first el. to the Leg. Ass. of Ont. at g. e., 1902; re-el. 1905, 1908. *Address:* Bethany, Ont.

PRESTON, Thomas H.; Proprietor of the Brantford *Expositor; b.* Mount Vernon, Ind., 22 Oct., 1855; *s.* of Rev. James Preston and Emeline A. Phelps; *m.* 1876, Lillian, *d.* of A. R. Macdonald, of Montreal; five c. *Educ.:* Pub. and Gram. Schs., of Belleville and Woodstock. Became a printer's apprentice in office of Woodstock *Sentinel;* completed his apprenticeship on the Stratford *Beacon;* worked as a compositor on Toronto *Globe,* 1871; removed to U.S.; returned to Can. 1874, and joined staff of Ottawa *Free Press,* and was mem. Press Gallery, H. of C.; night-editor, Toronto *Globe,* 1881; special corres. for the *Globe,* Press Gallery, H. of C.; was mng. dir. and chief shareholder of Winnipeg *Sun;* purchased Brantford *Expositor,* 1890. El. to Legis 1899; re-el. at g. e., 1902 and 1904; pres., Can. Press Assn., 1895, Brantford Bd. of Trade, 1900. Southern Fair Assn., 1899. *Address:* Brantford, Ont.

PRESTON, William Thomas Rochester; *b.* Ottawa, 6 Sept., 1853; *s.* of G. H. and M. A. Preston; *m.* Evelyn Harris, Port Hope, Ont.; one *s.* two *d.* Journalist; organizer for the Liberal party for 10 yrs.; Provincial Librarian for Ontario; Commissioner of Emigration to Great Britain and Europe, 1899-06; special Commissioner to South Africa and Commissioner of Trade to Japan and China, 1906-1909; at present Commissioner of Trade to Northern Europe. *Address:* Dept. of Trade and Commerce, Ottawa; and The Hague, Holland.

PREVOST, Jean, K.C., LL.B., M.L.A.; *b.* Ste. Scholastique, Que., 17 Nov., 1870; *s.* Hon. Wilfrid Prevost, M.L.C. and Angelique Marien; *m.* Gabrielle Gagnon; one *s.* *Educ.:* Jesuit Coll., Montreal, and Laval Univ.; admitted to practice law, 8 July, 1894; apptd. K.C., 1904. Pres. of the Lib. Assn. of the Co. of Terrebonne, 1899-1900. El. to Legis Ass., at g. e., 1900, 1904, 1908. Called to Prov. Cabinet as Min. of Colonization, Mines and Fisheries, 3 July, 1905; re-el. by accl. at bye-el. July 17. Pres. of North American Fish and Game Assn., 1906 07; resigned his portfolio, 30 Sept., 1907. *Address:* St. Jerome, Que. *Clubs:* St. Denis, Montreal; Garrison, Quebec.

PRICE, Herbert Molesworth, J.P.; *b.* at Ross, Herefordshire, Eng., 31 Aug., 1847; *s.* of Mr. and Mrs. William Price; *m.* S. A. Martha Hall, of Montmorency Falls, Que. (*deceased*); one *s.* two *d.* *Educ.:* Herefordshire and Croyden, Surrey, Eng.; arrived in Canada, April, 1869; resided in West of England and South Wales, Dist. of Ross, 1864 to 1869; with Bank of British North America from 1869 to 1879, in London, New York and various places in Canada; Manager of Merchants Bank of Canada, 1879 to 1884; since then lumber merchant, etc.; vice-pres., Quebec Electric Light Co.; vice-pres., Auditorium Co.; director, Lake Superior Corporation, Sault Ste. Marie. *Recreations:* gardening, fishing. *Address:* The Cottage, Montmorency Falls, Que. *Club:* Garrison, Quebec; Mount Royal, Montreal.

PRICE, William, M.P.; *b.* Talca, Chili, 38 Aug., 1867; *s.* of Henry Ferrier Price and Florence Stoker Rogerson; *m.* Aemilia Blanche Smith; four *s.* two *d.* *Educ.:* Bishop's Coll. Sch., Lennoxville, Que., and St. Marks Sch., Eng. Arrived in Canada, July, 1878; first elected to the H. of C. for Quebec West, 1908; a lumber merchant; vice-pres. Union Bank, and vice-pres. of various commercial enterprises; served as an officer in the 8th Royal Rifles, Quebec. *Address:* 145 Grande Allee, Quebec. *Clubs:* Garrison, Quebec; Rideau, Ottawa.

PRIMROSE, Alexander, M.B., C.M., Edin.; *b.* Pictou, N.S., 5 April, 1861; *e. s.* of Howard Primrose, and Olivia, *d.* of late Hon. Alexander Campbell; *m.* 1889, Clara Christine, *d.* of late George Ewart, Toronto one *s.* three *d.* *Educ.:* Pictou Academy; Edinburgh Univ.; Middlesex Hospital, London. Fellow, Royal Medical Soc. of Edinburgh, and member of the Pathological Soc. of London; Pathologist and Chloroformist, Paddington Green Children's Hospital, London, 1888, Assistant Demonstrator of Anatomy, Surgeon's Hall, Edinburgh, 1885; Professor in Anatomy, Royal Coll. of Surgeons of England, 1887; Demonstrator of Anatomy, 1889; Associate Professor of Anatomy, 1892, Univ. of Toronto; pres., Pathological Soc. of Toronto, 1898; Pres. Toronto Medical Society, 1900; mem. Examining Board, Ontario Coll. of Physicians and Surgeons, 1889-1902; Secy of the Medical Faculty, Toronto Univ. *Publications:* The Anatomy of the Orang-Outang, 1898-99; Tuberculous Disease of the Bones and Joints; The American Practice of Surgery, vol. iii., 1907; papers in scientific journals. *Recreations:* golf, cycling. *Address:* 100 College Street, Toronto. *Clubs:* Toronto, Golf, Royal Canadian Yacht, Toronto.

PRINCE ALBERT, Bishop of; *see* Rt. Rev. Albert Pascal.

PRINCE, Edward Ernest, F.R.S.C.; Commr. of Fisheries for Canada; *b.* Leeds, Eng., 23 May, 1858, *s.* George Augustus Prince, and Harriette Rothery; *m.* Bessie Morton, *d.* of the late Hugh Morton Jack, Scot.; one *s.* two *d.* *Educ.:* Univ. of St. Andrews', Edinburgh, and Cambridge. Fishery Expert on Irish Government Survey of Fishery Grounds, 1890; Secretary of Lord Tweedmouth's Scottish Bait Commission, 1891; Professor of Zoology, Royal Infirmary Medical Coll., Glasgow, 1890-3; apptd. Commissioner of Fisheries, Canada, 1902; International Fisheries Commission, under treaty with U.S., 1908-9; vice-pres., International Fisheries Congress, Wash., D.C.,

1908; vice-pres., Zoological Section, Brit. Assn., Winnipeg, 1909. *Publications:* Life History of British Food Fishes (28 plates) Trans. Soc. of Edinb., Vol. xxv; Inaugural address as Professor in Glasgow, 1890; Scientific articles in Transactions and Magazines. *Address:* 206 O'Connor St., Ottawa.

PRINCE, Hon. Joseph Benjamin; Senator; *b.* St. Gregoire, Que., 29 April, 1885; *s.* Benjamin Prince and Mary Louise Bordages; *m.* Ernestine Brassard; one *s.* four *d.* *Educ.:* Nicolet Coll., Que.; went west in 1878 and started farming. In 1883, entered flour and lumbering business. Fought during N. W. Rebellion of 1885; from 1892 to 1904, was cattle exporter to G. B.; opened gen. store in Battleford, 1898; first el. to Territorial Legis., 1899; re-elec., 1904; Mayor of Battleford since 1906, and pres. Bd. of Trade since its organization; called to Senate of Can., July, 1909. *Address:* Battleford, Sask.; The Senate, Ottawa.

PRINGLE, Robert Abercrombie; *b.* Cornwall, Ont., 15 Dec., 1855; *s.* of J. F. Pringle (of Scotch descent) and Isabella Pringle; *m.* 1884, Ada Vanarsdale; two *s.* *Educ.:* Pub. and High Schs., Queen's Univ., Kingston; entered Civil Service in Ottawa as Asst. Sec. to Minister of Militia; went to the Northwest Territories with staff of Lindsay Russell, C.E., who had charge of the Peace River Survey; studied law in office of Carman & Leitch, 1876-1878, and completed his term in Toronto. Treas. Town of Cornwall for over sixteen yrs. El. to H. of C. at g. e., 1900; re-el. at g. e., 1904; unsuccessful 1908. *Address:* Cornwall, Ont. *Clubs:* Rideau, Ottawa; Albany, Toronto.

PRIOR, Lieut.-Col. Hon. Edward Gawler, P.C.; *b.* Dallowgill, Yorkshire, Eng., 21 May, 1853; 2nd *s.* of late Rev. Henry Prior, who was Rector of that Parish, and afterwards Vicar of Boston, Lincolnshire; *m.* (1st) 1878, Suzette (*d.* 1897), *y. d.* of Hon. John Work, of Hillside, Victoria; (2nd) 1899, Genevieve, *e. d.* of Capt. J. Wright, San Francisco; one *s.* three *d.* *Educ.:* Gram. Sch., Leeds, Yorkshire; served his articles as a mining engineer with the late J. Tolson White, M.E., at Wakefield. Went to Vancouver Island, 1873, as mining engineer and surveyor for the Vancouver Coal Mining and Land Company; was Government Inspector of Mines, 1878-80, resigned to commence business as an iron and hardware merchant, and still continues as such; Lieut.-Col. commanding the 5th Regt. Canadian Artillery, 1888-96; Hon. A.D.C. to the Governors-General of Canada, Lords Stanley and Aberdeen; commanded the Canadian rifle team at Bisley, 1890; was twice Pres. of the Dominion Artillery Association; one of the Canadian contingent present at the late Queen's Jubilee, 1897; mem. of Leg. Ass. of British Columbia, 1886-88; resigned, and was elected by acclam. the same day to H. of C.; re-el. 1891 and 1896; Controller of Inland Revenue in the administrations of Sir Mackenzie Bowell and Sir Charles Tupper; Minister of Mines in Local Legislature of British Columbia, 10 March, 1902 to 31 May, 1903; Premier of B.C. from 21 Nov., 1902 to 31 May, 1903; a Conservative. *Recreations:* riding, driving, motor boating. *Address:* The Priory, Victoria, B.C. *Clubs:* Union, Victoria, B.C.; Vancouver, B.C.

PROCTOR, Alexander Phimister; *b.* Ont. 27 Sept., 1862; *s.* Alexander and Tirza Smith Proctor; *m.* 1893, Margaret Gerow. Studied sculpture under Puech and Ingalbert, Paris; awarded Winehart Paris scholarship; exhibited at Paris Exp'n, 1900 (mem. sculpture jury), received gold medal. Member Nat. Acad. Design; mem. Nat. Sculpture Soc., Soc. Am. Artists, Am. Water Color Soc., Architectural League. Furnished quadriga for U.S. Pavilion, Paris Exp'n, 1900; groups for Pan-Am. Exp'n, 1901. Represented in public parks, New York and Denver, in Zool. Park, New York, in Pittsburgh, and colossal lions, McKinley Monument, Buffalo. Mem. Art Comm'n., New York, 1903-6. Permanent works at St. Louis Art Gallery, Mary's Inst., St. Louis, and Met. Mus. of Art. *Address:* Bedford, N.Y. *Club:* Century, New York.

PROUDFOOT, William, K.C.; M.L.A.; *b.* Colborne Tp., Huron Co., Ont., 1 Feb., 1889; *s.* of Robert Proudfoot and Margaret Darlington; *m.* Marion F. Dickson; one *s.* one *d.* *Educ.:* Goderich, Ont.; practiced law for 27 years; was Reeve of Goderich for 10 years; at present head of the law firm of Proudfoot, Hays and Blair, Goderich, and Proudfoot, Duncan, Grant and Skeans, Toronto; first elec. to represent Centre Huron in the Ontario Leg. Ass., June, 1908. *Address:* Goderich, Ont., and Confederation Life Building, Toronto, Ont. *Clubs:* Victoria, Ontario, Toronto.

PROULX, Edward, M.P.; *b.* St. Hermas, Que., 21 May, 1875; *s.* of Isidore Proulx and Philomene Lalonde; *m.* Renee Audette of Quebec; two *s.* *Educ.:* Bourget Coll., Rigaud, and Univ. of Ottawa; first el. to the H. of C., 1904; re-el. in 1908. *Address:* L'Original, Ont.

PROWSE, Lemuel E., M.P.; Pres. Prowse Bros., Ltd.; *b.* B. P. Road, P.E.I., 2 Feb., 1858; *s.* of Wm. and Helen Prowse; *m.* 29 July, 1879, Frances J. Stanley; three *s* one *d.* *Educ.:* In County Sch.; a member of the P.E.I. Legislature from 1893 to 1897; first el. to H. of C. for Kings Co., P.E.I., 1908; a Methodist; a Liberal. *Address:* Charlottetown, P.E.I.

PUFFER, William Franklin, M.L.A.; *b.* North Crosby, Leeds Co., Ont., 1 Nov., 1861; *s.* of Asa Puffer and Louisa P. Root; *m.* Charlotte A. Gilmour; four *s.* three *d.* Parents moved to Peterborough Co. from Leeds Co., when 8 years of age, then to Dresden, Ont., when 13 years of age; thence to Illinois at 14 and to Michigan at 16 yrs.; went to Alberta early in 1890; worked at farming and lumbering; was a pioneer in Alberta; homesteading and farming spring of '95; started in the meat and cattle trade at Lacombe, and for several years also conducted a lumber yard and machine business; elec. to the first Alberta Legislature, Nov., 1905; re-el. by acclam., 1909. *Address:* Lacombe, Alta.

PUGSLEY, Hon. William, B.A., K.C., D.C.L., P.C.; Minister of Public Works for Canada; *b.* Sussex, Kings Co., N.B., 1850; *s.* of William and Jane Pugsley; *m.* Fannie J. Park; two *s.* two *d.* *Educ.:* Sussex Com. Schs. and Univ. of New Brunswick. El.

N.B. Leg. Ass., 1885; Speaker of Ass., 1887; resigned 1890; became Solicitor-Gen.; retired from politics, 1892; re-el. 1899; apptd. Attorney-General, 1900; became Premier and Attorney Gen., 1907; resigned same yr., when apptd. Minister of Pub. Works for Canada; el. by accl. to H. of C. for St. John, N.B., Aug., 1907; re-el. at g. e., 26 Oct., 1908. *Address:* Aylmer Apts., Ottawa. *Clubs:* Rideau, Country, Laurentian, Hunt, Ottawa, Union, St. John, N.B.

PURDOM, Thomas Hunter, K.C.; *b.* London, Ont., 25 July, 1853; *s.* of Alexander Purdom and Margaret Hunter; *m.* (1st) 1884, Belle, (*d.* 1885), *d.* of the late John Craig; (2nd) 1893, Nellie, (*d.* 1900), *d.* of David Davies, of London, Ont.; (3rd) 1902, Marion, *d.* of David Davies; one *s.* one *d.* *Educ.:* Pub. and Gram. Schs. of London. Studied law in office of E. Jones Parke, K.C., of London, Ont.; became Attorney-at-Law and Solicitor, 1875; called to the Bar at Osgoode Hall, 1876; Bencher of the Law Soc. of Ont., 1884-1890, apptd. Q.C., 1898, and is now head of the firm of Purdom & Purdom; vice-pres., Northern Life Assur. Co. of Can.; pres., Dom. Savings and Investment Soc.; dir., Canada Trust Co., of London; pres., London Advertiser Co., Ltd.; dir., Masonic Temple Co.; trustee, Western Ontario Law Soc.; pres., London Press Club. *Address:* London, Ont.

PURVIS, David; *b.* Scarboro tp., York Co., Ont., 14 May, 1845; *s.* of Henry Purvis. *Educ.:* Dist. and pub. schs. In 1867, commenced working a farm for himself; opened an agricultural implement warehouse, with his brother, in Barrie, Ont., 1875; removed to North Bay, 1888, to take charge of their branch stores; the firm now has branches at Sudbury and Webbwood; mem. of the Barrie Town Council, 1877-1882; mem. of municipal council of North Bay, 1891; unsuccessful candidate for Ont. Legis., 1890; for many yrs. mem. of Pub. and High Sch. Bds. of North Bay; chn. of the Bd. of Trade, 1894-1902. *Address:* North Bay, Ont.

PYNE, Hon. Robert Allan, M.L.A., M.D., Minister of Education for Ontario; *s.* of Thomas Pyne, M.D., and Hester Jane Roberts, *cousin* of Field-Marshal Earl Roberts, both of Waterford, Ireland; *b.* Newmarket, Co. York, Ont., 29 Oct., 1855. Registrar of College of Physicians and Surgeons of Ont.; has been Chairman of Toronto Sch. Board and Toronto Free Library Board; Member of the first Board of Health, Toronto; member of the High Sch. Board, Toronto; member of the 37th Haldimand Rifles for years; late Assistant Surgeon 10th Regt. Royal Grenadiers; first el. to Ont. Leg. Ass., 1898; re-el. 1902, 1905, 1908; apptd. Min. of Education in the Whitney Admn., 8 Feb., 1905. *Address:* Cor. Sherbourne St. and Wilton Ave., Toronto. *Club:* Albany, Toronto.

Q

QU'APPELLE, Bishop of; *see* Rt. Rev. John Grisdale.

QUEBEC, Archbishop of; *see* Most Rev. L. N. Begin.

QUEBEC Bishop of; *see* Rt. Rev. Andrew H. Dunn.

QUIGLEY, Most Rev. James Edward, R. C. archbishop of Chicago; *b.* Oshawa, Ont., 15 Oct., 1854. *Educ.:* St. Joseph's Coll., Christian Brothers, Buffalo, N.Y.; went with parents to Lima, N.Y., 1856; studied Sem. of Our Lady of Angels (now Niagara Univ.); grad. Univ. at Innsbruck, Austrian Tyrol; grad. Coll. Propaganda, Rome, 1879; ordained priest, 1879; pastor St. Vincent's Ch., Attica, N.Y., 1879-84; St. Joseph's Cathedral, Buffalo, 1884-96; St. Bridget's Ch., Jan., 1896-Feb., 1897; bishop of Buffalo, 1897-1903; installed archbishop of Chicago, Mar., 10, 1903. *Address:* 623 N. State St., Chicago, U.S.A.

QUINLAN, Joseph; Dist. Passr. Agent. G.T.R., Montreal; *b.* Lacolle, Que., 10 Aug., 1859; *s.* Wm. Quinlan and Philomene, *d.* of Capt. Bary, an English officer who came to Canada during the rebellion of 1837; *m.* (1st) Mary Morrow (*dec.*); (2nd) Blanche B., *d.* of M. P. McGammon, pres. of the Merchants Bank of Aurora, Ind., U.S.A.; one *s.* *Educ.:* Lacolle and St. Valentine, Que. Entered the service of the G.T.R., in 1877, as telegraph operator; employed successively as station agent, express agent, travelling passenger agent, 1890-1902; district passenger agent at Montreal, 1902 to date. Has supervision of all immigrants landing, for the G. T. R. and its connections at Montreal, Halifax, St. John and Portland Me. *Recreation:* work. *Address:* 440 Mt. Stephen Ave., Westmount, Que.

R

RACE, Thomas Henry; Police Magistrate, Mitchell, Ont.; *b.* Durham Co., Eng., 1 May, 1848; *s.* of Thomas Race and Elizabeth Thompson; *m.* Margaret Ballentine, of Guelph, Ont.; two *s.* two *d.* *Educ.:* Port Hope Gram. Sch. and Victoria Univ. Came to Canada with parents, 1853, and worked on farm for some yrs. Thirty yrs. in journalism as editor of Mitchell *Recorder*. Exhibition Com. for Canada since 1904 to U.S., England, New Zealand, Australia, and Scotland. *Recreations:* fruits, flowers and agriculture. *Address:* Mitchell, Ont.

RACINE, Damase, M.L.A.; *b.* Crysler, Stormont Co., Ont., 28 May, 1855; *s.* of J. B. Racine, and A. Charlebois; *m.* Corina Benoit; six *s.* four *d.* *Educ.:* Crysler Pub. Sch. Has been Councillor, Dep. Reeve, Reeve, Co. Councillor and Warden of the U. C. of Prescott and Russell. First el. to Leg. Ass. at g. e., 1905; re-el. 1908. *Address:* Casselman, Ont.

RAINVILLE, Hon. Henri B., K.C., B.C.L. (McGill); *b.* Ste. Angele de Monnoir, 5 April, 1852; *s.* of Felix Rainville, farmer, and Marie Daignault; *m.* 1876, Eugenie, *d.* of the late Alexandre Archambault. *Educ.:* St. Hyacinthe Coll., Ste. Marie de Monnoir Coll. Grad. B.C.L., McGill Univ., 1873. Admitted to the Bar, 14 Jan., 1874. Was for many yrs. an Alderman of the City of Montreal. First returned to Legis. for Montreal (St. Louis Div.) g. e., 1890; defeated at g. e., 1892, re-el. g. e., 1897, 1900; Speaker of the Quebec Legislature

1901-4; dir., Montreal Light, Heat & Power Co., Crown Life Insur. Co.; Royal Electric Co. *Address:* 382 Sherbrooke St. W., Montreal.

RANKIN, Colin; *b.* nr. Pictou, N.S., 26 July, 1826; *s.* of Colin Rankin and Mary Robertson; *m.* (1st) Rebecca Scott, of Quebec (*d.* 1871); (2nd) Annie Deacon, of Lindsay; four *s.* four *d.* *Educ.:* Bathurst, N.B. Entered the service of the Hudson's Bay Co. at Mattawa, March, 1849, and was stationed in subsequent yrs. at posts on the St. Maurice, north shore of Gulf of St. Lawrence, Lake Spperior, Saguenay, Simcoe Dist., and finally as chief factor in the Temiskaming Dist with headquarters at Mattawa; retired 1902, then being senior chief factor, after 52 yrs. continuous service with the H. B. Co. An ardent sportsman. Arranged moose hunting expeditions for Lords Minto and Grey, Governors-General; organized canoe brig. in connection with the lumbermen's entertainment of their Royal Highnesses, the Duke and Duchess of Cornwall and York on their visit to Ottawa, 1901; personally thanked by H. R. H.; organized the Kippewa Fish and Game Club, which has the largest hunting area of any similar club in Can.; organized the Wa-Wash-Keshi Fish and Game Club with headquarters on the Schyan River, Pontiac Co. *Recreations:* big game hunting, fishing. *Address:* Mattawa, Ont.

RANKIN, James Palmer, M.B., L.R.C., P. & S. (Edinb.) M.P.; *b.* County of Oxford, Ont., 30 April, 1855; *s.* of David Rankin and Jane Palmer Davis; *m.* Mary Jane McKee; one *s.* and two *d.* *Educ.:* Toronto Univ. and Edinburgh; a physician and surgeon; practiced his profession in the counties of Perth and Oxford since 1879; chairman of Sch. Board, Stratford, 1906; alderman, 1907-08; Major in 28th Regt., Stratford; grand Junior Warden of the G. L. of Can., A. F. & A.M.; first el. to H. of C., 1908. *Recreations:* military and rifle practice. *Address:* Stratford, Ont. *Club:* Ontario, Toronto.

RATZ, Hon. Valentine; Senator; *b.* St. Jacobs, Waterloo Co., 12 Nov., 1848; *s.* of Jacob and Mary Ratz; *m.* Mary Gager, of Hamburg; two *s.* three *d.* *Educ.:* Pine Hill Pub. Sch.; a lumberman and pres. of the South River Lumber Co.; el. to the H. of C. in 1896; defeated 1900; re-el. 1904; called to the Senate, 19 Jan., 1909. *Address:* Parkhill, Ont.

RAYMOND, Ven. William O., M.A., LL.D., F.R.S.C., Archdeacon of St. John, N.B.; *b.* Woodstock, N.B., 3 Feb., 1853; *s.* Lt.-Col. Chas. W. and Mary E. Raymond; *m.* Julia Nelson of St. John, N.B.; one *s.* one *d.* *Educ.:* Carleton Co. (N.B.) Gram. Sch. and Univ. of New Brunswick; in early manhood commanded the Woodstock Field Battery of Artillery; ordained by Bishop Midley in 1879; stationed for six years at Stanley, York Co.; for 25 years at St. Mary's Church, St. John, N.B.; Archdeacon, 1908; Secretary the N.B. Historical Soc. *Publications:*Kingston and the Loyalists, 1889, early days of Woodstock, 1891, U.E. Loyalists, 1893, the London Lawyer, 1894, the Old Fort, Windsor Papers, 1901, History of St. John River, 1905; story of Old Fort Frederick. *Recreation;* curling. *Address:* 57 Waterloo St., S, John, N.B.; The Park Rothesay, N.B. (summer).

READ, Hon. Joseph; *b.* Summerside, P.E.I., 31 Oct., 1849; *m.* Sarah Carruthers of North Bedeque, P.E.I.; two *s.* *Educ.:* Summerside, Gram. Sch., Ions Nautical Academy, Liverpool, Eng.; has been pres. local board of trade and pres. Maritime Board of Trade; elec. to the P.E.I. Legislature, 1900; member of the Cabinet without portfolio, 1903; re-elec. in 1904 and in 1908. *Publications:* one of the contributors to history of P.E.Island, past and present. *Recreation:* travel. *Address:* Summerside, P.E.I.

READE, John, LL.D., F.R.S.C.; *b.* Ballyshannon Co., Donegal, Ireland, 13 Nov., 1837; *s.* Joseph Reade and Frances Smyth; unmarried. *Educ.:* Enniskillen and Belfast Arrived in Canada, June, 1856; associate Editor of the Montreal *Gazette* for forty yrs.; has been mostly engaged in journalism and literature; has consistently advocated the conciliation of race and religion in Canada, Canadian Confederation and the unity of the Empire; one of the orginal members, Royal Society of Canada (1882); founded by Marquis of Lorne, and pres. of Hist. and Archæol. Section (English); with Prof. Penhallow, the late H. Beaugrand (Mayor of Montreal in 1885, ect.), and W. J. White, K.C., founded Canadian Branch of American Folk Lore Society. *Address:* Montreal.

REAUME, Hon. Joseph Octave, M.D., M.L.A., *b.* 13 Aug., 1856; *s.* of Oliver Reaume and Josette Dumont, French Canadians; *m.* 1887, Catherine L. Turner, Lockport, New York; two *s.* two *d.* *Educ.:* Assomption Coll., Sandwich; Windsor High Sch.; Detroit, Mich. Coll. of Medicine; Trinity Medical College; Minister of Public Works, Ontario, 1905; commenced as Sch. teacher, and afterwards for 18 years practised medicine in Windsor and Essex Co.; elec. mem. of Ont. Leg., 1902, 1905 and 1908; Conservative. *Recreations:* horses and baseball. *Address:* Toronto, and Windsor, Ont. *Club:* Albany, Toronto.

REDFERN, James Henry; lumber merchant; *b.* Douglas, Isle of Man, 1841; *s.* of George Redfern, a merchant of Douglas, and Margaret Quiggin; unmarried. *Educ.:* Completed his educ. in Liverpool; entered lumber business with his uncle in Troy, N.Y. Removed to Montreal, 1870, where he has since been in the lumber business. First Mayor of Westmount. Mem. Montreal Bd. of Trade; pres. of St. George's Soc. for two yrs. *Address:* 28 Rosemount Ave., Montreal. *Clubs:* St. James, Montreal Hunt, Forest and Stream, Montreal; Rideau, Ottawa.

REED, Hayter; Mgr. of the C. P. R. Hotel System; *b.* L'Orignal, Ont., 1849; *s.* of George Decimus and Harriet Reed; *m.* (1st) 1888 Georgina (*d.* 1889), *d.* of the late Lt.-Col. Ponton, of Belleville; (2nd) 1894, Kate, *d.* of the late Chief Justice Armour, of Toronto; one *s.* *Educ.:* Upper Can. Coll. and Model Gram. Sch., Toronto. Acted as Brigade Major 6th Military Dist., in 1870; transferred to North West Force, stationed at Fort Garry, acting as its Adjutant until its disbandment; transferred to Indian Dept., successive steps of agent, asst. commr., commr., and rose to position of Dep. Supt. of Indian Affairs for the Dom.; retired 1897; was a mem. of the original North West Council and for a time acted as Lieut. Gov. for the Territories; now mgr. in chief of the C. P. R. Hotel System. *Recreations:* yachting, polo, riding. *Address:* 116 Place Viger Hotel, Montreal. *Clubs:* St. James's, Montreal; Garrison, Quebec; Manitoba, Winnipeg.

REED, Mrs. Hayter (Kate); *b.* Cobourg, Ont.; *d.* of the late Chief Justice Armour and Eliza Clench; *m.* (1st) 1880, Grosvenor Lowrey, a mem. of the New York bar (one *s.* one *d.*;(2nd) 1904, Hayter Reed, Mgr. of the C. P. R. Hotel System (one *s.*) Of great artistic taste; selected and purchased and personally supervised the installation of the internal furnishings of the C. P. R. Empress Hotel at Victoria, B.C., whish is conceded to be one of the most beautiful hostelries for its size on the continent. *Address:* 116 Place Viger Hotel, Montreal.

REFORD, Robert; Pres. of the Robert Reford Co., Montreal; *b.* Belfast, Ireland. Arrived in Canada, 1845, and resided in Toronto until 1865, doing business as wholesale grocer. Removed to Montreal latter yr., and engaged in ocean shipping, the present business of his Co. Agents of Donaldson Line, Thompson Line, and several other Co's. Pres. of Mount Royal Milling and Mfg. Co.; director, Bank of Toronto, Lake of Woods Milling Co., Labrador Co., York Lumber Co., N.S. Steel and Coal Co., and Montreal Elevating Co.; a governor of McGill Univ. Chairman of Royal Com. on Transportation, 1904-5, which reported on improvements required for increase of shipping and transportation trade of country. *Address:* 260 Drummond St., Montreal. *Clubs:* Mount Royal, Canada, Montreal.

REGAN, John William; journalist; *b.* Dartmouth, N.S., 1872, *s.* of John Regan and Bridget Bowes; unmarried. *Educ.:* in the pub. Sch. A merchant for a number of years; eight years journalist, connected with the Halifax *Herald*; one year with *City News*, and *World*, New York; at present Maritime Provinces representative of the Associated Press, and managing editor of monthly magazine, *Industrial Advocate*. *Publications:* "sketches and traditions of the Northwest Arm," historical; in Summer Land, Illustrated. *Address:* Halifax, N.S.

REID, George Agnew, R.C.A.; *b.* Wingham, Ont., 1860, of Scotch and Irish parents; *m.* Mary Kieslae of Reading, Pa. *Educ.:* Toronto, Philadelphia, Paris and Madrid; exhibits in Paris Salon; medals World's Fair, Chicago and St. Louis; served on Jury of Awards Fine Arts Department, Pan American Exhibition, Buffalo; pres. of Ontario Society of Artists, 1898-1902; pres. of Royal Canadian Academy, 1906-1909. *Works:* include The Pioneers, 6 panels, City Hall, Toronto; Dreaming; Mortgaging the Homestead, and The Arrival of Champlain at Quebec, 1608, in National Gallery, Ottawa; Family Prayer; a modern Madonna; Lullaby; Lagging; A Story; The Clock Cleaner; The Foreclosure of the Mortgage; Homeseekers, etc. *Address:* Wychwood Park, Toronto; Ontario-in-the Catskills. *Clubs:* Arts and Letters, Toronto.

REID, James, M.P.; *b.* River Charlo, Restigouche Co., N.B., 14 Nov., 1839; *m.* 5 March, 1873, Lizzie McNair. *Educ.:* River Charlo, Restigouche Co.; elected to H. of C., 1900, 1904 and 1908; a Presbyterian; a Liberal. *Address:* Charlo Station, N.B.

REID, John Alexander; *b.* Liverpool, Eng., 4 March, 1862; *s.* of David Reid, and Elizabeth Miller Gordon; *m.* Mabel Victoria Laurie. *Educ.:* Liverpool Institute and Univ. Coll., Liverpool, Eng. Arrived in Canada, 22 Sept., 1883; Clerk of the Executive Council of the Province of Sask.; business training in England; journalism in Western Canada; public service, Dominion, 1884-9; service of the N. W. T., and Sask., 1895 to date. *Address:* Regina, Sask.

REID, John Dowsley, M.D., M.P.; *b.* Prescott, Ont., 1 Jan., 1859; *s.* of John and Jane Reid; *m.* Ephie Labatt, of London, Ont.; one *s.* one *d.* *Educ.:* Queen's Univ., Kingston, Ont.; was manager of Edwardsburg Starch Co. for seven years; manager of Imperial Starch Co. for four years; graduated in medicine, Queen's; elected to the H. of C., 1901, to 1909. *Address:* Prescott, Ont. *Clubs:* Rideau, Ottawa; Albany, and R. C. Y. C., Toronto.

REID, John Rogers; *b.* Brooklyn, N.Y., 9 Oct., 1855; *s.* John Reid (Irish) and Matilda Paterson (Scotch); *m.* Emma Kate Rusland; one *s.* one *d.* *Educ.:* early schooling in New York; finished at Brockville, Ont.; arrived in Canada, 1867; joint manager for Eastern Ontario, of the Sun Life Assurance Co., under firm name of John R. and W. L. Reid; has occupied present position for 20 years; pres. of the Ottawa Board of Trade; now Treasurer; Pub. Sch. Trustee; dir. of General Hospital; dir. of Home for Aged; has been Grand Master I. O. F., and Grand Senior Warden of Masons. *Recreations:* bowling and curling. *Address:* 300 Waverley St., and Sun Life Building, Ottawa.

REYNAR, Rev. Alfred Henry, M.A., LL.D.; Dean of the Faculty of Arts, Victoria Univ., Toronto, *b.* Quebec, 13 Oct., 1840; *s.* of James Reynar and Ellen Conner; *m.* (1st) Fanny M. Punshon; (2nd) Ida Hayden; seven *d.* *Educ.:* High Sch., Quebec, and Victoria Univ., Cobourg (Prince of Wales medalist, 1862). In 1862 grad. in Arts and entered the Ministry of the Methodist Church; in 1866 apptd. to Chair in Victoria Univ. as Prof. of Modern Languages; now Wm. Gooderham Prof. of English Literature and Dean of the Faculty of Arts of Victoria Univ.; mem. of Senate of Toronto Univ. *Publications:* "Over-Legislation in Church and State;" text books in History and Literature. *Address:* Cobourg, Ont.; Victoria Coll., Toronto.

REYNOLDS, His Hon. Edmund John, K.C.; *b.* Brockville, Ont., 13 Feb., 1855; *s.* Thomas Reynolds, M.D., and Eleanor Sara Sinkler; *m.* Margaret Crawford Smart; one *s.* two *d.* *Educ.:* Brockville pub. and Gram. Sch.; called to the bar, 1876; created Q.C., in 1899; Junior County Judge, Leeds and Grenville, 1902. *Address:* Brockville, Ont.

REYNOLDS, Martin Montgomery; *b.* Syracuse, N.Y.; *m.* Flora Livingston, 1894; *Educ.:* Syracuse, N.Y. Arrived in Canada, 1908. Fifth vice-pres., G. T. Ry. of Canada third vice-pres., G. T. Pacific Ry.; has 30 years experience in railroad accounts and finances; was comptroller Govt. Railways of Mexico for five years, and resigned in March, 1908, to join the Grand Trunk Ry. of Canada. *Address:* Linton Apartments, Montreal. *Clubs:* St. James, Canada, Montreal, Que.

RHODES, Edgar Nelson, B.A., LL.B., M.P.; *b.* Amherst, N.S., 5 Jan., 1877; *s.* of Nelson A. Rhodes and Sarah Davidson Curry; *m.* M. Grace, 2nd *d.* of late Hon. W. T. Pipes, Atty.-Gen'l., Nova Scotia; one *s.* one *d.* *Educ.:* Amherst Academy, Horton Coll. Academy, Acadia Univ., and Dalhousie Univ.; commenced practice at Amherst, 1 Jan., 1903; successful in first political contest, being returned from Co. of Cumberland, 1908, for many years represented by Sir Charles Tupper; Conservative whip for the Maritime Provinces. *Recreations:* motoring and tennis. *Address:* Amherst, N.S. *Clubs:* Halifax; Rideau, Ottawa.

RICHARDS, James W., M.P., *s.* of Wm. and Susan Richards. *Educ.:* Public Schs. and St. Dunstan's Coll., Charlottetown, P.E.I.; was a member of the Government of P.E.I.; for upwards of 30 years, continuously represented the second district of Prince Co., in the Provincial Legislature; first el. to H. of C., 1908; Church of England; Liberal. *Address:* Bideford, P.E.I.

RICHARDSON, Amos Augustus, M.L.A.; *b.* Co. of Lennox, Ont., 2 April, 1850; *s.* of Amos Richardson and Nancy Huyler; *m.* Jane Bigg; one *s.* one *d.* *Educ.:* in the Com. Sch.; was a farmer until 21 years of age; clerk and merchant from that time until the present; first el. to the Ont. Leg. Ass., at g. e., 1908. *Address:* Deseronto, Ont.

RICHARDSON, His Hon. Hugh; *b.* London, Ont., 21 July, 1826; *s.* of Richard and Elizabeth Sarah Richardson; *m.* (1st) Charlotte Houghson ;(2nd) Rachel Piper (both *deceased*); two *s.* five *d.* *Educ.:* London, Up. Can.. and Ontario. Arrived in Canada, Aug., 1831; called to the Bar, Osgoode Hall, Nov., 1847; practiced at Woodstock, Ont., until June, 1872; chief clerk, Department of Justice, Ottawa, until July, 1876; Legal adviser to Lt.-Gov. and member of N. W. Council at Battleford and Regina, to Feb., 1887; senior Judge, Supreme Court of N.W.T., now retired on pension; served in the active militia; private to Lieut.-Col., from 1860 to 1875; Frontier service, 1864-6 (medal); presided trial, Louis Riel and other rebels, 1885. *Address:* The Windsor, Ottawa.

RICHARDSON, Right Rev. John Andrew, M.A., D.D.; Bishop of Fredericton, N.B.; *b.* Warwick, Eng., 30 Oct., 1868; *s.* of Rev. John Richardson, Rector of Saddington, Eng., and Mary Watkins; *m.* Dora Lillian Fortin, 2nd *d.* of the Ven-Arch. Fortin, Rector Holy Trinity Church, Winnipeg; one *s.* three *d.* *Educ.:* Warwick, Gram. Sch., and St. Johns Coll., Winnipeg; Univ. of Manitoba. Arrived in Canada, 1 May, 1888; curate in charge St. Luke's Winnipeg, 1893-1897; Rector, 1897-1899; Rector, Trinity Church, St. John, N.B., 1899-1906; Bishop, Coadjutor, Fredericton, 1906-1907; Bishop of Fredericton, 1907. *Address:* Bishop's Court, Fredericton, N.B.

RICHARDSON, Robert Lorne; Editor and Prop. of the Winnipeg *Tribune;* *b.* Balderson, Lanark Co., Ont., 28 June, 1860; *s.* of Joseph Richardson and Harriet Thompson; *m.* Clara Jane Mallory, of Mallorytown, Ont.; five *d.* *Educ.:* Balderson Pub. Sch. Began newspaper career in 1878 as reporter on Montreal *Star;* joined Toronto *Globe* staff in 1880; removed to Winnipeg, 1882, and estbd. the Winnipeg *Tribune*, 1890, of which he is still ed. and prop. El. to H. of C., 1896; re-el. 1900; unsuccessful. 1904. *Publications:* two novels, "Colin of the 9th Concession," 1903; "The Camerons of Bruce," 1905. *Address:* Winnipeg, Man.

RIDDELL, Archibald, M.L.A.; *b.* Perth, Ont., 25 June, 1864; *s.* of George Riddell and Jane Campbell; *m.* Catherine Strachan; four *s.* four *d.* *Educ.:* in pub. sch.; went west, 1892, and was one of the pioneer settlers in Sask.; was councillor for five years; elec. to the Legislature of Sask. in 1908; dir., the Oxbow Farmers' Elevator Co. *Address:* Oxbow, Sask.

RIDDELL, Hon. William Renwick, B.A., B.Sc., LL.B., F.B.S.; *b.* Hamilton tp., Ont., 6 April, 1852; *s.* of Walter Riddell, Hamilton, and Mary Ann Herbert Renwick; *m.* Anna Hester Kersop Crossen, *y. d.* of James Crossen, Cobourg, Ont. *Educ.:* Cobourg Coll. Inst. and Victoria Univ.; for four years professor of Mathematics, Government Normal Sch., Ottawa; called to the bar of Ont., Hilary term 1883, Osgoode Hall; created Q.C., 1897; Bencher Law Society of Up. Can., elec. 1892, and continuously re-elec.; Victoria Univ. and Univ. of Toronto; elec. by graduates in law, 1884, and continuously re-elec.; apptd. Judge of the High Court of Justice, Ont., King's bench division, 1906. *Address:* 109 George St., Toronto. *Clubs:* Toronto, Ontario Jockey, Toronto, Ont.; London, London.

RILEY, Hon. George; Senator; *b.* St. Catharines, Ont., 1843; *m.* Mary N., *d.* of Hon. W. D. Balfour, Prov. Secy. of Ont., in the Hardy Administration; removed to British Columbia in the early days, and became identified with the interests of that province; an unsuccessful candidate for H. of C., 1900; returned at bye-elec-, 1902; re-elec., 1904; resigned from H. of C., Feb., 1906, and called to the Senate, March 22nd of the same year; a Liberal. *Address:* Victoria, B.C.

RILEY, Robert Thomas; *b.* Yorkshire, Eng., 1 July, 1851; *s.* of Thomas Riley, ship-owner, and Lavinia Bell; *m.* 1873, Harriet Murgatroyd; four *s.* two *d.* *Educ.:* St. Thomas' Charter House, London, Eng. Spent four yrs. as clerk in architects' and builders' offices; was clerk on staff of Adjutant-General's Dept., Horse Guards, London, Eng. for two yrs. Arrived in Canada, 1875, and lived in Wentworth Co., Ont., for nine yrs. engaging in farming and contracting; removed o Manitoba. 1881; was mgr. of the Manitoba Drainage Co.; organized and managed for thirteen yrs the Westbourne Cattle Co., of Westbourne, Man.; apptd. Mgr. Dir., on organization of Canadian Fire Insur Co., and is also Western Mgr. for the W. E. Sanford Mfg. Co., Ltd. of Hamilton, Ont. Dir., Canada Permanent & Western Canada Mortgage Corporation, of Toronto; Great West Life Assur. Co. of Winnipeg. *Address:* Winnipeg, Man.

RIMMER, His Hon. R.; *b.* Southport, Lancashire, Eng., 1865; *s.* of Edward Johnson Rimmer, J.P., and Sarah Frances Bookroyd; *m.* Leone, *d.* of W. Marchant; three *s.* three *d.* *Educ.:* Liverpool and London; arrived in Canada, 1891; member of the bar of N. W. T., Sask., Alta., and Man., 1892, 1898; solicitor, England, 1888; Legal Advisor to Governor of N.W.T., 1897; Dept. of Indian affairs, 1898; apptd. Judge of the District Court, Judicial Dist. of Cannington, Sask., 1907. *Address:* Arcola, Sask. *Club:* Assiniboia, Regina.

RIORDON, Charles Christopher, B.A. (Toronto Univ.); *b.* St. Catharines, Ont., 3 June, 1876; *s.* of Chas. Riordon and Edith Ellis, of Toronto; *m.* 1900, Amy Louise, *d.* of Rev. Chas. Paterson, of Port Hope, Ont.; two *s.* one *d.* *Educ.:* Upper Canada Coll.; Ridley Coll., St. Catharines; Toronto Univ. Has served in all branches of the paper making and pulp industries; asst. mgr. at Hawkesbury Mill; mgr. Merritton Mills; gen. mgr. of the Riordon Paper Mills, 1905. Was for a time Capt., 19th Regt., St. Catharines. Mem. of the Chapter of the Alpha Delta Phi Fraternity of Toronto Univ. *Recreation:* canoeing. *Address:* Cote des Neiges Rd., Montreal. *Clubs:* Engineers', Montreal; Toronto; Alpha Delta Phi, New York.

RITCHIE, Miss Eliza, B.L., Ph. D.; *b.* Halifax, N.S., 31 Jan., 1856; *d.* of Hon. J. W. Ritchie, Judge in Equity of the Supreme Court of N.S., and Amelia Rebecca Ritchie, *d.* of W. B. Almon, M.D. *Educ.:* privately; attended Dalhousie Coll. as soon as that institution was opened to women; apptd. Fellow of Philosophy at Cornell Univ., in 1887; in 1890, Instructor in Philosophy, Wesley Coll., Mass.; Asso. Professor, 1894; resigned this chair in 1900. *Publications:* The Problem of Personality, 1889. *Recreations;* reading, book collecting, chess. *Address:* "Winwick," Halifax, N.S.

RITCHIE, Philip Embury, B.A., B.C.L.; *b.* Montreal, 18 Aug., 1865; *s.* Thomas W. Ritchie, Q.C., and Jessie Torrance, *d.* of John Fisher, Esq., Quebec; *m.* Francis Jean McLean, *d.* of John McLean, of Lessamska House, Co. Mayo, Ireland. *Educ.:* Montreal High Sch., Heidelburg and Fredericskdorf (Germany), McGill Univ., Trinity Coll., and Osgoode Hall, Toronto; practiced law 12 years in Toronto; apptd. Registrar of Copyrights and Trade Marks, 1 Jan., 1906. *Recreations:* curling, lawn bowling. *Address:* 143 Cartier St., Ottawa.

RIVET, Louis Alfred Adhemar, B.A., LL.B., K.C., M.P.; *b.* Joliette, Que., 15 Sept., 1873; *s.* of Charles Rivet and Herminie Michaud; *m.* Rose de lenna Cypihot; two *s.* one *d.* *Educ.:* Joliette Coll. and Laval Univ.; admitted to the bar, Que., 1895; first elected to the H. of C., 1904, at bye-elec.; re-elec. in 1904 and 1908; represents Hochelaga; Liberal. *Recreation:* travel. *Address:* 610 Center St., Montreal. *Clubs:* St. Denis, St. George, Montreal.

ROBB, James Alexander, M.P.; *b.* Huntingdon, Que., 10 Aug., 1859; *s.* of Alexander Robb and Janet Smith, *m.* Mary Alma Mathe (*deceased* 1902); one *d.* *Educ.:* Huntingdon Academy; member of Valleyfield Council for 8 years; Mayor, 1906 to 1910; Trustee Valleyfield Schools from 1897 to the present time; first el. to H. of C. at g. e., 1908. *Address:* Valleyfield, Que.

ROBERTS, Charles George Douglas, M.A., LL.D.; *b.* Douglas, York Co., N.B., 10 Jan., 1860: *s.* of Rev. Geo. Roberts, M.A., LL.D., Rector of Fredericton and Canon of Christ Church Cadedral, and Emma Wetmore Bliss Roberts; grad. Univ. of New Brunswick, 1879; *m.* 1880, Mary I. Fenety, *d.* of the late George E. Fenty, Queen's Printer of N.B., Headmaster Chatham, N.B. Gram. Sch., and of the York St. Sch., Fredericton; editor *Week*, Toronto, 1883-4; prof. English and French literature, Kings Coll., Windsor, N.S., 1885-8; prof. English and economics, same, 1888-95; asso. editor Illustrated American and resided in New York, 1897-8. *Publications:* (verse) Orion and Other Poems; In Divers Tones; Ave—An Ode for the Shelley Centenary; Songs of the Common Day, The Book of the Native; New York Nocturnes; The Book of the Rose (prose) The Canadians of Old; Earth's Enigmas; The Raid from Beausejour; A History of Canada; The Forge in the Forest; Around the Campfire; Reube Dare's Shad Boat; A Sister to Evangeline, 1898; Appleton's Canadian Guidebook, 1899; By the Marshes of Minas, 1900 The Heart of the Ancient Wood, 1900; Poems (collective edit.), 1901; The Kindred of the Wild, 1902; Barbara Ladd, 1902; The Prisoner of Mademoiselle, The Little People of the Sycamore, 1905; The Return to the Trails, 1905; Red Fox, 1905; The Heart that Knows, 1906; In the Deep of the Snow, 1907; The Young Acadian, 1907; Haunting of the Silences, 1907; The House in the Water, 1908; The Backwoodsman, 1909; *Editor:* The Alastor and Adonais of Shelley (with intro. and notes), 1902. *Recreations:* canoeing, tennis, fishing, camping. *Address:* Fredericton, N.B.

ROBERTSON, David, M.D., C.M. (McGill); M.C.P. & S., Ont.; Registrar of Deeds for the Co. of Halton; *b.* Tp. of Esquesing, Halton Co., Ont., 9 July, 1841; *s.* of Alexander Robertson and Agnes Moore; *m.* 1867, Jeannette Sophia Morse, of Milton; one *s.* three *d.* *Educ.:* Milton Gram. Sch., and McGill Univ. Grad. in Medicine in 1864 and practiced until 1898, when was apptd. Registrar of Deeds. El. to Leg. Ass. of Ontario, 1879. Mayor of Milton for the yrs.; reeve fourteen yrs.; co warden, 1892. Pub. Sch. Trustee since 1870 and chn. of the Bd. for eight yrs.; treas. of Pub. Library, Milton for over 30 yrs.; treas. of Halton Agric. Soc. for five years; pres. of Halton Historical Assn.; pres. of the Milton Pressed Brick Co. *Recreations:* curling, boating. *Addresses;* Milton, Ont.; "Struan", Bala P.O., Muskoka, Ont. (summer).

ROBERTSON, Farquhar; *b.* North Branch, near Martintown, Glengarry Co., Ont., 14 April, 1850; *s.* of Hugh Robertson and Flora McLennan; *m.* Flora Craig, *y. d* of the late James Craig, M.L.A. for Glengarry Co.; two *d.* *Educ.:* Williamstown, Glengarry Co., Ont.; represented St. Andrew's ward in the Montreal City Council for six years and was representative of the Montreal City Council on the Protestant Board of Sch. Commissioners for the same period; vice-pres., Montreal Board of Trade, 1908, and pres., 1909. *Recreations:* curling and golf. *Address:* 30 Ontario Av., Montreal. *Clubs:* St. James, Hunt, and Outremont Golf, Montreal.

ROBERTSON, Hon. James Edwin, M. D., M.S., Senator; *b.* at New Perth, P.E.I., 8 Oct., 1840; *s.* of Peter Robertson and Ann McFarlane; *m.* Elizabeth McFarlane. *Educ.:* Com. Sch., Central Academy, P.E.I., and McGill Coll., entered the P.E.I. Legislature in 1870, and H. of C., in 1882; apptd. to the Senate, 1902. *Address:* Montague, P.E.I.

ROBERTSON, James Wilson, C.M.G., LL.D.; *b.* Dunlop, Ayrshire, 2 Nov., 1857; *s.* of John Robertson and Mary Wilson; *m.* 1896, Jennie, *o. d.* of John Mather, of Ottawa Arrived in Canada, 1875; Professor of Dairying, Ont. Agric. Coll., Guelph, Ont., 1886-90; first Dairy Commissioner for Canada, 1890; first Commissioner of Agri- and Dairying for Canada, at Ottawa, 1895-1904; principal of the Macdonald Coll. at Ste. Anne de Bellevue, but now on one yr's. leave of absence; Hon. Secretary of the Provisional Committee for establishing a fund for founding the Victorian Order of Nurses in Canada, 1897; apptd. one of the governors of the Order by the Governor-General of Canada, 1902; Chairman of the Central Board of the Aberdeen Association for the distribution of good literature to settlers in the newer and more remote parts of Canada; a member of the Executive Council of the Canadian Association for the Prevention of Consumption and other forms of Tuberculosis; a member of the federal commission for the conservation of the natural resources of Can. *Address:* Ste. Anne de Bellevue, Que.; Victoria Chambers, Ottawa. *Clubs:* Rideau, Ottawa; St. James's, Montreal.

ROBERTSON, John Duff, M.L.A.; *b.* Chesterfield, Oxford Co., Ont., 26 March, 1873; *s.* of the late Rev. Wm. Robertson, M.A., and Elizabeth Duff; unmarried. *Educ.:* Elora High Sch. and Ontario Coll. of Pharmacy; elec. to Legislature of Sask., 1908. *Address:* Camora, Sask.

ROBERTSON John Ross; proprietor of the Toronto *Telegram;* *b.* Toronto, 28 Dec., 1841; *s.* of John Robertson, of Nairn, Scot., and Margaret, *d.* of Hector Sinclair, of Stornoway, Isle of Lewis; *m.* (1st) Maria, *d.* of Edward E. Gillbee (*d.* 1886); (2nd) Bessie Elizabeth, *d.* of George D. Holland, Toronto; two *s.* *Educ.:* Upper Can. Coll.; at twenty yrs. of age, estbd. a newspaper, devoted to athletic sport. Reporter on staffs of different Toronto newspapers; London, Eng., correspondent of *Globe*, 1872-1875. In 1876, estbd. the *Evening Telegram*, which he still owns. Active in masonic circles; Grand Master of Canada, 1890-91; Grand Rep. of the Grand Lodge of Eng. Takes great interest in hospital work. Chn. of Bd. of Trustees of Toronto Hospital for Sick Children. Founded Lakeside Home for Little Children; was pres. of Can. Copyright Assn. for some yrs.; el. to H. of C. as Ind. Con. at g. e., 1896; retired, 1900. *Publications:* "A History of Canadian Free Masonry;" other works on masonic subjects. *Address:* 291 Sherbourne St., Toronto. *Clubs:* Toronto, National, Toronto.

ROBERTSON, William Fleet, B.A.Sc.; *b.* Montreal, 1859; *s.* of Wm. W. Robertson, Q.C.; *m.* Edith Mercer, Montreal; one *s.* *Educ.:* Galt Coll. Inst., High Sch., Montreal, and McGill Univ.; a mining engineer, and metallurgist; constructed several large copper works in U.S. and Canada; member Am. Inst. Min. Engineers; M.C.M.I., M.M. T.N.S.; now Provincial Mineralogist, British Columbia. *Recreations:* fishing, golf. *Address:* 1721 Rockland Av., Victoria, B.C. *Clubs:* Union, Golf. Victoria, B.C.

ROBERTSON, William John, B.A., LL. B.; *b.* Westmeath, Renfrew Co., Ont., 12 Sept., 1846; *s.* John Robertson and Amma Rudsdale; (Highland Scotch, and Yorkshire ancestry); *m.* Margaret K. Junkin, St. Catharines, Ont., two *d.* *Educ.:* Pub. Sch., Bathurst Tp., High Sch. Perth, Ont., Toronto univ.; gold medalist in metaphysics and logic; silver medalist in mathematics; Prince of Wales prizeman, Toronto Univ.; teacher of mathematics and History, St. Catharines Coll. Inst.; pres. of Ont. Library Assn., for one year; member of General Conference, Methodist Church, 24 years; Board of Education, Methodist Church and Secy. Superannuation Fund Board. *Publications:* High Sch. Algebra, Parts I and II (Robertson and Bechard); Public Sch. History of England and Canada; High Sch. History of England and Canada; (Benkly and Robertson); Pamphlet on Banking and Commerce. *Recreations:* golf and indoor bowling. *Address:* 96 King St., St. Catharines, Ont. *Club:* Golf, St. Catherines.

ROBIDOUX, His Hon. Joseph Emery, K.C., D.C.L., Judge of Superior Court, Que.; *b.* 10 March, 1844; *m.* 1869, Sophie, *d.* of James B. Sancer. *Educ.:* Montreal Coll.; St. Mary's (Jesuit) Coll.; McGill Univ. Called to the Bar, 1866; Q.C., 1879; has practised in Montreal; was Professor of Civil Law in McGill Univ. for over 10 years; pres. of the McGill Graduates' Society, 1884; Batonnier of the Montreal Bar, 1895, re-elec., 1896; Batonnier-General, 1896; pres. of first newly-organised Canadian Bar Association, 1896; Liberal Member of the Legislature for Chateauguay, 1884-92, and 1897; Provincial Secretary and afterwards Attorney-General, 1892; again Provincial Secretary, 1897-1900; Judge, 1900. *Address:* 151 University St., Montreal. *Clubs:* St. James's, St. Denis, Jockey, Montreal.

ROBINS, William; sec. and dir. of the Hiram Walker & Sons, Ltd., distillers; *b.* Cornwall, Eng., 1 Aug., 1850; *s.* of Rev. Matthew Robins, a dissenting minister, and Jane Phillips; *m.* 1874, Margaret Keighley, of Toronto; one *d.* *Educ.:* Pub. Schs. Engaged in clerical work in England. Arrived, Canada, 1870, and became employed as accnt. with business of J. C. Fitch, of Toronto; employed as office mgr. with Noxon Co., of Ingersoll, Ont., 1873; returned to Toronto, 1894, and in 1876, opened an office as pub. accnt.; became Insp. of the Mercantile Agency of R. G.

Dunn & Co., 1880, and removed to New York; return to Toronto, 1882 and in 1888, became mgr. of the business of Hiram Walker & Sons' distillery at Walkerville, which position he still holds. Vice-pres. of the Oil Exportation Co., of Canada; vice-pres., Canadian Trinidad Assn. *Address:* Windsor, Ont.

ROBINSON, Major-General Charles Walker, C.B., B.A., D.C.L.; *b.* Toronto, Ont., 3 April, 1836; *y. s.* of Sir John Beverley Robinson, Bt., C.B., and Emma, *d.* of Charles Walker of Harlesden, Middlesex, *m.* 1884, Margaret Frances, *d.* of Gen. Sir Archibald Alison, Bt., G.C.B.; one *s.* two *d.* *Educ.:* Up. Can. Coll.; Trin. Coll., Toronto. Joined Rifle Brig., 1857; passed through Staff Coll., 1865; served in the Indian Mutiny (medal); in Ashanti Expedition, 1875-74; Brigade-Major, European Brigade, medal with clasp and Brev. of Major; in Zulu War, 1879 (A.A.G. 2nd Div.), medal with clasp, and brevet of Lt.-Colonel, held appiontments of Brigade Major, D.A.A. Gen. and A.A.G. at Aldershot; Assistant Military Secretary Headquarters of the Army (1890-92); commanding the troops, Mauritius (1892-95); Lt.-Governor and Secretary Royal Hospital, Chelsea, 1895-98; retired April, 1898. *Publications:* Strategy of the Peninsular War; Life of Sir John Beverley Robinson, Bt.; Wellington's Campaigns, 1808-15. *Recreations:* cycling, riding. *Address:* Beverley House, Eaton Rise, Ealing, Eng. *Club:* Army and Navy, London, Eng.

ROBINSON, Christopher Blackett; editor and proprietor of *The Dominion Presbyterian;* *b.* Thorah, Ontario Co., Ont., 2 Nov., 1837; *s.* of Charles Robinson, J.P. (Eng.), and Annie Gunn (Scotch); *m.* (1st) Mary Burnside (*d.* 1875); (2nd) Frances Cameron; two *s.* three *d.* *Educ.:* Thorah pub. sch. Commenced journalistic career, 1857, as ed. and prop. of *The Post,* Beaverton, Ont., which was removed to Lindsay in 1861; went to Toronto in 1871 and commenced pub. of *Canada Presbyterian,* now *The Westminster.* Publisher and mgr. for some yrs. of the *Week,* a high class journal of which he was joint prop., with Dr. Goldwin Smith. Est. the *Dominion Presbyterian* in 1898, and is still ed and prop. Ex-pres. of the Can. Press Assn. Removed to Ottawa, in 1900. *Address:* 323 Frank St., Ottawa.

ROBINSON, Clifford William, B.A., M.L.A., *b.* Moncton, N.B., 1 Sept., 1866; *s.* of William J. Robinson and Margaret Trenholm; *m.* Annie M. Himson. *Educ.:* N.B. Com. Sch., and Mount Allison Coll.; alderman and mayor, Moncton, 1895-6-7; candidate for H. of C. for Westmoreland Co., 1896; first elec. to N.B. Legislature, 1897; re-elec. 1899-1903-1908; Premier of N.B., 1907, until the Government was defeated, March, 1908. *Address:* Moncton, N.B.

ROBINSON, James; *b.* 1 May, 1856; *s.* of Thomas Robinson and Elizabeth Seanor; *m.* 1887, Alice M. Robinson; two *s.* three *d.* *Educ.:* Montreal pub. schs. At age of fifteen entered employment of a shoe factory, in which line of business he has since been engaged, and is now head of the largest wholesale jobbing house in boots, shoes and rubber boots in Can. Pres. Maple Leaf Rubber Co., Wholesale Boot and Shoe Assn. of Can., Durham Rubber Co.; Chairman of the Ex. Committee of the Can. Consolidated Rubber Cos.; pres. Dom. Commercial Travellers' Mutual Benefit Soc., and has twice been pres. of the Dom. Commercial Travellers' Assn. Mem., Montreal Bd. of Trade; el. mem. City Council, 1906; re-el. by accl., 1908. *Recreations:* boating, fishing, travelling. *Address:* 626 Sherbrooke St. W., Montreal.

ROBINSON, William; *b.* nr. Montreal, 22 Dec., 1849; *s.* of William Robinson and Jane A. Paton; *m.* 1886, Kate A. Easton; three *c.* *Educ.:* Dist. Sch. of his native place, and Fergus Gram. Sch. At age of nineteen commenced ry. construction work; for some time engaged in construction of C.P.R. between Winnipeg and Rat Portage; began building steamboats 1878, and was first man to place a steamer for pub. traffic on Lake Winnipeg, and instituted a regular steamboat service on the rivers. Was one of the founders of the Northwest Navigation Co., of which he became mgr. and is now pres. He is also pres. of the Dominion Fish Co., which has seven branches and storehouses throughout the Dom.; a dir. for Manitoba of the Crown Life Insur. Co. *Address:* Winnipeg, Man.

ROBLIN, Hon. Rodmond Palen, M.L.A, Premier, Minister of Agriculture and Railway Commissioner for the Province of Manitoba; *b.* Sophiasburgh, Prince Edward County, Ont., 15 Feb., 1853; *s.* of James Platt and Devorah Roblin; of German descent; *m.* 1875, Adelaide Demill; four *s.* *Educ.:* Albert Coll., Belleville, Ont.; went west to Manitoba, 1880, and settled at Carman, where he has carried on farming upon a large scale; and also as a grain-dealer, with headquarters in Winnipeg; advanced through the usual channel; Sch. Trustee, Reeve, Warden and M.L.A.; contested Dufferin for the Legislative Assembly of Manitoba; twice elected 1888; formed a Govt. in 1900 and has been Premier, Minister of Agriculture and Railway Commissioner ever since. *Address:* 211 Garry St., Winnipeg. *Clubs:* Manitoba, Commercial, and St. Charles Country, Winnipeg.

ROBSON, May Waldron; *b.* Waldron, Hamilton, Ont., 1 Nov., 1868; *m.* 1894, to Stuart Robson (*died* Apr. 29, 1903); removed with parents to Chicago; mem. choir St. Paul's Ch.; joined Pinafore Co.; from that went to Augustin Daly's Co.; then Robson and Crane's Co., with which she played leading female roles of legitimate comedy. *Address:* Highlands, N. J., U.S.A.

ROCHE, Rev. J. O., LL.D.; *b.* P.E.I., 3 Jan., 1865; *s.* of Michael Roche and Hannah Murphy. *Educ.:* P. of W. Coll., Ottawa Univ., St. Mary's Seminary, Baltimore, Md.; ordained priest, 17 Dec., 1892; held parishes in the Western States; first vice-pres. of the Catholic Church Extension Society, when formed at Chicago, 16 Oct., 1906; editor of the *Catholic Register and Canadian Extension. Publications;* seven books," "Business Side of Religion," "The Ought-to-be's," "Obligation of Hearing Mass," etc. *Address:* The Catholic Church Extension Society, 119 Wellington St., Toronto.

ROCHE, Hon. William; Senator; *b.* Halifax, N.S., 1842; descended from an Irish family which first settled in N.Y., but on the breaking out of the Revolutionary War, removed to N.S., with the U.E. Loyalists in 1783. *Educ.:* Halifax. Vice-pres. of the Union Bank of Can.; Pres., Halifax Fire Ins. Co. Returned to Ho. of Assembly, g. e., 1886, 1890, 1894. Was a mem. of Executive Council, of N.S. without portfolio. El. to Ho. of Commons at g. e., 1900; re-el. at g. e., 1904; unsuccessful at g. e., 1908; called to the Senate, Jan., 1910. *Address:* Halifax.

ROCHE, William James, M.D., M.P.; *b.* Clandeboye, Ont., 30 Nov., 1860; *s.* of Wm. E. Roche and Maria Carter Roche; *m.* Annie, E. Cook, of Toronto; one *s.* one *d.* *Educ.:* Lucan Pub. Sch., London High Sch., Trinity Medical Coll., Toronto Univ., and Western Univ., London, Ont.; removed to Minnedosa, Man., 1883, where he practiced as a physician; Grand Master, I.O.O.F., Manitoba, 1893; Grand Representative to Sovereign Grand Lodge, 1894-95; member of Manitoba Medical Council for several yrs.; first el. to H. of C. 1896; re-el. 1900, 1904, 1908; Asst. chief whip of the Lib.-Conservative party. *Address:* Minnedosa, Man.

RODDICK, Thomas George, M.D., C.M. (McGill); *b.* Harbour Grace, 31 July, 1846; *s.* of the late John Irving Roddick and Emma Jane Martin; *m.* (1st) 1880, Urelia Marion (*d.* 1890), *d.* of the late Wm. McKinnon of Pointe Claire, Que., (2nd) Amy, *d.* of the late J. J. Redpath, of Montreal. *Educ.:* Model and Normal Sch., of Truro, N.S.; McGill Univ. (Holmes Gold Medal and Final Prize). For six yrs. House Surgeon of Montreal Gen. Hospital; apptd. Lecturer on Hygiene at McGill, 1873; Demonstrator of Anatomy, 1874; Prof. of Clinical Surgery, 1875; Prof. of Surgery, 1890; Dean of the Faculty of Medicine, 1901; resigned 1908, to accept governorship of McGill Univ., and is a trustee mem. of Royal Inst. for the Advancement of Learning; is consulting surgeon to General Hospital and Royal Victoria; pres. Medico-Chirurgical Soc. of Montreal,; Canadian Medical Ass.; vice-pres., Canadian Branch of British Red Cross Soc., Montreal branch of British Medical Assn. Cr. LL.D., Univ. of Edinburgh, 1898; el. an hon. F.R.C.S. of Great Britain, 1899. Joined Grand Trunk Artillery, 1868, and was Asst. Surgeon; apptd. Surgeon Prince of Wales Own Rifles; made Lieut.-Col. on retired list 1894; organized hospital and ambulance service during North-West Rebellion, 1885 (despatches, and recommended for C.M.G.) El. to H. of C. for St. Antoine div., Montreal, at g. e., 1896, 1900. *Address:* 705 Sherbrooke St. W., Montreal. *Club:* St. James's, Montreal.

ROE, James Sydney; *b.* Oundle, Northampton, Eng., 15 July, 1877; *s.* of Robert Garrett Roe, and Jane Hannah Browning. *Educ.:* Oundle Gram. Sch. In merchants office in London, for several years. Came to Canada, 1897, and took up journalism. Severally employed on staffs of Chatham *Banner*, Toronto *World*, Montreal *Star*. Has been for some years on staff of Montreal *Gazette*, as its parliamentary correspondent. *Publications:* "Songs of the Session," and fugitive verse in many publications. *Recreations:* angling, walking. *Address:* Gazette Office, Montreal.

ROGERS, Hon. Robert, Minister of Public Works for Manitoba; *b.* Lakefield, Que., 2 March, 1864; *s.* George Rogers; *m.* 1888, Aurelia Regina Medymer; one *s.* Started general business when he was 18 years of age at Charlevoix, Man., and remained at it for 16 years; then engaged in grain dealing and mining; unsuccessful candidate for H. of C., for Lisgar, 1896; elec. to Leg. Ass. of Manitoba, 1899; member of Executive Council, 29 Oct., 1900, without portfolio; Minister of Public Works, 20 Dec., 1900; re-el., 1903-1907. *Recreations:* riding, driving. *Address:* Winnipeg, Man. *Clubs:* Manitoba, Commercial, Advance and Country, Winnipeg.

ROGERS, Lieut.-Col. Samuel Maynard; *b.* Plymouth, Eng., 14 April, 1862; *s.* of Samuel Rogers and Elizabeth Maynard; *m.* 1886, Annie Woodburn. *Educ.:* Ottawa Pub. Schs. and Coll. Inst.; arrived in Canada, Jan., 1864; Lt.-Col., commanding 43rd Regt., The Duke of Cornwall's Own Rifles; Past Master Dalhousie Lodge, No. 52, A.F. & A.M.; ex-alderman, Ottawa; ex-pub. sch. trustee; ex-pres., Ottawa Amateur Athletic Assn., and Ottawa Hockey Club; served as Staff-Sergt., with Ottawa Sharpshooters, N.W. Rebellion, 1885; medal; served as Captain in D. Co., 2nd Batt., Royal Canadian Regt., South African War, medal with four clasps; participated in aid to Civil Power, Low, Que., D.A.A.G., under Lord Aylmer, also at J. R. Booth's Labour Riots, and E. B. Eddy Labour Riots; chief Staff Officer at Rockcliffe Camps, 1905-1906-1907; Colonial and Auxiliary Officers decoration; *Recreations:* rifle shooting, moose and deer hunting, fishing. *Address:* 221 Laurier Av. East, Ottawa, and Point Comfort, Que. *Clubs:* Laurentian, Golf, Elks', Ottawa.

ROLAND, Charles Franklin; Commr., Winnipeg Development and Industrial Bureau; *b.* St. Catharines, Ont., 29 Jan., 1870; *s.* of John Roland and Adeline Karr; *m.* Kayme A. Jones; three *s.* two *d.* *Educ.:* St. Catharines. Entered commercial life at age of sixteen; left Canada when twenty-one for nine yrs. in commercial life in U.S.; returned to Canada; engaged in journalism; owned and published trade papers; took charge of Bureau for Winnipeg in 1906. Pres., Winnipeg Camera Club. *Recreations:* lawn bowling, motoring. *Address:* Winnipeg, Man. *Clubs:* Winnipeg Camera, Men's Advertising.

ROLLAND, Hon. Jean Damien, M.L.C.; *b.* Montreal, 23 Feb., 1841; *s.* of the late Hon. J. B. Rolland, and Esther Dufresne; *m.* Arbena Parent; four *s.* four *d.* *Educ.:* Ste. Marie Coll. Pres. of the J. B. Rolland & Sons Co., wholesale stationers; pres. of the Rolland Paper Co., vice-pres. of the Northern Paper Mills; mem. of the Hochelaga town coun., 1872-1786; mayor, 1876-1879; mem. Montreal City Coun., 1882; for several yrs. chn. of the Civic Finance Com.; Pres., Can. Mfgrs. Assn.; founder and is pres. of the "Societe de Colonisation et de Repatriement," of Montreal; one of founders, and now mem. of Bd. of the Commercial Travellers' Assn., dir. of the Bank of Hochelaga; dir., Mfgrs'. Life Insur. Co.; pres. of "Le Cercle de la Librairie Franco Canadien;" gov., Laval Univ.; dir., L'Assomption d'Administration Generale; pres., Northern Colonization Ry. Co.; apptd. to Leg. Coun., 14 Nov., 1896. *Address:* 18 St. Denis St., Montreal. *Club:* Lafontaine, Montreal.

ROSAMOND, Bennett; *b.* Carleton Place, Ont., 10 May, 1833; *s.* of James Rosamond and Margaret Wilson. *Educ.:* Gram. Sch., Carleton Place, Ont., filled various municipal and sch. positions; represented North Lanark in H. of C. for 13 yrs ; pres., Rosamond Woolen Co., since 1866; pres., Almonte Knitting Co. *Address:* Almonte, Ont. *Clubs:* Rideau, Ottawa; St. James's, Country, Montreal.

ROSCOE, Lieut.-Col. Wentworth Eaton, M.A., K.C.; *b.* Kentville, Kings County, 21 Aug., 1849; *s.* Jacob Miner Roscoe and Prudence Rockwell; *m.* Annie E. Mortin; two *s.* two *d.* *Educ.:* Horton Coll. Academy, Wolfville, and at Dalhousie Coll., Halifax, N.S.; taught sch. for seven years in Kings Co.; later studied law at Kentville; admitted to the bar, May, 19, 1876; in August, 1878, began practice in Kentville on his own account; Warden of Kings Co., in 1891, 1893, 1896 and 1899; previously as Co. Councillor for two years. In 1889, was apptd. Commissioner of Schs.; since that year, has represented Ward Three in the Municipal Council; in 1896, was made Q.C.; lecturer on contracts in the affiliated law course at Acadia Univ. Apptd. one of the revisors of the Dominion Statutes in 1902, under the chairmanship of Sir Henry Strong; Mayor of Kentville in 1904-7. Lieut.-Colonel of the 68th Kings County Regiment of the Active Militia of Canada, 1905. *Address:* Kentville, N.S.

ROSE, Herbert Jennings, B.A. (McGill), B.A. (Oxford); *b.* at Orillia, Ont., 5 May, 1883; *s.* of Rev. S. P. Rose, D.D. and Jennie Andrews; unmarried. *Educ.:* private tuition; Ottawa Coll. Inst.; McGill Univ.; Balliol Coll., Oxford, Eng.; has had a distinguished carreer as a scholar. When sixteen yrs. old passed the ordinary matriculation exams., admitting him to McGill Univ. During the following yr. was a student at the Ottawa Collegiate, where he won medals in English and Classics. In 1900, entered McGill as a first year's man, having won, in open competition, a $200 exhibition. Each yr. of his course won exhibitions aggregating in all $575. At graduation, shared with Mr. John Archibald, now a Fellow of All Soul's, Oxford, the honor of winning the gold medal in classics. Was also the class-poet of the year. With Mr. Archibald, was chosen one of the first Rhodes scholars from McGill, entering Oxford, in the autumn of 1904. Secured a "first" in "moderations" at the end of his first yr., and in the December following, gained the blue ribbon in classics open to undergraduates in the Univ., the Ireland scholarship, worth £300 in money, but chiefly valued as a recognition of superior scholarship. Mr. Askwith, Goldwin Smith, and W. E. Gladstone, were former Ireland scholarship winners. In recognition of this achievement was el. as an hon. scholar of Balliol. Subsequently captured the Kingston-Oliphant prize, awarded for superiority in Fourteenth Century English and general philology. Prior to graduation, won the Chancellor's Latin essay prize, offered for competition among the senior students. "First in greats" in his finals; admitted B.A., Aug., 1907. On graduation was offered and accepted a tutorial fellowship in Exeter Coll., Oxford, and now one of its dons. *Publications:* magazine articles; contributor to Hastings' Dictionary of Religion and Ethics. *Recreations:* chess, boating. *Addresses:* 115 Wellesley St., Tronto; Exeter Coll. Oxford, Eng.

ROSE, Rev. Samuel P., D.D.; *b.* Muncey, Ont., 19 April, 1853; *s.* of the late Rev. Samuel Rose, D.D., and Mary Street; *m.* Jennie Andrews; two *s.* *Educ.:* Upper Can. Coll., Toronto; Toronto Gram. Sch., private study. Ordained as Methodist minister in 1877; pastor of churches in Brantford, Montreal, Ottawa, Hamilton, Winnipeg, Toronto. Chn. of Dist.; Pres. of Confce. *Publications:* regular magazine contributor. *Address:* 115 Wellesley St., Toronto.

ROSENROLL, Anthony S. de, J.P., M.L.A.; *b.* Castleman, Italy, 4 Dec., 1857; *s.* of Rudolph de Rosenroll and Margaret Thompson; *m.* Ida Eterhard (*dec.*); two *s.* one *d.* *Educ.:* Private tuition; formerly practiced as a land surveyor and civil engineer; pres. of the Rosenroll Lumber Co., of Wetaskiwin; pres., The Pigeon Lake Saw Mills Co., Ltd.; large land interests in Alberta; a Justice of the Peace since 1896; Notary Public since 1897; twice elected to the Leg. Ass. of the N.W.T.; elected a mem. of the first Provincial Legislature of Alberta. *Address:* Wetaskiwin and Rosenroll, Alberta.

ROSS, Crawford; *b.* Gould, Compton, Que., 4 Oct., 1856; *s.* James Ross and Anna Browne *m.* Elizabeth Christie; two *s.* three *d.* *Educ.:* Cookshire Acad., Lennoxville Coll,. and privately. Commenced business in Ottawa, 1876; now managing dir., The C. Ross Co. of Ottawa; dir., the Rideau Mfg. Co.; ex-pres., Ottawa Board of Trade and Gatineau F. & G. Club; vice-pres., Central Can. Exh. Assn.; mem. Can. Mfgrs. Assocn.; pres., Ottawa Amateur Athletic Assn., and Club. *Recreations:* golf, driving, hunting, fishing, curling. *Address:* 295 Metcalfe St., Ottawa. *Clubs:* Laurentian, Hunt, Golf, Ottawa.

ROSS, Donald Henry; *b.* Englishtown, St. Anns, Cape Breton, N.S., 20 April, 1864; *s.* of Hon. William and Eliza Ross.; *m.* Blanch Elizabeth Cordeteni, at Melbourne, Australia, 1 Jan., 1909. *Educ.:* Halifax pub. sch.; Commercial Commissioner of Trade and Commerce for Canada in Victoria Southern Australia and Tasmania, since March, 1903. *Address:* P. O. Box 140, Melbourne, Asutralia. *Club:* Melbourne.

ROSS, Duncan Campbell, B.A., M.P.; *b.* Strathroy, Ont., 16 Dec., 1871; *s.* of Hon. George W. Ross, formerly Prime Minister of Ont., now Senator, and Christina Campbell; *m.* 1900, Emily Amelia Biel; one *d.* *Educ.:* Strathroy Pub. and High Schs., Toronto Univ., and Osgoode Hall. A barrister. Dir. of the Cameron-Dunn Mfg. Co. El. to Ont. Legis. for West Middlesex, at bye-el., 20 Feb., 1907; el. for Middlesex

North at g. e., 1908; el. to H. of C. for West Middlesex, at bye-el., 1909. *Address:* Strathroy, Ont.

ROSS, Hon. George William, Senator, LL.D., barrister; *b.* near Nairn, Williams Tp., Middlesex Co., 18 Sept., 1841; *s.* of James Ross and Ellen McKinnon, natives of Ross-shire, Scotland. *Educ.:* Normal Sch., Toronto; Albert Univ.; St. Andrews, Scotland, Toronto Univ., Victoria Univ., McMaster Univ., Queen's Univ.; Teacher, Pub. Sch. Inspector; Model Sch. Inspector; barrister; called to bar, 1887; M.P. (L.) West Middlesex, 1872-74-78-82; Minister of Education, 1883-99; Premier and Treasurer Province of Ont., 1899-1905; called to Senate, 1907; F.R.S., Can.; has edited the Strathroy *Age*, the Huron *Expositor*, and the Ontario *Teacher*. *Publications:* The Life and Times of the Hon. Alex. Mackenzie, jointly with Wm. Buckingham; History of Public and Separate Schools; Patriotic Recitations for Public and High Schools; Reports on schools of England and Germany, etc. *Address:* 3 Elmsley Place, Toronto.

ROSS, James, C.E.; *b.* Cromarty, Scotland, 1848; *s.* of Capt. John Ross, merchant and shipowner, and Mary B. McKeddie; *m.* Annie Kerr; one *s.* *Educ.:* Inverness Academy, Scotland and also in England; arrived in United States in 1868 and settled in Canada a few yrs. later; held numerous appointments as engineer and manager on various railways and subsequently as railway contractor on C.P.R.; has been identified with street railway building in Canada and elsewhere; for many yrs., Presdt. of Dominion Coal Co., and other large industrial concerns; is director of a number of important institutions, including Bank of Montreal; a governor of McGill Univ. and of Royal Victoria Hospital, Montreal. *Recreations:* yachting, fishing, shooting. *Address:* 360 Peel St., Montreal; Drumbo, Sydney, C.B. *Clubs:* Mount Royal, St. James's, Montreal; Halifax; Union, St. John; Toronto; Manitoba, Winnipeg; Rideau, Ottawa; Royal St. Lawrence Yacht; Royal Yacht Squadron of N.S.; Royal Canadian Yacht; Royal C.B. Yacht; New York Yacht; Manhattan, New York; Constitutional, London, England.

ROSS, James Alway, M.L.A.; *b.* St. Ann's, Lincoln, Ont., 13 Jan., 1869; *s.* of Wm. N. Ross and Lydia Ross; *m.* Agnes Kay, of Wellandsport, Ont.; two *s.* two *d.* *Educ.:* Smithville High Sch., St. Catharines Coll. Inst., and Toronto Normal Sch. An insur. inspector. Taught sch. for ten yrs.; promoted and managed for three yrs., the Empire Store Co., Ltd.,Wellandsport; mgr', Sterling Bank of Can., at Wellandsport for two yrs. Recently apptd. inspr. for the Excelsior Life Insur. Co., Toronto. Dir., Central Securities, Toronto; provisional pres., Dunnville, Wellandsport and Beamsville Electric Ry. Co. Unsuccessful can. for Ont. Legis., 1902 and 1905; el. 1908. *Address:* Wellandsport, Ont.

ROSS, James F. W., M.D.; surgeon; *b.* Toronto, Ont., 15 Aug., 1857; *s.* of the late Dr. James Ross and Anne Jean McIntosh; *m.* 1882, Adelaide M., *d.* of George Gooderham; two *d.* *Educ.:* Toronto Model Sch., Gram. Sch., Upper Can. Coll., Toronto Univ. (Grad. M.D., 1878). Apptd. an asst. resident surgeon of Toronto Gen. Hospital, and in autumn of same yr., went to London, Eng., to continue his studies; became a Licentiate of Royal Coll. of Physicians, of London, 1880, and pursued a further course of studies in London, Berlin. Leipzig and Vienna; returned to Toronto, 1882, and began gen. practice; went abroad again for six mos., 1888; returned to Toronto, 1889, and resumed practice. Was pres., Toronto Med. and Toronto Clinical Socs.; mem., Medical Faculty of Toronto Univ. Is active on staff of number of Toronto Hospitals; el. hon. mem. Med. Soc., of State of N.Y., 1892, and pres., American Assn., of Obstetricians and Gynaecologists. Was for number of yrs., Lieut. in "I" Co., Queen's Own Rifles; retired as paymaster. Has contributed to many medical and surgical publications. *Address:* 481 Sherbourne St., Toronto.

ROSS, James George; sen. mem. of the firm of P. S. Ross & Sons, accountants, Montreal; *b.* Montreal, 1861; *s.* of Phillip Simpson Ross and Christine Dansken; *m.* 1901, Margaret Alice, *d.* of the late John Monk; two *d.* *Educ.:* Priv. sch., High Sch., Montreal and attended Guelph Agricultural Coll., where he grad. 1881. Entered partnership with his bro. in firm of P. S. Ross & Sons, and on death of his father, became head of the firm. Mem. Ont. Field Battery, 1879-1883; officer in Victoria Rifles, 1884-1891, when retired with rank of Captain. Joined 5th Royal Scots, 1898; promoted Major, 1906. Received Long Service Medal for officers, 1907; mem. Montreal Bd. Trade; Council of Montreal Assn. of Chartered Accts., and F.C.A., Dom. Assn., of Chartered Accts. *Address:* 393 Kensington Av., Montreal. *Clubs:* St. James's, Canada.

ROSS, Hon. James Hamilton; *b.* London, Ont., 12 May, 1856; *s.* of Scotch parents; *m.* 23 Nov., 1886, Barbara E. McKay (*deceased*, Aug., 1901). *Educ.:* London Gram. Sch., and High Sch.; a rancher; unsuccessful candidate for H. of C. for West Assiniboia, 1887; elec. to North West Ass., 1883, retaining seat until 1901; member of Executive Council; Treas., Commr. of Public Works, and Territorial Secretary; delegate to the Liberal Convention, held in Ottawa, 1893; apptd. Commissioner of the Yukon Territory, 1901; el. to H. of C., 1902, for Yukon Territory; apptd to the Senate, 30 Sept., 1904; Liberal. *Address:* Moosejaw, Sask.

ROSS, Howard Salter, B.A., LL.B.; *b.* Victoria Mines, Cape Breton Co., N.S., 13 April, 1872; *s.* of Alexander Charles Ross and Marian Ross; *m.* Susie Murray; one *s.* three *d.* *Educ.:* High Sch., North Sydney, N.S., and Horton Academy, Wolfville, N.S., Preparatory Sch.; Acadia Univ., Wolfville, Cornell Law Sch., Ithaca, N.Y., and Dalhousie Law Sch., Halifax, N.S.; admitted to the N.S. bar, 3 April, 1897; has been in general practice at Sydney, N.S., since 1899; member of Senate of Acadia Univ.; director of Sydney Cement Co., Ltd.; dir., Cape Breton Trust Co.; Commissioner for taking affadavits in the Superior Courts of Quebec and Newfoundland. *Recreations:* tennis, riding, and target shooting. *Ad-*

dress: 18 Park St., Sydney, N.S. *Club:* R. C. B. Y. C., Sydney.

ROSS, Jean Auguste, M.D., M.P.; *b.* Rimouski, Que., Sept., 1851; *s.* of the late John Ross and Caroline Talbot; *m.* 1875, Mary, *d.* of David Talbot, of Bic, Que.; one *s.* one *d.* *Educ.:* St. Anne's Coll., Rimouski; Laval Univ., Quebec. Was Mayor of the village of Mont Joli; coroner for the district of Rimouski and quarantine officer for the port. Returned to H. of C. at bye el., 1897 by accl.; re-el. 1900, 1904, and 1908. Dir. Matane and Gaspe Ry. Co. *Address:* St. Flavie, Que.

ROSS, John Theodore, B.A. (McGill); *b.* Quebec, 1862; *s.* of the late John Ross; *m.* 1896, Miss Burstall, of Quebec; two *s.* two *d.* *Educ.:* Quebec High Sch., Morrin Coll., Quebec; McGill Univ., Montreal. Grad. B. A., 1883. Joined father's wholesale bus., John Ross & Co.; partner 1887-1894, when concern liquidated. Vice-Pres., Quebec Bank; pres. since 1908; vice-pres., *Chronicle* Printing Co.; dir., Quebec Steamship Co.; mem. Quebec, Bd. of Trade. *Address:* St. Louis Rd., Quebec. *Club:* Garrison.

ROSS, John W.; mem. of the firm of P. S. Ross & Sons, accountants, Montreal; *b.* Montreal, Que., 1870; *s.* of Phillip Simpson Ross and Christine C. Dansken; *m.* 1894; Gertrude E. Holland, of Montreal; two *s.* three *d.* *Educ.:* High Sch., Business Col., Montreal. Entered firm of Messrs. James Walker & Co., hardware merchants; became associated with firm of P. S. Ross & Sons, 1892; mem. Montreal Assn. of Chartered Accts., Dom. Assn. of Chartered Accts.; pres., Y.M.C.A., Montreal; governor, Protestant Home of Industry and Refuge. *Address:* Montreal. *Clubs:* Montreal, Westmount Golf, Beaconsfield Golf.

ROSS, Philip Dansken B.A.Sc.; *b.* Montreal, 1 Jan., 1858; *s.* of Philip Simpson Ross, and Christine Dansken, both Scotch; *m.* Mary Littlejohn, of Toronto. *Educ.:* McGill Univ.; entered journalism 1879; Asst. editor Toronto *News*, 1882; managing editor, Montreal *Star*, 1885; founded Ottawa *Journal*, 1886; member Ottawa City Council, 1902-1903; vice-pres. Board of Trade; unsuccessful candidate for Ontario Leg. Ass., 1904; pres., Ottawa Conservative Association, 1908-10; pres., Royal Canadian Golf Association, 1909. *Recreations:* rowing, golf. *Address:* 421 Laurier Ave. E., Ottawa. *Clubs:* Rideau, Golf, Country and Hunt, Ottawa.

ROSS, Hon. William; Senator; *b.* Boulardarie, C.B., 20 Dec., 1825; *s.* of John Ross and Robina McKenzie; *m.* 27 Mar., 1855, Eliza *d.* of Capt. Moore, North Sydney, C.B.; four *s.* one *d.* *Educ.:* private sch., Boulardarie, C.B.; first el. to Leg. Ass. of N.S., 12 May, 1859; re-elec., 1863; elec. to the H. of C., 1867-72-74, three successive g. e. by acclam.; apptd. collector of Customs at Halifax, Nov., 1874, and served 14 and a half years; returned again to the Dominion Parliament; apptd. to the Senate, 1906; Minister of Militia in the Mackenzie Government, and introduced bill establishing the Royal Military Coll. at Kingston. *Recreation:* curling. *Address:* 43 Brenton St., Halifax, N.S.

ROSS, William Gillies; *b.* Montreal, 6 Aug., 1863, *s.* of Phillip Simpson Ross and Christine Dansken, *m.* Ida E. M. Babcock; three *s.* two *d.* *Educ.:* Montreal High School; pres., Quebec railway Light and Power Co.; managing dir., Montreal Street Railway Co.; dir., Dominion Iron and Steel Co.; chartered accountant, 1879 to 1888; private secretary until 1896; comptroller, secretary-treasurer and now Managing Dir., Montreal Street Railway. *Address:* 6 Alexander Av., Montreal.

ROWELL, Newton Wesley, K.C.; *b.* Middlesex Co., Ont., 1 Nov., 1867; *s.* Joseph and Nancy Rowell; *m.* Nellie Langford; one *s.* one *d.* *Educ.:* London, Ont.; barrister and solicitor; called to the bar, 1891; apptd. Kings Council, 1902. *Recreations:* riding. *Address:* 134 Crescent Road, Toronto. *Clubs:* National, Ontario and Lambton Golf, Toronto.

ROWLEY, William Horsley, J.P.; *b.* Yarmouth, N.S., 21 March, 1851; *s.* of Lt.-Col. John William Horsley Rowley, of London, Eng., and Anne Norman Farish, of Yarmouth, N.S.; a U. E. Loyalist on mother's side; *m.* Grace Richardson, of Windsor, Ont. (*dec.*); one *s.*; (*dec.*) *Educ.:* Yarmouth, N.S. Entered the Bank of Yarmouth, 1867; clerkship in St. John, 1868-70; entered the Merchants Bank of Canada, Montreal, 1871; came to Ottawa, 1875; manager, Merchants B. of C., Ottawa, 1880 to 1886; organized the E. B. Eddy Company, 1886, and has been president and treasurer thereof since 1906; member of Executive Council of The Canadian Mfgrs. Association since 1906, and now vice-pres.; an Anglican; has been for many years a delegate to Synod; is a member of the chapter and Treasurer-Seneschal of Christ's Church Cathedral, Ottawa. *Recreations:* angling, bowling, riding. *Address:* "Worfield," Ottawa. *Clubs:* Rideau, Country, Hunt, Golf, Laurentian, Ottawa; National, and Albany, Toronto; Mount Royal, Montreal.

ROY, Lieut.-Col. A., M.V.O., A.D.C.; Chief Staff Officer, Quebec Command; *b.* Montreal, 23 Sept., 1859; married. *Educ.:* Montreal. Some time an accountant. Joined 65th Batt. as Lieut., 1880; served North-West Rebellion, 1885. Present at relief of Battleford; action at Cutknife Hill; operations against Chief Big Bear's Band. Mentioned in despatches. Brigade Major No. 6 Dist., 1888. Promoted Lieut.-Col., to No. 5 Dist., Montreal, 1895. O. C., No. 6 Dist., St. John's Quebec, 1897; chief staff officer, 10 Aug., 08. Took musketry course at Hythe; cavalry course, Shorncliffe; tactical fitness for command, Aldershot. *Address:* 289 University St., Montreal.

ROY, Cyrias, M.P.; *b.* St. Francois de Montmagny, 6 July, 1864; *s.* of George Roy and Henrietta Corriveau; *m.* Alma Theberge, Practiced law at Montmagny, Que.; Mayor of the Town for 4 years; Prothonotary of the Superior Court at Montmagny; elec. to H. of C., 1908. *Address:* Montmagny, Que.

ROY, Joseph Alfred Ernest, B.A., M.P.; *b.* St. Valier, Bellechasse Co., Que., 3 Oct., 1871; *s.* of Nazaire Roy and Rose Therien; *m.* Marie M. Godbout; four *s.* three *d.* A lawyer; was for a short time journalist; Advocat, 1898; elec. to the Leg. Ass. of

Quebec, 30 Nov., 1900, for Montmagny; re-el. by acclam., 1904; first elec. to the H. of C., 1908. *Address:* 75 Lachevrotiere St., Quebec. *Clubs:* Garrison, St. Denis, Quebec.

ROY, Joseph Edmond, N.P., Lit. D.; *b.* Levis, Que.; *s.* of Leon Roy; *m.* Lucienne Carrier. *Educ.:* Levis Coll., Quebec Seminary and Laval Univ. Pres. of the Prov. Bd. of Notaries and Past Pres. of the Royal Soc. of Canada; formerly Mayor of Levis, and dir. of several prominent Cos. Now Prof. of Geography in Laval Univ., and chief of the Manuscripts Div. in the Dom. Archives. *Publications:* Le premier Colon de Levis, 1884; Monseigneur Deziel, sa vie, ses oeuvres, 1885; Voyage au pays de Tadoussac, 1886; L'Ordre de Malte en Amérique, 1888; Au Royaume du Saguenay, 1889; La réception de Monseigneur le Viscomte d'Argenson, 1890; Lettres du P. F. X. Duplessis, S.J., 1892; Claude de Bermen, Sieur de la Martiniere, 1891; Jean Bourdon et la Baie d'Hudson, 1896; L'Ancien Barreau au Canada, 1897; Histoire de la Seigneurie de Lauzon, 5 vols., 1897-1904; Notice Historique sur la famille de Rene la Voye, 1899; Histoire du Notariat au Canada; Tableau general des Notaries pratiquant dans la province de Quebec, 1906; Souvenirs d'une Classe, 1907; Essai sur Charlevoix (Premier part), 1908. *Address:* 131 Somerset St., Ottawa.

ROY, Hon. Louis Rodolphe; Provincial Secy. and Registrar of the Prov. of Que. *b.* St. Valier, Que., 7 Feb., 1859; *s.* of N. Roy and Marie Letellier; unmarried. *Educ.:* Quebec Seminary; Grad. D.C.L., Laval Univ., 1883. Called to Bar 1883. El. to Prov. Legis. for Kamouraska, and has continuously represented that Co. since; Prov. Secy., 23 March, 1905. *Address:* Quebec. *Club:* Garrison, Quebec.

ROY, Mgr. Paul Eugene; Coadjutor Bishop of Quebec; *b.* Berthier en Bas, 9 Nov., 1859. *Educ.:* Quebec Sem.; l'Ecole des Carmes, Paris, France. Ordained priest, 13 June, 1886; cure of Hartford, Conn., U.S.A.; cure, Jacques Cartier, Quebec; Prof. ,Quebec Sem.; dir. of *l'Action Sociale Catholique;* Bishop of Eleutheropolis and Coadjutor Bishop of Quebec, 1908. *Address:* Quebec.

ROY, Hon. Philippe, M.D.; Senator; *b.* St. Francois Co., Montmagny, Que., 13 Feb. 1868; *s.* of G. B. Roy and Josephine Valliers; *m.* 28 Dec., 1899, Helen Young, Edmonton. two *s.* two *d.* *Educ.:* College of Ste. Anne de La Pocatiere, and Laval Univ., Que.; Physician and Surgeon; Man. Dir., "*Le Courrier de l'Ouest* Pub. Co.; pres., Jaspers, Limited, Edmonton; Liberal; Catholic. *Address:* Edmonton, Alta.

RUDDICK, John Archibald; Dairy Commr. for Canada; *b.* Oxford Co., Ont., 3 Sept., 1862; *s.* of Lawrence Ruddick and Marion Moir; *m.* Harriet Congdon; one *d.* *Educ.:* Oxford Co. Sch.; connected with the Dairy industry since 1880; Dept. of Agriculture, 1891; Dairy Commissioner, New Zealand, 1898; Dairy Commissioner for Canada, 1905. *Publications:* various reports; papers in cold storage and dairy journals. *Address:* Dept. of Agriculture, Ottawa.

RUMBALL, Frederick George; Pres. of the Monarch Fire Insur. Co.; *b.* Clinton, Huron Co., Ont., 8 Dec., 1853; *s.* of Benjamin and Mary Rumball; *m.* Amelia Shannon; two *s.* two *d.* *Educ.:* Clinton. Manufacturer; was for a period Mayor of London, Ont. *Address:* 295 Dufferin Av., London, Ont. *Club:* London.

RUPERT'S LAND, Archbishop of; *see* Most Rev. Samuel Pritchard Matheson.

RUSSELL, Hon. Benjamin, M.A., D.C.L., a Puisne Judge of the Superior Ct. of Nova Scotia; *b.* Dartmouth, N.S., 10 Jan., 1849; *s.* Nathaniel and Agnes Russell; *m.* 1872, Louise E., *d.* of the late Capt. Coleman, of Dartmouth. *Educ.:* Halifax Gram. Sch. and Mount Allison Univ. Called to Bar of Nova Scotia, 1872; law reporter to Supreme Ct. of N.S., 1875; for many yrs. official reporter of the N.S. Legis. Assem.; Lecturer, 1885, in the Law Faculty of Dalhousie Univ. El. to H. of C., for Halifax, 1896; el. for Hants Co., 1900; apptd. to present position, 1904. *Address:* Halifax, N.S. *Club:* Halifax.

RUSSELL, Joseph, M.P.; *b.* Toronto, Ont., 1 April, 1868; *s.* of John Russell and Mary Smith; *m.* Nora Lorne; one *s.* three *d.* *Educ.:* Pub. Sch. and British American Business Coll.; a brick manufacturer; first elec. to the H. of C., 1908. *Recreation:* poultry farming. *Address:* 437 Jarvis St., Toronto, Ont.

RUSSELL, Samuel, B.A.; Registrar of Deeds for the County of Hastings; *b.* Newcastle, N.B., 29 Jan., 1848; *s.* of James and Anne Russell; *m.* Evelyn M. Davis. *Educ.:* Pub. and Gram. Sch., Newcastle, N.B.; Univ. of New Brunswick; Queens' Univ., Kingston; Glasgow Univ., Scotland. Editor of Deseronto *Tribune* for many yrs.; el. to Legis. Ass. of Ontario for East Hastings, 1898; re-el. 1902; apptd. Registrar of the Co. of Hastings, 1904. *Address:* Belleville, Ont.

RUTAN, William Winfield, M.P.; *b.* Le Suer Co., Minn., U.S.A., 28 March, 1865; *s.* of Andrew and Anna Jane Rutan (both *deceased*); *m.* Josie Lasley; one *s.* three *d.* *Educ.:* Mankato, Minn., and Battle Creek, Mich.; arrived in Canada in Aug., 1897; parents moved from Canada many years ago; father was physician by profession, and served in the Minnesota Leg.; left home when he was 12 years of age, and has been engaged in commercial business ever since; elec. to the H. of C., 1908. *Recreations:* hunting and travel. *Address:* Melfort, Sask.

RUTHERFORD, Hon. Alexander Cameron, B.A., B.C.L. (McGill), LL.D. (Toronto, McMaster and Alberta Univs.); M.L.A., Premier of Prov. of Alberta, Minister of Education, Provincial Treasurer; *b.* Osgoode, Co. of Carleton, Ont., 2 Feb., 1857; *s.* of James Rutherford and Elizabeth Cameron; *m.* M. Birkett, *e. d.* of late William Birkett, of Ottawa; one *s.* one *d.* *Educ.:* Ont. Pub. Sch., Metcalfe High Sch., Woodstock Coll., McGill Univ. A barrister of Ontario and Alberta; elected to the last Legislature of the N. W. Territories for Strathcona constituency in 1902; Deputy Speaker of Legislature. Called upon to form first government of Prov. of Alberta, 2 Sept., 1905; government sustained at election 9 Nov., 1905, and 22 March, 1909.

Recreation: curling. *Address:* Strathcona, Alta. *Clubs:* Edmonton; Strathcona.

RUTHERFORD, John Gunion, V.S., H.A.R.C.V.S., Live Stock Commissioner for Canada; *b.* Mountain Cross, Peeblesshire, Scot., 25 Dec., 1857; *s.* of Rev. Robert Rutherford, M.A., and Agnes Gunion; *m.* Edith, *d.* of Washington Boultbee, Ancaster, Ont.; three *d.* *Educ.:* High School, Glasgow, private tuition; arrived in Canada, 12 Sept., 1875; Veterinary Director General and Live Stock Commissioner; Veterinary practitioner, 1889 to 1901; member of Manitoba Legislature, 1892-6; el. to H. of C., 1897; chief Veterinary Inspector, 1907; Vet. Director General, 1904; Live Stock Comr., 1906. *Publications:* reports. *Recreations:* riding and driving. *Address:* Ottawa. *Clubs:* Rideau, Hunt, Golf, Ottawa.

RUTTAN, Lieut.-Col. Henry Norlande, C.E., mem. Am. Soc. C.E.; *b.* Cobourg, Ont., 31 May, 1848; *s.* of Henry Jones Ruttan and Margaret Pringle; *m.* Andonia Ballerie; four *s.* one *d.* Engineer and contractor in the construction of the Intercolonial and Canadian Pacific Railways; for the past 24 years, City Engineer of Winnipeg; pres., 1910 of the Can. Soc. of Civil Engineers; served in the Fenian Raids and North West Rebellion; medals; Long Service Decoration. *Address:* Armstrong's Point, and 223 James St., Winnipeg. *Club:* Manitoba, Winnipeg.

RUTTAN, R. P., B.A., M.D., F.R.S. Canada, 1896; Prof. of Organic and Biological Chemistry, McGill Univ., Montreal; *b.* 1857; *s.* of A. Ruttan, M.D., Napanee, Ont., and Caroline Smith, Montreal; unmarried. *Educ.:* Toronto Univ.; McGill Univ. (M.D., gold medal Chemistry, 1884); Univ. of Berlin (1885 and 1886, in Hofman's Laboratory, French and German Chem. Soc.) Lecturer Chemistry, McGill Univ., 1887-91; Prof. Practical Chemistry and Registrar Medical Faculty, 1891-1902; Fellow Corporation McGill, 1891-1910, F.R. S. Can., 1902; apptd. Professor of Chemistry McGill Univ., Montreal, 1902. *Publications:* Dimethyl-Triethyl Amines, Chemistry of O. Tolidin, 1887; a Diohinolin, 1890; Methods of Water Analysis; Methods in Clinical Chemistry; Artificial Alkaloids; Glycol Fats, etc. *Recreations:* golf, yachting. *Address:* "The Sherbrooke," Montreal. *Clubs:* St. James, Mount Royal, Royal Montreal Golf, Royal St. Lawrence Yacht, Montreal.

RUTTER, Arthur Frederick; *b.* Woodford, Essex, England, 1 Feb., 1856; *s.* Thomas Rutter and Maria Downing; *m.* Isabella Jane Bell; two *s.* one *d.* *Educ.:* Oil Springs, Ont. Came to Canada, with his parents in 1859. Clerk with Barclay and Herring, booksellers, stationers and printers, Petrolia, Ont., 1869; entered service of Wm. Warwick, Toronto, 1873, admitted a partner, 1884, and firm name changed to Warwick Bros. and Rutter. For many years the firm has printed the Ontario Govt publications; a member of the Toronto City Council for some years; ex-pres., C.A.A.A., Nat, Amateur Lacrosse Union; Toronto Lacrosse Ass.; Toronto Reform Assoc. *Address:* Woodford, Birch Cliff P.O., Ont. *Clubs:* National, Jockey, Royal Canadian Yacht, Toronto.

RYAN, Patrick Eugene; sec. to National Transcontinental Ry. Com. of Canada; *b.* Ottawa, Ont., 26 July, 1876; *s.* of Patrick Eugene Ryan and Mary Elizabeth Cullen; *m.* Geraldine, *d.* of J. R. E. Chapleau, M.D. and niece of late Sir Adolphe Chapleau, Lieut.-Gov. of Province of Quebec; one *s.* one *d.* *Educ.:* Ottawa Separate Schs., Ottawa Univ., clerk mechanical dept., C.P. Ry., Ottawa, 1892-1897; purchasing dept., C. P. Ry., Montreal, 1897-1899; private sec. to Minister of Public Works, Toronto, 1899-1902; sec. treas. Temiskaming and Northern Ont. Ry., Toronto, 1902-1904; sec., Trans. Ry. Com., Ottawa, 1904 to date. *Address:* 54 Russell Ave., Ottawa. *Clubs:* Royal Canadian Yacht, Toronto; Laurentian, Golf, Ottawa.

RYAN, Peter; Registrar of Deeds for East Toronto; *b.* Carlisle, Cumberland, Eng., 23 Aug., 1842; *s.* of Bernard Ryan of Conego, Co. Down, Irel., and Susannah Tait, of Carlisle, England; *m.* Margaretta Connell, Ormskirk, Lancashire; four *s.* six *d.* *Educ.:* St. Mary's Catholic School, Carlisle, Eng.; arrived in Canada, 1873; has been engaged in wholesale dry goods, lumbering, and various other industrial pursuits; now Registrar, East Toronto. *Address:* 51 Grosvenor St., Toronto.

RYERSON, Col. George Sterling, M.D., L.R.C.S. (Edinb.); *b.* Toronto, 21 Jan., 1855; *s.* of Rev. George Ryerson and Isabella D. Sterling, nephew of the Rev. Egerton Ryerson, founder of the Ontarie Sch. System, and grandson of Joseph Ryerson, a U. L. Loyalist; *m.* 1882, Mary A., *d.* of James Crowther, barrister, Toronto, four *s.* one *d.* *Educ.:* Galt Gram. Sch.; Coll. of Physicians and Surgeons, New York City; Trinity Medical Coll., Toronto; Royal Coll. of Physicians and Surgeons, Edinburgh; Moorfield's Eye Hospital, and London Hospital; also studied at Heidelberg, Paris and Vienna; returned to Canada in 1879, and established himself in Toronto; was apptd. surgeon of the Royal Grenadiers, 1881, serving in the North West Rebellion with that corps in 1885; (medal, and 3rd class decoration of St. John); was made deputy Surgeon General, 1895; organized ambulance corps of the Grenadiers, 1884, and was also instrumental in forming the Association of Medical Officers of the Militia, of which he was secretary, 1891, and president, 1907-08; one of the founders of the Toronto Clinical Society, president, 1894; an original member of the Ophthalmological Society of Great Britain, in 1880, since resigned; member of the Canadian Medical Association; hon. member of the Assn. of Military Surgeons of the U.S.A.; Professor of Eye and Ear diseases in Univ. of Toronto, and has been a member of the Senate of that institution; sat for one term as member for East Toronto in Ont. Leg. Ass.; on re-organization of Army Medical Corps, was apptd. Lieut.-Col.; founder and general secretary, St. John Ambulance Association in Canada; founder and chairman of Canadian Red Cross Society; Canadian Red Cross Commissioner in South African War, 1900; apptd. British Red Cross Commissioner at Lord Roberts' headquarters; war medal; mentioned in despatches; promoted to rank of Hon. Col.

A.M.C.; made Knight of Grace, Order of St. John of Jerusalem; delegate for Department of Militia and Defence to the International Congress of Medicine at Buda Pest, 1909. *Publications:* contributor to the Medical Press of the U.S. and Canada. *Recreations:* yachting and hunting. *Address:* 66 College St., Toronto; Oakhurst, Kawartha Lakes, Ont. *Clubs:* Toronto, R.C.Y.C., Toronto.

S

SAINT-PIERRE, Hon. Henri C.; Judge of the Superior Court for the Prov. of Quebec; Off. Ord Crown of Italy; *b.* Ste. Marthe de Rigaud, Que., 13 Sept., 1842; *s.* of Joseph Berrier Saint Pierre, and Domitilde Denis; *m.* Marie Adeline Lesieur, (*d.* 1908); five *s.* three *d.* *Educ.:* Montreal Coll. (Sulpicians). After leaving Coll., joined Northern Army, and took part in Civil War of U.S. Wounded and left for dead in the battle of Virginia, Nov., 1863. Picked up on battlefield by Southern Cavalry and carried off as prisoner until end of war. Returning to Montreal, studied law under Sir George Cartier and Sir J. J. C. Abbott, admitted to bar, July, 1870; Q.C., 1889; Judge of the Superior Ct., June, 1902. *Publications:* Many pleadings and addresses in Courts of Prov. of Quebec. *Address:* 144 Berri St., Montreal.

SANDERS, Lieut.-Col. Gilbert Edward, D.S.O.; *b.* Fort Yale, B.C., 25 Dec., 1863; *s.* of E. H. Sanders (formerly of the Austrian Service, and during the Crimea, adjutant of the British German Legion); *m.* Caroline, *s. d.* of Dr. Jukes, M.D. *Educ.:* King Alfred's Sch., Wantage, Berks; R.M. C., Kingston. Entered North West Mounted Police as Inspector, 1884; served throughout Riel Rebelllion, 1885 (medal); went to South Africa in command of squadron of Canadian Mounted Rifles, 1900 (twice wounded). *Decorated* for saving the life of Sergt. Tryon, whom he brought in on his own horse under a heavy fire, his horse being killed and he himself wounded; Supt. Royal North West Mounted Police, Canada, commanding Depot division and Regina District. *Recreations:* riding. *Address:* The Barracks, Regina, Sask.

SANDHAM, Henry, R.C.A.; *b.* Montreal, 1842; *s.* of John and Elizabeth Sandham, both of England; *m.* Agnes, *d.* of late John Fraser, of Scotland; one *d.* *Educ.:* Montreal. One of the charter members of the Royal Canadian Academy, 1880; removed to Boston, Mass., 1881, and twenty yrs. later to London, Eng; Medallist, Philadelphia Centennial Exhibition, 1876; London, 1886; Boston, 1881; Honours, Portugal 1901. Historical paintings and portraits now hanging in Parliament Buildings, Ottawa and Halifax; Smithsonian Institute, Washington; Town Hall, Lexington; State House, Boston; City Hall, Paisley, Scotland, etc.; exhibitor, Royal Academy, Salon, etc. *Address:* Quinta Lodge, South Parade, Bedford Park, London, W., England.

SANDYS, Edwyn Willis; journalist; *b.* Chatham, Ont., 9 June, 1860; *s.* Rev. Francis W. (D.D.) and Elizabeth A. B Moeran; unmarried. *Educ.:* privately. Was editor Canadian *Sportsman,* Toronto; journalist to Canadian Pacific Ry.; removed to New York and became editor *Outing,* and special writer for other publs. *Publications:* Upland Game Birds (Am. Sportsman's Library), 1902; Trapper Jim, 1903; Sportsman Joe, 1904; Sporting Sketches, 1905. *Address:* Care The Macmillan Co., New York.

SARGISON, Major Albert George, R.L.; *b.* Montreal, 1862; *s.* of George Andrew Sargison and Margaret Barnard; *m.* Fanny Adele Eugenie Jackson; four *s.* two *d.* *Educ.:* Victoria, B.C. pub. and High Sch. Joined staff of the *Colonist* on leaving Sch., in 1879; became half owner of that paper in 1890; managing director in 1902; retired from the firm in 1907. *Recreation:* yachting. *Address:* Victoria, B.C. *Club:* Pacific Coast, Victoria.

SASKATCHEWAN, Bishop of; *see* Rt. Rev. Jervois A. Newnham.

SAULT ST. MARIE, Bishop of; *see* Rt. Rev. David Joseph Scollard.

SAUNDERS, Charles Edward, B.A., Ph.D.; *b.* London, Ont., 2 Feb., 1867; *s.* of Dr. William Saunders and Sara Agnes Robinson; *m.* Mary Blackwell of Toronto. *Educ.:* London Coll. Inst., Toronto Univ., Johns Hopkins Univ., Baltimore, Md.; Harvard Coll., Cambridge; Cerealist of Dominion Experimental Farms since 1903. *Recreations:* photography, music. *Address:* Experimental Farm, Ottawa.

SAUNDERS, Miss Margaret Marshall; *b.* Milton, Queens Co., N.S., 1861; *d.* of Edward Manning Saunders, D.D., Baptist clergyman and author, Halifax, N.S., and Maria Kisboro Freeman; has traveled much in Europe and America; interested in philanthropic work. *Publications:* "My Spanish Sailor;" "Daisy;" "Beautiful Joe" (sold in 1909, 500,000 copies); has been translated into Swedish, German and Japanese languages; other books, novels and books for children, including The House of Armour, For the Other Boys' Sake, and other stories; Charles and his lamb; The King of the Park; Rose à Charlotte; Deficient Saints; Her Sailor; For His Country; Tilda Jane; Beautiful Joe's Paradise; The Story of the Graveleys; Nita; Princess Sukey; Alpatok, the story of an Eskimo Dog; Essay, the cause and prevention of Crime (awarded $300 prize by Am. Humane Educational Soc); Our Dumb Animals. *Address:* 28 Carleton St., Halifax, N.S.

SAUVALLE, Marc Paul, B.Sc. (France); translator, Geological Survey; *b.* Havre, France, 20 Feb., 1857; *s.* of Alphonse Sauvalle. and Aline Barbulee; *m.* Laure Lecomte; three *d.* *Educ.:* Lycee of Havre, St. Cyr Military Sch. Lieut. in French Army 5th Cuirassiers; editor "Trait d'Union," Mexico; arrived in Can., June, 1884; editor "*La Patrie,*" Montreal; special Parl. correspondent "*La Presse;*" editor "*Le Canada;*" now editor of French publications for the Geological Survey of Canada, Dept. of Mines; a former president of the Parl. Press Gallery. *Publications:* Louisiane-Mexique-Canada; Manuel des Assemblees Deliberances, Guide du Conciliateur; recueil de discours prepares. *Recreation:* fencing. *Address:* 375 Daly Ave., Ottawa.

SAVOIE, Francois T., M.P.; *b.* Plessisville, Que., 14 Feb., 1846; *s.* of Narcisse Savoie and Seraphine Cormier; *m.* (1st) Eugene Duplessis, (2nd) Sara Vigneault, (3rd) Alice Seguise. *Educ.:* Model Sch. of Plessisville, Que.; represents Megantic in the H. of C.; elected at g. e., 1904 and 1908. *Address:* Plessisville, Que.

SBARRETTI, Most Rev. Donatus, D.D., Archbishop of Ephesus, Apostolic Delegate to Canada; *b.* Montepranue, Umbria, Italy, 12 Nov., 1856; *s.* of Agostino Sbarretti, who is a brother of the late Cardinal Sbarretti. *Educ.:* Seminary of Spaleto and Apollinare Coll., Rome; ordained priest, 12 April, 1879; Professor of Ethics and Menutaute of the Propaganda for American Affairs; auditor of the Apostolic delegation in Washington, D.C., Jan., 1893; Bishop of Havana, Cuba, 14 Feb., 1900; Titular Archbishop of Ephesus, 1901; Apostolic Delegate to Canada, 26 Nov., 1902. *Address:* Apostolic Delegation, The Driveway, Ottawa.

SCHAFFNER, Fred. Lawrence, B.A., M.D., M.P.; *b.* South Williamstown, Annapolis Co., N.S., 18 Aug., 1855; *s.* of William C. and A. Schaffner; *m.* C. A. Allan, of Perth, Ont., 19 April, 1886. *Educ.:* Acadia Coll., N.S., and Trinity Coll., Toronto; a physician; has practiced medicine in Boissevain, Man., for 22 years; twice mayor; represented constituency of Souris, in Manitoba Leg. Ass., for five yrs.; first el. to H. of C., 1904; re-el. 1908. *Address:* Boissevain, Man. *Club:* Advance, Winnipeg.

SCHELL, Jacob Thomas; lumber manufacturer and contractor; *b.* Tp. of East Oxford, Oxford Co., Ont., 27 Dec., 1850; *s.* of Jacob Schell, and Catharine Smith; *m.* 1883, Sarah McIntyre, of Tilsonburg, Ont. *Educ.:* Pub. and Woodstock Gram. Schs. Was for many yrs. Town Councillor of Alexandria, Glengarry. Contractor for Canadian Northern Ontario Ry., between Hawkesbury and Ottawa. Unsuccessful can. for H. of C. at g. e., 1891; el. to H. of C. at g. e., 1900; re-el. at g. e., 1904; retired at g. e., 1908. *Address:* Alexandria, Ont.

SCHELL, Malcolm Smith, M.P.; *b.* County of Oxford, Ont., 13 Nov., 1865; *s.* of Jacob and Catharine Smith Schell; *m.* Josephine H.., *d.* of the Rev. A. E. Russ, Brantford; one *s.* two *d.* *Educ.:* Oxford pub. sch. and Woodstock Coll.; agriculturist, manufacturerer and wholesale dealer in lumber; also grower and exporter of apples; winner of prizes offered by the Dept. of Agriculture, Ont., for essays on "the advantages of rotation of crops treated from a practical and scientific standpoint, and "Apple culture and its importance as an article of commerce;" elected to the H. of C. in 1904 and in 1908; has taken a prominent part in all matters pertaining to agriculture and the marketing of Canadian products; Chairman of the Standing Committee on Agriculture and Colonization of the H. of C., 1909. *Address:* Woodstock, Ont.

SCHURMAN, Jacob Gould, M.A. (Lond.), D.Sc. (Edin.), LL.D. (Columbia, Yale, Edin.); Pres. of Cornell Univ., Ithaca, N.Y.; *b.* Freetown, P.E.I., 22 May, 1854; *s.* of the late Robert Schurman; *m.* 1884, Barbara Forest, *e. d.* of the late George Munro, of New York, three *s.* four *d.* *Educ.:* Frince of Wales Coll., Charlottetown, P.E.I.; Acadia Coll., N.S.; Univ. Coll., London; Univ. of Edinburgh, Heidelberg, Berlin, and Gottingen. Won Canadian Gilchrist Scholarship and Univ. Scholarship in Philosophy, Univ. of London; Hibbert Travelling Fellowship, 1878. Prof. of Eng. Lit., Political Economy, and Psychology, at Acadia Coll., N.S., 1880-84; Prof. of Philosophy, Dalhousie Coll., N.S., 1882-86; Sage prof. of Philosophy, Cornell Univ., 1886-92; pres. of U.S. Comn. to the Philippine Islands, 1899. *Publications:* "Kantian Ethics and the Ethics of Evolution;" "The Ethical Import of Darwinism;" "Belief of God;" "Agnosticism and Religion;" "The Genesis of the Critical Philosophy;" "Report of the First Philippine Commission;" "The Philippines, a Retrospect and Outlook." *Recreations:* golf, skating, tobogganing, walking. *Address:* Cornell Univ., Ithaca, New York, U.S.A.

SCHWEGEL, Dr. John; Consul of Austria-Hungary; *b.* Province of Carniola, Austria, 17 Feb., 1875; *m.* 1905, Angelina Keenly, of Brooklyn, N.Y., *Educ.:* Vienna (Orient Academy); dir. of the Univ. of Tyrol (Trenbruck); first Lieut. Dalmatia Mounted Rifles; arrived in Canada, 1909; in Consular Service since 1899, in Chicago, Pittsburg, Switzerland, Cape of Good Hope, Salonica (Turkey), New York. *Address:* Montreal.

SCOLLARD, Right Rev. David Joseph, S.L.T., Bishop of Sault St. Marie; *b.* Ennismore, Ont., 14 Nov., 1862; *s.* of John Scollard and Catharine O'Connor. *Educ.:* St. Michael's Coll., Toronto, and Grand Seminary, Montreal, Que.; ordained priest, 21 Dec., 1890; consecrated Bishop of Sault St. Marie, 24 Feb., 1905. *Address:* North Bay, Ont.

SCOTT, Lieut.-Col. B. A.; *b.* Quebec, 30 Sept., 1859; *m.* 1886, Josephine, *d.* of Hon. Joseph Shehyn, of Quebec, senator; five *s.* *Educ.:* Quebec High Sch.; a lumberman; commenced business in timber trade with the firm of Price Bros. & Co., at their mills on Saguenay River; Mayor of the Parish of Roberval for twelve yrs. and Mayor of the town of Roberval for two yrs. Acted as collector of H.M. Customs at Chicoutimi for several yrs., and Vice-Consul for Sweden and Norway and Republic of Uruguay, at same port. Pres., Saguenay Bd. of Trade; mem. Quebec Bd. of Trade. Joined company of infantry at Chicoutimi as Lieut.; became Capt.; joined 61st Regt.; retired with rank of Major to organize 18th Regt.; promoted command 10th Infantry Brigade. *Address:* 3 Genevieve Ave., Quebec. *Clubs:* Garrison, Quebec; New York Yacht, City, New York.

SCOTT, D'Arcy; Asst. Chief Commr., Bd. of Ry. Commrs. for Canada; *b.* Ottawa, 8 March, 1872; *s.* of Sir Richard W. Scott and Mary A. Heron; *m.* Mary Emma Davis; four *s.* two *d.* *Educ.:* Ottawa Univ.: Osgoode Hall Law Sch., Toronto. Called to Bar of Ont., 7 June, 1895; Mayor of Ottawa, 1907-8; apptd. Asst. Chief Commr., Bd. of Ry. Commrs. for Canada, Sept., 1908, when resigned mayoralty of Ottawa.

Pres. Can. Club of Ottawa, 1909-10. *Recreation:* golf. *Address:* 324 Chapel St., Ottawa. *Clubs:* Rideau, Country, Hunt, Golf, Ottawa.

SCOTT, Duncan Campbell, F.R.S.; *b.* 2 Aug., 1862; *s.* of Rev. William Scott, parents English and Scotch; *m.* 1894, Belle W. Botsford, a prominent violinist, *d.* of late Geo. W. Botsford, Boston, Mass.; one *d.* *Educ.:* Canadian Common Sch.; Stanstead Coll. Entered Canadian Civil Service, 1879; now chief accountant, Dept. of Indian Affairs, since 1893. *Publications:* The Magic House (poems); Labor and the Angel (poems); In the Village of Viger (fiction); The Life of Simcoe (Makers of Canada); New World Lyrics and Ballads; numerous short stories and poems in American and Canadian magazines; joint-editor with Pelham Edgar, Ph.D., of Makers of Canada, a series of historical biography. *Recreations:* music, canoeing, skating, etc. *Address:* 108 Lisgar St., Ottawa.

SCOTT, Rev. Frederick George, M.A., D.C.L., F.R.S.C.; *b.* Montreal, 1861; *s.* of late William Edward Scott, M.D. of Montreal, Professor of Anatomy, McGill Univ. for nearly forty years, and Elizabeth Sproston, both parents of English birth; *m.* 1887, Amy, *d.* of late George Brooks-Barnet, England; five *s.* one *d.* *Educ.:* Montreal High Sch.; Proprietary Sch., Mc Gill; Bishop's Coll., Lennoxville; Kings' Coll., London. Deacon, 1884; Master in St. John's Sch., 1884; priest, 1886; curate, of Coggeshall, Essex, 1886; rector of Drummondville, Que., 1887; curate of St. Matthew's ,Que., 1896; F.R.S.C., 1900; Rector of St. Matthew's, Quebec, since 1899; Canon of Quebec Cathedral since 1906. *Publications:* Soul's Quest, and other Poems, 1888; Elton Hazlewood, 1892; My Lattice, and other Poems, 1894; The Unnamed Lake, and other Poems, 1897; Poems Old and New, 1900; The Hymn of Empire and other Poems, 1906; The Key of Life, 1907, etc. *Address:* St. Matthew's Rectory, Quebec.

SCOTT, George Adam, J.P., M.L.A.; *b* Winnipeg, Man., 11 Dec., 1875; *s.* John Scott and Jane Bell; *m.* Etta M. Elliott, of Hamilton, Ont.; one *s.* two *d.* *Educ.:* Brandon Coll. Inst., and Winnipeg Normal Sch.; raised on a farm at Deloraine, Man.; sch. teacher at 20 years of age; principal, Wawanesa Sch. four years; elec. to the Sask. Leg. Assembly, 1908. *Recreation:* curling. *Address:* Davidson, Sask.

SCOTT, James Guthrie; *b.* Quebec, 13 Feb., 1847; *s.* of Hugh Erskine Scott and Margaret Chillas; *m.* (1st) Sophy Mary Jackson; (2nd) Cordelia Mary Jackson; three *s.* two *d.* *Educ.:* Quebec High Sch.; General Manager of the Quebec and Lake St. John Ry.; retired in 1908; built that road and also the Great Northern, 500 miles in all; both are now part of the Canadian Northern System; was chief promotor of the Trans.-Canada Ry., the surveys and agitation for which resulted in the selection of the Northern route for the National Transcontinental Ry. from Quebec to Winnipeg; member of Council, Quebec Board of Trade; director of the Quebec Geographical Society. *Address:* Quebec. *Clubs:* Garrison, Quebec; Rideau, Ottawa.

SCOTT, Miss Mary McKay; *b.* Ottawa, 17 Aug., 1851; *d.* of Alexander Scott and Alison McKay Scott. *Educ.:* Ottawa, private sch., Bute House, Montreal; a Sunday Sch. teacher for 30 years; Church work (St. Andrew's); Woman's Christian Temperance Union; Dom. Supt., Y.W.C.T.U.; editor Woman's *Journal* for nine years; vice-pres., Y.W.C.A.; ex-pres., Y.W.C.A.; pres., Supt. W.C.T.U. *Address:* Aberdeen Chambers, 291 Sparks Street, Ottawa.

SCOTT, Hon. Sir Richard William, K.C., LL.D., K.C.M.G., Senator; *b.* Prescott, Ont., 24 Feb., 1825; *e. s.* of William J. Scott, M.D., and Sarah McDonell; *m.* Mary A. Heron (*dec.*) *Educ.:* Prescott. Barrister, 1840; Mayor of Bytown, 1852; M.P. for Ottawa, 1857-63; mem. Ont. Leg. Ass., 1867-73; Speaker, 1871; Commr. of Crown Lands, 1872-53; apptd. to the Senate, 1874; Secretary of State, 1874-78, and again 1896-1908; Leader of the Opposition in Senate, 1879-96; carried through Parlt. School Bill giving Roman Ca holics right to establish separate schools, 1863; Canada Temperance (local option) Act known as "Scott Act," 1875; drafted address to Queen Victoria, giving reasons why she should select Ottawa as seat of Government; leader of the Govt. in the Senate, 1896-1908. *Recreation:* golf. *Address:*274 Daly Ave., Ottawa. *Clubs:* Rideau, Golf Ottawa.

SCOTT, Lieut.-Col. Robert Kellock, D.S.O.; *b.* Perth, Lanark Co., Ont., 20 Nov., 1871; *s.* of Col. Thomas Scott, Collector of Customs, Winnipeg, Man.; *m.* 1899, Edith, *d.* of G. Ferris W. Mortimer, of Romsey, Hants Co., Eng.; one *s.* one *d.* *Educ.:* Roy. Mil. Coll., Kingston, Ont. Apptd. 2nd Lieut., Royal Artillery, 16 July, 1891; Captain, R. A., 1899; served in North West Rebellion, 1885 (medal); served in South Africa, 1899-02 (despatches twice, brevet of Major, Queen's medal, 3 clasps, King's medal, 2 clasps, D.S.O.). Joined Army Ordnance Dept., 26 April, 1896; promoted Ordnance Officer, 2nd class, with rank of Lieut.-Col., 18 April, 1907; apptd. for service with Canadian Forses, 20 May, 1907; now holds appointment of Principal Ordnance Officer and Director of Clothing and Equipment. *Address:* 4 Rideau Apts., Ottawa.

SCOTT, Hon. Walter; Premier of Saskatchewan; *b.* London Tp., Co. Middlesex, Ont., 27 Oct., 1867; *s.* of George Scott and Isabella Telfer; *m.* 1890, Jessie Florence, *d.* of the late E. B. Read of Regina, formerly of Smith's Falls, Ont. *Educ.:* in the public schs.; a printer and journalist; partner in the *Standard*, Regina, 1892-93; proprietor and editor "*The Times,*" Moose Jaw, 1894-95; purchased in 1895, *The Leader*, Regina, from its founder, the late Nicholas Flood Davin; edited and managed the same until 1900; pres., Western Canada Press, 1899; pres., the Regina Land and Investment Co.; elec. to the H. of C. for Assiniboia West. 1900 and 1904; took part in negotiations and passage of Acts creating provinces of Alberta and Sask.; was invited 5 Sept., 1905, to form first Sask. Ministry, which was sustained at the Polls, 13 Dec., 1905; elec. for Lumsden District to

Assembly; on redistribution, 1908, Lumsden District disappeared; elec. for Swift Current 14 Aug., 1908, when administration was sustained with 27 seats against 14. *Address:* Regina, Sask.

SCOTT, William Duncan; Supt. of Immigration; *b.* Dundas, Ont., 7 Oct., 1861; *s.* of James Scott, and Margaret McEwan. *Educ.:* Dundas High Sch.; in C. R. Ry. land department for several years; later in service of Manitoba Government; Dept. of Agriculture, Dominion Government for 4 years, as exhibition Commr.; Supt. of Immigration, 1903 to date. *Address:* Aylmer Apartments, Ottawa. *Clubs:* Laurentian, Golf, Hunt, Ottawa.

SEALEY, William Oscar, M.P.; *b.* Waterdown, Wentworth Co., Ont., 26 Jan., 1879; *s.* of Charles Sealey and Mary Ann Eaton; *m.* Agnes Annie Forbes. *Educ.:* Waterdown pub. and high sch.; Reeve of East Flamboro; member of Wentworth County Council; unsuccessful candidate for H. of C., 1900; elec. in 1904, but was unseated; unsuccessful candidate in 1905; elec. in 1908 by a large majority; advocate of good roads, free roads, enlarged markets, higher tariff on agricultural products, and farmers' interests generally. *Address:* 61 Hunter St. W., Hamilton, Ont. *Clubs:* Ontario; Hamilton.

SEATH, Major David; Sec. and Treas. of the Harbor Commission of Montreal; *b.* Montreal, 9 May, 1847; *s.* of the late Robert Seath, a wholesale clothing merchant of Montreal, and Margaret Stephen. *Educ.:* Montreal High Sch. Entered employ of his father, 1864. Was with Tyre, Perkins & Lajoie, accountants, assignees, etc., afterwards becoming Thibaudeau & Seath, 1873-1895; pres. and mgr. of Perrault Publishing Co., 1895-1898,t when apptd. Sec. and Treas. of the Harbour Com. of Montreal, which position he still holds. Served in militia 1863-1905. Took part in Fenian Raid, 1866, 1870 (medal and two clasps). Attained rank of capt. in Sixth Fusiliers, and became paymaster of the Prince of Wales Fusiliers, retiring in 1905 with hon. rank of Major. Has the Colonial Auxiliary Forces Officers' Long Service Decoration. J.P. and Commr. for receiving affidavits outside the Prov. of Ont., to be used in Ont.; commr. Superior Ct. of Prov. of Que. *Address:* Montreal.

SEATH, John, M.A., LL.D.; Superintendent of Education for Ontario; *b.* Auchtermuchty, Fifeshire, Scotland, 6 Jan., 1844; *s.* of John Seath, Manager Gas Works, Monaghan, Ireland, and Isabel Hinkless; *m.* Caroline Louisa McKenzie; one *s.* two *d.* *Educ.:* Monaghan, Ireland; Glasgow Univ., and Queen's Univ., Belfast, Irel.; arrived in Canada, 1861; from 1861 to 1884, was principal of Brampton, Oshawa and Dundas High Schs., and St. Catharines Coll. Inst.; from 1884 to 1906, was Inspector of High Schs. and Coll. Insts.; apptd. in 1906 to his present position as Superintendent of Education for Ontario. *Publications:* High Sch. Gram., and reports on Education. *Address:* 86 Walmer Road, Toronto.

SEDGWICK, Rev. Thomas, D.D.; *b.* Aberdeen, Scot., 5 May, 1838; *s.* of Robert Sedgwick, D.D., Pastor of the Pres. Ch. at Musquodoboit, N.S., and Jessie Middleton; *m.* 1868, Christina Patterson, *d.* of the latet Roderick Macgregor, of New Glasgow, N.S.; one *s.* one *d.* *Educ.:* King's Coll., Aberdeen; Edinburgh; Coll. of the Pres. Ch. of N.S. Came to Canada, 1857. Ordained min. of the Pres. Ch. in Can., at Tatamagouche, N.S., 1860; Clerk of the Synod of the Maritime Provinces, 1885; Moderator of the Genl. Assem. of the Pres. Ch. in Can., 1903. *Address:* Tatamagouche, N.S.

SENKLER, John Harrold, B.A., K.C.; *b.* Brockville, Ont., 21 July, 1866; *s.* of Edmund John Senkler and Margaret McLeod Cumming; *m.* Margaret Hargrave Richards; two *s.* four *d.* *Educ.:* Up. Can. Coll., Toronto Univ., and Osgoode Hall; a barrister. *Address:* 1889 Harro St., Vancouver, B.C. *Clubs:* Vancouver, Commercial, Vancouver, B.C.; Union Club, Victoria, B.C.

SEQUIN, Paul Arthur, B.S., LL.B., M.P.; *b.* Charlemagne, Que., 2 Oct., 1875; *s.* of Felix Seguin and Vitaline Noiseux; *m.* Anna Rivest; one *s.* two *d.* *Educ.:* L'Assomption Coll., Montreal Coll., and Laval Univ., Montreal; apptd. Notary in Sept., 1898; practiced in Terrebonne, Que.; Sec.-Treas. of St. Paul Ermite; was for some time, Sec.-Treas. of the Mnuicipality; elec. M.P., 1908. *Address:* St. Paul Ermite, Que.

SERVICE, Robert W.; poet; *b.* Preston, Lancashire, Eng., 1876; of Scotch descent; removed at early age to Scotland. *Educ.:* Glasgow. Arrived Can., 1897; worked for several yrs. on Vancouver Island in variety of occupations; clerk in Canadian Bank of Commerce at Whitehorse branch; thence to Dawson; resigned clerkship in bank to devote himself to literature. *Publications:* Songs of a Sourdough, Ballads of a Cheechaco. *Recreations:* hunting, angling. *Address:* Dawson, Y.T.

SETON, Ernest Thompson; (nom de plume, Seton-Thompson); *b.* South Shields, Durham, 14 Aug., 1860; *m.* 1896, Grace Gallatin, of California (Sacramento); one *d.* *Educ.:* Toronto, London Royal Academy. Descended direct from George Seton, last Earl of Winton; went to Canada at age of 5, lived in the backwoods till 1870, then went to Toronto to be educated at the public schools and at the Collegiate Inst.; went to London for art training, 1879-81; went to Manitoba to follow natural history; became naturalist to the Government of that province; in 1898 he published his "Wild Animals I have Known", the biographies of 8 wild animals, 10 editions in 1 year; began lecturing on Wild Animals in 1899; started an Outdoor Life movement, called the Woodcraft Indians, which now has some 80,000 followers in the United States, 1901; Asso. mem. R.C.A.A. *Publications:* Wild Animals I have Known; Art Anatomy of Animals; Birds of Manitoba; Mammals of Manitoba; Trail of the Sandhill Stag; Biography of a Grizzly; Lives of the Hunted, 1901; Two Little Savages; Pictures of Wild Animals; Monarch, the Big Bear; Woodmyth and Fable; Animal Heroes; Birch Bark Roll of the Woodcraft Indians; Natural History of the Ten Commandments; Life Histories of Northern Animals; Biography of a silver fox, 1909. *Recreations:* camera-hunting, *i. e.* hunting big game with the camera; natural history and woodcraft. *Address:* Wyndygoul, Coscob, Conn. U.S.A.

SHAKESPEARE, Noah, J.P.; *b.* Brierly Hill, Staffordshire, Eng., 26 Jan., 1839; *s.* of Noah and Hannah Shakespeare; *m.* *m.* Eliza Jane Pearson; three *s.* one *d.* *Educ.:* at private sch.; arrived in Canada, 11 Jan., 1883, having sailed from London, Aug., 1862, around Cape Horn; in 1885, was pres. of the B.C. Agricultural Association; served as Municipal Councillor for four years; elec. Mayor of the City of Victoria, in 1882; elec. to the H. of C., 1882, and re-elec. in 1887; apptd. Postmaster, Victoria, 1 Jan., 1888. *Address:* Victoria, B.C.

SHALLOW, Francis Dominick; *b.* St. George, Iberville Co., Que., 3 Aug., 1853; *s.* of Thomas Shallow and Jane Sherry; *m.* Annie Hamall; five *s.* two *d.* Proprietor and publisher of "*Le Moniteur du Commerce*," the oldest land leading French Commercial Journal in Canada; proprietor, publisher and editor of the Magazine of Insurance and Epitome of Finance. *Address:* Montreal, and Senneville, Que. *Club:* Albany, Toronto.

SHANNON, Robert Walker, M.A., barrister; *b.* Portglenone, Co. Antrim, Irel., 2 Nov., 1856; *s.* of James Shannon, for many yrs. Postmaster of Kingston, Ont., and Letitia Leatham; unmarried. *Educ.:* Kingston Gram. Sch.; Queen's Univ., Kingston. Called to the bar of Ont., 1880, and practised his prof. there for some yrs.; was editor simultaneously of his brother's paper, the *Kingston News.* Member of the City Council of Kingston for 6 yrs.; unsuccessful can. for the Mayoralty. In 1892, with his brother, Major. L. W. Shannon, purchased the Ottawa *Citizen*, which he edited until 1897. Resumed practice of law, in Ottawa, and later at Dawson, Y.T. Has now large practice at Saskatoon, Sask.; town solicitor. *Recreations:* music, walking. *Address:* Saskatoon, Sask.

SHANNON, Samuel Leonard; *b.* Halifax N.S., 18 Jan., 1862; *s.* of the late Hon. Samuel Leonard Shannon, D.C.L., and Annie Fellows; *m.* Beatrice Maude, *d.* of late Lt.-Col. Thomas Bacon, of Ottawa; one *s.* four *d.* Comptroller and Treasurer Intercolonial Railway of Canada; Captain, R.O., Canadian Militia; entered Canadian Civil Service, Feb., 1880; apptd. to Dept. of Railways and Canals, Ottawa, Jan., 1881; chief accountant, Oct., 1889; transferred to Intercolonial Railway as Comptroller and Treasurer, Oct., 1906; served during the North West Rebellion, 1885, as Lieut., York and Simcoe Batt. (medal). *Address:* Moncton, N.B.

SHARPE, Major Samuel Simpson, B.A., LL.B., M.P.; *b.* Zephyr, Scott Tp., Ont. Co. 13 March, 1873; *s.* of George Sharpe, formerly of Suffolk, Eng., and Mary Ann Simpson, born near Londonderry, Irel.; *m.* 1903, Mabel Edith Crosby, *g. d.* of Joseph Gould, ex-M.P. *Educ.:* Uxbridge public and high sch., Toronto Univ., Osgoode Hall; grad. Toronto Univ. with first class honours, 1895; grad. in law from Osgoode Hall, taking two scholarships during the course, 1898; practices law in Uxbridge; first elec. to H. of C. for North Ontario, 1908; Major in 14th Regt., and has been in the Militia for over 20 years; an enthusiastic athlete, holding championships at Toronto Univ. and of the Province. *Address:* Uxbridge, Ont. *Club:* Albany, Toronto.

SHARPE, William Henry, M.P.; *b.* Scott. Tp., Ont. Co., 19 April, 1868; *s.* of George Sharpe, English, and Mary Ann Sharpe, Irish; *m.* 20 May, 1893, Cora A. Breston; one *s.* one *d.* *Educ.:* Uxbridge, Ont., and at Belleville Business Coll.; pres. of the R. A. Garrett Co., carrying on their general store, but sold out in 1907; has been councillor for the village of Manitou for six years, and Mayor, 1908; in 1904, ran against the late Hon. T. Greenway for the H. of C., and was defeated by 180; first elected to the H. of C. for Lisgar, 1908; Methodist; Conservative. *Address:* Manitou, Man.

SHARPLES, Hon. John, M.L.C., Quebec; *b.* Quebec, 1848; *s.* of the late Hon. John Sharples, M.L.C., one of founders of lumber firm of W. & J. Sharples of Quebec and Liverpool; *m.* Margaret, *d.* of the late Hon. Charles Alleyn, Sheriff of Quebec. *Educ.:* St. Mary's Coll., Montreal. Joined his father's firm, 1871, and has been connected with it ever since. Pres., Union Bank of Can. and *Chronicle* Printing Co.; director of Quebec Light and Power and Quebec Steamship Cos. Was Harbour Commr. for twenty yrs.; mem. Quebec City Council for five yrs. Apptd. to Legis. Council of Quebec, 1894. Made a Knight of St. Gregory the Great by Pope Pius X, Dec., 1907. *Address:* 65 Esplanade, Quebec. *Club:* Garrison, Quebec.

SHATFORD, Lytton Wilmot, M.L.A.; *b.* at Hubbards, Halifax Co., N.S., 14 Feb., 1873; *s.* of Henry A. Shatford and Cecelia Victoria Dauphine; *m.* 1897, Lavinia Bartlett; three *s.* one *d.* *Educ.:* Halifax Co., N.S., pub. sch.; was chairman of School Board and License Commissioner; elec. to B.C. Provincial Legislature in 1903; re-elec. in 1907 and 1909. *Address:* Hedley, B.C.

SHAUGHNESSY, Sir Thomas George. K.C.V.O., Knight; *b.* Milwaukee, Wis., 6 Oct., 1853; *s.* of Thomas Shaughnessy; *m.* 1880, Miss Nagle; two *s.* three *d.* Chicago, Milwaukee and St. Paul, from 1869 to 1882; General purchasing agent C.P.R., 1882; subsequently Assistant General Manager; vice-pres., 1891; pres. since 1899; knighted by H.R.H. the Duke of Cornwall and York, 1901; president and director of a number of Railway Companies, all of which are directly or indirectly connected with the C.P.R.; Knight of grace of the order of the Hospital of St. John of Jerusalem, 1910. *Address:* 905 Dorchester St. W., Montreal. *Clubs:* Mount Royal, St. James, Montreal; Rideau, Ottawa.

SHAW, Charles Lewis; barrister; *b.* Perth, Ont., 16 Feb., 1863; *s.* of Wm. McNairn Shaw, M.L.A., and Eliza J. Dunham; *m.* 1905, Isabelle, *d.* of J. H. Thompson, of Toronto. *Educ.:* Trinity Coll., Toronto. Called to bar of Man., 1884, and practised in Edmonton. Nile voyager, 1884 and correspondent in Egypt for Winnipeg *Times;* afterwards saw service in Turkey. Returned to Canada, 1886, and resumed law practice and journalism; war correspondent, S. Africa for syndicate Can. newspapers.

Resident of Winnipeg past five years; engaged in legal practice and frequent contrib. to magazines and daily press. *Publications:* short stories (McClure); Random reminiscences of a Nile Voyager. *Address:* Osborne St., Fort Rouge, Winnipeg.

SHAW, William; *b.* Quebec, 1841; *s.* of the late John Shaw, of English descent; unmarried. *Educ.:* Quebec High Sch. Joined firm of his uncle, S. J. Shaw, wholesale hardware merchants, as junior clerk; admitted a partner 1870; incorporated The Chinic Hardware Co., 1887, of which he is now pres. and mng. dir. Dir., Union Bank of Can., Light and Power Co., Quebec Ry., Leboutilller Bros. Co.; gov. Jeffery Hale Hospital, Quebec. *Address:* Maple Av., Quebec. *Club:* Garrison.

SHEARER, Rev. John G., B.A., D.D.; *b.* Oxford, Ont., 9 Aug., 1859; *s.* of John Shearer and Margaret Cowan; *m.* Elizabeth A. Johnston, Burford, Ont. *Educ.:* Western High Sch., Brantford Coll. Inst., Toronto Univ., and Knox Coll.; ordained Presbyterian Minister, 1888; Pastor Caledonia, Ont., and Erskine Church, Hamilton, till 1900; seven years general secretary, Lord's Day Alliance of Canada; now general secretary of Moral and Social Reform and of Evangelism of the Presbyterian Church in Canada, and of the Moral and Social Reform Council of Canada. *Address:* Toronto. Ont.

SHEHYN, Hon. Joseph; Senator; Kt. Com. of St. Gregory the Great; Officer of the Order of Leopold; *b.* Quebec, 10 Nov., 1829; of Irish and Canadian extraction; *m.* (1st) 1858, Marie Zoe Virginie, *e. d.* of Ambroise Verret, (2nd) 1892, Mrs. Josephine Leduc, *nee* Beliveau. *Educ.:* Quebec Seminary and by priv. tuition. Ex-pres. of the Quebec Bd. of Trade and ex-mem. of the Quebec Harbour Com. Was Prov. Treas. in the Quebec Legis., in Mr. Mercier's Admn., 1887-1891; apptd. Minister without portfolio in Mr. Marchand's Admn., 26 May, 1897. El. to Legislature at g. e., 1875; re-el. at each succeeding el. up to time of being called to the Senate, 5 Feb., 1900. *Address:* 75 Grand Allée, Quebec. *Club:* Garrison, Quebec.

SHEPHERD, Francis J., M.D., C.M., LL.D., F.R.C.S., Edin.; surgeon; *b.* Como, Que., 1851; *s.* of the late Robert W. Shepherd and Mary C. de Les Derniers; *m.* 1878, Lilias G. Torrance (*dec.*); one *s.* two *d.* *Educ.:* Montreal High Sch., McGill Univ., Univ. of Vienna. Apptd. demonstrator of Anatomy at McGill, 1875; Prof. of Anatomy, 1883; now Dean of the Medical Faculty and Prof. of Anatomy, McGill Univ.; Senior Surgeon, Montreal Gen. Hospital. Mem. of Congress of American Physicians and Surgeons; was vice-pres., American Dermatological Assn. and pres. of Canadian Medical Assn. and Montreal Medico-Chirurgical Soc. Is a Fellow of American Surgical Assn. and International Soc. of Surgery; pres. Montreal Art Assn. Cr. Doctor of Laws at Edinburgh, 1905, and by Harvard Univ., 1906; F.R.C.S.E., 1905. *Publications:* One of the authors of the American Text Book of Surgery (The American System of Surgery), and the Quarterly Retrospect of Surgery, and has contributed to numerous medical papers. Has written largely on anatomy and surgery for Woods' Reference Hand Book of the Medical Sciences. *Address:* 152 Mansfield St., Montreal. *Clubs:* Mount Royal, University, Montreal Hunt.

SHEPPARD, John Albert, M.L.A ; *b.* Mount Forest, Ont., 1 Sept., 1875; *s.* of John Sheppard and Margaret Reid; *m.* Florence Herring of Belfontain, Ont.; one *s.* one *d.* Taught sch. in Ont., two years, and eight years at Moosejaw, Sask.; farmed for five years; at present in partnership with H. E. Anderson, Insurance and Real Estate, Moosejaw; went west in 1897; elec. to represent Moosejaw in first Legislature of Province of Sask., 1905; re-elec. 1908, and apptd. Deputy Speaker. *Address:* Moosejaw, Sask.

SHERBROOKE, Bishop of; *see* Rt. Rev. Paul LaRocque.

SHERWOOD, Lieut.-Col. Arthur Percy, M.V.O., C.M.G., A.D.C.; *b.* Ottawa, 18 March, 1854; *s.* of Edward Sherwood, of Mount Sherwood, Ottawa, and Isabella P. Turner; *m.* 1883, Esther Alberta, *d.* of James Dyson and Esther Slater of Ottawa; two *s.* four *d.* *Educ.:* Ottawa Gram. Sch. Dep. Sheriff of Carleton, 1877; Chief of Police, Ottawa, 1879; Supt. of Dominion Police, 1882; Commissioner of Dominion Police for Canada since 1885; has charge of Secret Service; officially thanked by the Government of Canada for special services rendered in connection with obtaining certain evidence for the Behring Sea Arbitration (Order in Council, 13 Oct., 1893); was responsible to the Government for the safety of Their Royal Highnesses the Prince and Princess of Wales during their stay in Canada, and directed the police arrangements at the various points visited, accompanying the royal party throughout, 1901, and again in connection with the visit of the P. of W. to Quebec in 1908; specially mentioned by His Royal Highness in a letter to the Governor-General published in the Canada Gazette, 26th Oct., 1901; military career began 1884, as 2nd Lieut., Governor General's Foot Guards; Lieut., 1885; transferred to 43rd Rifles as Captain, 1886; Major, 1889; Lieut.-Col., 1898; at present O. C. 8th Infantry Brigade; Hon. A.D.C. to H.E. the Earl of Minto, Governor Gen., 1899; and to H. E. Earl Grey, 1905; member of the Canadian rifle teams which competed at Wimbledon, 1885 and 1889; President Canadian Military Rifle League and Commandant Canadian Rifle Team at Bisley, 1903. *Address:* 81 Laurier Avenue West, Ottawa. *Clubs:* Rideau, Laurentian, Country, Golf, Hunt, Ottawa.

SHERWOOD, Wm. Albert, A.R.C.A., O.S.A.; *b.* Omemee, Ont., 1 Aug., 1855; father, English; mother, Irish; unmarried. *Educ.:* Omemee Gram. Sch. Began the study of portrait painting at an early period of life; has painted many Can. genre pictures, amongst which are The Gold Prospector, in the possession of the Ont. Government; The Canadian Rancher; The Canadian Backwoodsman, exhibited at the British Colonial Exhibition, London, England, 1902; The Negotiation, in the possession of Dominion Government. Chief portraits.—Hon. G. W. Ross, Premier of Ontario, Rev. Chas. Scadding, D.D., Rev.

Geo. F. Sherwood, Dr. Samuel Passmore May, G.L.H., Art Superintendent of Ontario Col. Gunsaulus, and others. Life member Can. Inst. *Publications:* articles in the leading magazines of Canada; in the Encyclopædia of Canada; and Lectures upon the National Spirit in Art. *Recreations:* walking, swimming, canoeing. *Address:* 2½ Queen St., East., Toronto.

SHORTT, Adam, F.R.S. (Can.); *b.* near London, Ont., 24 Nov., 1859; *s.* of George S. Short and Mary Shields, both from Scot.; *m.* 1887, Elizabeth Smith, M.D., of Hamilton, one of the first women in Canada, who obtained the degree of M.D.; one *s.* two *d.* *Educ.:* Queen's Glasgow and Edinburgh Univ. Has specially devoted himself to a study of Canadian economic and political development, involving a close study of French and British colonial policies; after his return to Canada, became lecturer and afterwards professor of Political Science in Queen's Univ., Kingston; apptd. in 1908, one of two Commissioners of the Canadian Civil Service. *Publications:* a series of papers on the History of Canadian Currency, Banking and Exchange, published in the Journal of the Canadian Bankers' Association; Imperial Preferential Trade, from a Canadian point of view; among numerous articles and reviews may be mentioned, Social Life of Canada, The Nicaragua Canal and the Clayton-Bulwer Treaty, In Defence of Millionaires, Some Aspects of the Imperial Problem, in the Canadian Magazine; edited with Dr. Doughty, "Documents relating to the Constitutional History of Canada, 1759-1971;" "Life of Lord Sydenham," (makers of Canada series). *Recreations:* gardening and boating. *Address:* 5 Marlborough Ave., Ottawa.

SHORTT, Mrs. Elizabeth Smith, M.D.; *b.* Winona, Ont., 18 Jan., 1859; *d.* of Sylvester Smith and Isabella Magee; *m.* Prof. Adam Shortt, Civil Service Commissioner; one *s.* two *d.* *Educ.:* by Governess, also Hamilton Coll. Inst., and Queen's Univ.; one of the first women in Canada to obtain the degree of M.D. *Publications:* newspaper articles. *Address:* 5 Marlborough Ave., Ottawa.

SHUTT, Frank Thomas, M.A. (Tor.), F.R.I.C., F.R.S.C.; *b.* London, Eng., 15 Sept., 1859; *s.* of William D. and Charlotte Shutt. *Educ.:* by private tuition and Toronto Univ.; arrived in Canada 1870; trained in laboratory of Professor Ellis, Public Analyst, Toronto, previous to taking Univ. course; Fellow in Chemistry; Toronto Univ.; Chemist to the Dominion Experimental Farms since 18 July, 1887; *Recreations:* music, photography. *Address:* Central Experimental Farm, Ottawa.

SICOTTE, Louis Wilfrid; Stipendiary Magistrate, Montreal; *b.* Boucherville, Que., 10 Dec., 1838; *s.* of J. B. Sicotte, and Josephte Cere; *m.* Marie Malvina, *d.* of Dr. Louis Giard, Sec. of Prov. Bureau of Educ.; five *s.* six *d.* *Educ.:* St. Hyacinthe Coll. Was prop. and ed. of the *Colonisateur;* priv. sec. to late Sir George Cartier; employed in Montreal Registry Office. Registrar of the cos. of Hochelaga and Jacques Cartier; pres. of the Numismatic Soc. of Montreal; pres. of the Historical Soc. of Montreal. *Publications:* Extracts from the Registers of Montreal and adjacent counties; sketch of Michel Bibaud. *Addresses:* 23 Laval Av., Montreal; Dorionville and Fraserville (summer).

SIFTON, Hon. A. L., M.A., LL.B., K.C.; *b.* 26 Oct., 1858; *s.* of Hon. John W. and Kate Sifton; *m.* 1882, Mary H. Deering. *Educ.:* various public sch.; Wesley Coll., and Victoria Univ. Called to Bar, 1883; practised law; first elected to Territorial Legislature, 1898; re-elected by accl., 1901, on taking office as Treasurer and Commissioner Public Works; Chief Justice of Alberta since 1905. *Address:* Edmonton, Alta.

SIFTON, Hon. Clifford, B.A., P.C., M. P.; *b.* Tp. of London, Middlesex, Ont., 10 Mar., 1861; *s.* of John W. Sifton, formerly Speaker of the Manitoba Assembly, and Kate Sifton; *m.* 1884, Elizabeth Arma, *d.* of H. T. Burrows, late of Ottawa; five *s.* *Educ.:* Victoria Coll., Cobourg, Ont., Prince of Wales' Medal, 1880. Called to the Man. bar, 1882; practised in Brandon; created Q.C. by Dominion patent, 1895; elected to Man. Legislature for North Brandon, 1888, and continued member until 1896; Attorney-General and Minister of Education Greenway Administration, 1891; codified laws relating to civil procedure in Man.; conducted negotiations on behalf of Man., with Dominion authorities in reference to the Man. school question; retired from Manitoba Government and entered Sir Wilfrid Laurier's Administration as Minister of the Interior and Superintendent-General of Indian Affairs, 1896; resigned 1905 on account of disagreement with Sir Wilfrid Laurier regarding educational clauses of bills to establish the provinces of Alberta and Sask.; agent of the British Government before the Alaska Boundary Tribunal, 1903; Chairman of Commission on Conservation of natural resources of Canada 1909; first elected to H. of C., for Brandon, Man., 1896; re-elected, 1900, 1904, 1908. *Address:* 215 Metcalfe Street, Ottawa; Assiniboine Lodge, Mallorytown, Ont. (June to Oct.) *Clubs:* Manitoba, Winnipeg; Rideau, Ottawa.

SIMMONS, Thomas Lockwood, C.E., B.A., (Univ. N.B.); *b.* Lakeville, Sunbury Co., N.B., 17 Jan., 1872; *s.* of James Edward Simmons and Hannah Burpee; *m.* Winifred M. Dick; one *s.* *Educ.:* Coll. Sch., Fredericton, and Univ. of N.B.; grad. in 1893; on railway work from that time until 1898; from 1898 to 1901, in charge of work deepening channel on river reaches of Lake St. Francis; in 1901, apptd. inspecting engineer of Dept. of Railways and Canals; in 1904 apptd. inspecting engineer Board of Railway Commissioners for Canada. *Recreation:* golf. *Address:* 92 James St., Ottawa.

SIMPSON, Louis, J.P.; *b.* Manchester, Eng., 15 Feb., 1853; *s.* of Thomas Simpson and Maria Gillett; *m.* Ellen Ashton, of Darwin, Lancashire, Eng.; two *s.* *Educ.:* Great Ealing School, primary; completed education under tutelage of the Rev. W. W. Wilson, B.A., Oxford; learned the business of cotton spinning and manufacturing at the mills of his elder brother, Albert Simpson, of Preston, Lancashire; came to Canada in 1887 and assumed management of the Nova

Scotia Cotton Co.; management of the Montreal Cotton Co., 1 June, 1888 for twelve years; spent 5 years in furtherance of the electric smelting of iron ores; resumed management of the Montreal Cotton Co., 1 Sept., 1905; resigned 30 Jan., 1909, to complete the work commenced on electric smelting of iron ores. *Address:* Fitzroy Harbor, Ont. *Club:* Rideau, Ottawa.

SINCLAIR, John Howard, LL.B., M.P.; *b.* Goshen, Guysboro Co., N.S., 27 May, 1848. *s.* Donald Sinclair and Jane McNeil; *m.* Jessie M. Carmichael, *d.* of the late Senator J. W. Carmichael of New Glasgow, N.S.; one *s.* *Educ.:* Com. Sch., Goshen, Guysborough Acad., and Dalhousie Coll., Halifax; Mayor of New Glasgow, 1900-1901; elec. to N.S. Legislature for Guysboro Co., 1894, and held the seat until 1904; elec. to the Federal House at a bye-elec., 1904; re-elec. 1904, and 1908. *Address:* New Glasgow, N.S. *Club:* Rideau, Ottawa.

SINNOTT, Very Rev. Mgr. Alfred Arthur, B.A., D.C.L.; *b.* Morell, P.E.I., 22 Feb., 1877; *s.* of John Sinnott and Jane McAuley; *Educ.:* St. Dunstan's Coll., Charlottetown, P.E.I., Grand Seminary, Montreal, and a post graduate course in Rome. Ordained priest 18 Feb., 1900; was for two years professor in St. Dunstan's Coll., Charlottetown, P.E.I., when in Nov., 1903, was named to present position as Private Secretary to His Excellency the Apostolic Delegate in Ottawa. *Address:* Apostolic Delegation, The Driveway, Ottawa.

SIROIS, Louis Philippe, N.P., LL.D. (Laval Univ.); Prof. of Constitutional Law at Laval Univ.; *b.* Kamouraska, Que., 4 May, 1851; *s.* of Theodore Sirois and Justine Pelletier; *m.* (1st) 1877, Atala Blais, of Montmagny (*d.* 1883); (2nd) 1889, Atala Fournier; five children. *Educ.:* Ste. Anne's Coll., Laval Univ. Grad. LL.L., 1875 (gold medal donated by Lord Dufferin the then Gov.-Gen. of Can.), LL.D., 1886. Apptd. Prof. of Constitutional Law, Laval Univ., 1887; apptd. mem. of Com. for Revision of the Statutes of the Dom. of Can. Admitted a N.P., 18 May, 1876. Pres., Bd. of Notaries 1900-1903. Vice-pres. La Caisse d'Economie de Notre Dame de Quebec; sec. and gov. Le Syndicat Financier, Laval Univ., Quebec. *Recreations:* yachting, travelling. *Address:* 21 Couillard St., Quebec.

SKELTON, Oscar Douglas, M.A., Ph. D.; *b.* Orangeville, Ont., 1878; *s.* of Jeremiah and Elizabeth Skelton; *m.* Isabel Murphy; two *s.* *Educ.:* Cornwall and Orangeville High Sch., and Univ. of Chicago; in journalism in the United States, 1901-1904; post graduate work, Univ. Chicago, 1905 1908; professor of political sicence, Queen's Univ., Kingston, 1908. *Publications:* Socialism; a critical analysis. *Address:* Queen's University, Knigston. *Club:* Frontenac, Kingston.

SLADEN, Arthur French; *b.* Woolwich, Eng., 30 April, 1866; *s.* of Col. Sladen, late Royal Artillery, and Caroline Mary French; *m.* Kathleen Hume Powell, of Ottawa; four *s.* *Educ.:* Haileybury Coll., Royal Naval Coll., Grenwich; arrived in Canada, 1887; formerly in Royal Marine Artillery; afterwards farming; entered Governor General's office in 1891; private secy. to three Governors General. *Recreations:* shooting, fishing, golf. *Address:* 182 Daly Ave., Ottawa. *Clubs:* Rideau, Golf, Ottawa.

SLOAN, William; capitalist; *b.* Wingham, Ont., 10 Sept., 1867; *s.* of Dr. R. J. Sloan and Elizabeth McMichael; *m.* Flora McGregor Glaholm; *Educ.:* Pub. Sch. and Coll. Inst., Seaforth, Ont. Spent two yrs. in Customs service at Shanghai, China; returned to B.C. in 1888, and resided in Victoria, Vancouver and Nanaimo; was unsuccessful can. for H. of C. for Vancouver at g. e., 1900; el. for Comox-Atlin, at g. e., 1904; re-el. 1908, but resigned seat in favour of Hon. Wm. Templeman, Min. of Inland Revenue. Treas. of B.C. Liberal Assn. and Liberal Organizer for Vancouver Island; ex-pres. of the Nanaimo Caledonian Soc. *Address:* Nanaimo, B.C. *Clubs:* Rideau, Ottawa; Union, Victoria, B.C.

SMALL, Henry Beaumont, M.D., C.M. (McGill); *b.* Toronto, 1856; *s.* of Henry Beaumont Small; *m.* Minnie Macpherson, of Kingston, Ont.; one *s.* two *d.* *Educ.:* Durham Coll. Sch., Montreal; McGill Univ. Practises prof. in Ottawa. Hon. treas., Dom. of Can. Medical Assn. *Publications:* Contributions to "Reference Handbook of Medical Science," "25th Century Pract. of Medicine," and medical journals. *Recreations:* golf, curling. *Address:* 150 Laurier Ave., W., Ottawa.

SMALLFIELD, William Elgood; editor and proprietor of the Renfrew *Mercury;* *b.* Brooklyn, N.Y., 22 Oct., 1861; *s.* of Albert Smallfield and Martha Ann Elgood; *m.* Ida J. Hamilton; two *s.* Came to Canada, 1863, and educ. at the Renfrew Pub. and High Schs. Taken into business partnership in "The Renfrew *Mercury*," before reaching majority. Served as Town Councillor for several yrs.; reeve one yr.; Mayor three yrs. Pres., Pub. Library, Bd. of Trade; mem. of Hospital Bd.; mem. of Executive of Can. Press Assn. for seven yrs.; sec.-treas. of Renfrew Agric. and Industrial Fair. *Publications:* Special articles on "Municipal Ownership in Canadian Towns." *Recreations:* municipal and local activities. *Address:*: Renfrew, Ont.

SMALLPEICE, Henry Edward, J.P.; *b.* Guildford, Surrey, Eng., 28 Jan., 1848; *s.* of Henry William and Harriett Smallpeice; *m.* Eliza 2nd *d.* of John Wickson, 7 June, 1869; two *s.* five *d.* *Educ.:* West Camberwell Coll., Denmark Hill, London, Eng.; arrived in Canada, July, 1862; newspaper man all his life; started on Toronto *Globe;* was owner of the late Toronto *Sun* and *National;* member of the Board of Education for the City of Toronto for many yrs.; at present represents several leading Canadian newspapers in Toronto. *Recreations:* horticulture and horses. *Address:* 156 Dunn Ave., Toronto.

SMART, Lieut.-Col. Charles Allan; *b.* Montreal, 23 March, 1868, of Scotch descent; *m.* 1893, Ella Maud, *d.* of William McWood, for many yrs. supt. of car dept. of G.T.R.; one *d.* *Educ.:* Montreal pub. and high schs. Was in employ of stationery firm of Buntin, Boyd & Co., for three yrs.; Tellier, Rothwell & Co., dealers in oils for seven yrs., and Dom. Bag Co., Ltd., then Consumers' Cordage Co. In 1906, organized the Smart Bag Co., Ltd., of which he became pres. and mgr. dir. Served for a number of yrs. with the Sixth Hussars. Organized the Thirteenth Scottish Light Dragoons, 1904, and became Lieut.-Col.; retired 1906. Mem. Montreal Military Inst., St. Andrew's Soc., Caledonia Soc., Carnarvon Chapter, R.A.M.; a Knight Templar and a Shriner. *Address:* 33 Sussex Ave., Montreal. *Club:* Canada.

SMART, George Bogue; *b.* Brockville, Ont., 30 May, 1864; *s.* of James Smart and Annie Bogue; *m.* Annie Lindsay Page; three *s.* *Educ.:* Pub. Sch., Brockville, and Woodstock Coll.; on the staff of the Molson's Bank; joined the Immigration service in June, 1899; now inspector of Immigrant Children. *Publications:* Annual reports on Juvenile Immigration. *Address:* 60 McLaren St., Ottawa.

SMART, James Allan; *b.* Brockville, Ont., 6 June, 1858; *s.* of James Smart, manufacturer, and Anne Bogue; *m.* E. Frances Jones, Prescott; five *s.* two *d.* *Educ.:* at Com. and Gram. Sch. Brockville, and Woodstock Coll.; lived in Manitoba for 17 years, 1880 to 1897; merchant at Winnipeg and Brandon; alderman and Mayor of Brandon for four years; represented East Brandon in Provincial Legislature from 1886 to 1888, and Brandon, from 1888 to 1892; Minister of Public Works in Greenway Government for five years; Deputy Min. of Interior, 1897-1904. *Address:* Lachine, Que., and 260 St. James St., Montreal.

SMITH, Alexander, B.A., barrister, *b.* Tp. of Saugeen, Bruce Co., Ont.; *s.* of Peter Smith and Christina Bell (both Scotch). unmarried. *Educ.:* Port Elgin pub. sch., Walkerton high sch., Toronto Univ., Ontario law sch. Taught sch. while studing for matriculation. Graduated B.A. (1889), at Toronto Univ. with honours. In journalism for four years while taking law course; called to bar of Ontario, 1893; shortly after commencing practice, was offered and accepted the position of Secretary to the Liberal Party in Federal and Provincial affairs, and election organizer with headquarters alternating between Ottawa and Toronto. While occupying this important confidential post, the Liberals were successful in the Federal General Elections of 1896, 1900 and 1904, and in the Ontario Provincial General Elections of 1894, 1898 and 1902. Immediately after the Federal Election of 1904, resumed the practice of law in the City of Ottawa, as senior member of the firm of Smith & Johnston, and in the Federal Elections of 1908, acted in the capacity of general adviser to the Liberal organization with particular reference to matters of legal importance. Has an extensive knowledge of every constituency in Ont., and by frequent visits to the Western Provs. is also in close touch with their development. For many yrs. a mem. of 2nd Q. O. Rifles, Toronto; is now chn. of the Ottawa Committee of ex-members of the Regt., who will participate in Jubilee celebration of Regt., June, 1910. *Recreations:* rowing, curling, lawn bowling. *Addresses:* 132 O'Connor St.; Trust Building, Ottawa (bus. *Clubs:* Laurentian, Elks', Ottawa; National, Ontario, Toronto.

SMITH, Alexander Wilson, M.P.; *b.* Victoria, York Co., Ont., 12 Nov., 1852; *r.* of James S. Smith, who represented North Middlesex, in Ont. Legis., 1867-1875, and who was born in Thurso, Caithness, Scotland, and Agnes Wilson Smith, born in Elderslie, Lanark, Scot. *Educ.:* Pub. Sch., Rockwood Acad., and Canadian Literary Inst., Woodstock, Ont.; pres. Prov. Winter Fair, Guelph, at its beginning and for four years following; pres. Dom. Cattle Breeders' Association, the Dom. Sheep Breeders' Assn., the American Leicester Breeders' Assn., and Dom. Shorthorn Breeders' Assn.; first elected to H. of C., 1908; Presbyterian; Liberal. *Address:* Maple Lodge, Ont.

SMITH, Charles James; Gen. Mgr. of the Richelieu & Ontario Navigation Co.; *b.* Hamilton, Ont., 10 March, 1862; *s.* of John and Sarah A. Smith; *m.* Jessie L. Brown; one *s.* three *d.* *Educ.:* Hamilton High Sch., and Wentworth Coll. Entered Ry. service 1879, since when he has been consecutively clerk local frt. office, Hamilton & Northwestern Ry., at Hamilton, 1879-1880; with audit and purchasing dept., Chicago and Alton Rd., 1880-82; in construction dept., C. P. Ry., 1882-1885; in traffic dept., New York Lake Erie & Western Rd., 1885-86; chief clerk to gen. mgr., Chicago & Atlantic Ry., 1886-88; traffic dept., "Soo" line, 1888; in traffic dept., St. Paul Minneapolis & Manitoba Ry. (Great Northern), 1888-90; gen. frt. and passenger agt., Canada Atlantic Ry., 1890-98; gen. traffic mgr., same rd. and Canada Atlantic Transit Co., 1898-1904; apptd. gen. mgr., Richelieu & Ontario Nav. Co., 1 April, 1904. *Address:* 31 Ontario Ave., Montreal. *Clubs:* Rideau, Ottawa; Garrison, Quebec; R. C. Y., Toronto; St. James, Forest and Stream, Hunt, Montreal.

SMITH, E. Norman; managing editor Ottawa *Free Press;* *b.* Manchester, Eng., 3 Feb., 1871; *s.* of John Walker Smith and Annie Bourne; *m.* Bessie Irving of Dundas, Ont.; one *s.* one *d.* *Educ.:* British Sch., Croyden, Eng.; arrived in Canada, 1873; reportorial staff, Press Association, London, Eng.; Chicago *Tribune*, Toronto *World;* editorial staffs Woodstock *Sentinel Review;* Toronto *Mail and Empire*, and Toronto *Globe;* became managing director and editor, Ottawa Daily *Free Press*, Dec., 1905, subsequently becoming principal owner. *Address:* Ottawa, *Clubs:* Rideau, Ottawa; Ontario, Toronto.

SMITH, His Hon. George, M.A.; *b.* Newton Farm, Cambuslang, Lanarkshire, Scot., 1852; *s.* of John Douglas Smith, and Margaret Paton; *m.* Emily Irvine Smith, M.B.; two *d.* Arrived in Canada, 1859; First Blake Scholarship and M.A., Toronto Univ.; Latin Master, Woodstock Baptist Coll.; barrister; elected member of H. of C. for North Oxford, 1905; apptd. County Judge of Essex, 1909. *Address:* Windsor, Ont.

SMITH, Goldwin, D.C.L.; *e. s.* of Richard Smith, M.D., Reading, Berks, and Eliza Breton; *m.* Harriet E. M. Boulton (*nee* Dixon). *Educ.:* Eton; Farley, near Bath; Univ. Coll., Oxford. Gained Hertford Scholarship, 1842; Ireland, 1845; Chancellor's Prize for Latin Verse, 1845; Latin

Essay, 1846; English Essay, 1847; Fellow Univ. Coll., 1846; barr. Lincoln's Inn; Regius Prof. Modern History, Oxford, 1858-66; prominent champion of the North during American Civil War, 1864; went to U.S., 1868; became honorary Prof. of English and Constitutional History in Cornell University, U.S.A.; took up residence in Canada, 1871; active in Philanthropic work in Toronto. *Publications:* Irish History and Irish Character; Three English Statesmen; The Empire; Lectures on the Study of History; The Reorganisation of the University of Oxford; A Plea for the Abolition of Tests; Does the Bible sanction American Slavery? The Civil War in America; Letter on Southern Independence; Rational Religion and Rationalistic Objections; Canada and the Canadian Question; The Political Destiny of Canada; Loyalty, Aristocracy, and Jingoism; False Hopes; Lectures and Essays; Cowper; Jane Austen; The United States; Essays on Questions of the Day; A Trip to England; Oxford and her Colleges, William Lloyd Garrison; Bay Leaves; Specimens of Greek Tragedy; Guesses at the Riddle of Existence; The United Kingdom; Commonwealth or Empire; In the Court of History; the Founder of Christendom; Lines of Religious Inquiry; My Memory of Gladstone; Irish History and the Irish Question; In Quest of Light; Revolution or Progress?; Labour and Capital; etc. *Address:* The Grange, Toronto. *Club:* Press. (hon. presdt.) Toronto.

SMITH, Lieut.-Col. Henry Robert, I.S.O., A.D.C., J.P., Sgt.-at-Arms of the H. of C. of Canada; *b.* Kingston, Ont., 30 Dec., 1843; *s.* Sir Henry Smith, K.B.; Q.C., and Mary, *d.* of Robert Talbot, Kingston; *m.* Mary Gurley, widow of Major R. W. Barrow, R. C. R., of Syndope Hall, Derbyshire (*dec.* 1907). *Educ.:* Gram. Sch., Kingston; Deputy Sergt.-at-Amrs, H. of C., 1872; Sergt.-at-Arms, 1892; A.D.C. to successive Governors General since the time of the Marquis of Lorne. *Recreations:* shooting and fishing. *Address:* 118 William St., Kingston, and House of Commons, Ottawa. *Clubs:* Rideau, Country, Ottawa; Frontenac, Kingston.

SMITH, James Frederick, K.C., LL.D., *b.* Barrie, Ont., 6 Nov., 1840; *s.* of James Frederick Smith and Mary Sanford; *m.* Alice Jeffery, Carters Corner Place, Hailsham, Sussex, Eng.; four *s.* three *d.* *Educ.:* Up. Can. Coll., and Univ. of Toronto; called to the bar, 1862; Q.C., 1885. *Publications:* editor of Ontario Law Reports, 1885-1909. *Recreations:* walking, travelling. *Address:* Westholm, May Street, Toronto.

SMITH, J. Obed; Asst. Supt. of Emigration at London, England; *b.* Warwickshire, Eng., 22 Sept., 1864. Called to the Manitoba Bar, 30 Nov., 1891; for many yrs. in the service of the Manitoba Govt.; apptd. Dominion Commissioner of Immigration at Winnipeg, 18 Jan., 1901; Asst. Supt. of Emigration at London, England, Jan., 1908. *Address:* 11-12 Charing Cross, London, S.W. Eng.

SMITH, Ralph, M.P.; *b.* nr. Newcastle-on-Tyne, England, 8 Aug., 1858; *s.* of Robert and Margaret Smith; *m.* M. E. Spear; five *s.* *Educ.:* Newcastle and District Sch. Arrived in Canada, 1 Oct., 1892; went into the mines at Newcastle, at 11 years of age; worked up into official position; prominent Methodist layman, associated with G. Finwick, M.P., John Wilson, M.P., T. Burt, M.P., and other labour Liberals; prominent with co-operative societies; delegate to Glasgow Congress; left England for his health; became agent for B.C. coal miners; elec. 1898 to Leg. Ass. of B.C.; elec. to the H. of C., 1900; re-elec. 1904; and 1908. *Address:* Nanaimo, B.C.

SMITH, Lieut.-Col. Robert, K.C., M.P.; *b.* Tp. of Ramsay, Lanark Co., Ont., 7 Dec., 1858; *s.* of William Smith and Jane Neilson; *m.* Florence Parker Pettit, *d.* of the late Rev. Canon Pettit; one *s.* one *d.* *Educ.:* Almonte High Sch.; called to the bar, 1885; apptd. K.C., 1908; is a director of the Montreal and Cornwall Navigation Co., Ltd.; practices in Cornwall; is Lieut.-Col., Commanding the 59th Regt.; unsuccessful candidate for H. of C., 1904; elec. 1908. *Recreations:* shooting and yachting. *Address:* Cornwall, Ont. *Club:* Cornwall.

SMITH, Robert Cooper, B.C.L., K.C.; *b.* Montreal, 13 June, 1859; *s.* of Robert Smith, and Annie Reynolds; *m.* 1890, Charlotte Florence Elizabeth, *d.* of Milton Pennington. *Educ.:* Montreal High Sch.; McGill Univ. Called to Bar, 1882; Q.C. 1897; some years on council of the Bar; practising as senior member of legal firm of Smith, Markey, and Skinner. Professor of Commercial Law, McGill Univ., since 1899; at present Batonnier of the Bar of Montreal; Commodore, R. St. L. Y. C. *Recreations.* yachting, golf. *Addresses:* Montreal and Dorval. *Clubs:* St. James, Mount Royal, R. St. L.Y.C., Dorval, Forest and Stream, Montreal; Garrison, Quebec; Rideau, Ottawa.

SMITH, William; *b.* Tp. of East Whitby Ont., 16 Nov., 1847; *s.* of William Smith and Elizabeth Laing; *m.* Helen Burns; two *s.* one *d.* *Educ.:* Pub. Sch. and Up. Can. Coll.; Trustee of Public Sch. since 1869; Deputy Reeve of East Whitby five years; Reeve for four years; member of the H. of C. for South Ont., from 1887 to 1896; president of Maple Leaf Insurance Co. for over 14 years; farmer and stock breeder. *Address:* Township of East Whitby, Ont.

SMITH, William, B.A.; Secy. P. O. Dept.; *b.* Hamilton, Ont., 31 Jan., 1859; *s.* of Thomas and Margaret Smith; *m.* Mabel McHenry, of St. John, N.B.; five *s.* one *d.* *Educ.:* Hamilton Coll. Inst., and Toronto Univ.; entered Hamilton Post Office in Nov., 1876; was transferred to mail contract branch of P. O. Dept., 1886, and became Secretary of the Department on 1 July, 1902; takes great interest in cable matters, wrote chapter on a "Postal Cable Service" in Johnson's "Annals and Aims of the Pacific Cable." *Address:* 93 Fourth Ave., Ottawa.

SMITH, William Richmond; *b.* Ottawa, Ont., 26 Feb., 1868; *s.* of John Smith and Martha Smith. *Educ.:* Ottawa. In journalism for many yrs. Was on the staff of the Ottawa Journal, and Montreal *Star;* rep. latter paper throughout South African campaign; rep. London, Eng. *Standard,* and American Associated Press during Russo-Japanese War. Spent several months in England investigating municipal affairs, subsequently published result of his enquiries. For the past three yrs. on the editorial staff of the New York *Tribune*, as such made exhaustive enquiry into finances of City of New York, which led to radical charges in civic bookkeeping. *Publications:* "Siege and Fall of Port Arthur;" "Municipal Trading in Great Britain." *Address:* The Tribune, New York. *Club:* National, Toronto.

SMITH, Rev. William Wye; *b.* Jedburgh, Scot., 1 March, 1827; *s.* of John Smith, Crailing, Roxburghshire, and Sarah Veitch, Yetholm, Roxburghshire; *m.* (1st) Margaret Chisholm, Lancaster, Ont., (2nd) Catharine R. Young, Hamilton, Ont.; one *s.* three *d.* Arrived in Canada, 1837; worked on his father's farm, S. Dumfries, Brant.; sch. teacher; store keeper; clerk of court; editor; now Congregational Minister. *Publications:* poems 1888; "New Testament in Braid Scotch," 1901; (2nd edition, 1904); selected poems, 1908. *Address:* 151 Halley Ave., Toronto, Ont.

SMYTH, William Ross, K.C., M.P.; *b.* Thomroan, Aberdeenshire, Scot., 3 Jan., 1857; *s.* of Francis and Isabella Smyth, Scotch; *m.* 17 Oct., 1879, Nancy Burden, Tp. of Plummer; four *s.* seven *d.* Pres., Nancy Helen Mine, Ltd.; elec. to the Ont. Legis., 1902, 1905, 1908; resigned from local Leg. and elected to the H. of C., 1908, for Algoma E.; Presbyterian; Conservative. *Address:* Rydal Bank, Ont.

SNIDER, His Hon. Colin George, B.A., Judge of the County Court, Wentworth, K.C.; *b.* Norfolk Co. Ont., 21 May, 1850; *s.* of George Snider, and Elizabeth M. Hamel; *m.* Helen B. Grasett; one *s.* five *d.* Judge of the County Court of the County of Wentworth. *Address:* Hamilton, Ont. *Clubs:* Hamilton, Oakville.

SNOWBALL, William Bunting; *b.* Chatham, N.B., 12 Jan., 1861; *s.* of Hon. Jabez Bunting and Margaret Snowball; *m.* Bertha B. Harris of Hamilton, Ont., five *s.* two *d.* *Educ.:* Gram. Sch., Chatham, N.B., and Up. Can. Coll., Toronto; alderman of Chatham, 1898, 1899, 1903-1904, 1905; Mayor, 1901, 1902; President, J. B. Snowball Co., Ltd.; President, Canadian Forestry Assn., 1908; President, Maritime Board of Trade, 1909. *Recreations:* fishing and hunting. *Address:* Chatham, N.B.

SOPER, Warren Young; *b.* Oldtown, Maine, 9 March, 1854; *s.* of Albert Webster Soper and Eleanor Young; *m.* Annie, *d.* of Lt.-Col. Newson; three *s.* one *d.* *Educ.:* Ottawa; arrived in Canada, 1856; pres., Ahearn & Soper, Limited; Dunlop Tire Company; Ottawa Building Companv; director, Ottawa Electric Railway Company Ottawa Light Heat and Power Co.; Imperial Life Assurance Co. *Address:* Lornado, Rockcliffe Park, Ottawa. *Clubs:* Rideau, Golf, Hunt, Ottawa; Engineers, Montreal.

SORMANY, Alphonse, M.D., M.L.A.; *b.* Shippigan, Gloucester Co., N.B., 31 March, 1880; *s.* of H. A. Sormany and Virginia Hacké; *m.* Eva Couillard, of Quebec; one *s.* *Educ.:* Caraquet College and Laval Univ. A physician; pres. of Gloucester Navigation Co., Ltd.; elec. member Provincial Legislature, Mar. 2, 1908; youngest member in the House; Roman Catholic; Liberal. *Address:* Shippigan, N.B.

SOUTHAM, William; Pres. of Southam Ltd.; *b.* Montreal, 23 Aug., 1843; *s.* of William and Mercy Southam; *m.* Wilson, *d.* of James Mills, of Ayr, Scot.; six *s.* one *d.* *Educ.:* London, Ont. Pub. Sch. A master printer in Hamilton and Toronto for many yrs., also in Montreal,; different businesses consolidated in company known as Southam Ltd.; also controls the Hamilton *Spectator*, Ottawa *Citizen*, and Calgary *Herald;* a dir. of the Canadian Transmission Co.; dir. of the Caledonian Power Co.; dir., of the Mercantile Trust Co., of Hamilton. *Recreations:* lawn bowling, curling. *Address:* Pinehurst, Hamilton, Ont. *Clubs:* Hamilton, Golf, Hamilton.

SOUTHAM, Wilson Mills; *b.* London, Ont., 2 Oct., 1868; *s.* of William Southam and Wilson Mills; *m.* Henrietta A. Cargill, 3rd *d.* of late Henry Cargill, Cargill, Ont., and member of H. of C. for East Bruce; two *s.* two *d.* *Educ.:* Hamilton Pub. Sch. and Coll. Inst. In journalism for many yrs.; formerly business mgr. of the Hamilton *Spectator*; now managing dir. Ottawa *Citizen*. *Address:* Ottawa, Ont. *Clubs:* Rideau, Golf, Country and Hunt, Ottawa, Ont.

SPENCE, Francis Stephens; Chn. of the Toronto Harbour Comn.; *b.* Donegal, Irel., 29 March, 1850; *s.* of Jacob Spence and Elizabeth Stephens; *m.* Sara Violet Norris; two *s.* two *d.* Came to Can., in 1861, and educ. at Toronto Normal Sch. Taught sch. at Drummondville, Prescott and Toronto; mem. of the Toronto Sch. Bd. for two yrs.; mem. Toronto City Coun. as Alderman for six yrs.; Controller four yrs.; hon. pres., Ont. Branch, Dom. Alliance; mng. ed. Canada *Citizen*, *Pioneer*, etc.; Chn., of the Harbour Comn. *Publications:* "The Facts of the Case;" "The Vanguard;" "The Campaign Manual. *Addresses:* Confederation Life Bldg. (Bus.); 554 Spadina Ave., Toronto.

SQUAIR, John, B.A. (1883); *b.* Bowmanville, Ont., 1850; *s.* of Scotch parents; *m.* Laura Prout; one *d.* *Educ.:* Pub. Sch. of Clarke, High Sch. of Newcastle and Bowmanville, and Univ. of Toronto; head of the Department of French in Univ. Coll., since 1883; active in work of Ontario Educational Association, and Dominion Educational Association; examiner in Modern Languages (chiefly French) for Ontario Educationa, Department, and Univ. of Toronto. *Publications:* in colloboration with various persons edited many vols. and translations of French literature; ready for press, a selection from the poetry of Victor Hugo, also a French Reader, a French Grammar, and Exercises in French prose (all three in colloboration). *Address:* 61 Major St., Toronto.

STAIRS, Major Henry Bertram, D.S.O.; *b.* 29 Apr., 1871; *s.* of late John Stairs, Halifax, N.S.; *m.* 1903, Judith, *d.* of late George Henderson. Barrister, Supreme Court, N.S., 1893. Served South Africa; present at Paardeberg, 18-27 Feb., 1900 (despatches, Queen's medal, 4 clasps, D.S.O., Brevet Majority), Driefontein, Hout Nek, Sand River, Johannesburg, etc.; Capt. and Brevet Major and Adjutant, 60th Regt.,

Princess Louise Fusiliers, Canada. *Address:* 14 Lucknow Street, Halifax, N.S. *Club:* Halifax.

ST. ALBERT, Bishop of; *see* Rt. Rev. Emile J. Legal.

STANFIELD, John, M.P.; *b.* Charlottetown, P.E.I., 18 May, 1868; *s.* of Charles Edward Stanfield, and Lydia Dawson; *m.* 1902, Sadie Yorston, Truro, N.S., one *s.* *Educ.:* Truro; Pres., Stanfield's Limited, operating the plant formerly known as the Truro Knitting Mills Company, elec. to the H. of C. at bye-election, 28 Nov., 1907; re-elec. 1908; Church of England; Conservative. *Address:* Truro, N.S. *Club:* Laurentian, Ottawa.

STANSFIELD, Prof. Alfred, D.Sc., A.R. S.M.; *b.* Bradford, Yorks, Eng., March, 1871; *e. s.* of Frederic Stansfield; *m.* 1905, Ethel Ernestine, *d.* of F. E. Grubb, formerly of Cahir Abbey, Co. Tipperary. *Educ.:* Ackworth Sch.; Bradford Technical Coll.; Royal Coll. of Science, London. Carried out researches on alloys for Sir Wm. Roberts-Austen, 1891-98; Doctor of Science of the London Univ., 1898; in charge of Metallurgical Laboratories of the Royal Sch. of Mines, 1898-1901; Prof. of Metallurgy, McGill Univ., Montreal, since 1901. *Publications:* papers on Pyrometry, the Solution Theory of Carburised Iron, the Constitution of Alloys, the Burning of Steel, Metallurgical Teaching and the Electric Furnace. *Address:* 214 Park Ave., Montreal. *Club:* Engineers, Montreal.

STAPLES, William D., M.P.; *b.* Fleetwood, Tp. Manvers, Ont., 10 Nov., 1868; *s.* of James Staples and Jane Evans; *m.* 26 May, 1892, Nellie Metcalf, *d.* of Thomas A. Metcalfe of Treherne, Man., *Educ.:* pub. sch., Fleetwood; High Sch., Lindsay, and Coll. Inst., Winnipeg; holds 2nd Class Teacher's Certificate; was twelve years in municipal council as councillor and reeve; elec. to the H. of C., 1904, and 1908, for Macdonald, Man.; Methodist; Conservative. *Address:* Treherne, Man.

STEELE, James; Registrar of Deeds for North Perth; *b.* Avonbank, Tp. of Downie, Perth Co., Ont., 8 Aug., 1864; *s.* of Thomas Steele and Joan Todd; *m.* Emily Rutledge Custed; one *s.* one *d.* *Educ.:* St. Mary's Coll. Inst. and Osgoode Hall, Toronto. Called to bar of Ont., June, 1892, and practiced law in Stratford, until apptd. to present pos., Aug., 1908. Took an active part in politics on Cons. side; mem. of Public Sch. Bd. and Public Liby. Bd. for several yrs. *Recreations:* curling, lawn bowls, golf, gardening. *Address:* 137 Mornighton, St., Stratford, Ont.

STEELE, Col. Samuel Benfield, C.B., 1900; M.V.O. (4th Class), 1900; *b.* Medonte, County Simcoe, Ont., 5 Jan., 1849; 4th *s.* of Captain Elmes Steele, R.N., of Coleford, Gloucestershire, and 2nd wife, Anne, *y. d.* of Neil MacIan Macdonald, of Islay; *m.* 1890, Marie Elizabeth, *e. d.* of Robert Harwood, Seigneur of Vaudreuil, Que., one *s.* two *d.* *Educ.:* Orillia, Co. Simcoe; British American Commercial Coll., Toronto. 35th Batt. Simcoe Foresters, 1866; qualified with 2nd Batt. 17th Regt., (now the Leicestershires); served Fenian Raids, 1866-70; Red River Expedition, 1870 (medal with three clasps); joined Canadian Permanent Artillery on the return of the expedition; joined the North-West Mounted Police, 1873; Inspector, 1878; Superintendent, 1885; served campaign of 1885 in North-West Terr. and was present at action of Frenchman's Butte; commanded the Mounted Force in pursuit of Big Bear's Band and the Wood Crees (despatches, medal with clasp); commanded "D" Division of the North-West Mounted Police in an expedition into Kootenay, British Columbia, to restore order (thanked in General Orders); commanded the North-West Mounted Police posts on the summits of the White and Chilkoot passes during the rush of the miners into the Klondyke, 1898; was magistrate and had charge of the Customs (thanked by the Governor-General in Council); commanded the North-West Mounted Police in the Yukon territory during the organization of the same in 1898-99, and was a member of the Council of the territory; commandant of the Strathcona Horse in Boer War (despatches twice, Queen's medal, three clasps, King's medal, two clasps); regiment presented with King's Colours and medals by King Enward VII; Commanding Military District, No. 11, Canada. *Recreations:* riding, shooting big game, swimming, walking, boating; takes an interest in all sports. *Address:* Fort Osborne Barracks, Winnipeg, and 353 Broadway, Winnipeg, Man.

STEPHENS, Major George Washington; Chn. of the Montreal Harbour Comn.; *b.* Montreal, 1866; *s.* of the late Hon. George Washington Stephens; married. *Educ.:* Montreal high sch., McGill Univ., and completed his education in Univs. of France, Germany and Switzerland. Commenced his business carrer with the firm of Steidtman & Co., importers, of Hamburg, Germany, later was with J. and H. Taylor, and subsequently with Thos. Robertson & Co., Ltd., steel merchants, Montreal. Has been administrator of the Stephen's estate for ten yrs. Vice-pres. Consolidated Rubber Co., Pres., Montreal Harbor Comn. El. a mem. of the Legis. Assembly for St. Lawrence div., by acclam. Was commanding officer, Montreal Third Field Battery. Accompanied Minister of Militia to Eng. as a mem. of the Montreal and Canadian contingent, at time of Jubilee celebration. Apptd. chairman of new harbour comn., Jan., 1907. *Address:* 597 Sherbrooke St. W., Montreal.

STEPHENSON, Hon. Isaac; a mem. of the U.S. Senate for the State of Wisconsin; *b.* nr. Fredericton, N.B., 18 June, 1829. Is a lumberman, farmer and banker. *Educ.:* at Pub. Sch., N.B. Moved to Wisconsin, 1845. Engaged in lumber trade at Escanaba, Mich., for twelve yrs.; moved to Marinette, Mich., 1858. Mem. of Wis. Leg., 1866-68. Mem. of House of Rep. from 9th Dist. of Wis. in the 48th and 49th Congresses. El. to U.S. Senate, May, 17, 1907, to fill out unexpired term of Hon. J. C. Spooner. Term of service will expire 1915. *Addresses:* The Senate, Washington, D.C.; Marinette, Wis., U.S.A.

STEWART, Thomas Joseph, M.P.; *b.* Oxford, Ont., 26 July, 1849; *s.* of Molby and Mary Stewart; *m.* Maria Jane Pollock; one *d.* *Educ.:* Com. Sch.; thirteen years a member of Bruce Co. Council; nine years a member of Hamilton City Council; two years (1907-1908), Mayor; first el. to the H. of C., Oct., 1908. *Address:* 85 Robinson St., Hamilton, Ont. *Club:* Commercial, Hamilton, Ont.

STEVELY, Samuel; *b.* Wardsville, Ont., 12 Aug., 1865; *s.* of William and Eliza Stevely; *m.* Maude Tackabury of Canastota, N.Y.; three *d.* *Educ.:* London, Ont.; in business in London, Ont., since 1889; Alderman for 9 years, and Mayor, 1908-9; *Recreations:* curling, golf, tennis, and lawn bowling. *Address:* London, Ont. *Clubs:* London, Travelers, Hunt and Country, London, Ont.

STEVENSON, Elliott G.; Supreme Chief Ranger, Independent Order of Foresters; *b.* Middlesex Co., Ont., 18 May, 1856; married. *Educ.:* Pub. Sch. and Seminary, Komoka, Ont. Taught school near Strathroy for two years; removed to Port Huron, Mich., 1871; studied law and admitted to Bar of Michigan as Attorney and Counsellor in 1874, when only 18 years of age; Prosecuting Attorney of St. Clair County, 1878-9, 1882-3; Mayor of Port Huron, 1885; nominated (1886) on democratic ticket for Congress, but declined; removed to Detroit, 1887, and became law partner of Hon. Don. M. Dickinson, Postmaster General of the United States. In 1892, became chairman of the Democratic State Central Committee of Michigan; del. 1896 to Democratic National Convention at Chicago, which first nominated Wm. Jennings Bryan as can. for the Presidency of the U.S.; joined Indpt. Order of Foresters in 1896; el. Sup. Counsellor of the Order, 1898; succeeded the late Dr. Oronhyatekha as Sup. Chief Ranger, 1907. *Addresses:* Temple Bldg., Toronto, Ont.; Detroit, Mich. U.S.A.

STEVENSON, John James, M.L.A.; *b.* Russell, Ont., 11 May, 1873; *s.* of John and Eliza Stevenson; *m.* Jennie Wallace Canning; one *s.* one *d.* *Educ.:* Russell and Ottawa, Ont.; worked for W. C. Edwards Co. for 12 years, during which time he spent one year exploring in the wilds of Labrador; then went west and entered into lumbering and horse raising; elec. to Sask. Legis., Aug., 14, 1908. *Recreations:* motoring, horseman. *Address:* Tyvan, Sask.

STEWART, Douglas; *b.* Williamsdale, N.S., 20 June, 1850; *s.* of Wm. Stewart, J.P., formerly of Blair Athol, Scot.; *m.* Alma, *d.* of Thomas R. Thompson, founder of the Oxford Woolen Mills, Oxford, N.S. *Educ.:* Public Sch. and Amherst Acad. Entered Civil Service, 1879, as clerk in Accts. Branch, Dept. of Public Works; apptd. Asst. Acct., with rank of 1st class clerk, Dept. Rys. & Canals, May, 1882; Private Secretary to Minister of Justice, Feb., 1886, Nov. 1894; attached to staff Canadian Plenipotentiary during Chamberlain-Bayard negotiations, Washington, 1887. Accompanied several Ministers to Washington on subsequent missions connected with pending commercial questions; accompanied Minister of Justice to London, 1890, in connection with copyright negotiations; Secretary, Canada-Newfoundland Convention, Halifax, 1892; Secretary to Canadian Arbitrator, Behring Sea Arbitration Tribunal, Paris, 1893. Prepared daily official report of proceedings for special Canadian Press cables, for which service was specially complimented and thanked by British Attorney-General. Joint Secretary, Intercolonial Conference, Ottawa, 1894; apptd. Inspector of Penitentiaries for Canada, Jan. 31st, 1895. Honorary Vice-President and member of Board of Directors, American Prison Association. Has contributed papers on "The object of imprisonment" and "Prison Discipline," embodied in proceedings of that Association. *Address:* Kenniston Apts., Ottawa. *Club:* Rideau.

STEWART, Elihu, D.L.S., C.E.F.E., *b.* Co. of Lambton, Ont., 17 Nov., 1844; *s.* of Lionel and Catherine Stewart; *m.* Ellen Noble; three *s.* one *d.* *Educ.:* Toronto Normal Sch.; practiced for several years as Dominion and Provincial Land Surveyor, and Civil Engineer on various Government Surveys; acted as Commissioner for determining the Boundary between Ontario and Manitoba; organized Dominion Forestry; Service, and founded the Canadian Forestry Assn.; supt. of Forestry Branch Dept. of Interior; resigned 1907, to assume managership of lumber Co. *Recreations:* curling and golf. *Address:* Montreal and Collingwood, Ont. *Clubs:* Rideau, Ottawa.

STEWART, Hugh Alexander, K.C.; *b.* Tp. of Elizabethtown, Leeds Co., Ont., 29 Sept., 1871; *s.* of Alexander Stewart and Jane Morrison; *m.* Estelle L. Wiltsir; two *s.* *Educ.:* Rural Pub. Sch., Brockville High Sch. and Osgoode Hall, Toronto. A barrister and solicitor. Mayor of Brockville, 1905-1906; Lieut., Corps of Guides. *Address:* Brockville, Ont. *Clubs:* Brockville; Albany, Toronto.

STEWART, John Alexander, LL.B.; *b.* Renfrew, Ont., *s.* of Robert Stewart and Barbara Stewart; *m.* Jessie M. Henderson. *Educ.:* Perth Pub. Sch. and Coll. Inst., Ottawa Univ., Osgoode Hall. A barrister and solicitor; Mayor of Perth, 1900-1904. H.C.R., C. O. Foresters. *Address:* Perth, Ont.

STEWART, John Duncan, M.L.A.; *b.* Perth Co., Ont., 16 Oct., 1859; of Canadian parents; unmarried. *Educ.:* Perth Co. Pub. Sch.; manager for three years of the Arcola Farmer's Elevator Co.; first el. to Sask. Leg. Ass., 1905; re-el. 1908. *Address:* Arcola, Sask.

STEWART, McLeod; barrister-at-law; *b.* Ottawa, Ont., 6 Feb., 1847; *s. e.* of William Stewart and Catharine Stewart; *m.* 1874, Linnie Emma, *d.* of Col. Walker Powell, late Adjutant-Gen. of Militia. *Educ.:* Ottawa Gram. Sch., Toronto Univ. (B.A., 1867, M.A., 1870), called to the bar in 1870, and commenced practice of his profession in Ottawa. Was one of the early advocates of the building of the Canada Atlantic Ry., and was associated with J. R. Booth and the late W. G. Perley in forming the Canada Atlantic Ry. Co., of which he was the first pres.; was pres. of the Stewart Ranching Co.; also a dir. of the city of Ottawa Agricultural Soc., Can. Granite Co., and other enterprises; Mayor of Ottawa, 1887-1888; was a dir. of the Co. of Carleton Protestant General Hospital, and Protestant Home for the Aged.; was vice-pres. of the Art Sch., pres. St. Andrew's Soc., and of the Soc. for Prevention for Cruelty; opened the first anthracite coal mine in the Rocky Mountains, and was pres. of the Co.; promoter of the Montreal, Ottawa and Georgian Bay Canal. *Address:* 383 Frank St., Ottawa.

STEWART, Robert J.P.; insurance agent; *b.* Ottawa, 7 April, 1850; *s.* of William Stewart and S. J. Donaldson; *m.* Mary Louisa Sharp; four *s.* four *d.* *Educ.:* Ottawa . Ottawa mgr. for fifteen insur. Cos. For several yrs. mem. of the Ottawa Pub. Sch. Bd. and City Council. Unsuccessful can. for H. of C., 1900; el. at g. e., 1904. Formerly in Ottawa Rifles; served in Fenian Raid, 1870 (medal). *Recreation:* whist. *Address:* 220 Maclaren St., Ottawa. *Club:* Laurentian, Ottawa.

STEWART, Robert Meldrum, M.A.; Astronomer at Dominion Observatory, Ottawa; *b.* Gladstone, Man., 15 Dec., 1878; *s.* of Rev. J. S. Stewart and Margaret Meldrum; *m.* May Dickson; three *d.* *Educ.:* Toronto Univ. Graduated in 1902, and joined staff of Dom. Observatory. *Publications:* various scientific papers in journal of R.A.S.C., and in proc. R. S. Can. *Address:* 991 Carling Ave., Ottawa.

STEWART, William Grant, M.D.; *b.* Oro, Ont., 1860; *s.* of Rev. James Stewart and Christina Grant; *m.* 1894, Jennie, *d.* of the late David McFarland, of Montreal. *Educ.:* McGill Univ. from which he grad. B.A., 1885, and M.D., 1888. Apptd. House Surgeon in Montreal Gen. Hospital, and then practiced his prof. in Montreal. Went abroad and continued his studies in medicine in Berlin and London, returning to Montreal, and resuming practice. For a number of yrs. lecturer in Medical Dept., of Univ. of St. Bishop's Coll., Lennoxville, and attending physician of Montreal Western Hospital. Vice-Pres. Medical Chirurgical Soc.; mem. Corporation of McGill Coll. and Univ., Canadian Medical Assn. *Recreation:* music. *Address:* 61 Sherbrooke St. W., Montreal. *Club:* University.

STEWART, William James; Chief Hydrographer; *b.* Ottawa, Ont., 23 Jan., 1863; *s.* of Lt.-Col. John and Mary Stewart; *m.* Clara Lasher; two *d.* *Educ.:* Ottawa Pub. Schs., Coll. Inst. and Royal Military Coll., Kingston. Grad. from latter Inst., 1883. Apptd. asst. to Capt. Boulton, R.N., on Canadian Hydrographic Survey, March, 1884; succeeded Capt. Boulton, 1893 Apptd. Chief Hydrographer, July, 1904, when survey was enlarged; apptd. a commr. for Canada on International Waterways Com., March, 1907. *Recreation:* curling *Address:* 56 Lisgar St., Ottawa.

ST. JOHN, Bishop of; *see* Right Rev. Timothy Carey.

STOBART, F. W.; *b.* Durham, Eng., 27 Jan., 1859; *s.* of William Stobart; married. *Educ.:* privately and at Wellington Coll., with view to becoming marine engr. Sent to Canada in 1880 to look after interests of his father who had established business in western Can. as fur and gen. trader. In 1899 business turned into limited liability Co., with F. W. Stobart as pres. and gen. mgr. Vice-pres. of the Canadian Fire Insur. Co.; a mem. of the Advisory Bd. for Manitoba of the Edinburgh Life Insur. Co.; a dir. of the Winnipeg Gen. Hospital. *Address:* Winnipeg.

STONE, Henry Athelston; *b.* Londan, Eng., 5 Aug., 1861; *s.* of the late Wm. Stone, of London, Eng.; *m.* Beatrice Hetty, 3rd *d.* of the late Charles Philps, of London, Eng.; one *s.* two *d.* *Educ.:* England. Apprenticed to Daniel Nicholson, of St. Paul's Ch. Yd., London; went to Toronto, when 21 years of age, and after being in business there for some yrs., proceeded to Vancouver to manage Gault Bros. business; made a director of the company three yrs. ago; now managing director; president, Vancouver Board of Trade; director the Heaps Lumber Co. *Recreations:* gardening and yachting. *Address:* 1249 Davie St., Vancouver, B.C. *Club:* Terminal City, Vancouver.

STONE, William; *b.* Birmingham, Eng., 8 July, 1856; *s.* of William and Harriett Stone; *m.* Ellen M. Bungay; three *s.* two *d.* *Educ.:* Birmingham, Eng. Arrived in Canada, 1869; now President of Stone, Limited, lithographers and publishers; director, Bank of Toronto; vice-president National Life Assurance Co.; vice-pres., National Club, Toronto; pres. of the Ontario Motor League. *Address:* 661 Huron St., Toronto. *Clubs:* Toronto Hunt, National, Lambton, Toronto.

STRANG, Andrew; *b.* Montreal, 9 March 1849; *s.* of Struthers Strang and Janet Ferrie; *m.* 1870, Ann Harriett Sinclair, of St. Andrews, Man.; ten *c.* *Educ.:* Hamilton. At sixteen yrs. of age, entered the office of the G. T. R. at Toronto. In 1868, went to Winnipeg as representative of a syndicate of Hamilton merchants, and has remained there ever since, engaged in mercantile life. El. to the first Council of Winnipeg 1874; an active mem. of the Winnipeg Bd. of Trade, and treas. for six yrs. Pres. of the Exhibition Bd. for two yrs.; a dir. of the Winnipeg Gen. Hospital; at one time pres. of the Winnipeg Liberal Assn. *Address:* Winnipeg.

STRATHCONA AND MOUNT ROYAL; 1st Baron; (Donald Alexander Smith,) G.C.M.G., G.C.V.O., F.R.S., LL.D., P.C., D.L.; High Commissioner for Canada since 1890; *b.* Scotland, 1820, *s.* of the late Alexander Smith, of Archieston, and Barbara, *d.* of Donald Stuart, of Leanchoil; *m.* Isabella Sophia, *d.* of the late Richard Hardisty; one *d.* *Educ.:* Scotland. Last resident gov. and chief commr. at Montreal, of the Hudson's Bay Co.; special commr. during first Riel Rebellion in Red River Settlement, 1869-70; mem. first Ex. Council of N. W. Territory, 1870; mem. for Selkirk in Dom. Parlt., 1871-2, 1874, and 1878; for West Montreal, 1877-96; represented Winnipeg and St. John in Manitoba Legis., 1871-84; dir., St. Paul, Minneapolis, and Manitoba Ry., Hon. pres., Bank of Montreal; Chancellor of Aberdeen Univ., since 1903, and of McGill Univ.; Cr. K.C.M.G., 1886; Lord Rector of Aberdeen Univ., 1899; hon. LL.D., of Cambridge, Yale, Glasgow, Aberdeen, Toronto, Laval and Victoria (Manchester); hon. D.C.L. of Oxford and Dublin; F.R.S., 1904; apptd. High Commr. for Canada, 1896; pres., Quebec Rifle Assn.; *Address:* 28 Grosvenor Square, London W.; 17 Victoria

St., S.W.; Glencoe, N.B.; Colonsay, N.B.; Debden Hall, Newport, Essex; Norway House, Pictou, N.S.; 911 Dorchester St. W., Montreal. *Clubs:* Athenaeum, London, Eng.; Mount Royal, St. James', Montreal; Rideau, Ottawa.

STRATHCONA, Baroness (Isabella Sophia); *d.* of late Richard Hardisty; *m.* Hon. Donald A. Smith, who was cr. K.C.M.G., in 1886; G.C.M.G., 1896, and was raised to the peerage 1897; one *d.* (Hon. Margaret Charlotte Howard). *Educ.:* Edinburgh, Scot. In conjunction with her daughter, gave $100,000 to McGill Univ. for the erection of a new wing to its Medical Bldg. *Address:* 28 Grosvenor Square, London, W., England.

STRATHY, Stuart; Gen. Mgr. The Traders' Bank of Canada; *b.* Toronto, 26 Jan., 1860; *s.* of Dr. George W. Strathy, Mus. Doc., and Mary Cornwall Strathy; *m.* Elizabeth Ford; one *s.* two *d.* *Educ.:* Toronto Coll. Inst.; entered banking office in 1878; and passed through all grades to gen. mgr. *Recreation:* golf. *Address:* 54 Clarandon Ave., Toronto. *Clubs:* Toronto, Golf, Toronto.

STRATTON, James Robert, M.P.; proprietor of the Peterborough Daily *Examiner* *b.* Millbrook, Ont., 3 May., 1858; *s.* of James Stratton and Rosanna Stratton; *m.* Eliza Jane Ormond. *Educ.:* Peterborough Coll. Inst. Assumed ownership and publication of the Peterborough *Examiner* while yet a minor, Daily *Examiner* 1885, and still publishes it. Mem. Bd. of Educ. for the City of Peterborough for several terms. First el. to Ont. Legislature for West Peterborough, 1886, and at each succeeding el.; was Prov. Sec. in Ross Govt. from 8 Oct., 1899 until 1905, on its retirement from power. Vice-pres. of the Traders' Bank; pres., The Trusts & Guarantee Co.; The Dominion Permanent Loan Co., Home Life Assn., Peterborough Lock Co.; dir., Canada Starch Co., Imperial Cotton Co. Returned to H. of C. for West Peterborough, at g. e., 1908. *Address:* Peterborough, Ont. *Clubs:* National, Toronto; Peterborough.

STREET, Lieut.-Col. Douglas Richmond; Commanding the Governor General's Foot Guards, Ottawa; *b.* Fredericton, N.B., 19 June, 1864; *s.* of Charles Frederick Street, and Lucy A. Kendall; *m.* Elizabeth Bauld Christie, of North Sydney, N.S.; two *s.* one *d.* *Educ.:* Univ. of Ottawa For the past 18 yrs. has been associated with the electric lighting interests of Ottawa; sec.-treas. of the Ottawa Light, Heat & Power Lt.-Co.; Col. commanding the Gov.-Genl's. Foot Guards. *Address:* 327 Somerset St., Ottawa. *Clubs:* Rideau, Golf, Hunt, Ottawa.

STREET, Miss Evelyn de Latre; *b.* London, Ont., 5 April, 1874; *d.* of the late Hon. W. P. R. Street, Justice of the High Court of Ontario, and Mrs. Street. *Educ.:* Germany; graduate of the Royal Leipzig Conservatory; soloist with the Damrosch Orchestra of New York; is now 2nd violin of the American String Quartette of Boston, Mass., organized and coached by Ch. M. Laeffler, the eminent violinist and composer. *Address:* Midfield, Mass., and 10 Mackenzie Ave., Rosedale, Toronto.

STREETON, Mrs. Arthur (Nora Clench) *b.* St. Mary's, Ont., *d.* of Leon M. Clench; *m.* 1908, Arthur Streeton, a well-known Australian landscape painter. Studied at Hellmuth Coll., London, Ont., and after at Leipsic Conservatory under Brodsky, the famous Russian violinist. Has played in nearly all the countries of the world. *Address:* c|o Concert Soc., 2 Hill Road, London, N., Eng.

STRINGER, Arthur; poet, novelist; *b.* London, Ont., 26 Feb., 1874; *m.* 1900, Jobyna Howland, of New York. *Educ.:* Toronto Univ., Univ. of Oxford, Eng. Editorial writer on Am. Press Assn., 1898-1901; lit. editor of Success, 1903-4. *Publications:* Watchers of Twilight; Pauline and Other Poems; Epigrams; A Study In King Lear; The Loom of Destiny; The Silver Poppy; Lonely O'Malley; Hephaestus and Other Poems; The Wire Tappers, 1906; Phantom Wires, 1907; The Occasional Offender, 1907; The Woman In The Rain, 1907; The Gun Runner, 1909; a frequent contributor to mags. *Address:* Cedar Springs, Ont.

STUART, Hon. Charles Allan, B.A. (Toronto Univ.) LL.B. (Toronto Univ.), Chancellor of Univ. of Alberta; *b.* Tp. of Caradoc, Co. of Middlesex, Ont., 3 Aug., 1864; *s.* of Charles Stuart and Hannah Campbell; *m.* Beatrice Roxborough, *d.* of late Wm. E. Roxborough, of Norwood, Ont.; three *s.* *Educ.:* Strathroy Collegiate Ins ., Univ. of Toronto; graduated Univ. Toronto 1891; called to Bar of Ont., 1896; called to Bar of Northwest Territories, 1898; elected to first legislature of Alberta for constituency of Gleichen, 1905; Judge Supreme Court of North West Territories for provs. of Alberta and Saskatchewan, 8 Oct., 1906; Judge Supreme Court of Alberta, Sept., 1907; Chancellor of Univ. of Alberta, 15 March, 1908. *Address:* 718 7th Ave. W., Calgary, Alta.

STUPART, Robert Frederic, F.R.S.C., F.R.A.S.C.; *b.* Toronto, 24 Oct., 1857; *s.* of Capt. R. D. Stupart, R.M.; *m.* Marion Dallas; three *s.* one *d.* *Educ.:* Upper Can. Coll., Toronto; entered Metereological service early in life; apptd. director, of the Toronto Magnetic Observatory in 1894. *Publications:* various articles on the climate of Canada. *Recreation:* golf. *Address:* 15 Admiral Road, Toronto. *Clubs:* R.C.Y.C., Victoria, Massissauga Golf, Toronto, Ont.

STURDEE, Lieut.-Col. Edward Thankful, (R. O. Militia); *b.* St. John, N.B., 2 Sept., 1854; *s.* of the late Henry Parker Sturdee, London, Eng., and Emily Lawrence, London, Eng.; *m.* Gertrude C. Scovill, *d.* of the late Richard C. Scovill, in 1889; one *s.* two *d.* *Educ.:* St. John, N.B., private sch.; received business training in a bank and was for some years accountant in water dept.; atty. of St. John; for the past 20 years has been in business as a broker and manufacturers' agent; has always been an enthusiast in military matters, and served in the 62nd St. John Fusiliers for over 30 years, rising to the rank of Lieut.-Col., and to the command of the regiment; has several times acted on the staff and was for three years Brigade Major of the 13th Brigade; now on the Reserve of Officers; long service decoration; past pres., St.

George's Society; a Director of the Fernhill Cemetery Co.; Liberal; Church of England. *Publication:* a History of the Union Jack. *Address:* Germain St., St. John, N.B. *Club:* Union, St. John.

SULLIVAN, Hon. Michael, M.D.; senator; *b.* Killarney, 13 Feb., 1838; *s.* of late Daniel O'Sullivan, formerly of Killarney, Co. Kerry, Ireland; *m.* June, 1867, Mary Brown, Kingston. *Educ.:* Regiopolis Coll. and Queen's Univ.; grad. M.D., 1858; arrived in Canada, 1842; apptd. Prof. of Surgery and Anatomy, Royal Coll. of Physicians and Surgeons, Kingston, 1870; pres., Dom. Medical Assn., 1883; was purveyor general during the N. W. Rebellion, 1885; Mayor of Kingston, 1874; unsuccessful candidate for H. of C. for Kingston, 1882; called to the Senate, 29 Jan., 1884; Catholic; Liberal. *Address:* 116 Rideau St., Kingston, Ont.

SULMAN, George William, M.L.A.; *b.* Burford, Brant Co., 4 July, 1866; *s.* of Wm. Sulman and Sarah Cooper; *m.* Mary Agnes Meekeson; two *s.* two *d.* *Educ.:* Burford and Brantford; alderman in Chatham for six years; Mayor for two years, 1901-02 first el. to Ont. Leg. Ass., 1908. *Address:* Chatham, Ont. *Clubs:* Chatham (President)

SULTE, Benjamin, F.R.S.C., LL.D.; *b.* Three Rivers, Que., 17 Sept., 1841; *s.* of Benjamin Sulte, navigator, and Marie Antoinette Lefebvre; *m.* 1871, May Augustine, *d.* of Etienne Parent, Under Secretary of State; one *s.* one *d.* (*dec.*) *Educ.:* Friars' School, Three Rivers. Engaged in commerce and lumbering business; served as a volunteer at the frontier, 1865; military school certificate, 1865; served at the frontier, 1866 (medal); translator in Parliament, 1867; Private Secretary to Minister of Militia and Defence, 1870-73; Clerk in same department, 1874; Chief Clerk and Acting Deputy Minister, 1889; retired on superannuation, 1903; President, Institut Canadien, Ottawa, 1874; President, St. John Baptist Society, Ottawa, 1883; Pres. of St. Joseph Society, 1877; Pres. of the Royal Society of Canada, 1904; Corresponding member of several historical societies. *Publications:* Les Paurentiennes (poems), 1870, Les Chants Nouveaux (poems), 1876; Melanges d'Historie, 1876; Histoire des Canadiens-Francais (8 vols.), 1882-84; Pages d'Histoire, 1891; Histoire de la Milice Canadienne, 1897; La Langue Francaise en Canada, 1898; La Bataille de Chateauguay, 1899; besides many small publications; has translated the National Anthem, into French, and delivered many lectures on historical subjects. *Address:* 304 Wilbrod Street, Ottawa.

SURVEYER, Edouard Fabre, B.A., LL.M., B.C.L., K.C.; *b.* Montreal, 24 March, 1875; *s.* of Louis Joseph Arthur Surveyer, and Hectorine Fabre, sister of His Grace Archbishop Fabre, of Montreal, Lady Costelo, Hon. Hector Fabre, C.M.G., Canadian Commissioner in Paris; *m.* Elodie *d.* of the late Edmond Barnard, Q.C., Montreal; one *d.* *Educ.:* St. Mary's Coll., Laval Univ., McGill Univ., Montreal; called to the bar of Quebec, July, 1896; lecturer on Pleading and Practice, McGill Univ., since 1905; pres., Junior Bar Assn., 1903-04; K.C., July, 1909; pres., Canadian Club of Montreal. *Publications:* The Bench and the Bar of Montreal (1907). *Address:* 161 Ste. Famille St. and 112 St. James St., Montreal. *Clubs:* University, Lafontaine, M.A.A.A., Montreal.

SUTHERLAND, Rev. Alexander, D.D.; Missionary Sec. of the Methodist Church in Canada; *b.* Tp. of Guelph, 17 Sept., 1833; *y. s.* of Capt. N. Sutherland, and Mary Henderson (both Scotch); *m.* Mary Jane, *e. d.* of Hugh Moore, of Dundas, Ont. *Educ.:* Pub. Sch., Guelph. Commenced life as a printer, but later studied for the Methodist ministry, and was ordained in 1879. Held pastoral charges in many towns and cities in Ontario and Quebec. In 1874, was apptd. gen. sec. of Methodist Missions, and Clerical Sec. of the Missionary Soc.; del. from the Canadian Church to the Gen. Conference of the M. E. Church of the U.S. at Brooklyn, 1872; del. to the Meth. Ecumenical Conference in England, 1881; fraternal del. to the British Wesleyan Conference, 1880, declined the principalship of Mount Allison Univ., N.B., 1891; has held present position since union of Methodist Churches consummated at Belleville, 1884. *Publications:* A Summer in Prairieland; Methodism in Canada, its Project and Study. *Address:* 437 Sherbourne St., Toronto.

SUTHERLAND, Donald; *b.* West Zorra tp., Co. Oxford, 8 April, 1863; *s.* of Robert Sutherland and Elizabeth Hutchison; *m.* Minnie Pearl Hossack; four *s.* one *d.* *Educ.:* in the pub. schs.; Councillor and Reeve of the Tp. of North Oxford; Co. Councillor Division No. 1 Co. of Oxford, two years; elec. member of Ontario Legislature for S. Oxford, 1902; re-elec. in 1905; defeated in 1908; director of Colonization for Ont. *Address:* Humewood Ave., Toronto, Ont.

SUTHERLAND, Hugh; chief executive officer of the Canadian Northern Ry.; *b.* New London, P.E.I., 22 Feb., 1845; *m.* May, only *d.* of Hon. R. D. Banks, of Baltimore, Md. Removed to Oxford Co., Ont., while still a child, with his parents, and educ. there. Commenced business in lumbering and contracting. In 1874 was apptd. Dom. Supt. of Pub. Works in the Northwest, but retired from the office 1879 and established first saw mill in Winnipeg. El. to H. of C. for Selkirk, Man., 1882, but was defeated for Winnipeg at g. e., 1887. A warm advocate of Hudson Bay Ry. Has been largely instrumently in development work in Canada, and associated with Messrs. Mackenzie and Mann for some yrs. *Address:* Winnipeg. *Club:* Manitoba, Winnipeg.

SUTHERLAND, Hon. Robert Franklyn, B.A., K.C., P.C., Judge of the High Court of Justice for Ontario; *b.* Newmarket, Ont., 5 April, 1859; *s.* of Donald Sutherland and Jane Boddy; *m.* Mary Bartlett; two *d.* *Educ.:* Newmarket, Windsor and Toronto; called to the bar of Ont., 1887; created K.C., 1899; elec. for the constituency of North Essex, 1900 to the H. of C., re-elec. 1904 and 1908; Speaker of the H. of C., 1905 to 1909; sworn in as Privy Councillor, 1909; apptd. Judge of the High Court of Justice for Ont., 1909. *Recreations:* cricket and golf. *Address:* Toronto, Ont. *Clubs:* National, Toronto; Windsor.

SUTHERLAND, Hon. William Charles, B.A., M.L.A.; *b.* Embro, Oxford Co., Ont., 7 June, 1865; *s.* of Thomas and Isabella Sutherland, (Scotch); *m.* Alice Mary Walker, of Shelburne, Ont., one *s.* one *d.* *Educ.:* pub. sch., Orangeville High Sch., McGill Univ.; studied law in Manitoba; called to the bar in Manitoba; moved to Saskatoon, Sask., in 1903; elec. to the Legislature in 1905, and apptd. deputy speaker; re-el. in 1908, and apptd. speaker of the Legislature; owns a large wheat farm near Saskatoon. *Recreations:* motoring and tennis. *Address:* Saskatoon, Sask. *Club:* Saskatoon.

SWEENEY, Right Rev. James Fielding, M.A., D.D., Bishop of Toronto; *b.* London, Eng., 15 Nov., 1857; *s.* of Col. James Fielding Sweeney; *m.* Catherine Boomer; two *d.* *Educ.:* Montreal High Sch., McGill Univ., McGill Normal Sch., Trinity Univ.; arrived in Canada, 1868; pursued his theological studies at the Montreal Diocesan theological Coll., and was ordained deacon by the late Archbishop, then Bishop Bond, in 1880, and priest in 1881; became rector of St. Luke's, Montreal, and chaplain to the Montreal General Hospital; in 1882, went to Toronto to become rector of St. Philip's; apptd. Honorary Canon of St. Alban's Cathedral 1889. In 1895 was elected Rural Dean of Toronto, and was later apptd. Archdeacon of York and Simcoe; was assistant to the late Archbishop, and took an active part in the administration of Diocesan affairs; consecrated Bishop of Toronto, March 25th, 1909. *Address:* See House, 68 Howland Ave., Toronto.

SWIFT, James; *b.* Kingston, Ont., 20 Feb., 1843; *s.* of Michael Swift and Katherine Haughey; *m.* 1876, Helen A. Hogan, of Troy, N.Y.; two *s.* *Educ.:* Christian Brothers' Sch., Kingston; entered Kingston office of Montreal Telegraph Co., 1857; and later became an operator; employed by Western Union Tel. Co. at Cincinnati, Ohio, 1862-1865; transferred to Buffalo, 1865, and returned to Kingston the same yr. In 1866, purchased the St. Lawrence wharf at Kingston and started in business for himself. Is interested in mining; a stockholder in the Richelieu & Ontario Navigation Co., and was for several yrs. a dir.; a dir., of the Kingston & Pembroke Ry., until it was leased to the C.P.R.; mem., Kingston City Council for three yrs. *Address:* 254 King St., Kingston, Ont.

SYLVESTRE, Joseph Israel, LL.B., M.L.A., K.C.; *b.* St. Barthelemy, Que., 26 Feb., 1870; *s.* of Naubert and Elise Sylvestre; *m.* Laetitia Corsin; four *s.* two *d.* *Educ.:* Coll. of L'Assomption, and Laval Univ.; elec. to the Quebec Leg. Ass., June, 1908, for the Co. of Montcalm. *Address:* St. Julienne, Que.

SYMONS, Harry, K.C.; *b.* Dartmouth, Eng., 5 March, 1854; *s.* of John Darnell Symons and Agnes Dashper Hamaford; *m.* Florence Theresa *d.* of Samuel Hesson, ex-M.P., Stratford, Ont.; four *d.* *Educ.:* London, Eng., and York Co. Gram. Sch., Toronto; arrived in Canada, July, 1866; solicitor in 1874; called to the Bar of Ont., 1875; advocate, N.W.T., 1890; apptd. Q.C., 1894; pres., St. George's Soc., Toronto, 1885-6; Hon. member Royal Society of St. George, London, Eng.; life member, Imperial Institute; presented at Court of St. James', London, June, 1907. *Recreations:* walking, bowling. *Address:* 98 Madison Ave., Toronto. *Club:* National, Toronto.

SYMONDS, Rev. Herbert, M.A., D.D.; *b.* Rickinghall, Suffolk, Eng., 28 Dec., 1860; *s.* of George Symonds and Hannah Wright; *m.* Emma B. Boyd, 4th *d.* of the late Mossom Boyd of Bobcaygeon, Ont.; three *s.* four *d.* *Educ.:* Framlingham Coll., Suffolk and Trinity Univ., Toronto; arrived in Canada, in 1881; first class honors in theology in 1885; ordained deacon, 1885; priest, 1887; fellow and lecturer, Trinity Univ., 1887-1890; professor of Theology, 1890-92; rector of Ashburnham, Peterboro, 1892-1901; headmaster, Trinity Coll. Sch., Port Hope, Ont., 1901-1903; vicar of Christ Church Cathedral, Montreal, 1903; Honorary D.D., Queen's, 1897. *Publications:* "Lectures on Christian Unity," various pamphlets. *Recreations:* gardening, curling. *Address:* 145 Metcalfe St., Montreal; "Beau Bocage," Knowlton, Que. (summer).

T

TAILLON, Hon. Louis Olivier, K.C., D.C.L.; *b.* Terrebonne, Que., 26 Sept., 1840; *s.* of Aime Taillon and Josepthe Daunais; *m.* 1875, Marie Louise Georgina (*d.* 1876), *d.* of the late Hon. P. U. Archambault, M.L.C. *Educ.:* Local Schs., and Masson Coll. Called to Quebec Bar. 1865. Commenced practice in Montreal, and is now head of the firm of Taillon, Bonin & Morin. Cr. Q.C. by Marquis of Lorne 1882; apptd. a Commr. under the Municipal Loan Fund Act. 1880-82; offered a Judgeship, 1888 and 1889 but declined and el. Batonnier of Bar in 1892; D.C.L., Laval Univ., 1900, and by Univ. of Bishop's Coll., Lennoxville, 1895; one of originators of French-Canadian National Congress at Montreal, 1874; mem. for Montreal East in Quebec Legis., 1875-86; Speaker of the Leg. Ass., 1882-84; became Attorney-Gen., 1884; resigned portfolio after Prov. g. e., 1886; Leader of the Opposition 1886-1890; mem. for Chambly, 1892; Premier of Que., 1892-1896; apptd. Postmaster-General, 1896; unsuccessful at g. e., 1896 and 1900; has now retired into private life. *Address:* 180 St. James' St., Montreal.

TAIT, Hon. Sir Melbourne McTaggart, Kt., D.C.L.; Chief Justice of the Superior Ct. of the Prov. of Quebec, at Montreal; *b.* Melbourne, Que., 20 May, 1842; *s.* of late Thomas Tait, *m.* (1st) 1863, Monica (*d.* 1876), *d.* of late James Holmes, of Montreat; (2nd) 1878, Lydia, *d.* of Henry B. Kaighn, of Newport, R.I. *Educ.:* St. Fransic Coll. Sch., Richmond, Que.; Univ.Mc. Gill Coll., Montreal. Called to the Bar June, 1863; practised at Melbourne in partnership with the late Hon. W. H. Webb, Q.C., M.L.C.; removed to Montreal 1870, and joined the late Sir J. J. C. Abbott, later becoming head of the firm of Tait, Abbott & Campbell; cr. Q.C., 1882; cr. Kt. 1897; apptd. a Puisne Judge of the Superior Ct., 1887; acting Chief Justice, Montreal, 1894; Chief Justice, 1906. *Address:* 614

Sherbrooke St. W., Montreal. *Clubs:* Montreal, St. James, Montreal.

TAIT, Thomas James; Chairman of the Victorian Rly. Commission, Australia; *b.* Melbourne, Que., 24 July, 1864; *s.* of Sir Melbourne Tait, Chief Justice of the Superior Court for the Province of Quebec, and Monica (*deceased*), *d.* of the late Thomas Holmes, Montreal; *m.* Emily St. Aubert, *d.* of G. R. R. Cockburn, Toronto; one *d.* *Educ.:* High Sch., Montreal; in 1880, entered the Audit Office of the G. T. Ry.; secretary to Sir Wm. Van Horne, then vice-pres. and general manager C. R. Py. in 1882; afterwards Asst. Supt., Moose Jaw; General Supt., Ontario Division at Toronto; General Supt. of Ontario and Quebec Division; Asst. General Manager of the whole system; manager of lines east of Port Arthur; Manager of Transportation east of Port Arthur; Manager of Transportation over the entire system; went to Australia in the spring of 1903 to be chairman of the Victorian Railway Commission; has converted the Ry. System of Victoria from a nonpaying to a paying basis, the surplus last year being £200,000, representing a profit of £550 a day, as compared with a deficit of £1,000 a day before assuming chairmanship of Comn. *Recreations:* golf, tennis. *Address:* Victorian Railway Commission, Melbourne, Australia. *Clubs:* St. James., Montreal; Toronto, Toronto; Melbourne, Australia.

TALBOT, Lieut.-Col. Onesiphore Ernest *b.* St. Arsene, Temiscouata Co., Que.; *s.* of J. F. Talbot and Marguerite, *d.* of E. R. Frechette; *m.* 1887, Mary Ann Law Guilmartin, of Savannah, Georgia, U.S. *Educ.:* St. Michael and Quebec Seminary; a member of the Agric. Council of Prov. of Que.; Lieut.-Col. of the 17th Regt of Levis and Bellechasse; was Adjutant of the Bisley Team, 1906; elec. to H. of C. at g. e., 1896; re-el. at g. e., 1900, 1904, 1908; a Liberal. *Address:* St. Michel de Bellechasse, Que.

TALBOT, Hon. Peter; senator; *b.* Eramosa, Wellington Co., Ont., 30 March, 1854; *s.* of Henry Talbot and Margaret Stewart; *m.* 1879, Clara, *d.* of John Card, of Guelph, Ont. *Educ.:* Rockwood Acad., and Ottawa Normal Sch. Holds teacher's first-class certificate. A farmer. El. to the Leg. Ass. for the North-West at g. e., 1902. El. to the H. of C. at g. e., 1904; resigned 8 March, 1906, and called to the Senate. A Liberal. *Address:* Lacombe, Alta.

TANGUAY, G. Emile; architect; *b.* St. Gervais, Qoe., 8 Oct., 1857; *m.* 1888, Clara Trudel; five *s.* *Educ.:* Quebec Normal Sch. At age of eighteen, entered office of J. F. Peachy, architect; has practiced in Quebec since 1880; designed and constructed Hotel-Dieu Hospital, City Hall, Garneau Block, Daily Telegraph Office, Quebec, and St. Roch's branch of Quebec Bank, Cathedral at Three Rivers, Cathedral and Bishop's Palace at Alexandria, Ont., and many other important institutions. Was the third pres., Architects' Assn. of the Prov. of Que.; dir. Council of Arts and Manufacturers of same prov.; dir., Plessisville Foundry, Matabetchouan Pulp Co., Lake St. John Dist., Canada Cement Co., mem. Quebec Bd. of Trade, Knights of Columbus, Que. *Address:* 20 d'Aiguillon St., Quebec. *Club:* Hunt, Quebec.

TANNER, Charles Elliott, K.C.; Recorder and Stipendiary of Pictou, N.S.; *b.* Pictou, N.S., 7 Oct., 1857; *s.* of Richard Tanner and Jane Brown; *m.* Alice May McDonald; one *s.* *Educ.:* Pictou Acad. Admitted to the Bar, 1878; cr. K.C., 1896; recorder and stipendiary of Pictou since 1888. First el. to N.S. Legis., 1894; defeated 1897; re-el., 1900, 1901 and 1906; resigned 1908 to run for Fed. Parlt., but unsuccessful. Tendered prov. leadership by provincial convention, 1909. *Address:* Pictou, N.S.

TARTE, Louis Joseph; *b.* L'Assomption Que., 25 Dec., 1872; *s.* of J. Israel Tarte and Georgina Sylvester; *m.* Bertha Gauthier one *s.* and two *d.* *Educ.:* Quebec Commercial Acad. In journalism for many years; pres. and gen'l. mgr. "*La Patrie,*" Montreal. *Address:* 716 St. Hubert St., Montreal, Que. *Clubs:* St. Denis, Lafontaine, Montreal Jockey, Montreal.

TASCHEREAU, Rt. Hon. Sir Henri Elzear, Kt., P.C., LL.D.; Dean of the Law Faculty, Univ. of Ottawa; *b.* St. Mary's, Beauce Co., Que., 7 Oct., 1836; *s.* of P. E. Taschereau, M.L.A., and Catherine H. Dionne; *m.* (1st) Marie Antoinette, *d.* of late Hon. R. U. Harwood, M.L.C.; (2nd) 1897, Marie Louise, *d.* of late Charles Panet, of Ottawa; five *s.* three *d.* *Educ.:* Quebec Seminary. Called to the Quebec Bar, 1857; cr. Q.C., 1867; sat in Can. Legis. Assem. for Beauce Co., 1861-67; Judge of the Superior Ct. of Quebec, 1871-1878; Judge of the Supreme Ct. of Can., 1878-1906; Chief Justice 1902-1906; Administrator of Govt. in 1904; cr. Kt., 1902; P.C., 1904. *Publications:* "Criminal Law of Canada" (3 eds.); "Code Civil Procedure of Prov. of Quebec." *Recreations:* tennis, whist. *Address:* 265 Laurier Av. E., Ottawa. *Clubs:* Rideau, Country, Ottawa; Fraserville.

TASCHEREAU, Hon. Louis Alexander, M.L.A.; Minister of Public Works, Quebec; *b.* Quebec, 5 March, 1867; *s.* of Hon. Jean Thomas Taschereau, Judge of the Supreme Court, and Josephine *d.* of R. E. Caron, some time Lieutenant Governor of Quebec; *m.* Adene Dionne; three *s.* two *d.* *Educ.:* Quebec Seminary; an advocat; was elec. to the Quebec Legislature, 1900 and 1905; sworn in as Minister of Public Works, 17 Oct., 1907. re-elected in 1907 and 1908. *Address:* 66 St. Louis St., Quebec. *Club:* Garrison, Quebec.

TAYLOR, Andrew Thomas, R.C.A., F.R.I.B.A.; *s.* of late James Taylor, publisher, Edinburgh, and Agnes Drummond; *b.* Edinburgh, Oct., 1850; *m.* 1891, Mary, *d.* of Acct. Commissary-General Elliott, H.M.'s Ordnance. *Educ.:* Edinburgh; Royal Academy Sch., London. Pursued professional studies in Edinburgh, Aberdeen London, Italy, and the Continent; practised in London for a short time; came to Canada, 1883, on professional work, and has since practised in Montreal; gained numerous architectural competitions and medals, and designed and erected many important buildings all over Canada; is architect to the Bank of Montreal, McGill Univ., Royal Victoria Hospital, and the Montreal General

Hospital; Prof. of Ecclesiastical Architecture in Presbyterian Coll., Montreal; past president, Province of Que. Assn. of Architects; Hon. Secy. for Canada, R.I.B.A. *Publications:* Towers and Steeples of Sir Christopher Wren; Dominion Drawing Books; various lectures upon art subjects. *Recreation:* golf. *Address:* 19 Essex Avenue, Montreal. *Clubs:* Mount Royal, Montreal.

TAYLOR, Rev. Andrew Todd, M.A., D.D.; *b.* in Ireland, 1866; *s.* of Robert and Mary Leach Taylor; *m.* Lauretta M. Brownson; one *s.* four *d.* *Educ.:* Grove City Coll., Pa., and Princeton Univ., New Jersey, U.S. Arrived in Canada, 1908; in business for six years; teacher for two years; clergyman for 16 years. *Recreations:* golf and tennis. *Address:* 118 Pembroke St., Toronto. *Clubs:* North Toronto Golf, Toronto; Friars, Princeton, N.J.

TAYLOR, Frederick William; *b.* Moncton, N.B., 1863; *s.* of Ezekiel Taylor and Rosalie Beatty; *m.* Jane Fayrer Henshaw, of Montreal; one *s.* one *d.* *Educ.:* High Sch. and privately at Moncton; entered service of Bank of Montreal, 1878; manager, Deseronto, 1896; Asst. Inspector, 1898; Manager, Chicago, 1902; manager, London, Eng., 1905. *Recreations:* tennis, golf, skating. *Address:* Hans Court, Hans Road, S.W., Fairfield, Sunninghill, Ascot, or Bank of Montreal, 47 Threadneedle St., London, Eng. *Clubs:* St. James, Montreal; City of London, and Bath, Eng.

TAYLOR, George, M.P.; *b.* County of Leeds, Ont., 31 March, 1840; *s.* of William Taylor and Ann Graham; *m.* Margaret Ann Latimer, 10 Sept., 1863. *Educ.:* Com. Sch. in the Tp. of Lansdowne, Ont.; a manufacturer; was reeve of Gananoque for seven years; also Warden of United Co. of Leeds and Grenville; Co. auditor; a general merchant for 25 years; has been a manufacturer for 20 years; first elec. to the H. of C. in 1882, and has represented Leeds constantly since that time, being re-el. at every election; chief whip of the Lib.-Cons. party. *Address:* Gananoque, Ont.

TAYLOR, Hon. Hedley Clarence, M.A. (Mount Allison Univ., N.B.), LL.B. (Michigan Univ., U.S.A.); *b.* Sheffield, N.B., 20 Sept., 1864; *s.* of Samuel Taylor and Charlotte Jane Hunter; *m.* Bessie Perley Taylor; two *s.* *Educ.:* pub. sch., N.B., Mount Allison Academy and Univ. Studied law in St. John, N.B.; admitted to bar of N.B. in 1891, and to bar of North West Territories same yr.; apptd. Judge of District Court of Alberta, 21 Nov., 1907. *Address:* 417 Fifth St., Edmonton, Alta. *Club:* Edmonton.

TAYLOR, James Davis, M.P.; *b.* Abenaqui Mills, Dorchester Co., Que., 2 Sept., 1863; *s.* of Thomas Taylor and Mary Humphrey Henderson; *m.* Janie Hay, *d.* of the late Rev. J. H. Jenkins, Rector Three Rivers, Que. *Educ.:* Quebec and Ottawa Public Schs;. apprenticed to the printing trade, and followed newspaper business in Montreal and Ottawa; for many yrs on staff of Ottawa *Citizen* and mem. of Parlty. Press Gallery; removed in 1892, to Victoria, B.C., and thence to New Westminster, 1900; Managing director, *Columbian* Co., Ltd., New Westminster, B.C.; unsuccessful candidate for H. of C., 1904; elected 1908. *Recreation:* rifle shooting. *Address:* 212 Third Av., New Westminster, B.C. *Club:* Westminster.

TAYLOR, Louis Denison; *b.* Ann Arbor, Mich., U.S.A.; *s.* of Gustavus Adolphus and Amy Taylor; *m.* Annie Louise Pierce, Chicago, Ill., U.S.; two *s.* Arrived in Canada, Sept., 1895; was in business until 1897; employed in office of Vancouver Daily *Province* in that year; became owner and editor Daily *World*, June, 1905, which has grown to be the largest newspaper published in Western Canada, averaging 30 pages daily; Independent Liberal in politics; defeated candidate for Mayor of Vancouver, 1909. successful 1910. *Address:* Granville Mansions, Vancouver, B.C. *Clubs:* Terminal City and Commercial, Vancouver, B.C.

TAYLOR, Hon. Thomas, M.L.A.; Minister of Public Works for B.C.; *b.* 4 Feb., 1865, London, Ont.; *s.* of Thomas Taylor and Ann Talbot; *m.* Georgia Larson. *Educ.:* Pub. Schs. and Commercial Coll., London. Removed to Winnipeg 1885, and entered service of C.P.R. Moved to Trout Lake, B.C., 1894, and engaged in mercantile pursuits; apptd. mining recorder, 1895, for the Trout Lake Mining div. El. to B. C. Legis., March, 1900. Sworn as Min. of Pub. Works upon institution that office, 21 Dec., 1908. A mining broker; dir. of the Great Western Mines, Ltd.; vice-pres., Prince Mining Co. *Address:* Revelstoke, B.C.

TELFORD, Robert Taylor, M.L.A.; *b.* Shawville, Pontiac Co., Que., 19 June, 1860; *s.* of Robert and Ann Telford; *m.* Belle Howard, of Shamrock, Wis., U.S.; one *s.* *Educ.:* Public Sch.; went West during the rebellion and served four years in the Royal North West Mounted Police; a lumber dealer; elec. for Leduc, in the first legislature of Alberta, 1905. *Address:* Leduc, Alta.

TELLIER, Hon. Louis; Pusine Judge of the Superior Ct. of the Prov. of Quebec; *b.* Berthier, Que., 25 Dec., 1844; *s.* of Zephirin Tellier, of Ste. Melanie Daillebout, and L. Ferland, *d.* of V. Priskue Ferland; *m.* (1st) 1868, Hermine (*d.* 1878), *d.* of the late Dr. A. Malhiot; (2nd) 1882, Elzire (*d.* 1906) *d.* of G. A. Hamel; three *s.* five *d.* *Educ.:* Joliette Coll.; studied law under the late Mr. Baby, and later under Mr. Chagnon. Called to the Bar, 1866; practiced prof. in St. Hyacinthe; for some yrs. Dep. Prothonotary of the Superior Ct. and Dep. Clerk of the Circuit Ct. for Dist. of St. Hyacinthe; apptd. Crown Prosecutor for same dist., 1873. El. to H. of C. for St. Hyacinthe riding, at g. e., 1878; unsuccessful can. at g. e., 1882; became Puisne Judge of the Superior Ct. of the Prov. of Quebec, 1887; an administrator of Laval Univ., Montreal. *Address:* Montreal.

TEMPLEMAN, Hon. William, P.C., M.P., Minister of Inland Revenue for Canada; *b.* Packenham Village, Ont., 28 Sept., 1844; *s.* of Wm. Templeman and Helen Taylor; *m.* Eva Bond, of Almonte. *Educ.:* Pub. Sch., Pakenham, Ont.; established the Almonte *Gazette*, 1867; moved to Victoria, B.C., in 1884, establishing the *Times*, which he has since published; an unsuccessful candidate for the H. of C., 1891, and twice in 1896; called to the Senate in 1897; sworn of the Privy Council, and entered the Government 22 Feb., 1902, without portfolio; apptd. Minister of Inland Revenue, 6 Feb., 1906, and Minister of Mines upon creation of the Department, 3 May, 1907; elec. to the H. of C. for Victoria, B.C., 1906; unsuccessful in 1908, but elec. by acclam. for Comox-Atlin, in bye-election, Feb., 1909. *Address:* Victoria, B.C. *Clubs:* Rideau, Ottawa; Pacific, Victoria, B.C.

TESSIER, Hon. Auguste; Judge of the Superior Court of Quebec; *b.* Quebec, 20 Nov., 1853; *s.* of Hon. Ulric I. Tessier, Judge of the Court of King's Bench, and Adele Kelly; *m.* Corinne Gauvreau; three *s.* two *d.* His ancestors arrived in Canada at the time of the French régime; member of the Quebec Leg. Assem. for Rimouski, from 1889 to 1907; Speaker of the Assembly 1905; Minister of Agriculture, and Treasurer of the Province of Quebec in the administration of Premier Gouin; apptd. Judge of the Superior Court. *Address:* 3 Ursuline Lane, Quebec. *Clubs:* Garrison, Quebec.

TESSIER, Lieut.-Col. Joseph Adolph, K.C.; *b.* St. Anne de la Perade, Champlain Co., 17 Dec., 1862; *s.* of Louis de Gouzague Tessier, and Rose De Lima Laquerre; *m.* Marie Elmire Guillet; three *d.* Officer Commanding the 86th Regt.; City Attorney of Three Rivers, from 1896 to 1907; elec. to Quebec Legis. Assem., 1904 and 1908. *Address:* Three Rivers, Que.

TESSIER Hon. Jules; senator; *b.* Quebec, 16 April, 1852; *s.* of the late Hon. U. T. Tessier, Judge of the Court of Queen's Bench; *m.* 1882, Francois Mathilde Barnard, *Educ.:* Quebec Seminary, Jesuits Coll., Montreal, and Laval Univ. Called to the bar 1874; apptd. K.C., 1900; for several years editor of Quebec Law Reports;" Secretary of the National Convention, 1880, of the St. Jean Baptiste Soc. of Quebec, and also pres.; a director of the Lake St. John Co., pres., Quebec Colonization Soc.; a member of the Quebec City Council; elec. to Quebec Legis. Assem., 1886, 1890, 1892, 1897 and 1900; speaker, 1897-1900; was one of the founders and editors of *Le Clarion;* apptd. to the Senate, 12 March, 1903, Liberal. *Address.* Quebec.

THOBURN, William, M.P.; *b.* Portsmouth, Eng., 14 April, 1847; *s.* of John and Mary Thoburn; widower; two *d.* *Educ.:* Co. of Carleton; arrived in Canada, 1857; a woolen manufacturer; a director of the Almonte Knitting Co., Almonte; director of the Trust and Guarantee Co., Toronto, Ont.; was Mayor of Almonte for seven yrs.; first el. to H. of C., 1908; a Conservative. *Recreations:* boating, curling. *Address:* Almonte, Ont. *Club:* Rideau, Ottawa.

THOMAS, Chester Ashley; resident mgr Yukon Gold Co.; *b.* Los Angeles, Cal., Dec., 1874. *Educ.:* Stamford Univ., Cal. Entered service Yukon Gold Co., 1905. *Address:* Dawson, Y.T.

THOMPSON, Alfred, M.D., C.M.; *b.* Nine Mile River, Hants Co., N.S., 6 June, 1869; *s.* of James A. Thompson and Jane Thompson; *m.* Elsie Miller; one *s.* one *d.* *Educ.:* Univ. of Dalhousie, Halifax, N.S. Graduated in 1898; removed to Dawson, Y.T., 1899, where he has since practiced the medical profession. Served as mem. of the local legislature known as Yukon Council for two yrs. First el. to H. of C. at g. e., 1904; served for four yrs. and then retired from pub. life to continue practice of medicine. *Address:* Dawson, Y.T.

THOMPSON, Alfred Burke, B.A., M.L. A.; *b.* Penetanguishene, Ont., 18 July, 1862; *s.* of Alfred Andrew Thompson and Sarah Burke; *m.* Kate Worthington May (*dec.*) *Educ.:* Upper Can. Coll., Toronto Univ. Served in N. W. Rebellion with Q. O. R.; now Capt. of the 36th Regt. An unsuccessful can. in Simcoe Co. for the Legis. at g. e., 1894; el. at g. e., 1898; defeated 1902; re-el. at g. e., 1905 and 1908. *Recreation:* curling. Church of England. A Conservative. *Address:* Penetanguishene, Ont.

THOMPSON, Lieut.-Col. Andrew Thorburn, B.A., LL.B.; *b.* "Ruthven Park," Haldimand Co., Ont., 27 May, 1870; *s.* of David Thompson, M.P., and Elizabeth Stinson; *m.* Violet Isabel, *o. d.* of the late James Hepburn Burns, M.D., Toronto; two *s.* one *d.* *Educ.:* Cayuga High Sch., Up. Can. Coll., Toronto Univ., and Osgoode Hall; called to the bar in 1893; elected to the H. of C. in 1900; sat until 1904, during which time he was liberal whip for Ontario; was second in command of Canadian Coronation Contingent, and now in command of 5th Infantry Brigade; practicing in Ottawa as a parliamentary lawyer. *Publications:* articles on the Canadian Militia for the Encyclopedia American; editor of the Canadian Military *Gazette.* *Address:* 309 Frank St., Ottawa, and Ruthven Park, Cayuga, Ont. *Clubs:* Rideau, Country, Ottawa.

THOMPSON, Hon. Frederick Pemberton; senator; *b.* Douglas, York Co., N.B.; *s.* of Alexander Thompson and Hannah Pickard; *m.* 1876, Eliza Snowball, *d.* of Rev. John Snowball, (*dec.* 30 Nov., 1900). *Educ.:* Fredericton and Sackville Inst.; was a member of the firm of Thompson and Anderson, established in 1871; and lately re-organized as a joint-stock Co., under the name of McFarlane, Thompson Mfg. Co.; also interested in lumbering and milling; was a member of York Council for six years, and Warden three years; elec. to N.B. Legis. Assem., 1890, and continued a member until called to the Senate, 8 Feb., 1902; was vice-pres., the People's Bank of N.B., absorbed by the Bank of Montreal; pres., of the McFarlane Neill Manfg. Co.; man., dir., N.B. Telephone Co.; dir., Fredericton Gaslight Co., and pres., Victoria Hospital (founded by Lady Tilley); Methodist; Liberal. *Address:* Fredericton, N.B.

THOMPSON Frederick William; Vice-Pres. and Managing Dir., Ogilvie Flour Mills Co., Ltd.; *b.* Montreal, 1862; *s.* of the late Andrew Thompson and Josephine De Lesperance; *m.* 1882, *d.* of James Reid, formerly of Bedford, Que.; one *s.* three *d.* *Educ.:* Montreal and Brooklyn, N.Y. At age of fifteen entered service of the old Exchange Bank of Montreal; resigned to join the Ogilvie Milling Co. six yrs. later. became gen. mgr. of the business in the North-West, 1889; gen. mgr. of the entire concern, 1900; in conjunction with Mr. C. R. Hosmer, 1902, purchased and re-organized the business under style of the Ogilvie Flour Mills Co., Ltd., and became vice-pres.

and mng. dir. Vice-pres. of Kaministiqua Power Co.; pres., Canadian Appraisal Co.; dir., Royal Bank of Canada, the Liverpool, London and Globe Insur Co., Manitoba Insur. Co. *Address:* 80 Redpath St., Montreal. *Clubs:* Mount Royal, St. James, Forest and Stream, Montreal, Canada, Royal Montreal Golf and Jockey; Manitoba, Commercial, Winnipeg; Rideau, Ottawa; Constitutional, London, Eng.

THOMSON, Edward William, C.E., F. R.S.L.; *b.* Toronto Tp., Ont., 12 Feb., 1849; *s.* of William Thomson and Margaret Hamilton Foley; *m.* A. L. G. St. Denis; one *s.* *Educ.:* Pub. Sch., Caledonia and Brantford; Trinity Coll. Gram. Sch., Weston, Ont.; served in the U.S. Army last year of the Civil War; in Queen's Own Rifles, Toronto, 1866; Land Surveyor, 1872; civil engineer, 1875-1878; editorial writer, Toronto *Globe*, 1878-1891; editor *Youths' Companion*, Boston, 1891-1901; Free Lance and author since 1901; Ottawa Correspondent, Boston *Transcript*. *Publications:* "Old Man Savarin," "Between Earth and Sky," "Walter Dibbs," "Smoky Days," "Collection of Short Stories," "Versifier in M. S. Henry's translation of Ancassin and Nicolette"; "The Many Mansioned House," "When Lincoln Died," "Collection of Poems," fugitive stories, poems and press articles. *Recreations:* fishing and walking. *Address:* 360 Concession St., Ottawa. *Clubs:* Authors, London, Eng.; International, Boston, Mass.

THOMSON, Henry Broughton, M.L.A.; *b.* Newry, Co. Down, Ireland; 21 July, 1870; *s.* of the late Capt. William Thomson, 78th Highlanders, and Alice Groughton. *Educ.:* Bedford Gram. Sch., Bedford, Eng. Arrived in Canada, 1893; has followed a general commercial business in British Columbia; lived for five years in Nelson, Kootenay Dist., and two years in Cariboo; went to Victoria, in 1902, as manager of the Turner-Beeton Co.; elec. as one of the Conservative members for Victoria City in provincial Legislature, 1907. *Address:* Victoria, B.C. *Clubs:* Union, Victoria.

THORBURN, John M.A., LL.D.; *b.* Quothquan, Lanarkshire, Scot., 10 Oct., 1830; *s.* of John Thorburn and Mary Wilson; *m.* Maria J. I., *d.* of Dr. Henry G. Parish, of Yarmouth, N.S. *Educ.:* Quothquan and Liberton Schs., and Edinburgh Univ. Taught in the Gram. Sch., Musselburgh, and in the Western Inst., Edinburgh. Came to Can., 1856; taught sch. for a short time in Yarmouth, N.S., and was then apptd. Principal and Prof. of Classics in St. Francis Coll., Richmond, Que.; Head-master of the Ottawa Gram. Sch. (now the Coll. Inst.), 1862-02; apptd. Librarian of the Can. Geol. Survey, and a few months later apptd. Chn. of the Bd. of C. S. Examiners, which position he held for 27 yrs.; hon. mem. of Am. Acad. of Political and Social Science, Philadelphia; of Trinity Historical Soc., Dallas, Texas; hon. corr. Fellow of the Geol. Soc. of Australasia, Melbourne, etc. Was pres. of the St. Andrew's Soc., of the Literary and Scientific Soc. of Ottawa, of the Univ. Extension Scheme of Lectures; was for many yrs. Trustee of the Ottawa Coll. Inst., and Chn. of the Bd. for five yrs. *Publications:* Lectures on various subjects; "Counting and Time Reckoning," published in Trans. of Can. Inst. *Address:* 211 Daly Ave., Ottawa.

THORNE, William Henry; *b.* St. John, N.B., 12 Sept., 1844; *s.* of E. Thorne; unmarried. *Educ.:* St. John, N.B.; Iron and Hardware Merchant; commenced business 1867; pres. of W. H. Thorne Co., Limited; director of Royal Bank of Canada, and Cornwall and York Cotton Mills Co.; two years president Board of Trade. *Recreations:* salmon fishing, shooting. *Address:* St. John, N.B. *Clubs:* Union, St. John; St. James, Montreal.

THORNELOE, Rt. Rev. George, M.A., D.D., D.C.L., Bishop of Algoma; *b.* Coventry, Eng., 4 Oct., 1848; *s.* of James and Catherine Thorneloe; *m.* Mary E. Fuller, of Lennoxville, Que.; one *s.* one *d.* *Educ.:* Bishops Coll., Lennoxville, Que.; arrived in Canada, 1858; Rector of Stanstead, Que., 1874 to 1885; Rector of Sherbrooke, Que., 1885 to 1897; Bishop of Algoma, 1897. *Address:* Sault St. Marie, Ont.

THORNTON, Charles Jonas, M.P.; *b.* Tp. of Clarke, Durham Co., Ont., 30 May, 1850; *s.* of Thomas Thornton, Yorkshire, Eng., and Susannah Powers, U. E. L. descent; *m.* Eleanor Hughson; two *s.* two *d.* *Educ.:* Pub. Sch., of his native co., and Coll. at London, Ont.; seven years Tp. Councillor, and five years in the Co. Council; el. for West Durham in 1900, but lost seat because deposit was made by marked cheque instead of cash; elec. in 1908. *Address:* Kirby P. O., Ont.

TIFFIN, William Richard; Supt. North Division, G. T. Ry.; *b.* Hamilton, Ont., Sept., 1844; *s.* of Samuel Tiffin and Anne Tiffin; *m.* Susan Amelia Oakley; three *s.* *Educ.:* Hamilton. Entered railway service, 1860, since which he has been consecutively to 1875, clerk in office at Hamilton and in general superintendent's department, Great Western Ry. of Can.; 1875 to 1880, asst. supt. same road at Palmerston; on amalgamation of Great Western Ry. with Grand Trunk Ry. in 1890, apptd. asst. supt. latter road in charge of Northern division at Stratford, Ont., which position he held until July, 15, 1896, when he was assigned to other duties; Jan. 1, 1897, to date, Supt. of G. T. R., Northern Divn. *Address:* Allandale, Ont.

TILTON, Col. John; *b.* Lancaster. N.B., 27 March, 1837; *s.* of Barnabas Tilton (native of Boston, Mass.) and Anne Wylie (English); *m.* Roberta E., *d.* of late Daniel J. Odell, for many yrs. British consul at Eastport, Me., U.S.A. *Educ.:* St. John Gram. Sch. and Kingston, N.B. For some years in business as a merchant in St. John; joined the public service of Canada, 1867; promoted to Deputy Minister of Fisheries, 1884; retired on the union of the departments of Marine and Fisheries, 1892; a member of the Royal Commission, 1880, to enquire into and report on the organization of the Civil Service. Was Lieut.-Col., commanding the Governor-General's Foot Guards, Ottawa; commanded the Canadian team at Wimbledon, 1892, and at Bisley, 1901. Has devoted the greater portion of his life to the encouragement of rifle shooting. A warm advocate of the Rockcliffe site for the Dom. Rifle Range, and after site selected by Govt., took great interest as chairman of the Executive of the Dom. Rifle Assn. in the construction of the range; promoted to be Hon. Col., 1901. General agent for Canada, for the Metropolitan Life Ins. Co., since 1897. *Address:* 37 Gloucester St., Ottawa. *Club:* Rideau, Ottawa.

TISDALE, Lieut.-Col. Hon. David, P.C., K.C.; *b.* 8 Sept., 1835; *s.* of Ephraim Tisdale (great grand-parents as U.E. Loyalists, emigrated from United States in 1783 to what is now St. John, N.B.); *m.* Sarah Araminta *d.* of James Walker; two *s.* two *d.* *Educ.:* Pub. Schs. and Gram. Sch., Norfolk Co., Ont.; Toronto Univ.; barr., Ont., 1858; senior member firm Tisdale, Tisdale and Reid, Simcoe, Ont.; Q.C. 1872; extensively engaged in financing and construction of railways; in lumbering, mining, sheep-farming and cattle-ranching; assisted in raising a rifle company, 1861; was its first Captain, on service with it at the time of the Trent difficulty, and the Fenian Raid, 1866; subsequently other Companies were raised and 39th Norfolk Rifles formed (8 Companies); gazetted Lieut.-Col.; retired but retaining rank; was a delegate with others from all parts of Canada who met at Ottawa and formed the Dominion Rifle Association, 1868; Chairman Standing Committee on Railways and Canals in H. of C., 1891-96; Minister of Militia and Defence, 1896. Pres. Crown Life Assurance Company; Pres., St. Clair and Erie Ship Canal Company; Vice-Pres. of the U.E. Loyalist Association for Ontario. *Recreation:* organized the "Long Point Shooting Club." *Address:* Simcoe, Ont.

TOBIN, Edmund William; *b.* Brompton Falls, Que., 14 Sept., 1865; *s.* of Patrick Tobin and Helen Hanley; *m.* 24 April, 1893, Bessie E. Nott. *Educ.:* Elementary schs.; general merchant and lumber dealer; Mayor of Brompton Falls, and Warden of the Co. of Richmond,; elec. to the H, of C., 1900, 1904 and 1908; Roman Catholic; Liberal. *Address:* Bromptonville, Que.

TODD, Frederick G.; landscape architect; *b.* Concord, N.H., 11 March, 1876; *s.* of G. W. Todd and Mary E. Cole; *m.* Beatrice E. Pinkerton, one *s.* one *d.* *Educ.:* High Sch., Andover, Mass., and Agricultural Coll., Emherst, Mass.; arrived in Canada, 6 June, 1900; is a fellow of the American Soc. of Landscape Architects; principal work—plans of Winnipeg Park; plans for Ottawa Improvement Commission; plans for parks and location of Parliament Buildings for the Governments of Alberta and Sask.; plans for National Battlefields' Commission. *Address:* 10 Phillips Place, Montreal. *Clubs:* Engineers', Montreal.

TODD, Percy R.; *b.* Toronto, Ont., 4 Dec., 1859; *s.* of Alfred and Katherine Todd; *m.* Fanny S. Folker of New York; two *d.* *Educ.:* Coll. Inst., Ottawa, Ont. Began Ry. service as telegraph operator until 1875; Canadian agt., Ogdensburg & Lake Champlain R. R., 1875-82; gen. travelling agt., Nat. Despatch Line at Chicago, 1882-5; commercial agt., N. Y. , West Shore & Buffalo R. R. at Albany, 1885; chief clerk gen. freight dept., same at New York, 1885-6 gen. freight and passenger agt., Canada Atlantic R. R. at Ottawa, 1886-9; gen. freight agt., 1889-92; gen. traffic mgr., West Shore R. R., 1892-1901; 2d v.-p., 1901-3, 1st v.-p., 1903-7; dir., 1905-7; N. Y. New Haven & Hartford R. R.; v.-p., Bangor & Aroostook R. R., since Jan., 1907., *Address:* Bangor, Me. *Clubs:* Tarratine Golf, Bangor, Maine; Union League and Transportation, New York.

TODD, William F., M.P.; *b.* St. Stephen N.B., 2 May, 1854; *s.* of Freeman H. Todd, and Adeline Boardman; *m.* 1879, Ethel J. Bolton, *d.* of John Bolton, member of H. of C. shortly after Confederation; three *d.* A merchant; memb. of N.B. Legis., 1899; first elec. to H. of C., 1908; Universalist; Liberal. *Address:* St. Stephen, N.B.

TOLMIE, John, M.P.; *b.* Balgowan, Parish of Laggan, Scot., 30 Aug., 1845; *s.* of Alexander Tolmie and Mary Fraser; *m.* (1st) Maggie Patterson; (2nd) Alice Robertson; one *s.* one *d.* *Educ.:* Balgowan Sch., Scot.; arrived in Canada, 30 July, 1868; sixteen years on a farm; last 25 years a manufacturer of salt; was two years Councillor for Bruce Tp. and three years Reeve; Deputy Reeve of Kincardine, for one year, and two years Mayor; first el. to H. of C., 1896; has been returned four times. *Recreations:* fond of Scottish poetry and music. *Address:* Kincardine, Ont.

TORONTO, Bishop of; *see* Right Rev. James Fielding Sweeney.

TORRINGTON, Mrs. Rosaline Rebecca; wife of Dr. F. H. Torrington, of Toronto, Ont.; *b.* Ireland; two *s.* *Educ.:* Ireland; arrived Canada 1869; has written number of articles on social questions. Pres., Local Council of Women, Toronto; mem., Women's Canadian Club, Women,s Historical Soc., Women's Art Assn. of Can., Toronto. *Address:* 12 Pembroke St., Toronto.

TOTZKE, Albert Frederick, Phm. B., M.L.A.; *b.* Berlin, Ont., 20 Dec., 1882; *s.* of E. L. Carl and Louise Totzke; *m.* Evelyn Lynch; one *d.* *Educ.:* Berlin, Ont., and Toronto; went to Sask. in 1904, and entered the drug business at Vonda, 1905; elec. to the Provincial Legislature in 1908. *Recreations:* shooting and curling. *Address:* Vonda, Sask.

TOURIGNY, Hon. Francois Simeon, K.C., B.L., LL.L., LL.D.; Judge of the Superior Ct. of the Prov. of Quebec; *b.* Becancourt, Nicolet Co., Que., 3 Nov., 1858; *s.* of Olivier Tourigny and Olive Comeau; *m.* Eugenie Arcandy; one *d.* *Educ.:* Nicolet Coll. Practised law at Three Rivers. Took an active interest in municipal affairs; alderman of Three Rivers, 1898-1906; Mayor 1906-08; one of the promoters of the St. Maurice Valley Ry. Co. Apptd. Judge, 1908. *Address:* Three Rivers, Que.

TOUT, Charles Hill; *b.* Cyland, Devonshire, Eng., 28 Sept., 1858; *s.* of John Tout and Elizabeth Hill; *m.* Edith Mary Stothert; five *s.* four *d.* Arrived in Canada, 1884. *Educ.:* partly at Oxford and Lincoln, Eng., for the Church, but took up educational work, by preference, and later scientific investigation among the native races of Canada and the United States for the B.A. A.S. *Publications:* The American volume of "The Native Races of the British Empire," series. *Recreations:* farming, stock raising. *Address:* Bucklands, Abbotsford, B.C.

TOWNLEY, Mrs. Charles Robert (Alice Ashworth); *b.* Quebec, 26 Nov., 1870; *d.* of William Henry Ashworth and Jane Moray Askworth; *m.* Charles Robert Townley. *Educ.:* Canada. Before her marriage wrote number of short stories, verse, descriptive articles for Canadian and American newspapers and magazines, as "Alice Ashworth," but now writes as "Alice Ashworth Townley." Mem., National Council of Women. *Publications:* "Just a Little Boy," 1897; "Just a Little Girl," 1907; "Opinions of Mary," 1909. *Address:* 944 Hastings St. W., Vancouver, B.C. *Clubs:* Women's Canadian, Press, Vancouver.

TOWNSHEND, Hon. Charles James, B.A., B.C.L., Chief Justice of the Supreme Ct. of N.S.; *b.* 22 March, 1844; *s.* of Rev. Canon Townshend; Rector of Christ Church, Amherst, N.S., and Elizabeth Stewart; *m.* (1st) 1867, Laura, *d.* of J. D. Kinnear; (2nd) 1887, Margaret, *d.* of John McFarlane; three *s.* two *d.* *Educ.:* Coll. Sch. and King's Coll., Windsor, N.S. Bar., Canada, 1866; Q.C., 1881; elected M.L.A. for Cumberland, 1878 and 1882; to H. of C., 1884; M.E.C., 1878-82; Judge of the Supreme Court of N.S., 1887-1907; chief Justice, 1907 to date. *Address:* Halifax, N.S., and Wolfville, N.S. (summer). *Club:* Halifax.

TRANT, William, J.P.; Police Magistrate of Regina, Sask.; *b.* Leeds, Yorkshire, Eng., 13 March, 1844; *s.* of William Trant, chemist, of Leeds, and Isabella Hirst, of Dewsbury; *m.* Jane, *d.* of Edward Trood, of Bridgewater, Eng.; three *s.* one *d.* *Educ.:* Leeds Mechanics' Inst., Leeds Free Gram. Sch.; founder of the Leeds Astronomical Soc. For some yrs. was engaged in journalism; on staffs of the Yorkshire *Post* and several London newspapers; special corr. at Paris during the Commune; went on journalistic missions to Ireland, Spain, Algeria, Morocco, U.S.A., and Mexico, 1878-88. Came to Can., 1889. Called to the Bar of Sask., 1904; apptd. Police Magistrate at Regina, 1907. *Publications:* "Financial Reform," 1874; "Trades Unions," 1876; 2nd ed. 1882; a novel, "Daisy Baines" (now in the press); contributions to mags. and newspapers in England, Canada, and U.S. *Address:* 2108 Lorne St., Regina, Sask. *Club:* Assiniboia, Regina.

TRENHOLME, Hon. Norman William, M.A., D.C.L. (McGill Univ.); Puisne Judge of the Court of King's Bench of the Prov. of Quebec; *b.* Kingsey Tp., Drummond Co., Que., 18 Aug., 1837; *s.* of Edward Trenholme and Mary Ann Ridley; *m.* (1st) 1868, Lucy Wilkes (*d.* 1885), *d.* of the late Samuel Hedge, of Montreal; (2nd) 1886, Grace Low, *d.* of the late Robert Shaw, of Quebec; five *s.* two *d.* *Educ.:* McGill Univ., Montreal (Henry Chapman Medal, 1863; the Elizabeth Torrance Gold Medal, 1865). Called to the Bar, 1865, and commenced practice of prof. in Montreal. 1872-1882, in partnership with J. J. McLaren, now Judge of the Ont. Ct. of Appeals.; apptd. prof. of Roman and Public Law in McGill Univ., 1868, and Dean of Faculty of Law, 1888, but resigned in 1905. Created a Q.C., 1889; apptd. Puisne Judge of the Superior Court of the Prov. of Que., 1901, and Puisne Judge of the Ct. of King's Bench, 1904. *Address:* "Rosemount," 65 Rosemount Av., Montreal, Que. *Club:* University, Montreal.

TROOP, Rev. George Osborne, M.A.; *b.* Bridgetown, N.S., 6 March, 1854; *s.* of the late William Henry Troop, barrister-at-law, and Georgina Coster; *m.* Suzette Lawe Hill, *d.* of the late Rev. G. W. Hill, D.C.L., formerly rector of St. Paul's Halifax. *Educ.:* King's Coll., Windsor, N.S.; ordained deacon, 1877; priest, 1878; curate of St. Paul's, Halifax, 1877-1881; rector St. James. Church, St. John, N.B., 1882-1886; rector, St. Martin's Church, Montreal, 1886 to the present. *Recreations:* walking, reading. *Address:* 738 St. Urbain St., Montreal.

TROTTER, Major Gerald Frederick, D.S.O., M.V.O. (4th class); *b.* London, Eng., 21 July, 1871; *s.* of Maj-Gen. Sir Henry Trotter, G.C.V.O., and Hon. Eva Gifford; unmarried. *Educ.:* H.M.S. Britannia. Joined Grenadier Guards, June, 1892; served in South Africa with 3rd Brig. Grenadier Guards, from Nov., 1899, until April, 1900; invalided to England on account of wounds; returned to South Africa, March, 1902, and remained until close of Boer War; arrived in Canada, Dec., 1904, as A.D.C. to Lord Grey, Governor General of Can. and remained until 1906; again A.D.C. in 1909-10. *Recreations:* fishing, hunting, shooting, racing. *Addresses:* Government House, Ottawa; 126 Sloane St., London, Eng. *Clubs:* Guards, Turf, Beefsteak, M.C.C. and Prince's Racquet, London, Eng.; Rideau, Ottawa.

TROTTER, Rev. Thomas, B.A., D.D., LL.D.; *b.* Thurlaston, Leicestershire, Eng., 11 Aug., 1853; *s.* of Edwin and Hannah Trotter; *m.* Ellen Maud, *o. d.* of the late Rev. David Freeman, M.A., Canning, N.S., 5 May, 1887; two *s.* and two *d.* *Educ.:* Woodstock Coll., Woodstock, Ont.; Univ. of Toronto, McMaster Univ. Arrived in Canada, 13 Sept., 1870; Pastor of the Baptist Church, Woodstock, Ont., 1885-1889; Pastor of the Bloor St. Baptist Church, Toronto, 1889-1890; professor of Homeletics and Pastoral Theology, McMaster Univ., Toronto, 1890-1895; pres., Acadia Univ., Wolfville, N.S., 1896-1906; pastor, Ashland Av. Baptist Church, Toledo, Ohio, 1907-1909; re-apptd. professor of Homeletics and Pastoral Theology, McMaster Univ., Toronto, 1909. *Address:* McMaster University, Toronto, Ont.

TULLY, Miss Sydney Strickland, A.R.C.A.; *b.* Toronto, Ont.; *d.* of late Kivas Tully, I.S.O. *Educ.:* Toronto, London, and Paris. Artist; portrait painter; member of Ontario Society of Artists. Studied at the Slade Sch., London, under Professor A. Legros, 1884-86; and Paris, studied under the late Benjamin Constant; exhibited in the Salon of 1888; studied also under T. Robert-Fleury and Gustave Courtois, etc.; exhibited in the Royal Academy ,1886-87; World's Fair, Chicago, and at the Pan-American at Buffalo, where received honourable mention; at St. Louis Exhibition, bronze medal. *Address:* 36 Toronto Street, Toronto, Ont.

TUPPER, Hon. Sir Charles, 1st Bt., *cr.* 1888; G.C.M.G., *cr.* 1886; K.C.M.G., *cr.*

1879; C.B., 1867; M.A., D.C.L., hon. LL.D. Camb., Edinburgh, Acadia, and Queen's; M.D.; *b.* 2 July, 1821; *s.* of late Rev. Charles Tupper, D.D., Aylesford, N.S.; *m.* Frances Morse, Amherst. *Educ.:* Acadia and Edinburgh Univ. Was fourteen consecutive times returned as M.P. for his native county Cumberland, N.S., and represented it for thirty-one years; Premier of province of N.S. at time of Confederation, 1867; declined seat in first Dominion Cabinet; sworn of Privy Council, 1870; President of Privy Council, 1870-72; Minister of Inland Revenue, 1872-73; Minister of Customs, 1873; Minister of Public Works, 1878-79; Minister of Railways and Canals, 1879-84; High Commissioner for Canada in England, 1883-87; Minister of Finance, 1887-88; reappointed High Commissioner, 1886-96; was one of H.M.'s Plenipotentiaries on Fishery Commission, Washington, 1887-88; and to negotiate treaty between Canada and France, 1893; Prime Minister, 1896; leader of Opposition , Canadian H. of C., 1896-1900. *Address:* Broomwood, Bexley Heath, Kent, Eng. *Clubs:* Manitoba, Winnipeg; British Empire, Colonial, London, Eng.

TUPPER, Hon. Sir Charles Hibbert, K.C.M.G., *cr.* 1893; LL.B.; K.C.; *b.* 1855; *s.* of Sir C. Tupper; *m.* Janet, *d.* of Hon. James Macdonald, C.J., of N.S.; four *s.* three *d.* *Educ.:* McGill Coll., Montreal (Gov.-Gen. Scholarship); Harvard Law Sch. Barr., N.S., 1877; Ont., 1895; B.C., 1898; elected to H. of C., 1882, 1887, 1888, 1891, 1896-1900; Minister of Marine and Fisheries, 1888-95; Minister of Justice and Attorney-General for Canada, 1895-96; Agent of H.B.M. Paris Tribunal of Arbitration, 1899; created K.C.M.G. in recognition of services there; senior member of legal firm Tupper and Griffin, Vancouver, B.C. *Recreation:* tennis. *Address:* Vancouver. *Clubs:* Albany, Toronto; Union, Victoria, B.C.; Vancouver, Country, Vancouver.

TUPPER, J. Stewart, B.A., K.C.; *b.* Amherst, N.S., 26 Oct., 1851; *e. s.* of the Rt. Hon. Sir Charles Tupper, Bt., G.C.M.G., C.B., and Lady Tupper; *m.* (1st) 1875, Marie Wilson (*d.* 1876), *d.* of the late Andrew Robertson, of Montreal; (2nd) Ada Campbell, *d.* of the late Sir Thomas Galt, Chief Justice of Common Pleas, Ont.; one *s.* three *d.* *Educ.:* McGill Univ., Montreal (grad. B.A. with First Rank Honors). Called to Ontario Bar, 1875; Manitoba Bar, 1882; cr. Q.C., 1890; Bencher of the Law Soc., 1900; treas. of the Law Soc., 1906; senior mem. of the firm of Tupper, Galt, Tupper, Minty & McTavish, barristers and solicitors, Winnipeg; solicitors for the Bank of Montreal, Bank of B.N.A., Merchants, Royal, Traders' and Home Banks, H.B. Co., C.P.R., and many other corporations. *Recreation:* riding. *Address:* Ravenscourt, Winnipeg. *Clubs:* Manitoba, St. Charles Country, Winnipeg.

TURCOTTE, Gustave Adolphe, M.D., M.P.; *b.* at Three Rivers, Que., 19 Nov., 1848; *s.* of Jos. Ed. Turcotte and Flora Buteau; *m.* (1st) Jean Le Blanc, *d.* of the late Dr. J. Le Blanc; (2nd) Emma Houde, *d.* of C. E. Houde, ex-M.L.A.; one *s.* two *d.* *Educ.:* St. Mary's Coll., Montreal and St. Joseph's Coll., Three Rivers; a physician; was Registrar of Nicolet Co., Division No. 2, for 10 years; was unsuccessful candidate for parliament six times from 1877 to 1907; elec. to the H. of C. for Nicolet, 1907; re-elec., 1908. *Address:* Nicolet, Que.

TURCOTTE, Joseph Pierre, M.P., *b.* St. Jean, Isle d'Orleans, 21 May, 1857; *s.* of F. K. Turcotte, and Elizabeth Rousseau; *m.* 7 May, 1895, Marie Eva Dick; four *c.* an advocate; was twice a candidate for Quebec Legislature, in 1886 and 1896; first elec. to H. of C. 1908; Roman Catholic; Liberal. *Address:* Quebec.

TURGEON, Hon. Adelard, C.M.G., C.V.O., B.C.L. (Laval Univ.); President Leg. Coun. of Quebec; *b.* Beaumont, Que., 19 Dec., 1863; *s.* of Damase Turgeon and Christine Turgeon; *m.* 1887, Augene, *d.* of the late Etienne Samson, of Levis. *Educ.:* Levis Coll., Laval Univ., Que. Called to the bar, 12 July, 1887, and commenced practicing his prof. in Levis. He is now in partnership with the Hon. L. R. Roy, Prov. Sec. and Registrar, and Mr. Ernest Roy, M.P. for Dorchester, in Quebec. Returned to the Que. Legis. for the Co. of Bellechasse at g. e., 1890; re-el. in yrs. 1892, 1897, 1900 and 1904; apptd. Minister of Colonization and Mines, in the Marchand Govt., 26 May, 1897; held same portfolio in the Parent Admn., which was formed 3 Oct., 1900; resigned his seat in Parent Ministry, and re-el. by his constituency, March, 1905; accepted portfolio of Minister of Lands, Mines and Fisheries in Gouin Admn., 23 March, 1905; resigned seat, 1907, but el. 4 Nov., 1907, and again resumed his seat in the Gouin Govt., with portfolio of Lands and Forests; now pres., Leg. Coun., 1909; is one of the founders of "Union Liberale," a governor of Laval Univ.; was made a Companion of the Most Distinguished Order of St. Michael and St. George, 1906, and created a Knight of the Legion of Honor by the Pres. of the French Republic, and C.V.O. by His Highness the Prince of Wales during Tercentenary celebrations at Que., July, 1908. *Address:* Parlt. Bldgs., Quebec. *Club:* Garrison, Quebec.

TURGEON, Onesiphore, B.A., M.P.; *b.* St. Joseph de Levis, Que., 6 Sept., 1849; *s.* of Simon Turgeon and Pelagie Paradis, *m.* (1st) Margaret Eulalie Baldwin, of Bathhurst, N.B., 20 Aug., 1876 (*dec.* 7 Sept., 1896); (2nd) Mary Loretta Meahan, of Bathurst, N.B., 27 Sept., 1905; one *s.* two *d.* *Educ.:* Christian Brothers' Sch., Levis, and Quebec Seminary; a member of the Gloucester Municipal Council for three yrs.; unsuccessful candidate in g. e. for H. of C., 1896; elec. in 1900, 1904 and 1908. *Address:* Bathurst, N.B.

TURGEON, Hon. William Ferdinand Alphonse, B.A., K.C., M.L.A.; Attorney Gen. of Saskatchewan; *b.* at Bathurst, N. B., 3 June, 1877; *s.* of Onesiphore Turgeon, M.P., and Margaret Baldwin; *m.* Gertrude Boudreau; two *d.* *Educ.:* New York City and Laval Univ., Quebec; admitted to the bar of Quebec, but moved shortly afterwards to Prince Albert, Sask., where he entered into partnership with Hon. J. H. Lamont, now a Judge of the Supreme Court of Saskatchewan, whom he succeeded in the Legislature of the Province; Attorney General of Sask., 23 Sept., 1907; elected in

1908 for Duck Lake. *Address:* Regina, Sask.

TURNER, Hon. J. H.; *b.* 7 May, 1834; *s.* of John and Martha Turner, Ipswich, Suffolk, England; *m.* 1860, Elizabeth Eilbeck, of Whitehaven, Cumberland; one *s.* *Educ.:* Whitstable, near Canterbury, Eng. Merchant; commenced in Victoria, 1863; elec. to the City Council, 1877; Mayor of Victoria, 1879, 1880, 1881; elected Legislative Assem. of province, 1886 (city of Victoria); Minister of Finance and Agriculture, 1887-98 and 1899-1901; Premier, 1895-98; introduced the Budget for thirteen years, and Acts for encouragement of fruit growing, dairying, and formation of Farmers' Institutes and Farmers' Banks, etc.; joined the first company of volunteers, 1864; retired into Canadian Reserve Militia, 1881, as Lieut.-Col.; agent General for British Columbia in London, since 1901. *Recreations:* riding, fishing, cricket. *Address:* Salisbury House, Finsbury Circus, E.C.; 15 Hereford Square, South Kensington, S.W. *Clubs:* Union, Victoria; United Empire, London, Eng.

TURNER, Hon. Richard, M.L.C.; *b.* Quebec, 15 Aug., 1843; *s.* of James Turner, of Rochester, Eng., and Susan Frizelle; *m.* 1867, Emily Maria Ellis; four *s.* two *d.* Established firm of Whitehead & Turner, wholesale grocers, 1870. Dir. of the Imperial Bank of Can.; ex-pres., St. George's Soc. of Que.; pres. or dir. of National Telephone Co., Quebec Cartage and Transfer Co., Turner Lumber and Pulp Wood Co., Bouthillier Co., Levis County Ry., and other important mercantile institutions. Served three terms on the Que. City Council; Pres., Que. Bd. of Trade; hon. vice-pres., Quebec Lib. Club; apptd. to Que. Legis. Council, 1897; chairman, Bd. of dirs. of the Que. High Sch.; mem. National Battlefields Com. *Address:* 55 D'Auteuil St., Quebec. *Club:* Garrison.

TURNER, Lieut.-Col. Richard Ernest William, D.S.O., V.C.; *b.* Quebec, 25 July, 1871; *s.* of Hon. Richard Turner and Emily Maria Ellis; *m.* Harriet Augusta Goodday of London, Eng.; one *s.* two *d.* *Educ.:* Quebec; a member of the wholesale grocery firm of Whitehead & Turner; served in South African War, 1889-1900. Operations in the Orange Free State, Feb. to May, 1900, including actions at Vet River (5 and 6 May), and Zand River (10 May.) Operations in the Transvaal in May and June, 1900, including actions near Joannesburg (29 May), Pretoria (4 June), and Diamond Hill (11 and 12 June). Operations in the Transvaal, east of Pretoria, July to 21 Nov., 1900, including actions at Reit Vlei (16 July), Belfast (26 and 27 August, 1900). Operations in Cape Colony, south of Orange River, 1899-1900. Operations in the Transvaal between 30 Nov., 1900 and 31 May, 1902. Intelligence Officer at Wonderfontein, Transvaal, 20 Sept. to 22 Oct., f1900. (Severely wounded.) *Despatches.* Lord Roberts 2 April, 1901; Lord Kitchener, 8 March, 1902; *London Gazette,* 16 April, 1901; April and 23 April, 1901. Victoria Cross, *D.S.O.* Brevet of Lieut.-Colonel. Medal with six clasps. Commanded the King's Royal Colonial Escort at the Coronation, 1902; now commands the 3rd Cavalry Brigade, Can. Mil. *Address:* 26 St. Ursule St., Quebec. *Club:* Garrison, Quebec.

TURRIFF, John Gillanders, M.P.; *b.* Little Metis, Que., 14 Dec., 1855; *s.* of Robert Turriff and Jane Gillanders; *m.* (1st) Eva Louise Josephine Bartlette Buchanan, in 1884; (2nd) Catherine Mary Wilson; one *s.* three *d.* *Educ.:* Little Metis and Montreal; represented Moose Mountain District in N.W. legislature for three terms, 1884 to 1891; unsuccessful candidate in East Assiniboia for H. of C. in 1891, against Hon. E. Dewdney, Minister of Interior; Commissioner of Dominion Lands at Ottawa, 1898-1904; elected to the H. of C., 1904, 1908. *Address:* 61 Cartier St., Ottawa.

TWEEDALE, John Fletcher, M.L.A.; *b.* Fredericton, N.B., 18 Dec., 1858; *s.* of Matthew and Martha Tweedale; *m.* Joan Campbell; two *s.* four *d.* *Educ.:* Fredericton, N.B.; m0mber of the Municipal Council, Co. of Victoria for 18 Consecutive years; Warden of the Co.; member of the N.B. Legislature for the past 8 years. *Address:* Arthurette, Victoria County, N.B.

TWEEDIE, Hon. Lemuel John, K.C., LL.D.; Lieut.-Governor of New Brunswick; *b.* Chatham, N.B., 30 Nov., 1849; parents Irish and Scotch; *m.* Agnes, *d.* of the late Alexander Loudon, of Chatham; four *s.* two *d.* *Educ.:* Chatham, Gram. Sch. and Presbyterian Academy. Called to the bar of New Brunswick, 1870. El. to Legis. Assem., 1874; defeated 1878; re-el., 1886, and at every g. e., until apptd. to his present position. Became surveyor-general and head of the Crown Lands Dept., 1890; Prov. Sec., 1896; Premier of New Brunswick, 1900; apptd. Lieut.-Governor, 2 Mar., 1907. *Recreations:* shooting, fishing, curling. *Address:* Chatham, N.B. *Club:* Union, St. John.

TYE, William Francis, C.E.; *b.* 5 March, 1861. *Educ.:* Ottawa Univ. and Sch. of Practical Science. Entered ry. service, 1882, since which he has been consecutively to 1885, rodman, leveler, transitman on location and asst. engr. on construction, C. P. Ry.; transitman on location and asst. engr. on construction St. Paul Minneapolis & Manitoba Ry., 1886-87; engr. of track and bridges Tampico branch Mexican Central Ry. 1888-89; location engr. Great Falls & Canada Ry. in Montana, 1890; engr. in charge of location and div. engr. Pacific extension Great Northern Ry., 1891-92; engr. in charge of change of gauge Alberta Ry. and Coal Co., 1893-94; chief engr., Kalso & Slocan Ry. and Trail Creek Tramway, 1895; chief engr., Columbia & Western Ry., 1896-1900; chief engr. of construction, C. P. Ry., 1900-02; asst. chief engr., 1902-04; chief engr., 1904-6; in private practise since; pres. The Sterling Coal Co. *Address:* 64 Rosemount Av., Toronto.

TYRRELL, James Williams, C.E., D.L.S.; *b.* Weston, Ont., 10 May, 1863; *s.* of William and Elizabeth Tyrrell; *m.* Isabel Macdonald; two *s.* two *d.* *Educ.:* Weston, and Toronto Univ.; an explorer of Canadian wilds. *Publications:* "Across sub-arctics of Canada," etc. *Address:* 7 Hughson St. S. Hamilton. *Club:* Hamilton.

TYRRELL, Joseph Burr, M.A., B.Sc.; *b.* Weston, Ont., 1 Nov., 1858; *s.* of William

Tyrrell, of Kildare Co., Ireland, and Elizabeth Burr; *m.* Mary Edith Carey, of St. John, N.B.; two *s.* one *d.* *Educ.:* Weston High Sch., Upper Can. Coll., and Univ. of Toronto; after graduating from the Univ. of Toronto in 1880, joined the staff of the Geological Survey of Canada and from that time onwards for seventeen years explored and searched for mineral wealth in the Provinces of Manitoba, Saskatchewan, Alberta and British Columbia, and the Districts of Keewatin, Mackenzie and Yukon; survey of Lake Athabasca and of the Dubawant and Kazan rivers which drain large area to the west of Hudson's Bay; awarded diploma and the "Back Grant" by the Royal Geographical Society of London, England. In 1898, resigned from the Geological Survey and moved to Dawson, where he practised as a mining engineer and reported on many of the largest mining properties in the Klondyke; in 1906, moved to Toronto where he is now practising as a consulting mining engineer. *Publications:* Published numerous papers on mining and scientific subjects in the *American Journal of Science*, the *American Geologist*, *Bulletin of the American Geological Society*, *Canadian Record of Science*, *Science*, *Geological Magazine*, *Journal of Geology*, *Economic Geology*, *Engineering and Mining Journal*, *Geographical Journal*, *Journal of the Royal Scottish Geographical Society*, *Transactions of the Institution of Mining Engineers* (England), *Transactions of the Institution of Mining and Metallurgy*, *Canadian Journal*, *Journal of the Canadian Mining Institute*, *Canadian Mining Journal*, *&c.* *Recreations:* shooting and photography. *Address:* 518 Huron St., Toronto; Weston, Ont. (summer). *Clubs:* National, Albany and Victoria, Toronto; Rideau, Ottawa.

TYRWHITT-DRAKE, Brian Halsey; *b.* Victoria, B.C., 6 Oct., 1866; *s.* of late Montague W. Tyrwhitt-Drake, Puisne Judge of the Supreme Ct. of B.C., and Joanna, *d.* of James Tolmie, of Ardersier, N.B. *Educ.:* Charterhouse, Eng. Called to the Bar of B.C., 1890, and commenced practice as barrister and solicitor in B.C.; registrar of Supreme Ct. of B.C., 1895; registrar of B.C. Admiralty Dist., 1895. *Address:* Pleasant St., Victoria, B.C. *Club:* Union, Victoria.

U

USSHER, Charles E. E.; Asst. Passngr. Traffic Manager, C.P.R.; *b.* Niagara Falls, Ont., 29 Dec., 1857. Entered ry. service as clerk in auditor's office, Great Western Ry., 1874; clerk, gen. passngr. dept. same rd., 1876-80; chief ticket clerk, Wabash St. Louis & Pacific Ry., 1880-83; for seven mos. rate clerk, Chicago & Atlantic Rd.; in commercial business at Hamilton, Ont., 1883-86; chief ticket clerk, C. P. Ry., 1886-69; asst. gen. passngr. agt., 1889-98; gen. passngr. agt. Eastern Lines same rd., 1898-08; asst. passngr. traffic mgr., 1908 to date. *Address:* Winnipeg, Man. *Club:* Manitoba, Winnipeg

V

VANCOUVER, Archbishop of; *see* Right Rev. Neil McNeil.

VAN DER SMISSEN, William Henry, M.A.; *b.* Toronto, Ont., 18 Aug., 1844; *s.* of Henry Van der Smissen of Altona in Holstein; *m.* 1878, Elizabeth Sara Mason, *d.* of J. Herbert Mason, of Toronto; one *s.* two *d.* *Educ.:* Up. Can. Coll. and Univ. of Toronto. B.A., with Classical Honours, 1864; apptd. Lecturer in German at Univ. Coll., Toronto, 1866; Librarian of the Univ. of Toronto, 1873-1890; Associate Professor of German, 1890; Professor of German, 1902; Captain of University Company, Queen's Own Rifles of Canada, 1876. *Publications:* High School German Grammar and Reader; Shorter Poems of Goethe and Schiller; several translations of German classics. *Recreation:* golf. *Address:* University College, Toronto.

VANDRY, George Alfred; *b.* Quebec, Oct., 1866; *s.* of Joseph Vandry and Matilda Tremblay; *m.* Florence Turcott; two *s.* six *d.* *Educ.:* Quebec; Pres. of the Quebec Board of Trade; Pres. and Managing dir. of the Paquet Co., Ltd., Quebec. *Recreation:* fox hunting. *Address:* 50 Ste. Ursule Street, Quebec. *Clubs:* Hunt (Master), Quebec.

VAN HORNE, Sir William Cornelius, K.C.M.G.; Chairman of the Bd. of Directors of the Canadian Pacific Ry. Co.; *b.* nr. Joliette, Ill., 3 Feb., 1843; *s.* of the late Cornelius Cavenhoven Van Horne; *m.* 1867, Lucy Adeline, *d.* of Erastus Hurd, of Galesburg, Ill.; one *s.* one *d.* At age of fourteen entered office of the ry. station of his native town, and later became a telegraph operator on the Illinois Central Ry.; joined Michigan Central Ry., 1858; apptd. ticket agent and telegraph operator on the Chicago and Alton Ry., 1864; train despatcher for three yrs.; supt. of telegraphs for one yr.; divisional supt. for three yrs.; became gen. supt. of the St. Louis Kansas City and Northern Ry., 1872; gen. mgr. of the Southern Minnesota Ry., 1874, and later el. pres.; became gen. supt. of the Chicago and Alton Ry., 1878, retaining at the same time the presidency of the Southern Minnesota Ry.; apptd. gen. supt. of the Chicago, Milwaukee and St. Paul Ry., 1 Jan., 1880; became gen. mgr. of the C. P. R., 1881; el. vice-pres., 1884; apptd. pres., 1888; retired from active responsibility, 1899, and became chairman of the Bd. of Governors. Pres. of the Cuba Co., the Cuba Railroad Co., the Canadian Salt Co., Ltd.; Canada North-West Land Co., Ltd., Laurentide Paper Co., Ltd.; dir., Dom. Iron and Steel Co., Ltd., of the Royal Trust Co., of the Duluth, South Shore and Atlantic Ry. Co., the Minneapolis, St. Paul and Sault Ste. Marie Ry. Co.; ex-dir., Rio de Janeiro Tramway, Light and Power Co., Ltd., Equitable Life Assur. Soc., Winnipeg Electric Ry. Co.; mem. of the committee of management, Montreal Homoepathic Hospital; gov., McGill Univ.; vice-pres., Montreal Art Assn. Cr. K.C.M.G., May, 1894. *Recreations:* painting, travel. *Address:* 513 Sherbrooke St. W., Montreal. *Clubs:* Mount Royal, St. James, Montreal; Toronto; Century Association, Manhattan, Metropolitan, Lawyers', New York.

VENNING, Robert Norris; Supt of Fisheries for Canada; *b.* St. John, N.B., 14 Feb., 1854; *s.* of W. H. Venning and Adelaide Georgina Pottee; *m.* Francis Cecelia Magee; three *s.* one *d.* *Educ.:* St. John Gram. Sch. Entered Dept. of Marine and Fisheries, 1869; chosen as British Agent, under Imperial appointment, to report upon the Russian sealing operations on the Komondorski Islands in 1893; asstd. the British Commrs. and Counsel at the sittings of the Behring Sea Claims Com.; accompanied Sir John Thompson and other Can. dels. to Halifax in 1892 at the Intercolonial Conference with Nfld.; went to Washington with Sir Charles H. Tupper in 1894, to negotiate a settlement of the Behring Sea Claims; Joint Sec. of the Conference of Experts on the Behring Sea Seal Question, at Washington, 1896-1897; on staff of Joint High Com. at Quebec and Washington, 1898-1899; promoted to Chief Clerk, 1895; apptd. Asst. Commr. of Fisheries, 1903; accompanied Can. del. to London, Eng. at the Conference on the Russian seizures of sealing schooners in the North Pacific Ocean; accompanied Can. Ministers to Colonial Conference in London, 1907; apptd. supt. of Fisheries, 1909. *Publications:* special official reports. *Address:* 237 Chapel St., Ottawa.

VERVILLE, Alphonse, M.P.; *b.* Cote St. Paul, Que., 28 Oct., 1864; *s.* of Alfred Verville and Pamela Leduc; *m.* 1 Jan., 1884, Josephine Mailhot. *Educ.:* Sault-au-Recollet, Que.; unsuccessful candidate in Provincial election 1904; first elec. H. of C., bye-elec., Maisonneuve, 23 Feb., 1906, to fill vacancy caused by death of Hon. R. Prefontaine; re-elec., 1908. Roman Catholic. *Address:* Maisonneuve, Que.

VICTORIA, B.C., Bishop of; *see* Right Rev. Alexander Macdonald.

VINCENT, Swale, M. D., D.Sc.; *b.* West Bromwich, Eng., 24 May, 1868; *s.* of Joseph and Margaret Vincent; *Educ.:* King Edward's High Sch., Birmingham, Eng., Univ. of Birmingham, London, Edinburgh and Heidelberg; arrived in Canada, Oct., 1904; member R.C.S.; L.R.C.P., F.R.S.C.; Prof. of Physiol., Univ. of Manitoba; formerly asst. professor of Physiol., Univ. Coll., London; British Medical Association research scholar; Sharply physiological scholar; Mason research scholar; research Fellow, Univ. of Edinburgh. *Recreation:* music. *Address:* Univ. of Manitoba, Winnipeg, Man.

VOGT, Augustus Stephen, D.M.; *b.* Washington, Oxford Co., Ont., 14 Aug., 1861; *s.* of John George Vogt and Mariana Ling Vogt.; *m.* Georgia Adelaide McGill; one *s.* one *d.* *Educ.:* Elmira, Waterloo Co.; organist of German Lutheran Church at Elmira, Ont., at the age of twelve; organist and choir master First Methodist Church, St. Thomas, Ont., at the age of 17; studied in Boston, Mass., 1881-1882; Leipsig, Germany, 1883-1888; organist and choirmaster Jarvis Baptist Church, Toronto, 1888 to 1906; member of Piano faculty, Toronto Conservatory of Music, and Toronto Univ.; conductor of Mendelssohn Choir of Toronto, an organization which has attained to international fame, and which has been acclaimed by leading critics of New York, Buffalo, and Chicago in which cities the choir has appeared, as being unsurpassed amongst the great choirs of the world. *Publications:* "Modern Pianoforte Technique," 1900; now in its 12th edition. *Recreations:* travel, golf. *Address:* 331 Bloor St. W., Toronto, Ont. *Clubs:* Lambton Country and Golf Club, Deutscher Verein, Golf Club, Toronto, Ont.

VOWELL, Arthur W.; *b.* Clonmell, Ireland, 1841; of Irish parentage. *Educ.:* Gram. Sch., Clonmel, Ireland; arrived in Canada, 1861; settled in B.C.; on attaining manhood, obtained a commission with Irish Militia in 1858, and retired senior Lieutenant, 1860; Esquimalt, 1862; Civil Service in 1864, and 1866, was apptd. Chief Constable at Big Bend during the excitement there; removed to the Kootenay district as gold commissioner and stipendiary magistrate; seven years later was transferred to the Omineca dist., where he served in a similar capacity; from there went to Cassiar. Resigning from the government service in 1875 was elected to the provincial legis. Assem. for the Kootenay district; the following year resigned his seat and re-entering the government service proceeded to the Cassiar district where he acted as gold commissioner and stipendiary magistrate until 1884, when he removed to the Kootenay. During the construction of the C. P. R. in that district, he was stipendiary magistrate. *Address:* Victoria, B.C.

VROOM, Rev. Frederick Williams, M.A., D.D., Hon. D.C.L.; *b.* St. Stephen, N.B., s. of William Vroom and Frances Eliza Foster; *m.* in 1885, Agnes Jessie Campbell, *d.* of Colin Campbell, of Weymouth, N.S.; one *d.* *Educ.:* King's College, Windsor, N.S.; ordained deacon, 1881; priest, 1882, by Bishop Medley, Fredericton; curate of Peticodiac, N.B., 1881; rector of Richmond, N.B., 1883; rector of Shediac, N.B., 1885; Professor of Divinity at King's Coll., Windsor, 1888. *Address:* King's College, Windsor, N.S.

W

WADDELL, John Alexander Low, B.A.S., D.Sc., LL.D.; *b.* Port Hope, Ont., 15 Jan., 1854; *s.* Robert Heedham and Angeline Esther Jones; *m.* July 13, 1882, Ada, *d.* late Horace Everett, Council Bluffs, Ia. Prep. ed'n Trinity Coll. Sch., Port Hope; grad. Rensselaer Poly. Inst., C. E., 1875; and M. Eng'ring, 1882, McGill Univ., 1904; Univ. of Mo., 1904; in engineering work, C. P. R., 1876-7; asst. prof. rational and tech. mechanics, Rensselaer Poly. Inst. 1878-80; chief eng'r Raymond & Campbell, bridge builders, Council Bluffs, Ia., 1881-2; prof. civ. eng'ring, Imperial Univ. of Japan, 1882-6; consulting bridge eng'r since 1887; now sr. mem. of Waddell & Harrington, Kansas City. Mem. Am. Soc. Civ. Eng'rs, Inst'n of Civ. Eng'rs, Great Britain, La Societe des Engéniers Civils de France, Canadian Soc. Civ. Eng'rs, Am. Soc. for Testing Materials, Rensselaer Soc. Eng'rs, Soc. for Promotion of Eng'ring Ed'n, Geog.

Soc. of France; hon. mem. Kogaku Kyokai (Japanese Eng'ring Soc.); hon. mem. Tau Beta Pi Assn. and Phi Beta Kappa Soc.; decorated by Emperor, 1888, Knight Commdr. Order of the Rising Sun of Japan; by the Grand Duchess Olga, of Russia, First Class Order of her Société de Bienfaissance for service as prin. eng'r of Trans-Alaska-Siberian Ry.; at present consulting engr. for the Alberta and Gt. Waterways Rly. *Publications:* The Designing of Ordinary Iron Highway Bridges, 1884; A System of Iron Railroad Bridges for Japan, 1886 (Japanese Govt.); De Pontibus, 1898; Specifications for Steel Bridges, 1900; Engineering Specifications and Contracts, 1907. Extensive contb'r to engring socs., en'ring journ. and to Forest and Stream. A compilation of 22 of his professional papers edited by John Lyle Harrison, 1905. *Address:* 2708 Forest Av., Kansas City, U.S.A.;

WADE, Frederick Coate, K.C.; *b.* Bowmanville, Ont., 26 Feb., 1860; *s.* of William Wade, formerly mgr. of the Ontario Bank at Ottawa; *m.* 1886, Edith Mabel, *d.* of D. B. Read, K.C., Toronto; one *s.* one *d.* *Educ.:* Ottawa, Owen Sound, Toronto Univ. (grad. 1882). While at the Univ., was editor of Varsity and later was editorial writer of the Toronto *Globe*. Removed to Winnipeg, 1883; called to bar of Manitoba, 1886; editorial writer Manitoba *Free Press*, 1886-7. First pres. of the Young Liberal Assn. of Winnipeg; a mem. of the Provincial Bd. of Education; mem. of the Council of Manitoba Univ. Commr. 1897 (to investigate certain charges made in connection with Manitoba Penitentiary). Apptd. 1897, Registrar of the Yukon Land Registration Dist., Crown Prosecutor for the Yukon and Clerk of the Supreme Ct. for the territory. Legal advisor to the Yukon Council, 1898; resigned 1902, all positions except that of Crown Prosecutor, in order to devote himself to law practice; removed to Vancouver, 1907; unsuccessful candidate for Prov. Legis., 1909. *Publications:* "National Schools of Manitoba," 1892; and "The Manitoba School Question," 1895. *Address:* Vancouver, B.C. *Club.* Union, Vancouver.

WADMORE, Lieut.-Col. Robinson Lyndhurst; *b.* London, Eng., 6 Jan., 1855; *s.* of James Foster Wadmore, of Tonbridge, and Anna Elizabeth Wadmore; *m.* Annie Skead, *d.* of the late Hon. James Skead, of Ottawa; three *d.* *Educ.:* Tonbridge Sch., Eng.; Officer Commanding the Royal Canadian Regiment; studied architecture; was a Lieut. in the (then) 2nd London Rifle Volunteers; in 1883, was given a commission in the Infantry School Corps (now the Royal Canadian Regiment); served with C. Company, R.C.R., in North West Rebellion, 1885; Relief of Battleford (24 April); action at Cut Knife Hill (2 May); operations against Chief Big Bear's Band (June-July); medal with clasp; was present with detachment at opening Imperial Institute by Her late Majesty Queen Victoria, in 1893; Commandant of Royal School of Infantry at St. Johns Que.; afterwards Commandant Royal School of Infantry, at Fredericton, New Brunswick. *Recreations:* fishing boating, yachting, riding, painting. *Address:* Halifax, N.S.

WAINWRIGHT, William; 4th Vice-Pres. of the G. T. Ry. System; 2nd Vice-Pres., Grand Trunk Pacific Rly. Co.; *b.* Manchester, Eng., 30 April, 1840; *s.* of Abraham Wainwright, a native of Lancashire; *m.* (1st) 1867, Rosabelle Hilda (*d.* 1876), *d.* of Richard Arnold, of Toronto; (2nd) 1878, Mary Emily, sister of his first wife. *Educ.:* Manchester. Joined service of the Manchester, Sheffield and Lincolnshire Ry., 1851, and eventually became gen. mgr. Arrived Can., 1862 and took position as a senior clerk and shorthand sec. in chief accnt's office of the G. T. R., at Montreal; sec. to man. dir.; senior clerk in charge of the car mileage dept.; gen. passngr. agt.; asst. mgr., 1881; asst. gen. mgr., 1890; gen. asst., 1896, and in addition comptroller, 1900; 4th vice-pres., 1907; gen. mgr., North Shore Ry., 1883-1885. Dir. Montreal Telegraph Co., Guarantee Co. of North America; vice-pres., Richelieu and Ont. Nav. Co., and Grand Trunk Ins., and Provident Soc.; 2nd vice-pres., Grand Trunk Pacific Ry.; dir. Canadian Express Co., and of various subsidiary lines of the G.T.R.; governor Montreal Gen. Hospital. Retired with rank of Capt. from Co. of Artillery in the old Grand Trunk Brigade, upon its disbandment, which he commanded for eight yrs. *Address:* 156 Metcalfe St., Montreal, Que. *Clubs:* St. James, Canada, Montreal; Rideau, Ottawa; Garrison, Quebec.

WAKEHAM, William, M.D., C.M.; Inspector of Fisheries for the Gulf of St. Lawrence; Commr. of Police for the Prov. of Quebec; *b.* Quebec, 30 Nov., 1844; *s.* of late George Wakeham, for many yrs. prop. of The Belmont Retreat, Quebec, and Mary Wakeham; unmarried. *Educ.:* High Sch., Quebec; McGill Coll. Practiced medicine in Gaspe until apptd. to his present position as Inspr. of Fisheries for the Gulf of St. Lawrence, 1878. In 1893 was selected to be H.M.'s Comnr. under the agreement with the U.S., for enquiring into the preservation of the fisheries in waters contiguous to Can. and the U.S., the report of which was presented to both Govts. in Jan., 1897; in 1898, was apptd. a commr., with Judge Lavergne and F. Gourdeau, to enquire into the alleged grievances of the St. Lawrence pilots. Commissioner to investigate conditions of lobster industry, 1909. *Address:* Gaspe, Que.

WALKER, Byron Edmund, D.C.L., LL.D., C.V.O.; *b.* Hamilton, Ont., 14 Oct., 1848; *s.* of the late Alfred Edmund Walker, Hamilton, Ont.; *m.* Mary, *d.* of Alexander Alexander, Hamilton, Ont.; four *s.* three *d* Entered the Canadian Bank of Commerce in 1858 at Hamilton; agent in New York in 1881; gen. mangr., in 1886; dir. in 1906 and president in 1907; has been chairman of the bankers' section of the Toronto Board of Trade and vice-pres. and pres. of the Canadian Bankers' Association, holding the last named office for two terms. In 1897, local secretary in connection with the meeting of the British Association for the Advancement of Science in Toronto. At the Universal Exposition held at St. Louis in 1904, he acted as Chairman of the Section of Money and Credit in the Department of Economics of the International Congress of Arts and Sciences. He has been for a number of years a trustee and senator of the University of Toronto, and when, in 1905, the Provincial Government of Ontario apptd. a Royal Commission to report upon the administration of the University, he was selected as a member of the Commission; was nominated by the Ontario Government as a member of the first Board of Governors of the University apptd. under the reorganization which took place; chn. of the Board of Governors, 1910; pres. of the Canadian Institute for two years; Fellow of the Geological Society of England and of the Institute of Bankers of England, and a dir. of the Canada Life Assurance Company and of the Toronto General Trusts Corporation; mem. of the Quebec Battlefields Commission; mem. of the Federal Commission to select art works for the National Gallery. *Publications:* Books and addresses on banking. A paper on Early Italian Art. *Address:* Long Garth, Toronto, and Broadeaves, De Grassi Point, Lake Simcoe. *Clubs:* Toronto, T.C.Y.C., Hunt, Lambton Golf and Country Club, Toronto; St. James, Montreal; Rideau, Ottawa; Devonshire, London, England.

WALKER, Edward Chandler; Pres. Hiram Walker & Sons, Ltd., distillers; *b.* Detroit, Mich., 7 Feb., 1851; *s.* of the late Hiram Walker and Mary Williams; *m.* 1896, Mary, *d.* of Thomas F. Griffin, of Detroit. *Educ.:* Detroit; entered office of his father's firm, the Hiram Walker & Sons, Ltd., and upon retirement of his father became pres.; also pres., Walkerville Malleable Iron Co., Walkerville Brewing Co., Walkerville Land and Bldg. Co.; dir. 2f several other Cos. *Address:* Walkerville, Ont.

WALKER, Francis Austin, M.L.A.; *b.* Lucan, Ont., 17 Nov., 1871; *s.* of William Walker and Catherine Spences; *m.* Emma J. Curry, of Belleville, Ont. *Educ.:* Lucan, Ont., and Edmonton, Alta.; went to Western Canada in 1882; settled near Edmonton in 1883; farming; travelled to Klondyke by overland trail from Edmonton, Alta., 1898; elected to the first Legislative of Alberta in 1905; a Liberal. *Address:* Edmonton, Alta.

WALKER, Herbert Barber; *b.* Hamilton, Ont., 25 Sept., 1858; *s.* of Alfred and Fanny Walker; *m.* Anna Fraser, *d.* of the late Alexander Fraser of Cobourg, Ont.; one *s.* one *d.* *Educ.:* Pub. Schs., Hamilton, Ont.; entered service of Canadian Bank of Commerce in 1877; manager at Windsor, 1888; agent in Chicago, 1897; joint agent in New York, 1902; manager at Montreal, 1908; director of the Canadian Life Assurance Co., and of the National Trust Co., Ltd. *Address:* The Linton, Montreal. *Clubs:* Mount Royal, Montreal, Montreal; Toronto.

WALKER, John Bruce; *b.* Ayrshire, Scotland, 13 Dec., 1861; *s.* of Andrew Walker, shipmaster, of Ayrshire, and Jeannie Crosbie Bruce of the same place; *m.* Mary Alice Will, of Brant Co., Ont.; one *d.* Arrived in Canada, 10 April, 1882; in journalism for 20 years before entering emigration service; now asst. supt. of immigration at Winnipeg. *Recreations:* curling, bowling, golf. *Address:* 446 Maryland St., Winnipeg, Man. *Club:* Manitoba, Winnipeg, Man.

WALKER, T. L., M.A., Ph.D., F.G.S.; *b.* Co. of Peel, Ont., 30 Dec., 1867. *Educ.:* Queen's Univ., Kingston; Univ. of Leipzig, Germany; with honours in Chemistry and Mineralogy, 1890; granted a scholarship of £150 per year by H.M. Commissioners for the Exhibition of 1851; studied in Leipzig, 1895; Assist. Superint. Geol. Survey of India, 1897-1902; while in India made a scientific expedition across the high passes of the Himalayas into Thibet; Professor of Mineralogy, Univ. of Toronto. *Publications:* numerous scientific papers from 1894 onward, in publications of the Geological Survey of India, American Journal of Science, and Zeitschrift fur Krystallographie. *Address:* Dale and Maple Ave., Toronto, Ont.

WALLACE, Rev. Prof. Francis Huston, M.A., B.D.; *b.* Ingersol, Ont., 1851; *s.* of Rev. Robert and Marianni Wallace; *m.* Joy Wilson, *d.* of Bishop Wilson, R. E. Church, New Jersey; two *s.* three *d.* (two *d. deceased*). *Educ.:* Up. Can. Coll., and Univ. of Toronto; Dean of the Faculty of Theology, Victoria Coll., Toronto, Ont.; for about ten yrs. was pastor of the Methodist Church; one year professor of New Testiment Exegisis in Victoria Coll.; about 10 years dean of the Faculty of Theology. *Recreation:* boating. *Address:* 95 Bedford Road. Toronto.

WALLACE, Malcolm William, B.A., Ph.D.; *b.* Essex Co., Ont., 1 May, 1873; *s.* of William Wallace and Elizabeth Thompson; *m.* May Pitkin; one *s.* *Educ.:* Windsor High Sch., Univ. Coll., Toronto; Univ. of Chicago; grad. from Univ. of Tronto, 1896; fellow in English, Univ. of Chicago, grad. Ph.D., 1897-1899; professor of Rhetoric and English Literature in Beloit Coll., Beloit, Wis., 1899-1904; lecturer in Univ. Coll., Univ. of Toronto, 1904; Registrar, 1906; Associate professor of English, 1909. *Publications:* "The Berth of Hercules;" "Goldings' Tragedie of Abraham's Sacrafice;" *Recreation:* golf. *Address:* 171 Robert St., Toronto, Ont. *Club:* Rosedale Golf, Toronto.

WALLACE, Capt. Thomas George, M. P.; *b.* Ottawa, Ont., 7 May, 1879; *s.* of late Hon. N. Clarke Wallace and Belinda Gilmour. *Educ.:* Woodbridge pub. sch. and Weston High Sch., Ont.; merchant and flour miller; gazetted Captain, 36th Regt., 15 Dec., 1897; served as private in the Royal Canadian Regiment, during the South African War, 1900 (medal and three clasps), including Driefontein and Paardeberg; unsuccessful candidate for H. of C. in bye-elec. in Centre York, 1907; elected, 1908. *Address:* Woodbridge, Ont.

WALLIS, Arthur Frederick; chief ed. of the Toronto *Mail and Empire;* *b.* London, Eng., 1854; *m.* 1882, Sarah Kennedy, of Toronto; three *s.* Came to Can. with his parents when 16 yrs. of age. Learned printing, and then took up journalism; reporter on Toronto Mail; chief ed. 1890; chief ed. *Mail and Empire,* 1895. Rep. *Mail* in Press Gallery, H.of C. for many yrs.; pres. of Press Gallery, 1887. *Pub-*

lication: "Journalism as a Profession." *Address:* 27 St. Patrick St., Toronto.

WALLIS, Herbert; *b.* Derby, Eng., 10 March, 1844; *s.* of the late William Wallace Wallis and Sarah Campion Wallis; *m.* (1st) Mary Ellen, *e. d.* of the late Thomas Walklate, goods manager, Midland Ry., of Derby, (2nd) Ida Shaw Boulter, of Montreal, one *s.* one *d.* *Educ.:* Private Sch. in England; arrived in Canada, 16 May, 1871; member Inst. C.E.; M.I. Mech. Eng.; past pres., Can. Soc. C.E. *Educ.:* as an engineer; pupil of the late Matthew Kirtley, Locomotive Supt., Midland Ry. Co.; eleven years with that Company; twenty years with the G. T. Ry. Co., as asst. and chief mechanical supt.; retired, May, 1896. *Address:* 230 Drummond St., Montreal. *Club:* St. James, Montreal.

WALSH, Edmund Joseph, C.E., F.R. Met. Soc. (England); Engineer in charge of Trent Canal Surveys, Dept. of Rys. and Canals, Ottawa; *b.* Canada, 10 Dec., 1860; *s.* of Robert and Marjorie Walsh; *m.* Margaret, *d.* of the late Hon. William Wilkin, mem. of the Ex. Coun. of Montserrat, W.I.; one *d.* *Educ.:* Pub. Schs. and by private tuition. Asst. Engr. on municipal works, Prov. of Ont., 1877-80; Asst. Engr., C. P. Ry., Rocky Mountain Div., 1881; Asst. Engr., Northern Pacific Ry. and O. T. Ry., 1882; Asst. Engr., C. P. Ry., 1883-84; Asst. and Res. Engr., on surveys and construction of the Cape Breton extension of the Intercolonial Ry. for the Dom. Gov., 1885-89; Chief Govt. Engr. and Dir. of Pub. Works of the Leeward, (West India) Islands, carrying out special comprehensive works for the Dept. of the Sec. of State for the Colonies and the Leeward Islands Govt.; in Nov., 1890, carried on special mission to Ottawa, on behalf of Leeward Islands Govt., to negotiate for establishment of money order system and parcel post between the two countries; immediately successful in case of former, and discussed basis upon which latter arranged at later date; returned to Can., 1896; consulting engr. with headquarters at Ottawa, 1896-1904; apptd. engr. in charge of Trent Canal Surveys, Dept. of Rys. and Canals, 1 Aug., 1904. *Recreations:* golf, boating, curling, skating, snow-shoeing. *Address:* 402 O'Connor St., Ottawa. *Club:* Rideau Curling, Ottawa.

WALSH, James E.; *b.* Ormstown, Que., 10 July, 1862; *s.* of Peter Walsh and Eleanor Boudreau de Gravelene; *m.* Anna Roger; one *s.* one *d.* *Educ.:* Huntingdon Acad., Joliette, and Varennes Coll., Que.; engaged in transportation work since graduating from coll; for many yrs. with the Canada Atlantic Rly. Co.; after leaving railroad work, was for a time assistant to the General Manager of the Richelieu and Ontario Navigation Co.; from there went to the Department of Public Works, Federal Government, in connection with the Georgian Bay Ship Canal survey; now manager, Transportation Department, Canadian Manufacturers' Association. *Address:* 86 Bedford Rd., Toronto.

WALTON, Frederick Parker, B.A., LL.D., *b.* Nottingham, Eng., 1858; *s.* of Isaac Walton, Buxton, England; *m.* Mary, *d.* of Rev. D. Parker of Brampton, Derbyshire. *Educ.:* Oxford; Edinburgh; Lincoln Coll., Oxford, first class Cl. Moderations; second class Lit. Hum.; B.A., 1883; Edinburgh Univ., LL.B., 1886; Aberdeen, 1906; Scottish Bar, 1886; Lecturer in Roman Law, Glasgow University; legal secretary to Lord Advocate (Right Hon. J. B. Balfour), 1894; Dean of the Faculty of Law; professor of Roman Law, McGill Univ., Montreal, since 1897. *Publications:* Handbook of Law of Husband and Wife in Scotland; Scotch Marriages, Regular and Irregular; articles on Husband and Wife, Married Women's Property, etc., in Green's Encyclopædia of Law of Scotland, Historical Introduction to the Roman Law; Scope and Interpretation of Civil Code of Lower Canada; and contributions to legal journals. *Recreations:* cycling, travel. *Address:* 552 Pine Avenue W., Montreal. *Clubs:* St. James's, University, Montreal.

WANKLYN, Frederic Lamb, M.I.C.E.; *b.* Buenos Ayres, Argentine, S.A., 25 Feb., 1860; *s.* of Frederick Wanklyn and Elizabeth Riestra Lumb; *m.* Edith Margaret Angus (*deceased*, 1907); three *s.* one *d.* *Educ.:* Marlborough Coll., Wilts, Eng. Arrived in Canada, I Jan., 1881; member Inst. C.E., London; member Can. Soc. C.E. (Council); articled to Chasler Savie C.E., M. S. & L. Ry. Co.; served apprenticeship in locomotive works of A. Gorton, Manchester, Eng.; formerly president engineer, Lombardy Ry. Co., Milan, Italy; Asst. Locomotive Supt., G. T. Ry.; Manager Locomotive Works, G. T. Ry.; Manager of Toronto Ry. Co.; General Manager and vice-president, Montreal Street Ry. Co.; vice-pres., Dominion Coal Co. until its amalgamation with the Dominion Steel Co. *Recreations:* shooting and fishing. *Address:* 241 Drummond St., Montreal, and St. Anne de Bellevue, Que. *Clubs:* St. James, Mount Royal, Montreal; Forest and Stream, Dorval, Que.

WARBURTON, Alexander Bannerman, B.A., D.C.L., K.C., M.P.; *b.* Charlottetown, P.E.I., 5 April, 1852; *s.* of Hon. James Warburton, fo merly of Garryberch, Portarlington, Ireland, and Miss Green, *d.* of Hon. Samuel Green, formerly of St. Eleanor, P.E.I.; *m.* (1st) 23 Aug., 1883, Helen, *o. d.* of Hon. Daniel Davies (*deceased*, 1884), (2nd) Mabel C., *y. d.* of the late Hon. J. Longworth, of Charlottetown, P.E.I.; three *d.* *Educ.:* Summerside (P.E.I.) Gram. Sch., St. Dunstan's Coll., Charlottetown; King's Coll., Windsor, N.S., at Edinburgh and at Walter Wren's, London, Eng; studied law with Mr. (now Sir) L. H. Davies; a dir. of the *Patriot* Pub. Co., and a frequent contributor to the columns of that paper; is a governor of King's Coll.; unsuccessful candidate in Provincial elections for City of Charlottetown, Jan., 1891; was first elec. to Prov. Legis. for 1st Dist. of Queen's, bye-election, May, 1891; re-elected 1908 and 1897; was Premier of P.E.I. in 1897-98; was judge of King's Co. Court from 1898 to 1904, resigning to contest Queen's County in Liberal interests; unsuccessful for H. of C., 1904; first elec. 1908; Church of England; Liberal. *Address:* Charlottetown, P.E.I.

WARD, Lieut.-Col. Henry Alfred, K.C.; *b.* Port Hope, Ont., 20 Aug., 1848; *s.* of George Charles Ward, and Harriet Amelia

Brent; *m.* Annie B. Goodwin, of Savannah, Georgia, U.S.; two *d.* *Educ.:* Pub. Sch., Port Hope, Ont.; called to the bar of Ont., 1872; Mayor of Port Hope, 1885, 1903, 1904; elec. member of H. of C., 1885, 1887-1900, 1904; Lieut.-Col. Commanding the 46th Regt., Canadian Militia, 1903-1909. *Recreations:* fishing, shooting, golf. *Address:* Ganeraska, Port Hope, Ont. *Club:* Toronto.

WARD, Hon. James Kewley, M.L.C.; *b.* Peel, Isle of Man, 19 Sept., 1819; *m.* (1st) 1848, Eliza King, of London, Eng. (*d.* 1854); (2nd) Lydia, *d.* of William Trenholme, of Kingsey, Que. (*d.* 1900); three *s.* seven *d.* *Educ.:* May's Academy, Douglas, I. of M. Landed in New York, 1842, and was employed at his trade as a carpenter; engaged in lumber operations in Steuben Co., N.Y. State, 1850; removed to Prov. of Que., 1853, and purchased a lumbering establishment, with timber lands, on the Maskinonge River; removed to Three Rivers, Que., 1863, and purchased a mill on St. Maurice River; removed to Montreal, 1873, and estbd. the Mona saw mills on the Lachine Canal; retired from business, 1900. Mem. Montreal Bd. of Trade since 1887; mem. Cote St. Antoine Council for eighteen yrs., and Mayor nine yrs.; life mem. and past pres., St. George's Soc.; life mem. Mechanics' Inst.; life gov. Montreal Gen. Hospital, Western Hospital, House of Refuge and Industry, Montreal Dispensary; life gov. and hon. pres., Protestant Hospital for Insane. Unsuccessful candidate for H. of C. at Dom. g. e., 1882, 1887; apptd. to Quebec Legis. Council, June, 1888. Has been a mem. of the Council of Pub. Instruction since Oct., 1903; J.P. for dist. of Montreal. Donated a pub. library costing $10,000 to Peel, Isle of Man., which was erected over the spot where he was born. *Address:* 18 Rosemount Ave., Montreal. *Club:* St. James, Montreal.

WARD, Major Walter Reginald; *b.* Saltash, Cornwall, Eng., 24 Oct., 1869; *s.* of Commander H. Purcell Ward, R.N.; *m.* Irene Silver Payzant, of Halifax, N.S., 2nd *d.* of John Y. Payzant; one *s.* one *d.* *Educ.:* Christ's Hospital, London, Eng;. served in Royal Navy from 15 Jan., 1886 until 1904, when he resigned commission and subsequently joined Canadian Permanent Staff at Ottawa; now Asst. Paymaster-General, Canadian Army Pay Corps. *Address:* The Kenniston, Elgin St., Ottawa.

WARE, Arthur Buller ("Doc."); *b.* Exeter, Eng., 3 Feb., 1864; *m.* Jean Semple; one *s.* one *d.* *Educ.:* Exeter. Came to Canada in 1883, and was engaged on the staffs of different newspapers as reporter; wrote military column for Montreal Gazette for many yrs. under nom-de-plume of "Cartridge Box," Was a public entertainer for ten yrs.; travelled with Hermann, the great conjurer, as card trick expert; was also with Barnum's circus for some yrs. Is now advertising expert; pres. of the Ware Co. (outdoor advertisers.) *Recreations:* curling, snowshoeing. *Address:* 20 Hanover St., Montreal. *Clubs:* Elks, Press.

WARMAN, Cy.; *b.* Greenup, Ill., U.S.A. 22 June, 1855; *s.* of John Warman, and Nancy Askew; *m.* Myrtle Marie Jones; three *s.* two *d.* *Educ.:* Public Schools; arrived in Canada, 1897; farmer; wheat merchant; railway man; publisher of Western Railway (Denver) Daily *Chronicle*, Creedo, Cal. *Publications:* Tales of an Engineer," "Express Messenger," "The White Mail," "Short Rails," "Frontier Stories," (Scribners); "Snow on the Headlight," "Story of the Railroad," (D. Appleton & Co.); "Weiga of Temagami," (H. M. Caldwell & Co.) *Recreation:* The Woods. *Address:* P. O. Box, 1181, Montreal. *Club:* Chicago Press, Chicago, Ill.

WARNOCK, Miss Amelia Beers; *b.* Galt, Ont., 1878; *d.* of James Warnock and Katherine Hale Bayard; *Educ.:* Galt, Toronto and New York; sang in public when very young girl; adopted journalism as a career shortly after leaving school; well known as a literary and musical critic; poet and magazine writer; staff writer on the *Mail and Empire*, Toronto. *Address:* 66 Charles St., Toronto. *Clubs:* Canadian Women's Press Club, Toronto.

WATSON, Major David; *b.* Quebec, 7 Feb., 1869; *s.* of William and Jean Grant Watson; *m.* Mary Browning; three *d.* *Educ.:* in Quebec; in newspaper work for 20 years; mgn. dir. of the *Chronicle*; was a delegate to the Imperial Press Conference 1909; takes great interest in Militia affairs; Capt. and Brev. Major, 8th Royal Rifles, Quebec. *Address:* 35 Ursule St., Quebec. *Club:* Garrison, Quebec.

WATSON, Harrison; *b.* Montreal, 13 June, 1864; *s.* of Charles Standhop Watson and Eleanor Rebecca Underwood; *m.* Ruth Appleton Blake; one *s.* *Educ.:* Canada, England, France and Germany; in business in Canada for a number of years, the greater portion of which with the Montreal Rolling Mills Co., alternately as secretary and sales agent; subsequently in charge of Canadian section of the Imperial Institute London, Eng., and now in charge of the Canadian Government Trade Branch in the City of London, Eng. *Address:* 73 Basinghall Street, London, E.C., England. *Clubs:* Junior Atheneum, London, Eng.; St. James, Montreal.

WATSON, Harry Holgate, M.L.A.; *b.* Milton, Ont., 26 Dec., 1867; *s.* of Henry Watson and Jane Elizabeth Holgate; *m.* Kathleen Constance Black; one *d.* *Educ.:* Milton Pub. Sch., and Up. Can. Coll.; druggist; pres., McDowall Aikens Watson Co.; first el. to the B.C. Legis. Ass., 1909; an active member of the Masonic fraternity; 33° A. & A. S. R. *Recreations:* rowing and football. *Address:* 1230 Burnaby St., Vancouver, B.C. *Club:* Vancouver.

WATSON, Hugh; *b.* Maryhill, Glasgow, Scotland, 23 Jan., 1839; *s.* of John Watson and Ann Goodwin; *m.* 1879, Eleanor, *d.* of the late Jas. Schearer. *Educ.:* Parish Sch., Maryhill, Glasgow. Arrived Canada, 1860, in partnership with his brother and Mr. F. S. Foster (both deceased); started the manufacturing of wall papers in Montreal; business formed into a joint stock Co., the Watson-Foster Co., Ltd., of which he now is pres. Mem. Montreal Bd. of Trade; life governor, Montreal General Hospital; the Homeopathic Hospital, Protestant House of Industry and Refuge; life mem. Natural

History Soc. *Address:* "Hillcrest," 478 Mt. Pleasant Ave., Montreal.

WATSON, John, M.A., LL.D., F.R.S.C., Prof. of Moral Philosophy at Queen's Univ., Kingston; *b.* Glasgow, Scot., 25 Feb., 1847; *s.* of John Watson, and Elizabeth Robertson, both Scotch; *m.* Margaret Patterson Mitchell, Glasgow, 1874; one *s.* three *d.* *Educ.:* at Kilmarnock and Glasgow Univ., 1866; arrived in Canada, 1872; professor of Logic, Metaphysics and Ethics, Queen's Univ., Kingston, 1872, afterwards professor of Moral Philosophy. *Publications:* Kant and his English critics; Schelling's Transcendental Idealism, 1882; Comte, Mill and Spence, 1885; Hedonistic Theories, 1895; Christianity and Idealism, 1896; Philosophy of Kant Explained, 1908. *Recreations:* golf, bowling. *Address:* Union St., Kingston, Ont.

WATSON, Hon. Robert; Senator; *b.* Elora, Ont., 29 April, 1853; *s.* of late George Watson, Edinburgh, and Elizabeth McDonald of Inverness, who came to Canada, 1847; *m.* July, 1880, Isabella, *d.* of Duncan Brown, of Lobo, Ont. A millwright by trade; moved to Manitoba, 1876, and built mills at Portage la Prairie, and Stonewall; was a municipal councillor; elected to H. of C. for Marquette, 1882, and 1887, and was the only Liberal member from West of Lake Superior in those parliaments; re-elec. 1891, but resigned to accept portfolio of Minister of Public works in Greenway Administration, 26 May, 1892, an office he held until the resignation of that Govt., 6 Jan., 1900; elec. to Legislature for Portage la Prairie, 1892, 1896, but defeated 1899; called to the Senate, 29 Jan., 1900; Presbyterian; Liberal. *Address:* Portage la Prairie, Man.

WATT, Mrs. A. T. (Madge Robertson); *d.* of Henry Robertson, K.C., of Collingwood, Ont.; *m.* A. T. Watt, of Victoria, B.C. The first woman in Canada to obtain the degree of M.A. Was engaged in newspaper work in New York, and contributed stories and articles to *Judge, Life, Vogue, Truth,* etc. For some yrs. since her marriage did the reviewing for the Victoria *Times. Publications:* A series of articles on "Outdoor Sports for Girls," for different syndicates; a pamphlet descriptive of the south part of Vancouver Island, to be published by the Prov. Govt.; a Year Book for the King's Daughters (now being prepared.) *Recreation:* horticulture. *Address:* Victoria, B.C.

WATT, David A.; *b.* Ayrshire, Scotland, 1830; *m.* 1857, Frances MacIntosh (*d.* 1876); one *s.* three *d.* *Educ.:* Gram. Sch., Greenock, Scotland. Arrived Canada, 1846; and has ever since been associated with Messrs. Allan, the well-known shipowners, Montreal. Mem. Montreal Bd. of Trade; one of the organizers of the Montreal Corn Exchange; life mem. Natural History Soc., and formerly editor of "The *Canadian Naturalist.*" Life gov.. Art Assn.; one of the founders of the Good Govt. Assn. *Address:* 285 Stanley St., Montreal.

WATTS, John William Hurrell, R.C.A., F.R.A.I.C.; *b.* Teignmouth, Devon, Eng., 16 Sept., 1850; *s.* of John Watts and Susan Hurrell; *m.* Elizabeth Blanche Morris; two *s.* one *d.* *Educ.:* Priv. Sch., London, Eng Was a student of the Arch. Assn. of London, Eng., and afterwards practised there a short time; left England for Canada, 1874; shortly after arrival was associated with arch. branch of Dom. Govt., and for fifteen yrs. was asst. architect of Pub. Works. Dir. of National Gallery, 1880. In 1897, severed connection with Govt. and has since practiced his profession in Ottawa. *Recreations:* fishing, boating. *Addresses:* 62 Robert St.; Central Chambers, Ottawa.

WAUGH, Richard Deans; controller of the City of Winnipeg; *b.* Melrose, Scot., 23 March, 1868; *s.* of Richard Waugh, and Janet Deans (both Scotch); *m.* Harriet L., *d.* of the late Alexander Logan, ex-Mayor of Winnipeg; four *s.* two *d.* *Educ.:* Highfield Acad., Melrose, Scot. Arrived Can., 6 April, 1883. For six yrs. in office of Glass & Glass, barristers, Winnipeg; entered real estate business, 1890; now mem. of firm of Waugh & Beattie, real estate agts.; chn. of Pub. Parks Bd., Winnipeg; el. controller of Winnipeg, 1908-9-10; ex pres., Manitoba Branch, Royal Caledonian Cur-l ing Club. A patron of all healthful amateur sports. *Recreation:* curling. *Address:* 1398 Portage Ave., Winnipeg.

WEATHERBE, Hon. Sir Robert Linton, Kt.; *b.* Bedeque, P.E.I., 7 April, 1836; *s.* of late Jonathan Weatherbe and Mary, *d.* of John Baker; *m.* 1864, Minnie, *y. d.* of Lewis Johnston, of Annandale, N.S.; six *s.* *Educ.:* Prince of Wales' Coll.; Acadia Coll., Wolfville. Edited the Acadian Recorder; called to Bar, N.S., 1863; Judge of Supreme Court, N.S., 1878; Chief Justice of N.S., 1905-7; Q.C., 1876; Kt., 1906. *Address:* St. Eulalie, Grand Pre, N.S. *Club:* Halifax.

WEAVER, Miss Emily Poynton; authoress; *b.* Manchester, Eng., 1865; *d.* of Richard T. and Elizabeth D. Weaver. *Educ.:* Priv. Schs. nr. Manchester. Came to Canada with parents, Sept., 1880; lived for some yrs. on a farm in Ontario; removed to Toronto, 1889; was winner of a prize in the Dominion History Competition; removed to Halifax, N.S., 1898; returned to Toronto, 1905. *Publications:* A Canadian History for Boys and Girls; Builders of he Dominion; My Lady Nell; Prince Rupert's Namesake; The Rabbi's Sons, also other stories and articles in various periodicals. Mem. Women's Canadian Club. *Address:* 26 Bernard Ave., Toronto.

WEBSTER, Robert Edward, M.D., C. M., M.R.C.P. & S.; *b.* Brockville, On ., 25 March, 1870; *s.* of Robert Webster and J. C. Moles; *m.* Irene Jones; one *s.* *Educ.:* McGill Univ., grad. in 1891; post grad. course in London and New York in surgery; Clinical professor of Surgery in Western sch. of Medicine, 1893 to 1898; apptd. chief consulting surgeon C. C. General Hospital, Ottawa, 1901; takes a great interest in horses and dogs; is present master of hounds of the Ottawa Hunt Club; a frequent and successful exhibitor at Canadian horse shows; active in organisation of first horse held in Ottawa. *Recreations:* hunting, golf. *Address:* 196 Metcalfe St., Ottawa. *Clubs:* Rideau, Hunt, Golf and Country, Ottawa.

WEDDERBURN, His Hon. William; Judge of the Co. Ct. for King's and Albert Cos.; *b.* St. John, N.B., 12 Oct., 1834; *s.* of the late Alexander Wedderburn and Jane

Heaviside; *m.* 1878, Jennie, *d.* of C. C. Vaughan, of St. John. *Educ.:* Gram. Sch. of St. John, and also took up study of law. Called to Bar of N.B., 1858; cr. Q.C. by Earl of Dufferin, 1873; apptd. Commr. of Prov. Statistics of N.B. same yr. El. to N.B. Legis., 1870; el. Speaker of the Prov. Assem., Feb., 1876; apptd. Prov. Sec. of N.B., 1878; apptd. to his present position, 28 June, 1882. Past Supreme Chief Ranger of the I.O.F. *Address:* Hampton, N.B.

WEIR, Hon. William Alexander, B.C.L., Superior Court Judge of the Prov. of Quebec; *b.* Montreal, 15 Oct., 1858; *s.* of William Park Weir and Helen Craig Smith; *m.* Adelaide Sayers Stewart; one *s.* and one *d.* *Educ.:* High Sch. and McGill Univ., Montreal; created Queen's Counsel in 1899; apptd. Minister without portfolio in Parent admn., Oct., 1903; elec. Speaker, April 25, 1905; on August 31, 1906, was sworn as Minister of Public Works and Labour, and re-elec. by accl.; was one of the representatives of Quebec at the interprovincial conference of Oct., 1906, to consider the readjustment of Federal subsidies to the provinces; on Oct. 17, 1907, was sworn in as provincial treasurer of Quebec; resigned Jan., 1910, to accept Judgeship of Superior Court. *Publications:* Code of civil procedure and Municipal Code of Province of Quebec. *Address:* 957 Dorchester St., Montreal. *Clubs:* Garrison, Quebec; University, Montreal.

WETHERALD, Miss Agnes Ethelwyn; *b.* Rockwood, Ont., 26 April, 1857; *d.* of William Wetherald and Jemima Harris. *Educ.:* Union Springs Boarding Sch., New York State, and Pickering Coll., Ont. A well known Canadian poetess. *Publications:* Four books of verse, The House of the Trees, Tangled in Stars, The Radiant Road, and The Last Robin. *Address:* Chantler, Welland County, Ont.

WETMORE, Hon. Edward Ludlow, B.A., LL.D., Chief Justice of Saskatchewan; *b.* Fredericton, N.B., 24 March, 1841; *s.* of Charles Peters Wetmore and Sara Burr Ketchum; *m.* 1872, Eliza Jane, *d.* of Charles Dickson of St. John, N.B.; two *s.* one *d.* *Educ.:* Gram. Sch., Fredericton, and Georgetown; King's Coll., Fredericton (now the Univ. of N.B.); called to the bar, 1864; for some years deputy clerk of the crown; Queen's Council, 1881; Mayor of Fredericton, 1874-1876; pres. of barristers' society, N.B., 1886-1887; representative of Alumini Assn. in Senate of Univ., 1886-1887; representative of County of York in New Brunswick Legislature, 1885-1884, during which time he was leader of the opposition; Puisne Judge of the Supreme Court, N.W.T., 18 Feb., 1887; a commissioner of Consolidated Ordinances of N.W.T., 1898; chief Justice of Saskatchewan, 16 Sept., 1907; Chancellor, Univ. of Saskatchewan, 16 Oct., 1907; Chairman of Committee for consolidating the laws of Saskatchewan, 1907-1908. *Recreations:* cricket, fishing, and shooting. *Address:* Regina, Sask. *Club:* Assiniboia, Regina.

WHITE, Albert Scott, B.A., LL.B., D.C.L., Judge of the Supreme Court of New Brunswick; *b.* Sussex, N.B., 12 April, 1855; *s.* of James E. White, descendant of William White, a U.E. L., and Margaret Scott, *d.* of Daniel Scott, Perthshire. *Educ.:* Varley Sch., St. John; Mount Allison Univ. (grad. in Arts, 1873). LL.B. Harvard, 1877; began the practice of law at Sussex, where he has since continued to reside; elected a member of the Legislature in 1886, and has been five times re-elec, twice by accl., as representative of King's Co.; was unanimously elected Speaker of the House of Assembly of New Brunswick, 1890; three years later became Solicitor-General; Attorney-General of the Province, 1897-1900; apptd. under an Act passed in 1900, chairman, to revise and consolidate the laws of the Province; resigned, 1900, and contested Queens-Sunbury for Dominion Parliament; Chief Commissioner of Public Works for some months, resigned 1900. *Address:* Fredericton, N.B.

WHITE, Aubrey; Dep. Minister of Lands and Forests for Ontario; *b.* Omagh, Tyrone, Irel., 19 March, 1845; *s.* of David White and Margaret Mackenzie; *m.* Mary Bridgland; one *s.* four *d.* *Educ.:* Royal Schs., Raphoe and Dungannon, and Dunbars, Dublin. Came to Can., April, 1862. Engaged in lumbering until 1876; forest ranger of Ontario, 1876-78; Crown Lands agt., Bracebridge, 1878-82; clerk, Woods and Forests Branch, Crown Lands Dept., Ont., 1880-87; apptd. Deputy Minister of Lands and Forests, 1887. D.G.M., Grand Lodge of Can., A. F. & A.M. *Addresses:* 35 Admiral Rd., Crown Lands Dept., Toronto. *Club:* Royal Canadian Yacht, Toronto.

WHITE, Lieut.-Col. Frederick, C.M.G.; Comptroller of the Royal Northwest Mounted Police; *b.* Birmingham, Eng., 16 Feb., 1847; *m. e. d.* of the late R. W. Cruice, of Ottawa; three *s.* five *d.* *Educ.:* Birmingham, Eng. First employed in rly. work in Montreal; removed to Ottawa and apptd. clerk in Dept. of Justice, 1 March, 1869. was entrusted with the administrative work in connection with the raising of the N.W.M.P.; promoted chief clerk, 23 Sept., 1878; comptroller, Nov. same yr.; Priv. Sec. to Rt. Hon. Sir John A. Macdonald, 1880-82; accorded the status of a Dep. Min., July, 1883. Served in the ranks of the 3rd Victoria Rifles while residing in Montreal; later held comn. in the Gov. Gen's Foot Guards, Ottawa, attaining rank of Captain. In 1901, accorded rank of Lieut.-Col. in the militia as a special case in recognition of his services in connection with the raising and equipment of Can. Contg. for South Africa; cr. C.M.G., 1902; apptd. Comnr. of the N.W.T., 1905. *Address:* 368 Besserer St., Ottawa. *Club:* Rideau, Ottawa.

WHITE, Gerald Vernon, B.Sc., M.P.; *b.* Pembroke, Ont., 6 July, 1879; *s.* of late Hon. Peter White, P.C., and Janet Reid Thompson; *m.* Mary Elizabeth Tretes; one *d.* *Educ.:* Pembroke Pub. and High sch., and McGill Univ., Montreal. Elec. at bye-elec. in Oct., 1906 to represent North Renfrew in the H. of C.; re-elec. in Oct., 1908; successor to his father in the constituency. *Address:* Pembroke, Ont. *Club:* Rideau, Ottawa.

WHITE, James; secy. of the Conservation Commission of Canada; *b.* Ingersol, Ont., 3 Feb., 1863; *s.* of David White and

Christina Hendry; *m.* Rachel Waddell; two *d.* *Educ.:* Aikens Private Sch., Ingersol Coll. Inst., and Royal Mitilary Coll.; apptd. topographer on the staff of the Geological Survey of Canada, Jan., 1884; made surveys in the Rocky Mountains, 1884-85; in the Madoc, Ont. gold district, 1886; in the Ottawa Co., Que. phosphate district, 1887-1890; Kingston and Pembroke, Ont., district, 1891-1893; apptd. Geographer and Chief Draughtsman to the Geological Survey in 1894; apptd. Chief Geographer of the Department of the Interior in 1899; employed on the Alaska Boundary Commission in 1903; made investigations respecting fast trans-Atlantic passenger steamships in 1906; apptd. Secy. of the Commission on conservation of Natural resources, 1909; is a Fellow of the Royal Geographical Society, Member of the National Geographical Society, Canadian Society of Civil Engineers, Champlain Society, American Academy of Political and Social Science, etc. *Publications:* Atlas of Canada, 1906; Altitudes in Canada, 1901; Dictionary of Altitudes, 1903; "Maps and Map-making in Canada" (Can. Soc. Civil Engineers, 1905); "Ashburton Treaty" (University Magazine, Oct., 1907); "Oregon & San Juan Boundaries" (University Magazine, Oct., 1908); "Ashburton Treaty-an afterword" (University Magazine, Dec., 1908); "Labrador Boundary" (University Magazine, April, 1909; "Altitudes in Canada," 2nd edition, revised and enlarged; "Derivations of Place-names in Ontario;" "Derivations of Place-names in Manitoba, Saskatchewan & Alberta;" "Derivations of Place-names in Northern Ontario." *Recreation:* travel. *Address:* 243 Chapel St., Ottawa.

WHITE, Peter, B.A., LL.B., K.C.; *b.* Pembroke, Ont., 28 Jan., 1872; *s.* of Andrew T. White and Mary Ranson; *m.* Katie Ethel Lloyd; two *d.* *Educ.:* Pembroke Pub. and High Sch.; Toronto Univ.; Law Sch., Osgoode Hall. Practices law in Pembroke. was an officer in Queen's Own Rifles, Toronto for six yrs. Can. for Leg. Ass., 1902; Mayor of Pembroke; reeve, Tp. of Pembroke, since 1901; vice pres. Dom. Shorthorn Breeders' Assn.; pres. Eastern Ontario Livestock and Poultry Assn.; dir. of various industrial cos.; a wellknown breeder of shorthorn cattle. *Recreations:* lacrosse, football, hockey. *Address:* Pembroke, Ont. *Clubs:* National, Can. Mil. Inst., Toronto.

WHITE, Richard, D.C.L.; *b.* Montreal, 14 May, 1834; *s.* of Thomas White and Dorothea Smeaton; *m.* 1859, Jean Riddel; six *s.* four *d.* *Educ.:* High Sch., Montreal; removed to Peterboro in 1850; engaged in large lumber concerns for nearly five years; took charge of the Peterboro *Review* 1 Jan., 1855, and in 1856, joined by his brother, Hon. Thos. White, purchased the "*Review,*" continued to manage it until Sept., 1864, when the firm of T. and R. White, purchased the Hamilton *Spectator* and conducted it until July, 1870; purchased the Montreal *Gazette* that year; in 1878, on Mr. Thomas White entering parliament, the concern was converted into a joint stock company of which Mr. Richard White has been pres. ever since; has been a member of the City Council of Montreal; of the Board of Harbour Commissioners; vice-pres. of the Board of Trade, and on almost every protestant board in connection with the hospitals and other charitable institutions. *Address:* 298 Stanley St., Montreal.

WHITE, Robert Smeaton; Collector of Customs, Montreal; *b.* Peterboro, Ont., 15 March, 1856; *s.* of Hon. Thos. White and Eleanor Devine; *m.* Annie H. Barclay. *Educ.:* Hamilton, Ont., and Montreal. In the service of the Bank of Montreal, 1872-1874; in journalism on the staff of the Montreal *Gazette,* 1874 to 1895; chief editor, 1885 to 1895; member of the H. of C. for Cardwell, his father's constituency, from 1888 to 1895; apptd. Collector of Customs, Montreal, 31 Dec., 1895. *Publications:* annual review, trade of Montreal. *Address:* 465 Roslyn Ave., Westmount, Que.

WHITE, Smeaton; man. dir. of the Montreal *Gazette*; *b.* Hamilton, Ont., 17 March, 1865; *s.* of Richard White and Jean Riddel; unmarried. *Educ.:* Montreal High Sch., Bishop's Coll. Sch., Lennoxville. In journalism, on staff of Montreal *Gazette* since leaving college; business mgr. of Gazette for many yrs. *Recreations:* angling, camping. *Address:* Gazette, Montreal. *Clubs:* St. James, Montreal, Canada, Hunt, Royal St. Lawrence Yacht, Montreal.

WHITE, William, C.M.G., J.P.; *b.* London, Eng., 6 Jan., 1830; *s.* of William and Anne Alice White; *m.* Elizabeth (*dec.,* 1892), *d.* of Geo. Keen; three *s.* one *d.* *Educ.:* Burlington House Sch., Hammersmith; clerk, Gen. P. O., London, Feb., 1846; clerk, P. O. Dept., Canada, Dec., 1854; Secretary P. O. Dept., Canada, Jan., 1861; Deputy P. M. Genl., Canada, July, 1888; Commissioner to enquire into organization of Canadian Civil service, 1880; Canadian delegate to Postal Union, Washington, 1897; chairman pub. sch. board, Ottawa, 1909; has been president of the Ottawa Atheneum; Ottawa Field Naturalists' Club; Ottawa Horticultural Society and Ottawa St. George's Society; entered Canadian Militia as Lieut. in 3rd Batt., Toronto Militia, 1859; Captain, Civil Service Regiment, 1866; Major, Governor-General's Foot Guards, 1872; Bt. Lieut.-Col., 1877; Lieut.-Col., 43rd Ottawa and Carleton Rifles, 1881; Hon. Lieut.-Col., 43rd O. & C. Rifles, 1898; Commandant, Canadian Team to Wimbledon, 1884; Chairman of the Executive Committee of Dom. of Canada Rifle Assn., 1886-96. *Recreations:* horticul ture, rifle shooting. *Publications:* Post Office Gazette, Annals of Canada. *Address:* Whitehurst, Ottawa, Ont. *Club:* Rideau, Ottawa.

WHITE, William James; *b.* Stouffville, Ont., 26 June, 1852; *s.* of John White and Margaret Miller; *m.* Wilmatte Clung Templeton; four *s.* three *d.* *Educ.:* Stouffville and private tuition; went to Brandon, Man., Aug., 1881, and established the "Brandon *Sun,*" in January, 1892, in the interests of the Liberal party; took charge of Canadian Immigration work in the United States in 1897; is also in charge of the publicity work of the Immigration branch. *Address:* 138 Somerset St., Ottawa.

WHITE, William John, M.A., D.C.L., K.C.; *b.* Peterboro, Ont., 29 Jan., 1861; *s.* of Richard White and Jean Riddel. *Educ.:*

High Sch., Montreal; McGill Univ.; a prominent member of the bar of the Prov. of Quebec; has frequently appeared before the Judicial Committee of the Privy Council in England; senior partner in the firm of White & Buchanan. *Publications:* Canadian Company Law. *Address:* 95 Crescent St., Montreal. *Clubs:* St. James, Montreal, University, Outremont Golf, Montreal; Rideau, Ottawa; Garrison, Quebec; Constitutional, London, Eng.

WHITE, William Robert, K.C.; *b.* Pembroke, Ont., 16 Sept., 1843; *s.* of the late Lt.-Col. White and Cecilia Thompson; *m.* 1871, Jennie, *y. d.* of the late Lt.-Col. M. Wilson, of Onondago, Ont.; three *s.* *Educ.:* local schs., by private tuition, and Victoria Coll., Cobourg. Called to the bar, 1868, and commenced practice of his profession in Pembroke, where he estbd. the firm of White & Williams in 1895; Mayor of Pembroke for three yrs., mem. of the County Council for twelve yrs.; Warden of Renfrew Co. for one yr.; pres., Pembroke Navigation Co.; solicitor in Renfrew Co. for C. P. R.; the Pembroke Electric Light Co., the Quebec Bank. Cr. Q.C., 1889; el. a Bencher of the Law Soc. of Ont., 1901. P.G.M. of the Masonic Order. *Address:* Pembroke, Ont.

WHITNEY, Albert; *b.* Williamsburg tp., Dundas Co., Ont., June, 1841; *s.* of Richard L. Whitney and Clarissa Farrman; *m.* 1872, Charlotte Coursselles, *d.* of Alpheus Jones, of Prescott; one *s.* four *d.* *Educ.:* Pub. Sch., and Matilda Gram. Sch. Engaged in mercantile life in Prescott, and since 1883 has been sec. of the firm of J. P. Wiser & Sons, Ltd., distillers. A mem. of the Town Coun. of Prescott for 21 yrs.; chn. of Finance Committee for nine yrs. Pres. of the Reform Assn. of South Grenville, 1901. *Address:* Prescott, Ont.

WHITNEY, Lieut.-Col. Hon. Sir James Pliny, Kt., LL.D., D.C.L., K.C.; President of Executive Council and Premier of Ontario; *b.* Williamsburgh, Ont., 2 Oct., 1843; *s.* of Richard Leet Whitney and Clarissa J. Farrman; *m.* 1877, Alice, third *d.* of Wm. M. Park, of Cornwall, Ont.; one *s.* two *d.* *Educ.:* Cornwall Gram. Sch. Called to the bar, 1876; cr. Q.C., 1890. Took part in Fenian troubles as N.C.O. Is Lt.-Col. of the Militia Reserve. Unsuccessful can. for Ont. Legis., 1886; returned at bye-el., 1888; returned at each subsequent g. e.; chosen Leader of the Opposition, 1896; on defeat of Ross Govt., at g. e., Jan., 1905, formed a govt. on Feb. 8th, and assumed office of Attorney-Gen. in addition to that of Prime Minister; re-el. by accl.; became Pres. of the Ex. Coun. in June, 1905, relinquishing office of Attorney-Gen. Received degree of LL.D. from Toronto Univ., June, 1902; D.C.L., from Trinity Univ., Toronto, 1902, and LL.D., from Queen's Univ., Kingston, 1903; cr. Kt. by H.R.H. the Prince of Wales, July 23, 1908, on the occasion of the Quebec Tercentenary. Has been a del, to General Synod of Church of England in Canada, and to the Diocesan Synod. *Address:* 113 St. George St., Toronto. *Clubs:* Toronto, Albany, Royal Canadian Yacht, Toronto.

WHYTE, William; 2nd Vice-Pres. of the Canadian Pacific Ry., Winnipeg; *b.* Fifeshire, Scot., 15 Sept., 1843; *s.* of William Whyte and Christian Methven; *m.* Jane, *d.* of Adam Scott, of Toronto; one *s.* four *d.* *Educ.:* Scotland. Junior clerk in office of factor of Lord Elgin's estate in Scot. for two yrs. In May, 1862, commenced ry. work as station agt. on the West of Fife Ry. Came to Can., June, 1863, and secured position on G.T.R., for which Co. he worked for twenty yrs.; eight months brakeman; two yrs. frt. clerk, Cobourg; five mos. frt. clerk, Toronto; one yr. foreman frt. dept., Toronto; one yr. yardmaster, Toronto; two yrs. conductor; six mos. night stationmaster, Toronto; over three yrs. stationmaster, Stratford; six yrs. stationmaster and frt. and passngr. agt., London, Ont.; eight mos. frt. agt., Toronto; and over one yr. div. supt.; 1883-1884, gen. supt. Credit Valley Ry.; 1883-1884, gen. supt., Ontario and Quebec Ry., which also included Credit Valley and Toronto Grey & Bruce Rys.; 1884-85, gen. supt. Ontario Div. of C.P.R., which embraced all lines in Ont., west of Smith's Falls Junction, Ont.; 1885-1886, gen. supt., Eastern Div. as well as Ont. Div.; 1886-97, gen. supt., Western Div.; 1897-1901, mgr. Western lines including all lines west of Lake Superior, same rd.; 1901-04, asst. to pres. same rd.; Jan. 1, 1904, to date second vice-pres., same rd. Has been prominently identified with every public movement in the city of Winnipeg since taking up his residence there; ex-pres. of the Canadian Club. *Recreations:* shooting, golf. *Address:* 603 River Ave., Winnipeg. *Clubs:* Manitoba, St. Charles' Country, Winnipeg; St. James, Montreal; Vancouver; Union, Victoria, B.C.

WICKETT, Samuel Morley, B.A., (Toronto), Ph.D.; *b.* Brooklin, Ont., 17 Oct., 1872; *s.* of Samuel Robert Wickett, and Margaret Cowle; unmarried. *Educ.:* Toronto and Leipzig; Lecturer in Political Economy, Univ. of Toronto, 1898-1902; Univ. of Toronto Literary and Scientific Society, 1898; member of National Municipal League; Pres., Secretary-Treasurer, and Managing Dir., Wickett and Craig, Ltd., 1902 to the present time; member of the Executive Can. Manuf. Assn., from 1901, to the present. *Publications:* Municipal Government in Canada; Buchers Industrial Evolution (translation from German); Reports to C. M. A. on Trade conditions in the Yukon (1903), and to the Federal Government in connection with the Alaska Boundary Case (1904). *Recreations:* golf, tennis, motoring. *Address:* 124 Isabella St., Toronto. *Clubs:* National, R.C.Y.C., Lambton Golf and Country, Toronto.

WICKSON, Alexander Frank; architect; *b.* Toronto, 30 March, 1861; *s.* of John Wickson and Eliza Chilver; *m.* Annie E. Fisher; one *s.* *Educ.:* Upper Can. Coll. Studied and practised in Toronto; worked in U.S., and travelled in England and part of continent. Mem. of Ont. Assn. of Architects; Fellow of the Roy. Architectural Inst of Can. *Recreation:* golf. *Address:* 62 Forest Hill Rd., Toronto. *Club:* High Park Golf and Country, Toronto.

WICKSON, Paul Giovanni; *b.* Toronto, Ont.; *s.* of Rev. Arthur Wickson, first classical tutor and rector, Toronto Gram. Sch. and Coll. Inst., and Mary Ann, *d.* of

William Thomas, architect; *m. o. d.* of Norman Hamilton, of Paris, Ont.; one *s.* one *d.* *Educ.:* Gram. Sch., Toronto; South Kensington Sch. of Arts, England; silver medalist for painting. Spent 12 yrs. in Eng. in study and travel; exhibited at Royal Acad., London and other galleries; painted, "March of Civilization," a series of Canadian subjects for the Dominion Govt. Bldgs. at St. Louis, Liege and other exhibitions. "The Promised Land," purchased by Dept. of Interior, 1909. Many pictures of Canadian subjects have been reproduced by magazine publishers, etc. *Recreations:* gardening, horses. *Address:* Hamilton Place, Paris, Ont.

WIDDIFIELD, His Hon. Charles Howard, LL.B.; Judge of the Ct. Court and local master High Court of Justice, Co. Grey; *b.* Uxbridge, Ont., 21 Jan., 1859; *e. s.* of the late J. C. Widdifield, whose father was a U. E. L.; *m.* Emma M. Gillespie, *o. d.* of James Gillespie, Sheriff of the County of Prince Edward; two *s.* two *d.* *Educ.:* Uxbridge High Sch., and Up. Can. Coll.; studied law with H. M. Howell, K.C.; now chief Justice of Manitoba; called to the bar in 1881, and practiced in Picton, Ont., apptd. Judge, County of Grey, and local Master High Court of Justice, 1905. *Publications:* Widdifield on "Law of Costs" (Carswell, 1892). *Recreations:* cricket, golf. *Address:* The Gables, Owen Sound, Ont. *Club:* Sydenham, Owen Sound.

WILCOX, Charles Seward, Ph.B., (Yale); *b.* Painesville, Ohio, U.S.A., 16 March, 1856; *s.* of Aaron Wilcox, and Jane Morley Wilcox; *m.* Margaretta Morley. *Educ.:* Yale Univ Came to Can., 1879. Pres. of the Hamilton Steel & Iron Co.; dir. of the Traders Bank. *Recreations:* golf, curling, yachting. *Address:* 69 Herkimer St., Hamilton, Ont. *Clubs:* Hamilton, Thistle, Royal Hamilton Yacht, Golf, Hamilton.

WILCOX, Oliver James, M.P.; *b.* South Woodslee, Essex Co., Ont., 1 Sept., 1869; *s.* of John Wilcox (Irish) and Mary Tollen (English); *m.* 1892, Mary Rachel Hamilton, of Chesterville, Ont.; one *s.* one *d.* *Educ.:* South Woodslee Pub. Sch. and Essex High Sch. El. mem. of Rochester Council, 1899 and sat for four yrs. as reeve. Pres., North Essex Farmers' Inst., 1904-05. First el. to H. of C. for N. Essex at bye-el. 11 Nov., 1909. *Address:* South Woodslee, Ont.

WILGRESS, Arthur Trollope, prop. and ed., the *Times*, Brockville, Ont.; *b.* Sheerness, Kent, Eng., 28 Dec., 1867; *s.* of Geo. Wilgress and Caroline Boulton; *m.* Meta Carleton, *d.* of Geo. Acheson, of Tandragee, Irel; one *s.* one *d.* *Educ.:* Up. Can. Coll., Toronto. Came to Can. with parents in 1872; after leaving coll., studied law at Cobourg and then ent. service of Bank of Toronto (5 yrs.); engaged in private banking at Clarksburg, Grey Co.; acquired Brockville *Times*, 1895. Capt., Corps of Guides; a governor, Brockville Gen. Hosp.; mem. Brockville Coll. Inst. Bd., 5 yrs.; member of Town Council, 1910; an ardent Imperialist. *Recreations:* camping, cricket, riding, curling. *Address:* Brockville, Ont. *Clubs:* Brockville, Albany, Toronto.

WILKIE, Daniel Robert; president of the Imperial Bank of Canada; *b.* Quebec, 17 Dec., 1846; *s.* of Daniel Wilkie and Angelica Graddon; *m.* Sara Caroline, *d.* of the Hon. J. R. Benson, St. Catharines, Ont.; two *s.* one *d.* *Educ.:* Quebec High Sch., Morren Coll.; entered service of Quebec Bank at Quebec, 1862; became manager Toronto branch, 1872; general manager Imperial Bank of Canada, 1875; pres., 1906. *Recreations:* golf, curling. *Address:* 432 Sherbourne St., Toronto. *Clubs:* Union, London, Eng.; Albany, National, Toronto, Hunt, Toronto Golf, Lambton Golf, Toronto; Mount Royal ,Montreal.

WILKINSON, William Carr; Sec.-Treas Board of Education, Toronto; *b.* Toronto, 1 Aug., 1841; *s.* of Christopher and Hannah Wilkinson; *m.* Maria Jewell; one *s.* four *d.* *Educ.:* Toronto public sch., and private tutor; has been Secretary-Treasurer, Board of Education since Nov., 1874; an active mem. of the Masonic fraternity. *Recreation:* travel. *Address:* 121 Parliament Street, Toronto.

WILLEY, Arthur, M.A., D.Sc. F.R.S., Professor of Zoology in McGill Univ., Montreal; *b.* Scarborough, Yorks, Eng., 1867; *s.* of late Rev. William Willey; *m.* 1902. *Educ.:* Kingswood Sch., Bath; Univ. Coll., London. Tutor in Biology, Coumbia Univ., New York, 1892-94; Balfour Student of the University of Cambridge, 1894-99; Lecturer in Biology, Guy's Hospital, 1899-1901. *Publications:* papers in technical journals, principally in the Quarterly Journal of Microscopical Science; Amphioxus and the Ancestry of the Vertebrates, 1894; edited Zoological Results, 1898-1902; editor of Spolia Zeylanica; director of Colombo Museum and Marine Biologist to the Ceylon Government, 1907; apptd. Prof. of Zoology, McGill Univ., 1910. *Address:* McGill Univ., Montreal.

WILLIAMS, Right Rev. David, M.A. (Oxon), S.D. (Western Univ.), LL.D. (Toron o Univ.); Bishop of Huron, Ont.; *b.* Silian, nr. Lampeter, Cardiganshire, Wales, 14 March, 1859; *s.* of John and Margaret Williams; *m.* Alberta Eliza Burwell, of Seaham Lodge, London, Ont.; three *s.* three *d.* *Educ.:* Lampeter Gram. Sch., St. David's Coll., Lampeter and Oxford Univ. Curate of Nestinlog, 1883-1887; Prof. at Huron Coll., London, On ., 1887-1892; Rector of Stratford, 1892-1905; Archdeacon of Perth, 1903-1905; Bishop of Huron, Jan. 6, 1905. *Publication:* "What the Church Stands for." *Address:* Bishopstowe, London, Ont.

WILLIAMS, Frederick George Hilary; *b.* London, Eng., 13 Jan., 1863- *s.* of Charles and Georgina Gould Williams; *m.* Aley Mary Shonfeld, of Croyden, Eng.; one *s.* one *d.* Was secretary to his father before coming to Canada in 1882; employed on Montreal newspapers until 1893; went to Australia; returned in 1896; since then on Montreal, Toronto and Ottawa newspapers; now political correspondent at Ottawa; served in Montreal Garrison Artillery during the North West Rebellion, 1885 (medal). *Recreation:* walking. *Address:* "Free Press", Ottawa.

WILLISON, John Stephen, LL.D. (Queens), journalist; *b.* Stanley, Huron Co., Ont., 9 Nov., 1856; *s.* of Stephen and Jane Willison; *m.* Rachel Turner, of Bruce Co.,

Ont.; two *s.* *Educ.:* Pub. Sch.; for many yrs. editor "*The Globe,*" Toronto; now editor "*The News;*" apptd. correspondent in Canada for "*The Times,*" 1910. *Publications:* "Sir Wilfrid Laurier and the Liberal Party;" The Railway Question in Canada; and various pamphlets. *Recreation:* bowling (winner Dominion and Ontario Championships). *Address:* 10 Elmsley Place, Toronto. *Clubs:* Toronto, National, R.C.Y. C., Toronto.

WILLSON, Beckles; *b.* Montreal, 26 Aug., 1869; *s.* of Henry Willson and Henrietta Gall; *m.* 1899, Ethel Grace, *d.* of the late Albert White Dudley, of Colborne, Ont. two *s.* one *d.* *Educ.:* Montreal and Kingston. *Publications:* a number of books on subjects relating to Canada. *Recreations:* golf, riding, cycling, foreign travel. *Addresses:* Quebec House, Westerham, Eng.; 8 Southampton St., London, W.C. *Clubs:* Royal Societies, Authors, London, Eng.

WILLSON, Thomas Leopold; *b.* Princeton, Oxford Co., Ont., 14 March, 1860; *s.* of Thomas Whitehead, *y. s.* of late Hon. John Willson, and Rachel Sabina Bigelow; *m.* Mary Parks, *e. d.* of late William H. Parks, of Marysville, Calif.; two *s.* one *d.* *Educ.:* pub. sch., Hamilton, Ont.; discovered in May, 1892, Commercial Calcium Carbide; which gave to the world a new lighting medium—acetylene gas, and thereby established a new industry which flourishes today in a dozen different countries; inventor of the Willson Acetylene Gas Buoy, and the Willson gas beacon; since adopted by the Govts. of Gt. Britain, U.S.A., Brazil, Colombia, Argentina, India, Korea, Guatemala these inven ions being controlled and manufactured in Ottawa, by the International Marine Signal Co., of which Mr. Willson is president. *Recreations:* motoring, gardening. *Addresses:* 188 Metcalfe St., Ottawa, Ont., and Meaches Lake, Que. *Clubs:* Rideau, Golf, Hunt, and Country, Ottawa.

WILSON, Arthur; administrator of Yukon Territory in absence of Commr.; *b.* British Columbia, 1872. Has been a resident of Yukon Terr. for several yrs.; a mining operator. Del. to Ottawa on behalf of Yukon to present grievances of people to Govt. Was one of the two first el. members of the Yukon Govt.; license inspector until office amalgamated with others. *Address:* Dawson, Y.T.

WILSON, Charles, K.C.; *b.* London, 5 Feb., 1841; twice *m.*; one *d.*; member of B. C. Legislature, 1882 and 1890-1907; Attorney-Gen., 1903; senior partner in legal firm of Wilson and Bloomfield; barrister. *Address:* Vancouver, B.C. *Clubs:* Union, Victoria; Vancouver.

WILSON, Charles Avila, B.A., K.C., M.P.; *b.* Ile Bizard, 10 Dec., 1869; *s.* of Antoine Stanislas Wilson and Odile St. Pierre; *m.* Imilda L. Lanctot of Montreal. *Educ.:* St. Therese Coll., Montreal, graduating in 1891, B.A.; admitted to the bar of Quebec, in 1895; LL.B., Laval; secretary Grain Inspection Committee, Montreal, 1902; Liberal candidate in Laval, 1902; defeated by 8 votes in June, 1908 was candidate for Legis. Assem., but was defeated; first el. to H. of C., 1908. *Address:* Place Viger Hotel, Montreal; St. Vincent de Paul (summer). *Club:* St. Denis, Montreal.

WILSON, Lieut.-Col. Erastus William; *b.* Belleville, Ont., 1 July, 1860; *s.* of James Wilson; *m.* Sara E. L. Bricker, Berlin, Ont.; two *s.* one *d.* *Educ.:* High Schs., Belleville and Oshawa; now officer commanding 18th Infantry Brigade, Montreal; joined the 3rd Regt., Victoria Rifles of Canada in 1882; Lieut., 1892; Captain 1894; Major, 1899; Lt.-Col., 1903; retired in 1907 with rank; apptd. to the Brigade command, 1 March, 1909. *Address:* 4035 Dorchester St., Montreal, Que. *Clubs:* St. James, Forest and Stream, Montreal.

WILSON, George Samuel; Asst. Sec., Union of Canadian Municipalities; *b.* Montreal, 23 April, 1846; *s.* of Samuel Wilson and Elizabeth Crocket; *m.* Edith A. Alport, of Belleville, Ont.; one *s.* two *d.* *Educ.:* Montreal. Started life as a clerk in a book store; for 20 yrs. engaged in the paper trade. In 1905 estbd. the Canadian Municipal Journal, the organ of the federal and provincial Municipal unions in Canada; also conducts the Bureau of Municipal Information. *Address:* 6 Durocher St., Montreal.

WILSON, Maj.-General James Frederick; *b.* Kingston, Ont., 23 Jan. 1852; *s.* of William and Sarah A. Wilson; *m.* Florence Adelaide, *d.* of late Sir Hugh Allan; *Educ.:* Trinity Coll. Sch., and Trinity Coll., Toronto; for many yrs. an officer in Canadian regular forces; served in campaigns with Gordon relief column in the Soudan 1884-5; North-West rebellion, 1885-6; hon. A.D.C. to His Excellency the Gov.-Gen.; retired from Can. mil. service, 15 Nov., 1907. *Address:* 141 Crescent St., Montreal. *Clubs:* Garrison, Quebec; St. James, Montreal.

WILSON, James Lockie, J.P.; *b.* Alexandria, Ont., 12 Nov., 1856; *s.* of Robert Wilson, J.P., and Agnes Logie, both Scotch; *m.* Mary, *d.* of Andrew Hodge, of Cornwall, Ont.; one *s.* four *d.* *Educ.:* Alexandria pub. sch. and high sch.; notary public; supt. of Fairs and Exhibitions for Ontario; supt. of Horticultural Societies of Ontario; secy., Ontario Association of Fairs and Exhibitions; secy. and man. dir. of Ontario Vegetable Growers' Assn.; secy. and editor Ontario Horticulture Assn.; director of Ontario Horticultural Exhibition, and also Canadian National Exhibition; farmer and pedigreed cattle raiser; one of the largest exhibitors in Eastern Ontario; was pres., Glengarry Agricultural Society; pres. of the Patrons of Industry; pres. of Farmers' Association of Canada; and farmers' candidate for H. of C. in 1896. *Publications:* Reports of Ontario Vegetable Growers; Ontario Horticultural Assn., and Assn. of Fairs and Exhibitions. *Recreation:* lawn bowling. *Address:* 582 Huron St., Toronto.

WILSON, John Edwards, M.L.A.; *b.* St. John, N.B., 16 Aug., 1862; *s.* of John Edwards Wilson, and Elizabeth Young; *m.* Beatrice J. Orr; one *s.* three *d.* *Educ.:* St. John, N.B.; pres., H. Wilson, Ltd., Iron Foundry and Sheet Metal Works., St. John, N.B.; alderman for the city of St. John, 1896, retiring for business reasons; el. to N.B. Legis. Assem. in 1908. *Address:* 208 Waterloo St., St. John, N.B. *Club:* Union, St. John.

WILSON, Hon. John Henry, M.D.; senator; *b.* near Ottawa, Ont., 14 Feb., 1834;

s. of Jeremiah and Mary Wilson; *m.* Amelia A. Williams, of Toledo, Ohio. *Educ.:* pub. sch. and Victoria Coll.; a physician and lecturer on anatomy; member of the Ontario Legislature from 1871 to 1879, first elected to the H. of C., 1882; re-elected 1887; apptd. to the Senate, 8 March, 1704. *Address:* St. Thomas, Ont.

WILSON, Matthew, K.C.; *b.* Harwich, Ont., 28 Aug., 1854; *s.* of Robert and Isabella Wilson; *m.* Anna Marden, *e. d.* of Charles R. Atkinson, K.C.; one *s.* two *d.* *Educ.:* Chatham, Whitby and Toronto; a law student with Harrison, Osler and Moss, Toronto; special honours at Osgoode Hall; barrister in 1879; Q.C., 1889; elected a bencher of the Law Society, two years in succession; senator of the Western University; member of council, Huron Divinity College; director of the Trust and Guarantee Co., and of the Northern Life Assurance Co.; member of Supreme Court of Appeal for the Church of England in Canada. *Recreation:* horseback riding. *Address.* 325 Wellington St. West, Chatham, Ont.

WILSON, His Hon. Peter Edward, B. A. LL.B., County Court Judge for East Kootenay; *b.* Bond Head, Ont., 28 Aug., 1871; *s.* of Charles and Rachel Wilson; *m.* Christine Brown; two *s.* four *d.* *Educ.:* Brampton high sch., Toronto Univ. and Osgoode Hall; practiced law in Nelson, B.C., for nine yrs.; city solicitor there for six yrs.; county judge for East Kootenay. *Recreations:* curling, bowling. *Address:* Cranbrook, B.C.

WILSON-SMITH, Richard; *b.* Ireland, 1852; one *s.* two *d.* *Educ.:* Ireland. Arrived Canada, 1878 and estbd. himself in business in Montreal as an investment broker. Proprietor of the *Insurance Chronicle;* pres. of the Canada Accident Co.; dir. of the Lachine Rapids Hydraulic and Land Co., the Montreal Trust and Deposit Co., and the National Surety Co., of New York; trustee of the Guardian Fire and Life Assur. Co.; a mem. of the Montreal Bd. of Trade, and Montreal Stock Exchange. Sat in City Council of Montreal, 1892-1896 as alderman, mayor 1896-97; is hon. treas. of the Montreal Diocesan Theological Coll.; governor of the Montreal Gen. Hospital, Protestant Hospital for Insane, Notre Dame Hospital, Western Hospital; a trustee of the Mount Royal Cemetery Co.; hon. pres. the Irish Protestant B.S.; hon. Lieut.-Col. of the 2nd Regt., C.A. *Recreations:* hunting, golf. *Address:* 580 Sherbrooke St. W., or Guardian Bldg., Montreal. *Clubs:* St. James, Montreal, Canada, Hunt, Royal Montreal Golf, Montreal.

WILSON, Uriah, M.P.; *b.* Township of North Fredericksburgh, nr. Napanee, Ont., 17 March, 1841; *s.* of James Wilson, of Yorkshire, Eng., and Harriet Worthington, Co. Tyrone, Irel.; *m.* Mary Moyle, Napanee, Ont., 16 Oct., 1867; four *s.* *Educ.:* Napanee pub. sch., a merchant; entered mercantile pursuits in 1863; town councillor of Napanee; deputy reeve, 1879 to 1882; Warden of Co. Lennox and Addington, 1882; reeve of Napanee, 1884; Mayor, 1886; elected to the H. of C., 1887; defeated in 1891; re-elected at bye-election 1892, and at each g. e. since. *Address:* Napanee, Ont.

WINKLER, Valentine, M.L.A.; *b.* Neustadt, Ont., 18 March, *s.* of David Winkler and Barbara Lang; *m.* Josephine, *d.* of M. B. Rombough, D.L.S.; one *s.* three *d.* *Educ.:* pub. sch. in Ont.; a lumber merchant; first reeve of the municipality of Stanley; member of the Legislature of Manitoba for Rhineland continuously since 1892; unsuccessful candidate for the H. of C., 1900. *Address:* Morden, Man.

WISER, John Philip; Pres., J.P. Wiser & Sons, Ltd., Prescott; *b.* Trenton, Oneida Co., N.Y., U.S.A.; *s.* of Isaac John Wiser and Mary Egert; *m.* Emily, *s. d.* of Hon. H. Godard, of St. Lawrence Co., N.Y.; four *s.* two *d.* *Educ.:* Oneida schs. Came to Canada as mgr. for Egert & Averall, who were then conducting a distillery business in Prescott; purchased an interest in the firm, 1857; acquired his partners' interests, 1862; was pres. of the Dom. Cattle Co., mem. of the Ontario Agricultural Commission, 1880; is pres. of the Prescott Elevator Co.; dir. Montreal Stock Yards Co., Imperial Starch Co., Montreal Lighterage Co.; el. to H. of C., 1878, but did not took ro ol. *Address:* Prescott, Ont.

WOLFENDEN, Lieut.-Col. Richard, I.S.O. 1903; V.D.; *b.* 20 March, 1836; *s.* of late Robert Wolfenden, of Rathmell, Yorkshire; *m.* (1st) 1865, Kate 2nd *d.* of late Henry Cooley, of Ashford, Kent; (2nd) 1879, Felicite Caroline, *e. d.* of late John Bayly, supt. of police, Victoria, B.C.; five *d.* *Educ.:* Arkholme, Lancashire; Kirkby Lonsdale, Westmoreland. Served eight yrs. in the Royal Engineers, three years in England, five in British Columbia; served in New Westminster, B.C., and Victoria, B.C. Rifle Volunteers with the rank of Ensign, 1864-74; joined the Active Militia of Canada on formation in British Columbia, 1874, and served with the respective ranks of Ensign, Lieutenant, Captain, Major, and Lt.-Col. until retirement, 1888; mem. of Wimbledon team, 1874; King's Printer for British Columbia for many yrs. *Recreations:* all outdoor sports. *Address:* 125 Menzies Street, Victoria, B.C.

WOOD, Edwards Rogers; *b.* Peterboro, Ont., 14 May, 1866; *s.* John Wood (Irish); *m.* 1891, Agnes Euphenia Smart; one *d.* *Educ.:* Peterboro. Commenced life as a telegraph operator; joined staff of Central Canada Loan and Savings Co., on its formation in 1884, and rose gradually to position of vice-pres. and gen. mgr. of company; is also gen. mgr. of the Dominion Securities Corporation; vice-pres., National Trust Co.; dir. Crow's Nest Pass Coal Co., Canadian Bank of Commerce, Western Assurance Co., Canada Life Assurance Co., Sao Paulo Tramway, Light and Power Co.; Mexican Light and Power Co., and other industrial enterprises. *Address:* Queen's Park, Toronto. *Clubs:* Toronto, National, Toronto.

WOOD, Hon. Josiah, M.A.; Senator; *b.* Sackville, N.B., 18 April, 1843; *s.* Mariner Wood, merchant; *m.* 1874, Laura S., *d.* of Thompson Trueman, Sackville. *Educ.:* Mt. Allison Wesleyan Coll., Sackville, (grad. 1863); called to the bar of N.B., 1866; afterwards entered mercantile business, and became chief partner and man. of M. Woods & Sons; was for some years interested in shipping; in lumbering and in several manufacturing industries; also in farming and stock raising; mayor of Sackville from its incorporation for five years (until 1908); is treas. of the Board of Regents of Mt. Allison Coll.; unsuccessfully contested Westmoreland for Legislative Assembly, N.B., 1878; elected to the H. of C., 1882-1887-1891; called to the Senate, 5 Aug., 1895; Conservative. *Address:* Sackville, N.B. *Clubs:* Rideau, Ottawa; Union, St. John, N.B.

WOOD, Hon. Samuel Casey; *b.* Village of Bath, Ont., 27 Dec., 1830; *s.* of Thomas S. and Frances Wood; *m.* Charlotte Maria Parkinson; five *s.* five *d.* *Educ.:* common sch.; County Clerk and Treasurer, Co. of Victoria, for 16 years; chairman of high sch. board in Lindsay; representative of pub. sch. Inspectors in the Council of Public Instruction; elected to Parliament in 1871; apptd. Provincial Secretary and Registrar in 1875; held the office of Commissioner of Agriculture from that date until 1883; in 1877 was apptd. Provincial Treasurer; retired from public life in 1883; is at present vice-pres. of the Toronto General Trusts Corporation and vice-pres. of the Imperial Life Assurance Company. *Address:* 97 Avenue Road, Toronto.

WOOD, Lieut.-Col. Wm., F.R.S.C.; *b.* Quebec (of British, French and American descent.) *Educ.:* England and Germany. pres. of the Literary and Historical Society of Quebec, 1900-1, and 1904-5; F.R.S.C., 1905; D.C.L. of Lennoxville, 1907; pres. of the Historic Landmarks Association, 1907-9; Commanding officer of the 8th Royal Rifles, 1907-10; vice-pres., the Quebec Tercentenary, 1908. *Publications:* The Fight for Canada, 1904; definitive edition in England, 1905, Canadian and American editions, 1906. The Logs of the Conquest of Canada (for the Champlain Society), 1909. R.S.C. monographs on French-Canadian Folksongs and the Quebec Ursulines, and various contributions to encyclopædias and periodicals in England, Canada and the United States. Is editing a series of original documents of the War of 1812, for the Champlain Society; and will afterwards write a new history of the war, based on sources of information which are now for the first time becoming complete enough to justify an attempt at finality. *Recreations:* animals, scenery, canoeing, sailing, mountaineering, reading, poetry and listening to music. *Address:* 59 Grande Allée. Quebec.

WOOD, Major Zachary Taylor; asst. commr. of R. N. W. Mounted Police, Dawson; *b.* Nova Scotia, 27 Aug., 1860; *s.* of Capt. Wood, of the U.S. Army. Grad. R. M. Coll., Kingston, 1882; joined Mounted Police as insptr., 1 Aug., 1885. Went to Yukon with first detachment of Mounted Police, 1897, and stationed at Skagway; promoted asst. commr. 1 July, 1902. *Address:* Dawson, Y.T.

WOODRUFF, Miss Anne Helena; *b.* St. David's, Ont., 28 Dec., 1850; *d.* of William Henry and Mary D. Secord Woodruff; attended pub. sch. until 14, Brockport (N. Y.) State Normal Sch., 6 mos. Resident of Chicago, since 1897. *Publications:* Betty and Bob, 1903; The Pond in the Marshy Meadow, 1906; Three Boys and a Girl, 1906; contb'r. verse and prose to religious press. *Address:* 524 Garfield Av., Chicago.

WOODS, George B.; Pres. and Gen. Mgr. of the Continental Life Insur. Co.; *b.* nr. Ely, Norfolk Co., Eng., 16 June, 1866; *s.* of James Woods and Hannah Howlett; *m.* Annie Isabell, *d.* of Chas. Dash, of Woodstock, Ont.; one *d.* *Educ.:* Northampton and Lincolnshire, Eng. Came to Can., 1885. Was engaged in lumber business in Woodstock for some yrs.; then joined staff of Manufacturers' Life Insur. Co.; organized Continental Life Insur Co., 1900; now pres. and gen. mgr. *Recreations:* curling, bowling, golf, cricket. *Address:* 410 Huron St., Toronto. *Clubs:* National, Victoria, Lambton Golf, Granite Curling, Canada Bowling, Royal Canadian Yacht, Toronto.

WOODS, Henry Wellington, M.L.A.; *b.* Welsford, Queen's Co., N.B., 17 Dec., 1864; s. of Hon. Francis Woods, M.L.C., and Jane Eliza Armstrong; *m.* Hannah Z. Gorham, 30 Sept., 1899; three *s.* two *d.* member of Queen's County Council 1895-08; Warden of County, 1904; first elec. to Legis. Assem. of N.B., March, 1908. *Address:* Welsford, N.B.

WOODS, James Hossack; managing director of the Calgary *Herald;* *b.* Quebec, 12 July, 1867; *s.* of Alexander Woods and Elizabeth Banfield; *m.* Leonora C., *d.* of J. F. Eby, of Toronto; one *d.* *Educ.:* Quebec High Sch., McGill Univ., Manitoba Univ. A journalist. Worked on staffs of Toronto *Mail.* and Montreal *Herald;* now managing director of the Calgary *Herald.* *Publications:* contributions to magazines and newspapers. *Recreations:* motoring, golf, curling. *Address:* Calgary, Atla. *Clubs:* Ranchmen's, Calgary; Tennis, Curling, Golf, Royal Canadian Yacht, Toronto.

WOODS, James W.; President Woods Ltd., Ottawa, Hull and Winnipeg; *b.* Kildare, Que., 10 April, 1863; *s.* of Russell Woods and Anne J. Davis; *m.* Ida E. Edwards; three *s.* two *d.* *Educ.:* privately and at Montreal Coll.; two years with the late W. W. Ogilvy; ten years with the Hodgson Sumner Co., representing the firm in Ottawa district; started Woods Limited in 1896; Woods Western, Winnipeg, 1903; director Smart Bag Co., Ltd.; pres. and genl. mgr. Imperial Realty Co.; dir., Kildare Mining Co.; ex-director Crow's Nest Pass Coal Co.; Captain Gov. Gen. Foot Guards, Ottawa; attached to Coldstream Guards for special course during winter 1909-10, London, Eng.; pres., County Carleton General Hospital; ex-pres., Ottawa Board of Trade; dir. of Ashbury Coll., Ltd.; chairman of Finance Committee, Earl Grey Musical and Dramatic Competition. *Address:* Chapel St., Ottawa. *Clubs:* Rideau, Hunt (pres.), Ottawa; Mount Royal, Montreal; Manitoba, Winnipeg.

WOODS, Sydney Brown, K.C., B.A., LL.B.; *b.* Quebec, 23 June, 1872; *s.* of Alexander Woods, and Elizabeth Banfield; *m.* Ethel Brown, Hamilton, Ont.; one *s.* one *d.* *Educ.:* Quebec High Sch., Toronto Coll. Inst., and Univ. of Toronto, Ont.; was a reporter and correspondent for Toronto *Mail,* Toronto *News;* practiced law 1897 to 1906 in Toronto; became Deputy Attorney General for Alberta on formation of the Province, 1905; resigned 1910. *Recreations:* golf, whist, chess. *Address:* 315 Fifth St., Edmonton, Alta. *Club:* Edmonton.

WOOLLCOMBE, Rev. George Penrose, M.A.; *b.* Londwater, Bucks, Eng., 21 May, 1867; *s.* of Rev. W. P. Woollcombe and Henrietta Jacob; *m.* (1st) Julia D. Acres, Liverpool, Eng., (2nd) Jessie Mickle, Toronto, Ont.; three *s.* two *d.* *Educ.:* the Gram. Sch., High Wycombe, Bucks, and Christ Church, Oxford; arrived in Canada 1888; assistant master at Bishop's Coll. Sch., Lennoxville, Que.; assistant master at Trinity Coll. Sch., Port Hope; now headmaster of Ashbury Coll., Ottawa, Ont. *Recreation:* golf. *Address:* Ashbury Coll., Rockcliffe., Ottawa. *Clubs:* Rideau, Golf, Ottawa.

WORRELL, Rt. Rev. Clarendon Lamb, M.A., D.D., D.C.L., Bishop of Nova Scotia; *s.* of Rev. Canon Worrell; *b.* Smith's Falls, July 20, 1853; *m.* Charlotte Ann, *d.* of Surgeon-Maj. General J. W. Ward, F.R.C.S. one *s.* three *d.* *Educ.:* Trinity Sch., Port Hope and Trinity Coll., Toronto. Deacon, 1880; Priest, 1884; Math. Master, Bishops Coll., 1873; Headmaster Gananoque High Sch., 1877; Principal Brockville Coll. Inst., 1879; Prof. Royal Military College, Kingston, 1891; Curate of Gananoque, Ont., 1881; Holy Trinity, Brockville, and Head Master of High School, Brockville, Ont., 1882-84; Rector of Williamsburg, Ont., 1884-86; Morrisburg, Ont., 1886-91; Professor of English Literature, Royal Military Coll., Kingston, 1891-1904; Rector of St Mark's, Barriefield, Ont., 1891-1903; Rector St. Luke's, Kingston, 1903-1904; Chaplain to Archbishop of Ontario, 1896; Archdeacon of Ontario, 1900; Prolocutor, Provincial Synod of Canada, 1904; Bishop of Nova Scotia, 1904. *Address:* Bishop's Lodge, Halifax, N.S.; Hubbards, N.S. (summer).

WORTHINGTON, Lieut.-Col. Arthur Norreys, M.D., C.M., M.P., P.M.O. (Que. Com.); *b.* Sherbrooke, Que., 17 Feb., 1862; *s.* of Dr. E. D. Worthington and Frances Smith; *m.* 1887, May, *d.* of H. H. Cook, Toronto, ex-M.P. for Simcoe. *Educ.:* Bishop's Coll. Sch., Lennoxville, and McGill Univ. (first class honors). Surgeon to Sherbrooke Protestant Hospital; gov. Coll. of Physicians and Surgeons, Prov. of Que.; principal medical officer, Quebec Command. Served with Field Hospital during N. W. Rebellion, 1885; and mentioned in despatches; Brig. Surgeon-Major, C.F.A., in South Africa, 1900; was present at battles of Faber's Farm, Belfast, Lydenberg (despatches). Brevet Lieut.-Col. and commanded Can. Field Hospital in S. A. during operations in Transvaal, again mentioned in despatches. El. to H. of C. at g. e., 1904 and 1908. *Recreations:* riding, shooting. *Address:* Sherbrooke, Que. *Clubs:* Rideau, Ottawa; Albany, Toronto; St. George's, Sherbrooke.

WRIGHT, Alexander Whyte; *b.* Markham tp., Ont., 17 Dec., 1845; *s.* of Geo. Wright and Helen Whyte; *m.* Elizabeth R. Simpson, one *d.* *Educ.:* New Hamburg sch. Learned the woollen mfg. business which he followed for some yrs.; then took up journalism, editing among other newspapers, the Stratford *Herald*, Guelph *Herald*, Toronto *National*, *Journal* of the Knights of Labour, New York; *Craftsman*, New York; for several yrs. secy. of the Can. Mfgrs. Assn.; was secy. of the Executive Bd. of the K. of L.; one of the Canadian reps. for the Antwerp, Colonial and Indian exbns.; commercial agt. for Can. at the Colonial exbn.; Dominion commr. (1896) to examine into and report upon the sweating system in Canada. Has taken an active part in politics and spoken frequently in several provs. of Canada; one of the earliest advocates of the N. P.; unsuccessful can. for Ont. Leg. Assem. in West Lambton and West Toronto; organizer of the Lib.-Cons. party, through three general elections; active in the campaign for public ownership and at present Pres. of the Can. Public Ownership League. *Address:* 105 Macdonell Ave., Toronto. *Club:* Albany, Toronto.

WRIGHT, William, M.P.; *b.* Township Egremont, Co. Grey, Ont., 29 Oct., 1853; *s.* of David Wright and Susana Foster; *m.* Mary Elizabeth Quirt; one *s,* three *d.* *Educ.:* Pub. Sch.; has been farmer, blacksmith, manufacturer and merchant in succession. Elected to H. of C., 1906; re-elec., 1908. *Recreation:* travel. *Address:* Huntsville, Muskoka, Ont.

WRONG, George McKinnon, M.A.; *b.* Gravesend, Co. of Elgin, Ont., 25 June, 1860; *s.* of Gilbert Wrong, of Aylmer, Ontario, and Christina Mackinnon; *m.* 1886, Sophia Hume, *d.* of Hon. Edward Blake, three *s.* two *d.* *Educ.:* Univ. Coll., Toronto; Wycliffe Coll., Toronto; Univ. of Toronto; Oxford, etc.; M.A., Univ. of Toronto. Took orders in the Church of England, 1883, but has since been engaged continuously in academical work, succeeding in 1894 the late Sir Daniel Wilson as Professor of History in the Univ. of Toronto. *Publications:* The British Nation; a History, 1903; The Earl of Elgin, 1905; The Review of Historical Publications relating to Canada (annually). *Recreation;* golf, *Address:* 467 Jarvis Street, Toronto; summer—Pointe au Pic, Que. *Club:* Toronto Golf.

WYLIE, David James, M.L.A.; *b.* Shrewsbury, Eng., 1 July, 1859; *s.* of D. Wylie, C.E., and Elizabeth Wylie; *m.* Rachel M. Bathelll, three *s.* three *d.* *Educ.:* Cheltenham Coll., England; arrived in Canada, 1880; rancher; dir., Maple Creek Cattle Co.; el. to Sask. Legis. Assem., 1908. *Address:* Maple Creek, Sask.

Y

YATES, Henry Brydges, B.A. (Cantab), M.D.C.M. (McGill); *b.* Montreal, May 10, 1865; *s.* of the late Henry Yates, C.E., and Emily Sapey; *m.* 1896, Alice Mary, *o. d.* of the late C. W. Bunting, of Toronto; two *s.* one *d.* *Educ.:* Charterhouse; Jesus Coll., Cambridge; McGill Univ., Montreal. Major (M.O.) 3rd Regt., Victoria Rifles of Canada; Lecturer on Bacteriology, McGill Univ.; alderman of Montreal, 1906-10; Norwegian Consul General for Canada, 1906-8; Kt. of the Order of St. Olaf; Esquire of the Order of St. John of Jerusalem, 1910. *Recreations:* cricket, golf, tennis. *Addresses:* 257 Peel

St., Montreal; Gaywood, Cacouna (summer) *Clubs:* St. James', Mount Royal, Montreal.

YEIGH, Frank; *b.* Burford, Brant Co., Ont., 21 July, 1860; *s.* of Edmund Lassing and Eliza Yeigh; *m.* Annie L. Laird; one *s.* *Educ.:* Burford; was on the staff of the Brantford *Expositor*; private secretary to the Hon. Arthur S. Hardy, Premier of Ontario; now registrar of Crown Lands Department, Toronto; well known as a magazine writer and illustrated lecturer. *Publications:* Ontario Parliamentary Buildings, 1792-1892; compiler of "5000 facts about Canada." *Recreation:* golf. *Address:* 667 Spadina Ave., Toronto.

YEO, Hon. James; senator; *b.* Port Hill, P.E.I., 29 June, 1837; parents from Devonshire, Eng. *Educ.:* at Uxbridge, Eng. A ship owner and farmer; sat in the Legislative Assembly of P. E. I. for the second district of Prince from 1858 to 1891, when he resigned to run for the House of Commons; apptd. to the Executive Council of P.E.I. in 1870; speaker, 1871; re-apptd. to Executive, 1873, and again in 1876; resigned in 1879; elected to the H. of C. for Prince County, 1896; elected Grand Master of the Free Masons in P.E.I., 1875, and annually until 1889; apptd. to the Senate. 19 Nov., 1898; Liberal. *Address:* Port Hill, P.E.I.

YOKOME, Ferman Richardson; editor of the Peterborough *Daily Examiner; b.* Crowland, Welland Co., Ont., 1844; *s.* of Jesse and Margaret Yokome; *m.* Louvenia Eyre, of Brockville, Ont.; one *s.* one *d.* *Educ.:* Welland High Sch., Toronto Univ., Toronto Sch. of Medicine (under graduate). Has been engaged in journalistic work for 36 yrs.; for 28 yrs. editor of the Peterborough *Daily Examiner*, which position he still holds. *Recreations:* tree planting, Dickens. *Address:* Peterborough, Ont.

YORSTON, Frederic, B.A.; *b.* Pictou, N.S., 30 July, 1871; *s.* of James Yorston, of Orguil, Orkney, Scot., and Mary McDonald, of St. John, N.B.; unmarried. *Educ.:* Dalhousie Univ.; took honors in English literature and history, the new Shakespere Society's prize, Arts Valedictorian, editor Dalhousie Univ. Magazine; was city editor of the Montreal *Star*, 1902-1905; London Daily *Mail*, Montreal *Star* and Associated Press correspondent;—Royal Tour in Canada, 1901; vice-pres. of Standard Publishing Co., and managing editor *The Standard*, 1905, to the present time. *Publications:* editor of Shelley's Poems; many magazine articles; descriptive work, etc. *Recreation:* curling. *Address:* 171 St. James St., Montreal.

YORSTON, John MacKay, M.L.A.; *b.* Orkney, Scot., 11 Oct., 1867; *s.* of Robert and Mary Yorston; *m.* Janet Mary Robertson. *Educ.:* Scot.; arrived in Canada, June, 1890; farmer; elected to represent the district of Cariboo in Legislature of B.C., 1907. *Recreation:* hunting. *Address:* Australian Ranch, Cariboo, B.C.

YOUNG, Charles W.; Editor and Prop. of the *Freeholder*, Cornwall; *b.* Georgetown, Ont., 17 May, 1849; *s.* of James and Hester Young; *m.* Caroline Carthew, of Guelph; one *s.* one *d.* Acquired a knowledge of printing under T. &. R. White, Peterboro, and in office of the Toronto *Leader:* employed on editorial staff of several newspapers in the U.S.; later joined staff of the Stratford *Beacon;* in 1885 purchased the Cornwall *Freeholder*, of which he has since published. Was press agt. for the Ont. Govt. at the Chicago World's Fair, 1893. *Recreations:* hunting, fishing. *Address:* Cornwall, Ont. *Club:* Cornwall.

YOUNG, Hon. Henry Esson, B.A., M.D. C.M., LL.D.; Provincial Sec. and Minister of Education for B.C.; *b.* English River, Que., 24 Feb., 1867; *s.* of Rev. Alexander Young (Scotch) and Ellen McBain (Canadian); *m.* 1904, Rosalind Watson. *Educ.:* Queen's Univ., Kingston (B.A.), McGill Univ., Montreal (M.D., C.M.) Spent a yr. and a half in England in post grad. studies. Received hon. degree of LL.D. from Toronto Univ., 1 Oct., 1907. A physician. first el. to B.C. Legis. at g. e., 1903; re-el. at g. e., 1907, 1909. Sworn of the Ex. Coun. as Prov. Sec. and Min. of Education, 27 Feb., 1907. Re-el. by accl. at bye-el., 12 March, 1907. *Address:* Victoria, B.C.

YOUNG, Mrs. Rosalind Watson, M.A., A.M.I.M.E.; *b.* Huntingdon, Que., 19 April, 1874; *d.* Rev. James Watson, D.D., and Margaret Fyvie, *d.* of Rev. Adam Lind; *m.* Hon. H. E. Young, Provincial Secy. and Minister of Education for B.C.; one *d.* *Educ.:* Huntingdon Academy and McGill Univ. President of the University Woman's Club, of Victoria, B.C.; member of the Can. Min. Inst. *Publications:* a geography of B.C.; articles on mining, especially in the Atlin dist. *Address:* Victoria, B.C. *Club:* Alexandra, Victoria.

YOUNG, Hon. James; *b.* Galt, Ont., 24 May, 1835; *s.* of John Young, of Melrose, and Janet Bell, of Ledburg, Scot., who settled in Galt in 1834; *m.* Margaret, 2nd *d.* of John McNaught, of Brantford, Ont. *Educ.:* public sch. of Galt; went into the printing business at 16 yrs. of age; at 18 was publisher and editor of Galt *Reformer;* elec. to H. of C. for S. Waterloo, 1867; re-elec. by acclam., 1872 and 1874; defeated in 1878; elec. for North Brant to the Ontario Legislature, 1879; re-el. by acclam. in 1883; became a member of the Mowat Government in June, 1883; re-elec. after accepting office. *Publications:* "Reminiscences of the Settlement of Galt and the Township of Dumfries;" "Public Men and Public Life in Canada." *Recreations:* shooting and fishing. *Address:* "Thornhill," Galt, Ont.

YOUNG, Robert Evans, D.L.S.; Supt. of Ry. Lands, Dept. of the Interior, Ottawa; Chief Geographer of Dom. of Canada; *b.* Georgetown, Ont., 17 March, 1861; of Scotch and English parentage; *m.* 1887, Winifred Frances, (*dec.*) *d.* of Henry Lawe D.L.S., formerly of Dunnville, Ont., now of Ottawa; four *d.* *Educ.:* High Schs. of Stratford and Belleville; Albert Coll., Belleville. Passed exams. as Dom. Land Surveyor and Prov. Land Surveyor of Manitoba in Winnipeg, 1882; Prov. Land Surveyor of B.C. in Victoria, 1899; spent about 20 yrs' in surveying in Man. and B.C.; 1890-04; made special survey of the entire city of Winnipeg, which was rendered necessary by the introduction of the Torrens system of Land Transfer, and was carried out under the Prov. Govt. and the City Council of Winnipeg, jointly. *Publications:* several articles on the "Northland of Canada." *Recreation:* photography. *Address:* 644 Rideau St., Ottawa.

Z

ZAVITZ, Charles Ambrose, B.S.A.; Prof. of Field Husbandry, Ontario Agric. College, Guelph; *b.* Coldstream, Middlesex Co., Ont., 25 Aug., 1863; *s.* of Daniel and Susan Zavitz; *m.* Rebecca Wilson; one *s.* *Educ.:* Coll. Inst., Strathroy, Ont.; Agric. Coll., Guelph. Received college diploma in 1886, and degree in agric. at Toronto Univ., 1888. Brought up on farm in Middlesex Co. Has been at Ontario Agric. Coll. for over 25 yrs., principal work being for the improvement of agric. and especially the farm crops of Ontario. Has lectured at Agric. Colleges in Canada, the U.S., England and Scotland; Sec., Ontario Agric. and Experimental Union; vice-pres., Canadian Seed Growers. Assn., dir., Co-operative Experiments in Agric.; chn. of Committee on Cereal Breeding of American Breeders' Assn.; experimentalist, Ont. Agric. Coll. *Publications:* reports and bulletins in connection with the Ontario Agric. Coll. and Ontario Experimental Union. *Recreation:* lawn bowling. *Address:* Ontario Agricultural Coll., Guelph, Ont.

ZIMMERMAN, Adam; *b.* Harrisburg, Pa., U.S.A., 14 Aug., 1852; *s.* of Isaac and Otellia Zimmerman; *m.* 1873, Isabelle Campbell, of Hamilton, Ont. *Educ.:* Delaware, Ohio. A merchant. Mem. Bd. of Education for ten yrs.; now Chairman; on Bd. of License Commrs. for 14 yrs. El. to H. of C. at g. e., 1904; unsuccessful, 1908. A Presbyterian. A Liberal. *Address:* Hamilton, Ont.

Printed by R. J. Taylor, 134 Queen Street, Ottawa, Canada.